▨ Let's Go writers travel on your budget.

"Guides that penetrate the veneer of the holiday brochures and mine the grit of real life."

—*The Economist*

"The writers seem to have experienced every rooster-packed bus and lunar-surfaced mattress about which they write."

—*The New York Times*

"All the dirt, dirt cheap."

—*People*

▨ Great for independent travelers.

"The guides are aimed not only at young budget travelers but at the independent traveler; a sort of streetwise cookbook for traveling alone."

—*The New York Times*

"Flush with candor and irreverence, chock full of budget travel advice."

—*The Des Moines Register*

"An indispensible resource, *Let's Go*'s practical information can be used by every traveler."

—*The Chattanooga Free Press*

▨ Let's Go is completely revised each year.

"Only *Let's Go* has the zeal to annually update every title on its list."

—*The Boston Globe*

"Unbeatable: good sightseeing advice; up-to-date info on restaurants, hotels, and inns; a commitment to money-saving travel; and a wry style that brightens nearly every page."

—*The Washington Post*

▨ All the important information you need.

"*Let's Go* authors provide a comedic element while still providing concise information and thorough coverage of the country. Anything you need to know about budget traveling is detailed in this book."

—*The Chicago Sun-Times*

"Value-packed, unbeatable, accurate, and comprehensive."

—*Los Angeles Times*

Let's Go Publications

Let's Go: Alaska & the Pacific Northwest 2001
Let's Go: Australia 2001
Let's Go: Austria & Switzerland 2001
Let's Go: Boston 2001 **New Title!**
Let's Go: Britain & Ireland 2001
Let's Go: California 2001
Let's Go: Central America 2001
Let's Go: China 2001
Let's Go: Eastern Europe 2001
Let's Go: Europe 2001
Let's Go: France 2001
Let's Go: Germany 2001
Let's Go: Greece 2001
Let's Go: India & Nepal 2001
Let's Go: Ireland 2001
Let's Go: Israel 2001
Let's Go: Italy 2001
Let's Go: London 2001
Let's Go: Mexico 2001
Let's Go: Middle East 2001
Let's Go: New York City 2001
Let's Go: New Zealand 2001
Let's Go: Paris 2001
Let's Go: Peru, Bolivia & Ecuador 2001 **New Title!**
Let's Go: Rome 2001
Let's Go: San Francisco 2001 **New Title!**
Let's Go: South Africa 2001
Let's Go: Southeast Asia 2001
Let's Go: Spain & Portugal 2001
Let's Go: Turkey 2001
Let's Go: USA 2001
Let's Go: Washington, D.C. 2001
Let's Go: Western Europe 2001 **New Title!**

Let's Go *Map Guides*

Amsterdam	New Orleans
Berlin	New York City
Boston	Paris
Chicago	Prague
Florence	Rome
Hong Kong	San Francisco
London	Seattle
Los Angeles	Sydney
Madrid	Washington, D.C.

Coming Soon: *Dublin* and *Venice*

Let's Go

PERU, BOLIVIA, & ECUADOR
2001

Micaela Root editor
Megan I. Creydt associate editor
Marla B. Kaplan associate editor

researcher-writers

Alvaro Bedoya
Michelle Bowman
Helen Gilbert
Page McLean
Daryk Auran Pengelly

Geraldine Rosaura Slean
Frances Tilney
Katherine R. Ünterman
Elizabeth D. Wilcox

Daisy Stanton map editor

Macmillan

HELPING LET'S GO

If you want to share your discoveries, suggestions, or corrections, please drop us a line. We read every piece of correspondence, whether a postcard, a 10-page email, or a coconut. Please note that mail received after May 2001 may be too late for the 2002 book, but will be kept for future editions. **Address mail to:**

**Let's Go: Peru, Bolivia, & Ecuador
67 Mount Auburn Street
Cambridge, MA 02138
USA**

Visit Let's Go at **http://www.letsgo.com,** or send email to:

**feedback@letsgo.com
Subject: "Let's Go: Peru, Bolivia, & Ecuador"**

In addition to the invaluable travel advice our readers share with us, many are kind enough to offer their services as researchers or editors. Unfortunately, our charter enables us to employ only currently enrolled Harvard students.

Published in Great Britain 2001 by Macmillan, an imprint of Macmillan Publishers Ltd, 25 Eccleston Place, London, SW1W 9NF, Basingstoke and Oxford.
Associated companies throughout the world
www.macmillan.com

Maps by David Lindroth copyright © 2001, 2000, 1999, 1998, 1997, 1996, 1995, 1994, 1993, 1992, 1991, 1990, 1989, 1988 by St. Martin's Press.

Published in the United States of America by St. Martin's Press.

ISBN: 0-333-90139-8
First edition
10 9 8 7 6 5 4 3 2 1

Let's Go: Peru, Bolivia, & Ecuador is written by Let's Go Publications, 67 Mount Auburn Street, Cambridge, MA 02138, USA.

Let's Go® and the thumb logo are trademarks of Let's Go, Inc.
Printed in the USA on recycled paper with biodegradable soy ink.

HOW TO USE THIS BOOK

To anyone who's ever ridden roof-top through the Avenue of the Volcanoes, tracked Butch Cassidy to his grave, tasted a new part of the chicken, discovered hot springs at 3am, drifted down the Ucayali for eight days—and all those who are about to—welcome. Here's to traveling. Here's to South America. And here is *Let's Go: Peru, Bolivia, and Ecuador 2001.*

ORGANIZATION

INTRODUCTORY MATERIAL. Discover gives an overview of travel in our three favorite countries. **A Regional Overview** provides general introductions to the land, people, history, and culture of the region. (Shorter introductions before each country provide more specific cultural information, as well as accounts of the country's recent history.) **Essentials** outlines the practical information you'll need to prepare for and execute your trip.

COVERAGE. Our book begins with coverage of **Peru,** then gives way to coverage of **Bolivia** and, finally, coverage of **Ecuador** (including the Galapagos Islands). Within each country's section, we start with the **capital** (Lima, La Paz, or Quito); the rest of the section then follows a vague west-to-east pattern. Most of the time. Actually, the **Table of Contents** could probably explain this better—it's on the next page.

APPENDIX. The appendix contains a calendar of **regional holidays and festivals,** a **climate** chart, and a **phrasebook** of handy Spanish, Quechua, and Aymara phrases.

LET'S GO FORMAT

RANKING ESTABLISHMENTS. Each town (or city, or national park) write-up begins with an introduction. Then there is a **Transportation** section. Then comes: **Orientation and Practical Information, Accommodations, Food, Sights** and/or **Beaches** or **Outdoor Activities, Entertainment** and/or **Nightlife.** Towns that have a large trekking or tour industry than have what we call an **"Into the"** section—for example, "Into the Jungle from Rurrenabaque" or "Into the Mountains from Huaraz." **Daytrip** destinations follow; **"near"** destinations (like daytrips, but you're more likely to stay overnight) follow that. In each section, we list establishments in order from **best to worst.** Our absolute favorites are denoted by the highest honor given out at Let' s Go, the thumb (🕮).

PHONE CODES AND TELEPHONE NUMBERS. The **phone code** for each region, city, or town appears opposite the name of that region, city, or town, and is denoted by the ☎ icon. **Phone numbers** in text are also preceded by the ☎ icon.

GRAYBOXES AND WHITEBOXES. Grayboxes at times provide wonderful cultural insight, at other times crude humor. **Whiteboxes,** on the other hand, provide important practical information, such as warnings (**M**), helpful hints and further resources (**🛈**), and border crossing information (**✈**, a symbol that also shows up on **maps,** in a somewhat modified form).

CONTENTS

MAPS

RESEARCHER-WRITERS

Alvaro Bedoya   *Central and Eastern Bolivia, Bolivian Oriente*

With a pen that moved faster than a bus on the road to Rurrenabaque, Alvaro hurtled into Bolivia. We could have published *seven* books with the meticulous work that Alvaro sent back in each of his 200-page copybatches—and we would have, if only we didn't think they might reveal too much. You see, over the course of the job, our sweet-faced native Peruvian learned to live cheap (navigating Santa Cruz with five cents to his name), to sleep naked (in Torotoro), to dress dirty (if bemoaning the lost whiteness of his shirts), to cross borders illegally (while researching a crossing into Brazil)—and then to convince the officials to let him back in. We could not have asked for anything more.

Michelle Bowman   *Cordillera Blanca, Central Highlands, Amazon Basin, Cusco*

Mighty Mouse Michelle saved the day; we needed a reliable researcher to trek, bounce, and push her way through remotest northern Peru—and this *Let's Go: Eastern Europe 2000* veteran jumped at the chance. Her cheery phone calls (what part of the *pollo* was that again?) brightened up many a day back here in Cambridge. Although, to be perfectly honest, we suspect her smile brightened the skies of the Peruvian jungle somewhat more—particularly around one strapping young suitor in Iquitos... Not that such dallies ever affected Wonder Woman Michelle's copy. Neither rain, nor snow, nor 24-hour bus ride, nor stolen backpack—nay, nor marriage proposal—could block this researcher's path; it continued long after *her* itinerary had ended, and aren't we glad it did.

Helen Gilbert   *Southern Bolivia*

We didn't think it was possible to be perfect. We didn't think it was possible to follow every instruction, to fulfill every request, to capture and record every single fact. Helen proved us wrong. Helen rented a dirt bike to reach towns ordinary mortals would have declared unreachable. Helen found phones when locals told her there were none, and she spent hours trying to call from the barren heights of the altiplano, just to make sure we wouldn't worry. Helen vomited on her copy to keep the floor clean. Most incredible of all, Helen crafted pages upon pages of perfect new coverage—and brought the words "on time" to southern Bolivia.

Page McClean   *Quito, Central Ecuador, Ecuadorian Oriente*

We had to wrench this rosy-cheeked hiker out of the hills before we could pack her off to Quito, but the effort was well worth it. After months spent bushwhacking through Southern Patagonia, Page took the Ecuadorian Andes by storm. She checked out hike after hike, sending back the most complete safety information for trekkers and volcano-scalers the world has ever seen. But her itinerary was no walk in the woods—poor Page found love in all the wrong places—to be more specific, everywhere she went. Luckily, she was able to wax philosophical about the situation, and when things looked particularly bleak, to pull a vegetarian restaurant out of her left pocket (the right one held that pencil).

Daryk Pengelly   *Western Ecuador, Galapagos*

This Galapagos guru promised us hard-core research and did he ever pull through. Whether shimmying in Salinas or snorkeling off the Devil's Crown, our hard-core, hard-core (and addendums), HARD-CORE (speak up, Daryk, what was that?) researcher will be grinning for years to come after all the blue-footed boobies on his itinerary. Vanquishing El Niño with a single swipe of his highlighter ("down with that bad boy!"), Florida's favorite son spent the summer getting in touch with his inner surfer and his inner shrimp-lover to revolutionize *Let's Go's* coverage of Western Ecuador. His copy was a joy to edit, his style notes a tremendous help; his letters reminded all of us in the office why we do this again.

Geraldine Slean   *Northern Peru, Southern Highlands, Ecuadorian Oriente*

A veteran of many summers of South American travel, Geraldine was no ordinary researcher; she said her batches would be typed and, goshdarnit, typed they were. A trained archaeologist, she then hit every ruin in Northern Peru—including some still wearing a fresh coat of soil—and typed them up with fresh zeal and fresh insight into the region's ancient cultures. A native Spanish speaker, she toiled to bring our readers the inside scoop, the best of the best in whatever form it came: ruin, mountain, or hostel two miles out of town. We are sad to report, however, that Geraldine, a senior, has graduated to bigger things—or at least to bigger digs.

Frances Tilney   *Cusco and the Sacred Valley, Central Highlands, Amazon Basin*

Climaxing from the very start, Frances "former editor of *Let's Go: Mexico 2000*" Tilney climbed through Peru's central highlands with a copy of *Let's Go* in one hand and her trusty short-wave radio in the other. She discovered new hot springs, made new friends, and, like Bingham before her, put a new town on the map. Ever-cheerful, Frances made an art of dodging demonstrations in Ayacucho (and a fallen bridge in San Luis Rey); put her formidable vocabulary toward the lioniza-tion of Peru's people (and places); conquered Cusco (and environs) in record time; and still, though not-quite-tan after a *friaje* took over Puerto Maldonado during her research there, managed to be home in time for dinner.

Kate Ünterman   *Lima, Arequipa, Northern Coast, Southern Coast*

A veteran like no other, this original (1997!) *Let's Go: Ecuador and the Galapa-gos* editor stunned us with perfection and taught us a thing or two about format. With visions of former researching routes (through Costa Rica and Los Angeles) dancing 'round in her head, Kate set out to clean up Peru's coast; to say that she did so would hardly do her justice. In the midst of her mastery, even Lima seems a jewel, since to happy happy Kate, it was. We did, however, have two problems with this former editor of *Let's Go: Middle East 2000*. First, we couldn't take credit for discovering her; second, we couldn't thank her enough.

Elizabeth Wilcox   *La Paz, Lake Titicaca, the Yungas*

The smiley faces that dotted Liz's copy hid the tortured path that this mean, green cleaning machine traversed from Puno to La Paz and back again. Then again, so did her work; unfazed by the dangers and scams that seemed to throw themselves in her path, Liz blazed her way through Bolivia and never once let us down. She hewed a capital chapter from scratch, and—despite everything—managed to smile her way through doing it. Her poet's prose introduced art to the copyflow process; her frequent mail introduced her many friends to us. We will miss her check-in phone calls; Bolivia, we are sure, will miss her.

ACKNOWLEDGMENTS

PBE thanks: Our stupendous RWs, for taking the responsibility and running with it, farther and faster than we could have dared hope. Olivia, for friendship, for patience, for pulling it all together—for whom our keyboards will forever be missing a B. Daisy, for mapping it all out. Valerie, for being the bestbestbest—there was supposed to be an ode, but, then, there was supposed to be a deadline. Ben W., Marly, Anup, and Rachel for incredible generosity, and most of all Meredith, for redefining the concept. Don Montague and the South American Explorers for piles upon piles of information. nickgrossman for the typists, the proofers, and the pep talk. The typists and the proofers for typing and proofing—props to Paula, wherever she may be. The basement brighteners. Anne Chisholm. Rosa, Melissa, and John. Sarah J., Sobi, Ankur, for the eleventh-hour help. Thank you.

Mica thanks: My wonderful AEs, my wonderful ME, my wonderful friends, my most wonderful family, and, last but hardly least, this wonderful organization, for three wonderful, wonderful summers.

Megan thanks: To Mica, for the opportunity and the inspiration; may Cornershop motivate you to all corners of the globe. To Marla, for sunny days of paper edits and for keeping some of my jokes in the book. Aaron, for the welcome  distractions. Em, Michal, you guys are the best—thanks for having schedules just as crazy. To Mom and Dad and Jacob, for support and for comic relief (even when I didn't find it funny). Hey Al (can I call you Al?), this is why I didn't return many calls. To Tony, for always keeping my ego in check (and for the summer tan). Love you all!

Marla thanks: Mica, for her superhuman effort and dedication. It's all worth it. Megan for always being there, for her expertise in transferring phone calls, and for loving food almost as much as me. The salsa pod for loving Shakira. Mere for understanding that "half" isn't always possible. Smoothieqn, toy4080, and yaap for providing ample distraction. Kim, Lisa, Emily, Naomi, Darya, Claire, Rachel, and Mary for putting up with me and my warped schedule—it's really not *that* weird go into work at 11pm. Dad and Jonah for being there. Aunt Paula for always supporting me every step of the way, and the rest of my family for the past 19 years.

Editor
Micaela Root
Associate Editors
Megan I. Creydt, Marla B. Kaplan
Managing Editor
Olivia L. Cowley
Map Editor
Daisy Stanton

Publishing Director
Kaya Stone
Editor-in-Chief
Kate McCarthy
Production Manager
Melissa Rudolph
Cartography Manager
John Fiore
Editorial Managers
Alice Farmer, Ankur Ghosh,
Aarup Kubal, Anup Kubal
Financial Manager
Bede Sheppard
Low-Season Manager
Melissa Gibson
Marketing & Publicity Managers
Olivia L. Cowley, Esti Iturralde
New Media Manager
Daryush Jonathan Dawid
Personnel Manager
Nicholas Grossman
Photo Editor
Dara Cho
Production Associates
Sanjay Mavinkurve, Nicholas
Murphy, Rosalinda Rosalez,
Matthew Daniels, Rachel Mason,
Daniel Visel
(re)Designer
Matthew Daniels
Office Coordinators
Sarah Jacoby, Chris Russell

Director of Advertising Sales
Cindy Rodriguez
Senior Advertising Associates
Adam Grant, Rebecca Rendell
Advertising Artwork Editor
Palmer Truelson

President
Andrew M. Murphy
General Manager
Robert B. Rombauer
Assistant General Manager
Anne E. Chisholm

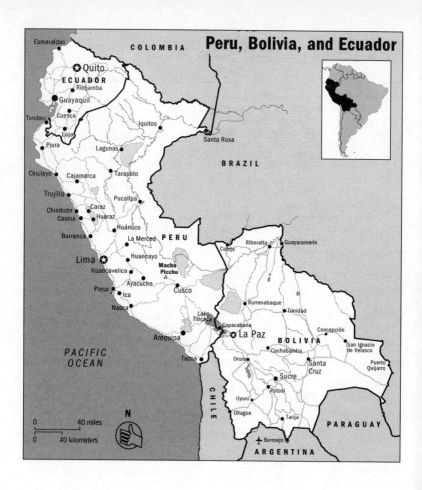

Peru, Bolivia, and Ecuador

Esmeraldas
COLOMBIA
Quito
ECUADOR
Riobamba
Guayaquil
Tumbes
Cuenca
Loja
Piura
Lagunas
Iquitos
Santa Rosa
BRAZIL
Chiclayo
Cajamarca
Tarapoto
Trujillo
Pucallpa
Chimbote
Caraz
Casma
Huaraz
Huánuco
Barranca
La Merced
PERU
Riberalta
Guayaramerín
Cobija
Lima
Huancayo
Huancavelica
Machu
Picchu
Ayacucho
Cusco
Rurrenabaque
Trinidad
Pisco
Ica
Concepción
Nasca
Lake
Titicaca
Copacabana
San Ignacio
de Velasco
Arequipa
La Paz
BOLIVIA
Cochabamba
Santa
Cruz
Puerto
Quijarro
Tacna
Oruro
Sucre
PACIFIC
OCEAN
Potosí
Uyuni
Ollague
Tarija
PARAGUAY
CHILE
Bermejo
ARGENTINA

0   40 miles
0   40 kilometers
N

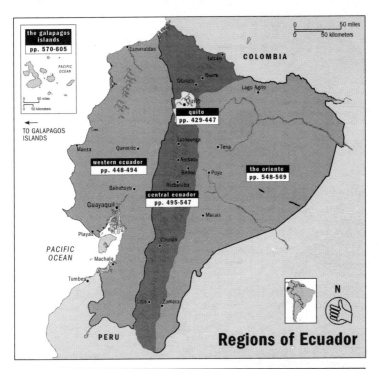

Regions of Ecuador

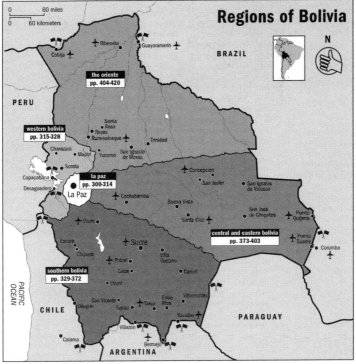

Regions of Bolivia

Regions of Peru

COLOMBIA

⊗ Quito

ECUADOR

● Guayaquil

Tumbes

● Piura

● Chiclayo

Cajamarca ●

● Iquitos

Santa Rosa

Lagunas ●

● Moyobamba

● Tarapoto

● Juanjuí

BRAZIL

Trujillo ●

Chimbote ●

Casma ●   ● Huaraz

Barranca ●

● Pucallpa

Tingo
María ●

● La Oroya

Lima ⊗

● Pisco

Ayacucho ●

Machu
Picchu   Cusco ●

Puerto
Maldonado ●

● Nasca

PACIFIC
OCEAN

Arequipa ●

Juli ●

BOLIVIA

N

Tacna ●

Arica ●

Regions of Peru

0   200 miles

0   200 kilometers

CHILE

XIV

DISCOVER PERU, BOLIVIA, & ECUADOR

PERU FACTS AND FIGURES

CAPITAL Lima

PRESIDENT Alberto Fujimori

POPULATION 26½ million

AREA 1,285,220 sq km

DECLARED INDEPENDENCE July 28, 1821

HIGHEST POINT Huascarán 6768m

VARIETIES OF POTATOES 3500

BOLIVIA FACTS AND FIGURES

CAPITAL La Paz (government seat), Sucre (judiciary seat)

PRESIDENT Hugo Banzer

POPULATION 8 million

AREA 1,098,580 sq km

DECLARED INDEPENDENCE August 6, 1825

HIGHEST POINT Sajama 6542m

KM OF UNPAVED ROAD PER KM OF PAVED ROAD 17¼

ECUADOR FACTS AND FIGURES

CAPITAL Quito

PRESIDENT Gustavo Noboa

POPULATION 12½ million

AREA 283,560 sq km

DECLARED INDEPENDENCE May 24, 1822

HIGHEST POINT Chimborazo 6267m

RATIO OF FOREIGNERS TO RESIDENTS IN THE GALAPAGOS 3 to 1

Peru, Bolivia, and Ecuador are extreme sorts of places. In their west, Andean slopes plummet into the wet, wet Amazon basin; in their east, those snow-crowned peaks fall to the driest desert in the world. Once home to one of the world's wealthiest empires, Bolivia holds the word's highest forest and highest lake, Ecuador houses the world's largest tortoise population, and Peru forms the shore onto which the world's longest and tallest waves crash. They are superlative places, these countries, and they are both beautiful and very, very interesting. Of course, if you look at the foreign media, the three appear even more extreme than they are. If CNN told the whole story, almost every day in the last year has seen mass turmoil—against dollarization in Ecuador, against coca eradication in Bolivia, against President Fujimori's third term in Peru. In reality, once one leaves the major city centers, life is progressing as usual: calmly, coolly, slowly. Peru, Bolivia, and Ecuador are places where everything gets done in its own time, or at least *mañana, sin falta.*

WHEN TO GO

Despite the region's proximity to the equator, its climate varies greatly across three geographical regions. As a result, there are many great times to visit the area, but none perfect. (In the **jungle**—called the Amazon Basin in Peru and the Oriente in Bolivia and Ecuador—and along Peru and Ecuador's Pacific **coast,** the sweltering heat reflects tropical norms, but bring a sweater or twelve for trips into the **highlands.**) The seasons here don't cycle from summer to winter as in temperate regions; instead, they go from wet to dry. The currents of the Pacific govern coastal and lowland weather; warm waters bathe the western shores from January to April, bringing torrential downpours and daytime temperatures around 31°C (88°F). Cooler currents arrive in May and mean less heat and rainfall for the rest of the year. Despite the rains, sun worshippers and those seeking solace from high temperatures crowd the Peru and Ecuador's **beaches** from **December to April,** especially on weekends and holidays. The rest of the year, skies are cloudy, temperatures are cooler, and you'll most likely have the beach to yourself. In the mountains, temperatures remain more or less constant all year, averaging 21°C (70°F) during the day and 8°C (47°F) at night, but the driest time lasts from **June to September.** In the Amazon Basin and Oriente, it rains year-round. It may be especially damp from June to August, but precipitation does not vary much across the year; year-round temperature and humidity approximates that of the coast during the wet season. Out by the **Galapagos,** the warm waters of El Niño and the cold ones of the Humboldt Current battle to keep temperatures on the warm side—but replete with rain, rain, and more rain. The first half of the year is the wet season; the air dries out and cools off noticeably during later months, when temperatures fall below 21°C. For a **climate chart,** see p. 606.

Local **festivals and holidays** are another seasonal variation to keep in mind when planning your trip. The most important nation-wide holidays are Christmas, Semana Santa (Easter week), and Independence Day (July 28-29 in Peru, August 6 in Bolivia, and May 24 in Ecuador). For a chart detailing area festivals, see p. 606.

WHAT TO DO

Peru, Bolivia, and Ecuador really do offer something for everyone. Not at every time of year, and not in every hamlet or port, but somewhere and someplace, you'll find what you're looking for. The headers below highlight some of the reasons we'll be visiting these countries again; for more specific regional attractions, see the **Highlights of the Region** section at the beginning of each chapter.

THE ROAD TO RUIN(S)

As the sky grows light behind them, the Andean foothills appear haloed. Up by the Sun Gate, a weary band of trekkers holds their collective breath, and the new day's sun carries away the shadows that had obscured the valley below. For many, this is why they came to Peru. This is the Incas' magical, incomparable unfound city. This is **Machu Picchu** (p. 120). Few places can match Machu Picchu's setting, but the nearby fortresses of **Ollantaytambo** (p. 115), **Pisac** (p. 113), and **Sacsayhuamán** (p. 110) give it a good shot. Up north, vast **Huánuco Viejo** (p. 229) bills itself as "the second-best" Inca ruin in Peru, but this little-visited site is overshadowed by the north's copious other ruins, most from cultures older than the Inca. The ruins of **Chavín de Huántar** (p. 208) housed eight generations of the Chavín people within the Cordillera Blanca. Where the mountains meet the rainforest, the Chachapoyas constructed the huge, limestone fortress that is **Kuélap**

(p. 225). The fascinating exhumed graves of the **Sipán** (p. 189) housed a mummy hailed, when discovered, as the "Peruvian King Tut." And farther up the coast, outside Trujillo, **Chan Chan** (p. 194), once the capital of the Chimú Empire, is the largest preserved mud brick city in the world. Nor does Peru have a monopoly on ruins. Not far from La Paz lies **Tiahuánaco** (p. 314), former capital of one of the area's longest-ruling people. Farther east, **El Fuerte** (p. 396) is, incredibly, hewn from a single rock. The site's unfillable hole provides ample discussion topics. And while not perhaps as impressive in stone work as the sites above—being ruins that live up to their category—the still-used Inca terraces and crumbling stone ceremonial sites on **Isla del Sol** (p. 319) inhabit a lake-enclosed landscape as serene as any. Finally, though Ecuador's offers may pale in comparison with those to the south, the Inca Trail that runs from **Ingapirca** (p. 534) to Cuenca's Pumapungo ruins is certainly a trip worth taking.

HIKING AND TREKKING

Peru, Bolivia, and Ecuador offer great opportunities for both hiking and trekking. After all, the Andes—the highest tropical peaks in the world—do cut a swath through their middles. Anyone considering a trek in Peru should first consider the stunning **Inca Trail** (p. 116), much of which follows an Inca stone road. The walk begins near Ollantaytambo and passes several interesting ancient *tambos* (rest stops) before reaching South America's number one tourist site, Machu Picchu. But the Inca Trail is hardly the only option. Farther north in Peru, the Cordillera Blanca's **Parque Nacional Huascarán** (p. 199) holds the country's highest peak and any number of stunning and snow-capped others. In Ecuador, the **Avenue of the Volcanoes** (p. 505) allows for many a risky climb, as well as some more mellow ones. Particularly popular climbs scale volcanoes **Cotopaxi** (p. 511), **Chimborazo** (p. 527), and, right near Quito, **Pichincha** (p. 443). Of course, Ecuador has its own **Inca Trail** (p. 534) as well—it runs from sacred Ingapirca to other ruins in Cuenca, several kilometers away. In Bolivia, there's **Sajama** (p. 354), the country's highest peak, for those feeling particularly muscular. For those feeling less so, the country's best trekking probably takes place in the Yungas, a beautiful never-neverland in the vast green lands between the altiplano and the jungle. The most common bases for exploration, **Sorata** (p. 322) and **Coroico** (p. 326), are also charming towns in their own right.

URBAN EXPLOITS

Hiking boots are not a prerequisite for adventure. You could explore **Quito's** (p. 429) colonial Old Town or **La Paz's** (p. 300) witch market in high heels, although *Let's Go* does not recommend high heels. (Except in **Lima** (p. 68), where the red velvet ropes go up around 11pm.) While off-the-beaten-track is certainly a great place to get to, there's also great stuff to see and do on the best-beaten tracks around: big cities. There's charming if gringo-infested **Cusco** (p. 98) and its calmer lookalike in the north, **Cajamarca** (p. 217). Slightly north sits erudite **Ayacucho** (p. 249), at one point thought lost to the Shining Path. In Bolivia, travelers who tire of La Paz's fascinating, current-focused museums—or just the cold—head to **Sucre** (p. 331), Bolivia's white-walled second capital and one of three so-called "garden cities." The countries other two "garden cities" are the bustling commercial center of **Cochabamba** (p. 373) and beautiful **Tarija** (p. 365), which lies deep in wine country. Everyone loves **Cuenca** (p. 528), Ecuador's southern hub, and **Arequipa** (p. 153), Peru's refined "white city." Finally, other favorites include the indigenous center of **Otavalo** (p. 496), the cosmopolitan though jungle-bound, **Iquitos** (p. 258), and **Trujillo** (p. 191), which some describe as Lima's good points packaged and placed farther up on the Pacific Coast.

DISCOVER

WET AND WILDLIFE

If wet's what you want, your best bet's probably either **surfing** or **rafting. Puerto Chicama** (p. 197) has the world's longest wave; down by **Punta Hermosa** (p. 127), South America's tallest wave (up to 24ft.) rolls in April through May. **Montañita** (p. 470) is where all the surfers hang out. For rafting, the **Río Cañete** (p. 127), by Lunahuaná, is a sure thing (Dec.-Mar.). The many rivers around **Tena** (p. 557) offer Ecuador's best; near Cusco, the **Río Apurímac** (p. 112) has Class V rapids. For those who just want to swim, Ecuador's secluded **Suá** (p. 453) and **Same** (p. 453) are some of the continent's prettiest beaches. And, of course, there's always **Lake Titicaca**, whose clear blue water looks more inviting than its temperature. Still, from **Copacabana** (p. 315), you can row or kayak your way through its oh-so-blue waters.

For animals, nothing compares to the **Galapagos Islands** (p. 570), but such quantity has a high price. Two alternatives, both Ecuador's **Isla de la Plata** (p. 469) and the **Islas Ballestas** (p. 132) off the coast of Peru have earned themselves the nickname "poor man's Galapagos." Bolivia's flat **pampas** is the area to visit for firsthand encounters with caiman and such; **Rurrenabaque** (p. 404) is the most popular town from which to take a tour. Of course, if birds are your bag, you'll have many options. Among the best spotting sites are the lake that will never escape Titicaca's shadow, Peru's second-biggest, the **Lago de Junín** (p. 234); and the macaw licks around **Puerto Maldonado** (p. 288) and the **Manú Bioshere Reserve** (p. 286).

▓ LET'S GO PICKS

BEST HIGHS: Lake Titicaca (p. 166 and p. 315), the world's highest navigable lake; **Parque Nacional Sajama** (p. 354), the world's highest forest; **Cotopaxi** (p. 511), the world's highest active volcano; the **Lima-Huancayo Railway** (p. 239), the world's highest train tracks; **cocaine** (p. 11).

BEST EXPLOITATION OF A GEOGRAPHICAL FEATURE: Mitad del Mundo (p. 444), an equatorial theme park.

BEST RELIGIOUS INTERPRETATIONS: According to paintings in Quito (p. 440) and Cusco (p. 104), Christ ate **cuy** (guinea pig) for his Last Supper; according to a statue in Huánuco (p. 233), San Sebastián had **smallpox**.

BEST SIGN: "Today for me, **tomorrow for you**" at the Sucre city cemetery (p. 337).

BEST PHALLIC SYMBOLS: Chucuito (p. 172); **Valle de los Machos** (p. 362).

BEST MISNOMERS: Pisco (p. 137), an alcohol actually from Ica; **Panama hats** (p. 463), hats actually from Ecuador; **Vilcabamba** (p. 122), ruins that were actually Machu Picchu. That last one has been straightened out.

BEST KITSCH: Tours to **Butch Cassidy and the Sundance Kid's** graves (p. 363).

BEST COLOR-COORDINATED CITIES: Arequipa (p. 153) and **Sucre** (p. 331), Peru's and Bolivia's "Ciudades Blancas."

BEST VIRTUAL GALAPAGOS: Isla de la Plata (p. 468) and **Islas Ballestas** (p. 132), the "poor person's Galapagos" of Ecuador and Peru, respectively.

BEST LANDSCAPING: The **Nasca lines** (p. 142). Who's *their* gardener?

BEST GRAFFITI: In the hospital laundry room where **Che Guevara** was laid out after his death (p. 397).

BEST EVIDENCE OF MONOPOLY: Computación e Informática Bill Gates (p. 131), an Internet cafe in Pisco.

BEST PAMPERING: Baños (p. 516), where the hot water never runs out.

BEST EIFFEL NON-TOWERS: Fountains in Moquega (with water-spitting frogs, p. 147) and Tacna (p. 152); the **Iron House** in Iquitos (p. 264). It seems Gustave got around.

BEST SECOND BEST: Huánuco Viejo (p. 229), which the local tourist office has dubbed "the second best Inca ruins" in Peru.

BEST COUNTRIES: Peru (p. 62); **Bolivia** (p. 292); **Ecuador** (p. 421). Naturally.

WHAT TO READ

What follows is a list of our favorite books about (in one way or another) Peru, Bolivia, or Ecuador—in print, available in English, and never, ever dull:

At Play in the Fields of the Lord, by Peter Matthiessen. A compelling thriller set in the Amazon basin. An honest and powerful depiction of clashing motives and cultures.

The Beak of the Finch: A Story of Evolution in Our Time, by Jonathan Weiner. About finches in the Galapagos, yet somehow engaging enough to interest non-scientists.

The Bridge of San Luis Rey, by Thornton Wilder. A Pulitzer Prize-winning novel about five people who die when a bridge collapses in Peru's central highlands in the 18th century.

Broad and Alien is the World, by Ciro Alegria. A many-layered tale of a Peruvian town by one of the nation's foremost writers.

The Celestine Prophecy: An Adventure, by James Redfield. Controversial best-seller. Purports to be the true story of the "author's" spiritual self-discovery in Peru.

Chasing Che: A Motorcycle Journey in Search of the Guevara Legend, by Patrick Symmes. A gritty account of the 10,000-mile road trip Symmes undertook, which retraced Che's route through Peru, Bolivia, Argentina, and Chile.

Che Guevara: A Revolutionary Life, by Jon Lee Anderson. The most complete biography of the legendary revolutionary who died in La Higuera, Bolivia in 1967.

Death in the Andes, by Mario Vargas Llosa. A surreal and haunting story of an isolated Andean village plagued by avalanches and Shining Path terrorists. By the pre-eminent Peruvian author and one-time presidential candidate.

The Heights of Machu Picchu, by Pablo Neruda. Considered to be one of Nobel laureate Neruda's greatest poems, "Alturas de Machu Picchu" portrays a pilgrimage—and captures the Lost City of the Incas as no photograph can.

Living Poor: A Peace Corps Chronicle, by Moritz Thomson. An unsentimental autobiographical account of the author's stint in a coastal village in northern Ecuador.

The Old Patagonian Express: by Train through the Americas, by Paul Theroux. An amusing log of this respected travel writer's rail journey from Boston to Chile.

Paddington, by Michael Bond. The first in a series concerning the London adventures of a most endearing bear "from darkest Peru."

The Storyteller, by Mario Vargas Llosa. Another by Vargas Llosa. A modern fable that weaves cultural questions into an engrossing mystery.

Sweat of the Sun, Tears of the Moon: A Chronicle of an Incan Treasure, by Peter Lourie. The captivating true story of a treasure hunt in the Andes.

Touching the Void: The Harrowing First Person Account of One Man's Miraculous Survival, by Joe Simpson and Chris Bonington. The true story of a climbing disaster in Peru.

The Voyage of the Beagle: Charles Darwin's Journal of Researches, by Charles Darwin. From 1831 to 1836, as the official naturalist of the Royal Navy Ship HMS Beagle, Darwin surveyed the coast of South America and observed phenomena which would later lead to his theories of evolution through natural selection. Yet this book records far more than scientific observations; it reveals Darwin's personal revelations and observations well—and the combination is, perhaps surprisingly, fascinating.

DISCOVER

SUGGESTED ITINERARIES

BEST OF ECUADOR, PERU, AND BOLIVIA

BEST OF (ECUADOR, PERU, AND BOLIVIA IN 3 MONTHS) Fly into **Quito** (p. 429, 3 days), where you can ease into life in South America and then head out to **Mindo** (p. 446, 3 days), a nature-lover's paradise. Head north next, to the Saturday market in **Otavalo** (p. 496, 1 day), where *everything's* for sale. Backtrack south and explore the **Latacunga Loop** (p. 509, 3 days); rent a horse in Chugchilán and ride to Laguna Quilotoa. Head west to **Parque Nacional Machalilla** (p. 468, 3 days) and you may encounter the wildlife that's earned the park the moniker "poor man's Galapagos." Join the barefoot parade in nearby **Montañita** (p. 470, 3 days); grab a surf board—or just a drink—and relax. Back inland, luxury awaits in **Baños** (p. 516, 2 days), Ecuador's hot-springs capital. Hop back on the Panamericana and head to **Riobamba** (p. 522, 1 day), where you can catch the spectacular Nariz del Diablo train to **Alausí** (p. 527, 1 day). Farther south, **Cuenca** (p. 528, 3 days) may be the most attractive city in Ecuador; the nearby Ingapirca ruins are the country's finest. Next-stop **Vilcabamba** (p. 544, 5 days) has room for native groups, vacationing Cuencans, resident ex-pats, roaming backpackers, *and* horses—which you can use to explore Parque Nacional Podocarpus. Continue south to **Macará** (p. 494, 1 day), proof that nice border towns do exist. Come morning, you're in Peru—from Piura, hop on a bus to historic **Cajamarca** (p. 217, 3 days), which is a lot like Cusco, only less crowded. Then it's off to **Trujillo** (p. 191, 3 days), Peru's second city, which—while we're making comparisons—is just like Lima, only pleasant. While you're there, check out Chan Chan, the largest preserved mud-brick city in the world. From here it could be a straight shot down the coast to the capital, but the Cordillera Blanca beckons. Heed its call— get yourself some camping paraphenelia and head for the hills near **Huaraz** (p. 199, 4 days). After the mountains' blue skies, **Lima** (p. 68, 1 day) may come as a bit of a shock. You'll likely see some other escapees on the next morning's bus to **Pisco** (p. 130, 1 days), where you can join a boat to the Islas Ballestas. Another short ride down the Panamericana and hey! you're in **Nasca** (p. 139, 1 day). An early-morning flight's the best way to view the mysterious lines, but for serious budgeteers, the lookout tower will have to do. After the desert coast, **Arequipa** (p. 153, 3 days) seems an oasis. Take in its pale churches and fascinating Santa Catalina Monastery, but leave time to watch a condor soar over the fathomless **Colca Canyon** (p. 162, 2 days). Then catch a train to Puno, where you'll get your first glance of Lake Titicaca as you cross the border to **Copacabana** (p. 315, 2 days). From here, it's an easy trip to the Inca ruins and rustic quietude that constitute **Isla del Sol** (p. 319, 2 days). Then, three hours from Copacabana, **La Paz** (p. 300, 4 days) opens up beneath your bus window, near-vertical in places. Just *try* to exhaust its options. When you give up, take a trip south to **Uyuni** (p. 355, 1 day) and find yourself a tour jeep with which to explore the as-cool-as-the-hype **Salar de Uyuni** (p. 357, 4 days). Cold yet? The Chaco's not far away; even if the local smiles and temperate climate in **Tarija** (p. 365, 3 days) don't warm you up, the fruits of the area's vineyards will. Then it's back north, to pursed-lipped **Potosí** (p. 340, 2 days), where a descent into the mines will put almost anything in persepective. In contrast, nearby second-capital **Sucre** (p. 331, 3 days) shines its white, white smile all day long; it's a pleasure just to walk the streets. From here, the road back to the real capital isn't much fun; some choose to fly. There's another, scarier bus ride waiting—but **Coroico** (p. 326, 3 days) is worth it; just make sure you lounge around a bit before braving the journey to **Rurrenabaque** (p. 404, 4 days), the best and the cheapest town from which to tour the Amazon basin. Save your heart and fly back to La Paz. Then get an overnight bus to **Cusco** (p. 98, 3 days), gateway to the Sacred Valley. And now (drumroll please) it is time to hike the **Inca Trail** (p. 116, 4 days) to **Machu Picchu** (p. 120). Afterward, return to Cusco and sleep through the long ride to **Ayacucho** (p. 249, 3 days), city of a thousand churches. Continue north through the central highlands and admire the *artesanía* of **Huancayo** (p. 238, 2 days). From here, it's just one more day's travel, and you're catching a flight home from Lima.

CHOOSE YOUR OWN ADVENTURE (PERU AND BOLIVIA IN 2 MONTHS)

Start in **Lima** (p. 68, 2 days), where watch-snatchers and violent demonstrations define urban adventure. Get some rest; these next two months will take your breath away. Take a night bus to **Huaraz** (p. 199, 3 days), where you can snowboard down the Pastoruri Glacier one day and hike up to the Lagunas Llanganuco the next. Next stop: **Puerto Chicama** (p. 197, 2 days), home to the longest wave in the world; bring your own surf board and wetsuit. **Huancabamba** (p. 185) lies less than a day farther north, and its environs offer an altogether different sort of adventure. Spend a night with a *maestro* (shaman) and some assorted substances, and go on an internal escapade—a trip, if you will. Head south again to **Cajamarca** (p. 217, 2 days), a lovely colonial city, before you veer completely off the beaten track on a multi-day pilgrimage to the mouth of the Amazon. Get a bus to **Chachapoyas** (p. 223, 2 days), from where you can explore any number of impressive pre-Inca ruins. Head down into the jungle on a bus to **Tarapoto** (p. 271, 2 days), then get another bus to **Yurimaguas.** From here, it's a short, cheap ride on a tiny aircraft to **Iquitos** (p. 258, 3 days). Enjoy the Iberian-tiled buildings, the sweeping views of the Amazon, and the floating village of Belén. Then sling your hammock on deck a **cargo ship** (see Getting Around, p. 51) and spend 4-9 days floating down the Río Ucayali on one of the least expensive cruises the world has to offer. Hop off the boat in **Pucallpa** (p. 273, 2 days) and check out nearby Laguna Yari-

nacocha. From Pucallpa, it'll take a full day to reach **Puerto Bermúdez** (p. 280, 4 days), one of the best spots in the area from which to explore the jungle. Join the other backpackers on the bus back to **Lima** (p. 68, 1 day); the next morning, get an early bus to **Lunahuaná** (p. 127, 1 day) and raft the Río Cañete. Follow the Gringo Trail to **Nasca** (p. 139, 1 day) and to **Arequipa** (p. 153, 2 days). Leave your stuff there while you set out on a week-long trek from **Cabanaconde** (p. 166) to the **Valle de los Volcanes** (p. 164). Head to **Cusco** (p. 98, 3 days) and explore the Sacred Valley. Then hike the **Inca Trail** (p. 116, 4 days); it may not be remote, but man is it stunning. Take the train back to Cusco and get some sleep; the next day, head to **Copacabana** (p. 315, 2 days), crossing the uneventful border (p. 168) at Yunguyo en route. Rent a kayak and explore the coastline one day; the next, walk to the end of the peninsula and row yourself to **Isla del Sol** (p. 319, 2 days). Explore the hills that—legend has it—spawned the Inca Empire, then head back to the mainland and make for **La Paz** (p. 300, 3 days). A few days later, hop on a mountain bike and ride down the "Most Dangerous Road" in the world to **Coroico** (p. 326, 3 days), a warm relief from the altiplano and a hiker's dream. Later, take the harrowing bus journey to **Rurrenabaque** (p. 404, 4 days) and join a tour of the pampas—if your group doesn't object, your guide may capture a baby crocodile for you to hold. Head to **Trinidad** (p. 416, 30min.) and then leave the city for the intriguing **Last Frontiers** (p. 420, 2 days). Then it's off to the **Jesuit Missions** (p. 399, 3 days), a little-visited but fascinating series of small, church-filled villages. Spend a night in **Santa Cruz** (p. 385) en route to **Cochabamba** (p. 373, 1

CHOOSE YOUR OWN ADVENTURE

Huancabamba · Iquitos
Chachapoyas
Yurimaguas
Tarapoto
Cajamarca
Pucallpa
Puerto · Huaraz
Chicama · Puerto · San Javier
Bermúdez · San Ignacio
Lima · **PERU** · **BOLIVIA** · de Velasco
Lunahuaná · Cusco · Santa Ana
Nasca · Rurrenabaque
Trinidad
Coroico
Arequipa · Cochabamba
La Paz · Santa
Isla del Sol · Torotoro · Cruz
Copacabana · San José de
Chiquitos
San Rafael

day). From Cochabamba, head to the wonderful **Parque Nacional Torotoro** (p. 383, 3 days), where you can play in dinosaur tracks. From Cochabamba, it's a short journey back to La Paz.

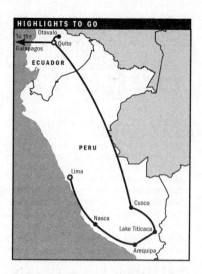

HIGHLIGHTS TO GO

HIGHLIGHTS TO GO (ECUADOR AND PERU IN 16 DAYS) Fly into **Lima** (p. 68, 1hr.); try to get a flight that arrives in the morning so you can catch a bus to **Nasca** (p. 139, 2 days) the same day. Visit the Cemetery of Chauchilla, get some rest, and the next morning, take a flight over the lines. Then get thee to a nunnery—a 9-hour bus ride away, the vast Santa Catalina Monastery is like a city within a city—**Arequipa** (p. 153, 2 days). A short trip to the **Colca Canyon** (p. 162, 1 day)—almost the world's deepest—involves a lot of driving but will leave you more time to explore Arequipa's white-walled streets. It's a 12-hour train trip to **Puno** (p. 166, 30min.), so it may make sense to do it overnight—you'll wake up to the incomparable blue of Lake Titicaca, stretching out to the horizon. Puno's not the best place from which to see it, however; head down to the port and hop on a boat to **Islas Taquile and Amantaní** (p. 173, 2 days). Here, you can stay with a Quechua family and, of course, have Titicaca on all sides. Then it's back to Puno, where you can get a night bus or train to **Cusco** (p. 98), once the capital of the Inca Empire and Peru's current tourist center. Take a day to explore the city (or lounge in its many cafes), a day for the **Sacred Valley** (p. 113), and then, the best at last: a day for **Machu Picchu** (p. 120). From Cusco, fly to **Quito** (p. 429, 2 days); compare intricate Old Town and cosmopolitan New Town. If you're feeling energetic, hike Volcán Pichincha on a very long daytrip. The next day—particularly if it's a Saturday—visit **Otavalo** (p. 496, 1 day) and the best and biggest Andean market in existence. Head back to Quito to catch your flight to the **Galapagos** (p. 570, 3 days). It'll be expensive, but traveling fast ain't cheap.

A REGIONAL OVERVIEW

THE LAND

The **Andes** span the western side of South America, from Venezuela to the southern tip of Chile. The extraordinary mountain range was formed by the brutal collision of two tec tonic plates several million years ago. Its relatively young age has prevented wind and water from working their erosive magic on the rugged peaks, but the region's geology is far from static; the entire South American coast lies on the edge of a continental plate that is being subducted by the oceanic plate of the Pacific. The interaction of the two plates causes volcanic activity and relatively frequent **earthquakes.** All along the Peruvian, Bolivian, and Ecuadorian Andes, active and extinct **volcanos** mingle with long stretches of arable highlands (**sierra**), which are cultivated with barley, wheat, and corn. The southern highlands of Ecuador and the Sacred Valley in Peru feature the typical sierra landscape of patchwork fields dominated by snow-capped mountains, with an occasional sparkling lake thrown in for good measure. Farther south, Peru and Bolivia contain extraordinarily desolate high altitude plains (**altiplano,** also called **puna** in Bolivia), too high to support anything but scrub grass. This altiplano, however, is highly populated (70% of Bolivia's population) and also supports **Lake Titicaca,** the highest navigable lake in the world. Bolivia lacks Peru and Ecuador's coastal landscapes, but has its own unique features: the **pampas,** an area of very wet plains, and the **salt fields of Uyuni** (on the Bolivia-Chile border).

All three of the Andean countries, along with their rocky peaks, contain **lowlands** where coffee and bananas thrive. In Ecuador, swampy areas that were once breeding grounds for many species follow the coastline, though some are being replaced by shrimp and fish farms. Closer to the Peruvian coast, the Andes become scorched foothills, then arid **desert.** In some sections (like Nasca along the southern coast), the surrounding desert is among the driest in the world.

Most of the three countries' land area is occupied by hot, humid, and sparsely populated rainforest, east of the central corridor formed by the Andes. Called the **Oriente** in Ecuador and Bolivia and the **Amazon basin** in Peru, this is where much of the region's extraordinary biodiversity can be found. In Peru and Bolivia, the high jungle is the choice climate for growing coca, a sacred crop since Inca times, but lately also used for less holy purposes—to produce cocaine for export.

The **Galapagos Islands** (controlled by Ecuador) are in an ecological niche all their own. Formed over the past five million years from the eruptions of underwater volcanoes, the islands began as barren lava masses. Today, they swarm with the animal and plant species that have crossed the water from the continent to the islands. (For more information on the land and life of the Galapagos, see **The Galapagos: Geology,** p. 571).

FLORA AND FAUNA

The region encompassed by Peru, Bolivia, and Ecuador hosts an extremely diverse range of plants and animals. The rainforest has by far the greatest biodiversity: of the two million plant and animal species known to exist in the world today, half live exclusively in **rainforests.** Activists around the world have recently stepped up efforts to protect the biodiversity of these forests, where tall trees form a several-story-high canopy under which smaller ferns, palms, and other plants grow. Thousands of animal species thrive in the Amazon basin, from the familiar deer, squirrels, and bats, to the powerful tapirs and jaguars, to the comically exotic guatusa, capybaras, and three-toed sloths. The high-altitude **cloud forests** of the **sierra** are remarkable for their strange combinations of cool, moist air and fairy tale flora. The only species of bear found in South America, the spectacled bear, resides in the highland region, as do domesticated llamas and alpacas. The *vicuña*, a relative of these latter two, can only be found in areas above 3500m altitude. Ecuador has over 1600 bird species, Peru has over 1700, and Bolivia over 1300; each country also boasts several hundred species of mammals and fish. Within the six distinct zones of vegetation on the Galapagos (supporting mangroves, cacti, ferns, orchids, coffee plants, pineapple trees, and much more), numerous animal populations evolved in isolation, becoming unique to these islands. Some 30 endemic species of birds, various iguanas, sea lions, penguins, and the endangered giant tortoise from which the archipelago derives its name are all unique to the islands.

THE PEOPLE

The first peoples to inhabit the region of present-day Peru, Bolivia, and Ecuador migrated from the north to the coastal regions over 12,000 years ago. The most notable migration of the modern era was the 15th-century conquest of much of the region by the Cusco-based **Incas**. The Incas spread their language (Quechua) and culture to many previously disparate social groups. No external invasions occurred, however, until Francisco Pizarro's momentous 1526 invasion. Since the infusion of **Spanish** blood and culture, other groups, too, have been mixed into the picture: **African slaves** were brought to work plantations on the coast, and small but thriving communities of **Chinese** and **Japanese** live in the region today. The majority of Peru's 26 million and Ecuador's 12 million inhabitants live in the highland and coastal regions, and 70% of Bolivia's 8 million inhabitants live in the highlands; the Amazon remains little populated. A significant percentage of the region's population is centered in the urban centers of Lima (with a population surpassing 7 million), Quito and Guayaquil (home to over 2 million), and La Paz (home to 700,000 people). Issues of race and ethnicity are closely intertwined; an individual's identity as white, black, *mestizo* (mixed white and indigenous), or *indígena* (indigenous) is a combination of biological and social factors. Since the elite class has always been predominantly white and the working class mainly *mestizo* and *indígena*, a biological *mestizo* of high social rank may be called white, while a biological white with a low social rank may be called *mestizo*. The current ethnic breakdown estimate for Peru is 45% *indígena*, 37% *mestizo*, 15% white, and 3% black, Japanese, Chinese, and other ethnicities; Ecuador is 55% *mestizo*, 25% *indígena*, 10% white, and 10% black; Bolivia's most recent estimate is 55% *indígena*, 25-30% *mestizo*, and 5-15% white.

Descendants of slaves who arrived in the 17th and 18th centuries, the **black population** of the region clearly maintains a distinct culture and ethnicity. Peru's small black population is centered along the coast between Lima and Ica. The black peoples of Ecuador live in the northern coastal province of Esmeraldas and in the Chota Valley of the northwest. (Bolivia's black population is negligent.) The countries' **white population** is predominantly made up of descendants of Spanish conquistadors and colonists. Like their ancestors, they make up the majority of the country's elite and are concentrated in urban centers. **Mestizos** make up the bulk of Peru, Bolivia, and Ecuador's urban populations but also inhabit rural zones, often overlapping with indigenous communities. The cultures and lifestyles of various *mestizo* groups are the complex result of varying influences, and resulting cultures vary greatly from the coastal lowlands to the highlands to the jungle.

COCA: SACRED AND PROFANE

In most countries, the coca plant is notorious for one reason; it is the base element in the production of cocaine. However, the stigma associated with the plant doesn't extend to Peru, Bolivia, or Ecuador, where coca in its original form is not only legal, but used commonly for a wide variety of purposes. Many tourists drink coca tea (*mate*) which helps alleviate altitude sickness and maintains the rhythm of respiration. A more common form is *chaccheo*, or chewing coca. The *indígenas* of these countries use coca to cure just about everything, from toothaches and digestion to diarrhea. *Llipta* and *tocra*, mixtures of lime, potash, and coca, supposedly combat fatigue, while coca leaves themselves are chewed as an appetite suppressant.

Besides being a highly practical cure-all, coca has long been used in the Andean region for **spiritual purposes;** it has been telling the future since before the Incas. Anthropological evidence dates the coca leaf back to as early as 1300 BC. Ancient Moche art shows that people were chewing the plant as early as 200 BC, and the Inca culture continued the dependence on this staple; they used it as a sign of nobility, as well as a tribute to the sun god, **Inti.** The Spanish conquistadors restricted access to the valuable plant, deciding that coca and its sacramental practice did not fit into their "Christian world." Ironically, the Spaniards soon began making a hefty profit by selling the precious plant to the Indians, who needed it to survive the high-Andes life.

Coca continued to be an important part of the Peruvian economy, but took on a whole new set of implications when European scientists isolated the cocoa element of the plant in 1855. In 1880, the concept of coca **addiction** was discovered and the plant began developing the significance (and reputation) it now has in much of the world. The crop continued to be incredibly fruitful, because unlike more traditional crops such as maize and potatoes, coca takes no care, grows on the steep fields of the Andes, and produces six harvests per year. Furthermore, by the mid-1970s, consumption of cocaine, especially in the United States, created an incredible market for the plant. Today, Peru and Bolivia produce the second- and third-most of this **oro blanco** (white gold) in the world, respectively. (Colombia holds the current title.)

Nations such as the United States now spend billions of dollars each year on the war against drugs. However, in fighting this battle, these powerful nations tend to forget that highly profitable coca production is the only way for many *indígenas* to make a living. The **Plan Colombia,** in which the United States has promised to fund the Colombian military with over 1 billion dollars to fight its country's cocaine industry, will very likely affect its neighbors, Peru, Bolivia, and Ecuador.

INDIGENOUS IDENTITY

INDIGENOUS PERU

The majority of Peru's indigenous people come from the highland Andean regions in the central and southern parts of the country. They number approximately nine million, or 38% of Peru's total population. Of indigenous people in the highlands, 30% speak **Quechua** and 22% speak **Aymara** (or local variations of these languages). Both Aymara and Quechua are officially recognized languages of the government in areas where they are predominantly spoken, but Spanish is the official national language. Social prejudice in society leads many indigenous people to resort to speaking their native tongue at home, while speaking Spanish in public. There are clear differences between the indigenous people of the Andes and the coastal region from those indigenous of the **Amazon.** All have different languages, customs, and lifestyles, and, because they lived in relative isolation for many centuries, even neighboring tribes are likely to have little in common. Traditionally, the Andean peoples were referred to by outsiders as "indios," while those from the Amazon were referred to as "savages." As in many societies in Latin America, most of the indigenous people of Peru are in the lowest socio-economic and political tier. Most earn their incomes from agricultural work, mining, and heavy industrial labor. Illiteracy is high; they are often taught in Spanish (not their native tongue) and the school year is not coordinated with the agricultural labor cycle.

From 1919 until 1930, the government modernized the economy and tried to include indigenous groups in the market. In 1926, 59 indigenous communities were officially recognized; this number steadily increased throughout the next several decades. In 1958, the first indigenous union was formed to mobilize against the selling of indigenous territories. During the 1960s many Quechua speakers protested the government through marches and various acts of vandalism. Since 1969, indigenous people have been given autonomy regarding internal organization and the administration of their own communities. In 1979, the Peruvian constitution was reformed to include the protection of all ethnicities in the country and recognize the right of people to adhere to their own "cultural identities." By the 1980s, peasant organizations had formed, composed of both Indians and non-Indians, as a form of grassroots mobilization against agrarian reform and development of indigenous lands. These include the **Peasant Confederation of Peru** and the **National Agrarian Confederation,** which offer small loans and credit to indigenous farmers.

Despite the political gains of the last few decades, the indigenous people of Peru still suffer from widespread discrimination and, at times, outright persecution by *mestizos* or Peruvians of European descent.

INDIGENOUS BOLIVIA

With the greatest percentage of indigenous population in South America (over 50%), one might infer that Bolivia is well-integrated. In a way, it is; skin color and actual nationality matter much less than education and lifestyle when it comes to acceptance. Unfortunately, the 4.1 million indigenous people of Bolivia rarely have opportunities to acquire the education and money necessary to afford the lifestyle of *"gente decente/refinado,"* those in the upper class. Bolivian *indígenas* can be easily separated into two main categories: highland and lowland. The highland Indians are primarily Quechua-speakers (30%) and Aymara-speakers (25%), while the lowlanders have many dialects, the most common being Panoan, Tacanan, Moxoan, and Guaranian. Bolivia's indigenous are similar to those of Peru, both in structure (highland/lowland groups) and in subsequent socioeconomic ranks.

Bolivia's indigenous population formed its first national organizations in the 1940s and 1950s, though these early unions had little chance of effecting change; upper-class landowners controlled over 92% of Bolivia's land by the 50s, and 1953 Agrarian Reform Laws which granted Indian suffrage and citizenship only served to attempt assimilation of indigenous peoples.

The **CSUTCB** (Unitary Union Confederation of Bolivian Workers and Peasants), **MITKA** (Tupac Katari Indigenous Movement), and **MRTK** (Tupac Katari Revolutionary Movement) began to exercise independent operation in the 1970s and 80s, and though little was first accomplished, the late 1980s incited a new, more effective round of indigenous representation, possibly beginning with the consecutive mayoral elections of Aymaran Carlos Palenque (of the CONDEPA party) as mayor of La Paz and El Alto. In 1992, Bolivian President Paz Zamora granted over 1 million hectares of land to the indigenous population, and Agrarian Laws today continue to disperse millions of hectares of land to its indigenous peoples. Unfortunately, much of Bolivia's land is being exploited by foreign oil and mining companies, and the issue continues to be a major one among the indigenous.

Also a major issue is the Bolivian military's organized destruction of coca fields; funded by United States anti-drug efforts, their aim is to combat Bolivia's illegal **coca market** (the country is third in the world in cocaine production), but along with the destruction of crops comes destruction of many indigenous farmers' livelihoods. In 1999, cocaine exports profited more than all legal Bolivian exports, and one in five *indígenas* was believed to be somehow dependent on its profits. To compensate, large amounts of foreign aid (intended for the promotion of alternate crops and exports) accompany the coca eradication projects.

INDIGENOUS ECUADOR

Each of Ecuador's indigenous groups has a distinct ethnic identity, and many members identify more strongly with their ethnicity than with the Ecuadorian state. Indeed, until the middle of the 20th century, the government mainly catered to the needs of the white and *mestizo* majority of its population. Exploitation of *indígena* labor, begun in colonial times, continued after Independence until a more liberal government in the early 1900s made a move to incorporate *indígenas* into the national community. In the name of fighting for equality, the liberals attempted to pass legislation that would free *indígenas* from ties to the church or private landholders by dissolving their communal holdings. However, some interpreted this as an attempt by politicians to claim indigenous land and labor for themselves. Indigenous groups resisted these measures, and in 1937 two laws were enacted to reinforce indigenous rights to own land communally.

One of Ecuador's most successful and well-known indigenous groups founded the **Shuar Federation** in response to new pressures from outside forces (including missionaries, colonists from the highlands, and later, oil companies). The Shuar organized into groups of about 30 families, called *centros*, which hold land communally in order to prevent the breakup and loss of indigenous property. They have also instituted a health care program and radio schooling system independent from the government. Their new practices have helped the Shuar prosper financially while maintaining their ethnic identity.

Attempts by the state to integrate local, ethnic identities into a national one have met resistance. Some groups recognize a government agenda behind such events and criticize them as fictionalized versions of indigenous culture. One example is Otavalo's festival of Yamor, boycotted by a group of *indígenas* in 1983 and 1984. Originally a celebration of the corn harvest, the tourism industry had begun promoting it with parades and fireworks.

Indígenas have developed a number of organizations to voice their desires and complaints. In 1989, these groups came together under an umbrella organization called the **Confederation of Indigenous Nationalities of Ecuador** or **CONAIE** (http://conaie.nativeweb.org/brochure.html). In 1990, CONAIE organized the largest indigenous uprising in Ecuador's history, paralyzing the country for a week. Their rallying cry, "500 years of resistance and survival," protested the upcoming 1992 quincentenary celebration of Columbus's landing in the Americas. Their agenda included demands to help create a satisfactory relationship between *indígenas* and the state, including more indigenous autonomy and a proposed constitutional amendment making Ecuador a multinational state. The interim government (which ruled in place of ousted Bucarám) joined forces with CONAIE to establish **The People's Mandate,** in which a National Constituent Assembly of 400 was presented as an alternative governing body. In January 1998, the assembly released a suggested new constitution for Ecuador, its demands resonating with those of the original 1990 declaration. Not all of CONAIE's suggestions were adopted in the new constitution that went into effect in August 1998, and in March 1999, CONAIE led an 11-day *levantamiento* (uprising) against the Mahuad regime.

In January 2000, Mahuad was ousted after 5000 CONAIE-led (and military-supported) Indians marched to Lima, overtook Congress, and demanded his resignation. Their immediate concern was Mahuad's plan to dollarize the Ecuadorian currency (which they believe will only increase the gap between rich and poor), but CONAIE leaders believed Mahuad would not make many of the changes they believed necessary to indigenous well-being. They replaced him with General Carlos Mendoza, though upon international pressure against a military government, Mahuad's vice-president, Gustavo Noboa, was put in office. CONAIE and many Ecuadorians are unhappy about this change, however, as Noboa has continued many of Mahuad's policies (see p. 426 for more information). This next year will be a test of Noboa's ability to pull Ecuador through its economic and political woes—perhaps the bigger struggle will be staying in office.

HISTORY

THE EARLIEST INHABITANTS

While the Inca culture has left the most visible mark on the region today, earlier pre-Hispanic civilizations thrived in the area long before the Incas arrived. Archeological evidence shows that the earliest cultures lived over 12,000 years ago in the coastal regions of present-day Peru and Ecuador. In general, the ancient coastal inhabitants were hunter-gatherers and fishermen whose descendants gradually learned to practice sustainable agriculture. Auspicious ocean currents and winds made the coast ideal for farming, and for 8000 years industrious settlements thrived there. There are few remains from these early civilizations, so little is known of them today. The oldest extensive archeological findings are from the **Valdivia** culture, a people who lived along the coast of Ecuador's Santa Elena Peninsula roughly between 3500 and 1500 BC. The earliest known site is **Loma Alta,** where impressive pottery and female figurines were produced as early as 3500 BC. Another ancient town, **Real Alto,** reached its peak by 1500 BC. The site is scattered with more female figurines and remnants of over 100 households. Villages consisted of wood and straw huts arranged in a semi-circle around a central plaza, paved with shells for ceremonial purposes. By the variety of the materials used in their construction, these sites suggest the existence of trade networks connecting the coast, highlands, and jungle.

Other cultures also arose in the coastal areas over time, including the **Esmeralda, Manta, Huancavilca, Puná, Paracas, Mochica, Nasca,** and **Chimú** tribes. These groups also traded with tribes from the sierra, and as they eventually developed oceanic travel, trans-coastal trade became increasingly important. Several of these groups left remarkable accomplishments. The Nasca are famous for the gigantic, cryptic etchings they left on the dry soil of southern Peru (see p. 142), as well as for the high quality of their pottery. The Mochica of Northern Peru constructed lofty pyramids to their gods and an extensive irrigation system that allowed an otherwise barren valley to sustain a population of more than 50,000. In the same region, the Chimú built the great city of Chan Chan, which still stands outside Trujillo and was also once home to about 50,000 residents. The **Tiahuanuco** empire, having spanned Bolivia, Peru, Chile, and Argentina, disappeared mysteriously in AD 1172. Farther north, **La Tolita,** a civilization that reached its peak around 700 BC, produced some of the most remarkable gold work known from Ecuador, most notably the famous mask of the Sun god whose image is frequently replicated in Ecuadorian literature and culture. Slowly, these early coastal cultures expanded and developed, creating a background against which later cultures would flourish.

By about the first century AD, various erstwhile coastal tribes had moved into the Andes region. These sedentary and mainly agricultural tribes—among them the **Pasto, Cara, Quitu, Cañari, Palta, Chavín, Huari,** and **Paititi**—used irrigation to cultivate corn, quinoa, beans, many varieties of potatoes and squash, and fruits such as pineapples and avocados. Local chieftains raised armies, distributed communal lands, and united different villages in political confederations headed by a single monarch. Several of these highland cultures have left lasting impressions on the region. The Cañari culture, which occupied the Cuenca region of southern Ecuador, developed an extensive irrigation system that came to support large cities and a military strong enough to fiercely resist the Inca expansion of the 15th century. In the Ancash region of northern Peru, the Chavín culture diffused its own set of ideas, rituals, and religious art across a fairly extensive empire. They are best known for their stylized religious iconography, which included depictions of various animals—particularly the jaguar. These early cultures persisted and maintained their autonomy for over 1000 years, but that independence was destined to end with the rise of an overwhelmingly powerful military force based in the southern sierra.

THE INCA EMPIRE

The Inca culture made a more extensive and profound impact on the region than did any other pre-Hispanic society. With meager beginnings as a small tribe centered around **Cusco** (or *Qosqo* in the Inca tongue of Quechua) in southern Peru, the Inca Empire expanded rapidly in the mid-15th century; within a century, it controlled nearly one-third of South America and more than 10 million people. In the process of expanding their empire from its capital in Cusco, the Incas moved north through Peru and into Ecuador in the late 15th century. The Inca conquest was executed mostly under the leadership of the warrior **Pachacuti Inca Yupanqui** (1438-71). Several tribes, including the Cañari from southern Ecuador, met the Inca troops with fierce resistance, and it took nearly four decades before both the sierra and coastal populations surrendered. **Huayna Cápac,** grandson of Pachacuti Inca Yupanqui and son of a Cañari princess, became ruler of the entire extended Inca empire, **Tawantinsuya** ("four corners" in Quechua), which spanned from present-day Northern Chile to what is now Southern Colombia.

A few aspects of life among the conquered tribes, such as their traditional religious beliefs, were left largely intact, but most areas of society were significantly changed by the conquering Incas. In addition to new foods (such as yucca, sweet potatoes, and peanut) and agricultural techniques (such as irrigation and terracing, in a planned exportation known as the *mitmaq* system), new land-ownership patterns were also introduced by the Incas. Instead of the previous system of private ownership, land became property of the Inca emperor (referred to as "the Inca") and was divided up into units for collective farming by **ayllu,** kinship-based clans. Each *ayllu* consisted of a number of individual families who, though allowed to consume a portion of their produce, were required to give tribute payments to an Inca **kuraka,** or chieftain.

Huayna Cápac grew up in the area occupied by modern-day Ecuador. Enamored of his homeland, he named Quito the second capital of the Inca empire. Fearful of unrest in his ever-expanding kingdom, he traveled all over the empire putting down uprisings and strengthening unions whenever he could—sometimes by marriage, other times by replacing troublesome populations with colonists from more peaceful parts of the empire. These colonizations helped spread the traditional Inca language of Quechua, which is still widely spoken today in many indigenous communities throughout Peru and Ecuador (now called "Quichua" in the latter).

Huayna Cápac's sudden death in 1526 (possibly from measles introduced by European explorers) brought on a bitter power struggle that became a devastating civil war. Rather than leaving the empire to one heir, he split the kingdom between two sons: Cusco and the southern empire were left to **Huáscar,** a son by Huayna Cápac's sister and therefore the legitimate heir; while Ecuador and the northern empire went to **Atahuallpa,** born by a lesser wife but his father's favorite. In 1532, Atahuallpa decisively defeated Huáscar near Riobamba in central Ecuador. Though the civil war was over, the Inca empire was left weakened and divided, unprepared for the arrival of the Spanish conquistadors a few months later.

THE SPANISH CONQUEST

As the Inca empire thrived in South America, Spain was rising in prominence and power in the New World. After pillaging and subjecting the peoples of Mexico and Central America, Spanish *conquistadores* moved south to the vast continent beyond. One of these conquerors was **Francisco Pizarro,** who had become a rich *encomendero* (landowner) in Panamá after leading the conquest of Nicaragua in 1522. Starting in 1524, he began leading several financed expeditions to the west coast of South America. After several failed journeys, Pizarro solicited King Carlos I for more funding and manpower from Spain. His request was granted, and the reinforced Spanish troops landed on the shores of northern Peru late in 1531. They reached Tumbes in mid-1532, where Pizarro left **Sebastián de Benalcázar**—who would later lead the conquest of Ecuador—to develop the Spanish base of San Miguel. Although the Incas received news of the foreigners' arrival, they failed to realize the threat they represented.

Fueled by stories of great Inca riches, Pizarro pushed inland to Cajamarca, the Inca summer residence in the highlands of northern Peru. He arrived in November 1532, and immediately demanded an audience with recently victorious Inca ruler **Atahuallpa,** who was resting in the Baños del Inca thermal baths (see p. 219). Accompanied by several thousand troops, Atahuallpa met the Spanish explorers in the plaza of Cajamarca. There, he was confronted by a priest, who ordered him to renounce his gods and swear allegiance to the King of Spain. He refused and threw a Spanish prayer book to the ground, an offense that inflamed the tempers of the Spanish soldiers surrounding the plaza. They opened fire on the Inca envoy, killing several thousand of Atahuallpa's men and taking the Inca emperor captive. Atahuallpa feared that the Spanish planned to depose him in favor of his brother, so he ordered the execution of Huáscar along with several hundred military leaders and members of the ruling family. Ironically, this action further weakened the Inca empire and facilitated the Spanish conquest in the months and years to come. According to legend, Pizarro offered to free Atahuallpa if he could raise a **King's ransom,** filling his prison cell once with gold and twice with silver (yielding a total of nearly 15,000kg of precious metals). Atahuallpa complied, but instead of releasing him, the Spanish held a mock trial that called for the Inca emperor's execution.

The strength and cohesion of the Inca nation died with Atahuallpa. Nevertheless, some Inca warriors continued to defend their empire. In Quito, the general **Rumiñahui,** with the help of Cañari tribesmen from southern Ecuador, engaged in a struggle with the Spanish. Sebastián de Benalcázar, one of Pizarro's lieutenants, defeated Rumiñahui near Mount Chimborazo and began pushing the Incas north. In mid-1534, when Rumiñahui realized that the Spaniards would soon conquer Quito, he set it ablaze, preferring to destroy this secondary Inca capital rather than surrender it to the conquistadors. Quito was refounded by the Spaniards on **December 6, 1534,** a day still celebrated with parades, bullfights, and dances in the modern city.

Meanwhile, the Spanish initiated a march of conquest on the Inca capital of Cusco. To aid in their assault, they enlisted the support of other native groups eager to end years of subjugation by the Incas. Even Manco Capac II, half-brother of the slain Inca leader, agreed to collaborate with the Spanish after Pizarro promised to install Manco as the ruling Inca. Eventually Manco realized that he was little more than a puppet, and instigated an indigenous revolt against his erstwhile ally in 1536. Though they had superior numbers, the Inca forces were unable to eject the conquistadors, and set their sacred capital ablaze in desperation. Following his defeat, Manco Capac II retreated to Vilcabamba, a town deep in the rugged Andean interior, and established an Inca kingdom that would remain autonomous and continue to resist Spanish rule until 1572.

THE COLONIAL ERA

After the Conquest, Pizarro assumed the role of governor of **New Castile,** as the area was first known. Unfortunately, he had neither the vision nor the ability to establish a peaceful society, and fighting and civil strife prevailed. During this time, the native population was grossly exploited, serving as a slave labor force for **encomenderos,** conquistadors given control of the land and (in exchange for Christianizing them) its residents. These *encomenderos* created huge plantations for themselves on land obtained by making deals with the *kurakas* (local chieftains). The *kurakas* acquiesced to the more powerful Spaniards and agreed to hand over their *ayllu*'s tribute payments, supposedly in exchange for the order brought by Spanish Christianity. The era of *encomiendas* was one of extreme civil unrest, with fighting between *indígenas* and colonists as well as violent power struggles among the Spanish landowners.

Originally, Peru, Bolivia, and Ecuador were part of the **Viceroyalty of Peru,** administered by the *audencia* (high court) and *cabildo* (municipal court) in Lima. As the colonial population grew, the *audencia* in Lima could no longer exert adequate control over its sprawling area of responsibility, so in 1563 the **Audencia de Quito** was established. This allowed Spain to better exercise its control of the entire region and finally bring a civil order that would last for several centuries. In

1720, in a further attempt to tighten Spanish control over the colonies, Ecuador was made part of the **Viceroyalty of Nueva Granada,** and central authority shifted from Lima to Bogotá, Colombia. The viceroy and *audencias* enforced the New Laws of 1542, which officially abolished slave labor and *encomiendas*, though both continued throughout most of the colonial period. Later viceroys established a social system known as the *repartamiento de indios*, which made the entire indigenous population vassals of the Spanish crown. They also introduced the *mita*, a system of forced labor that required all men between the ages of 18 and 50 to work for the Spanish crown for at least two months each year. Overseen by *corregidores*, new Spanish officials in charge of administering the *mita*, *mitayos* (workers) labored on huge agricultural *haciendas* or in *obrajes* (primitive textile sweatshops). As treacherous as the *mita* was for Ecuadorian workers, they were fortunate relative to their Peruvian counterparts (including those residents of Upper Peru, which would soon become the Republic of Bolivia). In Peru, where there were much heftier deposits of valuable minerals, miner *mitayos* experienced even more brutal conditions in the dark and dangerous quarries. The largest threat to the *indígenas*, however, was disease. **Smallpox** and **measles** brought by the colonists virtually wiped out the coastal population and drastically reduced the population of the sierras, especially during an epidemic in the 1690s. In the first century of Spanish rule, the indigenous population of the area was reduced by 80%, plummeting from over 20 million to around four million.

RELIGION

One important repercussion of the Spanish Conquest was the conversion of the *indígenas* to **Catholicism.** The earliest colonists were granted the labor of indigenous groups by the Spanish monarchy on the condition that they convert them to Christianity before working them to death. The Spanish justified this cruelty by reasoning that they had saved the *indígenas'* souls before they took their lives. As indigenous labor became more scarce, missionaries headed into the wilderness and established missions there. This often resulted in peaceful conversion, but conquistador landowners often used the newly blazed trails to enslave and exploit the native populations. Today's Peru, Bolivia, and Ecuador, like the rest of Latin America, have mostly Roman Catholic populations. As a result of missionary activities during this century, a small percentage of the population is also **Protestant.** Even modern-day missions can be quite coercive, offering medical services or other aid only to those who visit their churches. In recent years, **Mormon** and **Seventh Day Adventist** missionaries have been traveling to the region in ever greater numbers.

In many cases, the indigenous populations have not given up their own traditions but have simply incorporated Catholicism into their earlier belief systems. The resulting **hybrid religions** intertwine identities of indigenous gods and spirits with those of Christian saints. Indigenous celebrations are now often held on Saints' Days; for instance, the June 24 festival of St. John the Baptist is thought to have replaced the Inca festival of Inti Raymi, held on the summer solstice. In other cases, a given situation (e.g. an illness) requires an offering to a certain saint instead of to an indigenous spirit. Other traditions have remained completely distinct from Catholicism. Many indigenous peoples in the Andes still worship mountains, which they believe are the homes of mighty spirits (or *apus*) that control fertility and the rain. In addition, **shamans** (*curanderos* in Spanish) are often called upon to cure the sick.

CUSTOMS AND MANNERS

Traveling in the region of Peru, Bolivia, and Ecuador, it doesn't take long to figure out that local customs and manners aren't always what you're used to. No one bats an eye when an elderly woman spits a huge blob on a public bus, but a traveler might be frowned upon for having a stubbly beard. The people you encounter will pay particular attention to you, as a foreigner, and you'll be more likely to earn their respect if you take a moment to familiarize yourself with their social norms.

Foreign visitors are often shocked by the overwhelming **machismo** in some parts of Latin America. Women in bars—and foreign women in general—are often regarded as lascivious. Females who drink and act rowdy, or even just express their opinions, will shock men who prize meekness in women. Whether you're male or female, be sensitive to rising testosterone levels. Never say anything about a man's mother, sister, wife, or girlfriend.

Personal hygiene and **appearance** are often difficult to maintain while traveling, but they are very important in Peru, Bolivia, and Ecuador. Your appearance affects how you are treated by locals: clean-shaven men with short hair and women who don't show much skin are more likely to receive respect than scruffies and smellies or women without bras. Men should remove hats when entering a building.

Punctuality isn't as important as it is in Europe and the US (as that bus schedule will quickly confirm), but there are, of course, limits. A different perspective on time is apparent during meals, which are rarely hurried. After a big meal, enjoy the ingenious tradition of *siesta*, a time in the afternoon when it's just too hot to do anything but relax, have a drink, or nap; don't expect much to happen during the mid-afternoon, as banks and shops often shut their doors. Latin Americans hold **politeness** in high esteem, both in acquaintances and strangers. Jaded travelers who consider urban indifference the highest virtue need to adjust if they expect to be treated with respect. When meeting someone for the first time, shake hands firmly, look the person in the eye, and say *"Mucho gusto de conocerle"* ("Pleased to meet you"). When entering a room, greet everybody, not just the person you came to see. Females often greet each other with a peck on the cheek or a quick hug. Sometimes men shake hands with women in a business situation, but the standard greeting between a man and a woman—even if they are meeting for the first time—is a quick kiss on the cheek.

Salutations in passing are considered common courtesy in small towns, particularly in the Oriente. *"Buenos días"* in the morning, *"buenas tardes"* after noon, and *"buenas noches"* after nightfall should be said to almost anyone with whom you come into contact. This charming Latin American custom epitomizes a general feeling of *amistad* on the streets, even between strangers. A similar custom is saying *"buen provecho"* ("enjoy your meal") to everyone in a restaurant upon entering or leaving. The American "OK" symbol (a circle with the thumb and forefinger) is considered vulgar and offensive—move your hand rapidly toward and away from yourself, and you'll understand why. Finally, be sensitive when taking **photographs.** If you must take pictures of locals, first ask permission—they may object strongly to being photographed.

FOOD

From conventional standbys to exotic local dishes, Peru, Bolivia, and Ecuador satisfy people of all tastes. The fruits encountered here are some of the most succulent in the world. Distinctive grains and tubers abound, and a plethora of vegetables are cultivated and cooked. As for meat, just about any animal—and any part of its body—is considered fair game, from hoof to heart, tentacle to testicle. For the most part, your culinary experience will be determined by the region you're in and the type of restaurant you choose to visit.

Eating in a hotel or in a pricier restaurant allows you to sample finely prepared cuisine native to regions other than the one you're visiting, as well as hard-to-find desserts like the exquisite *dulce tres leches* (three-milk dessert). But chances are you'll do most of your eating in small, family-owned local diners, sometimes referred to as **comedores.** Unequivocally the most economical way to acquire your daily sustenance, and certainly the most popular way to eat out among locals, is to order the **menú del día** (meal of the day) that most *comedores* offer. Sometimes referred to as *el almuerzo* (lunch) during the day or *la merienda* or *la cena* (dinner) at night, this is a set platter, usually with two courses and various extras. It is prepared in advance and served at a special price (US$1-3). The first course consists of soup; you may be served a succulent *chupe de pescado* (a popular fish and vegetable soup), a hearty *caldo de res* (beef stew), *caldo de patas* (pig- or cow-hoof stew), or *llunca* (wheat soup). The second course (*segundo* or *plato fuerte*) is almost always based upon some kind of *carne* (meat), often smothered in a savory sauce appealing to the tastes of the locals. Popular traditional *platos fuertes* include *lomo saltado* (a stir-fried meat dish), *seco de pollo* (a thick chicken stew), *chicharrón* (deep-fried meats, usually pork), and *pescado sudado* (traditionally flavored steamed fish; mainly eaten along the coast), *charqui* (dried pork) or *picante de cuy* (spicy guinea pig). Along with the *carne* generally comes rice, fried potatoes, vegetables, or *menestre* (lentils or beans). Occasionally you'll luck into *choclo* (large-kernel native corn), yucca, a *tamal* (like a tamale), or an *humita* (also like a tamale; sometimes sweet). Fancier restaurants sometimes offer a *menú del día* as well, always at significantly higher prices, often with extras like coffee, dessert, cloth napkins, and uniformed waiters. If the *menú del día* doesn't do the trick, check out the menu for **a la carte** selections. These will almost always cost more and provide less nourishment, but sometimes it's worth the extra cash to be able to choose your own meal.

To diversify your diet you may decide to dine at three other types of restaurants that are both inexpensive and abundant. **Chifas** (Chinese restaurants), present in even the smallest of towns, are generally very clean and serve scrumptious and filling *chaufas* (fried-rice dishes) and *tallarines* (noodle dishes). **Parilladas** (grills) serve meat—and nothing but meat—of all kinds: steak, pork chop, liver, and more unusual but very popular cuts such as intestine, tripe, udder, heart, and blood sausage. **Cevicherías** (sometimes called *picanterías* in Peru) serve seafood, especially ceviche (or *cebiche*), a popular dish made from raw seafood marinated in lemon and lime juice (whose acids partly cook the meat), with cilantro and onion (served extra spicy in Peru). Larger and more touristed cities also offer all the fast food, international food, and vegetarian options you're accustomed to at home.

Of course, ceviche and blood sausage just don't satisfy first thing in the morning. Luckily, breakfast food can be found in most any *comedor*, though *desayuno* (breakfast) is usually light. Most common are bread, juice, coffee, eggs, and sometimes rice and beans, as well as plantain dishes such as *chirriados* in certain regions. Well-touristed areas may offer a *desayuno americano*, which includes a bit more food for voracious American appetites. If you don't mind a light breakfast or want a midday snack, a quick and easy way to grab a bite is to buy fruit at the local **mercado** (market): papayas, passion fruit, avocados, tangerines, pineapples, tamarinds, *naranjilla*, and *tomate de árbol* are just a few of the possibilities. Or visit a **panadería** (bakery): *empanadas de queso* (bread stuffed with cheese), *pan dulce* (sugar-coated rolls), and *pan de sal* (salted rolls) all go unbelievably cheap.

TRADITIONAL FOODS

PERU. Most dishes popular in Ecuador or Bolivia can be found in Peru and vice-versa, but some foods are more particular to one country or the other. Peru has a culinary history equaled in richness only by its assortment of delectable **desserts:** *picarones* (deep-fried bread in a golden syrup); *mazamorra* (a sweet purple pudding); *helado de lúcuma* (ice cream made with a local fruit); and, in Lima, *suspiro de limeña* ("sigh of a Liman woman," made with sugar and condensed milk). But resist, if you can, the temptation to skip right to the sweets. Start instead with the ubiquitous **papas a la huancaína** (potatoes covered in a special creamy sauce). Originating in Huancayo, this simple but delicious dish is wildly popular throughout most of the country. Another light and simple plate loved by locals is **palta rellena,** consisting of an avocado stuffed with a chicken and vegetable mix. For something a bit heartier, try **anticuchos de corazón** (kabob of cow heart). Equally scrumptious is **encocado de mariscos** (seafood in coconut milk), often served in a coconut shell. Peruvians also enjoy a good plate of *cuy* (see Ecuador, below). If you don't have the cash to eat these relative delicacies, sample a **bistec a lo pobre,** "poor man's steak," mixed with bananas and egg. Maximally filling and a perennial side dish is the national specialty, **tacu-tacu,** a dense mix of mashed beans and rice served with anything and everything: don't leave Peru without trying it.

BOLIVIA. Bolivians are exceptional meat eaters. Nearly every restaurant serves up a basic *menú* involving some sort of meat—unless you're a vegetarian, expect every meal to be rich with chicken, pork, beef, or fish. People here break out the meat even before their breakfast **pañuelos** (doughnut-like pastries) and **pasteles** (fried dough stuffed with cheese) settle. Sidewalk stands and restaurants alike cater to the throngs of business people, market-goers, and tourists that come in search of a mid-morning **salteña**—a small, pouch-like pastry (similar to an *empañada*) filled with any combination of spicy beef or chicken, eggs, potatoes, or onions. Certain regional specialties test even the most adventurous carnivores, such as Oruro's local favorite—**sheep's head,** served boiled *(cabeza)* or fully baked *(rostros asados)*. A variety of other meat dishes come fried, such as **chicharrón** (fried chicken or pork), especially popular in the altiplano. Vegetarian options are fairly hard to find, although the larger cities have their share of vegetarian restaurants. The popular breakfast drink, **api** (a thick, chunky drink made from corn), can be found in markets, while chocolate, rich pastries, and ice cream fill dessert menus countrywide.

ECUADOR. Tronquito (bull penis) and **yaguarlocro** (soup with blood-sprinklings) are among Ecuador's most exotic (and erotic) dishes. Equally shocking to foreigners but extremely popular among locals is the mouth-watering delicacy known as **cuy** (guinea pig). A specialty dating back to Inca times, the dish gets its name from the sound the animal makes just before getting skewered and roasted: "cuy, cuy, cuy...." The more vegetarian-friendly **llapingachos** (Andean potato and cheese pancakes) also date back to ancient times and get their name from the sound the potatoes make when being boiled and mashed: "llapingacho, llapingacho, llapingacho...." Andean natives really know their potatoes, first cultivated in the Andes before becoming a starch staple the world over. Perhaps the easiest way to get your daily intake of non-meat foods, though, is to order a few of the myriad banana and plantain dishes that constitute a mainstay of the *costeño* (coast-dweller) diet. **Patacones** (deep fried plantain slices) are a favorite side dish, divine as an accompaniment to ceviche.

DRINK

If urgent visits to the nearest restroom are not your idea of fun, avoid drinking tap water. Water advertised as **purificada** (purified) may have only been passed through a filter, which does not necessarily catch all of those diarrhea-causing demons. Water that has been boiled or treated with **iodine** is safe to drink; otherwise, **bottled water** is best. Make sure the cap is sealed and wipe the rim before taking a sip.

Sweeter, more effervescent options also abound. Popular soft drinks, always called *colas*, include the worldwide brands Coca-Cola, Sprite, and Fanta, as well as **Fioravanti** in Ecuador (with strawberry, apple, and pineapple flavors) and **Inka Kola** (see An Uncommon Kola, below). **Juices** made from the region's abundance of exotic fruits are common and delicious, but almost always made with water; before drinking up, make sure the water used was purified. **Coffee** is not as good as it should be, considering that the beans come from the region. It is usually served as *esencia* (boiled-down, concentrated grinds mixed with water or milk). You might also be served hot water with a can of Nescafé instant coffee. **Milk** is also readily available, but is much creamier than the low-fat milk to which many foreigners may be accustomed. A favorite dairy drink is **yogur,** a cold drink made with thin, sweetened yogurt, often flavored with fruit. Before downing a tall, cold glass, however, make sure it's been pasteurized.

If you're looking for something a bit more intoxicating, sample a local lager. **Cristal** and **Cusqueña** abound in Peru; try some Bolivian **Paceña,** said by some to be the best on the continent; **Pilsener** and **Club** predominate in Ecuador. One of these beers will set you back a fraction of a US dollar—at these prices, why hold back? If you really want to drown your sorrows, liquor is readily available at almost every corner store at absurdly cheap prices (around US$2 for a liter of decent rum). If you wish to imbibe in a nice bar or restaurant, prices rise dramatically.

AN UNCOMMON KOLA The fluorescent yellow glow envelops the country; the sweet, sweet aroma of bubble gum crowds small restaurants. As any visitor to Peru will soon discover, the omnipresent Inka Kola is more than a soda; it's a national symbol. After hitting the markets in 1935, Inka Kola has dominated Peruvian soda culture for over 61 years, never once altering its secret, fruity, "lemon-glass" formula. The overwhelming, artificial drink may be an acquired taste, but it instills a sense of national pride in the many Peruvians who gulp it by the liter. In fact, Peru is one of the few countries where Coca-Cola is challenged as the number one soft drink. (Most Inka Kola officials claim that they dominate the market, while, not surprisingly, the folks at Coke say that their product's slightly in the lead.)

This inter-cola competition took on a new flavor in the mid-nineties, when the Coca-Cola Corporation purchased fifty percent of Inka Kola from original owner J.R. Lindley, and another twenty percent from the bottler. Coke officials attempted to appease disgruntled Peruvians by promising not to change Inka Kola in any way—instead, they pledged to spread Peru's national drink throughout the world. Now, several years later, advertisements affirm that Inka Kola remains the "national drink of Peru." But, true to Coca-Cola's word, it also shows up in several other Latin American countries, in Europe and Japan, and in 18 of the United States. Look for it in a *tienda* near you.

Many a tasty drink is made from **aguardiente,** an extremely potent sugarcane alcohol. **Caneliza,** made by boiling water, aguardiente, cinnamon, and lemon juice, will warm your insides on cool, misty highland evenings. Another enticing intoxicant is Peru's **pisco,** a clear, white grape brandy with a tequila-like kick. You'll most often find it in the form of a pisco sour, a mixed drink made with pisco, lemon juice, and sugar. In the valleys surrounding Tarija, Bolivia, **singani** reigns supreme; made from white grapes, this powerful liquor packs more of a wallop than its weaker wine relative. And then, of course, there's the omnipresent **chicha,** a liquor made from the yucca plant and fermented with the saliva of the women who brewed it. Look for it in houses that fly white or red flags over their doors. **Non-alcoholic chichas** (also non-saliva) come in myriad varieties throughout the region. Especially popular in Peru is **chicha morrada,** a sweet purple beverage made from corn.

THE ARTS

Peruvian, Bolivian, and Ecuadorian arts reveal a complex blend of influences—indigenous and European, ancient and modern. The legacy was laid down by the Incas and other pre-Hispanic groups through **artesanía** (arts and crafts) and distinctive Andean music. When the Spanish arrived, the artistic influences and technology of the Old World mixed with indigenous art styles. In particular, the religious art so well known in the Old World developed a distinct new style, and this region's art followed more and more trends. Indigenous artisans, combining ancient and modern techniques, began making products for an international market. A number of talented painters, in touch with worldwide artistic currents, started producing modern art with South American subject matter. Today's Peruvian, Ecuadorian, and Bolivian art scenes are as active as ever, and numerous museums, festivals, and markets celebrate the countries' artistic traditions.

ARTESANÍA

Crafts of all kinds are produced in Peru, Bolivia, and Ecuador, but the region is best known for its large variety of **handmade textiles,** almost all of which are produced by various indigenous groups.

In Peru, the best textiles can be found in the highlands, particularly in the **Ayacucho** area (known for its weavings) and in **Huancayo** and the surrounding **Río Mantaro** region. On **Lake Titicaca,** the **Isla Taquile** is the place to go for famous fine-spun products. The most common medium is wool, whether from sheep (generally referred to simply as *lana*, sometimes as *lana de oveja*), llama, or alpaca. Occasionally, soft *vicuña* wool is also used; however, because *vicuña* are extremely difficult to raise domestically, their wool is rare and quite expensive. In addition to the practical items of clothing that many tourists buy as protection from the cold, artisans sell a wide selection of tapestries with scenes of the mountains or local life.

Bolivia's best-known textiles might be the woven goods of the **Tarabuco** and **Jalq'a** peoples, whose crafts can be found and purchased in and around Sucre, in Bolivia's southern region (for more information on the Jalq'a, see p. 336). Bolivia's **Lake Titicaca** territory hosts an array of straw and reed crafts, and La Paz's **Mercado de Brujos** sells more than everything a souvenir-shopper could want, including the customary alpacas and tapestries as well as llama fetuses and coca tea.

In Ecuador, the most prolific and well-known center of textile production is **Otavalo**, an indigenous community 96km north of Quito. *Otavaleños* have been in the textile business for centuries. When the Incas conquered the area in the late 15th century, they forced the inhabitants to pay tribute with their textiles. A few decades later, the Spanish brought new technologies in the forms of treadle looms and hand carders, and new materials like silk and sheep's wool. Under one guise or another, they forced the *indígenas* to work under horrible conditions in *obrajes* (textile workshops) well into the 19th century. In the early 1900s, the *otavaleños* got their start in the modern textile industry by producing imitations of British tweeds (called *casimires*). Since then, the region has continued to produce quality textiles, with almost all production taking place in indigenous households. Most weaving is done with the treadle loom, but some families still use the backstrap loom, a pre-Hispanic design, with one end attached to the weaver's back. All kinds of indigenous products, from ponchos to belts and tapestries, are exported to markets around the world.

A major center for **leatherwork** exists in **Cotacachi**, Ecuador, just north of Otavalo. Wallets, purses, belts, whips, and even leather underwear can all be found in the many shops lining the town's main street. The handiwork of the Cotacachicans is of excellent quality. The people of the Andes carve **wood products** of all kinds, from intricate wooden boxes and sculptures to furniture. Many artisans work and sell goods right out of their homes, hence the sounds of saws and chisels, and the trails of sawdust. In Peru's Río Mantaro region, **carved gourds** known as *matés burilados* also make popular gifts.

Pre-Hispanic **metalwork** was highly skilled, and in some places the tradition of hand-crafting jewelry lives on. Elaborate shawl pins (called *tupus*) are made and worn by *indígenas*, often as family heirlooms passed from one generation to the next. Much current area jewelry incorporates beads into its design, a tradition that began before the Spanish conquest. Beads made of red Spondylus shell were traded throughout the Andes, and to this day, red is the favored bead color. **Ceramics** are also made throughout the region. The Quichua *Sacha Runa* (jungle people) who inhabit the Ecuadorian Oriente produce fine hand-coiled pots with paintings of Quichua life and mythology on the sides. Other well-respected Ecuadorian ceramics are made in the area around Latacunga. The small town of **Pujilí** is known for its painted ceramic figurines. In Peru, ceramics are produced all along the coast, displaying the same designs and made with techniques similar to those used by the region's ancient cultures. **Ayacucho** and **Cajamarca** are good places to find reputable ceramics, as are many shops in Quito and Lima.

MUSIC

The music of Peru, Bolivia, and Ecuador resulted from the confluence of two distinct musical streams: Spanish and pre-Hispanic. This tranquil hybrid music of the Andes, rife with fife, strings, and other things, has been popularized around the world by traveling musicians from all three countries. Often the music is just instrumental, but when there's singing, it is usually in Quechua. One of the most popular songs in the Andes is "El Cóndor Pasa," whose tune was made internationally famous by **Simon and Garfunkel**. Bands frequently play at festivals, and recently music competitions are becoming more popular. Get into the groove at one of the many folk music clubs (called *peñas*), where locals get together to celebrate and have a good time. Indigenous contributions to the typical Andean band include wind instruments, drums, and rattles. The first instrument that pops into most people's minds when thinking of Andean music is the **panpipe** or *rondador*, which is believed to be over 2000 years old. A relative of the *rondador*, originating from the southern Andes, is the **zampoña**, with two rows of pipes instead of just one. This instrument, along with the five-note scale on which the tunes are based, gives Andean music its distinctively haunting sound. Two flutes of different sizes are also quite often used—the larger **quena** and the smaller **pingullu.** The flutes and panpipes are both carved from bamboo. Bells, drums, and **maracas** (rattles made from gourds) comprise the rest of the indigenous contribution to the modern Andean band. (But, catchy as those Andean strains are, the area's largest musical contribution of late has to be **Azul Azul,** the Bolivian pop sensation who spawned the brilliant "La Bomba," one of the best dance songs the world has ever heard.)

When the Spanish arrived, they brought with them **stringed instruments** of all shapes, sounds, and sizes, including the *guitarra* (guitar), *violín, bandolín* (mandolin), *charango* (a ukulele-type instrument commonly made from an armadillo shell), and *arpa* (harp). These added more variety and texture to the already rich local music, and today's sounds reflect the continued use of both breeds of sound. **Jesuit missionaries** in Bolivia made a significant, and unique, contribution to the Andean music scene; they taught Indians to play and manufacture violins and many other classical music instruments. The area most influenced by the Jesuits— Chiquitania—still demonstrates its classical proficiencies through performances and instrument manufacturing.

ARCHITECTURE

The oldest large-scale architecture in the region is that which the Incas left behind. **Machu Picchu,** near Cusco in Peru, reigns as the most famous and majestic example of Inca ruins in all of South America. Unknown to the outside world until 1911, the site may have been a ceremonial center. The ruins of **Ingapirca,** just north of Cuenca, are Ecuador's best. Located on an old Inca road, the complex is believed to have served as an inn, a fortress, a temple, or some combination of the three. In Bolivia, the ruins of **Tiahuanuco** are thought to have been the center of the Tiahuanuco civilization (1580 BC to AD 1172), which once spanned Bolivia, Peru, Chile, and Argentina, and had a population equivalent to Bolivia's today. Parts of this ancient capital are still being explored.

Many of the area's ruins no longer stand, primarily because the Spanish either destroyed or co-opted their buildings. A number of important towns are built on the rubble of the Inca civilization; in many cases, the Spaniards even reused Inca building stones. Many colonial churches are on hilltops because they were built over foundations of Inca temples.

Colonial architecture is a blend of the Old and New Worlds; the style of religious art and architecture that resulted from the mix is called the **Quito School.** The Spaniards commissioned works to be done in the popular Baroque style, but the indigenous peoples who executed them added their own distinctive touches. Churches and convents in older towns are decorated with intricately carved facades, ornate interiors sparkling with gilt, and leafy stone vines wrapping around classically styled columns. Municipal buildings and private residences are usually more modest. Large wooden doors open onto blocky two-story buildings with high ceilings, interior courtyards, and covered verandas. Simple stonework and elegant wrought iron decorate white-washed interiors, while ancient wooden beams and weathered red tiles make up the roofs above. Much of the region's built environment has been erected in the 20th century, a time when building costs assumed primary importance in the architectural mind. Blocky concrete and rebar buildings predominate the downtown areas of the region's larger cities.

SPORTS AND RECREATION

When they're not working, the people of Peru, Bolivia, and Ecuador love to play. As is the case in the rest of Latin America (and the world, for that matter), soccer, or **fútbol,** reigns supreme. Fútbol fields dot the countryside and urban areas and are heavily used by *jugadores* (players) of all shapes, sizes, and ability levels. For a slightly less strenuous activity, many people also enjoy **foosball,** the analogous table sport that relies more on hand-eye coordination than strength and stamina. But don't be fooled by its tranquil appearance; although the game involves minimal physical movement, matches can become as heated as any World Cup final.

Basketball has become quite popular in Latin America in recent years. This is largely because of the global attention that the sport receives and the hero-god role its finest players and teams have assumed in North American pop culture. Perhaps harder to explain is the increasing popularity of **volleyball** in some parts of the region. The courts are usually rather makeshift, often marked off by articles of clothing in an open lot or field, but the rules are basically the same as elsewhere in the world. The play of the games differs slightly; since most residents are under six feet tall, most of the action takes place *below* the net.

For the slightly more adventurous (and wealthier) visitor, there is a multitude of activities that will quench any adrenaline craving. Because of the, well, *extreme* geography of the region, thrill-seeking opportunities abound. The Andes mountain range, which bisects the region from north to south, provides not only incredible scenery but also some of the best **trekking** and **mountaineering** in the world. With dozens of peaks over 5000m high, Peru, Bolivia, and Ecuador have become prime destinations for serious mountain climbers from across the globe. **Skiing** and **snowboarding** have become popular around Huaraz, Peru; the Cordillera Blanca's snow-capped peaks provide every opportunity for adventure. For more sedate activity, the passes and valleys created by volcanic peaks provide perfect conditions for short- or long-distance **hikes** through pristine countryside.

If you'd rather swim than walk, check out the excellent **whitewater rafting** and **kayaking.** Raging rivers run rapidly from the mountains to either the Pacific or the tropical Amazon basin, creating plenty of aquatic turbulence along the way. A word of caution: since rafting is a fairly new industry in Latin America, those interested should check equipment ahead of time and ask tourist authorities to recommend reputable operators. Some companies just want to attract tourists, even if it means using outdated equipment, incompetent guides, or dangerous rapids. At the very least, make sure they provide everyone with a life jacket and helmet. Try to find out which rivers are safe during the rainy or dry seasons and plan your trip accordingly.

The accomplished will find surprisingly good **surfing** along most of the Pacific coast. The central coast of Ecuador, especially Montañita, and most of the Peruvian coast have recently developed local surfing communities, with the occasional foreigner "dropping in" with little or no problem. Some surf shops have sprung up, many of which repair dings and rent boards to visitors. If you bring your own equipment, consult with the airline first to make sure that you can check it as regular baggage or sporting equipment rather than freight. Because of the Humboldt current, the water in central and southern Peru may be surprisingly chilly despite the latitude. Hate the water, but want to surf? You can do it in Peru. Try **sandboarding** in Huacachina; "surf" shops there will rent out sandboards and wax, and even give your first lesson on the enormous dunes surrounding the area.

ESSENTIALS

FACTS FOR THE TRAVELER

DOCUMENTS AND FORMALITIES

PERUVIAN, BOLIVIAN, AND ECUADORIAN EMBASSIES AND CONSULATES ABROAD

PERU

Australia: Embassy of Peru, 43 Culgoa Cct., O'Malley, ACT 2606 (☎(02) 6290 0922; fax (02) 6290 0924; email emperuau@dynamite.com.au). Consulate General of Peru-Sydney, Level 3 De la Sala House, 30 Clarence St. Sydney NSW 2000 (☎(02) 9262 6464; fax (02) 9290 2939; email conper@mail.magna.com.au).

Canada: Embassy of Peru, 130 Albert St. #1901, Ottawa, ON K1P 5G4 (☎(613) 238 1777; fax (613) 232 3062; email emperuca@magi.com).

United Kingdom: Embassy of Peru, 52 Sloane St., London SW1X 9SP, United Kingdom (☎(020) 7235 1917; fax 7235 4463).

United States: Embassy of Peru, 1700 Mass. Ave. NW, Washington, DC 20036 (☎(202) 833-9860; fax (202) 659-8124; www.peruemb.org; email peru@peruemb.org). Consulate General of Peru, 1625 Massachusetts Ave. NW #605, Washington, D.C. 20036 (☎(202) 462 1084; fax (202) 462 1088; email conwash@erols.com).

BOLIVIA

Australia: Consulate-general of the Republic of Bolivia, GPO Box 53, Brisbane QLD 4001 (☎(07) 3221 1606); Consulate of the Republic of Bolivia, Level 6, 74 Pitt St., Sydney, NSW 2000 (☎(02) 9235 1858).

Canada: Embassy of the Republic of Bolivia, 130 Albert St., Suite 416, Ottawa, Ontario K1P 5G4 (☎(613) 236-5730; fax 236-8237; email bolcan@iosphere.net).

United Kingdom: Embassy and consulate of the Republic of Bolivia, 106 Eaton Square, London SWIW 9AD (☎(020) 7235 4248 or 7235 4255 for visa enquiries; fax 7235 1286).

United States: Embassy of the Republic of Bolivia, 3014 Massachusetts Ave., NW, Washington, D.C. 0008-3603 (☎(202) 483-4410; fax 328-3712; email bolembus@erols.com).

ECUADOR

Australia: Consulate of Ecuador, Suite 1702-A, American Express Tower, 388 George St., Sydney NSW 2000 (☎(06) 273 4437; fax 273 4279).

Canada: Embassy of Ecuador, 50 O'Connor St. #131, Ottawa, ON K1P 6L2 (☎(613) 563 8206; fax 235 5776).

United Kingdom: Embassy of Ecuador, Flat 3B, Hans Crescent, London SW1X OOI, United Kingdom (☎(020) 7584 1367; fax 7823 9701).

United States: Embassy of Ecuador, 2535 15th St. NW, Washington, D.C. 20009 (☎(202) 234 7200; fax 265-6385; email mecuawaa@erols.com; www.ecuador.com).

ENTRANCE REQUIREMENTS FOR PERU, BOLIVIA, AND ECUADOR

Passport (p. 26). Required for all visitors.
Visa (p. 27). Required for stays of over 90 days; required anytime for citizens of Ireland and South Africa.
Inoculations (p. 35).
Work Permit (p. 27). Required for all foreigners planning to work.
Driving Permit (p. 53). Required for all those planning to drive.

CONSULAR SERVICES IN:

PERU

Australia: Victor Andrés Belaúde 147, Edificio Real 3, Office 1301, San Isidro (☎222 82 81; fax 221 49 96). Open M-F 8:30am-5:30pm.

Canada: Libertad 130, Miraflores (☎444 40 15; fax 444 43 47). Open M-Tu and Th-F 8am-noon and 2-4pm, W 8am-noon.

Ireland: Santiago Acuña 135, La Aurora, Miraflores (☎/fax 445 68 13; email mgrperu@pol.com.pe). Open M-F 10:30am-2:30pm.

South Africa: Via Principal 155, Office 801, San Isidro (☎440 99 96; fax 422 38 81). Open M-F 9am-noon.

United Kingdom: Natalio Sánchez 125, off the 5th block of Arequipa, 12th floor, on the Plaza Washington, just south of Lima Centro (☎433 50 32; fax 433 47 35). Open M and Th-F 8am-1:30pm, Tu-W 8am-4:15pm. Also handles affairs for **New Zealand.**

United States: Encalada Block 17, in front of Jockey Plaza Mall, Monterrico, Surco, Lima (☎434 30 00; fax 434 30 37). Open M-F 8am-5pm.

BOLIVIA

Canada: 20 de Octubre, on the Plaza Avaroa, La Paz 2475 (☎(02) 432 838 or 433 550; fax 430 250; email cida-lapaz@mail.megalink.com). Open M-Th 8am-12:30pm, 2-6:30pm, F 8am-1:30pm.

United Kingdom: Arce 2732, La Paz 694 (☎(02) 433 324, 433 424, or 431 338; fax 431 073; email ppa@mail.rds.org.bo). Sells visas for Bs330. Open M-F mornings and 1:30-4:30pm.

United States: Arce 2780, La Paz 425 (☎(02) 430 251 or 430 120; fax 433 900; www.megalink.com/usembalapaz). Sells visas for US$45. Open M-F 8:30am-12:30pm and 1:30-5:30pm.

ECUADOR

Canada: 6 de Diciembre 2816 and Paul Rivet, 4th floor, Quito (☎(02) 232 114; fax 503 108; email quito@dfait.maeci.gc.ca). Open M-F 9am-noon.

Ireland: Antonio de Ulloa 2651 and Rumipamba, Quito (☎(02) 451 577; fax 269 862). Open M-F 9am-1pm.

United Kingdom: Gonzales Suárez 111 and 12 de Octubre, Quito (☎(02) 560 670; fax 560 730; emergencies ☎(09) 723 021). Open M-F 8:30am-12:30pm and 2-5pm.

United States: Patria 120 and 12 de Octubre, Quito (☎(02) 562 890; fax 502 052; 24hr. emergency ☎561 749). Open M-F 8am-12:30pm and 1:30-5pm.

PASSPORTS

All visitors need valid passports to enter Peru, Bolivia, and Ecuador and to re-enter their own country. Peru, Bolivia, and Ecuador do not allow entrance if the holder's passport expires in under six months; returning home with an expired passport is illegal and may result in a fine.

PHOTOCOPIES. It's important to photocopy the page of your passport that contains your photograph, passport number, and other identifying information, along with other important documents such as visas, travel insurance policies, airplane tickets, and traveler's check serial numbers, in case you lose anything. Carry one set of copies in a safe place apart from the originals and leave another set at home. Consulates also recommend that you carry an expired passport or an official copy of your birth certificate in a part of your baggage separate from other documents.

LOST PASSPORTS. If you lose your passport, immediately notify the local police and the embassy or consulate of your home government. To expedite its replacement, you will need to know all information previously recorded and show identification and proof of citizenship. In some cases, a replacement may take weeks to process, and it may be valid only for a limited time. Any visas stamped in your old passport will be irretrievably lost. In an emergency, ask for temporary traveling papers that will permit you to re-enter your home country. Your passport is a public document belonging to your nation's government. You may have to surrender it to a foreign government official, but if you don't get it back within a reasonable amount of time, inform the nearest embassy or consulate of your home country.

NEW PASSPORTS. All applications for new passports or renewals should be filed in advance of your departure date. Most passport offices offer emergency passport services for an extra charge. Citizens residing abroad who need a passport or renewal should contact their nearest embassy or consulate.

VISAS AND WORK PERMITS

VISAS. For most tourists, visas are not required for visits of 90 days or fewer. For information about who needs a visa to enter or information regarding visas for stays longer than 90 days, contact your nearest consulate. US citizens can take advantage of the **Center for International Business and Travel** (CIBT; ☎ (800) 925-2428), which will secure visas for travel to almost all countries for a variable service charge.

WORK PERMITS. Admission as a visitor does not include the right to work, which is authorized only by a work permit, and entering Peru, Bolivia, or Ecuador to study requires a special visa. For more info, see Alternatives to Tourism, p. 57.

IDENTIFICATION

When you travel, always carry two or more forms of identification on your person, including at least one photo ID; a passport combined with a driver's license or birth certificate is usually adequate. Many establishments, especially banks, may require several IDs in order to cash traveler's checks. Never carry all your forms of ID together; split them up in case of theft or loss. It is useful to bring extra passport-size photos to affix to the various IDs or passes you may acquire along the way.

STUDENT IDENTIFICATION. Although international student discounts are not as common in Peru, Bolivia and Ecuador as in the US or European countries, it is still worthwhile to flash your student ID whenever you get the opportunity, even if no discount is advertised. The **International Student Identity Card (ISIC),** is the most widely accepted form of student ID. The ISIC is preferable to an institution-specific card (such as a university ID) because it is more likely to be recognized (and honored) abroad. All cardholders have access to a 24-hour emergency helpline for medical, legal, and financial emergencies (in North America call ☎ (877) 370-ISIC, elsewhere call US collect ☎ (715) 345-0505), and US cardholders are also eligible for insurance benefits (see Insurance, p. 39). Many student travel agencies issue ISICs, including STA Travel in Australia and New Zealand; Travel CUTS in Canada; usit in the Republic of Ireland and Northern Ireland; SASTS in South Africa; Campus Travel and STA Travel in the UK; and Council Travel (www.counciltravel.com/idcards/default.asp) and STA Travel in the US (see p. 48). The card is valid from September of one year to December of the following year and costs AUS$15, CDN$15, or US$20. Applicants must be degree-seeking students of a secondary or post-secondary school and must be of at least 12 years of age. The **International Teacher Identity Card (ITIC)** offers the same insurance coverage as well as similar but limited discounts. The fee is AUS$13, UK£5, or US$22. For more info, contact the **International Student Travel Confederation (ISTC),** Herengracht 479, 1017 BS Amsterdam, Netherlands (☎ +31 (20) 421 28 00; fax 421 28 10; email istcinfo@istc.org; www.istc.org).

YOUTH IDENTIFICATION. The International Student Travel Confederation issues a discount card to travelers who are 25 years old or under but are not students. This one-year **International Youth Travel Card** (**IYTC;** formerly the **GO 25** Card) offers many of the same benefits as the ISIC. Most organizations that sell the ISIC also sell the IYTC for the same prices (see above).

CUSTOMS

When entering Peru, Bolivia, or Ecuador, customs is generally a pretty laid-back process. Officials are more likely to stop Ecuadorian, Peruvian, or Bolivian nationals returning with loads of foreign merchandise than backpacking gringos. Nevertheless, they do sometimes search bags, and you don't want to get busted. You may not enter or leave with firearms, ammunition, narcotics, fresh meat, or live plants or animals. At customs, travelers are occasionally required to pay a fee on all electronic items they bring, not including laptop computers.

Upon returning home, you must declare all articles acquired abroad and pay a **duty** on the value of those articles that exceeds the allowance established by your country's customs service. Goods and gifts bought at **duty-free** shops abroad are not exempt from duty or sales tax at your point of return; you must declare them as well. "Duty-free" means that you need not pay a tax in the country of purchase. Coca leaves, legal throughout the Andes, are not generally appreciated by customs officials in countries of lower altitudes.

MONEY

If you stay in hostels and prepare your own food, expect to spend anywhere from US$10-15 per person per day in Peru. Accommodations average about US$6 per night for a single, although many hostels are substantially less, while a basic sit-down meal costs US$2-3. Ecuador (not including the Galapagos) and Bolivia are slightly less expensive: expect to spend from US$8-12 per person per day. Accommodations in Ecuador and Bolivia start at about US$4 per night for a single, and a basic sit-down meal goes for around US$2.

CURRENCY AND EXCHANGE

DOLLARIZATION IN ECUADOR

As a result of constant economic trouble, the Ecuadorian government has begun the process of dollarization; by September 2000, all circulating currency should be United States dollars. Because this book was researched as the transition took place, some prices in the Ecuador chapters are direct conversions from the listed price in *sucres* to their corresponding US$ amount (the exchange rate of *sucres* to dollars was formerly fixed at 25,000/1). Otherwise, all prices in this book are listed in local currency, except where payment is expected or preferred in US dollars. Prices were updated in the summer of 2000, but due to high inflation rates and frequent devaluation, they may have changed since and should be used for comparative purposes only. A useful currency converter website is www.oanda.com/cgi-bin/ncc.

THE PERUVIAN NUEVO SOL

NUEVO SOL		
	US$1 = 3.47 SOLES	1 SOL = US$0.29
	CDN$1 = 2.28 SOLES	1 SOL = CDN$0.44
	UK£1 = 5.45 SOLES	1 SOL = UK£0.18
	IR£1 = 4.58 SOLES	1 SOL = IR£0.22
	AUS$1 = 2.19 SOLES	1 SOL = AUS$0.46
	NZ$1 = 1.76 SOLES	1 SOL = NZ$0.57
	SAR1 = 0.56 SOLES	1 SOL = SAR1.77
	10,000 SUCRES = 1.38 SOLES	1 SOL = 7,229.26 SUCRES
	1 BOLIVIANO = 0.56 SOLES	1 SOL = 1.79 BOLIVIANOS

THE ECUADORIAN SUCRE

SUCRE		
	US$1 = 25,000 SUCRES	10,000 SUCRES = US$0.40
	CDN$1 = 16,936 SUCRES	10,000 SUCRES = CDN$0.59
	UK£1 = 37,758.8 SUCRES	10,000 SUCRES = UK£0.27
	IR£1 = 30,375.3 SUCRES	10,000 SUCRES = IR£0.33
	AUS$1 = 14,726.4 SUCRES	10,000 SUCRES = AUS$0.67
	NZ$1 = 11,728.3 SUCRES	10,000 SUCRES = NZ$0.85
	SAR1 = 3,550.84 SUCRES	10,000 SUCRES = SAR 2.81
	1 SOL = 7,229.26 SUCRES	10,000 SUCRES = 1.38 SOLES
	1 BOLIVIANO = 4009.26 SUCRES	10,000 SUCRES = 2.49 BOL.

THE BOLIVIAN BOLIVIANO

BOLIVIANO		
	US$1 = 6.16 BOLIVIANOS	1 BOLIVIANO = US$0.16
	CDN$1 = 4.19 BOLIVIANOS	1 BOLIVIANO = CDN$0.24
	UK£1 = 9.30 BOLIVIANOS	1 BOLIVIANO = UK£0.11
	IR£1 = 7.52 BOLIVIANOS	1 BOLIVIANO = IR£0.13
	AUS$1 = 3.68 BOLIVIANOS	1 BOLIVIANO = AUS$0.27
	NZ$1 = 2.91 BOLIVIANOS	1 BOLIVIANO = NZ$0.34
	SAR1 = 0.88 BOLIVIANOS	1 BOLIVIANO = SAR1.14
	1 SOL = 1.79 BOLIVIANOS	1 BOLIVIANO = 0.56 SOLES
	10,000 SUCRES = 2.49 BOLIVIANOS	1 BOLIVIANO = 4009 SUCRES

In Peru, Ecuador, and Bolivia, as in many Latin American countries, US currency is widely accepted and, in many cases, is even preferred over the local currency. Other foreign currency is difficult or impossible to change. Even dollars with rips or stains may not be accepted. Upon arrival it is a good idea to have mostly US dollars and then convert them gradually. Despite the versatility of US dollars, consider avoiding using them (except in newly-dollarized Ecuador). First, there is a potential risk of being overcharged if you don't pay in *soles* or *bolivianos*. Second, throwing dollars around to gain better treatment is offensive and can attract theft. Bolivians often call *bolivianos* "pesos," as do visitors that have been around longer. Longstanding gringos will often say "b"s.

As a general rule, it's cheaper to convert money once you get to Peru, Ecuador, and Bolivia, although it's good to bring enough foreign currency to last for the first several days of a trip to avoid being penniless after banking hours or on a holiday. Travelers living in the US can get foreign currency from the comfort of their home; **International Currency Express** (☎ (888) 278-6628) will deliver foreign currency or traveler's checks overnight (US$15) or second-day (US$12) at competitive exchange rates, but of Peru, Ecuador, and Bolivia, only *soles* can be exchanged.

THE SOL STOPS HERE Peru's currency, the *nuevo sol*, may have stabilized in recent years, but not without a price: increased counterfeiting. Beware of shoddily molded and hammered "*cinco soles*" coins passed back at the market. Fake bills, in particular, are easy to avoid. Real ones printed relatively recently have iridescent drops painted on the front, and all bills should feature an inner plastic strip with a serial number. Also, hold the paper up to light in order to spot the watermark copy of the face (e.g. Raúl Porras Barrenechea on the 20). Dodge a phony right from the start; no savvy Peruvian will later accept it for payment.

Watch out for commission rates and check newspapers for the standard rate of exchange. Banks generally have the best rates. A good rule of thumb is only to go to banks or *casas de cambio* that have a 5% margin or less between their buy and sell prices. Also, using an ATM card or a credit card (see p. 30) will often get you the best possible rates. If you use traveler's checks or bills, carry some in small denominations (US$50 or less), especially for times when you are forced to exchange money at disadvantageous rates. However, it is good to carry a range of denominations since charges may be levied per check cashed.

TRAVELER'S CHECKS

Traveler's checks are one of the safest and least troublesome means of carrying funds, since they can be refunded if stolen. Several agencies and banks sell them, usually for face value plus a small percentage commission. (Members of the American Automobile Association and some banks and credit unions can get American Express checks commission-free.) **American Express** and **Visa** are the most widely recognized. If you're ordering checks, do so well in advance, especially if you are requesting large sums. Each agency provides refunds if your checks are lost or stolen, and many provide additional services, such as toll-free refund hotlines in the countries you're visiting, emergency message services, and stolen credit card assistance. In order to collect a **refund for lost or stolen checks,** keep your check receipts separate from your checks and store them in a safe place or with a traveling companion. Record check numbers when you cash them, leave a list of check numbers with someone at home, and ask for a list of refund centers when you buy your checks. Never countersign your checks until you are ready to cash them, and always bring your passport with you when you plan to use the checks. In many cases, banks will cash traveler's checks in the local currency for free but charge a hefty fee for dollars.

American Express: Call ☎(800) 251 902 in Australia; in New Zealand ☎(0800) 441 068; in the UK ☎(0800) 521 313; in the US and Canada ☎(800) 221-7282. Elsewhere, call US collect ☎ (801) 964-6665; www.aexp.com. Checks are available for a small fee (1-4%) at American Express Travel Service Offices and banks, commission-free at AAA offices. American Express offices cash their checks commission-free (except where prohibited by national governments), but often at slightly worse rates than banks.

Visa: Call ☎(800) 227-6811 in the US; in the UK ☎(0800) 89 50 78; from elsewhere, call UK collect ☎ +44 (1733) 31 89 49. Call for the location of their nearest office.

CREDIT CARDS

Credit cards are generally accepted in all but the smallest businesses and very rural areas. Major credit cards—**Visa** is welcomed most often, with **Mastercard** a distant second—can be used to extract cash advances in *soles*, dollars, and *bolivianos* from associated banks and ATMs throughout Peru, Ecuador, and Bolivia. Credit card companies get the wholesale exchange rate, which is generally 5% better than the retail rate used by banks and other currency exchange establishments. **American Express** cards also work in some ATMs, as well as at AmEx offices and major airports. AmEx cardholders have access to an emergency medical and legal assistance hotline (24hr.; in North America call ☎(800) 554-2639, elsewhere call US collect ☎ (202) 554-2639) and can enjoy American Express Travel Service benefits (including baggage loss and flight insurance, mailgram and international cable services, and held mail). You must ask your credit card company for a **Personal Identification Number (PIN)** before you leave; without it, you will be unable to withdraw cash with your credit card outside your home country. If you already have a PIN, check with the company to make sure it will work in Peru, Ecuador, and Bolivia. Credit cards often offer an array of other services, from insurance to emergency assistance. Check with your company to find out what is covered.

ATM CARDS

ATMs (Automated Teller Machines)—known as *cajeros automáticos*—are common in urban areas of Peru, Ecuador, and Bolivia. If headed to a small town, bring plenty of cash, as ATMs are most likely non-existent and banks may have extremely limited services and hours. Most ATMs offer English directions and the option of withdrawing dollars or local currency. Depending on the system that your home bank uses, you can probably access your personal bank account whenever you need money. ATMs get the same wholesale exchange rate as credit cards, but there is often a limit on the amount of money you can withdraw per day (usually about US$500), and your bank might charge a hefty service fee per withdrawal. Memorize your PIN in numeric form since machines elsewhere often don't have letters on their keys. Also, if your PIN is longer than four digits, ask your bank whether the first four digits will work, or whether you need a new number.

The two major international money networks are **Cirrus** (US ☎ (800) 424-7787) and **PLUS** (US ☎ (800) 843-7587 for the "Voice Response Unit Locator"). **Bank Hapoalim** ATMs take bank cards affiliated with Cirrus and often Plus networks for free, but your home bank may charge you. Inquire before you go.

GETTING MONEY FROM HOME

AMERICAN EXPRESS. Cardholders can withdraw cash from their checking accounts at any of AmEx's major offices and many of its representative offices (up to US$1000 every 21 days; no service charge, no interest). AmEx "Express Cash" withdrawals from any AmEx ATM in Peru, Ecuador, and Bolivia are automatically debited from the cardholder's checking account or line of credit. Green card holders may withdraw up to US$1000 in any seven-day period (2% transaction fee; minimum US$2.50, maximum US$20). To enroll in Express Cash, cardmembers may call ☎ (800) 227-4669 in the US; outside the US call collect ☎ +1 (336) 668-5041.

WESTERN UNION. Travelers from the US, Canada, and the UK can wire money abroad through Western Union's international money transfer services. In the US, call ☎ (800) 325-6000; in Canada ☎ (800) 235-0000; in the UK ☎ (0800) 833 833. The rates for sending cash are generally US$10-11 cheaper than with a credit card, and the money is usually available at the place they're sending it to within an hour. For agent locations and services call: in Peru ☎ (01) 421 9089 or (01) 422 0014; in Ecuador ☎ (02) 565 059 or (04) 287 044; in Bolivia ☎ 0800 4020 (toll free).

US STATE DEPARTMENT (US CITIZENS ONLY). In dire emergencies only, the US State Department will forward money within hours to the nearest consular office, which will then disburse it according to instructions for a US$15 fee. Contact the Overseas Citizens Service, American Citizens Services, Consular Affairs, Room 4811, US Department of State, Washington, D.C. 20520 (☎ (202) 647-5225; nights, Sundays, and holidays 647-4000; www.travel.state.gov).

TIPPING, BARGAINING, AND TAXES

Generally, tipping is not common and not expected, although some fancier restaurants include a small (5-10%) tip on the bill. It is also rare to tip for services, but on occasion it is appropriate to tip for maid service or for a guide or porter; in many cases, these people count on a small bonus.

In some places it's okay to **bargain,** and a little practice can make it worth the effort. Bargaining for rooms works best in the low season, and it's not hard to get prices lowered at markets or from street vendors. It is also acceptable to bargain with taxi drivers, though an excessively low first bid may send the *taxista* on his way without you. The basic technique is to expect the first offered price to be higher than what the seller actually wants; pick a lower price, and marvel at the magic of compromise. However, it is vulgar for travelers to bargain down to a price that is clearly unreasonable. In countries where the cost of living is already dirt cheap, the discount of pennies or a dollar received by a foreigner might mean a lot more in the pocket of a local vendor.

Upscale restaurants, hotels, and shops often charge a **sales tax (IVA),** which you should expect to appear on the bill. The real whammy, though, hits the traveler on the way out—there are **airport/departure taxes** in Ecuador (US$25), Peru (US$10 from regional airports, US$25 from Lima), and Bolivia (US$20).

SAFETY AND SECURITY

PERSONAL SAFETY

> **FURTHER INFORMATION** The following government offices provide travel information and advisories by telephone, fax, or the web.
> **Australian Department of Foreign Affairs and Trade:** ☎(2) 6261 1111; www.dfat.gov.au.
> **Canadian Department of Foreign Affairs and International Trade (DFAIT):** In Canada call (800) 267-6788, elsewhere call ☎(613) 944-6788; www.dfait-maeci.gc.ca. Call for their free booklet, *Bon Voyage...But.*
> **New Zealand Ministry of Foreign Affairs:** ☎(04) 494 8500; fax 494 8511; www.mft.govt.nz/trav.html.
> **United Kingdom Foreign and Commonwealth Office:** ☎(020) 7238 4503; fax 7238 4545; www.fco.gov.uk.
> **US Department of State:** ☎(202) 647-5225, auto faxback (202) 647-3000; http://travel.state.gov. For *A Safe Trip Abroad,* call (202) 512-1800.

EXPLORING. Extra vigilance is always wise, but there is no need for panic when exploring a new city or region. Find out about unsafe areas from tourist offices, from the manager of your hotel or hostel, or from a local whom you trust. You may want to carry a **whistle** to scare off attackers or attract attention. Whenever possible, *Let's Go* warns of unsafe neighborhoods and areas, but there are some good general tips to follow. When walking at night, stick to busy, well-lit streets. Do not attempt to cross through parks, parking lots, or other large, deserted areas. Buildings in disrepair, vacant lots, and unpopulated areas are all bad signs. The distribution of people can reveal a great deal about the relative safety of the area; look for children playing, women walking in the open, and other signs of an active community. Keep in mind that a district can change character drastically between blocks. If you feel uncomfortable, leave as quickly and directly as you can, but don't allow fear of the unknown to turn you into a hermit. Careful, persistent exploration will build confidence and make your stay in an area much more rewarding.

TERRORISM. The **Sendero Luminoso** and the **Tupac Amaru Revolutionary Movement,** the two major terrorist organizations active in Peru, are a less potent force now than they have been in previous years, and terrorist attacks have not occurred in traditional tourist destinations for a number of years. But the US Department of State warns that these organizations are still capable of terrorist actions. The Sendero Luminoso continues to operate in rural provinces of the Junín, Huanuco, San Martín, and Ayacucho of Peru. Adventure travelers are encouraged to contact the US Embassy in Lima for current security information.

GETTING AROUND. Traveling within Peru, Bolivia, and Ecuador can be dangerous. Roads are often in very poor condition, especially since the El Niño weather phenomenon, and potholes, sharp curves, lane ends, and construction sites are often unmarked. Travel only by day if possible, and use bus companies that take special precautions, such as frequent driver-changing, to ensure your safety. The extra money you pay to travel with the slightly better bus lines could be the most important investment you make. Drivers should not travel alone in rural areas, even during the day; sticking with convoy travel is the safest way to go. If you do choose to rent a **car,** learn local driving signals and wear a seatbelt. If you plan on spending a lot of time on the road, you may want to bring spare parts, carry a cellular phone if service exists, and invest in a roadside assistance program (see p. 53). Park your vehicle in a garage or well-traveled area, and use a steering wheel locking device in larger cities. **Sleeping in your car** is one of the most dangerous (and often illegal) ways to get your rest. If your car breaks down, wait for the police to assist you. *Let's Go* does not recommend **hitchhiking** under any circumstances, particularly for women—see **Getting Around,** p. 51 for more information.

SELF-DEFENSE. There is no sure-fire set of precautions that will protect you from all the situations you might encounter when you travel. A good self-defense course will give you more concrete ways to react to different types of aggression. **Impact, Prepare,** and **Model Mugging** can refer you to local self-defense courses in the US (☎ (800) 345-5425) and Vancouver, Canada (☎ (604) 878-3838). Workshops (2-3hr.) start at US$50; full courses run US$350-500. Both women and men are welcome.

FINANCIAL SECURITY

Visitors to Andean countries often return with magical tales of unexpected theft: handbags carefully slit and emptied of valuables, hats deftly snatched from the tops of heads, cameras that vanished into thin air. Quito and Guayaquil in Ecuador, and Lima and Cusco in Peru have the worst reputations. Bolivian cities tend to have better records, although theft is still a threat, particularly in La Paz and Santa Cruz. While most victims of robbery are not physically harmed, almost everybody sustains wounded pride. When packing, weigh the necessity of each object against the anguish you'll experience should it be taken.

PROTECTING YOUR VALUABLES. Theft is a danger throughout Peru, Bolivia, and Ecuador, but its prevalence varies greatly with location. To prevent easy theft, don't keep all your valuables (money, important documents) in one place. **Photocopies** of important documents allow you to recover them in case they are lost or filched. Carry one copy separate from the documents and leave another at home. Label every piece of luggage both inside and out. Carry as little money as possible, keep some aside to use in an emergency, and never count your money in public. **Don't put a wallet with money in your back pocket.** If you carry a purse, buy a sturdy one with a secure clasp, and carry it crosswise on the side, away from the street with the clasp against you. Secure packs with small combination **padlocks** which slip through the two zippers. A **money belt,** a nylon, zippered pouch with a belt that sits inside the waist of your pants or skirt, combines convenience and security; you can buy one at most camping supply stores. A **neck pouch** is equally safe, though far less accessible. Refrain from pulling out your neck pouch in public. Avoid keeping anything precious in a fanny-pack (even if it's worn on your stomach): your valuables will be highly visible and easy to steal.

CON ARTISTS AND PICKPOCKETS. Among the more colorful aspects of large cities are **con artists.** They often work in groups, and children are among the most effective. They possess an innumerable range of ruses. Beware of certain classics: sob stories that require money, rolls of bills "found" on the street, mustard spilled (or saliva spit) onto your shoulder to distract you while they snatch your bag. Don't ever hand over your passport to someone whose authority you question (ask to accompany them to a police station if they insist), and **don't ever let your passport out of your sight.** Similarly, don't let your bag out of sight; never trust a "station-porter" who insists on carrying your bag or stowing it in the baggage compartment or a "new friend" who offers to guard your bag while you buy a train ticket or use the restroom. Beware of **pickpockets** in city crowds, especially on public transportation. Also, be alert in public phone booths. If you must say your calling card number, do so very quietly; if you punch it in, make sure no one can look over your shoulder.

ACCOMMODATIONS AND TRANSPORTATION. Never leave your belongings unattended; crime occurs in even the most demure-looking hostel or hotel. Bring your own padlock for hostel lockers if you want to store clothing during the day, but never leave valuables or money in lockers. Be particularly careful on **buses,** carry your backpack in front of you where you can see it, don't check baggage on trains, and don't trust anyone to "watch your bag for a second." If possible, avoid storing luggage on the roof of a bus, or underneath. Thieves thrive on **trains;** professionals wait for tourists to fall asleep and then carry off everything they can. When traveling in pairs, sleep in alternating shifts; when alone, use good judgement in selecting a train compartment: never stay in an empty one and use a lock to secure your pack to the luggage rack.

DRUGS AND ALCOHOL

A meek "I didn't know it was illegal" will not suffice. Remember that you are subject to the laws of Peru, Bolivia, or Ecuador, not to those of your home country, and it is your responsibility to familiarize yourself with these laws before leaving. Those caught in possession of drugs can expect **extended pre-trial detention** in poor prison conditions and a **lengthy prison sentence** if convicted. If you carry **prescription drugs** while you travel, it is vital to have the prescriptions themselves and a note from a doctor, both readily accessible at country borders. Also beware that some prescription drugs and traditional herbal remedies readily available in Peru, Bolivia, or Ecuador may be illegal in your home country. Coca-leaf tea, for example, though easy to acquire in Peru, is highly illegal in many nations.

Drinking in Latin America is not for amateurs; non-gringo bars are often strongholds of *machismo*. When someone calls you *amigo* and orders you a beer, bow out quickly unless you want to match him glass for glass in a challenge. **Avoid public drunkenness;** it can jeopardize your safety and earn the disdain of locals.

HEALTH

Common sense is the simplest prescription for good health while you travel. Travelers complain most often about their feet and their gut, so take precautionary measures: drink lots of fluids to prevent dehydration and constipation, wear sturdy, broken-in shoes and clean socks, and use talcum powder to keep your feet dry.

BEFORE YOU GO

Preparation can help minimize the likelihood of contracting a disease and maximize the chances of receiving effective health care in the event of an emergency. For tips on packing a basic **first-aid kit** and other health essentials, see p. 40.

In your **passport,** write the names of any people you wish to be contacted in case of a medical emergency, and also list any allergies or medical conditions of which you would want doctors to be aware. Matching a prescription to a foreign equivalent is not always easy, safe, or possible. Carry up-to-date, legible prescriptions or a statement from your doctor stating the medication's trade name, manufacturer, chemical name, and dosage. While traveling, be sure to keep all medication with you in your carry-on luggage.

IMMUNIZATIONS. Take a look at your immunization records before you go. Travelers over two years old should be sure that the following vaccines are up to date: MMR (for measles, mumps, and rubella); DTaP or Td (for diptheria, tetanus, and pertussis); OPV (for polio); HbCV (for haemophilus influenza B); and HBV (for hepatitus B). Adults should consider an additional dose of Polio vaccine if they have not already had one during their adult years. Travelers are required to have a certificate of **yellow fever vaccination** that is between 10 days and 10 years old at many borders in South America.

INOCULATIONS. The Centers for Disease Control (CDC) maintains a very comprehensive and detailed database of information for people traveling abroad. As of August 2000 they recommend protection against the following diseases:

Hepatitis A: ask your doctor about Harvix or an injection of **Immune Globulin.**

Hepatitis B: if you might be exposed to blood, have sexual contact on the road, stay more than 6 months in the region, or be exposed through medical treatment. The vaccine is also now recommended for all infants and children ages 11-12 who did not complete the series as infants.

Malaria: travelers to the coast, jungle, or rural areas, may want to take weekly **anti-malarial** drugs.

Rabies: if you might be exposed to animals through your work or recreation.

Typhoid: particularly if you are visiting rural areas in this region.

Yellow fever vaccination: if you will be traveling outside urban areas.

Tetanus-diptheria and **measles:** booster doses as needed.

ESSENTIALS

USEFUL ORGANIZATIONS AND PUBLICATIONS

The US **Centers for Disease Control and Prevention** (**CDC;** ☎(877) FYI-TRIP; www.cdc.gov/travel), which is an excellent source of information for travelers, maintains an international fax information service. The CDC's comprehensive booklet *Health Information for International Travelers*, an annual rundown of disease, immunization, and general health advice, is free on the website or US$22 via the Government Printing Office (☎(202) 512-1800). The **US State Department** (www.travel.state.gov) compiles Consular Information Sheets on health, entry requirements, and other issues for various countries. For quick information on health and other travel warnings, call the **Overseas Citizens Services** (☎(202) 647-5225; after-hours 647-4000), contact a US passport agency or a US embassy or consulate abroad, or send a self-addressed, stamped envelope to the Overseas Citizens Services, Bureau of Consular Affairs, #4811, US Department of State, Washington, D.C. 20520. For information on medical evacuation services and travel insurance firms, see http://travel.state.gov/medical.html. The **British Foreign and Commonwealth Office** also gives health warnings for individual countries (www.fco.gov.uk).

For detailed information on travel health, including a country-by-country overview of diseases, try the *International Travel Health Guide*, Stuart Rose, MD (Travel Medicine, US$20; www.travmed.com). For general health information, contact the **American Red Cross** (☎(800) 564-1234, M-F 8:30am-4:30pm).

MEDICAL ASSISTANCE ON THE ROAD. The quality of medical care in Peru, Bolivia, and Ecuador varies enormously. The best hospitals in major urban centers offer well-trained doctors, some of whom know English, and have much better resources than their small-town counterparts. Even in cities, however, the quality of the care will likely not be on a par with the care you have become accustomed to at home. The caliber of the medical care in smaller towns is often significantly lower, and an English-speaking doctor is by no means guaranteed. In both major cities and smaller towns the best health care locally available is generally provided by private **clínicas** (clinics). Public hospitals are often less expensive but less reliable. Many hospitals and clinics will not accept your insurance from home and will demand cash or, in urban centers, credit cards.

If you are concerned about access to medical support while traveling, there are support services you may employ. The *MedPass* from **Global Emergency Medical Services (GEMS),** 2001 Westside Dr., #120, Alpharetta, GA 30004 (☎(800) 860-1111; fax (770) 475-0058; www.globalems.com), provides 24-hour international medical assistance, support, and medical evacuation resources. The **International Association for Medical Assistance to Travelers** (**IAMAT;** in the US ☎(716) 754-4883, in Canada (416) 652-0137, in New Zealand (03) 352 2053; www.sentex.net/~iamat) has free membership, lists English-speaking doctors worldwide, and offers detailed info on immunization requirements and sanitation. If your regular **insurance** policy does not cover travel abroad, you may wish to purchase additional coverage (see p. 39).

Those with medical conditions (diabetes, allergies to antibiotics, epilepsy, heart conditions) may want to obtain a stainless-steel **Medic Alert** ID tag (first-year US$35, $15 annually thereafter), which identifies the condition and gives a 24-hour collect-call number. Contact the Medic Alert Foundation, 2323 Colorado Ave., Turlock, CA 95382 (☎ (800) 825-3785; www.medicalert.org).

ENVIRONMENTAL HAZARDS

Heat exhaustion and dehydration: Heat exhaustion, characterized by dehydration and salt deficiency, can lead to fatigue, headaches, and wooziness. Avoid it by drinking plenty of fluids, eating salty foods (e.g. crackers), and avoiding dehydrating beverages (e.g. alcohol, coffee, tea, and caffeinated soda). Continuous heat stress can eventually lead to **heatstroke,** characterized by a rising temperature, severe headache, and cessation of sweating. Victims should be cooled off with wet towels and taken to a doctor.

Sunburn: Bring sunscreen with you, and apply it liberally and often to avoid burns and risk of skin cancer. If you get sunburned, drink more fluids than usual and apply Calamine or an aloe-based lotion.

Hypothermia and frostbite: A rapid drop in body temperature is the clearest sign of over-exposure to cold. Victims may also shiver, feel exhausted, have poor coordination or slurred speech, hallucinate, or suffer amnesia. *Do not let hypothermia victims fall asleep,* or their body temperature will continue to drop and they may die. To avoid hypothermia, keep dry, wear layers, and stay out of the wind. When the temperature is below freezing, watch out for frostbite. If skin turns white, waxy, and cold, do not rub the area. Drink warm beverages, get dry, and slowly warm the area with dry fabric or steady body contact until a doctor can be found.

High altitude: The extreme variation in altitude in Peru, Bolivia, and Ecuador means that altitude sickness *(soroche)* is a risk. Travelers to high altitudes must allow their bodies a couple of days to adjust to lower oxygen levels in the air before exerting themselves. Ignoring this advice can result in symptoms such as headaches, nausea, sleeplessness, and shortness of breath, even while resting. It is best treated with rest, deep breathing, and moving to a lower altitude. If the symptoms persist or worsen, or if the victim begins to turn blue, **immediately descend to a lower altitude** and proceed to a hospital if necessary. Those planning to climb some of the region's taller peaks should take a week in the Sierra to adjust to the altitude before attempting the climb.

PREVENTING DISEASE

INSECT-BORNE DISEASES

Many diseases are transmitted by insects—mainly mosquitoes, fleas, ticks, and lice. Be aware of insects in wet or forested areas, while hiking, and especially while camping. **Mosquitoes** are most active from dusk to dawn. Use insect repellents that contain DEET, and soak or spray your gear with permethrin (licensed in the US for use on clothing). Consider natural repellents that make you smelly to insects, like vitamin B-12 or garlic pills. To stop the itch after being bitten, try Calamine lotion or topical cortisones (like Cortaid), or take a bath with a half-cup of baking soda or oatmeal. Wear long pants and long sleeves (fabric need not be thick or warm; tropic-weight cottons can keep you comfortable in the heat) and buy a mosquito net. Wear shoes and socks, and tuck long pants into socks.

Malaria: Transmitted by *Anopheles* mosquitoes that bite at night. The incubation period varies from 6-8 days to as long as months. Early symptoms include fever, chills, aches, and fatigue, followed by high fever and sweating, sometimes with vomiting and diarrhea. See a doctor for any flu-like sickness that occurs after travel in a risk area. Left untreated, malaria can cause anemia, kidney failure, coma, and death. It is an especially serious threat to pregnant women. To reduce the risk of contracting malaria, use mosquito repellent, particularly in the evenings and when visiting forested areas, and take oral prophylactics, like **mefloquine** (sold under the name Lariam) or **doxycycline** (ask your doctor for a prescription). Be aware that these drugs can have very serious side effects, including slowed heart rate and nightmares.

Dengue fever: An "urban viral infection" transmitted by *Aedes* mosquitoes, which bite during the day rather than at night. Dengue has flu-like symptoms and is often indicated by a rash 3-4 days after the onset of fever. Symptoms for the first 2-4 days include chills, high fever, headaches, swollen lymph nodes, muscle aches, and in some instances, a pink rash on the face. If you experience these symptoms, see a doctor, drink plenty of liquids, and take fever-reducing medication such as acetaminophen (Tylenol). **Never take aspirin to treat dengue fever.**

Yellow fever: A viral disease transmitted by mosquitoes; derives its name from one of its most common symptoms, the jaundice caused by liver damage. While most cases are mild, the severe ones begin with fever, headache, muscle pain, nausea, and abdominal pain before progressing to jaundice, vomiting of blood, and bloody stools. While there is no specific treatment, there is an effective vaccine that offers 10 years of protection.

Other insect-borne diseases: Leishmaniasis is a parasite transmitted by sand flies. Common symptoms are fever, weakness, and swelling of the spleen. There is a treatment, but no vaccine. **CHAGAS disease (American trypanomiasis)** is another relatively common parasite transmitted by the cone nose or kissing bug, which infests mud and thatch. Its symptoms are fever, heart disease, and later on, an enlarged intestine. There is no vaccine and limited treatment.

FOOD- AND WATER-BORNE DISEASES

Prevention is the best cure: be sure that everything you eat is cooked properly and that the water you drink is clean. Peel your fruits and veggies and avoid tap water (including ice cubes and anything washed in tap water, like salad). Watch out for food from markets or street vendors that may have been cooked in unhygienic conditions. Other culprits are raw shellfish (used in ceviche), unpasteurized milk, and sauces containing raw eggs. Buy bottled water, or purify your own water by bringing it to a rolling boil or treating it with **iodine tablets.** Always wash your hands before eating, or bring a quick-drying purifying liquid hand cleaner. Your bowels will thank you.

Traveler's diarrhea: Results from drinking untreated water or eating uncooked foods; a temporary (and fairly common) reaction to the bacteria in new food ingredients. Symptoms include nausea, bloating, urgency, and malaise. Try quick-energy, non-sugary foods with protein and carbohydrates to keep your strength up. Over-the-counter anti-diarrheals (e.g. Imodium) may counteract the problems, but can complicate serious infections. The most dangerous side effect is dehydration; drink 8 oz. of water with ½ tsp. of sugar or honey and a pinch of salt, try uncaffeinated soft drinks, or munch on salted crackers. If you develop a fever or your symptoms don't go away after 4-5 days, consult a doctor. Consult a doctor for treatment of diarrhea in children.

Dysentery: Results from a serious intestinal infection caused by certain bacteria. The most common type is bacillary dysentery, also called shigellosis. Symptoms include bloody diarrhea (sometimes mixed with mucus), fever, and abdominal pain and tenderness. Bacillary dysentery generally only lasts a week, but it is highly contagious. Amoebic dysentery, which develops more slowly, is a more serious disease and may cause long-term damage if left untreated. A stool test can determine which kind you have; seek medical help immediately. Dysentery can be treated with the drugs norfloxacin or ciprofloxacin (commonly known as Cipro). If you are traveling in high-risk (especially rural) regions, consider obtaining a prescription before you leave home.

Cholera: An intestinal disease caused by a bacteria found in contaminated food. The disease has recently reached epidemic stages in South America. Symptoms include diarrhea, dehydration, vomiting, and muscle cramps. See a doctor immediately; if left untreated, it may be deadly. Antibiotics are available, but the most important treatment is rehydration. Consider getting a (50% effective) vaccine if you have stomach problems (e.g. ulcers) or will be living where the water is not reliable.

Hepatitis A (distinct from B and C, see below) is a high risk in this region. Hep A is a viral infection of the liver acquired primarily through contaminated water, ice, shellfish, or unpeeled fruits, and vegetables, but also from sexual contact. Symptoms include fatigue, fever, loss of appetite, nausea, dark urine, jaundice, vomiting, aches and pains, and light stools. Ask your doctor about the vaccine called Havrix, or ask to get an injection of immune globulin (IG; formerly called gamma globulin). Risk is highest in rural areas and the countryside, but is also present in urban areas.

ESSENTIALS

Parasites such as microbes and tapeworms also hide in unsafe water and food. **Giardia,** for example, is acquired by drinking untreated water from streams or lakes all over the world. Symptoms of parasitic infections in general include swollen glands or lymph nodes, fever, rashes or itchiness, digestive problems, eye problems, and anemia. Boil your water, wear shoes, avoid bugs, and eat only cooked food.

Schistosomiasis is another parasitic disease, caused when the larvae of the flatworm penetrates unbroken skin, and is a risk when swimming in fresh water, especially in rural areas. If your skin is exposed to untreated water, the CDC recommends immediate and vigorous rubbing with a towel and/or the application of rubbing alcohol. If infected, you may notice an itchy localized rash; later symptoms include fever, fatigue, painful urination, diarrhea, loss of appetite, night sweats, and a hive-like rash on the body. Schistosomiasis can be treated with prescription drugs once symptoms appear.

Typhoid fever is common in villages and rural areas. While mostly transmitted through contaminated food and water, it may also be acquired by direct contact with another person. Symptoms include fever, headaches, fatigue, loss of appetite, constipation, and a rash on the abdomen or chest. Antibiotics can treat typhoid, but the CDC recommends vaccinations (70-90% effective) if you will be hiking, camping, or staying in small cities or rural areas.

OTHER INFECTIOUS DISEASES

Rabies: Transmitted through the saliva of infected animals; fatal if untreated. By the time symptoms appear (thirst and muscle spasms), the disease is in its terminal stage. If you are bitten, wash the wound thoroughly, seek immediate medical care, and try to have the animal located. A rabies vaccine, which consists of 3 shots given over a 21-day period, is available but is only semi-effective.

Hepatitis B: A viral infection of the liver transmitted via bodily fluids or needle-sharing. Symptoms may not surface until years after infection. Vaccinations are recommended for health-care workers, sexually-active travelers, and anyone planning to seek medical treatment abroad. The 3-shot vaccination series must begin 6 mo. before traveling.

Hepatitis C: Like Hep B, but the mode of transmission differs. IV drug users, those with occupational exposure to blood, hemodialysis patients, and recipients of blood transfusions are at the highest risk, but the disease can also be spread through sexual contact or sharing items like razors and toothbrushes that may have traces of blood on them.

AIDS, HIV, STDS

Acquired Immune Deficiency Syndrome (AIDS) is a growing problem around the world. The World Health Organization estimates that there are more than 30 million people infected with the HIV virus, and women now represent 40% of all new HIV infections. The easiest mode of HIV transmission is through direct blood-to-blood contact with an HIV-positive person; never share intravenous drug, tattooing, or other needles. The most common mode of transmission is sexual intercourse. Health professionals recommend the use of latex condoms. Since it isn't always easy to buy condoms when traveling, take a supply with you. For more information on AIDS in Peru, Ecuador, and Bolivia, call the **US Centers for Disease Control's** 24-hour hotline at ☎(800) 342-2437, or contact the **Joint United Nations Programme on HIV/AIDS (UNAIDS),** Appia 20, CH-1211 Geneva 27, Switzerland (☎+41 (22) 791 36 66, fax 791 41 87). Council's brochure, *Travel Safe: AIDS and International Travel,* is available at all Council Travel offices and on their website (www.ciee.org/lsp/safety/travelsafe.htm).

Sexually transmitted diseases (STDs) such as gonorrhea, chlamydia, genital warts, syphilis, and herpes are easier to catch than HIV and can be just as deadly. **Hepatitis B** and **C** are also serious STDs (see Other Infectious Diseases, above). Though condoms may protect you from some STDs, oral or even tactile contact can lead to transmission. Warning signs include swelling, sores, bumps, or blisters on sex organs, the rectum, or the mouth; burning and pain during urination and bowel movements; itching around sex organs; swelling or redness of the throat; and flu-like symptoms. If these symptoms develop, see a doctor immediately.

WOMEN'S HEALTH

Women traveling in unsanitary conditions are vulnerable to **urinary tract** and **bladder infections,** common bacterial diseases that cause a burning sensation and painful and sometimes frequent urination. To try to avoid these infections, drink plenty of vitamin-C-rich juice and plenty of clean water, and urinate frequently, especially right after intercourse. Untreated, these infections can lead to kidney infections, sterility, and even death. If symptoms persist, see a doctor.

Women are also susceptible to **vaginal yeast infections,** a treatable but uncomfortable illness likely to flare up in hot and humid climates. Wearing loosely fitting trousers or a skirt and cotton underwear will help. Yeast infections can be treated with an over-the-counter remedy like Monostat or Gynelotrimin. Bring supplies from home if you are prone to infection.

Tampons are almost impossible to find in Peru, Bolivia, and Ecuador, and **pads,** although not hard to find, are of the thick, uncomfortable type. Chances are, your preferred brand won't be available, so you might want to take supplies along. **Reliable contraceptives** may also be difficult to find in some areas. Women on the pill should bring enough to allow for possible loss or extended stays. Bring a prescription, since forms of the pill vary a good deal. Though condoms are increasingly available, bring your favorite brand along as availability and quality vary.

Women considering an **abortion** abroad should contact the **International Planned Parenthood Federation (IPPF),** Regent's College, Inner Circle, Regent's Park, London NW1 4NS (☎ (020) 7487 7900; fax 7487 7950; www.ippf.org), for more information.

INSURANCE

Travel insurance generally covers four basic areas: medical/health problems, property loss, trip cancellation/interruption, and emergency evacuation. Although your regular insurance policies may well extend to travel-related accidents, you may consider purchasing travel insurance if the cost of potential trip cancellation/interruption or emergency medical evacuation is greater than you can absorb.

Medical insurance (especially university policies) often covers costs incurred abroad; check with your provider. **US Medicare** does not cover foreign travel. **Canadians** are protected by their home province's health insurance plan for up to 90 days after leaving the country; check with the provincial Ministry of Health or Health Plan Headquarters for details. **Homeowners' insurance** (or your family's coverage) often covers theft during travel and loss of travel documents (passport, plane ticket, railpass, etc.) up to US$500.

ISIC and **ITIC** (see p. 27) provide basic insurance benefits, including US$100 per day of in-hospital sickness for up to 60 days, US$3000 of accident-related medical reimbursement, and US$25,000 for emergency medical transport. Cardholders have access to a toll-free 24-hour helpline for medical, legal, and financial emergencies overseas (US and Canada ☎ (877) 370-4742, elsewhere call US collect +1 (713) 342-4104). **American Express** (US ☎ (800) 528-4800) grants most cardholders automatic car rental insurance (collision and theft, but not liability) and ground travel accident coverage of US$100,000 on flight purchases made with the card.

INSURANCE PROVIDERS. Council and **STA** (see p. 48 for complete listings) offer various plans that can supplement your regular coverage. Other private insurance providers in the **US and Canada** include: **Access America** (☎ (800) 284-8300); **Berkely Group/Carefree Travel Insurance** (☎ (800) 323-3149; www.berkely.com); **Globalcare Travel Insurance** (☎ (800) 821-2488; www.globalcare-cocco.com); and **Travel Assistance International** (☎ (800) 821-2828; www.worldwide-assistance.com). Providers in the **UK** include **Campus Travel** (☎ (018) 6525 8000) and **Columbus Travel Insurance** (☎ (020) 7375 0011). In **Australia,** try **CIC Insurance** (☎ 9202 8000).

ESSENTIALS

PACKING

PACK LIGHT. Lay out only what you absolutely need, then take half the clothes and twice the money. The less you have, the less you have to lose (or store, or carry on your back). Any extra space left will be useful for any souvenirs or items you might pick up along the way. If you plan to do a lot of hiking, also see Outdoors, p. 41.

LUGGAGE. If you plan to cover most of your itinerary by foot, a sturdy **frame backpack** is unbeatable. (For the basics on buying a pack, see p. 42.) Toting a **suitcase** or **trunk** is fine if you plan to live in one or two cities and explore from there, but a very bad idea if you're going to be moving around a lot. In addition to your main piece of luggage, a **daypack** (a small backpack or courier bag) is a must.

CLOTHING. No matter when you're traveling, it's always a good idea to bring a **warm jacket** or wool sweater, a **rain jacket** (Gore-Tex® is both waterproof and breathable), sturdy shoes or **hiking boots,** and **thick socks. Flip-flops** or waterproof sandals are crucial for grubby hostel showers. You may also want to add one outfit beyond the jeans and t-shirt uniform, and maybe a nicer pair of shoes if you have the room. Peru, Bolivia, and Ecuador are all fairly conservative countries—visitors should respect local customs and dress accordingly. Women should avoid revealing clothing (like tank tops and shorts), although more is acceptable in large cities. Men should stick to simple, solid shirts and slacks—bright, flashy clothing will attract unnecessary attention.

SLEEPSACK. Some hostels require that you either provide your own linen or rent sheets from them. Save cash by making your own sleepsack: fold a full-size sheet in half the long way, then sew it closed along the long side and one of the short sides.

CONVERTERS AND ADAPTERS. In Peru, Bolivia, and Ecuador electricity is 110V. This is the same as in North America, but is not compatible with Europe and Australia. Ask first though, as some places might have alarm-clock-melting 220V outlets. If necessary visit a hardware store for an adapter (which changes the shape of the plug) and a converter (which changes the voltage). Don't make the mistake of using only an adapter (unless appliance instructions explicitly state otherwise).

FIRST-AID KIT. For a basic first-aid kit, pack bandages, aspirin or other painkiller, antibiotic cream, a thermometer, a Swiss Army knife, tweezers, moleskin, decongestant, motion-sickness remedy, diarrhea or upset-stomach medication (Pepto Bismol or Imodium), an antihistamine, sunscreen, insect repellent, burn ointment, and a syringe for emergencies (get an explanatory letter from your doctor).

FILM. If you are not a serious photographer, you might want to bring a **disposable camera** or two rather than an expensive permanent one. Despite disclaimers, airport security X-rays *can* fog film, so buy a lead-lined pouch at a camera store or ask security to hand inspect your film. Always pack film in your carry-on luggage, since higher-intensity X-rays are used on checked luggage.

OTHER USEFUL ITEMS. For safety purposes, you should bring a **money belt** and small **padlock.** Basic **outdoors equipment** (plastic water bottle, compass, waterproof matches, pocketknife, sunglasses, sunscreen, hat) may also prove useful. Quick repairs of torn garments can be done on the road with a needle and thread; also consider bringing electrical tape for patching tears. Doing your **laundry** by hand (where it is allowed) is both cheaper and more convenient than doing it at a laundromat—bring detergent, a small rubber ball to stop up the sink, and string for a makeshift clothes line. **Other things** you're liable to forget: an umbrella; sealable **plastic bags** (for damp clothes, soap, food, shampoo, and other spillables); an **alarm clock;** safety pins; rubber bands; a flashlight; earplugs; and a small calculator.

ACCOMMODATIONS

HOTELS AND HOSTELS

Most budget accommodations in Peru, Bolivia, and Ecuador are in the form of basic hotels and hostels. Rooms are usually small and simple, bathrooms may be private or communal, and there is often a lounge area. Some accommodations offer **matrimonials**—rooms for two people with a double, queen, or king-sized bed rather than the two twin beds, and these often cost less than a traditional double. Hostels are occasionally dorm-style accommodations. They sometimes have kitchens and utensils for your use, bike or moped rentals, storage areas, and laundry facilities. Both hotels and hostels may offer laundry service for a fee, they may have a place where guests can do their own laundry (sometimes a washtub and a clothes line), or there may be no laundry facilities at all. It is expected everywhere that after you've finished your business, you throw your toilet paper into the waste basket—*not* the toilet. It's also a good idea to carry a small roll of toilet paper with you; many places don't provide it. Otherwise, the rules vary. There is occasionally a lockout time before which you must return to the hotel or hostel. If you get locked out, you can try to wake the owner or receptionist, but don't expect a cheerful greeting. An average room will cost about US$3-8. The general hierarchy for accommodations is hotels, the most expensive option, followed by hostels, residencials, and *alojamientos*.

HOSTELLING INTERNATIONAL. Joining the youth hostel association in your own country (listed below) automatically grants you membership privileges in **Hostelling International (HI)**, a federation of national hosteling associations that guarantees a certain level of quality in terms of cleanliness, comfort, and friendliness. HI cards, however, may not be extremely useful in Peru, Bolivia, and Ecuador—there are very few affiliated hostels, and the discount you'll receive may not be worth the price of the card. Most student travel agencies (see p. 48) sell HI cards, as do national hosteling organizations. HI's umbrella organization's web page (www.iyhf.org) lists the web addresses and phone numbers of all national associations; contact the one nearest you to join.

CAMPING AND THE OUTDOORS

Camping is definitely possible in Peru, Bolivia, and Ecuador, but it is most frequently an option for hikers along trails or in national parks for free or a minimal fee rather than in established campsites in towns. Some parks and reserves have designated camping areas, and some more frequently climbed mountains have *refugios* (rustic shelters) at various elevation levels. Some landowners may allow camping on their property, but be sure to ask. Be cautious when camping in non-designated spots, especially in isolated areas.

The non-profit **South American Explorers (SAE)** is widely recognized as a wonderful source of travel information on Peru, Ecuador, and Bolivia. This well-respected outfit (with clubhouses in Lima and Cusco, Peru; Quito, Ecuador; and Ithaca, New York) is the ultimate resource for information about outdoor experiences in the region, providing members with reliable, up-to-date information on discount airfares, trip planning, and travel conditions. There is no clubhouse in Bolivia, but the SAE offers information on the country. Contact them at 126 Indian Creek Rd., Ithaca, NY 14850 (☎(607) 277-0488; fax 277-6122; email explorer@samexplo.org; www.samexplo.org).

USEFUL PUBLICATIONS AND WEB RESOURCES

A variety of publishing companies offer hiking guidebooks to meet the educational needs of the novice or expert. For information about camping, hiking, and biking, write or call the publishers listed below to receive a free catalog.

Sierra Club Books, 85 Second St., 2nd fl., San Francisco, CA 94105, USA (☎(415) 977-5704; www.sierraclub.org/books). Publishes general resource books on hiking, camping, and women traveling in the outdoors.

The Mountaineers Books, 1001 SW Klickitat Way, #201, Seattle, WA 98134, USA (☎(800) 553-4453 or (206) 223-6303; www.mountaineersbooks.org). Over 400 titles on hiking, biking, mountaineering, natural history, and conservation.

CAMPING AND HIKING EQUIPMENT

WHAT TO BUY...

Good camping equipment is both sturdy and light. It's best to bring equipment with you, since buying it in Peru, Bolivia, or Ecuador will be much more expensive. There are shops in most major cities if you need to replace or fix equipment.

Sleeping Bag: Most sleeping bags are rated by season ("summer" means 30-40°F at night; "four-season" or "winter" often means below 0°F). Sleeping bags are made either of **down** (warmer and lighter, but more expensive, and miserable when wet) or of **synthetic** material (heavier, more durable, and warmer when wet). Prices may range from US$80-210 for a summer synthetic to US$250-300 for a good down winter bag. **Sleeping bag pads** include foam pads (US$10-20), air mattresses (US$15-50), and Therm-A-Rest self-inflating pads (US$45-80). Bring a **stuff sack** to store your bag and keep it dry.

Tent: The best tents are free-standing (with their own frames and suspension systems), set up quickly, and only require staking in high winds. Low-profile dome tents are the best all-around. Good 2-person tents start at US$90, 4-person at US$300. Seal the seams of your tent with waterproofer, and make sure it has a rain fly. Other tent accessories include a **battery-operated lantern,** a **plastic groundcloth,** and a **nylon tarp.**

Backpack: Internal-frame packs mold better to your back, keep a lower center of gravity, and flex adequately to allow you to hike difficult trails. **External-frame packs** are more comfortable for long hikes over even terrain, as they keep weight higher and distribute it more evenly. Make sure your pack has a strong, padded hip-belt to transfer weight to your legs. Any serious backpacking requires a pack of at least 4000 in^3 (16,000cc), plus 500 in^3 for sleeping bags in internal-frame packs. Sturdy backpacks cost anywhere from US$125-420—this is one area in which it doesn't pay to economize. Fill up any pack with something heavy and walk around the store with it to get a sense of how it distributes weight before buying it. Either buy a **waterproof backpack cover,** or store all of your belongings in plastic bags inside your pack.

Boots: Be sure to wear hiking boots with good **ankle support.** They should fit snugly and comfortably over 1-2 pairs of wool socks and thin liner socks. Break in boots over several weeks first in order to spare yourself from painful and debilitating blisters.

Other Necessities: Synthetic layers, like those made of polypropylene, and a **pile jacket** will keep you warm even when wet. A **"space blanket"** will help you retain your body heat and doubles as a groundcloth (US$5-15). Plastic **water bottles** are virtually shatter- and leak-proof. Bring **water-purification tablets** for when you can't boil water. Although most campgrounds provide campfire sites, you may want to bring a small **metal grill** or **camp stove** (the classic Coleman starts at US$40) and a propane-filled **fuel bottle** to operate it. Also don't forget a **first-aid kit, pocketknife, insect repellent, calamine lotion,** and **waterproof matches** or a **lighter.**

...AND WHERE TO BUY IT

The mail-order/online companies listed below offer lower prices than many retail stores, but a visit to a local camping or outdoors store will give you a good sense of the look and weight of certain items.

Campmor, P.O. Box 700, Upper Saddle River, NJ 07458 (US ☎(888) 226-7667; elsewhere call US +1 (201) 825-8300; www.campmor.com).

Discount Camping, 880 Main North Rd., Pooraka, South Australia 5095, Australia (☎(08) 8262 3399; www.discountcamping.com.au).

Eastern Mountain Sports (EMS), 327 Jaffrey Rd., Peterborough, NH 03458, USA (☎(888) 463-6367 or (603) 924-7231; www.shopems.com)

L.L. Bean, Freeport, ME 04033 (US and Canada ☎(800) 441-5713; UK ☎(0800) 962 954; elsewhere, call US +1 (207) 552-6878; www.llbean.com).

Mountain Designs, P.O. Box 1472, Fortitude Valley, Queensland 4006, Australia (☎(07) 3252 8894; www.mountaindesign.com.au).

Recreational Equipment, Inc. (REI), Sumner, WA 98352, USA (☎(800) 426-4840 or (253) 891-2500; www.rei.com).

YHA Adventure Shop, 14 Southampton St., London, WC2E 7HA, UK (☎(020) 7836 8541). The main branch of one of Britain's largest outdoor equipment suppliers.

WILDERNESS SAFETY

Stay warm, stay dry, and stay hydrated. The vast majority of life-threatening wilderness situations can be avoided by following this simple advice. Prepare yourself for an emergency, however, by always packing raingear, a hat and mittens, a first-aid kit, a reflector, a whistle, high energy food, and extra water for any hike. Dress in wool or warm layers of synthetic materials designed for the outdoors; never rely on cotton for warmth, as it is absolutely useless when wet.

Check **weather forecasts** and pay attention to the skies when hiking, since weather patterns can change suddenly. Whenever possible, let someone know when and where you are going hiking, either a friend, your hostel, a park ranger, or a local hiking organization. Do not attempt a hike beyond your ability—you may be endangering your life. See Health, p. 34, for information about outdoor ailments and basic medical concerns.

Don't leave food or other scented items (trash, toiletries, the clothes that you cooked in) near your tent. Hanging edibles and other good-smelling objects from a tree out of reach of hungry paws, is the best way to keep your toothpaste from becoming a condiment. Animals are also attracted to any perfume, as are bugs, so cologne, scented soap, deodorant, and hairspray should stay at home.

For more information, consult *How to Stay Alive in the Woods*, by Bradford Angier (Macmillan Press, US$8).

JUNGLE TOURS

Tourists mainly visit Peru, Bolivia, and Ecuador's rainforests to take a jungle tour through the Amazon basin. While the different tours vary greatly, they typically include treks through dripping rainforests, canoe rides down muddy rivers, visits to remote indigenous communities, and overnight stays in cabaña outposts or jungle lodges. Some regions of the jungle have less primary growth and smaller wildlife populations than others, mainly because oil companies have built roads opening the jungle up to colonization, deforestation, and the destruction of native habitats. Other sections remain more or less intact, but this is precisely because they are more isolated, harder to reach, and thus more expensive to visit.

Tours operate out of just about every town in and around Ecuador's Oriente, but to reach the most remote parts, you'll want to head out of either **Coca** or **Lago Agrio,** which provide access to the country's most undeveloped, impressive, and protected jungle areas, including the prominent **Cuyabeno Reserve** and the enormous, remote **Parque Nacional Yasuní.** To the south and west of Coca, the pleasant town of **Tena** and the tourist village of **Misahuallí** send trips into the less pristine but still impressive jungle wilderness that stretches out just to the east of them. The undisputed base for southern Oriente jungle tours is **Macas,** which offers access to remote Shuar villages, the nearby Cueva de los Tayos, and the rugged expanse of the *zona baja* of **Parque Nacional Sangay.** A number of jungle tours can also be taken from cities in Peru. Although not actually situated in the jungle, Cusco promises numerous touring options out to Peru's highly revered **Manu Biosphere Reserve.** Within the rainforest, **Iquitos** makes a fabulous base for tours to the Pacaya-Samiria Reserve. **Tambopata-Candamo Reserve** is another promising area for exploration and is accessible from Puerto Maldonado. Seventy percent of Bolivia is comprised of the Amazon Basin, making it easy to venture into the jungle. **Rurrenabaque** is the best place to start a tour, but numerous agencies operate out of other towns, including Santa Cruz and Trinidad. Popular destinations from Rurrenabaque include the **Beni Biological Reserve** and the **Alto Madidi National Park.**

After deciding which area you want to explore, you must make the equally important decision of who will guide you through it. You might end up having an excellent time with a tour guide who knows what he's doing, points out interesting wildlife, and respects the land and the people—or you could go along silently as your guide mentally counts his profits and stares out into a jungle he doesn't know much about. SAE (see p. 41) can be helpful in avoiding such a situation; they provide trip reports that offer recommendations and warnings about various companies. The companies listed in this guide are generally quite reliable, but they don't come guaranteed. In general, it pays to ask a lot of questions and follow your gut feeling; after all, there are plenty of companies to choose from. If you plan on visiting any nationally protected areas, make sure the company is approved by the National Park Administration (INEFAN) in Ecuador or the appropriate licensing board in Peru and Bolivia.

KEEPING IN TOUCH

MAIL

SENDING MAIL TO PERU, BOLIVIA, AND ECUADOR

Envelopes should be marked "airmail" or "por avion" to avoid having letters sent by sea. The more remote the destination, the longer mail will take to arrive.

Australia: Allow at least 20 days for regular airmail to Lima, Quito, or La Paz. Postcards and letters up to 20g cost AUS$1; packages up to 0.5kg AUS$9, up to 2kg AUS$45. **EMS** can get a letter to Peru in 5-6 days, Ecuador in 3-5 days, or Bolivia in 4-5 days for AUS$32. www.auspost.com.au/pac.

Canada: Allow 7 to 20 days for regular airmail to Lima, Quito, or La Paz. Postcards and letters up to 20g cost CDN$0.95; packages up to 0.5kg CDN$10.45, up to 2kg CDN$39.20. www.canadapost.ca/CPC2/common/rates/ratesgen.html#international.

Ireland: Allow 15 to 20 days for regular airmail to Lima, Quito, or La Paz. Postcards and letters up to 25g cost IR£0.32. Add IR£2 for Swiftpost International. www.anpost.ie.

New Zealand: Allow at least 20 days for regular airmail to Lima, Quito, or La Paz. Postcards NZ$1.10. Letters up to 200g cost NZ$1.80-7; small parcels up to 0.5kg NZ$58, up to 2kg NZ$112. www.nzpost.co.nz/nzpost/inrates.

UK: Allow 4-8 days for airmail to Lima, Quito, or La Paz. Letters up to 20g cost UK£0.65; packages of 0.5kg UK£9.05, of 2kg UK£35.30. UK Swiftair delivers letters a day faster for UK£2.85 more. www.royalmail.co.uk/calculator.

US: Allow at least 7-10 days for regular airmail to Lima, Quito, or La Paz. Postcards/aerogrammes cost US$0.55/0.60; letters under 1 oz. US$1. Packages under 1 lb. cost US$7.20; larger packages cost a variable amount (around US$15). US Express Mail takes 6 days and costs US$19/23 (0.5/1 lb.).

Additionally, **Federal Express** (Australia ☎ 13 26 10; US and Canada ☎ (800) 247-4747; New Zealand ☎ (0800) 73 33 39; UK ☎ (0800) 12 38 00) handles express mail services from most of the above countries to Peru, Ecuador, and Bolivia. They can get a letter from New York to Lima or Quito in 2 days, or to La Paz in 3 days, for US$43.

RECEIVING MAIL IN PERU, BOLIVIA, AND ECUADOR

General Delivery: Mail can be sent to Peru, Bolivia, and Ecuador through **Lista de Correos** (or by using the international phrase **Poste Restante**) to almost any city or town with a post office. Address letters to: Anup <u>KUBAL</u>, *Lista de Correos*, Quito, ECUADOR. The letter should also be marked *Favor de retener hasta la llegada* (please hold until arrival). The mail will go to a special desk in the central post office, unless you specify a post office by street address. As a rule, it is best to use the largest post office in the area, since mail may be sent there regardless. When picking up your mail, bring a form of photo ID, preferably a passport; occasionally there is a small fee (if there is, it should not exceed the cost of domestic postage). If the clerks insist that there is nothing for you, have them check under your first name as well. *Let's Go* lists post offices in the **Practical Information** section for each city and most towns.

American Express: AmEx's travel offices offer a free **Client Letter Service** (mail held up to 30 days and forwarding upon request) for cardholders who contact them in advance. Address the letter in the same way shown above. Some offices offer these services to non-cardholders (especially AmEx Travelers Cheque holders), but call ahead to make sure. AmEx has offices in Lima and Cusco in Peru, Quito and Guayaquil in Ecuador, and La Paz and Santa Cruz in Bolivia; *Let's Go* lists the office info in the **Practical Information** sections of those cities; for a complete, free list, call ☎(800) 528-4800.

DHL: The most reliable, and fastest way to send packages world-wide from Peru, Bolivia, and Ecuador is DHL. For a hefty price, DHL can get mail anywhere in the world within a few days. See the **Practical Information** sections of most mid- to large-sized cities; most have a DLH office or affiliate.

SENDING MAIL HOME FROM PERU, BOLIVIA, AND ECUADOR

Airmail from Peru, Bolivia, and Ecuador to North America averages 7 days; to Australia or New Zealand 14 days; to the UK or Ireland 7 days; to South Africa 14 days. Mark envelopes "por avion." **Aerogrammes,** printed sheets that fold into envelopes and travel via airmail, are available at some post offices. Most post offices will charge exorbitant fees or simply refuse to send aerogrammes with enclosures.

Post offices in larger cities tend to have the quickest and most consistent service—if you need something to reach its destination in a reasonable amount of time, don't send it from a tiny post office in a remote jungle town.

Surface mail is by far the cheapest and slowest way to send mail. It takes one to three months to cross the Atlantic and two to four to cross the Pacific—good for items you won't need to see for a while, such as souvenirs or other articles you've acquired along the way that are weighing down your pack.

TELEPHONES

CALLING HOME

A **calling card** is probably your cheapest bet. Calls are billed either collect or to your account. **To obtain a calling card** from your national telecommunications service before leaving home, contact one of the following:

Australia: Telstra Australia Direct (☎13 22 00)

Canada: Bell Canada **Canada Direct** (☎(800) 565-4708)

Ireland: Telecom Éireann **Ireland Direct** (☎(800) 25 02 50)

New Zealand: Telecom New Zealand (☎(0800) 00 00 00)

South Africa: Telkom South Africa (☎09 03)

UK: British Telecom **BT Direct** (☎(800) 34 51 44)

US: AT&T (☎(888) 288-4685); **Sprint** (☎(800) 877-4646); or **MCI** (☎(800) 444-4141)

To **call home with a calling card,** contact the operator for your service provider by dialing the appropriate toll-free access number below:

	PERU	ECUADOR	BOLIVIA
AT&T	0800 50 000	999 199	0800 1112
Sprint	0800 50 020	999 171	0800 3333
MCI WorldPhone Direct	0800 50 010	999 170	0800 2222
Canada Direct	0800 50 295	N/A	0800 0102
BT Direct	0800 50 080	999 178	0800 0044

ESSENTIALS

You can also make **direct international calls** from some pay phones, but if you aren't using a calling card, you may need to drop your coins as quickly as your words. Where available, prepaid phone cards can be used for direct international calls, but they are still less cost-efficient. Placing a **collect call** (*llamada con cobro revertido*) through an international operator is even more expensive, but may be necessary in an emergency. You can typically place collect calls through the service providers listed above even if you don't possess one of their phone cards. Although incredibly convenient, in-room hotel calls invariably include an arbitrary and sky-high surcharge.

FROM ECUADOR. Ecuador's infamous national phone company, known as **PacificTel** on the coast and **ANDINATEL** in the interior, has inspired fury for being slow and unreliable. Public phones are nonexistent, even in Quito, and many phone offices are not equipped to handle calling card, collect, or even international calls. Those offices that can handle international calls sometimes do them for exorbitant rates, others allow collect and calling cards calls for a fee or with the use of tokens (*fichas*), and a very few kindly allow collect and calling card calls for free.

FROM PERU. Things get easier in Peru, where the whole wondrous show is run by the Spanish firm **Telefónica del Perú.** To make a calling card call, keep your eyes peeled for the newer blue public phones that often have slots for both phone cards and coins. These public phones are a better bet than the telephone offices which sometimes only have old phones unable to cope with the concept of toll-free calls. **Prepaid phonecards** are available in various denominations starting at s/5.

PLACING INTERNATIONAL CALLS. To call Peru, Bolivia, or Ecuador from home or to place an international call from Peru, Bolivia, or Ecuador, dial:

1. The **international dialing prefix.** To dial out of **Australia,** dial ☎0011; **Canada** or the **US,** ☎011; the **Republic of Ireland, New Zealand,** or the **UK** ☎00; **South Africa** ☎09. Peru, Bolivia, and Ecuador do not have dialing prefixes.
2. The **country code** of the country you want to call. To call **Australia,** dial ☎61; **Canada** or the **US** ☎1; the **Republic of Ireland** ☎353; **New Zealand** ☎64; **South Africa** ☎27; the **UK** ☎44; **Peru** ☎51; **Bolivia** ☎591; **Ecuador** ☎593.
3. The **city** or **area code.** *Let's Go* lists the phone codes for cities and towns in Peru, Bolivia, and Ecuador opposite the city or town name, alongside the following icon: ☎. If the first digit is a zero (e.g., 04 for Cochabamba, Bolivia), omit it when calling from abroad (e.g., dial ☎011 591 4 from Canada to reach Cochabamba).
4. The **local number.**

FROM BOLIVIA. In Bolivia, **ENTEL** is the national phone company. To use ENTEL public phones, located in most major cities, you must buy a calling card from the main office or at stands throughout the city. Cards come in increments of Bs10 and Bs50, buying 10 and 50 minutes of local phone time respectively. **Cotel** phones (generally orange), used primarily for local calls, are coin-operated and cost Bs8 per minute. ENTEL phones on the street are ENTEL card- or credit card-operated. Snap off the indicated corner of the card before inserting it into the phone. While ENTEL phones can be used for long-distance calls, they eat up *bolivianos* pretty quickly. Note that La Paz cell phone numbers (commonly beginning with 01) cannot be called from Cotel or vendor-owned phones; only ENTEL provides such connections. Phone cards usually do not work, as many public phones cannot be used to call toll-free numbers, but phone offices are the best place to try.

CALLING WITHIN PERU, BOLIVIA, AND ECUADOR

The simplest way to call domestically is to use a coin-operated phone. **Prepaid phone cards** (available at newspaper kiosks and tobacco stores), which carry a certain amount of phone time depending on the card's denomination, usually save time and money in the long run. The computerized phone will tell you how much time, in units, you have left. Phone rates tend to be highest in the morning, lower in the evening, and lowest on Sunday and late at night. In Peru, Bolivia, and Ecuador, those who know use the red coin-only Comteco phones for local calls. It costs almost as much to call between cities in Bolivia as to call internationally.

TIME DIFFERENCES

Greenwich Mean Time (GMT) is five hours ahead of New York time, eight hours ahead of Vancouver and San Francisco time, two hours behind Johannesburg time, 10 hours behind Sydney time, and 12 hours behind Auckland time. **Bolivia** is four hours behind GMT and **Peru** and **Ecuador** five hours behind. All three countries ignore **daylight savings time.**

EMAIL AND INTERNET

Fax service and email are widespread in Peru, Bolivia, and Ecuador. Not only are these services increasingly common in the larger cities, but it is even possible to now find e-communication opportunities in rural areas. Places like the SAE, embassies, and Internet cafes can all provide a good fix for your online addictions. In all large cities, and in some smaller ones, there are also shops that cater especially to those needing computer and Internet access. Though in some places it's possible to forge a remote link with your home server, in most cases this is a much slower (and more expensive) option than taking advantage of free web-based email providers, including Hotmail (www.hotmail.com), RocketMail (www.rocketmail.com), and Yahoo! Mail (www.yahoo.com). In general, Internet access is cheaper and faster in the morning, and there is no correlation between connection speed and price.

GETTING THERE

BY PLANE

When it comes to airfare, a little effort can save you a bundle. If your plans are flexible enough to deal with the restrictions, courier fares are the cheapest. Tickets bought from consolidators and standby seating are also good deals, but last-minute specials, airfare wars, and charter flights often beat these fares. The key is to hunt around, to be flexible, and to ask persistently about discounts. Students, seniors, and those under 26 should never pay full price for a ticket.

DETAILS AND TIPS

Timing: Airfares to Peru, Bolivia, and Ecuador peak between mid-June and early September; holidays are also expensive. Midweek (M-Th morning) round-trip flights run US$40-50 cheaper than weekend flights, but they are generally more crowded and less likely to permit frequent-flier upgrades. Traveling with an "open return" ticket can be pricier than fixing a return date when buying the ticket and paying later to change it.

Route: Round-trip flights are by far the cheapest; "open-jaw" (arriving in and departing from different cities) tickets tend to be pricier. Patching one-way flights together is the most expensive way to travel.

Round-the-World (RTW): If Peru, Bolivia, or Ecuador is only one stop on a more extensive globe-hop, consider RTW ticket. Tickets usually include at least 5 stops and are valid for about a year; prices range US$1200-5000. Try **Northwest Airlines/KLM** (US ☎(800) 447-4747; www.nwa.com) or **Star Alliance,** a consortium of 13 airlines including United Airlines (US ☎(800) 241-6522; www.star-alliance.com).

Gateway Cities: Flights between capitals or regional hubs will offer the cheapest fares. The cheapest gateway cities in the region are typically Lima and Quito. Flights to La Paz tend to be expensive; it is often cheaper to book a flight to Lima and then a separate one to La Paz; most "direct" flights to La Paz involve layovers in Lima anyway. Cheaper still would be to fly to Lima, then book a flight to Juliaca (outside of Puno), and cross the border to Bolivia at Copacabana, a 3½ bus ride from La Paz.

Boarding: Confirm international flights by phone within 72hr. of departure. Most airlines require that passengers arrive at the airport at least 2hr. before departure. One carry-on item and 2 checked bags is the norm for non-courier flights.

Fares: Round-trip from gateway cities in the US to Quito or Lima can be as low as US$350-700. Flights to La Paz (starting around US$700) and the Galapagos are substantially more. Connections are usually made through New York, Atlanta, Miami, Houston, Los Angeles, or Mexico City.

BUDGET AND STUDENT TRAVEL AGENCIES

While knowledgeable agents specializing in flights to Peru, Bolivia, and Ecuador can make your life easy and help you save, they may not spend the time to find you the lowest possible fare—they get paid on commission. Students and those under 26 holding **ISIC and IYTC cards** (see p. 27), respectively, qualify for big discounts from student travel agencies. Most flights from budget agencies are on major airlines, but in peak season some may sell seats on less reliable chartered aircraft.

usit world (www.usitworld.com). Over 50 **usit campus** branches in the UK (www.usitcampus.co.uk), including 52 Grosvenor Gardens, **London** SW1W 0AG (☎(0870) 240 1010); **Manchester** (☎(0161) 273 1721); and **Edinburgh** (☎(0131) 668 3303). Nearly 20 **usit now** offices in Ireland, including 19-21 Aston Quay, O'Connell Bridge, **Dublin** 2 (☎(01) 602 1600; www.usitnow.ie), and **Belfast** (☎(02890) 327 111; www.usitnow.com). Offices also in Athens, Auckland, Brussels, Frankfurt, Johannesburg, Lisbon, Luxembourg, Madrid, Paris, Sofia, and Warsaw.

Council Travel (www.counciltravel.com). US offices include: Emory Village, 1561 N. Decatur Rd., **Atlanta,** GA 30307 (☎(404) 377-9997); 273 Newbury St., **Boston,** MA 02116 (☎(617) 266-1926); 1160 N. State St., **Chicago,** IL 60610 (☎(312) 951-0585); 931 Westwood Blvd., Westwood, **Los Angeles,** CA 90024 (☎(310) 208-3551); 254 Greene St., **New York,** NY 10003 (☎(212) 254-2525); 530 Bush St., **San Francisco,** CA 94108 (☎(415) 566-6222); 424 Broadway Ave. E., **Seattle,** WA 98102 (☎(206) 329-4567); 3301 M St. NW, **Washington, D.C.** 20007 (☎(202) 337-6464). **For US cities not listed,** call ☎(800) 2-COUNCIL (226-8624). In the UK, 28A Poland St. (Oxford Circus), **London,** W1V 3DB (☎(020) 7437 7767).

CTS Travel, 44 Goodge St., **London** W1 (☎(020) 7636 0031; fax 7637 5328; email ctsinfo@ctstravel.com.uk).

STA Travel, 6560 Scottsdale Rd. #F100, Scottsdale, AZ 85253 (☎(800) 777-0112; fax (602) 922-0793; www.sta-travel.com). A student and youth travel organization with over 150 offices worldwide. Ticket booking, travel insurance, railpasses, and more. US offices include: 297 Newbury St., **Boston,** MA 02115 (☎(617) 266-6014); 429 S. Dearborn St., **Chicago,** IL 60605 (☎(312) 786-9050); 7202 Melrose Ave., **Los Angeles,** CA 90046 (☎(323) 934-8722); 10 Downing St., **New York,** NY 10014 (☎(212) 627-3111); 4341 University Way NE, **Seattle,** WA 98105 (☎(206) 633-5000); 2401 Pennsylvania Ave., Ste. G, **Washington, D.C.** 20037 (☎(202) 887-0912); 51 Grant Ave., **San Francisco,** CA 94108 (☎(415) 391-8407). In the UK, 11 Goodge St., **London** WIP 1FE (☎(020) 7436 7779 for North American travel). In New Zealand, 10 High St., **Auckland** (☎(09) 309 0458). In Australia, 366 Lygon St., **Melbourne** Vic 3053 (☎(03) 9349 4344).

Travel CUTS (Canadian Universities Travel Services Limited), 187 College St., **Toronto,** ON M5T 1P7 (☎(416) 979-2406; fax 979-8167; www.travelcuts.com). 40 offices across Canada. Also in the UK, 295-A Regent St., **London** W1R 7YA (☎(020) 7255 1944).

COMMERCIAL AIRLINES

The commercial airlines' lowest regular offer is the **APEX** (Advance Purchase Excursion) fare, which provides confirmed reservations and allows "open-jaw" tickets. Generally, reservations must be made seven to 21 days ahead of departure, with seven- to 14-day minimum-stay and up to 90-day maximum-stay restrictions. These fares carry hefty cancellation and change penalties (fees rise in summer). Book peak-season APEX fares early; by May you will have a hard time getting your desired departure date. Use **Microsoft Expedia** (www.expedia.com) or **Travelocity** (www.travelocity.com) to get an idea of the lowest published fares, then use the resources outlined here to try and beat those fares.

FLIGHT PLANNING ON THE INTERNET. The Web is a great place to look for travel bargains—it's fast, it's convenient, and you can spend as long as you like exploring options without driving your travel agent insane.

Many airline sites offer special last-minute deals on the Web. Other sites compile the deals for you—try www.bestfares.com, www.onetravel.com, www.lowestfare.com, and www.travelzoo.com.

STA (www.sta-travel.com) and **Council** (www.counciltravel.com) provide quotes on student tickets, while **Expedia** (msn.expedia.com) and **Travelocity** (www.travelocity.com) offer full travel services. **Priceline** (www.priceline.com) allows you to specify a price, and obligates you to buy any ticket that meets or beats it; be prepared for odd routes. **Skyauction** (www.skyauction.com) allows you to bid on both last-minute and advance-purchase tickets.

Just one last note—to protect yourself, make sure that the site uses a secure server before handing over any credit card details. Happy hunting!

TRAVELING FROM NORTH AMERICA

Round-trip airfare from the US fluctuates greatly depending on season, although Internet specials and student discounts make it possible to find affordable flights at any time of the year. Both Latin American and US commercial airlines fly to Peru, Bolivia, and Ecuador. While the US airlines are typically more expensive, they allow you to fly from anywhere in United States, although the cheapest flights involve connections through one the major hubs (Miami, Houston, Los Angeles, and sometimes New York). Latin American airlines fly only from those cities.

The major US carries that fly to Peru, Bolivia, and Ecuador are: **American** (☎(800) 433-7300; www.aa.com), **Continental** (☎(800) 231-0856; www.flycontinental.com), **Delta** (☎(800) 221-1212; www.delta-air.com), **Northwest/KLM** (☎(800) 225-2525; www.nwa.com), and **United** (☎(800) 538-2929; www.ual.com). The major Latin American options are **AeroContinente** (☎(305) 436-9400; www.aerocontinente.com.pe), **LASCA** (☎(800) 225-2272; www.flylatinamerica.com), and **SAETA** (☎(800) 827-2382).

AIRCRAFT SAFETY. Developing nations do not always meet safety standards for domestic flights. The *Official Airline Guide* (www.oag.com) and many travel agencies can tell you the type and age of aircraft on a particular route. The **International Airline Passengers Association** (US ☎(972) 404-9980; UK ☎(020) 8681 6555) provides region-specific safety information. The **Federal Aviation Administration** (www.faa.gov) reviews the airline authorities for countries whose airlines enter the US. **US State Department** (☎(202) 647-5225; travel.state.gov/travel_warnings.html) travel advisories sometimes involve foreign carriers, especially when terrorist bombings may be a threat..

TRAVELING FROM THE UK AND IRELAND

Few carriers fly direct to Peru, Bolivia, or Ecuador from the United Kingdom or Ireland. To get to La Paz, one must first fly to either the United States or Mexico City, then change airlines. **AeroMexico** (US ☎(800) 237-6639; www.aeromexico.com) and **AeroCalifornia** (US ☎(800) 237-6225) provide the most convenient and inexpensive connections through Los Angeles and Mexico City.

Travelers to Lima don't have to change airlines, but will make several stops along the way. **Avianca** (London ☎(087) 0576 7747; www.avianca.com) flies from London to Colombia, then to Lima; **Iberia** (London ☎(44) 02078 30 0011; www.iberia.com) stops in Madrid; **Northwest/KLM** (London ☎(087) 0507 4074; www.klm.com) stops in Amsterdam; and **Varig** (US ☎(800) 468-2744; www.varig.com) goes through Brazil. Various US carriers (see above) fly from the UK and Ireland to Houston or Miami then to Lima.

Both **Avianca,** via Bogota, and **Northwest/KLM** fly from the UK to Quito, while **Continental** takes passengers to Houston first before continuing south.

TRAVELING FROM SOUTH AFRICA

Flights from South Africa to Peru, Bolivia, and Ecuador are extremely limited; the most common way to get there involves several stopovers and/or airline changes in Europe, the United States, or Mexico. **Northwest/KLM** is the best option for travel to Bolivia. **Varig** flies via San Paulo, Brazil, to Lima, while **Iberia** flies via Madrid to both Lima and Quito (see above for contact information).

GETTING AROUND

BY BUS

While bus travel is the cheapest and most reliable way to get around Peru, Bolivia, and Ecuador, it can still be daunting. Buses along the well-paved Panamerican Highway that hugs the Peruvian coast promise a reasonably tame journey. Elsewhere, prepare for anything. Coaches crammed with people and luggage whip around hairpin turns through thick clouds on the edges of cliffs. And once you muster up enough courage to open your eyes again, another bus coming in the opposite direction swerves past on a one-lane dirt highway overlooking oblivion. Because of the mountainous terrain, there are virtually no paved highways inland, and the quality of dirt roads varies from smooth to non-stop bumps.

Buses leave town from the **terminal terrestre** (bus station) or from a particular street with a high density of bus companies. Departure times are usually approximate, and buses run between most destinations frequently enough that it is practical just to show up at the terminal and board the next bus headed your way. The destination is usually indicated on the bus itself, as well as advertised by a man yelling the town's name over and over and over again. The vehicles themselves vary greatly in quality, from open-air trucks to second-hand school buses to sparkling new Mercedes-Benz mega-buses. A general guideline: the longer the route, the nicer the bus will be, so it may be worthwhile to board a long-distance bus even if you plan to get off before the final destination. Some bus companies, like Peru's Cruz del Sur, offer different classes of travel, ranging from the most basic, to middle-of-the-line with videos, bathrooms, and air conditioning, to the most luxurious with reclining seats and meals. One peculiar aspect of bus travel is that the buses rarely get "full." Drivers are often happy to pack as many passengers/chicken crates as they can into the aisles or even hanging out the doors and windows. If the buses get really full, drivers will occasionally let passengers ride on the roof, an especially amazing (and certainly dangerous) experience in the mountains. It is a good idea to keep your bags and belongings with you if at all possible, although luggage is usually stored on the roof or below the bus. On buses where passengers are assigned seats, be sure to request a seat that is not *al fondo* (at the back)—the difference in bumpiness will make your ride that much more enjoyable. There are no scheduled stops on colectivos; when you want to get off, simply say *"bajo aquí."*

BY PLANE

Air travel within and between Peru, Bolivia, and Ecuador is more expensive than bus or train travel, but it's also much quicker and more comfortable. Moreover, flights on the mainland are usually cheap (US$40-90), though they can cost more between the capital cities. Flying to Cusco, and then traveling overland back to Lima is a particularly common itinerary. Expect flights to the Galapagos to be very expensive (US$350-450). As a general guideline, purchase tickets a few days before departure (at least a week ahead of time for flights between large destinations), and call to confirm the booking shortly before the flight. Often, flights are overbooked and, despite holding a *billete* (ticket), a passenger may be bumped off the flight for not having *cupo*, roughly translated as "a reservation." Ask the ticketing agent if you have both. If you don't have *cupo*, it is still possible to fly standby if you arrive three hours early and hope for the best. Flights tend to leave extremely early in the morning, and it's always best to arrive a few hours early to guarantee a seat. Airlines often offer lower "promotional fares" from November to March. For specific flight, airline, and airport information, see the **Practical Information** section in individual cities with access to an airport.

PERUVIAN AIRLINES

AeroContinente (US ☎ (305) 436-9400; www.aerocontinente.com.pe) is Peru's largest national airline. Other national companies include **AeroCondor** (Lima ☎ (1) 442 5215; www.ascinsa.com.pe/AEROCONDOR/index.html); **TANS** (www.tans.com.pe); and **LanPeru** (Lima ☎ (12) 151 800, US ☎ (800) 735-5590; www.lanperu.com).

BOLIVIAN AIRLINES

AeroSur (La Paz ☎ (02) 375 152; www.angelfire.com/on/aerosur/) and **Lloyd Aereo Boliviano** (Bolivia ☎ 0800 3001, US ☎ (800) 327-7407; www.labairlines.com) serve Bolivian cities along with a limited number of other South American destinations.

ECUADORIAN AIRLINES

The three major Ecuadorian airlines for service within the country and limited international flights are: **TAME** (US ☎ (800) 990-0600; www.tameairlines.com); **Ecuatoriana** (US ☎ (800) 328-2367; www.ecuatoriana.com.ar); and **SAETA** (US ☎ (800) 827-2382; www.saeta.com/ec).

BY TRAIN

Railroad travel is not the most convenient, cheapest, or quickest way to get around, but is a valid alternative to buses. Not only do the trains travel through some of the most spectacular terrain in the world, but in Ecuador roof-riding is also permitted. While the tracks run the length of Ecuador, much of this distance is in disrepair due to mudslides, El Niño, and other natural damage. Nevertheless, there are several stretches that have been repaired and maintained. The most well-traveled stretches lie between Guayaquil and Alausí in the south, which travels from the coast into the Sierra and give passengers the opportunity to see the land change with the altitude. In Peru, trains cover the route from Arequipa to Cusco through Puno and Juliaca and from Cusco to Machu Picchu. Trains run every day, but weather sometimes causes the tracks to be inoperable for a day or two. In Bolivia, tracks connect Oruro and the Chilean and Argentinian borders, and Santa Cruz and the borders with Paraguay and Argentina. For info on prices and travel times, check the **Practical Information** sections of these towns.

BY BOAT

Large **cargo ships** travel the rivers that connect many towns in the jungle. These usually have two decks: a lower one for cargo and an upper one for passengers. The latter features a few toilets and showers, several cramped and windowless cabins (bedding is not provided), and often a canteen selling biscuits, soda, toilet paper, and other "necessities." The **kitchen** can be found below, where the cook often scoops water straight from the river to prepare the rice, fish, or soup—many passengers become ill from the food, so it may be wise to bring your own. Either way, you'll need your own bowl and utensils as well as enough water to last you more days than the captain projects. Every passenger also makes use of his or her own **hammock** and hanging rope, which are best installed as far from the bathrooms, the engine, and the lights, as possible. Hammocks are available in markets all over the jungle, in both string and cloth varieties. The cloth sort—though somewhat more expensive—provides far greater protection against intrusive elbows or feet. Other useful items include toilet paper, a chain with which to attach your bag to a pole while you sleep, a clothesline on which to hang wet towels, and a sleeping bag or blanket—constant wind makes sleeping on deck quite chilly at night.

Boats accepting passengers hang **chalkboards** from their bows, announcing their intended destination and departure times. However, while most reach their destinations, few depart on time. They often hang around the port for weeks, stuffing themselves with cargo; the boat that looks most ready to sink under the weight of its load will probably be the next to leave. There's no need to arrange a "ticket" ahead of time, as these boats don't take reservations; but it may be a good idea to establish a price with the captain. Someone will collect the passage fee (depends on length of journey and usually includes 3 meals per day) once the boat has embarked. The fee may be reduced if you wish to bring your own food. However, a tiny private cabin will raise the price—again, arrangements should be made with the captain before departure. It's also worth going down to the port beforehand to search for a boat without your backpack; travelers who arrive at the ports with their luggage often find themselves being pulled in every direction by touts. And should your chosen vessel not depart the day you board? Sling your hammock anyway and spend the night in port. The first people on board may have to wait the longest, but they also receive first choice in hammock location. Trips such as this are particularly common on waterways that flow to and from **Iquitos.**

BY TAXI AND CAR

Taxis can be a convenient way to get around, especially when you are in a hurry or traveling to places where buses don't venture. They are commonly used for travel between towns or to outlying destinations. It is usually cheaper to arrange for a taxi to drop you off and pick you up at an out-of-the-way spot than it is to rent a car yourself. When taking a taxi, always agree on the price before entering—few, if any taxis have meters, and drivers often charge more for unsuspecting tourists. You can also travel by **colectivo,** often a VW van that travels regular routes and pick up numerous passengers, falling in-between taxis and buses in price, speed, and size. Beware of advice given by taxi drivers—their recommendations are often biased; in particular, they may be lying if they tell you your chosen lodging is full.

Car rental can be a real nightmare. It will cost between US$30-80 per day (try Budget for good deals), the roads and drivers can be very scary, and a car is one more thing to worry about getting stolen. If you plan to drive you should have an **International Driving Permit** (IDP). It will be indispensable if you're in a situation (e.g. an accident or being stranded in a smaller town) where the police do not speak English, as information on the IDP is printed in Spanish. Your IDP, valid for one year, must be issued in your own country before you depart. An application for an IDP usually must include one or two photos, a current local license, an additional form of identification, and a fee.

Australia: Contact your local Royal Automobile Club (RAC) or the National Royal Motorist Association (NRMA) if in NSW or the ACT (☎(08) 9421 4444; www.rac.com.au/travel). Permits AUS$15.

Canada: Contact any Canadian Automobile Association (CAA) branch office or write to CAA, 1145 Hunt Club Rd., #200, K1V 0Y3. (☎(613) 247-0117; www.caa.ca/CAAInternet/travelservices/internationaldocumentation/idptravel.htm). Permits CDN$10.

Ireland: Contact the nearest Automobile Association (AA) office or write to the UK address below. Permits IR£4. The Irish Automobile Association, 23 Suffolk St., Rockhill, Blackrock, Co. Dublin (☎(01) 677 9481), honors most foreign automobile memberships (24hr. breakdown and road service ☎(800) 667 788; toll-free in Ireland).

New Zealand: Contact your local Automobile Association (AA) or their main office at Auckland Central, 99 Albert St. (☎(9) 377 4660; www.nzaa.co.nz). Permits NZ$8.

South Africa: Contact the Travel Services Department of the Automobile Association of South Africa at P.O. Box 596, 2000 Johannesburg (☎(11) 799 1400; fax 799 1410; http://aasa.co.za). Permits SAR28.50.

United Kingdom: To visit your local AA Shop, contact the **AA Headquarters** (☎(0990) 44 88 66), or write to: The Automobile Association, International Documents, Fanum House, Erskine, Renfrewshire PA8 6BW. To find the location nearest you that issues the IDP, call ☎(0990) 50 06 00 or (0990) 44 88 66. For more info, see www.theaa.co.uk/motoringandtravel/idp/index.asp. Permits UK£4.

United States: Visit any American Automobile Association (AAA) office or write to AAA Florida, Travel Related Services, 1000 AAA Drive (mail stop 100), Heathrow, FL 32746 (☎(407) 444-7000; fax 444-7380). Permits US$10. AAA Travel Related Services (☎(800) 222-4357) provides road maps, travel guides, emergency road services, travel services, and auto insurance.

CAR INSURANCE

Most credit cards cover standard insurance. If you rent, lease, or borrow a car, you will need a **green card,** or **International Insurance Certificate,** to certify that you have liability insurance and that it applies abroad. Green cards can be obtained at car rental agencies, car dealers (for those leasing cars), some travel agents, and some border crossings. Rental agencies may require you to purchase theft insurance in countries that they consider to have a high risk of auto theft.

BY THUMB

Let's Go urges you to use common sense if you decide to hitch and to seriously consider all possible risks before you make that decision. Let's Go does not recommend hitchhiking as a means of transportation.

There are some remote areas in Peru, Bolivia, and Ecuador where buses don't travel. In such places, trucks will often pick up passengers to make a little extra money. Usually they cost about the same as taxis, but may charge a little more; settle on a price before getting in. If hitchhiking, use common sense and go with your gut; if something does not feel right or safe, chances are you're better off waiting.

ADDITIONAL INFORMATION

SPECIFIC CONCERNS

WOMEN TRAVELERS

Women exploring on their own inevitably face some additional safety concerns, but it's easy to be adventurous without taking undue risks. If you are concerned, you might consider staying in hotels which offer single rooms that lock from the inside or in religious organizations that offer rooms for women only. Communal showers in some hostels are safer than others; check them before settling in. Stick to centrally located accommodations and avoid solitary late-night treks. When traveling, always carry extra money for a phone call, bus, or taxi. **Hitchhiking** is never safe for lone women, or even for two women traveling together. Look as if you know where you're going (even when you don't), and consider approaching older women or couples for directions if you're lost or feel uncomfortable.

Generally, the less you look like a tourist, the better off you'll be. Dress conservatively, especially in rural areas. Shorts and t-shirts, even if unrevealing by Western standards, will clearly identify you as a foreigner. As it is, many Latin Americans believe foreign women have looser sexual morals and will consider skimpy clothing an invitation. Wearing a conspicuous **wedding band** may help prevent unwanted overtures. Some travelers report that carrying pictures of a "husband" or "children" is extremely useful to help document marriage status. Even a mention of a husband waiting back at the hotel may be enough in some places to discount your potentially vulnerable, unattached appearance.

In cities, you may be harassed no matter how you're dressed. *Machismo* is very common among Peruvian, Bolivian, and Ecuadorian men, and they will often express their manliness with a kind of stuttered hissing or, sometimes, by yelling vulgarities. The best answer to such harassment is no answer at all; feigning deafness, sitting motionless, and staring straight ahead at nothing in particular will do a world of good that reactions usually don't achieve. The extremely persistent can sometimes be dissuaded by a firm, loud, and very public "*¡Déjame!*" (DEH-ha-me, "leave me alone!") or "*¡no molestes!*" (no mole-EST-ace, "don't bother me!"). If need be, turn to an older woman for help; her stern rebukes will usually be enough to embarrass the most determined jerks. Don't hesitate to seek out a police officer.

Let's Go lists emergency numbers in the Practical Information listings of cities. Memorize these numbers in the places you visit. Carry a **whistle** or an airhorn on your keychain, and don't hesitate to use it in an emergency. An **IMPACT Model Mugging** self-defense course will not only prepare you for a potential attack, but will also raise your level of awareness of your surroundings as well as your confidence (see Self Defense, p. 32). Women also face some specific health concerns when traveling (see Women's Health, p. 39).

TRAVELING ALONE

There are many benefits to traveling alone, including independence and greater opportunities to interact with residents of the region you're visiting, who are generally enthusiastic about making a new foreign *amigo*. On the other hand, any solo traveler is a more vulnerable target of harassment and street theft. Lone travelers need to be well-organized and look confident at all times. Try not to stand out as a tourist, and be especially careful in deserted or very crowded areas. If questioned, never admit that you are traveling alone. Maintain regular contact with someone at home who knows your itinerary.

For more tips, pick up *Traveling Solo* by Eleanor Berman (Globe Pequot, US$17) or subscribe to **Connecting: Solo Travel Network,** P.O. Box 29088, Delamont RPO, Vancouver, BC V6J 5C2 (☎/fax (604) 737-7791; www.cstn.org; membership US$25-35), or the **Travel Companion Exchange,** P.O. Box 833, Amityville, NY 11701, USA (☎(631) 454-0880 or (800) 392-1256; www.whytravelalone.com; US$48).

OLDER TRAVELERS

Agencies for senior group travel are growing in enrollment and popularity. These are only a few:

ElderTreks, 597 Markham St., Toronto, ON, Canada, M6G 2L7 (☎(800) 741-7956 or (416) 588-5000; fax 588-9839; email eldertreks@eldertreks.com; www.eldertreks.com). Adventure travel for the 50+ traveler in Peru, Bolivia, and Ecuador.

Elderhostel, 75 Federal St., Boston, MA 02110 (☎(617) 426-7788 or (877) 426-2166; email registration@elderhostel.org; www.elderhostel.org). Organizes 1- to 4-week programs at colleges, universities, and other learning centers in Peru and Ecuador on varied subjects. Must be 55 or over (spouse can be of any age).

Walking the World, P.O. Box 1186, Fort Collins, CO 80522 (☎(970) 498-0500; fax 498-9100; email walktworld@aol.com; www.walkingtheworld.com), organizes trips for 50+ travelers to Peru.

BISEXUAL, GAY, AND LESBIAN TRAVELERS

Homosexuality is not socially accepted in Peru, Bolivia, or Ecuador, partly due to the influence of the Catholic church. The derogatory term, "*maricón*," is used more frequently than the proper "*homosexual*," and homosexuals are sometimes subject to ridicule. For more information, contact **Movimiento Homosexual de Lima,** Mariscal Miller 828 (☎(01) 433 63 75; fax 433 55 19) in Jesús María, Lima. Listed below are contact organizations, mail-order bookstores, and publishers which offer materials addressing some specific concerns. **Out and About** (www.planetout.com) offers a bi-weekly newsletter addressing travel concerns.

Gay's the Word, 66 Marchmont St., London WC1N 1AB (☎(020) 7278 7654; email sales@gaystheword.co.uk; www.gaystheword.co.uk). The largest gay and lesbian bookshop in the UK, with both fiction and non-fiction titles. Mail-order service available.

Giovanni's Room, 345 S. 12th St., Philadelphia, PA 19107, USA (☎(215) 923-2960; fax 923-0813; www.queerbooks.com). An international lesbian/feminist and gay bookstore with mail-order service (carries many of the publications listed below).

International Gay and Lesbian Travel Association, 4331 N. Federal Hwy., #304, Fort Lauderdale, FL 33308, USA (☎(954) 776-2626; fax 776-3303; www.iglta.com). An organization of over 1350 companies serving gay and lesbian travelers worldwide.

International Lesbian and Gay Association (ILGA), 81 rue Marché-au-Charbon, B-1000 Brussels, Belgium (☎/fax +32 (2) 502 24 71; www.ilga.org). Not a travel service; provides political information, such as homosexuality laws of individual countries.

FURTHER READING
Spartacus International Gay Guide, Bruno Gmunder Verlag (US$33).
Ferrari Guides' Gay Travel A to Z, Ferrari Guides' Men's Travel in Your Pocket, Ferrari Guides' Women's Travel in Your Pocket, and *Ferrari Guides' Inn Places.* Ferrari Guides (US$14-16). For more information, call ☎(602) 863-2408 or (800) 962-2912 or check their website (www.q-net.com).

TRAVELERS WITH DISABILITIES

Traveling with a disability through Peru, Bolivia, and Ecuador may be difficult. The more upscale hotels will generally be able to meet your needs, but public transportation systems and most hostels are ill-equipped. Those with disabilities should inform airlines and hotels of their disabilities when making arrangements; some time may be needed to prepare special accommodations. Call ahead to restaurants, hotels, parks, and other facilities to find out about the existence of ramps, the widths of doors, the dimensions of elevators, etc., keeping in mind that handicapped-accessible places are scarce. The following organizations provide information or publications that might be of assistance:

USEFUL ORGANIZATIONS

Mobility International USA (MIUSA), P.O. Box 10767, Eugene, OR 97440, USA (☎(541) 343-1284 voice and TDD; fax 343-6812; email info@miusa.org; www.miusa.org). Sells *A World of Options: A Guide to International Educational Exchange, Community Service, and Travel for Persons with Disabilities* (US$35).

Moss Rehab Hospital Travel Information Service (☎(215) 456-9600 or (800) CALL-MOSS; email netstaff@mossresourcenet.org; www.mossresourcenet.org). An information resource center on travel-related concerns for those with disabilities.

Society for the Advancement of Travel for the Handicapped (SATH), 347 5th Ave., #610, New York, NY 10016 (☎(212) 447-7284; www.sath.org). An advocacy group that publishes the quarterly travel magazine *OPEN WORLD* (free for members, US$13 for nonmembers). Also publishes a wide range of info sheets on disability travel facilitation and destinations. Annual membership US$45, students and seniors US$30.

DIETARY CONCERNS

In larger cities, vegetarians shouldn't have too much trouble finding amenable cuisine. However in smaller towns—where every restaurant seems to serve a fixed *menú*—vegetarians may have to resort to a monotonous diet of rice. Still, many restaurants will serve a vegetarian dish upon request–eggs are a popular option. When ordering, request a dish *sin carne* (without meat). Another option is to visit the local market and to stock up on fruits and vegetables. Those planning to keep kosher, will probably find most meat unsuitable, so vegetarian dishes are the best bet. **The Jewish Travel Guide** lists synagogues, kosher restaurants, and Jewish institutions in Peru, Bolivia, and Ecuador. It is available from Vallentine-Mitchell Publishers, Newbury House 890-900, Eastern Ave., Newbury Park, Ilford, Essex, UK IG2 7HH (☎ (020) 8599 8866; fax 8599 0984); in the US ($16) from ISBS, 5804 NE Hassallo St., Portland, OR 97213-3644 (☎ (800) 944-6190).

ALTERNATIVES TO TOURISM

For an extensive listing of "off-the-beaten-track" and specialty travel opportunities, try the **Specialty Travel Index,** 305 San Anselmo Ave., #313, San Anselmo, CA 94960, USA (☎ (888) 624-4030 or (415) 455-1643; www.spectrav.com; US$6). **Transitions Abroad** (www.transabroad.com) publishes a bimonthly on-line newsletter for work, study, and specialized travel abroad.

STUDY

Many students come to Peru, Bolivia, and Ecuador to learn Spanish from one of the language schools around the region. Programs vary, but they generally include four to seven hours of daily instruction and a homestay with a local family. In Quito, these schools are as abundant as shoeshiners, and they flourish in Lima, Cusco, and La Paz as well. Sifting through the available opportunities can be a daunting task. Cost, duration, intensity, and availability of extracurricular programs are a few of the variables to be considered. The **South American Explorers** (see p. 41) can help narrow down the options, as can the resources listed below. Arrangements can be made before leaving your home country or after you arrive. In addition to local language schools, American universities and other more global organizations have different academic programs in Peru, Bolivia, and Ecuador. Local libraries and bookstores can be useful sources for current info on study abroad. The Internet has a study abroad web site at www.studyabroad.com. You will need to acquire a student visa for stays longer than 90 days.

LANGUAGE SCHOOLS

Programs vary significantly in cost, duration, and inclusions. A few are listed below. See **Further Reading** and the **Practical Information** sections in individual cities to find out about more.

American Field Service (AFS), 310 SW 4th Ave., #630, Portland, OR 97204 (☎(800) 237-4636; fax (503) 241-1653; email afsinfo@afs.org; www.afs.org/usa). AFS offers summer, semester, and year-long homestay exchange programs in Ecuador and Bolivia for high school students and graduating high school seniors. Financial aid available.

Amerispan Unlimited, P.O. Box 40007, Philadelphia, PA 19106 (☎(215) 751-1100; fax (215) 751-1986; email info@amerispan.com; www.amerispan.com), offers 2-week to 6-month language immersion programs (ranging in price from US$400-4500, not including airfare) in Peru, Bolivia, and Ecuador. Also offers educational travel programs and volunteer and internship opportunities.

School for International Training, College Semester Abroad, Admissions, Kipling Rd., P.O. Box 676, Brattleboro, VT 05302 (☎(800) 336-1616 or (802) 257-7751; fax 258-3500; www.sit.edu). Runs semester- and year-long culture and development and comparative ecology programs in Quito and the culture and development program in Cochabamba, Bolivia. Programs cost US$10,000-12,000, all expenses included. Scholarships are available, and US financial aid is transferable. Prerequisite of 3-4 semesters of college-level Spanish. Also runs the **Experiment in International Living,** Summer Programs (☎(800)-345-2929; fax (802) 258-3428; email eil@worldlearning.org; www.usexperiment.org). Founded in 1932, it offers cross-cultural, educational homestays, community service, ecological adventure, and language training throughout Ecuador for high school students. Programs are 5 weeks long and cost around US$4500. Positions as group leaders are available worldwide for college graduates with strong in-country experienced language skills for the host country and experience working with students. Applications available online.

FURTHER READING.
Academic Year Abroad, Institute of International Education Books (US$45).
Vacation Study Abroad, also from the Institute of International Education Books (US$40).
Peterson's Study Abroad Guide, Peterson's (US$30).
Peterson's Summer Study Abroad 2001, Peterson's (US$30).

VOLUNTEER AND WORK

Volunteering is an excellent way to immerse yourself in Latin American culture, becoming familiar with the people and language while giving back to the place you are visiting. The good news is that it's very easy to find volunteer positions, especially if you are willing to shell out a few bucks for program fees; the bad news is that paid work can be exceedingly difficult to find. Countries are reluctant to give up precious jobs to traveling gringos when many of their citizens are unemployed. It's not impossible, though. Friends in Peru, Bolivia, or Ecuador can help expedite work permits or arrange work-for-accommodations swaps, and some businesses are eager to hire English-speaking personnel for prestige or for the convenience of their patrons. The following is a list of useful publications and organizations.

TEACHING ENGLISH

For the most part, it is easiest for foreigners to find employment teaching English in Peru, Bolivia, and Ecuador, where many professionals and students are eager to learn but there is often a shortage of instructors. Pay is meager, but bilinguals with some teaching experience or certification can earn considerably more.

International Schools Services, Educational Staffing Program, P.O. Box 5910, Princeton, NJ 08543 (☎(609) 452-0990; fax 452-2690; email edustaffing@iss.edu; www.iss.edu). Recruits teachers and administrators for American and English schools in Peru, Bolivia, and Ecuador for a 2-year commitment. All instruction in English. Applicants must have a bachelor's degree and 2 years of relevant experience. Nonrefundable US$150 application fee, US$200 to register for a recruitment center in the US. Publishes the *Directory of Overseas Schools* (US$35).

Office of Overseas Schools, US Department of State, Room H328, SA-1, Washington, D.C. 20522 (☎(202) 261-8200; fax 261-8224; www.state.gov/www/about_state/schools/). Keeps a comprehensive list of schools abroad and agencies that arrange placement for Americans to teach abroad.

World Teach, Center for International Development, Harvard University, 79 JFK St., Cambridge, MA 02138 (☎(800) 483-2240 or (617) 495-5527; fax 495-1599; email info@worldteach.org; www.worldteach.org). Volunteers teach mostly English, but also math, science, and environmental education to students of all ages in Ecuador. Bachelor's degree required for 6-month and year-long programs. Room, board, and a living stipend are provided, but volunteers must pay a fee covering transportation, health insurance, and training. (There is currently no progam in Peru or Bolivia.)

OTHER VOLUNTEER OPPORTUNITIES

Volunteer jobs are readily available, and many provide room and board in exchange for labor. You can sometimes avoid high application fees by contacting the individual workcamps directly.

Earthwatch, 680 Mt. Auburn St., Box 403, Watertown, MA 02272 (☎(800) 776-0188 or (617) 926-8200; www.earthwatch.org). Arranges 1- to 3-week programs in Ecuador to promote conservation of natural resources. Programs average US$160.

Habitat for Humanity International, 121 Habitat St., Americus, GA 31709 (☎(800) 334-3308; www.habitat.org). Offers international opportunities in Peru, Ecuador, and Bolivia to live and build houses in a host community. Costs range US$1200-3500.

Peace Corps, 1111 20th St. NW, Washington, D.C. 20526 (☎(800) 424-8580; www.peacecorps.gov). Opportunities in 78 developing nations including Ecuador and Bolivia (there is currently no program in Peru). Volunteers must be US citizens, age 18+, and willing to make a 2-year commitment. A bachelor's degree is recommended.

Service Civil International Voluntary Service (SCI-IVS), 814 NE 40th St., Seattle, WA 98105 (☎/fax (206) 545-6585; www.sci-ivs.org). Arranges placement in workcamps in Ecuador and Bolivia for those 18+. Registration fee US$65-150.

Volunteers for Peace, 1034 Tiffany Rd., Belmont, VT 05730 (☎(802) 259-2759; fax 259-2922; email vfp@vfp.org; www.vfp.org). A nonprofit organization that arranges speedy placement in 2-3 week workcamps in Peru, Ecuador, and Bolivia comprising 10-15 people. Programs vary by year, so call for more information. Most complete and up-to-date listings provided on the website or in the annual *International Workcamp Directory* (US$20). Registration fee US$200. Free newsletter.

Archaeological Institute of America, 656 Beacon St., Boston, MA 02215 (☎(617) 353-9361; fax 353-6550; email aia@bu.edu; www.archaeological.org), puts out the *Archaeological Fieldwork Opportunities Bulletin* (US$16 for nonmembers), which lists field sites in Peru, Ecuador, and Bolivia. This can be purchased from Kendall/Hunt Publishing, 4050 Westmark Dr., Dubuque, IA 52002 (☎(800) 228-0810).

OTHER RESOURCES

Let's Go tries to cover all aspects of budget travel, but we can't put *everything* in our guides. Listed below are books and websites that can serve as jumping off points for your own research.

USEFUL PUBLICATIONS

Latin American Travel Consultants, P.O. Box 17-17-908, Quito, Ecuador (fax (32) 562 566 or USA/CDA toll-free fax (888) 215-9511; email latc@pi.pro.ec). Publishes quarterly newsletter on 17 countries in Latin America (Latin American Travel Advisor), focusing on the public safety, health, weather, natural phenomena, travel costs, politics, and economy of each country. US$39 for one-year newsletter subscription. Sells road, city, and topographic maps. Organizes small-group expeditions and multilingual private guides. Complete travel information service.

Specialty Travel Index, 305 San Anselmo Ave., #313, San Anselmo, CA 94960 (☎(415) 455-1643 or (800) 442-4922; fax 459-4974; email info@specialtytravel.com; www.specialtytravel.com). Published twice yearly, this is a listing of specialty travel opportunities through adventure tour operators. One copy US$6, one-year subscription (2 copies) US$10 (US$15 to Canada and US$22 overseas), but information is also available for free on the website.

TRAVEL BOOK PUBLISHERS AND BOOKSTORES

Hippocrene Books, Inc., 171 Madison Ave., New York, NY 10016 (☎(212) 685-4371; orders (718) 454-2366; fax 454-1391; www.netcom.com/~hippocre). Free catalog. Publishes travel guides, foreign language dictionaries, and language learning guides.

Hunter Publishing, 130 Campus Dr., Edison, NJ 08818 (☎(800) 255-0343; www.hunterpublishing.com). Has an extensive catalog of travel books, guides, language learning tapes, and quality maps.

Rand McNally, 150 S. Wacker Dr., Chicago, IL 60606 (☎(800) 234-0679 or (312) 332-2009; www.randmcnally.com), publishes road atlases (each US$10).

Adventurous Traveler Bookstore, 245 S. Champlain St., Burlington, VT 05401 (☎(800) 282-3963 or (802) 860-6776; www.adventuroustraveler.com).

Travel Books & Language Center, Inc., 4437 Wisconsin Ave. NW, Washington, D.C. 20016 (☎(800) 220-2665 or (202) 237-1322; www.bookweb.org/bookstore/travel-bks). Over 60,000 titles from around the world.

THE WORLD WIDE WEB

Almost every aspect of budget travel (with the most notable exception, of course, being experience) is accessible via the web. Even if you don't have Internet access at home, seeking it out at a public library or at work would be well worth it; within 10 minutes at the keyboard, you can get advice on travel hotspots or experiences from other travelers who have just returned from South America, find the latest news from the region, and learn about the people and the culture.

Listed here are some budget travel sites to start off your surfing; other relevant web sites are listed throughout the book. Because website turnover is high, use search engines (such as www.yahoo.com) to strike out on your own. But in doing so, keep in mind that most travel web sites simply exist to get your money.

LEARNING THE ART OF BUDGET TRAVEL

How to See the World: www.artoftravel.com. A compendium of great travel tips, from cheap flights to self defense to interacting with local culture.

Rec. Travel Library: www.travel-library.com. A fantastic set of links for general information and personal travelogues.

Shoestring Travel: www.stratpub.com. An e-zine focusing on budget travel.

INFORMATION ON PERU, BOLIVIA, AND ECUADOR

CIA World Factbook: www.odci.gov/cia/publications/factbook/index.html. Vital statistics on the geography, government, economy, and people of Peru, Bolivia, and Ecuador.

Foreign Language for Travelers: www.travlang.com. Provides free online translating dictionaries and lists of phrases in Spanish.

MyTravelGuide: www.mytravelguide.com. Country overviews, with everything from history to transportation to live web cam coverage.

Geographia: www.geographia.com. Describes the highlights, culture, and people of the Andean countries.

Atevo Travel: www.atevo.com/guides/destinations. Detailed introductions, travel tips, and suggested itineraries.

Columbus Travel Guides: http://www.travel-guides.com/navigate/world.asp. Helpful practical information.

LeisurePlanet: www.leisureplanet.com/TravelGuides. Good general background.

TravelPage: www.travelpage.com. Links to official tourist office sites throughout Peru, Ecuador, and Bolivia.

PlanetRider: www.planetrider.com/Travel_Destinations.cfm. Subjective list of links to the "best" websites about the culture and tourist attractions of Peru, Bolivia, and Ecuador.

Peru Online Networks: www.peruonline.com. Provides a very comprehensive set of links and search engines for everything Peruvian.

Peru.com: www.peru.com. Contains Spanish-language tourist information along with current national and international news.

Ecuaworld: http://ecuaworld.com. Provides historical, cultural, geographical, and other useful information about Ecuador. Includes chat room and links to all kinds of resources useful to travelers.

Embassy of Ecuador: www.ecuador.org. A detailed resource for tourists, run by the Embassy of Ecuador in Washington, D.C.

Bolivia Web: www.boliviaweb.com. The site to visit for the latest on all aspects of Bolivian life and tourism.

Latinworld: www.latinworld.com. Provides information on Latin America with links to specific countries including Peru and Ecuador.

World Travel Guide: www.wtgonline.com. Gives comprehensive travel, historical, practical, and cultural information on Peru, Ecuador, and Bolivia.

South American Explorers: www.samexplo.org. Has all you'll ever need. For a list of services, see p. 41.

AND OUR PERSONAL FAVORITE...

Let's Go: www.letsgo.com. Our recently revamped website features photos and streaming video, info about our books, a travel forum buzzing with stories and tips, and links that will help you find everything you could ever want to know about Peru, Bolivia, and Ecuador.

ESSENTIALS

PERU

HISTORY SINCE INDEPENDENCE

FALTERING FIRST STEPS (1824-1886)

CAUDILLISMO. After Independence, power transferred from the *peninsulares* (Spanish mainlanders) to elite Peruvian *criollos* (people of European descent born in Peru), who tried to increase their social and economic privileges. Following liberation, Simón Bolívar maintained power for two years before events in Colombia led him to return to Bogotá. There followed several short-lived military administrations headed by *caudillos*, military strongmen who often seized power by force or manipulation of the populace's most divisive issues. Heated struggles between rival *caudillos* made 1826 to 1845 a time of great instability and economic stagnation in Peru.

In the late 1830s, after a five year interlude of stability under **General Agustín Gamarra** (1829-34), the struggle for power incited a series of short but politically debilitating civil wars. Bolivia invaded its weakened neighbor in 1836 and forced it into the hated **Peru-Bolivia Confederation,** which lasted until Chile ended the confederation by military force in 1839.

GUANO BOOM AND BUST. Two events transpired in 1845 to usher in a period of relative peace and stability. The first was the so-called "guano boom." A huge deposit of the potent fertilizer, guano (Quechua for "bird droppings") was discovered on the Chincha Islands, and over the next few decades Peru accrued close to US$500 million from its exportation. **General Ramón Castilla** rode the guano economic boom tide to power and used his popular support to end the factional conflict that had wracked Peru since independence. Castilla also instituted a number of social and economic reforms, including the abolition of the remaining vestiges of slavery, the termination of native tribute, and the rapid repayment of Peru's internal and external debt.

Unfortunately, Castilla and his successors committed a number of economic policy blunders and failed to capitalize on the opportunities presented by the guano boom and the early repayment of all foreign debt. The sound credit rating established by Castilla was used for massive borrowing of funds from Great Britain, which—in combination with revenue from guano—were invested in an overly ambitious program of railroad- and road-building. Castilla and his successors were also unable to prevent the elite business class from securing the majority of the profits brought in from guano sales. Elected in 1865 and again in 1875, military hero **Mariano Ignacio Prado** attempted to undo the economic damage, but Prado's reforms came too late. Insufficient returns on the massive investment in transportation infrastructure, two successful but costly wars with Ecuador and Spain, and the world-wide depression of 1873 forced Peru to default on its newly accumulated foreign debt. A final blow was struck to the economy by the **War of the Pacific** (1879-83), a war with Chile over a border region rich in nitrates (another fertilizer in high demand). Peru suffered a humiliating defeat and was forced to sign the **Treaty of Ancón,** which committed Peru to ceding economically important provinces to Chile and only receiving half of them back ten years later. A three-year period of economic and civil unrest followed the signing of the Ancón Treaty.

Peru

PARTY POLITICS AND MILITARY RULE (1886-1990)

ECONOMIC RECOVERY AND DEVELOPMENT. From 1875-1919, Peru was ruled by a Lima-based elite and governed through small elections.

In the late 1880s British creditors cast out a life-raft to the sinking Peruvian economy in the form of the **Grace Contract.** British creditors would cancel Peru's foreign debt in exchange for complete control over Peru's railroad system for sixty-six years and annual payments of funds and goods for thirty years. General **Andrés Avelina Cáceres** (1886-90, 1894-95) seized the opportunity for economic salvation and made it the core of his relatively successful program for initiating export-led economic growth.

In what has been dubbed the **Revolution of 1895, José Nicolás Piérola** seized power from an increasingly dictatorial Cáceres. Piérola quickly forged an alliance with the **Civilista Party (PC),** a party supported primarily by guano-enriched elite merchants and businessmen who came to power in what was dubbed the "Aristocratic Republic." The Republic remained in complete control until WWI, when an economic slump sent the PC tumbling to the ground.

POPULARIZATION OF POLITICS. As the case in other Latin American countries, Peru saw the rapid transformation from rule by the elite to rule by the masses, which is known as populism.

The post-WWI period was one of intense intellectual ferment. Writers such as Manuel González Prada and Clorinda Matto de Turner and thinkers like José Carlos Mariátegui and Víctor Raúl Haya De La Torre advanced new, liberal thought and helped increase awareness of and sympathy for the extreme poverty of rural Peru. This movement for radical social change and greater equality became known as the **Indigenista movement.**

The economic development of the 1900s and 1910s initiated and propelled mass migration from rural areas in the Sierra to urban centers along the coast. This massive influx of rural poor into the cities helped facilitate the rise of mass-based labor and social-reform movements. Tapping energy and guided by the new wave of liberal ideas, Haya De La Torre founded the **Alianza Popular Revolucionaria Americana (APRA)** in 1924, seeking to incorporate the rural masses into the move for social and economic change.

In the 1919 presidential election, the first election after the fall of the Civilista Party, **Augusto Leguía** came to power on a tide of support from lower- and middle-class workers. Leguía initiated his *oncenio*, or "eleven-year rule," by drafting a new, progressive **constitution** (1920) that centralized political power. Leguía's social programs included reforms in education, banking, and urban housing, which improved the condition of the middle class but failed to provide significant relief to the most impoverished sectors of society.

Leguía sought to attract foreign capital by granting virtual *carte blanche* to overseas investors. This initiated a long period of export-led economic growth. The benefits of this growth were, again, distributed very unevenly; the wealthiest classes reaped the greatest rewards. During his rule, Leguía dissolved Congress, creating a dictatorship, and ran unopposed in the 1924 and 1929 elections. In the face of temporary economic decline engendered by the **Great Depression** in 1930, the *oncenio* of the increasingly dictatorial Leguía came to an abrupt halt when the military overthrew him in a coup. Democracy was essentially nonexistent for nearly 30 years (1930-1956) during a period of extensive military governments.

THE "CONVIVENCIA". In 1956 the APRA and the conservative **Manuel Prado** forged an awkward, opportunistic alliance dubbed the *Convivencia* ("living together") to ensure the election of Prado and to guarantee the legitimation of the previously outlawed APRA. Many supporters became severely disaffected and shifted their support to smaller, more militant groups that had been overshadowed by the mammoth APRA. **Fernando Belaúnde Terry** of the newer party, **Acción Popular (AP)**, took advantage of general frustration with the APRA to gain power in 1963. Both Belaúnde and the AP proved too moderate for their own constituency and relinquished power at the end of Belaúnde's term.

RADICAL MILITARY REGIMES (1968-80). In 1968 a group of radical military officers trained at the prestigious Center for Advanced Military Studies and committed to radical change decided the time was ripe for the establishment of a new order. Taking advantage of increasingly ardent popular dissatisfaction, they staged a coup under the leadership of General **Juan Velasco Alvarado** (1968-75). Velasco instituted a revolutionary socialist program that was nationalistic, reformist, and anti-oligarchic. Velasco's program soon lead to over-bureaucratization, corruption, economic stagnation, and soaring inflation. General **Francisco Morales Bermúdez Cerrutti** (1975-80), Velasco's appointed successor, reversed much of Velasco's legislation, but proved incapable of halting the downward spiral.

GUERRILLAS IN THE MIST The bombing of ballot boxes on May 17, 1980 in Chuschi, Peru was the first of many terrorist acts committed by the **Sendero Luminoso (Shining Path).** Founded and led by **Abimael Guzmán,** a philosophy professor in Ayacucho, the Sendero has directed a brutal campaign against all vestiges of bourgeois capitalism, seeking to advance its own Maoist, communist ideology. In all, 30,000 people have died in Sendero violence. While most deaths have occurred in the Central Sierra near the towns of Ayacucho and Huancayo, in July of 1992, a car bomb on Tarata in Lima's affluent suburb of Miraflores killed 23 people. Other Sendero attacks targeted the city's electrical transformers, leaving the city in the dark. The Peruvian government under Fujimori captured Guzmán in 1992 and eventually (after a much-televised manhunt in July 1999) captured his successor, Oscar Alberto Ramírez Durand (a.k.a. **Feliciano**), in Jauja, a small town near Huancayo. Since these events, the influence of this and similar factions have been minimal.

In the early 1990s, near the end of the Shining Path's reign of terror, Peru constructed an enormous cross on the edge of a cliff in Barranco. **La Cruz de Morro,** which separates Barranco from Chorrillos, was constructed from scrap debris collected from the bombing sites. Brightly lit at night, the cross serves as a conspicuous reminder of the country's recent bloodshed. The experience is captured by Peru's most famous author, Mario Vargas Llosa, in *Death in the Andes.* Gustavo Gorriti gives an excellent historical account in *The Shining Path: A History of the Millenarian War in Peru.*

RETURN OF DEMOCRACY AND CAPITALISM. Acknowledging the failure of their program, the military arranged for democratic elections in 1980. The relatively conservative ex-president **Fernando Belaúnde** (1980-5) emerged victorious and began laying the foundations for a return to a free-market system. Unfortunately, some misguided policy, several natural disasters, and a dire international economic situation triggered soaring inflation (163% per year by 1985).

Victory in the 1985 election went to the APRA's **Alan García Pérez** (1985-90). For the first time in its history the APRA ruled the country by itself, but it once again proved unable to meet the high expectations aroused by decades of radical rhetoric. The program of *concertación* ("national understanding") managed to curtail inflation and mitigate the trade imbalance created under Belaúnde, but only temporarily. In 1987, with the economy already severely stressed, García nationalized the country's banking system. Private investment plummeted, inflation continued its upward swing, and by the 1990 election the economy lay in ruin.

FUJIMORI AND REFORMS (1990-PRESENT)

In 1990, the APRA was eliminated in the first round of elections. Conservative **Mario Vargas Llosa** (see p. 67), a prominent writer and head of a political party called the Liberty Movement, and **Alberto Fujimori,** a university president of Japanese decent, remained for a run-off; the latter finally won thanks to support from a diverse but strong grass-roots campaign conducted by **Cambio '90.** Profound distaste for all things representative of the status quo was probably the primary contributor to the relatively unknown Fujimori's success. Fujimori, referred to as "El Chino," seemed untainted by politics and representative of the common man.

The most pressing concern for the newly elected Fujimori was Peru's skyrocketing inflation, and he responded with **"Fujishock,"** which sought to control inflation by expanding and eliminating controls on the private sector while increasing prices in the public sector. The program was Fujishockingly successful: inflation fell from 2300% to 10% from 1990 to 1992. Growth was very uneven, however, and Fujishock resulted in severe hardship for the nation's poorest. Despite this, broad support for the new president continued long after his election.

EL AUTOGOLPE: FUJIMORI'S COUP. Cambio '90, an eclectic hodge-podge of interests, failed to maintain unity and secure seats in Congress following Fujimori's election. Fujimori held an awkward alliance with the APRA through 1991, but without a stable basis of political support in the Congress, he was forced to rely ever more heavily on the military. Fujimori staged a successful coup—the *autogolpe*—on April 5, 1992, dissolving the Congress and suspending the constitution to rule by personal decree.

Fujimori was quickly forced to restore democratic rule by foreign forces. In November 1992, he held elections for an entirely new congress, his "Democratic Constituent Congress," composed of 120—instead of the previous 240—members. The new Congress quickly drafted a new **constitution,** which, in accordance with the president's wishes, centralized power, increased presidential authority, and allowed a single person to hold the presidency for two consecutive terms. Fujimori continued to maintain popularity despite his Machiavellian manipulation of the governmental structure, and the newly drafted constitution was approved by a referendum on October 31, 1993. With sanctions lifted and with the powers of the presidency augmented, Fujimori continued to promote his orthodox economic policy popular with big business at home and major capitalist economies abroad.

FUJIMORI'S SECOND TERM. In 1995, with a growing economy and a high approval rating, Fujimori was vindicated by a free election that resoundingly demanded his continued occupation of the presidency, thus beginning his second term (1995-2000). One outstanding triumph of the Fujimori regime has been the campaign against radical, terrorist guerrilla organizations such as the **Sendero Luminoso** (Shining Path) and the **Tupac Amaru Revolutionary Movement.** Critical victories included the arrest of Abimael Guzmán, leader of the Sendero (see **Guerrillas in the Mist,** p. 65) and the recovery of all 72 occupants of the Japanese embassy taken hostage on December 17, 1997. In October 1998, Fujimori negotiated with Ecuadorian president Jamil Mahuad for a peace treaty ending a long-standing border dispute with Ecuador. A somewhat lesser known success is the Fujimori administration's war against drug cultivation and export, which is considered one of Latin America's most successful anti-drug campaigns.

In 1997-98, Peru was left devastated by a period of massive, destructive flooding (and subsequent infectious disease epidemics that killed thousands) brought on by the weather pattern known as **El Niño.** In combination with the Asian recession and the worldwide crisis provoked by turmoil in Russia, El Niño made 1998 a year of economic stagnation and decline. The economic outlook was much brighter in 1999, but all is not completely well. Unequal growth has preserved and fostered extreme inequality, unemployment remains high, and a burgeoning trade imbalance has forced Peru to increase its borrowing from abroad.

The past year was a tumultuous one for Peru. After having changed Peru's constitution and declared it legal for a president to seek a third term in 1996, Fujimori ran in a heated race against **Alejandro Toledo** of the "Possible Peru" party. Neither candidate won the majority of votes. Runoff elections were to be held in May, 2000, but Toledo boycotted them, claiming electoral fraud. Although officially out of the race (with Fujimori running unopposed), Toledo amassed 25.67 of the vote, and another 29.93 of the ballots were left blank or defaced in protest, meaning that if counted, the race would have been close. Because only complete ballots were counted, Fujimori was declared the winner, with 74.33% of the votes. **Mass protests** resulted, including one, on Fujimori's third inaugural day, in which six people died—and the press reported that there were many more tens of thousands of protesters in attendance.

FINE ARTS

The people of Peru have been producing exquisite works of art since long before the arrival of the Europeans. Much pre-Columbian art was destroyed in the Conquest—including the priceless pieces of gold and silver that were acquired by the

Spaniards as Atahuallpa's ransom—or were stolen by looters or *huaqueros* (grave robbers). Along the coast, beautifully decorated pre-Inca ceramics and textiles reveal much about the lifestyles of the ancient Chimú, Moche, Paracas, and Nasca cultures, while in the Huaraz area the Chavín left detailed carved rock figures.

In the 17th century, Spanish colonization was accompanied by the arrival of European art to the New World, especially Flemish, Italian, and Spanish religious paintings that were used to illustrate the teachings of Christianity. In the highlands, newly converted natives were trained in contemporary styles of painting but soon began to add local touches to their works of art. The tradition that developed, known as the **Cusco School,** reflects the mixture of European and Peruvian influences. A famous painting of *The Last Supper* by acclaimed artist **Marcos Zapato,** for example, depicts the well-known religious scene with a distinctly Andean twist—the subjects of the painting are feasting on *cuy* (guinea pig). Groups of indigenous and *mestizo* painters continue to mix the traditional with the Peruvian to produce unique works of art.

One interesting example of the Peruvian fascination with historical and cultural artistic roots is the world-renowned **Usko-Ayar Amazonian School of Painting** in Pucallpa. The works produced by the artists of Usko-Ayar ("Spiritual Prince" in Quechua) exist as a celebration and documentation of the flora, fauna, and culture of the Amazon and its native peoples. Founded in 1988 by visionary painter and *shaman* Pablo Amaringo, the school is made up of local artists aged 8 to 24.

LITERATURE

The ancient civilizations of Peru had a long tradition of storytelling, but stories and historical accounts were passed down to future generations only in oral and pictographic forms. After the Spanish Conquest, a rich body of literature developed out of the folklore and history of the region. One important chronicler was **Garcilaso de la Vega,** the son of an Inca noblewoman and a Spanish conquistador whose writing recorded the last days of the Incas. Inca folklore, mythology, and history continue to play major roles in the literary traditions of modern-day Peru. These foundational elements and the country's diverse ethnic make-up have led to an equally diverse (and difficult to quantify) body of literature that has long been the subject of intense intellectual and academic interest.

MARIO VARGAS LLOSA. Easily the most famous—and most notorious—of the Peruvian writers in the 20th century is Mario Vargas Llosa. His first novel, *La ciudad y los perros* (1963), used conflicts rising between school boys and the faculty of a Peruvian boarding school to comment indirectly on unjust political treatment. Many of his works have been stylistically experimental as well as controversial (e.g. *Conversión en la catedral* (1969) and *La casa verde* (1966). Along with Gabriel García Márquez, Carlos Fuentes, and Julio Cortázar, Vargas Llosa is one of the Latin American Boom novel pioneers. In 1990, representing the Liberty Movement Party, Llosa unsuccessfully ran against Alberto Fujimori for the presidency of Peru (see p. 65). In his 1993 memoirs, *El pez en el agua*, Vargas Llosa refers to this campaign as seeking "the most dangerous job in the world." The election has not affected the quality of his writing—one of his newer works, *Lituma en los Andes* (1993), is regarded as one of his best. In 1999, Vargas Llosa received an honorary degree from Harvard University.

CÉSAR VALLEJO. The most celebrated poet from Peru is César Vallejo (1892-1938), whose modernist works deal with issues of humanity and historical realism. Born in Santiago de Chuco, Peru, Vallejo published his first book of poetry, *Los heraldos negros,* in 1918. The nature of his writing changed following a 112-day incarceration in 1920; the influences of his experiences are reflected in his widely acclaimed *Trilce,* published in 1922. Vallejo left Peru for Paris shortly thereafter, where he became involved in politics and was ultimately exiled from France. His final collection of *Poemas humanos* was published posthumously in 1939.

LIMA

☎ **01**

Lima began its life as a quiet, affluent Inca city on the banks of the Río Rímac; it was not the center of the empire, but it did house large quantities of gold, silver, and architectural masterpieces. When the Spanish conquered the area, they stripped it of its gold and destroyed most of the Inca buildings—before Francisco Pizarro decided to establish the new colonial capital here in 1534. Even then, though, Lima wasn't safe; a 1746 earthquake wiped out nearly the entire city. Forced to recreate itself, Lima did so in a manner as ornate as it believed European cities to be, and many of Lima Centro's elaborate buildings and immense plazas were constructed during this time. Then, over the course of the 19th century, the newly sophisticated Lima prospered as Peru's main port. The good times couldn't last forever, though—in the last half of this century, Lima has suffered political and economic crises, rising poverty, and overly rapid urbanization. The problems of overpopulation—smog, strained public utilities, and scarce jobs—have taken their toll. In the first half of the 1990s, Lima was pounded by terrorist bombs, shamed by a hostage crisis at the Japanese Embassy, impoverished by hyperinflation, overwhelmed by immigrants from Peru's interior provinces, and beset by a cholera epidemic. The results of these events—aggressive street vendors, highly visible poverty, and frequent petty crime—earned the city the reputation of a necessary evil: a gateway to Peru, but not a great place to visit.

This is a reputation the city wants to shake. With over 10 million residents— one-third of Peru's total population—Lima is the nation's only true metropolis, and as such finds itself in an awkward position. To the rest of the nation, it is the "big city," so foreign to provincial Peru that it might as well be a different country. Yet to the rest of the world, Lima represents Peru: not as sophisticated or wealthy as other world capitals (or even other South American capitals), its appearance defined more by its pollution and overpopulation than by its colonial monuments. Perhaps both views are correct—Lima may not always be pretty (though it does have its moments), but it is unstoppably vibrant. The historical city center, Lima Centro, sets gilded 17th-century churches and old colonial houses within walking distance of each other, near open plazas where one can watch the country's most diverse cross-section scurry past, or even join forces in one of the city's frequent political rallies. To the south, the posh seaside districts of Miraflores, Barranco, and San Isidro harbor some of the best dining and nightlife in the country. And as the new millennium creeps in, Lima's fortunes are again on the rise: the historic center is being restored, terrorist activity has nearly been eradicated, police vigilance has increased, and the cholera plague has retreated. At the same time, the impassioned but generally peaceful protests against fraud in the 2000 presidential elections confirm that *limeños* still care deeply about their freedom, their future, and their role in the political process.

HIGHLIGHTS OF LIMA

EXPLORE the catacombs, which contain the bones of more than 25,000 skeletons, in the 17th-century **Convento de San Francisco** (p. 84).

TRACE the history of all the civilizations that have lived in Peru at the extensive archaeological exhibits at the Museo de la Nación (p. 85).

MARK the city's historical center in Lima Centro's grandiose Plaza de Armas (p. 87), where Spanish colonial masterpieces stand on Inca foundations.

BALANCE on cliffs that fall to the Pacific Ocean in glitzy **Miraflores** (p. 89), home to Lima's trendy and affluent citizens, as well as many fine shops and restaurants.

PARTY until dawn—Lima's **nightlife** (p. 92) puts the rest of the region's to shame.

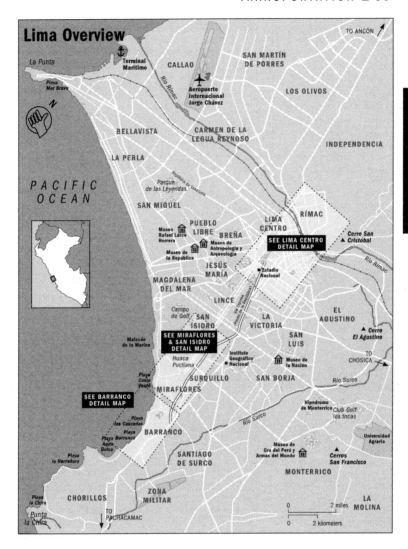

Lima Overview

La Punta

Playa
Mar Brava

CALLAO

Terminal
Marítimo

Aeropuerto
Internacional
Jorge Chávez

Río Rímac

SAN MARTÍN
DE PORRES

LOS OLIVOS

TO ANCÓN

BELLAVISTA

LA PERLA

CARMEN DE LA
LEGUA REYNOSO

INDEPENDENCIA

PACIFIC
OCEAN

SAN MIGUEL

Parque
de las Leyendas

República de Venezuela

PUEBLO
LIBRE

Museo
Rafael Larco
Herrera

Museo de
la República

Museo de
Antropología y
Arqueología

BREÑA

LIMA
CENTRO

RÍMAC

SEE LIMA CENTRO
DETAIL MAP

Cerro San
Cristóbal

Río Rímac

JESÚS
MARÍA

Estadio
Nacional

MAGDALENA
DEL MAR

LINCE

Campo
de Golf

SAN
ISIDRO

LA
VICTORIA

EL
AGUSTINO

Paseo de la República

Malecón
de la Marina

SEE MIRAFLORES
& SAN ISIDRO
DETAIL MAP

Huaca
Pucllana

Instituto
Geográfico
Nacional

SAN
LUIS

Museo de
la Nación

Cerro
El Agustino

TO
CHOSICA

Playa
Costa
Verde

SEE BARRANCO
DETAIL MAP

SURQUILLO

MIRAFLORES

SAN BORJA

Río Surco

Playa
las Cascadas

Playa
Barranco
Agua
Dulce

BARRANCO

Río Surco

Hipodromo
de Monterrico

Club Golf
los Incas

Universidad
Agraria

Playa
la Herradura

SANTIAGO
DE SURCO

Museo de
Oro del Perú y
Armas del Mundo

Cerros
San Francisco

MONTERRICO

Playa
la Chira

Punta
la Chira

CHORILLOS

ZONA
MILITAR

TO
PACHACAMAC

LA
MOLINA

0   2 miles

0   2 kilometers

LIMA

⊑ TRANSPORTATION

GETTING THERE AND AWAY

Airport: Aeropuerto Internacional Jorge Chávez (☎575 14 34, domestic flight information 574 55 29, international flight information 575 17 12; www.corpac.gob.pe/ jchavez), 11km north of Lima Centro, on Elmer Faucett in the suburb of Callao, a relatively unsafe area. **Currency exchange** booths in the international terminal change US dollars at poor rates. 24hr. **V/MC ATMs** in the domestic terminal, to the left as you exit the international terminal. A secure new bus service (US$6) shuttles travelers to their lodgings; ask the women in blue suits at the terminal doors for help finding it. However, the "Official Taxi Distributor" outside the international terminal has traditionally been the safest way to get to the city (US$15 to Lima Centro, US$25 to Miraflores). You can

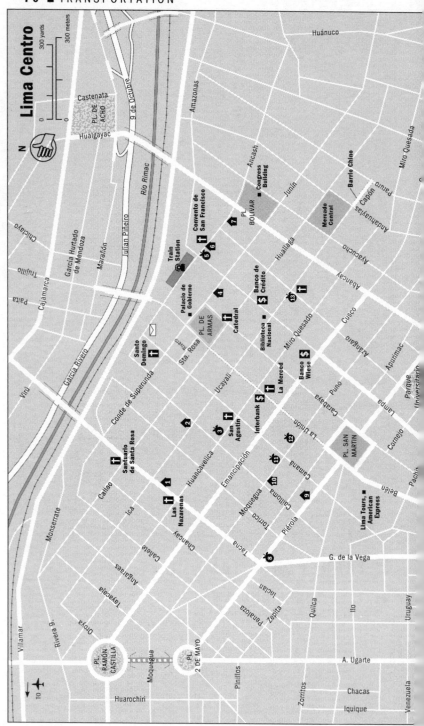

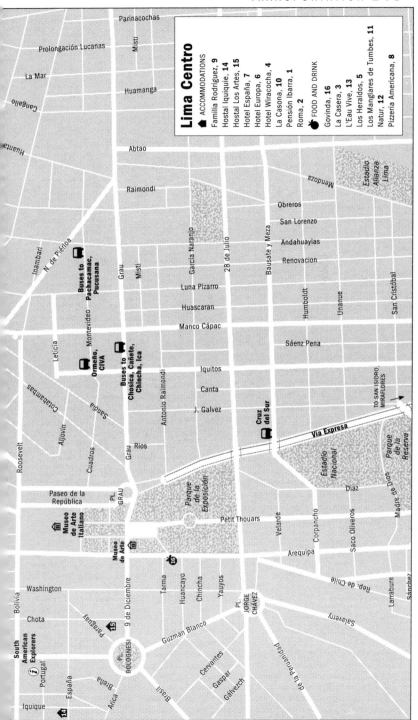

Lima Centro

▲ ACCOMMODATIONS
Familia Rodríguez, 9
Hostal Iquique, 14
Hostal Los Artes, 15
Hotel España, 7
Hotel Europa, 6
Hotel Wiracocha, 4
La Casona, 10
Pensión Ibarra, 1
Roma, 2

● FOOD AND DRINK
Govinda, 16
La Casera, 3
L'Eau Vive, 13
Los Heraldos, 5
Los Manglares de Tumbes, 11
Natur, 12
Pizzeria Americana, 8

also take your chances with the unofficial taxi drivers who congregate outside the domestic terminal. Don't hesitate to bargain; a taxi to Lima Centro should cost s/10-20, to Miraflores or Barranco s/20-30. Finally, several of the colectivos (s/1) that run along Benavides, Brasil, and Javier Prado go to the airport's outside gate.

International Airlines: Copa, 2 de Mayo 741, Miraflores (☎444 78 15); **Iberia,** Camino Real 390, 9th fl., San Isidro (☎421 46 16); **LanChile,** José Pardo 805, Miraflores (☎446 42 72; www.lanchile.com); and **Varig,** Camino Real 456-803, San Isidro (☎442 43 61) fly to other Latin American countries. **American,** Canaval y Moreyra 380, 1st fl., San Isidro (☎211 70 00; www.aa.com); **Continental,** Victor Andrés Belaúnde 147, Edificio Real 5, Office 101, San Isidro (☎221 43 40); **Delta,** Victor Andrés Belaúnde 147, Vía Principal 155C, Torre Real, Office 701, San Isidro (☎211 92 11; www.delta-air.com); **KLM/Alitalia,** José Pardo 805, Miraflores (☎242 12 41); and **United,** Camino Real 390, Torre Central, 8th and 9th fl., San Isidro (☎421 33 34, toll-free outside Lima 0800 40 380) serve the US and Europe but usually have higher prices for flights within Latin America.

Domestic Airlines:

AeroContinente, Torrico 981 (☎232 46 18 or 424 97 13; reservations in Lima 242 42 42 or 0800 42 421 outside Lima; www.aerocontinente.net). Open M-F 9am-7pm, Sa 9am-5pm. Flies to: **Arequipa** (1¼hr., 6am and 3pm) via **Juliaca; Ayacucho** (45min.; M, W, F, Sa 6am); **Cajamarca** (1¾hr., 6:30am); **Chiclayo** (1hr.; 7am, noon, and 4:30pm) via **Piura; Cusco** (1hr.; 6, 6:30, 10am) via **Puerto Maldonado** (M, Th, Sa, Su); **Iquitos** (1½hr., 11am and 4pm); **Pucallpa** (1hr., 11am); **Tacna** (1½hr., 9am and 5pm); **Tarapoto** (1hr., 3:30pm); and **Trujillo** (1hr., 7:45am and 5:40pm). All US$44-89.

Tans, Belén 1015 (☎426 91 18, reservations 241 85 10). Open M-F 9am-7pm, Sa 9am-5pm. Flies to: **Iquitos** (2½hr., 1-2 per day); **Tarapoto** (1hr.; Tu, Th, Sa, Su 10am); **Pucallpa** (1hr.; M, W, F 10am); **Tumbes** (2¼hr., 1 per day); **Piura** (2¼hr.); **Chiclayo** (1hr., 1 per day); **Trujillo** (1hr., 1 per day); **Ayacucho** (55min., Th and Sa 6:15am); **Puerto Maldonado** (2hr., 1 per day); **Cusco** (1hr; 5:45, 6am, 8pm); **Arequipa** (20min., 11:30am and 5pm); **Juliaca** (2½hr.); and **Tacna** (1hr., 5pm). All US$58.

LanPerú, José Pardo 805, Miraflores (☎215 18 00; www.lanperu.com). Flies to **Arequipa** (1½hr.; 6, 9:30am, 5pm; US$59) and **Cusco** (1¼-2½hr.; 6am, one bus via Arequipa; US$59).

Trains: Train service from Lima has been suspended indefinitely. Call Perurail (☎440 73 73 or 440 22 22) for more information.

International Buses: Ormeño Expreso Internacional, Carlos Zavala 177 (☎427 56 79), 2nd fl., has the only international bus service out of Lima. To: **Quito, Ecuador** (1½ days, M and F 10am, US$60); **Guayaquil, Ecuador** (1¼ days, M and F 10am, US$50); **Santiago, Chile** (2½ days, Tu and Sa 1:30pm, US$90); **Buenos Aires, Argentina** (3¾ days; Tu, Th, Su 1pm; US$160, includes 1 night in a hotel); **Bogotá, Colombia** (3 days, M and F 10am, US$140); and **Caracas, Venezuela** (4¼ days, M and F 10am, US$170). Passengers may take up to 20kg of luggage, US$1-3 for each additional kg. Soles, US dollars, and Visa accepted.

Domestic Buses: There is no single terminal, so you'll have to go to the individual agencies. Many are on or around Carlos Zavala, just north of Grau in Lima Centro, though most agencies that serve central Peru are around Luna Pizarro. It's best to buy tickets in advance, especially for overnight rides. Call to confirm times.

Ormeño, Carlos Zavala 177 (☎427 56 79), in Lima Centro, with a smaller terminal at Javier Prado Este 1059 (☎472 17 10), in San Isidro. To: **Arequipa** (14hr.; 8:30am, 1:30, 3:30, 6:30, 9pm; s/50); **Ayacucho** (12-14hr.; 7, 9:30am, 8:15pm; s/35); **Chiclayo** (12hr.; 6:30, 9:30am, 12:30, 4, 8pm; s/40); **Cusco** (36hr., 6:30 and 9pm, s/70); **Huaraz** (8hr.; 7am, noon, 9pm; s/25); **Ica** (5hr., every hr. 6am-11:30pm, s/12); **Nasca** (8hr., 13 per day 6am-10:30pm, s/20); **Pisco** (4hr., 9 per day 6:30am-8pm, s/10); **Tacna** (20hr.; 9:30am, 3, 9:30pm; s/50); **Trujillo** (8-9hr.; 7 per day 6:30am-10:30pm; s/30); and **Tumbes** (21hr., 9:30am and 12:30pm, s/60).

CIVA, Carlos Zavala 217 (☎426 49 26), at Montevideo in Lima Centro. To: **Arequipa** (14hr., 3:30 and 8:45pm, s/40); **Cajamarca** (14hr., 6:30pm, s/50); **Cusco** (35hr., 8pm, s/60); **Nasca** (7hr., 9:15pm, s/15); **Piura** (14hr.; 3, 4, 5:30, 7pm; s/40-50); **Tacna** (18hr.; 11am, 2:15, 7:15pm; s/50); **Trujillo** (8hr., 1 and 10:30pm, s/30); and **Tumbes** (20hr., 1pm, s/50).

Cruz del Sur (☎424 10 05 or 362 41 10), at 28 de Julio and Paseo de la República (ticket sales and departures) and Carlos Zavala 211 at Montevideo (ticket sales only), both in Lima Centro. To: **Arequipa** (14hr.; *ideal* 7 per day 9:45am-8:15pm, s/40; *imperial* 4pm, s/70; *crucero* 6:30 and 8:15pm, s/85-100); **Ayacucho** (12hr., *imperial* 10am and 9pm, s/50); **Cajamarca** (12-13hr.; *imperial* 4:30pm, s/50; *crucero* 7pm, s/75-95); **Chiclayo** (11hr.; *ideal* 8pm, s/35; *imperial* 8pm, s/60; *crucero* 8pm, s/70-90); **Cusco** (30hr., every hr. 11am-8pm, s/80); **Huaraz**

(8hr., *imperial* 9:15am and 9:15pm, s/35); **Tacna** (18-20hr.; *ideal* 10:30am and 7:30pm, s/ 50; *imperial* 1:45pm, s/80; *crucero* 6pm, s/95-115); **Trujillo** (8hr.; *ideal* 9:15pm, s/30; *imperial* 9:45pm, s/50; *crucero* 11:45am and 11pm, s/60-85); and **Tumbes** (20hr., 2pm, s/80).

Leon de Huánuco, 28 de Julio 1520 (☎ 424 38 93). To: **Huánuco** (8hr.; 9am, 8, 8:45, 9pm; s/30-35); **Tingo María** (10hr.; 8:30am, 6:30, 7pm; s/40); **Pucallpa** (22hr., 4:30pm, s/55); **La Merced** (8½hr., 9:15pm, s/25); and **Satipo** (10hr., 7:15pm, s/35).

Empresa Paz, Montevideo 1064 (☎ 428 50 95). To: **La Oroya** (4hr.; 6:45am, 1:30, 2:30pm; s/20) and **La Merced** (8hr.; 6:35am, 8, 9pm; s/35) via **Tarma** (6hr., s/30).

Empresa Merced, Luna Pizarro 255 (☎ 423 36 67). To: **La Merced** (8hr.; 8, 11am, 9, 9:30pm; s/ 18) via **La Oroya** (4hr., s/15) and **Tarma** (6hr., s/15); **Oxapampa** (12hr., 5pm, s/27); and **Satipo** (12hr., 6:40pm, s/25).

TransInter S.A., Luna Pizarro 240 (☎ 330 42 86). To: **Huánuco** (8hr., 9pm, s/25-30); **Tingo María** (12hr., 7pm, s/35); and **Pucallpa** (20hr., 4pm, s/45).

Expreso Huamango, Luna Pizarro 396 (☎ 332 82 57). To: **Yurimaguas** (42hr., 6:30am, s/80) via **Trujillo** (10hr., s/40) and **Tarapoto** (36hr., s/70).

GETTING AROUND

Public Transportation: Buses and colectivos (s/1-1.20) are the cheapest way to get around the city between 6am and 1am, though usually not the fastest. Colectivos (also called combis) are easy to use—all post stickers on their windshields that specify their routes (ignore the often-misleading destinations painted on the sides of vehicles). There are no fixed stops; just say "bajo aquí" when you want to get off. The main colectivo route is **Arequipa/Tacna/Wilson** from Larco in Miraflores, along Arequipa through San Isidro, to Lima Centro; to return to San Isidro or Miraflores from Lima Centro, catch a colectivo marked "Todo Arequipa" on Garciliaso de la Vega. The **Brasil/La Marina/ Faucett** route runs from Parque Kennedy in Miraflores to the market on La Marina, and then to the airport. Buses marked **Barranco/Chorrillos** go to the southern nightlife district in Barranco via Larco or Arequipa. Many colectivos run east-west along Javier Prado from La Molina to San Isidro and Magdalena del Mar.

Taxis: Ubiquitous and generally cheap. No meters, so you'll have to bargain—a ride from Lima Center to Miraflores should cost s/5-7, within the Miraflores/San Isidro/Barranco area s/3-4. Official taxis are yellow, but the independent VW bugs and white Ticos with fluorescent stickers are cheaper alternatives. Of course, calling a taxi is the safest way to go, especially for rides outside the city limits or to the airport; **Taxi Miraflores** (☎ 446 39 53), **Taxi Real** (☎ 470 62 63), and **Taxi Seguro** (☎ 438 72 10) operate 24hr.

Car Rental: Avis (☎ 434 11 11); **Budget** (☎ 441 04 93); **Dollar** (☎ 452 67 41); **Hertz** (☎ 442 44 75); and **National** (☎ 433 37 50); all at the airport. US$40-50 per day for a compact car. But rates change frequently; Dollar often has specials as low as US$22 per day. Min. age 25, but younger drivers can sometimes rent for an extra fee.

▓ ORIENTATION

Lima is huge—if you spend any time here, it's well worth your soles to buy a map. *Guía 2000* or *Guía Inca de Lima* (s/40 in any bookstore) are both detailed, laminated, and easy to carry. While it's possible to get around on foot in any one part of town, Lima is so spread out that a taxi or colectivo is usually necessary to travel throughout the various parts of the city.

The main tourist districts are **Lima Centro** and, to the south, San Isidro, Miraflores, and Barranco. In the maze that is Lima Centro, the main landmark is the **Plaza de Armas,** Lima's main square, bounded by the streets **La Unión, Junín, Carabaya,** and **Huallaga.** East-west streets change names when they cross La Unión. Streets in Lima Centro are often labeled with plaques on the side of corner buildings; the street's historical nickname is in big, fancy script, while its real name (the one useful for navigation) is in smaller letters underneath. Heading southwest from the Plaza de Armas, La Unión's busy **pedestrian walkway** leads to the center's second largest square, the **Plaza San Martín.** This plaza intersects one of Lima Centro's biggest streets, **Nicolás de Piérola.** Another major street, a few blocks west of Plaza San Martín, is the north-south **Garciliaso de la Vega.** East-west streets change names when they cross G. de la Vega. Heading south, both Piérola and G. de la Vega intersect the major east-west thoroughfare, **Grau.** Most of the long-distance colectivos and buses depart from on or just north of Grau, between Iquitos (which turns into Carlos Zavala) and Piérola.

From Lima Centro, there are two direct ways to reach the southern districts. First, south of Grau, G. de la Vega changes its name to **Arequipa** and becomes an enormous boulevard that stretches southeast for nearly 10km, traversing San Isidro and crossing that suburb's other main boulevard, **Javier Prado** (it's the only time Arequipa dips under an overpass), before ending up in Miraflores. When streets in San Isidro or Miraflores have an "Este" or "Oeste" suffix, it means that that portion of the road lies east or west of Arequipa. The second and quicker way to head south from Lima Centro uses the **Paseo de la República,** parallel to and just east of G. de la Vega, which turns into the speedy highway known as the **Vía Expresa.** The Vía Expresa continues all the way to Barranco, but Arequipa ends at the Ovalo in Miraflores, where **Larco** (Arequipa's southern continuation), **José Pardo,** and **Diagonal** all intersect. Diagonal (also known as Oscar R. Benavides, not to be confused with the Benavides a few blocks south of the Ovalo) provides the easiest direct access down the Miraflores cliffs to the beach. To get to Barranco, head south on Larco until it meets the seaside LarcoMar shopping center, then bear east as it merges into Armendariz; Armendariz leads (circuitously) to San Martín, which heads south to Barranco's main Parque Municipal.

⏻ PRACTICAL INFORMATION

TOURIST AND FINANCIAL SERVICES

Tourist Information: Lima's official **tourist office,** Pasaje Santa Rosa 168 (☎427 60 80, ext. 222), just off the Plaza de Armas in Lima Centro. Basic (though not necessarily up-to-date) information on attractions and tour companies. Open M-F 9am-6pm, Sa-Su 11am-3pm. **PROMPERÚ,** Calle 1 Oeste 50 (☎224 31 25), in the Ministerio de Industria building, 14th fl., Corpac, San Isidro, has a much more informative binder full of tourist information. You must bring some form of ID to enter. Open M-F 9am-6pm. **Biblioteca Nacional,** on the 4th block of Abancay in Lima Centro. More in-depth on Lima's history (Spanish only). A 1-year library card (s/8, necessary even for a 1-day visit) requires a valid passport. Open M-Sa 8am-8pm, Su 8:30am-1:30pm. **South American Explorers (SAE),** República de Portugal 146 (☎/fax 425 01 42; email montague@amauta.vcp.net.pe), off Ugarte near the 13th block, just up from the Plaza Bolognesi. Advice and information on all things Peruvian and South American. English-speaking staff. Message boards. Book exchange. Equipment storage. Membership US$40 per year. Open M-F 9:30am-5pm, until 8pm on 1st and 3rd W of each month.

Tour Agencies: Lima Tours, Belén 1040 (☎424 75 60), sets the standard for travel agencies. Wide selection of city and department tours. Open M-F 9am-5pm, Sa 9am-noon. There's high density of agencies on Larco near the Ovalo in Miraflores. Beware of unbelievably cheap packages. **Intej,** San Martín 240, Barranco (☎247 32 30; fax 477 41 05; email intej@amauta.rcp.net.pe; www.intej.org), 5 blocks up from the park. The official ISIC site. Fines for changing travel dates must be paid in cash. Open M-F 9:30am-12:30pm and 2-6pm, Sa 9:30am-1pm.

Embassies and Consulates: For **Australia, Canada, Ireland, South Africa, UK,** and **US,** see p. 26. The British embassy handles affairs for **New Zealand. Argentina,** Arequipa 121, Santa Beatriz (☎433 33 81). Open M-F 10am-12:30pm. **Bolivia,** Los Castaños 235, San Isidro (☎422 82 31; fax 222 46 94). Open M-F 9am-1pm. **Brazil,** José Pardo 850, Miraflores (☎421 56 60; fax 445 24 21). Open M-F 9:30am-1pm and 3-5pm. **Chile,** Javier Prado Oeste 790, San Isidro (☎221 28 17 or 221 20 80; fax 221 28 16; email eglimape@mail.cosapidata.com.pe). Open M-F 9am-1pm. **Colombia,** Jorge Basadre 1580, San Isidro, 4th block of Eucaliptos (☎441 09 54; fax 441 98 06). Open M-F 8am-2pm. **Ecuador,** Las Palmeras 356, off the 6th block of Javier Prado Oeste, San Isidro (☎442 41 84; fax 442 41 82). Open M-F 9am-2pm. **Netherlands,** Principal 190, 4th fl., Santa Catalina, La Victoria (☎476 10 69; fax 475 65 36; email negovlim@hys.com.pe).

LIMA

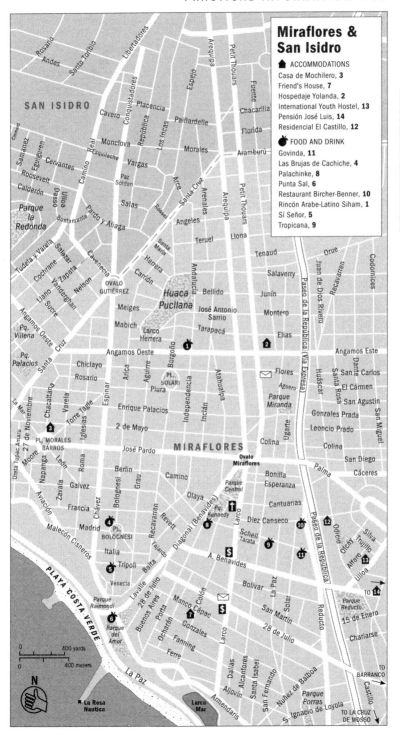

Miraflores & San Isidro

⌂ **ACCOMMODATIONS**

Casa de Mochilero, **3**
Friend's House, **7**
Hospedaje Yolanda, **2**
International Youth Hostel, **13**
Pensión José Luis, **14**
Residencial El Castillo, **12**

🍎 **FOOD AND DRINK**

Govinda, **11**
Las Brujas de Cachiche, **4**
Palachinke, **8**
Punta Sal, **6**
Restaurant Bircher-Benner, **10**
Rincón Arabe-Latino Siham, **1**
Sí Señor, **5**
Tropicana, **9**

Immigration Office: Dirección de Inmigración, España 700, 3rd fl. (☎330 41 14 or 330 40 74), 2 blocks west of Ugarte at Huaraz. 30-day visa extension (US$20), up to 3 times in a 1-year period; the process takes about 20min. Replacement tourist card s/ 11. Open M-F 8:30am-1pm.

Currency Exchange: There are *casas de cambio* and money changers all over the city, but the best place to do on-the-street banking is in central Miraflores, where the money changers (spot them by their blue vests) are regulated, so you're less likely to be ripped off. They congregate on Tarata, the pedestrian walkway 1 block south of Schell.

Banks: Banco de Crédito, Lampa 499, Lima Centro; also Larco 1099, Miraflores, makes Visa cash advances and has Visa/PLUS **ATMs. Banco Wiese,** Cusco 245 at Carabaya, Lima Centro; also Alfonso Ugarte 1292, Breña; and Larco 642, Miraflores, gives MC cash advances, as does **Banco Latino,** Paseo de la República 3505, San Isidro. All open M-F 9:15am-6pm, Sa 9:30am-12:30pm.

Traveler's Checks: Interbank, La Unión 600 at Huancavelica, Lima Centro; also Larco 690 at Benavides, Miraflores. Exchanges AmEx, Visa, Thomas Cook, and Citibank traveler's checks. No commission if exchanging for soles, 5% commission for US dollars. They also sell AmEx and Citicorp traveler's checks at a 1% commission. Open M-F 9am-6pm. **Banco de Crédito** (see above) sells AmEx traveler's checks (0.5% commission) as well as exchanging AmEx and Visa.

ATM: Red Unicard ATMs accept all major international cards: Visa, PLUS, Cirrus, MC, and Maestro. You can find these 24hr. miracle machines at: **Banco de Comercio,** at Lampa and Ucayali, Lima Centro; **Bancosur,** on Larco at 28 de Julio, Miraflores; **Banco Wiese Sudameris,** on Larco at Tarata, Miraflores; and **Banco de Lima,** Grau 422 in Barranco.

American Express: Belén 1040 (☎424 75 60), Lima Centro, in the Lima Tours office (see Tour Agencies, above). Sells AmEx traveler's cheques, but does not exchange them for cash. Open M-F 9am-1pm.

Western Union: Call (☎422 00 14) to find out which of the over 100 locations in the greater Lima area is nearest you. Locations include: Correo Central, Calle de Superunda Block 1 (☎427 93 70), just off the Plaza de Armas in Lima Centro; and Larco 826 (☎/ fax 241 12 20), at 28 de Julio, Miraflores.

LOCAL SERVICES

English-Language Bookstores: In Miraflores, **Mosca Azul,** Malecón de la Reserva 713 (☎241 06 75), next to Kentucky Fried Chicken on the east side of LarcoMar, sells used non-Spanish books, mostly of the paperback romance variety (s/4-8). Open M-Sa 10am-9pm, Su 3-10pm. A few blocks away, **La Casa Verde,** Larco 1144 (☎446 21 49), at Fanning, has high prices (US$13-30) to go with their highbrow novel selection. Open M-Sa 10:30am-10:30pm. **Revistería Mallco,** Larco 175, in an inconspicuous building on the Ovalo in Miraflores, sells 2- to 7-day old American and European newspapers (s/6) and international magazines. Open daily 7am-9pm. In Lima Centro, the **South American Explorers Club** (see tourist information, above) has a varying selection of English books for exchange and an extensive library with 2-week check-out. Services available to members only. The **Instituto Geográfico Nacional,** Aramburú 1190 (☎475 30 85), near the 9th block of República de Panamá in Surquillo, sells the best selection of maps and has a library, though books cannot be checked out. Some form of ID required. Open M-F 8:30am-5:30pm.

Cultural Centers: Find home-country newspapers, magazines, film screenings, and cultural events at the **Instituto Cultural Peruano-Norteamericano** (ICPNA), Cusco 446 (☎428 35 30), in Lima Centro, or Angamos Oeste 160 (☎241 19 40), at Arequipa in Miraflores; the **British Council,** Alberto Lynch 110 (☎221 75 52), near the Ovalo Gutiérrez at the Miraflores-San Isidro border; **Goethe-Institut,** Nasca 722 (☎433 31 80), in Jesús María; **Alliance Française,** Arequipa 4595 (☎241 70 14), in Miraflores.

Jewish Centers: 3 synagogues: the conservative **Unión Israelita Sharon,** Maimonides 610 (☎440 02 90), in San Isidro by the 14th block of Pezet; the reform **Sociedad de 1870** (☎445 10 09); and an **Orthodox congregation** (☎471 72 30). Also: **Club Hebraica** (☎437 23 95), farther from the city, and **Delicatessen Minimarket Kosher,** Pezet 1472 (☎264 21 87), around the corner from the synagogue.

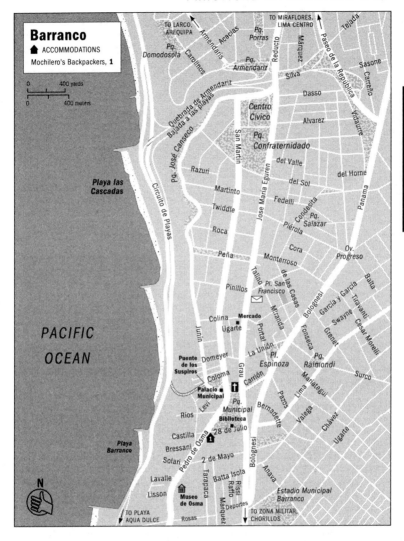

Barranco

▲ ACCOMMODATIONS
Mochilero's Backpackers, 1

PACIFIC
OCEAN

Gay and Lesbian Organizations: Movimiento Homosexual de Lima, Mariscal Miller 828 (☎433 6375; fax 433 5519), in Jesús María. Provides lots of information. *Taller libre* (discussion group) for women on Mondays and for men on Tuesdays (7:30-9pm). Open M-F 9am-1:30pm and 3-6:30pm.

Supermarkets: Santa Isabel, Benavides 481 (☎444 00 87), 1 block east of Larco in Miraflores, and José Pardo 715 (☎446 59 31), in Miraflores; and **E. Wong,** Santa Cruz 771 (☎422 33 00), at Ovalo Gutiérrez in Miraflores, and (☎421 09 99) in the Centro Comercial San Isidro on the 22nd block of Arequipa, just north of Javier Prado. All open daily approximately 9am-9pm; Santa Isabel's Benavides 481 location open 24hr. **Hipermercado Metro,** at Venezuela and Ugarte in Breña, is one of the few megamarkets near Lima Centro. Open M-Sa 9am-10pm, Su 9am-9pm.

Laundromats: Laundromats are common in Miraflores, but scarcer in Lima Centro. Many hostels also offer laundry service. A good price is s/12-14 per 4kg. **Laverap,** Schell 601 (☎241 07 59), at Solar in Miraflores, will wash everything you can cram into their big baskets for s/16; same-day service s/20. They also do dry cleaning (4 shirts for s/12). Open M-Sa 8am-10pm, Su 10am-6pm. **Lavandería Suprema,** Ica 699 at Cañete (☎423 97 24), in Lima Centro. s/14 per 4kg. Open M-Sa 10am-8pm, Su 10am-6pm.

Pharmacies: Well-stocked **Boticas Fasa** has 24hr. locations at La Unión 616 (☎222 26 62), in Lima Centro; and Larco 129 (☎444 05 11), on Parque Central in Miraflores.

EMERGENCY AND COMMUNICATIONS

Emergency: Police ☎105. **Fire** ☎116.

Police: Miraflores: ☎445 65 83, 445 42 16, or 445 35 37; San Isidro: ☎421 25 00; Barranco: ☎477 00 88; Breña: ☎431 14 25. Also **Policía de Turismo,** Javier Prado Este 2464 (☎225 86 98), next to Museo de la Nación in San Borja.

Tourist Protection Bureau: INDECOPI, Calle de la Prosa 138 (☎224 78 88, toll-free outside Lima 0800 42 579), works to protect tourists' consumer rights. Helps tourists who need advice in the event of lost or stolen documents and valuables. All operators speak English. Lima hotline 24hr., toll-free number M-F 8:30am-4:30pm.

Medical Services: The following clinics have English-speaking doctors. **Clínica Internacional,** Washington 1471 (☎433 43 06), between 9 de Diciembre and España, Lima Centro. Consultations s/20. Lab tests s/80-100. Open M-F 8am-8pm, Sa 8am-1pm and 1-6pm. **Clínica Anglo-Americana** (☎221 36 56), on Salazar in San Isidro, has the best selection of immunizations (though no typhoid). Consultations s/150-180. Open M-F 9am-noon and 3-7pm, Sa 9am-noon.

Telephones: You can dial home-country operators from most Telefónica del Perú phones, found on many street corners. The call occasionally requires a small fee (s/0.3). For regular international calls, dial ☎108 to reach an operator. Local calls s/0.5, but an increasing number of pay phones accept phone cards only. s/5-40 Telefónica del Perú or Telepoint cards are sold in most small markets and pharmacies. Directory assistance ☎103. National Operator Assistance ☎109. **Telefónica del Perú,** La Unión 620 (☎433 16 16), allows collect calls. Open daily 8am-11pm.

Internet Access: All over the city, especially concentrated in Lima Centro on La Unión Block 8, 1 block north of the Plaza San Martín, and in Miraflores on Tarata, the pedestrian walkway just off Larco. s/3-4 per hr. in Lima Centro, s/4-6 per hr. in Miraflores. Most open daily 8am-10pm; some on Tarata open 24hr. If you see incredibly low prices posted in the window, they may only be valid during certain off-peak hours. Die-hard cheapskates can get 1hr. of free Internet access at the Congress building (☎426 07 69), at Junín and Lampa, 2 blocks east of the Plaza de Armas in Lima Centro. You must call ahead to book time and show a foreign passport upon arrival.

COMMON CROOKS Lima: the capital of Peru, a jewel on the edge of the sea, the gateway to the ancient Inca Empire—and one of the best places in the world to get things stolen. The city has certainly cleaned up its act in the last few years, but it still suffers a large amount of street crime. As a tourist, the first step to preventing victimization is to be aware of the risk. The second is to know what to call the guy who ran off with your wallet. Oh, of course he's a *ladrón* (thief). Most likely he's a *carterist* (one who specializes in stealing wallets). Were his friends with him? Maybe he's part of a *pandilla* (gang of thieves). Be especially careful on busy streets, where a *lancero* (one who works crowds) may be right at your side; those guys are capable of all kinds of *pillo* (roguish behavior). Others will pounce as you sit quietly on your colectivo; these *pungas* (people who pick pockets on public transportation) like to catch people unaware. Speaking of unaware: a *tombero* (one who picks padlocks) can always find his way into a hostel. Who knows, he may be helping his friend, and every *gemilero* (one who steals lightbulbs) knows that hostels are the best places to attack. No need to be paranoid—just watch out for those *rateros* (crooks).

Post Office: Correo Central (☎427 93 70), on Conde de Superunda, ½ block from the Plaza de Armas. Open daily 8:30am-9:30pm. The **Poste Restante** office is around the corner at Camaná 189; address letters to: Isabel MEBARAK, Poste Restante, Lima 1, PERU. Open M-Sa 8am-8:30pm. Main **Miraflores** post office, Petit Thouars 5201 (☎445 06 97). Open daily 8am-10pm. Main **Barranco** branch, Grau 610, Office 101 **Pensión Ibarra,** Tacna 359, #1402 and 1502 (☎/fax 427 86 03), on the 14th and 15th fl. Spacious and comfortable, with impressive views of the city. The amiable owner believes in giving travelers personal attention; she offers breakfast (US$2), laundry facilities, and free kitchen access. Ask for a room off the street if you plan to sleep. Dorms and singles US$7; doubles US$10; triples US$15. Discounts for longer stay.

NEAR LIMA CENTRO: BREÑA

Though not smack in the center of it all, Breña hotels are a short 15- to 20-minute walk to the sights in Lima Centro. This neighborhood is less hectic than the area around the Plaza de Armas, and hotels offer more substance for your *soles;* rooms are generally cleaner, larger, and better decorated than those in Lima Centro.

Hostal de Las Artes, Chota 1460 (☎433 00 31; email artes@terra.com.pe), near the Museo de Arte and the SAEC. Decorated with Old World touches, including colored glass mosaics. Spacious rooms. Unbelievably high ceilings. Helpful English-speaking staff. Small but growing book exchange. Singles s/20; doubles with bath s/30.

Hostal Iquique, Iquique 758 (☎/fax 433 47 24; email hiquique@net.telematic.com.pe), around the corner from the SAEC. Even the common bathrooms are spotless in this recently renovated house, lined with plants and bright blue tiles. Free kitchen use. Book exchange. Lobby TV. Matrimonials s/25, with bath s/36; doubles s/32, with bath s/48.

Machupicchu Guest House, Juan Pablo Fernandini 1015 (☎424 34 79; fax 447 73 25), parallel to Brasil Block 10. This hostel may be narrow, but the rooms (doubles, triples, and dorms, all with bath) are ample and the TV lounge is comfy. Kitchen use. Laundry service. Breakfast included. Rooms s/12 per person.

SAN ISIDRO, MIRAFLORES, AND BARRANCO

Hotels get more modern and more expensive as you move south from Lima Centro. San Isidro, Miraflores, and Barranco are also generally safer, quieter, and cleaner, as well as closer to nightlife and many good restaurants. Then again, you'll have to take a bus or cab to see the sites in Lima Centro.

▨ Friend's House, Manco Capac 368 (☎446 62 48), 2 blocks west of Larco, in Miraflores. You may meet people who claim to be your friend, but none means it as sincerely as Nancy Palacios, who runs her hostel like a home and treats her guests like family. Time here passes over the foosball table, in front of the TV, or in the kitchen (free use for all guests), but the central location is also ideal for going out. Doubles, triples, and dorms. Breakfast included. Rooms US$5 per person. Discounts for longer stays.

▨ Pensión José Luis, Francisco de Paula Ugarriza 727 (☎444 10 15; fax 446 71 77; email hsjluis@terra.com.pe), off 28 de Julio between República de Panamá and Paseo de la República, in Miraflores. The low price of a hostel without any of the institutional feel. A quiet old house with fish ponds, sunny patios, a kitchen, reading rooms, cable TV, and washing machines. All rooms have baths and phones. Breakfast included. Must call in advance. US$12 per person.

Casa del Mochilero, Cesareo Chacaltana 130-A (☎444 90 89; email casamochilero@hotmail.com), 2nd fl., near the 10th block of José Pardo, in Miraflores. The young Israeli-Peruvian couple who run this place know how to make backpackers feel comfortable. Their formula? Find a nice house on a quiet street and add lots of armchairs around a cable TV/VCR. Locked storage facilities. Free kitchen access. Tight but comfortable 5-person dorms US$4 per person.

Mochilero's Backpackers, Pedro de Osma 135 (☎477 4506; email backpacker@amauta.rcp.net.pe), 1 block from Parque Municipal, in Barranco. A great deal for students, this converted mansion has 40 beds, mostly in dorms that are so big, you'll forget you're sharing a room. Internet access. Fully-equipped kitchen. Excellent security. Close to nightlife. Breakfast included. The adjoining pub, **Dirty Nelly's,** gets rowdy on weekends (open M-Sa 9pm-3am). Dorms US$10 per person, with ISIC US$6.

Youth Hostel Malka, Los Lirios 165 (☎442 01 62; fax 222 55 89), in San Isidro. From Arequipa, head 4 blocks up Javier Prado Este, turn right on Las Camelias (just before Bembo's Burgers), then right on Los Lirios. Small climbing wall and ping pong. A bit out of the way, but popular. Cafeteria. Laundry service. Single sex dorms US$6 per person.

(☎477 58 37), in the Galerías Gemina complex. Open M-F 8:30am-6pm, Sa 8:30am-1pm. Most of the smaller Serpost branches open M-Sa 9am-5pm. It's quicker and more secure to send packages via **DHL,** Los Castaños 225 (☎954 43 45), in San Isidro (open M-F 8am-9pm, Sa 9am-5pm); **EMS** (☎511 51 10), inside the Correo Central (open M-Sa 8am-8pm); or **FedEx,** Pasaje Olayo 260 (☎242 22 80), in Miraflores (open M-F 8:30am-6pm).

▛ ACCOMMODATIONS

LIMA CENTRO

Staying in Lima Centro is convenient, though the area can be unsafe at night and noisy during the day. Still, there's no better place to get a real sense of the capital's colonial history and tumultuous present. *Casas antiguas,* rambling 17th-century mansions that have been converted into hotels, are by far the most attractive and affordable options in Lima Centro. If you ignore the concave iron beds, uneven floor boards, and occasional errant paint chip, you can live like a conquistador in rooms with private balconies, elaborately painted ceilings, and arched doorways.

Hotel España, Azángaro 105 (☎428 55 46). This statue-filled colonial house echoes with constant backpacker commotion. Plants grow, birds fly, staircases wind, and travelers plan future adventures from the rooftop cafe. Shared baths with hot water. Laundry service. Message board. Locked storage facilities. English-speaking staff. Dorms US$2.75; singles US$5.55; doubles US$8; triples US$11; quads US$12.50.

Familia Rodríguez, Nicolás de Piérola 730 (☎423 64 65; fax 424 16 06; email jjrart@mail.cosapidata.com.pe), on the 2nd fl. This comfortable apartment, equipped with 2 6-person dorm rooms, is almost as congenial as the caring family that runs it. Breakfast included. US$6 per person.

La Casona, Moquegua 289 (☎/fax 426 65 52). This *casa antigua* has the most authentically colonial feel of Lima's budget hotels, thanks to high ceilings, hallway lanterns, ornate wooden furniture, and a marble staircase. All rooms with hot baths. Restaurant. Singles s/25; doubles s/30; triples s/40. Discounts for longer stays.

Residencial Roma, Ica 326 (☎427 75 76; fax 427 75 72; email resroma@peru.itete.com.pe). Pass into Roma's airy courtyard and leave Lima chaos behind. Rooms vary greatly in size and attractiveness—try for one with skylights. TV lounge. Singles US$10; doubles US$15, with bath US$20; triples US$22, with bath US$28. Prices 20% lower Jan.-May and Nov.-mid Dec.; 7-10% SAEC discount.

Hotel Europa, Ancash 376 (☎427 33 51). This *casa antigua* could use some windows in its sparsely decorated bedrooms but remains backpacker-friendly nonetheless. TV lounge. Luggage storage. Singles s/16; doubles s/23; triples s/30.

Hotel Wiracocha, Junín 284 (☎427 11 78), ½ block from the Plaza de Armas. For such a large place with such a central location, Wiracocha's quiet rooms feel quite private. Cheerful hallway murals depict Peru's finest sights and plazas. Singles s/18; matrimonials s/24, with bath s/30; doubles s/31, with bath s/35; triples with bath s/48.

International Youth Hostel, Casimiro Ulloa 328 (☎446 54 88; fax 444 81 87), off Benavides, in Miraflores. The largest hostel in the area. Laundry facilities. Enormous backyard. Kitchen access s/2. The sterile dorm rooms aren't quite as charming as the old colonial house they're in. You don't need to be an HI member; just flash your international passport. Dorms US$11.80; doubles with bath US$36.

Residencial El Castillo, Diez Canseco 580 (☎446 95 01). A quiet, antique-filled house. Simple but sufficient rooms all have baths. Breakfast included. Dorms US$10; singles US$12; doubles US$24; triples US$30. Discounts for longer stays.

◘ FOOD

LIMA CENTRO

Lima Centro's lunchtime *menús* (around s/5) offer the most calories per sol. Many vendors also set up food stalls on Lima Centro's streets, particularly at night.

▨ **L'Eau Vive,** Ucayali 370 (☎427 56 12). This 3-course lunch *menú* (s/12) is one of the best bargains in central Lima—such carefully prepared French delicacies can't be found for this price (or any price) anywhere else in Peru. Run by friendly Carmelite nuns who donate all profits to charity. A la carte lunch s/8-12, dinner s/25-30. Open M-Sa 12:30-3pm and 7:30-9pm.

Los Manglares de Tumbes, Moquegua 266 (☎427 14 94). Nothing's subtle at this campy combination of fisherman's wharf and Las Vegas showroom. It's a bit disconcerting to eat ceviche (s/13-25) under the watchful gaze of the larger-than-life sea creatures painted on the walls, but this restaurant is one of the less risky places to get seafood in Lima Centro. Live music after 3pm. Open daily 9am-midnight.

Natur, Moquegua 132 (☎427 8281), 1 block off La Unión. A diverse selection of vegetarian cuisine. All dishes are made-to-order, and can be modified to suit particular dietary restrictions or picky palates. Soups s/3.50. Vegetable stir-fries s/6-7. Rice and lentils s/6. Open M-Sa 8am-9pm, Su 10am-5pm.

Los Heraldos, Ancash 306 (☎427 40 44), across from the Convento de San Francisco. The English menu lists the ingredients in every dish. Beef dishes s/10-15. Fixed *menús* as low as s/4.50. Karaoke F nights and Su afternoons. Open Su-F 8am-10pm.

Pizzería Americana, Nicolás de Piérola 514. A predominantly Peruvian crowd munches internationally themed pizzas. It makes sense that the German pizza bears sausage and the Greek one olives, but since when has Australia been the country of bacon or Peru the tuna nation? Large pizzas s/22-27. Open daily 10am-2am.

SAN ISIDRO, MIRAFLORES, BARRANCO

With a few exceptions (for the most part listed below), there are four types of restaurants in the San Isidro-Miraflores-Barranco area: cheap fast food; economical but unexceptional chifas; expensive international cafes where the people are more beautiful than the food; and finally, excellent criollo restaurants and *cevicherías*. In Miraflores, San Ramón (more commonly known as Pizza Street), radiating from Diagonal on the west side of Parque Kennedy, attracts many diners. There's fierce competition in this row of nearly identical Italian restaurants (large pizzas around s/25); if you shop around long enough, someone's sure to offer you a free pitcher of beer or *sangría*, and/or complimentary garlic bread.

▨ **Govinda,** Schell 630 (☎444 28 71), in Miraflores. The flagship location for this colorful chain of Peruvian Hare Krishna restaurants. Govinda's healthy vegetarian cuisine offers a refreshing, if somewhat bland, alternative to the standard meat and fish fare. Entrees s/6-9. Lunch *menú* s/7. Divine juices s/3-4. Open M-F 11am-7:30pm, Su 11am-4pm. A **smaller branch,** G. de la Vega 1670 (☎433 25 89), in Lima Centro, serves snacks and a limited lunch *menú*. Open daily 11am-8pm.

▨ **Javier,** Bajada de Baños 403-B (☎477 53 39), in Barranco. Go down the stairs to the left of Puente de los Suspiros and turn left; it's in a yellow building on the left. Javier guarantees the freshness of his seafood—after all, you can see the ocean where it's caught. Rooftop tables offer a particularly breathtaking view at sunset. Huge portions. Ceviche s/12. *Anticuchos* s/7. Open M-Th 4pm-1am, F-Su noon-2am.

LIMA

Restaurant Bircher-Benner, Diez Canseco 487 (☎444 42 50), between Larco and Paseo de la República in Miraflores. Another popular vegetarian restaurant. The dining room verges on elegant. Most of the menu is devoted to their pizzas (individual s/ 12.50-19.50). Open M-Sa 8:30am-10:30pm.

Punta Sal, Conquistadores 948 (☎441 74 31), in San Isidro; also at Malecón Cisneros Block 3 (☎445 96 75), across from Parque del Amor in Miraflores. Famous for its fresh ceviche (s/28)—deservedly. Entrees s/30-35. Both locations open daily 11am-5pm.

Palachinke, Schell 120 (☎447 92 05), on Parque Kennedy in Miraflores; also in Centro Comercial El Polo, Surco (☎437 77 64; open daily 1pm-1am). Like a cozy Swiss cha-let, with the best crêpe-style pancakes in town. The misnamed *"chico"* size is easily large enough for a meal (s/11-16). Open Tu-Sa noon-11pm, Su-M 3-11pm.

Palacio Beijing, Benavides 768-B (☎444 35 69), between Solar and Paseo de la República, in Miraflores. Lives up to its imperial name with unpretentious elegance and enormous meals. Vegetarian-friendly. The multilingual manager entertains guests with piano solos. 4-course dinners s/15-20. Open daily noon-4pm and 6:30-11pm.

Tropicana, Schell 492 (☎444 56 26), at La Paz in Miraflores. Low-key tropical-hut-styled eatery. *Menú* s/6. Open M-Sa 8am-11pm.

INTERNATIONAL CUISINE

In a country where "international" cuisine rarely means anything beyond Chinese, Italian, or McDonald's, taste buds can start to crave something a little more exotic. Lima does offer food from all over; it's just a little harder to find than in most cap-ital cities. Predictably, however, rarities like sushi or samosas can be expensive.

Rincón Arabe-Latino Siham's, Independencia 633 (☎447 52 29), in Miraflores. Pales-tinian-born owner Siham Giha has cooked Middle Eastern favorites at this 8-table cafe for the past 30 years. Falafel s/6. Hummus s/6.50 Shwarma s/7.80. Stuffed grape leaves s/12. Open daily noon-10pm.

Namaskar, Benavides 2711 (☎271 14 56), in Miraflores. Namaskar's owner was born and bred in Delhi; he welcomes patrons with authentic Indian dishes, both vegetarian and otherwise. Samosas s/6-8. Entrees s/20-38. Open daily noon-midnight.

Sí Señor, Bolognesi 706 (☎/fax 445 37 89), in Miraflores. A festive cantina serving Mexican favorites at a price (tacos s/18-22, quesadillas and burritos s/20). Colorful flags make no secret of their allegiance to José Cuervo (tequila shots s/5-8), but don't get too carried away—there's a 10-margarita (s/12.50 each) maximum per customer per hr. Happy hour 5-9pm. Open daily 5pm-midnight.

Makoto Sushi Bar, on the bottom level of LarcoMar (☎444 50 30), in Miraflores; and Las Casas 145, off Petit Thouars Block 31, in San Isidro (☎442 91 83; open M-Sa 12:30-4pm and 7-11:30pm). Of Lima's overpriced sushi bars, Makoto is the most rea-sonable. The interior emulates a Japanese garden. Sashimi platter for 2 s/39. Rolls s/ 12-15. Open M-Th 12:30pm-midnight, F-Sa 12:30pm-1am, Su 12:30-11pm.

Europa, Ugarte 242 (☎247 57 52), off San Martín in Barranco. There may be an abun-dance of Italian restaurants in Lima, but few can claim a trained chef from Italy. From the quality of the food and atmosphere, one would expect higher prices. Pastas s/13-18. Open M 6pm-2am, Tu-Sa noon-4pm and 6pm-2am, Su noon-4pm.

CAFES

Feast your eyes, not your stomach, at Miraflores's overpriced cafes. A slice of tasteless quiche will cost more than a full meal in Lima Centro, but the espresso is affordable. Ovalo Gutiérrez, where Comandante Espinar, Conquistadores, and Santa Cruz converge, has several overpriced, yuppified gathering places. More cof-fee-oriented cafes congregate around Parque Central; a posh favorite is **Café Haiti,** at an ideal people-watching spot next to Cinema El Pacífico. (Cappuccino s/8. ☎445 05 39.) **Pasaje Nicolás de Rivero** (also called Pasaje de los Escribanos), a pedestrian walkway off the west end of the Plaza de Armas, is a little slice of Mira-flores cafe culture transplanted into Lima Centro. But the best deal on hot caffein-ated drinks is at the espresso stand on Larco in Miraflores, next to the cathedral on

CENTRAL AMERICA   MIDDLE AMERICA

AT&T Direct Service access numbers are the easy way to call home from anywhere.

AT&T Direct® Service

The easy way to call
home from anywhere.

AT&T Access Numbers

Anguilla ✦ ..1-800-USA-ATT1	British V.I. ✦ 1-800-USA-ATT1
Antigua ✦ ..1-800-USA-ATT1	Cayman Isl. ✦ 1-800-USA-ATT1
Argentina ...0-800-555-4288	**Chile 800-225-288**
Argentina ...0-800-222-1288	**Colombia......980-911-0010**
Aruba ▲ 800-8000	Costa Rica ...0-800-0-114-114
Bahamas...1-800-USA-ATT1	Dominica ✦ 1-800-USA-ATT1
Barbados✦ 1-800-USA-ATT1	Dom. Rep. ...1-800-USA-ATT1
Belize ▲ ....811 or 555	**Ecuador ▲ 999-119**
Bermuda ✦ 1-800-USA-ATT1	Grenada ✦ .1-800-USA-ATT1
Brazil 000-8010	Guadaloupe ▲ 0800-99-00-11

 AT&T

AT&T Direct® Service

The easy way to call
home from anywhere.

AT&T Access Numbers

Anguilla ✦ ..1-800-USA-ATT1	British V.I. ✦ 1-800-USA-ATT1
Antigua ✦ ..1-800-USA-ATT1	Cayman Isl. ✦ 1-800-USA-ATT1
Argentina ...0-800-555-4288	**Chile 800-225-288**
Argentina ...0-800-222-1288	**Colombia......980-911-0010**
Aruba ▲ 800-8000	Costa Rica ...0-800-0-114-114
Bahamas...1-800-USA-ATT1	Dominica ✦ 1-800-USA-ATT1
Barbados✦ 1-800-USA-ATT1	Dom. Rep. ...1-800-USA-ATT1
Belize ▲ ....811 or 555	**Ecuador ▲ 999-119**
Bermuda ✦ 1-800-USA-ATT1	Grenada ✦ .1-800-USA-ATT1
Brazil 000-8010	Guadaloupe ▲ 0800-99-00-11

 AT&T

The best way to keep in touch when you're traveling overseas is with **AT&T Direct® Service**. It's the easy way to call your loved ones back home from just about anywhere in the world. Just cut out the wallet guide below and use it wherever your travels take you.

For a list of AT&T Access Numbers, tear out the attached wallet guide.

AT&T

Guatemala ● ▲.....**99 99 190**	Peru ▲ 0-800-500-00
Guyana ○ 165	**Spain 900-99-00-11**
Honduras 800 0 123	St.Kitts/Nevis ✦ 1-800-USA-ATT1
Jamaica ● ..1-800-USA-ATT1	St.Lucia ✦ ..1-800-USA-ATT1
Mexico ● ..01-800-288-2872	**St.Pierre 0800-99-0011**
Mexico ● ▽ .001-800-462-4240	St.Vincent ✦ 1-800-USA-ATT1
Neth.Ant. ▲❂ 001-800-USA-ATT1	Trinidad/Tob. 0800-USA-ATT1
Nicaragua ● 174	Turks/Caicos ✦ 01-800-USA-ATT1
Panama 00-800-001-0109	**U.K. 0800-89-0011**
Paraguay ✦▲▶ ...008-11-800	Uruguay 000-410
Venezuela 800-11-120	

FOR EASY CALLING WORLDWIDE
1. Just dial the AT&T Access Number for the country you are calling from.
2. Dial the phone number you're calling. *3.* Dial your card number.

For access numbers not listed ask any operator for **AT&T Direct®** Service.
In the U.S. call 1-800-331-1140 for a wallet guide listing all worldwide AT&T Access Numbers.
Visit our Web site at: **www.att.com/traveler**
Bold-faced countries permit country-to-country calling outside the U.S.
- ● Public phones require coin or card deposit to place call.
- ✦ Public phones and select hotels.
- ▲ May not be available from every phone/payphone.
- ○ Collect calling only.
- ▽ Includes "Ladatel" public phones.
- ❂ From St. Maarten's or phones at Bobby's Marina, use 1-800-872-2881.
- ▶ City of Asuncion only.

When placing an international call *from* the U.S., dial 1 800 CALL ATT.

CALA   © 8/00 AT&T

Guatemala ● ▲.....**99 99 190**	Peru ▲ 0-800-500-00
Guyana ○ 165	**Spain 900-99-00-11**
Honduras 800 0 123	St.Kitts/Nevis ✦ 1-800-USA-ATT1
Jamaica ● ..1-800-USA-ATT1	St.Lucia ✦ ..1-800-USA-ATT1
Mexico ● ..01-800-288-2872	**St.Pierre 0800-99-0011**
Mexico ● ▽ .001-800-462-4240	St.Vincent ✦ 1-800-USA-ATT1
Neth.Ant. ▲❂ 001-800-USA-ATT1	Trinidad/Tob. 0800-USA-ATT1
Nicaragua ● 174	Turks/Caicos ✦ 01-800-USA-ATT1
Panama 00-800-001-0109	**U.K. 0800-89-0011**
Paraguay ✦▲▶ ...008-11-800	Uruguay 000-410
Venezuela 800-11-120	

FOR EASY CALLING WORLDWIDE
1. Just dial the AT&T Access Number for the country you are calling from.
2. Dial the phone number you're calling. *3.* Dial your card number.

For access numbers not listed ask any operator for **AT&T Direct®** Service.
In the U.S. call 1-800-331-1140 for a wallet guide listing all worldwide AT&T Access Numbers.
Visit our Web site at: **www.att.com/traveler**
Bold-faced countries permit country-to-country calling outside the U.S.
- ● Public phones require coin or card deposit to place call.
- ✦ Public phones and select hotels.
- ▲ May not be available from every phone/payphone.
- ○ Collect calling only.
- ▽ Includes "Ladatel" public phones.
- ❂ From St. Maarten's or phones at Bobby's Marina, use 1-800-872-2881.
- ▶ City of Asuncion only.

When placing an international call *from* the U.S., dial 1 800 CALL ATT.

CALA   © 8/00 AT&T

Parque Central, where you don't pay extra for ambience. (Cappuccino s/4. Open M-Tu 6am-8pm, W-Su 6am-11pm.) After all, man cannot live on Nescafé alone.

▨ **Café Café,** with 3 locations: Mártir Olaya 250, off Parque Kennedy in Miraflores (☎445 11 65; open M-W 8:30am-1am, Th 8:30am-2am, F-Sa 8:30am-3am); Pasaje Nicolás de Rivero 106-112, off the Plaza de Armas in Lima Centro (☎428 26 65; open daily 8am-11:30pm); and at LarcoMar (☎445 94 99; open Su-Th 8:30am-1am, F-Sa 8:30am-3am). The blatant yuppie-pandering may leave a bad taste in your mouth; the fabulous coffee and pastries will not. Each location has its own feel: Mártir Olaya is supremely popular among chic 20-somethings, LarcoMar boasts a staggering ocean panorama, and the Plaza de Armas attracts Lima's corporate power lunchers.

▨ **Gelatería Laritza D.,** Comandante Espinar 845, off Ovalo Gutiérrez, in Miraflores; Pasaje Nicolás de Ribero 148, off the Plaza de Armas, in Lima Centro; and at LarcoMar. A popular hangout with some of the best ice cream in Lima (s/4 for 2 scoops). Try the *lúcuma,* a local fruit with a honey-like flavor, or the divine caramel-esque *manjar.* Open Su-Th 8am-midnight, F-Sa 8am-1am.

Quattro D., Angamos Oeste 408 (☎447 15 23), in Miraflores, serves it all—tasty gelato, rich desserts, and decent espresso drinks. Pleasant calla lily-filled interior. Small gelato s/3.50. Tiramisu s/10. Open M-F 7:30am-12:15pm, Sa-Su 8:30am-12:15pm.

CHEAP EATS

Many of Lima's cheap food options are fast food joints. One notable exception is the Hare Krishna-run ▨**Vrinda,** Javier Prado Este 185, off the overpass at the 30th block of Arequipa, in San Isidro. They serve a daily vegetarian *menú* (s/5) and arrange Sunday excursions to "ecological communities" for yoga sessions. (☎421 00 16. Open M-Sa 9am-9pm.) At the other end of the spectrum, fast food chain **Bembo's Burgers,** on both La Unión in Lima Centro and Larco across from Parque Central in Miraflores, will stuff you full of greasy morsels (s/5-15). The popular **Norky's,** La Unión 750 (☎428 57 63), in Lima Centro; Abancay 210 (☎521 05 26), in Lima Centro; or on José Pardo at Bellavista, in Miraflores, features bright neon lights that contrast oddly with the slow-roasting rotisserie chicken. Such details matter little once you taste their *pollo a la brasa.* (Chicken combo meals s/4-9.50. Open daily 11am-11pm.) According to some carnivores, **El Peruanito,** Angamos 391, near the Vía Expresa, has the best sandwiches (s/3-6) in metropolitan Lima. (Open daily 7am-midnight.) If you're in the mood to order in, try **Dinno's Pizza,** a fresher, locally-owned alternative to Domino's. (Large pizzas s/19-40. ☎242 06 06; www.pizza.com.pe. Free delivery.)

THE BIG SPLURGE

It's definitely worth visiting one of the costlier criollo restaurants to sample Peru's signature cuisine prepared with every care.

▨ **Manos Morenas,** Pedro de Osma 409 (☎467 04 21), in Barranco. Criollo food at its best, in a 19th-century mansion near the ocean. If you want to chow on their *cau-cau* (a fish stew) but lack the cash, check out their stand at the LarcoMar food court; the food isn't as carefully prepared, but it's loads cheaper. Live criollo music or dance shows accompany dinner W-Sa after 10:30pm (s/35 cover). Entrees s/20-40. Open Su-W 12:30-4:30pm and 7pm-midnight, Th-Sa 12:30-4:30pm and 7pm-1am.

El Señorio de Sulco, Malecón Cisneros 1470 (☎445 66 40), near José Pardo. The Incas would have been obese had their food been anything like Señorio's. Only traditional tools (e.g. earthen pots) are used to prepare regional meat, chicken, and fish specialties (s/30-45). Open daily noon-midnight.

Las Brujas de Cachiche, Bolognesi 460 (☎444 53 10), at Plaza Bolognesi in Miraflores. Bewitches the clientele with tamales verdes (s/8) and traditional Andean platters. Have no illusions, however; the bill for the meal will not disappear. Entrees s/20-40. Live peña band F and Sa nights. Open M-Sa 12:30pm-1am, Su 12:30pm-4pm.

Wa Lok, Paruro 864-878 (☎427 26 56), to the right at the end of Capón in Lima Centro. Generally considered the finest of Lima's many chifas. Entrees average s/32. Dim Sum served all day (most dishes s/7.50). Open M-Sa 9am-11pm, Su 9am-10pm.

◉ SIGHTS

Most of Lima's historic sights—plazas, *casas antiguas*, museums, and churches—cluster in the complicated maze that is Lima Centro. This district, bounded roughly by 28 de Julio to the south, Alfonso Ugarte to the west, Río Rímac to the north, and Abancay to the east, was built on top of the old Inca city, though today almost nothing remains of that pre-Hispanic architecture. A small part of Lima's historical center spills over into Rímac to the north of the river, across the 17th-century bridge, the Puente de Piedra. While the center shows what Lima was, the glittering southern districts of Miraflores, San Isidro, and Barranco demonstrate what Lima might be.

LIMA CENTRO

CHURCHES

The Spanish quest to save Inca souls resulted in the construction of numerous visible reminders of the three great motivators: gold, glory, and God. Lima's churches are artistic masterpieces almost invariably filled with ornate wood carvings, gold- and silver-covered altars, and ethereal paintings.

■ **CONVENTO DE SAN FRANCISCO.** One of the finest examples of viceroyal architecture in Peru, this 17th-century church holds priceless colonial treasures: cedar choir stalls adorned with finely carved portraits of saints; a Franciscan library containing over 25,000 rare books, including the first dictionary published by the Royal Spanish Academy; and a main cloister inlaid with Sevillian tilework illustrating the life of St. Francis of Assisi. But that's not why people come here. Most visitors rush through the religious riches to visit a different sort of stash—the famous **catacombs,** narrow underground passageways that contain the skulls and bones of over 25,000 bodies. Until the city cemetery was opened in 1808, *limeños* tossed the corpses of natural disaster and epidemic victims into this subterranean crypt, though today the whitewashed bones are arranged in neat, photogenic patterns. The passageways supposedly lead to the Catedral de Lima a few blocks away. *(Ancash 471, at Lampa, a 5min. walk from the Plaza de Armas. ☎427 13 81. Free guided tours in English, M-F every hr. 10am-noon and 3-5pm, Sa-Su every 15-20min. Open daily 9:30am-5:45pm. s/5, students s/2.50.)*

LA CATEDRAL DE LIMA. Resplendent in gold and silver glory, Lima's central cathedral was first constructed in 1555, completely destroyed by a severe earthquake in 1746, then faithfully rebuilt in the exact same spot according to the original plans. The Catholic cardinal lives in the attached Palacio Arzobispal, and his Sunday mass at 11am is broadcast to the entire country. The glass coffin in the sacristy contains some human remains which, after years of debate and DNA testing, are now generally agreed to belong to Francisco Pizarro, who died in Lima in 1541. The attached **Museo de Arte Religioso** contains more carved-wood furniture, including choir stalls by artesanía master Pedro Noguero, and a large collection of gilt-encrusted 17th- and 18th-century paintings. *(On the east side of the Plaza de Armas. Cathedral open M-Sa 7-10am and 4:30-8pm, Su 7am-noon. Free. Museum open M-Sa 10am-4:30pm. ☎427 59 80, ext. 6. s/5, students s/3.)*

IGLESIA DE LA MERCED. Home to the massive, much-kissed silver cross of miracle-maker Padre Pedro Urraca, this church boasts an impressive, elaborately carved stone facade. First built in 1534, before the city's actual founding, this church was the site of Lima's first mass. It has since been destroyed twice by earthquakes and once by fire, but the current incarnation (built in the 18th century) mimics its original appearance. *(La Unión, Block 6. ☎427 81 99. Open M-Sa 7am-12:30pm and 4-8:30pm, Su 7am-1pm and 4-9pm. Free.)*

IGLESIA Y CONVENTO DE SANTO DOMINGO. This 16th-century church houses the relics of sainted *limeños* San Martín de Porres, the first black Catholic saint, ever-virginal Santa Rosa (see below), and lesser-known San Juan Masias. Inside the monastery, well-preserved Sevillian tile mosaics represent the life of Santo Domingo de Guzmán, founder of the Dominican order. The dark cloisters and blooming central garden offer a pleasant retreat from the streets outside. The church also houses a private chapel dedicated to San Martín de Porres. *(Camaná 170, across from the Correo Central. ☎427 67 91. Guided tours in English and Spanish; tip expected. Open M-Sa 9am-1pm and 3-6pm, Su 9am-1pm. s/3, students s/2.)*

SANTUARIO DE SANTA ROSA. Constructed over the site where Isabel Flores de Oliva (better known as Santa Rosa de Lima) was born in 1586, this sanctuary glorifies the life of Peru's only female saint. Visitors can see the small adobe meditation/prayer hut she and her brothers built with their own hands, the tree trunk bed where she allowed herself two hours of sleep with a stone for a pillow, and the well where she chucked the key to her chastity belt. There is also a small church on site. *(On the 1st block of Tacna. ☎425 12 79. Open daily 5:30am-noon and 3-8pm. Free.)*

LAS NAZARENAS. Las Nazarenas contains one of the oldest—and some say most miraculous—walls in Lima. During the colonial era, many freed African slaves lived in this area of town, known then as Pachacamilla. When the original church on this site crumbled in a 1655 earthquake, one wall with a large mural of Christ on the cross, painted by an ex-slave, survived unharmed. Since then, a cult has formed around the image, known as El Señor de los Milagros (Lord of the Miracles). In mid-October, devotees dressed in purple lead processions through the streets with a replica of the painting. The wall is currently under heavy construction. *(At Huancavelica and Tacna. ☎423 57 18. Open M-Sa 6:30am-noon and 4:30-9pm, Su 6:30am-1pm and 4-9pm. Free.)*

OTHER CHURCHES. The Jesuit-built, 17th-century **Iglesia de San Pedro**, Azángaro 451, at Ucayali, harbors gilded altars with Moorish-style balconies as well as the oldest bell in Lima, called "La Abuelita." *(☎428 30 17. Open daily 8:30am-1pm and 2-4pm. Free.)* Home to the barefooted friars, the **Iglesia de San Agustín**, on Ica at Camaná, is full of carved wooden effigies; the most famous, Baltazar Gavilán's *La Muerte* (Death), is currently in storage. *(☎427 75 48. Open M-F 7:30-10am and 4:30-7pm. Free.)* The **Convento de Los Descalzos** displays the spartan cells in which pious Franciscan friars once lived and worked. It also contains an **art museum** with examples of the Cusco, Quito, and Lima schools as well as a weighty gold altar. *(Alameda de los Descalzos, in Rímac. ☎481 34 33. Open W-M 9:30am-1pm and 2-6pm.)* Originally constructed in 1544, the **Iglesia de San Sebastian**, on the 5th block of Ica, was Lima's first parish, and is the site where religious and military bigshots from Santa Rosa de Lima to Francisco Bolognesi were baptized.

MUSEUMS, ETC.

Lima is home to some of the country's finest museums. Most have an archaeological slant, focusing on the history and handicrafts of the various pre-Columbian civilizations living in Peru. When that thousandth piece of ceramics becomes too much, though, there are also some fine art museums to take off the edge.

■ MUSEO DE LA NACIÓN. This museum's three floors offer an overview of Peru's archaeological heritage, tracing the various civilizations that have inhabited the area over the centuries. The museum's staggering collection of pre-Columbian artifacts dates to 10,000 BC, and the fact that the Inca relics don't begin until the middle of the top floor emphasizes just how much history Peru has. The free, English-speaking tour guides can point out the highlights and supplement the few explanatory signs. Detailed replicas of Peru's archaeological highlights—scale models of the Nasca Lines (see p. 142) and Machu Picchu (see p. 120), among others—give newcomers to Peru a taste of what's to come. *(Javier Prado Este 2465, San Borja. From Arequipa, take a colectivo marked "Todo Javier Prado" towards Jockey Plaza. Free 45min. guided tours in English leave every hr. ☎476 98 92. Open Tu-Su 9am-5pm. s/6.)*

MUSEO DE ARTE. Dedicated solely to art created by native Peruvians, this collection spans over 3000 years of history. The museum houses everything from Chavín ceramics and textiles to colonial silverware in its huge 19th-century palace. The paintings' style and subject matter change drastically over the years, from 17th- and 18th-century religious themes (excellent examples of the Cusqueño school), to 19th-century upper-class portraits, to more abstract 20th-century scenes of everyday life in Andean villages. Downstairs, the Sala de Arte Contemporáneo contains abstract art from the past 50 years, much of it political in nature. The museum also shows films and has short-term classes in subjects from singing to sculpture to computer literacy. (At G. de la Vega and Grau, in the unmistakable palatial building. Colectivos from Miraflores marked "Arequipa-Tacna-Wilson" pass right in front of the museum. ☎ 423 51 49. Open Tu-Su 10am-1:20pm and 2-5pm. s/8, students s/6; free W.)

CASAS ANTIGUAS. Although most of the old mansions in Lima Centro have gradually rotted away or been converted into cheap hotels, some have been preserved in their original grandeur. Built in 1735, the **Palacio Torre Tagle,** widely considered the finest example of colonial architecture in Peru, retains its glory as the headquarters of the Ministry of Foreign Affairs. (Ucayali 358. ☎ 427 38 60. Open M-Sa 9am-5pm. Free.) The **Casa de Aliaga,** La Unión 224, was built in 1535 and is the oldest standing colonial house in Lima today. The **Casa de las Trece Monedas,** Ancash 536; **Casa Oquendo,** Conde de Superunda 298; and **Casa de Riva Agüero,** Camaná 459, are a few more impressive *casas antiguas* now open to the public.

MUSEO DE ORO DEL PERU Y ARMAS DEL MUNDO. As its name suggests, this museum displays Peruvian gold and weapons of the world. The basement vault overflows with an impressive hodge-podge of pre-Columbian gold—used for ear plugs, jewelry, ornate metal-plated capes, and tumis (ceremonial knives)—as well as pottery, masks, and even mummies. However, little effort is made to show how these treasures were used before they were looted, and many of the repetitive exhibits overwhelm rather than educate. A prior visit to the Museo de la Nación is crucial to understanding many of the artifacts' significance. Upstairs, though, the improbable shapes and wild decorations of the world's largest collection of firearms will intrigue even the most gentle of people. (Alonso de Molina 1100, off Primavera Block 18, in Monterrico. Taxis s/8-10. ☎ 345 12 92. Guides (Spanish only) s/35 per group; English-language catalog s/45. No cameras. Open daily 11:30am-7pm. s/20, children s/7.)

MUSEO ARQUEOLÓGICO RAFAEL LARCO HERRERA. Opened in 1927, this museum holds the world's largest private collection of pre-Columbian art from Peru. Nearly 50,000 pieces reside in this beautiful, early 18th-century colonial mansion—most items on display are ceramics (mostly from the Moche and Chimú cultures), gold and silver jewelry, and textiles, with explanatory signs in English and French. Hidden downstairs, out of view of visiting elementary school groups, is the popular Sala Erótica, a collection of ceramics that confirms that ancient Peruvians did indeed get it on, and quite creatively—the best part are the awkwardly worded English captions describing the acts depicted on each ceramic piece. (Bolívar 1515, Pueblo Libre. ☎ 461 13 12. Open daily 9am-6pm. s/20, students s/10.)

MUSEO NACIONAL DE ANTROPOLOGÍA, ARQUEOLOGÍA, E HISTORIA. Although it lost some of its best pieces to the Museo de la Nación, this museum still retains an impressive collection of ceramics and other archaeological finds. While yet another pottery collection may not seem like Lima's most pressing need, the displays here (with frequent Spanish and sporadic English captions) give the exhibit an interesting twist, using the scenes depicted on the pieces to help figure out how the artists lived. The titillating *paleopatología* room features trepanned and other deformed skulls, as well as a mummy that indicates that tuberculosis existed in the Americas before 1492. The adjoining historical gallery features colonial furniture and paintings of many of the men who have streets named after them. (On the Plaza Bolívar in Pueblo Libre. ☎ 463 50 70. Guided tours in English available; s/10-15 tip expected. Open Tu-Su 9am-6pm. s/10.)

PRE-INCA RUINS. Huaca Huallamarca, on El Rosario at Nicolás de Riviera in San Isidro, and **Huaca Pucllana,** off the 4th block of Angamos in Miraflores, were pre-Inca centers of administration and ceremony for the Cultura Lima (AD 200-700). These ruins, minor and visually unimpressive compared to other sites in Peru in the mountains above, have their strong points: admission is free, and they are conveniently located near Lima Centro. The free English tours of Huaca Pucllana include a look at the excavation site and a small museum. *(Huaca Pucllana* ☎ *445 86 95. Entrance on Borgoño. 45min.-1hr. tours for groups only; tip expected. Call ahead to reserve a guide who speaks English. Open W-M 9am-5pm. Free.)* The ruins of **Puruchuco** (Quechua for "plumed helmet") consist of an adobe dwelling that once served as a home for a pre-Inca noble. Visitors can explore the labyrinth where the chief and his servants lived, restored perhaps a little too well in the 1960s—the floor and many of the walls have been plastered with smooth concrete, and some of the ancient bedrooms now have electrical outlets. The complex also contains a small but informative museum. *(Take a colectivos marked "Chosica" from the Plaza Grau. Ask the driver to stop at "las ruinas de Puruchuco" (45min., s/ 1.50), and look for the zona arqueológica sign on the right. Open Tu-Su 9am-5pm. s/6.)*

BANK GALLERIES. Small galleries seem to be today's accessory of choice for Lima banks, and it is worth calling to see what special collections they have on display. **Banco Central de Reserva del Peru** has a permanent ceramics collection. *(Ucayali 299, at Lampa, Lima Centro.* ☎ *427 62 50, ext. 2660. Open Tu-F 10am-4:30pm, Sa-Su 10am-1pm. Free.)* The **Museo Numismático del Banco Wiese** is a coin collector's dream. *(Cusco 245.* ☎ *428 60 00. Open M-F 9:30am-5pm. Free.)*

OTHER MUSEUMS. There are smaller, more specific art museums scattered throughout the city. The **Museo de Arte Italiano** houses early 20th-century European art in an imposing neoclassical building. *(Paseo de la República 250, across from the Sheraton.* ☎ *423 99 32. Open M-F 10am-5pm. s/3, students s/2.)* The **Museo de Artes y Tradiciones Populares** displays folk art such as weavings and dolls by 20th-century Peruvian artisans. *(Camaná 459, 2nd fl., Lima Centro.* ☎ *427 92 75. Open Tu-Su 10am-1pm and 2-7:30pm. s/2, students s/1.)* Barranco's **Museo de Arte Colonial Pedro de Osma** focuses on paintings, sculptures, furniture, and artisanry from colonial Peru. *(Pedro de Osma 421, Barranco.* ☎ *467 09 15. Open Tu-Su 10am-1:30pm and 2:30-6pm. s/10, students s/5.)* The **Museo Amano** specializes in pieces from the Chancay culture. *(Retiro 160, off Angamos Oeste Block 11, Miraflores.* ☎ *441 29 09. Tours in Spanish M-F 3, 4, and 5pm; by appointment only. Free.)* The **Museo Nacional de la Cultura Peruana** offers a smaller mix of pre-Columbian archaeological findings and contemporary art. *(Alfonso Ugarte 650, Lima Centro.* ☎ *423 58 92. Open Tu-F 10am-4:30pm, Sa 10am-2pm. s/2, students s/1.)* The gory **Museo de la Inquisición** exhibits torture instruments from the Inquisition, many with mannequins strapped on in demonstration. *(Junín 548, in the Plaza Bolívar, Lima Centro.* ☎ *426 03 65. Free tours in Spanish, English, French, German, or Portuguese depart every 15-20min. Open daily 9am-5:30pm. Free.)*

PLAZAS

THE PLAZA DE ARMAS. Where an Inca temple and the last palace of the Inca prince once stood, Lima's main square now glorifies Spanish culture. The plaza has been the city's administrative and political center since the its founding and has witnessed some of the most important events in Peru's history: it was here that victims of the Inquisition were hanged in the 16th century, that Peruvians declared their independence in 1821, and that, just last summer, six people died during protests questioning Fujimori's third presidential victory. Flanked by colonial-style buildings with elaborately carved cedar balconies, the plaza revolves around a bronze **fountain** topped by a trumpeting angel, crafted by legendary artisan Pedro de Noguera in 1651. This fountain is actually the oldest standing object in the square—all of the surrounding buildings are 20th-century replicas of the originals, which collapsed in various earthquakes over the years. Nevertheless, colonial power relations still hold here: a larger-than-life statue of Francisco Pizarro on horseback dominates one corner of the plaza while a granite monument to the last pre-Hispanic ruler of this valley, Inca leader Tauri Chusko, is hidden on Pasaje Santa Rosa, a side alley.

The two most spectacular buildings on the plaza are the **Catedral de Lima** on the east side (see Churches, above) and the **Palacio de Gobierno** on the north. The Palacio de Gobierno, a replica of Pizarro's residence that stood on this spot, today houses the Peruvian president. A popular photo shot, the changing of the guard in front takes place Monday through Friday at 11:45am. The **Palacio Municipal**, or City Hall, on the west side of the plaza, has a small Pancho Fierro art gallery that highlights the work of colonial Peruvian artists. *(Free guided tours of the Palacio from the entrance on La Unión. Open M-F 11am-8pm. Free.)* Since the privatization of the postal system, Lima's Correo Central, just off the plaza on Conde de Superunda, has become more a stamp collector's museum than an important mail center. *(Museo Postal y Filatélico del Peru open M-F 8:30am-1pm and 2-6:30pm, Sa 8:30am-12:30pm. Free.)*

OTHER PLAZAS. The Plaza de Armas sits at the northern end of the hectic pedestrian mall La Unión; flanking its southern end is the lesser of Lima's two main squares, the **Plaza San Martín.** This plaza was inaugurated on July 28, 1921, to celebrate Peru's centennial, and its architecture shows a French Baroque influence, though some of the beautiful buildings now serve as movie theaters that screen porno flicks. The plaza is an attractive place to stroll or sit—or protest: tourists who want a glimpse of Lima's politics can often find some sort of demonstration here. The grassy **Plaza Bolívar,** at Abancay and Junín, serves as front yard to the Parliament Building. The **Plaza Grau,** at the end of Paseo de la República, offers little more than a park between the Sheraton Hotel and Palacio de Justicia with shrubs, flowers, and life-size animal statues. Three smaller plazas with similar equestrian statues lie along Alfonso Ugarte (from south to north): the **Plaza Bolognesi,** where Ugarte meets 9 de Diciembre and Brasil; the **Plaza 2 de Mayo,** where Ugarte and Piérola intersect; and the **Plaza Castilla.**

OUTSIDE LIMA CENTRO

BARRIO CHINO

Lima's small Chinatown (Barrio Chino) is in the eastern part of the city center, mainly along Calle Capón. While the term *chino* has come to refer to anyone of Asian descent (President Fujimori, whose parents were born in Japan, is known as "El Chino"), a sizable Chinese population has existed in Peru since the mid-19th century, when landowners first brought Chinese laborers to the country. Though assimilated to Peruvian life in many ways, today's thriving community maintains its distinct ethnic identity. Calle Capón has recently been renovated and both a traditional gateway and street tiles illustrating the different symbolic animals of the Chinese calendar now further distinguish the area. Barrio Chino has no specific sights, but the many chifas and import shops that line Calle Capón, as well as the signs and chatter in Chinese, provide an interesting look into another sort of Lima life. **Chinese New Year** (mid-Feb.) adds a lively parade and fireworks to the mix. *(Calle Capón is the eastern end of Ucayali. Barrio Chino begins 2 blocks east of Abancay.)*

SAN ISIDRO

Though there are a few budget hostels in San Isidro, backpackers are unlikely to spend much time in this affluent suburb. Full of luxury hotel complexes, corporate skyscrapers, and the sleek apartments of yuppies who work there, this financial center is more about business than pleasure. The district has a few discos and overpriced cafes, but they are scattered and not as pleasant as those in Miraflores or Barranco. San Isidro's biggest attraction is its mall, **Centro Camino Real,** at Camino Real and Paseo de la República. Global mall rats won't want to miss the piped-in music or overhyped international boutiques.

MIRAFLORES

Miraflores fills the land between San Isidro and the Pacific coastline with modern high-rises, glittering casinos, and well-kept oceanside parks. Its name has become synonymous with the well-to-do, though the many residential areas are more likely to be populated by families than by San Isidro's young urban professionals; it's not uncommon to see packs of teenagers roaming the streets, looking every bit as blond and tan as California surfers. Much of Miraflores was either built or rebuilt in the last two decades, and its modern thoroughfares, lined with cafes and international shops (as well as their home-grown look-alikes), wouldn't be out of place in the US or Europe.

Flanked by a large cinema complex and every fast food joint under the sun, the traffic circle known as the Ovalo Miraflores, at the end of Arequipa, marks the northern end of the district's activity. Just south of the Ovalo, **Parque Central** and **Parque Kennedy,** busy with vendors selling all manner of homemade goods, are prime spots for people-watching, cafe-lounging, and partying. You'll have to head farther south along Larco to lose your money in a casino, though the street's trendy clothing shops and shoe stores could eat it up just as well. **LarcoMar** (www.larcomar.com.pe), at the southern end of Larco, is a three-story, open-air shopping mall. Built into the side of an ocean-front cliff, the center is nearly undetectable from the street above. Beyond the myriad first-world shops, restaurants, bars, and movie theaters, the complex offers breathtaking views of the sea below (and an underground bowling alley). At the northwest end of town, where Comandante Espinar, Santa Cruz, and Conquistadores converge at the Miraflores/San Isidro border, Ovalo Gutiérrez offers another homage to US imperialism with some large American chain restaurants and the Peruvian joints that emulate them.

The beach along the southern end of Miraflores, **Playa Costa Verde,** is almost always crowded with sunbathers, swimmers, and surfers, despite the fact that the shore is mostly rocky and the water may not be the cleanest around. It's easiest to descend the seaside cliffs and access the ocean via Diagonal, which runs along the west side of Parques Central and Kennedy. Surfers generally head a few kilometers north to **Playa Waikiki,** or south to **Herradura,** which has the largest swells (6-15ft.) in the area. If you'd rather admire the water than enter it, the parks along Malecón Cisneros provide the sorts of vistas that keep postcard companies in business. And St. Valentine would have a field day with **Parque del Amor's** enormous statue of lovers embracing, real-life couples mimicking the statue, and love-poem-inscribed mosaics. Farther up the malecón, the flowers in Parque Maria Reiche grow in patterns that resemble the famous ones of the Nasca Lines.

BARRANCO

A century ago, Barranco was an isolated seaside enclave accessible only by train from Lima Centro and populated mainly by artists and writers. Over the years, however, suburban sprawl turned the no-man's-land to the north into Miraflores, and Barranco is now fully connected to the rest of Lima. The walk along the beach from Miraflores to Barranco takes about 15 minutes, but at night the area below the cliffs—except for the luxurious La Rosa Nautica restaurant on the pier—is dangerous and deserted. Barranco's reputation has shifted from bohemian to bacchanalian; with the highest concentration of clubs and bars in the city, this district is nightlife central. The old mansions and seaside promenades that fan out from Parque Municipal are pleasant for walks during the day, but the crowds really come out at night—to drink, dance, see, and be seen. A few vestiges of Barranco's artsy past remain, thanks to the artisans who sell their wares at the far end of Parque Municipal, and to the artists' workshops (many of which are open to the public) on the blocks between the park and the ocean. Facing the parkside church, Barranco's walkway to the water starts behind the smaller plaza to the left, and leads down the stone steps and over the **Puente de los Suspiros,** a bridge named for the love-lorn who sigh (*suspiran*) as they gaze at the twinkling lights and waves below. *(Taxi from Miraflores s/4. Colectivos marked "Chorrillos" or "Barranco" can also get you there, but you'll have to jump off at the gas station at Grau and Piérola, five blocks north of the park (about a 10min. walk). Getting back is easier; the colectivos marked "Todo Arequipa," on Grau along the park, go all the way to Lima Centro via Miraflores and San Isidro.)*

OTHER SUBURBS

The string of parks along the Malecón Cisneros in Miraflores continues west to the middle-class suburbs of **Magdalena del Mar, Pueblo Libre,** and **San Miguel.** Lima's zoo, **Parque de Las Leyendas,** is in San Miguel on La Marina. *(Take a colectivo marked "La Marina" running along Benavides or Javier Prado. Open daily 9am-5pm. s/4, students s/2.)* Farther west, the industrial port of **Callao** houses Lima's airport and the Pilsen brewery. To the east, Javier Prado heads from San Isidro to the suburbs of **San Borja** and **Monterrico.**

SHOPPING

Lima markets feature *artesanía* from all over Peru, but the markets in the goods' cities of origin often have wider selections at lower prices; most tourists who buy handicrafts in Lima are on last-minute souvenir shopping sprees. That said, the best *artesanía* **markets** in Lima lie along blocks 700 to 900 of La Marina in San Miguel. Still, as always, the quality of the alpaca sweaters, woven wall hangings, and gold, silver, and turquoise jewelry varies. None of the prices are fixed and bargaining is expected. (Most booths open M-Sa 9:30am-8pm, Su 10:30am-6pm. From Lima Centro, take a colectivo marked "La Marina" from Javier Prado.) Other artisans hawk their wares at more expensive (but also more convenient) markets in Lima Centro, near the Plaza de Armas at Carabaya 319 (open M-Sa 10am-9pm, Su 10am-6pm); and in Miraflores, around the 5200 to 5400 blocks of Petit Thouars, north of Gonzales Prada (open M-Sa 9am-8pm, Su 10:30am-7pm).

The city's glitziest **shopping centers** are Jockey Plaza (also called Centro Comercial El Polo) in Monterrico and LarcoMar in Miraflores (see Miraflores, above); they are filled with goods imported from the US and Europe. (To get to Jockey Plaza, take a colectivo marked "Jockey Plaza" down Javier Prado Este. LarcoMar is at the end of Larco, the southern continuation of Arequipa; take a "Todo Arequipa" colectivo heading to Miraflores.) Alternatively, you can find all that imported stuff under one roof at the South American department store chain **Saga Falabella,** with locations on the second block of La Unión in Lima Centro and at the Centro Camino Real in San Isidro. There are also a number of trendy clothing stores around Parque Kennedy and down Larco in Miraflores.

For more local character and better bargains, head to pedestrian walkway **La Unión,** which runs between the Plaza San Martín and the Plaza de Armas. This crowded mall teems with street performers, tattoo parlors, drug dealers, and vendors hawking everything from shoes to more shoes. Get the best deals on electronic goods, watches, brand-name tennis shoes and hiking boots, t-shirts, sweatshirts, and just about anything else it's possible to get one's hands on at the **Polvos Azules flea market.** Just keep your money close to your body and don't bring any valuables, or you might find your watch on a sales table. (Just off the Vía Expresa at 28 de Julio, slightly south of Lima Centro. Open daily 9am-9pm.)

 ENTERTAINMENT

Lima is a haven for all forms of entertainment. The newspaper *La República* has a Friday supplement, *Viernes Sábado Domingo*, which lists the upcoming weekend's concerts, sporting events, plays, films, and other diversions.

SPORTS

Fútbol (soccer) is more than a sport in Peru; it is a religion with the power to empty the streets, halt traffic, and drag even policemen away from their work. The **Estadio Nacional,** off Blocks 7-9 of Paseo de la República, and the nearby **Estadio Alianza Lima** host most of the important matches. Matches between the two Lima-based teams, reigning champion **Universitario** (or simply La U) and bitter rival **Alianza** are almost guaranteed to get rowdy; be aware that no one can innocently wear cream or blue to such games. If you can't make the match, you can listen to it in a colectivo, park, or pretty much any other venue with a loudspeaker. (National match seats s/25-45. Professional match seats as little as s/5.) **Volleyball,** also played in the Estadio Nacional, comes in a distant second.

When you've tired of watching humans play, turn to the animals: bullfighting, cockfighting, and horse racing are all popular spectator events. The **Plaza de Acho,** Hualgayoc 332, across the bridge from Lima Centro in the northern suburb of Rímac, hosts bullfights during the **Fiestas Patrias** in the last week of July, as well as from October to December. (☎481 14 67. Look in newspapers for exact dates and times. Tickets from s/20.) Chickens battle to the death in **La Chacra,** at the end of Tomás Marsano in Surco, and **Coliseo El Rosedal,** near the Plaza de Armas. (Tickets s/10 for national championships.) Horses and jockeys run in circles at the **Hipódromo de Monterrico,** on Javier Prado Este at the Panamericana Sur. (☎436 56 77. Races Sa, Su, Tu, Th. Tickets s/2-10. Min. bet s/1.)

If spectator sports aren't your thing, create the spectacle yourself. Many gringos come to Peru to get high, but no one succeeds better than those who hook up with the extreme sports company **PerúFly,** Jorge Chávez 658, in Miraflores. **Bungee jump** from a hot air balloon 100m over the ocean, or **paraglide** with an instructor over the Miraflores beach. To paraglide solo, you'll have to take their five-day course (US$280), which includes practice runs over sand dunes and the Pachacamac ruins. (☎444 50 04. Bungee jumps every Sa or Su; US$49 per person, min. 4 people. Tandem paraglide flights daily; US$20 per 20min. Office open daily 8am-8pm.) The **Lima Hash House Harriers** (www.geocities.com/Colosseum/Track/8302), a group of expatriates devoted to the British cross-country running game of Hares and Hounds, organizes frequent group runs around the city.

FILM

In Lima, high-budget Hollywood movies—in English with Spanish subtitles—are as cheap as a video back home (s/6-15). Oddly enough, it's harder to find theaters that show Spanish-language films. Most movies take three to six months after their US release to make it to Peru. Screenings and times are listed daily in the "Luces" section of *El Comercio.* Some of the biggest theaters (with the largest screens, cleanest seats, and best sound quality) are: **El Pacífico,** José Pardo 121, on Parque Kennedy, in Miraflores (☎445 69 90; s/15, M and W s/10); **Cinemark Jockey Plaza,** Javier Prado Este 4200, in the shopping center of the same name in Surco (☎434 00 34; s/15, before 6pm s/12); **Orrantia,** Arequipa 2701, at Javier Prado, in San Isidro (☎221 60 08; s/10); **Excelsior,** La Unión 780, Lima Centro (☎426 35 47; s/6); **Adán y Eva,** La Unión 819, Lima Centro (☎428 84 60; s/7); and **UVK Multicines LarcoMar,** in the LarcoMar shopping center in Miraflores (☎446 73 36; s/15, M and W s/10). And then there's ▧**CineBar,** Sala 12 of UVK Multicines LarcoMar, perhaps the only theater of its kind in the world. Viewers sit in plush armchairs around cafe-style tables, receive a free beer or soda with the price of admission, and can press a buzzer during the movie to call a waiter over and order more food or drink (s/21, M and W s/16). Older, international art house films are shown at *cine clubes* such as: **Julieta,** Porta 139 (☎444 01 35), on the south side of Parque Kennedy, in Miraflores; **Filmoteca de Lima** (☎331 01 26), in the Museo de Arte (see Sights: Museums, p. 85) in Lima Centro; **Cine Club Arcais,** Coronel Zegarra 162, Jesús María; and **Cine Club Miraflores,** Larco 770 (☎446 39 59), in the Centro Cultural Ricardo Palma.

THEATER

The week's theater performances are listed in the "Luces" section of *El Comercio*. The **Instituto Cultural Peruano-Norteamericano** and the **British Council** (see Practical Information: Local Services, p. 76) put on frequent plays in English. Spanish-language theater, often with local actors, takes place at the **Auditorio Museo de la Nación**, Javier Prado 2475, San Borja; **Centro Cultural PUCP**, Camino Real 1075 (☎222 68 09), in San Isidro; **Teatro Auditorio Miraflores**, Larco 1150, in Miraflores; **Teatro Canout**, Petit Thouars 4550, in Miraflores; and **Centro Cultural Casa Abierto**, Petit Thouars 5390, Miraflores. The **Teatro Mocha Graña**, Saenz Peña 107 (☎247 62 92), Barranco, puts on more experimental local plays.

🎵 NIGHTLIFE

Lima comes alive at night and stays wide-eyed until 5 or 6am. The parks, large and small, fill with strolling families, cruising teenagers, smooching couples, and attentive snack sellers. The clubs blare all varieties of music, and the energetic salsa away while the sedentary imbibe one *jarra* of beer after another. While you can find "nightlife" and liveliness all over the city, it's safer to stick to the bars and clubs in Miraflores and Barranco. *Limeños* refer to some discos in Lima Centro as *mala muerte* (bad death) because of the prostitution, drugs, and violence they sometimes contain. If going out in this area, take a cab, know the club's address, and don't bother people you didn't come with.

LIMA CENTRO

Las Brisas del Titicaca, Wakulsky 168 (☎332 18 81), off the 1st block of Brasil. A relatively inexpensive *peña* that attracts nationally-known folk, Andean, and criollo acts. F and Sa shows 1:30pm; cover s/20. Open M-Th noon-9pm, F-Sa noon-4am.

Cerebro, Emancipación 119 (☎427 71 28), at La Unión. The biggest and most widely-known club in Lima Centro. Move to rock and Latin music on the dark, underground dance floor. *Jarras* s/15. Show your international passport and not only will you get in free, they'll also give you a free drink. Open daily 6pm-6am.

MIRAFLORES

Slick locals, clad in designer attire, swarm to Miraflores's hotspots to groove to Latin, rock, and techno beats into the wee hours. Some locals spend their weekend nights loitering at the outdoor LarcoMar shopping center, but Miraflores's real nightlife centers around Parque Kennedy. Most of Lima's gay and lesbian nightlife is in this area as well (see Gay and Lesbian Nightlife, p. 390).

🖼 Valkyria, Benavides 571 (☎927 16 11), 1 block east of Larco, in a complex that looks vaguely like a Swiss chalet. Popular with everyone from teenagers to tourists, due in large part to its 2-for-1 drink specials. A bit cramped, but people always make room to dance. *Jarras* s/17. Mixed drinks s/11-18. 2-for-1 specials include all drinks Su and Tu, chopps M, cocktails W, *jarras* Th, all beer F. Open daily 8pm-8am.

Bizarro, Lima 417, above El Parque D'Onofrio on Parque Kennedy. Breaking new ground in the use of fluorescent paint, Bizarro has 2 dance floors with 2 different DJs and moods—a trance/house room decorated with glowing stars, and an electronica room made to look like a graffiti-covered alley. Cover Tu-Th s/6, F-Sa s/15; includes 1 beer. Open daily 11pm-5am.

Tequila Rock, Diez Canseco 146 (☎444 36 61), near Parque Kennedy. Full of young women who are there to be seen by gringos and older businessmen; dancing with one's reflection in the mirror is the groove of choice. The music is unremarkable and the lights tacky, but there are booths for getting cozy with the special someone you met. Beers s/ 1 after 2am. Cover Su, W, Th s/10; F-Sa s/20; F includes 1 drink. Open daily 9pm-7am.

O'Murphy's Irish Pub, Schell 627 (☎242 45 40), at Solar. Fulfills all the duties of an Irish pub except one: there's no Guinness on tap. Drown your sorrows in a can (s/15) instead. Live music Th and Sa. Happy hour 7-10pm. Open M-Sa 6pm-4am.

Bauhaus, Bellavista 362 (☎448 96 23), off Parque Kennedy. Plays 1980s and industrial music in a dark room to an even darker-souled crowd. Rave night (Th) is especially popular. Cover W-Th s/6, includes 1 drink; F-Sa s/10. Open W-Sa 10pm-5am.

BARRANCO

The best way to choose where to go in Barranco is to stand in the middle of Parque Municipal and follow the music of your choice. You'll hear everything from classical music, jazz, techno, and folk, to romantic whispers and drunken gibberish. **Pasaje Sánchez Carrión,** just off the park, is a pedestrian walkway lined with nothing but bars and discos. They all play identical dance hits, normally have no cover, and often offer cheap beer (*jarras* as low as s/10). Most also lack a distinctive character, but there are still plenty of cafes and bars off the walkway that value substance. Cross over the **Puente de los Suspiros,** and pounding surf replaces music. The bars near this seaside lookout are more romantic (and expensive) than elsewhere. Hungry late-night revelers can always find a sandwich (s/5) along the first and second blocks of **Piérola,** a few blocks up Grau at the traffic light.

▩ **El Dragón,** Nicolás de Piérola 168 (☎477 54 20). Full of hip 20-somethings who take their style cues from underground jazz clubs instead of Ricky Martin videos. Wander through the rooms comparing funky color schemes, lounge on a couch with Absolut and tonic (s/11) in hand, notice you're the only tourist there, and feel cool. Music runs the gamut from James Brown to Moby. Occasional live shows. Open Tu-Sa 10pm-3am.

▩ **Kafe Kitsch,** Bolognesi 743 (☎247 33 25). Fulfills its name: a mermaid mannequin greets guests at the door, ABBA Gold holds a permanent place in the CD rotation, and drag queens regularly climb onto the bar to perform. Everyone is welcome. Try to arrive before midnight on the weekend, or you might not get in. Open W-Sa 9pm-5am.

La Noche, Bolognesi 307 (☎477 41 54), at the far corner of Sánchez Carrión. Whether you feel like dancing, listening to live bands, or engaging in a round of toasts, this enormous 3-story bar has the room. *Jarras* s/18. Live music M-Th from 11pm. Frequent poetry readings and art shows; check calendar. Open M-Th 7pm-3am, F-Sa 8pm-4am.

Juanito's, Grau 234, an unlabeled doorway next to Domino's Pizza. Founded in 1937, this hole-in-the-wall is the oldest bar in Barranco and the legendary watering spot of various Peruvian artists. But the real reason to come is El Famoso Cucharita, who can do the unimaginable with beer bottles, teaspoons, and cigarettes (performances nightly sometime 10pm-midnight). *Jarras* s/14. Open Su-W 11am-2am, Th-Sa 11am-4:30am.

Las Terrazas de Barranco, Grau 290 (☎477 55 33), on the park. Offers a more civilized, tree-screened, candlelit dining spot during the day, but watch out—when the sun goes down, it morphs into a towering, 4-story disco. Surrender to the rhythms of Latin pop. *Jarras* s/15. Restaurant open daily 9am-7pm. Disco open daily 7pm-4am.

La Posada del Ángel, with 3 eerily identical locations: Pedro de Osmas 164 and 222 (☎247 03 41), and San Martín 157 (☎247 55 44). Decorated with lots of antiques, these small bars attract a tranquil crowd. Live Cuban folk music. There's often a wait for a table on weekends. Pitchers of *sangría* s/25. Open M-Sa 7:30pm-3am.

De Parranda, Grau 622 (☎247 20 36), features a rousing 18-piece salsa orchestra. You can't help but get down at this gigantic salsa extravaganza. Many patrons dress to the nines, so get those dancing shoes shined. Cover s/20. Open Th-Sa 9pm-4:30am.

GAY AND LESBIAN

Although homosexuality isn't widely accepted in Peru, Lima is home to the most visible gay community in the country. The capital has some excellent resources (see Practical Information: Local Services, p. 76) and great nightlife. For the latest in Lima's ever-changing gay scene, check out www.gaylimape.tripod.com. When looking for gay-friendly night-life, the key phrase is *"al ambiente."* Many of the buildings are unmarked on the outside but rocking inside, and most are not exclusively frequented by gays or lesbians. The biggest, flashiest, and by far most popular disco-bar is **Gitano,** Berlin 231, off Parque Kennedy in Miraflores. With a classy lounge, lively dance floor, and fabulous DJs, straight bars only wish they had it this good. (☎446 34 35. Open W-Su 10:30pm-6am. Cover W-Th s/10 after midnight, F s/20 includes 1 drink, Sa s/25.) One of the only exclusively gay spots in Lima Centro, **Imperio,** Camaná Block 9, near the Plaza Francia, isn't as posh as Gitano, but it fills up on the weekend and features occasional shows. The area can be unsafe, so take a taxi. (Open W-Sa 11pm-5am. Cover s/5.) While not exclusively gay, **Splash,** Los Pinos 181 in Miraflores, attracts an "open-minded" mixed crowd in a more upscale establishment. (☎444 24 00. Open W-Su 11pm-6am. Cover Sa s/15, s/20 after midnight; includes 1 drink.) Similarly, **Voglia,** Ricardo Palma 336, also in Miraflores, attracts a mixed crowd and treats them to techno and salsa throughout the night. (☎864 31 34. Open Tu-Su 10pm-6am. Cover s/5, F-Sa s/10.) One of Lima's most popular bars is gay-friendly **Kafe Kitsch** (see In Barranco, above), second home to many a drag queen. Gay men also frequently meet in the city's private **Baños Turkos** (saunas), though not all baths are exclusively homosexual. The most popular mainly-gay baths are **Baños Pardo,** José Pardo 182, in Miraflores (☎445 50 46; s/37); **Oupen Sauna,** 28 de Julio 171, in Miraflores (☎242 30 94; M-Th s/25, F-Su s/30); and **Baños Tivoli,** Petit Thouars 4041, in San Isidro (☎222 17 05; s/20).

⚑ DAYTRIPS FROM LIMA

There are three main escape routes from Lima's honking horns, constant fog, and urban bustle: north to the ruins of the Chancay Valley, the beaches of Ancón, and the Lomas de Lachay wildlife reserve; east (and inland) to Chosica and the Marcahuasi ruins; and south to the Pachacamac ruins and surf spots along the coast.

ANCÓN

To get to Ancón, take a colectivo (45-90min., s/1.5) from the Plaza 2 de Mayo to the end of the line, then walk downhill to reach the beach.

For the most part a quiet seaside town, Ancón teams with visitors come summer (Nov.-Jan.). Compared to Lima, however, Ancón remains tranquil throughout the year, although on a nice day you will usually have to share your sand. The **beaches** are relatively clean, but check the ratings posted on large signs by the beach, and avoid any *muy malo* (very bad) water. Ancón's oceanfront is divided into two parts by the huge *Fuerza Aerea del Peru, Escuela de Supervivencia en el Mar* (Armed Forced of Peru, School of Ocean Supervision). Facing the water, head right from the *Fuerza Aerea* to reach a wide stretch of sand. To the left, the area is more commercial. Numerous **pre-Inca ruins** lie in the Chillón Valley near Ancón, but they have not been developed for inquisitive tourists; it's best to ask around in Ancón for a guide to visit the three pyramids of the **Templo El Paraíso.**

THE CHANCAY VALLEY

To reach Huaral, take a bus from the Plaza de Acho in Lima (1½-2½hr., 15 per day, s/3). From Huaral, buses leave from the dirt parking lot between the river and the freeway.

The Chancay Valley harbors a wealth of rarely visited ruins. Start your journey in **Huaral,** the valley's gateway town, where you can ask around for a guide to the ruins in any shop. From Huaral, you can embark on a day trek to see the **Huampon Ruins** (US$50 for one person, US$150 for four people; negotiable) or on longer journeys to the **Anay ruins** near Huayopampa, the **Rupac** ruins near La Flonda, or the **Chiprac** ruins near Huasloy. Guides have information about rafting, rock climbing, and bicycle trips. There is not a lot to do in Huaral proper. If you're stuck in town overnight, try the **Hostal del Sol,** R. Morales-Bermúdez 345. From the Plaza de Armas, follow signs pointing down Morales-Bermúdez; the hostel is on the left. You may have to maneuver to fit all your baggage in the room, but cleanliness and all-day hot water will be your rewards. (☎246 1235. Singles s/20, with bath s/25.)

QUID PRO QUO? Peru's blossoming Hare Krishna community has left an indelible mark on Lima's landscape, from vegetarian restaurants to the myriad herbal medicine stores. Unlike Peru's small Buddhist community, most Hare Krishnas are ethnic Peruvians, many raised Catholic, who converted to this form of Hinduism as adults. The story begins tens of thousands of miles away, in a land where Indian is not a politically incorrect term. Born in Bombay in 1896, His Divine Grace A.C. Bhaktivedanta Swami Prabhupada emigrated to the United States in 1966 with the intention of spreading Krishna consciousness throughout the world. During the 1970s, his disciples spread the faith through South America. Though things got off to a slow start when the first Hare Krishna center opened in Lima in 1977, the movement grew over the years, attracting terrorism-scarred Peruvians with its non-violent philosophy of clean living. Today, the Hare Krishna population in Peru numbers in the thousands, and adheres to a few basic principles: strict vegetarian eating habits; no drinking, smoking, or using drugs; and a lack of attachment to material objects. Though they pay tribute to the Hindu god Krishna, devotees (as they call themselves) emphasize that they are not Hindus; rather, they are simply adherents to "Krishna consciousness."

To at least one scholar, the Hare Krishna philosophy's popularity in Peru makes perfect sense. V. Ganapati Sthapati, an Indian architect who designed hundreds of Hindu temples according to strict religious guidelines, discovered something strange when he visited Machu Picchu: the Inca structure conforms exactly to all the design principles prescribed by the Vastu Shastras of India, as does the masonry at the Sacsayhuamán complex in Cusco. After finding the same similarities in Chichen Itza, Tikal, and other Latin American architectural masterpieces, Sthapati theorized that Mayan, the creator of Indian architecture, originated from the Maya people of Central America, and that the Hindu planning principles actually originated in Latin America centuries ago. Perhaps Prabhupada and his disciples didn't introduce Krishna consciousness to Peru; maybe they brought it home.

CHOSICA

Colectivos marked "Chosica" (1½hr., s/3.5) run inland from the Plaza Grau in Lima Centro. The temple is at Km32 of the Carretera Central. Open daily 9am-8pm.

Chosica sees sun nearly 365 days a year, making it a choice spot for a *limeño's* weekend getaway. And although travelers cannot enter the grounds of Chosica's many resorts, they can visit a different sort of nirvana. The **Templo Védico,** the main place of worship for Peru's Hare Krishnas, was constructed in Chosica in 1991, and its painted domes and beautiful garden look like sacred sites in India. Visitors are welcome—the monks give free tours of the grounds. Every Sunday at noon the temple hosts a festival with music and vegetarian food, free to the public.

MARCAHUASI AND SAN PEDRO DE CASTA

Getting to Marcahuasi is a full day's journey. Take a colectivo to Chosica and ask to be let off at Parque Echenique (1½hr., s/4), the town's central bus depot. From there, take a colectivo up to the small mountain village of San Pedro de Casta (3-4hr., 9am and 4pm, s/5). The Marcahuasi plateau is an uphill 3km hike from here, which could take 4hr. or longer for those not yet acclimatized—the altitude leaps from 3200 to 4000m. Those camping at the top should come prepared; bring a tent, a sleeping bag, food, rain gear, and a compass in the rainy season (since a dense fog rises by early afternoon).

An enigmatic collection of rock formations 90km east of Lima and 4000m up, Marcahuasi makes for an excellent camping excursion. These massive chunks of spookily eroded granite resemble sphinxes, tortoises, judges, and even the Egyptian fertility goddess Thueris (with the head of a hippo and the belly of a pregnant woman). Their source is unclear, but Marcahuasi sees many a weekend pilgrimage by Peruvians who speak of a powerful spiritual presence and can feel "magnetic forces" coursing through their fingertips. (Cynics might call this altitude sickness.) Nevertheless, the plateau's dead silence invites meditation, provided one gets there before the weekend crowds. Obtain a map (s/5) after registering at the **tourist office** in San Pedro de Casta, located in the central plaza along with a clinic and a store with the town's only telephone. The tourist office also rents horses and mules for the hike up (s/15). Those low on provisions can stay in the friendly and hard-working community of **Casta,** at the lavender-colored house of Manuel Olivares, directly behind town hall. Sr. Olivares keeps two rooms with bunk beds, wool blankets, and one of the town's only flushable toilets. (Rooms s/ 10 per person). The tourist office also rents rooms upstairs without beds or running water. (Rooms s/5 per person.) Next door, a store has canned staples, and a local woman will cook rice, chicken, and eggs upon request. On the plaza, ask at the school for a key to Casta's one-room collection of **mummified human remains** recovered from an ancient burial spot at Marcahuasi. They retain the fetal position in which they were buried as well as the ghastly looks they had on their faces when they died.

PACHACAMAC

Catch one of the frequent brown and white colectivos marked "Lurín" (1hr., s/2) heading east on Grau in Lima Centro. Colectivos that pass Pachacamac (1hr., every hr. 5am-10pm, s/2.7) also leave from the corner of Montevideo and Andahuaylas. Ask the driver for "las ruinas;" if you simply say "Pachacamac," you may be dropped of at a small town about 1km past the entrance to the ruins.

Limeños head south for one reason—the beaches. Tourists head south for the Pachacamac ruins. On the way there, colorful make-shift huts dot the hillsides of Lima's southern outskirts; they constitute Villa El Salvador, the most publicized of Lima's *pueblos jóvenes* (shanty-towns built to accommodate the city's burgeoning population). Pachacamac, roughly translated as "creator of land and time," was a Huari god with the power to destroy the world through earthquakes and to see the past as well as the future—hence the two faces on either side of his head. The Lima Culture began the sacred city dedicated to this deity between AD 200-600 and the Huari later supplemented it, after AD 650, with pyramids accessible by huge stone ramps. When the Incas razed the rest of the Huari settlement in 1470, they feared the sacredness of this complex so much that they left it intact. Instead, the Incas added their own theological input in the form of the Temple of the Sun, and affiliated Pachacamac with their own creator-god. When the Inca emperor Atahualpa tried to convince the Spanish conquistadors to set him free by tempting them with tales of his kingdom's treasures, he named two gold-laden spots in particular: the Sun Temple in Cusco and Pachacamac. With visions of precious metals dancing in his eyes, Hernando Pizarro (brother of Francisco) led an expedition to Pachacamac in 1533; the men stormed into the sacred temple and tore it apart looking for riches, but found nothing. Driven by rumors that the high priests had hidden their gold, the Spaniards raided Pachacamac a few more times over the next decade, but always came out empty-handed. Most of the complex has fallen into disrepair, but the largest structures still stand—the Huari pyramids and the temple and palaces built by the Incas. The ruins lie along an unshaded loop that takes at least an hour to walk, so bring water and wear a hat or sunscreen. A small **museum** at the entrance, as well as signs (in Spanish and English) in front of each structure, are quite informative. All of the ruins are off-limits to visitors except the **Inca Temple of the Sun,** the top of which offers an incredible view of the ruins, the nearby ocean, and the Valle El Salvador. (English-speaking guides s/15. Ruins and museum open daily 9am-4pm. s/6, students s/3.)

CUSCO AND THE SACRED VALLEY

The Inca Manco Capac founded Cusco around AD 1100, back when the Incas were just one of many small Andean states vying for control. Things changed in 1438, when the soon-to-be ninth Inca Pachacuti defeated the fierce Chanka people, opening the way for a massive expansion of the empire. Cusco became the center of Inca Peru, the building ground of great palaces and temples, and an administrative and religious headquarters. However, Pachacuti's influence extended far beyond his capital; that era saw the construction of great military and religious complexes at Pisac and Ollantaytambo, not to mention the extraordinary city of Machu Picchu. Today, the name "Cusco" applies to both the city and this surrounding department, often considered the archeological capital of South America. As in Inca times, the region revolves closely around its capital—only now, the connection is based on a thriving tourist industry. But the undeniable comforts of Cusco (the city) should not dissuade anyone from spending time in Cusco (the department). Exploring the serene Sacred Valley allows visitors to observe a lifestyle that the hustle and bustle of tourism still hasn't (for the most part) touched.

HIGHLIGHTS OF CUSCO AND THE SACRED VALLEY

PRAY in one of the best colonial cathedrals (**P. 104**) in Peru.

SCRUTINIZE the comprehensive displays at the **Museo Inka** (p. 106).

BOOGIE with the other backpackers at one of Cusco's many **clubs** (p. 109).

OVERLOOK the city's red rooftops from awe-inspiring **Sacsayhuamán** (p. 110).

BUY souvenirs at **Pisac's market** and then make the scenic hike up to its glorious and well-preserved **ruins** (p. 113).

COMPLETE the **Inca Trail,** an enchanting pilgrimage to the sacred city of the Incas and one of the best treks in South America (p. 116).

GO to **Machu Picchu** (p. 120). Come along, hurry up.

The term **Sacred Valley** ("Valle Sagrado" in Spanish; p. 113) refers to the area around the Río Urubamba, which flows northeast from Cusco. With its rolling, maize-resplendent hills, the Urubamba Valley was the breadbasket of imperial Cusco, particularly after Inca engineers solved the region's problem with landslides and soil erosion by constructing agricultural terraces. These steps, a few meters in width and height, were sculpted from the earth and retained by stone walls; thousands still exist today. Another dazzling Inca achievement was the redirection of the Río Urubamba—the straightening of the waters near Pisac in order to allow for more efficient crop irrigation. The result of this labor was the longest pre-Columbian canal in the Americas. Besides this agricultural legacy, the Incas left a valley replete with sacred structures: the fortresses of Pisac and Ollantaytambo, and the sprawling city of Machu Picchu. Coupled with their valley's rustic splendor, these ruins manage to lure most visitors away from Cusco at least once.

CUSCO
☎ 084

There are Peruvians who live in Cusco. There are *cusqueños* who do things other than run hostels or tour agencies. You'd just never know it from hanging around the Plaza de Armas, where, nowadays, fleece is a fashion statement. Welcome to the tactical center of the Sacred Valley's gringo invasion, part two. Once upon a time, Cusco was the capital of Tawantinsuyo, the vast Inca Empire that stretched from southern Colombia to Chile and Argentina. Then came the original gringo invasion in 1533 (also called the Spanish Conquest), when Francisco Pizarro and his men arrived. But after squashing the final Inca resistance in 1572, the conquistadors let Cusco slip into colonial obscurity. The city was forgotten to the rest of the world until 1911, when the American Hiram Bingham "discovered" nearby Machu Picchu and put Cusco on the international tourist map.

Yet it would take more than overexposure to diminish Cusco's cobblestoned charm. Narrow streets lead past balcony cafes, majestic colonial churches, the artisan dens in San Blas, and the hottest discos this side of Lima. Furthermore, the Sacred Valley, home to South America's greatest collection of Inca ruins, sits in Cusco's backyard. It is crowded, yes. At 3400m, it's cold, too. In many ways, Cusco is prepackaged and overly primped. But tourists and those elusive locals alike love this city, a thriving integration of cultures deep within the incredible Andes, and you'd be a fool not to visit.

In recent years, Cusco has experienced a rash of **strangle muggings,** particularly around San Cristóbal, San Blas, and other quiet areas. The muggers work in gangs, and can, with alarming speed, find the right pressure point in the neck to knock someone unconscious. A victim wakes up seconds later stripped of all valuables, but otherwise unharmed. A similar surprise technique involves pouring water on unsuspecting tourists from balconies above. A group of thieves then comes from behind and takes the sodden victims' wallets. Men and women, even in groups, are advised to take a taxi after dark and not pay the driver until the front door of their hostel is opened. Unfortunately, this is not a cure-all: some taxi drivers have been known to work with the thieves. The best prevention is to stay aware at all times and carry only small amounts of cash.

◪ TRANSPORTATION

Airport: Aeropuerto Alejandro Velasco Astete (☎222 611), in the southeastern part of the city. To get there, take one of the frequent colectivos along Sol marked "Aeropuerto," s/0.5. Taxi s/10. International departure tax s/25; national departure tax s/10.

Airlines: AeroContinente, Carnes 245 (☎243 031), on the Plaza de Armas. Open M-F 8am-7:30pm, Sa 8am-6pm, Su 9am-noon. To: **Lima** (1hr.; 7:30, 8:30, 9:30am, 12:30pm; US$59); **Arequipa** (30min.; M, Tu, F, Su 8:30am; US$59); and **Puerto Maldonado** (30min.; Tu, Th, Sa, Su 7:30am; US$59). **Tans,** Almagro 133 (☎227 101 or 242 727). Open M-Sa 9am-1pm and 4-8pm, Su 9am-noon. To **Lima** (1hr.; 7:40, 9, and 10:30am; US$68) and **Puerto Maldonado** (30min., 9am, US$58). **LanPerú,** Portal Mantos 114 (☎225 552 or 255 554; fax 255 555). Open M-F 8:30am-7pm, Sa 8:30am-6pm, Su 9:30am-12:30pm. To **Lima** (55min.; 7:40, 8:55, 11:10am, 12:25pm; US$79) and **Arequipa** (35min., 11:10am, US$59). **Taca Perú,** Sol 226 (☎249 921, reservations 0800 482 22). Open M-Sa 8am-1:30pm and 3-7pm. To **Lima** (1hr., 7:50am, US$43). **Star Up,** Sol 800 (☎249 697), at Garcilaso. Open M-F 8:30am-1pm and 4-7pm, Sa 8:30am-1pm. To **Lima** (1¼hr.; Tu, Th, Sa 8:30am; US$55) via **Ayacucho** (40min., US$55). **Lloyd Aero Boliviano (LAB),** Santa Catalina Angosta 160 (☎222 990). Open M-F 9am-7pm, Sa 9am-1pm. To **La Paz, Bolivia** (50min.; Tu 11:15am, Th 9:30am, Sa 10am; US$100).

Trains: Reservations for all trains should be made at least a day in advance, especially Jun.-Sept. **Estación San Pedro** (☎224 552). From the Plaza de Armas, walk 7 blocks

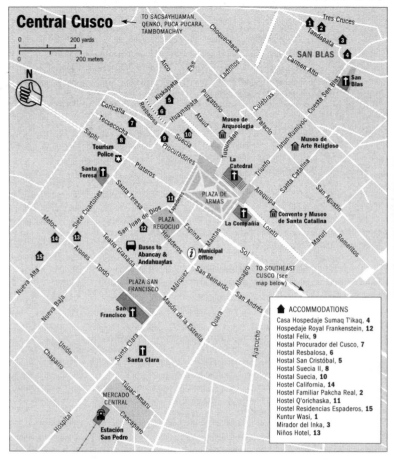

Central Cusco

TO SACSAYHUAMAN, QENKO, PUCA PUCARA, TAMBOMACHAY

0   200 yards
0   200 meters

N

Tres Cruces

SAN BLAS

San Blas

Choquechaca
Arco
Ese
Ladrillos
Kiskapata
Coricalla
Resbalosa
Huaynapata
Ataud
Puyatorio
Tecsecocha
Saphi
Tourism Police
Santa Teresa
Platiaros
Santa Teresa
Suecia
Procuradores
Museo de Arqueologia
Tucumán
La Catedral
Triunfo
Palacio
Culébras
Carmen Alto
Tandapata
Cuesta San Blas
Jatun-Rumiyoc
Museo de Arte Religioso
Santa Catalina
Arequipa
San Agustín
Maruri
Romeritos
Loreto
Convento y Museo de Santa Catalina
La Compañia
PLAZA DE ARMAS
Espaderos
San Juan de Dios
PLAZA REGOCIJO
Heladeros
Espinar
Mantas
Sol
Municipal Office
Buses to Abancay & Andahuaylas
Teatro Granada
Meloc
Siete Cuartones
Arones
Nueva Alta
Tordo
Nueva Baja
Unión
Chaparro
Santa Clara
Santa Clara
PLAZA SAN FRANCISCO
San Francisco
Mansón de la Estrella
Márquez
San Bernardo
Quera
San Andrés
Almagro
Ayacucho
TÚpac Amaru
Cascaparo
MERCADO CENTRAL
Estación San Pedro
Hospital

TO SOUTHEAST CUSCO (see map below)

ACCOMMODATIONS

Casa Hospedaje Sumaq T'ikaq, **4**
Hospedaje Royal Frankenstein, **12**
Hostal Felix, **9**
Hostal Procurador del Cusco, **7**
Hostal Resbalosa, **6**
Hostal San Cristóbal, **5**
Hostal Suecia II, **8**
Hostal Suecia, **10**
Hostel California, **14**
Hostel Familiar Pakcha Real, **2**
Hostel Q'orichaska, **11**
Hostel Residencias Espaderos, **15**
Kuntur Wasi, **1**
Mirador del Inka, **3**
Niños Hotel, **13**

CUSCO

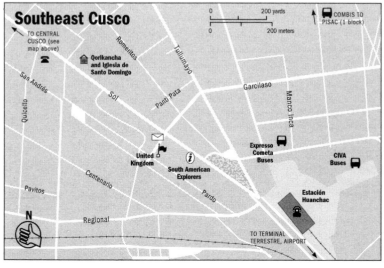

Southeast Cusco

0   200 yards
0   200 meters

COMBIS TO PISAC (1 block)

TO CENTRAL CUSCO (see map above)

Qorikancha and Iglesia de Santo Domingo

Romeritos
Tullumayo
Garcilaso
Manco Inca
San Andrés
Quicello
Sol
Panti Pata
United Kingdom
South American Explorers
Expresso Cometa Buses
CIVA Buses
Centenario
Pavitos
Pardo
Estación Huanchac
Regional
N

TO TERMINAL TERRESTRE, AIRPORT

along Mantas, Márquez, and Santa Clara. Ticket window open daily 8-11am and 3-4pm. Local train to **Machu Picchu** (4-5hr., 7:45am, s/15) via **Ollantaytambo** (3hr., s/15) Tourist trains to **Machu Picchu** (3½hr.): Turismo Económico (7:30am, US$30), Autovagon (6:30am, US$50), Inca (7am, US$80). Times and prices change frequently. **Estación Huanchac** (☎233 593), at the downhill end of Sol. Ticket window open M-F 7am-noon and 2-5pm, Sa 7am-noon, Su 8-10am. To **Puno** (11hr.; M, W, F, Sa 8am; Económico s/25, Pullman US$19, Turismo Inka US$23) and **Arequipa** (23hr.; M, W, F, Sa 8am; Económico s/45, Pullman US$29) via **Juliaca** (10½hr.; Económico s/25, Pullman US$19).

Buses: Terminal, several kilometers southeast of the center, at the end of Sol. Taxi s/7. E.T. Power (☎247 515) to **Puno** (7hr.; 7, 8am, noon, 7, 8, 8:30pm; s/15). San Jéronimo (☎261 142) to **Quillabamba** (8hr., 7pm, s/15) and **Andahuaylas** (12hr., 6 and 7pm, s/25) via **Abancay** (6hr., s/15). Turismo Ampay (☎227 541) to **Tacna** (16hr., 6pm via Arequipa and 8pm via Puno, s/5); and **Quillabamba** (8hr., 6 and 8pm, s/15). Ormeño (☎228 712) to **Lima** (25hr., 5 and 6pm, s/60) and **Nasca** (24hr., 5 and 6pm, s/55). Romeliza (☎252 994) to **Lima** (26hr., 5 and 6pm, s/60). Chaski Tours (☎229 784) to **Arequipa** (12hr.; 6am, 2, and 5:30pm; s/20). Global (☎234 300) to **Abancay** (6hr., 5 and 6pm, s/13). Turismo Abancay (☎224 447) to **Abancay** (6hr.; 6am, 1, and 8pm; s/15). Transportes Turismo Colca (☎227 535) to **Colca** (6:45am and 5pm, s/20). Expreso Wari to **Ayacucho** (24hr., 7pm, s/50). Turismo San Luis to **La Paz, Bolivia** (15hr., 8pm, s/100) and **Arequipa** (12hr., 5:30 and 6pm, s/25). Libertad (☎247 174) to **Copacabana** (10hr.; 8am, 7:30, 8pm; s/25).

Taxis: Taxis surround the Plaza de Armas. Bus terminal s/7. Airport s/10. Within the city center s/2, after dusk s/3. Slightly more expensive when called ahead (☎222 222).

Colectivos: Run along Sol, Pardo, and Tullumayu. s/0.5. Colectivos to **Pisac, Chinchero,** and **Urubamba** run along Tullumayu 7am-6pm (s/2-3).

■✳🛈 ORIENTATION AND PRACTICAL INFORMATION

A tourist's Cusco revolves around the **Plaza de Armas.** From the plaza's right-hand (if you're facing downhill) downhill corner, Cusco's main avenue, **Sol,** runs toward the post office, bus terminal, Huanchac train station (service to Puno and Arequipa) and airport. From the western part of town, the Santa Ana station sends trains to Machu Picchu. **Procuradores** and **Plateros** head uphill from the Plaza de Armas and contain many hostels, restaurants, and tour companies. The streets behind the cathedral lead uphill from the plaza to **San Blas,** an area that houses numerous restaurants and artisan shops.

TOURIST, FINANCIAL, AND LOCAL SERVICES

Tourist Information: Municipal Office, Mantas 188 (☎263 176), at Heladeros, across from Iglesia de La Merced. Maps of Cusco and the Inca Trail available. They also sell tourist tickets (see p. 104). Open M-F 8am-6:30pm, Sa 8am-2pm. **South American Explorers (SAE),** Sol 930 (☎/fax 223 102; email saec@wayna.rcp.net.pe), at Garcilaso, 6 blocks down Sol from the Plaza de Armas. Recommendation lists, trip reports, bulletin boards, luggage storage, safe boxes, library, book exchange, free email, updates on train schedules. Open M-Sa 9am-5pm, Su 10am-1pm. Membership US$40 individuals, US$70 couples (see HARDGI about SAE, p. 390).

Tour Agencies: See Guided Tours from Cusco, p. 111.

Consulates: United Kingdom, Pardo 895 (☎226 671). Open M-F 9am-1pm and 3-6pm. **United States,** Tullumayo 127 (☎224 112). Open M-F 8am-noon and 3-6pm.

Currency Exchange: Banks cluster 2 blocks down Sol from the Plaza de Armas, and the streets around the Plaza de Armas harbor many casas de cambio.

ATMs: Banco Continental, Sol 352 at Puluchapata; **Banco de Crédito,** Sol 189 at Almagro; and **Bancosur,** Sol 459 at Arrayanniyoq, have Visa **ATMs. Banco Latino,** Sol 395 at Puluchapata, has a MasterCard **ATM.**

Language Schools: Amauta Cultural Spanish School, Suecia 480 (☎241 422; email info@amautaspanish.com). The largest Spanish school around. Offers a variety of language programs in Cusco and Urubamba. Group classes US$190 per week; private lessons US$7.50 per hr.; week-long package US$240, includes family stay, 20hr. of class, and activities such as salsa dancing, city tours, and cooking lessons. Office open M-F 8am-6pm, Sa 9am-noon. **Excel Language Center,** Cruz Verde 336A (☎235 298). Another school, with similar programs. Private lessons US$7 per hr. Office open M-F 9am-noon and 3-8pm. **Cusco Spanish School,** Garcilaso 265 (☎226 928; email cuscospan@webcusco.com/cuscospan; www.webcusco.com/cuscospan).

Supermarkets: Buy snacks for the Inca Trail at **El Chinito,** at Sol and Almagro, or the larger **El Chinito Grande,** Matar 271 at Ayacucho. Both open daily 8am-2pm and 3-8pm. There are also several small markets on Plateros.

Laundromats: Along Procuradores and Suecia—you shouldn't pay more than s/3 per kg.

EMERGENCY AND COMMUNICATIONS

Police: Tourism Police, Saphy 510 (☎232 221), at Siete Cuartones. English spoken. Open 24hr. To file complaints against fraudulent businesses or seek help if robbed, see the **Tourist Protection Bureau,** Carrizos 250 (☎252 974, 24hr. emergency ☎(01) 224 78 88), on the Plaza de Armas. English spoken. Open daily 8am-8pm.

Hospitals: Hospital Regional (emergency ☎223 691), Cultura. **Clínica Pardo,** Cultura 710 (☎240 387). **Dr. Oscar Tejada** (☎233 836) is available for emergencies 24hr.

Dentist: Dr. Virginia Valcarel Velarde, Panes 123 (☎231 558, emergency ☎246 220), on the Plaza de Armas.

Internet Access: Internet Station, Teqsicocha 400. s/3 per hr. Open daily 8:30am-midnight. **Ukukus** (s/2 per hr.) and **Mama Africa** (s/2.50 per hr.) have the cheapest and cushiest access if you don't mind music while typing (see Clubs, p. 109).

Post Office: Serpost (☎224 212), at Sol and Garcilaso, 5 long blocks from the Plaza de Armas. Open M-Sa 8am-8pm, Su 8am-2pm.

▐▌ ACCOMMODATIONS

Cusco swells with over 100 places to stay. Nevertheless, it can be difficult to find vacancies during July, August, and the Inti Raymi festival in late June. High season reservations (and reservation confirmations) are recommended.

AROUND THE PLAZA DE ARMAS

The location proves ideal but good deals are few and far between. Beware the *cusqueño* enemy to peaceful slumber: the all-night *disco-pub* on the second floor.

■ **Hostal Suecia II,** Teqsicocha 465 (☎239 757). Make a left at the top of Procuradores and follow the street around the corner. Cushier than the original (see below), with welcoming rooms, hot water, and a bright interior courtyard. Singles s/20, with bath s/30; doubles s/30, with bath s/50; triples s/45, with bath s/70.

Hostal Suecia, Suecia 332 (☎233 282). Simple rooms surround a plant-filled courtyard and share hot-water baths. Dorms s/14; singles s/20; doubles s/30; triples s/51.

Hostal Felix, Teqsicocha 171 (☎241 949). Tons of exposed stone make Felix feel like a cave, but fireplaces warm its rooms. Decent baths. Hot water most of the time. Singles s/15, with bath s/20; doubles s/20, with bath s/24; triples s/30, with bath s/33.

Maison de la Tennesse (HI) (☎235 617), on a little street off the 5th block of Sol. A tidy, family-run link in the worldwide HI web. Rooms may be a little cramped given the price. Hot water 24hr. Kitchen access. Rooms US$8 per person, with bath US$10.

Hospedaje Magnolia II, Regional 898 (☎224 898), at Centenario, is actually nowhere near the Plaza de Armas. We just didn't have anywhere else to list it. From the Plaza, walk down Sol, take a right on Garcilaso (which turns into San Miguel), then left on Centenario. In a circular psychedelic-blue building near the bus terminal. Clean, with large windows. Hot water 24hr. Singles s/20, with bath s/25; doubles s/35, with bath, s/35.

AROUND THE PLAZA REGOCIJO

Plenty of cheap beds wait in colonial houses on the streets around this leafy plaza, one block southwest of its larger friend. Shop around on Nueva Alta, Siete Cuartones, and Tambo de Montero.

◪ **Niños Hotel,** Meloq 442 (☎231 424; email ninos@correo.dnet.com.pe; www.target-found.nl/ninos), at Siete Cuartones. All revenues assist in the upbringing of 12 boys, formerly homeless, who now live with the Dutch owner. Each large, art deco room bears the name of a boy and his sponsor. Hot water 24hr. Chic cafe and restaurant. Singles US$10, with bath US$15; doubles US$20, with bath US$25; triples with bath US$35.

Hostal California, Nueva Alta 444 (☎/fax 242 997), at Meloq. A lovely place, despite floppy mattresses. Any time of year, you can find hot water here. Live it up with kitchen access. Dorms s/15 per person; doubles with bath s/20-25.

Hostal Q'orichaska, Nueva Alta 458 (☎228 974). Plain, dim rooms surround the seating area and flower pots in the inner courtyard. The furniture has seen better days. 24hr. hot water. Kitchen access. Breakfast included. US$5 per person, with bath US$7.

Hospedaje Royal Frankenstein, San Juan de Dios 260 (☎236 999), off the Plaza Regocijo. Lively lounges and a social kitchen add some spice to the clean but cell-like rooms dubbed "Mary Shelley" and "Frank 'n stoned." Laundromat. Singles US$10; doubles US$20, with bath US$30; triples US$30. Prices often halved in the low season.

AROUND SAN CRISTÓBAL

Getting to the following places requires a bit of an uphill hike, but outstanding valley views, which include snow-capped Ausangate on clear days, reward the effort. Better yet, prices here remain relatively low. On the downside, there have been strangle muggings in this area; take taxis and caution after dark.

◪ **Hostal Resbalosa,** Resbalosa 494 (☎240 461). Comfortable rooms with warm blankets, parquet floors, and big windows. Rooftop terrace complete with sun porch and laundry basins. Shiny-clean bathrooms, occasional hot water. Breakfast available. Singles s/10; doubles s/25, with bath s/30; triples s/30, with bath s/36.

Hostal San Cristóbal, Kiscapata 242 (☎223 942). Make a right halfway up Resbalosa. Ramshackle but pleasant, run by sweet old ladies. A happy semi-dorm experience. Some rooms—as well as the upstairs terrace—have great views. Hot water most of the time. Kitchen access. 1-6 bed rooms s/10 per person.

Hostal Procurador del Cusco, Coricalle 425 (☎243 559). Spacious rooms. Hot water 24hr. An upstairs terrace takes in the neighborhood's usual sweeping views. Singles s/15; doubles s/30; triples s/40, with bath s/60; quads s/60.

IN SAN BLAS

This attractive whitewashed neighborhood on the hill behind the cathedral, a five-minute walk from the Plaza de Armas, is one of the calmest areas in Cusco. In recent years San Blas has welcomed many new family-run hostels where hospitality accompanies the slightly higher price. Unfortunately, the streets become shady and deserted at night. It's a good idea to take a taxi.

Hostal Familiar Pakcha Real, Tandapata 300 (☎237 484). The cheapest of the many family-run hostels on Tandapata. Hot water 24hr. Kitchen access. Sitting rooms. Clean quarters. Family dog. Rooms s/15 per person, with bath s/20.

Kuntur Wasi, Tandapata 352-A (☎227 570). A kind family runs this clean *casa* with great beds and electric showers. US$5 per person, with bath US$10.

Casa Hospedaje Sumaq T'ikaq, Tandapata 114 (☎229 127). The outgoing landlady takes exceptional care of her visitors. Quiet patio. Kitchen access. Breakfast included. Large rooms with bath US$10 per person.

Hostal Choquechaka, Choquechaka 436-B (☎237 265). One of the cheaper options among Choquechaka's inexpensive hostels. Slightly dingy baths have 24hr. hot water. Kitchen access. 1-4 bed rooms s/12 per person.

Mirador del Inka, Tandapata 160 (☎261 384). A lovely place to stay. Courtyards and stone walls add to the charm of this family's hostel. US$5 per person, with bath US$15.

Hospedaje Sambleña, Carmen Alto 114. A 3rd-floor *mirador* yields great views. All rooms with hot bath (and hardwood floors). Singles s/30; doubles s/60; triples s/60.

🍴 FOOD

Cusco is known for its *cuy* (guinea pig), *trucha* (trout), *lechón* (roast suckling pig) and *rocoto relleno* (chili pepper stuffed with meat, vegetables, and spices, then fried in dough). Of course, many visitors don't quite make it that far. Streets around the Plaza de Armas tempt diners with international cuisine, and many a backpacker has been known to spend all his *soles* at the Mexican, Italian, Japanese, and vegetarian establishments. Should you be among those who grow tired of such pricey—if often tasty—options, a few-block walk down Loreto leads to rows of typical joints serving s/2-4 *menús*.

🍴**Macondo,** Cuesta San Blas 571 (☎229 415). Oh-so-cool. The sign says "Come into my world," and after trying this amazing twist on Peruvian cuisine (*alpaca mignon a les parisiennes* s/21.50; "Amazonic Salad" s/15), it may be hard to leave. Breakfast s/7-15. Lunch s/6-12. Dinner s/12-22. Dinner reservations recommended. Open daily 11am-10pm, after which the place transforms into a trendy bar.

🍴**Govinda,** Espaderos 128 (☎252 723). Hare Krishna in inspiration, vegetarian in cuisine, and very mellow in outlook. Delicious whole wheat bread (s/0.5), fruit salads (s/5-7), and yogurt (s/5-7) fill hungry tourists to the brim—cheaply. Open daily 8am-10pm.

🍴**Green's,** Tandapata 700 (☎651 332), behind the church in the Plaza San Blas. Green's menu lists steaks and curries for the most discriminating palates. The fireplace, couches, backgammon, and magazines ensure that diners stay a while. Entrees s/14-24. Open daily noon-midnight. Food served noon-3pm and 6-11pm.

La Quinta Eulalia, Choquechaka 384 (☎241 380). Specializing in *cuy* (s/20), *lechón* (s/14), and *rocoto relleno* (s/8), La Quinta Eulalia has been serving local regulars since 1941. Enjoy it for yourself in the tented outdoor seating. Open daily 11am-6pm.

Chez Maggy, Plateros 339 (☎232 478). One of Cusco's many pizzerias, this small restaurant is a crossroads for wacky waiters, itinerant musicians, and travelers of every origin and ilk. Eating at the long tables in these cramped quarters, you'll meet them all. Small pizzas s/10-12. Open daily 11am-4pm and 6pm-midnight.

Pacha Papa Cafe Restaurant, Plazoleta San Blas 120 (☎241 318), across from the Iglesia San Blas, serves traditional food in a classy atmosphere. Alpaca s/12-18. ¼ *cuy* s/15. Entrees s/12-30. Open daily 10am-9pm.

Kin Taro, Heladeros 149 (☎226 181), off the Plaza Regocijo. A splendid array of Japanese dishes (the cooked kind). Teriyaki s/10-15. Open M-Sa noon-10pm.

Al Grano, Santa Catalina Ancha 398 (☎228 032). An experiment in Pan-Asian cuisine, Al Grano rotates a healthy, healthy menu of vegetarian curries, identified by country of origin (s/13.50). Open M-Sa 10am-9pm.

Don Lucho, Pardo 789 (☎237 343). From the Plaza de Armas, 7 blocks down Sol and 1 to the right on Garcida 50. No sign. Locals pack this simple spot, where the s/3.50 lunch *menú* proudly includes soda. At night the fare switches to fried chicken and *salchipapas*. The ample portions are worth the walk. Open daily noon-10pm.

Kusikuy, Plateros 348 (☎262 870). A popular first testing ground for Peruvian dishes, Kusikuy specializes in *cuy al horno* (s/38). After about an hour, the chewy little critter emerges from the kitchen wearing a little hat of tomatoes—and is promptly greeted by the flash of tourists' cameras. None of the other dishes is as elaborate (or as expensive). Trout s/17-19. Sandwiches s/4-6. Open M-Sa 8am-10:30pm, Su 7-10:30pm.

Restaurant Delicatessen, Afligaros 124 (☎249 785), 2 blocks down Sol and ½ block to the left. The food, the atmosphere, and—perhaps most importantly—the prices are all more typically "Peru" than the at tourist cafes that line the plaza. Lunchtime *menú* s/3.5. Entrees s/6-12. Open M-Sa 8am-10pm.

CAFES

The foreign invasion of Cusco has made java brewing, java selling, and java consumption top priority—praise the lord and say goodbye to Nescafé. By day, the city's cafes serve breakfast and sandwiches. At night, they turn into smoky, multilingual conversation parlors.

▓ **La Tertulia,** Procuradores 44 (☎241 422), 2nd fl. The best breakfast place in town, with several tremendous all-you-can-eat options (s/7-15). Salads, pizzas, and Peruvian dishes, too. Book exchange. Open daily 6:30am-3pm and 3-11pm.

▓ **Café Ayllu,** Carnes 208 (☎232 357), on the Plaza de Armas, beside the cathedral. Peruvians and foreigners flock to cool, calm Ayllu for serious coffee (s/2-5) and straightforward breakfasts (s/6-10). Open M-Sa 6:30am-11pm, Su 6:30am-1:30pm.

Café Varayoc, Espaderos 142 (☎232 404). An angsty cafe-bar. Sandwiches s/4-10. Cheese fondue s/30. Crepes s/16. Open daily 8am-11pm.

El Buen Pastor, Cuesta San Blas 579 (☎240 586). Exceptional pastries, croissants, and *empanadas* s/1-2. All profits go to a local orphanage. Open daily 7am-8pm.

◉ SIGHTS

Most sightseeing in Cusco requires a **tourist ticket** (*boleto turístico;* US$10), which includes admission to the cathedral, Iglesia de San Blas, Museo de Arte Religioso del Arzobispado, Museo de Arte y Monasterio de Santa Catalina, the site museum at the Qorikancha, Museo Municipal de Arte Contemporáneo, Museo Histórico Regional (Casa Garcilaso), and the nearby ruins of Sacsayhuamán, Qenco, Puca Pucara, Tambomachay, Pisac, Ollantaytambo, Chinchero, Tipón, and Pikillacta. The ticket *does not* include admission to the part of the Qorikancha that belongs to Convento de Santo Domingo, Convento de la Merced, or Museo Inka at the Casa del Almirante. Paying individual entrance fees is not possible at most locations included in the tourist ticket, but one can buy a **partial ticket** (*boleto parcial*) for just museums and churches or just ruins (US$6). Tickets are available at the **OFEC office** (☎226 919), at Garcilaso and Heladeros, on the Plaza Regocijo, or at the **tourist office** (see Practical Information, p. 100), and sometimes at the sights themselves, especially the churches. Carrying an ISIC entitles students to discounts in many museums and tour agencies. Many of the city's museums feature paintings from the **Cusco school.** This prominent colonial school of art lasted 200 years and included *mestizo* as well as indigenous painters. As a result of this mixed heritage, even paintings on Christian themes incorporate a great deal of Andean symbolism: backgrounds are painted with local flora and fauna and biblical figures wear Inca costumes. Though not a conventional sight, many women and children roam Cusco wearing fine ceremonial garments and leading **well-primped llamas**–definitely camera-worthy. However, since most of these characters are models and their costumes rented, photographers are expected to pay a *sol* or two in tip.

CATHEDRAL

On the Plaza de Armas; its the one with the big steps. Open M-Sa 10-11:30am and 2-5:30pm, Su 2-5:30pm. Admission with tourist ticket only, except during mass.

Built upon the foundations of the Inca Wiraccocha's palace, Cusco's cathedral was begun in 1550 and took nearly a century to complete. The church sustained serious damage in the 1986 earthquake; inside, some areas are still blocked off or obscured by scaffolding. Regardless, the cathedral is fascinating in its subtle incorporation of Inca symbolism, an element attributable to the large number of indigenous craftspeople who helped build it. It also boasts a collection of several hundred paintings from the Cusco school.

CAPILLA DE LA SAGRADA FAMILIA. Visitors enter through the Capilla de la Sagrada Familia. Passing into the nave, one encounters the Renaissance-style main **altar,** which is covered in silver plating. Next to it sits the oft-discussed **Last Supper,** attributed to Marcos Zapata of the Cusco school. A *mestizo* artist of the

18th century, Zapata borrowed from sacred Inca feasts when he made Christ's final meal a guinea-pig roast. Behind the altar stands the cathedral's finely carved wooden **choir,** considered one of the best in the Americas. The choir was used as a didactic tool for the evangelization of the natives. Curiously, each seat has an armrest supported by a pregnant-bellied carving of **Pachamama,** the Inca Earth goddess—yet another example of indigenous artistry.

CAPILLA DEL TRIUNFO. Passing into the Capilla del Triunfo, next door, one encounters the **Altar de Señor de los Temblores** (Altar of the Lord of the Tremor). According to legend, a procession that carried this Christ image through the Plaza de Armas brought a swift end to a 1650 earthquake. Blackened by centuries of candle smoke, el Señor repeats his performance (or at least his appearance) in the plaza on the Monday of Semana Santa. His altar is a magnificent stone work covered in gold. A number of the other altars incorporate painted carvings of Peruvian jungle fauna. In a crypt under the chapel, you can view the ashes of Garcilaso de la Vega, the *mestizo* chronicler of the Incas. The El Triunfo chapel itself was the first Christian church built in Cusco. It had been the site of **Suntur Wasi,** an Inca armory where Spanish troops took refuge during Manco Inca's attack in 1536. During this attack, the Incas set much of Cusco on fire. Miraculously, however, El Triunfo did not burn. Inside, the Spaniards had visions of the Virgin Mary and St. James fighting back the flames (though it was more likely just slaves with buckets of water). After the "miracle," the Spanish broke out and subdued the Incas; in honor of their victory, they dragged stones from Sacsayhuamán (see p. 110) to build El Triunfo. Later, the chapel was joined to the cathedral.

QORIKANCHA AND IGLESIA DE SANTO DOMINGO

On the grassy expanse 2 blocks down Sol from the Plaza de Armas, at Arrayan. Archaeological museum open M-Sa 10am-6pm. Admission with tourist ticket only. Santo Domingo and Sun Temple open M-Sa 8am-6pm, Su 2-4pm. s/3; not included in Cusco tourist ticket.

HISTORY. When Atahuallpa was held prisoner in Cajamarca in 1533, the Incas promised his captor, Francisco Pizarro, roomfuls of ransom in gold and silver from Cusco. Impatient, Pizarro sent three of his men to the Inca capital to hurry matters along. These soldiers quickly found the Qorikancha ("Court of Gold"), a massive, gold-covered temple that at that time extended from its present site to Sol's intersection with Tullumayu, and looted some 3150 pounds of pure gold plating from the its walls. In subsequent trips, Pizarro and his army joined the mayhem, dumping tons of precious silver and gold objects into the melting pot.

Years later, Dominicans built a baroque church on the site. When much of the church crumbled in a 1950 earthquake, unsympathetic archaeologists cheered, for the Inca foundations had emerged again. Subsequent findings give an idea of the marvel that the Qorikancha must have been. It accommodated some 4000 priests and attendants, who made daily offerings to gods and deceased royal ancestors. A great golden disc once deflected morning sunlight into a sun temple lined with gold. A silver-lined moon temple had its own silver disc. Other temples paid homage to thunder, lightning, the rainbow, and various stars. At least one room held the captured idols of conquered tribes, so that if subjugated peoples ever rebelled, the Incas could publicly desecrate their gods. The Qorikancha also acted as an astronomical observatory where the *amautas* (priests of a learned caste) plotted the solstices and equinoxes and predicted eclipses, all of which were intricately tied to sacred and agricultural practices. Indeed, the Qorikancha was the center of a geographical zodiac wheel that encompassed 327 sacred sites.

THE SITE. Enter through the underground museum on Sol to see a small collection of ceramics, tools, jewelry, and some interesting old photographs of Cusco. Models give an idea of what the Qorikancha used to look like. Exit past the bathrooms to the grounds upstairs, a graveyard of Inca building blocks. The remains of a pre-Inca fountain date to AD 800. Far more interesting (though unfortunately not included in the tourist ticket) is the part of the complex that belongs to the Church of Santo Domingo. This section is commonly called the **Sun Temple,** although its largest surviving shrines probably belonged to the Moon and Stars. Across the courtyard from these shrines stand temples to Lightning and the Rainbow. A large stone receptacle in the center of the courtyard, formerly covered in 55kg of gold, is said to have held chicha to quench the Sun God's thirst. The church's sacristy holds other treasures, including ornate religious vestments. Qorikancha's walls, with it finely-fitted stones, provide great examples of Inca masonry.

SAN BLAS

Known in Inca Cusco as the district of Tococache, San Blas is one of Cusco's oldest and most picturesque neighborhoods. It is also a thriving artistic community that produces both traditional and contemporary works. Its winding streets and footpaths extend uphill from behind the cathedral; wandering them allows for window shopping and yields spectacular views of the city below.

ARTESANÍA. A number of famous workshops surrounds the Plaza de San Blas. **Antonio Olave** creates fine ceramics and oil paintings with Andean and religious themes. *(Plaza San Blas 651. ☎231 835. Open daily 8am-6pm.)* **Pancho Mendivil** produces beautiful painted wood, ceramics, and mirrors, as well as his trademark long-necked ceramic dolls. *(Plaza San Blas 619. ☎233 247. Open daily 8:30am-9pm.)* The plaza itself hosts a small **craft market** on Saturdays. But perhaps the most rewarding part of visiting San Blas is the opportunity to poke inside its shops and discover the obscure, bizarre, and beautiful for yourself.

IGLESIA DE SAN BLAS. A small, attractive church dating from 1562, the Iglesia de San Blas is unremarkable except that it holds perhaps the best **wood-carved pulpit** in the Americas. The symmetrical pulpit is crafted from a single cedar trunk and features images of the Virgin Mary, Apostles, and numerous angels and cherubs—all supported by the gut-wrenching efforts of eight heretics on the pulpit's underside. Legend has it that the carving was done by a leper named Juan Tomás Tuirutupa, and that the skull at St. Paul's feet was his own. *(On the Plaza San Blas. Open M-Sa 10-11:30am and 2-5:30pm and during mass. Admission with tourist ticket only.)*

OTHER CHURCHES AND MUSEUMS

▧ MUSEO INKA (PALACIO DEL ALMIRANTE). Beautifully organized, transporting visitors from pre-Inca peoples to the rebellious years after conquest, Museo Inka is a must-see for anyone curious about Andean civilization. The Universidad Nacional de San Antonio Abad maintains the collection, which is housed in the magnificent 17th-century **Palacio del Almirante.** The museum's first floor exhibits some remarkably well preserved ceramics and tools from the pre-Inca Nasca, Chimu, Mochica, Pukara, Tiahuanuco, and Huari cultures. Some neat pieces include large **Pukara monoliths** and a **funerary blanket** dating from 900 BC. The second floor features colorful dioramas that depict Inca agricultural practices, as well as Inca jewelry, clothing, weapons, and ceremonial vases. Peek into a replicated burial crypt containing real **mummies.** A map demonstrates the vastness of the Inca Empire (Tawantinsuyo) by superimposing it on top of Europe. Another room exhibits furniture from a salon that belonged to post-conquest Inca royalty, including wooden tables and chests inlaid with tortoise shell and mother-of-pearl. Early copies of Garcilaso de la Vega's *Comentarios Reales* introduce an exhibit on Inkanismo, a cultural preservation movement. *(Cuesta del Almirante 103, uphill and to the left of the cathedral. ☎237 380. Open M-Sa 8am-5pm. s/5; not included in tourist ticket.)*

MUSEO DE ARTE RELIGIOSO DEL ARZOBISPADO. Before this mansion belonged to the archbishop (who lives in the wing next to the museum), it was the Marqués de Buenavista's home; in turn, that home had been built on the foundations of Inca Roca's palace. One of the palace's immense walls survives along Hathrumiyoq, or "Street with the Big Stone." This name refers to the great **12-sided stone** that fits harmoniously into the center of the wall. The exceptional courtyard is a sight in itself, covered in blue-and-white tiles from Seville and featuring beautifully carved wooden doorways and grilles. The paintings within the building belong to the Cusco school, and although they're a smaller collection than others in town, they tend to be in better condition. One of the most interesting rooms is filled with paintings by **Marcos Zapata,** the 18th-century *mestizo* artist who often included native elements in his religious works (see Cathedral, p. 104). Zapata's *Circumcisión* portrays the Christ child facing the blade. *(At Hathrumiyoq and Herrajes. ☎ 225 211. Open M-Sa 8-11:30am and 3-5:30pm. Admission with tourist ticket only.)*

IGLESIA DE LA COMPAÑÍA AND MUSEO DE HISTORIA NATURAL. The *other* large church in the Plaza de Armas, La Compañía was constructed over Amarucancha, the palace of Inca Huayna Capac; one of the palace's walls survives along Loreto. During the church's 17th-century construction, a controversy broke out among *cusqueño* clergy when La Compañía's size threatened to match that of the cathedral. Eventually, even Pope Paul III turned against the building, but by then most of the church had been built. *(Open for mass M-Sa 7am, noon, 6, and 6:30pm; Su 7:30, 11:30am, 6, and 7pm. Free.)* The adjoining **Museo de Historia Natural** displays sveral hundred stuffed animals from the region. *(Open daily 9am-noon and 3-6pm. s/1.)*

THE CONVENTO DE SANTA CATALINA. The Convento de Santa Catalina currently houses nuns, but its foundations once belonged to a different kind of female residence; it was the **Acllahuasi** ("House of Chosen Women"). These women acted as the Inca's concubines or as virgin priestesses for sun god Inti, and were responsible for preparing the ruler's chicha and woven garments. Weaving clothes made out of alpaca and vicuña was an interminable affair, as the Inca tended to burn his garments after one wearing. The Sun Virgins also tended the Sun Temple (see Qorikancha, p. 105); they prepared offerings to Inti, served as his liaison to the Inca, and dressed for him in bird feathers. Today, in addition to cloistering nuns, the convent shelters a **Museo de Arte.** A series on the ground floor captures the life of another "chosen woman," the self-flagellating **Santa Rosa de Lima** (see **Lima: Sights: Churches,** p. 84). The collection includes religious colonial paintings from the Cusco school. *(At Santa Catalina and Arequipa. Museum open M-Th 9am-6pm, F 9am-3pm, Sa 9am-6pm. Admission with tourist ticket only.)*

IGLESIA DE LA MERCED. The Iglesia de La Merced keeps a **Museo de Arte Religioso** around its dilapidated (though charming and soon-to-be-restored) courtyard. The collection may be small, but it includes notable works such as two Virgins by the *cusqueño* painter Bitti and a crucified Christ by the Spanish Renaissance artist Zurbarán. Most impressive is the **Custodia de La Merced,** an 18th-century monstrance rendered from 22kg of gold and encrusted with 1518 diamonds and 615 pearls, among other precious stones. The remains of Diego de Almagro, conquistador of Chile, rest under the church. *(Art museum open M-Sa 8am-noon and 2-5pm. s/3.)*

OTHER MUSEUMS. The **Museo Histórico Regional** is housed in the Casa Garcilaso de la Vega, former home of the important chronicler of the Incas. Within, there's an uninspiring collection of pre-Inca ceramics and a mummy with braids that extend a full 1½m. *(On Plaza Regocijo at Garcilaso and Heladeros. ☎ 223 245. Open M-Sa 8am-5:30pm. Admission with tourist ticket only.)* Across the Plaza Regocijo sprawls the **Museo Municipal de Arte Contemporáneo,** which displays regional handicrafts and some modern painting. *(On San Juan de Dios. ☎ 240 006. Open M-Sa 9am-6:30pm. Free.)*

ENTERTAINMENT

FESTIVALS

The most exciting festivals in Cusco are **Semana Santa** (Apr. 8-15), when El Señor de los Temblores processes through the Plaza de Armas (see Cathedral, p. 104); **Corpus Christi**, in early June, with its own fine processions and abundant feasting; and most importantly **Inti Raymi**, at the winter solstice (June 24), the world-famous festival of the sun god. Cusco goes crazy as thousands of people fill its plazas to witness dancing, parades, and hundreds of pounds of flower petals. Meanwhile, an elaborate pageant up at Sacsayhuamán reaches new heights in debauchery.

SHOPPING

Cusco is the central exchange for handicrafts from all over Peru: carved gourds from Huancayo, *retablos* and tapestries from Ayacucho, weavings from the coast, sweaters from all over the Andes, erotic ceramic keychains from—well, no one will admit where. Cusco's **mercado central** is devoted to quotidian goods (and pickpockets). A better bet for quality *artesanía* is one of the many enclosed markets, which appear on **Espinar** (next to the tourist office and in Plaza Regocijo), **Palacios,** and **Plateros.** Bargaining is expected. Stores in **San Blas,** the neighborhood uphill from and behind the cathedral, may be more expensive, but they often feature the work of neighborhood artists—which includes oil paintings, delicate ceramics, and lively painted masks and religious objects.

MOVIES

Many restaurants and discos around the Plaza de Armas screen films in the afternoon and early evening. They aren't just 80s hits, either—somehow Cusco manages to snag very recent releases. **Ukukus** and **Mama Africa** (see p. 109) and the **Andes Café** on the Plaza de Armas are among the most popular viewing locations.

MUSIC AND THEATER

Cusco specializes in collecting aspects of various Peruvian regional cultures and wrapping them up for gringo consumption. At night, restaurants and bars around the Plaza de Armas host musicians playing traditional tunes. For a more formal exhibition of local performance, head to the **Centro Q'osqo,** Sol 604. (☎227 901. Daily shows 6 or 7pm. s/10.) The **Teatro Municipal,** Mesón de la Estrella 149, also puts on occasional concerts. (☎221 847. Shows 7 or 7:30pm. s/10.) But Cusco's best music and drama displays take place in the streets, during festivals—especially Inti Raymi at the end of June (see Festivals, above).

 NIGHTLIFE

BARS

You'll never go thirsty for a beer in Cusco—if your beer of choice is Cusqueña, that is. Although the city's many foreign-owned pubs have brought international brews such as Guinness, Bass, Foster's, and Budweiser to the Plaza de Armas, only you can decide if a hometown high is worth those prices. Hey, if you grab enough of the **free drink coupons** that local club promoters thrust at plaza-strollers, maybe you'll be able to afford it. However, those suffering from altitude sickness should be careful; alcohol tends to make acclimation worse.

Los Perros, Teqsicocha 436. Australian Tammy and Peruvian Guillermo own this young, artsy bar. Fine food, dope couches, and Cyprus Hill in da house. On Sunday nights Tammy sings with her jazz band. Open daily Sept.-May 1pm-1am, June-Aug. 11am-3am.

The Cross Keys, Confiturías 233, on the Plaza de Armas. An established Pommie pub, Cross Keys fills nightly with expats and travelers. Grub available. Good pisco sour s/8. Happy hour 6-7pm and 9-9:30pm. 10% SAE discount on beer. Open daily 11am-1am.

Paddy Flaherty's, Triunfo 124 (☎246 903), right of the cathedral. Small and warm. The faithful gather to watch rugby and "other sports." Pint of Guinness s/12. Draft beer s/5-7. Happy hour 7-8pm and 10-10:30pm. Open daily noon-1am.

Norton Rat's Tavern, Loreto 115 (☎246 204), to the left of La Compañía, overlooking the Plaza de Armas. US-owned, the Tavern still manages to count Peruvians among its clientele. Spectacular balconies capture the nighttime lights. Long Island Iced Tea s/6. Domestic beer s/4-7. Happy hour usually 7-9pm. Open daily noon-1am.

Rosie O'Grady's, Santa Catalina Anch 360 (☎247 935), 2 blocks from the cathedral. This Irish watering hole eschews dark wooden interiors for light, upscale decor. TVs show live *fútbol* or rugby. 10% SAE discount. Guinness s/12, Cusqueña s/4. Live music Th-F. Happy hour 1-2pm, 6-7pm, and 11-11:30pm. Open daily 11am-1am.

Bar Fly, on the Plaza de Armas, at Procuradores. A welcoming new bar-cafe complete with crackling fire, rocking chairs, and balcony. Pisco sour s/7. Open daily 11am-1pm.

CLUBS

Most nights of the week (especially June-Aug.), the streets around the Plaza de Armas thump to the beats of Cusco's 15 discos. Some charge covers on Fridays and Saturdays, but these are usually waived for tourists. If not, check around the plaza for free passes. Meanwhile, leave the blue suede shoes at home—where foreigners hit the floor, gore-tex and fleece dominate the dress code. And don't expect to get to bed while it's still dark out.

Mama Africa, Espaderos 135 (☎241 979), 2nd fl. Part of a multi-level disco complex, playing a reggae-rock mix to scrubby backpackers and beautiful young *cusqueñas*. Email (s/2.50 per hr.) and excellent food in a separate room. Afternoon movies. Beer s/6. Live music 10:30pm. Happy hour 8-9:30pm. Open just about all the time.

Ukukus, Plateros 316 (☎242 951). Plenty of seating and a spacious floor accommodate crowds. DJs play rock, pop, salsa, and techno. Afternoon movies. Email access s/2 per hr. Cusqueña s/5. Live music 11pm-midnight. Happy hour 8-9:30pm. Open late.

Uptown, Suecia 302 (☎227 241), 2nd fl. Very popular with Peruvians. Latin music. Thatched hut motif. Secluded tables filled with amorous couples. Happy hour 9-10 and 11-11:30pm. Open most of the night.

XCess, Carnes 298, in the same complex as Uptown. So packed with international youngsters that dancing becomes difficult. Cristal s/5. Two cuba libres s/10. Happy hour 9-10 and 11-11:30pm. Open late.

Kamikase, Plaza Regocijo 274 (☎233 865), 2nd fl. The oldest disco-pub in town, now in its 16th year. Standard reggae, disco, and 80s tunes. Balcony over the plaza. Cusqueña s/5. Live music 11pm-midnight. Happy hour 8:30-9:30pm. Alive until dawn.

Eko, Plateros 334, 2nd fl. Cusco's newest club. Trance, trance, and more trance. Huge dance floor, with a fluorescent bar at one end. Beer s/5. Happy hour 7:30-9pm.

▶ DAYTRIPS FROM CUSCO

Most of the Sacred Valley could qualify as daytrips from Cusco. However, the area is so rich, so full, so worthy on its own terms, that it gets its own section (p. 113). Which is not to say that the following ruins are not worthy on their own terms; they're just closer to the city. Along the paved road to Pisac, they make excellent day-hike destinations; prominent signs direct the way to each. Some like to view the ruins in reverse by taking a taxi (s/20) to Tambomachay, the farthest of the four, then walking downhill; you can also catch a Pisac-bound colectivo on Tullumayu and ask to get off at Tambomachay (s/2.50). Agencies in Cusco offer horseback tours of the route; you can also rent horses at the Corcel Ranch just outside Sacsayhuamán for the ride up to the other sites. (☎245 878. s/25 for 5hr.)

SACSAYHUAMÁN

Sacsayhuamán is a steep hike from the center of town, up either Choquechaka from San Blas or Resbalosa (a sort-of-continuation of Suecia) from the Plaza de Armas (30min.). Open daily 7am-5:30pm. Admission with tourist ticket only.

Sacsayhuamán (pronounced "sexy woman") is believed to form the head of the Cusco puma, and the name itself may come from the words "Sacsa Uma," Quechua for "speckled head." Sacsayhuamán was the site of a key 1536 battle during the Inca **Manco Capac II's** rebellion against the Spanish. The Incas claimed the fortress early in the struggle, using it as a headquarters from which to attack the city of Cusco below. They seemed successful at first—in an attempt to win the area, conquistador **Juan Pizarro** (Francisco's half-brother) died from a slingshot wound. But the bitter fighting that followed claimed thousands of lives and came to a close with a Spanish victory and Manco's retreat to Ollantaytambo (see p. 115). Many historians believe that this battle was a major turning point in the Spaniards' quest for conquest and that Manco's loss of Sacsayhuamán sealed his empire's doom.

As a result of this grim history, people often think of Sacsayhuamán as little more than a fortress, but the original complex contained many buildings and towers that likely served functions besides the defensive. After the Spanish victory, however, most of these structures were demolished. The site then served as a municipal stone quarry until excavations halted the looting in 1935—but by that point, most of the smaller structures had disappeared as well. Nevertheless, the parts that do still exist are among the most impressive Inca ruins in existence. Three tiers of giant **zig-zag stone ramparts** were too massive to be carried off (one estimate measures the biggest stone at 8.5m and 360 tons); they now amaze visitors with their precise interlocking edges. Three towers—**Muyucmarca, Sayacmarca,** and **Paucarmarca**—once stood on the hill behind these ramparts. The first two still have foundations intact. Few structures remain on the opposite hill, but just over it lies a round depression and clearing that may have served as a reservoir or site for water worship. A couple of short tunnels at the edge of the clearing dare tourists to stumble through their pitch-black interiors.

QENCO

Near Km7 on the road to Pisac. Open daily 7am-5:30pm. Admission with tourist ticket only.

Qenco ("zig-zag") is a large limestone outcropping that the Incas altered for religious purposes, probably to serve as a shrine. The site gets its name from the **zig-zag channels** carved into the top of the rock. Inca priests may have poured chicha or animal blood down the channels and predicted the future according to the path the liquid took. Some interesting carvings on top of the outcropping include a small llama in relief and an even smaller headless condor, both located on the side closest to the road. Closer to the plateau's interior sits a mysterious stone topped with two fat cylinders and a small replica of a house. At the edge of the rock, a large 19-niche **amphitheater** surrounds a tall, vaguely phallic rock. The caves underneath the outcropping probably held **mummified remains** of Inca nobility.

PUCA PUCARA AND TAMBOMACHAY

About 5km beyond Qenco on the road to Pisac, on opposite sides of the road from each other. Open daily 7am-5:30pm. Admission with tourist ticket only.

"Puca Pucara" means "red fort," but the building more likely served as a *tambo* (resting house), or perhaps as the hunting lodge of the Inca Pachacuti. "Tambomachay" means "cavern lodge," but is actually an ancient site of **ritual bathing.** Evidently, a water cult directed the hillside's underground stream through a series of stone fountains, which continue to work today. Trees and gardens may have surrounded the site back in its glory days.

🏔 GUIDED TOURS FROM CUSCO

At the hub of the Peruvian travel network, Cusco tour agencies offer tons of trips, ranging from the easy and cheap (city and Sacred Valley tours) to the more rugged (Inca Trail) and expensive (Manú Biosphere). The longest guided treks head to the little-visited pre-Inca ruins at Vilcanota or snow-capped Ausangate (each usually 7 days), and along the Inca Trail from the glacier of Salcantay (also 7 days). Intrepid explorers can tackle these trips without an agency's help—look for maps, directions, and possible companions at the South American Explorers Club or the tourist office (see Practical Information, p. 100).

THE INCA TRAIL

The standard three-night, four-day Inca Trail trek (see p. 116) travels from Ollantaytambo to the gates of Machu Picchu. A few agencies also do shorter or longer versions. Many companies offer similar packages and prices; it is important to ask specific questions and get all answers in writing. Some concerns include: group size (fewer than 20 is preferable); food (some agencies only supply bread and water); porters' responsibilities (most budget companies have you carry your own pack); equipment (you'll probably have to supply a sleeping bag—make sure it's a warm one); and guide experience and language ability. Ask if the guide for the Inca Trail and Machu Picchu will be the same person. Some agencies save money by sending a less experienced guide on the Inca Trail, then hiring a new one at Machu Picchu, since only certified guides are allowed into the ruins. Finally, make sure that porters and cooks will have a place to sleep each night (a tent, not a cave); treat them with respect and tip them well—they deserve it.

SAS Travel, Panes 143 (☎/fax 237 292), on the Plaza de Armas. A favorite among budget travelers, SAS promises to be eco-sensitive and treats its staff well. Groups generally 15-18 people. Daily departures. All guides are Machu Picchu-certified; Kenny and Hilbert have been recommended. US$88, students US$80. Other tours include: Sacred Valley, city, rafting, horseback riding, and mountain-biking. Open daily 6am-10pm.

United Mice, Plateros 351 (☎221 139). Another premier budget agency. Efraín, Hamilton, and Salustio are certified to guide Machu Picchu; others aren't. Groups generally 10-22. Departures M, W, and F. US$85, students US$76. US$5 SAE discount. Rafting, horseback riding, and city tours available as well. Open daily 9am-8:30pm.

Q'ente Adventure Trips, Plateros 365 (☎238 245), 2nd fl. Groups 8-18 people in high season, 8-12 in low. All guides certified for Machu Picchu; Roberto has received rave reviews. Daily departures. US$80, students US$71. 2-day, 1-night hike US$65, students US$60. Also runs treks to Ausangate and Salcantay. 5% SAE discount. Open daily 9am-2pm and 3-8pm.

Inca Explorers, Suecia 339 (☎239 669). One of the best that offers a "Class B" Inca Trail. "Class B" means guides are more experienced, porters carry everything but you and your daypack, and groups are no more than 10 people. Guide Santiago has gotten a thumbs-up. US$220, students US$212. 8% SAE discount. Open daily 7am-9pm.

MANÚ BIOSPHERE RESERVE

Most of the nine companies that head to Manú (see p. 286) offer similar packages, with tours ranging from four to nine days. Trips that bus in and out cost less and witness all the heights of Manú's forest. A trip that involves flying to Boca Manú, a town near the mouth of the reserve zone, saves only time. The companies below have fixed departure schedules from May to December; from January to April, the reserve zone often closes due to flooding.

Pantiacolla Tours, Plateros 360 (☎238 323; www.pantiacolla.com). More affordable and comparably good. Run by a biologist who worked for several years in Manú, Pantiacolla sends out camping tours as well as posher lodge-based ones. Camping tours: 9-days, 8-nights US$725; 7-days, 6-nights US$795; 5-days, 4-nights US$725. 10% SAE discount, discounts for groups of 4 or more.

Manú Nature Tours, Pardo 1046 (☎252 721; www.manuperu.com). One of the original groups to send trips to Manú. Nature Tours' trips spend more time than most in the reserve zone, although trips to the macaw lick at Blanquillo (included at most other companies) cost extra. Mountain biking and whitewater rafting options. 8-days, 7-nights US$2095 in high season, US$1633 in low season. 5-days, 4-nights US$1625-2000.

Manú Expeditions, Pardo 895 (☎226 671). The other original organization. Maintains a partnership with the non-profit Selva Sur Conservation Group. Owner Barry Walker also runs the Cross Keys pub. 9-days, 8-nights US$1695. 6-days, 5-nights US$1119.

Manú Ecological Adventures, Plateros 365 (☎261 640; www.cbc.org.pe/manu), sends the most visitors to the park. As befits a cheaper alternative, their boats and tents tend to be crowded. Most clients, however, report relative satisfaction. 8-days, 7-nights US$550-600. 7-days, 6-nights US$646. 6-days, 5-nights US$724. 10% SAE or student discount.

MISCELLANEOUS ADVENTURES

Of the various expeditions that run out of Cusco (mountain biking, rock climbing, horseback riding, kayaking), **rafting** on the **Río Urubamba** (Class II-III May-Sept., III-V Oct.-Apr.) is the most popular. The **Río Apurímac** offers riskier, lengthier expeditions (usually 3 days, May-Sept. only, Class IV-V). Rafting comes with ample thrills—and ample risks. Beware companies that cut costs that might also compromise safety. Raft with reputable agencies only, and make sure they cover the basics; life jackets and emergency preparations are a must.

Instinct, Procuradores 50 (☎233 451; email instinct@chavin.rcp.net.pe; http://ekeko.rcpip.net/instinct/), at the Plaza de Armas. Head down the Río Urubamba on Class II and III rapids (1 day US$20) or the Apurimac on Class I-V rapids (4 days US$199). All rafting guides are paramedics. 3 days kayaking US$120. Mountain biking, horseback riding, and rock climbing excursions. Open daily 9am-1pm and 4-9pm.

Perol Chico (☎624 475; fax 252 696; email perolchico@hotmail.com). Dutch owner leads Peruvian Paso horses through Quechua communities and trout farms. More difficult 5-6 day rides across the Urubamba Valley to the Las Salineras and Moray. 1-12 day routes. All trips leave from Urubamba. 1 day US$55, 2 days US$195-200, 12 days US$2500; 10% SAE discount.

Mayuc, Confituria 211 (☎232 666; www.mayuc.com), has led adventures into the wild since 1978. Spend a day rafting Class II and III rapids on the Urubamba (US$25) or 3 on the more intense Apurimac (US$130-250). Rapelling daytrips US$30. Office open M-Sa 9am-9pm, Su 9am-noon and 7-9pm.

Loreto Tours, Medio 111 (☎236 331). 1-day rafting trip on the Urubamba US$35. 3 days on the Apurimac US$150. Mountain bike tour of Moray and Las Salineras US$20, includes quality bikes. Open M-Sa 9am-1pm and 5-10pm, Su 5-10pm.

Eric Adventures, Plateros 324 (☎228 475), a long-time provider of rafting tours. Daily rafting trips on the Urubamba US$25-35, students US$20. 2-day kayaking lessons also US$80. Inca Trail US$75, students US$65. Open daily 8:30am-1pm and 4-10pm.

NEAR CUSCO: PAUCARTAMBO

To get to Paucartambo, take a minibuses (4hr.; leaving when full, usually around 8 or 9am; s/15) from Huáscar off Garcilaso (where the minibuses to Pisac leave). To get to Tres Cruces by sunrise, take a taxi from Paucartambo's plaza around 1:30 or 2am

Small and out of the way, beautiful Paucartambo receives few visitors most of the year; large trucks rumble across its cobblestones on their way down to the jungle, but that's about it. In mid-July, however, the **Celebración de la Virgen del Carmen** deposits hordes of revelers in this sleepy colonial town. For several days, locals and visitors dance, don outrageous masks and costumes, act out folk tales, and consume beer and chicha by the liter. That there's no place for them to stay serves as little deterrent—who's going to bed? The party doesn't end until the village plazas reek of urine and everyone has visited nearby **Tres Cruces** to watch the legendary sunrise over the cloud forest. Tres Cruces, a rocky plateau 44km from Paucartambo, was a sacred place for the Incas, primarily because of the beauty of its winter sunrises. At dawn, rainbows glow through the mist that cascades over the green, green Manú forest. And although the festival's undeniably cool, such amazing sunrises occur throughout June and July. If you visit at a less hectic time, you may actually get a bed somewhere—perhaps at the basic **La Quinta Rosa,** right off the plaza (1 bed s/12).

THE SACRED VALLEY

PISAC ☎ 084

Back in the day, Pisac's **Sunday market** happened once a week. Then the event outgrew its time slot, and now it takes place on Tuesdays and Thursdays as well. The weekend market remains the largest affair, but all three feature hundreds of canopied stands selling silver jewelry, ceramics, woven blankets, and old coins. One end of the market still caters mostly to villagers, who come, dressed in traditional garb, to exchange bags of potatoes or fruit according to the centuries-old *trueque*, or bartering system. Local notables join the fanfare when they emerge from morning mass (11am), a service performed entirely in Quechua. But the town's charms extend beyond its famous market. Its hills hold the Pisac **ruins,** well-preserved buildings enhanced by stunning mountain views, and the destination of one of the area's most popular day-hikes.

The Pisac ruins constitute the largest standing **Inca fortress**—perhaps because, unlike their counterparts at Sacsayhuamán and Ollantaytambo, no famous battles took place here. Although in its heyday this inaccessible fort city occupied a key strategic point overlooking the valley, Pisac seems to have been abandoned before the Spanish Conquest. From the Plaza de Armas, two trails lead up to the ruins. The one leading uphill from the right side of the plaza (when coming from the bus stop by the river) leads to a paved road used by tour groups. Most hikers take the steep path that leads uphill from the plaza's left side. The path is fairly well-marked and weaves through a number of complexes, the most impressive of which is the **Intihuatana** (Temple of the Sun) sector, a triangle-shaped plateau. The Intihuatana itself is at the center; it probably served as an astronomical observatory. Nearby lies a set of water channels and a ritual bath, which feed into the residential sector just downhill, called the **P'isaca.** Some say Pisac was designed to look like a massive condor—its agricultural terraces built as feathers. As the

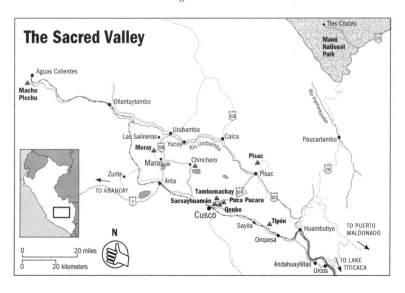

The Sacred Valley

condor symbolized travel between the mortal and spiritual worlds, it seems appropriate that these hills hold the largest known **Inca cemetery.** Most of the graves have been robbed, however, leaving small holes in the mountainside (1½hr.; US$6, free with tourist ticket). A taxi from the river to the ruins should cost s/2. A third alternative, horses are available for rides up to the ruins; inquire at Hotel Pisaq; prices vary depending on season and availability.

Colectivos from Cusco drop passengers off at the edge of town, next to the police station just after crossing the Urubamba. A three-minute walk uphill leads into the **Plaza de Armas** and the **market. Minibuses** return frequently to **Cusco** (1hr., every 15min. 7am-8pm, s/2). Others head to **Yucay** (30min., s/1), **Urubamba** (30min., s/1), and **Ollantaytambo** (1hr., s/2). Most people make Pisac a half-day trip; however, the beautiful rooms at **Hotel Pisaq** might be worth an overnight splurge. (Sauna. Breakfast included. Doubles US$10, with bath US$13.) **Kinsa Cocha Hospedaje,** Arequipa 307, on a street parallel to the Plaza de Armas, keeps tidy dorm rooms and can supply hot water upon request. (☎203 101. Beds s/10 per person.)

YUCAY   ☎084

Yucay was once the Inca Sayri Tupac's royal estate; the grounds occupied the sites of the present-day Plaza de Armas and Plaza Manco II. At one end of the Plaza Manco II remain the Inca Sayri Tupac's **palacial walls;** across from these, in the Plaza de Armas, stand the walls that belonged to his princess. Meanwhile, the beautiful hacienda that houses the Posada del Inca Hotel also holds an interesting chapel and the small **Museo Posada del Inca,** a collection of Inca artifacts, weapons, and ceramics from the Sacred Valley. (2nd fl. Open most of the time.) To get from **Cusco** to Yucay, catch a colectivo (1½hr., s/2) along Tullumayu or take a Caminos del Inca bus (1½hr., every 20min. 5am-7pm, s/2.50) from the terminal at Huáscar and Garcilaso. From Yucay, you can travel to **Urubamba** by taxi (s/2), mototaxi (s/1), or colectivo (s/0.5), all of which pass frequently along the highway. The best budget lodging option is **⬛Hostal Y'llary,** Plaza Manco II 107, part of the same 300-year-old hacienda as the next-door Posada del Inca Hotel. Y'llary offers much of the hotel's grandeur at a fraction of the price, with gorgeous rooms, glorious gardens, and a wonderfully welcoming owner. (☎/fax 226 607. Singles US$25; doubles US$30; triples US$40; breakfast included. Camping US$3 per person.)

URUBAMBA   ☎084

Despite the tour groups that roll through nearly every day, Urubamba remains a community of quiet neighborhoods where women still summon their children in Quechua and men still plow their fields with oxen. In fact, it provides a markedly less gringo-ridden base than Cusco from which to explore the Sacred Valley. It also provides a wider range of services than many nearby towns. Most of these services revolve around Mariscal Castilla, perpendicular to the highway and recognizable by the taxis and mototaxis which congregate at its foot. **Buses** arrive and depart from the bus station, 500m beyond Castilla on the highway. From the station, walk uphill on the dirt road about five blocks to reach the **Plaza de Armas.** Combis go from the bus station to **Ollantaytambo** (30min., s/1) and **Chinchero** (1hr., every 20min. 5am-7:30pm, s/2.50). To get to **Yucay,** catch a taxi (s/2), mototaxi (s/1), or colectivo (s/0.5) along the highway. To get to Urubamba from **Cusco,** take a colectivo (1½hr., s/2) from Tullumayu or a Caminos del Inca bus (1½hr., every 20min. 5am-7pm, s/2.50) from the terminal at Huáscar and Garcilaso. The **Banco de la Nación** on Castilla may change cash. Other services include: the **police** (☎201 092), at Palacio and Bolognesi; a **clinic** (☎201 334), along the highway at the end of Castilla; and a **post office,** on the Plaza de Armas. On Tuesdays, a sprawling **market** lies to the left of the Plaza de Armas. The basic **Hostal Urubamba,** Bolognesi 605, off Palacio between Castilla and the plaza, has thin mattresses and cold communal baths. Private baths have hot water in the mornings. (☎201 400. Dorms s/5 per person; singles s/10, with bath s/20; doubles s/16, with bath s/30; triples s/24.)

CHINCHERO ☎084

Technically, a 3762m plateau lifts Chinchero (the mythical birthplace of the rainbow) out of the Sacred Valley. Of course, it also allows for incredible views of the surrounding plains and mountains. Chinchero could have been a major city in Inca times; the most striking remnant of the period is the great stone wall in the main plaza. However, the town's sole current claim to anything approaching majorness is its large **Sunday market,** Pisac's main competitor. To get to Chinchero from **Cusco,** catch a colectivo (1½hr., s/2.50) along Tullumayu. Combis run to and from **Urubamba** (1hr., every 20min. 5am-7:30pm, s/2.50).

MORAY AND LAS SALINERAS ☎084

Moray's Inca terraces and the salt pans of Las Salineras (sometimes called Salinas) may be hard to get to, but they are well worth the effort. Moray consists of two sets of concentric **agricultural terraces** sculpted from natural depressions in the earth. The small changes in altitude among the steps create a variety of climatic conditions, allowing an assortment of crops to be planted in one place. Archaeologists believe that Moray was a site of agricultural experimentation even before the Inca; earlier Andean peoples may have used the terraces to develop corn that could grow at high altitudes (s/5). Las Salineras also took advantage of natural phenomena to produce something useful: salt. These **Inca salt pans,** used to this day, are forged from shallow pools dug into the hillside. Over time they fill with salty water from the mountain in underground streams. Then, in the dry season, the water evaporates, leaving a thin layer of sparkling white salt (s/5).

Unfortunately, public **transportation** serves neither Moray nor Las Salineras. To reach Moray, catch a Chinchero-bound colectivo from Urubamba (from the bus station; every 20min. 5am-7:30pm, s/2.50) and ask to get off at the *"desvío a Maras."* From this turn-off, it's a one-hour walk to the tiny village of Maras, then another two hours on a trail that leads to Moray. Ask a local to point out the trailhead in Maras—it's slightly obscure. One could also commission a taxi or mototaxi from Maras (about s/20 round-trip). Las Salineras are a couple of kilometers downhill from Maras, on the way to Pichingoto; from Moray, you must go through Moras to reach the salt pans. From the salt pans, a footpath leads farther downhill to the paved road between Ollantaytambo and Urubamba, along the river. Cross the river and turn right onto the highway; from there, frequent colectivos can take you the rest of the 2km to Urubamba. Alternatively, a number of agencies in Cusco can arrange mountain biking excursions to the two sites (US$25, see Guided Tours from Cusco, p. 112). These tours approach Moray and Las Salineras from a different direction, often passing the picturesque **Laguna Huaypo** along the way.

OLLANTAYTAMBO ☎084

In its day, Ollantaytambo's now-ruined fortress witnessed many great conflicts and was, as such, a source of myriad tragic tales. Today, the fortress enchants invading gringos with its colossal stone walls and fabulous valley vistas. However, as the best surviving example of an Inca town's appearance, Ollantaytambo village is a sight in itself. Streets preserve a perfect grid pattern and are kept clean by waters diverted from the Río Patacancha into stone channels. Houses are arranged in enclosed blocks called *canchas*, and local men, who cherish their strong Quechua identity, wear the poncho typical of the region. One can imagine the Spanish soldiers' fright as they rode up to the **fortress** at Ollantaytambo. Perched atop a set of steep terraces, the Inca army rained arrows and dropped boulders on the invaders and their horses, helpless below. During one battle, the Inca Manco Capac II flooded the courtyard at the foot of the fortress by diverting water from the Río Patacancha; Pizarro and his men retreated. Eventually, though, Ollantaytambo was abandoned. Enormous granite blocks were dragged from the Cachicata quarry, 6km away, form the fortress' foundation. Three similar stones were abandoned mid-haul and now lie along the road into town. The stone court-yard (known as the **Plaza Manyaraqui**) where Pizzaro's men met watery failure now holds a tribute to Inca engineering: a gushing channel that leads into the **Baño de la Ñusta** (Bath of the Princess), where locals sometimes soak their feet. From here, over 200 stone steps climb the terraces at the front of the fortress. At the top of the stairs to the left stands the unfinished complex known as the **Temple of the Sun,** with a number of tremendous stones notable for their carved faces. (Open daily 7am-5:30pm. Admission with tourist ticket.) **Museo CATCCO,** off Principal, was opened by a British group responsible for much of the archaeological excavation in the area. The collection is small but provides informative displays on local customs. (Open Tu-Su 10am-1pm and 2-4pm. s/5.)

Buses arrive in Ollantaytambo's **Plaza de Armas.** The **ruins** lie at the end of **Principal,** which runs downhill from the plaza and across the **Río Patacancha.** The road to the left before crossing the river leads to the **train station** (a 10min. walk). Trains go to **Machu Picchu** (1½hr., 4 per day 8-11am and 4:30-10pm, s/15) and **Cusco** (2½hr., 8pm, s/15). The schedule and prices shift constantly; ask for current information at the station or hostels. **Buses** to **Cusco** (2hr., leaving right after the train arrives—follow the running Peruvians, s/10) leave from the train station. Buses to **Urubamba** (30min., s/1) leave from the Plaza de Armas. There is **no bank** in Ollantaytambo, although local businesses might be able to exchange dollars. Services include: the **police** (☎204 086), on the plaza; a **Centro de Salud** (☎204 090), next to the river on Principal; and a **post and telephone office,** on Principal off the Plaza de Armas in the opposite direction of the ruins (open daily 7am-9pm).

Ollantaytambo has some excellent lodging options. **Hospedaje Miranda,** on Principal, toward the ruins, appears fairly grotty at the entrance, but inside the rooms are lovely. A sunbaked terrace yields fabulous views of the ruins. (☎204 091. Singles s/12, with hot bath s/15; doubles with hot bath s/30.) The warm rooms at **Hostal Restaurant La Nusta,** on Principal, open onto a sunny terrace above the river. (Rooms US$8 per person. Breakfast included.) Next to the train station, **El Albergue** features handsome gardens and a sauna. (☎/fax 202 014. Rooms US$15 per person. Sauna US$5.) **Hostal Munay Tika,** a block toward the train station from Principal, is brand-new and shiny. The owner, Ascencio Flores, owns a shop that sells hand-carved masks. (☎/fax 204 111. Rooms s/50 per person.) **Café Alcazar,** down a cobbled street off the plaza, has great, mostly vegetarian, food and an attractive atmosphere. (Open daily 8am-8pm.)

THE INCA TRAIL

Admission from Km88 US$50, students US$25; from Km104 US$12, students US$6, expected to increase sometime this year.

Peru's most famous hike, the Inca Trail weaves up mountainsides and winds down into cloud forests just like many other Inca highways throughout the Sacred Valley. But only this Inca Trail leads to the stony gates of Machu Picchu, which most consider the climax of the trek, many the highlight of their experience in Peru, and some the most incredible site in South America. Little can match the wonder of reaching the final pass at daybreak, then descending on the sacred city to wander its temples and terraces. Yet spectacular moments fill the two to four days preceding this point, too. The trail swings past a grand diversity of landscapes—jungle vegetation hung with moss, llama-dotted mountain stretches, rushing rivers and potable streams—and a number of impressive ruins that build anticipation for what lies ahead. Any reasonably fit person should be able to complete the route, although the drastic altitude changes ensure that it will be challenging for many; doing some preparatory hiking around Cusco is a good idea. Given the trek's awe-inspiring properties and supreme accessibility, it comes as no surprise that many, many people attempt the Inca Trail—and become impossible to avoid from June to August.

HIKING THE TRAIL INDEPENDENTLY. As the number of tour groups on the Inca Trail multiplies, a heated debate has broken out among visitors to Cusco: follow the crowds or go it alone? While most hikers elect to do the hike with a guided tour from Cusco (see p. 111), another faction has made a strong case for the independent route. Solo hikers can do the trail at their own pace, make their own food, avoid the mindlessness and noise of large groups, make sure that campsites are left intact, and perhaps even save money. However, non-conformity has potential drawbacks. Independent hikers must carry their own equipment (although porters can be found in the nearby town of Ollantaytambo (see p. 115) or at the village of Huayllabamba, along the trail). They will get the worst campsites, since agencies reserve the best ones ahead of time. (This is only really a problem June-Aug., and even then, "worst" is relative. Independent hikers' campsites might be rocky, but at least they're not crowded.) Those short on time or experience may prefer the organization of a tour and the knowledge of a guide. Finally, the money one saves by not buying into a tour might be offset by transportation, admission, and equipment rental costs often included with the price of a group tour.

Those not discouraged by these last considerations should hike prepared: don't leave Cusco without a tent, a sleeping bag (preferably down), raingear, rainproof coverings, warm (preferably wool or polarfleece) clothing, good hiking boots, a knife, a flashlight, matches, a water bottle, water purification tablets, a first-aid kit, toilet paper, bags for garbage, sunscreen, insect repellent, a stove and fuel canisters, cooking utensils, and a change of clothing (since wet clothing won't dry). You can buy light plastic ponchos (s/3-5) in Ollantaytambo. Food is rarely found along the trail; where it is, it's expensive, so hikers should bring enough for four to five

days. A map and detailed guide to the trail are recommended. The classic source for the trail's historical background is Peter Frost's excellent *Exploring Cusco*. Many of these items can be purchased or rented from outfitters around the Plaza de Armas. Daily rental prices run US$2-3 per equipment piece. Occasional robberies suggest that hikers should camp in groups, not alone. There are always other travelers in Cusco looking for hiking partners; check the bulletin boards at the tourist office, the SAE, and hostels around town.

TRAIL ETIQUETTE Thousands of people walk the Inca Trail each month and, especially in the high season, it shows. You can help preserve the Machu Picchu Sanctuary's delicate ecosystem by following a few simple rules. Campfires are strictly prohibited. Trash should be deposited in designated places or carried away in plastic bags, never buried. Human waste should be disposed of away from the trail or in a public latrine; never leave toilet paper behind. Finally, it goes without saying that every hiker should **treat the trail porters with respect.** These men (and a few women) scramble along the trail, setting up tents, hauling equipment, sometimes carrying as much as 60kg on their backs. When hiring porters, either individually or through an agency, make sure they will have adequate food and places to sleep on the trail. Then tip them well.

THE TRAIL

Traditionally, the Inca Trail begins at **Km88,** scales four mountain passes, runs through several stretches of jungle, and climbs up and down several thousand stone steps. Most tour companies cover the trek in three nights, spend the fourth morning at Machu Picchu, and return to Cusco by train in the evening; fleet-footed independent hikers sometimes make it to Machu Picchu halfway through the third day. An alternative to taking the Km88 route is to ride the train from Cusco as far as **Km104,** where what is called the **Royal Trail** begins. The fastest hikers on this trail don't hike at all: they run—in a race held every September in which participants traverse the 33km to Machu Picchu in about four hours.

DAY I. The independent Inca Trail begins with the local train from Cusco (see **Cusco: Transportation,** p. 98) to Km88; most tour agencies choose to bus their groups to Km82 instead. Hikers cross the Río Urubamba and pass the ruins of **Llactapata** ("Town on the Hill"), which appear on the right. The ascent to this point is the first steep hike on the trail. The clearly marked path then crosses the Río Cusichaca ("River Happy Bridge") and follows the river's bank before beginning the 2½km climb toward the village of **Huayllabamba** ("Grassy Plain"), where many tour groups spend the night. There are a number of good campsites before and after the village, many with running water and toilets. In Huayllabamba, you can hire porters to carry your stuff up the towering first pass on the second day. Porters generally charge s/25-35 per pack per day.

DAY II. The main order of the day is scaling the steep incline to the **Abra de Huarmihuañusca,** better known as **Dead Woman's Pass,** the highest point on the Inca Trail. At a dizzying 4200m, the air feels much thinner up here than at the 3000m where most hikers woke up that morning. From Huayllabamba, it's a 2½hr., mostly uphill walk to a campground at **Llulluchapampa.** On the way, a stone stairway leads into a small patch of jungle with a green canopy that offers momentary relief from the sun. At Llulluchapampa, one can finally see the course of the daunting climb ahead, along the left flank of the mountain. The gentle U-shape at the top is the pass. The next three hours expose hikers to the elements: first, scorching sun, then, closer to the pass, freezing winds. Huarmihuañusca is met with great celebration, although hail and snow sometimes cut the celebration short. Past the summit, it's a two-hour descent on stone steps to the Pacamayo Valley floor, where some groups spend the night. Other groups choose to continue up the second big pass on the same day rather than staying in the valley. This does make the second day grueling, but it gets the hardest passes over with right away.

DAY III, PART I. Halfway up to the second pass rest the **Runkuracay ruins,** which Hiram Bingham discovered in 1915 as he traced the stone path from Machu Picchu. Runkuracay is noteworthy for being the only circular complex on the Inca Trail. Another 40 minutes uphill leads to the second pass: **Abra de Runkuracay** (4000m). Just over the pass, there's another official campsite. From this point on, 80% of the Inca Trail is the real thing, original and unrestored. The footpath leads downhill through a natural tunnel and onward toward the **Sayacmarca** ("Inaccessible Town," 1hr.), an appropriate name given the sheer cliffs surrounding the town on three sides. The lack of nearby agricultural terracing suggests that no one actually lived here. Given the four ritual baths—three of which are found across the middle of the complex—Sayacmarca may have been a sacred spot for meditating pilgrims. Walk to the far end of the ruins to a triangular balcony overlooking the Aobamba valley. The sweeping view of the surrounding territory gives a hint at Sayacmarca's additional role: that of a control point for passing cargoes or persons on the highway. Backtrack and rejoin the trail as it passes **Conchamarca,** which probably once served as a resting house for weary travelers. If you're feeling a bit weary yourself, you can camp at the small site.

From Conchamarca the path descends into dense jungle, meandering past orchids, wild daisies, bromeliads, and hanging mosses. This section is among the best preserved parts of the Inca Trail. An hour later, the trail passes a 20-meter-long **tunnel.** The trail then climbs, very gradually, to the third pass, **Abra de Phuyu-patamarca** (3720m, 2hr.), which yields exceptional views of Aguas Calientes below, the back side of Machu Picchu mountain (with its rainbow flag), and several snow-capped peaks including **Palcay** (5600m), **Salkantay** (6180m), and **Verónica** (5750m).

DAY III, PART II. Descending, one arrives at the ruins of Phuyupatamarca ("Town in the Clouds") and passes its six working ritual baths. The surrounding terraces, too high up for crops, probably functioned as retaining walls. The top of the complex is dominated by a large slab of rock pocked with mysterious dents. Some think these held sacrificial offerings, but locals like to say that Hiram Bingham pitched his tent here on stilts for fear of snakes. More likely, this was the base of an important building that was never completed. Some choose to camp here too, though the rocky plateau is very windy and cold.

A trail leads up and away from Phuypatamarca, bypassing the next two ruins, and heading directly to Machu Picchu. Most hikers take a 2250-step stone staircase down instead. After one to two hours, the path levels off some and forks near an electricity tower. The left path continues along the side of the mountain toward the terraces of **Intipata.** The right path descends to the ruins of Huiñay Huayna, which is next to a popular campsite and **hostel** that offers hot showers (s/5), food, and beer. However, especially in high season, the grounds can end up looking (and smelling) like something akin to a Lima shantytown. As an alternative, there are some coveted spots at the foot of Intipata, accessible from the main trail (as described above) as well as from a short path that leads uphill from Huiñay Huayna. **Huiñay Huayna** ("Forever Young") was the last of the major complexes to be discovered (by Paul Fejos in 1941) and is named for the perpetually flowering orchid which grows nearby. Here, the number of ritual baths, all with flowing water, increases to ten. Huiñay Huayna must have been a center of agricultural production, as dozens of steep terraces cling to the mountainside.

DAY IV. The Inca Trail is almost over. Groups attempt to wake at 3:30am in order to scramble to the pass over Machu Picchu in time for the legendary sunrise. To reach the pass, hikers must negotiate another hour of Inca stone pathways, which culminate in a brief but near-vertical set of 50 steps, probably a defensive measure to secure this vulnerable edge of the sacred city. It's a few minutes' climb to the fourth and final pass, **Intipunku** ("Sun Gate"), from which one can watch the morning's first rays of sunlight fall on Machu Picchu below. (The sky starts getting light by 6am; Machu Picchu is illuminated 1hr. later.) On the morning of the summer solstice, the sun's rays shine directly through a large stone "gate," and during the winter solstice they shine through another. Now the celebrating begins as you, weary pilgrim, descend to the promised sacred city of the Incas—Machu Picchu.

MACHU PICCHU

Open daily 5am-4:30pm. US$10, students US$5, children US$2. Repeat admission US$5.

Clinging to a vertiginous hillside, surrounded by towering green mountains, and bathed in a near-constant stream of sunshine, the Inca ruins of Machu Picchu are among the most awe-inspiring sights in South America. The structures are as intact as Inca ruins come, for they had to contend only with natural forces; the invading Spaniards never knew Machu Picchu existed. One can only imagine what the city looked like when neighborhoods of adobe buildings occupied the site. Luckily for visitors, Machu Picchu's massive size comes close to absorbing the mobs of sunburnt tourists who visit annually. On average, 1000 people visit Machu Picchu each day; this number is much greater in July and August.

A DISCOVERY LONG OVERDUE. The American Hiram Bingham is commonly touted as the discoverer of Machu Picchu, even though locals living nearby knew about the ruins long before Bingham explored the area and variations of the words "Machu Picchu" appeared all over property deeds and explorers' maps before the 20th century. Nevertheless, Hiram Bingham was the first person with the resources needed to expose the city's significance to the rest of the world. Ironically, he completely mistook it for the long lost Inca capital of Vilcabamba, the city he had set out to find (see **Bingham's Blunder,** p. 122).

However, what Hiram Bingham discovered in 1911—whether he knew it or not—turned out to be far more wondrous and enigmatic than even the lost city of Vilcabamba. Despite numerous excavations over the years, it is still unclear who built Machu Picchu, who lived there, and why. Nor can one say with any authority why it was abandoned or forgotten. This last detail may be the most disconcerting. The Spanish never got to Machu Picchu because they did not know it existed, but they failed to learn of the site because even the *last Incas* did not know it existed. Adding to the mystery, Bingham and others discovered several ruins near Machu Picchu—now found on the Inca Trail—which are similar in style. Like Machu Picchu, these were carefully constructed, inhabited, abandoned, and subsequently forgotten. Machu Picchu seems to have been the administrative center of this network of complexes, an entire region never preserved in Inca memory, despite the existence of royal oral historians whose duty it was to remember it.

FIGURING IT ALL OUT. The style and function of Machu Picchu's buildings place it within the reign of the **Inca Pachacuti,** also responsible for Cusco's success and the empire's extension toward Ecuador and Chile. The city was probably constructed shortly after the Incas defeated the rival Chanca people in 1438, an event which marked the beginning of the great Inca expansion. And yet, if one accepts that Machu Picchu had been laid to waste before the Conquest, that leaves less than a century for the city to have been built, populated, and left behind. Almost no one who has seen Machu Picchu's buildings, temples, and terraces is satisfied with this time frame, but few can offer a coherent alternative account.

Hiram Bingham's mistaken view that the city was built as a defensive post popularized the notion that Machu Picchu was a citadel. Its many lookout towers and one drawbridge seem to support this view. However, archaeologists have of late considered Machu Picchu more a religious center than a fortress. Bingham's excavation crew's studies of human remains revealed a large majority of women in Machu Picchu's population, suggesting the prominence of virgin priestesses. Machu Picchu may have been a holy city at the end of a long walk of pilgrimage. Evidence of habitation suggests that only around 1000 people ever lived there at one time. Yet the surrounding terraces—in Machu Picchu and nearby at Huiñay Huayna and Intipata—would have fed thousands. Perhaps then, Machu Picchu was a site of agricultural experimentation (intricately tied to sacred ritual), or maybe the city served as a jungle outpost guaranteeing a secure and constant supply of coca leaves. Given all of coca's uses in sacrifice, divination, and medicine, the Inca Empire would have stood still without it.

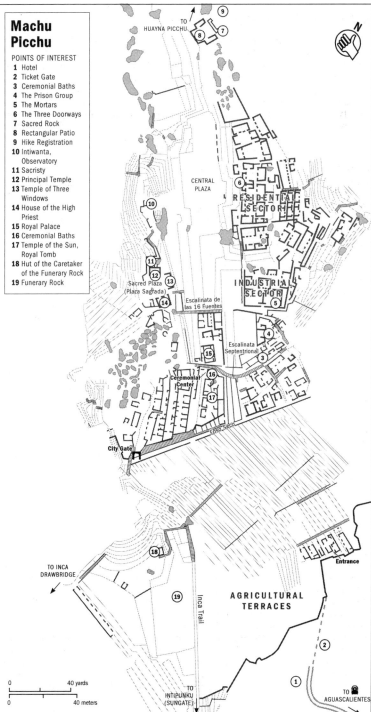

Machu Picchu

POINTS OF INTEREST
1 Hotel
2 Ticket Gate
3 Ceremonial Baths
4 The Prison Group
5 The Mortars
6 The Three Doorways
7 Sacred Rock
8 Rectangular Patio
9 Hike Registration
10 Intiwanta, Observatory
11 Sacristy
12 Principal Temple
13 Temple of Three Windows
14 House of the High Priest
15 Royal Palace
16 Ceremonial Baths
17 Temple of the Sun, Royal Tomb
18 Hut of the Caretaker of the Funerary Rock
19 Funerary Rock

SACRED VALLEY

TO HUAYNA PICCHU

N

CENTRAL PLAZA

RESIDENTIAL SECTOR

INDUSTRIAL SECTOR

Sacred Plaza (Plaza Sagrada)

Escalinata de las 16 Fuentes

Escalinata Septentrional

Ceremonial Center

Caso Seco

City Gate

TO INCA DRAWBRIDGE

Entrance

AGRICULTURAL TERRACES

Inca Trail

0   40 yards
0   40 meters

TO INTIPUNKU (SUNGATE)

TO AGUASCALIENTES

BINGHAM'S BLUNDER Hiram Bingham, Machu Picchu's "scientific discoverer," was a doctor in philosophy and history at Yale when he decided to try his luck at finding the "lost Inca ruins." In 1911, after the young son of a local family showed Bingham kilometers of terracing and walls of unmistakable Inca stonework, who could doubt the American when he declared Machu Picchu the very place he had set out to find, the long lost Inca city of Vilcabamba the Old?

After the Spanish Conquest, the rebellious **Inca Manco Capac II** retreated into the jungle and built a town called Vilcabamba, which the last Incas used as a base from which to attack the Spaniards. The Spanish finally put an end to this pesky Inca resistance with a brutal invasion in 1572. They sacked Vilcabamba, brought the very last Inca ruler, **Tupac Amaru** (Manco's half-brother) back in chains, executed him in Cusco, and dispersed his relations, putting an end to the Inca dynasty for good. In time, Vilcabamba was abandoned and all but forgotten; no Spanish chronicler could even pinpoint its location on the map. But then Bingham announced its discovery to the international press, brought in his team of scientists and archaeologists, and carted their findings back to Yale. Vilcabamba the Old had been found.

Or had it? Bingham's "discovery" stood unchallenged for 50 years. Never mind that it didn't hold up to the simplest scrutiny. "Vilcabamba" means "Sacred Plain" in Quechua, but Machu Picchu is far from flat. Vilcabamba was attacked by the Spaniards, but Machu Picchu shows no signs of Spanish invasion. Vilcabamba was built after the Conquest, but Machu Picchu's architecture shows no Spanish influence. Finally, Vilcabamba was constructed in a hurry by a renegade set of Inca warriors. Machu Picchu was no rush job. Bingham's mistake was affirmed by American explorer **Gene Savoy** in 1964, when he discovered what most people agree are the true ruins of Vilcabamba the Old at **Espíritu Pampa,** four or five days by truck, horse, and foot into the jungle. Ironically, Hiram Bingham actually found part of these ruins in 1909, but passed over them, judging them unimportant. Bingham never lived to learn the tremendous significance of what he found at Machu Picchu.

The mystery of the region's abandonment inspires even more speculation. Some believe the site's population was decimated by an epidemic disease. Others point to hypothetical sieges by the Antis tribe from the jungle. It is possible that Machu Picchu was a vacation estate for the Inca Pachacuti and populated by his own clan. If true, the site's abandonment could be explained simply by the death of Pachacuti. One theory conjectures that the entire region rebelled against the empire, and that to prevent a major uprising the Incas swept in and moved the population out. Peruvian archaeologist Marino Sánchez offers a vivid narrative according to which Machu Picchu was struck by torrential rains, the gold-covered principal temple was hit by lightning, and seeing this as a bad omen, everyone fled in tearful grief. Guides to Machu Picchu will present these accounts with varying degrees of factuality, but it's all speculation. Happily though, the great mystery of these walls only adds to Machu Picchu's mystique.

LOGISTICS. The nearest **train station** is in **Aguas Calientes** (p. 123). **Shuttle buses** depart for Aguas Calientes from the Machu Picchu Hotel (20min., continually 12:30-5:30pm, US$5). **Luggage storage,** mandatory for backpackers fresh off the trail, is located near the admission booth (s/2 per bag, free for hikers with park ticket). **Guides** can be hired on site for around US$12 per person. There are **coin telephones** outside the Machu Picchu Hotel and **public toilets** beside the entrance. **Police** and **medical facilities** sit near the entrance as well. A terraced restaurant by the ticket booth sells overpriced, mostly Western food (s/10-25) and a daily lunch buffet (US$15 per person). The only hotel at the sacred city is the luxurious **Machu Picchu Ruinas Hotel,** outside the main entrance. **Camping** is permitted at the bottom of Machu Picchu mountain by the banks of the Urubamba.

EXPLORING THE RUINS. Spread between two mountains, the sacred city sprawls along Machu Picchu mountain and faces Huayna Picchu mountain. Even those coming off the Inca Trail must exit Machu Picchu and re-enter, getting their ticket stamped in the process. The front entrance leads into what is called the agricultural sector of the city, great terraces which supported enough crops for the entire population. Those llamas munching on the grass have been installed for the tourists—they actually prefer to live at higher altitudes. At the top of the terraces, one finds a carved granite slab known as the funeral rock, which may have been used to prepare the dead for burial; this upper part of the city seemed to function as a cemetery. Hikers emerge from the Inca Trail onto this hilltop. Those interested can follow the path in reverse to see **Intipunku** and the enormous terraces at **Huiñay Huayna** (admission US$2; see p. 119). Also from the cemetery hill, a road leads to the **Inca bridge,** a defensive drawbridge which has been restored with logs.

Back down the hill, starting at the front entrance, everyone walks across one of the large flat terraces to reach 16 lined-up ritual baths with water cascading down the side of the mountain. On the left just before the baths is the **Sun Temple,** notable for its U-shaped wall which hardly betrays a flaw in its fine masonry. On the winter solstice, sunlight shines through one of the windows and falls exactly on the center of the rock in the middle of the temple. This rock shares the Southern Cross's diamond shape, and many visitors hold their hands over it, to glean energy from its supposed power source. A carved cave underneath the temple might have held human remains. It is said that the large buildings across the baths on the other side of the Sun Temple once housed Inca nobility. Walk to the top of the staircase along the baths to reach the rock quarry.

Walking farther into the city on the same level of terrace brings you to the three-walled **Temple with Three Windows,** which is beautifully symmetrical and carved from immense stones. Opening onto the same plaza, the three-walled **Principal Temple** has one droopy corner that has partially sunk into an underground chamber. In one wall, find the building block that is counted to have at least 32 edges around its various faces. Beyond this, on top of a small hill, resides the **Intihuatana,** another carved rock which may have been used to measure the movements of the sun. Look over at the flat grassy area that divides the city like a parade ground.

On the other side of this clearing, at the far edge of the city on the way toward Huayna Picchu, another plaza with three-walled buildings centers on an erected rock. Called the **Sacred Rock,** it is shaped like the outline of the mountain behind it. A lot of visitors continue along this path in order to hike up the steep **Huayna Picchu,** which takes about two hours round-trip. The most interesting aspect of Huayna Picchu is its mountaintop terracing which seems to have been intended more for decoration than for agriculture. On the way up to Huayna Picchu, a trail splits off toward the fine **Temple of the Moon.** Walking back into the city, you'll find dozens of stone complexes, most of which likely comprised ordinary housing. Within one of these buildings, two circular pans are carved into the floor stone. Bingham called these **mortars** because he thought they were used to grind corn; others have speculated that they were filled with water and used as mirrors to observe the night sky. A nearby staircase leads to the multi-level, intricately carved **Temple of the Condor.** Bingham incorrectly thought its inner chambers served as a jail, leading to the misnaming as the "Prison Sector." The temple's more recent name stems from the triangular stone, thought to represent the condor's head, and a carved rock face that looks like an extended wing.

AGUAS CALIENTES ☎ 084

Aguas Calientes is one Sacred Valley town that everyone visits. Unfortunately, overpriced and artificial, it is hardly the introduction the valley deserves. The village derives its name from the warm waters of nearby mineral springs, but its main focus is that great tourist mecca up the hill, Machu Picchu. Tourists going to the sacred city lodge in Aguas Calientes, eat in Aguas Calientes, buy their souvenirs in Aguas Calientes, and at the end of the day, soak in Aguas Calientes's *aguas cali-*

entes—doing so falls second only to hiking the Inca Trail as the best way to beat the train's crowds to Machu Picchu. The *baños termales*, at the top of Pachacutec, consist of a couple of steaming pools and one cold pool. The mineral waters soothe aching muscles fresh off the Inca Trail. Gangs of gringos show up in the afternoon. A bar next to the pool serves pisco sours in the evening and has towels and swimsuits available for rent. (Open daily 5am-8:30pm. s/5.).

The only two real streets in town are **Imperio de Los Incas,** the stall-lined street along the old train tracks, and **Pachacutec,** which heads uphill to the hot springs. The **Plaza de Armas** is just uphill of the train tracks—its church is visible from below. The **local train** leaves from these old tracks; all **tourist trains** leave from Estación Nueva, uphill and through the market to the left of the tracks. **Tickets** can be purchased at the Estación Nueva by late morning. However, most tourists reserve tickets through a tour agency in Cusco. Times and prices change constantly. A local train goes to **Cusco** (4-5hr., 6pm, s/15) via **Ollantaytambo** (2½hr., s/15). Three classes of tourist trains go to **Cusco** (3½hr.): Backpackers (5pm, US$25), Autovagon (3pm, US$40), Cocha Inka (3:30pm, US$50). **Shuttle buses to Machu Picchu** (30min.; at least 1 per hr. 6:30am-5pm; US$4.50, US$9 round-trip) leave from the lower part of the market. The hike up to Machu Picchu is on the steep trail, not the road (2hr.). There are **no banks** in Aguas Calientes; businesses on Pachacutec and Imperio de las Incas buy dollars at decent rates. Services include: the **police** (☎211 178), on Imperio de Las Incas; a **telephone office** on Imperio de las Incas; **Internet access** at Café Internet Yanantin Masintin, off the train tracks (☎211 036; s/ 10 per hr.); and a **post office,** in Qosqo Service on Pachacutec.

From June to August, most rooms in Aguas Calientes seem to be booked most of the time. If you want to stay here, call well in advance. **Gringo Bill's,** Colla Raymi 104, on the Plaza de Armas, has comfortable, if sometimes dim, rooms decorated with trippy Andean murals. The bar is certainly happening; the expensive restaurant caters to famished hikers fresh from the Inca Trail. Make reservations in Cusco at Garcilaso 265-3 (☎241 545), off the Plaza Regocijo. (☎/fax 211 046; email gringobills@yahoo.com. Singles US$14, with bath US$24; doubles US$27, with bath US$40; triples US$49.50, with bath US$57.50.) **Hostal Don Guiller,** Parachutec 136, features bright and simple rooms, an accompanying restaurant, clean shared baths, and a fresh paint job. (☎211 128. Beds s/20.) A nice older man owns **Hospedaje El Mirador,** Parachutec 135, where the few rooms sparkle with clean and quiet. (☎211 194. Doubles with bath s/30; triples s/30.) **Hostal La Cabaña,** Parachutec 20-30, has lovely furnishings and cheerful owners. (☎/fax 211 048. Breakfast included. Singles US$15; doubles US$20; triples US$30.)

SOUTHERN PERU

When tourists—now coughing and cursing—hightail it out of Lima, most of them head this way. The route south from the capital takes in a variety of landscapes, many of which are conveniently joined by the paved Panamerican Highway. Along the **southern coast** (p. 125), sweeping desert expanses stretch among the well-known city oases. From Camaná, the road moves inland and ascends toward **Arequipa** (p. 153), a fantastic colonial city 2000m above sea level, which presents a drastic contrast to the flat desert attractions of the coast. The city's white buildings ooze cosmopolitan charm, but Arequipa appeals to more than just city-slickers. Destinations for mountain climbing and trekking, the most important being the extraordinarily deep Colca Canyon, lie at a short distance. The Panamericana abandons the tourist at this point, but thanks to a frequently running rail line, the shores of the world's highest navigable lake have become the next stop in the tourist circuit. The train from Arequipa climbs more than 1000m to the stark altiplano that surrounds **Lake Titicaca** (p. 166). More than a body of water, Lake Titicaca is a boundary—between Peru and Bolivia, of course, but also between two very different highland cultures, Quechua and Aymara. Still deeply influenced by their history, people in some of the region's villages preserve the methods, language, dance, and clothing of their ancestors.

HIGHLIGHTS OF SOUTHERN PERU

HANG with boobies and sea lions in the **Islas Ballestas** (p. 132).

GUZZLE the goods at the many **wineries** around Lunahuaná (p. 127) and Ica (p. 134).

TRY your skills at **sandboarding** on the Huacachina sand dunes (p. 138).

FLY over the fascinating **Nasca lines** (p. 142).

WANDER the serene streets of Arequipa's **Santa Catalina Monastery** (p. 158).

OBSERVE a majestic Andean Condor soar above one of the deepest ravines in the world, **the Colca Canyon** (p. 162).

WEAVE with the Quechua women on Titicaca's Islas Taquile and Amantaní (p. 173).

SOUTHERN COAST

PUNTA HERMOSA   ☎01

In the summertime, surfers and *limeños* longing for a day of sun head to Punta Hermosa, 45km from Lima. While the north coast's Puerto Chicama has the world's longest wave, Punta Hermosa boasts **Pico Alto,** South America's tallest wave, which ranges from seven to an incredible 24 feet (the biggest swells arrive Apr.-May). The town itself serves mainly as a getaway for wealthy *limeños*, whose luxurious beach houses line the *malecón* along the water. A few restaurants, discos, and hotels open for the busy summer season (Dec.-Mar.), but during the rest of the year Punta Hermosa is a veritable ghost town.

◼ **TRANSPORTATION.** Punta Hermosa is 2km off the Panamericana, so make sure that your bus or colectivo is going to the beach, not just dropping you off on the side of the highway. The most direct are the brown striped colectivos marked "Lurín" (1¼hr., frequently 6am-8pm, s/3) that head down Grau in Lima Centro; they drop passengers off at the top of a hill 200m from the beach. To get to one of the nearby **beaches** or back to **Lima,** catch a colectivo at the same spot. You'll need to take a taxi to get to and from the **San Bartolo discos** (s/10 each way).

◪◨ ACCOMMODATIONS AND FOOD. Since the majority of Punta Hermosa's visitors are either daytrippers or vacation homeowners, the hotel selection is limited and generally expensive. **Hotel Sol y Mar Coconut,** Bolognesi 551, just up from the water, is by far the cheapest, but lets in little light. (☎870 43 12. M-F rooms s/10 per person, Sa-Su rooms s/15 per person.) Both price and comfort increase at **La Isla Hostel,** Malecón Central 943, on the main beach; perks include hot showers, free breakfast, **surfboard rental** (US$5 per day), Internet access, and English-speaking owners. (☎230 71 46; email islasurf@terra.com.pe. Rooms US$10-15 per person.) Hard-core surfers gather at **Hostal Pico Alto International Surf Camp,** a 15-minute walk north of town, just in front of the Pico Alto wave. Owner Oscar Morante, a former surfing champion, can pick guests up from Lima with advance notice. (☎230 72 97; fax 230 78 69; email surfcamp-peru@terra.com.pe.) He also rents **surfboards** (US$10 per day) and **wetsuits** (US$5 per day). Doubles, triples, and quads US$28 per person. Hot bath and three meals included. Most restaurants in Punta Hermosa are wildly overpriced (meals start around s/20) and even more inconvenient (closing by 6pm). The simple but satisfying seafood *menús* (s/6) at **Pikalos,** Bolognesi 524, are the most economical. (Open 9am-6pm.)

◪◪ BEACHES AND NIGHTLIFE. Punta Hermosa isn't the only beach in the area; there are somewhat more secluded beaches with great waves a few kilometers north and south. At Panamericana Km42, the calm waters of **El Silencio** are popular with swimmers, sunbathers, and snack food vendors. Just to the south, waves reach up to nine feet at the **Señoritas** and **Caballeros** beaches. At the southern end of Punta Hermosa, **La Isla's** swells can top 4m, though the surfing's even better (with waves up to 5m) at secluded, spectacular **Punta Rocas,** 2km south of town. The international Copa del Pacífico surf championship usually takes place at Punta Rocas in early March, though it was cancelled in 2000 due to lack of sponsorship. The waves get smaller and the nightlife better as one moves south to the town of **San Bartolo,** 4km south of Punta Hermosa at Km49. **El Huayco Discoteca,** 150m in from the entrance to San Bartolo, under the huge red Cristal sign, pumps dance music to an enclosed, open-air dance floor with three different bars. (Open Dec.-Mar. F-Sa 11pm-6am. Cover s/5.) **La Rumba,** at Panamericana Km48, does the same but with more Latin rhythms. (☎247 32 80. Open Dec.-Mar. Sa 11pm-6am. Cover s/10, includes 1 beer). There are also discos at Señoritas and El Silencio.

NEAR PUNTA HERMOSA: PUCUSANA

From Lima Centro, buses head to Pucusana (1½hr., 5am-10pm, s/3) from Montevideo and Andahuaylas. From Punta Hermosa, catch a colectivo at the stop on the top of Libertad (15min., s/1). Buses to Lima (s/3) leave Pucusana from Lima. Colectivos leave from the lot next to the church and go north to Lima (s/3) and south to Pisco (s/5).

The beaches aren't so nice in the small fishing town of **Pucusana,** 15km south of Punta Hermosa, but you'll find more permanent residents, practical services, and affordable accommodations. In an isolated bay about 1km away, **Naplo beach** offers no waves for surfing but is nice for swimming. No ATMs or banks in Pucusana change traveler's checks, but many stores will change dollars. **Emergency:** ☎105. Services include: the **police** (☎430 90 05), on Lima near the buses; and a small **hospital** (☎430 90 53). **Hostal Salón Blanco,** on the water, has spacious, well-lit rooms and a good restaurant. (☎430 95 42. Singles s/15, with bath s/20; doubles with bath s/30, with TV s/35.) Another good place to sleep and eat is the **Hostal Restaurant Las Delicias,** also on the water, lined with plants to keep the place cheerful. (☎430 91 01. Doubles with bath s/25.) The **Restaurant Turístico Bahía,** near the inlet with crashing waves, comes highly recommended for its excellent seafood. (☎430 90 23. Open daily 9am-10pm. Ceviche s/12.)

CAÑETE ☎034

A small, slow town that sees few tourists, dull but pleasant Cañete serves as little more than a stop en route to Lunahuaná, since there are no direct buses. Spending a night here, rather than switching buses immediately, may be a relaxing experience. The **Plaza de Armas** lies on 2 de Mayo, a few blocks from the spot on the Panamericana where **buses** pause for passengers to get on or off. From Lima Centro, direct buses for Cañete (2½hr., s/5) leave from Montevideo between Iquitos and Abancay. All buses heading south from Lima or north to Lima on the Panamericana also pass through Cañete; frequent buses to **Lima** (2½hr., s/5-7) and **Pisco** (1hr., s/3-5). **Plaza San Martín,** where colectivos to **Lunahuaná** stop, is also on 2 de Mayo, two blocks from the Plaza de Armas. Services include: **Interbank,** 2 de Mayo 451, with a Visa/PLUS **ATM** (open M-F 8:30am-6:15pm, Sa 9am-12:30pm); the **police** (☎581 20 83), on 2 de Mayo at the Plaza San Martín; and the **Hospital Rezola,** Bolognesi 222 (☎581 20 10), next to the Municipalidad building. **Hostal Casablanca,** 2 de Mayo 689, has nice rooms in a comfortable house. (☎581 20 40. Doubles with hot water s/40.) **Hostal La Casona,** on the Plaza de Armas, livens up its concrete rooms with Peruvian wall hangings and pictures of tourist sites. (☎581 31 30. Singles with bath s/20; doubles with bath s/30.)

LUNAHUANÁ ☎034

Two things bring visitors to Lunahuaná: wine and whitewater—both of which are celebrated at the **Fiesta de la Uva, el Vino, y el Canotaje** during the first weekend in March. Highlights of the *fiesta* include free wine tastings and collective grape-stomping, when the town sheds its shoes and jumps into an enormous vat. While the high seasons for wine and rafting run roughly December through March, both can be enjoyed the rest of the year as well. In fact, scenic Lunahuaná—only a one-hour diversion off the Panamericana—is one of the most underappreciated gems of the southern coast.

Southern Coastal Peru

SOUTHERN PERU

☎☷ TRANSPORTATION AND PRACTICAL INFORMATION. Lunahuaná isn't so much one town as it is a series of small *anexos* (or neighborhoods) spread out along the road that runs above the **Río Cañete.** The largest *anexo* is called Lunahuaná, and its **Plaza de Armas**—where most of the *fiesta* events take place—sits two blocks up from the main road. Frequent **combis** travel the main road between the *anexos* (s/1). To get to Lunahuaná from Cañete—through which one *must* pass to get to Lunahuaná—take a colectivo from the *ovalo* near Plaza San Martín to the small village of **Imperial** (10min., s/70); from there, catch another colectivo to Lunahuaná (1hr., s/2.50). Lunahuaná's **tourist office,** on the Plaza de Armas, distributes maps of the area. (Open W-F 9am-1pm and 2-5pm, Sa-Su 10am-1pm and 2-6pm.) **City Tours Lunahuaná** (☎868 05 99), in Hostal Los Andes, two blocks from the Plaza de Armas, gives a good deal on tours of the town, vineyards, and minor ruins nearby (3hr., daily 10am and 3pm, s/15 per person).

☎☷ ACCOMMODATIONS AND FOOD. It's worth it to pay a little more for a hotel in Lunahuaná; few dirt-cheap ones exist, and the quality of the rooms usually plunges with the price anyway. The best hotel value—as well as some of the cheapest food—can be found at the **Restaurant Hostal Campestre Mi Rosedal,** on the main road in the *anexo* of Uchupampa, at Km41.7. All rooms are clean and welcoming, with hot-water baths (☎284 11 77. Matrimonials s/35; doubles s/50.) The restaurant downstairs specializes in shrimp. (*Chupe de camarones* s/4. Open daily 8am-9:30pm.) **Las Viñas,** at Km41.5 in the nearby *anexo* of Condoray, offers beautiful cabanas with a tropical feel, pleasant balconies, and tastefully decorated rooms. Las Viñas also offers campsites, horseback riding on their enormous grounds, and rafting trips. (☎(01) 437 31 87. Campsites s/10, with tent rental s/15; matrimonials s/60; doubles s/90; s/10 discount M-Th.) **El Guanabo,** in the Juta *anexo,* also offers camping, and their sites have views of the river. (Campsites s/10, with tent rental s/20.) **Sol & Río Restaurant,** overlooking the river, on the main road in Lunahuaná proper, serves excellent food, but service can be slow. (Ceviche s/15. ☎284 10 78. Open daily 8am-7pm.)

☎☷ SIGHTS AND ACTIVITIES. The best season for **whitewater rafting** is January through March, when the rapids reach a respectable Class IV. The rest of the year, the rapids are Class II-III—good for beginners but less exciting for more experienced paddlers. **Kayaking** is also possible if you can convince the agencies that you know what you're doing; there is no kayak instruction. Many hotels and restaurants (see above), as well as agencies around the Plaza de Armas, offer whitewater rafting trips on the Río Cañete; Las Viñas's are renowned for their emphasis on safety. Most companies charge US$10-15 for 30-40 minutes spent on the 6km of whitewater, although this varies with the seasons.

Several small **bodegas** in the Lunahuaná Valley produce pisco, a white brandy-like alcohol, and cachina, a naturally fermented wine. The best time to visit the bodegas is from February to April, the season of the *vendimia,* when tourists can shed their shoes, roll up their pants, and help with the wine-making. Arrive as early as possible—the grape-stomping takes place in the morning. The tourist office can give you a list of all the bodegas in the area, but the best are **La Reyna de Lunahuaná** (☎449 99 17), in the *anexo* of Catapalla, 7km across the river, and the closer **Viña Los Reyes,** in the *anexo* of Condoray (☎284 12 06. Spanish or English tours s/10. Pisco s/15, and wine s/8-10, available all year. Open daily 7am-7pm. Free.)

CHINCHA ALTA ☎034

Though Chincha Alta is one of the larger and more culturally interesting towns on the southern coast, few tourists visit on their way to Pisco or Nasca. During the 17th and 18th centuries, local plantations relied on African slave labor; after the slaves were freed, many chose to remain in the Chincha area. Their influence remains highly visible in and around the city, in the skin tone, music, art, and dance. Chincha is famous in Peru for being a city that knows how to party, though its various *fiestas*, once elaborate productions, have decreased in size and attendance due to financial strains. The two most famous are **Verano Negro** ("Black Summer," Feb. 18-Mar. 4)—a celebration of art and culture featuring contests, dancing, and lots of local pride—and the similar **Fiesta de Chincha** (end of Oct.).

Chincha Alta's main street is the busy **Mariscal Benavides,** which runs between the palm tree-laden **Plaza de Armas** and the bus-laden **Plazuela Bolognesi.** Halfway between the two plazas, **Mariscal Castilla** runs perpendicular to Benavides. The Ormeño bus station (☎261 301), also in the *plazuela*, sends buses to: **Marcona** (5:30, 9am, noon, and 9pm; s/15) via **Pisco** (s/2), **Ica** (s/3), **Palpa** (s/10), and **Nasca** (s/12); **Arequipa** (12hr.; 11:30am, 4:30, 6:30, and 9:30pm; s/35) via **Camaná** (s/30); **Ilo** (1:30pm, s/45) via **Moquegua** (s/45); **Tacna** (19-20hr., 12:30 and 6pm, s/50); and **Lima** (3hr., every hr. 6am-9pm, s/6). Other bus companies and colectivos leave from the same area. Services include: **tourist information,** in the Municipalidad building on the Plaza de Armas (open M-F 8am-3pm); **Banco Wiese Sudameris,** Benavides 194, on the Plaza de Armas, with a 24-hour Red Unicard **ATM** (open M-F 9am-1pm and 4:30-6:45pm, Sa 9:30am-12:30pm); the **police** (☎261 261), on the Plaza de Armas; **Hospital San Jose** (☎ 269 006), several blocks from the center of town on Alva Maurtua; **Internet access** at Future Net, Benavides 114, just before the Plaza de Armas (s/4 per hr.; open daily 9am-11pm); and a **post office** (☎261 141), on the Plaza de Armas (open M-Sa 8am-8pm).

There are plenty of hotels in Chincha, so chances are that you won't have trouble finding a room at a reasonable price, even during festivals. **Hotel Sotelo,** Benavides 260, has three floors of basic but clean pale-blue rooms off long hallways. (☎261 681. Doubles s/25, with bath s/45, with bath and TV s/50.) **Hostal Oriente,** Mariscal Castilla 211-223, may be a bit sterile, but all rooms have warm baths and soft beds. (☎263 008. Singles s/35; doubles s/45; s/10 off-season discount.) When in Chincha, eat as the *chinchanos* do; a local favorite is *tacu tacu* (a scramble of rice, beans, onions, meat, and spicy ají). **Restaurante Cevichería Costa Marina,** Plaza de Armas 148, is the best place in town for seafood and traditional *chinchano* cuisine. (*Tortuga a lo macho,* turtle in a seafood sauce, s/17; *tacu tacu* s/16. ☎262 700. Open daily 7am-midnight.)

NEAR CHINCHA ALTA: CASA-HACIENDA SAN JOSÉ

To get to Casa-Hacienda San José, catch a combi marked "El Carmen" (35min., every 15min., s/1.30) from Caqueta, on the side of Chincha's market closest to the Plaza de Armas. Alternatively, take a taxi from Chincha (25min., s/13-15). Combis back to Chincha pass in front of the main entrance to the Hacienda.

A taste of what it would have been like to have lived in the era of cotton and sugar plantations, the Casa-Hacienda San José, which dates to 1688, waits just 30 minutes southeast of Chincha in the district of El Carmen. The state originally produced only sugar and honey; during the late 18th century, they planted cotton as well. At the height of productivity, more than 1000 African slaves worked at the hacienda, and in 1879, many of them organized a large-scale revolt in which they murdered their master. Cotton, asparagus, and citrus fruits are still harvested in the fields, but now San José is primarily known as a resort hotel. The beautiful grounds include a swimming pool, stables, tennis courts, ping-pong tables, and *sapo*, a traditional game similar to horseshoes. Anyone can take a guided tour of the estate, which includes an excursion, lit only by hand-held candles, into the underground catacombs of the Salazar and Carillo families. (Open daily 9am-5pm. 40min. tours in Spanish only, s/10.) The hotel isn't exactly "budget," but their all-inclusive three-day packages are a pretty good deal. (US$80 per person M-Th, US$100 F-Su.) For information or to make reservations, contact the Lima office (☎(01) 444 52 42; fax (01) 444 55 24; email hsanjose@terra.com.pe.)

PISCO ☎ 034

When most Peruvians hear the word "pisco," this small coastal town isn't the first thing that comes to mind. Poor town—a powerful white-grape brandy produced in the region shares its name, and most people find it far more exciting. Still, although the town of Pisco is not itself particularly interesting, nor its beach particularly inviting, dozens of Peruvian and foreign tourists veer off the Panamericana every day with Pisco as their destination. Are pisco sours so good that people should come simply to pay homage to the town that shares their name? Well, yes, but the pisco is not especially cheap or plentiful here. Most tourists have another reason for visiting: fascinating nearby sights such as the wildlife at the Islas Ballestas, the beaches in the Paracas Reserve, and the ruins of Tambo Colorado.

▐ TRANSPORTATION

Buses: Pisco is 3km west of the Panamericana, so relatively few buses go directly to town. However, any bus heading to a destination beyond Pisco can drop you off at the turn-off (tell the bus driver, *"Bajo en la cruce para Pisco"*). From there, frequent **colectivos** leave for the center of town (10min., s/0.5). **Ormeño** (☎532 762), at San Francisco and Ayacucho, serves: **Arequipa** (12hr.; 11am, 3:30, 6:30pm; s/30); **Ayacucho** (8hr., 9, 11am, 10, 11pm, midnight; s/30); **Ica** (1hr., 9am and 12:30pm, s/2); **Lima** (4hr.; 8 per day 9am-6:30pm, Su also 8:10pm; s/10; royal service 2 and 4:45pm, s/30); **Nasca** (3hr., 9am and 12:30pm, s/10; royal service 4:30pm, s/35); and **Tacna** (18hr., 11am and 5pm, s/40). **Transportes Saky,** Pedemonte 190 (☎534 309), sends the most frequent buses to **Ica** (1hr., every 20 min. 6am-8pm, s/2.50). **Colectivos** to **Paracas** (30 min., s/1) leave from the market area at Fermín Tanguis and B. de Humay whenever full. Colectivos to **Chincha** (1hr., s/2) leave regularly from 2 blocks south of the Plaza Belén.

Bicycle Rentals: Ask nicely at **The Zarcillo Connections** (see **Tour Agencies,** below), which rents bikes as a side business. Bikes s/10-15 per day.

▐ ORIENTATION AND PRACTICAL INFORMATION

Most services cluster around the **Plaza de Armas.** On the north side of the plaza runs **San Francisco,** home to most of the travel agencies. On the southwest side of the plaza, the busy pedestrian walkway of Comercio (called **Boulevard** by locals), leads to the smaller **Plaza Belén.**

Tour Agencies: Everywhere you look, especially on San Francisco between the Ormeño station and the Plaza de Armas, there are agencies advertising trips to the Islas Ballestas, Paracas Reserve, and, less frequently, Tambo Colorado. While most agencies offer similar tours at the same price (Islas Ballestas s/25, Ballestas-Paracas combo s/35), only 3 are officially registered tour agencies: **The Zarcillo Connections,** San Francisco 111 (☎536 543; email zarcillo@post.cosapidata.com.pe. Open daily 6:30am-10pm); **Ballestas Travel Service,** San Francisco 249 (☎/fax 533 095; email jpacheco@net.telematic.com.pe. Open daily 7am-10pm); and **Paracas Tours,** San Francisco 257 (☎/fax 533 630. Open daily 8am-8pm).

Banks: Banco de Crédito, Pérez Figuerola 162 (☎532 340) on the Plaza de Armas, will change AmEx or Visa traveler's checks. **ATM** accepts Visa. Open M-F 9:15am-1:15pm and 4:30-6:30pm, Sa 9:15am-12:30pm.

Laundry: Lavandería Iris, Pedemonte 170 (☎532 285), has next-day service (shirts s/2, pants s/3). Open M-Sa 8am-noon and 3-8pm, Su 8am-noon.

Emergency: ☎105.

Police: (☎532 884), on the Plaza de Armas.

Hospital: Hospital Antonio Skrabonja A. (☎532 784), on San Francisco's 3rd block.

Telephones: There are a few **Telefónica del Perú** booths around the Plaza de Armas. For more privacy, head to **Telefax Services S.R.L.,** Progreso 123 (☎534 055 or 533 994), on the Plaza de Armas. Open daily 8am-11pm.

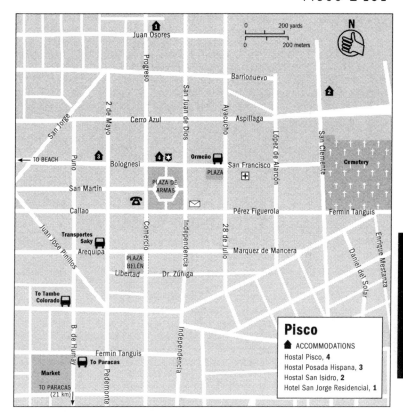

Pisco

▲ ACCOMMODATIONS

Hostal Pisco, **4**
Hostal Posada Hispana, **3**
Hostal San Isidro, **2**
Hotel San Jorge Residencial, **1**

Internet Access: Computación e Informática Bill Gates, San Francisco 290 (☎533 616), charges a whopping s/10 per hr. Open daily 7am-11pm. Fortunately, it no longer holds a monopoly. **Interworld,** Comercio 147, 2nd fl. (☎536 155), on the pedestrian walkway, costs s/8 per hr.

Post Office: Serpost, San Juan de Dios 108 (☎432 272), on the Plaza de Armas. Open M-Sa 8am-9pm.

▛ ACCOMMODATIONS

The large number of budget travelers who pass through Pisco ensures the existence of many clean, comfortable, and low-priced options in town. Camping is free on the beaches in the Paracas Reserve (bring your own supplies), but do not camp on the Pisco beach; many robberies have been reported there, especially at night.

▧ **Hostal San Isidro,** San Clemente 103 (☎533 217), past the cemetery. The rooms, many with TVs, are clean and cheerful. Guests may use the laundry and kitchen facilities, or just lounge in the courtyard and play foosball or billiards. The friendly owners provide free coffee in the morning—necessary since the Islas Ballestas tours usually leave before 8am. Rooms s/12 per person, with bath s/15.

▧ **Hostal Posada Hispana,** Bolognesi 236 (☎/fax 536 363; email andesad@ciber.com.pe). A better name might be "Pasado Hispano," as this quaint hostel evokes memories of a colonial past—complete with the Castilian accents (the owners are from Barcelona). The two-story dorms and private rooms are immaculately maintained, and Internet (s/5 per hr.), free laundry and kitchen access, and a backyard garden add to the charm. Singles and dorms US$10; doubles US$15; triples US$19; quads US$24.

Hotel San Jorge Suite, Comercio 187 (☎/fax 534 200), on the pedestrian walkway, and **Hostal San Jorge Residencial,** Juan Osores 267-269 (☎532 885), 3 blocks behind the Plaza de Armas. It doesn't take much eye-squinting to imagine you're living in luxury here. All rooms have TVs and baths with soap and towels, though San Jorge Residencial isn't quite as plush as its sibling. Singles at San Jorge Residencial s/30; doubles s/50; triples s/65; quads s/70. San Jorge Suite s/10-30 more.

Hostal Pisco Playa, Jose Balta 639 (☎532 492), 3 blocks from the ocean. As close as you can get to Pisco's beach, not that Pisco's beach is something you'd want to be particularly close to. Still, it's cheaper, cleaner, and calmer than many of the options in the center of town. Rooms with bath s/12 per person, with breakfast s/15.

Hostal Colonial Jr., Comercio 194 (☎532 035), on the walkway near Plaza Belén. The location's good, if a bit noisy, and it's one of the cheapest places in town. Posters of heartthrobs past and present spice up the rooms. Rooms s/10 per person.

◘ FOOD

The tourist industry can take credit for a plethora of good, affordable hotels in Pisco, but it hasn't made much of an impact on the restaurants. Still, the nearly identical eateries lining the pedestrian walkway with decent, economical tourist *menús* ensure that nobody goes away hungry.

Restaurant Turistico Ch'Reyes, Comercio 167 (☎534 678), on the pedestrian boulevard. Smaller and simpler than its neighbors, Ch'Reyes serves tasty food at low prices. *Menú de casa* s/5-6; vegetarian *menú* s/10. Open daily 6am-10pm.

Restaurant Pizzeria Catamaran, Comercio 162-166 (☎680 327), across from Ch'Reyes on the pedestrian walkway. Their s/7 *menú* offers a vast selection of fish, pasta, and vegetarian dishes—stick to it, as a la carte entrees are pricey (s/13-20) and the pizzas barely recognizable as such. Open daily 8am-11pm.

Don Manuel, Comercio 187 (☎532 035), also on the pedestrian boulevard, across from Hostal Colonial, specializes in foods beginning with the letter C—ceviche (s/9-17), *conchas de abanico* (scallops; s/12-15), *churrasco* (s/13-19), and chicken (s/11-13). Slightly more upscale than its neighbors. Open daily 6am-11pm.

▐ DAYTRIPS FROM PISCO

ISLAS BALLESTAS AND EL CANDELABRO

Even the most independent travelers must resign themselves to a guided tour if they wish to visit the Islas Ballestas; private boats are not allowed to go to the islands. Instead, 12-tourist motorboats depart from El Chaco port with a guide. Tours usually last 2-3hr., cost US$8 (US$10 including an afternoon visit to the Paracas Reserve) and leave early (7-8am), since morning is the best time to see the wildlife. Sign up with an agency the night before to reserve a spot, and wear layers, since the temperature varies greatly. For information on specific agencies, see Tour Agencies, p. 130.

They may not be the Galápagos, but only the most seasoned critics will be disappointed by the wildlife here. Off the coast of the Paracas peninsula, the Islas Ballestas house sea lions and birds, including Peruvian boobies, three types of cormorants, Inca terns, pelicans, turkey vultures, Humboldt penguins, and a number of other migratory species. There's no way you'll miss them; even if there were someplace for them to hide from the tour boats, the islands' coat of *guano* (bird droppings) would give them away. Every few years, locals collect the heaps of excrement and export it as a fertilizer. Other than these *guano*-collectors, nobody may set foot on the islands, so all visiting with the marine animals happens at a distance, from tour boats.

Before reaching the islands, most tours stop in front of *el candelabro*, a mysterious figure etched in the sand on the northeast side of the Paracas Bay. The three-pronged geoglyph is 177m high, 54m wide, and up to 60cm deep. Nobody knows who made the figure or what its significance was. Some believe that it dates back to the Paracas culture (circa 700 BC) and represents a hallucinogenic variety of cactus which was used in religious ceremonies. Others believe that it is related to the Nasca lines (see p. 142), which were probably constructed around 500 BC. Another theory posits that it wasn't created by any ancient culture, but rather by the pirates who raided the area in the 17th century: it either marked the location of buried treasure or was used as an orientating landmark. Supporting this theory is the fact that early explorers in the region never mentioned the figure in any of their reports; the first record of the geoglyph dates from 1863.

RESERVA NACIONAL DE PARACAS

Though many visitors choose to visit the Reserve as part of an organized tour—often combined with the Islas Ballestas tour to make a full-day excursion—it is also possible to visit the area alone. Colectivos leave regularly from the market area on B. de Humay in Pisco for the port of El Chaco, just outside the entrance to the reserve (30 min., s/1). Taxis from Pisco to El Chaco cost around s/8. You can walk the 5km from El Chaco to the museum—stick close to the water, and you'll probably see some flamingos in the bay—or just take a taxi (s/7, round-trip s/10). As there is no public transportation within the reserve, you'll have to rely on taxis to reach farther sights and beaches.

In 1975, the Reserva Nacional de Paracas was established to protect the ecological and archaeological splendor of the Paracas peninsula and the Islas Ballestas. The reserve extends down more than 25km of coastline with the highest concentration of marine birds in the world. The shores are ideal for camping, but rough water and a strong undertow preclude swimming. Tours to Paracas involve spending most of the afternoon on a bus with occasional photo stops; those short on time might stick with the morning Ballestas boat trip. After visiting the Tello Museum (see below), they stop at a bay where flamingos flock from April to December. Most tours also include a visit to **La Catedral,** a naturally eroded rock structure that attracts many birds and an occasional sea otter; allow time to explore some of Peru's prettiest beaches. Conclude with an hour or so in **Lagunillas,** a small port with fresh seafood restaurants.

The Paracas peninsula has a very long history; the first inhabitants arrived in the region about 9000 years ago and thrived from around 500 BC to AD 200. Their remains can be seen at the **Julio C. Tello Museum** in the reserve (s/2, students with ID s/1; open daily 9am-5pm), named for the man often referred to as the "father of Peruvian archaeology." Tello (1880-1947) led excavations at the sites of **Cerro Colorado** and **Cabezas Largas** in Paracas from 1924 to 1930, uncovering much of what we now know about the Paracas culture. Cabezas Largas gets its name from the unusual custom of skull deformation practiced by the Paracas culture (see **Beauty is Only Skull Deep,** p. 133). Both elongated and trepanned skulls are on display in the museum. However, the most impressive and important artifacts from Paracas culture have been taken to the Museo de la Nación and the Museo Arqueológico in Lima (see **Lima: Museums,** p. 85).

SOUTHERN PERU

BEAUTY IS ONLY SKULL DEEP

Archaeological investigations in the Reserva Nacional de Paracas have revealed that Paracas culture had some ideas about physical beauty and health that today might strike one as rather unusual. Skulls unearthed in the region suggest that infants of upper-class birth had boards and pads tied around their foreheads so that as they grew, their skulls became elongated. A long, sloped cranium probably signaled ethnic identity, beauty, and prestige. In addition to cranial elongation, the Paracas people also practiced an early form of brain surgery known as trepanation. The procedure involved removal of a piece of skull to relieve pressure on the brain following a severe head trauma. However, the large number of trepanned skulls discovered in Paracas suggests that this practice was used not just to cure head-trauma patients, but also to treat psychological or behavioral problems, perhaps by providing an escape route for evil spirits thought to be residing in the brain. Astonishingly, a large majority of the patients survived the procedures, as evidenced by the signs of healing around the holes.

Camping at Paracas is permit- and cost-free (except for the s/5 to enter the reserve). Although the reserve is safer than other beaches, never camp alone; the local police in Pisco recommend pitching tents in groups of four or more. Bring all supplies with you and don't leave anything behind. Because of the lack of public transportation, hire a taxi and arrange for a pickup the next day, or for a tour agency to leave you at the beach and let you return with them the following day. Alternatively, there are a few hotels just outside the reserve at El Chaco. Make a left at the end of the row of seafood restaurants to reach **Hostal El Amigo**, with clean rooms and a mellow rooftop terrace (doubles s/35, with bath s/50; triples with bath and a view s/60). Across the small plaza, **Hospedaje El Chorito** is clean and comfortable, although on the expensive side. Ask for a discount if your room doesn't have hot water or a view (☎ 665 024. Doubles s/70).

TAMBO COLORADO

Colectivos marked "Humay" leave from the corner of B. de Humay and 4 de Julio on Pisco, one block north of the market area, whenever full (1.5hr., s/2.50). Travel agencies in Pisco also organize tours during the high season with a minimum of three people (US$8).

About 45km from Pisco, Tambo Colorado is the site of some of the best-preserved Inca ruins on the Peruvian coast. Although they are not as frequently visited as the Islas Ballestas or Paracas Reserve, they're easily accessible from Pisco, either with an organized tour or on your own. The name alone says a lot about the 700-800 year-old complex. "Tambo" indicates that it was a resting spot for the Inca; in this case, he would spend five to seven days sunbathing on the banks of the Río Pisco when traveling between Cusco and the coast. The complex also included a market for merchants from the respective regions to trade their local wares. "Colorado" refers to the color of the buildings; traces of red, yellow, and white paint still adorn the adobe walls of these distinctly coastal buildings. (In the sierra, they fit rocks together like a a jigsaw puzzle. It never rains on the coast, though, so the ancient architects could use *barro*, a natural cement, to hold their buildings together.)

Just inside the gate is the **main courtyard,** where the Inca made business deals with important officials. To the left are the Inca's quarters, including the roped-off **dormitorio del Inca** (bedroom) and the adjacent **cusi** (Quechua for bathroom), into which water was poured from the opposite side of the wall so that the Inca could shower. Beyond are the smaller dorms of the Inca's closest male companions. Up the stairs to the second courtyard and to the left stand the similar quarters of the Inca's concubines; about 15 traveled with each at a time. The large spaces to the right of the courtyard contained the **granary** and **market**. (Open daily 7am-5pm. Gatekeeper Ferry Losa can give guided tours in Spanish; tip expected. s/3.)

ICA   ☎ 034

A major transportation hub, Ica (pop. 245,000) is capital of the Ica department. The city itself is dusty, hot, and crowded, and recent El Niño-related destruction hasn't helped matters much. The surrounding region, however, offers more pleasant diversions. In addition to the sandboarding at nearby Laguna Huacachina, the area is well-known for its wine and pisco bodegas—about 85 small *bodegas artesanales* and three industrial bodegas keep the region's bars well-stocked. The bodegas still make wine by stomping on grapes; the industrial bodegas have replaced traditional methods with impressive looking machines. The wine harvest takes place around the beginning of March and is celebrated throughout the city during the Fiesta Internacional de la Vendimia.

Ica is more dangerous than many of the surrounding areas. Exercise considerable caution with all of your belongings, especially around bus terminals. It is not uncommon for hats and glasses to be snatched right off tourists' heads.

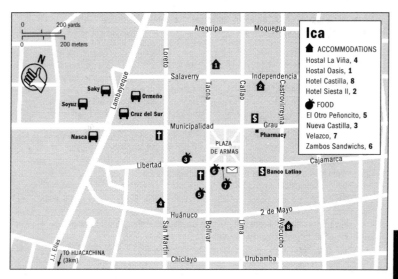

TRANSPORTATION

Airplanes: AeroCondor runs a small, private **airport** (☎522 424), from which you can take expensive flights over the Nasca lines. Inquire at **Inca Baths Tours,** Lima 171 (☎234 127), on the Plaza de Armas.

Buses: Transportes Soyuz, Matías Manzanilla 130 (☎224 138), sends buses to **Lima** (4hr., every 15min., 24hr., s/13). **Cruz del Sur** (☎223 333), on Lambayeque at Municipalidad, goes to: **Arequipa** (11hr.; 3, 5:30, 9, 10pm; s/30; imperial service 8:30pm, s/65); **Tacna** (16hr., 3:30pm, s/40; imperial service 6pm, s/70); and **Moquegua** (imperial service 7pm, s/70). **Ormeño** (☎215 600), at Lambayeque and Salaverry, serves **Nasca** (3hr., 10:45am, 3, 10:30pm; s/5) and **Lima** (4hr., every hr. 6:30am-7:45pm and 12:30am, s/10). **Transportes Saky,** on Lambayeque, across from the Ormeño station, sends buses to **Pisco** (1hr., every 20min. 6am-9:30pm, s/2.50). **Colectivos** also leave for **Pisco** or **Nasca** from the intersection of Lambayeque and Municipalidad whenever full.

ORIENTATION AND PRACTICAL INFORMATION

Ica is a fairly large city, but, as in most Peruvian cities, much of the activity centers on the **Plaza de Armas.** Most of the bus terminals are on **Lambayeque** near its intersection with **Municipalidad,** which leads to the north side of the Plaza de Armas. Streets running north-south change names after Municipalidad, while those running east-west switch names after **Callao,** which forms the plaza's eastern border.

Tourist Information: The **tourist office,** Jerónimo de Cabrera 426 (☎235 409), is a 15min. walk from the Plaza de Armas. Walk 9 blocks down Ayacucho and turn left at Cutervo; Cabrera is the street behind the gas station. Provides maps and basic info about the entire department. Open M-F 7:30am-6:30pm. **Inca Bath Tours,** Lima 171 (☎234 127), on the Plaza de Armas, also gives maps and leads city tours (3½ hr., 9:30am and 3pm, US$9).

Banks: Banco Latino, Cajamarca 178. Open M-F 8:45am-1:30pm and 4-7pm, Sa 9am-1pm. 24hr. Cirrus/MC **ATM.** There's a Visa/PLUS **ATM** on the Plaza de Armas at Bolívar.

Emergency: ☎105.

Pharmacies: Farmacia Ayacucho, Grau 112. Open daily 8am-11pm.

Hospital: Hospital Felix Torrealva Gutierrez, Bolívar 1065 (☎234 450).

Internet Access: ELW Services, Lima 276 (☎213 370), charges s/4 per hr. Open daily 9am-midnight.

Post Office: Serpost, Libertad 119-A (☎233 881), on the Plaza de Armas. Open M-Sa 8am-8pm.

▌ ACCOMMODATIONS

Most backpackers who spend the night in the area choose to snooze in Huacachina (see **Daytrips from Ica,** p. 138) rather than in Ica proper; most hotels, therefore, cater more to Peruvians than to international travelers. Still, staying in the city means more selection and a chance to get out of the tourist loop for a night.

Hostal Oasis, Tacna 216 (☎234 767). Oasis's rooms are open, airy, and clean, with TVs provided upon request. Most rooms have baths blessed with toilet paper. Singles s/25; doubles s/35; triples s/40.

Hotel Siesta II, Independencia 160 (☎231 045), feels like a 70s motel with its plaid blankets and plastic furniture, but given all the dust and dirt outside, its sterility is nothing to complain about. Breakfast included. Attached cafeteria and travel agency; laundry service available. Rooms with bath s/20 per person.

Hotel La Viña, San Martín 256 (☎218 188). Though slightly worn for the wear, La Viña offers five breezy floors of rooms with baths and electric hot water. Quarters on the upper levels are quieter, but brick-wall views are equally scenic from every floor. Singles s/25; doubles s/30; triples s/34; s/5 low season discount.

Hotel Castilla, Ayacucho 317 (☎233 712), has a secure front gate and an attractive plant-lined main passage, but rooms are quite basic and have only cold water. Singles s/10, with bath s/15; doubles s/20, with bath s/25.

▐ FOOD

▒ Zambos Sandwiches, Libertad 173 (☎228 074), on the Plaza de Armas, decorated with posters of the Doors and Madonna. Scrumptious hamburgers and chicken sandwiches. Combo meals with fries s/7. Open Su-Th 8am-midnight, F 8am-2am, Sa 8am-4am.

Velazco, Libertad 137 (☎218 182), next to the post office on the plaza. A bakery and a breezy cafeteria. A decent selection of local and international food at affordable prices. *Palta rellena* (stuffed avocado) s/5. Omlettes s/6. Open daily 8am-11pm.

Nueva Castilla Restaurant Café Bar, Libertad 252 (☎213 140). A more upscale, exclusively *criollo*-cooking establishment adorned with scattered abstract art. Dine inside or out on the front patio for s/10-17. Open daily noon-4pm and 7pm-midnight. Morphs into a disco/pub F-Sa 10pm-2am.

El Otro Peñoncito, Bolívar 255 (☎233 921), has an enormous selection of food (including vegetarian options) and alcohol, served by candlelight, sometimes to live music. Entrees s/12-24; house specials about s/5 more. Open daily 7am-midnight.

▗ SIGHTS

▒ MUSEO CABRERA. Brilliant scholar or deranged lunatic? You be the judge. Dr. Javier Cabrera, who holds a degree in medicine from Lima's prestigious Universidad de San Marcos, has been collecting petroglyphs (carved rocks) since 1966, and insists that these two jam-packed rooms are a "library of books in stone" rather than a museum. According to Dr. Cabrera, his collection of over 10,000 stones—ranging from baseball-sized rocks to boulders weighing over a ton—provide conclusive proof that the pre-Incas performed such amazing feats as brain transplants, the domestication of dinosaurs, and the discovery of the theory of relativity. Despite the fact that the locals who sold him the petroglyphs later confessed to carving them themselves, Dr. Cabrera insists on the authenticity of his collection—even though he has never had them carbon tested to determine their exact age. Nevertheless, the stones are, in the words of renowned Nasca Lines archaeologist Maria Reiche, "engraved by some of the most talented artisans of our time," and Dr. Cabrera's eloquent, scientific explanations of the rocks' significance are fascinating, to say the least. If you can't get enough, he sells his 1976 book, *The Message of the Engraved Stones of Ica*, for s/50. *(Bolívar 170, on the Plaza de Armas. ☎231 933. Open daily 9am-1pm and 4-8pm. s/10, includes a 1hr. guided tour (Spanish preferred). If no one is there, try Dr. Cabrera's home next door at Bolívar 178.)*

EL CATADOR. Though not the best maintained or most romantic of the Ica Valley's three major bodegas, El Catador is the most easily accessible spot to taste the wine- and pisco-making process. Free tours include a look at the small **Wine Museum,** an explanation of the winery's traditional wooden distillery instruments, and a taste of the various finished products: pisco and semi-dry *(seco)* red wine. If you come between the harvest months of January and March, kick off your shoes and help out with the grape stomping (don't worry, all foot grime is killed in the fermentation process). More a tourist attraction than a productive bodega nowadays, the complex also houses a restaurant and a weekend disco. *(In the Subtanjalla district, 5km north of the city center, a 15min. drive. Taxis s/5, colectivos s/1. Tours in Spanish, and occasionally English daily 10am-9pm. Free. Restaurant open daily 10am-6pm.)*

MUSEO REGIONAL MARIA REICHE DE ICA. This museum has a small but interesting collection of artifacts from the region, including a "bioanthropology hall" with mummies and deformed and trepanned skulls. Many exhibits have English explanations. Behind the museum is a 1:500 scale model of the Nasca lines. *(On the 8th block of Ayabaca, a short taxi ride (s/2) from the Plaza de Armas. ☎234 383. Open M-Sa 8am-7pm, Su 9am-6pm. s/5; camera permit s/4.)*

OTHER SIGHTS. Honoring Ica's patron saint, the neoclassical **Sanctuary of Luren** stands out among the city's primarily colonial-style cathedrals. Built in 1556, the church predates the founding of the city of Ica by seven years—back then, it was just the settlement of Villa Valderve. *(On the 10th block of Ayacucho, at Piura.)* Surrounded by ancient *huarango* and date palm trees 4km from Ica, the village of **Cachiche** is famous for its legendary *brujas* (witches), beautiful sorceresses with the power to cure illness and cause grievous bodily harm. Though a few folk healers still practice there today, there are no tourist-oriented sights in town. *(Taxis s/5.)*

A CASE OF MISTAKEN IDENTITY

Pisco sours may go down easy, but the history of the drink hasn't been such a smooth ride. As native as pisco may seem to Peruvians today, the pre-Columbian societies actually didn't have this white grape. It was the Spanish, scouring the Peruvian coastline in the early 1500s in search of the right spot to cultivate the home wines they missed so much, who deemed the dry, fertile Ica Valley vine-worthy. The powerful brandy (at 45 proof, stronger than rum or vodka) was invented later in the century—not as a drink, but as a disinfectant for the conquistadores to treat their wounds. Until one day when there was nothing else to imbibe...before long, the Spanish settlers wanted to send their new concoction home to be sampled by friends and family! And when the first barrels went out, they were stamped with the name of the port from which they departed—Pisco. When the liquor arrived in Spain, the name on the barrels stuck, despite the fact that pisco had been born and bred in the Ica Valley. Iqueños held a grudge for years, but nowadays they have a bigger problem on their hands. Chilean cultivators have far surpassed Peruvians in pisco production and export, and many are now promoting the drink overseas as their own home-grown invention.

DAYTRIPS FROM ICA

HUACACHINA

Taxis travel the 8km from Ica in 10min. (s/3). Colectivos leave from the corner of Munici-palidad and Lambayeque whenever full (15min., s/1).

Surf's up! But hey, where are the waves? At Huacachina, the sport of choice is **sandboarding,** an exhilarating experience that will leave you covered in sand and gasping for breath. Rent sandboards (available at the slopes and at Hostal Rocha; s/2 per hr., s/10-15 per day) and get some instruction (s/3 per hr.). Then spend the next 30-40 minutes huffing and puffing up the enormous dunes, stick your feet in the loops, and take off down the steep slopes. Be sure to bring plenty of wax (included with sandboard rental); thrill-seekers who can't muster up sufficient speed to make it down the dunes may find the whole experience anticlimactic. As tempting as the panoramic vistas may be, don't bring your camera, as there have been a number of **armed robberies** at the top of the dunes. Rental agencies can provide a safe place to lock up valuables, including watches and wallets. Those looking for relaxation can lounge around **Laguna Huacachina,** a small lake that supposedly has curative properties; locals sometimes swim in it, though the water is not particularly inviting. You can rent pedal boats (s/6 per 30min.) or row boats (s/5 per 40min). After the adventure, wash off in the lukewarm showers past Restaurante Moran (s/1 per person). A clean alternative is the swimming pool at the very fancy **Mossone Hotel** (☎213 630), which they'll let you use for s/15—sometimes they throw in a complimentary sandwich and drink.

Most backpackers find a haven at **☒Hostal Rocha,** the huge old house behind the Mossone with big rooms, even bigger lounging terraces that almost look onto the lake, and free kitchen and bike use. They also rent sandboards. (☎222 256. Rooms s/10 per person, with hot water bath s/12, with balcony s/15). By the lagoon, the (not so) **Gran Hotel Salvatierra** has basic rooms with cold-water baths (☎232 352. Rooms s/10 per person). **Camping** by the lake is free, but lock up your things at one of the sandboard rental agencies for the night.

OCUCAJE

Blue sedans serve as colectivos to Ocucaje (30min., s/2.50). They leave from one block east of the Plaza Barranca whenever full. From the Plaza de Armas, walk two blocks up Cajamarca, then turn right onto La Mar and continue another three blocks.

Meaning "between hills" in Aymara, Ocucaje could also be described as "in the middle of nowhere." A 30-minute drive from Ica (including some off-road maneuvering through sand dunes), the small desert town is best known for its **winery,** the most traditional and scenic of Ica's three industrial bodegas. In addition to the standard pisco and *cachina* (wine aged for only half of the normal 25-28 days), the Ocucaje winery has produced a variety of white and red wines, dry and sweet, since 1898. Some of their older wines have been aging since 1940. They offer a tour of the winery with wine sampling. (1hr. tours leave M-F 11am and 3pm, Sa noon. s/10 per person.) Ocucaje also boasts the a beautiful **Hotel Ocucaje** (☎408 001; fax 408 003; email rubitours@ocucaje.com; www.ocucaje.com), next door to the winery, featuring a large, inviting swimming pool, horseback riding, a tennis court, ping-pong, foosball, and pool tables. All-inclusive package deals, including a tour of the winery (with sampling), are worth it if you can afford to splurge (2 nights with food US$100-130 per person). Even for non-guests, the hotel offers a unique way to get the adrenaline pumping—one-hour stints on **areneros** (four-wheel-drive dune buggies) over dunes as high as 25m, with a couple sandboarding runs thrown in. (US$25. Trips leave daily every 1½hr. 8am-5pm. Reservations recommended.)

PALPA
☎ 034

There's a legend that the ancient inhabitants of Palpa once captured the sun and would only agree to release it on two conditions: that it would always shine on Palpa, and that the town's oranges would be the best in the country. It seems the sun kept its promise on both counts; Palpa is now known as "*la tierra del sol y las naranjas*" (the land of sun and oranges). Yet almost no tourists stop in Palpa. Palpa officials are hoping this will change as the town develops more of a tourism infrastructure, and indeed, it is not without attractions—the town publishes a map marking 28 sights that might be of interest to travelers, including geoglyphs (lines in the earth) and petroglyphs (lines in rock) that archaeologists consider to be nearly as important as their counterparts in Nasca. If you don't believe it, check out Palpa's web page (www.concytec.gob.pe/palpa-ica/index.htm), which features photos and descriptions of the attractions.

The sights most worthy of a visit are the **Petroglifos de Chichictara,** anthropomorphic figures carved into volcanic rocks scattered across a mountainside 11km east of Palpa. The petroglyphs are believed to be the work of the Charin, a pre-Paracas culture, and have various astrological and religious meanings. Go with a knowledgeable guide who can explain the significance of the different designs and symbols; ask in the Municipalidad building on the Plaza de Armas, or call ahead to make arrangements (☎404 256. "El Profesor" Pedro Giurfa Fuentes has been highly recommended). Also impressive are the **Líneas de Palpa,** constructed between 100 BC and AD 600, which, like those in Nasca, were also studied by Maria Reiche. Flights over the lines have been suspended ever since a plane crash in 1987, but the **Reloj Solar,** a large, double-lined spiral, possibly used as a sun dial, is visible from a *mirador* (lookout spot) 3km from town (taxis recommended rather than the steep climb by foot, s/4). Outside Palpa, you can also visit the lost city of **Huayuri,** ruins from the Nasca period with influences from the Paracas culture. At its entrance stands **El Arbol Milenario,** a famous *huarango* tree that is over 1000 years old and has come to serve as a symbol of ancient medicine. Full-day tours of all the sites, including transportation and guide, run around US$40, whether arranged in Palpa or through an agency in Nasca.

Colectivos to Palpa (45min., s/2.50) leave from in front of the Ormeño station in Nasca whenever full. From the north, any vehicle heading to Nasca passes through Palpa. Palpa's food and accommodation options are somewhat limited. The **Hostal San Francisco,** Lima 181, one block north of the Plaza de Armas, offers simple rooms and cold-water baths. (☎404 043. Singles s/10; doubles s/15, with bath s/20.) On the next block is the comparable **Hostal Villa Sol,** Lima 200, with only common baths. (☎404 149. Singles s/8.) The best place to eat is the hospitable **El Monterrey,** on the Panamericana next to the Mobil station. (☎404 126. Open daily 6am-9pm).

NASCA
☎ 034

It's impossible to speak of Nasca without mentioning the Nasca lines; they're certainly the reason most tourists visit. And while its plenitude of hotels and services will make short stays comfortable ones, the shabby town of Nasca is not as spectacular as the nearby attractions. Since a 6.4 earthquake devastated the area in 1996, it seems that Nasca's residents have spent more time building up the tourist infrastructure than building up their own homes. It would be a mistake, though, to think that the lines are all that Nasca has to offer. The town is a convenient base for one of the most archaeology-rich regions in the country; indeed, Maria Reiche isn't the only scientist who came here and never left.

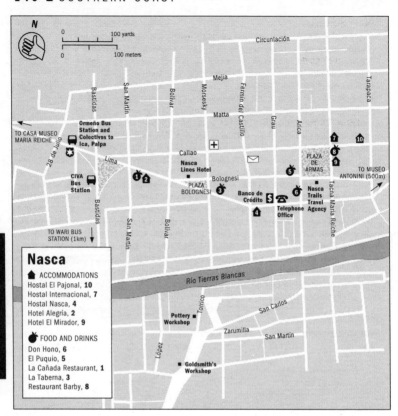

Nasca

⌂ **ACCOMMODATIONS**
Hostal El Pajonal, **10**
Hostal Internacional, **7**
Hostal Nasca, **4**
Hotel Alegría, **2**
Hotel El Mirador, **9**

🍅 **FOOD AND DRINKS**
Don Hono, **6**
El Puquio, **5**
La Cañada Restaurant, **1**
La Taberna, **3**
Restaurant Barby, **8**

TRANSPORTATION

Airplanes: The small **airport** in Nasca is primarily used only for flights over the Nasca lines, but it is occasionally possible to get expensive flights between Lima and Nasca on **AeroCondor,** Lima 187 (☎521 440).

Buses: Buy a ticket fast, especially for night buses to Arequipa, since they often sell out. **Ormeño** (☎522 058) serves: **Lima** (7hr.; 7:15, 9, 10:45am, 6:45, 11pm; s/18); **Arequipa** (9hr.; 3:30, 6, 8, 10pm, 1, 3am; s/35; bus cama (with bed) 10pm, s/60); **Ica** (3hr., 6 per day 7:15am-6:45pm, s/5); **Pisco** (3½hr., 4:15 and 6:45pm, s/10); and **Tacna.** On the far end of the *ovalo,* **Civa** (☎523 019) also sends buses to **Lima** (7hr., 10:45pm, s/20) and **Arequipa** (8hr., 11pm and 3am, s/35; *servicio ejecutivo* at midnight, s/45). **Transportes Wari** (☎523 746), a 5min. taxi ride on the road to the airport, sends buses on the much-improved and now safe road to **Cusco** (18-22hr.; 4, 6, 11pm; s/50). **Colectivos** to **Ica** (2½hr., s/5) via **Palpa** (45min., s/2.50), **Chala** (2½hr., s/10), and other locations leave from near the Ormeño station.

ORIENTATION AND PRACTICAL INFORMATION

The small city has a simple layout: most hotels and restaurants are on either Lima or Bolognesi, which splits off from Lima and heads to the Plaza de Armas.

Tourist Information: Unfortunately, there is no official tourist office in Nasca, so you'll have to rely on one of the private tour agencies. **Nasca Trails Travel Agency,** Bolognesi 550 (☎/fax 522 858), on the Plaza de Armas, gives information on sights and transportation without aggressively trying to sell their tours.

Tour Agencies: If you arrive in Nasca's bus station, be prepared to meet a dozen representatives of hotels and tour agencies. While it is often perfectly fine to trust them, there are always exceptions—people who lie about which agencies they represent, prices, their guides' ability to speak English, and tour availability. Even reputable agencies have been known to charge different prices for the same tour, depending on how much cash a customer seems to have. Ideally, you should go personally to the agencies' offices and speak to the owner and to other backpackers who have taken the tour. Only four of Nasca's tour companies are officially registered; three are listed below. **Alegría Tours,** Lima 168 (☎/fax 523 775; email alegriatours@hotmail.com; www.nazcaperu.com), run by the same owner of the Hotel Alegría next door, runs the most varieties of tours to nearby sights. Try to make arrangements directly through friendly owner Efraín Alegría, who speaks several languages including English, Hebrew, French, and German. They also show a Time/Life video about the lines every morning and night. **Nanasca Tours,** Lima 160 (☎/fax 522 917; email nanascatours@yahoo.com), is a fairly new agency run by the owners of the La Cañada restaurant. People who sign up for tours here receive a complimentary pisco sour. **Nasca Trails Travel Agency,** Bolognesi 550 (☎/fax 522 858; email nasca@correo.dnet.com.pe), on the Plaza de Armas, is a helpful, straightforward agency. Cockney-accented owner Juan Tohalino Vera lived in England for many years.

Currency Exchange: Banco de Crédito, at Grau and Lima, changes AmEx traveler's checks and gives Visa cash advances. Open M-F 9:30am-1:15pm and 4:30-6:30pm, Sa 9:30am-12:30pm. It also has a 24hr. Visa/PLUS **ATM,** the only ATM in town. There are plenty of **money changers** wandering the streets.

Police: (☎522 442), on Lima, across from the Ormeño station.

Hospital: Hospital Apoyo de Nasca (☎522 586), on Callao at Morsesky.

Telephones: Local and international calls can be made from the **Telefónica del Perú booths** around town. Phone services at the **Telefónica del Perú** office, Lima 545 (☎523 758; fax 523 757). Open daily 8am-10:30pm.

Internet Access: The **Hotel Alegría** and **La Cañada Restaurant** (see below) offer Internet access (s/5 per hr.). Get a cheaper connection at **Informática San Isidro** (☎522 349), at Arica and Lima, 2nd fl. (s/4 per hr.). Open daily 8am-1am.

Post Office: Fermín del Castillo 379 (☎422 016). Open M-Sa 8am-8pm.

▛ ACCOMMODATIONS

For those in a hurry, it's possible to arrive in Nasca early, take a flight over the Nasca lines, tour the cemetery, and leave town that evening. However, you'll get a better deal if you arrive in town the night before.

▩ **Hotel Alegría,** Lima 168 (☎/fax 522 444; email alegriatours@hotmail.com), is the most popular option among budget travelers—so popular that they recently opened a second branch, **Hotel Alegría II,** across from the Ormeño station. If you take a tour with Alegría Tours you can use the hotel's services—including a luggage storage room, hot shower, Internet access, and book exchange—even if you don't spend the night. Clean and comfortable, and the pleasant garden courtyard is a great place to hang out while you wait for a bus. Rooms s/10 per person, with bath s/20, with bath and TV US$10.

Hostal El Pajonal, Callao 911 (☎521 011), 1 block from the Plaza de Armas. Decorated with old velvet sofas and lots of bamboo, El Pajonal provides a welcome respite from aggressive travel agents. Small kitchen and laundry areas. Free luggage storage. Singles s/15; doubles with bath s/25; triples with bath s/35.

Hostal Internacional, Maria Reiche 112 (☎522 744). Internacional's interior rooms are less attractive than their bungalows, but they're also less expensive. All well-kept rooms have baths; bungalows also have TVs. Laundry service. Restaurant. Single bungalows s/45; double bungalows s/60; single interior rooms s/25; double interior rooms s/35.

Hostal Nasca, Lima 424 (☎/fax 522 085), has basic concrete rooms and bare-bones common bathrooms. The owners are congenial and the atmosphere calm, maybe because there's no common room to congregate in. s/10 per person; breakfast s/4.50.

Hotel El Mirador, Tacna 436 (☎/fax 523 741), the unmistakable modern building on the Plaza de Armas, has a sterile, luxury-class feel and a rooftop restaurant with a view. All rooms come with TV, fan, phone, hot-water bath, and some of the most comfortable beds in Nasca. Breakfast included. Singles s/40; doubles s/60.

◖ FOOD

Plenty of Nasca's restaurants cater to tourists, which means a good selection, but also relatively high prices. Places that offer affordable set *menús* (s/5) are still common, though.

La Cañada Restaurant, Lima 160 (☎522 917), next to the Hotel Alegría, builds romance with a thatched roof and live Peña music Th-Su at 10pm. Entrees aren't cheap (s/15-25), but they come with a complimentary pisco sour (though you may have to ask for it). Open daily 6am-11pm.

La Taberna (☎521 411), on Lima between Morsesky and Fermín de Castillo, serves a wide selection of pastas, meat, and fish (*menú turístico* s/8.2) in a dining room with walls covered in multilingual graffiti (look for the green "LG 2001"). Grab a marker and add your own signature or sketch of the Nasca lines. Open daily 8am-3pm and 6-11pm.

El Puquio, Bolognesi 481 (☎522 137). This popular pizzeria serves creative pies—try a "*hawayana*" (ham, pineapple, and peach; medium s/17.5). Open daily 12:30-11:30pm.

Don Hono, Arica 251 (☎523 066), just off the Plaza de Armas. A small, simple spot that serves only the freshest fruits and fish. Don't pass up their personal-sized pitchers of juice (made with mineral water; s/2.5). Fruit salad with yogurt, honey, and cereal s/3; catch of the day around s/10. Open daily 8:30am-10pm.

Restaurant Barby, (☎522 363), at Tacna and Callao, at the northeast end of the Plaza de Armas. This no-frills establishment is popular with locals, and for good reason—it achieves tasty, filling *menús* (including soup, entree, and hot drink) for only s/2.5. Not vegetarian-friendly. Open M-Sa 6am-2pm and 4-8pm, Su 6am-4pm.

◉ SIGHTS

THE NASCA LINES

Flights leave regularly throughout the day on 3-5 person planes. You can arrange a trip either at the airport or through a group in town, for about the same price. It's best to go in the morning, as the cooler air means a smoother ride. Flights 35-45min. US$30 per person. Departure tax s/5. If you don't have the money—or just want a different perspective, you can see two of the figures from a mirador on the Panamericana, built by Maria Reiche herself in 1976. Take any northbound bus or colectivo out of Nasca, 15min., s/2; taxis s/10.

Etched into the desert over 1000 years ago by clearing away the surface rocky soil to reveal the white-colored dirt underneath, these curious figures have become Peru's second-biggest tourist attraction—in 1994, they were named a UNESCO World Heritage Site. The lines, which have been attributed to both the Paracas and the Nasca cultures, are best described as **geoglyphs,** hundreds of squiggles and drawings that represent birds, hands, monkeys, sharks, spiders, flowers, and elongated trapezoids. The desert surface has stayed nearly unchanged, thanks to its unique thermal air cushion and its position in one of the driest places on earth, with only a few minutes of rain each year; some conjecture that even a footprint in this desert would survive 1000 years. Most amazingly, the designs extend hundreds of feet in length, making them indiscernible except from above. So it was that the lines only gained international attention in the 1930s, by which time one of the ancient lizards had already been cut in half by the Panamericana.

Since then, though, it seems like everyone's advanced a theory about the purpose of the lines. The most esteemed authority on Nasca is **Maria Reiche** (see Our Lady of the Lines, p. 144), who lived at the site for over 50 years, and believed that the lines were intended to map the movements of **celestial bodies** as a way of directing land cultivation. She posited that the Nasca culture used long ropes and sophisticated mathematics to create their extraordinarily straight figures and magnify their designs to a gargantuan scale. Some designs seem to depict constellations, and Reiche demonstrated that many lines point toward where the sun and moon would have risen and set 1000 years ago. However, several scholars have shown that this kind of correspondence doesn't occur frequently enough to be statistically significant. The British documentary-maker Tony Morrison has championed the theory that Nasca was a predecessor to the extensive Inca zodiac system, or **ceque.** The Incas conceived a great conceptual wheel centered on the Qorikancha in Cusco (see p. 105), with sight lines radiating out towards the horizon. Each line ran through some sacred spot, or **huaca.** Similarly, the Nasca lines may have delineated shrines of great importance. Anthropologist Johan Reinhard, best known for his work in the Arequipa area (see p. 390), believes that the lines were connected to a **mountain/water/fertility cult,** and that the straight paths led to spots where fertility rites were performed. Each of the animal figures relates to water. Reinhard argues that their artists meant for them to be seen by deities residing on the mountain top. Viktoria Nikitzki, who worked with Maria Reiche for many years, gives nightly **lectures** about these theories with a scale model of the Nasca lines, as long as at least four people show up (San Martín 221, 1hr., 7pm, s/10).

The incredible notion that an ancient people with no aeronautical technology would spend so much time and energy constructing something they would never be able to see has led some observers to other hypotheses. In 1969, Erich von Daniken asserted that the lines were actually constructed by extraterrestrial life forms who wished to mark a landing site for their aircraft. Since then, many have regarded Nasca as an other-worldly energy center, attracting mystics who sometimes try to camp directly on the lines in order to absorb some of their power. (This is prohibited, not to mention foolish and irresponsible. Driving or walking over the lines will help erase them permanently.) Critics of the alien theory include those who are offended by the assumption that the indigenous people could not have had the intelligence to build the formations themselves. Others argue that the lines were not meant for mortal eyes; they were drawn at their huge size as a direct message for deities who, according to much pre-Columbian mythology, often peered down from above.

OTHER SIGHTS

CEMETERY OF CHAUCHILLA. Here you'll find mummies with bones and skulls bleached so white by the sun that they almost look fake. Nasca's dry climate has preserved the bodies—including the still-attached hair, skin, and cotton textiles on some—for over 1000 years. The bones' placement in the deep tombs is not quite as authentic. When *huaqueros* (grave robbers) looted jewelry and pottery from these tombs, they left the bodies scattered around the desert; only a few years ago did archaeologists place them back in the graves as they might have originally been found, crouched in the fetal position and facing east, toward the rising sun. *(Round-trip taxis s/30. Tours from Nasca US$10. Admission s/3.)*

CANTALLOC AQUEDUCTS. Built between AD 400 and AD 600, these ingenious underground canals tapped into subterranean rivers coming from the sierra in order to direct water to the fields of the dry Nasca Valley. They are still used by local farmers today. The blowholes located every few kilometers allowed people to enter the aqueducts in an annual cleaning ritual. Some guides allow tourists to climb down into the canals during the dry season (Apr.-Dec.), but low oxygen levels make this risky. While there are more than 30 aqueducts in the Nasca Valley, each beautifully lined with small stones, the Cantalloc is the most frequently visited. The nearby **Ruinas de Paradones** are well-preserved walls from an ancient administrative center. *(Round-trip taxis s/15. Tours from Nasca US$10. s/3.)*

OUR LADY OF THE LINES When German mathematician **Maria Reiche** went to Peru in the 1940s to work as the tutor of a diplomat's son, she hardly expected to make South America a permanent home. But when a colleague introduced her to the enigmatic **Nasca lines**—hundreds of enormous designs of animals, symbols, and abstract figures etched into the nearby desert—Reiche began to see a mystery so great, it would consume all of her energies until the day she died. Reiche spent years in the desert alone, eating little besides fruit and sleeping under the stars, during which she measured the lines and cleaned the debris obscuring them. She became the major advocate of the **astronomical calendar theory:** the lines—marking celestial paths or copying the designs of constellations—were used by farmers when planting their crops.

Besides wrestling with ancient puzzles, Reiche also tackled the threat posed by a number of unsympathetic interests. This mathematician-turned-archaeologist became Nasca's fiercest guardian, thwarting plans to irrigate the desert for agriculture, construct highways through the plain, or "reconstruct" the lines. Revenues from Reiche's published works supported research projects and hiring a team of guards to patrol the grounds and keep vandals out.

In June 1998, at the age of 95, Maria Reiche died of ovarian cancer, leaving many to wonder who could possibly step in to continue her work. Since then, the occasional disturbance of the lines by careless tourists and treasure hunters has heightened fears. Fortunately, the extraordinary nature of the woman and her mission did not go unrecognized among most locals. Reiche is regarded as a national hero—some have even suggested that the Nasca site be renamed the Reiche Lines.

CAHUACHI. A current center of attention in the archaeological community, the 24 sq. km Cahuachi was once the largest religious ceremonial center and pilgrimage site of the Nasca culture. The site was constructed between 500 BC and AD 200 and abandoned around AD 359, perhaps because of a strong earthquake. Which temples and pyramids are open to the public varies from month to month, as archaeologists generally rebury their excavations to protect them from the high winds in the area. Tours include visits to **Pueblo Viejo,** a residential settlement from the pre-Nasca Paracas culture (800 BC-AD 100), and the **Estaqueria,** a mysterious grouping of *huarango* tree trunks placed over adobe brick platforms. The two dominant theories about its function are that it was a ritual mummification site where dead bodies were dried, and that it served as some sort of a sundial. *(The only way to visit these sights is with a guided tour from Nasca, US$10.)*

MUSEO DIDÁCTICO ANTONINI. Even if you don't have time for any excursions, you can get a good taste of the archaeological and anthropological wonders of the region here. The museum, opened in July 1999, has excellent displays of ceramics, textiles, and other artifacts discovered by Italian archaeologists, as well as an authentic Nasca aqueduct in the back. *(Av. de la Cultura 600, a 10min. walk down Bolognesi from the Plaza de Armas. ☎ 523 444. Open daily 9am-7pm. s/10.)*

OTHER SIGHTS. Organized tours from Nasca often include a visit to a **pottery workshop** and a **goldsmith's workshop,** which some tourists find quite interesting and others find too commercial. The **Casa Museo Maria Reiche,** on the Panamericana 26km north of town, is the local legend's former home. Her body's buried in the back, and there is also a small collection of charts and artifacts. About three hours out of town, the **Pampas Galeras Reserve** is one of the best places in Peru to see vicuña. True lovers of the cameloid won't want to miss the Vicuña Festival held there at the end of June. *(To get there, hop on an early bus heading north to Puquio or Cusco, or take a guided tour from Nasca, US$35.)*

CHALA AND PUERTO INCA ☎054

Three hours south of Nasca, Chala is basically a one-road town (the one road being the Panamericana) with a large, clean beach. Just north of the town is Puerto Inca, home to some remarkable Inca ruins overlooking the ocean, relatively unknown among tourists but well-loved among regional archaeology buffs. As the name implies, this was an Inca seaport; constructed from AD 1300 to 1500, it also served as a ceremonial center and a favorite resort of the Inca. A road (still visible in places) connected it to Cusco, 240km away, with runner stations every few kilometers so that messages and supplies, including fresh fish, could speed between the coast and the highlands. The small circular caves around the complex, called *chullpas*, were used to store fish and agricultural products. Getting to the ruins from Chala, 10km downhill, can be pricey.

Colectivos to Chala (2½hr., s/10) leave from the *ovalo* in Nasca, in front of the Civa station, whenever full. Buses coming from the south along the Panamericana also pass through town. To catch a **bus** or colectivo out of Chala, wait in front of the gas station *(grifo)* at the north end of town. **Taxis** and **combis** to the ruins, which depart from the market area across from the Hotel de Turistas, demand s/ 10-15 each way. If arriving from the north, it's easiest to get off at the turn-off to the ruins, then walk the 2km from the highway. Today the small village next to the ruins is gone, and in its place is the resort-like **Hotel Puerto Inka,** with comfortable rooms and plenty of amenities, including water sports, and prices not *too* far out of budget travelers' range (☎/fax 272 663. Rooms US$24 per person, including food). In Chala, there are several less expensive places to stay, including the basic **Hostal Grau** (☎501 009) and **Hostal Evertyh** (☎501 095), both with ocean views and cold-water bath (rooms s/10-15 per person), though Grau also offers a cafeteria and kitchen. There are a number of good seafood restaurants across from the Hotel de Turistas; **Restaurant Chimoni** serves big portions. (☎501 017. Entrees s/9-14. Open daily 7am-4pm and 7-9:30pm.)

CAMANÁ ☎054

Another three hours down the Panamericana will bring you to Camaná, a much bigger town with nice beaches nearby at **La Punta**—to which Arequipan youths flock during the summer months of December-March. Locals, however, take more pride in their gastronomical than their recreational achievements. Camaná's soil produces the highest amount of rice per hectare in the world, a feat celebrated at the **Festival de Arroz** in mid-February. The even more boisterous **Festival de Camarón** (shrimp festival) takes place on the second Sunday in November. Proud *camanaños* also never fail to mention that their town was the first Spanish settlement south of Lima, founded on November 9, 1539.

The main streets in Camaná are **Lima** and **Mariscal Castilla,** neither of which borders the fairly quiet **Plaza de Armas.** Transportes Flores, Lima 319, sends **buses** to and from Arequipa (3hr., every hr. 4:30am-6:30pm, s/7). The Ormeño office, Lima 346 (☎571 376) serves as the stop for buses to: Lima (12hr., s/35); Nasca (6hr., s/ 20); and Arequipa (3hr., s/6). **Tourist information** is available through the Relaciones Públicas department of the Municipalidad building on the Plaza de Armas. (☎571 044. Open M-F 7:30am-2pm.) However, the real expert on all things local is Augusto Mogrovejo Argote, who works in **Bazar Librería D'Amory's,** Piérola 256, just off the Plaza de Armas. (☎571 135. Open daily 8:30am-1:30pm and 4-9:30pm.) The **Banco de Crédito,** also on the plaza, changes dollars and traveler's checks and has a 24hr. **Visa/PLUS ATM.** (Open M-F 9:15am-1pm and 4:30-6:30pm, Sa 9:30am-12:30pm.) **Emergency:** ☎105. **Police:** Castilla 600 (☎572 988). **Post office:** Castilla 223. (☎571 157. Open M-Sa 8am-1pm and 4-7pm.)

During the summer, there are plenty of fun places to stay and eat by the beach at La Punta (see below). The rest of the year, however, the beach area is deserted, and it's better to stay in Camaná. The **Hostal Plaza,** 28 de Julio 317, on the Plaza de

Armas, has comfortable rooms with TV and hot-water bath, as well as a rooftop restaurant. (☎571 051. Breakfast included. Rooms s/20 per person M-F; weekend prices are higher.) The cheaper **Hotel Lima,** Lima 306, has simple but clean rooms and electrically-heated showers. (☎572 901. Singles s/12, with bath s/15; doubles s/20, with bath s/25.) One of the best places to eat in Camaná is **Pollos Willy,** Lima 137, which serves delicious chicken and anticuchos (☎571 028. Combo meals with fries and salad s/6. Open daily 4pm-midnight).

NEAR CAMANÁ: LA PUNTA

Colectivos to La Punta (15min., s/0.5) leave from Camaná's market area, one block west of Lima, and also pass through the Plaza de Armas; those going back to Camaná are marked "El Chorro." Taxis travel the 6km for s/3. La Punta also has a Transportes Flores office, where buses stop on their way to Arequipa (3hr., every hr. 4:30am-7:30pm, s/7).

But why stay in Camaná during the summer, when **La Punta** gets right to the point—non-stop beach merriment, day and night. The water is better for swimming than surfing, and the crowds grow sparser north of the main strip. The big man of the beach is Sr. Hans, whose **Hostal-Restaurant Hans,** on the main strip, offers simple, shared-bath rooms; free use of umbrellas, showers, dressing rooms, and lockers even to non-guests; and boogie board (s/10 per hr.) and surfboard (s/15 per hr.) rental. (☎572 288. Rooms s/15 per person.) The quality of the quarters, however, gets better around Plaza Grau to the north, where **Santa María del Mar Hostal** offers a pristine, scenic setting. (☎572 553. Doubles s/30, with bath s/40.) At any hostel, reservations are a good idea during the summer, especially if you want to stay over the weekend. Also on Plaza Grau, **El Cangrejo** serves seafood with a criollo twist. (☎572 359. Entrees s/10-15. Open daily 10am-9pm.) Nightlife only gets going on weekends, but once it starts, it doesn't stop until dawn. There are a number of bars around Plaza Grau, near three of La Punta's most popular **discos** (often with live music)—El Cangrejo, **Blues Beach,** and **Cálido.** (All open F-Sa 10pm-5am.)

MOLLENDO

During the summer months (Jan.-Mar.), *arequipeños* flock to Mollendo for its attractive beaches and calm currents. The rest of year, the small town (pop. 15,000) is more subdued, but can be a blessing for tourists looking to relax on quiet beaches or to explore the nearby Mejía bird sanctuary.

🖃🛪 TRANSPORTATION AND PRACTICAL INFORMATION. The city center has two plazas, **Plaza Grau** and **Plaza Bolognesi.** Grau is on the beach at the southern edge of town, and Bolognesi is two blocks up. Both are formed by the parallel north-south streets of **Arequipa** and **Comercio.** Buses and **colectivos** leave from Mariscal Castilla, north of Plaza Bolognesi. Santa Ursula, Castilla 824 (☎533 040), and Carpio, Castilla 818 (☎532 743), send buses to and from the terminal in **Arequipa** (2hr., every hr. 6am-7pm, s/5). A **taxi** ride downhill to the beach should cost s/1. **Banco de Crédito,** Arequipa 330, has a Visa/Plus **ATM** accessible on Comercio. (☎534 260. Open M-F 9:15am-1:15pm and 4:30-6:30pm.) Other services include: the **police** (☎534 242), on Comercio along Plaza Grau; **Farmacia Milagros,** Arequipa 374 (☎534 601; open daily 8am-10pm); **Serpost,** Arequipa 530 (☎532 264; open M-Sa 8am-1pm and 4-8pm); **Internet S.A.,** Comercio 235, on Plaza Bolognesi (s/3 per hr.; open daily 9am-11pm); and the **telephone office,** Arequipa 412 (☎535 045; open daily 6:30am-10:30pm).

🖙🛏 ACCOMMODATIONS AND FOOD. **Hostal Villa,** Castilla 366, four blocks uphill from Plaza Bolognesi, is the most attractive place in town—it even has a swimming pool. Inviting rooms have baths, telephones, cable TV, and large windows, but the added luxury comes at a price. (☎535 051. Singles s/69; doubles s/85.) **Hostal La Cabaña,** Comercio 240, 2nd floor, on the Plaza Bolognesi, is less elegant but offers better views from its rooftop terrace and similar amenities (though no pool)—every room has a bath, phone, and TV—for a humbler price. (☎/fax 534 671. Singles s/10, with bath s/40; doubles s/20, with bath s/40.) As far as food goes, fresh fish wins hands

SOUTHERN PERU

Here's your ticket to freedom, baby!

**Wherever you want to go...
priceline.com can get you there for less.**

- Save up to 40% or more off the lowest published airfares every day!

- Major airlines serving virtually every corner of the globe.

- Special fares to Europe!

If you haven't already tried priceline.com, you're missing out on the best way to save. **Visit us online today at www.priceline.com.**

down. There are lots of seafood restaurants around Plaza Bolognesi, but the best is **Restaurant Marco Antonio,** with two locations: the posh one at Castilla 366, in front of Hostal Villa (☎533 712; open M-F 11am-2:30pm and 7-10pm, Sa-Su 11am-10pm); and the more popular one on Comercio 258 (☎534 258; open M-Sa 8am-1am, Su 8am-7pm). *Corvina* (s/17) is the real delicacy, but the fish of the day (s/11) is tasty as well.

🔲 **ENTERTAINMENT.** Mollendo's **beach,** which extends in either direction from town, is inviting and convenient but fails to compare to the calmer, cleaner beaches to the south, such as **Mejía** (see below) and **La Punta,** 20min. beyond Mejía. **Nightlife** around the two plazas can get rowdy on summer weekends, especially when the young naval officers stationed nearby come to town. The drinking starts before the sun goes down and doesn't stop until it comes up again.

NEAR MOLLENDO: MEJÍA

Combis from Mollendo to Mejía (marked "El Valle") leave from the PetroLube gas station (grifo) next to the bus stop on Castilla (25min., s/0.9). The sanctuary is 4km beyond the small town of Mejía. Get off 1km past the sign marking the sanctuary, at the visitors center, the brown house on the left.

One of the most serene jewels of Peru's southern coast only a few years ago, today the warm waters of Mejía's beaches are just as calm, but the sand is dominated by the huge **Club Mejía** resort, where rich *arequipeños* come to relax between January and March. The exclusive club only lets members stay there, but you'll be saving *soles* anyhow by sleeping at the agreeable **Hostal El Chunchito,** Tambo 406, which is surprisingly quiet for being on the Panamericana. (☎555 061. Doubles with common bath s/25.) The resort does allow outsiders to eat and lounge at its restaurant, **El Sombrero,** the unmissable edifice shaped like a Panama hat. (*Ceviche mixto* s/17. Daiquiris s/6. ☎213 654. Open M-Sa 11am-4pm, Su noon-4pm.) El Sombrero is also the center of action after the sun sets, with a *discoteca* and Friday night karaoke. (Open Th-Sa until 1am, Jan.-Feb. only.)

The beauty of the Mejía beach, however, pales in comparison to the natural splendor of the nearby **Mejía bird sanctuary** (Santuario Nacional Lagunas de Mejía), 3km to the south. The 8km strip of unspoiled coastal marshlands is home to over 100 species of tropical birds, including the protected *parihuana* (Andean flamingo). The best time to visit is when the migratory flocks come en masse from the western coast of North America (Oct.-Nov.), a journey of over 2500 miles. The **visitors center** can provide guides to take you to the seven *lagunas* and various *miradores;* you're free to use their motorcycles, but otherwise you'll have to hire a taxi or arrange other transportation, as the sanctuary is too large to navigate by foot. Call ahead so that they'll have a guide ready. (☎555 003. Open daily sunrise-sunset. s/5. Guide service included; tip expected.)

MOQUEGUA ☎054

Moquegua (pop. 10,000) sits on the border of the driest desert in the world, the Atacama. This charmingly sleepy town lives up to its name ("Quiet Place" in Quechua), with cobblestone streets, a quaint and attractive center, and sun that offers respite from the coastal fog. Nearby ruins and a fascinating museum make Moquegua worth a visit for anyone interested in archaeology. At one corner of the plaza, the **Iglesia de Santo Domingo** holds the remains of 13th-century Italian martyr Santa Fortunata. (Open daily 6:30am-noon and 3-7:30pm.) Fireworks honor Fortunata's legacy every October 14.

📧🔲 **TRANSPORTATION AND PRACTICAL INFORMATION.** The **Plaza de Armas,** centering on an interesting fountain of water-spitting frogs designed by the famous Gustave Eiffel, marks the center of town. **Ayacucho, Moquegua, Ancash,** and **Tacna** border the plaza. Two blocks west of the plaza, **Piura** leads downhill to the traffic circle, and its name changes to **La Paz.** Ormeño (☎761 149) has its bus terminal at the traffic circle; the terminals for Cruz del Sur (☎762 005), Flores, and other bus companies lie a five-minute walk farther down La Paz. **Buses** go to: **Lima** (18hr., 6 per day 3:15-6:45pm, s/50-80); **Tacna** (2hr., 16 per day 5:30am-8:30pm, s/5-7); **Arequipa** (3½hr., 10 per day 6:45am-11:30pm, s/10-18); and **Ilo** (1½hr., 10 per day 5:30am-12:30am, s/4-5). The **Oficina de Información Turística,** Ayacucho 1060, hands out an informative Spanish brochure and map. (☎762 236. Open M-F 7:30am-4:30pm.) **Banco de Crédito,** Moquegua 861 (☎761 325), has the only 24-hour Visa **ATM.** (Open M-F 9:15am-1:30pm and 4:30-6:15pm, Sa 9:15-12:30pm.) Other services include: the **police,** Ayacucho 808 (☎761 271); the **post office,** Ayacucho 560, on the plaza (☎762 551; open M-Sa 8am-12:30pm and 2:30-6:30pm); and **Internet access** at Systems Service E.T.R.L., Moquegua 332 (☎763 758; s/3 per hr.; open daily 8am-11pm).

▐▞▛ ACCOMMODATIONS AND FOOD. Moquegua's accommodations come in all types. Higher on the spectrum is **Hotel Los Limoneros,** Lima 441, designed around a courtyard with a colorful flower garden. (☎761 649. Singles s/24, with bath s/42; doubles s/36, with bath s/55.) On the lower end is **Hostal Carrera,** Lima 320, with bare but sufficient rooms and cold-water common baths. (Rooms s/10 per person.) A comfortable medium, the **Hostal Piura,** Piura 255, offers handsome rooms with orthopedic mattresses, oriental rugs, big mirrors, baths, and cable TV. (☎763 974. Singles s/25; doubles s/35.) Moqueguan restaurants serve all the local specialties— *palta* (avocado), wine, and pisco—and a surprising number of restaurants also serve Italian food. **Choclo's,** Moquegua 686 (☎762 111), prepares *criollo* dishes (entrees s/8-10) as well as the popular "Pizza Hot" (with the works, s/18). (Open M-Sa 8am-10pm.) **Casa Vieja Pizzeria Bar,** Moquegua 326, serves delicious, well-priced Italian food, including vegetarian dishes, in a quaint old brick house. (Lasagna s/6. ☎761 647. Open M-Th 6-11pm, F-Sa 6pm-1am.)

▨ SIGHTS. The dry desert has preserved the possessions of earlier cultures— and sometimes their bodies—perfectly. The environment's conduciveness to the preservation of ancient remains makes Moquegua and the surrounding lands an area of intense archaeological interest. A good source of initial information on the region and its history is the **Museo Contisuyo,** Tacna 294, entrance on Moquegua on the plaza. Its interactive exhibit (with excellent signs in English) traces cultural development from as far back as the Archaic period, 12,000 years ago. (☎761 149. Open W-M 10am-1pm and 3-5:30pm, Tu 10am-noon and 4:30-8pm. s/1.50.) A trip to the museum may pique your interest for a visit to one of the nearby archaeological sites. Most interesting are the **Paleolithic caves of Toquepala;** a visit to the caves must be arranged through the museum. (Guided trips in Spanish s/50 per person, must arrange own transportation.) **Cerro Baúl** ("Storage Trunk Hill"), named for its boxy appearance, is a large hill 12km from town where the pre-Inca Huari constructed a city in the years AD 600-750. The city's ruins, which burned down mysteriously around AD 950, sit on the flat summit. This excursion, which involves an uphill hike, is most pleasant in the morning—it becomes very hot later in the day. (Frequent colectivos from the corner of Balta and Ancash, two blocks downhill from the Plaza de Armas, pass Cerro Baul; 30min.; s/1.5.)

ILO
☎054

The tankers and fishing boats one sees upon arriving in Ilo are emblematic of this busy industrial town's importance to the region; it's a major port not only for Peru but also for Bolivia, since Peru granted its landlocked neighbor a duty-free zone here in 1992. Two of the largest mines in South America are nearby, controlled by the Southern Peru Copper Corporation (SPCC), whose logo adorns many of the tankers in the bay. For the tourist, Ilo's a place to get away from the backpacker scene, eat fresh seafood, and watch the smoke curl out of fishmeal factories.

Buses arrive at the corner of Ilo and Matará. The **Plaza de Armas** lies two blocks downhill from the bus stop, the **water** is an additional two blocks. **Moquegua,** street of many hostels and restaurants, borders the Plaza de Armas. **Buses** go to: **Tacna** (2hr., 18 per day 6am-8pm, s/8); **Arequipa** (5hr., 12 per day 8am-8pm, s/10); and

Moquegua (1½hr., 16 per day 5:30am-midnight, s/5). The **tourist office**, Venecia 222, gives brochures and advice about the region. (☎781 347. Open M-F 7:30am-4pm.) **Banco de Crédito** (☎781 024), at the corner of Zepita and 28 de Julio, one block down from the plaza, has a 24-hour Visa **ATM**. Other services include: the **post office**, Marina Lino 311, a 10-minute walk from the town center (open M-Sa 8am-1pm and 4-7pm); and the **police**, Pichincha 327 (☎781 021), at Moquegua.

The best lodging value in town is the **Hotel San Martín**, Matará 325. This two-star, three-story hotel offers ocean views, spacious common areas, comfortable rooms with baths, and a pool in the summer. (☎781 082. Singles s/30; doubles s/40.) The busy **Hotel Paraíso**, Zepita 749, has more character but fewer amenities, though rooms are also very well kept. (☎781 432. Singles s/20, with bath s/35; doubles s/25, with bath s/45.) Seafood in town is about as fresh as it gets; try the *parahuela* (a pungent fish soup). **La Estancia**, Moquegua 445, doesn't have a fixed menu—just talk to the server about what's fresh, and they'll serve you a heaping plate of it at a reasonable price. (Catch of the day s/6-10. Open M-Sa 6pm-midnight.) **Los Corales**, Abtao 401, is generally considered the best restaurant in town, and although it's more expensive, it has a spectacular view of the water. (Entrees around s/18. ☎782 505. Open daily 11am-3pm and 6-11pm.)

The **Museo Eduardo Jiménez Gómez**, Moquegua 447, on the Plaza de Armas, displays artifacts of the pre-Inca Chiribaya, who lived in the area 1000 years ago. (Open Tu-Su 9am-8pm. s/6.) **Museo de Sitio El Algarrobal**, 6km to the east in the suburb of El Algarrobal on the main highway (taxi s/6), exhibits a larger collection of Chiribaya weavings and jewelry. (☎781 989. Open Tu-Su 9am-1pm and 2-5pm. s/10.) The **beaches** to the north and south of Ilo are much cleaner than the shoreline in town. The most popular, especially during the summer season (Dec.-Mar.), is the easily accessible Pozo de Lizos, 8km south of town (taxi s/8). To the north, the Waikiki and Platanales beaches are more remote (taxi 30min., s/20). Camping on all beaches is free, and no permit is necessary. Just before Pozo de Lizos, the **Punta de Coles Nature Reserve** hosts 6000 sea lions, a variety of aquatic birds, and many large reptiles. Access to the park is a little difficult; the park officials (☎781 191) are happy to open the reserve to tourists free of charge, but they need a few days notice to make arrangements.

TACNA   ☎054

Peru's southernmost city and principle crossing point into Chile, Tacna (pop. 170,000) lies only 36km from the border and actually became part of Chile when Peru lost it in the 1879 War of the Pacific. On August 28, 1929, Tacna's citizens voted themselves back into Peru, earning the city the nickname "Heroic Tacna." But Tacna's well-maintained streets, relatively high prices, and good health care probably all stem from Chilean influence. Few gringos stay more than a day in their rush to cross to Chile or pass deeper into Peru, but for those with a yen to explore or some time before crossing into Chile, the city and its periphery offer good shopping, hot springs, and remarkable petroglyphs.

▐ TRANSPORTATION

Flights: Aeropuerto Carlos Ciriani Santa Rosa, 5km south of town. Taxi s/10. **AeroContinente,** Apurimac 265 (☎713 042). To **Lima** (1½hr.; 1, 5:30, and 7pm; US$89).

Trains: The **Estación Ferroviaria** (☎724 981), at Albarracin and 2 de Mayo. Follow Blondell beyond the cathedral in the Plaza de Armas, turn right onto Cusco just before the railroad tracks, and continue 2 blocks. Trains are the slowest and most infrequently used way to get to **Arica, Chile** (1½hr.; M, W, F 6am; US$1).

Buses: Terminal, a 20min. walk north of the Plaza de Armas on Hipolito Unanue. Taxi s/2. Ormeño (☎723 292) has service to: **Lima** (20hr.; 1, 4, 7pm; s/40. *Servicio especial* 2pm, s/70); **Arequipa** (6hr.; 7am, 2, 9:30, 10pm; s/12); and **Moquegua** (2hr.; 7am, 2, 4pm; s/5). **Cruz del Sur** (☎746 149) also has a ticket office in town at Ayacucho

96, though all buses leave from the terminal to: **Lima** (standard 20hr.; 12:30, 6:30, 8pm; s/40; imperial 17hr., 3 and 5:30pm, s/70-110); and **Arequipa** (6hr.; 6:45, 10am, 1:30, 4:45, 9, 9:45pm; s/15) via **Moquegua** (2hr., s/6). **Flores** (☎726 691) has the most frequent service to: **Ilo** (2hr., 17 per day 5:30am-8pm, s/8) and **Arequipa** (6hr., 16 per day 5:30am-10:15pm, s/15) via **Moquegua** (2hr., s/8).

International Colectivos: Colectivo sedans to **Arica, Chile** (1hr., whenever full 5am-8pm, s/10) also leave from the bus terminal.

> **BORDER CROSSING: INTO CHILE**
> The only way to cross the border to Arica is in one of the giant 1970s American sedans that leave, when full, from the bus terminal (1hr., 5am-8pm, s/10). If the driver tries to overcharge you, be firm and point to the signs above the ticket counter. All you need is your passport, tourist card, a terminal departure tax ticket (s/1), and patience. Don't be alarmed if the driver takes possession of your passport during the ride; it's standard procedure for him to present all passports to customs. The worst time to cross is during the middle of the day when lines at the two immigration offices are longest. Expect your bags to be searched; the Chilean officials are meticulous. **Arica** is a lively, active coastal town well connected to Chile's transportation infrastructure. If you plan to move on immediately, ask the sedan driver to drop you off at the bus terminal. From there, buses depart for: **Santiago** (30hr., 10:30am-11pm, US$25-30) via **Iquique** (4hr., US$7), **La Serena** (24hr., US$20), and **Valparaiso/Viña del Mar** (28hr., US$25); **La Paz, Bolivia** (8hr., 3am, US$20); and **Buenos Aires, Argentina** (23hr., W 11pm, US$84). There is a Visa/MC **ATM** in the shopping complex next to the terminal. Arica has a wide range of accommodations, abundant seafood, and popular beaches, but be forewarned: everything is more expensive in Chile. It is wise to get rid of your *soles* before entering the country. Even Chilean wine is cheaper in Tacna than Arica.

ORIENTATION AND PRACTICAL INFORMATION

The main street in town, **San Martín** houses most of Tacna's tourist services. San Martín runs into the **Plaza de Armas,** where it splits at the cathedral into **Callao** and **Blondell.** Another major street is Bolognesi, parallel to San Martín and two blocks to the south. Hipolito Unanue, which intersects San Martín at the Plaza de Armas, runs north to the **bus terminal** and the Panamericana.

Tourist Office: (☎/fax 713 501), Blondell 50, 4th fl., in the municipal building behind the cathedral. Open M-F 7am-4pm.

Consulates: Chile (☎723 063), on Presbitero Andia at Albarracin, 100m past the train station. Open M-F 8am-1pm. **Bolivia,** Bolognesi 1721 (☎711 960), about 1km east of the Plaza de Armas. Open M-F 9am-noon.

Currency Exchange: Banco de Crédito, San Martín 574 (☎722 541), exchanges AmEx and Visa traveler's checks, gives Visa cash advances, and has Visa **ATM.** Open M-F 9:15am-1:15pm and 4:30-6:30pm, Sa 9:30am-12:30pm. There is a Red Unicard **ATM,** which accepts Visa, MC, and Maestro, at Banco Santander on Apurimac between San Martín and Bolívar. The best casa de cambio is **Cambios Tacna,** San Martín 612 (☎743 607). Open M-Sa 8:30am-8pm.

Markets: Shopping opportunities abound in Tacna. The most convenient public market is the **Mercado Central,** on Bolognesi at Paillardelli. Open daily 6am-8pm. But the mother of all Tacna markets is the rambling **Polvos Rosados,** on Pinto just past Industrial. Taxis s/2. Find everything from athletic shoes to chocolates, liquor to electronic goods, at prices 35-60% lower than in Lima. Open daily 8am-8pm.

Folice: Callao 121 (☎ 714 141), on San Martín at the Plaza de Armas.

Pharmacy: Inka Farma, San Martín 547 (☎ 746 821).

Hospital: Hospital Hipolito Unanue (☎ 723 361), on Blondell beyond the cathedral.

Telephones: Telephone office, San Martín 442 (☎ 728 157; fax 742 161). Open daily 7am-11pm. There are also Telefónica del Perú **pay phones** around the plaza.

Internet Access: *Tacneños* have no problem paying the local s/3 per hr., so the many cafes tend to be full, especially at night. **InfoRed Internet,** San Martín 735 (☎ 727 573), has a fast connection. Open daily 8am-midnight.

Post Office: Serpost, Bolognesi 361 (☎ 724 641). Open M-Sa 8am-8pm.

ACCOMMODATIONS

Tacna offers underwhelming accommodations at prices higher than in the rest of Peru, though many rooms include perks like baths with hot water. Most mid-range hotels are centered around the Plaza de Armas and up San Martín, while the bare-bones places cluster at the southern end of town, across Bolognesi. It can be hard to find a free room in mid-December, when Chileans arrive en masse to do their Christmas shopping.

El Sol Hospedaje, 28 de Julio 236 (☎ 727 711). In an Inca-like homage to the sun, this hotel centers on a courtyard with a translucent yellow plastic roof. Rooms with baths have balconies or big windows; those without are smaller and darker, but all are spotless and have cable TV. Singles s/20, with bath s/25; doubles s/30, with bath s/35.

Lido Hostal, San Martín 876-A (☎ 721 184). At least the basic rooms are well-maintained, the baths are hot, and the price is right. Often fills up later in the day. Singles s/20; doubles s/30.

Hospedaje Lima, San Martín 442 (☎ 744 229), presents some of the trappings of an elegant place: a red carpet leads up the stairs and beds have faux-leather headboards. Don't be fooled by first impressions, though; rooms aren't particularly luxurious. Adjoining restaurant. Singles with bath s/28; doubles with bath s/38; color TV s/5 extra.

Hostal Lider, Zela 724 (☎ 715 441), at the end of the walkway off San Martín between Vizquerra and Varela. Clean but unremarkable rooms in a quiet building with an emphasis on safety and solitude. Singles with bath s/25; doubles with bath s/40.

FOOD

Most of Tacna's restaurants cluster on the main drag, San Martín, just up from the Plaza de Armas. The regional specialty, *picante a la tacneña*, is a spicy mix of potatoes, beef, and *ahí* sautéed in oil. True to Tacna's position on the border with more cosmopolitan Chile, there are also lots of Italian restaurants, particularly on Libertad, the pedestrian street just before the 600 block of San Martín. The suburb of Pocollay is known for its excellent regional cuisine (taxis s/3).

El Viejo Almacén, San Martín 577 (☎ 714 471). The curved blue walls and plush seats may be ultra-modern, but food here is strictly traditional. *Criollo* and seafood entrees s/10-28. Large *menús* s/10-15. Open daily 7:30am-1am.

Café Genova, San Martín 649 (☎ 744 809). Where Tacna's most sophisticated come to mingle at outdoor tables on the hectic main street. Spend your last *soles* on elaborate salads (s/9-18) and exquisite pasta dishes (s/15-18). Open daily 8am-midnight.

Sebastiano's, San Martín 295, across from the cathedral. The smell of *anticuchos* (s/3) grilling in the window lures passersby into this intimate local favorite. The menu features purely *típico*, meat-intensive food—your 1st introduction or last goodbye to the wonder that is *lomo saltado*. Nothing over s/10. Open daily 7am-11pm.

⚑ SIGHTS

PLAZA DE ARMAS. The plaza features a fountain known as the **Pileta Ornamental,** designed by **Gustave Eiffel** (of tower fame) in the 19th century but only completed in 1955, and similar in design to the fountains Eiffel created for Buenos Aires, Lisbon, Paris, and nearby Moquegua (see p. 129). Facing the plaza, the neo-Renaissance **cathedral,** finished in 1854, is simple but elegant. The yellow interior displays a giant chandelier over the altar and small, round stained-glass windows lining the nave. *(Open mornings and evenings.)* On the other side of the plaza, an 18m high **commemorative arch** honors two heroes from the War of the Pacific: Miguel Grau and Francisco Bolognesi.

OTHER SIGHTS. The **Museo Ferraviario** consists of two exhibit rooms right along the tracks at the train station. It's debatable whether the newspaper clippings and retired train parts are worth the admission fee; it's more interesting to climb into the old locomotives on the other side of the tracks and explore. *(Knock at the green door on 2 de Mayo, to the right of the clock.* ☎ *215 350. Open M-Sa 7am-5pm. s/1.)* **La Casa de Cultura,** above the public library, displays cases with local pre-Inca artifacts and paintings representing the War of the Pacific, though without explanatory signs. *(Apurimac 202, at Bolívar. Open 9am-1pm and 3-6pm. Free.)* Francisco Antonio de Zela y Arizaga, the Peruvian patriot most famous for his voice (he shouted the first cry for independence in 1811), lived and died in the Casa de Zela, one of the oldest colonial houses remaining in Tacna, with a recently attached archaeological museum. *(Zela 542. Open daily 10am-1pm and 3-6pm. Free.)*

🎵 ENTERTAINMENT

Tacna has a few places to drink and dance. One is **La Taberna de 900,** San Martín 577, where old saloon doors and an antique cash register contrast with trendy splotched walls. They also offer some light bar food. (☎ 726 657. Open daily 11pm-1am.) **Monako's,** San Martín 781, is the most popular disco in town, but it only gets going around 2am. There's an 11-sided dance floor in the center and a mural of John Lennon on the wall. (Cover s/5. Minimum bar tab s/5. Open Th-Sa 7pm-6am.)

IN AREQUIPA WE TRUST Some *arequipeños* might argue that there's a mistake on the cover of this book, that the title should be *Let's Go: Peru, Bolivia, Ecuador—and Arequipa.* Many residents consider their department an independent nation, a sentiment that dates back to colonial times. While a mixed-race *mestizo* population emerged in other Peruvian cities during the Spanish occupation, Arequipa remained largely empty of *indígenas*—giving new meaning to the city's "La Ciudad Blanca" nickname. Colonial Arequipans felt themselves culturally removed from the northern and highland regions, and didn't hesitate to act when José de San Martín liberated their city in July 1821, one week before declaring the rest of Peru independent. In those seven days, *arequipeños* elected their own federal government, issued their own passports, and minted a new currency. Memories of that week of glory remain strong in the hearts of the city's residents; the Municipalidad still displays a list of the names of every citizen of La República de Arequipa who applied for a passport.

Even today, *arequipeños* refuse to blend in with the rest of Peru; they are infamous for their frequent objections to the management and internal abuses of the government in Lima. Historically, presidential candidates who have held overwhelming popularity in Arequipa have been defeated nationally. *Arequipeños* today joke that the two things a republic needs (besides independence) are an international airport and a local saint. But with Aeropuerto Internacional Rodríguez Ballón indefinitely suspending all flights to Chile, and Beata Ana de Los Angeles Monteagudo still lacking two miracles (see Santa Catalina Monastery, p. 158), it looks like Arequipa still has a long way to go.

⛰ DAYTRIP FROM TACNA

CALIENTES AND MICULLA

To get to Calientes or Miculla, catch a colectivo (45min., every 15min. 6am-7pm, s/1.50) from central Tacna at Leguea and Kennedy, about 1km north of the Plaza de Armas. Round-trip taxi s/25-30. Baths open daily 6am-6pm. s/8 per 30min.

The town of Calientes, 22km east of Tacna, rests in a valley warmer and sunnier than the city's. The town has eight private **thermal baths,** kept very clean and at a steaming 38°C. From the Miculla, you can walk 3km east to an area full of **petroglyphs,** where there are 400 rocks with over 2000 engravings of animals and people, estimated to be at least 1500 years old. To get there, you have to cross a 70m long and 1m wide suspended bridge—don't look down.

AREQUIPA AND AROUND

AREQUIPA   ☎054

Arequipeños take great pride in their city's rich and unique cultural and culinary traditions. Attracted by its warm climate, job opportunities, and excellent universities, Peruvians are moving to Arequipa en masse; the population has recently exploded, growing from 300,000 to over one million in the last 30 years. While this has resulted in some sprawling suburbs, the city's colonial center maintains its intimacy, which boasts several beautiful churches and the enormous, 16th-century Santa Catalina monastery. The historical center gains most of its charm from the colonial houses and churches made from *sillar*, a white volcanic rock, hence the city's nickname: "La Ciudad Blanca." Even before these dignified buildings were constructed, however, the Incas could tell that there was something special about this place; when they settled here nearly 600 years ago, they deemed the spot sacred for its nearby volcanos. Three of the fire-spewers are visible on the horizon from nearly everywhere in the city: El Misti (5825m), which is still active, Pichu Pichu (5664m), and the higher and extinct Chachani (6075m). The run-off from the peaks' icecaps create the headwaters of the mighty Amazon, thousands of kilometers away. At 2325m, Arequipa is well above the coastal fog of Lima, and many recently-arrived tourists come here to relax and acclimatize before moving on to the higher Cusco. The city is a convenient location from which to visit the nearby Colca and Cotahuasi canyons, two of the deepest in the world. The adventurous attempt trekking and rafting trips, while most are content just to view the canyon's depth and wildlife from *miradores.*.

 Although most of the city is safe during daylight hours, Arequipa has recently experienced a rash of **strangle muggings** at night. See the very-similar-to-this-one **box,** p. 98, for an explanation of strangle muggings. Men and women, even in groups, are advised to take taxis after dark and not to pay the driver until the front door of their hostel is opened.

⛐ TRANSPORTATION

Airplanes: The **Aeropuerto Internacional Rodríguez Ballón** (☎443 464) is 7km northwest of the *centro* and can be reached by taxi (s/5-8). **AeroContinente,** Portal 113 (☎204 020; fax 219 914), offers flights to: **Lima** (6 per day 7:45am-8:15pm); **Cusco** (7:45am); **Juliaca** (10:45am, 2:45, 4:45pm); and **Tacna** (6:30pm). **Tans,** Portal 119 (☎/ fax 203 517), goes to **Lima** (1 per day) and **Juliaca** (1 per day); and **LanPeru,** Portal 109 (☎201 100; fax 218 555), goes to **Lima** (3 per day) and **Cusco** (1 per day). All airline offices are located on the Plaza de Armas. Domestic one-way flights normally cost US$44, but last-minute prices can rise to US$59, and holiday fares to US$79. Despite its name, there are **no longer any international flights from Arequipa.**

SOUTHERN PERU

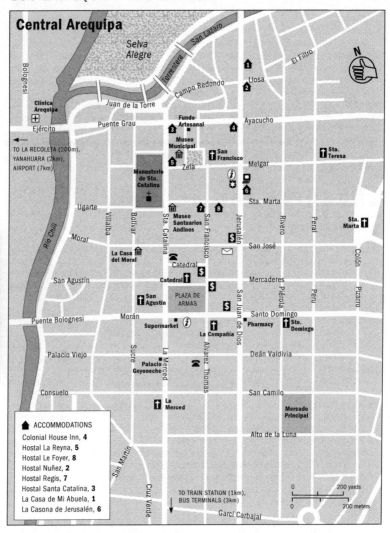

Central Arequipa

ACCOMMODATIONS
Colonial House Inn, **4**
Hostal La Reyna, **5**
Hostal Le Foyer, **8**
Hostal Nuñez, **2**
Hostal Regis, **7**
Hostal Santa Catalina, **3**
La Casa de Mi Abuela, **1**
La Casona de Jerusalén, **6**

TO TRAIN STATION (1km),
BUS TERMINALS (3km)

Trains: The **train station** (☎215 350), 1km downhill from the *centro,* can be reached by taxi (s/2 from the *centro*). Though buses are faster and cheaper, trains are safer and more comfortable, and chug to: **Cusco** (21hr., W and Su 9pm, s/40) with stops in **Juliaca** (9hr., s/18.50) and **Puno** (11hr., s/22). The most comfortable option is to take the Pullman car (with reclining seats) to Juliaca (s/30), then switch to economy class to Cusco (s/21.50). **Ticket office** open M-Tu and Th-F 7am-noon and 12:45-3:45pm; W and Su 8am-noon, 2-5pm, and 7-10pm; Sa 8am-noon. Travel agencies shouldn't charge more than a s/5 commission per ticket.

Buses: The bus terminals, 3km south of the *centro,* can be reached by taxi (s/3). The **Terminal** hosts the majority of bus companies, but long-distance or luxury coaches leave from the neighboring **Terrapuerto,** including all of the following buses: Ormeño (☎424 187) goes to **Lima** (13-15hr.; 7am, 3, 9pm; s/35; Royal class 12hr., 4 and

10pm, s/90) via **Nasca** (7hr., s/30) and **Tacna** (6hr.; 8am, 2, 4:30, 9:30pm; s/15). San Cristóbal (☎232 567) huffs up to **Cusco** (12 hr., 4pm, s/25) and **Puno** (8-10hr., 7am and 4:30pm, s/25) via **Juliaca.** Cruz del Sur (☎216 625) sends its land cruisers to **Lima** (17hr., 9 per day 8:30am-8:30pm, s/35; Imperial class 13hr., 4:30 and 7:30pm, s/70). All journeys from Arequipa require an **exit ticket** (s/1), available from booths inside the terminals.

🔲 🔟 ORIENTATION AND PRACTICAL INFORMATION

Arequipa feels much smaller than it really is, as most services of interest to the tourist are concentrated in the handsome and compact *centro antiguo*, the historical center of Arequipa that is home to colonial *sillar* buildings. The *centro* extends north from the **Plaza de Armas,** and has three major thoroughfares, which run parallel to each other and uphill from the plaza. If you're facing the **cathedral** in the plaza, **Santa Catalina** forms the left-hand border and runs past the **Santa Catalina Monastery** and beyond. The plaza is bound on the right by **San Francisco,** and hosts the largest concentration of tour agencies. Half a block north of the Plaza de Armas, just behind the church, the pedestrian walkway of **Catedral** contains some of the higher-quality souvenir shops. Beware—most streets change names east of Jerusalén or south of the Plaza de Armas, but the city's regular grid pattern prevents much confusion. There are two separate **bus terminals** located next to one another 3km to the south of the city center.

TOURIST, FINANCIAL, AND LOCAL SERVICES

Tourist Office: (☎211 021) on the Plaza de Armas, across from the cathedral. Offers maps and advice on how to get to nearby sites alone. Open M-F 8:30am-3:45pm.

Consulates: Bolivia, Mercaderes 212, office 405. (☎213 391. Open M-F 8:30am-3:30pm.) **Chile,** Mercaderes 202, office 402. (☎226 787. Open M-F 9am-2pm.) **UK,** Tacna y Arica 145 (☎241 340. Open M-F 8:30am-1pm and 2:30-6:30pm.)

Banks: Banco de Crédito, Morán 101 (☎212 112), a block away from the Plaza de Armas, has a VISA/Plus **ATM.** Open M-F 9:15am-1:15pm and 4:30-6:30pm, Sa 9:30am-12:30pm. **Banco Continental,** San Francisco 108 (☎215 060), one block uphill from the Plaza de Armas, offers identical services. Open M-F 9:15am-1pm and 4:30-6:30pm, Sa 9:30am-12:30pm.

ATMs: There are two clusters of Red Unicard ATMs; at **Banco Sur,** at the corner of Moral and Jerusalén; and next to the Plaza de Armas at San Francisco and Mercaderes.

Money Exchange: Vendors on the street offer the best rates. There are several *casas de cambio* on the first block of San Francisco. Most open daily 9am-7pm.

Markets: The hectic **mercado principal** is located indoors at the corner of Piérola and San Camilo, 2 blocks downhill from the Plaza de Armas and across San Juan de Dios. Here, you can purchase exotic fruit (piled 3m high), puppies, and fresh fish, but be especially careful of pickpockets. Open daily 6am-7pm. There are two **artesanía markets** in town, rife with woven and leather wares. The larger is the **Centro Artesanal Fundo El Fierro,** with its entrance on Grau between Santa Catalina and the alley leading to Parque San Francisco. Open M-Sa 9am-8pm. The **Casona Coronel Flores del Campo,** Portal de Flores 136, on the Plaza de Armas, also offers local foodstuffs. Open daily 10am-9pm. Stores selling high-quality but expensive **alpaca goods** can be found on Pasaje Catedral, the pedestrian street ½ block up from the Plaza de Armas.

Supermarket: El Super, Municipal 130 (☎284 313), on the south side of the Plaza de Armas, is Arequipa's only real supermarket. Open M-Sa 9am-2pm and 4:15-8:30pm, Su 9:30am-1:30pm.

Laundromat: Magic Laundry, Jerusalén 404-B and La Merced 125, #136. Wash and dry s/5 per kg. Same-day service. Open M-Sa 9am-7pm.

SOUTHERN PERU

EMERGENCY AND COMMUNICATIONS

Emergency: ☎105.

Police: ☎254 020.

Fire: ☎213 333.

Tourist Police: Jerusalén 315 (☎239 888). Open 24hr.

Pharmacies: Bótica del Pueblo, San Juan de Dios 200 and Santo Domingo (☎213 691).

Medical Services: The principal hospital is **Hospital General** (☎233 812), on Carrión, 1km to the south of Plaza de Armas. **Clínica Arequipa** (☎253 424, emergency 253 416), just over Puente Grau at the intersection with Bolognesi, charges s/60 for consultations. **Es Salud,** Santa Catalina 118-C (☎222 162), is a national health service with a 24hr. hotline, but no English. Office open daily 7am-9pm.

Telephones: Make international and local calls from the **Telefónica del Perú Office,** Alvarez Thomas 209 (☎281 112). Open M-Sa 7am-9pm, Su 7am-8pm. Or use one of several private agencies, such as **Cell Star,** Santa Catalina 118. Open daily 8:30am-1pm and 2-7pm. Most public phones are inside small shops; there's also a group of them at the corner of Catedral and San Francisco.

Internet: Internet cafes are sprouting up all over the place. Most people go to **La Red,** Jerusalén 306 (☎287 700), for its speedy access and employees clad in tight plastic clothing (s/3 per hr.; free soda, cigarettes, or candy after 1hr.). **Chips Internet,** San Francisco 202-A (☎203 651), has the same hourly price, but charges s/1 per 15 min. Open daily 9am-midnight.

Post Office: Serpost, Moral 118 (☎215 245). Open M-Sa 8am-8pm, Su 9am-1pm.

▐ ACCOMMODATIONS

Arequipa has a plethora of excellent hostels, hotels, and *casas de alojamiento*, many of which inhabit well-maintained *casas antiguas* with a similar central courtyard-rooftop terrace layout. There are a host of places that, while slightly more expensive, offer an exponential increase in comfort and security. Most hostels are affiliated with a travel agency, so if you're in a rush, you can arrange Colca Canyon tours without leaving home.

▨ **La Casa de Mi Abuela,** Jerusalén 606 (☎241 206; fax 242 761; email casadmiabuela@lared.net.pe), uphill from the city center. A full-service resort with 2 restaurants, multilingual library with Internet access, travel agency, and almost 50 rooms, from singles to 6-person suites. Beautiful swimming pool, ping-pong table, fountain, and pet alpaca. Breakfast (s/5) in one of the gardens. Singles begin at US$13, with bath US$26; doubles US$17, with bath US$33. Reservations recommended.

▨ **Hostal La Reyna,** Zela 209 and Santa Catalina (☎286 578). An attractive *casa antigua* reincarnated as a popular hostel. Sunny rooms around rooftop terrace. Inside rooms are simple but clean. Shared and common baths have hot water. *Desayuno americano* in the cafeteria (s/3). Helpful owner arranges tours to the Colca Canyon (US$20), buys and rents camping equipment, provides laundry service and kitchen access (stove s/2), and offers free luggage storage. 1am curfew. Rooms s/13 per person, with bath s/15.

▨ **Colonial House Inn,** Grau 114, 2nd fl. (☎223 533). Bed and breakfast with 6 spacious and eclectic rooms (one has a piano). English-speaking hosts offer washing facilities, a large library and book exchange, email, kitchen access, and scrumptious breakfast omelettes (s/5). Singles s/25; dorms and doubles s/17 per person.

Hostal Santa Catalina, Santa Catalina 500 and Grau (☎243 705). Spacious rooms around a courtyard. Warm showers. The genial owner serves breakfast in an attached cafeteria every morning and will purchase bus tickets and medication for ailing travelers. Singles s/15, with bath s/25; doubles s/25, with bath s/35.

Hostal Nuñez, Jerusalén 528 (☎218 648). Swing seats and rocking chairs in this lovely, plant-filled colonial-era house. Larger rooms have hot-water baths and cable TV; common bathrooms are spartan but clean, but singles are cramped. In-house beauty salon, laundry service, and free tourist info. Attached cafeteria serves breakfast and dinner, and has a terrace. Singles s/20, with bath s/35; doubles s/35, with bath s/60.

Hostal le Foyer, Ugarte 114 (☎286 473). Spacious rooms open onto a sunny courtyard. Ask for one with a balcony. Hot water, laundry service (s/5 per kg), and book exchange. Singles s/18, with bath s/27; doubles s/28, with bath s/40.

Hostal Regis, Ugarte 202 and San Francisco, 2nd fl. (☎226 111). Overwhelming marble staircase, chandeliers, and elaborate friezes in a colonial mansion. Unfortunately, the rooms are small and bare. Book exchange, video rental, huge lobby TV. Maps and info on nearby sights. Rooms US$5 per person.

La Casona de Jerusalén, Jerusalén 306 (☎214 221), 2nd fl. Sparse but attractive—airy rooms, all with sinks and comfy mattresses, surround a homey courtyard. Laundry service, breakfast (s/4-6), and an on-site travel agency. Singles s/18, with bath s/40; doubles s/36, with bath s/60. Discounts offered during low season.

◖ FOOD

There are an overwhelming number of outstanding restaurants in the center of town. Regional specialties include *rocoto relleño*, meat and vegetables stuffed into a spicy red bell pepper; *palta rellena*, the vegetarian version; *adobo de chancho*, a spicy pork stew; and *soltero de queso*, chunks of fresh cheese mixed with potatoes and vegetables. For the open-minded: *bistek de alpaca* (alpaca fillets) or *cuy chactao* (stone-grilled guinea pig). Try typical desserts at **Antojitos de Arequipa,** Morán 125-129, where they churn their own *queso helado* (cheese ice cream) and prepare *alfajores* (cookies stuffed with coconut, nuts, or a sweet sauce called *manjar*) and *cocadas*, similar to marzipan. (☎282 599. Open daily 8am-9:30pm.)

▧ **Sol de Mayo,** Jerusalén 207 (☎254 148), in the nearby suburb of Yanahuara. Sample succulent *arequipeño* appetizers (*rocoto relleño* s/12.50) at this long-time favorite; it's been around since 1897. Typical Peruvian entrees (s/15-32) served in the beautiful outdoor courtyard. On the street leading to Yanahuara's *mirador* (see Outside the City Center, p. 160). Open M-Sa noon-10pm, Su noon-6pm.

▧ **Govinda,** Jerusalén 400-B (☎285 540). Govinda is an exceptional installation of the national Hare Krishna vegetarian consortium. Healthy variety of fixed-price *menús* (s/7 and up) are light, unlike the more meaty traditional fare. Open daily 7:30am-9:30pm.

▧ **El Turko,** San Francisco 216-A. The chicken döner kebab (s/3.50) is truly something special, either as a snack or light meal. Try one with chef Ibrahim's special *salsa picante*. Entrees s/6-8. Open M-Th 8am-10:30pm, F-Sa 8am-11:30pm, Su 1:30-8pm.

Are Quepay, Jerusalén 502 (☎672 922). This quaint hut serves up well-prepared traditional Arequipan specialties such as *rocoto relleno* (s/10), *cuy chactao* (s/18; the timid should request it without head and paws); and *adobo* (s/12) to the sounds of a *peña* band at night. Vegetarian options around s/10. Open daily 11am-1am.

Lakshmivan Restaurant, Jerusalén 402 (☎228 768). Its menu is less comprehensive than Govinda's, but this Hare Krishna eatery is still excellent. Hearty breakfasts taste even better under the morning sun in the charming courtyard. 5-dish buffet includes soup, salad, bread, and juice (lunch s/4, dinner s/6). Open daily 7am-10pm.

Pizzería Los Leños, Jerusalén 407 (☎289 179), at Cercado. Generous, piping-hot pizzas from a wood-brick oven soar through a graffiti-decorated, picnic-tabled dining room to land on the plates of hungry backpackers and locals alike. Large pizzas s/20-50. Pastas s/10-13. Open daily 5:30pm-2am.

Déjà Vu's Terraza, San Francisco 319-B (☎ 221 904). Come lounge on a hammock over a delicious *desayuno* on the rooftop terrace ("surprise breakfast" s/6), then return at 7pm for the free English movie screening and s/8 *menú*. Return even later for a dance club (see Arequipa Nightlife, below). Open daily 8am-3am.

Snack Veinticuatro Horas, Portal de Flores 122 (☎218 777), on the east side of the Plaza de Armas. Small and cheerful. The specialty is the *pollo al spiedo*, maybe the tastiest rotisserie chicken in Peru (s/5). Sandwiches (s/4), omelettes (s/5), *conejo al ajo* (rabbit with garlic s/10), and *bisteck de alpaca* (s/10). Open 24hr.

SIGHTS

CITY CENTER

SANTA CATALINA MONASTERY. A functioning Dominican convent, this enormous 20,000 square-meter complex of cobblestone streets, chapels, artwork, and residences seems more like a city within walls. A population of 500—including 175 nuns, maids, and students—once lived here; now only 20 nuns live in a small, isolated section with the relative comforts of cable TV, modern kitchens, and washing machines. Santa Catalina was first constructed in 1579 (though subsequent earthquakes necessitated many renovations); most of the nuns took their vows as teenagers and were forbidden to leave the complex for the rest of their lives. The rules of the convent were so strict that if a nun accidentally smelled a flower or saw her own reflection in water, she had to flagellate herself as penance. Yet despite this extreme asceticism, worldly riches still held an important place here; only the wealthiest families could pay the expensive dowry for their daughter to "marry God," and the size of a nun's room also depended on how much money her parents donated. For the first 300 years of the convent's existence, the nuns even lived in relative isolation from each other, with personal maids to do their cooking and cleaning, tasks that would interrupt a purely contemplative life (hence the smaller cells and kitchens behind many of the larger rooms). Santa Catalina's routine was shaken up in 1871 when **Madre Josefa** was elected head mother; as Madre Priora, she sent the maids packing and initiated a communal lifestyle (including a common kitchen, refectory, and dormitories). The biggest shake-up in the convent's history, though, occurred in 1960, when an earthquake measuring 8.0 on the Richter scale damaged much of the complex beyond repair. A private company bought 60% of Santa Catalina in 1968, opening it to the public in 1970.

Closest to the entrance is the **novice cloister,** restored in the early 19th century, where initiates would train for up to four years before taking their vows. Historically, Santa Catalina's nuns have been the best-educated women in Arequipa; as novices, they were required to learn to read and write. Many parents placed their daughters in the convent as young as 12 years old, hoping to save the souls of the entire family; other girls entered voluntarily rather than face an arranged marriage. A highlight of the main complex is the narrow **Calle Toledo,** the oldest and longest street in the convent. The street ends at the **Lavandería,** 20 huge stone basins on an incline, from where the nuns could see other buildings but the high walls kept outsiders from peering in on them while they did laundry. Uphill from and parallel to Toledo, Calle Burgos passes a beautiful flower garden before reaching a *cafetería,* a good spot to grab a quiet snack. The large communal kitchen was constructed in Madre Josefa's time in a space that once held the convent's first chapel (destroyed in an earthquake). Continuing to the right, Calle Granada leads to the fish-filled fountain at the **Plaza Socodobe,** a market area where the nuns bartered for goods before the initiation of a communal lifestyle, and an area where the nuns used to bathe. Calle Granada then leads to the *coro alto* and a beautiful view of Volcán Chachani. Along the way are the former quarters of **Ana de Los Angeles Monteagudo,** beatified by Pope John Paul II in 1985, after a cancer-stricken woman was cured upon praying to her. The shrine in her room is littered with written requests for favors; two more miracles, and she could become the second female Peruvian saint. Further along, the large confessionary cloister leads to the curtained-off main chapel in the domed *sillar* building visible from most of the complex. Still in use today, the chapel is open to the public for daily mass at 7:30am. Tours conclude in the religious **art gallery,** which once served as a dormitory for the nuns and now houses many excellent examples of Peruvian artistic styles, including the syncretistic fusion of the Cusco School. (*Santa Catalina 301.* ☎ *229 798. Open daily 9am-5pm; last admission 4pm. Excellent tours in English last 1¼ hr. (tip expected), but the monastery is also navigable on your own with the several explanatory English signs. s/12.)*

ICE MAIDENS OF THE ANDES In an expedition up Volcán Ampato in September 1995, high-altitude anthropologist Johan Reinhard and his climbing partner, Miguel Zárate, noticed something strange—bright red feathers protruding from a slope on the summit. When they excavated the site, they discovered something beyond their wildest dreams. The feathers belonged to a headdress on an Inca statue from the grave of a mummified **Inca sacrifice**, preserved by the sub-freezing temperatures at the peak of the extinct volcano. Tests revealed that the body was that of a 13- or 14-year-old girl killed by a severe blow to the head over 500 years ago.

Later named **Juanita**, Ampato's ice maiden was hardly the only one of its kind. The heat given off by the eruption of Volcán Sabancaya in 1990 melted the caps of other volcanos around Arequipa, and over the next five years Reinhard discovered 13 more mummies exposed on the summits of Ampato and nearby peaks Pichu Pichu, Sara Sara, and El Misti (where the most mummies—six—were found). These sacrifices were part of the Inca ritual of *Capac Cocha*, in which the purest, most beautiful pre-pubescent girl in the empire was chosen to be handed over to the mountain deities in times of crisis, usually after an earthquake or during a drought. Being selected for *Capac Cocha* was one of the greatest honors possible, as the girl would live with the gods eternally, but such a privilege also demanded extreme effort. Accompanied by priests, the chosen girl first had to walk a pilgrimage of over 200 miles from Cusco, then climb a 6000m peak wearing only sandals on her feet. By the time they reached the summit, most girls were already half-dead of exhaustion and frostbite, but the show went on; priests gave the chosen one a potent mix of alcohol and hallucinogenic drugs, performed the sacred rites, then killed her by strangulation or with a sharp blow to the head. The gift to the gods was finally put to rest in a grave filled with valuable objects of symbolic significance, such as spondylus shells from Ecuador and small statues of gold and silver, as well as bags of food and coca leaves for her journey to immortality. Today, Juanita and five other mummy sacrifices have a new home—Arequipa's **Museo Santuarios Andinos** (see p. 158), where they are currently on display to the public.

PLAZA DE ARMAS. Arequipa's tree-lined, well-groomed Plaza de Armas is one of the most attractive in Peru. The bronzed **Tuturutu,** named for the toot-toot of his horn, sits in the central fountain. On the north side of the plaza is the twin-towered **cathedral,** constructed out of white volcanic *sillar* in the 17th century. Since then, it has been damaged in earthquakes, gutted by an 1844 fire, and rebuilt in the late 19th century. However, the former highlight of the facade—a tower with an elaborate carving of the Last Supper, destroyed in the 1868 Santa Ursula earthquake— was never reconstructed. Inside the ornate interior, the marble altar was fashioned in an Italian neo-Renaissance style with French Baroque influences. The enormous Belgian **organ** is the second largest in South America; two or three people can play at once. *(Open M-Sa 7:30-11:45am and 4:30-8pm, Su 7am-8pm.)*

MUSEO SANTUARIOS ANDINOS. This archeological museum, maintained by the Universidad Católica de Santa María, specializes in mummies found on the summits of nearby volcanos. The best-preserved and most famous is **Juanita,** a 14-year-old girl sacrificed in the Inca ceremony of *Capac Cocha.* Discovered in the crater of Volcán Ampato by anthropologist Johan Reinhard and Miguel Zárate in September 1995, "Juanita" has just returned from a July 2000 tour of Japan (see p. 159). The museum screens a 20-minute National Geographic documentary on the discovery, followed by a mandatory 25-minute tour through displays of Inca metals, ceramics, textiles, and several other mummies. *(Santa Catalina 210. ☎ 200 345. Open M-Sa 9am-5:45pm. Mandatory tours in English or Spanish; tip expected. s/15.)*

LA COMPAÑÍA. This Jesuit church, just off the Plaza de Armas, is an excellent example of the Baroque-Mestizo style. First constructed in 1573, its original facade was destroyed by an earthquake and rebuilt in 1698, in an imitation of the contemporary style popular in Spain. Local influences, however, are apparent in the intricately carved *sillar* adorning the entrance, and even more clearly in the **San Ignacio Chapel** to the left of the altar. This *cupula* was painted with a jungle motif, including tropical birds, fruits, and flowers, in a style similar to the 17th-century Cusco School. Though still impressive, after the 1868 earthquake the church was never properly restored. Adjacent to the chapel, **cloisters** were constructed in 1738. The original cloisters now house high-quality and high-priced *artesanía* and alpaca shops, accessible through the huge wooden doors a few shops up from La Compañía. *(Open daily 9-11:30am and 3-5:30pm. Chapel admission s/1.)*

LA CASA DEL MORAL. Named for the 200-year-old *mora* tree in its central courtyard, this *casa antigua* was built in 1730 for a Spanish viceroy, and its design and decoration are promoted as good examples of the fusion of colonial and *mestizo* influences. But it's not that simple. When British silver moguls Arthur and Barbara Williams bought the house in 1948, they added *sillar* fireplaces, personal minibars, and European and Asian furniture. Tour guides can tell you which pieces are originals. The highlights are the Cusco school paintings; one in the bedroom shows Virgin Mary shaped like a mountain, with a halo resembling the sun. *(Moral 318. Open M-F 9am-5pm, Sa 9am-1pm. s/5, students s/3. Tours in Spanish or English included.)*

LA RECOLETA. Originally a Franciscan convent constructed in 1651, La Recoleta now contains a **museum** with exhibits on the Amazon River, pre-Columbian pottery, textiles, and ceramics. Most interesting is the 20,000-volume **library,** with a number of *incunables*, books printed during the 15th century. *(Recoleta 117. In a bright red building visible from the center of Arequipa, a 10min. walk over the Río Chili. ☎270 966. Open M-Sa 9am-noon and 3-5pm. s/5, students s/3.)*

OUTSIDE THE CITY CENTER

YANAHUARA. This neighboring suburb has a stunning *mirador* made of *sillar* archways with engraved republican and revolutionary slogans and affords excellent views of the city center, El Misti, and Pichu Pichu. Along the small park behind the *mirador*, the **Lejo Parroquial de Yanahuara church** is noted for its elaborate principal door. Below the *mirador* is a series of narrow alleys and old family orchards for which the neighborhood is known. *(A 15min. walk from the center of town. To reach the mirador, cross the Río Chili on Puente Grau from its intersection with Santa Catalina. Take Ejército until Jerusalén, 2 blocks after the statue of the bulls; turn right and continue uphill.)*

YURA. Visitors come to Yura for the four **thermal baths,** which vary both in temperature (up to 34°C) and odor, and reputedly have the power to heal various ailments. *(30km northeast of Arequipa. Buses to Yura leave from Puente Grau, at the bridge to Yanahuara (1hr., every 20min., s/2). Or go by taxi (25min., s/20). Open daily 7am-6pm.)*

SABADÍA. Sabadía is a tranquil town 7km southeast of the city. The main attraction is the **water-powered mill** *(molino)*, Cesca 1621, which still grinds wheat. The surrounding grounds are pleasantly decorated, and a lone alpaca patrols the grass. Nearby, in the smaller town of Huasacache, the **Mansión del Fundador** is one of the best examples of a 17th-century colonial estate. *(Buses to Sabadía leave from Independencia and Paucarpata, the eastern continuation of Mescaderes. Taxis s/10 round-trip. The mill is to the right of the main road, on the same road as the Holiday Inn. Open daily 9am-5pm. s/5.)*

🎵 ENTERTAINMENT

Most people come to Arequipa with a specific agenda, whether it's sightseeing in the city, visiting the Colca Canyon, or climbing the nearby volcanos. But if you find yourself in town with a few hours to kill, there are plenty of ways to pass them. **Club Internacional Arequipa** has excellent sports and recreational facilities, including two swimming pools; basketball, racquetball, and tennis courts; a soccer field; and a bowling alley. To get there, cross Puente Grau and turn right; the main entrance is about a 10-minute walk along the river. (☎253 384. One-day passes s/ 10, weekends s/15, 8-day passes s/50. Open daily 6am-8pm.) For that Hollywood fix, catch the free 7pm screening of an English-language movie at **Déjà Vu's Terraza** (see Arequipa Food, above), or try one of the local theaters. **Cine Fenix,** Morán 104, and **Cine Portal,** Portal de Flores 112 (☎203 485), both screen recently-released international movies (s/8), many in English with Spanish subtitles.

Arequipeños take great pride in their unique **bullfights** (*peleas de toro*), which, instead of pitting man against beast, match up two bulls of equal weight (categories range from 300-1500kg). Unlike traditional bullfights, these don't get too bloody. First, a fertile female is led in front of the macho males; after the two *varones* go at it, the loser is simply the first one to run away. (Location alternates between the Cerro Juli stadium near Sabadía and the Zarracola Bolaunde "El Azufral" near the airport. Taxis to either stadium s/8. Apr.-Dec. Su 2pm. s/10.)

◪ NIGHTLIFE

Though it is Peru's second-largest city, Arequipa's nightlife tends to disappoint when compared to its capital counterpart or the ever-raging Cusco. Don't be discouraged; this city still knows how to party in its own highland manner, especially on weekends and holidays. There is a pretty healthy assortment of *discotecas, peñas,* and gringo rock clubs, mostly centered around the intersection of San Francisco and Zela. If you're planning to make a night of it, it's worth your while to seek out the ubiquitous **free drink cards** distributed in hostels and touristy restaurants. Several local restaurants, especially near the Plaza de Armas, occasionally have live traditional music on weekend evenings; **Are Quepay** (see Arequipa Food, above) and **Las Quenas** (below) feature *peña* acts nightly.

◪ **Jenízaro,** Melgar 119, near the intersection with Rivero. Tourists who want to dance and the locals who dance with them. Mostly international music, with a fair amount of Latin flavor. Comprehensive bar. Happy hour 10-11pm (s/1-2 off all drinks). Avoid F-Sa s/8-10 cover with a free pass (found all over the city). Open Th-Sa 10pm-4am.

◪ **Ad Libitum,** San Francisco 300, behind Café Biblioteca. This hole-in-the-wall boasts something the other bars can't match—cuba libres for only s/1.50 (the s/12 pitchers tend to be stronger). The mood is always mellow, with trance, alternative, and 60s rhythms to match the trippy paintings and posters of rock idols. Open daily 7pm-5am.

Forum, San Francisco 317 (☎202 697). This enormous exercise in tropical tackiness includes a functioning waterfall. On weekend nights, it feels like all of Arequipa is in its 6 bi-level bars and gigantic dance floor. Live Latin cover bands F-Sa. Occasional s/10-15 weekend cover. Open M-Th 6pm-3am, F-Sa 10pm-4am.

Kibosh, Zela 205 (☎626 218), promotes itself as the biggest bar in town. It may not live up to that claim, but there's plenty of room in its 3 bars to drink up or get down. Not too in-your-face kitschy. No cover for tourists. Open Th-Sa 9pm-4am.

Las Quenas, Santa Catalina 302 (☎281 115). Intimate venue where authentic *música folklorica* (at deafening levels) tempts visitors. Arequipeña beer (s/4), *comida típica,* and pricey mixed drinks. Live music begins 10pm. Cover s/5. Open M-Sa 10am-1am.

Déjà Vu, San Francisco 319-B (☎221 904). At night the menu is replaced with a long list of house drinks ("chastity belt" s/10) and music videos take the screen. Especially popular on weeknights, when the other clubs are closed. Open daily 10pm-3am.

Dady O, Portal de Flores 112 (☎215 530), on the Plaza de Armas. This is a cheesy, Americanized bar. If you can overlook that, it's a lot of fun. Warps you back to the 70s, with the brightly tiled dance floor, shimmering disco ball, neon lights, and beer for only s/2. Cover s/10; women free Th until midnight. Open Th-Sa 9pm-4am.

The Hooka, Zela 202. A smaller club with multiple personalities—sometimes its dance floor can barely contain the raging techno beats, other times it hosts traditional *folklórico* groups. Occasional live music on Sa. No cover. Open Th-Sa 8pm-5am.

◪ INTO THE WILDS FROM AREQUIPA

The region around Arequipa hits all the extremes. Climb above the clouds by hiking up the El Misti or Chachani volcanos, or delve into the depths of the earth by trekking down into the Colca and Cotahuasi canyons, the two deepest in the world; get soaked in whitewater rapids, or venture into the desert to visit the Toro Muerto Petroglyphs. Tour agencies in town offer nearly every trip permutation, but it is possible to make the most of these excursions on your own. If you choose the independent option, try to find as many people as possible to go with you; smaller groups have been assaulted on El Misti and in the Colca Canyon.

THE COLCA CANYON

Although no longer considered the world's deepest canyon—nearby Cotahuasi Canyon has that honor—the Colca is visited much more frequently by tourists. Often touted as being twice as deep as the Grand Canyon in the US with a profundity of 3400m, the cavernous fissure was formed by a 100km long seismic fault between the Coropuna (6425m) and Ampato (6325m) volcanos. Incredibly, the canyon was unnavigated by Westerners until a Polish group explored it in 1986. Along the ridge of the canyon are a number of traditional Andean villages and scenic *miradores*, the most popular of which is the **Cruz del Cóndor.** As its name suggests, it is home to some of the boldest, most exhibited condors in the world. Watching groups of them rise up the canyon and surf the morning air currents in the early morning is quite a beautiful show. The best time to see the soaring condors is between 8:30 and 10am during the drier months (Apr.-Dec.). At other times of the year, the show is less reliable. It is possible to hike down into the canyon from any of the *miradores*, though some trails may sporadically be closed due to reforestation projects.

VISITING WITH A TOUR AGENCY. Most tours of the Colca Canyon last two days and one night. If you're in a hurry, many agencies offer a one-day trip, but it means arriving at Cruz del Cóndor in the afternoon (not the optimal time to view the condors) and is no cheaper than the two-day package (if anything, it can often be more expensive). A standard two-day tour (US$20-35, depending on the quality of the hotel) leaves Arequipa before 9am, stopping in the **Reserva Nacional de Salinas y Aguada Blanca** to watch *vicuña* and view the bizarre rock formations of the Bosque de Piedras, then continuing to the town of Chivay (p. 165). Groups spend the night in Chivay, first visiting the La Calera hot springs in the afternoon, then stopping at a restaurant with traditional *peña* music at night. The next morning, groups depart early to see the main attractions, the canyon and the condors, at Cruz del Cóndor. After about an hour, the tour bus heads back, stopping in small villages such as **Yanque** (with a colonial church) and **Maca** (where tourists can get their picture taken with a condor on their shoulder), and arriving back in Arequipa around 6pm. When shopping for a tour, make sure the agency covers all these standard attractions. The price of the tour should also include all transportation, an English-speaking guide, the US$2 entrance fee into the Colca Valley, the hotel room, and breakfast. Take along at least s/50 (to cover lunches, dinner, and admission to the hot springs), warm clothing, and of course, a camera.

DOING IT YOURSELF. It is quite easy to visit the Colca Canyon on your own using public transportation, and is a popular option with tourists who want to camp or hike in the canyon. Buses leave Arequipa for **Chivay** (4hr., 2am and noon, s/11) and **Cabanaconde** (6hr., s/15; for more information, see Chivay, p. 165). There are a number of hotels and services in Chivay and somewhat fewer in Cabanaconde; **camping** is also free and permitted everywhere in the canyon except Cruz del Cóndor. Cruz del Cóndor is an easy 14km (1½hr.) walk from Cabanaconde on the road back toward Chivay; buses to and from Arequipa also pass the site when traveling between the two towns. If you have your own camping equipment, the most popular **trek** is a three to four hour hike from Cruz del Cóndor to the bottom of the can-

Arequipa Area

yon, where there is a small, swimmable **oasis** that makes a good camping spot (6-7hr. hike back up). For those with more time to spare, it is also possible to hike from Cruz del Cóndor down to the Río Colca (3hr.); then west to the town of **Tapay,** where there are some pre-Inca ruins and small *hospedajes* (3hr. more); and finally down to the oasis (3hr. more).

EL MISTI

Buses to Chiguata leave from Espinar at its intersection with Sepúlveda, in the Miraflores district (45min., every 30min. 5:30am-7pm,s/1; taxis to bus stop s2.5). The more convenient Carros de Adrenales service goes to the higher town of Cachamarca, saving about half an hour of climbing time; cars depart from the same location daily at 6:30am (s/1). Alternatively, you can travel the 30km to Chiguata by taxi (30min., s/40).

El Misti (5825m) towers conspicuously over Arequipa and is a popular two to three day climb. The summit affords spectacular views of Lake Salinas and Pichu Pichu, as well as the yellow sulfur bubbling in the crater below. The ascent is demanding, but can be undertaken by anyone in fair shape. Do not attempt the climb unless you have been acclimatized for at least three or four days. There are four routes up El Misti, but three can only be accessed by private four-wheel drive vehicles, and are normally undertaken with tour agencies. The path from the **Aguada Blanca** reservoir is the least strenuous and can easily be done in two days; it begins at 4100m and curves around the northwest side of the volcano. The **Selva Alegre** and **Grau** routes begin at 3320m and 3000m respectively, and traverse the southern side of the peak. The trail beginning at the town of Chiguata (2980m) is the only one that can be reached by public transportation; unfortunately, it also happens to be the longest of the four trails; while it is possible to make the ascent in two days, most people stretch it out to three. If you choose to make the trip on your own from Chiguata without an agency or guide, be sure to obtain a topography map and instructions from Campamento Base (see p. 165), as the route is somewhat unclear. **Volcán Chachani** (6067m) is a challenging and isolated two-day climb. Private transport is required, and it is not advisable to make the ascent without a guide. For information on guided climbs, see p. 161.

OTHER EXCURSIONS

WHITEWATER RAFTING. The Río Colca snakes for over 400km around the department of Arequipa, changing its name, direction, and rafting difficulty along the way. The rapids range from Class II to V, but all pass through gorgeous mountain scenery. The most popular trip for beginners is a 7km stretch of **Río Chili** just north of the city center; the Class II-III rapids are navigable in the dry season (Apr.-Dec.) only, and trips takes up to four hours. The **Río Majes,** north of Camaná, is navigable year-round, but requires instruction first (Class II-III; full day trip, with about 3hr. on the water). Only experienced rafters should take on the **Río Colca,** in the highlands around the Colca and Cotahuasi Canyons; its rapids range from Class III-V (strongest on the stretch between Canco and Majes) and are navigable April to December only. Tour agencies can put together three to 12-day packages to Río Colca. **Kayaking** is also possible on all of these rivers. Normally, double kayaks (with a guide in one seat) are used; to take a single kayak, tour agencies require a three-day course (US$120-150). As always, the larger the group, the lower the price. Four hour trips down the Río Chili can be as little as US$25 per person.

TORO MUERTO PETROGLYPHS. Before the Colca was "discovered," this was the original Arequipa tourist attraction, consisting of more than 5000 black volcanic rocks (remnants from eruptions as far back as 50 million years ago) engraved with petroglyphic images thought to be more than 1000 years old, the work of the Huari and Chuquibamba cultures. The zoomorphic subjects vary from dancing people to the sun to animals such as dogs and snakes.

The easiest route to the petroglyphs is with a one-day tour with an agency (US$25-60 per person), though it's much cheaper and relatively simple to go solo. **Transportes del Carpio** (☎430 941) sends **buses** from Arequipa's terminal to **Corire,** the closest town to the petroglyphs (3hr., every hr. 4:45am-5:30pm, s/7.50; return times same). Get off about 1½km before town, at a sign marking the turn-off for Toro Muerto; if you miss the sign, just head from Corire by foot (30min.) or taxi (10min.). From the turn-off, the petroglyphs are a 1-1½hr. walk (s/5). Although it is possible to make the return trip in the same day, it's easier just to spend the night in Corire; **Hostal Willy's,** on the Plaza de Armas, has rooms for s/10 per person.

VALLE DE LOS VOLCANES. More than 80 small volcanic craters, none of which is more than 300m high, line this 65km valley, creating the appearance of a lunar landscape. The craters are believed to be the cones of the extinct fire-spewers that were the legendary "Valle del Fuego," almost completely buried under hardened lava from the nearby Volcán Coropuna 2000 years ago. They can be visited in a multi-day trip with a tour group from Arequipa or on your own from the town of **Andagua** (also spelled Andahua). The hard way to get to Andagua is via the five- to seven-day trek from Cabanaconde (see p. 166); the easy way is with **Transportes Reyna** (☎426 549), which sends **buses** from Arequipa's terminal (10hr., 4pm, s/28; return 4pm). From Andagua, Valle de los Volcanes is a two hour walk.

COTAHUASI CANYON. Colca canyon may have all the publicity, but with a depth of 3354m, Cotahuasi narrowly beats it out for the title of **deepest canyon in the world.** Because of its remote location, however, fewer tourists visit this canyon than visit Colca. The town of Cotahuasi makes a good base from which to explore the canyon if you make the trip independently. From town, there are a number of hikes to various *miradores,* as well as a 3hr. walk to the **Cataratas de Sipia,** waterfalls up to 150m high. **Transportes Cromotex** (☎421 555) sends buses from Arequipa's terminal to Cotahuasi (12hr., 5:30pm, s/30; return 4:30pm).

GUIDES AND TOURS

Some of the most exciting excursions around Arequipa may require special equipment or the expertise of a guide. When signing up with an agency, ask lots of questions and get answers in writing. If you have a specific tour company in mind, ask for some form of identification; many guides lie about which agency they represent. All companies should be able to provide guides who speak fluent English.

Campamento Base, Jerusalén 401-B (☎202 768; email jsoto@aasa.com.pe). With possibly the best mountain equipment in Arequipa (for rental and purchase), "base camp" leads climbs and treks in the Colca and Cotahuasi canyons. Do-it-yourself mountaineers can buy topographic maps of the volcanos (US$6 per page) which have trail descriptions. Vlado Soto is recommended. Open M-F 9:30am-1pm and 4-7pm, Sa 9:30-1pm; Vlado's home phone number is posted on the door in case of emergencies at any hour.

Pablo Tour, Jerusalén 400-A (☎203 737; email pablotour98@mixmail.com), are specialists in trekking trips to the Colca. Organizes climbing and rafting trips in the Colca during the dry season (2-day camping trips, with equipment and guide, US$55 per person; 1-day rafting trips US$35 per person). Excursions to Toro Muerto and Valle de los Volcanos also offered. Good source of multilingual advice. Open daily 8am-8pm.

Cusipata, Jerusalén 408-A (☎203 966; email gvellutino@Lared.net.pe). With trips led by the 3 Vellutino brothers, the rafting champions of Arequipa, Cusipata leads the pack in rafting and kayaking excursions down all the major rivers in the regions, ranging from 3hr. trips (US$25-40 per person) to 12-day journeys (US$600 per person). To kayak solo you must take their 3-day course (US$120). Open M-F 9am-1pm and 3-7:30pm.

Eco Tours, Jerusalén 402-A (☎200 516; email ecotur@peru.itete.com.pe). A multilingual tour agency with the standard Colca trip (US$20), rental gear (bicycles US$15 per day), and a 2-day trip that includes Toro Muerto and Valle de los Volcanos (US$80). Also a three-day whitewater kayaking course (US$120). Open daily 8:30am-10pm.

Santa Catalina Tours, Santa Catalina 219 (☎284 292). This agency leads the market with their conventional Colca Canyon trips (1-day US$25; 2-day US$23-26), English-speaking guides, and comfortable buses. 3hr. city (s/48, includes admission to all museums) and *campiña* (s/30) tours also. Open daily 8:30am-7pm.

Wasi Tour, Santa Catalina 207 (☎200 294; email wasitour@lettera.net; webs.demasiado.com/wasi/index.htm), offers the best deal on standard 2-day and 1-night Colca trips. Quality guides and groups of no more than 10 (US$19 per person). Trips can be extended a day to include the canyon (US$40). Open M-Sa 8am-8pm, Su 8am-5pm.

CHIVAY   ☎054

A green oasis after the grueling bus ride from Arequipa, the highland hamlet of Chivay (3633m) is the night stop for tour groups headed to the Colca Canyon. Independent canyoneers without their own camping equipment may want to spend the night here as well, as Chivay has many more resources than the smaller town of Cabanaconde, 35km farther along the road to Colca. More than just a pit stop, Chivay is not without its charms, including stunning scenery, opportunities for short hikes, and most notably the **Calera Hot Springs** 3km from town. Heated by nearby volcanos, the sulfuric springs are very warm (up to 45°C at midday) and surprisingly clean (open daily 4:30am-7:30pm; s/4).

The tiny town of Chivay is centered around the **Plaza de Armas,** where buses arrive and affordable restaurants and hostels congregate. Information about the town and Colca Canyon is available at the **tourist office** on the plaza. (Open daily noon-9pm.) **Transportes Cristo Rey** (☎254 326) sends buses to Chivay from Arequipa's terminal (4hr., 2am and noon, s/11). They continue from Chivay's Plaza de Armas to **Cabanaconde** via **Cruz del Cóndor** (2hr., 6am and 4pm, s/3). Return buses to **Arequipa** also leave from the plaza (4hr., 11am and 11pm, s/11). To get to the **hot springs,** catch a *colectivo* (5min., s/1) or taxi (s/3) in front of the church. **Hostal Anita,** Plaza de Armas 607, offers simple rooms with hot-water baths centered around a flowering courtyard. Though there is no shortage of stones in town, the hostel's manager has inexplicably decided to paint pictures of rocks on the walls instead. (☎521 114. Rooms s/15 per person.) **Colca Inn,** Salaverry 307, features recently renovated, carpeted rooms with the feel of a ski lodge, and is very popular with tour groups. (☎521 088. Singles US$12; doubles US$18.) **Casablanca,** Plaza de Armas 705, is a cozy choice for *rocoto relleno* or various vegetarian options. (*Menú* s/13. ☎521 019. Open daily 8am-9pm.)

NEAR CHIVAY: CABANACONDE

For information on how to get to Cabanaconde, see Chivay, p. 165. Buses leave from Caban-aconde's Plaza de Armas for Arequipa (6hr., 9am and 9pm, s/15) via Chivay (2hr., s/3).

A two-hour drive down the road from Chivay, Cabanaconde (3287m) is a very small town that is a good base for expeditions into the canyon; unlike Chivay, it is within walking distance of Cruz del Cóndor (14km; 1½hr.). There are many relaxing and scenic **hikes** from Cabanaconde, including a 10 minute hike leading to a *mirador* that, locals claim, offers the best view of the Colca Canyon. A good one-day trip is to the bottom of the canyon, where there's an **oasis** perfect for swimming (see Colca Canyon: Doing it Yourself, p. 162). Another popular trek is to **Andagua** (5-7 days) and the spectacular **Valle de los Volcanes** (see p. 164). July 14-18 is the most eventful time of the year to visit Cabanaconde, as it brings dances, fiestas, and **bullfights** to the specially constructed arena just outside of town. In town, **Hostal Valle del Fuego,** on Los Palacios and Grau, provides lodging, meals (s/5), and general information about treks into the canyon. The friendly owners also rent equipment and make arrangements with local guides and partners. (☎280 367. Rooms s/10 per person.) **La Posada del Conde** offers more comfortable quarters with private baths. (☎/fax 440 197. US$6.50 per person, includes breakfast.)

LAKE TITICACA

PUNO   ☎054

Tourist authorities like to promote Puno as the Folkloric Capital of Peru, a title forged by the city's unique confluence of cultures: Aymara from the south, and Quechua from the north. This city, on the edge of Lake Titicaca, is proud of its region's many traditional dances—numbering in the hundreds—though few tourists get to see the dances performed except during festival days. However, the local color is impossible to ignore; it appears in the form of bright traditional dress, bustling markets, and cheerful local musicians. To many visitors, however, Puno (3827m) is a bitterly cold, oxygenless place, and little more than a necessary stop on the way to the Titicaca islands or before crossing the border into Bolivia.

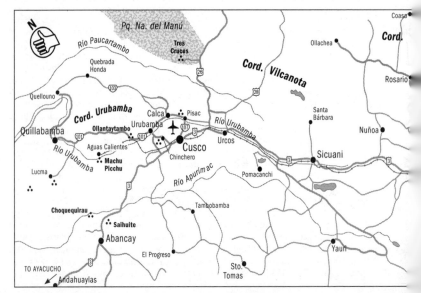

TRANSPORTATION

Airplanes: Airport, 45km away in Juliaca. "Aeropuerto" buses leave along Tacna (45min., s/5-7). **AeroContinente,** Tacna 301 (☎354 870), at Melgar. To **Lima** (2hr., M-F 2:30 and 5:30pm, US$89) via **Arequipa** (1hr., US$59). Open M-F 8am-noon and 2-6pm. **Tans,** San Román 153 in Juliaca (☎321 272). To **Lima** (M-F 4:30pm, US$58).

Trains: Estación La Torre (☎351 041). Open M and F 7-11am and 4-8pm, Tu-Th 7-11am and 2-6pm, Sa 7-10am, Su 4-7pm. Tickets sold 1 day in advance. To **Cusco** (10-11hr.; M, W, F, Sa 8am; economy s/25, *Turismo Ejecutivo* US$19, *Turismo Inka* US$23). Some shorten the ride to Cusco and save money by taking a *colectivo* to **Juliaca** (30min., along Tacna, s/2) and catching the train there (8hr., M-Sa 8:55am, s/21.5). Trains to **Arequipa** ride directly from Puno (10-11hr.; M and F 7:45pm; economy s/22, *Turismo Ejecutivo* s/30), or catch a *colectivo* to Juliaca and take the train from there (8-9hr., M-Sa 9:15, s/18.5).

Buses: Buses leave from the streets around Melgar to: **Lima** (24-30hr., 6:30am and 5pm, s/45-60); **Cusco** (6hr., M-F 7am and 6pm, s/30-35); **Arequipa** (11-12hr., M-F 6:30pm; s/25-30, or by omnibus s/15); and **La Paz** (4hr.; M, W, and F 7:30am; s/20). Or, arrange for any of these journeys through a travel agency; many line Lima and Tacna. Prices are roughly the same, but departure times are more punctual and many make pick-ups at hotels. Agencies can also arrange trips to **Copacabana** (2hr., s/10) with a border passport stop in Yunguyo.

Boats: Motorized *lanchas* leave from **Puerto Lacustreon** at the edge of town (s/5 by taxi or a 15min. walk from the center). *Lanchas* to **Los Uros** leave all day; to **Taquile** and **Amantaní,** they depart early in the morning (see p. 173). Trips can be arranged with a guide through one of numerous tour agencies, or even through hotel owners. Visits are also possible without guides by simply speaking to the boat owners at the port.

ORIENTATION AND PRACTICAL INFORMATION

Trains from Arequipa and Cusco drop off their passengers just outside the *centro* on La Torre, which leads into Tacna, one of the main roads in town. Most **buses** stop along Melgar, which is perpendicular to Tacna. The **Plaza de Armas** marks the center of town and lies three blocks from Tacna along Puno and Deustua. The plaza is connected to the creatively landscaped **Parque Pino,** three blocks away, via lively pedestrian street Lima. Roughly eight blocks from the center of town, **Lake Titicaca** can be seen from many streets in the *centro*.

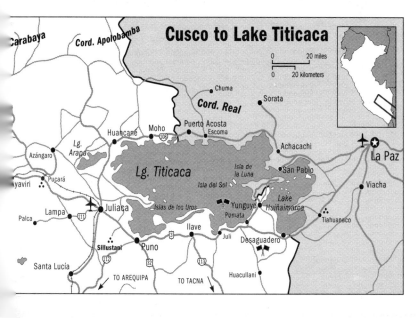

Cusco to Lake Titicaca

BORDER CROSSING: INTO BOLIVIA

At Yunguyo: The most popular crossing between Peru and Bolivia, **Yunguyo**'s en route to Copacabana. To get to Yunguyo from Puno, arrange with one of the agencies along Tacna or hop on an omnibus at the 14th block of Sol (departing all day, s/5). Buses drop their passengers off a few km from the border, where a number of colectivos and taxis await to shuttle individuals to the "frontera" itself (s/2). Stamps are required on passports from the immigration offices on both sides of the border. Both offices are open 24hr. (though the agent may be asleep in the back). Customs officials in Kasani (on the Bolivian side) can only grant clearance for 30 days. For longer clearance, speak to officials in La Paz. Change money at the little stand right outside of the immigration office in Kasani, as banks in Copacabana do not buy *soles,* and rates at casas de cambio are unreliable. From Yunguyo, catch a colectivo for the short but bumpy ride to **Copacabana** (45min., Bs2.5). If you end up staying overnight in Yunguyo, **Residencial Isabel,** on Grau at the corner of Plaza Castilla, has wood floors, firm beds, and beautiful armoires—unfortunately, the common baths are dark and dank. (☎866 019. Singles s/10; doubles s/20; triples s/30.) Another option is Hotel San Andres, Grau on the Plaza Mayor. Rooms are closet-like but warm and boast great views of the sunset on the lake. Common bathrooms do not have showers. (Singles s/10; doubles s/20; triples s/30.)

At Desaguadero: For those interested in a direct route to La Paz, the border destination is Desaguadero. From Puno, Desaguadero-bound omnibuses leave all morning and early afternoon from the 14th block of Sol (2.5hr., s/5). A cluster of people with individual tables, calculators, and piles of soles and bolivianos are prepared to change your money (all offer roughly the same rates). A large dirt parking lot dominates the entrance to Desaguadero, a small town at the border that few tourists visit for long. Listen carefully to the cries and shouts—one of them probably corresponds to your next destination. Agencies on Panamericana, across from the parking lot, send **buses** to: **Moquegua** (6hr., s/15); **Ilo** (7½hr., s/15-18); **Tacna** (9hr., s/15-18); **Arequipa** (10hr., s/25); **Juliaca** (3hr., s/5); and **Puno** (2hr., s/4). Departure times vary by agency, but range throughout the day, mainly between 7am and 6pm. Colectivos and omnibuses also depart for these destinations at all hours from the parking lot. Services on Panamericana include a customs office, Panamericana 302, near the parking lot, immediately before the port (open 24hr.). If you do end up here overnight, **Hostal Corona,** Panamericana 248, boasts a common area with cushy chairs and cable TV to compensate for basic rooms. (Hot shower s/2. Singles s/10, with bath s/16; doubles s/20, with bath s/24.) **Hostal,** 28 de Junio 322, one block from Panamericana, is as generic as its name, with extra amenities available for a fee. (☎851 040. 10min. hot shower s/3. Singles s/15, with bath and TV s/30; doubles s/25.)

Tourist Information: Tourist Office, Lima 549 (☎363 337), on the Plaza de Armas. A young, helpful, mostly Spanish-speaking staff can provide a map and suggest a few sights to visit. Open M-Sa 8am-7pm. Alternatively, one of the many tourist agencies along Lima and Tacna will be happy to answer queries with their own personal options.

Consulate: Bolivia, Arequipa 120, 3rd fl. Citizens of North America, most of Europe, South Africa, New Zealand, Australia, and numerous other countries do not need a visa to travel to Bolivia. Those who do need one can purchase it here (prices vary by nationality), available immediately. Open M-F 9am-3pm.

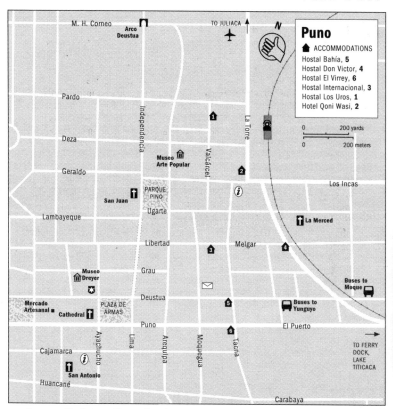

SOUTHERN PERU

Currency Exchange: Banco Continental, Lima 398 (☎351 080), open M-F 9:15am-12:45pm, 4-6:30pm. **Banco de Trabajo,** Lima 550, open M-F 9am-1:30pm, 3:45-7pm, Sa 9:30am-1pm. In addition, a number of *casas de cambio* are open in the mornings and afternoons, and offer low rates of commission cashing traveler's checks.

ATMs: Located primarily along Lima, though there are a few scattered about. Try **Banco Continental** for Visa cards, and **Telebanco** for MasterCard.

Laundromat: Don Marcelo Lavandería, Lima 427 (☎352 444). s/5 per kg. Drop off clothes in the morning and they'll be ready the following afternoon. Open 24hr.

Police: Tourist Police (☎357 100), on the Plaza de Armas.

Hospital: (☎353 780 or 369 286), 10th block of Sol. **ProMujer,** Libertad 345, 3rd fl. Half a block east of Lima. A center of operations for a variety of women's programs, including child care and meetings to reflect on the role of women in the Peruvian community. Open M-Sa 9am-noon, 3-5:30pm.

Telephones: Telefónica del Perú, Lima 439 (☎369 180). Open M-Su 7:30am-10pm.

Internet Access: A number of places sit on Lima, and more are scattered throughout town. Look for brightly painted signs on storefronts. Average s/3 per hr. **SurNet,** Lima 378, has plenty of fast computers and a cheerful staff. s/1 per 15min., s/1.5 per 30min., s/2.5 per 1hr. Open daily 8am-11pm. **Internet Cyber Club Puno,** Lima 428 (☎365 064), has the largest collection of computers around, and charge s/1.5 for 15min., s/2 for 30min., s/3 per hr. Open daily 8:30am-11pm.

Post Office: Serpost, Moquegua 269 (☎/fax 351 141). Open M-F 8am-8pm.

ACCOMMODATIONS

Even in high season, Puno seems to have more than enough room to house visitors. Hostels here are inexpensive, and when business is slow, most will offer hefty discounts. Rates jump a little (about s/10) during July and August.

Hostal Los Uros, Theodoro Valcárcel 135 (☎352 141). 1 block from La Torre. These cozy, wooden-floored rooms are cheery, with bright comforters and fuzzy towels. All rooms have baths and hot water. Singles s/19; doubles s/30; triples s/45.

Hotel Qoni Wasi, La Torre 119 (☎353 902), across from train station. Wood-paneled walls give the finishing touch to this clean, well-lit hotel. Bathrooms sparkle and carpeting provides extra comfort on cold nights. Singles s/35; doubles s/25, with bath s/35.

Hostal Don Victor, Melgar 166 (☎366 087), near the train tracks. This bright, well-kept hostel and its friendly management can fulfill nearly every desire, down to a clean towel and a bar of soap. All rooms are comfortable, with baths and broad views of the city and lake. Singles s/30; doubles s/50; triples s/65; TV s/5 extra.

Hostal Bahía, Tacna 409 (☎352 655), at Titicaca, 3 blocks from the plaza on Deustua. Aged but functional rooms boast generous windows. Almost all rooms have baths with hot water 6:30am-10:30pm. Singles s/20, with bath s/25; doubles s/40; triples s/60.

Hostal Internacional, Libertad 161 (☎352 109; e-mail internacional@netaccessperu.net), 2½ blocks from Lima. Large windows. Lounges on the landings provide an ideal atmosphere for mingling with other guests and glimpsing breathtaking views of Puno and Lake Titicaca (as well as catching up on the news with cable TV). All rooms have baths. Singles s/45; doubles s/75; triples s/90.

Hostal El Virrey, Tacna 510 (☎354 495), at Puno, 3 blocks down Puno from the Plaza de Armas. Spiffy carpeted rooms have firm beds, flowery bedspreads, and, in some cases, views of the lake. All rooms have cable TV and baths (though some of the bathrooms are actually directly across the hall, not in the suite). 24hr. hot water. Singles s/25-35; doubles s/70; extra bed s/15.

FOOD

The always busy pedestrian strip, Lima, which connects the Plaza de Armas and Parque Pino, has a high concentration of decent (if somewhat touristy) restaurants. Sitting on the shore of Lake Titicaca has its culinary advantages, namely delicious fresh fish, particularly *trucha* (trout) and *pejerrey* (kingfish).

Ukuku's Pizzería Restaurant, Lima 332 (☎355 690). A greenhouse-style structure ensures warmth in this spacious, welcoming restaurant. An extensive menu, including fish, pasta, and pizza, is accompanied by a *menú* whose variety exceeds that of most other restaurants. The manager is attentive and involved, though the service can be a bit slow. *Menú* s/4.5-10, entrees s/8-16. Open M-Sa 9am-10pm.

Café Restaurant Vegetarian Delisse, Moquegua 200. As the name would suggest, Delisse offers protein-packed vegetarian meals that could fill any empty stomach, and fresh juice to top it off. Children do most of the scurrying around and serving, making the experience all the more delightful. Meals s/3-8, drinks s/1-3. Open M-Th and Su 6am-6pm, Sa 6-10pm.

Restaurant El Portón Colonial, Lima 345 (☎351 214). Reed-covered walls and sheep-skin-covered chairs give a rustic feel to this touristy but tasty restaurant. On some nights, a local band might add its own native flavor. An extensive menu of seafood platters and quick service makes one wonder if there's an army in the kitchen. Most entrees s/11-15. Savory ceviche s/6-8. Open daily 8am-11pm.

Apu Salkantay Restaurant and Bar, Lima 419 (☎363 955). A very friendly staff serves a wide variety of hearty international dishes. Patrons also take advantage of a full bar and large selection of coffees. The atmosphere is warm, the crowd upbeat. Entrees s/0.6-16, drinks s/0.2-12. Open 3pm-1am.

Govinda, Deusta 310 at Arequipa. At this Hare Krishna restaurant, the food is satisfying and, of course, vegetarian. The clientele all seem to know each other and are very open and friendly. Set *menús* average s/5. Open M-Sa 7am-9pm.

SIGHTS AND ENTERTAINMENT

Little in the town of Puno should distract visitors from sights on the lake. A brief visit is sufficient to see the small collection in the **Museo Municipal Dreyer,** Conde de Lemus 289, across Deustua from the cathedral. The two-room edifice houses a variety of pre-Inca remains, including pots, jewelry, and some shocking mummies. (Open M-Sa 7:30am-3:30pm. s/0.5.) The **Arco Deustua,** though a bit of a hike from the center of town, is worth its spot on the map. The arch itself is pretty and historic; it was constructed in 1847 as a monument to the heroes of battles at Junín and Ayacucho. But what makes the walk truly worthwhile is the combination of fantastic views and open space in a quiet spot to read, rest, or write postcards. The **Plaza de Armas** is a sight in itself, always filled with people, and commonly interrupted by marching bands. If you can find a seat on one of the crowded benches, it's good for a few hours of people-watching.

Even on high-season weekends, **nightlife** in Puno is relatively tame. Streets in the center of town clear out after 10pm, as locals return to the true population-center, Juliaca. However, seemingly in the interest of keeping tourists entertained, a few nightspots remain lively into the night on the ever-busy Lima. For the young at heart, arcades offer a well-lit haven of diversions, and there are almost always a number of young locals strolling down the pedestrian street. **Ekeko's Pub,** Lima 355, starts pumping music early, followed closely by happy hour (7-9pm), which is populated mostly by tourists watching soccer games on a big-screen TV. Eventually, though, the crowd grows as locals file in, and the small dance floor gets frisky. (Beer s/5, mixed drinks s/5-13.)

FESTIVALS

The **Fiesta de la Virgen de la Candelaria** (Feb. 2-22) is identified by its vast concourse of typical native dances, some of which are performed by people in suits made of lights. **Puno Week** (Nov. 1-7) is characterized by daily parades put on by the students of the town's high schools and universities. There are also a number of demonstrations in the Plaza de Armas of games and fights, as well as lots of music. **Adoración del Sol** (June 22-23) is a religious celebration in which *brujas* (witches) from all over South America gather and dance traditional sun-worshipping dances all through the night in order to absorb the energy of the sun as it begins its decline into the coldest months of the year.

DAYTRIPS FROM PUNO

SILLUSTANI

To get to Sillustani, most opt for an agency tour. These usually leave around 2:30pm and cost as little as s/15, including admission. Alternatively, one could catch a colectivo bound for Juliaca and ask to be let off at the "desvio a Sillustani" (s/1.5). From this fork, colectivos cover the remaining 14km to Sillustani (s/1.5). A warning, though, for those going the colectivo route: catching a colectivo to the fork is relatively easy, and the ride takes about 20min. However, once at the fork, it can be up to an hr. before the next colectivo is full enough to leave. From there, the trip is another 30min. Catching a colectivo back to the fork can also be difficult. Once there, however, catching a ride back to Puno is relatively easy. Locals with totora reed boats give rides (s/8) to the island. Open daily 8am-6pm. s/5.

Sillustani, 34km north of Puno, is a peninsula jutting into the Laguna Umayu, a salt lake surrounded by the stark altiplano. It was a sacred burial site of the Colla people, who constructed numerous stone tombs, called **chullpas,** in which whole families were buried accompanied by their riches. Most of the towers have since been broken open, either by lightning or by grave-robbers. It's a beautiful stroll through the park, among various types of *chullpas*, from the early "rustic" variety to more ambitious ones built by the Incas. Wild *cuy* (guinea pig) peek out from behind the stones, but don't try to make a meal of these ones—hunting is forbidden on this sacred ground. An island in the lake serves as a reserve for **vicuña.**

CHUCUITO

To get to Chucuito, catch a colectivo marked "Acora" around the 14th block of Sol (20min., s/0.8). Walking uphill from the road, Santo Domingo is the first church. Turn right to find the enclosed lot where the temple awaits. Children play among the phalluses and can act as amateur guides. Some agencies offer tours for under s/5.

Chucuito, 18km south of Puno along Titicaca, is a very small Aymara village. (But really, does size matter?) Aside from two colonial churches and a nearby fish farm, Chucuito is the proud site of the **Inca Uyo,** a pre-Columbian fertility temple housing some **80 large stone phalluses,** which range from one to three feet in height. All shock with their anatomical detail. About half point straight up (as a potent tribute to the Sun god, Inti), while the rest are rammed into the ground (to fertilize the Earth goddess, Pachamama). At the center stands the principal stone penis, about five feet in length. What appears at first glance to be its simple stone base is actually a carved figure lying down—a head, arms, and legs—the phallus's virile owner. As the story goes, the Inca's wife and concubines would sit atop the giant phallus's mushroom head for three hours at a time to improve their chances of having male children.

Six years ago, this temple was incomplete, and the phalluses were stored in a museum in town. However, a number of archeologists persuaded the mayor to put them back into the temple—a rectangular area enclosed by stones with the marks of the Incas. Many were stolen once they were exposed, but the rest remain. However, the rocks that form the walls are perhaps more intriguing than the main attraction—on them, a sensitive hand can still trace faint imprints of important Inca images: puma paws, serpents, and suns.

Unfortunately, many discerning observers consider the Inca Uyo a fake. Several other Inca ruins feature large erect stones, possibly with phallic significance, but never with the kind of verisimilitude seen at Chucuito. Furthermore, the Spanish settled the area in the 17th century and probably would not have left such a temple intact. Even structures never seen by Spanish eyes—Machu Picchu for instance—don't look as complete as the Uyo. And if what locals say is true— that the Uyo has pre-Inca origins—Machu Picchu is more recent, and should be more intact. Nevertheless, *puneños* don't even crack a smile when they insist that the penises are legit. Literature from the tourist office speaks of the temple belonging to a fertility cult, tour guides mention it freely, and Puno's **Museo Dreyer** has one of the phalluses on display. The walls of the Uyo are undoubtedly Inca or Inca-influenced: the massive stones show fine interlocking corners typical of sacred buildings.

LOS UROS

Many tour agencies charge little (around s/15) for a guided tour of the islands. Most leave by 9am and rarely last more than an hr. A variety of package deals are also available, combining a trip to Amantaní and Taquile with a brief stop on Los Uros. It is also possible to make the trip to Los Uros without a guide: lanchas (motorboats) leave the port at Puno frequently 8am-5pm. The 35min. ride can cost anywhere from s/5-15, depending on the number of people on the boat. On some larger islands, locals offer short rides between individual islands of Los Uros on their long totora reed gondolas (s/3). Guided tours offer more information about the lives of the island people. Those who visit without guides are often left to wander around the small islands and their museos, which are usually just collections of stuffed birds. The gondola rides provided by locals are also more difficult to arrange without the presence of a guide and a tour group.

Centuries ago, the Uros people lived along the shores of Titicaca. But, faced with the gradual infiltration of the Aymaras and later the Incas, the Uros saw only one means of cultural preservation. They isolated themselves by constructing islands out of the totoro reeds which grow throughout the lake. Today, 45 islands still float in a cluster just a half-hour's motorboat ride from Puno. The inhabitants build everything out of totoro—houses, boats, souvenirs for tourists—and constantly need to stack more reeds on the surface of the islands as old reeds rot underneath. During the wet season, this process takes place at least once, sometimes twice a week. In the dry season, it is done about twice a month. Walking across an island is an eerie experience—the surface sinks slightly under each step. Many Uros people support themselves by fishing, just as their ancestors did. However, for many, tourists provide the steadiest source of income. About half of the islands are visited daily during the high season (June-Aug.) by a barrage of tourists. True Uros customs, including the language, were lost long ago as inhabitants intermarried with Aymaras. Many people on the islands don't actually live there, but commute each morning to sell souvenirs. Upon landing at Los Uros, the visitor is immediately surrounded by local children asking for candy and peddling drawings. Adults hawk cheap souvenirs they couldn't have made on the island—how can one make ceramics when there's no earth?

NEAR PUNO: ISLAS TAQUILE AND AMANTANÍ

Motorboats to Taquile and Amantaní leave the port in Puno early (4hr., 8am, s/10). Boats returning to Puno leave each island from their main port at 1 and 2pm. A few boats travel between the two islands in the morning only, usually departing at 8am to embark on the 1hr. journey. Almost all Puno agencies can arrange transportation, accommodations, some meals, and tours for the two islands (sometimes combined with a tour of Los Uros) for s/35; the tours are the easiest way to see the islands. Independent travelers may have difficulty finding a boat from Puno; it's a long trip and boat owners want a large group to ensure the cost-effectiveness of the journey. Tour guides will also have an easier time arranging accommodations and meals, since they communicate regularly with the families on the island and thus can fit into the rotation system more efficiently.

ISLA TAQUILE. This small island (pop. 3000) is far enough from the shore that it has maintained a good deal of authenticity, despite the occasional interruption by curious visitors. People on Taquile speak Quechua but many of the ancient traditions have faded over time. Women wear brightly colored skirts and cover themselves with black headscarves, a practice initiated by the conquistadors. Men don floppy woolen caps with colors that depend on the marital status of the wearer— unmarried males, even children, wear caps that are red on bottom and white on top, with the tips folded over to one of the sides. Married men wear caps of red, with the tips folded to the back. Some married men may also decide to wear the white and red caps, with the tips folded to the side, depending on their mood.

The people of Taquile subsist on agriculture; quinoa and potatoes are their main crops. The only animals found on the island are sheep and cows, as well as an occasional chicken. Aside from that, *taquileños* support themselves with the sale of exquisitely well-crafted **textiles.** All around the island, women can be seen spinning wool by using the drop-spool method, while men do all of the knitting. These textiles are a very important part of life for the inhabitants of Taquile. Not only are they a main source of income, the commonly woven belts and small bags play a key role in daily island life: the belts offer support when carrying heavy loads (which happens often since there are no load-bearing animals such as donkeys or llamas), and the small bags are worn as satchels in which to carry the coca leaves that are essential to life at such an altitude. During high season (June-Aug.), islanders set up stands in the Plaza de Armas (a breathless walk up hundreds of stone steps) to sell fine scarves, hats, belts, and gloves. Given the soundless customs of the people, this may be one of the more quiet markets you'll see. All items are sold on a communal basis: the families sell their handicrafts in the plaza on a rotating schedule, and all earnings are pooled.

As boats arrive on the island, local women meet them by the shore in order to offer tourists a place to stay; most locals speak some Spanish. **Accommodations** tend to be rudimentary—no running water or electricity. If staying on the island, bring a flashlight and warm clothing or a sleeping bag. Families generally charge around s/10 for lodging and a little bit more for meals; it is also customary to bring a gift of fruit to the family. As for food, islanders are chiefly vegetarian and limit themselves to a diet of eggs and potatoes. However, a slew of restaurants around the island can prepare seafood dishes as well.

The island itself is a large circuit of rocky paths. While the amount of terrain is limited, there is a very intricate web of walkways, so that one may be busied for most of the afternoon. Fantastic views of the lake provide plentiful excuses to pause and breathe in the fresh (thin) air.

ISLA AMANTANÍ. As pristine as Taquile is, Amantaní (pop. 4000) is even more so, though it has gradually begun to cut into Taquile's share of the tourism industry. Also Quechua-speaking, and the third largest island in Lake Titicaca, Amantaní possesses its own set of customs, more strongly influenced by Aymara ancestry than those of Taquile. A common display of the local culture comes in the form of an evening of dancing, to which all visitors are invited. In the island's central hall, men, women and children gather to listen to the town's young men play music. While the men and women observe, the girls invite the foreigners to dance in simple but lively steps long into the night. Amantaní is rocky and barren—the majority of agricultural energy is focused on a few grains, especially quinoa, which is a staple of all meals. Animals are present in greater numbers and variety than on Taquile; in addition to cows and sheep, there are pigs, donkeys, and alpacas. The inhabitants have utilized the rockiness to create a complex web of rectangles across the island, all bounded by stone walls. In particular, the eight small communities are all distinguished by the stone walls that encapsulate them.

Amantaní provides a good opportunity for hiking. The island is dominated by two hills crowned by temples, the taller hill being devoted to the **Pachatata** (Father Earth) and the shorter one to **Pachamama** (Mother Earth). No one is allowed to enter either temple except on the annual feast day (January 20), when the island's population splits in two, each half gathering at its own temple. A race is held from the summit of each to a designated point between them. One representative from each hill runs—if Mother Earth wins, the harvest will be a success; otherwise, the coming year will be stricken with scarcity. Pachamama always seems to end up victorious. The hike up both hills follows a path created by Inca ancestors, including still-intact stone archways, and the views at the top of both the island and the surrounding lake are well worth the gasping. Beware the wind at the top: it may snatch your already-scarce breath away. As on Taquile, accommodations are basic and arranged by local families as boats arrive in the morning. Room and board normally costs about s/10, and some gift of food is expected. Unlike Taquile, very few restaurants exist on Amantaní, so you will probably eat whatever your family prepares, which will be vegetarian unless you request otherwise.

NORTHERN PERU

The attractions of Peru's **northern coast** (p. 175) range from the natural to the architectural. This is where to find the country's most rugged and pristine beaches, and towns characterized by well-swept plazas and gleaming white churches. Yet the long stretches of desert that extend from Lima to the Ecuadorian border see few foreigners. Instead, most of Peru's economic activity happens here; locals occupy themselves with fishing and fish farming. Farther inland, the **Cordillera Blanca** (p. 199) is the most spectacular expanse of mountains in Peru and the second highest range in South America—19 of its summits are over 6000m in elevation. Most of the cordillera lies within the formidable 340,000-hectare Parque Nacional Huascarán, a nature reserve named for and centered around Nevado Huascarán, the country's highest peak. Among the park's other attractions are brilliant alpine lakes, sprawling mountain passes left by the receding glaciers, and unlimited opportunities for outdoor adventure. Between the Cordillera Blanca and the smaller Cordillera Negra lies El Callejón de Huaylas, a glacial valley that separates the mountain ranges and houses many towns. There are countless treks to be made and mountains to be climbed in this area, all of them best attempted during the dry season (May-Sept.). Travelers witness a distinct change in climate and vegetation after crossing the Río Marañon. This physical boundary marks the end of the Cordillera, the beginning of the elevated jungle, and, where the desert gives way to mountains, the edge of the **northern highlands** (p. 216). These distinct areas blend together to create a highland region of natural and archaeological wonders.

HIGHLIGHTS OF NORTHERN PERU

SURF the country's prettiest beaches: **Huanchaco** (p. 195), near Trujillo, and **Máncora** (p. 181), between Piura and Tumbes.

REJUVENATE in **Huancabamba** (p. 185), Peru's mystical faith healing capital.

HIKE around the **Lagos Llanganuco,** raised high among the towering peaks of the Cordillera Blanca (p. 206).

CONTEMPLATE the symbolism of the ancient engravings at the 3000-year-old **Chavín de Huantar** ruins (p. 208).

RELISH Cajamarca (p. 217), a lovely colonial town that's yet to be tourist-trampled.

NORTHERN COAST

TUMBES   ☎074

In Tumbes, the sun shines, and shines, and shines some more. It was shining on Pizarro when he sacked the then-Inca city—though as proud *tumbesinos* will remind you, the Spanish conquistadors weren't able to conquer it (that's why the city's main square is called the Plaza Principal rather than the Plaza de Armas). It was shining on the oil prospectors who discovered South America's first oil here in 1862; it was still shining on the Ecuadorians who ruled the city for the first part of this century; and it continued to shine on the Peruvians who took it back during the Border War of 1941. Tumbes is a sun-lover's paradise, and the nearby beaches, many still unspoiled by hordes of oil-smeared bathers, are some of the finest in South America. While most travelers see Tumbes as little more than a pit stop when crossing the Ecuadorian border, the city also provides a perfect base for exploring the area's warm mineral mud baths, mangrove swamps, and tropical rainforest. The center of town is lined with lovely pedestrian *paseos* overspread with myriad brilliantly colored tiles, lined by pastel buildings, and filled with shining mosaic-covered fountains and monuments.

⌐ TRANSPORTATION

Flights: Airport (☎525 102), 8km north of Tumbes. Take a colectivo (s/1) from the market on the corner of Ugarte and Mariscal Castilla to the turnoff on Panamericana Norte. Taxi s/10. Travel agencies-arranged shuttle s/10. **Tans,** Tumbes 293 (☎526 065). Open M-Sa 8am-8pm, Su 8am-noon. To **Lima** (2hr.; M, W, Th, Sa 10:45am; US$69) via **Chiclayo** (45min., US$20).

Buses: Terminals cluster around the intersection of Tumbes and Piura. Ormeño, Tumbes 314 (☎522 288), sends buses to **Lima** (18hr., 11:30am and 6pm, s/40; *servicio especial* 16hr., 1pm, s/70); and **Quito** (12hr., Tu and Sa 5am, US$30) via **Guayaquil** (6hr., US$20). Cruz del Sur, Tumbes 319 (☎524 001). To **Lima** (18hr., 1:30 and 7pm, s/40; imperial service 16hr., 5pm, s/75, includes dinner and breakfast). The normal-service **Lima** buses from both companies also stop in all major towns along the Panamericana, including **Piura** (4½hr., s/15), **Chiclayo** (7hr., s/20), **Trujillo** (10hr., s/25), and **Chimbote** (14hr., s/35). El Dorado, Piura 459 (☎523 480), sends buses to **Piura** (4½hr., 8 per day 7:30am-12:45am, s/15) via **Sullana** (4hr., s/15) and **Trujillo** (11hr.; 7:30am, 6, 9pm; s/25) via **Chiclayo** (8hr., s/20). Combis to the beaches south of Tumbes (marked "los Organos") also leave from the intersection of Tumbes and Piura, to: **Zorritos** (25min., s/1.5); **Máncora** (1½hr., s/5); and **Cabo Blanco** (2hr., s/6). Auto-colectivos to **Piura** (3½hr., s/20) via **Sullana** (3hr., s/20) leave around the clock from Terminal Tumbes, Tumbes 306, at the corner with Piura.

Taxis: Mototaxis s/1-2 for locations in town.

BORDER CROSSING: INTO ECUADOR

Tumbes-Huaquillas is the most popular place to cross the Peru-Ecuador border. Because of this, there are often substantial waits and unpleasant hassles; it is much easier (but less convenient) to cross between Sullana and Macará (p. 183). If you still want to cross here, catch one of the **Aguas Verdes**-bound auto-colectivos (30min., 6am-9pm, s/2) on Tumbes at Piura. Get your passport stamped at Peruvian Immigration, then take a mototaxi to the bridge (3km, s/1) and walk across it to **Huaquillas, Ecuador.** You must then pass through Ecuadorian Immigration (see p. 493)

◢⁊ ORIENTATION AND PRACTICAL INFORMATION

The **Plaza Principal,** on the southern edge of town, is the center of Tumbes's social activity, and **Tumbes,** the main thoroughfare, is the center of its vehicular activity. Two busy pedestrian walkways, **Bolívar** (also called **Paseo Las Libertadores**) and **San Martín** (also called **Paseo La Concordia**), radiate from the cathedral end of the plaza. Just south of the plaza, the **Malecón Benavides** offers a shady walk along the **Río Tumbes.** Artisans and fruit-sellers hawk their wares at the **market** on **Mariscal Castilla** near the corner of **Ugarte.** At night, stick to the well-lit plaza and pedestrian zones; the *malecón* and side streets are known for their pickpockets and sometimes even armed robbers.

Tourist Information: The **tourist office** (☎523 699), in the **Centro Cívico,** on the Plaza Principal, room 204, has maps. Open M-F 7:30am-7pm. Government-sponsored **Pro-Naturaleza,** Tarapacá 4-16 (☎523 412), an organization committed to conservation and sustainable development, gives tips about ecotourism in the area and occasionally organizes trips to nearby wildlife refuges. Open M-F 8am-1:30pm and 4-7pm.

Tour Agencies: Tumbes Tours, Tumbes 341 (☎526 086; fax 524 837). City tours US$6. Trips to the *manglares* or Hervideros mud baths US$20. Full-day tours of the Zona Reservada de Tumbes US$45. All led by the enthusiastic Emilio Mendoza Feijoo in Spanish only. Open M-Sa 8am-7:30pm. **Preference Tours,** Grau 427 (☎525 518), near the Plaza Principal, offers similar tour packages in Spanish or English and sells domestic plane tickets. Open M-Sa 7am-9pm, Su 7am-4pm.

Consulates: Ecuador, Bolívar 129 (☎525 949), on the Plaza Principal, can arrange tourist visas (though most Westerners don't need them). Open M-F 9am-1pm and 4-6pm.

Currency Exchange: Money-changers are more common than banks near the Plaza Principal. **Banco de Crédito,** behind the cathedral on the Paseo Los Libertadores. **Visa ATM.** Open M-F 9am-1:15pm and 4:30-6:30pm, Sa 9:30am-12:30pm.

Emergency: ☎ 524 036 or 105.

Hospital: Hospital de Apoyo, 24 de Julio 565 (☎522 222), at the northern end of Tumbes.

Telephones: Telephone/fax office, at Bolívar 250 (☎526 389), on Paseo Los Libertadores. Open daily 8am-10pm.

Internet Access: Modern Systems, Bolognesi 109 (☎522 081), in the blue building on the far corner of the Plaza Principal, behind the mural. s/5 per hr. Open daily 8am-9pm.

Post Office: Serpost, San Martín 208 (☎523 866). Open M-Sa 8am-8:15pm, Su 8am-3:15pm.

▐ ACCOMMODATIONS

Tumbes's safest budget hotels are within a few blocks of the Plaza Principal. Hot water comes at a price in Tumbes, and the cheapest hotels even have their cold water shut off at midday. While all hotel owners post their rates at the front desk, most will bargain for a discount of up to s/5.

Hotel César, Huáscar 311 (☎522 883). The tastefully furnished 3-star César has inlaid wooden floors, ceiling fans, hot baths, and cable TV, though the views of concrete walls leave something to be desired. Singles s/40; doubles s/50.

Hostal Tumbes, Grau 614 (☎522 203). A family-run bargain with simple but clean rooms with fans. Water in the morning and night only. Singles s/17; doubles s/25.

Hostal Chicho, Tumbes 327 (☎522 282), by the bus terminals. Offers the most amenities: hot water, refrigerator, radio/cassette player, TV, fan, mosquito net, and geriatric mattress pad. Singles s/35; matrimonials s/43; doubles s/50.

Northern Coastal Peru

NORTHERN PERU

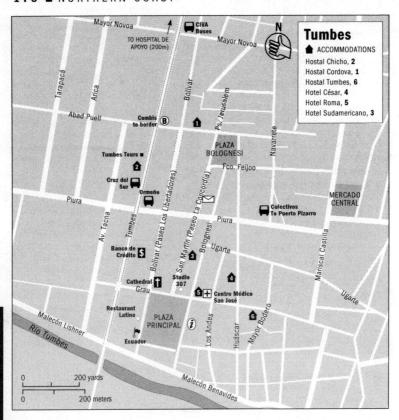

Hostal Cordova, Abad Puell 777 (☎523 981). A bit farther from the center of town, the spacious rooms lining Cordova's long hallways evoke the 1970s with their decor and linoleum floors. Laundry service, private baths. Singles s/19; doubles s/28.

Hotel Sudamericano, San Martín 130 (☎523 415), one block from the Plaza Principal. Bare-bones, with dimly-lit rooms and flimsy beds—but the owner is friendly, the location convenient, and the price a steal. Sporadic water. Doubles s/12, with bath s/17.

⌣ FOOD

You'll have no trouble finding *comida típica* in Tumbes. The *conchas negras* (black clams, for which the region is famous), ceviche, and other seafood specialties are universally fresh and well-prepared. **Panaderías** abound; many even wheel their goods around on street carts. **Mabrasa,** at Grau and Huáscar, offers fresh, warm rolls for mere *centavos.* (Open M-Sa 8am-8pm, Su 9am-noon and 6-9pm).

■ **Classic Restaurant,** Tumbes 179 (☎523 188). It's a shame it's only open through lunch, as this elegant eatery serves Tumbes's greatest hits with a gourmet twist, including *ceviche conchas negras* (s/11). Open Su-F 8am-5pm.

Studio 307 (☎524 052), at Grau and Bolognesi. Offers creative pizzas (large vegetarian s/34) on its huge patio overlooking the Plaza Principal. A bar with a large TV and a sound system blasting dance hits keeps the atmosphere lively, as does the *sangría,* which locals imbibe by the pitcher (s/20). Open daily 6pm-1am.

Restaurant Latino (☎523 198), on the Plaza Principal. Pleasant outdoor tables. Huge menu and even larger portions of local specialties like ceviche and *cau cau de mariscos* (s/10-15). Open daily 7am-11pm.

Chifa Danton, Bolívar 245 (☎521 566), on the Paseo Los Libertadores. The biggest chifa in a town full of chifas, with enormous *menú* portions to match (wonton soup, fried rice, and a noodle dish, s/6-10). Open daily noon-1am.

▣ ♫ SIGHTS AND ENTERTAINMENT

The area surrounding Tumbes covers four completely different ecological zones. First, there are the beaches—100km of them. The second ecological zone, the **manglares** (mangroves), begins north of Tumbes at Puerto Pizarro. The third and fourth regions comprise vast dry and tropical forests. To view all of these zones at once and get a sense of the abrupt contrast between them, check out the stunning 360° panorama from the top of the **Mirador Turístico Palo Santo,** 2km outside of town. From a height of 178m, you can see over 600 sq. km of surrounding landscape. (Taxi s/2. ☎524 837. Open daily 9am-5:30pm.)

Residents emphasize that Tumbes is *muy tranquilo*, which translates not only as "safe and clean" (at least in the plaza and well-lit pedestrian *paseos*) but also as "dead at night." There are a few small discos and karaoke bars near the Plaza Principal that are lively only on weekend nights, and even then most empty out by 1am. Instead, most locals amuse themselves with a stroll through the plaza or down the *paseos*. Tumbes's murals are doubly stunning when they sparkle and shimmer at night, especially that of **Chilimasa,** the legendary Tumpi leader who fought off the Spanish for 15 years, on the Plaza Principal across from the cathedral. Also on the plaza, the **Iglesia Matriz** does things with neon lights that seem almost blasphemous, and the **Matacojudo** tree in front of the Centro Cívico is said to drop its heavy gourd-like fruit on the head of any idiot (*cojudo*) who stands under its branches. Chess aficionados congregate on the Paseo Los Libertadores, and every Sunday night, the **Banda Militar Retreta** plays tunes from 8:30pm on.

▣ DAYTRIPS FROM TUMBES

NATURE RESERVES

Any of the travel agencies in Tumbes can arrange tours, but Tumbes Tours (see Practical Information, p. 176) offers a great daytrip to both reserves that includes transportation, a box lunch, and an informative Spanish-speaking guide (US$45 per person, less for larger groups). If you want to visit the reserves on your own, you'll have to rent a four-wheel drive vehicle (US$50-70 per day), as the roads are unpaved and hard to navigate—the Tumbes tourist office strongly recommends hiring a guide as well. They have a list of experienced guides (s/20-30 per day, Spanish-speaking only) and can make arrangements. Independent visitors also need a permit from the Ministry of Agriculture (INRENA), located at Tarapacá 401 in Tumbes (☎526 489); permits are currently free, but may soon cost s/5-10.

The nature reserves near Tumbes offer a chance to quickly and relatively cheaply get a sense of South America's biological diversity. Two hours southeast of Tumbes await the orchids, butterflies, birds, and beasts (including jaguars, tigers, and armadillos) of the tropical rainforest known as the **Zona Reservada de Tumbes,** quite similar in flora and fauna to the Amazon basin. Many wildlife enthusiasts come here to see two unique species: a breed of *mono coto* (howler monkey) much larger than those found around the Amazon, and the *cocodrillo americano,* a freshwater crocodile common in the Río Tumbes. The Zona Reservada is most easily accessible between May and December. Just across the Río Tumbes, the ecosystem changes drastically from lush vegetation to dry desert-forest in **Parque Nacional Cerros de Amotape.** The spiny flora is less dense here, but the diversity of fauna is still impressive—pumas, anteaters, red-headed monkeys, foxes, iguanas, and condors all thrive in this arid ecosystem.

NEAR TUMBES: PUERTO PIZARRO

Buses for Puerto Pizarro (20min., s/1.50) leave from Ponce. Taxis s/10.

Puerto Pizarro, a small fishing village 13km north of Tumbes, comes alive on weekends and holidays. There isn't much of a town—just a few neighborhoods on either side of the sandy road that leads to the water—but it's the water that brings people to Puerto Pizarro anyway. Hop on a small boat (s/15 per island) and head over to any of the nearby islands. **Isla Hueso de Ballena, Isla de los Pajares,** and **Isla del Amor** are the most frequented for their varieties of natural wildlife. The crocodile farm on **Isla Criadero de Crocodillos** can also be observed in action for a small fee (s/5). **Hotel Puerto Pizarro** (☎543 045) is the only place that offers resort-like perks (swimming pool, kayaking, and trips to the islands). Their clean but run-of-the-mill rooms have bath, fan, and TV (US$20 per person).

NEAR TUMBES: BEACHES

Getting to any of these beaches from Tumbes is simple; hop on a combi from the intersection of Tumbes and Piura or get on any Piura-bound bus and ask the driver to drop you off. Not all buses go all the way to Cabo Blanco; you may have to get off at the El Alto turn-off, then take a pick-up truck taxi to the water (15min., s/2).

Two major marine currents intersect here, the cold Humboldt from the south and the tepid El Niño from the north, generating warm water and sizable waves year-round. Along with the currents, two different schools of marine life meet by these 100km of beach south of Tumbes, and this water sees some of the hugest fish banks in Peru. Unlike the barren beaches of the southern coast, these tropical *playas* thrive with swaying coconut and carob trees, as well as colonies of pelicans, egrets, and other migratory birds. While many of the most spectacular spots lack overnight accommodations or only offer expensive resort hotels, a visit to the northern coast would be incomplete without watching a golden sunset over the finest ocean vistas Peru has to offer.

ZORRITOS. Zorritos, 27km south of Tumbes, is a fishing town with a clean beach and the most consistently warm water on the coast. Though its decent-sized waves pale in comparison to those farther south, the absence of a rip tide makes Zorritos ideal for swimming. The lack of a sizable surfer scene actually works to Zorritos' advantage; the beach here is safer than in hotspots like Máncora. The main attraction off the Panamericana are the hot springs in the nearby town of Bocapán. Tour agencies in Tumbes (p. 176) charge US$20 for trips to the springs, but you can also hike there on a marked trail from Zorritos (1-1½hr. each way; ask in Hostel Casa Grillo if you can't find the start of the trail). On the way from Tumbes, Caleta La Cruz, 10km north of Zorritos, is the spot where Pizarro first landed on the Peruvian coast in 1532. By taxi from Zorritos, you can also visit the **Aguas Termominero Medicinales,** a relaxing and nutrient-rich experience.

While there are a few small hotels or seafood restaurants in the village itself, it's well worthwhile to head 2km south to ▨**Hostel Casa Grillo (HI),** Los Pinos 563, at Panamericana Km1236. Spanish-born owner José Leon Millau designed this ecological ranch with Mother Nature in mind—rooms are in bamboo-roofed huts built by hand; the entire place runs on solar power (with a generator in case of cloudy days); and the open-air shower run-off nourishes the gorgeous bougainvillea gardens. By day, guests can rent horses (s/20 per hr.), use the bicycles, or relax on the hostel's private beach; by night, drinks flow until the last person quits (happy hour 6-8pm). The hostel also arranges daytrips and overnight camping excursions to nearby sights, and offers safe campgrounds by the beach as well as kitchen access (s/2) and laundry facilities. (☎/fax 544 222. Rooms US$6 per person, with bath US$8; camping US$2 per person, with tent rental US$4; non-members US$1-2 more.) Casa Grillo's amenities are outstanding, but perhaps the most noteworthy part of the place is its excellent, vegetarian-friendly **restaurant**, open even to non-guests. In addition to fresh seafood (s/9-12), fruit salads (s/7-10), and blended fruit drinks (s/3-5), the cooks use the wood-fire stoves to prepare Andalucian specialties like paella (vegetarian s/1, with seafood s/15), gazpacho, and the highlight, *langosto con pollo* (lobster with chicken, s/20).

MÁNCORA. Due to a fortuitous confluence of stunning scenery, killer waves, and an overall chilled-out attitude, Máncora's beaches have developed a legendary reputation among travelers. Attracted by hollow waves that reach heights of 3m between November and March, surfers come in throngs to partake in this small town's most popular tourist pastime. The second most common activity in Máncora is none at all—unless lounging on a hammock counts as an activity. Although the Panamericana (called **Piura** here) cuts through the center of town, the clean beach is completely isolated from the highway; one of the most serene spots is a natural rock formation known as **Las Pocitas.** Come nightfall, things stay just as mellow. Most opt against going to the few discos in town and instead sip *cervezas* while doing exactly what they came to do—relax in their hammocks.

There are plenty of hotels and restaurants in town, but other services are in short supply—head to Tumbes to take care of any pressing business. **Banco de la Nación,** Piura 527, exchanges dollars. (Open M-F 8am-2:30pm.) If you come unprepared, rent a surfboard or body board at **Soledad,** Piura 316. (s/10 per day. Open daily 8am-9pm.) The most crowded hostel in town is the beachfront **Sol y Mar,** off the second block of Piura. Basic rooms are heavy on the concrete (those on the upper floors are safer and cleaner), and all have baths with water that the owner calls warm. However, the location can't be beat, and most guests spend their time relaxing on the enormous fence-enclosed patio that faces the ocean. (☎868 106. Rooms s/10 per person, with ocean view s/15.) On the main street, **Casablanca,** Piura 232, has bigger, better maintained rooms, also with private cold-water baths. (☎858 337. Rooms s/10 per person; doubles with ocean view, TV, and fan s/40). Not all seafood restaurants are created equal; notice that the crowds head for **Restaurant Máncora,** Piura 664, for its huge selection. (Ceviches s/8-15 *Langostinos al ajo* s/15.☎858 236. Open daily 7am-midnight.) Sunny cafe-boutique **La Bajadita,** Piura 424, serves mainly sandwiches (BLT s/5.50, vegetarian s/4.50) and specialty seafood (sashimi s/8) to reggae rhythms. (☎687 784. Open Tu-Su 8:30am-9:30pm.)

CABO BLANCO. Most backpackers probably recognize Cabo Blanco from the labels on Peru's most popular economy rum. But in an unexpected union, surfers and literary buffs alike revere this fishing center, 109km south of Tumbes, as something more. Ernest Hemingway made frequent visits here in the 1950s, and supposedly wrote *The Old Man and the Sea* in the Cabo Blanco Hotel; the 1955 movie version was also shot here—not in Cuba. With all the oil pumps crowding the water nowadays, Cabo Blanco hardly looks like a place that inspires great novels, but its radical waves bring surfers running. The quiet town and sheltered nearby beach of **Restin** pick up only for the marlin (deep sea fishing) competitions held sporadically between October and May; for exact dates and entry requirements, contact the **Fishing Club** (☎(01) 445 4588). **Camping** on the beach is free and no permit is required; otherwise, accommodation options are limited to **El Merlín.** Ask for a room with a view. (☎856 188. Rooms US$20 per person.)

PIURA
☎074

Piura's placement on the map can be deceiving; though 200km east of Ecuador, it serves as a border town—and little more. Founded in 1532 by Francisco Pizarro, Piura enjoys the distinction of being Peru's oldest colonial city. Originally located in the Tangarará Valley, the town, evading pestilence and pirate attacks, moved three times before settling at its present site in 1588. Today, as the capital of its department and the closest major city to the Macará/La Tina border crossing, Piura is a convenient place to exchange money or catch a long-distance bus, but unless you're longing for a quiet night with nary a gringo in sight, you'd be best off moving on. Though the tree-lined streets and shady plazas invite peaceful strolls, Piura's climate can be oppressive—the landlocked city shares the same debilitating heat as the coast, but lacks the relief of the ocean breezes.

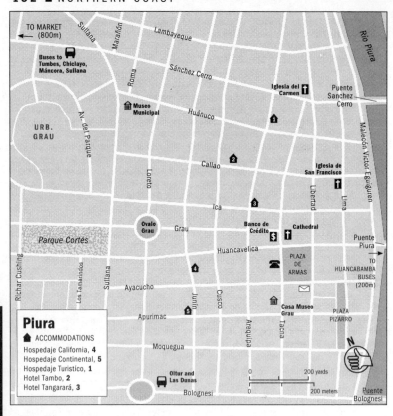

Piura

▲ ACCOMMODATIONS

Hospedaje California, **4**
Hospedaje Continental, **5**
Hospedaje Turístico, **1**
Hotel Tambo, **2**
Hotel Tangarará, **3**

▐ TRANSPORTATION

Flights: Airport (☎344 506), 2km south of town. Taxi s/4. **AeroContinente,** Grau 110 (☎310 080). To **Lima** (1¼hr.; 9:15am, 2:15, and 7pm; US$44-79) via **Chiclayo** (20min.). Open M-Sa 8:30am-1:30pm and 4-8pm, Su 9am-noon. **Tans,** Libertad 415 (☎306 886). To **Lima** (2hr., 6:30pm, US$44-49) via **Trujillo** (45min., US$20). Open M-F 8:30am-7:30pm, Sa 8:30am-6:30pm, Su 9:30am-12:30pm.

Buses: Those arriving on the night bus from Ecuador should know that there are no buses to Lima until the following evening. Many choose instead to spend the day in Chiclayo, 3hr. to the south, where there are more sights and better bus options. In Piura, most buses to Lima leave from the southern end of town, on Bolognesi at Sullana. Oltur S.A., Bolognesi 801 (☎326 666), sends direct luxury buses (with video, bathroom, dinner, and breakfast) to **Lima** (13-14hr., 6 and 6:30pm, s/60-80), as does Las Dunas (☎307 352), across the street (12-13hr.; M-Sa 6pm, Su 5:30pm; s/45). Most other bus companies leave from Sánchez Cerro west of Sullana. Vulkano/Linea, Sánchez Cerro 1215 (☎327 821), goes to **Trujillo** (6-7hr., 10:30pm, s/20) and **Cajamarca** (6hr., every hr. 5:30am-7:30pm, s/20) via **Chiclayo** (2½hr., s/10). El Dorado, Sánchez Cerro 1119 (☎325 875), sends buses to **Tumbes** (4½hr., 7 per day 8:30am-midnight, s/15) via **Máncora** (2½hr., s/12). The easiest way to cross the border is with Cooperativo de Transportes Loja (☎322 251), with direct service to **Loja, Ecuador** (9hr., 1 and 10pm, s/25). Buses to **Huancabamba** leave from Castilla, across the Puente Peatonal Piura; Turismo Express (☎345 382) and Etipthsa (☎473 000), both on Huancavelica, send daily buses (8hr., 8am and 7pm, s/15). If heading to points north along the Panamericana, it's easier (though more expensive) to take one of the frequent combis. Vehicles head to **Sullana** (from where you can get to the Peru/Ecuador border crossing at Macará/La Tina) from Sánchez Cerro and Sullana (30min., every 20min. 4:30am-8pm, s/1.5). Auto-colectivos to **Tumbes** (4hr., s/20) and **Máncora** (2½hr., s/20) leave from outside the El Dorado terminal on Sánchez Cerro.

BORDER CROSSING: INTO ECUADOR

The easiest way to cross the Peru-Ecuador border is on one of the direct buses between Piura and **Loja, Ecuador,** provided by Cooperativo de Transportes Loja. The border is open 24 hours. To officially enter or exit Ecuador or Peru, you must cross the bridge between the two countries by foot, passing through the immigration offices located on either side to receive entrance and exit stamps and to surrender or receive your tourist T3 card. From Sánchez Cerro and Sullana in Piura, catch a bus to the nearby town of Sullana (30min., every 30min. 4:30am-8pm, s/1.5). From José de Loma, Sullana's main street, take a mototaxi (s/1) to Calle 4, where taxi-colectivos depart for the border ("la frontera") at **La Tina** (2hr., 4am-7pm, s/10). Once you cross the bridge, pickup truck colectivos can drive you the 3km to **Macará** (see p. 494; 5min., s/1 or US$0.3), where multiple daily buses leave for Loja.

ORIENTATION AND PRACTICAL INFORMATION

Piura centers socially, if not geographically, around the **Plaza de Armas.** The always-busy **Grau** runs west from the cathedral to the Grau Monument. The two major north-south streets are **Loreto,** which intersects the Ovalo Grau, and **Sullana.** Most buses leave from **Sánchez Cerro,** west of Sullana. The **market** lies farther west on Sánchez Cerro. Of the two main bridges in the city, **Puente Sánchez Cerro** is to the east and **Puente Peatonal Piura** (also called Puente Viejo), to the south.

Tourist Information: Consult with one of the many private agencies, which can also arrange pricey tours of Piura and nearby towns. **Piura Tours,** Ayacucho 585 (☎328 873; email piuratours@mail.udep.edu.pe). Open M-F 8:30am-1pm and 4-7:30pm, Sa 8:30am-1pm. **Tallán Tours,** Tacna 258 (☎334 647; email tallantours@perumix.com). Open M-F 8:30am-1:30pm and 4-7pm, Sa 8:30am-1:30pm.

Currency Exchange: Banco de Crédito (☎323 712), at Grau and Tacna. **Visa ATM.** Open M-F 9:15am-1:15pm and 4:30-6:30pm, Sa 9:30am-12:30pm. There are 2 red Unicard **ATMs,** which accept all major international cards, on the block of Libertad just north of the Plaza de Armas.

Emergency: ☎113 or 105.

Hospital: Clínica San Miguel, Cocos 153 (☎335 913).

Internet Access: Cyber Solutions S.A. (☎327 471), at Libertad and Callao. s/3 per hr. Open M-Sa 8am-10pm, Su 9am-4pm.

Post Office: Serpost (☎327 031), on the Plaza de Armas. Open M-Sa 8am-8:30pm, Su 8am-2:45pm.

ACCOMMODATIONS

Apparently someone was expecting a lot of visitors—Piura today has a plethora of mostly empty budget hotels. Many offer both rooms with views of the street and rooms with views of a cement wall. Usually there is no difference in price. Few offer hot water, which isn't really necessary given Piura's sweaty climate.

Hospedaje California, Junín 835 (☎328 789). Bright and cheerful, with a sunny rooftop gazebo, friendly owners, and a fan in every room. Still, those who can't stomach ruffles, pastels, fake flowers, and obsessive color coordination should stay far, far away. Even the common baths are trimmed with lace. Singles s/13; doubles s/22.

Hotel Tambo, Callao 546 (☎322 312). The breezy building feels a few degrees cooler than the rest of town; fans in every room cool things down even more. A bit sterile, but comfortable. All rooms have baths. Singles s/20; doubles s/30; TVs s/4.

Hospedaje Turístico, Arequipa 481 (☎334 520), above Arnold's Gym. A group of grand-motherly *señoras* runs this hostel full of character and incongruous interior design. All rooms have baths. Singles s/20; doubles s/30; TVs s/5.

Hostal Tangarará, Arequipa 691 (☎326 450; fax 328 322), at Ica. Central. Functioning water heaters. Additional perks include personal TVs and phones, big windows, and lounges on each floor. Singles s/30; doubles s/40.

◖ FOOD

Since Piura's not exactly on the coast, there's less seafood served here than travelers to the region may have gotten used to. Most of the small chifas and restaurants serving *comida típica* are nearly identical.

Picantería la Santitos/Carburmer, Libertad 1014 (☎332 380) Elegant and high-quality Italian food. Enclosed outdoor courtyard. Personal pizza primavera s/15. Ravioli in fresh mushroom sauce s/11. "Gorden blue" *de lomo* s/27. Open daily 6pm-1am.

Ganímedes Vegetarian Restaurant, Lima 440 (☎329 176). A tropical hut stuck incongruously in the center of Piura. Soy meat seafood s/7-10. Over 20 types of fruit juices s/1-4. Open M-Sa 7:15am-10pm, Su 11am-8pm.

Tradiciones Piuranas, Ayacucho 565 (☎322 683). Pass a cast-iron gate and tiled patio to enter this alluring restaurant, decorated in the style of a traditional Piuran home and serving traditional Peruvian cuisine. Stuffed avocado s/8. Pisco sour s/4. Open daily noon-3pm and 7-11pm.

◖ ♫ SIGHTS AND ENTERTAINMENT

CHURCHES AND PLAZAS. Piura is perfect for long walks among colonial buildings and squares. The city takes great pride in its picturesque **Plaza de Armas,** home to a liberty statue nicknamed **La Pola.** Off the plaza, the somewhat run-down **cathedral** was built in 1588 and contains a gilded altar. At the end of Tacna, the more attractive **Iglesia del Carmen** serves as a **religious art museum.** *(Open M and W-Sa 10am-1pm and 4-7pm, Su 10am-1pm. Free.)* Piura's independence was declared at the small, simple **Iglesia de San Francisco,** at Lima and Callao, on January 4, 1821.

MUSEUMS. Casa-Museo Gran Almirante Grau, Tacna 662, displays the photographs, documents, and personal effects of the man who was born there, Admiral Miguel Grau (1834-79), a naval hero from the 1879 war with Chile—and Piura's pride and joy. *(Free tours; tip expected. Open M-F 8am-1pm and 3:30-6pm, Sa-Su 8am-noon. Free.)* The recently renovated **Museo Municipal,** at Sullana and Huánuco, has a little bit of everything: anthropological, archaeological, and geological exhibits; modern art; old photos of Piura; even a small gift shop. *(Open daily 7am-7pm. Free.)*

CATACAOS. This village, 12km from Piura, has an excellent **artesanía market** known for its *filigrana* work, thin strands of gold and silver elaborately woven into jewelry and wall hanging. The gold is generally of high quality (at least 18 carats), and prices are surprisingly low. Many wood carvings and cotton and straw weavings, including Panamá hats, are also sold in the market. *(Colectivos to Catacaos leave from Plaza Pizarro; 15min., s/1. Market open daily 9am-5pm.)*

NIGHTLIFE. Piura may not have the most exciting nightlife, but there are a number of **discos** and **peñas** in town. Piura's younger set goes for the pounding beats on Ayacucho between Cusco and Arequipa, at places such as **Flamingo's,** Ayacucho 534 (open Th-Sa 7pm-5am), and **Bohemio's,** Ayacucho 585 (open Th-Su 8pm-2am). Those with a few more years under their belts prefer the all-inclusive restaurant-peña club-discos on Guardia Civil, the eastern continuation of Sánchez Cerro on the other side of the bridge; the biggest are **Tony's,** at Guardia Civil and Cayetano Heredia (☎328 001), and **La Granja,** Guardia Civil Km1 (☎325 351).

🔁 DAYTRIP FROM PIURA

PAITA AND COLÁN

Buses to Paita leave frequently from Sánchez Cerro opposite the market, 6 blocks up from Sullana. Transportes Dora, Sánchez Cerro 1387 (☎326 670), has the most frequent service (1hr., every 20min. 6am-8pm, s/2.5). From Paita, it is a 20min. colectivo ride to Colán (s/2). Piura Tours (see p. 183) offers free transportation to Colán for Playa Colán Lodge guests.

The small town of **Paita,** 57km northeast of Piura, is the landlocked city's port. Located in a natural bay, Paita is also a major fishing center, and the combination of small fishing boats and large cargo ships can be somewhat disconcerting. In contrast to the port's prosaic present, its past was filled with drama and romance. British pirates, including adventurer Sir Francis Drake, repeatedly sacked Paita during the 16th century. The town also served as home to Manuela Sáenz, Simón Bolívar's mistress, after her lover's death in 1850. The activity around Paita's pier can be interesting to watch, but the real scenery lies in the unspoiled beaches to the north and south. The most notable is **Colán,** 16km to the north, a serene beach resort town. The community's houses sit on wooden stilts near the water line, where gentle waves lap the blindingly white sand. The town is also famous for the crumbling **Iglesia San Lucas,** the oldest church in Peru, built by Dominican friars in 1536. (10min. from town. Round-trip taxi s/8.)

HUANCABAMBA   ☎074

As if consciously defying miles of coastal flatlands, the first towering peaks of the Andes shoot up with startling abruptness. Only by braving the narrow dirt road that winds up through a dense plain of clouds can one reach the lofty valley that cradles Huancabamba, Peru's major center of traditional medicine. It would be enough to visit Huancabamba for the landscape and town, but most come in search of spiritual and medical healing. Huancabamba is renowned for its chamanes (spiritual healers, also known as *brujos, curanderos,* and *maestros*) and for the supposedly salubrious qualities of the nearby Lagunas de Las Huaringas.

■🔁 TRANSPORTATION AND PRACTICAL INFORMATION. Huancabamba's action centers around the colorful **Plaza de Armas,** bordered by **Grau, General Medina, San Martín** and the **Iglesia San Pedro.** The town's **bus terminal** is as the end of **Centenario,** three blocks uphill from the Plaza de Armas. From there, the two main bus companies, Etipthsa (☎473 000) and Turismo Express, send **buses to Piura** (8hr., 7:45am and 6pm, s/15); Etipthsa also serves **Chiclayo** (12hr.; Su, Tu, and Th 5:45pm; s/25). **Combis** to **Salalá** (2hr., 3-5am and 4-5pm, s/10) and other nearby towns also depart from the terminal. The incredibly helpful **tourist office** is in the terminal; they have a list of all registered maestros and free **luggage storage.** (Open daily 8am-noon and 3-7pm.) Other services include: **Banco de la Nación,** at Grau and Lima (no traveler's checks or ATM; ☎473 004; open M-F 8:30am-2:30pm); the **police,** on the plaza (☎473 010); **Hospital Rural de Huancabamba,** at the entrance to the city; and **Telefónica del Peru,** San Martín 124 (☎473 144; open daily 7am-10pm).

■🔁 ACCOMMODATIONS AND FOOD. All of Huancabamba's accommodations leave something to be desired. **Hospedaje Danubio,** Grau 208, on the Plaza de Armas, offers good views of the mountains from some rooms. The common baths are quite clean; there's only sporadic water at night, but it comes out warm. All rooms have TVs; prices depend on the floor. (☎473 200. Singles s/8-12, with balcony s/15; doubles s/12-20, with balcony s/20.) Considered Huancabamba's "luxury hotel" because of the 24-hour warm water in its shared baths, **Hostal Dorado,** Medina 116, on the plaza, has small rooms with water marks on the worn walls. (☎473 016. Rooms s/10 per person). **Hospedaje San Pedro,** Centenario 206, next to the bus terminal, offers large rooms that are much cleaner than the common baths, which have limited water. (☎473 178. Singles s/10; doubles s/20, with bath s/25.) Restaurants in town are small and simple. **Poker de Aces,** around the corner from Hospedaje San Pedro, offers *criollo* food and *rompopes* (s/1), a local libation made from caña (a strong sugarcane alcohol) with egg, sugar, honey, lemon, and vanilla, traditionally drunk at midday (open daily 8am-11pm).

■■ **SIGHTS AND FESTIVALS.** Inside the bus terminal, the small **Museo Munic-ipal Mario Polia Meconi** houses pottery from pre-Inca civilizations such as the Huancapampa, Chimú, Vicus, and Mochica, as well as two **mummies** found in Suc-chil. (Open daily 8am-noon and 3-7pm. If it's locked, ask someone in the tourist office to let you in. Free.) The **Plaza de Armas** provides an excellent view of the hills above. For an even better view, ask someone in the church or tourist office to let you into the **mirador** at the top of the bell tower. There are also some inter-esting sights outside of town. The nearby ruins at the **Templo de los Jaguares** include four large rocks sacred to the local Huancapampa culture. The boulders lie in and near a ceremonial temple built around AD 1200 for a jaguar cult, then converted to a Temple of the Sun when the Inca Tupac Yupanqui conquered the area around 1480. (Take a combi to Mitupampa (2hr., 6am-5pm, s/3) from the bus terminal, then walk another 30min. to the ruins.) South of Huancabamba, the tra-ditional village of **Sondor** is known for its leatherwork and its *alfañiques* (peanut sweets), prepared in special adobe jars called *mocaguas*. A 15-minute walk away, the 45m tall waterfalls of **Citán** and **Los Peroles** are best seen between June and August. (Take a combi to Sondor (45min., s/2) from the bus terminal.) The **Baños del Inca** is a natural rock formation in the shape of a chair, large enough for three people. A cold subterranean river shoots out overhead, creating a refresh-ing, shower-like stream. (Take a camioneta headed to Chulucanitas Bajo (3-3½hr., s/6) from the bus terminal.) The rock formations at **El Valle de los Infierni-llos** are only accessible by taxi (3½hr., round-trip s/70). Although admission is not generally charged at any of these sights, the Huancabamba tourist office can sell you a **Boleto Turístico** (s/3), ensuring free entrance to all attractions in case any-one gives you a hard time. With advance notice, the tourist office can also arrange for a Spanish- or English-speaking **guide** to accompany you; the service is free, but you must pay for the guide's transportation and food during the day. The best times to visit Huancabamba are between June and November, particu-larly during their *fiestas*. The most important of these is the **Festividad de la Vir-gen de Carmen,** a four-day celebration beginning July 16, which features performers in elaborate costumes who do dances that represent the struggle between good and evil.

⬛ DAYTRIP FROM HUANCABAMBA: VISITING THE MAESTROS. Whether you suffer from arthritis or unrequited love, financial difficulty or fevers, the maestros of the **Huaringas** promise to provide a cure. The Huaringas are com-prised of about 250 lakes of varying size, the largest of which is **El Shimbe**, at 3818m above sea level, while the most powerful is supposedly **Laguna Negra**, at 3957m. The ceremony begins at the lakes, a three- to four-hour horse ride away, where the maestro takes his patients to bathe in the purifying waters. The main part of the ritual takes place at night and is known as *la mesada* or *la mesa*. First, patients take a *remedia*, prepared from the hallucinogenic cactus known as the San Pedro or *huachumba*. After that has started to take effect, it is sup-plemented by *aguardiente* (sugarcane alcohol) and tobacco juice (absorbed through the nose). Finally, various spirits and saints are invoked with the help of perfumes, incense, and special staffs, swords, and amulets, depending on the nature of the ailment. This part of the ceremony lasts until 5am. While curious visitors are welcomed by locals, scorn or skepticism is not—these ceremonies are taken very seriously.

If you want to visit a *maestro*, check the official register in the tourist office to find out which one best suits your needs—not all of them work all the time, and some only treat certain ailments. Some *maestros* charge as little as s/50, but beware of untrained pseudo-shamans. The most respected, sought-after mae-stros charge between s/150 and s/3000 (less with larger groups). People in Huan-cabamba may offer to serve as guides to take you to your maestro of choice, but if you want to avoid paying a commission of up to 50%, you're better off finding

NORTHERN PERU

him on your own. Have a few back-up *maestros* in mind in case your first choice isn't working that night. Combis leave from the bus terminal for **Salalá**, the remote village where the maestros live (2hr., 3-5am and 4-5pm, s/10); tell the driver whom you want to see, and he'll drop you off at the right house. It's better to arrive in the morning to talk to a few maestros, as they can't be reached by phone. Once you've made a deal, you can spend the day relaxing in the *maestro's* house, or travel to the lakes by horseback (2½-4hr., s/20 each way). If you're in a hurry, there's enough time to take an afternoon *combi* and arrive in Salalá before nightfall.

CHICLAYO   ☎074

Most people visit Chiclayo for its prime location, close to several important archeological sites. The nearby pre-Inca ruins, which include remnants of the Moche and local Lambayeque cultures, are among the oldest in South America, and the famed **Señor de Sipán,** discovered nearby in 1987 and hailed as the Peruvian King Tut, is considered one of the most significant archaeological discoveries of the past century. In addition to its excellent nearby beaches, Chiclayo lives up to its nickname of "La Ciudad de La Amistad" ("The City of Friendship"). The city's wide streets and well-maintained plazas buzz with a disproportionately high number of amicable, curious, and outgoing locals who just want to welcome you to town.

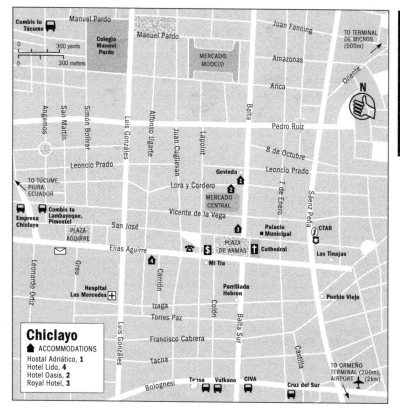

Chiclayo

🛏 ACCOMMODATIONS
Hostal Adriático, 1
Hotel Lido, 4
Hotel Oasis, 2
Royal Hotel, 3

NORTHERN PERU

▐ TRANSPORTATION

Flights: Aeropuerto José A. Quiñones (☎233 192), 2km south of the city. Taxi s/3. **Aerocontinente,** Elias Aguirre 712 (☎209 916). Open M-Sa 9am-7:45pm, Su 9am-12:30pm. To **Lima** (1hr.; 10am, 3, and 8pm; US$44-69) and **Piura** (20min.; 8:15am, 1:15, and 6:45pm; US$15). **Tans,** Balta Sur 611 (☎205 867). To **Lima** (1hr.; M, W, Th, Sa noon, F and Su 7pm; US$44) and **Tumbes** (45min.; M, W, Th, Sa 9:30am, F and Su 4:30pm; US$20). Open M-Sa 9am-8pm, Su 9am-noon.

Buses: Chiclayo contains about a dozen "terminals terrestres," each serving 1-10 bus companies, which are spread out along a 2km stretch south of town (mostly along **Bolognesi**). One of the few agencies not located on Bolognesi, Ormeño, Rail Haya de la Torre 242 (☎234 206), on the southern continuation of Saenz Peña, serves **Lima** (11hr., 7:30 and 9:30pm, s/30; *servicio especial* 10hr., 8pm, s/40). From the same building, Lit Peru (☎234 343) sends buses to **Chimbote** (5hr., every hr. 8am-7pm, s/15) via **Trujillo** (3hr., s/10). Direct luxury buses to **Lima** (10hr.; M-Sa 8pm, Su 8 and 9:30pm; s/55) leave from Cruz del Sur, Bolognesi 888 at Balta Sur (☎225 508). Trans Linea/Vulkano, Bolognesi 638 at Colón (☎233 497), serves: **Piura** (3hr., 13 per day 6am-8pm, s/10); **Cajamarca** (5-6hr., 10 and 10:30pm, s/18-22); **Jaén** (5½hr., 11pm, s/15); and **Lima** (11hr., 8 and 8:30pm, s/35-45). TransServis Kuélap, in the Terminal Tepsa at Bolognesi 536 (☎271 318), just west of Colón, has the best service to **Chachapoyas** (9hr., 6pm, s/25); reserve a seat well in advance. Etipthsa (☎229 217), also in the Terminal Tepsa, runs to **Huancabamba** (11hr.; M, W, F 4:45pm; s/25).

▐ ▐ ORIENTATION AND PRACTICAL INFORMATION

Activity centers around the **Plaza de Armas,** although Chiclayo is so spread out that many people rely on taxis (around town s/1-2) to get around. **Balta** is the major north-south street running through the plaza; **Elias Aguirre** intersects Balta on the southern end of the plaza. The **Mercado Central** is on Balta two blocks north of the plaza; the **Mercado Modelo** lies five blocks north of the plaza at Balta and **Arica.**

Tourist Information: Centro Informático de Turismo, Saenz Peña 838 (☎208 501). Open M-F 8am-1pm and 2:30-6pm.

Tour Agencies: Given that the sights around Chiclayo are easily accessible by public transportation and that inexpensive guides can be hired on location, guided tours are not necessary. **Quality Service Tours,** Balta 847 (☎221 963; fax 271 339; email quality@kipu.rednorte.com.pe), sells domestic and international plane tickets, has **Western Union** service, and arranges pricey city tours (US$30) and trips to Sipán, Túcume, and the Brüning museum (US$30-70). Open M-F 9am-1pm and 4-7pm, Sa 9am-1pm.

Currency Exchange: Interbank, Elias Aguirre 680 (☎238 361), on the plaza. Open M-F 9am-1pm and 4-6:15pm, Sa 9am-12:30pm. There is a **Red Unicard ATM** which accepts all major international cards on Elias Aguirre at the Plaza de Armas.

Markets: Mercado Central, Balta 961, 1½ blocks north of the Plaza de Armas. Open M-Sa 7am-7pm, Su 7am-2pm. Larger and more lively is **Mercado Modelo,** on Balta between Arica and Pardo, 4 blocks north of the plaza. In the back, the *mercado de brujos* (witch market) has one of the best selections of traditional medicine in Peru, including hallucinogens like *ayahuasca* (s/20 per bottle) and the San Pedro cactus (s/2). Open daily 6am-7pm.

Emergency: ☎233 152 or 114. **Fire:** ☎116.

Tourist police: Saenz Peña 830 (☎236 700, ext. 311).

Medical Services: Private **Clínica Lambayeque,** Vicente de la Vega 415 (☎237 961). **Hospital Las Mercedes,** Gonzales 635 (☎237 021).

Post Office: Serpost, Elias Aguirre 140 (☎237 031). Open M-F 8am-9pm, Sa 8am-8pm, Su 8am-2pm.

Internet Access: Most of Chiclayo's *cabinas de Internet* cluster around the Plaza Aguirre. **Efe Net,** Elias Aguirre 181 (☎234 951). s/3 per hr. Open daily 8am-midnight.

Telephones: Telefónica del Peru, Elias Aguirre 631 (☎232 225). Open daily 8am-11pm.

ACCOMMODATIONS

Chiclayo's very cheapest, bare-bones accommodations (rooms s/10 per person) are on Balta near the Mercado Modelo.

Royal Hotel, San Jose 787 (☎233 421), in a grand old building with a winding staircase and a perfect location. Rooms have generous windows that open onto the plaza, as well as private, hot-water baths. Singles s/23; doubles s/32.

Hotel Oasis, Lora y Cordero 858 (☎272 700). A newer establishment in a tall apartment building that could really use an elevator. Brightly-decorated rooms have spotless hot baths. Singles s/20; doubles s/40; cable TV s/10 extra.

Hostal Adriatico, Balta 1009 (☎221 873), is somewhat more worn but loaded with character. The lobby has a huge vestibule with a crystal chandelier, and large doubles have colonial-style balconies overlooking bustling Balta. Rooms s/10 per person.

FOOD

Chiclayo beats all other Peruvian cities in having the highest number of *pollerías* per capita; many lie along Balta. Those with a sweet tooth will delight in the *alfajores* sold on nearly every street corner; the local special is the **King Kong,** two cookies held together by *piña* (pineapple), *maní* (peanut), and *manjar blanco.*

Pueblo Viejo, Izaga 900 (☎229 863). One of the classiest restaurants in town, Pueblo Viejo serves exquisite *comida criolla* at affordable prices. The staff recommends the popular *tollito a la panca* (a fish native to the region; s/15). Open daily noon-5pm.

Parrillada Hebrón, Balta Sur 605 (☎222 709). Vegetarians beware—this carnivore's paradise isn't for you. *Menú ejecutivo* (roasted meat served with fresh juice and dessert) s/6. Ribs with french fries and salad s/12. Tell the manager you're a tourist, and he'll give you a souvenir. Open daily 7:30am-midnight.

Govinda, Balta 1029 (☎227 331). A branch of the national Hare Krishna-run vegetarian consortium, uncharacteristically featuring "Especialidades Hindus" such as Alu Panir Sak (a spinach and cheese dish; s/6). Open M-Sa 8am-9:30pm, Su 8am-4pm.

SIGHTS

Chiclayo's sights are all accessible by public transportation, though if you want to cram them all into a single day, you may want to hire a private taxi (s/80 per day).

SIPÁN. In early 1987, anthropologists realized that they had overlooked an important Moche burial site in the town of Sipán, 28km east of Chiclayo, when valuable artifacts from that area began popping up on the black market. Many feared that the most important sites had already been looted, but in September a team headed by Peruvian archaeologist Walter Alva discovered a tomb that the *huaqueros* had somehow missed, far surpassing all others in its riches. The warrior-priest known as the **Señor de Sipán** probably governed this area around AD 250. Replicas of his tomb and nine others at the Sipán site provide a fascinating glimpse of how the untouched graves appeared. Though his grave measures only five square meters, it was packed with the bodies of those sacrificed to join the Señor in his journey to the after-world. Also at the Sipán complex are a small museum (inferior to the Brüning) and various *miradores* from the top of barely recognizable ceremonial pyramids. *(Colectivos leave every 45min. from the Terminal Terrestre de Micros at Oriente and Piérola (45min., s/1.5), or hire a private taxi (round-trip s/40). Guides (in Spanish only) cost s/7 for groups of up to 10; tip expected. Site open daily 8am-6pm. s/5.)*

LAMBAYEQUE. The main attraction in Lambayeque, 12km northeast of Chiclayo, is the outstanding **Brüning Museum,** where the pieces found in the Señor de Sipán's tomb are displayed. The artifacts include over 1150 ceramics and numerous pieces of jewelry, *tumis* (ceremonial knives), idols, scepters, and breastplates made of gold, silver, bronze, and precious jewels, all beautifully presented with English captions. After a long stay in Lima's Museo de la Nación, the actual decomposed bones of the Señor himself returned to the Brüning in 1999. The museum also displays the tomb of the Viejo Señor, an older dignitary found intact beneath the Señor de Sipán, as well as Moche and Chimú artifacts from other nearby sites. If you have more time, check out Lambayeque's two mammoth architectural monuments, the **Iglesia San Pedro,** built around 1700, and the 16th-century **Casa de la Logia.** *(Combis to Lambayeque (12min., 6am-10pm, s/0.7) leave from Vicente de la Vega and Angamos. Get off at the market area on Castilla, Lambayeque's main street. To get to the Brüning, turn left on Atahuallpa and walk 1 block; the museum is at the corner of Huamachuco. Taxi s/8. ☎282 110. Guides in English or Spanish s/10. Open M-F 8:30am-6pm, Sa-Su 9am-6pm. s/5.)*

TÚCUME. Often called El Valle de los Pirámides, the complex of 26 ceremonial adobe pyramids here was perhaps larger than Chan Chan when constructed around AD 1000. At 700m long, 280m wide, and 30m tall, the largest pyramid, **Huaca Larga** is the single largest adobe structure in South America. You can climb up to *miradores* as high as 140m to get a bird's-eye view of the unrestored complex, but erosion has taken its toll on the pyramids. The pyramids were the work of the Lambayeque culture, whose history is outlined in the adjacent **Museo de Sitio.** *(Combis to Túcume (30min., s/2) leave from Angamos near Pardo. The pyramids and museum are another 2km from town; combis cost s/0.5. Guided tours in Spanish only (45min., s/10 per group). Wear sturdy shoes and insect repellent, as Túcume is overrun with mosquitos. Salas is 20min. farther north on the old Panamericana. Site open daily 8am-4:30pm. s/5.)*

NEAR CHICLAYO: PIMENTEL

Combis to Pimentel (30min., 6am-10:30pm, s/1) leave from the corner of Vicente de la Vega and Angamos. From Pimentel, head to Santa Rosa (10min.; colectivo s/0.8; taxi s/4)and then to Eten (15min., s/1), where you'll again have to switch vehicles to get to Puerto Eden, 2km away (combi s/0.5; mototaxi s/1). Direct combi from Puerto Eden to Chiclayo s/1.2.

In a city as hot as Chiclayo, few things are as refreshing or relaxing as a day at the beach. Fortunately, the fishing town of **Pimentel** is a mere 14km away. During the summer (Jan.-Mar.), Pimentel is less a beach resort than a popular daytrip for locals, where speakers on the lampposts set the mood by blasting beachy tunes. Pimentel is dominated by its 730m long pier, where fishermen busily reel in the catches of the day each morning (admission s/1). Many will rent out their small motorboats and guide trips to the nearby islands **Lobo de Afuera** and **Lobo de Tierra** (about s/30 for 3-4hr., ask around on the pier in the morning). It's also possible to rent horses for rides along the beach. (☎453 054. s/15 per hr.) The water is too calm for surfing, but in March the town hosts beach sport tournaments, fishing contests, and races with *caballitos de totora,* traditional fishing boats woven out of reeds. Accommodations in Pimentel are limited. Fortunately, the one budget hotel fulfills its duties well. **Hostel Garuda,** Quiñones 109, one block inland from the pier, has clean singles in a big yellow house. Guests are free to use the kitchen and body boards, and play with the pet dog. (☎452 964. Singles s/25; doubles s/45-60.) The best food in town—seafood with an Asian twist—hides within the zebra-meets-teepee exterior of ▩**Yomiuri,** on the beach 10m past the Casino de Pimentel. Entrees average s/10. (☎979 695. Disco F-Sa. Open Su-Th 11am-4pm and 9pm-2am, F-Sa 11am-4pm and 9pm-4am.) South of Pimental lie some smaller and more secluded shores. **Playa Las Rocas,** 2km away, is an empty stretch of beach with better waves for surfing. **Santa Rosa,** 6km from Pimentel, is a traditional fishing village dominated by a hectic public market. Colorful wooden fishing boats cover the sand, while *caballitos de totora,* still used by local fisherman, bob up and down on the water. About 18km from Pimentel, **Puerto Eden** may be remote (combis drive through a river to get there), but it's far from isolated—during the summer, sunbathers pack the seemingly endless 6½km of shore, while a DJ pumps dance tunes from a makeshift stage on the beach.

TRUJILLO   ☎044

Trujillo, Peru's third-largest city, lacks the vices of most major cities: the pedestrian-filled plazas are safer, the streets less disorienting, and the size less overwhelming. Colonial *casas antiguas* appear brighter than those in Lima, thanks, ironically, to a severe 1970 earthquake that necessitated their restoration. And Trujillo's un-Lima-like absence of choking pollution bodes well for its surrounding beaches. Founded in 1534 by conquistador Diego de Almagro and named for the birthplace of Francisco Pizarro, Trujillo was populated long before the arrival of the Spanish: the Mochica, Chimú, and Inca civilizations all inhabited these parts at one time or another. Remnants of their past splendor shine at the archaeological sites of the Huacas del Sol y de la Luna, El Brujo, and the enormous mud-brick city of Chan Chan. Of course, Trujillo doesn't surpass Lima in all respects. Its clubs and cafes are pale imitations of those found in the capital, and women report more incidents of verbal harassment here. Trujillo fosters its own traditions, most notably in its unique celebrations, like the Festival de la Marinera (last two weeks of January), featuring spirited competitions in the regional dance of the same name.

⌐ TRANSPORTATION

Flights: Aeropuerto Carlos Martínez de Pinillos, 20min. from town. Taxi s/10 (s/5 from Huanchaco). **AeroContinente,** Orbegoso 582 (☎200 775). Open M-Sa 9am-1pm and 4-8pm. To **Lima** (1hr., 9:15am and 7pm, US$44-69) and **Tarapoto** (1¼hr.; Tu, F, Su 1:45pm; US$35-59). **Tans,** Orbegoso 324 (☎207 181). Open M-F 9am-1pm and 2:30-7:30pm, Sa 9am-1pm and 4-6pm, Su 10am-noon. To **Lima** (1hr., 7:40pm, US$44-49) and **Piura** (45min., 5:20pm, US$20-25).

Buses: The main companies serving Lima and Tumbes have terminals around Ejército, just north of town center. Ormeño (☎259 782), on the 2nd block of Ejército, serves: **Lima** (8hr., 9, 11:30am, 9:30, 10pm, s/30; *especial* 10:30am, 1:30, 10:30, 11pm, s/45-55); **Tumbes** (11hr., 7pm, s/30; *especial* 10:15pm, s/45); and **Quito, Ecuador** (23hr., M and F 7pm, US$70) via **Guayaquil** (18hr., US$60). CIVA, Ejército 285 (☎251 402), sends buses with bathrooms, video, and A/C to **Lima** (8hr., 10:30pm, s/30) and **Tumbes** (9hr., 10pm, s/25). Around the corner, Cruz del Sur, Amazonas 437 (☎261 801), goes to **Lima** (8hr., 9:45 and 10:30pm, s/30; *bus cama* 12:30 and 11pm, s/60). Linea/Vulkano, Carrión 140 (☎235 847), off Mansiche, serves: **Chiclayo,** (3hr., every hr. 6am-7pm, s/10); **Cajamarca** (6hr., 10:30am and 10:30pm, s/18-25); and **Piura** (6-7hr., 11pm, s/20). Vulkano buses to **Huaraz** (8hr., 9pm, s/30) and **Lima** (8hr.; 10, 10:30, 10:45pm; s/25-50) leave from the terminal at Nicaragua 220 (☎243 847), southeast of town.

Taxis: Within town s/2-3. To Huanchaco s/8. Prices double after 11pm.

⬛⬛⬛ ORIENTATION AND PRACTICAL INFORMATION

Most of the popular plazas, hotels, restaurants, and colonial houses are enclosed in the **old town** by the circular **España,** which roughly follows the route of the wall that protected the city in colonial times. Remnants of that wall are located between blocks 11 and 17 of España. At the center of the old town lies the **Plaza de Armas.** The most frequented shopping and dining is along **Pizarro** past the plaza in the direction of rising street numbers. At the terminus of this street, **La Plazuela El Recreo** stands witness to the promenades of many a passerby. The main street out of the center, **Manische,** leads to the **Ovalo Coca-Cola,** center of all colectivo activity.

Tourist Information: Oficina de Turismo, Independencia 628 (☎258 216). Great maps and information on public transportation to local sights. Open M-S 9am-1pm and 4-8pm.

Tour Agencies: ▨ **Guía Tours,** Independencia 580 (☎245 170). Open M-F 9:30am-1pm and 4-8pm, Sa 9:30am-1pm. **Trujillo Tours,** Diego de Almagro 301 (☎233 091; email ttours@terra.com.pe). Open M-F 9am-1pm and 4-8pm, Sa 9am-1pm. Both have English-speaking staff and tours to nearby ruins. Guía Tours, however, has better prices (Chan Chan s/40, Huacas del Sol y de la Luna s/30) and the inimitable guide Pedro Puerta, who has been offering his original interpretations of the ruins for over 40 years.

Currency Exchange: Banco de Lima, Orbegoso 503 (☎261 030), off the plaza. 24hr. red Unicard **ATM,** which accepts all major international cards. Open M-F 9:15am-1pm and 3:30-6pm, Sa 9:30am-12:30pm.

Laundry: Lavandería La Moderna, Orbegoso 270. Next-day service s/6 per kg. Same-day service s/7.5 per kg. Open M-Sa 9am-1pm and 4-8pm.

Emergency: ☎105.

Tourist Police: Independencia 630 (☎291 705), in the 16th-century colonial house referred to as the Casa de la Portada de Leones.

Pharmacy: Botica Arcangel, Almagro 603 (☎291 805), at Bolívar. Open 24hr.

Hospital: Hospital Regional Docente (☎231 581).

Telephones: Telefónica del Peru, Pizarro 561 (☎231 287). Open M-Sa 8am-10pm, Su 8am-noon.

Internet: El Navegante, San Martín 626 (☎207 066). s/2.5-3.5 per hr. Open 24hr.

Post Office: Serpost, Bolognesi 410 (☎245 941), at Independencia. Open M-Sa 8am-8pm, Su 9am-1pm. **DHL/Western Union,** Almagro 579 (☎203 689). Open M-F 9am-1pm and 4-8pm, Sa 9am-1pm.

◤ ACCOMMODATIONS

Due to Trujillo's key location as the first major city north of Lima, accommodations are numerous. Places closer to the plaza are more convenient than elsewhere but are sometimes slightly noisier and more expensive. The best budget accommodations, however, rest in the nearby beach town of **Huanchaco** (see p. 195); even visitors more interested in sightseeing than sun worshipping may want to consider staying there, as it's a mere 20-minute colectivo ride from the city.

Hostal Americano, Pizarro 764 (☎241 361). With artwork, wall reliefs, and antique furniture that exude an air of past grandeur, Americano was probably once one of Trujillo's most upscale accommodations. Singles s/16, with bath s/20, with hot bath s/30; doubles s/26, with bath s/30, with hot bath s/40.

Hotel Trujillo, Grau 581 (☎243 921). This decaying house manages to turn age to its advantage with a 1950s charm. The bright pink facade gives way to blue rooms with clashing orange paisley bedspreads. Baths have hot water only during specific hours. Singles s/18, with bath s/22; doubles s/30, with bath s/35; TVs s/5 extra.

Hostal Central, Ayacucho 728 (☎205 745). Cell-like but sufficient. Ask for a fan if it gets too hot, or else you'll end up as lethargic as Juanito, the pet tortoise. Singles s/14, with bath s/20; matrimonials s/18, with bath s/24; doubles s/24, with bath s/30.

Hostal Lima, Ayacucho 718 (☎232 499). This basic budget find offers simple rooms with small windows and firm mattresses. The security gate provides extra peace of mind. Cold water only. Singles s/11; matrimonials s/14; doubles s/18.

◖ FOOD

Trujillo has plenty of delectable dining diversions, though some of the best food (especially seafood) is found in the nearby town of Huanchaco, a 20-minute bus ride away. If you'd like to try local dishes such as *cabrito de leche* (young goat cooked in milk), *arroz con pato* (rice with duck), or *shambar* (a wheat soup with beans and pork, traditionally served on Mondays), head to the inexpensive restaurants lining the Plazuela El Recreo at the end of Pizarro.

Demarco, Pizarro 725 (☎234 251). With chandeliers on the ceiling and elevator music tinkling over the sound system, this is one of the posher places in Trujillo. *Menús* s/5.5-8. Pastas s/10-15. Open daily 8am-midnight.

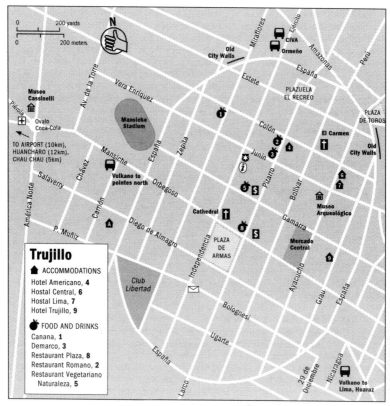

Trujillo

🏠 ACCOMMODATIONS
Hotel Americano, 4
Hostal Central, 6
Hostal Lima, 7
Hotel Trujillo, 9

🍎 FOOD AND DRINKS
Canana, 1
Demarco, 3
Restaurant Plaza, 8
Restaurant Romano, 2
Restaurant Vegetariano
    Naturaleza, 5

Restaurant Romano, Pizarro 747 (☎ 252 251). This cozy, European-style cafe serves the best coffee drinks in Trujillo (large cappuccino s/2.4). Meat and fish dishes s/10-20. Salads s/3-5. Vegetarian sandwiches s/3-4. Open daily 7:30am-1am.

Restaurant Plaza, Orbegoso 491 (☎ 262 589), at the plaza. A local favorite. ¼ chicken with salad and fries s/7. Open M-Sa 8am-3:30pm and 5-11:30pm, Su 2-11:30pm.

Canana, San Martín 791 (☎ 257 788), presents tasty *comida criolla,* including many varieties of *lomo* (grilled beef s/15-20). Traditional music and dancing take over on Fridays and Saturdays after 11pm. Open M-Sa 7pm-4:30am.

Restaurant Vegetariano Naturaleza, Gamarra 455 (☎ 292 055), makes up for its tiny interior with enormous portions. Vegetable omelettes s/4. *Menú* s/5. They also sell natural medicinal products such as bee pollen and *uña de gato.* Open daily 7am-10pm.

🔭 SIGHTS

IN THE CITY CENTER

CHURCHES. Trujillo's churches and cathedrals invite visitors to gawk over their fancy facades. The **Basílica Menor** of the **Catedral de Trujillo,** at the corner of the Plaza de Armas, was built in the mid-17th century and is the most important religious building in town. The attached **Museo Catedrálico** houses a collection of religious art and costumes, and its underground crypts contain the bones of *martiros degollados* (decapitated martyrs). (*Museum open M-Sa 8am-2pm and 4-8pm. s/5, students s/3. Tours in English, Spanish, or French included.*) The gilded interior of the **Monasterio El Carmen,** at Colón and Bolívar, is breathtaking. Next door, **Pinacoteca Carmelita** houses religious paintings from the colonial era. (*Open M-Sa 9am-1pm. s/3.*)

CASAS ANTIGUAS. A number of beautiful colonial houses are scattered throughout old Trujillo. Some, such as the **Casa Bracamonte,** Independencia 441—the oldest and most ornate of the houses—are closed to the public and can only be appreciated for their spectacular facades. Perhaps the most impressive *casa antigua,* **Palacio Iturregui,** Pizarro 688, has been converted into a private club, but much can be seen from the front court. The easiest to visit are those now occupied by banks, which are open to the public during business hours. Trujillo's independence was declared in 1820 inside the **Casa de la Emancipación,** Pizarro 610, which now houses a photo exhibit and a brilliant garden in back. **Casa Calonge,** Pizarro 446, displays republican relics like Bolívar's writing desk. The restoration of **Casa Garci Holguin,** Independencia 527, next to the cathedral, should be finished by 2001.

MUSEUMS. There are two decent archaeological museums in town. **Museo Arqueológico de la Universidad Nacional de Trujillo** has the most varied collection of pre-Columbian artifacts, including a detailed exhibit on the restoration of Huaca de la Luna, with modern and informative displays in Spanish. *(Junín 682, at Ayacucho. ☎ 249 322. Open M 9:30-2pm, Tu-F 9:15am-1pm and 3:30-7pm, Sa-Su 9:30am-4pm. s/5, students s/1.)* **Museo Cassinelli** has an incredible collection of over 10,000 ceramic pieces spanning 2500 years: from the Paleolithic age to the arrival of the Spanish. The impressiveness of the exhibit, however, is diminished both by its location (basically in the basement of a gas station) and by the realization that many of the pieces were unearthed by *huaqueros. (Nicolás de Piérola 601, behind the Mobil Station. ☎ 231 801. Open M-Sa 9:30am-1pm and 3:30-6:30pm, Su 10am-12:30pm and 4-6pm. s/5.)*

OUTSIDE THE CITY CENTER

The archeological sites around Trujillo trace the rise and fall of two of the most important pre-Hispanic cultures on the northern coast. While the **Huaca Prieta** and **Cupisnique** cultures lived in the Trujillo area as far back as 3000 years ago, the first civilization to leave a major mark was the militaristic **Mochica** (Moche) culture, which extended its empire as far as modern-day Piura in the north and Chimbote in the south between 100 BC and AD 600. The Mochica built the first major temple complexes in the area, but they are most often noted for their artistic achievements in metalwork, weaving, ceramics, and pottery. After the Mochica Empire declined between AD 600-700, the burgeoning **Chimú** culture consolidated in the Moche and Chicama valleys, and by 1400 had expanded their territory along the coast from modern-day Tumbes to Lima. A confederation of dynastic families with their central capital at **Chan Chan** (see below), the Chimú Empire was conquered and sacked by the Incas around 1460, 80 years before the Spanish arrived. Although travel agencies in Trujillo offer **tours** in English of the major Mochica and Chimú ruins in the area, a guide is only really necessary for Chan Chan. Guides can be hired at the sites themselves for a fraction of the tour agency price.

CHAN CHAN. Touted as the **largest preserved mud-brick city in the world,** Chan Chan was once the glorious capital of the **Chimú** Empire, which extended 1000km along the coast from Tumbes to Lima. The mud metropolis consists of 15 citadels, nine of which are believed to have been the personal palaces of individual rulers. Following their deaths, rulers were elaborately interred in their respective royal residences along with some of their subjects. Apart from the funerary function, excavations also suggest administrative, storage, metalworking, and residential sectors in the numerous palaces. Today, visitors can explore the winding passages, symbolic carvings, and grand halls of the L-shaped **Tschudi Palace.**

Though Tschudi is definitely the main attraction, the other, significantly smaller structures are worth a visit and are accessible by taxi. **Huaca Esmeralda** can be best appreciated for its detailed fish imagery, and **Huaca Arco Iris,** also referred to as **El Dragón,** is named after the intricate depictions of rainbows and "dragons" that line the two-story structure. The Chan Chan admission fee includes entrance to these three sites as well as the small **Museo de Sitio de Chan Chan.** The museum highlights the advanced technology and specialization achieved by the Chimú and uses ceramics to demonstrate outside influences. *(The Esmeralda ruins are 10min. from Trujillo by taxi (s/10) or bus (s/1, take any bus headed to Huanchaco from the corner of España and Independencia or the Ovalo Coca Cola). To visit the Museo, hop on another bus (s/0.5-1) going to Huanchaco, and then walk 1km to the Tschudi Palace. The Arco Iris complex is in an unsafe area, so tourists are advised to arrange a visit with a private guide or one from the museum. Guides s/10-15. Sites and museum open daily 9am-4pm. s/10, s/5 with ISIC.)*

MOCHICA RUINS. Just 5km south of Trujillo, at the foot of Cerro Blanco, lies the impressive mud-brick remains of the ceremonial capital of the Moche State (BC 100-AD 600), which at its peak extended from Piura to the Huarmey River. The site is defined by two massive structures, **Huaca del Sol** and **Huaca de la Luna,** which are separated by an elite residential sector. Following the El Niño-related collapse of the Moche, this central area was used as an elite cemetery by later civilizations. During the Colonial period, the Huaca del Sol was partially destroyed when the Spanish attempted to loot the mound by diverting the nearby Moche River. To the west, the 32m high Huaca de la Luna is in better shape. The building techniques preserved the polychrome decorations; of particular importance is the repeated presentation of the anthropomorphic dragon deity, the Decapitator God, which appears frequently on the pottery and frescos of other sites. *(The temples are a 30min. bus ride from the corner of Suárez and Los Incas in Trujillo or a 20min. taxi ride (s/10). Guided tours free with ticket. Guidebook s/10. Open daily 9am-4pm. s/5.)*

EL BRUJO. This remote site, 60km from Trujillo in the Chicama Valley, consists of three pyramidal temples: the 5000-year-old Huaca Prieta, Huaca del Brujo, and Huaca Cao Viejo. The polychromatic reliefs inside show scenes from Mochica life featuring prisoners, warriors, dancers, and human sacrifices. The area also includes burial sites and smaller Mochica and pre-Mochica ruins. *(El Brujo is hard to reach without private transportation or an expensive guided tour. Buses to the two closest town, Cartavio and Chocope, leave from the intersection of Gonzalez Prado and Los Incas (1½hr., s/3). From there, it is easiest to take a taxi to the site, and arrange for the driver to pick you up.)*

🎵🎭 ENTERTAINMENT AND NIGHTLIFE

Trujillo's nightlife is dead during the week but shows vital signs on the weekend. Discos smoke all over town but pale in comparison to Lima's. **Crack Discoteca,** América Sur 2119, at the Luna Rota complex, looks flashy but caters to a painfully young crowd (☎242 182. Cover Sa s/6. Open daily 9:30pm-3:30am.) Upstairs are a **casino** and the mellow **Luna Rota Pub,** with an older, salsa-loving crowd. (Pub cover Th s/5, Sa s/7. Open Th-Sa 10pm-5am.) With its eclectic mix of baroque art and a balcony overlooking the Plaza de Armas, the chic **Las Tinajas,** Pizarro 383-389, is more hip but also more expensive. On weekends, the attached underground dance club comes closer to matching Lima's bright lights, big mirrors scene. (Pub open M-Sa 9pm-2am. Disco open F-Sa 10pm-4am. Cover F s/5, Sa s/10.) **Millenium Drive Inn** (☎241 003), San Isidro, offers a novel concept: people come in their cars to enjoy big-screen music videos over a pitcher of beer (s/18). For the pedestrians who just wanna dance, Millenium also has a disco in the big, barn-like building in back with UFO-like lights and a bubble machine on Fridays. (Cover s/5. Open Th-Su 8pm-5am.) Trujillo also has two **movie theaters** that often show English language movies; one is at Pizarro 748 (shows 4:15, 7:15, and 10pm; s/6), and the other at Orbegoso 245 (4:15, 7:15, and 10:15pm; s/7). Near Trujillo: Huanchaco

To get to Huanchaco, take a colectivo from in front of the Shell station at the Ovalo Coca-Cola (15-20min., s/1). To get back to Trujillo, catch a colectivo on Rivera. Taxis normally cost s/8, but prices skyrocket to s/12-15 after 11pm, when the colectivos stop running.

NORTHERN PERU

Tourists passing through Trujillo venture north just to spend a relaxing few days in this serene beach town. Once a party hotspot, these days Huanchaco only gets busy during the high season (Feb.-Mar.) or when Trujillans flood the shores on weekends. Huanchaco offers a long, clean beach, good-sized waves (beware the ubiquitous sea urchins), an alluring artisan market, magnificent seafood, and plenty of tourist facilities. Huanchaco is also one of the few places left where you can find *caballitos de totora* (fishing boats made from bundles of totora reeds) still in use. If you'd like to try this alternative method of "riding the waves," just approach any of the fishermen near the pier (s/5 per 40min., s/10 with instruction).

Huanchaco certainly doesn't suffer from a shortage of excellent accommodations. ▨**La Casa Suiza,** Los Pinos 451, two blocks up from the water near the entrance to town, offers more options than a swiss army knife: 24-hour hot water, a book exchange, laundry service, Internet access, free boogie boards, reasonably priced wetsuit and surfboard rentals, and a rooftop terrace. (☎461 285. Dorms US$4; rooms with bath US$5 per person.) **Naylamp,** on Victor Larco, near the end of the beach to the right when facing the water, has clean, bright rooms. Amenities include a communal kitchen, laundry, and relaxing hammocks. (☎461 022; email naylamp@computextos.com. Dorms s/10; singles s/20; doubles s/30.) Naylamp also offers clean, safe **campsites** with a view of the beach (s/5, s/8 with tent rental). **Hospedaje Huanchaco's Garden,** Circunvalación, Lote 3, set back from the beach (look for the sign on the main walk), provides quiet two-room matrimonial suites with private baths and cable TV, as well as smaller, simpler singles. (☎461 194. Singles s/20; suites s/40, with kitchenette s/50.)

Another thing not in short supply in Huanchaco is fresh seafood. The street along the beach is lined with inexpensive *picanterías*, but when you order a s/5 ceviche, you just might get what you pay for. For some of the best seafood and beach views in town, stop in at **Lucho del Mar,** Victor Larco 600. The delicious *ceviche mixto,* which contains at least five types of fish, may be pricey (s/20), but it's easily big enough for two. (☎461 460. Open daily 10am-7pm.) **Mama Mía,** Victor Larco 538, offers a good selection of burgers (s/8) and Italian dishes. (Ravioli filled with ricotta, mozzarella, and spinach s/16. Open Tu-Su 7:30am-11pm.)

WHATEVER FLOATS YOUR BOAT Watching the Huanchaco fishermen bob over the waves in their **caballitos de totoro,** it seems amazing that they stay afloat. The reed boats get heavier as they absorb water and start to sink, making a morning fishing excursions a constant race against time. Peruvians have been constructing similar boats for more than 3000 years, but generally only use them for a few hours at a time, venturing just a couple miles offshore. However, in the 1940s, a Norwegian named **Thor Heyerdahl** bet that these vessels could stay afloat even longer—as long as it took to sail across the Pacific. A young botanist researching in Polynesia, Heyerdahl discovered that many species of Polynesian flora originated in Latin America, and became obsessed with the question of how those islands became inhabited by humans. He argued that Polynesian natives originally came not from Asia, but from the western coast of South America, and were descendants of the pre-Inca peoples of Peru. Scientists scoffed at the theory, arguing that ancient Peruvians lacked the technology to sail across the Pacific, so Heyerdahl set out to prove them wrong. In 1947, he set off from Callao, a port just outside Lima, in a raft made of the same type of Ecuadorian balsa reed used in the *caballitos de totoro.* Over the next 101 days, Heyerdahl and his crew of five successfully crossed more than 8000km and landed on the shores of the Tuamotu Islands in Polynesia, confirming that ancient Peruvians had the ability to cross the Pacific in their reed vessels.

NEAR TRUJILLO: PUERTO CHICAMA

Make sure the bus you catch is going to Puerto Chicama—not the town of Chicama, 20min. outside Trujillo. El Milagro sends buses to Puerto Chicama from Santa Cruz 290 in Trujillo (1½hr., every 30min., s/3), or flag down the red buses (often with a sign saying "Paiján") as they pass the Ovalo Coca-Cola. It may be faster to take a colectivo from the "Ovalo Coca-Cola" to Paiján (1hr., s/2) and then another to Puerto Chicama (½hr., s/1). Colectivos return from Chicama whenever full from Tarapaca and Ugarte between 5am and 8pm. If you're lugging a surfboard, it's easiest to travel the whole way by taxi (1hr., s/70 from Huanchaco or Trujillo).

Surfing is Puerto Chicama's *raison d'être*—the beach (also referred to as **Mala-brigo**) has one of the longest left-hand waves in the world. Rides of almost 2km are not unusual on a good day. Bring your own board and wetsuit, as there are no places to rent equipment here (though there are in Huanchaco) and the water may be quite chilly during the non-summer months (Apr.-Dec.). Non-surfers are better off staying in Huanchaco, as the town of Puerto Chicama is tiny and the beach dominated by fish-processing equipment. Accommodations in Puerto Chicama are strictly basic—you're expected to spend your time in the water, not in your room. **Hostal El Hombre**, Arica 803, at the end of the beach to the left when facing the water, has traditionally been the most popular among surfers, though its age shows. Basic rooms are just large enough for you and your surfboard. (☎977 6923. Rooms s/15 per person.) A better value is the brand-new **Hostal El Naipe** at Grau and Tacna, one block up from the beach. Even the shared cold-water bathrooms are super clean. (☎643 568. Singles s/15; doubles s/25.)

CHIMBOTE ☎044

The largest city between Lima and Trujillo, Chimbote sits by a natural bay that, while pleasant to the eyes, is not nearly so kind to the nose. The area's many fish-meal processing plants have made its waters some of the most polluted in Peru, and the smell is often overpowering. A few minor ruins and natural attractions in the area are the only (not very compelling) reasons to get off the bus.

Chimbote's main street is **Victor Haya de la Torre** (though most locals and street signs still use its former name, **José Pardo**), two blocks from the water and parallel to the shore. The **Plaza de Armas** lies between Pardo and **Leonicio Prado**. Almost all long-distance **buses** enter and depart from the new **terminal,** 8km from the center of town (taxi s/4). Ormeño (☎353 515) has buses heading south to **Lima** (6-7hr.; 11am, 3, 11:30pm; s/20) and north to **Tumbes** (13hr., 5 and 8pm, s/35) via **Trujillo** (2hr., s/7). Linea (☎354 000) goes to: **Lima** (6-7hr., 11pm, s/15); **Chiclayo** (5hr., 9:15am and 3:30pm, s/16); **Trujillo** (2hr., every hr., s/5); and **Cajamarca** (6hr., 7am and 7pm, s/25). Transportes Yungay Express (☎353 642) runs to **Huaraz** (8hr.; 6, 8am, 1, 9pm; s/20) via the stunning Cañon del Pato valley. Micros (s/2) and auto-colectivos to **Casma** (50min., s/3.5) leave from the intersection of Pardo and Tumbes, five blocks from the plaza. Services include: **Interbank,** Bolognesi 670, with a **Visa ATM** (☎321 411; open M-F 9am-6:15pm, Sa 9am-12:30pm); the **police** (☎321 651), at the corner of Prado and Bolognesi on the plaza; a **telephone office,** on the plaza at Villavicencio 346 (☎324 182; open daily 7am-11pm); the **post office,** at Pardo 294 (open M-Sa 8am-8pm, Su 9am-1pm); and **Internet access** at Computer House, Prado 509 (☎324 491; s/3 per hr.; open M-Sa 8am-midnight).

Hostal Bolognesi, Bolognesi 596, offers oddly-shaped but well-kept rooms with TV (upon request), and private baths. (☎336 510. Rooms s/15 per person.) **Hostal Chimbote,** Pardo 205, is cheaper but has only cold water. The lack of a breeze through the miniscule windows can be a mixed blessing on hot nights. (☎344 721. Singles s/10; doubles s/15.) With an artificial fishpond and gold lanterns, **Chifa Canton,** Bolognesi 498, is the most elegant restaurant in town. (Entrees s/10-16. ☎344 388. Open Su-F noon-3pm and 6-11pm, Sa 11am-3pm and 6:30pm-midnight.) Chimbote's renegade sandboarder community fuels up on tasty thin-crust pizza at the tiny **La Pizza Nostra,** Prado 593. Cheese or pepperoni slices with a cup of soda go for s/2.50. (☎325 654. Open daily 5:30-11:30pm.)

Most of Chimbote's sights lie out of town. **Helen Tours,** Ugarte 693 (☎322 921), at Manuel Ruiz, specializes in day trips to Chimbote's main tourist sight, the **Isla Blanca.** Part of the Fauna Marina ecological reserve, the island gives ample opportunity for visitors to go rock climbing, admire marine wildlife, or simply relax on the many unspoiled beaches. Though less than an hour offshore, the Isla Blanca is inaccessible by public boats; private tours cost only s/15 per person, but generally only leave with groups of 10 or more. If you call Helen Tours in advance and ask when the next group is scheduled to leave, you can generally go along. For more of an adventure, find a taxi driver willing to take you up to the top of the nearby mountain, **Cerro de la Juventud** (20min., s/15-20). Near the summit, the **Santuaría Señor de la Vida,** an impressive church built into the side of the mountain and walled only with windows, offers incredible views. You can reach the crypts beneath the sanctuary by walking 15m in darkness through a tunnel dug into the mountain. A damaged statue of Christ resides there, left unrepaired to symbolize the terrorism's effects on Peru. From the church, it's a 30-minute climb to the summit and the **Cruz de la Paz,** which affords even more spectacular views. To get back to town, walk down the road to the highway (1hr.) and flag down a passing bus or taxi. Hiking from Chimbote to the church is not recommended without a knowledgeable guide, as the road is unmarked and a wrong turn could quickly get you lost in the surrounding high desert. **Aventurs Peru,** Enrique Palacios 317, on the Plaza de Armas, leads three-hour city tours that include the Cerro de la Juventud (s/40 per person for groups of 4), as well as trips to the pre-Inca rock constructions at **Siete Huacas** and **Paredones.** (☎320 288. Open M-Sa 8am-10pm.)

CASMA ☎044

The small town of Casma has been completely rebuilt since its utter devastation in the 1970 earthquake centered just off the coast. Of course, most tourists don't visit Casma for its post-1970 architecture, but for its proximity to something much older: the 3500-year-old **Sechín** ruins, 3km from town. The site's age makes it of vital importance for archeologists trying to gain an understanding of the region's ancient cultures. The two main buildings in the center, one of adobe and the other of stone, are connected to the rest of the complex by a series of passageways lined with over 300 carvings of half-naked warriors engaged in gory battle and victory scenes. To learn more about the history of the ruins and those who built them, visit the **Museo Sechín,** at the site; knowledgeable guides (s/15) can also explain the site in detail. To get to the ruins, take a mototaxi (s/2-3); ask the driver to wait for you or return to pick you up later, or take your chances and hope that a taxi or colectivo will stop to pick you up on the road to get back to Casma. (Site and museum open daily 8am-6pm; s/5.) The less-visited **Chanquillo** ruins consist of three enormous concentric oval walls built on top of a hill overlooking the Río Sechín. Their purpose remains enigmatic, but some anthropologists hypothesize that the geometric figures were somehow related to astronomy. From the gas station at the edge of town, take a combi headed to San Rafael and ask to be let off "frente al castillo" (30min., s/1). From there, the ruins are a one-hour walk. Leave early and bring plenty of water. **Tortugas,** a beach 20km north of town, was adopted by wealthy vacationers from Lima and Chimbote 20 years ago. Today, the bay still laps a clean beach; there's plenty of swimming, water sports, fishing, and yachting in the summer (Dec.-Mar.), but resort-level prices preclude stays of longer than a day for most budget travelers. Tortugas-bound colectivos (20min., 5am-7pm, s/2) leave from Mejía, just off the plaza, past the intersection with Nepeña.

The main road in town, **Huarmey,** sits one block behind the tranquil **Plaza de Armas.** All **buses** traveling between Lima and the north pass the gas station at the edge of town and will stop if they have empty seats; to get there, follow Nepeña up from the Plaza de Armas for about 10 minutes. Turismo Las Dunas, Tarapacá 439 (☎711 381), serves **Lima** (5hr., 12:15am and noon, s/20) and **Piura** (8hr., 12:45am, s/30) via **Chiclayo** (6hr., s/25). Tepsa, Luis Ormeño 505 (☎711 226), goes to **Lima** (5hr., midnight, s/15) and to **Tumbes** (22hr., 2pm, s/35) via **Trujillo** (5hr., s/10), **Chiclayo**

(6hr., s/15), and **Piura** (8hr., s/28). Empresa Tamara (☎724 362), across the street from the gas station, sends buses to **Huaraz** (5hr., 9am, s/15). Colectivos to **Chimbote** (50min., s/3.50) leave when full from Nepeña and Mejía, just off the plaza. Services in town include: **Banco de la Nación,** on Nepeña behind the Municipalidad building (☎711 508; no traveler's checks; open M-F 8:10am-2pm); the **police,** Magdalena 201 (☎712 340), at the plaza; **Hospital de Apoyo Casma** (☎711 299), on Mejía; and the **post office,** which also has **telephone** facilities, on Lomporte by the plaza (☎711 067; open M-Sa 8am-8pm). For a comfortable room near the plaza, head to **Hostal Indo Americano,** Huarmey 130, which is safe and clean. (☎711 395. All rooms with bath. Singles s/20; matrimonials s/30; doubles s/40.) Nicer rooms are farther up the street at **Rebecca Hostal,** Huarmey 370, next to the Farmacia San Carlos, where well-decorated rooms all have hot baths, TVs, and firm beds. (☎711 143. Singles s/30, doubles s/45.)

BARRANCA   ☎034

Barranca is a small town that serves primarily as a base camp for exploring nearby ruins. In this case, the main attraction is the ancient **Paramonga Fortress,** built by the pre-Inca **Chimú Empire** at the southernmost extent of their expansive empire. Paramonga is a large ruin with walled passages that wind their way up a somewhat steep incline. At the top, one can still find traces of colored murals. Although referred to as a fortress, the compound was most likely used as a ceremonial center. A helpful information sheet can be purchased at the entrance (two very full pages in Spanish; s/0.5). The official who works at the office is quite knowledgeable. (Open daily 8am-6pm. s/3, students s/2.) The site lies on the Panamericana 17km north of Barranca, so any northbound bus can drop you off there (ask the driver to let you off at "la fortaleza"). Alternatively, take a colectivo from the corner of Lima and Ugarte in Barranca to the small village of Paramonga (25min., s/1) and then take a mototaxi the remaining 6km to the ruins (10min., s/3). In town, the main streets are **Lima** (the Panamericana) and the parallel **Gálvez,** one block away. **Alfonso Ugarte** leads between Gálvez and the **Plaza de Armas.** To catch a northbound bus from Barranca, go up to Lima and wait for one to come by. Several small companies clustered around the corner of Lima and Ugarte send buses south to **Lima** (3hr., every 30min. 4am-8pm, s/8). Services in town include: **Banco de Crédito,** Gálvez 330 (open M-F 9:15am-1:15pm and 4:30-6:30pm, Sa 9:30am-12:30pm), with a **Visa ATM;** the **Hospital de Apoyo** (☎235 2241), on the second block of Nicolás de Piérola; the **post office,** Ugarte 114 (☎235 4530; open M-Sa 8am-8pm); and the **telephone office,** Ugarte 161 (☎235 2020; open daily 7am-11pm). In general, accommodations in Barranca are basic and inexpensive. **Hostal Pacífico,** Gálvez 115, has simple rooms with lumpy beds and tiny windows too high to see out, but the old building is freshly painted and the water is hot. (☎235 2526. Singles s/10, with bath s/13; doubles s/16, with bath s/19.) The higher-end **Hostal Continental,** Alfonso Ugarte 190, resides in a modern building near the plaza. The halls are a bit dark, but the rooms have large windows onto the street. All rooms have a fan and hot bath. (☎235 2458. Singles s/25; matrimonials s/30; doubles s/40; cable TV s/5 extra.)

THE CORDILLERA BLANCA

HUARAZ   ☎044

As a primary gateway to the Cordillera Blanca, Huaraz buzzes with constant chatter about alpine adventures. Among older locals, however, talk is not always so lighthearted: Huaraz residents refer to any event in the region's history as *"antes de"* (before) or *"después de"* (after) the catastrophic earthquake that shattered all but one street and killed half the city's population in 1970. Huaraz recovered, of course, but hasty post-quake reconstruction led to a city that appears to have been built almost entirely of cement. Still, urban splendor—or lack thereof—isn't what draws so many backpackers to Huaraz from May to September, the regional dry season. Instead, the area's popularity with travelers interested in outdoor experiences, combined with residents' amicable and enthusiastic dispositions, makes it easy to find climbing, hiking, rafting, and traveling companions, not to mention others who want to set out for the Wilcahuaín and Chavín ruins nearby.

▐ TRANSPORTATION

Buses: Bus companies flank Raymondi. Newcomer Etti, Raymondi 800 (☎726 645), provides clean service for cheap prices. To: **Lima** (8hr., 10pm, s/15); **Chimbote** (6hr., 9pm, s/18); and **Trujillo** (8hr., 9pm, s/20). Maril Tours, Bolívar 452 (☎722 555), to: **Lima** (8hr.; 1, 10, and 11pm; s/25-35); **Chimbote** (6hr., 9pm, s/25); and **Trujillo** (8hr., 9pm, s/30). Cruz del Sur, Lucar y Torre 446 (☎724 390), goes to **Lima** (8hr., 10am and 10pm, s/30). Civa Cial, San Martín 502 (☎721 947), goes to **Lima** (8hr.; 10am, 2 and 9:30pm; s/20). To eastern and southern Cordillera towns, look for combis on Cáceres and Tarapaca. Chavín Express, Cáceres 338 (☎724 652), and Rápido, Cáceres 312 (☎726 437), also go to **Chavín** (4hr., s/10), **Huari** (6hr.; 7am, 11am, and 2pm; s/13), **Chiquián** (3hr.; 6am, 2 and 7pm; s/10), **Huallanca** (4hr., 7am and 1pm, s/12), and **Llaclla** (4hr.; Tu, Th, and Sa 1pm, s/15). Combis depart from the bridge over the Río Quilcay and head north to **Wilcahuaín** (1hr., s/1-1.5) and **Caraz** (2hr., every 30min. 6am-8pm, s/5), via **Carhuaz** (1hr., s/2) and **Yungay** (1½hr., s/4).

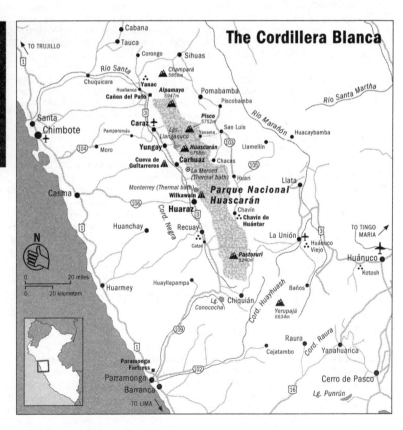

The Cordillera Blanca

Taxis: Taxis cruise up and down **Luzuriaga.** A ride between any two points in Huaraz generally costs s/2. Colectivo taxis cost a little less than private taxis.

Bike Rental: Mountain Bike Adventures, Torre 530 (☎724 259; email alaza2mail.cosapidata.com.pe), at Lucar, between José de la Mar and Morales, 2nd fl. The best bikes in Huaraz, but you usually need to go on a guided tour (US$20 per day) to use them. Open daily 9am-1pm and 5-7pm. **Sobre Ruedas,** La Cruz Romero 593 (☎792 004), has lower prices (s/2-5 per hr.). Open daily 6am-7pm.

⚡🛈 ORIENTATION AND PRACTICAL INFORMATION

Snug between the Cordillera Blanca and the Cordillera Negra, Huaraz rests in the Río Santa Valley, which is also known as the **Callejón de Huaylas.** The city's main thoroughfare, **Luzuriaga** runs north-south and connects the principal highways. The **Plaza de Armas,** home to many businesses, hotels, and restaurants, lies on Luzuriaga, about seven blocks south of the **Río Quilcay.**

Tourist Information: OPTUR (☎721 551), on Luzuriaga in the Museo Arqueológico. Open M-Sa 8:30am-1pm and 2-6:30pm, Su 9:30am-2pm. For information on clmbing, consult the **Casa de Guías,** Parque Ginebra 28 (☎721 811), 1 block from the plaza. Open M-F 9am-1pm and 4-8pm, Sa 9am-1pm. The bulletin board outside is a great place to advertise equipment or the need for it and to find climbing or trekking partners.

Tour Agencies: In Huaraz, companies offer everything from driving tours to climbing packages, whitewater rafting, and hang gliding. Be careful with whom you go, and beware of back alley agencies without credentials. **Pyramid Adventures,** Luzuriaga 530 (☎721 864), specializing in adventure tours, is reputed to be a valuable source of info, equipment, and guides, but their office is rarely open. **Pablo Tours,** Luzuriaga 501 (☎721 145; email pablot@net.telematic.com.pe), and **Chavín Tours,** Luzuriaga 502 (☎721 578), are both recognized tourist agencies open daily 7:30am-1pm and 4-10pm. For hang gliding and horseback riding info, check out **Monttrek,** Luzuriaga 646 (☎726 976; email Monttrek@si.computextus.net), above Banco del Trabajo. They also rent climbing and trekking equipment. **Outdoor Expeditions S.A.,** Caceres 418 Parque Pip (☎728 725; email snowk20@yahoo.com; www.peruoutdoorexpeditions.com), through the tunnel on Luzuriaga's 4th block, specializes in treks and climbs and rents high-quality equipment at fair prices. Open daily 8am-1pm and 3-10pm.

Banks: Banks cluster around the Plaza de Armas and have Visa **ATMs. Banco de Crédito** (☎721 170), at the corner of Sucre and Luzuriaga. Open M-F 9:15am-1:15pm and 4:30-6:30pm, Sa 9:30am-12:30pm. **Banco Wiese Sudameris,** on Sucre, changes traveler's checks for the lowest fee around. Open M-F 9am-1pm and 4:30-6:45pm, Sa 9:30am-12:30pm. **Chris and J.P. Casa de Cambio,** Luzuriaga 631-02 (☎721 160), offers **MoneyGram** services. Open M-Sa 9:30am-1pm and 4:30-7pm, and occasionally Su, for urgent callers. Banco del Trabajo, Luzuriaga 646 (☎725 606), supplies **Western Union** services. M-F 9am-1:30pm and 3:45-7pm, Sa 9:30am-12:45pm.

Market: Indoor market, at Raymondi and La Cruz Romero, with all the fruit, dry food, and shoe repair specialists you could ever need, be it for trekking or on-site consumption. Open daily 6am-7:30pm. Outdoor market, on the streets north of Raymondi from Confraternidad to San Martín. Open daily 7am-5pm. On Mondays and Thursdays, denizens from local communities congregate on Raymondi, just west of Confraternidad, to sell their goods. Local handicrafts on Luzuriaga and in the Feria Artesanal on the Plaza de Armas.

Laundromat: Lavandería Tintoreria B&B, La Mar 674 (☎721 719). s/4 per kg. Open M-Sa 9am-1pm and 3-8pm.

Equipment Rental: You can rent almost any piece of equipment in Huaraz. Bargaining is expected, especially if renting more than one item, or for more than one day. Inspect gear carefully before rental. **Outdoor Expeditions S.A.** (see Tour Agencies, above) is one source for quality outdoor gear. 4-person tent US$6 per day. Sleeping bags US$2.50-3 per day. Total camping equipment rental for 4 people, US$30 per day.

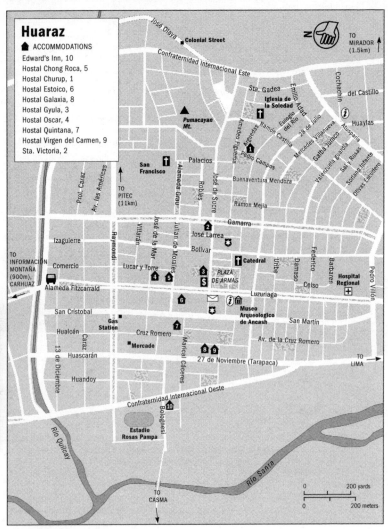

Huaraz

⌂ ACCOMMODATIONS

Edward's Inn, 10
Hostal Chong Roca, 5
Hostal Churup, 1
Hostal Estoico, 6
Hostal Galaxia, 8
Hostal Gyula, 3
Hostal Oscar, 4
Hostal Quintana, 7
Hostal Virgen del Carmen, 9
Sta. Victoria, 2

Police: Tourist Police, Loredo 716 (☎ 721 341 ext. 315), at Larrea, 2 blocks uphill from the Plaza de Armas. **PNP** (☎ 721 341 ext. 202), on the 5th block of Sucre, 1 block downhill from the plaza.

Emergency: ☎ 105.

Hospital: Regional Hospital (☎ 721 861; emergency 721 290 ext. 47), on Luzuriaga, near Pedro Villón.

Pharmacy: Botica 24 Horas, Luzuriaga 1224.

Telephones: Telefónica del Perú, at Bolívar and Sucre. Open daily 7am-11pm.

Internet Access: Parque Ginebra (☎ 727 480), on Parque Ginebra, offers full service (s/4 per hr.). Open daily 9am-11pm. **Avance S.R.L,** Luzuriaga 672 (☎ 726 690), offers private phone and Internet access (s/4 per hr.). Open daily 7am-midnight. **Chavin.com,** Gamarra 628 (☎ 691 722), offers cheaper service (s/3 per hr.) daily 8am-midnight.

Post Office: Serpost (☎ 721 031), on the Plaza de Armas, at the corner of Sucre and Luzuriaga. Open M-Sa 8am-8pm, Su 9am-1pm.

ACCOMMODATIONS

Huaraz sees a wide variety of travelers, and its wide variety of comfortable, affordable places to stay reflects this. Many of the following establishments can help guests arrange adventure tours.

Hostal Churup, Pedro Campos 735 (☎722 584; email churupalbergue@yahoo.com), directly below the Iglesia de la Soledad. Popular tourist hangout. Every morning, the family who runs this hostel invites guests to breakfast in their home, where the eager owner can share his encyclopedic knowledge of the region's attractions, as well as how best to see them. Spacious backyard. Book exchange. Dorms s/13-16 per person.

Hostal Virgen del Carmen, Cruz Romero 662 (☎721 729), off Parque Pip. A grand family home, transformed into immaculate rooms. Hot water all day. Singles s/15, with bath s/20; doubles s/25, with bath s/35.

Hotel Victoria, Gamarra 690 (☎722 422). A 3-star escape from the hustle of downtown. Comfortable rooms with spotless baths and color TV surround several lounges. Singles s/50; doubles s/80; triples s/120; quads s/160.

Hostal Residencial Galaxia, Cruz Romero 638 (☎722 230), off Parque Pip. Unadorned rooms overlook a patio. Laundry. Backpack storage. Singles s/20, with bath s/25.

Hostal Oscar, de la Mar 624 (☎722 720), just off of Luzuriaga. Somewhat comfortable. All rooms with private bath, hot water, and color TV. Choose a room away from the street to avoid early morning noise. Singles s/25; doubles s/30; triples s/40.

Hostal Chong Roca, Morales 661-687 (☎721 154), near Luzuriaga. Rooms without a shower cost a bit less, but still include a sink and toilet. Friendly, elderly owner. Hot water all day. High season rooms s/30 per person.

Hostal Estoico, San Martín 635 (☎722 371), on the other side of the tunnel where merchants sell handicrafts. Above a garden flourishing in its unkemptness, 2nd-fl. rooms have hot water all day. Low season singles s/12, with bath s/15.

Hostal Quintana, Mariscal Cáceres 411 (☎726 060), 2 blocks from Luzuriaga, through the merchant tunnel. Both sons in the family that runs this simple hostel are accomplished climbers; they rent equipment next door. Rooms s/15 per person.

Edward's Inn, Bolognesi 121 (☎722 692), near the stadium, down an unpaved road and quite out-of-the-way. Edward's Inn has been serving gringos in Huaraz for over 20 years. Spacious rooms. Expansive patio. And owner Eduardo's a font of climbing information. Evening hot water. Rooms s/25 per person, with bath s/35.

FOOD

Huaraz has enough restaurants to satisfy any hiker's cravings. Restaurants cluster on the streets around Luzuriaga, where numerous eateries offer lunchtime *menús*. Be sure to try the Cordillera's signature dishes: *llunca* (wheat soup), *charqui* (dried pork), *picante de cuy* (spicy guinea pig), and *trucha* (trout).

Siam de los Andes, Gamarra 419 (☎728 006), 3 blocks up from Luzuriaga. Thai chef Naresuan prepares exquisite curries (s/16) and stir-fries (s/16-20) with fresh meat and vegetables. The prices are high, but this is the best food in Huaraz. Naresuan also gives advice on cheap treks. Lunch service coming soon. Open daily 6-9pm.

Fuente de Salud, de la Mar 562, just below Luzuriaga. True to the name, this is the perfect place to cure whatever might be ailing you. Common prescriptions include vegetable soup (s/7) and yogurt (s/4), or the meatier *menú* s/4. Open daily 8am-11pm.

Crêperie Patrick, Luzuriaga 422 (☎723 364). Rich crepes (s/4) with all sorts of fillings (s/2-3). Patrick also offers standard dishes, which are about as budget as a Paris cafe (filet mignon s/29). Sophisticated decor. Open M-Sa 8am-12:30pm and 6-10:30pm.

Comedor Santa Victoria, Gamarra 690 (☎722 422), 3 blocks uphill from the Plaza de Armas. The scrumptious *menú* (s/5) deserves its popularity. Open daily 7:30am-10pm.

Bistro de Los Andes (☎ 726 249), on Julio de Morales. French cuisine meets Peruvian at this early-morning spot that serves excellent coffee to those just off the overnight bus from Lima. Later in the day, *trucha a la almendra* (almond trout s/18) is the house specialty. Book exchange. Vegetarian pastas s/8-14. Open Tu-Su 6am-11pm, M 5-11pm.

Alpes Andes, Parque Ginebra 28 (☎ 721 811), next door to the Casa de Guías. A relaxing cafe in which to discuss climbing plans with the guides who congregate here. Munch on garlic bread (s/2) while you catch up with world affairs from the variety of Spanish papers and magazines. Open daily 7am-11pm.

Pizzeria Chez Pepe, Raymondi 624 (☎ 726 482). The house specialty is pizza (large pie s/26-29), but its Pepe's quaint decorations that set his restaurant apart from the crowd. Also, he knows a lot about mountain climbing. Open daily 7am-11pm.

👁 SIGHTS

Some Huaraz tour agencies (see Practical Information, p. 201) offer **city tours** (3-5hr.) which take in several primary sights. (Tours should cost s/15, entrance fees another s/9.) However, many visitors elect to bypass the city's limited options and have more time for adventures in the Cordillera Blanca.

MUSEO ARQUEOLÓGICO DE ANCASH. This museum grapples with the task of representing all the cultures that have lived in Ancash province over the past 12,000 years. Of particular interest are the 75 Recuay monoliths that decorate the garden and the presentation of the Jancu tomb. Models of various sites (Cueva de Guitarreros, Wilcahuaín) are interesting, though they won't serve as adequate replacements to actual visits. Unfortunately, after all this, the crowded museum doesn't have much room left to explain its holdings. *(On the southeast corner of the Plaza de Armas. ☎ 721 551. Open M-Sa 8:30am-6:30pm, Su 9:30am-2pm. s/5.)*

MONUMENTO ARQUEOLÓGICO DE WILCAHUAÍN. Discovered in 1932 and dating to AD 1000, this complex of late Huari ruins consists of two sites, Chico and Grande, which were used as storage facilities and burial centers. Three principal stone structures with darkened inner rooms mark the two locations. Of course, if you've been to the nearby Chavín ruins (see p. 208), these might be a bit of a letdown. *(Combis marked "Wilcahuaín" leave from the bridge over the Río Quilcay to Chico (30min., s/1.50) via Grande (s/1). Visiting Chico first, then walking down to Grande and catching a combi home is probably the most efficient way to go. Alternatively, it is possible to walk the 6km to the ruins, either on the main road or through the town of Huanchuc. Children will give tours in exchange for a small tip. Open 24hr., but safer during the day. s/4, students s/2.)*

LOS BAÑOS DE MONTERREY. Two large pools and 27 smaller *pozas*, private chambers for one or two people, lure both Peruvians and tourists. The water is brown, but don't worry—that's just the minerals. *(7km north of Huaraz, just off the main highway. The green bus from Luzuriaga goes directly there (30min., s/0.5). Open daily 7am-6pm. Large pool s/3; private bath s/3.)*

OTHER SIGHTS. Calle Jose Olaya is all that remains of pre-1970 Huaraz. Its buildings' colonial influences and traditional green doors serve as reminders of the past and show what architectural tragedy the 1970 earthquake wrought. *(North of Confraternidad Este.)* Huaraz also shelters a small **Museo de Miniaturas,** but it is rarely open. *(Near the Hotel Huascarán. Take a colectivo (s/0.5) north from Luzuriaga. Erratic hours.)*

⛰ OUTDOOR ACTIVITIES

Nowadays there's more to do in the mountains than hike (although that's fun too—for information on **trekking** and **mountaineering**, see Into the Mountains from Huaraz, p. 206). Various tour agencies offer instructional **rock climbing** sessions near Monterrey. (Half-day US$10, includes equipment and guide.) The Río Santa presents great **rafting** opportunities all year, but particularly from May to October.

The Class III rapids on the route from Jangas to Anta (8km, US$15) may satisfy some, but risk-lovers will probably prefer the Class V Yungay to Caraz trip (17km, US$25). Only experienced fliers can attempt morning **hang gliding** runs in the Callejón—the climatic changes are too dangerous for novices. Those interested in gaining experience should contact Jorge Chávez in Lima. (☎ (01) 444 50 04; email airex@perufly.com; www.perufly.com.) **Horseback riding** gives visitors the opportunity to admire the scenery north of Huaraz as the Inca and Chavín once did. (Tours US$6 per hr.) **Skiers** and **snowboarders** can trek up to Pastoruri Glacier and squeeze in some downhill action. (Transportation with a tour company s/40 roundtrip.) Most of the prices quoted above include transportation and equipment. Talk to any of Huaraz's numerous tour operators (see **Tour Agencies,** p. 201) to arrange an excursion; Monttrek is the best for hang gliding and horseback riding.

FESTIVALS

As the capital of the Ancash department, Huaraz hosts several popular regional *fiestas*. The most important of these is the **Fiesta de Mayo** (May 2-9), which features dance festivals, ski races, and the traditional procession of the Señor de la Soledad. Other significant celebrations include the **Fiesta de Las Cruces** (Sept. 14), the **Fiestas Patrias** (July 28-29), **Semana Santa** (the week preceding Easter, Apr. 8-15 in 2001), and the **Semana de Andinismo** (mid-late June). This last festival involves rock climbing, biking, kayaking, rafting, hang gliding, golfing, and windsurfing competitions as well as many concerts and lots of partying. During festivals, transportation and lodging prices rise dramatically. In times of real overcrowding, ordinary residents may temporarily open their homes to accommodate guests.

NIGHTLIFE

Nightlife booms in Huaraz, where hopes of cashing in on the city's ongoing tourist influx increase every year. For those with extra energy or *soles*, the following are good places to dance and drink them away.

 El Tambo, José de la Mar 776 (☎ 723 417), 3 blocks up from Luzuriaga. It's smoky, it's crowded, and it's a really good time. *El DJ* presents an entertaining mix of top 40 hits, salsa, merengue, and of course *technocumbia*. Beer s/5. Pitcher of sangría. s/10. Peak season cover s/10-20. Open daily 8pm-6am.

Café Andino, Morales 753, 2 blocks up from Luzuriaga. A coffeehouse with a twist, Andino vends cuba libres (s/9) as well as fresh espresso (s/5). An eclectic, multilingual library and Scrabble boards ward off ennui. Open daily 9am-noon and 6pm-midnight.

Aquelarre, at Luzuriaga and Gadino Uribe. The owner, a local artist, has decorated this fun bar with his own interpretive paintings and sculptures. Open daily 7pm-1am.

El Sol, on Condor Pasa, off the 4th block of Luzuriaga. The current local hotspot. *Technocumbia*, guaranteed. Pitchers of beer s/20-25. Open daily 6pm-6am.

DAYTRIPS FROM HUARAZ

Visitors should be prepared to pay an admission fee (s/5 for the day) on any trip that enters Parque Nacional Huascarán, although park officials rarely collect it.

MIRADOR DE RATEQUENUA. This high (3650m) mountain pass provides spectacular views of Huaraz and the surrounding mountains. A short and scenic trip, the hike (about 3hr. round-trip) has helped many a trekker become properly acclimatized. Of course, there are also those who rent mountain bikes and enjoy a speedy descent. Sadly, the area has a dangerous reputation; tourists should not hike it alone or at night. *(To get to the mirador, head south on Luzuriaga from the Plaza de Armas to Villón; then follow the road that starts above the cemetery, at the uphill end of Villón.)*

NAMING NAMES The great Peruvian explorer **Antonio Raimondi** is best known as a 19th-century authority on the flora, fauna, and geography of his native country. Indeed, he relentlessly observed and catalogued the land's natural wonders, particularly in the mountainous Ancash department. Today, that region's gargantuan bromeliad, the **Puya Raymondi**, bears his name. What most visitors, and even many natives, don't know is that Raimondi coined names for more than just burly bromeliads. The explorer often personified towns that he visited according to events that transpired during his stay, giving them catchy nicknames that persist to this day. During a particularly eventful 1860 visit to the Callejón de Huaylas, Raimondi practically renamed the region based on his personal impressions. During his stay in the town of Recuay, one of his journals was stolen, leading him to condemn the entire community as **"Thieving Recuay."** He then continued north to Huaraz, where he became enamored with a local lass. Unimpressed by his credentials and confident swagger, the beauty dismissed him. His bravado bruised, Raimondi left **"Presumptuous Huaraz"** only to be further saddened by the intoxicated excesses on display at a fiesta in **"Intoxicating Carhuaz."** But the intrepid Raimondi continued north, where his outlook finally brightened. His spirits soared after witnessing a sensational sunrise in **"Lovely Yungay."** With a new spring in his step and a rumbling in his stomach, Antonio blissfully concluded his journey in **"Sweet Caraz,"** where he nursed himself back to full health with *manjar blanco*, the town's famous caramel sandwich spread.

LAGUNAS LLANGANUCO. On a clear day, these two spectacular alpine lakes shimmer and appear to stretch themselves toward some of the Cordillera Blanca's highest peaks, including Huascarán, which towers to their southeast. Tourists most often visit the lower lake, Chinacocha. Tours from Huaraz leave participants an hour of free time to rent rowboats or walk to the base of Huascarán. Another popular alpine lake, **Laguna Churup,** lies at the foot of Nevado Churup (5495m). *(To travel the 60km to the Lagunas LLanganuco independently, you're better off starting in Yungay (see Yungay, p. 210). However, many agencies in Huaraz offer tours (s/20-25). Park s/5. To reach Laguna Churup, take a combi from Raymondi to Unchus or Pitec and hike the rest of the way. Alternatively, agencies in Huaraz offer guided tours (US$20).)*

PASTORURI GLACIER. This popular excursion brings visitors for a walk on an Andean glacier—one that's relatively flat, as Andean glaciers go. No special equipment is necessary, but it's best to be already acclimatized, as the glacier is at 5240m. After a 45-minute hike (avid skiers and snowboarders trudging their equipment up behind them), travelers spend an hour of fun in the snow. Tour agencies often combine this trip (about 9hr., s/20-25 per person) with a visit to some of the Callejón's famous **Puya Raymondi** plants, which resemble giant (up to 13m), mutated cacti, but are actually more closely related to pineapples. Found between 3600 and 4300m, the plants live 100 years before they bloom once and then die. Most tour groups attempt to catch a plant in the midst of its brief flowering stage.

⚠ INTO THE MOUNTAINS FROM HUARAZ

It is the prospect of adventure in the Cordillera Blanca that calls people to Huaraz; such adventure can take any of several forms, but the most immersive are multiple-day **trekking** and **mountaineering**. Both offer breathtaking views—and breathtaking climbs. Although novices should leave summitting Huascarán to the experts, anyone in decent shape can trek many of the trails in the area as long as he does not attempt them solo and does bring clothing and equipment appropriate to the season (keeping in mind that rain, snow, and hail storms blow in throughout the year, although much less often May-Sept.). Also, in addition to the costs of equipment rental, initial transportation, and a guide, there is an **admission fee** (s/65) for multi-day excursions in Parque Nacional Huascarán.

Parque Nacional Huascarán receives heavy visitor traffic from around the world. When exploring the park, please do your part to preserve its natural beauty. Always pack out what you pack in, including all refuse and extra food, and try to stay on marked trails to avoid harming the fragile alpine vegetation.

TREKS. Hikers can undertake treks privately or with help from an *arriero*, a local muleteer who acts as guide and porter. You can commission *arrieros* at the Casa de Guías (see Practical Information, p. 201), as well as at individual trailheads; they charge about US$12 per day, not including food costs. Tour agencies in Huaraz and Caraz also guide trek-tours along the more popular trails during the dry season. (US$25 per day; equipment rental about US$10 per day.) Those who'd rather trek independently should obtain the following essential pieces of **equipment:** warm and waterproof clothing and tents, a camping stove and cookware, water purification tablets or a filter, a beveled-edge compass, a reliable topographic map of the region, and food.

Of the **more than 35 circuits** around Huaraz, the following enjoy current popularity: Huaraz to Laguna Llaca (27km, 2 days), Pachacoto to Carpa to Pastoruri (28km, 2 days), Pitec to Laguna Tullparaju (30km, 2 days), Pitec to Laguna Shallap (26km, 2 days), Huaraz to Laguna Palcacucha via Quebrada Cojup (20km, 2 days), Pitec to Laguna Cuchillacocha via Quebrada Quilcayhuanca (30km, 2 days), and Huaraz to Laguna Rajucolta via Quebrada Rajucolta (33km, 3 days). The most popular runs from **Llanganuco to Santa Cruz Valley** (4-5 days). Serene views of glacial peaks, tundra, and alpine lakes bless the route, which is not particularly strenuous. Moreover, due to the heavy traffic it receives, park officials have recently equipped the main trail with outhouses and designated campsites. Camionetas from **Caraz** run to both of the trek's possible starting points, Cashapampa (2hr., s/ 15) and Vaquería (2½hr., s/10). It's also possible to reach Llanganuco by starting in Marcará and walking along Quebrada Honda. For an extra five days' hike, the journey can be combined with a climb up **Nevado Pisco.**

Another fairly easy—but much less crowded—three-day trek that begins near Huaraz, the **Olleros to Chavín** trail winds through open fields and wide valleys, providing views of numerous snow-capped peaks along the way. It then veers uphill, to Punta Yanashallash (a 4680m pass between two glaciers) and passes several Quechua villages before ending at the Chavín de Huántar ruins (see p. 208), near the small town of the same name. (The trailhead is in the village of Olleros, 27km south of Huaraz.; s/1.50 by colectivo.) The more difficult **Los Cedros to Alpamayo** trek (9 days) allows a glimpse of the legendary 4th face of Nevado Alpamayo, considered to be one of the most picturesque in the world. (The journey begins at Cashapampa (2hr. from Caraz by camioneta, s/5), traverses six mountain passes along Quebradas Alpamayo and Yanacollpa, and ends in Pomabamba.

 Huaraz is full of "cowboy" guides, who "offer" their "services" at a "discount." Such shady characters rarely possess the proper training or equipment that their "services" require. **Every year, climbers in the Cordillera Blanca die due to human error, faulty equipment, and inadequate preparation.** If you don't know what you're doing, go with someone who does.

CLIMBS. Huaraz is the best place to find the appropriate equipment and a qualified guide with whom to attempt a glacier climb in the Cordillera Blanca. For serious technical climbing trips, head to the Casa de Guías for advice. The Casa maintains a list of certified mountain guides who have completed a rigorous three-year course to gain accreditation from the Peruvian Mountain Guide Association (UIAGM). An accredited guide's daily fee (US$50-70) is expensive by Peruvian standards, but most would-be mountaineers decide that their lives are worth it.

The most popular climbs are sometimes also the easiest, so climbers with little or no experience should not feel discouraged. **Nevados Pisco** (5752m), **Ishinca** (5534m), and **Uros** (5420m) require little more than a sense of adventure, well-acclimatized lungs, the proper gear, and a qualified guide. Moreover, these three-day climbs can help you acclimatize and give you the necessary knowledge and experience to tackle greater heights—like the mammoth **Huascarán** (6768m; 6- to 8-day climb). Alternatively, you can gain climbing experience in a three to five day course (US$40-70 per day, plus equipment rental) at **Pastoruri** (5220m). Depending on the height and difficulty of the mountain, equipment rental starts at about US$20 per day. Transportation is another variable cost, with public vehicles naturally being cheaper than privately organized transport.

NEAR HUARAZ: CHAVÍN DE HUÁNTAR

The ruins are a five-minute walk uphill from the town's Plaza de Armas on 17 de Enero Sur, the main street. Most visitors come with tours, arriving around noon and leaving around 4pm. Tours run s/25-30, not including the admission fee. To get to Chavín independently, catch a Huari-bound bus (4hr., s/10; see Transportation, p. 200) from Huaraz. s/5.

The intricate 3000-year-old Chavín ruins of the **Museo Arqueológico Chavín de Huántar** stand as a testament to the extraordinary culture which came to influence peoples as far north as the Ecuadorian border and as far south as Ica. The Chavín lived here from 1300 to 400 BC. Their stone ceremonial center, constructed over eight generations, endured the Recuay, Huaraz, and Inca cultures, not to mention the Spanish, until its formal protection by UNESCO in 1985. A guide can be very helpful in understanding the intricate culture behind this site; the map directly inside the gate is helpful in outlining the area. Even before it enters the ruins proper, the preordained path is interesting: it passes a row of San Pedro cacti; those that had seven columns were considered lucky by the Chavín, and thus consumed regularly. These plants also induce a hallucinogenic trance and studies show that most people were addicted. Seven was one of three special numbers in this ancient culture. The number two was spiritual because it represented duality (a recurring theme in the ruins). The number three was significant because it stood for one human and two animals. This combination of a human and two animal deities, the serpent (representing the underworld) and the jaguar (the mortal world), occurs frequently on Chavín's stone carvings. Look for human heads with jaguar teeth or legs, and serpents on the side. The third animal deity, the condor (representing the afterlife) is always pictured separately from the other two animals. Archeologists suggest that this may be because the condor is an animal of the mountainous Chavín area while the other two were native to the jungle, the original home of the Chavín people; because they existed in different environments, these three animals could never exist in the same field.

In order to build the temple, workers flattened a steep hill and constructed 14 well-engineered, labyrinthine **galleries** (only four of which are open to the public). Formerly above ground, they were covered by a landslide in 1945 and are now tunnels. The U-shaped temple has a sunken plaza, following ancient Andean architectural concepts. The nearby **pyramid structure,** built on a rectangular square, demonstrates the Chavín's philosophies of duality. Large canals, which once carried rushing water, are visible beneath; archaeologists speculate that those noisy canals might have mimicked the sound of thunder, which the Chavín revered. The most important artifact at Chavín, still in its original site inside a gallery, is the beautiful **Lanzón,** a tall, white granite carving of the feline, bird, and serpent. Two other famous artifacts, the Estela Raymondi and the Tello Obelisk, were moved to the Museo de Arqueología y Antropología in Lima (see **Museums,** p. 86).

Chavín de Huántar's many hotels are in bitter competition to accommodate the few overnight visitors. **La Casona,** Plaza de Armas 130, offers a wide variety of rooms, from clean-but-bare to beautiful. Located in a *casa antigua,* the hotel is sporadically decorated with antiques and animal hides. (☎754 048. Singles s/10, with bath s/15, with TV s/20; doubles s/18, with bath s/28.)

CARHUAZ   ☎044

Locals like to call it "Carhuaz Borrachera" ("Intoxicating Carhuaz"), and a visit to this hamlet 32km north of Huaraz proves the moniker to be no exaggeration. Boasting an enthusiastic nascent tourism as well as the Cordillera Blanca's characteristically beautiful mountain scenery, Carhuaz rewards visitors with charming townspeople and quiet accommodations. However, although for most of the year it's a great place to get away from the comparative hustle and bustle of Huaraz, this intoxicating town tends to get a bit tipsy itself during its yearly patronal fiestas, which take place throughout September.

TRANSPORTATION AND PRACTICAL INFORMATION. Small and easy to navigate, Carhuaz centers on its **Plaza de Armas,** which lies four blocks above the **Carretera Central,** the main road in the Callejón de Huaylas. Everything of importance is near the plaza. Combis to **Huaraz** (1hr., s/2) collect passengers at the corner of La Merced and Ucayali. Transportation to **Caraz** (1hr., s/2) via **Yungay** (30min., s/1.50) leaves from the corner of La Merced and Progreso. Between 6am and 8pm, you can also flag down combis on the Carretera Central. Buses to **Lima** (9hr., s/20) and **Chimbote** (6hr., s/20) leave from Progreso at the Plaza de Armas. For **tourist information,** talk to Felipe Díaz, who owns the Café Heladería El Abuelo (see Food, below) and designed the definitive tourist map of the region. A recently opened **tourist office,** Comercio 530, by the church, also answers questions. (Open M-F 7:30am-12:30pm and 1:30-4pm.) For **currency exchange,** visit Farmacia Señor de Luren, Buin 557, just north of the plaza, which also fills medicinal needs. (☎794 392. Open daily 8am-2pm and 3-10pm.) Other local services include: the **police** (☎794 197), on Buin just south of the plaza; a **hospital** (☎794 106), four blocks north of the plaza, on Union; and a **post office,** on Buin at the Plaza de Armas. (☎794 118. Open M-Sa 8am-1pm and 2-5pm.)

ACCOMMODATIONS AND FOOD. Carhuaz harbors several under-visited but quite handsome hostels. **Las Torrecitas,** on the sixth block of Amazonas, four blocks uphill and two blocks to the right from the Plaza de Armas, is the perfect example. The amicable owner rents spotless modern rooms with parquet floors and color TVs, and the well-decorated patio gives guests an alternative place to relax. (☎794 213. Rooms s/15 per person.) True to its name, the comfortable and tranquil **Las Bromelias,** Brazil 208, three blocks up from the plaza, has a beautiful flower garden. (☎794 033. Singles with bath s/20; doubles with bath s/30.) A third option, **Hostal Merced,** Ucayali 724, is comfortable, traditional, and undistinguished. (☎794 241. Rooms s/12 per person; rooms with bath s/15 per person.)

While Carhuaz may not be the culinary epicenter of Peru, there are certainly places to get a decent meal. **Café Heladería El Abuelo,** at Progreso and La Merced, on the Plaza de Armas, specializes in ice cream snacks (s/5-8) and tourist information, but also offers breakfast (s/8-13), simple sandwiches (s/4.50), and coming soon: Internet access. (☎794 144. Open daily 8am-9pm.) For something out of the ordinary, **Vio Chicken,** Santa Rosa 664 (quarter *pollo a la brasa* s/5.50; open daily 5:30-11pm), and **Las Retamas II,** at Aurora and Buin (*menú* s/3; open daily noon-3pm), aren't the places—but there's something to be said for the ordinary.

🔯 **SIGHTS.** A few quirky sights set Carhuaz's offerings apart from the average small Peruvian town. Several years ago, in the Cordillera Negra, American anthropologists discovered the **Cueva de Guitarreros**, a cave they believe may have been inhabited over 12,000 years ago—an idea that throws into question established theories on the population of the New World. To get to the cave, take a combi north to Mancos (30min., s/1). From Mancos, cross the Río Santa and walk south (30min.). The **Chancos Hot Springs** are famous for their caves that have been converted into private saunas. Take a colectivo to Marcará, 7km south of Carhuaz, and then walk or take a communal taxi (4km, s/1) uphill. (Open 6am-6pm. s/5 per 15min.) Closer to town, **Donde Se Baña la Bruja** (Where the Witch Bathes) provides a glimpse of the local vegetation and a small waterfall. Take Progreso south until it merges with the Central Highway. Turn right after passing Restaurante El Gran Sabor (20min.). Finally, a trip to icy **Punta Olímpica** (4890m), up by Laguna Auquiscocha, yields spectacular views. From the corner of Progreso and La Merced, take the Chacas-bound combi to Punta Olímpica (3hr., 1 per day 7-8am) via Laguna Auquiscocha (1½hr.; get off at the division of Quebrada Ulta and Quebrada Catay).

YUNGAY   ☎044

Yungay got its 15 minutes of fame tragically, 31 years ago, when a landslide destroyed its small settlement at the base of Nevado Huascarán. Today the rubble is something of a tourist attraction, and the town has moved—what few survivors there were rebuilt their homes 1km north of the original location. Now cowering in Huascarán's massive shadow, quiet Yungay has yet to assign most streets names. Otherwise, however, the town's catastrophic past seems to have faded to memory, and only its status as a regional crossroads distinguishes Yungay from other homely Andean villages.

Combis to **Caraz** (30min., s/1) leave from the market on the Plaza de Armas; those to **Carhuaz** (30min., s/1.50) and **Huaraz** (1½hr., s/4) leave from the corner of Graziani and 28 de Julio, one block south of the plaza. Alternatively, you can hail combis on the Central Highway (6am-8pm daily). Bus companies on Graziani at the plaza run buses to **Lima** (9½hr., s/18), **Chimbote** (6hr., s/18), and **Trujillo** (9hr., s/25). **Botica Santa Teresa,** Graziani 6, is on the plaza. (Open daily 7am-9pm.) Other services include: the **police** (☎793 300), at Graziani and 28 de Julio; a **hospital** (☎793 044), a few blocks north of the Plaza de Armas; **Telefónica del Perú,** in the Region Norte office, next to the Municipalidad; and the **post office,** on Graziani just south of the plaza (open M-Sa 8am-noon and 2-5pm).

The spotless rooms at **Hostal Gledel,** on Graziani two blocks down from the Plaza de Armas, surround an open patio. There's hot water at night, and the cafe serves traditional breakfast and dinner. (☎793 048. Internet access s/5 per hour. Rooms s/10 per person.) The cafe at **Las Rosas,** on Graziani after the arches that mark the southern entrance to Yungay, provides a tranquil area in which to write, eat, or watch TV. (☎793 337. Singles s/12, with hot bath s/15; TV s/5 extra.) **Hostal Yungay,** on Santo Domingo at the plaza, is pretty basic, but they do have hot water to chase away those mountain chills. (☎793 053. Singles s/10, with bath s/20; doubles s/25.) Outdoor restaurant **El Alpamayo,** on the northern outskirts of town on the highway, tends to fill up around lunchtime with tourists bound for the Lagunas Llanganuco. *Pachamanca* (tamales, meat, corn, potato, and sweet potato cooked in an underground oven, s/10) is available on weekends. (☎793 214. Open daily 7am-7pm.)

🔯 **SIGHTS.** Just south of the new city lies **Campo Santo,** site of the buried former Yungay. Intact traces of the original settlement, including a cemetery where many townspeople fled to escape the 1970 mudslide as well as four old palm trees and a church facade presiding over the past Plaza de Armas, still exist. Rosebushes now form a cross through the center of town and tourists wan-

HUASCARÁN'S WRATH On May 31, 1970, an enormous earthquake (measuring 7.8 on the Richter scale) brought a cascade of rock and ice down Nevado Huascarán, Peru's highest peak. The falling debris picked up water in its descent, eventually creating a deadly *alluvial* (landslide) that smothered Yungay. More than 80,000 residents of the Ancash region died in the disastrous seismic event, 20,000 in Yungay alone—many while watching the 1970 Mexico-hosted World Cup. Amazingly, a circus tent saved 260 children, who were attending the festivities within.

der among the eerie ruins. (A 20min. walk or s/0.5 colectivo ride from the new Plaza de Armas. Open daily 8am-6:30pm. s/1.) Far less depressing, the access road to the dazzling **Lagunas Llanganuco** begins in Yungay. Many tourists visit the lakes with a tour group from Huaraz (see Daytrips from Huaraz, p. 205), but it's easier to get there from Yungay. Take a Yanama-bound combi to Llanganuco (1hr.; leaving when full 6-10am, return 3pm; s/5) from the intersection of Santo Domingo and 28 de Julio.

CARAZ ☎ 044

Almost 1000m lower than Huaraz, Caraz enjoys a climate far more sweet than the bitter cold of the high Andes. Maybe this is why locals call it "Caraz Dulzura" ("Sweet Caraz," also see p. 206). Or perhaps the sugary sobriquet takes root in the region's renowned *manjar blanco*, a delightful concoction of milk, sugar, and cinnamon. In any case, this well-equipped yet tranquil terminus of the Callejón de Huaylas may prove the remedy for exhaustion, whether it results from hikes and bike rides in the nearby mountains, or merely too much hectic travel.

▐ TRANSPORTATION

Buses: Companies near the corner of Córdova and Villar send buses to: **Lima** (10hr., s/ 18), **Chimbote** (6hr., s/18), and **Trujillo** (8½hr., s/25). From the corner of Santa Rosa and Grau, buses run to **Parón** (1½hr., 5am and 1pm, s/3). The following colectivos and combis leave when full. From the corner of Bolognesi and Ugarte to **Pueblo Libre** (1hr., 6am-6pm, s/1.50) and **Huallanca** (1hr., 6am-6pm, s/5). From the corner of Santa Cruz and Castilla to **Cashapampa** (2hr., s/5). From the intersection of Grau and Galvez to **Huaraz** (2hr., s/4) via **Yungay** (30min., s/1) and **Carhuaz** (1hr., s/2).

Taxis: Rides anywhere in town should cost s/1-2.

▐▐ ORIENTATION AND PRACTICAL INFORMATION

The **Carretera Central** lies three blocks south of the **Plaza de Armas. Daniel Villar** and **Sucre** run perpendicular to the highway, and together help to form the plaza.

Tourist Information: (☎791 029), on San Martín, near the Municipalidad. Open M-F 8am-1pm and 2:30-5pm. **Pony's Expeditions,** Sucre 1266 (☎791 642; email ponyexp@terra.com.pe), on the Plaza de Armas, is often a better source of information. The proprietor, Alberto Cafferata, rents gear and bikes (US$25 per day with guide). He also arranges personalized and affordable tours, treks, and climbs. Internet access s/8 per hr. Open M-Sa 8am-1pm and 4-10pm.

Banks: Banco de Crédito, Villar 216 (☎791 012), just beyond the Plaza de Armas. 0.55% commission on traveler's checks. Open M-F 9:15am-1:15pm and 4:30-6:30pm, Sa 9:30am-12:30pm.

Market: The indoor market at Sucre and La Mar spills eastward along La Mar and Santa Cruz to Castilla. Merchants sell their wares daily 6am-6pm.

Police: (☎ 791 335), on 20 de Enero, near Córdova.

Hospital: (☎ 791 026), at Leonicio Prado and Sucre.

Pharmacy: Farmacia Santa Rosa, Grau 725 (☎ 791 196), in the market. Open daily 8am-9pm, but can offer service around the clock if you knock.

Telephones: Telefónica del Perú, Villar 109 (☎ 791 860), and Raymondi 410 (☎ 791 580). Both open daily 7am-11pm.

Internet: Both **Pony's Expeditions** (see Tourist Information, above) and **Albergue Los Pinos** (see Accommodations, below) charge s/8 per hr.

Post Office: San Martín 909 (☎ 791 094). Open M-Sa 8am-8pm, Su 9am-1pm.

▌ ACCOMMODATIONS

Caraz sees only a fraction of the travelers that tramp though Huaraz—which sometimes means lower lodging prices. Then again, hostels here can also be less tourist-friendly than in backpacker strongholds to the south.

▨ **Caraz Dulzura,** Saenz Peña 212 (☎ 791 523), about 10 blocks uphill from the plaza along Córdova. A comfortable hostel with all the amenities: relaxing lounge, full bar, restaurant, hot water, color TV. The tranquil location away from busy Caraz *centro* provides the perfect space to catch up on sleep. Rooms s/25 per person, with bath s/30.

▨ **Albergue Los Piños,** Parque San Martín 103 (☎ 791 130; email lospinos@terra.com.pe), 6 blocks down Villar from the plaza. A popular backpacker hangout with bonfires every Friday. Kitchen, laundry, Internet. Rooms s/15 per person, with bath s/20; camping s/7.

Hostal Perla de los Andes, Villar 179 (☎ 792 007), on the Plaza de Armas. This central, modern hostel's 2nd and 3rd stories yield plaza views. All rooms with comfortable bed and color TV. Restaurant. Singles with hot bath s/35; doubles with hot bath s/55.

Hostal Chavín, San Martín 1135 (☎ 791 171), on the Plaza de Armas. With its friendly staff and scrumptious breakfasts (s/5-7), Hostal Chavín is probably the best of the less-than-stellar lot. The owner, Señor Sotelo, gives lectures on the 1970 earthquake, complete with photos, documents, and a pointer, on request. Singles s/25; doubles s/35.

Alojamiento Caballero, Villar 485 (☎ 791 637). Well, it's cheap. Dorms s/10 per person; matrimonials s/17.

◖ FOOD

▨ **Café de Rat,** Sucre 1266 (☎ 791 642), above Pony's Expeditions (see Tourist Information, p. 211). Let's hope the name refers only to the *cuy* on the menu. At night, the lights dim, music pumps, and the restaurant morphs into a bar. Breakfast s/3.50-10. Pastas s/9. Crepes s/6. Great espresso s/2.50. Open M-Sa 8am-1pm and 4-10pm.

Restaurante La Punta Grande, Daniel Villar 595 (☎ 791 320), at the Carretera Central. Specializes in *comida típica* like *cuy* (s/9) and *trucha* (s/10). *Menú* s/4. At lunchtime, tour groups fill the 40 tables. Open daily 9am-7pm.

Restaurant El Mirador, Sucre 1202, on the Plaza de Armas, specializes in *pollo a la brasa* (¼ chicken s/6). *Menú* s/3.50. Open M-Sa 8am-10pm, Su 5-10pm.

La Estación, on the 9th block of Sucre, 2 blocks uphill from the Plaza de Armas. Although mainly an *anticucheria* (s/2.50 per stick), La Estación prepares other traditional dishes as well. Come nightfall, locals descend on this video pub to drink sangria or beer (s/4). *Menú* s/3.50. Open daily noon-3pm and 5-11pm.

◗ SIGHTS

The two-room **Museo de Arqueología,** in the Guarderia Infantil Nuestra Señora de Chiquinquirá, at Castilla and Pumacahua, shelters numerous artifacts from various area sites and cultures, though with little explanation. Of particular interest are the Cueva de Guitarreros remains and the deformed crania. (Open M-F 8am-1pm and 2:30-5pm. Free.) At the **Museo Amauta de Arte Ancashino,** on the third block of Bazán Peralta, by the Colegio 2 de Mayo, mannequins don costumes typical to Caraz, Yungay, Carhuaz, Huaraz, and Recuay. Ask the overseer to give you a brief tour. (Open Tu-Su 9am-1pm and 3-5pm. Free.) Part of a regional, pre-Chavín culture, excavations at the expansive **Tunshukaiko Ruins** have revealed some of the impressive stone architecture, although most structures are still concealed. (To get to the ruins, walk 1km north from the Plaza de Armas along Córdova and Saenz Peña. Cross the bridge and turn left at the end of the dirt road.)

DAYTRIPS FROM CARAZ

It's May, and the trekking's fine (see Into the Mountains from Huaraz, p. 206, for information on area treks). But Caraz has its fair share of shorter excursions—daytrips if you will. It's a great locale from which to spot a **Puya Raymondi** in bloom. (To see the plants, take a Pamparomás-bound colectivo to the Paso de Winchus (1½hr., 9am, s/5) from the corner of La Mar and Castilla. When you've had your fill, head down from to Pueblo Libre, where colectivos return to Caraz until 3pm.) The old highway from Pueblo Libre to Caraz makes another interesting trip. The journey yields Cordillera panoramas and ends with a walk across the suspension bridge over the Rio Santa. (About a 2hr. walk. From Caraz, combis to Pueblo Libre (1hr., s/1.50) leave from the corner of Bolognesi and Ugarte.)

LAGUNA PARÓN

From the corner of Santa Rosa and Grau in Caraz, colectivos run to Parón (1½hr., M-Sa 5am and 1pm, s/3). From the Parón sign on the road, it is a 9km (4hr.) hike up to the lake. It's possible to walk up and return to the descending colectivo (2:30pm) in a day, but staying overnight allows more time at the lake. Alternatively, you can rent bikes from Pony's Expeditions (US$25 per day; see p. 211), or take a taxi (round-trip s/80-100).

Laguna Parón (4140m) is the largest and deepest of the mountain lakes in the Callejón de Huaylas. During some parts of the year, drainage diminishes its grandeur—but this is necessary both to provide hydroelectric energy and to reduce the risk of water engulfing Caraz in the event of a natural disaster. A four-hour trek around the left side of the lake brings hikers to pleasant Laguna Artesancocha.

CAÑON DEL PATO

To travel to the far end of the Cañon del Pato, take a colectivo to Huallanca (2hr., s/10 round-trip). A taxi should cost about s/40 round-trip.

This canyon—sheer rock faces that follow the Río Santa as it cuts between the Cordillera Blanca and the Cordillera Negra—cradles a spectacular mountain highway that uses 35 tunnels to travel through the canyon. A hydroelectric plant, near the overlap of the Cordilleras, supplies power to the entire region.

POMABAMBA   ☎044

This mountain trek's starting and ending point takes visitors back to the basics. Despite its status as the largest town north of Huari on the eastern side of the Cordillera Blanca, Pomabamba often loses electricity, and the only hot water lies in thermal baths a good 10 minute walk away. The same one taxi circles the Plaza de Armas all day, and long, warm afternoons lull even the market to sleep.

TRANSPORTATION AND PRACTICAL INFORMATION. Located 579km northeast of Lima and 179km northeast of Huaraz, Pomabamba's center is the **Plaza de Armas.** Most markets and restaurants lie along **Huamachuco,** the main thoroughfare. Parallel, on the other side of the plaza, **Huaraz** also receives some traffic. Numerous **bus** companies on the plaza go to Huaraz or Lima: Virgen de Guadalupe/ Rosario, Huamachuco 350 (☎751 051), goes to **Huaraz** (8hr., 8am, s/20) and **Lima** (20hr., Th and Su 8am, s/35); Los Andes/El Solitario (☎751 133), on Centenario, also goes to **Huaraz** (8hr., 8pm, s/20) and **Lima** (20hr.; M, Th, F, Su 10am; s/40); Peru Andino, Centenario 260, sends buses to **Lima** (20hr.; M and F 8am, Th and Su 10am;

s/35). Down the road from the Plaza de Armas, Transportes San Francisco, Hua-machuco 776 (☎751 038), goes to **Chimbote** (15hr.; W, F, and Su 2am; s/30). Berisa Transport, Peru 255, will send colectivos anywhere. The Instituto Nacional de Cul-tura Pomabamba, on the Plaza de Armas at Peru, on the second floor of the bright blue building, is the closest this town gets to a museum—or to a **tourist office;** the staff can tell you everything you ever wanted to know about Pomabamba. **Banco de La Nación,** is at Huaraz 331. (☎751 181. Open M-F 8:10am-2:30pm.) **Serpost,** Huaraz 423, is the main post office. (Open M-Sa 8am-noon and 1-6pm).

⌐¦⌐ ACCOMMODATIONS AND FOOD. The quality of Pomabamba's lodgings reflects the fact that tourism has yet to hit big here. Still, **Alojamiento Estradavidol,** Huaraz 209, is blissfully quiet. Facing uphill from the Plaza de Armas, Huaraz is on your right; the hotel is one block down past the church. Some rooms are beautiful, with balconies and pictures; others, with cement walls and bare lightbulbs, are not. (☎751 048. Rooms s/10 per person.) **Hostal No Nos Ganan,** Huamachuco 245, a block uphill from the plaza, has one tragic flaw: its patio serves as a home for chickens en route to the restaurant next door, and, man, do those roosters make their presence known in the morning. (☎751 027. Singles s/8, doubles s/15.) Of the few restaurants in Pomabamba, **Restaurante Los Cedros,** Huaraz 357, draws the most customers with their s/4 *menú*. (☎751 002. Open daily 7am-10pm.) Chicken restaurants line Huamachuco; in the evening, street vendors join them. There are also two small daytime **fruit markets** on this main drag; one is uphill over the bridge, and the other is downhill, at Huamachuco 685.

◨ SIGHTS. Most travelers in Pomabamba are passing through at the beginning or end of a trek, unaware that this area also boasts several worthwhile short hikes. "Short," of course, is relative: a five to seven hour uphill walk will leave you at a set of largely intact **Yaino ruins.** Before a panoramic valley backdrop, the two buildings show off the large stones and straight organization characteristic in the architec-ture of the pre-Inca Yaino culture. To get to the ruins, take a right on Huamachuco from the Plaza de Armas. Take the first right after the bridge and walk along the river. At the intersection, turn right again and walk down the big hill. Cross the bridge and turn left. You'll probably appreciate the three **thermal baths** here on your way back; the cleanest is the green-walled structure next to the road on the right. (Open daily 5am-6pm. 20min. bath or shower s/1.) The stone baths across the road and by the river are more picturesque but also more deserted. At any rate, if you're still on your way to the ruins, go right on the first path leading uphill and carry on. Leave early if you plan to return the same day. From Yaino, it's about an hour farther to the ruins at **Carhuay.** A full-day hike leads to **Laguna Safuna,** reputed to change colors in the sunlight; camping supplies are essential.

HUARI   ☎044

Up the eastern side of the Cordillera Blanca, bus connections become less frequent and hot showers all but nonexistent. This, however, is no reason not to make the trip. A charming hillside, Huari is the perfect base for visits to nearby lakes. **Laguna Purhuay** is the closest, and this natural wonder makes a perfect daytrip. (Facing uphill, take a right on Luzuriaga and walk to the end of the street and up the steps. Turn right and follow the dirt road to the village of Acopalca; 45min. You can also take a colectivo to Acopalca from Huari. Pass the bridge in Acopalca and take a left onto the first major road; about 4 blocks later, a neon sign points to La Chosita. After an hour and a half walk, you will be sitting by the lake.) A longer hike goes past the lake and will bring you to **Chacas** after two to three days of walking. Other hikes lead to the Laguna Reparin or the ruins of Marca Jirca. Back in town, the central plaza is downhill, and Ancash extends from it uphill to the Parque Virgíl, which is the true city center. Most buses drop off passengers at this park. Finding transport in this area can be difficult, however, and it may be necessary to go down to the main road and flag down a bus en route to or from Lima, especially if you are attempting to go north. Peru Andino, Ancash 795, sends a bus to **Lima** (7-8hr., Su 7am, s/30) and **Huaraz** (6hr., 2 per day 3 and

10μm, s/13). El Solitario, Ancash 884 (☎753 113 or 753 155; the sign outside says "sandoral") sends various buses to **Lima** (14hr., 5 per week, s/30), as does Turismo Huari, on Parque Vigíl. Colectivos for nearby towns leave from the Parque Virgíl. Other services include: **Banco de la Nacíon,** San Martín 1001 (☎753 132; no traveler's checks; open M-F 8:10am-2:30pm); the **police,** uphill from Parque Virgíl on Ancash; **Centro Medico Huari,** 1105 San Martín (☎753 062); and **Serpost,** Luzuriaga 320, on the Parque Virgíl (open M-Sa 8am-5pm). The majority of Huari's accomodations lie on Simón Bolívar, which is off of the Plaza de Armas (to the left if you're facing uphill). The best deal is **Hostal Paraiso,** Bolívar 263, which offers two types of rooms. Those with a bathroom have white walls, a shower curtain, and toilet paper. Those *sin baño* have cement walls and floors and nary a window. (☎753 029. Singles s/10, with bath s/20; doubles with bath s/30.) **Hostal Huagancu,** Bolívar 387 (☎753 078), is as lovely as the native flower for which it is named. (Rooms s/15 per person.)

CHIQUÍAN ☎044

Deep in the Andes, the small village of Chiquían is a place where roads are used for soccer games instead of cars, where women wear traditional dress as they herd their pigs across the street, and where there are so few tourists that a gringo-sighting is a major event. Most travelers who venture to *chiquito* Chiquían use the town as a staging area for treks into the Cordillera Huayhuash, a range more rugged and isolated than its famous northern counterpart, the Cordillera Blanca.

▐▀▓ TRANSPORTATION AND PRACTICAL INFORMATION. Chiquían lies on a hill, sloping downhill from south to north. Almost everything of interest revolves around the **Plaza de Armas.** Most buses arrive uphill from the center and depart from the Plaza de Armas. The majority of the city's activity occurs on **2 de Mayo,** which lies parallel to Comercio. Most **long-distance buses** are based near the Plaza de Armas and go to either Huaraz or Lima. Buses will let you off at smaller towns along the way where you can make connections to even more remote areas. Several companies send buses to **Lima** (7-9hr.): Muscha, on the Plaza de Armas (☎747 070; 4pm, s/15); Cavassa, Bolognesi 421 on the plaza (☎747 036; 5 and 8pm, s/18); Transfysa, 2 de Mayo 1000, one block uphill from the plaza (☎747 063; 9am, s/15); and Rosario, Comercio 950, on the plaza (4am, s/14). El Rapido, 28 de Julio 400 (☎747 049), five blocks down Comercio and one to the left, goes to **Huaraz** (2¾hr.; 5am, s/7; 3pm, s/5), as does Chiquían Tours, 2 de Mayo 651 (☎747 157; 5:20am, s/6). **Colectivos** make the trip to **Huaraz** (2½hr., leaving when full, s/5) and can be found throughout the day near the Plaza de Armas. **Banco de La Nación** on the Plaza de Armas may frown upon traveler's checks. (☎747 031. Open M-F 8:10am-2:30pm.) There are no ATMs in town. Other services include: **Centro de Salud,** Guillermo Bracle 271 (☎747 085), several blocks downhill from the plaza, at the end of 28 de Julio; the **police** (☎747 124), uphill from the plaza; and **Serpost** (☎747 173), on the 2nd floor of the large white building on the Plaza de Armas.

▐▀▓ ACCOMMODATIONS AND FOOD. For such a tiny town, Chiquían offers a good variety of accommodations. The best bargain is the sparkling new **Gran Hotel Huayhuash,** 28 de Julio 400, upstairs from the El Rapido bus office, with private baths, cable TV, and amazing views from every room. Additional services include laundry, cash exchange, a restaurant, and porter arrangements. (☎747 049. Rooms s/15-80 per person.) **Hostal San Miguel,** Comercio 233, sits seven blocks downhill from the Plaza de Armas; tradition states that all tired backpackers sleep here. The hostel is basic but clean and friendly, with occasional hot water and the prettiest garden in Chiquían. (☎747 001. Rooms s/15 per person.) Chiquían's bargain hotel, **Los Nogules,** Comercio 1301, three blocks uphill from the plaza, has wooden floors, hot water, laundry, and a large corn garden in the middle. (☎747 121. Rooms s/10 per person.) Chiquianos seem to agree that **El Rincón de Yerupaja,** 2 de Mayo 803, a traditional restaurant near the plaza, offers the best food in town. Known as the best cook of the *alta montaña,* Yoder Bernabé will whip up a *menú* (s/3) of Peruvian specialties. (Entrees average s/7. Open daily 6am-10pm.)

NORTHERN PERU

📷 **OUTDOOR ACTIVITIES.** The **Cordillera Huayhuash** is deceptively large, encompassing 140,000 hectares of land, 115 glaciers, three regional departments (Ancash, Lima, and Huánuco), at least six rivers, and **Yerupaja,** the second tallest mountain in Peru (6634m). Numerous routes through these mountains offer genuine trekking experiences without the commercialism that haunts Huaraz and the neighboring Cordillera Blanca. However, hiking in the Cordillera Huayhuash can be long and arduous. Most trekkers hire an **arriero** (porter, US$8-10 per day) and at least one *burro* (mule, US$4-5 per day). Additionally, you may want to bring along a cook (US$20 per day) and/or an emergency horse (US$4-5). Make sure that your *arriero* is licensed by the Chiquían Provincial Touristic Service Association of the High Mountains; all members should have a photo ID card. Porters may or may not double as guides. Make arrangements at least a day or two in advance. Justo Nasario Prudenio, Maximo, and Catalino Rojas Carrera have all been recommended as *arrieros.* If you plan to end your hike prior to returning to Chiquían, you must pay for your *arriero*'s return transportation. You are responsible for bringing a tent and sleeping bag, as well as your own food (unless you hire a cook, in which case arrangements should be made with him). The best **map** of Cordillera Huayhuash is available from the South American Explorers Club in Lima (US$5; see **Lima: Practical Information,** p. 74). The principle route is a 12 to 15 day hike which begins in Chiquían, winds around the Cordillera Huayhuash, and ends back in Chiquían. To get to the trailhead, take a right on Figueredo. Walk to the cemetery, then take a left; the trail begins on the right after the cemetery wall ends. Bring warm clothes.

NORTHERN HIGHLANDS

HUAMACHUCO   ☎044

Between the coast and the highlands, tranquil Huamachuco is a good place to adjust to the altitude. When not admiring the carefully-shaped trees in the center of town, wander out to the variety of nearby ruins. The town's bullfighting coliseum stands empty except for the August 15-18 festival honoring the **Virgen de la Altagracia.** The impressive pre-Inca ruins of **Marcahuamachuco** reside on a hillside (3595m) 9.5km from Huamachuco. The fortified stone complex consists of **Cerro del Castillo** and **Cerro de las Monjas.** The latter was traditionally thought to house the Inca virgins of the Sun, but the function and occupation of the large, triple-walled, circular structures is unknown. Rectangular edifices comprise the more central Castillo. To get to the site (3hr.), walk down Bolívar, turn right after the bridge, and follow the highway to the summit. Combis (s/ 2.5 from the bridge) and taxis (s/30 round-trip from the Plaza de Armas) also make the trip. The closer, pre-Inca **Wiracochapampa** can be reached on foot (1hr.) or by combi (15min.) by heading downhill from the plaza along San Román. The **Baños de Yanazura** make an ideal spot for rest and relaxation. Combis (2hr., 4-10am, s/4; return by 3pm) leave from the hospital. Cheap lodging is available at the baths upon consultation with the priests. The beautiful **Laguna Sausacocha,** along the way to the baths, can be included in a daytrip to Yanazura if planned appropriately. Alternatively, the lake can be visited on foot (4hr. round-trip) or by combi (30min; s/1.5).

The life of this small town is focused around the **Plaza de Armas,** the **market,** and **Balta,** which connects the two. Bus companies arrive and depart from Balta, near the market, but offices can be found around the Plaza de Armas. Sanchez Lopez, Castilla 306, Transportes Agreda, Balta 348, and Palacios, Castilla 173, have early morning and evening service to **Trujillo** (9hr., s/15). Transportes Anita, 10 de Julio 700 (☎441 090), near the hospital, leaves daily for **Cajabamba** (3hr., 4am and noon, s/6). Services include: the **police,** San Román 513 (☎441 289), on the plaza; and the **post office,** Grau 454, (open M-Sa 8am-1pm and 2-4pm). For overnight stays, **Hostal Kaseci,** San Martín 756, has tidy, spacious rooms around a grassy, inner lawn. Hot water is available upon request. (Rooms s/10 per person.) **Noche Buena,** San Román 401, is more expensive, but provides cleaner and safer rooms on the Plaza de Armas. (☎441 435. Singles s/20, with bath s/35; TV s/5 extra.) Locals agree that the best restaurant in town is **El Caribe,** Carrion 537, on the plaza, where meals are carefully prepared. (*Menú* s/4. Open daily 7am-10:30pm.)

CAJAMARCA   ☎ 044

Up in the Sierra, the charming city of Cajamarca has been the feather in many a warrior's cap. First home to various pre-Inca civilizations, the land was conquered in 1465 by the Incas and 67 years later witnessed an epoch-changing event: the imprisonment and execution of the great Inca Atahuallpa by Francisco Pizarro, an event which sparked a chain of battles that would ultimately lead to the Spanish conquest of the region in 1534; remnants of these pre-Hispanic societies still remain and can be explored in the valley. The town itself, however, displays a far more Spanish influence, earning Cajamarca a reputation as one of the finest colonial cities in Peru. Cajamarca shares many of the qualities that tourists love about Cusco, yet the city remains relatively unvisited by travelers, giving it a more relaxed and authentic flavor than its more popular southern Andean cousin.

⌐ TRANSPORTATION

Flights: The **airport** (☎822 523) is 3½km east of town; take a taxi (5min., s/5), or catch a combi from El Batán, 5 blocks west of the Plaza de Armas (10min., s/0.5). AeroConti-nente, 2 de Mayo 574 (☎823 304), has a daily flight to **Lima** (1hr., 8:30am, US$69-99). Open M-Sa 8am-1pm and 3-7pm, Su 8am-noon. AeroCondor has its office at Cajamarca Tours (see below) and serves **Lima** (1¼hr., 8:45 and 9:10am, US$70) via **Trujillo** (20min., US$42). **AeroAndino,** Silva Santesteban 138 (☎822 228), on the Pla-zuela Belén, can leave at any time before 3pm with a min. of 5 passengers; destinations include **Chachapoyas** (US$65) and **Trujillo** (US$40). Open M-Sa 9am-2pm and 4-7pm.

Buses: All of the bus companies are stationed on Atahuallpa's 300 and 400 blocks. This is not the same Atahuallpa that appears on the map; this is 2km east of the center of town. Take a **taxi** (s/2) or a **colectivo** headed toward the **Baños del Inca** (s/0.5). Linea/Vulkano, Atahua-llpa 318 (☎823 956), serves: **Trujillo** (6hr.; 10am, 10, and 10:15pm; s/18-22; *bus cama* 10:30pm, s/25); **Chiclayo** (6 hr., 11pm, s/18; *bus cama* 10:45pm, s/22); and **Lima** (12hr., 7pm, s/50). Farther down the street, **Cruz del Sur,** Atahuallpa 600 (☎822 488), has direct buses to **Lima** (12-13hr., 5pm, s/50; *bus cama* 7pm, s/70-90). Combis depart from Atahua-llpa 299 (☎823 060), across from Grifo "El Che," for **Celendín** (4hr., 7am and 1pm, s/10), where it is possible to catch buses to **Chachapoyas** (10hr., Su and Th 2 and 4pm, s/25).

✖🛈 ORIENTATION AND PRACTICAL INFORMATION

At the heart of it all, the classical **Plaza de Armas** is large, green, and neatly kept. Most hotels and restaurants are nearby. **Amalia Puga, El Comercio, El Batán,** and **2 de Mayo** are the major streets passing the plaza.

Tourist Information: The moderately helpful **ITINCI,** Belén 600 (☎/fax. 822 903), on the 1st fl. of the Complejo Belén, has a few brochures and sells a detailed guidebook of the entire district in Spanish (s/15). Open M-F 7:30am-1pm and 2:15-7pm.

Tour Agencies: The reasonably priced tours offered by Cajamarca's many agencies are the easiest (and often the only) way to see the sights outside of town. Tours depart twice daily for the most popular destinations, at around 9am and 3pm, if enough peo-ple sign up; weekends are usually a safe bet. Standard prices are s/15-20 for Cumbe Mayo, Granja Porcón, Otuzco, city tours, or Colpa-Baños de Inca. Many agencies can also arrange trips to Kuntur Wasi for groups of at least 5 (s/40-50 per person). **Inca Baths Tours,** Amalia Puga 653 (☎/fax 821 828), is the best place for information in English. Open daily 7am-10pm. In addition to leading tours to nearby sights, **Cajama-rca Tours,** 2 de Mayo 323 (☎825 674), sells airline tickets and has Western Union and DHL service. Open M-Sa 7am-1pm and 2-7pm, Su 7am-noon. **Cumbe Mayo Tours,** Amalia Puga 635 (☎/fax 822 938), can provide English-speaking guides with advance notice. Open daily 7:30am-9pm.

Currency Exchange: Interbank (☎822 460), on 2 de Mayo at the Plaza de Mayo, has a Visa/Plus **ATM.** Open M-F 9am-6:15pm, Sa 9am-12:30pm.

Laundry: Lavandería Dandy, Amalia Puga 545 (☎828 067). s/4 per kg. Open M-Sa 8am-7:30pm.

Supermarket: Super Mercado San Francisco, Amazones 780, with perhaps the nicest facade of any supermarket in Peru. Open M-Sa 8am-9:30pm, Su 8:30am-1pm.

Police: Amalia Puga 807 (☎822 944), next to Hotel Casa Blanca on the Plaza de Armas.

Hospital: Hospital Regional Cajamarca, Mario Urteaga 500 (☎822 156).

Telephones: Telefónica del Peru, 2 de Mayo 460 (☎821 008), on the Plaza de Armas, handles international calls. Open daily 7am-11pm.

Internet Access: Atajo, El Comercio 716 (☎822 245). s/3 per hr. Open daily 8am-1am.

Post Office: Amazonas 443 (☎822 206). Open M-Sa 8am-9pm, Su 8am-3:15pm. **Cajamarca Tours** (see Tour Agencies, above) offers **DHL** and **Western Union** service.

ACCOMMODATIONS

The best values are found on the Plaza de Armas, and searching hotels for a room with a balcony onto the plaza is worth the effort. If you're in the mood for luxury, head to **Casa Blanca,** 2 de Mayo 442, the most upscale hotel on the plaza; it has every amenity one could possibly want, and smooth-talkers may be able to finagle a discount. (☎/fax 822 141. Singles s/59; doubles s/83.)

Hostal Residencial Atahualpa, Atahuallpa 686 (☎827 840), near the plaza. The friendly *señora* clearly put a lot of love into decorating the sunrise-yellow indoor courtyard. All of the large rooms have baths with hot water in the mornings, and some have big windows overlooking the quiet pedestrian street. Singles s/20; doubles s/35.

Hostal Peru, Amalia Puga 605 (☎824 030). Above a popular restaurant with live *peña* music on the weekends, Hostal Peru offers comfortable rooms for a lower price than other plaza hotels. All rooms have 24hr. hot-water baths. Singles s/20; doubles s/30.

Hostal Santa Apolonia, Amalia Puga 649 (☎827 207). Rooms surround a white-tiled courtyard filled with plants and couches. Carpeted rooms with TVs and pristine hot baths. Singles s/40; doubles s/70.

Hostal San Francisco, Belén 790 (☎823 070). Less character and an inferior location, but also costs less than its competitors. All rooms come with baths with limited water that is occasionally hot. Singles s/15; doubles s/25.

Hostal Plaza, Amalia Puga 669 (☎822 058), in a huge building above two busy courtyards. Some of the spacious but plain rooms have balconies on the plaza. Hot showers at certain hours of the day. Singles s/15, with toilet s/20, with shower and plaza view s/25; doubles s/28, with toilet s/35, with shower and plaza view s/45.

FOOD

Due to the high number of dairy farms in the area, Cajamarca abounds with *productos lacteos* such as fresh butter, yogurt, and *manjar blanco* (a sweet spread made with milk, sugar, and egg whites). Predictably, Cajamarca is also a cheeselover's paradise; in addition to the local *mantecoso*, *queserías* also produce Swiss varieties such as Emmenthaler and Gruyère.

El Batán, El Batán 369 (☎826 025; email kok.bolster@computextos.com.pe). Eat in the covered courtyard decorated with plants and paintings, or move inside the restored 18th-century house to find a fireplace and small stage where different groups perform on F and Sa (10pm, cover s/7). Choose from the fancy set menu (s/26), the more modest *menú ejecutivo* (s/12), or traditional *criollo* and original vegetarian a la carte items (s/10-19). Open Su and Tu-Th 10am-11pm, F-Sa 10am-1am.

El Cajamarqués, Amazonas 770 (☎822 128). Not quite as upscale as El Batán, but still popular and impressive. Walk under arches through an austere dining hall and into an interior garden courtyard filled with exotic birds. This is where to come for succulent *comida típica* and international dishes. Entrees around s/14. Open daily 8am-11pm.

Oscar's Restaurante Turístico, El Batán 149 (☎828 386). Oscar's offers a curious melange of food and atmosphere: barbecue, seafood, and Chinese fare is served between two big-screen TVs blasting music videos in a room with a strange country-western flare. No need to look at the menu—entree highlights (most s/6-12) are spelled out in neon lights. Open daily 10am-11:30pm.

Cascanuez Cafe-Bar, Amalia Puga 554 (☎826 089). This down-home café has hands-down the best mousse, chocolate cake, and fruit pie in town (slices s/3.50), as well as cappuccino (s/5), omelettes (s/4.50), and lasagna (s/10), in a dining room that looks just like grandma's. Open M-Sa 8am-1pm and 2:30-11pm, Su 2:30-9pm.

📷 SIGHTS

Though most of its tourist attractions lie outside of Cajamarca, the town itself is not without interest. One of the most noteworthy cathedrals, the beautiful 17th-century **Iglesia de San Francisco** on the Plaza de Armas, is covered with volcanic rock carvings and contains a museum of religious art. (Museum open daily 3-6pm.)

EL CONJUNTO MONUMENTAL BELÉN. A complex of colonial buildings in downtown Cajamarca, the *conjunto* includes the **Iglesia Belén,** built in the late 17th century, the small **Museo Médico** inside the Instituto Nacional de Cultura, and the **Museo Arqueológico y Etnográfico** across the street. While the vestiges of religious art might suggest that the Medical and Archaeological Museums were once churches, the 18th-century buildings were actually used as hospitals (for men and women, respectively) with small chapels for the infirm. The highlight of the *conjunto* is **El Cuarto del Rescate,** the room where Atahuallpa, the last Inca emperor, was held prisoner by the Spanish and which was to be filled with his ransom—once with gold and twice with silver. According to legend, Atahuallpa was ordered to stretch his hand as far up as possible to determine the required height of the treasures; the spot he touched, exactly 2m 40cm high, is still marked on the wall with a red line. The room, which used to be part of Atahuallpa's palace, is also the only remaining example of Inca architecture in Cajamarca; the rest of the Inca city was torn down by the Spanish conquistadors to make room and provide building material for their new colonial city. *(El Cuarto del Rescate is at Amalia Puga 750, across from the Iglesia de San Francisco. The rest of the complex is around the corner, surrounding the intersection of Belén and Junín. Open M-Sa 9am-1pm and 3-6pm, Su 9am-1pm. s/4; tickets good for 3 days. Spanish-speaking tour guides can be hired at the complex for about s/5 per site. For an English-speaking tour, go to one of the travel agencies listed above; prices are comparable, but guides are less specialized.)*

EL MIRADOR SANTA APOLONIA. For an excellent view of Cajamarca, visit this lookout looming high above the city. It lies in a trim garden park at the crest of an Andean mountain just above the Santa Apolonia cathedral. The vista overlooks the vast, flat valley, set 2700m above sea level amid towering peaks. Supposedly, Atahuallpa used to review his subjects here, and a natural rock formation resembling a throne is known as the Inca Chair. In addition to the well-groomed gardens, the park houses a number of caged owls, hawks, and a cute little monkey. *(Stairs begin at the end of 2 de Mayo. Park open daily 8am-11pm. s/1.)*

LOS BAÑOS DEL INCA. Just beyond Cajamarca's borders lie Los Baños del Inca, natural hot springs whose supposedly salubrious waters were the bathing place of the last Inca, Atahuallpa, shortly before his capture. Today, guests may enjoy private, indoor baths with water drawn from the springs (s/4), sit in the sauna (s/8), or go for a swim (s/2) in the outdoor pool. The actual springs are a scalding 78°C, but bathers can alter the temperature with knobs similar to shower faucets. *(To get to the baños, take a taxi (s/5) or a colectivo (15min., s/0.8) from Amazonas in Cajamarca. ☎821 563. Baños complex open daily 5am-8pm.)*

DAYTRIPS FROM CAJAMARCA

CUMBE MAYO

There is no public transportation to Cumbe Mayo, 20km southwest of Cajamarca. The easiest way to visit is with a guided tour (5hr., s/15-20). It is also possible to walk there along the winding mountain road from Cajamarca (3-4hr.); signs at Cerro Santa Apolonia mark the beginning of the road.

These rolling green hills (3700m), dotted with bizarre, mammoth rock formations, derive their name from the Quechua "humpi mayo," or "thin river." The "river" is actually a 9km long **aqueduct** built by the pre-Inca Caxamarca culture around 1000 BC, making it the oldest known man-made structure in South America. Amazingly, the canal was built by people with no knowledge of metal tools, and still functions (though is no longer used) today. The site also contains a number of ceremonial spots, or **santuarios,** for the Caxamarca nature cults; the most important, a perfectly semi-circular cavern resembling a human head, contains undecipherable petroglyphs inside. Dominating the tranquil landscape (3700m at its highest point) are the **bosques de piedra** (rock forests), gigantic volcanic rocks eroded by rain into bizarre shapes resembling phalluses or mushrooms, depending on your vice. Use your imagination and try to spot the dinosaur, contemplative iguana, military general, horny toad, chicken, and priest reading a book. **Camping** is permitted anywhere in the hills, though you'll either have to walk to and from town or make transportation arrangements with a tour company.

GRANJA PORCÓN

Agencies in Cajamarca charge s/15-20 for a 4hr. tour. Granja Porcón open to visitors daily 5:30am-7pm. If you want to stay in the albergue, the cooperativa can arrange for a private car to pick you up in Cajamarca.

Founded in 1985, this 9500-hectare collective ranch (formally called the **Cooperativa Agraria "Atahuallpa Jerusalén"**) is part of one of the world's largest reforestation projects. Technically, "reforestation" is a misnomer, since the coop's 10,500,000 trees (mostly pine, eucalyptus, and cypress) do not naturally grow at this 3700m altitude; instead, these trees are used for paper and furniture so that natural forests do not need to be decimated. With funding from the Peruvian government, the Universidad Nacional de Cajamarca, and various international environmental organizations, 51 families live here in a self-sufficient town that runs completely on hydroelectric power. Guided trips include a hike through the hilltop forests and a tour of the town and endangered animal sanctuary (which houses wildly-plumed rare birds, monkeys, tigrillos, a puma, an Amazon panther, and freely-roaming vicuña). Guests who aren't satisfied with a short visit can stay at the comfortable, hot-water **albergue** (☎/fax 825 631; s/20 per person); eat in the **restaurant,** where food's prepared exclusively with home-grown ingredients; and go on longer hikes to waterfalls and *miradores*.

VENTANILLAS DE OTUZCO

Tours through a Cajamarca agency cost s/15, but Otuzco is easily reached by public transportation and a guide is not necessary. Take a combi from El Batán, 5 blocks west of the Plaza de Armas (20min., s/0.5). Open daily 8am-6pm. s/3.

This necropolis consists of hundreds of niches or *ventanillas* (small windows), built in AD 800 by the Caxamarca as funeral tombs for the most important members of their society. All of the bones, along with any treasures that may have been inside, were sacked by the Incas when they conquered the land around 1470. A few of the *ventanillas* (on the left side) have been restored. Guided tours usually combine Otuzco with a trip to a flower farm growing some of the world's largest *hortensias* and a Swiss-style cheese factory.

LA COLPA AND LLACANORA

5hr. tours through agencies in Cajamarca cost s/15, and include a visit to the Baños del Inca.

Hacienda La Colpa is a cattle ranch situated in a gorgeous pastoral setting with an artificial lake. It is best known for its **"cow calling,"** an event in which ranch hands round up the ranch's cattle by summoning each animal by name. The nearby town of Llacanora has some 7000-year-old **cave paintings** and is a 20-minute walk from an impressive **waterfall.**

KUNTUR WASI

4hr. from Cajamarca. Full-day tours through an agency cost s/50 per person for a group of 5.

Less frequently visited because of the distance, this 3000-year-old stone complex consists of ceremonial plazas, terraces, and enormous petroglyphs with representations of anthropomorphic gods. The gold crowns and breastplates discovered in tombs here now reside in the nearby **Museo La Conga.**

CELENDÍN

Celendín is an optimal resting point for travel between the jungle and the coast. Various unexcavated ruins, such as La Chocta and La Lechuga, lie in the close vicinity. This Indiana Jones scenario has, unfortunately, led to an increasing amount of grave robbing. Not surprisingly, many locals keep some antiquities in their homes, and some even brag of their recent exploits as *huaqueros.*

TRANSPORTATION AND PRACTICAL INFORMATION. Transport companies have offices on the plaza, but most buses, combis, or camiones begin their journey from the blocks around the *ovalo.* Civa (☎855 163), at the corner of Galvez and Union on the plaza; Atahuallpa, at the corner of Pardo and 2 de Mayo on the Plaza; and Palacios, Union 333, go to **Cajamarca** (5hr., s/10-12); **Lima** (Atahuallpa 7am, s/40; Civa 7pm, *bus cama* s/60); and **Chachapoyas** (Virgen del Carmen; 12hr. in dry season; Th, Su 11am and noon; s/25) via **Leimebamba** (8hr., s/20).

The pale blue **church** with its towering spires marks the **Plaza de Armas** and the center of the city. The **monumento** at the *ovalo,* just five blocks uphill from the plaza, is the central departure point for buses. Although Celendín has a **Banco de la Nación,** changing money may be more successful at local shops like **Veterinaria Mersa,** Caceres 204, by the monument (open daily 7am-8pm). **Farmacia Zoila,** 2 de Mayo 697, just off the plaza, assists customers daily 6am to 10pm with health-related needs. Above the pharmacy is a **medical center** (☎855 457 or 855 003) that receives patients daily from 8am to 8pm. **Serpost** is located at Union 403, just off the plaza. **Telephone offices** are on the plaza at 2 de Mayo (☎855 270) and Union 309 (☎855 292). (Both open daily 7am-10:30pm.)

ACCOMMODATIONS AND FOOD. This small town offers travelers a surprising selection of budget accommodations. The newly opened **Hostal Imperial,** 2 de Mayo 566, two blocks from the plaza, has several immaculate rooms on the second floor. (Singles s/12, with bath s/15; doubles s/22, with bath s/25.) **Hostal Celendín,** Union 305, on the plaza, has ordinary rooms with hot-water baths around a beautiful fountain. More importantly, the staff is a great source of information, and the first-floor restaurant serves good dishes, including a *menú* (s/3). (☎855 239. Singles s/16.50; doubles s/28; TV s/5 extra.) **Hostal Galvez,** 2 de Mayo 344, is more interesting for its rock shrine to the Virgen del Carmen in the patio than for its run-of-the-mill rooms. Hot water is available for an extra s/2. (☎855 327. Rooms s/6 per person, with toilet s/8 per person.) **Hostal Amazonas,** 2 de Mayo 316, almost appears to reincarnate turn-of-the-century living, with wash basins and iron beds in each room. (☎855 283. Singles s/8, with bath s/10.) **La Reserva,** 2 de Mayo 549, is by far the most appetizing and luxurious restaurant in town. Patrons have the option of dining in the carefully decorated open-air section or watching TV in the more dull indoors. Try the sandwiches (s/1) and juices (s/1), or go all out with the lunch *menú* (*ejecutivo* s/5; *económico* s/3; ☎855 415; open daily 8am-11pm).

NORTHERN PERU

🔭 **SIGHTS.** The **Llanguat thermal baths** are a great place to kill time before the next bus or to soak away travel bruises (s/1.50). Transportes Araujo, Pardo 486, has service to Villanueva via Llanguat (s/4).) **La Chocta**, 44km from Celendín, is most famous for its various rectangular stone buildings *(chullpas)*, which were used as burial chambers. Apart from its funerary importance, the site also contains well-fortified residences and a plaza. (To get there, take a combi from the market to the town of Oxamarca (3-4 hr.), and then trek for an additional 3hr.)

LEIMEBAMBA

The recent discovery of over 200 mummies in the nearby archaeological site of Laguna de los Condores has brought a great deal of attention to this peaceful town. Having to cope with the recent surge of visitors interested in exploring the multitude of ruins left behind by the "Chachapoyas" culture, Leimebamba is in the rapid process of adopting an extensive tourist network.

📑 **TRANSPORTATION AND PRACTICAL INFORMATION.** Combis heading to **Chachapoyas** (s/7) via **Tingo** (s/5) park around the plaza daily after 7pm. Register with the driver for the following morning's departure (3:30-4:30am), and they will give you a wake-up visit. Service Kuélap, sixth block of 16 de Julio, just off the plaza, provides service to **Chiclayo** (9am, s/35) and **Lima** (Tu and Th 9am, s/65) via **Trujillo** (s/45). Chachapoyas is currently regarded as a better source of information and tour packages than Leimebamba, but that may change in the near future. **Tourist information** is available at San Agustin 407, on the plaza. (Open M-F 8am-noon and 2-5pm.) The office also contains a small **museum.** A larger museum, just out of town on the way to Celendín, was recently inaugurated thanks to Austrian sponsorship, and promises to give ample coverage to the numerous cultures that occupied the local ruins. (Open Tu-Sa 9am-noon and 2-5pm. Adults s/5, students s/2.)

Leimebamba has neither a post office nor a bank, but individuals are usually eager to **exchange dollars** for *soles.* This includes the **police,** Sucre 115 (☎778 024), on the plaza. The **hospital,** La Verdad 480, is three blocks from the plaza.

🏠 **ACCOMMODATIONS AND FOOD.** Accommodation and food selection is currently rather sparse, but promises to vary more in the upcoming months. The modern **Laguna de los Condores,** Amazonas 320, just off the plaza, offers comfortable rooms with super clean bathrooms. The relaxing first floor lounge and cafeteria are also great places to obtain tourist information from the knowledgeable owners. (Singles s/15, with bath s/30; doubles s/25, with bath s/40.) **Hotel Escobedo,** 16 de Julio 514, is the only other choice in town. Basic rooms (s/10 per bed) are available with communal, spacious baths that have hot water during the day. **Restaurante El Caribe,** 16 de Julio 712, offers select dishes of *comida típica* as well as a *menú* (s/3) for lunch. (Open daily 7am-11pm.) **Panaderia Jovita,** La Verdad 514, has good bread and cheese—ideal for daytrips.

🔭 **SIGHTS.** You better be pretty interested and pretty energetic if you want to see the original resting-place of the hundreds of mummies recently recovered from **Laguna de los Cóndores;** this trip takes nine hours walking, eight hours on horseback. The site contains seven stone towers, four polychrome *chullpas*, and about 200 circular structures near a beautiful lake. Well-preserved mummies were first interred in the *chullpas* over 1000 years ago, but it is believed these individuals underwent secondary burials as later cultures made room for members of their own society. By the time archaeologists visited the site in 1997, *huaqueros* had already sifted through the mummies and carelessly separated them from their original context. Ceramic remains indicate the influence of the Chimú and Cajamarca cultures, and the discovery of *quipus* emphasizes the presence of Inca administration. (To visit the ruins, tourists must be accompanied by a guide (s/20 per day). The journey begins near the new museum on the road to Celedín. Basic accommodations are available at the summit. A large **museum/research center** in town displays 220 mummies that once belonged by the lake.) **La Congona** is a much more accessible site that can be easily visited in a daytrip. The circular structures at the summit exhibit the three frieze types identified with the Chachapoyas culture: rhombus, zig-zag, and Greek-stepped. Apart from the archaeological ruins, the hilltop offers beautiful vistas of the nearby countryside. (The ruins are a 3hr. walk from the end of La Verdad in Leimebamba.) The less-explored region of **Tajopampa** also requires an overnight stay, but is well worth it. Primarily a funerary site, caves in a 500m cliff-face were used to inter the dead. The area also contains numerous red arches and petroglyphs. In particular, the image of a man holding a bleeding head supports theories concerning the bellicose nature of the Chachapoyas. Other nearby residential compounds can also be explored. (To get to the site, hire a guide (s/20 per day) and start from the path near the new museum.)

CHACHAPOYAS ☎ 044

As the capital of the Amazonas department, Chacha (as Chachapoyas is affectionately called) is home to some of the most impressive but least visited ruins in Peru. The extraordinary pre-Inca fortress of Kuélap, four hours away, is one of the largest architectural works in the Americas. A bustling highland city (2335m) with modern amenities—despite a population of only 15,000—Chachapoyas sees only a handful of foreign visitors. Even getting here is an adventure. Most opt for the bumpy eight-hour bus from Chiclayo, but true thrill-seekers take on the 20- to 24-hour journey from Cajamarca via Celedín, a spectacularly scenic ride not for the faint of stomach. If you're still thirsting for adventure after visiting Chachapoyas' most remote attractions, the crossroads to the jungle is only an hour away.

▐ TRANSPORTATION

Flights: The airport is 20min. outside of town. Flights from Chachapoyas are limited, but **Grupo Aereo No. 8,** with an office in Hotel Revash (see below), sends military planes to **Lima** (Tu, generally at 11am but confirm the night before; s/130). **La Vid Reina,** on the Plaza de Armas, also sends Sa flights to **Lima** Apr.-Dec.

Buses: Combis and taxis are concentrated around the market on Grau, and most buses arrive into or leave from Salamanca and Arrieta. TransServis Kuélap, Ortiz Arrieta 412 (☎778 128), has the most comfortable bus service to **Chiclayo** (8-9hr.; M and F 5pm, Tu-Th and Sa-Su 3pm; s/25). Transcar, La Libertad 690 (☎778 155), plays videos to help pass the time on the long ride to **Lima** (20-24hr.; 10am, W and Sa also 9am; s/60) via **Chiclayo** (9hr., s/30) and **Trujillo** (12hr., s/45). Civa, Ortiz Arrieta 279 (☎778 048) also sends buses (usually with video) to **Chiclayo** (10hr., 4pm, s/25) and **Lima** (22hr.; M, W and F 10:30am; s/60). Two buses to **Leimebamba** (4hr., noon-1pm, s/10) leave from the intersection of Grau and Salamanca. To **Pedro Ruiz** (1½hr.), combis (5am-6pm, s/6) leave from the 3rd block of Grau, or taxis (s/9) depart from the market on Grau. From Pedro Ruiz it is possible to hail down a bus headed to **Tarapoto** (9hr., s/20-25), but you probably will not be able to find a seat. The best place to hop on a bus is at the police checkpoint on the way out of town.

▐ ORIENTATION AND PRACTICAL INFORMATION

The main landmark in town is the **Plaza de Armas,** bordered by **Ayacucho, Grau, Amazonas,** and **Ortiz Arrieta.** The commercial center and **mercado** are on **La Libertad,** one block north of Ayacucho, between Grau and Ortiz Arrieta. Most combis to nearby towns leave from Grau between La Libertad and **Salamanca** (also called **San Juan de la Libertad**). Essential services can be found along **Amazonas** and **Triunfo.**

Tourist Information: The **official office** is located at Triunfo 852. Open M-F 8am-1pm and 3-8pm, Sa 8am-1pm. The **Cafe de Guías,** Ayacucho 755 (☎777 664), in the Gran Hotel Vilaya, is full of brochures, books, maps, guide referrals in English, and freshly brewed coffee. Open daily 7am-11pm. **Amazon Tours,** Arrieta 520 (☎778 294; fax 777 615), on the plaza, is another valuable source of information and supplier of tour packages. Choices include a guided trip to Kuélap (s/50), Karajia (s/50), or Revash (s/70).

Open M-Sa 8am-1pm and 3-7pm, Su 8am-2pm. **Hotel Revash,** Grau 517 (☎777 391), on the plaza, also offers tours to Kuélap for a similar price. **Hotel Gran Vilaya,** on the corner of 2 de Mayo and Ayacucho (☎757 664), provides more expensive tours for its ritzy clientele, but is also a great well of information. English-speaking guides available.

Currency Exchange: Banco de Crédito, Arrieta 580 (☎777 430), is on the plaza. Visa **ATM.** Open M-F 9:15am-1:15pm and 4:30-6:30pm, Sa 9:30am-12:30pm.

Laundry: Lavandería Clean, Amazonas 813 (☎777 078), just 1 block from the plaza, offers same day service if required. Open M-Sa 9am-1pm and 3-7pm, Su 9am-1pm.

Market: The busy **indoor market,** located at the corner of La Libertad and Grau, provides a cheaper option than restaurant dining. A good place to stock up on food before long daytrips is **Comercial Tito,** La Libertad 860 (☎777 123). Open M-Sa 7:30am-1:30pm and 2:30-7:30pm, Su 8:30am-noon.

Emergency: ☎105.

Police: The **Tourist Police,** Triunfo 592, **require that tourists register with them** upon arrival into Chachapoyas. The **National Police,** Ayacucho 1040 (☎777 176), can also be consulted in case of emergency.

Pharmacies: Botica Santa Rosa, Amazonas 717 (☎998 694), 2 blocks from the plaza. Open 24hr.

Medical Services: Clínica San Juan Bosco, Ayacucho 1231 (☎777 226).

Telephones: A **Telefónica del Perú** office (☎778 089 or 778 094) is located on Ayacucho on the plaza. Open daily 7am-11pm.

Internet: Ciber Club, Triunfo 761, charges s/6 per hr. Open M-F 8am-1pm and 3-9pm, Su 8am-12:30pm and 3-8pm. **Hotel Revash** and **Botica Santa Rosa** let individuals connect to the web on their personal desktops for slightly higher rates.

Post Office: Serpost, Grau 561 (☎777 019), on the plaza. Open M-Sa 8am-8pm.

ACCOMMODATIONS

Due to the recent increase in ecological and archaeological tourism, a number of comfortable hotels have sprung up to balance the more basic accommodations. The wide selection of hostels and hotels cater to all kinds of budgets.

Hostal Johumaji, Ayacucho 711 (☎777 279; fax 777 819; email olvacha@ddm.com.pe), 2 blocks from the plaza, offers day-, week-, or month-long stays. Singles with cold water s/10; rooms with hot-water baths s/15 per person.

Hostal Revash, Grau 517 (☎777 391), on the plaza, has cozy rooms with cable TV and 24hr. hot-water bathrooms. The hostel also offers a small cafeteria, gift shop, laundry service, and Internet access. Owner Carlos Burga is an expert on the region and eagerly helps arrange travel plans. Rooms s/35 per person, s/5-10 discount Dec.-Mar.

Hostal El Tejado, Grau 534, 2nd fl. (☎777 654), on the plaza. Comfortable and immaculate rooms are reasonably priced. Singles s/30; doubles s/50; s/5 less without TV.

Hotel El Dorado, Ayacucho 1060 (☎777 047), 1 block from the plaza. Colonial house. 2nd fl. rooms have hot baths, but are distinguished in price based on the type of floor present—wooden (singles s/20; doubles s/30) or tiled (singles s/25; doubles s/35). 1st fl. rooms share a cold bath (singles s/10; doubles s/20). Laundry service.

FOOD

Chacha's location has resulted in the influence of jungle cuisine in an otherwise highland diet. Rice-covered *juanes* are considered a tropical delicacy, but at higher altitudes, yucca is substituted for the water-needy white pellets. Elegant and modest establishments alike serve up these varieties of *comida típica.*

Chacha, Grau 545 (☎777 107), on the plaza, serves up heaping platters of comida típica. The bistek a lo pobre (s/9) is almost big enough for two. Lunch menús (s/3) are also available. Open M-Sa 7am-10pm.

El Tejado, Grau 534, 2nd fl. (☎ 777 654), on the plaza, delivers equally delicious dishes in a more elegant environment. The relaxing and quiet ambience is interrupted by the large screen TV, but that's exactly what attracts some locals. Open M-Sa 8am-10pm.

Panadería San José, Ayacucho 816, near the plaza. Beyond the varieties of bread, this small cafe sells inexpensive sandwiches, *humitas* (s/0.75), *empanadas,* and *juanes* (s/1). Open M-Sa 6:30am-1pm and 3-9:30pm, Su 7am-1pm and 4-9:30pm.

🖪 DAYTRIPS FROM CHACHAPOYAS

The most exciting times to be in Chachapoyas are during the **Fiestas Patrias,** the first two weeks of August and the **Semana Turística** in the first week of June, when an exposition of local foods and dances culminates with a procession of representatives from nearby villages. However, most people don't come all the way out here just to stay in town. While you can reach most of the outlying sights on your own, authorization is technically needed for all except Kuélap from the **Instituto Nacional de Cultura,** Ayacucho 1260, three blocks from the plaza. (☎ 777 045. Open M-F 8am-5pm.) The Instituto recommends venturing out in groups, preferably with a guide, as some of the remote areas can be dangerous. In addition to the trips provided by **Amazon Tours,** local experts **Martín Chumbe** (via Gran Hotel Vilaya) and **Carlos Burga** (via Hostal Revash) offer their services as Spanish-speaking guides (s/100-150 per day). For those interested in learning more about the nearby ruins and the cultures that once inhabited them, check out Keith Muscatt's *Warriors of the Clouds: A Lost Civilization in the Upper Amazon of Peru.*

KUÉLAP

To get to the ruins, catch the early-morning combi (2hr., s/12). Alternatively, the more fit and adventuresome can make trek up to the ruins (4-7hr.) from Tingo, a 2hr. bus ride from Chachapoyas. The path, indicated by occasional red arrows, starts near the bridge in Tingo and follows a level plain along the river before turning and becoming a steep mountain climb. Gates open daily 8am-4:30pm. s/10. Basic accommodations, lacking electricity or running water, are available in the INC dorm (s/7 per person).

If Chachapoyas is "the other Cusco," as it is sometimes called due to the size and scope of well-preserved ruins in the area, **Kuélap** is undoubtedly its Machu Picchu. Surrounded by a 30m high wall, this fortress measures 584m in length and 100m in width, and is often said (though the claim is unconfirmed) to contain three times more stone than the Egyptian pyramids at Giza. Though "discovered" in 1843, the complex remains a mystery to archaeologists. It is known that Kuélap was built by the Chachapoyas people roughly between AD 1100 and 1300, and its architecture and location—surrounded by sheer rock and cliffs on three sides—clearly indicate that it served as a defensive structure. But no one knows who the Chachapoyas were defending themselves against, nor where the massive quantities of stone came from and how it was transported to this remote location over 3000m above sea level. Despite erosion and the passage of time, the complex has remained amazingly intact. One of the most impressive structures is known as **El Tintero** (The Inkwell), a 6m-high inverted cone believed to have been used in religious ceremonies—some even claim that human sacrifices were thrown inside.

Thick vegetation still permits the identification of three visible levels that contain approximately 420 circular edifices and five rectangular structures. **Pueblo Alto** (the second level), supported by thick, fortified walls, is believed to be the location where the elite made their homes. Plazas and large rectangular structures on this level also indicate some public or ceremonial function. The **torreon** marks the northern tip and the third level. The recovery of axes and other weapons from this spot led archaeologists to theorize that it was a military lookout. The puzzling **tintero** (inkwell, 13.7m diameter, 5.5m high) in the southern portion has a conical outer form but a bottle-shaped inner compartment. Animal remains and offerings suggest that it served some religious function.

Although Kuélap was "discovered" by Crisostomo Nieto in 1843, it has been most recently studied by Alfredo Narváez and Arturo Ruiz. Only four round edifices (8m in diameter, 4m high) on the lowest level have been fully excavated. The resulting artifacts indicate that they served as residences before the Incas used them as burial chambers. Access to other circular structures on the first platform appears to have been impossible without ladders, further stressing the emphasis on fortification and protection. Although generally undecorated, some circular structures on this first platform have been adorned with geometric friezes.

OTHER RUINS NEAR CHACHAPOYAS

REVASH. This impressive funerary location consists of red, rectangular edifices built into the side of a cliff. The structures were erected as tombs and decorated with petroglyphs. Although you cannot enter the mausoleums, the view from below is still well worth the visit. *(Take a combi going to Leimebamba as far as Yerbabuena. Combis sporadically make the journey to Santo Tomás, saving an hr. of walking, but it is easier to walk (2hr.) directly to the site.)*

KARAJIA. Another spectacular funerary site, this location contains anthropomorphic wooden coffins that were carefully deposited under a cliff overhang between AD 800-1300. Crouched mummies were placed inside each coffin and skulls were perched atop each individual sarcophagus. The mummies have since been removed by archaeologists, but the coffins remain. *(Take a bus to Luya (between 7:30am-5pm) from Arrieta near Chachapoyas's marketplace, and then walk to the ruins (2½hr.). Occasional buses to Luya Viejo or Trita can also be taken from Luya, saving 1½hr. of walking.)*

JALCA GRANDE. This small town is the spot of the first founding of Chachapoyas in 1538, 74km from its present location. Today, it is popular as a folklore center that also attracts tourists to see the plaza's colonial stone tower and the nearby Ollape ruins (40min. walk). The circular structures at the Ollape archeological site were probably erected between AD 1150-1300 and display diamond friezes. Laguna Mamacocha (5hr. walk) can also be appreciated as a daytrip from Jalca Grande. *(Combis travel daily to Jalca (1½hr., noon-1pm, s/6) from Chachapoyas.)*

OLÁN. Of all the Chachapoyas residential complexes in the region, this is by far the most extensive. With approximately 600 circular homes, this is the best site to see the three frieze types: rhombus, zig-zag, and Greek-stepped. *(Take a combi from Salamanca in Chachapoyas to Montevideo (4hr., noon-1pm, s/8) and then trek 1½hr.)*

LEVANTO AND YÁLAPE. Levanto and Yálape are 22km and 14km, respectively, from Chachapoyas. The 4-hectare site of Yálape was constructed between AD 1110-1300, and contains circular buildings with diamond friezes. The Colla Cruz ruins, near the town of Levanto, contain an Inca foundation wall topped by a round structure typical of Chachapoyas. This construction typifies the perplexing relationship between the Inca and Chachapoyas peoples that archaeologists are trying to resolve. *(There is transportation to Levanto daily at 6am and 1pm from Chachapoyas, but the more athletic can walk (3hr.) to Levanto along a pre-Inca trail.)*

CENTRAL HIGHLANDS

In the 1980s and early 90s, Peru's spine was stricken from most travelers' itineraries because it was overrun with peasant-based terrorist groups. In recent years, however, the army's efforts—and shifting public opinion—have forced most group members underground, and the violence has nearly disappeared. Meanwhile, the lively, friendly towns of the central Andes, invigorated by growing tourism, have pushed past their violent history. The region presents the highlands at their most charming: artistry, history, and landscape, without all of the touristic excesses of Cusco. Traveling the region by bus—which is the only way to travel the region—can be arduous, particularly on the unpaved, 24-hour stretch between Ayacucho and Cusco. However, bus travel in the central Andes also gives an authentic taste of the Peruvian *campesino* lifestyle: locals overflow the aisles carrying goods both living and inanimate; stout women in their many-layered skirts hawk Inca Kola; and salsa tapes cycle endlessly.

HIGHLIGHTS OF THE CENTRAL HIGHLANDS

MARVEL at the Incas' prowess—their **Huánuco Viejo** (p. 229) once covered 2.5km.

GET AWAY from the crowds at Peru's *second*-largest lake, **Lago de Junín** (p. 234).

ADMIRE the **artesanía** in the craft villages around Huancayo (p. 242); it's some of the most beautiful in all of Peru.

STROLL among graceful colonial mansions and world-renowned tapestry workshops in the highland sun of **Ayacucho** (p. 249).

LA UNIÓN ☎064

La Unión is to Huánuco Viejo as Aguas Calientes is to Machu Picchu. But what's Huánuco Viejo, you ask? Just east of the Cordillera Blanca, Huánuco Viejo is the under-appreciated site of the "second-best Inca ruins" in Peru—at least that's what they say at the tourist office in La Unión. Like Aguas Calientes, this small town depends on its nearby ruins to attract tourists. But unlike in Aguas Calientes, this hasn't meant a whole lot for the tourist trade. The difficulties of getting to and communicating with the bustling market town of La Unión ensure that it won't be a backpackers' mecca anytime soon. Of course, that's also its charm.

▐▀ TRANSPORTATION

Buses: Cavassa, Unión 231, runs to **Lima** (20 hr., noon and 3pm, s/20). Turismo Armonia, on 2 de Mayo around 1000, also goes to **Lima** (13 hr., 2pm, s/20), as does Estrella Polar, Comercio 1471 (13hr., 2:30pm, s/18). Emp. de Automóviles Niño E.I.R.L., Comercio 1329, sends cars to **Huánuco** (4hr., leaving when full, s/25). Transporte Vitor, Comercio 1309, in the shop that says "Foto," sends buses to **Huánuco** (6hr., 7am, s/15). Combis leave from the market and the Plaza de Armas for **Huallanca** (30min., s/2.5) and **Iscopampa** (s/2).

✴️🛈 ORIENTATION AND PRACTICAL INFORMATION

The **Río Viscara** cuts through La Unión; everything of interest to the traveler lies east of the river. The busiest street in town, **2 de Mayo** runs parallel to the river. The **Plaza de Armas** lies one block over, on **Comercio,** a central thoroughfare that also runs parallel to the river. **Unión** bisects 2 de Mayo and Comercio before crossing the river via the town's major bridge.

Tourist Office: On the Plaza de Armas, in the **Municipalidad Provincial** building. The Spanish-speaking staff manages to be informative despite the office's lack of resources. Open daily 8:30am-noon and 2-5pm.

Currency Exchange: Banco de la Nación, 2 de Mayo and Unión. Open M-F 8:10am-2:30pm.

Market: Near the intersection of Comercio and Rios. It's very, very big.

Police: On Lourdes, near the Plaza de Armas.

Hospital: Hospital de Apoyo La Unión, 2 de Mayo 185.

Telephones: 2 de Mayo and Comercio house several phone booths, but these are often busy, as few people in La Unión have private lines. None accepts calling cards.

📷 ACCOMMODATIONS

"No hay Internet. No hay correos. Pero tenemos hoteles," comments a man waiting to use a phone booth on Comercio. True to his words—and despite the lack of tourists—La Unión has a plethora of budget accommodations.

Hostal Picaflor, 2 de Mayo 870 (☎510 222). From the Plaza de Armas, walk downhill to 2 de Mayo and take a left; Picaflor is on the right. Brand-spankin' new, with wooden floors, large windows, and hot water. Singles s/15; doubles s/20.

Gran Hostal Abilia Alvarado, Comercio 1196, between the market and the Plaza de Armas. It's no surprise that the Abilia complex is a local favorite, what with the bed-side lamps and large rooms. The large backyard, sink for hand washing clothes, disco (F-Sa only) and restaurant (see below) add to the allure. Singles s/15, with bath s/20; doubles s/30; triples s/30.

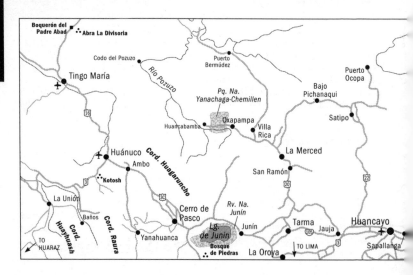

Hostal Ubertina, 2 de Mayo 978. Ubertina's large doubles have windows overlooking the river, but the singles lack windows and charm. Singles s/8; doubles s/12.

Hotel Domino, 2 de Mayo 359. The cheapest place in town, with cement walls, bare lightbulbs, and not-so-appealing communal bathrooms. Singles s/6; doubles s/8.

FOOD

Finding food is not a problem in La Unión. During the day, fresh fruit and bread appear everywhere, replaced after dark by vendors frying up french fries and mystery meat. Nearly identical restaurants line Comercio, especially near the market.

Restaurant Abilia Alvarado, on the 1000 block of 2 de Mayo, across from the gas station. Trees in the middle of the restaurant grow through the roof—they don't care to sample the yummy Peruvian food. Entrees s/6-8. *Menú* s/3. Open daily 7am-11pm.

Restaurant Vizcarra, Unión 100, next to the bridge. Locals love Vizcarra's s/3.50 *menú.* Open daily 7am-9pm.

Restaurant Pollería Chifa Caulang, on Comercio around 1440. You think you've seen big portions. Peruvian and Chinese entrees s/3-6. *Menú* s/5. Open daily 6am-11pm.

SIGHTS

HUÁNUCO VIEJO. The ruins of Huánuco Viejo, also called Huánuco Pampo, are thought to have been one of the major administrative areas of the Inca Empire. Building commenced in 1460 and continued until 1539, when the Spanish arrived. After two years of Spanish rule, the high altitude and severe climate (as well as frequent Inca uprisings) proved to be too much for the conquerors, and the Incas resumed control. At its height, Huánuco Viejo contained almost 4000 structures and extended more than 2.5km. Today, 7km south of La Unión, Huánuco Viejo remains a gargantuan reminder of the city's former glory. A thorough visit will take at least an hour, if not all day. Like so many of Peru's artifacts, though, the site lacks the funding for proper conservation or maintenance. Thus, at first glance, the ruins appear more a random pile of rocks than the seat of an ancient empire. But the lack of modernity or human activity in the area make it easy to step back in time. Unfortunately, though there's a map on a billboard at the complex entrance, the only further guidance consists of some rusty Spanish signs.

CENTRAL HIGHLANDS

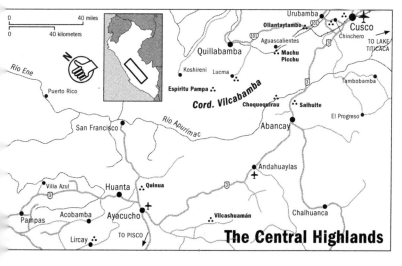

The Central Highlands

The Huánuco Viejo economy was based on textile production; **Acllawasi,** the primary production area, lies just beyond the complex entrance. Continue along the rapidly deteriorating path and you'll reach the **Plaza Central** (at 540m by 360m, the largest open space in the city). During Inca inhabitation, this area was empty except for the large **Ushno** in the middle; the other ruins in the plaza date from the period of Spanish rule. The Ushno was the center of Huánuco Viejo culture and the site of all its large ceremonies and calendar rituals. Constructed in a style which imitates Inca buildings in Cusco, the Ushno remains the most impressive (as well as the best preserved) building in the city. The top affords remarkable views of the ruins and surrounding pampa. The city's most complex structure lies just south (to the left as you walk in) of the Plaza Central; called the **Casa Inca,** it was only for Inca officials visiting from Cusco and was rarely used since they rarely came this far north. At the far end of the Casa sits a large platform that once overlooked an artificial lake, now just a stone-wall outline. To enter the Casa, one passes through **La Kallanka,** an impressive, largely intact building which probably housed a temporary hospital for soldiers, administration offices, or a market complex. *(To walk from La Unión (2½hr.) take Comercio past the market and turn left up Huánuco. Follow Huánuco uphill as it becomes a stone path; then take the trail that branches uphill to the left. Continue up this small but well-marked path for an hr. (even after you cross the highway). When you reach the top, walk straight ahead along the pampa; veer right to follow the wheel tracks. When you reach the road (about 40min. later), head right, toward the snow-covered mountains. Walk through the fields of grazing sheep and cattle; then go left toward the big blue sign and the entrance to the ruins. Alternatively, the colectivo to Iscopampa (s/2) can drop you off a 20min. walk away along the flat pampa, or a taxi (s/15) can take you right to the entrance. Open daily 6am-6pm. s/5.)*

THERMAL BATHS. The **Baños Termales de Tauripampa** constitute what is probably the most interesting natural sauna you'll ever enter. Visitors descend into a large room, then climb into a tiny (about 1m tall) stone cave. The temperature rises dramatically, the walls begin to sweat, all traces of light disappear. A 5m crawl leads to stone benches and small pools of boiling water—bring a bucket if you want to douse yourself. Not recommended for the claustrophobic or those afraid of the dark. *(From town, walk south along the main road to the 139km mark (about 20min.), where a large yellow sign marks the stone path that leads down to the baths. Colectivos (s/1) en route to Huallanca can also drop you off there. Open Apr.-Dec. M-F 5am-7pm, Sa-Su 4am-7pm. Adults s/ 1, children s/0.5 for 15-20min.)* The standard **Baños Termales de Conoc** offer baths, showers, and a large pool. *(From town, walk 30min. north on the road to Huánuco, or take a colectivo (s/1) en route to Pachas and ask to be let off at the baths. s/1.)*

▓ FESTIVALS

La Unión's **fiesta patronal,** also known as the **Semana Turística,** lasts from July 26-31. The festivities, which include traditional dances, adventure sports, food tasting, and bullfighting, reach their peak on July 28. A few months later, from November 5-12, the **Aniversario de la Fundación de La Unión** features similar events.

HUÁNUCO   ☎ 064

The Incas inhabited the original Huánuco, now a ruin 100km west of the modern city (see Huánuco Viejo, p. 229). Before them the Kotosh ruled the area, and their nearby temples may be the oldest in the Americas. But such historical currents wield little influence over present-day Huánuco, with its *video pubs* and burger joints and the concrete cathedral presiding over the Plaza de Armas. Only the ramshackle settlements climbing the hills on the outskirts of town seem like they too could have been here a long time ago. Still, leafy Huánuco retains an old-fashioned sort of peacefulness—it helps that the Gringo Trail has yet to discover the walkable city center, those whitewashed residential districts, or that aspect of their city of which residents are so proud: the ideal climate.

☞ TRANSPORTATION

Airport: The airport (☎513 066) is 6km north of the city center. A taxi there should cost s/5-10. **Star Up**, 28 de Julio 1015 (☎519 595 or 623 935) flies to **Lima** (50min.; W 1:20pm and F 4pm; US$59, round-trip US$98) and **Tingo María** (15min., W 1:20pm, US$10). **AeroCondor**, Abtao 519 (☎517 090) also flies to **Lima** (45min.; 1 per day Tu, Th, Sa, Su; US$69).

Buses: León de Huánuco, Malecón Aromias Robles 821 (☎512 996), runs to: **Lima** (8hr.; 10am, 8:30, and 9pm; s/20-25); **Satipo** (8-10hr., 7am, s/25); and **La Merced** (6-7hr., 7am, s/20). Trans Rey, 28 de Julio 1201 (☎513 623), goes to **Lima** (8-9hr.; 9am, 8:30, 9, 9:30pm; s/20-28) and **Huancayo** (6hr., 10:15pm, s/16). Transportes Perú, Tarapaca 449 (☎512 333), goes to **Tantamayo** (7-8hr., 7am, s/20) and **La Unión** (6hr., 8am, s/15). Transportes Vitor, Tarapaca 413 (☎513 347 or 512 226), serves **La Unión** (5-6hr., 7:30am, s/15). Leonicio Prado, Valdizan 235 (☎514 062), goes to **Pucallpa** (11hr., 8am, s/30) via **Tingo Maria** (3hr., s/5). Turismo Central, Tarapaca 560 (☎511 806), sends buses to **Huancayo** (6hr., 9:30pm, s/18). Estrella Polar, Tarapaca 536 (☎514 716), goes to **Lima** (8hr., 8 and 8:30pm; s/18-20). Comite de Automóviles 5, General Prado 1097 (☎518 346), sends colectivos to **Tingo Maria** (2hr., leaving when full 4am-7pm, s/13). ETNASA minibuses also head to **Tingo María** (3hr., every hr. on the hr. 6:30am-6pm, s/7). To get to ETNASA, walk down General Prado, cross the bridge and head left down the freeway. The company is 25min. down the road, in the Terminal Principal (taxi s/2).

Local Transport: Colectivos (s/1-1.5) have the run of the city; their routes are marked on the side—Mdo. is the abbreviation for Mercado. One of the more popular routes runs the length of 2 de Mayo.

Taxis: Taxis to anywhere in the city center should cost s/1.5; to the airport s/10; to the Kotosh temple s/3-5.

☀☞ ORIENTATION AND PRACTICAL INFORMATION

Bordered by the **Río Huallaga** to the east, the **Laguna Vina del Río** to the south and mountains all around, Huánuco rests approximately 300km northeast of Lima. Most streets follow a grid pattern. The principal ones border the **Plaza de Armas:** Damaso Beraun and General Prado run (almost) east-west, and 2 de Mayo and 28 de Julio interest them. Tarapaca, street of many bus stations, runs east-west (almost) four blocks south of the Plaza de Armas.

Tourist Office: General Prado 718 (☎512 980), on the Plaza de Armas. Small selection of photocopied maps and pamphlets. Spanish-speaking staff caters more to big-spending travelers. **Internet** available. (s/2 per hr.) Open M-F 8am-1pm and 1:45-8pm.

Currency Exchange: Banco de Crédito, 2 de Mayo 1005 (☎512 069), 1 block south of the Plaza de Armas. **ATM** accepts Visa/Plus. Open M-F 9:15am-1:15pm and 4:30-6:30pm, Sa 9:30am-12:30pm.

Markets: The **Mercado Modelo,** bordered by San Martín and Huánuco, and the **Mercado Antiguo,** 3 blocks away, fronting primarily on Huánuco and Valdizan, offer similar standards. Mercado Modelo tends to be more chaotic. Both open during daylight hours.

Laundry: Lavandería La Primavera, Beraun 530 (☎513 052). Shirts s/3, pants s/4-6. Open M-Sa 8am-noon and 3-8pm.

Emergency: ☎ 105

Police: Constitución 105 (☎513 115), at Abtao.

Hospital: Valdizan 950 (☎512 400), at Constitución.

Telephones: Telefónica del Perú has offices throughout the city, including one on the Plaza de Armas (see Internet Access, above). **Sermutel,** 28 de Julio 1135 (☎514 660 or 517 766; fax 512 093). Open daily 7:30am-10pm.

Internet Access: Telefónica del Perú, Beraun 749 (☎/fax 519 348), on the Plaza de Armas. Fairly speedy connection, s/5 per hour. Open daily 8am-11pm. (See also Tourist Office, above.)

Post Office: Serpost, 2 de Mayo 1157 (☎512 503), on the Plaza de Armas. Open M-Sa 8am-8pm, Su 8am-2pm.

ACCOMMODATIONS

There will be no bed shortage in Huánuco any time soon. Fairly decrepit yet inexpensive lodgings choke the Mercado Modelo area; pricier rooms dot the Plaza de Armas. The following accommodations fall somewhere in between.

Hostal Astoria, General Prado 984 at Bolívar, 2 blocks toward the river from the Plaza de Armas. Creaky floors and some initial mustiness are small prices to pay for a room in this charming old villa, with its mile-high ceilings and brightly tiled courtyards. Warm water in the morning. Singles s/10; doubles s/15; triples s/20.

Hotel Caribe, Huánuco 546 (☎513 645 or 510 708; fax 513 753), 2nd fl., next to the market. From the plaza, walk one block down 2 de Mayo (away from the Telefónico office), then turn right and walk 2 blocks on Huánuco. Caribe cultivates an air of professionalism despite its fake bricks and glowing electric lights. With 5 stories of rooms, it should be easy to get one facing away from the market. TV with cable, s/5. Singles s/7, with shower s/8; doubles s/10, with shower s/11, with bath s/15.

Hostal Kotosh, Ayacucho 560 (☎517 341). From the plaza, walk down General Prado (toward Serpost) and take a left on Abtao. After 2 blocks, turn right on Ayacucho. As crisp and impersonal as the hospital green of its walls and sheets implies. Back rooms get mountain views—and less noise from the market. All rooms have bath with hot water in the morning. TV s/5. Singles s/17; doubles s/26; triples s/36.

Hostal Trejo, Abtao 525, between Ayacucho and Aguilar. From the plaza walk down General Prado (toward Serpost), turn left on Abtao and keep walking for 2½ blocks. Some of the violet walls show scuffs, but otherwise the bright art-deco building seems in good condition. Close to Tarapaca and many bus agencies. All rooms with cold water bath. Singles s/18; matrimonial s/18; doubles s/25.

Hostal Huánuco, Huánuco 777 (☎512 050), between 28 de Julio and 2 de Mayo, is slightly more expensive, but its decor merits the price: particularly high ceilings and a manicured garden. Hot water mornings and evenings. Singles s/20, with bath s/25; doubles s/25, with bath s/30.

FOOD

Restaurants proliferate on the streets radiating from the Plaza de Armas. Several good bread stores line 2 de Mayo south of the Plaza. For chicken or Chinese food, try 29 de Julio.

Vegetariano, Abtao 897 (☎514 626). This cozy restaurant does serve meat, but as the name suggests, carnivores aren't their primary clientele. English menu available. Entrees s/2-7. Vegetarian *menú* s/3.50. Delicious fresh-squeezed juices s/2.5-4. Open daily 7am-10pm.

Lookcos Burger Grill, Abtao 1021 (☎512 460). With brightly colored tables, pictures of Marilyn Monroe on the wall, constant music videos, and a mini playground out back, Lookcos feels like a typical American burger joint. Burger meals s/4-6. Sandwiches s/3-7. Tacos s/4.5-5. Open daily 6pm-1am. V.

Rinconcita Huanuqueño, 2 de Mayo 175 (☎513 396), offers regional specialties at reasonable prices in their leafy courtyard. A rotating menu includes such Peruvian delights as ¼ *de cuy* (s/4.5). *Menús* s/4-8. Open daily 11am-5pm.

Cevichería el Piurano, Beraun 821 (☎516 451), near the Plaza de Armas. The cool white tile makes for pleasant meals, but it's the fresh ceviche (s/8-15) that draws crowds in spite of a certain priciness. Open daily 8:30am-3:30pm.

SIGHTS

KOTOSH TEMPLES. Only 5km from town, off the road to La Unión, the pre-Inca (4,000 years old in some parts) Kotosh Temples bake in the sun. One of the oldest Andean cultures, the Kotosh probably constructed their series of temples amidst cacti and butterflies similar to those surrounding the complex today. And while not much remains of the original structures, visitors can make out aspects of the temples' former stature. Following the marked path, the first site one reaches is thought to date from the Kotosh/Sajarupata period of around 300 BC. At that time the people lived communally, with many families sharing one building and yard— evident in the symmetrical compartments still visible in the bases of the walls. The complex's oldest structure rests at the top of the hill; its asymmetrical walls (now pretty crumbled) were 3m thick. Finally, the **Temple of the Crossed Hands** (the temple most people mean when they speak of "The Temple of Kotosh") sits under the archaeologists' shed. The temple actually housed two sets of crossed hands (representations of the Southern Cross constellation), a man's and a woman's; both are now in the National Museum in Lima (see **Lima: Museums,** p. 85). The crossed hands symbolized friendship, but the temple also contained a series of niches used for less friendly purposes—the Kotosh placed sacrificial animals in the niches after they had baked them to death. (*Both colectivos and camionetas can drop you off at Kotosh on their way to the mountains. Colectivos (s/0.5) depart from the corner of Aguilar and San Martín; camionetas (s/1) leave from the corner of Leonicio Prado and Aguilar. A taxi from the city center costs s/3-5. Open daily 8am-6pm. s/2.5, students with ID s/1.5, children s/1.*)

MUSEO DE CIENCIAS. This museum houses over 4000 stuffed animals native to Peru, all dissected and lovingly prepared by the curator, Nester Armas Wenzel, who learned his taxidermy in Spain and Japan. Señor Wenzel loves to give tours of his museum— watch for the case up front that displays a collection of deformed animals, including a cat with two mouths and a sheep with eight legs. Wenzel swears that they're all real. (*General Prado 495. Open M-F 9am-noon and 3-6pm, Sa-Su 10am-noon. s/1, children s/0.5.*)

CHURCHES. Huánuco shelters several beautiful churches. Three blocks down Beraun from the Plaza de Armas (going toward Serpost) waits the **Iglesia San Francisco,** which dates to 1560. Simple wooden benches lead back to an ornate gold altarpiece big enough to dwarf any priest. A great time to visit is during their children's mass (Su 10am). A joyful, song-filled event, the mass won't be wasted on anyone—no matter what age or religion. All the way down 2 de Mayo, overlooking the river near Quadra 200, is the 17th-century **Iglesia de San Sebastián.** Inside stands the world's only sculpture of San Sebastián covered with smallpox. (*Both churches open daily for mass 6:30-8am and 6:30-8pm. Free.*)

VICHAYCOTO'S DISTILLERIES. Modern-day earthly pleasures await at Vichaycoto's distilleries. The aguardiente (liquor) produced here is sold all over Peru, but workers at the factory will gladly give visitors a glass for free. And though the rusty old machines only set to work about once every fortnight, the huge metal vats keep a good reserve available all the time. It's not a traditional tourist destination but quite interesting nonetheless. (*To get to Vichaycoto take an Ambo-bound bus (25min., every 7min. 5:30am-9:15pm, s/0.5) from Cisne Aguilar 473. The entrance to the factory is on the right. ☎ 516 199. Open M-Sa 7am-1pm.*)

FESTIVALS

Huánuco's big event, the **Fiesta Patronal,** occurs annually on the anniversary of the city's founding. On August 15, 2001, the town will celebrate with parades, lots of music, traditional costumes, and a large commercial fair. Two weeks earlier, from July 27-31, the **Festival de Perricholi** features music, mountain biking, a motocross competition, and a bread fair.

JUNÍN   ☎ 064

Stretched flat along the Andes' barren plains, Junín does not see many visitors. The highway that passes through the center of town carries most of them along, far past the cold and sleepless nights one finds at 4105m. But most of them don't know what they're missing—the stunning Lago de Junín, with its attendant birds and neighboring village, lies a mere 20km away, just waiting to be discovered.

☰☷ TRANSPORTATION AND PRACTICAL INFORMATION. Buses and colectivos stop by the roadside market along **Manuel Prado,** the highway that divides Junín in two. The town's center lies downhill from the highway—the two paved streets that head down from either side of the roadside snack stalls, **Simón Bolívar** and **San Martín,** travel several blocks to the **Plaza de Libertad** and then another six to the **Plaza de Armas. Buses** drive through Junín all day; these can easily be flagged down. Buses with agencies in Junín go to: **Lima** (5-6hr., 10 per day, s/10) and **Cerro de Pasco** (1½hr., 3pm, s/3), where one can get another bus (1½hr., s/3) or a colectivo (1hr., s/12) to **Huánuco.** Colectivo cars leave when full and go to **Tarma** (1hr., 5am-8pm, s/6) and **La Oroya** (1hr., 5am-8pm, s/6). **Mototaxis** cruise the streets and should cost under s/1 in town. **Banco de la Nación,** Suárez 195, is two blocks downhill from the Plaza de Armas on San Martín, then a block to the left. (☎344 010. Open M-F 8:10am-2:30pm.) The **mercado modelo** resides in the huge building just uphill from the Plaza de Libertad, but on Tuesdays it moves into the streets, covering both San Martín and Bolívar. Other services include: the **police,** Bernardo Alcedo 170 (☎344 008), two blocks to the left of Plaza de Libertad on Ramón Castilla; a **hospital,** Saez Pena 650 (☎344 159), 1km to the right of Manuel Prado as you're coming downhill, parallel to the Plaza de Armas; and **Serpost,** in office 52 on the second floor of the mercado modelo, on the Plaza de Libertad (☎344 151; open M-Sa 8am-2pm and 3-7pm).

☰◌ ACCOMMODATIONS AND FOOD. Junín does not have many accommodation options. **Hostal San Cristóbal,** Manuel Prado 550, to the right if you're facing the town, is unfortunately far away from everything but the buses. However, it provides charmingly ascetic accommodations: concrete walls, rough wool blankets, and cold (if any) water down the hall. The back rooms have mountain views and the proprietors will heat up some water upon request, although it may take a couple of hours. (☎344 215. Singles s/12; doubles s/16.) **Hospedaje Libertad,** Bolívar 296, on the Plaza de Libertad, looks—with its small rooms and short ceilings—like it was built for a child. Windows in some rooms overlook the picturesque plaza, but the common baths lack showers. (☎344 337. Rooms s/8 per person.) For food, the **Plaza de Libertad** sports several places with cheap *menús* (s/2-3), and, starting around 6pm, food stalls by the market building.

◙ SIGHTS. A mere 40 minutes from Junín sits the **Lago de Junín,** the second largest lake in Peru (after Titicaca). The road through the **Reserva Nacional de Junín** passes many traditional stone houses and grazing alpacas before reaching the lake, an ideal locale for strolling or lolling (provided you have warm clothing and watch out for the llamas). While not particularly impressive at first sight, the lookout point near Km25 offers glorious views of the lake and landscape. Plenty of blue-billed, red-faced, and black-and-white spotted birds flap along the lake's periphery, but you should bring binoculars if you hope to glimpse one of the few remaining native *parihuana* birds. While the lake is renowned for its variety of feathered friends, however, it doesn't take a birding enthusiast to appreciate either the incredible scenery or the remote villages along its banks. The village of **Ondores,** at Km22, is the largest settlement on the shores of the lake and houses the lovely stone **Iglesia Matriz San Juan Batista** that locals claim dates from 1550; it's possible to enter this church on the Plaza de Armas, but you have to ask around for the key, which doesn't seem to have a permanent home. You can reach the Lago de Junín on Ondores-bound colectivos (35min., leaving when full, s/2-3), which leave from the end of Bolívar. A taxi or car can then take you from Ondores to the look-out point, though it's a pleasant walk. Colectivos head back to Junín every 20-30 minutes from Ondores.

LA OROYA ☎ 064

Nearly every bus that heads east from Lima passes through La Oroya. Luckily for them, most people won't do much more than glance out the window at this cold mining town. Oroya's barren white mountains are striking at first, but the novelty wears off around the time one feels the polluted air begin to infiltrate one's lungs. If you do somehow get stuck here, take a look around at the industrious scenery and get out early the next morning. Oroya is long and narrow, wedged between two mountain ranges along the **Río Mantaro.** The city follows a slight slope; at the bottom is **Oroya Antigua,** centered around the **Plaza Libertad** and the main street, **Dario León.** About 4km uphill sits central **Oroya Nueva,** and, at the top of the hill, the **Chuccis** district. One central street connects the entire city, but it changes names frequently; in Oroya Antigua it's **Malecón Odrio;** it becomes **Horacio Zeballos** after crossing the river and **Lima** after the railroad tracks until, finally, it's called **Grau** in Chuccis. **Buses** headed in all directions pass through Oroya. Those going uphill on Lima are going to Lima; those going downhill are headed to Huancayo. It's common practice to flag down buses, most of which roll through in the morning and evening; the best place to do so is at the divide in the road where Horacio Zeballos becomes Lima. The actual bus companies are located in Chuccis. Empresa Paz, Grau 519 (☎391 687), goes to **Lima** (4hr., every hr. 7:15am-5pm, s/10), Exp. America, Grau 619, goes to **Huancayo** (2hr., every 30min., s/5). Colectivo cars leave from between the two agencies for **Lima** (3hr., leaves when full 4am-10pm, s/20). Gran Terminal de Automoviles, Grau 622, sends cars, when full, to: **Huancayo** (2hr., s/15); **Tarma** (1hr., s/7); **Cerro de Pasco** (2hr., s/15); **Huánuco** (3hr., s/30); and **Lima** (2hr., 45min., s/25). Colectivo buses and cars cruise the main street; regardless of what it says on their sides, they move between Oroya Antigua and Chuccis (s/0.5).

Services in Oroya include: **Banco de Crédito,** Horacio Zeballos 421 (☎392 424; open M-F 9:15am-1:15pm and 4:30-6:30pm, Sa 9:30am-12:30pm); the **police,** Horacio Zeballos 209 (☎391 137, emergency ☎105); the **Centro de Salud MINSA,** Horacio Zeballos 431 (☎391 076); **Telefónica del Perú,** Horacio Zeballos 423 (☎392 232; open M-F 9:30am-1pm and 3-8pm, Sa 9am-2pm); and **Serpost,** Horacio Zeballos 303 (☎391 023; open M-F 8am-noon and 3-5pm). Oroya doesn't get many visitors, and its scarce accommodations are low in quality. The best of the worst is **Hostal Inti,** Arequipa 117, in Oroya Vieja. Walking down Horacio Zeballos, take a left on Dario León and the first right onto Arequipa. (☎391 098. Singles s/11; doubles s/15; triples s/21.) On the other side of town, **Hostal Roma,** Grau 611, in Chuccis, is closer to the bus companies. (Singles s/15; doubles s/20; TV s/5 extra.) Oroya's food selection isn't much better. Your best bet may be **Bodega Jusalini,** Horacio Zeballos 307, a small but well-stocked grocery store. (☎392 997. Open daily 7:45am-10pm.)

TARMA ☎ 064

Brown is the color of choice in Tarma. Nature coordinates with man in this sierra hamlet, where the packed mud of the surrounding hills coordinates well with the buildings' dull facade. Even the grandiose church on the plaza is a sedate light brown. Yet, despite this monotony, locals call Tarma "The Pearl of the Andes," and this optimistic nickname reveals the town's dormant vivacity. Currently a pilgrimage destination for Peruvian tourists who arrive to visit nearby villages of local importance—Acobamba, for example, with its sanctuary to El Señor de Murahuay—Tarma also contains such wonders as Peru's deepest explored cave.

▐ TRANSPORTATION

Buses: Agencies scattered throughout the city. San Juan, Odria 219 (☎321 677), near the stadium, goes to **Huancayo** (3hr., every hr. 5am-10pm, s/8) and **La Merced** (2hr., every hr. 5:30am-8pm, s/6). The not-yet-organized terminal terrestre, at Castillo and Veinrich, mainly houses buses to **Lima** (5-7hr., frequent in the morning and evening, s/10). Transportes Chanchamayo, Callao 1002 (☎321 882), goes to **Lima** (6hr.; 9am, 2, and 11pm; s/15). Transportes La Merced, Callao 960 (☎322 937), heads to **Lima** (6hr.; 11:15am, 1:15, 10:30, 10:45, and 11:15pm; s/15) and **La Merced** (2hr., 5:30am and 2:30pm, s/6), where connections can be made to **Oxapampa** and **Satipo.** Los Canarios, Juaja 524 (☎323 357), goes to **Huancayo** (3hr., every hr. 5am-6pm, s/7) and **Lima** (6hr., 9:30am and 9:30pm, s/12). Etraser, Veinrich 531 (☎322 888), sends colectivo cars, which leave when full, to **La Oroya** (1hr., s/7), **Junín** (1hr., s/6), **Cerro de Pasco** (2hr., s/13), **Huánuco** (3hr., s/30), and **La Merced** (1½hr., s/8).

■🎇🔔 ORIENTATION AND PRACTICAL INFORMATION

Buses from Lima arrive on Callao, which leads into the center of town. Tarma's focal point is its **Plaza de Armas,** framed by north-south streets **Moquegua** and **2 de Mayo** and east-west streets **Lima** and **Arequipa.** Most buses from Huancayo arrive on Manuel Odria; to get to the plaza from here, follow Manuel Odria toward the stadium, making a right to follow the **Río Tarma.** About three blocks later make a left onto 2 de Mayo, which leads to the Plaza de Armas.

Tourist Information: 2 de Mayo 775 (☎321 010), on the Plaza de Armas, facing the cathedral. Open M-F 8am-1pm and 3-6pm.

Currency Exchange: Banco de Crédito, Lima 401 (☎322 149), 1 block off the plaza. 24hr. Visa **ATM.** Open M-F 9:15am-1:15pm and 4:30-6:30pm, Sa 9:30am-12:30pm.

Police: Callao 118 (☎321 921).

Hospital: Pacheco 362 (☎321 400). 24hr **pharmacy.**

Telephones: Telefónica del Perú, Arequipa 293 (☎322 232), on the Plaza de Armas. Open M-F 8:30am-4:30pm.

Internet access: Centro de Servicios de Informática, Perene 290 (☎322 028). s/3 per hr. per person for 3 or more people, s/10 per hr. for one person. Open daily 9am-8:30pm.

Post Office: Serpost, Callao 356 (☎321 241), between Moquegua and Paucartambo. Open M-F 8am-1pm and 3-6pm.

🛏 ACCOMMODATIONS

Most lodgings in Tarma are either expensive or dilapidated and without hot water.

Hostal Tucho, 2 de Mayo 561 (☎323 483), which keeps newly painted rooms, all with neat bathrooms and dependably hot water, is the one exception to the rule above. Singles s/20; doubles s/30; TV s/5.

Residencial El Dorado, Huánuco 488 (☎321 598), at Paucartambo. Clean rooms and high ceilings create an airy atmosphere. Pleasant courtyard. Hot water in private baths. Singles s/15, with bath s/20; doubles s/20, with bath s/30; triples with bath s/40.

Hostal Ideal, on Moquegua 2½ blocks down from the plaza. Small rooms around a cement courtyard. Right in the center of the market. Singles s/8; doubles s/14.

🍴 FOOD

Cheap restaurants with set *menús* crowd the streets around the Plaza de Armas.

Lo Mejorcito de Tarma, Huánuco 190 (☎320 685), on 2 de Mayo, 3 blocks downhill from the Plaza de Armas and then a block to the right. Their dozen-page menu includes all manner of meat, seafood, and *comida criolla.* Sandwiches s/2-5. Entrees s/7-18. *Menú* s/5. Open daily 7am-11pm.

La Cabaña, Paucartambo 450 (☎321 087), near Huánuco, 2 blocks down Paucartambo from the Plaza de Armas. Typical. *Pachamanca a la olla* s/7. *Menú* s/3.5. Entrees s/6-12. Open daily 7am-10pm.

🧭 SIGHTS

Tarma's most important sights are actually closer to other towns.

LA GRUTA DE HUAGAPO. Going to Palcamayo, 28km from Tarma, brings one nearer to la Gruta de Huagapo, possibly the largest cave in Peru. It's hard to be sure, though, since no one has ever seen its end; even spelunkers using sophisticated underwater diving equipment have descended only (only!) about 2700m into the cave. Amateur explorers can walk in about 300m to look at stalagmites, stalactites, and an ancient cave painting. You'll need a flashlight and may also want a guide from Palcamayo—the easiest place to find one is by the mouth of the cave at the house of Modesto Castro. *(Minibuses to Palcamayo (1½hr., every 20min., s/2.5) leave from Otero, near Moquegua. Cars (s/1) can ferry you the remaining 5km to the caves. s/1.)*

SAN PEDRO DE CAJAS. At about 4000m high, San Pedro de Cajas is another important site on the Tarma tourist circuit. This small village produces and sells renowned **tapestries** woven from alpaca wool—see the Tarma tourist office for a beautiful example. *(Getting to San Pedro can be slightly difficult. The easy way is to get a taxi, which will cost roughly s/35. The less expensive option is to take a colectivo on its way to Junín or Cerro de Pasco and ask to be dropped off at Condorín (approx. 90min., s/7). From Condorín, flag down a micro to finish the journey to San Pedro (30min., s/0.5).)*

Huancayo

🏠 ACCOMMODATIONS
Hostal Baños y Sauna, 4
Hotel Confort, 3
Hostal Plaza, 2
La Casa de la Abuela, 1

EL SEÑOR DE MURHUAY. An important site of pilgrimage near **Acobamba**, 10km from Tarma, the sanctuary of **El Señor de Murhuay** sits on a hill where an image of Christ on the cross was etched into the rock, supposedly by a soldier during an independence battle. More religious locals hold that the carving appeared much earlier—around 1756—and that at various times it can be seen bleeding. Whatever the origin, paint now fills the holy outline, and nearby restaurants and food stands now feed *pachamanca* to hungry pilgrims. Throughout May, festivals honor of El Señor. *(To get to Acobamba, take a colectivo marked "Transrey" (30min., s/1) from the corner of Huánuco and 2 de Mayo. The sanctuary is 1½km away from Acobamba and visible from town.)*

CLOSER SIGHTS. A little less famous and much less overrun than its Sacred Valley cousin, a nearby 11km **Inca Trail** exhibits the flora and fauna of the sierra and a bit of Inca history. *(The trail runs from Huasci to Tarmatamba; to get to the trailhead, take a colectivo (15min., s/1) from the corner of Callao and Paucartambo. It's a 3hr. walk.)* History books may say that Manuel Odria was a dictator, but he was also a Tarmanian. The city honors their presidential representative with a **museum** that contains artifacts and materials that relate to him in one way or another. *(On the 2nd fl. of the Municipalidad. Free.)* The beautiful **Iglesia Catedral Santa Ana** is one of the most impressive churches in Peru. It is also one of the most unique, as it was constructed in the 20th century in a neo-classical style. *(Open in the morning.)*

᠁ FESTIVALS

Tarma's **Semana Santa** festivities, the week before Easter, consist of legendary processions over "the world's largest" carpet of flowers; the 1999 festival, with 12 tons of flowers covering 3200 square meters, is currently in the Guiness Book of World Records—and the size increases each year.

HUANCAYO ☎ 064

As the cradle of Huanca culture and the nucleus of the Río Montaro Valley, the city of Huancayo (pop. 350,000) has recently gained a reputation for being the mecca of Andean *artesanía*. During the 1980s and early 90s, however, tourism to the valley ceased as a result of rampant terrorism, culminating in the shutdown of the famed Lima-Huancayo rail line in 1991 (see Lima-Huancayo Railway, above). Huancayo itself tends toward the mundane, save its intriguing markets and easy accessibility to nearby artists' colonies. Due to these attractive options, Huancayo has become something of an alternative destination promising Andean authenticity.

⌐ TRANSPORTATION

Trains: Service to **Huancavelica** and **Izcuchaca** run from a station in the southeast portion of town at Libertad and Prado. From the Plaza de Armas, take Real to the right past Plaza Huamanmarca until you hit the train tracks. Turn right at the tracks and walk along the dirt road until the station looms in sight on the left. Otherwise, take a taxi from the Plaza (s/2). Train choices include: **Expreso** (5hr., M-Sa 6:30am, s/6-30), and **Ordinario** (6hr., M-Sa 12:30pm, Su 2pm, s/12-30). There's also a one-car train called the **Autovagon** (4hr., F 6:20pm, Su 6pm, s/12-30). Weekends, including Friday, get very crowded—it's a good idea to buy a ticket a day in advance. For other days, arrive at the station an hour in advance.

Buses: Cruz del Sur, Ayacucho 287 (☎235 650), goes to **Lima** (7hr, 8:30am, 2:30, 11:30pm, s/30). ETUCSA, Puno 220 (☎232 638), to **Lima** (11, 11:30, and 11:45pm; s/15-30). Mariscal Caceres, Real 1241 (☎216 633), to **Lima** (7:30, 10am, 1:30, 9, 11:30pm; s/15-20). Molina, Angaraes 334 (☎224 501), goes to **Ayacucho** (12hr., 5 per day, s/17). San Juan, Ferrocarril 161 (☎214 558), goes to **Tarma** (3hr., every hour 5:30am-6pm, s/7) and onto **La Merced.** Turismo Central, Ayacucho 274 (☎223 128), goes to jungle towns, including **Satipo** (8-10hr., 7pm, s/15); **Cerro de Pasco** (6hr.,

LIMA-HUANCAYO RAILWAY After being shut down in

1991, at the height of Shining Path activity in Huancayo, passenger service from Lima into the Andes was finally restored in late 1998. This extraordinary and famous train trip—the highest altitude standard gauge railway in the world—was considered one of the great feats of transportation technology when it was constructed between 1870 and 1908. President José Balta envisioned the **Ferrocarril del Centro** (F.C.C.) as a means of connecting the mining towns of La Oroya and the Mantaro valley to the coast.

The ride was stunning and severe in its scenery, winding around great rocky and snow-capped peaks and traversing numerous ecological zones, from coastal desert to Andean *páramo*. Around the town of Ticlio, temperatures drop some ten degrees below zero. The rail line reaches its apex on the pass through the Galera Tunnel—a startling 4780m above sea level. During its 12-hour journey to Huancayo, the F.C.C. passes through 27 stations, 58 bridges, 66 tunnels, and 9 switchbacks.

However, the Lima-Huancayo train now only carries cargo. After the line was privatized, the owners discovered that the infrequent tourist trips were completely unprofitable. The station is now gated, but a new mural stretches along its west wall depicting local customs, Inca mythology, and, most interestingly, a working train with passengers. A people's committee in Huancayo is currently attempting to restart passenger trips aimed at the tourist market, but their struggle remains difficult due to their opponents—the private, for-profit company.

2pm, s/12); **Tingo Maria** (12hr., 6:30pm, s/25); and **Huánaco** (8hr., 9pm, s/18). The cheapest way to get to **Lima** from Huancayo is to go to the 15th block of Mariscal Castilla (Real turns into Mariscal Castilla to the left of the plaza) where there are three terminal terrestres. You can show up there and catch a bus to Lima for s/5-10. The cheap price, however, comes with a few setbacks: buses seem to have no schedule and drivers might try to collect more than their quoted prices.

✴🛈 ORIENTATION AND PRACTICAL INFORMATION

Most services of interest to tourists revolve around the always-crowded **Plaza de Armas** (also called Parque de la Constitución), with gardens, fountains, and speakers playing a steady flow of Peruvian top-40 hits. Running more or less north-south through the city, **Ancash** to the north of the plaza on the cathedral side and **Real** on the bottom of the plaza, contain most banks, hostels, and restaurants. To the right of the Plaza, **Giraldez** runs east-west and becomes **Paseo La Breña** at the bottom of the Plaza. On the left hand side, also running east-west, **Puno** has a few bus stations. The light brown adobe towers of the cathedral on the plaza can be seen from most places in Huancayo. About five blocks on Real to the right of the plaza, **El Centro Comercial** or **Plaza Huanmanmarca** awaits with banks and a post office. The giant *mercado modelo* is on the right upper corner of the plaza behind a block of buildings. The **train station** is about 15 blocks down Real past Plaza Huanmanmarca—just follow the tracks to the right.

Beware of **scam artists** and **thieves** throughout Huancayo, especially on the side streets of Real, in the market area framed by Piura, Huánuco, Ancash, Amazonas, and at the bus stations.

Tour agencies: 🖼 **Incas del Perú,** Giraldez 652 (☎223 303; fax 222 395; email incacas&lucho@hys.com.pe), attached to Restaurante La Cabaña. Run by the inimitable Lucho Hurtado, who speaks near-flawless English and also owns La Casa de la Abuela and La Cabaña (see below). Dedicated to promoting authentic cultural experiences in Huancayo and the Río Mantaro Valley. Owner offers a crash course in Spanish, as well as classes in weaving, pan flute, and Quechua, and can offer tourist information. Open daily 9am-1pm and 2:30-7pm. Discounts for SAE members and students.

Currency Exchange: There are three reliable banks in town with **ATMs. Banco de Crédito**, Real 1003, accepts AmEx (open M-F 9:15am-1:15pm, 4:30-6:30pm, Sa 9:30am-12:30pm); watch out for the high commission rate here. **Banco Weise Sudameris**, Real 730, accepts MC. (Open M-F 9am-1pm, 4:30-6:30pm, Sa 9am-12:30pm.) **Intrabank,** Real 620, takes Visa. (Open M-F 9am-6:15pm, Sa 9am-12:30pm.)

Laundry: Lave-Rap, Breña 154 (☎231 107), 1 block down from the Plaza de Armas. An institutionally clean, self-service laundromat. Open M-Sa 8am-10pm, Su 10am-6pm.

Emergency: ☎105.

Police: ☎234 714. At Ferrocarril and Cusco near the Huacavelica train station.

Hospital: Clínica Ortega, Carrión 1124 (☎232 921), has ambulance service.

Telephones: Coin phones are located all around the Plaza de Armas; calling-card phones can be found inside and around the post office. For fair prices on calling cards for international calls, try "174", sold throughout the city.

Internet: ALPH@net, 282 Giraldez, charges s/2 per hr. Open daily 8am-11pm. **StarNet,** Giraldez 251 (☎291 804). s/2.50 per 80min. Open 24hr.

Post Office: Serpost, In the Plaza Huamanmarca, on the left with a big sign, 3 blocks to the right of the Plaza de Armas on Real. Open M-Sa 8am-8pm, Su 8am-2pm.

ACCOMMODATIONS

Hotels line Huancayo's downtown area; cheaper options and hostels surround the Plaza de Armas, especially on the top of Giraldez. On Ancash to the right of the Plaza de Armas, the hostels get dingier the closer they are to the *mercado modelo*.

La Casa de la Abuela, Giraldez 691 and Huancas (☎223 303; email incas&lucho @mail.hys.com.pe), 4 long blocks up on the right from the Plaza de Armas. The delightful *abuela* (Lucho Hurtado's mother) who runs this popular backpacker's hostel races around preparing glorious breakfasts and gossiping with travelers in her garden while jungle animals wander about. Game rooms, complete with darts, foosball, and ping pong are available for all guests. Immaculate rooms, sparkling communal baths and 24hr. hot water. Six-bed dorms s/15 per person; doubles s/20, with bath s/25.

Hostal Plaza, Ancash 171 (☎214 507), 2 blocks left of the top of the Plaza de Armas. Has dainty, well-swept rooms with new showers and occasional couches or dressing tables. 24hr. hot water. Singles s/30; doubles s/40; matrimonial s/40; triples s/50.

Hostal Paraíso, Huánuco 351, a short walk from the Plaza de Armas. Friendly women run this small hostel with new, flashy furniture and a little restaurant. Rooms have cable TV and baths with electric showers. Singles s/25; doubles s/45; triples s/65.

Hotel Confort, Ancash 237 (☎233 601), to the left and one block from the cathedral next to the Plaza de Armas. This enormous hotel with over 100 rooms and a decidedly pink motif has a restaurant in the front lobby (entrees s/5). Some rooms have baths, and 24hr. hot water kicks in eventually. Singles s/20; doubles s/30.

Hostal y Baños Sauna "Las Viñas," Piura 415, one block down Real from the Plaza Huamanmarca *Centro Cívico* and to the left ½ block from the pink building on the corner of Piura. Each room boasts a shower/bath, cable TV, telephone, and a fabulous view over Huancayo. Singles s/35; doubles s/45; triples s/55.

FOOD

Cheap *pollo a la brasa* joints (¼ chicken s/2-3) and chifas can be found up and down Real and Ancash. For traditional meals, one must go farther afield. Particularly good *típicos* await in the El Tambo district, a s/3 taxi ride up Real. Huancayo is the origin of *papa a la huancaína*, a cooked potato smothered in a dressing of butter, milk, and cheese, and is known for its *picante de cuy* (guinea pig).

▧ **La Cabaña,** Giraldez 652 (☎ 223 303), 4 blocks up from Plaza de Armas, across from la Casa de Abuela. This swinging dinner spot fills nightly with foreigners and well-dressed Peruvians. Candles throughout the multi-room restaurant set the mood for partaking in La Cabaña's strong sangría (s/3 per glass). Sandwiches and hamburgers s/3-7. Pizzas s/18-25. Fruit salad with ice cream s/5. Happy hour (5-7pm) features half-price drinks. Live folk bands play Th-Sa from 8pm. Open daily 5-12am, later on weekends.

Restaurante Vegetariano "El Paraíso," on the corner of Giraldez and Pachitea, 4 blocks up from the Plaza de Armas and across from the Texaco station. This dim, narrow locale serves up specialties such as *tortilla de verduras* and all manners of *soya* concoctions. Cool, natural juices and yogurt are welcome breaks from constant rice and chicken.

Panadería Koky, Jiron Puno 298, past the cathedral to the left and behind the Plaza de Armas. This glass-enclosed, spotless, and funky restaurant is lined with pisco, cold drinks, and towering cakes. Refreshing beers and *jugos* abound, while the towering glasses of hot *café* or chocolate will quench any thirst (s/2). Also features tasty and inexpensive sandwiches and pastries with tuna, egg, cheese, or ham (s/3). Open daily 7am-10pm.

Huancahuasi, Mariscal Castilla 2222 (☎ 244 826), in El Tambo, directly up Real (which changes into Mariscal Castilla). Located in a large colonial house with skylights and wrought-iron chandeliers, this is the place to go to satiate all *cuy* and *chicharrón* cravings. Peruvian families come here on Sundays and holidays for *pachamanca* (meat, beans, and grains wrapped in leaves and baked in an earthen oven; s/15), one plate of which could easily feed two or three. A heaping serving of *papa a la Huancaína* goes for s/5. Traditional music F-Sa. Open daily 8am-7pm.

▨ SIGHTS

Huancayo's main attraction is its vast collection of artisans and markets—the daily *mercado modelo*, filled with animals, vegetables, and dried frogs, is an unmatcheable experience. Parks and hikes into the surrounding countryside are not to be missed; panoramic views of the city, tiny workshops of *artesanías*, and abundant *campesino* life abound.

MARKETS. Mercado Artesanal, a winding, open-air market filled with alpaca sweaters, hats (s/5), and scarves, brightly-colored socks (s/6) and blankets, and traditional Peruvian gourd carvings with painted figures inside. Locally-made crafts mingle with ugly synthetic weaving—be careful to purchase real alpaca or wool. To test the material, take a fuzzball of the cloth and light it on fire. If it melts, your blanket was originally Tupperware. *(On the corner of Ancash and Piura, a block to the right of the upper right-hand corner of the Plaza Huamanmarca/Centro Comercial. Open daily.)* **Mercado Modelo,** past the Mercado Artesanal (there's a huge sign on top) to the left. Wander the streets full of cobblers, sewing machines, outdoor firepits with roasting chicken, and never-ending strands of mandarin orange rinds cascading in spirals from the *jugo* stands. Aisles of grains and beans, rows of hanging chickens, pig heads, towers of fruits and piles of vibrant vegetables await eager perusal. Live animals crowd in cages in the upper right-hand corner. *(Open daily 4am-9pm.)*

The **Sunday Market** is Huancayo's best-known attraction; a tradition since 1572, it now draws 50,000 from surrounding villages to hawk their wares. Most stands sell ordinary consumer goods, from cutlery to stationery to training bras, but good deals can be found on blankets and sweaters. *(The market stretches for dozens of blocks down Huancavelica. Head from the Plaza de Armas at the lower right-hand corner down Giraldez which immediately turns into Paseo la Breña. Five blocks down, Huancavelica runs perpendicular—the commotion will be hard to miss.)*

CERRITO DE LA LIBERTAD AND TORRE TORRE. This small church and park, along a path more than 10 blocks up Giraldez from the right side of the Plaza de Armas and up the hill, lend themselves to one of the more scenic views of the city of Huancayo below. It's best to hike in the late afternoon or early morning when the sun is bright and the air is cleaner. From Cerrito de la Libertad, the path continues upward to Torre Torre. Here, small boys will offer to guide you for a pittance and point out large scorpions and poisonous black widow spiders. At the top of the steep ascent, an even wider view of Huancayo and the surrounding mountains awaits. The snow-topped Corona de Fraile to the left dwarfs the countryside. Winding down the other side of Torre Torre, the trail to Parque de la Identidad makes for a relaxing downward descent. The entire hike from the city past Cerrito de la Libertad and Torre Torre to Parque de la Identidad takes 2½ hours.

PARQUE DE LA IDENTIDAD HUANCA. Once a rubbish dump, El Parque de la Identidad Huanca contains surreal statues, gardens, and bridges. The park was created on initiative from the last mayor and contains statues of the different people who influenced Peru, including famous painters, photographers, poets, and singers; locals proudly point out that there are no statues of politicians. Across the street, a market with very cheap traditional food keeps its wares in a striking two-tiered, stone, open-air structure. Any kind of *comida típica* is available here; try the rich *picarones* (doughnuts) made with lots of sugar. The park and the market fill with locals, especially on Sundays. *(If not arriving from Torre Torre by foot, take a trip to the Park during the early evening when the lights illuminate the fountains, statues, and tiny streams. From the Plaza de Armas, a taxi up Giralez takes about 10min (s/2).)*

⛰ DAYTRIPS FROM HUANCAYO

JAUJA
Buses to Jauja leave from Amazonas and Calixto in Huancayo (20min., s/1).

The small village of Jauja, north of Huancayo, makes a lovely half-day trip, especially if craving quiet streets and few cars. Several picturesque churches dot the various plazas, but the **Capilla de Cristo Pobre,** seemingly crafted from cake and icing, catches the eye. The best days to visit Jauja are Wednesdays and Sundays when the long **Parque Urbanización Olavegoya** fills with local crafts and typical manufactured goods.

Jauja does not have a simple layout nor easily accessible maps. **El Edificio Municipio,** on the top of the Plaza de Armas, has a map that visitors may photocopy. The buses from Huancayo stop in the long **Parque de Urbanización Olavegoya.** From the top of the park, **Junín** runs northwest and right by the Plaza de Armas. **Grau** runs northeast to the *mercado* and the leafy **Plaza Isabel.** Two blocks down from the Plaza de Armas and three blocks to the right on **San Martín,** lies the **Capilla de Cristo Pobre** and a large hospital.

Much of the reason to travel to Jauja is the gleaming **Laguna de Paca** northwest of the town. Though the shore is home to many a gaudy umbrella and blaring hi-fi stereo system, walking past the touristed area leads to blessed tranquility. Surrounded by mountains on both sides, the lake creates a surprising oasis from the small *campesino* farms and houses outside of Jauja.

The cliffs on the left-hand side of the road on one side of the lake are riddled with narrow paths. Laguna de Paca mostly aims its attractions at *peruvianos*; a small stretch of shoreline devotes itself to restaurants serving trout and hiring out launches (s/1), from which you can paddle near the infamous **Isla del Amor** where sirens reputedly lure men and women to their deaths. To get to the lake, flag down a taxi (5min., s/3-4) or make the 45min. walk from the Plaza de Armas, down Grau three blocks and left on Salvaterry seven blocks until you reach the hoardes of buses and the road widens into Paca. Keep walking straight until the lake glistens to your right. Walking back to Jauja might be your best bet, as it is mostly downhill. Buses constantly fly by, so it's possible to hop on for s/1.

CONVENTO DE SANTA ROSA DE OCOPA
It's possible to travel directly to the convent from Huancayo from the corner of Calixto and Amazonas (see directions to Jauja). Once the bus stops in Concepción (s/1.50), you will need to take a taxi (s/5) to the convent—they wait in a row across from the monument on the main road. The ride is about 15min and the drive takes you over the Río Quichuay and the tiny

Hmm, call home or eat lunch?

With  you can do both.

^{SM}

Nathan Lane for YOU^{SM}.

No doubt, traveling on a budget is tough. So tear out this wallet guide and keep it with you during your travels. With YOU, calling home from overseas is affordable and easy.

If the wallet guide is missing, call collect 913-624-5336 or visit www.youcallhome.com for YOU country numbers.

Dialing instructions:
Need help with access numbers while overseas? Call collect, 913-624-5336.

Dial the access number for the country you're in.
Dial 04 or follow the English prompts.
Enter your credit card information to place your call.

Country	Access Number	Country	Access Number	Country	Access Number
Australia **v**	1-800-551-110	Israel **v**	1-800-949-4102	Spain **v**	900-99-0013
Bahamas **+**	1-800-389-2111	Italy **+ v**	172-1877	Switzerland **v**	0800-899-777
Brazil **v**	000-8016	Japan **+ v**	00539-131	Taiwan **v**	0080-14-0877
China **+ ▲ v**	108-13	Mexico **u v**	001-800-877-8000	United Kingdom **v**	0800-890-877
France **v**	0800-99-0087	Netherlands **+ v**	0800-022-9119		
Germany **+ v**	0800-888-0013	New Zealand **▲ v**	000-999		
Hong Kong **v**	800-96-1877	Philippines **T v**	105-16		
India **v**	000-137	Singapore **v**	8000-177-177		
Ireland **v**	1-800-552-001	South Korea **+ v**	00729-16		

Service provided by Sprint

v Call answered by automated Voice Response Unit.   **+** Public phones may require coin or card.
▲ May not be available from all payphones.   **u** Use phones marked with "LADATEL" and no coin or card is required.
T If talk button is available, push it before talking.

Pack the Wallet Guide
and save 25% or more* on calls home to the U.S.

It's lightweight and carries heavy savings of 25% or more* over AT&T USA Direct and MCI WorldPhone rates. So take this YOU wallet guide and carry it wherever you go.

To save with YOU:
- Dial the access number of the country you're in (see reverse)
- Dial 04 or follow the English voice prompts
- Enter your credit card info for easy billing

Service provided by Sprint

town of Quichuay. Asking the taxi to wait while you visit the convent is a good idea if concerned about return transportation. The taxi will continue on to the town of Ingenio for another s/5, but it's more convenient to visit Ingenio first, travel to Concepción by bus (s/1) and then via taxi to the convent. Library open M, W-Su 9am-noon and 3-6pm. Guided tours in Spanish only. s/4 adults, s/2 students with IDs.

Near the town of Concepción—on peaceful, well-kept grounds—rests the Franciscan **Convento de Santa Rosa de Ocopa,** the starting point for the colonial settlement and Christianization of the Peruvian Amazon. There's an impressive **library** of over 25,000 books and manuscripts, some dating from the 1500s. The convent also hosts a number of stuffed jungle beasts and birds, as well as a collection of paintings from the Cusco school. The church itself has a lovely gilded interior. An interesting grotto with shining representations of the saints resides on the right-hand side. For a nice walk, exit the gates of the convent to the left and walk over the rippling river to the tiny plaza of **Santa Rosa de Ocopa,** with a pink church in its center. Further along the main road, Francisco Iratopa, lie some grassy escapes with miniature palm umbrellas. The **Bodéga Ocopa** across from the gas station serves cool sodas in the shade (s/1).

CHUPACA & THE AHUAC RUINS

To get to Chupaca, flag down a bus on the corner of Giraldez and Ferrocaril. From the Plaza de Armas, walk past the upper left corner of the Plaza, up Giraldez three blocks until you hit the train tracks running over the bridge. Walk under the bridge and stay on the left side. Across the street (Ferrocarril) will be a group of people waiting on the corner. Wait with them until a bus with the label "Chupaca" races by—someone will also be yelling out the destination (s/1). Once in Chupaca, get off at the lowest point to see the giant herd of bulls, cows, and calves.

Only 15min. by bus from Huancayo lies the hilly little town of Chupaca with its sprawling and fantastic **Saturday market.** Though the town itself is not terribly remarkable, the multi-level market with its neverending supply of live animals is a sight to see. Vendors hawk pieces of freshly-cooked *chanco* (pig) and women rapidly weave fiber rope. Above, sheep are killed and sheared in one fell swoop.

Nearby, on a high grassy plateau, the Inca and Wanka **ruins of Ahuac** tower on the summit. The exquisite row of Inca buildings, panoramic views of nearby mountainous red soil, small villages and glistening lake **Nahuinpuquino** are certainly worth the oxygen depravation on the way up. Perhaps the best aspect of Chupaca is its accessibility to the **ruins of Ahuac.** The drive to the foot of the small mountain is about eight minutes; a town member will be happy to point you in the right direction, but it is much better to hire a guide because the trail through the farmland is all but invisible. Once at the top of the mountain, 15-foot houses made of stone reach across the summit. Made by the Inca, then appropriated by the Huanca (1200-1400AD), the ruins are incredibly well-preserved; views of the surrounding countryside, fields, and houses can be seen through the miniature arched doorways. A newly-made pathway curves down the opposite side of the hill, leading to the eye-shaped lake on the right. Canoes are available to rent from the small homes lining the shore.

INGENIO

To get to Ingenio, catch a bus or combi on the corner of Calixta and Amazonas in Huancayo. (See directions to Juaja, above.) Take the bus to the very top of the hill—the trout farm is blue and on the right. The ride to Ingenio (30-45min, s/1.50) winds its way among beautiful hills and high roads.

If trout were a god, Ingenio would be its altar. The pride of this small, pleasant village is its trout farm or *criadero de trucha*, more formally known as the *Centro Pisicola del Ingenio;* the *criadero* produces 180,000kg of rainbow trout annually. Stroll along grassy paths winding among the many channels of swimming entrées-to-be. Spanish-only tours describe the 360-day reproductive cycle of rainbow trout in exhaustive detail. (Open daily 8am-noon and 1-5pm. s/1.) Stands outside the *criadero* cook up its former inhabitants. Down the hill, the **Restaurante Avila,** with a pond, waterfall, and two tree houses, serves trout to Alberto Fujimori when he comes to town. Included among the sundry *trucha* dishes (s/7-15) are the classic *trucha al ajo* (trout in garlic sauce), and the spicy *trucha a la mexicana* (trout stuffed with cheese, onions, and peppers). **Recreo las Brisas** and **Restaurante Sombras y Sol** both have beautiful, flower-filled gardens with mini footbridges and colorful tables. If desperate for a place to stay, try **Hospedaje Ingenio,** a low blue building with a grassy garden halfway down the hill and down the steps to the left on Juan Morales Bibanco (24hr hot water; singles s/20, doubles s/40). On your way back, keep an eye out for the breathtaking view of Ingenio and its lovely blue and white cathedral on the left. Llamas and sheep wind their ways down the hills to the right of the trout farm; it's possible to follow their paths up into the hills for another great view.

ARTESANÍA VILLAGES

Rather than taking the bumpy bus ride from Hualhaus to San Gerónimo up the main road, try taking the 1½hr. hike from Las Llamitas past the crossroad to Quilcas to the center of jewelry making. The road is rutted and lined with beautiful scenes of campesino life: children create adobe bricks on the right-hand side of the path and various animals graze in front of their owners' light brown homes. The mountains rise on either side of the road; once past the paved road, keep walking straight. The road to Quilcas is not terribly interesting—it is the center of the furniture trade. The dirt road will finally lead into a giant dusty plaza of San Gerónimo. Keep an eye out for a man on a bicycle tooting a rubber horn—he sells tasty flat bread to sustain you during the hike. The bottom right corner of the plaza turns into an uphill road that leads to the house of Sra. Nelly Vasquez. She crafts extremely intricate silver filigree earrings and rings in a tiny workshop with improvised tools. She'll be happy to show you how she accomplishes such intricate jewelrywork. Her house has a white sign on the left—just walk through the courtyard to the back workshop. To reach the ruins of the Inca at the top of the hill beyond San Gerónimo, follow the uphill path past Sra. Nelly's house to the town limits and follow the trail up. It's possible to see a line of ruins at the summit from the bottom of the trail. To leave San Gerónimo, follow the road past the church at the lower left-hand corner of the Plaza. It's another 200m to the main road back to Huancayo where you can catch a bus back for s/1. To get to San Gerónimo and avoid the 1½ hike, take a bus from Calixta and Amazonas in Huancayo marked either "Jauja" or "San Gerónimo." Get off on the right-hand side of the main road after 25min. (see directions to Jauja).

About 20 minutes from Huancayo lies the tiny village of **Hualhaus,** famous for its fine alpaca goods. Family-run, these tiny havens of *artesanía* offer the most beautiful and traditional pieces. Nobody speaks English, but mentioning the name of the artisan will prompt any town member to point you in the right direction. Worthy of a visit is the house and shop of **Simeon Guevara,** about 100m to the left of the main road from Huancayo. His tiny shop, Peru-Inkaiko, has lovely *matas, camas,* and *maletas.* In his courtyard garden, watch heaps of knotted wool transform into incredibly fine skeins of yarn, then upstairs, be woven on an old-fashioned loom into incredibly thick, tightly woven blankets. Sr. Guavera is partial to traditional designs reminiscent of geometrical Inca patterns in light brown, grey, and cream. The next artisan, about 25m down on the right, is **Faustino Maldonado.** His workshop, Tahuantinsuyo, specializes in alpaca clothing such as sweaters, hats, and the soft leggings Peruvian women wear under their thick skirts.

IZCUCHACA

The 6:30am train from Huancayo stops in Izcuchaca at about 8:30am. The 12:30pm train from Huancayo, due to its many stops, will arrive anytime between 4:30 and 5:30pm and continues toward Huancavelica. Likewise, the morning train from Huancavelica stops at 9am in Izcuchaca on its way to Huancayo and again in the late afternoon around 4pm. Wednesdays are good days to show up on the early train—the town plaza fills with makeshift restaurants and loads of market goods. The El Molino bus on the way from Huancayo to Ayacucho passes on the upper road next to the two restaurants and across the old bridge. Make sure to get a seat while all the passengers stop for their early lunch or luggage and sacks of potatoes in the aisles will have to do for the gruelling, unpaved journey to Ayacucho (8hr., 10am, s/17).

Hidden between two steep peaks, the tiny town of Izcuchaca (2800m) spills down the mountainside to the banks of the Río Mantaro. The land angles at such a degree that passengers jump a good three feet from the train to the platform. The gem of Izcuchaca arches over the river—the turretted "Izcuchaca" (meaning *bridge of stone* in Quechua) was built in the 18th century and runs parallel to a new steel bridge downstream. Sharp peaks and fertile landscape enshroud the town, and Izcuchaca retains simple charm as a true *campesino pueblito*.

A **pottery workshop** (fueled by a water-run turbine) sits at the egde of town and contains exemplary Mantaro Valley clay creations. The potter usually can be found working in his shop and has many jars, jugs, and bowls for sale. If you have time while waiting for the next Huancayo train, townspeople can point out the trail to the tiny **chapel** overlooking the valley (the hike is about 1hr. each way).

HUANCAVELICA   ☎064

If Huancayo is on the ground floor, Huancavelica is the slightly eccentric relative living in the attic. This remote and small city (pop. 35,000), capital of the region, floats among Andean mountaintops at a no-nonsense altitude of 3680m. Huancavelica got its colonial start when mercury deposits were discovered here in the 16th century. The indigenous population was ruthlessly exploited in the Santa Barbara "mines of death," where they found themselves exposed to noxious gases on a daily basis. Today, the railway constructed to haul the fruits of this morbid industry provides one of the few ways to access the town. The train from Huancayo chugs past picturesque farmland and dozens of rushing mountain streams. The town of Huancavelica itself, with the rustic feel of a still-young settlement, presents an interesting detour from the route through Huancayo.

▐ TRANSPORTATION

Trains: (☎752 898) run to **Huancayo** (6hr., 6:30am and 12:30pm, s/6-12). There is a faster one-car **Autovagon** (4hr., F 5:30pm, s/17).

Buses: A new bus station on the corner of Plaza Santa Ana and Muñoz (directly downhill from the train station) called Transportes Lobato has nice buses leaving daily for **Huancayo** (5hr., 6:30pm, s/20) and continue on to **Lima** overnight. Besides the cushy Transportes Lobato, there isn't much difference between the various services to Huancayo lining Plaza Santa Ana. Expreso Huancavelica, 516 Muñoz (☎752 964), with an orange and blue sign right as Muñoz runs into the Plaza Santa Ana. To **Huancayo** (4-5hr., 10pm, s/10). Oropresa, O'Donovan (☎353 181), with the red and white sign, diagonal to the church. To **Huancayo** (4-5hr., 3:45pm, s/10). Trans Yuri, O'Donovan, next to Oropresa with the blue, black, and red sign. To **Lima** (4pm, s/20) and **Huancayo** (5hr., 10pm, F, 6:30pm; s/10). Empresa Tiellas, O'Donovan (☎751 562), to the left of Trans Yuri. Buses to **Huancayo** (5hr.; 9, 10:30am, 1, 2:30, 10pm; s/10). Also, men holding "to Huancayo" signs in the Plaza de Armas provide rides on tiny buses throughout the day but leave haphazardly (5hr., s/5-10).

▓▐ ORIENTATION AND PRACTICAL INFORMATION

Exiting the train station, it's two blocks downhill on **Grau** to the main, shop-filled street, **Muñoz**. To the right lies the small **Parque Mariscal Castilla**, also called **Plaza San Ramón**. From the corner of Grau, turn left down Muñoz and walk for 6½ blocks to the red, yellow, and green Plaza de Armas. **Cathedral de San Antonio** sits at the top of the Plaza on Muñoz which also runs parallel to **Virrey Toledo** at the bottom of the Plaza. To the right of the cathedral, two blocks down **Arica** on the right, resides the **Instituto Nacional de Cultura**. The **Río Ichu** runs more or less parallel to Muñoz and the colonial bridge and pedestrian steps to the hot springs lie perpendicular— **Escalonado** runs by the left side of the Plaza de Armas and leads to the steps. Buses from Huancayo, Izcuchaca, and smaller surrounding towns gather in the **Plaza de Santa Ana,** which, to add to the confusion, is the same place as the Parque Mariscal Castilla and the Plaza San Ramón (see above).

Tourist Information: Ministerio de Industría, Nicolás de Pierola 180 (☎752 938), off the corner of Victoria Garma. From the lower right-hand corner of the Plaza de Armas, walk away from the Plaza down Virrey Toledo. Nicolás de Pierola is two blocks down on the left. The office has a free map of surrounding areas of interest and a street map available for copying. Spanish only. Open M-F 8am-1pm, 2:40-6pm. More tourist information can be found across the street from the **Instituto Nacional de Cultura** at Arica 202 (☎752 544; earhvca@net.telematic.com.pe), 3 blocks away from the upper right-hand corner of the Plaza de Armas. The Instituto itself is very helpful and informative.

Bank: Banco de Crédito, 383 Virrey Toledo, on the corner of Nicolás de Pierola and three blocks to the left away from the lower right-hand corner of the Plaza de Armas. Open M-F 9:15am-1:14pm and 4:30-6:30pm, Sa 9:30am-12:30pm.

Police: 173 Grau (☎753 041), on the left side of the Plaza de Santa Ana in a green building.

Hospital: On Cáceres (☎752 477), uphill from the Instituto Nacional de Cultura, about a 15min. walk. There are two blue-and-white **Es Salud** buildings on Muñoz.

Telephones: Telefónico del Perú, on Toledo and Carabaya. Various bodegas on Muñoz also have telephones.

Internet Access: Instituto Superior Pedagógico (☎752 959), on Toledo. s/7 per hr. Open M-F 10am-noon and 3-9pm, Sa 10am-noon and 3-6pm.

Post Office: Muñoz 759 (☎752 750), 3 blocks past the Plaza de Santa Ana, away from the center of town. Open M-Sa 8am-8pm.

▌ ACCOMMODATIONS

Cheap rooms can be found along Muñoz on the way to the Plaza de Armas, but nothing in the city will turn heads aesthetically-speaking. Check that a place has warm blankets since Huancavelica gets frigid at night.

Hotel Camacho, Carabaya 481 (☎753 298), five blocks up Muñoz from the Plaza de Santa Ana and intersection of Grau, is a left turn uphill and across from a school. Cell-like cement rooms are clean with wood furniture and very warm blankets. All bathrooms have 24hr. hot water (really only in the morning), but only the communal bathrooms are equipped with showers. Singles s/8, with bath s/13; doubles s/14, with bath s/22; triples s/21, with bath s/30; TV s/7 extra.

Hotel Ascensión, Manco Capac 481 (☎753 103). Look for a green sign on the left side of the Plaza de Armas (if standing at the bottom facing the cathedral). In a good location, but with mediocre rooms and communal showers only. Hot water 6am-9am. Singles s/10, with bath s/14; doubles s/18, with bath s/22; triples s/25.

◉ FOOD

Pollo certainly tends to be the food of the masses in Huancavelica; however, there are many oases of yogurt, fruit salads, and pizza tucked on side streets.

Pizzas Brother's Restaurant "El Americano," Muñoz 486, 1½ blocks toward the plaza de Armas from the Plaza de Santa Ana on the right. This new, clean little place offers typical fare alongside a generous list of pizzas ranging from *vegetariano* to Hawaiian, and individual to family size. Pizza s/5-22.

Restaurant Joy (pronounced "Yoy"), Toledo and Manuel Segura (☎752 826), right off the Plaza de Armas. Joy serves simple sandwiches (s/1-4) as well as many traditional dishes. Open daily 7:30am-10pm.

Casa Nuestra Bien de Salud, 591 Muñoz, 4 blocks from the Plaza de Santa Ana on the right on the way to the Plaza de Armas. One of many small health food and yogurt shops that line Muñoz and Virrey Toledo. Yogurt with fruit s/2. Open daily 8am-9pm.

SIGHTS

INSTITUTO NACIONAL DE CULTURA. The Institute, housed in a charming colonial building with a gurgling fountain in the courtyard, is dedicated to displaying the natural and cultural history of the region; the curator, Alfonso Zuashabar, is a veritable fountain of information. Several small rooms maintain an impressive collection of ancient Inca tools, clothing, weapons, and even mummies. A mural in the courtyard chronologically depicts the festivals and *fiestas* of Huancavelica. The mural leads into an interesting room demonstrating traditional multi-colored costumes (worn by disturbingly Caucasian mannequins) and a display of the native *danza de tijeras* (scissors dance), where outlandishly-clothed people cavort with giant metal scissors to create a cacophonous clacking during harvest season. *(On the corner of Arica and Juan García in the Plaza San Juan de Dios, one block to the right of the cathedral in the Plaza de Armas.)*

CATHEDRALS. Scattered throughout Huancavelica sit several colonial cathedrals, some desperately in need of renovation though nonetheless fascinating. Tourist visitation hours are unheard of—the curious sneak in with a curator or peek during mass. The yellow and red **Cathedral de San Antonio** was constructed in the 17th century in the Baroque style and has a collection of paintings from the Cusco school. *(Directly on the Plaza de Armas; open in the evenings and for Sunday mass.)* The squat **Iglesia de Santa Ana,** in the same plaza, is Huancavelica's oldest church, built in the 16th century. Supposedly, much of the interior decor remains similar to the style of El Greco. The altar peices retain vast ornamentation and historical value. The oft-closed 18th-century **Iglesia San Sebastian** lies diagonal to the **Claustero y Convento de San Francisco** in the same plaza, to the right and down 1½ blocks from the Plaza San Juan de Dios. The Claustero/Convento has altars of gold and silver and catacombs that are said to connect via tunnels to the seven other Huancavelican churches. In the 17th and 18th centuries, the priests met underground to combat the "unconventional" and "occult" religions of the *indígenas.* The **Iglesia y Convento de Santo Domingo,** on Virrey Toledo, two blocks to the left of the Plaza de Armas if looking at the cathedral, was constructed 30 years after the founding of Huancavelica in the 16th century. The church harbors the beautiful **Virgen del Rosario y al Patron Santo Domingo** which were brought from Rome.

MARKETS. The **Mercado Modelo,** a partially-covered building, houses a huge variety of wares. Alpaca sweaters, hats, and scarves, as well as the florid costumes of the Scissors Dance are available at good prices in various stalls. Also available are the standard potatoes, boots, and sheepskin. *(From the Plaza de Armas, take the pathway from the bottom right corner, opposite from the cathedral, that has large arches leading downhill. Two blocks down, the oblong market resides on Victoria Garma and Unanue. Open daily sunrise-9pm.)* Huancavelica also holds a significant **Sunday market,** mostly with food, fruits, and vegetables, but with many other goods as well. It stretches about seven blocks along Torre Tagle, the street parallel and uphill from Muñoz.

HOT SPRINGS. Huancavelica's own hot springs are also utilized as **thermal baths,** located in a blue-and-white building, a steep climb up Av. Escalonado. One can swim in the crowded pool or soak in private baths (though the water is not terribly hot). The baths are housed in concrete cubicles which rob the bather of mountain views ignored by the adolescent boys splashing in the pool. *(From the Plaza de Armas, walk down Manco Capac on the same side as Hotel Ascención for 4 blocks until you reach the bridge at Río Ichu; stairs continue to the baths on the other side. Open M-Th and Sa 5:30am-4pm, F 5:30am-noon. Pool s/1; private bath s/1.50. Towel, bathing suit, and soap rentals available.)*

DAYTRIPS FROM HUANCAVELICA

MINAS DE SANTA BARBARA

From the Instituto Nacional de Cultura (1 block to the right of the Cathedral in the Plaza de Armas on Arica), walk left down Juan García for two blocks and turn right on Agosto de Leguilla until you arrive at Colonial; cross the bridge with two arches. From Leguilla, it's a lazy 1hr. hike to the mines. Mines open daily sunrise to sunset. Free.

Discovered in 1566, the mines were exploited by the Spanish for their mercury deposits. The principle motive for the foundation of Huancavelica was the concept of a stable *indígena* workforce for the grueling labor. The mines, with the help of the natives, were enlarged to such a point that streets, chapels, buildings, and a bullfighting ring could fit within the walls and underground. The mine stands empty today, but represents a grandiose transition of cultures that doesn't necessarily leave a pleasant picture.

INKA WASI RUINS

To get to the ruins, catch a cab or a combi to the village of Sachapite (s/2). From there, a 1hr. hike winds around the ruins of Qorimina, Incañan, and Chunkana.

Many archeological zones from the Inca Empire reside nearby to Huancavelica. **Qorimina,** with strange constructions in the shapes of rectangles meant to carry water, has the shape of a giant bird.

Only 500m away, the giant arched doorway of **Incañan** greets the sun with religious ardor. A little higher up, the houses of the Inca community are visible in the ruins of **Chunaka**. In the central part, a geometrical figure (approx. 7m) engraved in the rock was meant to be an astronomical clock to show the precipitation and most productive times for farming.

AYACUCHO ☎064

Packed with students, overflowing with colonial churches, and surrounded by artisan villages, the city of Ayacucho is in many ways the cultural center of Peru. Conversations here always verge on political and social aspects of this area that has been so ravaged by terrorism. In the 1980s, Ayacucho spawned the violent activity of the Sendero Luminoso (Shining Path), masterminded by intellectual Abimael Guzmán, a professor of philosophy at the university who believed violence to be the only vehicle for revolution. The Shining Path swept through area villages, arming peasants and executing government officials in the name of a better life. The Peruvian army returned fire with secret missions and death squads. The total carnage—over 30,000 dead or disappeared—left a deep scar on the Ayacuchan way of life and state of mind. But after Guzmán's capture in 1992 and President Fujimori's considerable emphasis on police and military presence in Southern Peru, a new epoch of prosperity has found its way to Ayacucho, along with the hoardes of returning peasants reclaiming their land. Military occupation has dissipated, and the city's increased investment in their lovely colonial buildings have helped tourists once again find glory in the transformed city.

▐▌ TRANSPORTATION

Flights: Colectivos (s/0.5) run to the **airport,** 2km northeast of town, from opposite the cathedral on the Plaza Mayor. Taxis (s/3). **Aerocontinente,** 9 de Diciembre 160 (☎813 504; fax 817 504), 1 block from the Plaza Mayor, flies to **Lima** (M, W, F, Sa 7am; US$65). **StarUp,** 9 de Diciembre 118 (☎813 282), a few doors down from Aerocontinente, flies to: **Lima** (T, Th, Sa 10am; US$45); **Cusco** (T, Th, Sa 7:30am; US$49); and **Puerto Maldonado** (T, Th, Sa 7:30am; US$79).

Buses: Bus companies cluster on Andres Cáceres. From the corner of Cusco and the Plaza Mayor, walk 2 blocks down Asemblea away from the plaza and take a right on Cáceres. Some offices reside down the diagonal passage on the left, others by Tres Máscaras, 1 more block down Cáceres, on the right. **Antezana,** on the right of the diagonal passage off Cáceres, goes to **Huancayo** (9-10hr., 8:15pm, s/18). **Reybus,** next door to Antezana, sends cushy buses to **Lima** (10hr., 7 and 9pm, s/25). **Transmar,** Cáceres 896 (☎815 376), goes to **Lima** (9hr., 8pm, s/30). **Turismo Los Chankas,** across the street from Transmar on Cáceres, has service to **Cusco** (24hr., 7pm, s/25) via **Andahuaylas** (11hr.). **Turismo Nacional** (☎815 405), next door to Transmar, also travels to **Cusco** (24hr., 7pm, s/45) via **Andahuaylas** (11hr.). **Transportes Libertadores,** Tres Máscaras 490 (☎813 614), goes to **Lima** (9hr., 7 and 8:30pm, s/20). **Expreso Wari,** next door to Libertadores on Tres Máscaras goes to **Andahuaylas** (12hr., 5am, s/20). **La Molina,** 9 de Diciembre 450, under the pink and purple signs 4 blocks from the Plaza Mayor, runs buses to **Lima** (8hr.; 8am, 8, 9, 9:30, 10pm; s/30) and **Huancayo** (11hr.; 7am, 8, and 9pm; s/20-22).

◼✳▐ ORIENTATION AND PRACTICAL INFORMATION

Ayacucho's neatly gridded streets center on the **Plaza Mayor.** Almost everything of interest to visitors lies nearby. Most buses stop along **Mariscal Cáceres,** two blocks away. Streets change names as they pass the plaza.

Tourist Information: On the Plaza Mayor to the left of the cathedral. The staff can provide maps and suggest itineraries.

Tour Agencies: Urpillay Tours (☎815 074), on the Plaza Mayor. The agency the tourist office recommends for excursions to nearby sights. 4hr. trip to the Huari ruins and Quinua s/20 per person including transportation and admission fees. Also offers city tours and excursions to Vilcashuaman. Little English spoken.

Currency Exchange: Banco de Crédito, Portal Unión 28, on the Plaza Mayor. **ATM** accepts MC. Open M-F 9:30am-12:30pm and 4:30-6pm, Sa 9:30am-12:30pm.

Market: On 28 de Julio, 3½ blocks from the Plaza Mayor, across from the Iglesia San Francisco de Asis.

Police: (☎819 466), on 28 de Julio, 3½ blocks from the Plaza Mayor, to the right of the Iglesia San Francisco de Asis. **Policía de Turismo,** at 2 de Mayo and Arequipa on the Plaza Mayor. Open daily 7am-11pm.

Hospital: Hospital de Apoyo, Independencia 355 (☎812 380, **emergency** ☎812 181).

Internet Access: Internet C&V, Asemblea 255, 1½ blocks from the Plaza Mayor. 9:30am-3pm s/2 per hr., 3-11pm s/3 per hr. Open daily 9:30am-11pm. **Instituto Superior Technologicoprivado Lapontificia,** at Lima and 28 de Julio, on the Playa Mayor opposite the cathedral. s/2 per hr. Open daily 8am-10pm.

Post Office: Serpost, Asemblea 293 (☎812 224), at M. Cáceres. Open M-Sa 8am-8pm.

⌐ ACCOMMODATIONS

Mariscal Cáceres supports an assortment of rooms for s/10 per night, but shell out the few extra soles to stay by the Plaza Mayor and you'll find better values. Regardless, hot water often runs out by noon, and tour groups from Lima fill lodgings on weekends. Prices skyrocket during Semana Santa, when it can be hard to find vacancies; if necessary, the tourist office will place visitors in private homes.

Hotel La Colmena, Cusco 144 (☎811 318). Flowers climb the courtyard walls to La Colmena's bright, clean rooms, many of which have balconies. Restaurant. Singles s/15, with bath s/35; doubles s/25, with bath s/45; triples s/30, with bath s/60.

Hostal Central, Arequipa 188 (☎812 144), at Tres Máscaras. This lovely colonial house is chock full of large and comfortable chambers. Common baths have hot water (6-9am); private baths steam until evening. Singles s/12, with bath s/25; doubles s/24, with bath s/40; triples s/33, with bath s/60; quads s/44.

Hotel Los Alamos, Cusco 215 (☎812 782), at Tres Máscaras. Spacious 2nd-story rooms—each with firm bed and new bath—open onto a terrace above the superb restaurant downstairs. Singles s/20; doubles s/40; triples s/60.

Hotel Guzmán, Cusco 239-241 (☎816 262), at Sol. Brightly-painted, with wide beds and, in some rooms, a balcony or patio. The amicable staff promises 24hr. hot water, but lukewarm late morning tells a different story. TV s/5. Singles s/15, with bath s/24; doubles s/20, with bath s/30; triples with bath s/60; quads with bath s/70.

Hostal Mirador, Bellido 112 (☎812 338), at Sucre. A steep hike up Bellido, but the 6 rooms' outstanding views make the sweat worth it. Singles s/15, with bath s/20; doubles s/25, with bath s/35; triples s/35, with bath s/50.

Hotel Huamanga, Bellido 535. It's basic, but it's also clean and cheap. And with that nice restaurant and garden outside, the blue-walled rooms don't seem quite so dim. Singles s/10, with use of hot water s/12; doubles s/18, with hot water use s/22, with bath s/25; triples s/21, with hot water use s/27, with bath s/36.

Hostal San Marcos, 9 de Diciembre 143 (☎816 867), at Bellido and the end of a dark alley. Beautifully furnished rooms with varnished hardwood floors, hot-water baths, and cable TV. Breakfast included—and including fresh-baked bread still hot from the oven. Singles s/45; doubles s/70; triples s/90.

◯ FOOD

Ayacuchan cooks take pride in their *mondongo*, a soup of lamb or pork boiled overnight with peeled corn. Another favorite, *puca picante*, consists of potatoes in a spicy red sauce with rice and fried meat. Of course, on hot afternoons, most of Ayacucho heads instead for the ice cream vendors on the Plaza Mayor.

La Casona, Bellido 463 (☎812 733), at 9 de Diciembre. This cavernous colonial house, popular among locals and foreigners for 80 years, continues to serve its famed *bisteck a la casona*, a spicy concoction of cooked vegetables under a giant piece of beef, a fried egg, and strips of avocado (s/16.50). Entrees s/6-20. Open daily 7am-11pm.

Mía Pizza, San Martín 420 (☎815 407), near 2 de Mayo. Fresh and fabulous thick-crust pizzas join patrons at the wooden picnic tables. Personal pizzas s/10-14; family-sized pies s/20-28. Open daily 5:30pm-midnight.

Vegetariano El Madero, Asemblea 131, half block from the Plaza Mayor. Full of local students, gringos, and obsequious tourist officials, this bark-walled restaurant prepares delicious fresh juices, yogurts, and fruit salads (s/2.50-4), as well as hearty soy *"bistec"* and *"lomo saltado"* (s/6.50-8). Open daily 7am-11pm.

Chifa Taypa, Mariscal Cáceres 1131 (☎815 134), at Garcilaso de la Vega. Every night, Taypa whips up delicious shrimp and chicken stir-fry while patrons bask in the glow of the large-screen TV. Entrees average s/6. Open daily 6pm-midnight.

Restaurante El Portal, Bellido 593 (☎817 008). A sunny and flower-filled courtyard make this a pleasant option for lunch—as do the inexpensive traditional entrees (s/3-6). Open daily 7am-10pm.

◉ SIGHTS

Available for purchase at most churches and museums, Ayacucho's *boleto turístico* (s/5 or s/10) provides both admission to the city's attractions and good value for those planning heavy-duty sightseeing. The s/5 pass covers churches, colonial houses, and the Museo Mariscal Cáceres; the s/10 pass covers the above, the Huari Ruins, and the Museo Hipólito Unanue. If short on touring time, however, it might prove more economical to pay individual establishments' entrance fees (s/2). Many of the colonial houses are free anyway, as is a walk through the fascinating Barrio Santa Ana (see Shopping, p. 252).

CASONAS. Numerous restored **colonial mansions,** or *casonas*, occupy the streets surrounding the Plaza Mayor; many have been converted into municipal buildings or museums. The best way to view the *casonas* may be simply to wander the city and walk through the courtyard of any manse that strikes your fancy—particularly since there's often a knowledgeable guard keeping watch. **Casona Chacón** shelters both a Banco de Crédito and the **Museo Joaquín López Antay,** dedicated to popular art forms of the region. This is the place to find a full explanation of Ayacucho's most typical handicrafts, *retablos*, paper-machéd wooden boxes that depict all sorts of scenes, from bawdy merrymaking to the Nativity. The exceptional mansion itself dates from the 17th century. *(Facing the cathedral, Chacón is on the left side of the Plaza Mayor. Open M-F 9:30am-12:30pm and 4:30-6pm, Sa 9:30am-12:30pm.)* Immaculate 18th-century **Casona Ruíz de Ochoa y Monreal** has similarly bipolar tenants: a Banco Wiese and, on the second floor, a gallery. The courtyard opens onto a stone staircase full of contemporary art, preserved Huari artifacts, and Quinuan pottery. *(2 de Mayo 210, at San Martín. Open M-F 9:30am-1pm and 4:30-6:30pm, Sa 9:30am-12:30pm. Free.)* Built in 1740, **Casona Boza y Solís** now serves as the city's police headquarters. Patriot-martyr María Parado de Bellido was held captive here during the rebellion against the Spanish. *(On the Plaza Mayor, opposite the cathedral. Open daily 9am-5pm. Free.)*

CENTRAL HIGHLANDS

CHURCHES. In the 16th and 17th centuries, the Catholic Church built 33 outposts in Ayacucho. Most important of these is the baroque **cathedral** on the Plaza Mayor, first built in 1669, then partly destroyed and rebuilt after an earthquake in 1719. The silver artifacts in the small Museo de Arte Religioso on the right side of the narthex and the gold-leaf altars make the whole place shimmer. *(Open M-W and F-Sa 9am-noon and 3-5pm, Th 4-7pm. Mass daily 6pm, Su also 10am. Free.)* The intricately carved ceiling makes the **Iglesia Santa Clara** worth a trip. *(On Grau, behind the market. Open W-Su 6:30am-4pm. Free.)* The adobe **Iglesia San Cristóbal,** off the Plaza Mayor, was the first church built in Ayacucho (perhaps in all of South America).

MUSEUMS. Once home to former President (1886-90 and 1894-5) and General Mariscal Cáceres, the small, attractive mansion that houses the **Museo Mariscal Cáceres** displays a hodgepodge of colonial paintings, furniture, and Cáceres's personal articles. *(28 de Julio 508, at Chorro. ☎818 686. Open M-Sa 9am-12:30pm and 2-5pm.)* The **Museo Hipólito Unanue** exhibits hefty monoliths recovered from the nearby Huari ruins, among other artifacts. *(On Independencia, in the northern part of town. ☎812 056. Open M-Sa 8am-5pm and Su 8am-1pm. Free.)*

SHOPPING

Spilling down the slopes of the city's southern hills is the prolific artisan community of the **Barrio Santa Ana.** The narrow streets surrounding the plaza of this prolific artisan community contain fascinating workshops of intricate tapestrywork or painstaking chiseled creations. Crafts purchased here from the actual masters themselves are of much better quality and care than anything sold elsewhere.

Talleres open out from little doorways onto the Plaza Santa Ana, the most renowned, perhaps, being the many workshops of the **Sulca family.** Their gallery, at Plaza Santa Ana 83, has walls covered by large, awe-inspiring tapestries depicting Huari mythology, political beliefs, or poetic messages. To the left and downhill from the Sulca gallery, the husband-wife team of **Baljagui** toil, making immense tapestries and small, attractive decorative items of Huari or Inca design. A subterranean gallery to the right of **Srs. Sulca** combines a bustling weavery with an outstanding number of tapestries. **Alejandro Gallardo**, at Plaza Santa Ana 105-605, will lead awed observers to a brightly-lit group of rooms containing incredibly detailed tapestries, some over 20ft. long. All galleries are open from 8am to early evening. To get to Santa Ana, walk from the corner of the Plaza Mayor directly opposite the cathedral, walk one block up Lima and turn left on Grau. Follow Grau downhill through the noisy market and then uphill again until the streets change to dirt. The small paths leading upward eventually meet Plaza Santa Ana, identified by the countless workshops peeking out of doorways.

🌿 FESTIVALS

Ayacucho's **Semana Santa** festival draws record numbers of revellers. This year, officials expect more than 5000 onlookers at the magnificent procession of the Cristo de Resurrección through the plaza on Easter Sunday (April 15).

🎵 ENTERTAINMENT

Ayacucho's youth goes dancing on Friday and Saturday nights, often in converted apartments overwhelmed by flashing lights and blasting salsa. Disco-pubs **Los Balcones,** Asamblea 187, and **Caracol,** Arequipa 285, enjoy their current popularity. Live music club **Arco Blanco,** Asamblea 280, also packs a crowd. On clear days, locals gather to catch the breeze and sip beer at the **Mirador Acuchimaya,** on the hilltop to the left of the Barrio Santa Ana. This platform next to the large white cross affords sweeping views of the city below. (Taxi s/2-3.) In case of rain: the aptly-named **Cinema,** 9 de Diciembre, across from the green Plaza Hotel, plays subtitled American movies (and occasional pornos) in the late afternoon and evening.

BEAUTY AND THE BOLÍVAR

Legend has it that after Peru won its independence at the Battle of Ayacucho, **Simón Bolívar** visited the city to congratulate the victors. Musicians entertained at the banquet held in his honor, and the liquor flowed freely. As the merriment reached a heightened pitch, Bolívar noticed a group of local women and called over the famous beauty **Manuelita Toledo.** The two began to dance, and the great Latin American liberator, feeling especially liberated himself, swept the *señorita* into a passionate embrace. Not sufficiently impressed by her partner's military accomplishments, Manuelita resisted, sending a loud slap across his drunken face. Bolívar's men leapt to their feet and demanded that she be **executed** at once, but Bolívar raised his hand and said, "No. This woman has defended her dignity. I praise her for it." He then declared Ayacuchan women the most valiant in Peru.

🏃 DAYTRIP FROM AYACUCHO

HUARI RUINS

To get to the ruins, catch the minibuses or colectivos about 6 blocks downhill on the oval at Mariscal Cáceres. From the corner of Cusco and the Plaza Mayor, walk 2 blocks down Asemblea and turn right on Mariscal Cáceres. 30-45min., s/2.

Standing 22km from Ayacucho on the way to Quinua, the ancient capital of the Huari Empire lies in disarray after its flourishing success in 1000AD. The site extends some 1600 hectares across cacti-studded mountain deserts and is divided into 15 districts, of which only three have been excavated. Within the excavated area can be found a large slab of rock, on which animals might have been sacrificed, and the circular **Templo Mayor** where offerings were left for the god Wiraccocha. Also here are the **Monoachayoq** funerary chambers that once held the headless remains of the Huari's vanquished. Further uphill along the highway, in the chambers of **Cheqo Wasi,** whole noble households were buried. Mysterious holes in the stone may have released the souls of those inside or allowed caretakers to pour in preservative mercury. A small **museum** gives a good chronology of the Huari civilization and its Tiahuanuco roots. (Complex open daily 8am-5:30pm. Museum and site s/2.)

NEAR AYACUCHO: VILCASHUAMAN

Walk 5 blocks downhill on Ayachucho's Carlos Vivanco, which turns into Ramón Castilla. From the right-hand side of the rotary, unlabeled combis leave for the village quite frequently throughout the day (4-5hr., 5am-4pm, s/7). From the cathedral, walk 4 blocks down 2 de Mayo and turn left on Carlos Vivanco. To get back to Ayacucho, catch a minibus that's circling the plaza.

Entering the mountainous village of Vilcashuaman, 120km from Ayacucho, is a step into an ancient world only mildly affected by the pressures of modern life. Townspeople overwhelmed by the site of an outsider will eagerly accompany travelers to the many sites of the Inca Empire **Tawantinsayo.** The town remains overwhelmingly influenced by Inca culture; small stores and houses emerge from the earth alongside daunting tiered creations of stone. The sharp incline of the rocky road to Vilcashuaman leaves absolutely nothing to be desired in terms of phenomenal mountain scenery; this is an easy place to feel completely free of the noise, heat, and stench of urban life.

The tiny town centers itself on the plaza, which is undergoing construction into a park. The cathedral, constructed on top of the Inca Temple of the Sun, stands next to the plaza. Street names are mostly unused, and ruins pop up next to buildings all over town. The impressive **Temple of the Moon** lies to the right of the Plaza. *Combis* stop uphill, a few blocks above the Plaza. The **Banco de la Nación** lies opposite the cathedral on the plaza. (Open M-F 8:30am-2:30pm.) If in need of medical attention, **Es Salud** is in the blue-and-white building on the left of the plaza. For pharmaceutical needs, **Bótica Jonathan** is located next to the **police station,** next to the bank on the Plaza. The village has two **phones,** both next to the police station.

To appreciate the amazing surroundings in Vilcashuaman, it's best to stay in one of the three hostels on the plaza, **Hostal Pirámide, Hostal Turístio,** or **Hostal Fortaleza.** (All singles s/7; doubles s/10-14.) **Restaurants** operating out of locals' kitchens encircle the plaza; soup and meat staples go for s/2-3.

Vilcashuaman's **ruins** are considered to have been the center of the Inca Empire **Tawantinsayo.** The ruin retains the foundations of its Sun and Moon Temples and has the only known example of an *ushno*, or ceremonial pyramid. The Inca ruler and his queen supposedly gave orders from the double throne atop the *ushno*— the seats were gilded and shielded from the sun by multicolored bird feathers.

ANDAHUAYLAS ☎ 084

On the long road journey from Ayacucho to Cusco, all buses stop in the halfway point of Andahuaylas (pop. 35,000). The quiet inhabitants of Andahuaylas are largely Quechua-speaking and host a huge traditional market on Sundays in which locals use the old *trueque* system of bartering goods. Crammed between steep peaks, the city lies among snow-covered ridges and next to a tranquil lake where the Chanka created an imposing temple and city that was unearthed in 1997.

▌ TRANSPORTATION

Buses arrive and depart on Malecón Grau, which runs along the river and is the farthest point downhill from any location in the city. **Expreso Nacional Reymar,** Malecón Grau 232 (☎721 093), goes to **Lima** (22hr., 9am and 10am, s/50) and **Ayacucho** (10hr., 6:30pm, s/25). **Turismo Las Chankas** (☎722 441), to the left of Reymar, goes to **Ayacucho** (10hr., 6am and 6:30pm, s/20). **Expreso Wari** (☎721 936 or 721 381), to the left of Las Chankas, goes to **Lima** (20hr., 7am, s/45) via **Ayacucho** (10hr., s/20); and **Cusco** (12hr., 6pm, s/20). **San Jerónimo,** Andahuaylas 125 (☎721 400), on a street perpendicular to Grau and over from the Plaza de Armas, serves **Cusco** (12hr., 6pm, s/23) via **Abancay** (5hr., s/12). As a slow but frequent option, **Señor de Huanca,** Martinelly 170 (☎721 218), on the main street five blocks from the Plaza de Armas, sends cramped minibuses to **Abancay** (6hr.; 6am, 1, 8pm; s/15).

▐ ▌ ORIENTATION AND PRACTICAL INFORMATION

Buses stop on the lowest road in the city, **Malecón Grau,** which runs along the river. Uphill and to the left, the **cathedral** on the **Plaza de Armas** pokes its steeple into the sky. **Peru** runs parallel to **Grau** two blocks uphill, and contains the police, post office, phones, and banks. Five blocks down Peru from the Plaza de Armas runs the perpendicular main road of **Martinelly.** Two blocks closer to the plaza, **Andahuaylas** runs downhill also parallel to Martinelly.

Bank: Banco de Crédito, Peru, to the left of the police. Open M-F 9:30am-12:30pm and 4:30-6:30pm, Sa 9:30am-12:30pm.

Police: Peru 198 (☎721 671). About six blocks from the Plaza de Armas on the right in a pale green building.

Hospital: Located on Hugo Peze, one block away from the police station down Peru and to the right. **Es Salud,** Ayacucho in Barrio Salinas in the blue-and-white building.

Internet: Internet, Fax, and Phones, Francisco Ramos 317, downhill on Andahuaylas, 2 blocks from Peru and across the bridge on the right. s/3.50 per 30min.

Post Office: SerPost, Peru 243, across the street from the Banco de Crédito.

ACCOMMODATIONS

Cheap hostels cluster around the plaza, three blocks uphill from the river along Ricardo Palma.

Hotel "Los Celajes," Juan Antonio Trelles 210 (☎721 191), is the cheapest of the cheap. Cean rooms go for s/5 per bed if arriving on the late bus. Cement surroundings and grimy common baths aren't so bad considering the beds' comfort. Singles s/8-10, with bath s/15; doubles s/12-15, with bath s/20; triples s/20, with bath s/25.

El Encanto de Oro Hotel, Pedro Casafranca 424 (☎723 066; fax 722 555), uphill and to the left of Los Celajes in a pastel orange building. TVs, phones, hot water, immaculate bathrooms, and brand new furniture—for a price. Singles s/35, with bath s/45; doubles with bath s/60; triples with bath s/75.

FOOD

Though *pollo a la brasa* establishments stick out on every corner, a few places offer something more than *comida típica:*

Chifa El Dragón, Trelles 276 and Juan Ramos (☎721 641), downhill from Las Celajes (see **Accommodations,** above). Chicken, shrimp, and duck dishes (s/6-9) appear among the odd mix of Peruvian and Chinese decor. Open 8am-11pm.

El Mercado, Uphill on Trelles and to the right of Encanto de Oro (see **Accommodations,** above), three blocks downhill from the Plaza de Armas to the right of the municipal building. Upstairs in the sprawling market, luscious fruits await the blender at the many clean juice stands. Up a few more steps, families create makeshift kitchens, serving up filling *caldos* and fresh *ensaladas* (s/2-3). Open daily dawn to dusk.

SIGHTS

The most attractive aspect of Andahuaylas lies outside the city in the small region of Pacucha. *Combis* leave from the back of the market uphill on Trelles or five blocks down Peru from the Plaza de Armas and past the indoor concrete area. Continue past the Laguna de Pacucha on the bus until the impressive, many-tiered ruins appear on the right (1½hr., s/3). The **Sondor ruins,** an eight-level pyramid built by the Chankas for veneration and sacrifice, was the last major bastion of power against the Incas before the Spaniards appeared. The top of the ruin yields an unbelievable view of the mountains and lake (s/2). The lower part has been restored somewhat with thatched roofs, ready for the annual June festival of music, dancing, and *Chanka* traditions. Perhaps the nicest part of the ruins is the hike downhill to beautiful **Lake Pacucha.** Make sure to catch a minibus before 4pm; otherwise hike to the town of Pacucha on the other side of the lake (4hr.) and catch a truck heading toward Andahuaylas.

ABANCAY ☎084

The road from Andahuaylas emerges at the summit of a mountain and begins its winding descent to the valley town of Abancay though the small, hilly settlement is still three hours away. Once in the valley, the narrow streets of this steep little town teeming with people do not offer much in terms of tourist attractions—it is simply a convenient stop on the way to Cusco. The surrounding mountains frame the horizon with vertical cliffs, while deep canyons plunge into the river **Pachachacua,** yielding some rugged hikes.

▐ TRANSPORTATION

Buses: All buses to Cusco, Lima, and Andahuaylas stop in terminals on the left side of Arenas, one block uphill from the Plaza de Armas and two blocks to the right. Turismo Ampay, Arenas 210 (☎322 767), has buses to **Cusco** (5-6hr.; 5:45am, noon, 9pm; s/15; s/5 to the **Sahuite rock**). Empresa San Jéronimo (☎323 910), next door to Ampay on the right. To **Cusco** (5hr., 6 and 11:30pm, s/15). Turismo Abancay, Arenas 204 (☎322 910), to the right of San Jéronimo. To **Cusco** (5hr.; 5:45am, noon, 4pm; s/15). Expreso Wari (☎322 932), next door to Abancay, has sturdy, better-quality buses to **Lima** (20hr.; 3, 10am, 2, 3, 5pm; s/50) via **Andahuaylas** (5hr., s/15) and **Cusco** (5hr.; noon, 4, 6pm, midnight; s/15).

▐◪ ORIENTATION & PRACTICAL INFORMATION

Abancay bases itself on a hilly slope with the **Plaza de Armas** at the bottom. **Lima** runs across the top of the plaza with the **Cathedral Sagrario** to the right. **Cusco** runs perpendicular on the left while the **Parque Centenario** with its blue and orange benches and giant palms sits one block to the left. Parallel to Lima and uphill one block is **Arequipa,** which turns into **Arenas** to the right of the Plaza— this is where all the buses stop and cheap hostels spill out into the noisy street.

Bank: Banco de Crédito, Arequipa 218, 2 blocks to the left of the buses. Open M-F 9:30am-12:30pm and 4:30-6:30pm, Sa 9:30am-12:30pm.

Police: Lima 742(☎321 094), 7 blocks down Lima from the Plaza de Armas on the left, next to the statue of the Virgin Sta. Rosita.

Hospital: Es Salud, Arica 102 (☎322 525), one block uphill and to the left of the plaza between Arequipa and Barcenas. Another Es Salud can be found to the left of the big market at the end of Arequipa also to the left of the Plaza de Armas.

Market: Overflowing onto the streets surrounding Arequipa, 6 blocks left of the plaza.

Telephones: Telephone offices cluster near the bus stations.

Internet: Cabina Pública Internet, Díaz Barcenas 204 (☎321 605). s/2 per 30min. Open daily 8am-midnight.

Post Office: Serpost, Arequipa 221 (☎321 088), across the street from the Banco de Crédito. Open M-F 8am-8pm, Sa 8am-3pm.

▐ ACCOMMODATIONS

Cheap hostels line Arequipa on either side of the bus terminals. Quieter options are closer to the market.

Hotel Imperial, Díaz Bácenas 517 (☎321 578), uphill one block and to the left of the bus stations. Rooms overlook a flowery courtyard. All the modern accoutrements (think 24hr. hot water). Singles s/20, with bath s/45; doubles s/35, with bath s/70.

Hospedaje El Sol Arequipa 808 (☎321 434), 4 blocks to the left of the Plaza de Armas and down a passageway. Small rooms overlook the tiny courtyard of this economical and quiet hotel. Communal bathrooms have warm water through the late morning. Singles s/12; doubles s/18; triples s/24.

◖ FOOD

Surprisingly enough, some gems stick out among the oceans of *pollo braza* and *comida típica*. Abancay has endless inexpensive options as well as a fair share of attractive, relaxing establishments peppered around the city.

▨ **Luciano y Sebastian Pizzeria y Canto Bar**, Cusco 410, 2 blocks uphill from the Plaza de Armas. A scrumptious pizza place, decorated with tables and benches of darkly-stained wood. Usually crowded with students and well-dressed *hoipoloi*. Karaoke starts up by 9 or 10pm and is joined by live music on the weekends. Pizzas s/10-20.

Pollos Lafayette, Huancavelica 304, uphill and to the right of the Plaza de Armas upstairs in an orange building. The epitome of *pollo brazo* restaurants, Lafayette presents an extensive (and free) salad bar with the best and the brightest of vegetables, alongside filling chicken dishes (s/5-7). The bar, popular with 20-somethings, is shaded by palm trees. Open daily 11am-midnight.

Los Portales Video Pub, Arequipa 400, 4 blocks to the left of the bus stations. A brand new, glowing *comida típica* restaurant, boasting a giant mural on one side and a huge TV and wooden bar on the other. Good value and a great atmosphere. Set *menú* s/4.

NIGHTLIFE

Abancay's club scene may not rival Lima's, but there is plenty to do after sunset. One block uphill from the Parque Centenario, the flashing lights and whirling rides of a **mini amusement park** await.

Garabato, up Arenas on the right, one block past the bus stations and up a peach stairwell. The well-dressed student and professional clientele sit surrounded by animal skins, old saddles, and stirrups while tossing back *Cusqueñas* and the popular *calientitos* (s/3-4). Giant TV screen. Open daily 8pm-dawn.

La Chosa, across the street from Garabato. Packed with revelers of all ages. The swirling lights of this thriving *discoteca* mesmerize patrons dancing to US top 40, country, Latin music, and obscure 80s one-hit-wonders. Drinks s/4-10. No cover. Open 9pm-dawn.

NEAR ABANCAY: BAÑOS TERMALES DE CCONOC

From Abancay, ask to be let off the regular Cusco bus in Curahuasi and then hire a taxi to the hot springs (1hr., s/5). To continue on to Cusco, some travelers report catching a ride with other visitors or walking until someone drives by. Combis can be hailed at the peach-colored Bar Restaurant Apurimac, across the street from the fruit stands in Curahuasi. They go directly to Cusco with about 7 people in a car (3hr., s/10).

About 4 hours from Abancay on the road to Cusco (in a hidden valley near the little town of **Curahuasi**), lie the virtually unknown **hot springs** of Cconoc (pronounced "orno"). A popular spot for locals, the five pools of the medicinal springs are quite hot and extremely relaxing. Though there are rooms for rent (s/8 per person), the real fun comes from **camping** next to the river or staying up all night soaking in the springs. All night, people stay up dancing and singing around bonfires by the river or lying back watching the stars cluster near the snow-capped mountains. Though entrance to the springs costs s/2, it's free to camp and stay in the water as long as one desires. A little terraced **restaurant** nearby serves set *menús* (s/4) and hot tea and coffee.

CENTRAL HIGHLANDS

THE AMAZON BASIN

There are no Inca ruins here. Going to the Amazon Basin means leaving behind cobblestones and grand cathedrals; the jungle's hot and humid history is not the sort that people come to see. What has been recorded concerns systematic exploitation and depletion of resources: of oil, of timber, of rubber. It was in fact the foreign rubber barons who, at the turn of the 20th century, began the modern expansion of Peru's eastern frontier. And today the pattern of exploitation continues; commercial loggers and fishermen still threaten to destroy these rainforests. Nevertheless, it is the Amazon and its promise of outdoor adventure that lure tourists. Sadly, however, such adventure does not always agree with budget travel. Peru's rainforest hosts some 100%-guaranteed, class-act tour companies, but these cost substantial sums. Cheaper options, often in the shape of freelance guides, do exist, but it's nearly impossible to tell the gems from the con men, and thus signing up—not to mention handing over any money—can involve substantial risk. Moreover, even the "cheap" options aren't cheap—almost any jungle trip will cost upwards of $40 a day. To top it all off, many visitors have extensive misperceptions of what a jungle experience has to offer. The fact is, you're not going to encounter certain elusive animals no matter how or with whom you see the rainforest; there's simply too much vegetation for them to hide behind. Countless insects, yes. Incredible vegetation, yes. Many large mammals, no. Birds, however, do abound. At the end of the dry season, brightly colored parrots flock to the macaw licks in the south to eat clay, which neutralizes the poisonous seed acids they're forced to consume when the healthy seeds run out. And some contend that there is no better escape than the wilds of an area that has never been touched by humans, even if you're only sitting on a jungle lodge's porch. Furthermore, tourism, while not the ideal solution, does provide an alternative to the jungle's slow depletion—since, after all, nobody will pay to see a jungle that's been cut down.

HIGHLIGHTS OF THE AMAZON BASIN

CRUISE down the Río Ucayali on a **cargo ship** (p. 261).

TOUCH the vast, untouched **rainforest** around Iquitos (p. 267).

JUMP into the jungle from Puerto Bermúdez's **Albergue Humboldt** (p. 280), a paradisiacal oasis accessible from Lima.

DISCOVER a new plant in the **Manú Biosphere Reserve** (p. 286), one of South America's most pristine parks—it's only got 12,000 so far.

IQUITOS ☎ 094

Balanced at the mouth of the Amazon, Iquitos waxes remarkably cosmopolitan for an area accessible only by boat or plane. Intricate Iberian tiles, remnants of the rubber barons' turn-of-the-century residency, decorate buildings, and the prosperity they recall appears to be returning today as thriving commercial areas grow up around the Plaza de Armas. Their souvenir shops and money changers cater to the gringos who stroll Iquitos's streets en route to nearby jungle lodges. The tourist bureau has grand plans to maximize this trend, estimating that Iquitos will be a "bilingual city" in several years. Inevitably, though, there are people left behind: the floating shanty-town of Belén proves how little tourism means to many of the city's hardworking citizens. As for the 61 indigenous

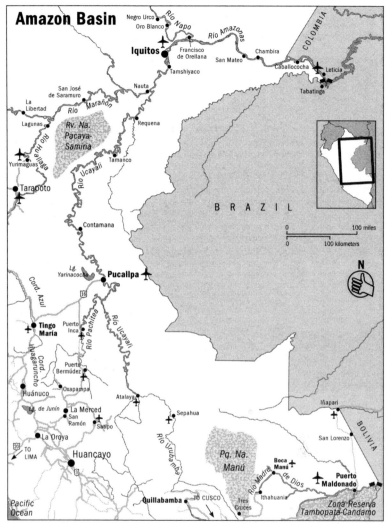

Amazon Basin

Negro Urco
Oro Blanco
Río Napo
Río Amazonas
COLOMBIA
Iquitos
Francisco de Orellana
San Mateo
Chambira
Caballococha
Leticia
Tamshiyaco
Tabatinga
San José de Saramuro
Nauta
La Libertad
Río Marañón
Requena
Lagunas
Rv. Na. Pacaya-Samiria
Río Huallaga
Tamanco
Río Ucayali
Yurimaguas
Tarapoto
B R A Z I L
Contamana
0   100 miles
0   100 kilometers
N
Lg. Yarinacocha
Pucallpa
Cord. Azul
16
Tingo María
Puerto Inca
Río Pachitea
Río Ucayali
Cord. Huaaruncho
Puerto Bermúdez
Huánuco
Oxapampa
La. de Junín
La Merced
San Ramón
Satipo
Atalaya
Sepahua
Iñapari
BOLIVIA
San Lorenzo
La Oroya
20
TO LIMA
Huancayo
3
Río Urubamba
Pq. Na. Manú
Río Madre de Dios
Boca Manu
Puerto Maldonado
Ithahuania
Pacific Ocean
Quillabamba
TO CUSCO
Tres Cruces
Zona Reserva Tambopata-Candamo

AMAZON BASIN

tribes living in the surrounding forest—it is the allure of viewing such ways of life, along with the accompanying flora and fauna of the "virgin jungle," that draws an increasing number of visitors to this region. And although tourism has its drawbacks, it causes the rainforest less harm than alternative commerces, like logging. However, travelers who come so far to see the *selva* in all its glory make a mistake if they overlook the heartbeat of Loreto province: Iquitos—a diverse, charming city safe enough to be the only one in Peru where police are not required to carry guns.

▐ TRANSPORTATION

Flights: Aeropuerto Francisco Secada V. Iquitos (☎260 147), 7km south of the city center. At the airport, city bus stops outside the gates and across the road; bus runs up Aguierre-Huallaga-Condamine and down Ocampo-Tacna-Grau (s/0.5, children s/0.3). Mototaxi s/7. AeroContinente, Próspero 232 (☎242 995), just south of Putumayo. Open M-Sa 8:30am-

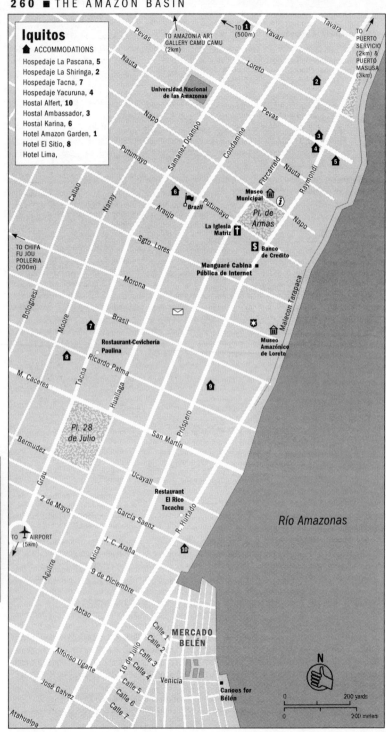

Iquitos

▲ ACCOMMODATIONS

Hospedaje La Pascana, **5**
Hospedaje La Shiringa, **2**
Hospedaje Tacna, **7**
Hospedaje Yacuruna, **4**
Hostal Alfert, **10**
Hostal Ambassador, **3**
Hostal Karina, **6**
Hotel Amazon Garden, **1**
Hotel El Sitio, **8**
Hotel Lima,

TO AMAZONIA ART GALLERY CAMU CAMU (2km)

TO ↑ (500m)

TO PUERTO SERVICIO (2km) & PUERTO MASUSA (3km)

Pevas

Nauta

Yavari

Loreto

Tavara

Universidad Nacional de las Amazonas

Napo

Samanez Ocampo

Condamine

Pevas

Putumayo

Fitzcarrald

Nauta

Raymondi

Callao

Nanay

Araujo

Putumayo

Museo Municipal 🏛 *i*

Napo

6

▷ **Brazil**

Pl. de Armas

La Iglesia Matriz ✝

TO CHIFA FU JOU POLLERIA (200m)

Sgto. Lores

$ Banco de Credito

Morona

Manguaré Cabina Pública de Internet ■

✉

Bolognesi

Moore

Brasil

7

✚

🏛 **Museo Amazónico de Loreto**

Malecon Tarapaca

Restaurant-Cevichería Paulina

8

Ricardo Palma

Tacna

M. Caceres

Hualiaga

9

Prospero

Pl. 28 de Julio

San Martín

Bermudez

Grau

Ucayali

Restaurant El Rico Tacachu

2 de Mayo

García Saenz

R. Hurtado

Río Amazonas

TO ↑ AIRPORT (5km)

Aguirre

Arica

J. C. Araña

10

9 de Diciembre

Abtao

Calle 1
Calle 2
Calle 3
Calle 4
Calle 5
Calle 6
Calle 7

16 de Julio

Alfonso Ugarte

José Galvez

MERCADO BELÉN

Venicia

Canoes for Belén ■

Atahualpa

N

0   200 yards
0   200 meters

AMAZON BASIN

7pm, Su 9am-noon. Offers flights to **Lima** (1½hr.; 8:30am, 1, and 6pm; US$44-59). Tans, Próspero 215 (☎231 086), is across the street from its competitor. Open M-Sa 8:30am-7pm, Su 8:30am-1pm. To: **Lima** (1½hr., 1pm, US$58); **Pucallpa** (45min.; M, W, F 1pm, Su 11am; US$58); **Tarapoto** (45min.; Tu, Th, Sa, Su 1pm; US$58); and **Trujillo** (1hr., F and Su 7:20pm, US$58). There is an airport tax of s/12 on all domestic flights.

The Iquitos airport is full of con men. Mototaxi drivers have been known to offer prices as low as s/1—they can afford to do this because they are planning to receive a commission when they take you to the hotel of their choice. Have a destination in mind before you arrive (or head straight to the tourist office) and be suspicious of taxi drivers who say that your hotel has burned down.

Boats: Depending on the height of the river, boats depart from either **Puerto Masusa** or **Puerto Servicio;** both are off La Marina in the north of the city. Aguirre-Guallaga-Condamine bus s/0.50, children s/0.30. Mototaxi s/2.5. Boats accepting passengers display signs to announce their destination and time of departure; however, few boats leave on schedule. Most departures take place around 4-5pm. Boats go to: **Pucallpa** (4-8 days, s/65); **Lagunas** (2-5 days, s/20); **Yurimaguas** (3-6 days, s/35-40); and **Leticia** and **Tabatinga** (1½-3 days, s/50). Prices are negotiable. **Speedboats** also leave daily for **Leticia** (10hr., around 6am, US$50); check at the speedboat agencies along Raymondi between Pevas and Loreto for current information.

OLD MAN RIVER A boat ride along the Ucayali offers as good a view of the jungle as—and far more local flavor than—any tour ship. The 150km boat journey from Pucallpa to Iquitos, or vice versa, can last anywhere from three to 10 days, depending on the height of the river, the speed of the current, and the strength of the vessel's engine. As most travelers have few means of gauging these variables beforehand, this trip is best not undertaken by those on a tight schedule. (For more on boat travel, see **Essentials: Getting Around, p. 52**.) The boat stops innumerable times en route. The three largest villages each house at least one basic hostel: Contamana lies 14 to 36 hours from Pucallpa; Orellana is about half-way to Iquitos; and Requena lies 12 to 22 hours from Iquitos. Inconveniently located control stations in the first two towns often demand a look at foreigners' passports; your captain should be able to inform you if this is necessary and point you in the right direction.

Local Transportation: During the day and evening, buses run down Ocampo-Tacna-Grau to the airport (although some deviate briefly to the west), and then back up Aguirre-Guallaga-Condamine to La Marina and the Masusa port. s/0.5, children s/0.3.

Taxis: Motorcycle rickshaws known as *motocarros* or *motos* are everywhere downtown. s/2 to anywhere in the town center, s/2.5 to the port, s/7 to the airport.

Motorcycle Rental: Park Motors, Tacna 621 (☎231 688), rents motorcycles (but not helmets). s/6-12 per hr. Limited cars (s/20 per hr.) and trucks (s/25 per hr.) are also available. Open daily 8am-12:30am. **Vision Motos,** Nauta 309 (☎234 759). s/6 per hr. or s/70 per day. Open daily 8am-10pm.

■★ 🛈 ORIENTATION AND PRACTICAL INFORMATION

Approximately 1860km northeast of Lima and technically an island, the large city of Iquitos is encompassed by rivers: **Río Mañon, Río Nanay,** and—most conspicuously—**Río Amazonas** to the east. **Malecón Tarapaca** (the **Boulevard,** as it is commonly called) is the pedestrian walkway that fronts the Amazon. One block inland, main drag **Próspero** runs from the **Plaza de Armas** eight long blocks south to the massive **Belén Market.** Many of the city's shops, services, and accommodations lie in the area between these landmarks and the **Plaza 28 de Julio,** south of the Plaza de Armas, north of the market, and two blocks farther from the river. Avenues that run north-south change names as they pass the two plazas.

BORDER CROSSING: INTO BRAZIL AND COLOMBIA
Crossing the border at **Tabatinga, Brazil** or **Leticia, Colombia** is a laid-back if slightly disorganized process. The entire area is considered a neutral, tri-national zone, so if you are not delving farther into Colombia or Brazil, it is acceptable to explore both cities without officially entering either country or getting your passport stamped. The two cities are so close together that they could easily pass as one; colectivos run between them (10min.; frequent until 7pm; 1000 Colombian pesos or 1 Brazilian real, about US$0.50). Most people in Tabatinga understand Spanish. They share one port, in Tabatinga. Boats from Iquitos stop in the Peruvian border town of Santa Rosa, where foreigners disembark, get their passports stamped, and turn in their tourist cards. **Once in Brazil,** the port has no tourist facilities; a taxi (10 Brazilian reals) can take you to change money and to the police office to get your passport stamped. US citizens need a visa to enter Brazil; most other western nationals need only a passport. Visas (US$40) can be purchased at the Brazilian consulate in Leticia. People entering also occasionally have to provide proof of inoculations, particularly for yellow fever. There are often health officials at the Peruvian border giving shots and inoculation cards to those without them. **To enter Colombia,** South Africans are some of the few people who need visas. Everyone must go to the Departamiento Administrativo de Seguridad office in Leticia, Calle 9 No. 962. (☎592 71 89. Officially open daily 8am-12:30pm and 2:30-6pm, but usually 24hr.).

Tourist Office: Napo 226 (☎235 621; email turismo.mpm@tvs.com.pe), on the Plaza de Armas. An excellent service run by an American. There's also a branch in the baggage claim area of the airport. Open M-F 8am-7pm, Sa 9am-1pm.

Currency Exchange: Banco de Crédito, Próspero 200 (☎234 501), on the Plaza de Armas. 24hr. Visa **ATM.** No commission if exchanging traveler's checks for *soles*, US$11.50 if exchanging for dollars. Open M-F 9:15am-1:15pm and 4:30-6:30pm, Sa 9:30am-12:30pm. **Banco Latino,** Próspero 330 (☎241 573), will change only AmEx traveler's checks into *soles* (for free) or into dollars (US$5 commission). MC **ATM.** Open M-F 8:45am-1:30pm and 4-7pm, Sa 9am-1pm. **Paucar Tours,** Próspero 652 (☎232 131), has Western Union and DHL service. Open M-Sa 8am-2:30pm and 3:30-7pm.

Market: The **Belén Market** sprawls for blocks between the river and Arica, south of Saenz. Open daily 3am-1am.

Laundromat: Lavandería Imperial, Putumayo 150 (☎231 768), between Próspero and Tarapacá. Self-service s/8 per load, up to 4kg. Full service s/10 per load. Open M-Sa 7am-9pm. **Lavacenter Lavandería,** Próspero 459 (☎242 136). Wash, dry, and fold s/ 2.9 per kg. Open M-Sa 7:30am-9pm.

Emergency: ☎105.

Police: Morona 123 (☎231 131), near Tarapacá.

Hospital: Hospital Apoyo Iquitos, Portugal 1747 (☎264 717), between Libertad and Leticia.

Telephones: Telefónica del Perú, Arica 200 (☎223 722), at Sargento Lores. Open M-F 8am-8pm, Sa 8am-1pm and 4-8pm.

Internet Access: Internet Sured, Próspero 392 (☎232 375). s/4 per hr. Open daily 9:30am-1am. **Cyber Internet,** Fitzcarrald 120 (☎223 608), half a block off the plaza. Open 24hr. **Internet Satellite,** Putumayo 188 (☎610 642), between the plaza and the river. s/4 per hr. Open daily 8am-midnight.

Post Office: Serpost, Arica 402 (☎234 091), at Morona. Open M-F 8am-1pm and 3-7pm, Sa 7:30am-6pm, Su 9am-1pm.

⌐ ACCOMMODATIONS

As tends to be the case with many prices in Iquitos, room rates are a bit inflated. Most of the following hotels offer such serenity, though, that the guest can almost forgive them the extra *soles*.

Hotel Lima, Próspero 549 (☎235 152; fax 234 111), between Brasil and Palma. A jaguar-print "Lima" behind the reception desk welcomes visitors. Rooms are squeaky clean; all have bath and fan. Great location. Singles s/20; doubles s/35; triples s/45.

Hostal Ambassador (HI), Pevas 260 (☎233 110). A great deal for HI members. Clean, modern rooms with cable TV, bedside lamps, phones, and hot water baths. Breakfast included. Reservations recommended. Singles US$20, US$10 with HI membership; doubles US$30, US$11 with HI membership. V, MC.

Hotel El Sitio, R. Palma 545 (☎234 932), between Tacna and Moore. Quiet but often full. Placid, plant-lined outdoor corridors lead to impeccably kept (if un-screened) sleeping quarters, complete with bath, fan, and TV. Singles s/25; doubles s/35.

Hostal Karina, Putumayo 467, 1½ blocks from the Plaza de Armas. Blue patterned wallpaper and carpets are so cheerful, you won't mind the dusty corners. Fan and hot bath in each room. Singles s/15; matrimonials s/25; doubles s/20; triples s/35.

Hotel Amazon Garden, Pantoja 417 (☎236 140), at Yavari. Mototaxi from center s/2.5. Gorgeous hotel in a residential neighborhood is a great post-jungle splurge. Bathtubs, soft beds, cable TV, hot water, hair dryers, and private water coolers. Sparkling pool outside. Discounts for long stays. Singles US$30; doubles US$40-45.

Hospedaje La Shiringa, Fitzcarrald 465 (☎243 293), between Yavari and Loreto. Spacious rooms are relatively bare but have bath and fan. Dark concrete hallways are a stark contrast to the floral bedspreads and teddy bear sheets. Singles s/20, with TV s/ 25; doubles s/30, with TV s/35.

Hospedaje La Pascana, Pevas 133 (☎231 418; fax 233 466; email pascana@lsicom.pe), between Raymondi and the Amazon. A perennial backpacker favorite, Pascana has 18 decent rooms, several thatched picnic tables, a book exchange, Internet access (s/7 per hr.), a travel agency, luggage storage, and some English-speaking staff. Singles US$9; doubles US$12; triples US$15.

Hospedaje Tacna, Tacna 516 (☎243 627), at Brasil. A bit noisy, and some faulty screening. Still, bright decors provides a colorful diversion. Rooms, all with bath, vary dramatically in terms of size and light. Singles s/15; doubles s/20; triples s/28.

Hostal Alfert, Saenz 01 (☎234 105), off R. Hurtado by the Amazon. Not in the most savory area, but where else could rooms have such panoramic views over Belén? Reports indicate that valuables might not be secure. Singles s/15; doubles s/20.

◖ FOOD

There's no need to flock to Ari's Burger (a.k.a. "Gringolandia") on the Plaza de Armas (burgers s/6-17); there are much less expensive, not to mention tastier, morsels to be had all over the city. Chifas line Grau on the blocks south of the Plaza 28 de Julio and cheap *típicos* cluster on Condamine north of the Plaza de Armas, and farther afield, on La Marina. Additionally, many stalls in the Belén market offer jungle specialties like *paiche* (giant river fish), amazing mixed-fruit juices (s/0.5-1), and *juanes* (rice, chicken, black olives, and egg wrapped in a banana leaf), at their best in Iquitos.

Restaurant-Cevichería Paulina, Tacna 591 (☎231 298), at Palma. Around lunchtime, Paulina's charming two-room restaurant hosts a rousing crowd, most awaiting her famous ceviche (s/10-20). Soups s/7-20. Steaks s/16-22. Noodles s/10-16. Juices s/3-5. Daily *menú* s/6 or s/10. Open daily 7am-10pm.

Don Pizza, Huallaga 204 (☎222 727), just south of Putumayo. The pick of Iquitos' pizzerias, Don's makes surprisingly chewy crusts. A wooden loft, decorated for Christmas year-round, doubles the tiny restaurant's size. Vegetarian pizzas s/10-30, pepperoni s/8-25. Jar of sangría s/18. Open daily 6pm-midnight.

El Chingon, Palma 145 (☎233 248), between Tarapacá and Próspero. Iquitos's attempt at Mexican food. What the concrete, four-table restaurant lacks in ambiance it makes up for with home-cooked Mexican morsels. All items have a meatless option. Burritos s/8-14. Fajitas s/15-19. Margaritas s/10. Open M-Sa 3-10pm.

Shambo, Morona 396 (☎231 357), at Próspero; also at Tacna 600, Grau 1048, and M. Cáceres 654. A city-wide chain serving amazing popsicles (s/1) made from local and more common fruits. A few licks reveal the real fruit inside. Open daily 9am-11pm.

La Palizada, Sargento Lores 791 (☎232 868), at Fanning. An uninspiring restaurant during the day, Palizada spills onto the street at night, cooking patrons' hand-picked fish over the coals. Entrees s/5-16. *Menú* s/5. Open daily 11am-3pm and 6-11pm.

Restaurant El Rico Tacachu, R. Hurtado 873, between Veayali and Saenz. The best place to get authentic jungle food if the market seems too hectic. Open daily 8am-2pm.

Snack Bar Antojitos, Napo 380 (☎234 631), near Condamine. Plain but popular, Antojitos serves salads (s/4-5), sandwiches (s/2-6), chicken (s/8-15), and fresh juices (s/2-3) for a fraction of the prices found on the plaza. *Menú* s/6. Open daily 8am-1am.

Restaurant Rajin, Nanay 775. An option for vegetarians. Vegetarian *menú* s/4. Standard *menú* s/3. Open daily 8am-4pm.

⊙ SIGHTS

BELÉN. One of the most vibrant (and poor) areas in Iquitos, the impoverished floating neighborhoods of and beyond Belén sit, literally, on the Amazon. Some houses rise and fall with the river on rafts that must be replaced every two years; others stand on longer-lasting stilts. The squalid area closest to land, Belén proper centers around a street called Venecia but has little in common with its Italian namesake. Adjacent *pueblos* such as San Francisco—with its many lily-pads—and San Andrés are cleaner and more tranquil. Each has its own church and primary school. You can hire a canoe, but in drier times, it may be necessary to walk on logs and planks over treacherously nasty mud to reach the port. There have been times when the settlements have rested on mud alone (generally Aug.-Nov.), making travel by canoe impossible. Farther inland lies the Belén market, a seemingly endless maze of wet piranhas, scrumptious juices, and overwhelming smells, where vendors sell many of the jungle remedies reputed to cure everything from cancer to arthritis. *(To hire a canoe (s/5-10 per hr.), head down Ugarte, through Belén market and past the small circular plaza. The market lies 8 blocks south of the Plaza de Armas.)*

MUSEO AMAZÓNICO DE LORETO. This relatively new museum (opened 1996) has already amassed a considerable collection of weapons, paintings, and turn-of-the-century pictographs. Look for the copy of the recent border agreement between Peru and Ecuador. Highlights include more than 70 detailed fiberglass sculptures of local tribespeople, made from old molds forcibly obtained from subjects who believed their souls might depart with the likenesses. While some exhibits could be better marked, the exquisitely restored government building dating from 1863 is a sight in itself. *(Malecón Tarapacá 386, at Morona. Look for the sign that says "Prefectura Loreto." ☎231 072. Open M-F 8am-1pm and 3-7pm, Sa 7am-1pm. s/3.)*

IRON HOUSE. The rubber tycoons' grand ambitions for a cosmopolitan city center ferried the Eiffel-designed Iron House across the Atlantic piece by piece. Now fully assembled, the much-hyped structure looks much like a house made out of tin foil. If tapped, the walls emit a profoundly hollow sound. *(On the Plaza de Armas, at Putumayo and Próspero.)*

IGLESIA MATRIZ DE IQUITOS. Builders laid the first brick on July 18, 1911, and the building was inaugurated in 1919. Many of the adornments that make the church so beautiful today, such as the tower and the temple, were added later, as were the intricate paintings on the roof, which depict various scenes starring the Virgin Mary. The church is named for San Juan, the city's patron saint, whose likeness also graces the main altar. *(At Putumayo and Arica, on the Plaza de Armas. Open Tu, Th 3-8pm; M, W, F-Su 6:30am-8pm. Mass daily 6:30am and 7pm; Su also 11am and 6pm. Free.)*

MUSEO MUNICIPAL. The tourist office is in the process of turning the third floor of their building—which once served as city hall—into a small museum. Under imported crystal chandeliers, city scale models mingle with embalmed *paiche* (giant river fish) in the room overlooking the Plaza de Armas, once used by the rubber barons for their weddings. The curators plan improvements (including a possible change of location) for the future; for now, inquire at the office downstairs. *(Napo 226, on the Plaza de Armas across from the cathedral. ☎ 235 621. Open M-F 8am-7pm, Sa 9am-1pm. Free.)*

BELLAVISTA NANAY. A small port on the Río Mañon, Bellavista sits at the northern edge of town. During the dry months of August and September, a beach emerges, and it's possible to swim in the river's black water. The rest of the year, the area serves only as a port and point of departure for nearby sites. A speedboat (s/30) can take a group to see the Boras and Yaguas Indians, two local indigenous groups that perform native dances for tourists. A cheaper option is to take a colectivo to Padrecocha (15min., s/1.50), from where the Boras are a 30-minute walk. The dancers usually expect payment (around s/10) for their performance. *(Any Huallaga bus with "Nanay" on the side terminates at Bellavista. 20min., s/2.)*

AMAZONIA ART GALLERY CAMU CAMU. This small gallery houses the work of Peruvian artist Francisco Grippa, who paints with a spatula. Although he was born in Tumbes and studied in the US and Spain, Grippa has made the jungle his home and the subject of his work; many of his paintings protest the destruction of the rain forest. Several other artists have paintings on display, too, and most are for sale—at high prices. *(Trujillo 498. Mototaxi s/1.5. ☎ 253 120; fax 250 047; email grippamazonpevas@yahoo.com; www.art-and-soul.com/grippa. Open daily 10am-1pm and 4-8pm. Free.)*

ASOCIACIÓN ARTESANOS IQUITOS SAN JUAN DE BAUTISTA. Just beyond the hustle and bustle of downtown Iquitos, San Juan vends a wide collection of *artesanía*. Over 20 booths sell necklaces, painted wooden butterflies, wood carvings, paintings, and hammocks, among other items. Furthermore, most of the vendors craft the goods themselves, so visitors can ask questions and, sometimes, watch them work. Has a more authentic souvenir shop than the ones downtown. *(Take an airport-bound bus (10min., s/0.5) along Tacna-Grau and ask to be let off at San Juan.)*

BIBLIOTECA AMAZÓNICA. More of a working library than a tourist attraction, the Amazónica revolves around a beautiful tiled and carved-wood reading room. Here, books and historical documents discuss the people, animals, and plants of Peru and, more specifically, the Amazon Basin. The library also possesses a wide collection of maps, which the staff will retrieve upon request. Tall double doors reveal a stupendous view of the river. *(Malecón Tarapacá 354, 2nd fl. ☎ 242 353. Open M 8:45am-12:15pm and 3:45-6:45pm, Tu-F 8:45am-12:15pm, Sa 9am-noon. Free.)*

■ NIGHTLIFE

BARS

Well-frequented, Iquitos bars often serve fun, exotic drinks. Most tourists stick to the breezy joints overlooking the Amazon on Tarapacá (especially between Nauta and Napo), but a dizzying array of options peppers the city.

- **Amauta Café-Teatro,** Nauta 250 (☎ 233 109), between Raymondi and Fitzcarrald. A lavish, artsy enclave watched over by a mammoth portrait of poet Cesar Vallejo Mendoza, this bar/theater/gallery hosts live music every night at 10pm. The enormous drink menu includes jungle classics such as *chuchuhuasi* and *clarohuasca* (small s/3.50, large s/6). Open M-Sa 6pm-5am.

Crazy, Tacna 173, packs a local crowd into its tiny interior. Serves some of the best and least expensive exotic drinks in town. Try the deliciously tropical *cola de mono* (s/3 per ½L, s/7 per 1½L). Outdoor seating. Open daily 8pm-late.

Arandú Bar, Tarapacá 113 (☎243 434). The gringos' pick, overlooking the Amazon and blasting American music. Pilsner s/4-10. Open Su-M 1pm-1am, Tu-Sa 1pm-2am.

Pushpa, Raymondi 341. Just off the beaten path. Straw roofs supply the requisite jungle charm. Live music F. Open daily 7pm-late.

CLUBS

A broad range of music, dance styles, and age groups makes Iquitos' small club scene exciting, if not extensive. The best information about hot happenings comes via the fluorescent banners around town. Two popular bands, **Explosion** and **Euforia,** play current salsa and merengue hits at clubs around the city.

◙ Noa Noa, Pevas 298, at Fitzcarrald. With flashing lights, smoke machines, a bi-level dance floor, and a gurgling waterfall, Noa Noa is everything a disco should be. Middle-aged tourists salsa beside hip young Peruvians. The salsa/pop mix is heavy on the salsa. Cover s/10. Open M 8:30pm-3am, Tu-Su 8:30pm-6am.

Agricobank, at Condamine and Pablo Rosell. On slow nights, Agricobank's a tent with cheap beer (s/10 for 3). But when groups like Explosion hit the stage, hundreds of salsaing teenagers pack the floor. Come to dance. Cover s/5-10. Open F-Su 9pm-3am.

Disco Kongo Bongo, Huallaga 365 (☎222 919). A traditional dance club. Tourists and locals get down with varying degrees of success. The salsa/pop mix is heavy on the pop. F-Sa cover s/18. Open daily 8pm-late.

Dreams, Ocampo 102 (☎234 155), at Napo. Small and chi-chi. Particularly popular among teenagers who enjoy US pop music. Open daily 9pm-late.

🔁 DAYTRIPS FROM IQUITOS

QUISTOCOCHA

Frequent combis (25min., s/2) leave from Próspero, just downhill from José Galuez, beyond Belén. Mototaxi s/10. Open daily 8am-6pm. s/3, children s/2. Other local swimming holes include Morona Cocha and Ruococha; both a s/5 mototaxi from the center.

Located 13km south of the city, the attractive waterside Quistococha resort offers rest, relaxation, and a chance to see all the animals you missed on your jungle trip. The main attraction at this complex is a pretty beach with a roped-off swimming area that beckons gringos and Peruvians alike—this is someplace where it's safe to enter the reddish water. Picnic tables, walking trails, lawn chairs, rowboats (s/5 per hr.), and volleyball courts make for a full day of play. Watch out for weekend crowds. Meanwhile, in a small but well-maintained zoo, monkeys and parrots frolic, a giant river otter flips for visitors, gargantuan *paiche* fish lurk just underwater, and pumas and jaguars yawn and pace. The snake house may call up second thoughts about jungle expeditions. A restaurant waits inside, but the booths just outside the complex gate serve less expensive fare.

SANTO TOMAS

To reach Santo Tomas, take any bus marked "aeropuerto" heading down Tacna/Grau and ask the driver to let you off at the road to Santo Tomas (s/0.5). From the intersection, taxi colectivos wait to take you the rest of the way to the village (15min., s/1 per person or s/5 to leave immediately in a private taxi).

A few kilometers off the route to Quistococha, a rutted dirt road leads to Santo Tomas. This small village is home to a coalition of 20 potters and other clay-molders who produce magnificent *artesanía* in their home studios. Behind their thin wood walls, these talented artists mold intricate pots in under five minutes. The organization's current president is the knowledgeable Emerito Pacaya Aricari (☎233 641), who can point visitors to interesting crafts. To find him, follow the main street several minutes to the school; he lives and works in the house directly to the left (Lote 08). You could also just walk down the street and peek into any open front door, as most artists set up their work in their front rooms. The craftspeople see few visitors, but most will gladly sell a pot (s/3-50) or knick-knack (s/2).

🐦 INTO THE JUNGLE FROM IQUITOS

The Iquitos tourist office delights in pointing out that Loreto, the jungle province of which Iquitos is capital, occupies an area roughly equivalent to the size of Germany. After all, this promise of vast virgin forest brings the city its visitors. However, the lay of the land ensures that Loreto's most pristine areas stay that way—almost entirely inaccessible. As is the case throughout Peru's *selva*, reaching anywhere even resembling untouched jungle requires lots of money and time. Your best bet lies in finding someone or something that will take you at least 80km away from Iquitos and preferably—though this is harder to find—off the main riverways. Of the various protected areas near Iquitos, the **Pacaya-Samiria National Reserve** and **Tamshiyacu-Tahuayo Community Reserve** provide the best looks at rainforest. But the romantic allure of "virgin jungle" should not make one forget that fascinating stuff happens all over the region; the native communities hawking goods to tourists are every bit as "real" as those who still make their clothes from tree bark. Three possibilities are open to the traveler: river cruises, lodges, and trips with independent guides. No budget options exist within the first group. The second option includes a wide range of opportunities, from deluxe resorts to simple and relatively inexpensive tours. Independent guides tend to keep the adventurous and budget-oriented traveler in mind. Whichever option you choose, make sure to sign up with your guide or company directly.

HIRING AN INDEPENDENT GUIDE

Unfortunately, of the legions of freelance guides operating in Iquitos, many have garnered **complaints** for lack of knowledge, stealing money, sexual harassment, and, most commonly, for not completing the trip as planned. At present, visitors arriving by plane enter an airport crammed with tour guides shouting for their attention. Gerald Mayeaux, the American Rotarian who took over the tourist office two years ago (and has made tour reform his mission) keeps records on all the guides and can let you know who has garnered complaints and whose record remains unblemished. Ask to see any potential guide's license and national ID card to check that the names coincide; then head to the tourist office (see Orientation and Practical Information, p. 262) to inquire about his record. Something to keep in mind, however, is that only one licensed guide is currently working. The majority of guides do not have licenses because licenses cost upwards of US$1000. A license may mean that a guide is reliable, but the lack of one does not dictate that he is not. Once you've decided on a guide, get the trip agreement in writing, and avoid paying in full up front. **Carlos Grandes** has 32 years of jungle experience and leads trips down the Ucayali and on five-day walks toward the Brazilian border and the Río Yavari. Carlos, who speaks some English, can shape any trip to fit travelers' desires. The trips get more interesting, adventurous, and cheaper as they get longer; three days is the minimum length. Trips usually cost US$40 per person per day; cost decreases with larger groups. Contact Carlos at his office in the Hotel Libertad, Arica 361 (☎235 763; email carlosgrandes@hotmail.com). Two other guides with sparkling reputations are **David Ríos** and **Richard Fowler,** a US expat.

JUNGLE LODGES

As a viable alternative to jungle tours, tourist lodges are a bit more predictable. Many of the affordable ones sit quite close to the city, however, and while they offer a few trails, visits to Yagua, Bora, Achuale, or Murato tribes, and sometimes even a swimming pool, any sort of excursion into the jungle generally costs extra. Such guided daytrips or overnights to explore the nearby jungle include options such as visiting native tribes, canoeing, fishing, and hiking; some lodges' trips have strict schedules while others can change to accommodate customers' interests. Make sure you understand what's included in your stay at the lodge (and what languages their trip guides speak) before you sign up; food, speedboat transport, daytrips, and lodging are all usually included—and get a written contract specifying these conditions. Finally, try bargaining—most people book these trips from home at set rates, but walk-in customers have far greater leverage.

▩ **Muyuna Amazon Lodge and Expeditions,** Putumayo 163B (☎242 858 or (01) 446 97 83; email muyuna@wayna.rcp.net.pe; www.muyuna.com). A relatively new lodge, 120km out of the city on the Río Yunayacu, that has received rave reviews. Lodge activities are fairly standard (birdwatching, native community visits, shaman ceremonies, piranha fishing) but also flexible. Eduardo is a guide of particular note. For more info, ask for Analía or her husband. Excursions into the Pacaya-Samiria Reserve, 5-person and 8-day min., US$100 per day. Accommodation in rustic bungalows with baths, mosquito nets, and kerosene lamps. US$50 per person per day; discounts for larger groups or Hostelling International members. Office open daily 7am-10pm.

Loving Light Amazon Lodge, Putumayo 128 (☎243 180; email info@junglelodge.com; www.junglelodge.com), 140km from the city on the Yanayacu River. US contact: 7016 248th Av. N.E. Redmond, WA 98053 (☎(425) 836 9431). Beyond the lodge, Loving Light arranges 5-day camping trips in the woods (US$60/day). Vegetarian food available. English-speaking local guides. US$50 per person per day with 2 people; group and longer trip discounts possible. Open daily 8am-8pm.

Paseos Amazónicos, Pevas 246 (☎233 110 or 231 618), between Fitzcarrald and Raymondi. In Lima: Bajada Balta 131-054, Lima 18 (☎241 7576; fax 446 7946; email postmast@p-amazon.com.pe). Maintains a variety of lodges in the area; the farthest, **Tambo Amazónico Lodge,** is 180km from Iquitos. From there, guests visit giant lilypads (*Victorias Regias*), make camping trips to the Pacaya-Samiria Reserve which lies 200km away, and hope to see pink dolphins. Trips tend to be more pre-planned than those of other companies. US$80 per person for 1½ days, US$600 for 3 days including camping excursion. Open daily 7am-7pm.

Heliconia, Próspero 574 (☎235 132; fax 232 499). In Lima: Las Camelias 511, Oficina 402 (☎442 4515). Resort-like accommodations at mid-range prices. Located just 80km from Iquitos, Heliconia's programs are very structured. Activities include birdwatching and native village visits. 2-day trip US$110 per person, 3-day trip US$165 per person. Their Zungarococha resort, only 20km from Iquitos, has a pool and slightly higher prices, and is more oriented toward rest and relaxation than jungle adventure. Office open M-F 8am-noon and 3:30-7pm.

Explorama, La Marina 340 (☎252 526; fax 252 533; US contact ☎(800) 707 5275; email amazon@explorama.com; www.explorama.com). The granddaddy of jungle trips from Iquitos. Organized, well-run, and expensive. Their three lodges each offer a slightly different program; the farthest is 160km from Iquitos. Explorama takes visitors to the ACEER environmental laboratory and the largest canopy walkway in the world. Prices start at US$100 per person per day. Office open daily 7:30am-12:30pm and 3-6pm.

Amazonas Tour Invest, Pevas 227 (☎223 801). A brand-new lodge 80km from Iquitos on the Yanayacu River. Emphasis on education and adventure; lodge stays are limited to 5 days, after which guests must embark on an adventure. Accommodations are rustic; participants are expected to help with preparations. US$50 per person per day; group discounts. Open daily 8am-8pm.

YURIMAGUAS   ☎094

At first glance, Yurimaguas offers little that is enticing or original. Sure, it's a nice little jungle town with nice excursions to some nearby lakes, but the city itself seems to be little but a cheap replication of Iquitos (notice the similarities between the two cathedrals). At second glance, you may realize that your first impression was correct. Yurimaguas is too large to be quaint and too small to be urban. However, it is a good place to get a taste of jungle life, start on a river journey to Iquitos, and see some of the most amazing sunsets in Peru.

⌐ TRANSPORTATION

Flights: Airport, on Libertad, 1km from the center. Servicios Aereos Tarapoto, Libertad 143 (☎352 121), sends a 6-person plane to **Tarapoto** (US$25 per person, 4 person min.) and on jungle tours to **Lagunas** (US$300 per hr.). **Aerolatino,** Libertad 137 (☎352 624), flies to **San Lorenzo** (s/139 per person, 3 person min.) and **Tarapoto** (US$200 per plane).

Buses: Transportes Paredes Estrella, Cácares 133 (☎351 307), heads to **Lima** (36hr., 7am, s/80) via **Tarapoto** (6½hr., s/12), **Chiclayo** (23hr., s/60), and **Trujillo** (27hr., s/70). Transportes Huamanga, Cácares 214, also sends buses to **Lima** (32hr., 6am, s/85) via **Tarapoto** (5hr., s/10), **Chiclayo** (24hr., s/50), and **Trujillo** (28hr., s/55). Turismo Ejetur, Libertad 355 (☎351 205), runs to **Trujillo** (28hr., 6am, s/60) via **Tarapoto** (6hr., 6am, s/10). Transportes New Image, Cesar López 615 (☎352 412), sends **cars** to **Tarapoto** (4hr., leaving when full 3am-5pm, s/25). To reach the company, walk 3 blocks down Jáuregui from the plaza, take a right onto Tacna, and the first left onto López. Yurimaguas Express (☎352 727), at Manco Capac and Huallaga, sends **trucks** to **Tarapoto** (5hr., leaving when full 3am-5pm, s/20), as does Oriente Express (☎352 122), at Tacna and Huallaga.

Boats: Yurimaguas has several ports. Boats to **Iquitos** (3 days; s/30-40, cabin s/60) via **Lagunas** (12-13hr., s/10) leave from **Puerto Zamora,** 7 blocks down Castilla from the Plaza de Armas. Boats leave almost every day, usually in the afternoon, but like most Peruvian river boats, few leave on schedule. Other ports send boats to more local destinations. **Puerto Abel Guerra,** between Zamora and the plaza, is one of the largest.

▛▜ ORIENTATION AND PRACTICAL INFORMATION

The **Ríos Shanusi, Paranapura,** and **Huallaga** form Yurimaguas's borders. The **Plaza de Armas** sits next to the Río Huallaga; **Jáuregui,** the main drag, extends from the plaza, perpendicular to the river. After five blocks, the street divides and Jáuregui heads to Tarapoto, while **Libertad** passes the **airport.** The **market** lies on Jáuregui, two blocks from the plaza.

Tourist Information: Lores 100 (☎352 676), in the large pink building on the plaza. Open M-F 8am-2pm. The **Oficina de Cooperación Técnica,** Plaza de Armas 114 (email mpaacooptec@usa.net), in the Municipalidad, distributes maps and advice.

Currency Exchange: Banco Continental, Lores 132 (☎352 070), half a block from the plaza. US$10 commission on traveler's checks. Open M-F 9:15am-12:45pm and 4-6:30pm, Sa 9am-noon. Visa **ATM.**

Market: Mercado Yurimaguas, 2 blocks from the plaza. Open daily 3am-noon.

Emergency: ☎ 105.

Police: (☎352 627), on the 2nd block of Condamine. Wants all foreign visitors to register with them upon arrival.

Hospital: Hospital Apoyo Santa Gema, Progreso 307 (☎352 135, emergency 352 142), 1 block down Jáuregui from the plaza, then 3 to the right.

Telephones: Telecomunicaciones y Servicios Yurimaguas, Bolívar 122-24 (☎/fax 352 020), 1 block from the plaza. Open M-Sa 7am-10pm.

Internet Access: Instituto de Educación Superior American System, Jáuregui 721 (☎352 141). s/10 per hr. Open 9am-11pm.

Post Office: Serpost, Arica 439 (☎352 172). Open M-Sa 7:30am-2pm and 3-5pm.

ACCOMMODATIONS

Quintas and *hostales* line the streets in Yurimaguas. Unfortunately, quantity does not ensure quality, and most options leave something to be desired.

Hostal de Paz, Jáuregui 429 (☎352 123), 5 blocks down from the plaza. Rooms include a table fan, television, and bath. Be careful—the rooms have mosquito screens, but the bathrooms do not. Singles s/20; matrimonials s/26; doubles s/28.

Hostal Jaen, Garcilaso 126 (☎351 576), by the port. Walk 3 blocks down Comercio; go left on Garcilaso. A near-shrine to hygiene. Rooms may be tiny, but the friendly family downstairs keeps them sparkling. Rooms s/10 per person.

Hostal Cesar Gustavo, Atahuallpa 102, 4 blocks down Jáuregui and one to the left. Fully equipped with fans, mosquito nets, and tiny private baths. Open bricks near the ceiling ensure that no rooms have secrets. Singles s/15; doubles s/20.

Quinta Lucy, Jáuregui 305 (☎352 139). One of many cheap *quintas* lining Jáuregui. Tall ceilings and cushy mattresses, but no fans or mosquito nets, and cement dominates the rustic decor. Singles with bath s/10; doubles s/12, with bath s/15.

FOOD

The majority of Yurimaguas's food options blend together. At night, small booths selling cheap hamburgers and jungle food line Capac between López and Huallago. The *pollo a la brasa* supply remains stable.

Cevichería El Dorado, Aguirre 126 (☎351 023), near the river, a short (s/1) mototaxi ride from the center. El Dorado's specialty is river fish, but it also serve all kinds of crazy jungle food. Most entrees s/8-15. Open daily 7am-5:30pm.

La Prosperidad, Próspero 101 (☎352 057), at Jáuregui. Slightly more conventional and preferred by locals. This double-decker snack bar serves up tasty morsels all day. Hamburger s/3. *Pollo a la brasa* dinner s/7. Juice s/2. Open 8am-1pm and 4-11:30pm.

FESTIVALS

The Yurimaguas **fiesta patronal** takes place from August 5-15. During these 11 days, a different neighborhood holds a fiesta each night. The dancing, food, *artesanía*—and in some cases a man reenacting Pamplona's running of the bulls—culminates in a big party in the Plaza de Armas on the final day.

DAYTRIP FROM YURIMAGUAS

LAGO CUIPARI

Colectivo boats to Lago Cuipari (2½hr.; leaving in the morning when full; s/5) depart from Puerto Garcilaso de la Vega, at the end of Garcilaso, to your right from the plaza if you're facing the river. The only return boats leave in the morning as well, so daytrips here often become 2-day trips; there are no hotels, but you can camp or stay in people's homes. From May-Sept., the dry season, the boats stop at Las Mercedes and it's a 2hr. walk to the lake. For more info check http://geocities.com/tarapoto-peru/cuipari.html.

Cuipari is a beautiful lake where one can canoe, visit orchid gardens, fish for piranhas, and experience some of the most beautiful sunsets in the world. A man named Orlando (a.k.a. *el hombre con el mono,* "the man with the monkey") knows the lake like the back of his hand and can serve as a guide for the region (email 0.2jungle@ole.com; US$50 per day).

🌴 INTO THE JUNGLE FROM YURIMAGUAS

Guides in the small pueblo of **Lagunas** serve as excellent resources for exploring the immense expanse of virgin jungle that is the **Reserva Nacional Pacaya-Simiria**. To reach Lagunas, take an Iquitos-bound boat (12-13hr., s/10) from Puerto Zamora, or a motorboat (8hr., s/10) from Puerto Abel Guerra. Alternatively, the area around **Balsa Puerto** holds native communities and waterfalls. From Puerto Boca in Yurimaguas, peke-peke boats (2 days, s/10) and motorboats (6hr., s/40) travel to Balsa Puerto; small airplanes (15min., US$100 round-trip) also make the trip. Inquire at the Municipalidad for more information on these options.

TARAPOTO   ☎094

Tarapoto's lush vegetation has earned it the tag "Ciudad de las Palmeras" ("Palm City"). After all, palm trees and medicinal extracts are among the few who appreciate the city's sticky air. As the commercial capital of the San Martín department, Tarapoto serves as a hub for traffic headed to and from the jungle. Within the city, however, vehicles as simple as mototaxis and motorcycles have become the businessman's vehicle of choice—renting one of your own facilitates both sightseeing and fitting in.

▐ TRANSPORTATION

Flights: Airport, a few blocks south of town. Mototaxi s/2. **Aerocontinente,** at San Pablo de La Cruz and Moyobamba (☎527 212 or 524 332), on the plaza. Open M-F 8am-1pm and 3-7pm, Sa 3-6pm, Su 8:30am-noon. To **Lima** (1hr., 4pm, US$59-79). **TANS,** San Martín 491 (☎525 339). Open M-Sa 8am-12:30pm and 3-7pm, Su 9am-noon. To **Lima** (Tu, Th, Sa, Su 2pm; US$58-68) and **Iquitos** (Tu, Th, Sa, Su 11:30am; US$58-68). **SAOSA,** Compagñon 468 (☎526 534). To: **Yurimaguas** (15min, US$25); **Pampa Hermosa** (s/180); **Contamana** (s/180-190); **Orellana** (s/180-190); and **Pucallpa** (s/200).

Buses: Agencies concentrated on Salaverry. Mototaxi s/2. Paredes Estrella (☎521 202), on the 8th block of Salaverry; Turismo Tarapoto, Salaverry 705 (☎523 259), Expreso Huamanga (☎527 272), and Guadalupe Express (☎528 038) run to **Lima** (32hr., s/70) via **Moyobamba, Rioja, Nueva Cajamarca, Chiclayo** (20hr., s/35-40), and **Trujillo** (24hr., s/50-55). Expreso Huamanga and Guadalupe Express also go to: **Bellavista** (s/10), **Juanjui** (s/12-15), and **Yurimaguas** (5hr., s/10) via the **Cataratas Ahuashiyaku** (1hr., 10-11am, s/3-5). *Combis* to **Lamas** (4am-10pm., 30min., s/3.5).

✳❓ ORIENTATION AND PRACTICAL INFORMATION

Agencies, banks, and other services line **San Martín, Pimentel,** and the **Plaza de Armas.** Transportation arrives and departs from **Salaverry,** near **Morales.**

Tour Agencies: Various agencies have sprung up to cater to the increasing interest in ecotourism. Among these are **Selva Tours,** San Martín 153 (☎526 668; open M-Sa 8am-1pm and 3-7pm), 1 block from the plaza; **Fomentours,** San Martín 148 (☎522 257), across the street; and **Demla Tours,** Moyobamba 253. All agencies coordinate tours to the **Cataratas Ahuashiyaku** (s/20), **Lamas** (s/20), **Laguna Sauce** (s/60), and **canoeing trips** (s/50) on the Mayo River.

Banks: Banco de Crédito, on Maynas off the plaza, has a **Visa ATM.** Open M-F 9:15am-1:15pm and 4:30-6:30pm, Sa 9:30-12:30pm. **Banco del Trabajo,** Hurtado 155 (☎527 000), provides **Western Union.** Open M-F 9am-1:30pm and 3:45-7pm, Sa 9:15am-12:45pm. The window at **Banco Continental,** Hurtado 149, is open daily 9am-9pm.

Markets: Mercado 1, on the 2nd block of Pimentel, south of the plaza. Larger **Mercado 2,** a few blocks downhill from the plaza.

Laundromat: Lavanderia y Tintoreria, San Pablo de la Cruz 248 (☎527 128), 2 blocks from the plaza. Machine-dried s/8 per kg. Line-dried s/3 per kg.

Emergency: ☎105.

Police: ☎522 141.

Pharmacy: Check the sign outside **Farmacia Popular,** San Martín 220 (☎522 079), to find the *farmacia en turno.*

Hospital: Clínica San Marcos, Leguia 604 (☎523 838). **Clínica San Martín,** San Martín 274.

Telephones: Telefónica del Perú, Castilla 167 (☎522 649), 1 block from the plaza. Open daily 7am-11pm.

Internet Access: San Martín 340 (☎523 601), s/4 per hr. San Martín 129, s/5 per hr. Both open daily 9am-1am.

Post Office: Serpost, San Martín 482 (☎522 021), 5 blocks from the plaza. Open M-Sa 8am-8pm, Su 8am-noon.

ACCOMMODATIONS

Alojamiento El Mirador, San Pablo de la Cruz 517 (☎522 177). As close as you can get to the jungle while still near the center of town. Tranquil environment encourages hammock-napping. First floor (includes private bath, TV, and fan) singles US$13; doubles US$16. Simpler 2nd fl. singles s/35; doubles s/40.

Hostal Edison (☎524 101 or 524 038), at Maynas and Pimentel, on the plaza. Party all weekend at the hostel's disco, casino, or karaoke bar, then crash in their spacious and comfortable rooms. Hot water. Breakfast s/5. Singles s/20; doubles s/30.

Hostal San Antonio, Pimentel 126 (☎525 563), off the plaza. Standard rooms, around a garden. Hot water. Restaurant. TV s/5. Singles s/20; doubles s/25.

Hotel Monte Azul, Morey 156 (☎522 443; fax 523 636). What's this? Mini-bars in each room? Singles s/75, with A/C s/109; prices negotiable.

FOOD

Tarapoto's fusion of highland and jungle cuisine has begot fabulous fruit juices and fish fillets (with *cecina* rather than *trucha*). Market vendors also advertise a variety of medicinal drinks.

Las Terrazas, Hurtado 183 (☎522 043), on the plaza. Delicious dishes, including typical plates such as *paiche* (s/6), *patarashca* (s/14), and *juanes* (s/7). *Menú* s/5. Open daily 7:30am-midnight.

Banana's Burger (☎523 260), at Morey and San Martín. Popular with locals, particularly at night. Specializes in burgers, chicken, and sandwiches. Open daily 7am-4am.

Real Grill, on Moyobamba, on the plaza. Chinese, Italian, and Peruvian plates in an atmosphere more elegant than most. Open daily 8:30am-midnight.

SIGHTS AND DAYTRIPS FROM TARAPOTO

MUSEO UNSM. The entrance to this one-room museum displays some startling examples of jungle wildlife, including anaconda snake skins. Inside, exhibits cover Tarapoto's long history in a circular fashion—first the fossilized shells, dinosaur bones, and mastodon jaw; then the archaeological remains and colonial artifacts; and finally newspaper clippings and photographs of 1940-1960 Tarapoto. *(Maynas 179. Open M-F 8am-noon and 12:30-8pm. s/1.)*

LAMAS. The descendants of the Chancas, or *Motilones,* who inhabit this town are renowned for their highland traditions and handicrafts, seemingly out of place in the jungle. The waterfalls Cascada de Chapawanki and Cascada de Mishquiyacu lie nearby. *(To get to Lamas, take a combi (30min., leaving when full 4am-10pm, s/3.50) from one of the bus company offices on Salaverry.)*

OUTDOOR ACTIVITIES. The spectacular Cataratas (Waterfalls) **Ahuashiyakuwa** make for an easy daytrip. Look for **Laguna Venezia** en route to the cascade. *(A 2hr. walk along the highway toward Yurimaguas. Alternatively, take a Yurimaguas-bound bus (1hr., 10-11am, s/3-5) or a mototaxi (round-trip s/15).)* **Laguna Sauce,** a beautiful lake also called Laguna Azul, requires a longer excursion. *(To get to the lake, take a mototaxi (s/1.5) to the Sauce bus stop in the Shilcayo district, then hop on a Sauce-bound combi (3hr., s/10). From Sauce, it's a 5hr. walk. Lodging (s/10) is available at the lake.)* Various tourist agencies in Tarapoto organize **canoeing** adventures (s/10) down the Río Mayo during the dry season (June-Nov.). *(For more information, visit Fomentours, San Martín 148 (☎522 257), or Demla Tours, Moyobamba 253.)*

✵ FESTIVALS

Highland customs are still practiced by descendents of the Chancas (*Motilones*) who live in Tarapoto. Travelers lucky enough to arrive during Tarapoto's main festival (July 7-19), in honor of the **Patrona de la Santa Cruz de los Motilones,** can witness these highland influences first-hand. Tarapoto's other major celebration is the week-long remembrance of **Tarapoto's anniversary** (Aug. 14-22), which includes typical *pandilla* dances.

PUCALLPA   ☎064

Pucallpa throbs with energy. Mototaxis crowd the streets, vendors push and pedal their goods, and even the shoeshine boys seem to have somewhere they need to be. Meanwhile, out by the port, the cargo-ferries continue their endless cycle of loading and unloading, and the vultures circle overhead, waiting to pounce on any scraps they leave behind. As Peru's largest jungle town accessible by road, Pucallpa's port forms an important link between the forest's resources and the rest of the country's markets. For visitors it is an Amazonian experience no one ever pays for: a realistic view of the frontier, hard at work.

▟ TRANSPORTATION

Flights: Airport (☎572 767), 5km northeast of the center. Mototaxi s/10. AeroConti-nente, 7 de Junio 861 (☎575 643), flies to **Lima** (45min., noon, US$69) and **Iquitos** (45min.; M, W, F, Su 11:50am; US$59). Tans, Arica 500 (☎591 852), at Arana, flies to **Lima** (50min.; M, W, F 2pm, Su noon; US$58) and **Iquitos** (45min.; M, W, F 11am, Su 9am; US$58).

Buses: Companies on 7 de Junio near Raymondi and San Martín send buses to: **Lima** (18-22hr., 5 per day 7:30-11am, s/35-40) via **Tingo María** (7-8hr., s/15-20), **Huá-nuco** (10-12hr., s/20-25), and **La Oroya** (12-18hr., s/25-30). Turismo Central, 7 de Junio 893 (☎577 168), goes to **Huancayo** (18hr., 6:30am, s/40). Selva Express, 7 de Junio 846 (☎573 219), and Turismo Ucayali, 7 de Junio 799 (☎577 158), run colectivos to **Tingo María** (5-6hr., leaving when full 4am-6pm, s/35). Transportes Palcazo, Centenario 142A (☎571 273), where 7 de Junio becomes Carretera Frederico B, sends colectivos to **Palcazú** (7hr., leaving when full 6-10am, s/35), where one can make connections to Puerto Bermúdez and Puerto Inco.

Boats: Passenger vessels wear chalkboards that announce their destinations and intended dates and times of departure; few leave on schedule. Even so, boats leave almost daily for **Iquitos** (3-8 days, s/60-70) from the ports at **La Hoyada** (Dec.-Mar.); **Cruze el Mangual** (Apr.-Jul.); and **Pucallpillo** (Aug.-Nov.), depending on the height of the river. All are near each other, about 3km northwest of the center. Mototaxi s/3. For more on the boat journey to Iquitos, see p. 261.

Public Transportation: The most popular **colectivo** route runs south down 7 de Junio toward the swamp and north up Ucayali toward the freeway and the Natural Museum. s/0.80-1. All colectivos announce their destination on their windshields.

Taxis: Mototaxis should cost under s/3 anywhere in town, s/10 to the airport and Yarina-cocha. To get a car (instead of a mototaxi) call **Empresa de Transporte** (☎575 026).

Car and Moped Rental: Rent-A-Moto Ruiz, unmarked at Tacna 601, at San Martín, rents bikes (s/6 per hr.). Open daily 7am-10pm. **Motos Virgen de Copacabana,** Ucayali 265, does the same (s/7 per hr.). Car rental s/100 per day. Car and driver s/20 per hr. Open 24hr., but you'll probably have to knock.

⬛🔃 ORIENTATION AND PRACTICAL INFORMATION

Pucallpa sits on the west bank of the **Río Ucayali,** 860km northeast of Lima. Its principal avenues are **Ucayali** and the parallel **7 de Junio** (along which stretch the town's two **markets**). These are intersected by **Raymondi** and **San Martín.** The **Plaza de Armas** is a block riverward from Ucayali, between Independencia and Sucre, which run perpendicular to Ucayali. Most **buses** come in on 7 de Junio or Ucayali. **Swampland** (or water in the wet season) marks the town's southern border.

Tourist Office: Dirección Regional Sectorial de Industria y Turismo, 2 de Mayo 111 (☎571 303; fax 575 110), near Mariscal Cáceres. From the plaza walk down Tarapaca toward the river and turn left on Portillo; after a few blocks this will become 2 de Mayo. A knowledgeable and friendly English-speaking staff has brochures, maps, and excursion information. Open M-F 7am-1pm and 2-6:45pm.

Currency Exchange: Banco de Crédito, Raymondi 404 (☎571 364), at Tarapacá. Visa **ATM.** Open M-F 9:15am-1:15pm and 4:30-6:30pm, Sa 9:30am-12:30pm.

Spanish Classes: The British Centre, Libertad 273-7 (☎/fax 578 682), can arrange private lessons. Approximately US$10 per person per hr. or US$30 per month for group classes. Open M-Sa 8am-9pm.

Markets: Pucallpa's larger market stretches along 7 de Junio. The smaller one, bordered by Tarapacá, Portillo, 9 de Diciembre, and Huáscar, sells hammocks (s/15-50).

Laundry: Lavandería Gasparin, Portillo 526 (☎591 147). s/1.25 includes detergent for self-service; min. s/6 per machine. Open M-Sa 9am-1pm and 4-8pm.

Emergency: ☎105.

Police: San Martín 466 (☎ 575 258). Open 24hr.

Hospital: Augustín Cauper 285 (☎575 209), between Diego Delunadro and Mariscal Cáceres.

Telephones: Telefónica del Perú, Tarapacá 540 (☎574 803; fax 590 343). Public telephones just outside. Open M-F 8:30am-4:30pm.

Internet Access: Trial Cabinas de Internet, Raymondi 399 (☎590 738; email trial_pucallpa@mixmail.com; www.geocities.com/trial_pucallpa), at Tarapacá, has A/C! Surf for 5hr., get 1hr. free. 8am-9pm s/4 per hr., 9pm-8am s/2 per hr. Open 24hr. **Eproima Net,** Tarapaca 725 (☎579 641; email epinet@eproima.com.pe; www.eproima.com.pe). s/4 per hr. Open 24hr.

Post Office: Serpost, San Martín 418 (☎571 382). Open M-Sa 8am-6:45pm.

🔃 ACCOMMODATIONS

Pucallpa's wide variety of accommodations will fit everyone's budget and expectations. The cheapest of the cheap cluster on 7 de Junio near Sucre. In this heat, a fan may be the most important feature of any room. None of these hotels has hot water, but you probably won't miss it.

Hostería Del Ray, Portillo 747 (☎575 815). With your back to the Plaza de Armas, walk south down 7 de Junio and take a right on Portillo. High-ceilinged rooms with bath and fan. Singles s/15; doubles s/20; triples s/25; TV s/5 extra.

Hospedaje Richard, San Martín 350 (☎572 242), sells Shipibo crafts in the lobby. All rooms have fans. Quite clean, besides the occasional hole in the paint. Singles s/10, with bath s/15; doubles with bath s/25.

Hospedaje Komby, Ucayali 360 (☎ 571 184; fax 577 081), 1½ blocks up from the Plaza de Armas. Pricey, but bath, fan, and TV in each room. Sparkling pool (non-guests s/5 per day). All rooms with bath. Singles s/35; doubles s/45; triples s/55.

Hospedaje Plaza, Independencia 420 (☎592 118). Right off the Plaza de Armas, this little hostel is still tranquil. Yellow walls brighten up rooms—but not as much as the fan. Singles s/10, with bath s/20; matrimonials s/15, with bath s/25; doubles s/18.

FOOD

A **fresh fruit market** appears daily along Ucayali between Independencia and Sucre. Farther along, at the intersection with San Martín, vendors sell irresistible, if too sweet, coconut patties (s/0.50). Another block down, Raymondi (between Ucayali and Tacna) plays host to a number of burger joints. For Italian food, head to Inmaculada between San Martín and Independencia. **Los Andes,** Portillo 553, is a well-stocked supermarket. (Open M-Sa 8am-1pm and 3-9pm, Su 10am-1pm.)

El Paraíso Naturista, Tarapacá 653, right off the Plaza de Armas. El Paraíso takes health food seriously. Entrees include Peruvian favorites served vegetarian-style. Soy *bistec* s/9. Yogurt s/2-4. Entrees s/3-9. *Menú* s/3. Open Sa-Th 7:30am-9pm, F 7am-4pm.

Don José, Ucayali 661 (☎572 865), between San Martín and Raymondi. This 34-year-old eatery isn't cheap, but its extensive menu yields large portions. Hamburgers s/9-12. Entrees s/4-19. *Menú* s/4. Open M-Sa 7am-11pm, Su 7am-3pm and 6-11pm.

Restaurant Las Margaritas, Tarapacá 250 (☎573 430). Like a trip into the jungle: plants climb the walls and the roof drips with straw. Also a bar. Entrees s/5-26. *Menú* s/4. Beer s/4-7. Live music F-Sa 7pm, karaoke Su-Th 7pm. Open daily 8am-late.

Polleria El Portal Chicken, Independencia 510 (☎571 771), on the plaza. The best of the city's many chicken restaurants. With such speedy service, who cares if the decor is fast food-esque? Quarter chicken s/6. Entrees s/6-24. Open daily 4:30pm-1am.

SIGHTS

PARQUE NATURAL-MUSEO REGIONAL. Most notable for its extensive **zoo,** the park features some beautiful animals in (somewhat-too-small) cages. Watch out for the friendly monkey which doesn't have a cage. Don't worry, it's a female; only males bite. Beyond the zoo and over the shark-head bridge sits the museum, which is worth a look. Four small huts outline aspects of local culture: one contains pottery from the Shipibo Indians; another an assortment of pelts and skins; the third bones, shells, and fossils; and finally a collection of Shipibo and other indigenous clothing. *(To get to the complex, take any combi marked "Pista" heading north. Ask to be let off at the "zoológico" (15min., s/0.8-1). Open daily 9am-5:15pm. s/2, children s/0.5.)*

ARTESANÍA. Internationally renowned painter **Pablo Amaringo** runs the Escuela de Pintura Usko Ayar. The pride of Pucallpa, Amaringo has developed a style known as "neo-Amazónico," mainly jungle landscapes created under the influence of the hallucinogenic Ayahuasca plant. More of a working school than a tourist attraction, the friendly teachers at Usko Ayar will show off students' work between classes. Amaringo's work is also on display. *(Sánchez Cerro 465-67. ☎573 088. The school is unmarked, with a large wooden platform overlooking the swamp. Mototaxi s/1.5. Open sporadically, generally daily 8-10am and 2-5pm. Free.)*

FESTIVALS

Pucallpa's primary festival, the **Fiesta de San Juan,** takes place June 17-25; the festivities reach their peak June 24. To honor San Juan, Pucallpa's patron saint, locals head to the river or lake to bathe in purifying water. And then they celebrate—traditional dances, music, boat and swimming races, and lots of San Juan *cerveza* are all part of the fun. The city's **anniversary,** October 1-18, provides another occasion to party, with parades, traditional dances, music, and *artesanía* displays.

AMAZON BASIN

JUNGLE TRIPPING Pucallpa's drug of choice comes from the hallucinogenic jungle plant Ayahuasca. Traditionally, only Shaman drank Ayahuasca, which gave them the ability to solve the others' problems. In recent years, however, most people interested in the plant's powers have started imbibing the substance themselves. Some users report developing a third eye, through which they can view the spiritual world, past and present united, the philosophy of nature, and the meaning of paradise. Painter Pablo Amaringo, whose neo-Amazonic pieces are inspired by his experience with the Ayahuasca plant, has said "This plant makes you see what others can't; it puts you in contact with deities, spirits, people from other worlds, and other dimensions." Groovy. Amaringo forsook Ayahusca in 1976 after finding himself injured by an emissary of the spirit world.

◩ NIGHTLIFE

Pucallpa's disco scene is extensive but not particularly distinguished. If a generic Latin pop mix and San Juan *cerveza* aren't to your liking, perhaps you should move on. Crowds are thin throughout the week, pick up on Thursday, and really swing Friday and Saturday. The majority of Pucallpa's clubs are tucked away in residential neighborhoods near the road to the airport. A mototaxi should cost s/2.

◪ **El Mandingo,** Bellavista 1050 (☎572 869). Disco-lovers of all shapes and sizes pack this popular club, enticed by the Latin pop, flashing lights, and smoke machines. Three dance floors, 3 bars, and a courtyard with fountain. Open Tu-Su 8pm-late.

La Granja, Leonicio Prado 451 (☎579 779). Salsa and merengue. Tables surround a cozy dance floor where younger partiers strut their stuff. Open W-Su 8pm-5am.

Las Brujas, Leticia 573 (☎574 955). Lives up to its spooky name with green lights and ghastly fake trees. M-Sa s/20 minimum consumption. Open daily 7pm-4am.

Tucho's Video Pub and Karaoke, Federico Basadre 708. Through the swinging wooden doors, a 20-something crowd sings along. Open daily 7pm-late.

NEAR PUCALLPA: LAGO YARINACOCHA

From time to time, a river changes its course when an easier route (e.g. through flood-weakened topsoil) becomes available. Some leave behind reminders of their former courses: oxbow lakes, which sometimes get re-flooded in the rainy season. Such is the case with Lago Yarinacocha, a "reminder" left by the Río Ucayali. Located 7km northeast of Pucallpa, Yarinacocha serves as a weekend retreat for the city's residents and a potential gateway into the jungle for wandering tourists.

◳◪ **TRANSPORTATION AND PRACTICAL INFORMATION. Puerto Callao,** the main town on the lake's shores, sees lots of activity. To get to Puerto Callao, take a colectivo marked "Yarina" (15min., s/1) from Ucayali. From here, colectivos and guided tour boats leave to plumb the area. The former are usually unmarked and decrepit, leave when full, and ferry groups to any destination on the lake. (1½hr. to San Francisco, 45min. to the botanical gardens, 20-30min. to jungle lodges. s/1-1.5.) The **tourist boats** are shiny and new; their guides flock to visiting gringos like vultures to Pucallpa. For s/15 per hour, they'll provide a guided tour to anywhere on the lake. The stated price is normally per group, so being a larger group ensures a better bargain. As usual, guides vary in knowledge and quality; talk to a guide before you hire him. Or ask for **Alligator Pepe**—he's been a guide for 18 years, speaks English and Italian, and knows everything about the jungle, from the habits of the Shipibo Indians to the constellations. Another recommended guide is **Gustavo Paredes Polonio,** whose boat is called "Poseidon." It is hard to find a boat of any kind after dark, around siesta, or during soccer games. **Cars** marked "Yarina" also head to San Francisco (30min., s/2) from the street parallel to the water in Puerto Callao. Santa Clara is a 30-minute walk from San Francisco.

ACCOMMODATIONS AND FOOD. There is very little reason to sleep in Puerto Callao. However, if you just can't leave, **Hospedaje Los Delfines,** on Aguatiya, has rooms so well-equipped with refrigerators, fans, and telephones that you may not notice that the ceiling is decaying. To get there, face the water, then follow the waterfront road all the way to the left. Turn away from the water at the end of the road; the hotel is one block up on the left-hand corner. (☎596 423. Singles s/18; doubles s/22; TV s/2 extra.) A cheaper option is **Hospedaje El Pescador,** Malecón 216, on the waterfront; enter through the Fuente de Soda Vanessa. There aren't any windows, though fans and vents in each room help compensate. (☎596 750. Rooms s/10 per person.) Countless restaurants line the waterfront, and at lunchtime everyone comes out to cook fresh fish along the street. The one restaurant worth a visit is the **Balsa Turistic Anaconda,** to the right when facing the water. It may cost a bit more, but it lies, literally, on the lake. Delicious seafood entrees cost s/10-22. (☎596 950. Live music Su 2pm. Open daily 9am-6pm.)

SIGHTS. Multiple destinations await around the lake. To the north (left if you're facing the water from Puerto Callao) sit **San Francisco** and, farther, smaller **Santa Clara,** both traditional Shipibo villages (or as traditional as you'll get this close to a city). Women sit outside their houses selling traditional *artesanía,* but this is not the place to bargain, as many people here live in poverty, and the prices are already dirt cheap. Closer to Puerto Callao, **Isla del Amor** is the best place to swim. Volleyball courts and shady trees stand nearby. Apparently, the lake's piranhas don't bother swimmers, but wear a swimsuit at all times or else an "orifice fish" could choose to make your body its new home (see Further Fearsome Fauna, p. 291). Boats to Isla del Amor (20min., s/1) depart frequently. On the right side of the lake (if you're facing the water from Puerto Callao) sits Yarinacocha's best **jungle.** The **Botanical Gardens,** 45 minutes by boat, houses over 2300 plants.

INTO THE JUNGLE FROM LAGO YARINACOCHA. Beyond daytrips, guides lead excursions (up to 5 days) around the lake and environs. After all, Yarinacocha still has direct aquatic connections to the Río Ucayali, and virgin jungle lies close at hand. Choose your guide carefully; check that he is knowledgeable and possesses adequate equipment. Establish all trip expectations (especially price) before setting out. **Alligator Pepe** (US$30 per person per day) and **Gustavo Paredes** (US$35 per person per day) lead similar trips that include all supplies, three meals a day, and which often involve alligator sightings and fishing for piranhas.

Jungle lodges in the area differ from those near other jungle towns. Yarinacocha's lodges are all within a 15-minute boat ride of Puerto Callao and are thus entirely connected to modern society. That said, they are all undeniably in the jungle, and they can arrange guides to lead you farther in. Perhaps more importantly, these jungle lodges are significantly cheaper than their equivalents to the north and south. But the most interesting option isn't really even a lodge at all—**Nueva Luz de Fatima,** actually a small village, lies just beyond the jungle lodges. There, townspeople Silvia Morales and Gilbert Reategui Sangamd open their home to travelers who wish to experience real life in a 20-family lakeside town. The accommodations are spartan—tourists stay in small bedrooms in a dark wood hut—but you can't get much more genuine than this. The rest of the village shares the common bathrooms out back, and showering means dumping buckets of river water over your head. Alligator Pepe also lives in Silvia and Gilbert's house, and is thus readily available for excursions. Boats head to Nueva Luz de Fatimo. You can also ask for Alligator Pepe in Puerto Callao. (Rooms s/25 per person, includes 3 meals.) Deeper into the jungle, **La Cabaña's** flashy sign and giant deck of lounge chairs overlooking the river make it hard to miss—clearly an experience distinct from Nueva Luz. A lakeside resort with individual cabins and a large restaurant, La Cabaña is clean and comfortable; ask for a cabin with a view of the lake. (☎615 009. Paddle boats available for loan; motorboats US$20 per hr. Singles with bath US$35 per person; doubles or triples with bath US$60 per person. Prices include 3

AMAZON BASIN

meals.) **La Perla,** somewhere between La Cabaña and Nueva Fatima both geographically and aesthetically, takes tourists in as one of the family. The German and Peruvian owners house visitors in rooms bedecked with Indian artifacts and animal skins. (☎616 004. Rooms US$30 per person, includes 3 meals per day and transportation to and from the airport.) To reach the jungle lodges, take a boat colectivo from Puerto Callao (20-30min., s/1).

TINGO MARÍA ☎064

Where the Andes give way to the jungle bustles little Tingo María, best known for its bottomless cave and bottomless cocaine supply. Steamy weather and incredible, impenetrable greenery cloak the town's already mysterious exploits in a cabalistic haze. Despite its reputation for unsavory behavior, however, Tingo María does have a splendid mountain backdrop, not to mention one of the grandest caves in the country. And give the burgeoning city a point for originality: it may well be the only one in northern Peru without a Plaza de Armas.

▰ TRANSPORTATION

Flights: Airport (☎562 003), on the far side of the river, 1km to the right after crossing the bridge. Mototaxi s/1.5. **T Double A** (☎562 806), on the right directly after crossing the bridge on the way to the airport, has flights to **Lima** (1-2hr., W and F 2pm, US$79).

Buses: Companies on Enrique Pimentel and Raimondi serve **Lima** (11-12hr.; 7:30am, 6, 6:30, 6:45, 7pm; s/25-40). Leonicio Prado, Enrique Pimental 127. To **Pucallpa** (8hr., 10:45am, s/20) and **Huánuco** (2½hr., 4pm, s/7). Turismo Central, Callao 135 (☎562 668). To **Huancayo** (10hr., 5:45pm, s/25). ETNASA, Callao 195. To **Huánuco** (3hr, every 30min. 7am-7pm, s/7). Comité 5, Raimondi 108 (☎563 602), sends colectivos to **Huánuco** (2hr., leaving when full 5am-8pm, s/13). Turismo San Juan, Callao 145, goes to **Huánuco** (2½-3hr., every hr. 6am-6pm, s/6-7). Turismo Unidas, at Cayumba and Raimondi, sends colectivos to **Pucallpa** (8hr., 2 per day, leaving when full 8-10am, s/20). In past years, night buses to Pucallpa have fallen prey to bandit attacks.

Mototaxis: Should not cost more than s/1.5 within the city limits.

❋▰ ORIENTATION AND PRACTICAL INFORMATION

Cradled in a curve of the **Río Huallaga,** Tingo María lies 545km northeast of Lima. Wide and grassy **Alameda Perú** bisects the city's primary square, the **Plaza Leonicio Prado.** Running parallel, two blocks away and next to the river, **Raimondi** houses the majority of practical spots in Tingo, including businesses and hotels. Most buses arrive at the southern end of Raimondi, where it turns into **Enrique Pimentel.** The city's pulse rests in the huge **markets** in the southern section of town.

Tourist Information: A new **tourist office,** Alameda Perú 525 (☎562 058), right off the plaza, distributes brochures, magazines, and maps. Open daily 8am-3:30pm.

Currency Exchange: Banco de Crédito, Raimondi 249 (☎562 110), is open M-F 9:15am-1:15pm and 4:30-6:30pm, Sa 9:30am-12:30pm. 24hr. Visa **ATM.**

Market: Mercado Modelo, bordered by Callao and Cayumba.

Emergency: ☎105.

Police: Raimondi 413 (☎562 533).

Hospital: Ucayali 114 (☎562 019, emergency ☎563 075).

Telephones: Telefónica del Perú, Tito Jaime 405 (☎563 450 or 563 426). Open daily 7am-11pm.

Internet Access: BeC@D, Raimondi 452 (☎561 852; email becad@latinmail.com.). Open daily 8:30am-midnight. **Internet Cartel,** Raimondi 272 (☎562 551; fax 561 611). Open daily 7am-11pm. Telephone service, s/5 per hr.

Post Office: Alameda Perú 451 (☎/fax 562 100), on the plaza. Open M-Sa 8am-8pm.

ACCOMMODATIONS

Super cheap lodgings (think s/7) abound in the streets around the markets, but most are downright frightening. Far better values wait close by.

■ **Hostal Palacio,** Raimondi 156 (☎562 319), near Callao, Doubles as a zoo, with a puma and a 3-toed sloth (among others) caged in the courtyard. Indoors, the decor is minimal but impeccable. Only rooms with private baths have fans. Singles s/10, with bath s/20; doubles s/20, with bath s/32; TV s/5 extra.

Hospedaje Cuzco, Raimondi 671 (☎562 095), may be dirt cheap, but there's no dirt in the bathrooms or showers. If you can ignore the musky smell and the fact that the reception area doubles as a funeral supply store, then these small but chipper rooms await you. Rooms s/5 per person—no kidding.

Hostal Viena, Lamas 252 (☎562 194), between Benavides and Raimondi. This rambling hostel could sleep an army. Keep looking till you find the best room. Singles s/10, with bath s/15; doubles s/15, with bath s/20; triples s/18, with bath s/25.

Hostal Falcon, Sucre 245 (☎561 817). From the plaza, with the river to your right, walk down Alameda Perú and take a left on Callao. Take the first right on Olaya, then a quick left onto 9 de Octubre. Sucre is the next right. Lovely rooms in a residential neighborhood, all with mirror, towel, soap, and toilet paper. The rooms on the balcony overlooking the street are the nicest. Singles with bath s/15; doubles with bath s/20.

FOOD

Most locals eat at the outdoor *fuentes de soda* that pop up at most intersections with Raimondi. The market area houses several similarly decrepit *menú* places.

La Tía Julia, Alameda Perú 374. A hole in the wall, but rumor has it that this is the best place around for *comida típica*. Entrees s/2-6. Open daily early-2pm.

El Mango Pizza and Sandwich Restaurant, Lamas 232 (☎561 671). No mangos, but: personal pizzas s/9-15; sandwiches s/2-3; and Peruvian entrees s/9-15. Open daily 8-10am, noon-3pm, and 7-11pm.

Comedor Vegetariano, Alameda Perú 353, between Pratoto and Monzón. Despite its name, this place serves *bistek* with the best of them. *Almuerzos* vegetarian and otherwise s/2.50. Open daily 7am-3pm and 7-10pm.

SIGHTS

PARQUE NACIONAL TINGO MARÍA. Reclining on the outskirts of the city, the **Bella Dormiente** (Sleeping Beauty) mountain, so called because its curves resemble those of a reposing woman, marks the location of the **Parque Nacional Tingo María.** The 18,000-hectare reserve maintains a few wooded trails and a refreshing river, but its most popular and interesting attraction is the **Cueva de las Lechuzas.** So immense that it's rumored to be bottomless, this cave could inspire a full day of exploration, although the extreme heat, the bats, and the cockroaches crunching underfoot make most visitors turn back well before that. But even the most fearful amateur spelunker can explore the cave's mouth, where wooden walkways provide security. There, magnificent rock formations hide flocks of parrots. Beyond the walkways, seemingly countless oil birds make their nests, and deeper still live the *lechuzas* (owls) for which the cave is named. Bring a flashlight and a hat to keep their various droppings off your head. If you plan to travel beyond the walkway, wear sturdy shoes. *(Park entrance 8km outside the city; cave less than 1km from the entrance. To get there, take a colectivo mototaxi from Pimentel 148 (30min., leaving when full, s/1.5). Guides with flashlights wait at the entrance of the cave and will lead visitors in for s/5. Park open daily 7am-5:30pm. s/5, children under 14 free.)*

PUERTO BERMÚDEZ ☎064

If Cusco is the tourist heart of Peru, then Puerto Bermúdez is the belly-button. So the locals claim, pointing out that their tiny village sits at Peru's exact geographical center. A plaque in the ground marks the spot—but the town's physical position is not the reason to visit. People travel to Puerto Bermúdez in search of a small albergue that has become the hottest budget jungle lodge in the country. This lodge runs excursions into the hungry jungle, where lush vegetation, indigenous communities and rolling hills await—all beyond the constant tourist flow that characterizes more established destinations like Iquitos and Manú.

In ▨**Albergue Humboldt,** two English-speaking men from Spain have created one of the most welcoming jungle experiences in Peru. Raúl and Jesús cook delicious Spanish food and organize treks into the nearby jungle while backpackers discuss travel experiences in their quiet library, comfortable hammocks, and spotless rooms. Humboldt's personalized trips range from a one-day waterfall visit to a week-long expedition to a 10-day boat trip to Cusco; Ashaninka Indians act as guides, as they know the jungle better than anyone else. Raúl and Jesús will also give you any information you need to arrange your own expedition. To reach Albergue Humboldt, walk all the way down Castillo; follow the road downhill and past the river. The Albergue is on the left, but it is unmarked and can be hard to find. (☎720 290 or 720 291; in Lima ☎427 91 96 or 428 55 46. Mototaxi s/ 1.5. Rooms s/15 per person; 3 meals s/15. Reasonable expedition prices vary according to the trip. Two days with 2 people US$30 per person per day; prices decrease with more people or longer treks.) There is little reason to spend the night elsewhere in Puerto Bermúdez, though the town does have some remarkably nice hotels. The best is the **Hostal Residencial Tania,** at Castillo and Oxapampa, 3 blocks down from the intersection. Villa-like inside and out, the hotel has clean white floral sheets, large windows, and shiny baths in each room. (Singles s/15; doubles s/20.)

Bus companies cluster at the intersection of **Remigio Norales** and **Alameda Ramón Castillo.** Transdife and Villa Rica, on opposite sides of Castillo above the intersection, both send trucks to **La Merced** (Oct.-Mar. 7-8hr., Apr.-Sept. 8-10hr.; 4am; s/25-35). Colectivos leave from the intersection to **Palcazú** (2½hr., leaving when full after 6am, s/10), where there are connections to **Pucallpa.** Castillo, the main street, shelters most of the town's services, few of which have addresses. There is **no currency exchange or post office** in Puerto Bermúdez. Services include: a **market,** on the third block on the right heading down Castillo; a **hospital,** 200m beyond the bus companies heading up Castillo; the **police,** 200m past the hospital on Castillo; and several **telephones,** two on Norales and a third at Hostal Pinto, on Oxapampa.

WOLFGANG, PERU; PERU, WOLFGANG. Once

upon a time, back in the 19th century, central Europe had a desperate situation on her hands. Up in the Tirol mountains, there wasn't enough land to go around. Even more serious, Austrian law prohibited the landless from marrying, which was leaving some young people very frustrated. Meanwhile, in a mountainous South American country worlds away, the government was trying to develop colonies in its jungle highlands. So, the government (Peru's, of course) hired a German baron living in Lima to bring his farmers to its land. The Baron returned home and gathered 200 landless Austrians and Germans, who were—by that time—more than happy to join his colonization project. The 300 embarked on a four-month journey across the Atlantic, stopping only briefly, for an on-board mass wedding. When they finally arrived in Peru, the settlers were dismayed to discover that there was no road to the jungle. Some decided to sample urban life and stayed in Lima. The rest set about building a road themselves. They reached Pozuzo two years later—in just a little more time than the trip takes now.

OXAPAMPA   ☎064

That little more than the surrounding mountain ridges produced prosperous Oxapampa comes as something of a surprise. It, after all, is no backwoods town, what with the cruising combis, elegant clothing stores, and—showing the influence of the German-Austrian settlement nearby—sporadically teutonic architecture. But while Oxapampa may surprise its surroundings, the mountains are no shock to the city. Farming and cattle industries support Oxapampa, and the backbone of its prosperity is its delicious yogurt and cheese, sold in markets around town but cultivated in the hills.

The **Río Chontabamba** and the **Río La Esperanza** border Oxapampa. Commercial **Bolognesi** runs past the **Plaza de Armas;** perpendicular **Bolívar** houses many bus agencies. Expreso Moderno, Bolívar 470, sends buses to **Lima** (12hr., 4:30pm, s/25) via **La Merced** (3hr., s/7), **Tarma** (5hr., s/12), and **La Oroya** (6hr., s/18). Empresa La Merced, Bolognesi 198 (☎762 133), on the Plaza de Armas, also sends buses to Lima (11hr., 5pm, s/25) via **La Merced** (3hr., s/8), **Tarma** (5hr., s/15), and **La Oroya** (8hr., s/20). Empresa Santa Rosa, San Martín Block 4 (☎762 516), sends colectivos to **Pozuzo** (3hr., 8:30am and 1pm, s/8), **La Merced** (3hr., every 35min. 4am-5pm, s/8), and **Chontabamba** (15min., leaving when full, s/1). Selva Central (☎762 033), 100m off the Plaza de Armas, on Bolognesi, sends colectivos to **Pozuzo** (3½hr.; 7, 10am, and 2pm; s/10). Transporte Oxapampa, Bolívar 248, sends cars to **Huancabamba** (1hr., leaving when full, s/3) and **Quillazu** (15min., leaving when full, s/1.5). In the same location, Perene sends combis to **La Merced** (3hr., every 30min. 3:30am-6pm, s/7) and Villa Rica sends combis to **Villa Rica** (4hr.; 11am, 3, and 5pm; s/8), from where one can connect to **Puerto Bermúdez.** Services include: a **tourist office,** offices 22-1 on the second floor of the galería (from the plaza, walk down Bolognesi toward the Banco and take the first right, and the galería is on the left after the market; ☎762 375; open M-Sa 8am-1pm and 3-5pm); **Banco de Crédito,** Bolívar 310 ($12 commission on traveler's checks; ☎762 213; open M-F 9:15am-1:15pm and 4:30-6:30pm); the **police,** 338 Bottger (☎762 217, emergency ☎105); a **hospital,** across from the police station on Bottger; a **24-hour pharmacy,** Bolognesi 218; **Serpost,** Castillo 205 (open M-Sa 9am-noon and 2-8pm); and a **telephone office,** Bolognesi 176, on the plaza (☎/fax 762 034; open daily 7am-11pm).

Pension Mama Zilia, Thomas Schauz 546, is the best deal in town—but hard to find. From the plaza, walk down Castillo toward the Municipalidad and take a left on Schauz; Mama Zilia is the unmarked, two-and-a-half-story building on the right with the triangular roof. You'll feel right at home as you settle into the cozy, eaved rooms in this large wooden house. (☎762 454. Rooms s/7 per person. 3 meals s/10, more for special diets.) **Hospedaje Don Calucho,** San Martín 411, is a more typical establishment. With green striped sheets, big windows, and private pink-tiled baths, Don Calucho leaves little to be desired—except, perhaps, for the removal of the roosters out back. (☎762 109. Rooms s/15 per person.) Just up the road, **Hospedaje Rocio,** San Martín 463, manages to be cheap without being sordid. Rooms are small but neat, and it's not hard to overlook the slightly blemished walls. The private baths, however, range from small to smaller. (☎762 163. Singles s/5, with bath s/10, with bath and TV s/20; doubles with bath s/15, with hot bath s/20.)

NEAR OXAPAMPA: PARQUE NACIONAL YANACHAGA-CHEMILLÉN

Pozuzo-bound colectivos pass through the park (1½hr., s/5).

Between Oxapampa and Pozuzo sits 122,000-hectare Parque Nacional Yanachaga-Chemillén, one of Peru's largest and most beautiful cloud forests. Host to countless waterfalls, birds, and flowers, the park is an excellent locale for birdwatching or hiking. Unfortunately, as it has no tourist resources, this is an area for independent exploration. The **park office** in Oxapampa can provide more information.

AMAZON BASIN

NEAR OXAPAMPA: POZUZO

Empresa Santa Rosa, San Martín Block 4, sends colectivos to Pozuzo (3½hr., 8:30am and 1pm, s/8), as does Selva Central, 100m off the Plaza de Armas, on Bolognesi (3½hr.; 7, 10am, and 2pm; s/10). Transport Pozuzo colectivos return to Oxapampa (4, 8, 11am, and 2pm); Selva Central (4, 11:30am, and 2pm).

Fertile Huancabamba River Valley mountains surround tiny, temperate Pozuzo, a beautiful village that attracts visitors for reasons besides its beauty. Pozuzo's draw is its novel position as the only German-Austrian community in Peru. Blond-haired, blue-eyed children play with their darker counterparts, and some of the older people still speak German. But it is the architecture, typical Peruvian houses dispersed among tall white buildings that look like they were transplanted from Bavaria, that is truly unique. Although Pozuzo has no tourist office, the **Museo Schafferer,** 400m past the plaza down Los Colonos, provides a thorough history of the region. The entrance is around back and on the 2nd floor, but you'll probably have to get the key from the woman who lives in the house behind the museum. Many of the displays are in German, the rest in Spanish. (Open daily 9am-5pm. s/2, Peruvian students s/1, children s/1.50.) Pozuzo comes alive during the last week of July, at the annual **festival** that celebrates the city's founding. Parades, typical food, characteristic clothes (typical and characteristic Peruvian-Austrian-German, that is), rodeos, and the crowning of the Queen of Pozuzo draw hoards of visitors—hotel reservations should be made in advance. Perhaps at **Hospedaje Maldonado,** one and a half blocks up Av. de los Colones from the plaza—the spacious rooms have floors so clean you could eat off them. (☎707 003. Rooms s/10 per person.) Another good option is **Recreo Hospedaje el Mango,** on Pacificación, three blocks down Av. de los Colones past the creek and take a right at the hospital, so named because of the mango tree in the yard. (☎707 028. Rooms s/10 per person.)

LA MERCED ☎064

For years isolated by the threat of terrorism, La Merced cultivated oranges and coffee (rather than hiking trails or tourist lodges) in the surrounding Chanchamayo Valley. As a result, today's city is too busy to worry about travelers. Motos race through the narrow, curving streets and the market swirls with activity, but visitors have not yet beaten a path through the leafy Plaza de Armas. Those now trickling in find a lively, orange-scented space on the border of the jungle—amid hills awaiting exploration.

▐ ◪ TRANSPORTATION AND PRACTICAL INFORMATION. La Merced sits on hills overlooking the **Río Tambopata**. The **Plaza de Armas** lies four blocks up from the river and is bordered by **Tarma** and **Palca** (parallel to the river) and **Junín** and **Ancash** (perpendicular to the river). Buses leave from and arrive at the **terminal,** seven blocks down the twisty Tarma. Many services lie along **2 de Mayo,** one block from the plaza, parallel to Junín. **Buses** from the terminal go to **Lima** (7hr., 9 per day 7:45-10am and 8-9:45pm, s/15-18) often via **Tarma** (1½-2hr., s/5-6) and **La Oroya** (3hr., s/10); **Huancayo** (4½-5hr., 7 per day 8:45-10:30am and 8:45-10pm, s/10-13); **Satipo** (2½-3hr.; 11:30am, noon, 11:30pm; s/8); **Huánuco** (7hr., 9:45pm, s/25); **Tingo María** (10hr., Tu and Sa 9:45pm, s/35); **Ayacucho** (14hr., 9:15am, s/35); **Puerto Bermúdez** (8hr., 3 per day 3:30-4:30am, s/30-35); and **Palcazu** (10hr., 3:30 and 4:30am, s/40), the place for connections to **Pucallpa.** Frequent **colectivos** leave when full and head to **Huancayo** (5hr., s/13) via **Tarma** (1½hr., s/6); **Satipo** (2½hr., 4am-9pm, s/13); **Oxapampa** (2½-3hr., s/8); and **Pichanaki** (2hr., s/4-5). Colectivos to **San Ramon** cluster on Junín, toward the hill. **Mototaxis** cruise the streets; most rides around town cost less than s/1. Services include: **Banco de Crédito,** on the plaza at Tarma and Junín (Visa **ATM; ☎**531 005; open M-F 8:15am-1:15pm and 4:30-6:30pm, Sa 9:30am-12:30pm); a **market,** two blocks downhill from the plaza between Ancash and Junín (open daily 6am-5pm); the **police** (☎531 292, emergency ☎105), three blocks down Junín, then two blocks to the left on Pirola; a **hospital,** Tarma 140 (☎531 002); a

telephone office, across from the post office (☎ 532 388; open M-F 8:30am-1pm and 2:30-6pm); **Internet access** at Cafe Internet Swiss System, Arica 409, office 301, two blocks up Junín and then two blocks to the right on Arica (s/4 per hr.; ☎ 531 661; open daily 8am-midnight); and **Serpost,** on 2 de Mayo between Arica and Pirola (☎ 531 174; open M-Sa 8am-1pm and 3-6pm).

███ **ACCOMMODATIONS AND FOOD.** There are many inexpensive hotels in La Merced but no great values. **Hostal Villa Dorada,** Pirola 265, three blocks up Junín and one block to the left, has good-sized rooms with similarly large windows. Unfortunately, some windows open onto the hostel's hallways, which offer little but a dim fluorescent glow. (☎ 531 221. Singles s/10, with bath s/20; doubles s/20, with bath s/25.) The modern facade at **Hotel Cosmos,** one block from Villa Dorada, on Pirola near Pauni, hides wooden bedframes and almost-parquet floors. (☎ 531 051. Doubles with bath s/20; triples with bath s/30.) **Hospedaje Santa Rosa,** 2 de Mayo 447, is one block down Palca (with the river on your left) and one to the left. Springing for a private bathroom will mean less time in Santa Rosa's dank corridors. Big windows and wooden furniture brighten up the rooms. (☎ 531 012. Singles s/10, with bath s/15; doubles s/15, with bath s/20; triples s/20, with bath s/25.)

La Merced's restaurant situation resembles its hotel situation: many contestants, but no prizewinners. There are a couple of chicken places along Tarma, and the Plaza de Armas houses a few touristy places that offer good traditional food in a clean setting. Cheap meals await at the **jugerías** in the market, two blocks down Tarma from the plaza (with the hill on your left). Sandwiches (s/1-2), juices (s/1-2), and desserts (s/1) are easy to find. (Open daily 6am-midnight.)

██ **SIGHTS AND ACTIVITIES.** La Merced is not laden with conventional sights. However, it is an aesthetically pleasing city; two blocks down from the Plaza de Armas, past the market, a **park** affords relaxation. Similar activities take place at the end of Lima (parallel to Palca), away from the terminal, where the street becomes a pedestrian walkway with benches that overlook a fantastic view of the river. Ashaninka natives usually sell their **artesanía** in the Plaza de Armas. **Tsiriski Tours,** Tarma 408 (☎ 689 656; email andrecaceres@hotmail.com), half block off the main plaza, offers three one-day excursions to **Oxapampa** (10hr., s/45), **Perene** (8hr., s/40) and the **Chanchamayo Valley** (5hr., s/35). Prices include all costs except food. The **La Merced Festival** is held the last week in September.

NEAR LA MERCED: SAN RAMÓN

Colectivos to San Ramón (15min., leaving when full, s/1) depart from Junín, one block uphill from the Banco de Crédito. In San Ramón, colectivos stop at the Plaza de Armas.

Slightly more than 10km back toward Lima, La Merced's sibling city isn't much different from its bigger sister. Though a little less vibrant, San Ramón holds potential points of interest for the traveler, and it's only a short colectivo ride away. A visit to the **Tirol Waterfall** near San Ramón provides a welcome excuse for a walk in the jungle, albeit not be a solitary one; the falls are popular among foreigners and Peruvians alike. A beautiful 30-minute walk takes you along a marked path next to the river (which can get prohibitively muddy during the rainy season). A mini-waterfall along the way foreshadows Tirol, but you'll know when you reach the actual falls, which are 60m high. It's possible to swim in the pool below. To get to the walk's starting point, take a mototaxi to *"Catarata Tirol"* (15min., s/4). There's a s/1 admission fee collected on the path. San Ramón's **tourist office,** Pardo 110, provides information about other waterfalls. (☎ 331 265. Open M-F 8am-1pm and 2:30-6pm). For more aquatic fun, Centro Recreacional Miguel Angel, at the end of Paucartambo, has a sparkling **swimming pool.** (☎ 331 769. Open Tu-Su 9am-6pm. s/2, children s/1; swimsuit rental s/1.) The best value in San Ramón is probably **Hostal Chanchamayo,** Progreso 291, two blocks from the Plaza de Armas. The rooms' wooden doors and windows almost make up for the lack of sunlight. (☎ 331 008. Singles s/10, with bath s/30; doubles s/20, with bath s/40; triples s/30.)

SATIPO
☎ **064**

Perched on the edge of the jungle 441km northeast of Lima, dusty Satipo offers little in the way of appearances—beyond its remarkably symmetrical Plaza de Armas, that is. With its prosperity level linked to current coffee prices, things haven't been looking too good for Satipo recently. Still, the city environs hide all sorts of natural treasures, and this market town can provide a glimpse of life along the frontier that is rapidly closing in on the Peruvian jungle.

⊞ℤ TRANSPORTATION AND PRACTICAL INFORMATION. Satipo rests along the **Río Satipo** and centers on the **Plaza de Armas.** Agusto Leguia and Francisco Irazto border the plaza and run (almost) parallel to the river; Colonos Fundadores and Manuel Prado intersect them. The **market** spans the area around Fundadores between the plaza and the river. **Combis** go to **Pichanaki** (1¼hr., leaving when full, s/4), where other combis leave for La Merced, from the river end of Fundadores. **Mototaxis** cruise the streets and charge under s/1 within the city. All **buses** go through La Merced on their way to other destinations. Molina Union, San Martín 468 (☎ 545 895), goes to **Lima** (9hr., 8pm, s/20) via **La Merced** (2½hr., s/12), **Tarma** (3½hr., s/12) and **La Oroya** (4½hr., s/18); and to **Huancayo** (7hr., 8:30pm, s/15). Selva Tours, Prado 425 (☎ 545 825), also goes to **Huancayo** (7-8hr.; 6, 7am, and 7pm; s/15) via **Tarma** (5hr., s/12). Libretadore, Leguia 330 (☎ 545 321), goes to **Lima** (10½hr., 7pm, s/22). Lobato (☎ 545 599), at Agusto Hilser and Los Incas, sends fancy buses to **Lima** (10hr., 7:30pm, s/20) and **Huancayo** (8hr.; 8:45am, 8, and 8:45pm; s/15). Turismo Central, Los Incas 325 (☎ 546 016), goes to **Huancayo** (6hr., 8pm, s/15) and **Lima** (8hr., 7pm, s/20). Leon de Huánuco, Prado 459 (☎ 545 291), goes to **Huánuco** (10-11hr., 7pm, s/30). Transfer, Prado 457 (☎ 545 401), goes to **Puerto Ocopa** (3hr.; 7am, 12:45, 3:30pm; s/8). The **tourist office,** Fundadores 312, is in the Municipalidad building on the Plaza de Armas. (Open M-F 8am-1pm and 2-4:30pm.) However, Henry Ginés, at **Expediciones Turísticas,** Fundadores 519, is the unofficial head of tourism in Satipo. (☎ 545 254; email henryginés@hotmail.com. Open daily 8am-8pm.) Other services include: **Banco de Crédito,** Prado 243, off the plaza ($12 minimum commission for traveler's checks; Visa ATM; ☎ 545 662; open M-F 9:15-1:15pm and 4:30-6:30pm, Sa 9:30am-12:30pm); the **police,** Leguia 638 (☎ 545 398 or 545 125); a **hospital,** Daniel Carrion 398 (☎ 545 045 or 546 015), three blocks down Leguia toward the Municipalidad, then one to the left; **Central Telefónica,** Irazola 253 (☎/fax 545 523 or 555 512; open daily 6am-11pm); **Internet access** at LGV Hardware and Software, Fundadores 450 (s/7 per hr.; ☎ 545 275 or 545 653; email lgvhys@terra.com.pe; open daily 8:30am-10:30pm); and **Serpost,** Fundadores 324, on the Plaza de Armas (☎ 545 963; open M-Sa 8am-1pm and 3-6pm).

▐▐▐ ACCOMMODATIONS AND FOOD. Some of Satipo's hotels are cheap in price and quality; others cost more—with good reason. **Hostal Residencial Colonos,** Fundadores 572, 2½ blocks down from the plaza, comes closest to combining the two categories. Sure there's paint chipping off the ceiling, but where else can you get private baths, cable TV, and embossed towels at this price? Ask for a room on the street if you mind stuffiness more than noise. (☎ 545 155. Singles s/16; doubles s/25.) **Hostal El Palmero,** Prado 228 (☎ 545 020), one block from the plaza, right over the market, counts noise potential as its only fault. Bright peach hallways lead to rooms with cable TV, baths, and some balconies—all spotless. (Laundry and restaurant services. Singles s/15, with bath s/25-30; doubles s/28, with bath s/45.) To get to **Hostal Trujillo,** Grau 277, one of the cheapest hotels in Satipo, take Leguia toward Serpost for two blocks, then go left. The house looks mid-construction, but the rooms themselves don't seem affected. (Singles s/8; doubles s/14.) Hungry? Countless chicken places radiate from the plaza, and cheap *menú* places stretch along Los Incas, near Irazola.

⊞ ⬛ SIGHTS AND ENTERTAINMENT. There's not much to do in Satipo, but **Recreo Turisto Laguna Blanca**, at Km2 on the road leading to La Merced outside of town, provides a nice way to spend a day. Have some *cuy* (s/10) or *cerveza* (s/ 4.5) on the picnic tables or next to the pool. Between the fields and the palm trees, it's easy to forget that the busy city exists. (☎ 545 796. Moto s/1. Entrees s/6-10. Open daily 11am-9:30pm. Pool s/2, children s/1. Camping s/5 per tent.) Other attractions lie outside the city. **Cataratas de Shiriari and Arco Iris** lie between Satipo and Puerto Ocopa. To get there, take a Puerto Ocopa-bound combi to the waterfalls (1½hr., s/6), then ask for directions for the short walk. In **Puerto Ocopa** itself there is a mission and a native community, as well as the Río Tumbo, which offers an additional set of attractions, including the 160m Catarata de Kaori two hours down river. Combis to Puerto Ocopa (3hr.; 7am, 12:45, and 3:30pm; s/8) leave from Transfer, Prado 457. In town, the one-room **Museo Particular Ruben Callegari,** Irazola 791, seven blocks from the plaza, displays Callegari's grand butterfly collection, some miscellaneous stuffed animals, and fossils. (☎ 545 152. Open daily whenever the family's awake. s/2.)

QUILLABAMBA ☎ 084

A panoramic mountain view dominates the sleepy city of Quillabamba, although the humid jungle air makes a joke of the snowy hills to the south. Despite its climate, however, some travelers remark that Quillabamba doesn't feel like a jungle town. After all, the tropical vegetation in the immediate area has long since been cleared away—one has to delve deeper into the *selva* to find that. The park at the base of Libertad does afford a glimpse of the **Río Vilcanota;** for a closer look, try the well-kept **Sambaray complex,** 2km north of town. Although the river rushes rapidly here, some swimmers brave the current for a dip in the Vilcanota's shining waters. Weekends can bring crowds. Colectivos (15min., s/0.50) leave frequently from the upper corner of the Plaza Grau. Open daily 7am-6pm.

Wedged between the **Río Chuyapi** and the **Río Vilcanota** (which flows into the Urubamba), Quillabamba's small center slopes down toward the east. Two central squares orient the city: the hectic, irregularly shaped **Plaza Grau,** and the shady **Plaza de Armas,** two blocks away. The terminal is on **25 de Julio,** several blocks south of the Plaza Grau. **Buses** run to: **Cusco** (9hr., 16 per day 8am-7:30pm, s/15) via **Ollantaytambo** (7½hr., s/12); **Abancay** (5hr., 6:30am, s/13); **Arequipa** (20hr., 6:30pm, s/ 35); **Juliaca** (10hr., 8am and 6pm, s/30); and **Puno** (10hr., 8am and 6pm, s/30); **Kiteni** (6-8hr., 10am and 5pm, s/10); and **Tinti** (8-12hr., 5pm, s/15). **Trucks** to **Kiteni** (8-10hr., s/7) and **Tinti** (11-15hr., s/10) also pick up passengers in the area. **Taxis** cost s/1-2 anywhere in town. Services include: **Banco de Crédito,** Libertad 545, one block uphill from the Plaza de Armas (open M-F 9:15am-1:15pm and 4:30-6:30pm, Sa 9:30am-12:30pm); the **police,** Libertad 545, on the Plaza de Armas; a **hospital,** on Gamarra, at Grau; 24-hour **Internet access,** at Hostal Don Carlos, Libertad 556, across from Banco de Crédito (☎281 150; s/10 per hr.); and **Serpost,** Libertad 115, on the Plaza de Armas (☎/fax 281 086; open M-Sa 8am-8pm, Su 8am-1pm).

Quillabamba's hotels cater more to traveling businessmen than to backpacking tourists, but at least they're cheap. **Hostal Cusco,** Cusco 223 (☎281 161), half a block from the Plaza Grau, features spacious—if somewhat spartan—chambers. (Singles s/15; doubles s/20; triples s/30.) Quieter and less central is **Hostal Alto Urubamba,** 2 de Mayo 333 (☎281 131; fax 281 570), a block north (right if you're facing uphill) of the Plaza de Armas, between Espinar and Pio Concha. (Singles s/18, with bath s/30; doubles s/25, with bath s/40; triples s/35, with bath s/60.)

NEAR QUILLABAMBA: EL PONGO DE MAINIQUE

To reach Ivachote, take a Tinti-bound bus (8-12hr., 5pm, s/7) or truck (11-15hr., s/10) from Palma, just off Grau. Alternatively, one could take one of the more frequent buses, also leaving from Palma, to Kiteni (6-8hr., 3 per day, s/10) and wait there (probably for a while) for a truck to Tinti (3-5hr., s/4). Most trucks depart Kiteni between 2 and 4am when they depart at all, leaving passengers at Tinti's dock (just downhill from where the trucks

AMAZON BASIN

stop) in time to catch a morning boat (45min., s/30) to Ivachote. Most returning canoes leave Ivachote in the morning as well, and buses and trucks to Quillabamba depart from Tinti around noon. The nearest hostels lie in Kiteni. It's possible to commission boats in Kiteni for the Pongo trip, but the extra distance (and the "little Pongo" along the way) will add to the cost.

Three hundred rough kilometers farther into the jungle, El Pongo's narrow gorge and boiling whitewater take a mere 15 minutes to navigate. The cheapest place to find boats to El Pongo is **Ivachote,** 200km from Quillabamba and 90km from the Pongo. There are no hostels in this tiny riverside village, but it should be safe to camp on the beach with a group. From here, occasional boats head to **Sepahua** (1-6 days, depending on the type of motor; 1-4 per month; s/30-100), the first large settlement beyond El Pongo. Boats back are just as infrequent, although Sepahua's small airport offers an alternate means of escape. In order to avoid waits longer that the duration of your visa, you can rent a canoe to take you through the rapids and then bring you back up (3hr. each way; the fuel for the journey costs about s/200—expect to pay more for the boatman's services). Keep in mind that the Pongo is dangerous at any time of year (prohibitively so in the rainy season) and that boats in Ivachote are unlikely to have helmets or life jackets for passenger use. Undeterred? Well, the gorge—30m at its widest point, its 60m high rock walls overhung with jungle flora—is stunning indeed. In Kiteni, the clean **Hostal Kamisea,** one of the last buildings on the road to Quillabamba, perches above an attractive river beach and features running water (although no lights: such is the case in all of Kiteni's lodgings) and clean common baths (doubles s/12). At the other end of town, **Hostal Kiteni's** sheetless, plant-and-plastic-partitioned chambers have the advantage of a view of the truck and bus stop (singles s/5).

MANÚ BIOSPHERE RESERVE

Situated at the confluence of the Manú and Alto Madre de Dios Rivers, Manú National Park has been declared both a World Biosphere Reserve (by UNESCO in 1977) and a World Heritage Site (by the International Union for Conservation of Nature in 1987) and is one of the largest reserve parks in all of South America. Its largely untouched primary and secondary forests contain 13 species of monkeys, 100 types of bats, 200 different mammals, 1000 kinds of birds, and an astounding 3228 named species of plants (with another nearly 12,000 species yet unlabeled). The fact that the area spans elevations from 300 to 3450m—encompassing lowland rainforest, cloud forest, and the scrubby vegetation of the high Andes—makes such a high variety of life forms possible.

HOT DAMN! Most people's jungle phobias revolve around lions and tigers and bears—or jaguars and pumas, at any rate. Contrary to tour company propaganda, however, your chances of encountering a cat strolling through the rainforest are about as great as a sudden cold spell. *Friajes* blow through... just not very often. But don't breathe easy yet; there are dangers in the jungle you never dreamed of. The skinny Tangarana tress looks innocuous enough from a distance. Get a little closer, and you may notice any eerie sort of clearing, perfectly circular, around the tree's base. Just don't get *too* close: a mere tap on its trunk will call out legions of fire ants. These tiny, sting-packing red critters live inside the Tangarana, and they work hard to protect it. They'll attack—and usually kill—any parasite or animal that dares scale their tree. In years past, the ants sometimes served as juries for indigenous communities, who would strap accused criminals to a Tangarana. If a criminal lived, he was guilty (and therefore needed to be executed). If the fire ants killed him (it's said to take 100 stings), alas! he was innocent. (For more bizarre jungle fauna, see Further Fearsome Fauna, p. 291.)

HISTORY. While most people know that the Spanish never conquered Machu Picchu, far fewer realize that one of the areas of Peru not conquered by the Incas was Manú. Few outsiders disturbed the native Machiguenguas, Kugapakoris, Amahuacas, or Wachipaeris, all tribes who still inhabit parts of Manú, until the **rubber barons** arrived at the end of the 19th century. Those less-than-socially-conscious men decimated much of the forest and many of the communities along its rivers—until the boom went bust and they left Manú to mend itself. Almost half a century later, an ambitious **Swede logger** built the first road into Manú, and the next cycle of exploitation began. The road brought not only loggers but poachers as well. Ironically, it was one of those poachers, a taxidermist named Celestino Kalinowski, who recognized Manú's precious **biodiversity** and petitioned the government to protect the area. In 1973, Peru declared Manú a national park.

Today, three "zones" combine to form Manú: the **cultural zone,** the **reserve zone,** and what is commonly referred to as the **impenetrable zone.** This last area occupies the space of the original national park, and only people native to the area and scientists with special permission may access it. Aerial photographic evidence suggests that it houses two tribes who have never had any (recorded) contact with other peoples. The other two zones joined Manú as buffer states at the time of UNESCO's 1977 declaration. In the inhabited cultural zone, there are few restrictions; residents may live (and hunt) as they please. Though uninhabited, the reserve zone welcomes visitors—provided they bring US$35 and a licensed guide. It is this zone that offers the best chance—maybe in all of the Peruvian jungle—to see animals, and it is this zone that makes Manú so prohibitively expensive.

TAKING A TOUR. Independent travelers cannot enter Manú's reserve zone; you can visit only with a **registered tour operator.** (For a list of registered tour operators, see **Guided Tours from Cusco,** p. 111.) And while this area does rank among the most pristine forests in the world, the expense may not be worth it, especially for those seeking isolation. In parts of July and August, the reserve zone gets downright **crowded.** Everyone pays through the nose for a "small" group, but many companies send out multiple "small" groups at once. And since Manú's reserve zone contains only one primary waterway and a limited trail system, groups meet frequently. Guides must rush their groups along to beat others to the best campsite, or to be the first boat on the river (for the best wildlife-spotting chances). At the busiest times, slow groups do suffer—guides must book sessions on the **Lake Salvador catamaran** and the 20m **Lake Otorongo observation tower** when entering the reserve zone; latecomers may find that there are no spaces left.

Aside from the occasional rush to get there first, trips to Manú move at a very, very slow pace. Travel time dominates the trips: many of them spend far more time in transit to the reserve than actually in it. Of course, this is guided travel time, and the hours on the river actually offer a greater chance to see animals than on a walk though the forest. In any case, trips to Manú involve a great deal of sitting still. Finally, although Manú probably does offer the best chance to see animals in all the Peruvian jungle, chances remain slim even here. Most visitors will see tons of **birds,** with **monkeys** and **caimans** (a type of alligator that can grow to 7m) possibilities as well. When they're not off hunting for food, the **giant otters** in Lake Salvador often greet passersby too. But it is the bird-watcher or botanist who will most enjoy Manú, and one thing the tours' high prices do provide is very knowledgeable guides, who can tell you all about the passing flora and avian life.

GOING IT ALONE. More adventuresome travelers (with a good deal of time to spare) can explore the Manú area, even though the reserve zone remains off-limits. From **Shintuya** (the end of the road from Cusco), cargo canoes head downstream to **Boca Manú** (6-9hr., no more than s/20) about once per week from May to November. From Boca Manú, similarly frequent canoes continue down the Madre de Dios to **Boca Colorado** (6-9hr., s/20), from where it's another day's journey to **Laberinto,**

near Puerto Maldonado. One could also commission a canoe (US$400-600 for 12m) and paddles (s/25 each) in the boat-building town of Boca Manú, although this might take up to a month. None of these towns possess very desirable, if any, accommodations; it's best to have a tent and sleeping bag. Beaches far more attractive than the few available hostels speckle the river banks. **Vampire bats** do live in this region, though, so it's not so wise to sleep outside.

At **Blanquillo,** a few hours downriver from Boca Manú, a series of trails winds through the jungle. Some lead to **Cocha Camungo,** on which floats a catamaran (actually more of a platform) similar to the one in the reserve zone at Cocha Salvador. As Blanquillo is unregulated, however, anyone with a few paddles can take this one out for a spin. (Do not swim: Camungo hosts both hungry piranhas and territorial giant otters.) Discerning the entrance to the trails can be difficult, but you may be able to find a boatman in Boca Manú who can point them out. On the downside, while independent travelers will undoubtedly spot hundreds of birds and trees, most won't understand much about them without a guide. One of the tour company Pantiacolla's most knowledgeable guides, **Tina Forster** (email tfold-spice@yahoo.com) runs tours for independent groups through the cloud forest, Manú cultural zone, and Blanquillo area—when she's free. Omitting the reserve zone enables cheaper prices (7-days, 6-nights US$320 per person with min. 5 people and max. 8) and more exploratory, off-trail trekking.

PUERTO MALDONADO ☎ 084

Billed as the "Biodiversity Capital of the World," Puerto Maldonado has built quite a name for itself in the tourism industry. The town's position as the primary jumping-off point for the vast Tambopata-Candamo Reserve Zone—which includes the Bahuaja-Sonene National Park and Las Pampas de Heath National Sanctuary—enables it to draw a larger proportion of visitors than any other corner of Peru's jungle. This heavy traffic, however, affects the 25km of park trails far more than the town's four paved streets. So many companies whisk their clients straight from the airport to waiting boats that Puerto Maldonado's humid languor remains largely undisturbed.

▐ TRANSPORTATION

Flights: Aeropuerto Internacional Padre Aldamiz Puerto Maldonado (☎571 531), 7km outside the city. Nurses with **needles** await disembarking passengers not vaccinated against the deadly yellow fever. **AeroContinente,** León Velarde 506 (☎573 702), south of 2 de Mayo. Open M-Sa 8am-9pm, Su 9am-noon and 5-8pm. To **Cusco** (30min.; Tu, Th, F, Sa, Su 8:30am; US$49-59). **AeroCondor,** León Velarde 545 (☎571 669), south of 2 de Mayo. Open M-F 7am-9pm. To **Cusco** (1hr., M-Sa 8:30am, US$39). **Santander,** 2 de Mayo 294 (☎573 120), near León Velarde. Open M-Sa 8am-9pm. To **Cusco** (1hr., 1 per day M-F 9:30-11:30am, US$39). **Tans,** at Cusco and Velarde. To **Cusco** and **Lima** (US$48). Open M-Sa 8am-9pm, Su 9am-1:30pm.

Trucks: Trucks to **Cusco** (2-4 days, 4-5 per week, s/20-30) leave from Ernesto Rivero, half a block south of the market.

Buses: Buses to **Laberinto** (2hr., every hr. 5:30am-6pm, s/5) leave from Ica, near Ernesto Rivero. From Laberinto, boats run to **Boca Colorado** (6-8hr., several per week, s/30-40) and from there to **Boca Manú** (4½hr., 1-2 per week, s/30-40).

Boats: Boats head from Puerto Maldonado's Río Madre de Dios port, at the end of Arequipa to **Puerto Paldo** at the **Bolivian border** (2hr. with outboard motor, 4hr. in a peke-peke canoe; several per week; s/15-20). The **Capitania de Puerto** (☎571 084), at the corner of Billinghurst and Arequipa, has destination and departure information.

Taxis: *Mototaxis* cost s/3-4 from the airport, s/1-2 anywhere in town.

Moped Rental: Take your pick on Prado, between Belarde and Puno. s/3.50 per hr.

BORDER CROSSING: INTO BOLIVIA

If you're planning to cross into Bolivia at **Puerto Pardo/Puerto Heath,** you need to get an exit stamp on your passport from the Peruvian police in Puerto Maldonado. From Puerto Maldonado, it's a five-hour peke-peke canoe ride down the Río Madre de Dios to Puerto Pardo (s/20-30). There is little bureaucracy (or infrastructure) at the Puerto Pardo crossing; just wait for the next canoe to Puerto Heath, Bolivia and then cross the border.

ORIENTATION AND PRACTICAL INFORMATION

Puerto Maldonado's streets form a straightforward grid pattern. The major roads are paved. **Leon Velarde** runs from the **Río Madre de Dios,** through the **Plaza de Armas,** past the post office, several kilometers farther southeast to a port on the **Río Tambopata.** Two blocks from the Plaza de Armas, **2 de Mayo** runs perpendicular to Velarde and goes all the way to the airport.

Consulate: Bolivia, on Loreto, at the Plaza de Armas. Open M-F mornings.

Currency Exchange: Banco de Crédito, Carrion 201 (☎571 001), on the Plaza de Armas. Open M-F 9:20am-1:30pm and 4:30-6:30pm, Sa 9:30am-12:30pm. **Banco de la Nación** gives MC advances. Open M-F 9:30am-1:30pm and 4:30-6:30pm, Sa 9:30am-12:30pm.

Market: Mercado Modelo, bordered by Ica, Ernesto Rivero, Fitzcarrald and Piura; 8 blocks from the Río Madre de Dios and 6 from the Tambopata.

Emergency: ☎105.

Police: Carrion 410 (☎571 022), at Puno, 1 block inland from the plaza.

Hospital: (☎571 127), on Cajamarca off Velarde.

Telephones: Phone booths cluster around the Plaza de Armas. **Telefónica del Perú,** Puno 670 (☎571 600), between Prado and Truncoso. Open M-F 8am-4:30pm.

Post Office: Serpost, Velarde 675 (☎/fax 571 088), at Truncoso. Open M-Sa 7:45am-8:15pm, Su 7:45am-3pm.

ACCOMMODATIONS

Hostal Moderno, Billinghurst 359 (☎571 063), at the end of Velarde, 1 block past the plaza. Clean clapboard rooms. Family-oriented. A little courtyard restaurant provides huge meals (s/3). Singles s/10; doubles s/17; triples s/25.

Hostal Cahuata, Fitzcarrald 517 (☎571 526), across from the market between Rivero and Piura. Dark, quiet, and tidy. Singles s/10, with bath and fan s/20; doubles s/20, with bath and fan s/30.

Hostal Tambo de Oro, 2 de Mayo 277 (☎572 057), between Velarde and Arequipa, 2 blocks from the plaza. Travelers ignore this *tambo's* slight deterioration and socialize on their way to the clean common baths. Singles s/10; doubles s/20.

Hospedaje Español, Prado 670 (☎572 381), between Rivero and Piura. Lit only with the barest fluorescence. Some of the cleanest common baths in the Amazon Basin. A bit out of the way. Singles s/10, with bath s/15; doubles s/20, with bath s/25.

FOOD

Über-cheap eats (s/2 *menús*) hang around the market, especially near the Piura-Ica intersection. Dos de Mayo (between Velarde and Puno) plays host to numerous *braserías*. And while Maldonado might not exhibit the same wealth of jungle specialty dishes as Iquitos, the profusion of exotic fruit juices makes up for it. Keep an eye out for the *cocona* (passionfruit).

AMAZON BASIN

Pizzoton, Velarde 315 (☎571 765), near the Plaza de Armas. Basket chandeliers, over-bearing landscape paintings, and leather tablecloths somehow pull off an unusual elegance. Crisp pizzas s/11-24. Sandwiches s/3-6. Beer s/3-6. Open Tu-Su 6:30-11pm.

Wasaí (☎572 290), on Billinghurst, 1 block toward the Río Madre de Dios from the plaza. This riverside gazebo offers the calmest dining in the area. Entrees s/15-25.

◪ NIGHTLIFE

Friday and Saturday nights in Puerto Maldonado bring out the city's young population. The clubs play great Latin music, there's no cover anywhere, and most spots stay open until dawn. The small **Discoteca Witite** (☎572 219), on Velarde off the Plaza de Armas, lives up to its motto, *"un buen motivo para no dormir"* ("the best reason not to sleep") **Garotas Night Club,** San Martín 173 (☎686 294), is the place to be if you want to boogie. The lights attract equally flashy patrons.

◪ DAYTRIP FROM PUERTO MALDONADO

LAGO SANDOVAL

Commission a canoe or motorboat (1hr., round-trip s/60) at the port where the Río Madre de Dios and the Río Tambopata converge. Boats let you off at a trailhead; follow the path 5km (1-1½hr.) through the jungle to the lake. There are two lodges along the way; both offer meals for s/7.

If you just can't stomach the exorbitant cost of jungle, perhaps a daytrip to the beautiful Lago Sandoval will be more to your liking. At the tranquil lake, **kingfishers, herons,** and **cormorants** swarm the area, and early in the morning, **giant otters** brave the sunlight from their murky depths. The serene atmosphere is perfect for a relaxing dip in the lake—just beware the tiny piranhas.

◪ INTO THE JUNGLE FROM PUERTO MALDONADO

The **Tambopata-Candamo** UNESCO reserve, whose 6000 sq. km include the Bahuaja-Sonene National Park and Las Pampas de Heath National Sanctuary, provides fields of play for the region's visitors. You probably won't see any large mammals here, but during most park tours it's not uncommon to see monkeys, caimans, perhaps a giant otter, and many brilliantly colored birds. The Tambopata-Candamo and other reserves in the area impose fees of US$20-30.

GUIDES

Freelance guides can offer less crowded, more adventurous, and more flexible trips than those based in lodges, though their services are often cheaper than a lodge only if there's a group to split costs. As always, be very cautious about whom you pick to accompany you into the wilderness; there are lots of con men in Puerto Maldonado. Below are some reliable options.

Willy Wither, Hotel Kross, Velarde 721 (email willywither@hotmail.com). Enthusiastic and knowledgeable. An expert on medicinal plants and local tribes, Willy's only weakness is his limited English. Lago Sandoval and Lago Valencia (4days, US$200 for 2 people). He's willing to go almost anywhere for any amount of time. Average trips cost US$25 per person per day (less with 6 or more people; includes all food, lodging, and transport but not the reserve fee).

Victor Yohamona (☎572 613; fax at Hotel Cabaña Quinta 571 045; email yohamona@pol.com.pe). Well-established and English-speaking. Victor leads piranha-fishing expeditions, searches for medicinal plants, and visits to indigenous communities as well as 4-day trips to Lagos Sandoval and Valencia or the Tambopata-Candamo Reserve and 8-day trips up the Las Piedras River. Trips for 2-3 people run US$35 per person per day to Sandoval and Valencia, US$50 to Tambopata-Candamo or the Las Piedras River (less with 4 or more people) and include food, most accommodations (though not tents for camping) and transport, but not the reserve fees.

AMAZON BASIN

Marco Linares-Pérez, Cusco 377, 2 blocks from the Plaza de Armas (email marcolinares-peres@yahoo.com). Precocious 16-year-old Marco, a Puerto Maldonado native, is always happy to show travelers every niche of his humid homeland. Besides running trips to Lago Sandoval and nearby indigenous villages, Marco knows all the *albergue* contacts in the area. Prices negotiable, but often cheaper than average.

Turismo De Los Angeles, Puno 657 (☎/fax 572 158), between Prado and Troncoso. Arranges tours with local boatsmen and guides (min. 4 people US$40 per person per day). The English-speaking owner is very helpful. Open M-Sa 8am-1pm and 4-9pm.

JUNGLE LODGES

A slew of expensive lodges, many hosting 40 to 60 guests per night in July and August, dot the Río Tambopata. Although there are more affordable ways to experience the area's 1234 species of butterflies and the world's largest macaw *colpa* (clay-lick), the lodges provide an opportunity to see the jungle in style.

Rainforest Expeditions, Galeón 120, in Lima, (☎(01) 421 8347; fax 421 8183), maintains the large and luxurious **Posada Amazonas** lodge in conjunction with the local Ese'eja community. While expensive, the fact that a native group both owns half of the lodge and makes up the majority of its employees sets Posada apart. Rainforest Expeditions can also arrange stays at the small **Tambopata Research Center,** 4-5hr. upstream and just 500m from the *colpa*. Both have private baths and transportation to and from the airport. 4 days, 3 nights all-inclusive at the Posada US$300; 5-days, 4-nights, half at the Posada and half at the Research Center, US$565.

Bahuaja Lodge (mailing address: Tina Smith, Lista de Correos, Serpost, Puerto Maldonado). Run by British biologist Tina Smith and her Peruvian husband Hilmar Huinga, Bahuaja offers a family-run, independently oriented lodge option. And with its organic food, lack of electricity and running water, and commitment to employing local guides, it operates far more responsibly than many others. Camping US$25 per person (with your own tent); beds US$35 per person per night. All meals included. Transport and expeditions to the macaw lick can be arranged at extra cost. 4 days, 3 nights all-inclusive US$165. Special prices may be available for Spanish-speakers willing to do manual or scientific work around the lodge (min. 3 weeks).

Tambopata Jungle Lodge (☎(084) 225 701; fax 238 911; www.cbc.org.pe/tambopata/tambopata.htm). A few hours from the *colpa* on the Tambopata River. The lodge organizes 3-5 day guided tours of the forest (US$150-230) and salt lick (US$510-630) that include transportation from Puerto Maldonado, food, lodging, and guides. They also have a lodge in town for easy access to nearby daytrips. Prices vary with season.

FURTHER FEARSOME FAUNA Unlike the terrifying **fire ants** (see Hot Damn!, p. 286), some jungle creatures don't wait for you to come to them; the **desmodus "vampire" bat** feeds on unconscious and unprotected mammals. One of the few bats that can walk, the desmodus lands near its prey, then—with great stealth—approaches on two legs and uses its razor-like teeth to cut off small layers of skin. There the bat perches, lapping blood that pours from the wound, the anticoagulants in its saliva assuring a constant flow. An **anaconda,** on the other hand, won't get to you without your noticing. This venomless boa constrictor, the largest snake in the world (up to 13m), kills by wrapping itself around its prey and strangling it to death. Later, he swallows it whole. People who know rainforests often advise that you watch what you touch, as snakes can resemble vines or branches—this guy looks more like a full-grown tree trunk. But perhaps the **candirú acu,** more commonly called the **orifice fish,** wins the prize for Most Frightening Jungle Animal. This miniscule, almost invisible river catfish has spikes on its tailfin. These spikes do not impede its swimming up *into* a bather's urethra, but they do prevent him from turning around and swimming back out. Without surgical removal, the pesky invader could cause death.

AMAZON BASIN

BOLIVIA

HISTORY SINCE INDEPENDENCE

CREATION OF A NEW COUNTRY (1825-39)

The liberation of Peru in the 1824 **Battle of Ayachuco** marked the end of **Simón Bolívar's** extended military campaign against the Spanish crown, but Upper Peru, the area around Chuquiscaca (modern-day Sucre), remained under the control of **General Pedro Antonio de Olañeta,** an area native who refused to accept Spain's concession of the highlands. Bolívar left Olañeta to his lieutenant **Antonio José de Sucre,** who won a decisive battle on April 1, 1825 and immediately convened a delegation in Chuquiscaca to determine the future of the region. Aware of the economic importance of the area's silver mines, many *criollo* elites in Upper Peru had long been frustrated with their subordinate status under colonial rule, and it took them only five days to decide upon a declaration of independence. In an effort to appease Bolívar, who was more interested in building alliances than weak new nation-states, the delegates named the new country Bolivia.

After writing a new constitution based upon land reform and equal citizenship, Bolívar handed the presidency of Bolivia to Sucre. Sucre's attempts to recover from war debts, which included tax reforms and confiscation of church wealth, threatened long-standing social and economic patterns and brought resentment from conservative *criollos*. In 1828 Sucre resigned, and after a series of short-term rulers, native-born **Andrés de Santa Cruz y Calahumana** was sworn into office in May 1829. A relatively competent ruler, Santa Cruz enacted Latin America's first civil and commercial codes and stabilized the Bolivian economy by instituting protective tariffs and reducing mining taxes. To secure the border with Peru, he intervened in the Peruvian civil war and established himself as protector of a **Peru-Bolivia Confederation.** Argentina and Chile, however, had no desire to deal with such a potential power block, and both nations declared war on the confederation. In January 1939, Santa Cruz was soundly defeated in the **Battle of Yungay,** the short-lived confederation was dissolved, and Santa Cruz went into exile in Ecuador.

CHAOS AND CAUDILLISMO (1839-79)

The 40 years following Santa Cruz's exile brought extreme political instability, continuous territory loss, and economic decline to Bolivia. Ten different leaders tried their hand at ruling the fragmented country, and while a few of them had good intentions, the majority were mere *caudillos*, ruthless military strongmen who stayed in power through a combination of sheer force and political maneuvering. Santa Cruz's direct successor, **General José Miguel de Velasco** (1839-41), failed to repel yet another invasion by Peruvian general **Agustín Gamarra** and was ousted in 1841. **General José Ballivián y Segurola** (1841-47) took his place, restored a degree of calm and reversed Santa Cruz's protectionist policies, but his continued reliance on taxing the Indian population only worsened agricultural output. **Manuel Isidoro Belzú** (1848-55), often seen as Bolivia's first populist, tried to appeal to artisans and peasants by limiting imports and seizing aristocratic land, but threats from Bolivian elites eventually exiled him to Europe. After a brief rule by Belzú's son-in-law, **José María Linares** (1857-61) took over the Bolivian presidency, reinstated free trade, and drew foreign investment in the mining industry; agriculture continued to lag, though, and taxes sparked peasant revolts in Copacabana.

Linares' overthrow in 1861 by a military coup marked the beginning of a period of extreme violence and remarkably incompetent leaders. **General José María Achá Valiente** (1861-1864) massacred more than 71 Belzú supporters during his time in office, and **General Mariano Melgarejo** (1861-1864), ceded 102,400 square kilometers of territory to Brazil in an attempt to secure rights to the Atlantic Ocean. He also signed treaties with Chile and Peru relinquishing rights to valuable *guano* and nitrate reserves in the coastal Atacama area; not even the country's most economically-minded elites intervened to prevent this mistake, as most of their capital was tied up in the newly-booming silver mines. By the time **Hilarión Daza Groselle** came to office in 1876, political unrest in Bolivia was so great that nothing short of international war could have patched together any sort of internal unity. Conveniently enough for Daza, Melgarejo had set the stage perfectly for just such a war.

WAR AND CONSERVATIVE RULE (1879-99)

THE WAR OF THE PACIFIC. Bolivia's first major war grew out of a long-standing conflict with Chile over the mineral-rich coastal area of the Atacama Desert. In the mid-1860s the two countries had almost gone to war over boundary-drawing, but in 1874 Chile agreed to fix the border at 24° latitude in return for Bolivia's promise not to increase taxes on Chilean nitrate companies for at least 25 years. Daza broke that promise only four years later in an attempt to raise money and spur nationalism, and on February 14, 1879, Chile declared war on both Bolivia and

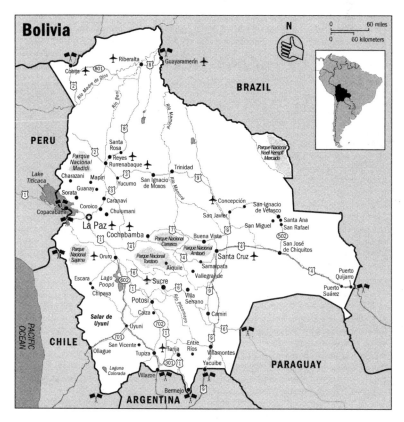

Peru. Thanks in part to Daza's military incompetence, Bolivian troops were almost immediately defeated, and Bolivia lost its entire coastal territory. Daza fled to Europe (with most of the national treasury) to avoid popular revolt, and Chile continued with a massive invasion of Peru (see **Guano Boom and Bust,** p. 62).

THE RETURN OF CIVILIAN RULE. The War of the Pacific marked a significant turning point in Bolivian history. To this day, Bolivia's lack of ocean access provides a sense of shared national loss, a rallying cry for campaigning politicians. But more importantly, the embarrassing military defeat discredited the armed forces just as the Bolivian upper class was reaping the benefits of increased silver production. Civilian elites heartily debated national politics and new parties were formed. The **Partido Conservardor** (Conservative Party), comprised mostly of mining entrepreneurs, favored a quick indemnity settlement with Chile in order to fund a railroad for Bolivian mining exports, while the **Partido Liberal** (Liberal Party) wanted to move away from dependence on British and Chilean financing. Both parties, however, shared an interest in economic modernization and a depoliticized, more professional army, and Conservative **Narciso Campero's** election as president in 1880 marked the beginning of 40 years of relative stability for Bolivia.

The Conservatives ruled with mixed success. High world prices for silver kept the economy afloat, profits grew from cash crops like rubber, and the Conservative governments did complete a rail line to the Chilean coast. Even agricultural production increased slightly. After Campero's term, though, fraudulent elections prompted several Liberal revolts, the expansion of wealthy farming *haciendas* at the expense of communal Indian lands alienated the lower classes, and the open economy created by the new railroad started to hurt local industry as imported goods, including Chilean wheat, began to replace domestic products.

THE RISE OF TIN AND LIBERALS (1899-1920)

THE FEDERAL REVOLUTION. Just as silver money and Conservative politics were highly intertwined in the late 19th century, Bolivia's switch to a Liberal government was closely tied to rapid growth in the tin industry (in 1900 it accounted for 50% of all national exports). Tin had always been readily available in Bolivia, but the ingredients for profit—a national railroad and major worldwide industrialization—did not arrive until the turn of the century. Once they did, it took no time at all for Sucre to fall from its privileged position as the financial center of the country. Major tin mines near La Paz drew international investors and migrating peasants, and by 1900 the city was not only wealthier than Sucre but also three times its size, with 72,000 people. This overt disparity provided the perfect justification for Liberal **José Manuel Pando** to lead the **Federal Revolution of 1899**, an armed ousting of the Conservatives on the grounds that La Paz, and not Sucre, should serve as the capital of Bolivia. The Federal Revolution was unique among Bolivian revolts in that Indian peasants, upset by wealthy landowners' encroachments on their land, actively participated in the fighting. (Pando secured their support by promising to stop the territorial assault but failed to keep his word once in office.)

LIBERALS IN CONTROL. The Liberal government brought substantial social and economic change to Bolivia. The Conservative party effectively died out completely and a new relationship developed between the government and industry: less personally tied to politicians than the old silver elite, powerful tin moguls like **Patiño, Aramayo,** and **Hothschild** steered clear of direct political involvement and were represented instead by lawyers and lobbyists not-so-fondly referred to as the *rosca.* Liberal leaders, especially **Ismael Montes** (1904-09 and 1913-17) wrested power from the Roman Catholic church, made significant efforts to professionalize the army, and finally settled long-standing border disputes; the **Treaty of Petrópolis** (1903) with Brazil ended skirmishes over rubber-producing territory, and Chile and Bolivia finally signed an official peace treaty. Liberal leaders brought Bolivia the calmest political period it would ever experience, but trouble was brewing just below the surface: Indian peasants, first betrayed by Pando and then displaced from their rural communities to crowded mining towns, became increasingly discontent with their social situation, and La Paz witnessed the **First National Congress of Workers** in 1912. International trade crises hurt mineral exports and helped prompt the formation of the **Partido Republicano** (Republican Party) in 1914. Liberals managed to defeat the Republicans at the polls in 1917, but **José Gutiérrez Guerra** (1917-1920) proved to be the end of the Liberal presidential line.

REPUBLICANS AND WAR AGAIN (1920-35)

MISFORTUNE FOR REPUBLICANS. The Republican party didn't have much of a chance in Bolivia. Almost as soon as their first president, **Bautista Saavedra Mallea** (1920-25) was elected, world tin prices began to fall drastically, and by 1930 the Great Depression had nearly destroyed the international tin market altogether. As the economy declined, Saavedra and his successor **Hernando Siles Reyes** (1926-30) were forced to rely heavily upon foreign loans, particularly from the United States, despite fierce opposition from Bolivian nationalists. Minor parties influenced by Marxist and socialist thought began to develop, and the labor unrest which had been growing under the Liberal government escalated in the 1920s; Saavedra was forced to resort to brutal violence to suppress a 1923 **miners' strike** in Uncia. Siles was more committed to improving the situation of workers and Indian peasants, but both presidents were severely crippled by the power of the *rosca*, and Siles's empty promises earned him the boot in 1930. A military junta took over until 1931, when **Daniel Salamanca Urey** (1931-34) was elected as a coalition candidate. Much like Hilarión Daza 50 years earlier (see Chaos and Caudillismo, p. 292), Salamanca inherited a Bolivia so fraught with social unrest and economic problems that only the distraction of war could possibly keep him in office.

THE CHACO WAR. Like all of Bolivia's international disputes, the Chaco War (1932-35) was sparked by a border disagreement, this one regarding the Chaco lowlands, where Standard Oil and Royal Dutch Oil had discovered reserves in both Bolivia and Paraguay. Paraguay was interested in access to oil fields beyond its border, while Bolivia hoped to use the Chaco to run a pipeline to the Paraguay River and South Atlantic Ocean. Bolivia's army had been significantly professionalized since the War of the Pacific, and in 1932 Salamanca decided that his country's German-trained, well-equipped troops were superior enough to make a quick war with Paraguay worthwhile. Three disastrous years of fighting proved him completely wrong; 65,000 people died, another 35,000 were wounded or captured, and Bolivia lost the Chaco, though it managed to keep its own petroleum fields. The military high command forced Salamanca to resign in 1934 when he refused to accept defeat, and his more peace-inclined vice-president, **José Luis Tejada Sorzano,** stepped into the presidential shoes until 1936.

LEGACY OF THE CHACO WAR (1936-46)

"MILITARY SOCIALISM". Bolivia's disastrous defeat in the Chaco War was the sharp spur needed to get an old horse running. Absolutely embarrassed military officials developed an acute political awareness and reformists and conservatives alike became poised to pursue their own political goals. Officers universally supported the overthrow of Tejada by **Colonel David Toro Ruilova** (1936-37) to avoid a civilian investigation of wartime leadership, and they created a powerful "police" legion to circumvent the army-reduction clause of the settlement with Paraguay. That was the extent of agreement among military leaders, however, and starting with Toro's brief rule, the government of Bolivia took a decidedly reformist bent.

Toro's main backers were disillusioned young veterans who wanted to bring profound change to their country, from the top down. He called his political program "military socialism" and hoped to achieve social justice and government control of natural resources. He was unable to secure lasting popular support, however, and in 1937 he was overthrown by an even more radical group of officers who wanted to challenge the *rosca* more directly. **Colonel Germán Busch Becerra** (1937-39) led the coup and ruled for two years, but he too failed to get enough support for his extremely radical goals, and in 1939 he committed suicide.

PENARAÑDA AND VILLARROEL. During the Toro and Busch years, a *concordancia* had formed among Liberals and Republicans disturbed by the rapid growth of the left, and **General Enrique Peñaranda Castillo** (1940-43) was elected to put a freeze on the status quo. The trend toward change could not be halted, however, and Peñaranda's Congress filled with several groups on the extreme left, including the **Partido Obrero Revolucionario** (POR; Revolutionary Workers' Party), the **Falange Socialista Boliviana** (FSB; Bolivian Socialist Falange), based on the Spanish model, and the **Partido de Izquierda Revolucionaria** (PIR; Leftist Revolutionary Party). The leader of the Congressional opposition, though, was the **Movimiento Nationalista Revolucionario** (MNR; Nationalist Revolutionary Movement), the first party in Bolivian history to have widespread support among varied social classes.

The openly anti-Semitic MNR returned to Toro and Busch's advocacy of total nationalization and far-reaching social reforms, and they communicated with the secretive **Razón de Patria** (Radepa; Fatherland's Cause), a group founded in 1934 by prisoners of war in Paraguay. In December 1943, the two parties formed an alliance to overthrow the Peñaranda regime, and **Major Gualberto Villarroel López** (1943-46) became Bolivia's next reformist president. He had little chance to enact lasting changes, however; despite his interest in the welfare of peasants and workers, the Bolivian people overwhelmingly accused Villarroel of fascism, and in 1946 mobs of students, teachers and workers captured and shot him in front of the presidential palace, then suspended his body from a lamppost.

THE "SEXENIO" (1946-52)

The six years preceding the **1952 National Revolution** are commonly referred to as the **sexenio.** For Conservatives, this period was a last-ditch opportunity to try to stem the growth of the left by simultaneously appeasing the upper class and the labor sector. For the MNR, it was a warm-up for revolution, as the party tried various tactics for gaining power. For everyone in Bolivia, the *sexenio* meant increasing inflation and economic instability as conservatives tried to maintain social spending without raising taxes, even in the face of plummeting tin prices.

Enrique Hertzog Garaizabal (1947-49) tried to bring together the conservative *concordancia* and the PIR in a coalition, but his government's severe suppression of a 1949 miners' uprising in Catavi squashed any potential for government/worker cooperation. The MNR made an unsuccessful coup attempt in 1949 and then sent legitimate representatives to the 1951 elections; **Paz Estenssoro** and **Siles Zuazo** actually won on a platform of nationalization and land reform, but the outgoing president called in a military *junta* to prevent the MNR from assuming power.

THE 1952 NATIONAL REVOLUTION (1952-64)

By March of 1952, economic decline, military demoralization and social unrest had reached such extremes in Bolivia that nearly every sector of society participated in a hunger march through La Paz. Paz Estenssoro and the MNR took the cue and tried once more to gain power by force, this time by arming civilian miners in La Paz. After three days of fighting and 600 deaths, the Bolivian army completely surrendered and Paz Estenssoro assumed the presidency on April 16, 1952.

The MNR wasted no time in implementing revolutionary political change. Within three months the government established unconditional universal suffrage, moved quickly to control and reduce the armed forces, nationalized the three largest tin companies, and created the **Corporación Minera De Bolivia** (Comibol; Mining Corporation of Bolivia) to run the newly state-owned mines. In 1953 the new government passed the **Agrarian Reform Law,** which abolished forced labor and laid out a program of land transfer from traditional landlords to the Indian peasants. Both the peasants and miners gained considerable influence under the new MNR regime; Paz Estenssoro actively encouraged the formation of miner militias to counterbalance the military, and miners immediately organized the **Central Oberea Boliviana** (COB; Bolivian Labor Federation), a powerful organization that would come to play a crucial role in Bolivia's long, slow road to democracy.

The MNR had an impressive start, but it lost momentum quickly. The party itself quickly divided between radical leftists and the more moderate majority, the nationalized mines consistently lost money, anarchy in the countryside led to major drops in agricultural production, and the government brought on high inflation with rampant social spending. Paz Estenssoro's successor, **Siles Zuazo** (1956-60 and 1982-85), alienated the far left and the COB by turning to a strict IMF stabilization program that froze wages and required heavy U.S. loans. In his own second term (1960-64) Paz Estenssoro spurred even deeper labor discontent, and was forced to lean more and more heavily on the military as a peacekeeping force.

MILITARY RULE AGAIN (1964-78)

The 1960s and 70s brought military rule back to Bolivia once more; after being elected as Paz Estenssoro's vice-president in 1964, **General René Barrientos Ortuño** (1964-69) announced himself president of Bolivia in a bloodless coup. Determined to suppress labor unrest, Barrientos continued the severe stabilization plan that had made Paz Entenssoro so unpopular in his final term. That aside, however, he reversed almost every single policy pursued by the MNR regime. He turned the military against the workers, placed Comibol under the control of a military director, abolished the COB, disarmed the miners' militias, and exiled union leaders. He also angered nationalists by inviting heavy American investment in Bolivia.

Barrientos was killed in a helicopter crash in April 1969. Following brief ineffectual rule by two different commanders, **General Alfredo Ovando Candia** (1969-70) and **General Juan José Torres** (1970-71), Bolivia's last important military ruler came to power, **Colonel Hugo Banzer Suárez** (1971-78). Banzer's regime was remarkably stable, and the 1970s brought unprecedented economic growth to Bolivia; foreign investment, oil reserves, good tin prices, and an increase in commercial agriculture all worked in the country's favor. Unfortunately for Banzer, the so-called "economic miracle" of the 70s turned out to be a short-lived mirage, and by 1978 he was faced with the same problems that had plagued those before him: state-owned mines that lost money, low tin and oil prices, and a heavy dependence on foreign aid. Under such conditions, Banzer's policy of courting the business community, mine owners, and loyal bureaucrats backfired, and labor unrest and hostility to his regime forced Banzer to agree to popular elections in 1978.

THE STRUGGLE FOR DEMOCRACY (1978-82)

The 1978 elections were carried out successfully, but the National Electoral Court annulled the results on suspicion of fraud by victor **General Juan Pereda Asbún.** Pereda responded by taking hold of the presidency anyway, and thus began Bolivia's tortuous path to democracy; in only four years the country would see two civilian rulers and seven military regimes before finally voting a legitimate president into office. The last military ruler, **General Luis García Meza Tejada** (1980-82), was one of the most corrupt in Bolivian history. García Meza and his supporters cooperated closely with neofascist terrorists and cocaine traffickers and ruled the country with overt, ruthless force. By 1982 García Meza's government had become so internationally isolated and internally threatened that he resigned and fled to Europe, and the **Congress of 1980** finally convened to elect a new president. Their choice was ex-MNR president Siles Zuazo, and on October 10, 1982, Bolivia officially achieved status as a democratic state, a title it still clings to today.

KEEPING DEMOCRACY ALIVE (1982-2000)

THE FIRST FIVE. The five presidents who have served Bolivia since 1982 have had more than enough to handle during their terms in office. **Siles Zuazo** (1982-1985) saw the country through disastrous crop failures caused by El Niño, inflation rates as high as 24,000%, and massive strikes in protest of his economic stabilization measures. **Paz Estenssoro** (1985-89) was faced with the collapse of the tin market and consequent unemployment, and he had to battle extreme public displeasure at his necessarily austere economic measures. The most recent presidents, **Jaime Paz Zamora** (1989-93), **Gonzalo Sánchez de Lozada** (1993-97) and **Colonel Hugo Banzer Suárez** (back again, 1997-present) have all dealt with similar economic issues but have also felt increasing international pressure to reduce annual borrowing and fight the cocaine trade.

THE WAR ON DRUGS. Bolivia is currently the third-largest producer of coca in the world, behind only Colombia and Peru. In 1997, the country exported 250 tons of the illegal leaf per year; today, after only three years of an intense anti-narcotics campaign, that number hovers around 70 tons per year. President Banzer has promised to eradicate the crop altogether by 2002 and thus far has been sticking to his word. He abolished the previous "voluntary eradication" program, which offered money for crop destruction but did not guarantee that farmers would stop planting. Instead, Banzer has offered growers credits, roads, technical help and even alternative crop seeds in exchange for promises to never grow coca again. So far about 75 agreements covering more than 7,000 farmers have been signed, according to officials, and many more are on the brink of completion. U.S. Secretary of State Madeleine Albright has promised $110 million in U.S. aid to help fund alternative crop development; she has also mentioned the distant possibility of lifting import duties on Bolivian textiles, a step which would bring $400 million to the Bolivian economy and provide a substantial replacement for lost coca jobs.

PROSPECTS FOR THE FUTURE. Bolivia is poised to enter its third decade of relatively stable democracy, a remarkable achievement considering that the country underwent more than 150 coups d'etat during its first 150 years. The road ahead is by no means smooth, however. Landlocked, isolated, and fragmented, Bolivia is still the second poorest country in Latin America, and its huge Indian population continues to suffer from severe discrimination. The country's political institutions are still far from mature; in particular, extreme factionalism—along lines of class, race, region and more—has necessitated complicated alliances and coalitions that make effective executive rule extremely difficult. Economically, Bolivia depends heavily on foreign loans, still has major inflation problems, and must find a way to compensate for the destruction of coca crops. Demonstrations and protests by growers have become weekly occurrences of late, and Bazner's finance minister estimates that Bolivia lost $500 million in drug revenues in 2000 alone. If Bolivia hopes to stabilize its economy and achieve Banzer's goal of coca eradication, it's going to have to find a way to employ its hundreds of thousands of starving citizens.

PAINTING

Early Bolivian painting dates from colonial times, when artists like **Gregoria Gamarra, Leonardo Flores,** and **Matías Sanjinés** depicted the Virgin Mary and the Trinity in the pieces now found in churches and museums. This school grew into the **Escuela Potosina Indígena** after the developments of Cochabamba-born **Melchor Pérez de Holguín,** who worked roughly from 1670 to 1732. The 19th century saw artists turn to the daily life around them, as in the watercolors of **Melchor María Mercado.** As the Bolivian populace began to fight against their post-war conditions, painting appropriately moved to more political themes; **Miguel Alandia Pantoja** created scenes of worker unrest and revolt in the 1940s as the exiled **Alejandro Mario Yllanes** invoked pre-colonization pride in murals and engravings. Modern Bolivian painting spans the entire thematic range: religion, in the colorful work of **Gilka Wara Libermann;** Bolivia in nature and in life, in the gorgeous scenes of **Mamani Mamani, Gil Imana,** and **David Darío Antezana;** and the continuing political struggles, in **Andrés Chambi** and **Alfred La Placa's** proud interpretations.

LITERATURE

As with most other Latin American countries, Bolivia's early indigenous literature took the form of an oral tradition. For an interesting study of **Aymara, Quechua, Kallahuaya,** and **Guaraní** oral tales, see the *Nueva historia de la liberatura boliviana* by Adolfo Cáceres Romeros. The most notable pre-independence writer in Bolivia was probably **Bartolomé Arzáns Orsúa y Vela** (1676-1736), whose *Historia de la villa imperial de Potosí* details nearly 200 years of the city's history, from its founding in 1545 to the author's death in 1736.

Bolivian literature grew substantially after the country gained independence in 1825. **Julio Lucas Jaimes** (1840-1914) wrote short-story versions of ancient oral narratives in an attempt to capture local, traditional culture. Turn-of-the-century writer **Adela Zamudio** (1854-1928) brought feminist poetry to Bolivia, and **Ricardo Jaimes Freyre** (1866-1933) became the first Bolivian author to gain international recognition. His famous story *Indian Justice*, a commentary on exploitation of the indigenous Bolivian population, is to this day one of the only Bolivian works translated into English. **Alcides Arguedas** (1879-1946), novelist, journalist, historian and sociologist, also focused on the problem of the South American Indian. His novel *Pueblo Enfermo*, published in 1909, is a major sociological statement on the Bolivian nation and its people. His 1919 *Raza de bronce* chronicles the travels of a group of Bolivian Indians that end in their extermination by white men. Arguedas's exploration of the Indian problem foreshadowed the popular Indianista novel of the 1930s and 40s. **Adolfo Costa de Rels** (1891-1980) spent most of his life in Europe and wrote an interesting novel about the different perspectives of an authoritarian *mestizo* landholder in Bolivia and his European-educated son. The first version, *Terres embrásees* (1932), was in French but was subsequently translated into Spanish as *Tierras hechizadas* and English as *Bewitched Lands*.

Bolivia's numerous wars and revolts have provided ample fodder for literary minds. **Augusto Céspedes** published the short story collection *Sangre de mestizos* in 1936 and poet and novelist **Jesús Lara** (1898-1980) is known for his diary-novel *Repete* (1937). The Revolution of 1952 inspired **Marcelo Quiroga Santa Cruz's** (1931-1980) novel *Los deshabitados*, an existential exploration of the meaning of life, as well as **Oscar Cerruto's** (1912-1981) short stories *Cerco de penumbras*.

One of the most notable contemporary writers in Bolivia was **Jaime Sáenz** (1921-86); his novel *Felipe Delgado* takes a piercing look at the underworld of La Paz. **Rentao Prado Oropeza** and **Manuel Vargas** have become important literary figures as well, and **Arturo von Vacano** has written an interesting autobiographical novel titled *Morder el silencio* (1980) that is now available in English as *The Biting Silence*.

BOLIVIA

LA PAZ

☎ 02

Originally founded as "La Ciudad de Nuestra Señora de La Paz," Bolivia's capital has had little time for peace. Spaniards first settled the city along the road to the ancient capital of Tiahuanuco, in a location now home to the town of Laja. However the cold and wind of the harsh altiplano surface was more than they could handle. So, instead, La Paz (3650m, pop. 2,500,000, est. 1548) lies nestled deeply and densely in the Chuquiago Marka Valley, enclosed by a wall of mountains that keeps the wind out and life's energy in.

HIGHLIGHTS OF LA PAZ

CAREEN down the "Most Dangerous Road" in the world—on a **mountain bike** (p. 305).

UNDERSTAND La Paz and her people, customs, and history after a visit to the **Museo Tambo Quirquincho** (p. 308).

CAST spells with coca leaves and llama foetuses from the **Mercado de Brujos** ("Witches' Market;" p. 309).

ABANDON the city for the hillside: the canyons and rock formations of the surrounding altiplano make for stunning area **daytrips** (p. 313).

CATCH a bus to the ruins (p. 314) of the **Tiahuanuco**, the area's original empire.

As early as 1781, the native Aymara attempted to eradicate Spanish control (finally succeeding in 1825, with the Declaration of Independence). Yet as recently as 1952, the aboriginal people still had to fight for even the most basic of political rights. Today, although La Paz's official language is Spanish and its boutiques display European fashions, the voices in the markets chatter in Aymara and the most prominent trend on the street is still the derby hat, voluminous skirt, and long braids that have characterized La Paz style for hundreds of years. Cars whiz by honking; pedestrians weave slowly up and down hills, stepping over the wares that spill out of vendors' stands. Shouts of "cómprame," blaring pop music, strong notes from the pipes of folk musicians, and screamed bus destinations create a cacophony that serves as tribute to La Paz's unique mix: the international feel of a big city and the traditions and history of an indigenous community.

⌐ TRANSPORTATION

GETTING THERE AND AWAY

Airport: El Alto Aeropuerto (☎810 120 or 810 123), in El Alto, 30min. from center. Information desk open daily 5am-8pm. Take an "Aeropuerto" microbus (Bs3.7) headed northwest from the Plaza Isabel la Católica or anywhere along El Prado, 16 de Julio, or Mariscal Santa Cruz. Radio-taxi Bs40. Tax on visitors who have been in Bolivia over 90 days Bs120. National flight exit tax Bs10; international flight exit tax US$25.

International Airlines: AeroContinente, 16 de Julio 1490 (☎310 707). Open M-F 9am-7pm, Sa 9am-noon. To **Lima** (1¾hr., US$262) and **Cusco** (1hr., US$142). **LanChile,** El Prado 1566 (☎358 377 or 322 370). Open M-F 8:30am-6:30pm, Sa 9:30am-noon. To: **Arica** (45min., US$110 round-trip); **Iquique** (2¼hr., US$123 round-trip); **Santiago** (5hr., US$276 round-trip). **Varig Airlines,** Mariscal Santa Cruz 1392 (☎314 040). Open M-F 9am-6:30pm, Sa-Su 9:30am-noon. To **Rio de Janeiro** and **Sao Paulo** also. **LAB** (see Domestic Airlines, below) flies to Peru and Ecuador.

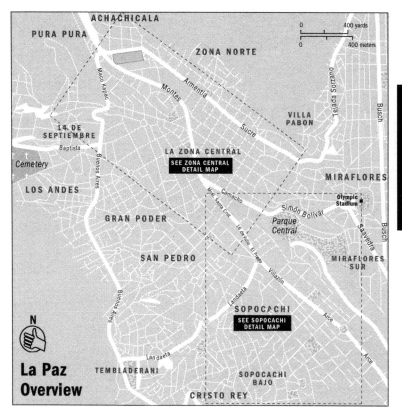

La Paz
Overview

Domestic Airlines:

AeroSur, 16 de Julio 1616 (☎313 233). To: **Sucre** (1hr.; M-F 10:45am, Sa 11:25am, Su 3:45pm; Bs414); **Cochabamba** (30min., 2 per day, Bs291); **Cobija** (1hr.; M-Th 7am, Su 12:40pm; Bs854); **Puerto Suárez** (3hr.; M, W, F, Su 1:30pm; Bs1030); **Santa Cruz** (1½hr.; 3 per day Sa-W, 5 per day Th-F; Bs646); **Tarija** (50min.; M, W, F 2:40pm; Bs647); **Trinidad** (4½hr., M-Sa 7am, Bs643); **Guayaramerín** (6½hr., M-Sa 7am, Bs971); **Riberalta** (1½hr.; M 12:30pm, Tu-F 12:10pm, Sa 12:40pm; Bs971); and **Yacuiba** (6hr., M 7am, Bs1033).

Lloyd Aero Boliviano (LAB), Camacho 1466 (☎371 020, customer service 0800 43 21, reservations and confirmations 0800 30 01). To: **Lima** (1¾hr., US$231); **Cusco** (1hr., US$107); **Quito** (3hr., US$381); and **Sucre** (1½hr., Bs414).

Transporte Aero Militar (TAM), (☎379 286), at Montes and Serrano. Open M-F 8:30am-6pm, Sa 9am-noon. To: **Cobija** (1¾hr.); **Cochabamba** (45min., Bs170); **Puerto Suárez** (4½hr.); **Reyes** (1hr.); **Riberalta** (3½hr.); **Roboré** (20¾hr.); **Rurrenabaque** (1hr., Bs320); **San Borja** (2hr.); **San Ignacio** (4½hr.); **San Matias** (3hr.); **Santa Cruz** (1½hr., Bs370); **Sucre** (1¾hr., Bs300); **Tarija** (3hr.); **Trinidad** (2½hr.); **Villamontes** (7¾hr.); **Yacuiba** (3¼hr.); and **Guayaramerín** (3½hr.).

Internacional Buses: Terminal de Buses (☎280 551), on Armentia. Expreso Cruz del Sur (☎282 077), to: **Puno** (6½hr., 8am, Bs50); **Lima** (2 days, 8am, US$50); **Quito** (4 days, 8am, US$135); **Guayaquil** (3½ days, 8am, US$130); and **Bogotá** (5 days, 8am, US$250). Chevas Internacional (☎281 748), to **Arica** (8hr., 7am, Bs80) and **Iquique** (12hr., 7am, Bs100). Chilebus Internacional (☎282 168), to **Arica** (8hr., 6:30am and 2pm, Bs80). Ramos Cholele (☎284 439), to: **Iquique** (12hr.; Tu, Th, Su 6am; Bs90); **Arica** (8hr.; Su, Tu, Th 6am; Bs80); and **Santiago** (36hr.; Su, Tu, Th 6am; Bs320). Cooperativo de Servicios Turisticos and Transporte 6 de Junio go to Peru; Expreso San Roque goes to Argentina; see Domestic Buses, below.

LA PAZ

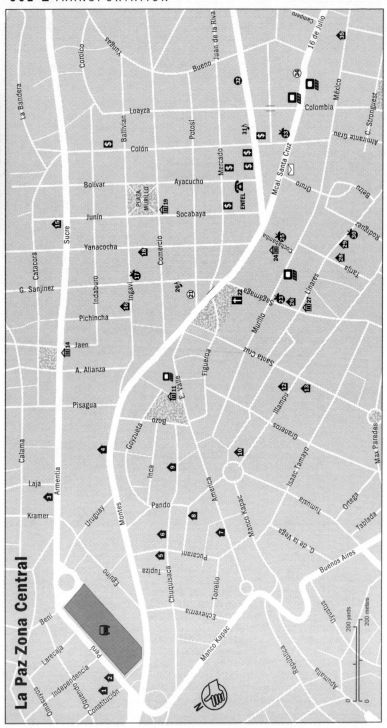

La Paz Zona Central

LA PAZ

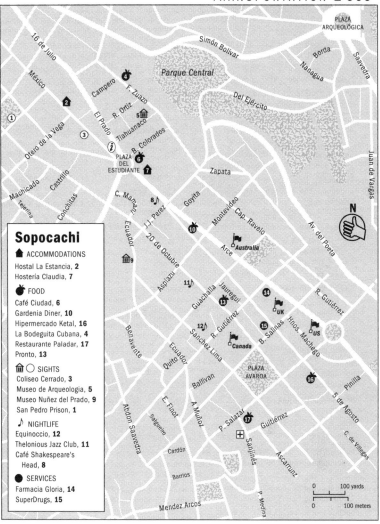

Sopocachi

🏠 ACCOMMODATIONS
Hostal La Estancia, 2
Hostería Claudia, 7

🍎 FOOD
Café Ciudad, 6
Gardenia Diner, 10
Hipermercado Ketal, 16
La Bodeguita Cubana, 4
Restaurante Paladar, 17
Pronto, 13

🏛 ◯ SIGHTS
Coliseo Cerrado, 3
Museo de Arqueologia, 5
Museo Nuñez del Prado, 9
San Pedro Prison, 1

♪ NIGHTLIFE
Equinoccio, 12
Thelonious Jazz Club, 11
Café Shakespeare's
 Head, 8

⬤ SERVICES
Farmacia Gloria, 14
SuperDrugs, 15

La Paz
Zona Central

🏠 ACCOMMODATIONS
Alojamiento 333, 7
Alojamiento Casero I, 1
Alojamiento La Ilajita, 5
Alojamiento la Riviera, 28
Alojamineto El Pasajero
 (Anexo 1), 9
Alojamineto Linares, 29
Hostal Austria, 18
Hostal Copacabana, 12
Hostal Ingavi, 16
Hostal La Estancia, 35
Hostal Montes, 4
Hostal Tambo de Oro, 3
Hotel Continental, 10
Hotel Happy Days, 26
Hotel Majestic, 13
Hotel Pando, 8
Residencial Florida, 6
Residencial Latino, 15
Residencial Riosinho II, 2

🍎 FOOD
Los Descudos, 33
Restaurant Alaya, 25
Restaurant Discoteca
 Jackie Chan, 17
Restaurant Romy, 30
Restaurant Vegetariano
 Laksmi, 23

🏛 MUSEUMS
Museo de la Coca, 27
Museo Etnografía, 24
Museo Nacional de Arte, 19
Museo Tambo Quirquincho, 11
Museos Municipales de la Paz, 14

🛈 ◯ SIGHTS
Casa de Cultura, 21
Iglesia de San Francisco, 22
McDonald's, 34

♪ ENTERTAINMENT
Soft Rock Café, 20
Wall Street Café, 31

⬤ SERVICES
Immigration Office, 32

Domestic Buses: La Paz has 3 long-distance bus terminals. The **Villa Fatima terminal,** at the far northeast tip of the city, sends buses to **Coroico, Chulumani, Rurrenabaque,** and **Guyaramerín.** Taxi Bs6. Micro Bs2. Almost constant departures (the company rotates) 7-11am; companies include: TransBolivia (☎2104690); Trans 10 de Febrero (☎210 146); Tourbus Total (☎212 526); Flota Yungueña (☎213 527). **El Cementerio terminal,** on Baptista, high above the Mercado de Brujas in the western pat of town, serves **Huatajata, Copacabana, Desaguadero, Sorata,** and **Tiahuanuco.** Most leave before 2pm. Finally, from the **terminal** (☎280 551), on Armentia:

Cooperativo de Servicios Turisticos (☎281 686). To: **Tiahuanuco** (2½hr., 8:30am and 3pm, Bs50); **Chacaltaya** (2hr., 8:30am and 3pm, Bs50); **Copacabana** (4hr., 8am, Bs20); **Arequipa** (18hr., Bs130); **Cusco** (15hr., Bs120); and **Lima** (2 days, US$50).

Cosmos (☎281 938). To **Cochabamba** (7hr., every hr. 7:30am-10:30pm, Bs25-30) and **Santa Cruz** (18hr., 8am and 5pm, Bs100).

El Dorado (☎281 672). To: **Cochabamba** (7hr., 8 per day 7am-10:30pm, Bs30); **Santa Cruz** (18hr., 5 and 7:30pm, Bs100); and **Potosí** (10hr., 8am, Bs40).

Expreso del Sur (☎281 921). To: **Tarija** (24hr., 4:30pm, Bs75-80); **Bermejo** (36hr., 4:30pm, Bs110-120); and **Yacuiba** (36hr., 4:30pm, Bs110-120).

Expreso Tupiza (☎282 153). To **Tupiza** (7:30pm, Bs70) and **Potosí** (10hr., 7:30pm, Bs50).

Expreso San Roque (☎281 959). To: **Camargo** (16hr., 4:30pm, Bs70); **Tarija** (22hr., 4:30pm, Bs90); **Yacuiba** (36hr., 4:30pm, Bs120); **Bermejo** (30hr., 4:30pm, Bs120); and **Buenos Aires** (2½ days, 4:30pm, US$120).

Express Tarija (☎282 009). To **Tarija** (22hr., 5pm, Bs90).

Flota Copacabana (☎281 596). To: **Cochabamba** (7hr., 10am and 10pm, Bs30); **Santa Cruz** (18hr., 5:30 and 8pm, Bs100); **Sucre** (18hr., 6:30pm, Bs90); and **Potosí** (10hr., 8:15pm, Bs60).

JumboBus 6 de Agosto (☎281 881). To **Oruro** (3½hr., 8 per day 7:30am-9:30pm, Bs20) and **Cochabamba** (7hr.; 7am, 9:30, 10pm; 2nd-class Bs25, 1st-class Bs30, with bed Bs45).

Jumbo Bus Aroma (☎281 894). To **Oruro** (3½hr., 8 per day 4:30am-9pm, Bs20).

Jumbo Bus Bolívar (☎281 963). To: **Cochabamba** (7hr.; 9, 11am, noon; Bs30); **Santa Cruz** (18hr., 5 and 7pm, Bs90); **Valle Grande** (26hr., 7:30am, Bs70); **Yacuiba** (35hr., 7pm, Bs90); **Sucre** (18hr., 7pm, Bs70); and **Trinidad** (30hr., 3pm, Bs120).

Jumbo Bus Cochabamba (☎284 222). To **Cochabamba** (7hr., 9:15am and 9:10pm, Bs40).

Jumbo Bus Urkupiña (☎281 725). To **Cochabamba** (7hr.; 9:30am, 8:30, 9pm; Bs20) and **Santa Cruz** (18hr.; 9:30am, 8:30, 9pm; Bs60).

Minera (☎281 685). To **Llallagua** (8hr., 7am, Bs20).

Panamericana (☎284 121). To **Uyuni** (13hr., 2:30pm, Bs50-70).

Pullman Suma Jorcko (☎281 644). To **Cochabamba** (7hr., 7:30am and 8pm, Bs25).

Super Jumbo Bolivia (☎281 832). To: **Oruro** (3½hr., 1:30pm, Bs25); **Cochabamba** (7hr., 9 per day 7:30am-10:30pm, Bs30); and **Santa Cruz** (18hr., 8 per day 7:30am-10:30pm, Bs100).

Trans Illimani (☎282 025). To: **Potosí** (10hr., 6:30am, Bs50); **Sucre** (18hr., 6:30am, Bs70); and **Villazón** (6:30am, Bs80).

Trans Imperial (☎281 661). To **Oruro** (3½hr., 8 per day 7:30am-8pm, Bs25).

Trans Imperio Potosí (☎281 769). To **Potosí** (10hr., 7pm, Bs40-50).

Trans Copacabana (☎282 135). To: **Oruro** (3½hr., 8 per day 7am-8pm, Bs15); **Cochabamba** (7hr.; 8:30am, 1, 8:45, 10pm; Bs30); **Santa Cruz** (18hr., 7:30pm, Bs150); **Potosí** (10hr., 7 and 8:30pm, Bs80); and **Sucre** (18hr., 6:45pm, Bs100).

Trans Naser (☎280 861). To **Oruro** (3½hr., 2:30pm, Bs15-20).

Transporte 6 de Junio (☎280 892). To: **Copacabana** (4hr.; 7 per day 8am-6pm; Bs20); **Puno** (6½hr.; 7 per day 8am-6pm; Bs40); **Cusco** (24hr.; 7 per day 8am-6pm; Bs110); and **Ilo** (24hr., 7 per day 8am-6pm, Bs110).

Tranportes Inquisiva (☎282 292). To **Tarija** (22hr., 5pm, Bs80) and **Yacuiba** (30hr., 5pm, Bs110).

Ponasur (☎281 708). To **Uyuni** (13½hr.; Tu and F 5:30pm, M, W, Th, Sa, Su 2:30pm; Bs50).

GETTING AROUND

Buses: Both **micro-buses** (large) and **mini-buses** (mini) run fixed routes all day, almost everywhere in the city. Destination on windshield. Pay upon boarding (Bs1 within the city, up to Bs3 outside) to get off yell "bajo aquí."

Taxis: Within the city Bs4-10; Bs30 outside. **Radio-taxis** (☎371 111 or 355 555).

Car Rental: American Rent-A-Car, Camacho 1574 (☎202 933). The selection is small (mostly 4-wheel-drive), but the safety standards are higher than most other places in town. US$49-89 per day; US$290-590 per week. V, MC, AmEx.

⚑ ORIENTATION

One of the biggest benefits to a city in the heart of a valley is that it is almost impossible to get lost: to re-orient, just walk downhill. There, the greatest activity lies along **El Prado,** the long main street that changes its name several times; in central La Paz, it's **Mariscal Santa Cruz, 16 de Julio,** or **El Prado;** toward the Armentia bus station, it becomes **Montes.** At its opposite end, it converts into **Villazón** briefly before splitting into **Arce** and **6 de Agosto**—in a neighborhood called **Sopocachi,** which is basically an extension of **La Zona Central.**

ⓘ PRACTICAL INFORMATION

TOURIST AND FINANCIAL SERVICES

Tourist Information: Tourist Office (☎371 044), at El Prado and Mexico. Open M-F 8:30am-noon and 2:30-7pm. **Angelo Colonial Tourist Services,** Linares 922-24 (☎360 199). Maintains a library of tour guides. Bulletin board. Internet access Bs7 per hr. Book exchange. Open M-F 9am-noon and 2:30-6:30pm, Sa 2:30-6:30pm.

Tour Agencies: ▓**Bolivian Journeys,** Sagárnaga 363 (☎357 848; email bolivian.journeys@mailexcite.com). Equipment rental. Experienced, multi-lingual guides. Maps. Open M-F 10am-12:15pm and 3:30-7pm, Sa 10:30am-12:15pm and 3:30-6pm. **America Tours SRL,** 16 de Julio 1490, Edificio Av., Office 9 (☎374 204; email AlistairM@hotmail.com; www.gamb.acslp.org). Incredible mountain biking experiences. Down the "World's Most Dangerous Road" US$49. Trekking and road maps. Book exchange. Open M-F 7am-7pm. **Inca Land Tours,** on Sagárnaga, Galeria Chuquiajo 10 (☎(01) 213 285); also at Pando 252 (☎457 908). Often has plane tickets to Rurrenabaque after the airlines have sold out. Open M-Sa 9am-7pm. **Fremen Tours,** Pedro Salazar 537 (☎416 336 or 414 069; fax 417 327; email vtfremen@caoba.entelnet.bo; www.andes-amazonia.com). Goes everywhere and anywhere in Bolivia. Open M-F 9am-12:30pm and 2:30-6:30pm, Sa 9am-noon.

Embassies and Consulates: Argentina, Sánchez Lima 497 (☎417 737), at Aspiazu. Open M-F 8:30am-5:30pm. **Brazil,** Capitan Ravelo 2334 (☎440 202). **Chile,** H. Siles 5873 (☎785 275), at Calle 13. Open M-F 9am-1pm and 3-5:30pm, Sa 9am-4:30pm. **Paraguay,** 6 de Agosto, Edificio Illimani II (☎432 201), at Salazar. Visas (US$30, within the day) for citizens of Australia, New Zealand, South Africa, and Canada, who need them. Open M-F 8:30am-1:30pm. **Peru,** 6 de Agosto, Edificio Allianza. Open M-F 9am-1pm and 3:30-5:30pm, Sa 9am-noon.

Immigration Office, Camacho 1433 (☎203 028). Visa extensions in under an hr. Open M-F 8:30am-4pm.

Currency Exchange: Casa de Cambios América, Camacho 1233 (☎204 369). Open M-Sa 9:30am-6:15pm. **Casa de Cambios,** Colón 330 (☎374 866 or 343 226). Bs1 commission. Open M-F 9am-6:30pm. **Casa de Cambio—International S.R.L.,** Mercado 990 (☎371 106). 2% commission. Open M-F 8:30am-2pm. **Sudamer Cambios,** Camacho 1311 (☎204 345). Open M-F 8:30am-12:30pm and 2-6:30pm, Sa 9am-noon. **Hotel Gloria** (☎341 457), at Potosí and Sanjinés, changes money on Sunday.

Banks: No banks in La Paz change traveler's checks—you'll have to use a *casa de cambio*. Banks can break large bills. **Banco Santa Cruz** (☎315 800 or 363 656), at Mercado and Socabaya. Open M-F 8:30am-6:30pm, Sa 8:30am-1pm. **Banco Económico,** Camacho 1245 (☎203 335). Open M-F 8:30am-noon and 2:30-6pm, Sa 9am-1pm. **Banco Nacional de Bolivia** (☎332 323), at Camacho and Colón. Open M-F 8:30am-noon and 2:30-6pm, Sa 9am-1pm.

American Express: Capitan Ravelo 2101 (☎442 727; fax 443 060; email magri_emete@megalink.com). Open M-F 9am-noon and 2-6:30pm, Sa 9am-noon.

LOCAL SERVICES

English-Language Bookstores: Los Amigos Del Libro, Mercado 1315 (☎320 742). Open M-F 9:30am-12:30pm and 2:45-7:30pm. **Libros del Amigo,** El Prado 1615 (☎318 164). Open M-F 9:30am-8:30pm, Sa 9:30am-noon.

Library: Biblioteca Publica de La Paz, at Mexico and Stronguest. Open M-F 9am-9:30pm, Sa 9am-1pm.

Language schools: La Casa de San Antonio, at N. Cordozo and Murillo 29, 2nd fl. (☎461 329; email escuespa@ceibo.entelnet.bo). Lessons US$7 per hr. Homestay option. Open M-F 8:30am-1pm and 3-8pm. **Centro Boliviano Americano,** Batallón Colorados, Edificio El Estudiante (☎441 508). 1-month course Bs500.

Cultural Centers: The following are great sources of information on upcoming cultural events. **Alliance Francaise,** Guachalla 399 (☎325 022). Open M and F 9am-1pm and 3-9pm, Tu-Th 7:30am-1pm and 3-9pm, Sa 9am-1pm. **Goethe Institut,** 6 de Agosto 2118 (☎442 453). Open M-F 9am-1pm and 3-7pm.

Supermarket: Hipermercado Ketal S.A. (☎335 433), at Arce and Pinilla. Its aisles can satisfy most cravings. Open daily 7am-10:30pm.

Laundry: Many accommodations offer laundry services. Average price Bs6 per kg.

EMERGENCY AND COMMUNICATIONS

Emergency: ☎110.

Police: Tourist Police, Edificio Olimpia 1314 (☎225 016, emergency ☎110), on the Plaza Tejada Sorazano.

Pharmacies: Farmacia Gloria, Arce 2670 (☎434 344). **SuperDrugs,** at Salinas and 20 de Octubre (☎434 442), on the Plaza Avaroa.

Hospital: AMID Clinic, Claudio Sanjinés 1558 (☎221 949 or 226 767). Ambulatory services available. V, MC.

Telephones: ENTEL, Ayacucho 267 (☎377 169). Open daily 7am-11:30pm. Only ENTEL can connect to La Paz cell phone numbers (commonly beginning 01).

Internet Access: Café Internet Pla@net, Murillo 914 (☎338 586). Bs4 per hr. 7am-noon, Bs6 per hr. noon-4pm, Bs8 per hr. 4-10pm. 1 free coffee per hr. Open daily 7am-10pm. **Café Internet Luntec,** Sorrano 27 (☎367 735). Bs6 per hr. Open daily 9am-9:30pm. **Centro de Informática Wiñay,** El Prado 1613 (☎331 341; www.entelnet.bo/winay.html). The fastest machines in town, but there's often a line. Bs6 per hr. Open M-Sa 24hr.

Post Office: Mariscal Santa Cruz 1278 (☎374 143 or 374 144). Open M-F 8:30am-8pm, Sa 9am-6pm, Su 9am-noon. **DHL/Western Union** (☎785 522), at Mariscal Santa Cruz and Loayza. Open M-F 8:30am-7pm, Sa 9am-noon. **FedEx,** Capitán Revelo 2401 (☎443 537). Open M-Sa 8am-8pm.

▐ ACCOMMODATIONS

Hotels in the center of the city tend to be the nicest. They can also be quite affordable, especially if an uphill walk doesn't bother you. Moving out of the center, the highest concentration of accommodations lies toward the bus station. These tend to be cheaper but more run-down.

CENTRAL LA PAZ

▨ **Hostal Austria,** Yanacocha 531 (☎351 140). The great backpacker meeting place. Laundry service Bs6 per kg. Safe box. Kitchen access. Bulletin board. Dorms Bs32; singles Bs36; doubles Bs72.

Alojamiento La Riviera, Tarija 325 (☎351 887). Colorful art and a bright red-tiled fountain offer a cheerful welcome. Large rooms. Volume controls in each room for the Latin pop that's piped in all day long. Rooms Bs30 per person, with bath Bs35.

Alojamiento Linares, Linares 1052 (☎364 282). Big, carpeted rooms; especially clean. Singles Bs20, with bath Bs35; doubles Bs40.

Residencial Latino, Socabaya 857 (☎370 947). Hidden at the top of the hill, these spacious rooms allow plenty of space to recover from the hike. Common baths a bit dark, but tidy. Rooms Bs20 per person.

Hotel Happy Days, Sagárnaga 229 (☎314 759; email happydays@zuper.net). The happy management does their best to make you happy. Firm beds. Shiny, happy bathrooms. All rooms with TV. Rooms Bs40 per person, with bath Bs45.

Hostería Claudia, Villazón 1965 (☎441 884). Attention to detail makes these rooms homier than most. Singles Bs55; doubles Bs72, with bath Bs126.

Hostal Copacabana, Illampu 734 (☎451 626). Plants create a foresty feel. Rooms— each with TV—are a bit small. Rooms Bs36 per person, with bath Bs60.

Hostal Tambo de Oro, Armentia 367 (☎281 565), across from the bus station, puts a premium on hygiene. All rooms with TV and bath. Singles Bs70; doubles Bs90.

Hotel Continental, Illampu 626 (☎451 176). The hip owners are too cool to worry that their beds are a little old and their bathrooms not the cleanest. Doubles Bs60.

Hostal Ingavi, Ingavi 735 (☎323 645). Functional. Perhaps the current construction will spruce it up. Rooms Bs30 per person, with bath Bs35.

Hotel Majestic, Santa Cruz 359 (☎451 628). Unbelievable views of the city (some including Mt. Illampu). All rooms with bath and phone. Cable TV Bs15. Breakfast included. Singles Bs70; doubles Bs90.

Residencial Riosinho II, Perú 129 (☎281 578). Limited space, but a motherly manager smiles brightly for every new arrival. Rooms Bs20 per person, with bath Bs35.

Hostal Montes, Montes 537 (☎378 960). Floor-to-ceiling windows. Towels. Breakfast included. Private baths only. Singles Bs60; doubles Bs80; triples Bs106.

Alojamiento Casero I, Constitución 102, off Perú, behind the bus station. Large windows allow an incredible view of the city. Bs15 per person.

Hotel Pando, Pando 248 (☎378 965). With an Internet cafe and tourist agency right downstairs, convenience is the name of the game. Cable TV, phone, and well-scrubbed bath in each room. Breakfast included. Singles Bs80; doubles Bs120; triples Bs150; quads Bs170; quints Bs190.

Residencial Flórida, Viacha 489 (☎455 239), off Pando. Spacious chambers have TVs and views of the surrounding hillsides. Rooms with bath Bs30 per person.

Alojamiento El Pasajero, Chuquisaca 579, off Pando. The rooms are showing their age, but the courtyard is gorgeous. Showers lack privacy. Rooms Bs20 per person.

⚀ FOOD

With so many restaurants in La Paz, it's a wonder *paceños* ever stop eating. From the wee morning hours until long after dark, **street vendors** dispense fresh, fresh fruit, hot, hot bread, and sausages grilled on the spot. Before noon, the **salteña** sells best—and with a cart every 10m, you won't have any problem finding a small pouch-like pastry (filled with spicy beef, chicken, or eggs and potatoes and onions) for yourself. Restaurants line both **El Prado** and the side streets that climb up from it. You can identify smaller, family-owned ones by the Coca-Cola advertisements perched above their doors. There, the *almuerzo* is likely fixed, cheap (Bs6-10), and quick. But those willing to pay for more variety in their meals should steer clear of flashy billboards and look for a restaurant that doesn't have "snack" in the title; try along **Arce** and **6 de Agosto.**

▧ **Restaurante Discoteca Jackie Chan,** Cochabamba 160 (☎339 231). Some of the tastiest Chinese food in Bolivia. Enormous menu. Fast, friendly service. Entrees Bs15-25. Appetizers Bs8-25. Open daily noon-11:30pm.

La Bodeguita Cubana, on Frederico Zuaza. Caribbean flavors with enough zest to inspire customers to write poems of praise on the walls. Entrees average Bs20. Don't leave without sampling the delectable passion fruit mousse (Bs4). Open M-Sa.

Restaurant Romy, Linares 1094. Traditional Bolivian dishes at a great price. *Almuerzo* Bs6. *Cena* Bs4. Open daily 9am-11pm.

Los Descudos (☎332 038), at Mariscal Santa Cruz and Colón. Oak tables, leather cushions, and vaulted ceilings make this massive hall look more Arthur's Court than La Paz. Dishes overflow with fresh vegetables. *Almuerzo* Bs12. Entrees Bs20-35. Open M-Sa 11am-3pm and 8pm-midnight.

Restaurant Alaya, Cochabamba 125 (☎315 152). Large portions and quick service. Their extensive selection of meat dishes will leave you drooling. *Almuerzo* Bs10. Entrees Bs25-40. Open daily 8:30am-10pm.

Restaurant Vegetariano Laksmi, Sagárnaga 239 (☎(01) 234 740). Creative vegetarian fare. All dishes under Bs15. Open M-F 9:30am-9pm, Sa 9:30am-6pm.

Café Ciudad (☎441 827), on the Plaza del Estudiante. Like other all-night diners the world over, Ciudad draws a varied crowd and serves food to satisfy most tastes, from pizza to kingfish. Entrees Bs10-30. Open 24hr.

Restaurante Paladar, Sanjinés 1538 (☎(01) 252 053). Brilliant Brazilian food. These chefs brought the best with them across the border: beans, rice, delectable beef, and good coffee. *Almuerzo* Bs10. Entrees Bs12-35. Open daily 11am-10pm.

Gardenia Diner, 6 de Agosto 2135 (☎444 037). A breakfast joint, all day long. Fantastic pancakes. Breakfast Bs3-15. Lunch and dinner under Bs25. Open daily 7am-11pm.

Pronto, Jáuregui 2248 (☎441 369), in the basement. A great Italian menu satisfies this smartly dressed, romantically inclined clientele. Pasta Bs18-30. Entrees Bs28-40. Open M-Sa 6:30-10:30pm.

👁 SIGHTS

MUSEUMS

La Paz's gallery assortment is as impressive as that of any commensurate city, but it proves of particular interest to travelers with short attention spans for ancient history or the traditional diorama—many of the city's museums feature lively and provocative exhibits that focus on customs and problems in the Bolivia of *today*.

MUSEO TAMBO QUIRQUINCHO. This museum documents La Paz's growth and development. From a startling collection of "then and now" photographs to an investigation of the *chola* persona, its varied displays neglect no aspect of *paceño* life. The exhibits also include some contemporary paintings and sculptures that allow deeper insight into the La Paz spirit. *(On Evaristo Valle at the Plaza Alonso de Mendoze. ☎390 969. Open Tu-F 9:30am-12:30pm and 3-7pm, Sa-Su 10am-12:30pm. Bs1.)*

MUSEO ETNOGRAFÍA. Home to an honest and respectful collection of displays that characterize daily Bolivian life, the museum maintains cases of sandals, food, tools, and clothing. An extensive video library provides further opportunity to learn about the themes explored in the museum's collection. *(Two blocks from the Plaza Murillo on Ingavi. Open Tu-F 9am-12:30pm and 3-7pm, Sa-Su 9am-1pm. Free.)*

MUSEO DE COCA. An honest and incredibly comprehensive analysis of the leaf that is so many Bolivians' livelihood. The museum challenges visitors to decide for themselves if coca provides a healthy life or a cycle of destruction. *(Linares 906, behind Iglesia de San Francisco. ☎333 032; www.coca-museum.magicplace.com. All information available in Spanish, English, French, and German. Bs7.)*

MUSEO DE ARQUELOGÍA. Discover the relics of an ancient empire in this castle-like building; treasures date back to the first known life in the Andes, the Tihuanacota culture. The collection holds mummies, stone jugs, metalwork, and figurines. *(Tiahuanuco 93, 1½ blocks from El Prado. ☎311 621. Open M-F 9am-12:30pm and 3-7pm, Sa 10am-12:30pm and 3-6:30pm, Su 10am-1pm. Bs5.)*

CASA MUSEO NUÑEZ DEL PRADO. Once a family mansion, this building now houses hundreds of excellently maintained stone and wood sculptures created by the late Narina Nuñez del Prado. Also on display are student works from nearby primary and secondary schools. The sculpture garden is one of the greenest nooks around. *(Ecuador 2034, 2 blocks up Pérez from Villazón. Open Tu-F 9:30am-1pm and 3-7pm, Sa-M 9:30am-1pm. Bs5, students Bs2, children under 10 and adults over 65 free.)*

MUSEOS MUNICIPALES DE LA PAZ. Also known as the Museos de la Calle Jaén, these four small museums warrant a short visit. **Museo Costumbrista** provides a thematic history of La Paz through small but colorful dioramas, masks, figurines, pictures, and scattered paintings. **Museo Litoral,** established in 1979 in honor of the 100th anniversary of the War of the Pacific, recreates one of the most important times in Bolivian history—the war that lost the nation's coastline—and has a fantastic collection of maps and historical documents. **Museo de Oro** displays the glittering metal that first drew the Spanish to Bolivia. The *Sala de Oro* ("Room of Gold") is a huge vault filled with tantalizing mobiles of the soft mineral that thousands died mining under the conquistadors' harsh rule. The *Salas de Plata* and *Cerámica* ("Rooms of Silver and Ceramics") recount the religious, decorative, and ceremonial uses of two more elements that were important in the Tiahuanuco and Inca cultures. **Museo Casa de Murillo** pays tribute to a hero of independence and indigenous medicine. Murillo's old home is now a shrine to a political history of the country. An additional small room presents local handicrafts, from masks to dolls to shoes shaped like dogs. *(Museo Costumbrista is on Sucre; the other three lie around the corner, on Jaén. Admission to all Bs4; ticket office in Museo Costumbrista. All open Tu-F 9:30am-12:30pm and 3-7pm, Sa-Su 10am-12:30pm.)*

MUSEO NACIONAL DE ARTE. In a building that was once a palace, three very distinct types of art come together. An eclectic collection of 20th-century Bolivian art and some contemporary paintings from other parts of Latin America rest on the top floor. The main floor is devoted solely to the La Paz school of art, united most strongly by a religious theme. The ground floor holds a small collection of *cuzqueño* paintings, a few sculptures, and old furniture. All exhibits surround a peaceful stone courtyard in the *barroco mestizo* style. The museum is considered one of the most important civil buildings in South America. *(At Comercio on the Plaza Murillo. Open Tu-F 9am-12:30pm and 3-7pm, Sa-Su 10am-1pm. Bs5, children under 18 free.)*

MARKETS

Walk a block down any street on a Saturday morning and you may start to believe that La Paz is just one big market. In some ways, it is. **Mercado de Brujos,** along Santa Cruz and Sagárnaga, behind Iglesia de San Francisco is for the superstitious and those in search of Bolivian kitsch. Indigenous women sell coca tea and dried llama fetuses to cure ailments and scare away bad luck. Meanwhile, hundreds of other merchants sell the staples most tourists just can't leave without: alpaca sweaters, reed pipes, silver and gold trinkets, and brightly colored bags. **Mercado Camacho,** at the end of Camacho, is a neverending farmer's market. **Mercado Negro,** along Max Paredes, is five department stores and a chain of pharmacies spilled onto the street. Anything you could want is here, balanced pyramid-style on tables.

OTHER SIGHTS

PLAZAS AND PARKS. With a nearly three-hour siesta every weekday afternoon, the people of La Paz need somewhere to rest their feet and enjoy the sun. A multitude of plazas scattered throughout the city provides just that. The **Plaza Avaroa,** on 20 de Octubre in Sopocachi, is a haven for the young at heart; children test-drive electric cars, dogs romp, and brilliant balloons fill the sky. **Las Velas,** on Bolívar on the way to the stadium, has a similarly youthful atmosphere, with go-carts, flying chairs, and loud Latin pop music. **Mirador Laikakota,** on El Ejército, another area that draws a mostly family crowd, is worth the walk for anyone who wants to see the bustle of La Paz laid out below them (Bs50). The **Plaza Murillo,** on Comercio, was founded as and still is the genuine center of town. The refined **cathedral** resides on its southern side; the presidential palace (also know as the Palacio Quemado, or Burnt Palace, because of the fires that have gutted it twice) sits next door. Come around 6pm to watch the crisp guards take down the flags; stay as shadows envelope the graceful yellow buildings. The **Plaza San Francisco,** impossible to miss from the top of Mariscal Santa Cruz, has become an activity center of its own—nearly every mode of transportation passes by it.

EL ALTO. A short ride up and out of central La Paz gives travelers an opportunity to look the Cordillera Real in the eye. Perched on the mountain rim that shadows the valley, the windswept district of El Alto looks across to Illimani and out over La Paz. The area—the capital's most prominent poor relation—centers around the airport; along its main street run combis, micro-buses, mini-buses, jumbo-buses, bicycles, and cars, all of which must pass through this area to enter or exit La Paz. Understanding this dynamic, the people of El Alto have lined their streets with car repair shops, oil change stations, and tire stores. Corrugated tin and plaster walls dominate the architecture here; Coca-Cola advertisements adorn the buildings. In many ways, the people who call this stretch of the altiplano home live outside the big city's complications; visiting the area, however, seldom simplifies a traveler's conception of La Paz. *(Catch any airport-bound bus on El Prado. About 20min. Bs3.7.)*

IGLESIA DE SAN FRANCISCO. Constructed in 1549, San Francisco imposes its presence on all who enter central La Paz, religiously inclined or not. Its enormous dome is visible from the highest points in town, its open plaza hosts all sorts of festivities, and its towering facade offers almost constant shade for those who rest on its steps. Thousands of feet pound its cobblestones throughout the day. Once inside, though, the city's ruckus fades away. Fresh flowers adorn every colorful altar, and devout worshipers kneel in the pews at all hours. This is not a place for flashing cameras, but for quiet visitors who wish to experience a taste of local religious life. *(Off Mariscal Santa Cruz. Open daily 7am-11pm. Free.)*

SAN PEDRO PRISON. A staggering opportunity to see inside a developing-world prison, this is an hour's activity for tourists, but the initial wait is a regular chore for hundreds of women and children who want to visit their husbands and fathers—except in the case of the most destitute families, who live in the cells with their imprisoned relatives. Bring your passport (or a copy) to leave with the guard; no cell phones or photographic devices allowed inside. *(Talk to the guards at the front desk about visiting one of the residents. Open Th and Su 9am-9pm. US$3.)*

MCDONALD'S. Anyone and everyone is welcome to tour their immaculate state-of-the-art kitchen. See the hidden stores of ketchup packets, the oven used only for toasting the burger buns, and the giant freezers that keep all the food safe and ready for preparation. Beware the stampede when the hand-washing bell rings— every employee is sanitized every half hour throughout the workday. *(On El Prado. Open Su-Th 10am-midnight, F-Sa 10am-1am. Free.)*

❄ FESTIVALS

If there's a street named after it, there's probably a parade or party on that date (and the day before, and the day after). Luckily for visitors, most holidays in La Paz provide a time for *paceños* to be with family and celebrate a rich history; they are not commonly a time of travel. Thus, accommodations remain readily available and prices unaffected. There are, however, certain celebrations that shake up the city. Throughout the last week of December and the first week of January, vendors pack every street and plaza, and the entire city center becomes an open-air market. The **Feria de Alasitas** (Jan. 24) is a time to make wishes; the most familiar face during this holiday is Ekeko ("dwarf" in Aymara), a chubby, jolly little man about whose neck every family hangs miniature versions of the things they most desire: cars, houses, food, etc. Later in the year, a preponderance of red and green La Paz flags, banners, and decorations mark the **anniversary** of the La Paz district (July 16). Dance troupes take over the evening, and the sidewalks fill to capacity with stands selling hot sausages, candied apples, and *ponche*, a hot drink made of milk and liquor. Along El Prado, the festivities last long into the night, and bands burst into song for days afterward. Most commercial establishments, banks, and restaurants close on this day and sometimes the next day as well. Transportation schedules are not in effect during the holiday; call for actual times. Finally, on

¡**BAILE!** Every year, the festival of **El Gran Poder** rolls into town at the beginning of summer. For most tourists who encounter it, it's a spectator event. But those who desire a more interactive experience should check out the **Entrado Folklórico Universitario.** The university students' version of El Gran Poder incorporates all the traditional dances—but it also provides free lessons in the afternoon and evening, on the plaza in front of the university. The parade takes place at the end of July, so be on the lookout for stamping feet and twirling ribbons throughout the month.

August 6, Bolivia's **Independence Day** is celebrated proudly and loudly. The parading starts the day before, with the Plaza Murillo in the spotlight. The drinking starts hot and strong as soon as darkness falls the day before, filling the Plaza San Francisco with people who are all too eager to celebrate anything they can. August 6th and 7th are both "feriados," so don'd expect to find much of anything open, and do expect to hear lots of bands and people screaming "Jesucristo" and see everyone carrying a red, yellow, and green flag.

ENTERTAINMENT

ARTS

The **Casa de Cultura,** on Mariscal Santa Cruz, across from Iglesia de San Francisco, has an information center for cultural events around town. A small theater upstairs sometimes hosts performances. (☎374 668. Open M-F 8:30am-noon and 2-7pm.) The weekly **Bolivian Times,** available at every newsstand in the city (Bs5), also offers a number of suggestions for cultural immersion, from art exhibits to the most recent films and plays. **Movie theaters** line El Prado, but most show foreign films with Spanish subtitles. For a taste of more traditional culture, look for signs in restaurants—many advertise live music on weekends. In particular, **Los Descudos** (see Food, p. 307) and **La Peña,** Sagárnaga 261, have reliable repertoires on Friday and Saturday nights. The restaurant at **Soft Rock Café** (see Nightlife, p. 311) is another good bet. The **Teatro Municipal,** at Sanjinés and Indaburo, puts on the most consistent and popular theatrical performances. **Cinemática Boliviana,** at Pichincha and Indaburo (☎325 346), is one of the few La Paz movie theaters that screens Spanish-language films.

SPORTS

Fútbol, anyone? The classic South American pastime doesn't disappoint in La Paz. *Fútbol* news dominates the sports section in almost every newspaper, which always has information on the next big game. Alternatively, head to the stadium and ask at the ticket window. Tickets for big matches (Bs50) often sell out, but it's usually possible to show up the day of the match and purchase them from hawkers, albeit at a slight mark-up. Another spot to check out for spectator events is the **Coliseo Cerrado** on México, by the Plaza de Estudiante. Common activities there include **wrestling** matches and cultural **festivals.**

LA PAZ

◪ NIGHTLIFE

Friday nights bring live music into clubs and restaurants and a *Paceña cerveza* into almost every hand. Saturday nights tend to be calmer—watch the cinema queues start to grow as early as 4pm.

Equinoccio, Sánchez Lima 2191 (☎(01) 245 667), between Aspiazu and Guachalla. A bar and dance club, Equinoccio constantly brings in fresh live music to please an excited and active crowd. The stage is big, the dance floor bigger. Cover Bs10-25.

Café Shakespeare's Head (☎(01) 292 589), on Villazón. An intimate crowd, loyal to its beer and small local bands. Live music most F and some Sa. Cover on nights with music Bs10. Beer Bs10. Mixed drinks Bs12-20. Open daily 8am-3am.

Beer's Pub, Sanjinés 2688 (☎411 668). One of the leaders in an attempt to bring Thursday nights to life in La Paz. Often hosts new bands. Well-dressed crowd. Cover Bs25. Open Th-Sa 9:30pm-2:30am.

Thelonious Jazz Club, 20 de Octubre 2172 (☎337 806). Cozy atmosphere and fantastic jazz, both traditional and with a Latin twist. Cover Bs20. Open W-Sa 9pm-1:30am.

Underground Club, Medinacelli 2234 (☎312 365). Underground's loud beats and flashing lights satisfy the raver in us all. Diverse international crowd. For a mid-week rush, try the Wednesday night Rave Party, when this place is the only one drawing a crowd. Cover Bs15. Open W-Sa 10pm-3am.

Soft Rock Café, Sanjinés 467 (☎314 455). Mellow food and atmosphere, with live local music on the weekends. A small theater hosts artists from all over Bolivia. Drinks Bs3-10. Snacks Bs5-18. Open M-Sa 9am-11pm.

Café Montmartre, Guachalla 363, off 20 de Octubre. Catch the big soccer game or nibble a dainty pastry, *en français*. The Alliance Francaise (the *official* French Cultural Center) is right next door. Open M-F noon-3pm and 4pm-2am, Sa 8pm-2am.

Wall Street Café, Camacho 1363 (☎316 090); also at Arce 2142 (☎338 619). Rounds out the array of odd cultural references. This one lives up to its name: coffee selection Bs3-15, desserts Bs3-20, meals Bs10-26. Open daily 8am-midnight.

⊠ INTO THE MOUNTAINS FROM LA PAZ

EL CHORO

This mainly-downhill **hike from Cumbre to Coroico,** the most popular trek in the La Paz area, promises spectacular views and a stunning variety of climates—you'll start in gore-tex and finish in shorts. Most of the trek follows a **pre-hispanic road,** remnants of which still pepper the trail. Because the weather and the trail are unpredictable, most people make the hike with a group and a guide; hikers who go without a guide should visit a travel agency that makes the trip often (see Tour Agencies, p. 305) to obtain an updated **map** of the trail and advice on conditions. If you're going it alone, transportation to the trail leaves every morning from Villa Fatima around 6am. Hiking during the dry season (Apr.-Oct.) is best, though snow stays in the high parts almost year-round. Prepare for all climates: bring a tent, a sleeping bag, raingear, clothing for all temperatures, a knife, cooking supplies, matches, flashlight, water bottle, water purification tablets, toilet paper, trash bags, and insect repellent.

Be prepared for about 70km of walking, all downhill but on a bad road. Villages along the route can provide food, water, batteries, and occasionally accommodations, but don't count on it. The trailhead is in **Cumbre,** a half-hour drive from La Paz, and the first day's travel follows an ancient road carved into a hillside. There is a small store that can be reached before dark to stock up on supplies if you are running low, but they tend to close early, so you shouldn't depend on them for that night. Most choose to spend the first night camping in the small community of **Chucura,** a five-hour hike from Cumbre, where a ranger camp is located. On the second day, the roads are worse but the vistas more breathtaking. Rivers and towns are more plentiful. Most choose to spend their second night in **Sandillani,** about eight-nine hours from Chucura. There are a number of camping areas here, and locals sometimes board hikers. The third day is long but rewards the tenacious with bountiful flora and fauna. Rare animals—including hummingbirds found only in Bolivia, spider monkeys, small tigers, and bicolored porcupines—inhabit the forest. There are camping sites in **Chairo,** where most choose to catch some sort of transportation either back to La Paz or into the bustling town of Coroico (p. 326).

▶ DAYTRIPS FROM LA PAZ

VALLE DE LUNA

Take Mallasa-bound micro 11 or minibus 231 or 237 (30min., Bs1.8) from the Plaza de Estudiante near the corner with México. Ask the driver to let you off at Valle de la Luna, right before Mallasa. There are formations and paths on both sides of the road. To head back to La Paz, hail a micro or mini from the side of the road.

Decades of erosion pattern have created the seemingly alien land forms found here today. Tall stone peaks are divided by deep gullies, each with its own unique perspective of La Paz. A slippery dirt path provides a means of navigation across, around, and between the incredible formations. The walk is brief but allows a relaxing insight into Bolivia's diverse terrain.

ZOOLÓGICO

Take Mallasa-bound micro 11 or minibus 231 or 237 (35min., Bs1.8) from the Plaza del Estudiante, off México. Tell the driver you're going to the zoo, just past Mallasa. Alternatively, from the Valle de la Luna, it's a 15min. walk down the main road. Buses back to La Paz leave from the zoo until closing. Open daily 10am-6pm. Bs3, children Bs1.

From the moment you step off the bus, you know you've left La Paz: Mallasa is about 5°C warmer, and its sun even brighter. Jaguars, placidly lapping water just 2m away, observe newcomers intently. Monkeys stretch tiny, human-like fingers through the fence for a taste of popcorn. Giant vultures bob by on their way to lunch, and ducks cry out to no one in particular. Such variety makes it easy to forget about the ordinary llamas and alpacas of the Bolivian countryside (although they, too, have their place at this zoo).

MUELA DEL DIABLO

Take minibus 288 (40min., Bs30) from the Plaza del Estudiante to the end of the line. From the parking lot, continue up the dirt road, to the right; when you reach a small cemetery, continue up and to the right (2hr.). Buses back to La Paz leave until around 4pm.

The hills that frame the path to the top of the Muela del Diablo ("Devil's Molar") rock change color every few meters. This provides an interesting contrast to the characterless modern architecture that lies below, in the village of Ovejuyo, where the trail begins. From the craggy rock's summit, La Paz appears in miniature. But don't get too caught up in the view; the path is known to be frequented by bandits—always exercise caution. Do not travel alone or in the dark.

VALLE DE ANIMAS

Take mini-bus or micro Ñ from the Plaza del Estudiante to Ovejuyo (40min., Bs2.3); ask the driver to alert you. There, a rocky path leads uphill. Passing minis and micros head back to La Paz until late afternoon.

On a hillside populated by enormous stone peaks, narrow paths lead up to where the views appear to belong on another planet. From the base, the path is not very well-defined; it becomes more difficult to discern as the walls of rock close in. One's foot falls on rocks pebbles, or sand that slips away with the lightest of pressure. As the track meanders its way around the needles of stone, a good handhold may be the only means of continuing upward. From the perch at the very top, the crumbling dirt is easy to forget as the world looks tiny and stable, nestled in the valley below. Beware crevices too narrow for broad shoulders or backpacks; step gingerly but plant your feet securely; and you'll be duly rewarded at the top. It's about a one-hour hike.

CAÑON DE PALCA

The few buses that serve Huni or Palca directly—the trail's two heads—leave before 9am. Catch one (45min., Bs4) at the corner of Boquerón and Luis Lara; ask to be let off at Huni. (The path leads downhill from Huni to Palca.) Or, take minibus 385 and ask to be let off at the fork that provides access to Huni. You can then trek up the hill (about 20min.), passing a small lake on your right, and descend into Huni. A faded black and white sign marks the beginning of the path; stay to the right. To return to La Paz, follow the main road to the plaza and take a minibus (1½hr., until 4pm, Bs6).

The Cañon de Palca's winding valley path sees some of the best possible views of Illimani. Starting from the brink of the canyon in Huni, the through-course makes for a leisurely stroll, the surrounding landscape becoming more incredible with each step. The hike takes about three hours. You can camp along most parts of the path and in much of the canyon, but look out for *"Propiedad Private"* signs.

TIAHUANUCO

Take a Guaqui-bound bus (1½hr., every 30min., Bs6) from the corner of José María Azin and Eyzagu. Ask the driver to drop you at Tiahuanuco. Head right from the fork where the bus stops, and look for a flat, orange building on the right, just off the railroad tracks, which is the museum. To get back to La Paz, catch a minibus in the plaza or along the main road. Open daily 7am-5pm. Bs15.

A trip to the ruins at Tiahuanuco offers numerous insights into how life once was on the barren altiplano. The Tiahuanuco Empire began around 1580 BC and ended, mysteriously, in AD 1172. Its empire stretched through Bolivia, Peru, Chile, and Argentina; this site was the capital. Historians believe that it was a warrior state, with a successful agricultural system that fed eight million people—a population equivalent to that of all of present-day Bolivia. The **Museo Regional de Tiahuanuco** pays tribute to the enormous archeological effort that has begun to explain these ruins over the past century. Its displays include maps that demonstrate the fallen empire's astounding size. In the ruins themselves, the **Pirámide de Akapana** was probably a religious temple, in honor of the mighty surrounding mountains; scientists estimate that it stood 18m tall, but little remains today. In **Kantat Hallita**, a half-underground temple, there's a stone map of the Tiahuanuco region. Distinctive stone heads emerge from the walls of the **Templete Semisubterraneo**, a large quadrangular temple. Archaeologists believe that at one point the Tiahuanucos may have displayed heads of their decapitated victims throughout this temple, but that as time passed, stone skulls replaced the real ones. **Kalasaya,** an enormous open-air temple, houses detailed structures that suggest it served as an agricultural calendar. Three stone statues therein—**monolito Ponce, monolito Fraile,** and **Puerta del Sol**—probably played important roles in measuring time. **Putuni,** also known as the Palacio de Los Sarcáfagos (Palace of the Sarcophagi), is still under excavation, but has already captured much attention with the hundreds of religious designs that decorate its polished stone floor. Finally, the wonders of **Pumapunku** are still being explored; massive stones, some weighing up to 130 tons, litter the site. Where they came from and how anyone moved them remains a mystery.

NEAR LA PAZ: URMIRI

Hotel Gloria La Paz, at Potosí and Sanjinés (☎ 370 010), runs a shuttle to Urmiri (2hr.; Tu, Th, and Sa 8am; Bs45 round-trip). Buy tickets in advance from the main desk. A min. of 6 people is necessary for the shuttle bus to make the trip.

In paradisiacal Urmiri, the sun is hot and the water hotter. Here, the owners of Hotel Gloria La Paz have created a resort by channeling the area's scalding **hot springs** into more accessible waters. Their **Hotel Gloria Urmiri** features hot-spring saunas, hot-spring swimming pools, and personal hot-spring bathtubs in every room. The colorful surrounding landscape invites short hikes—some of which lead to hidden hot springs. (Rooms M-F Bs40 per person, with bath Bs60; Sa-Su Bs60 per person, with bath Bs80. Camping Bs10 per person. Breakfast included. Pool and sauna use Bs15-25 per day.)

WESTERN BOLIVIA

According to Andean mythology, **Lake Titicaca** (p. 315) is the cradle of civilization, even of life itself. It's easy to see why Titicaca inspires such epic legends. At 3827m above sea level and extending across 8560 sq. km, it's the largest lake in South America and the largest in the world above 2000m. Traveling on its surface is like being on the open sea, except for the enormous peaks poking out of the horizon. The lake has 41 islands (not counting the floating ones made by the Uros people on the Peruvian side), the most significant of which, Isla del Sol and Isla de la Luna, are the mythic birthplaces of the Sun and Moon. The Aymara culture, descended from the Colla, Lupaca, and Tiahuanuco, once dominated the area. The expansion of the Inca Empire in the 14th and 15th centuries brought Quechua customs to Titicaca but never succeeded in supplanting what formerly existed. To this day, Quechua and Aymara people prefer to live separately—Quechua north of the lake, Aymara to the south.

HIGHLIGHTS OF WESTERN BOLIVIA

ROW across Titicaca's blue, blue waters—from the tip of the **Copacabana peninsula** to Isla del Sol (p. 319).

DRINK from the mystical Fuente del Inca on tranquil **Isla del Sol** (p. 319).

EMBARK on any number of excursions from the stunning green, green towns of **Sorata** (p. 322) and **Coroico** (p. 326).

PLUMMET down the "Most Dangerous Road" in the world (p. 327) and **live** to tell about it. (See also **Highlights of La Paz,** p. 300.)

Spanning the area between chilly La Paz and the steamy jungles of the Amazon lies a world stuck in the middle—though it's hardly complaining about its position. Here, the sun is hot, the flowers are brilliant, and the fruit is plentiful. This is **the Yungas** (p. 322), considered paradise by most visitors. North and south, the sunsets are limitless, the sunrises coated in a heavenly mist, and the land changes just as quickly as the scores in the soccer games that take place in every square, corner, and field. From rushing waterfalls to steep valley basins, every view is a wonder.**Fuente del Inca,** which remains, as it has since ancient times, the main source of water on the dry island

LAKE TITICACA

COPACABANA   ☎08

A town dependent on each passing wave of tourists, Copacabana must turn to its two ancient sources of stability. The first, Aymara culture, fills the air every day despite fervent attempts by both the Incas and the Spanish to eradicate it; it belonged to this lively port's original inhabitants and remains today in its language, lifestyle, and festivals. The second source, Lake Titicaca, possesses a serenity that offsets the tout-tout frenzy that chokes Copacabana's streets. And though even such old and powerful elements cannot shield pretty Copacabana from its tourist-trap reputation, they offer its many visitors deeper recesses to explore—indigenous influences peek out from among the Catholic relics, and boats of all shapes and sizes float by on the beach, waiting for passengers who wish to explore the highest navigable lake in the world from a comfortable base.

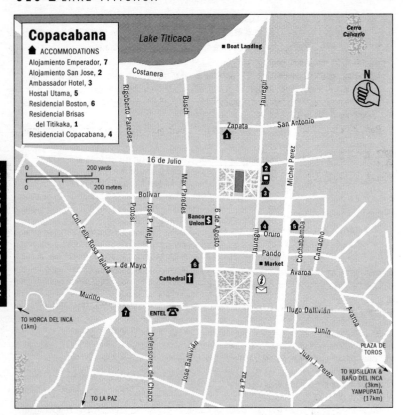

Copacabana

🏠 ACCOMMODATIONS
Alojamiento Emperador, **7**
Alojamiento San Jose, **2**
Ambassador Hotel, **3**
Hostal Utama, **5**
Residencial Boston, **6**
Residencial Brisas
  del Titikaka, **1**
Residencial Copacabana, **4**

⚡🔢 ORIENTATION AND PRACTICAL INFORMATION

Lake Titicaca marks Copacabana's western border. **6 de Agosto** leads uphill from the lake to the **Plaza Sucre** and, after a few more blocks, the **Plaza 2 de Febrero**. Most accommodations and services cluster around these landmarks.

Buses: All buses and colectivos deposit passengers along 16 de Julio or 6 de Agosto, near the Plaza Sucre. Trans Tur (☎622 233), on the Plaza 2 de Febrero, goes to **La Paz** (3½hr.; M, W, F 5 per day 8am-5pm; Tu, Th, Sa 3 per day 8am-5pm; Su 8 per day 8am-5pm; Bs14). Open daily 7am-7pm. Titicaca Tours/Lago Tours/Grace Tours, 6 de Agosto 100 (☎622 509), runs to: **La Paz** (3½hr., 1pm, Bs40); **Puno** (3½hr., 1pm, Bs15); and **Cusco** (15hr., 1:30pm, Bs80).

Tour Agencies: The conglomerate **Titicaca Tours/Lago Tours/Grace Tours** (see Buses, above) takes care of almost any travel need. Most hostel owners who arrange tours to the islands do so through these agencies. Full-day excursions to Isla del Sol including a stop at Isla de la Luna Bs25; half-day trips that stop only at the south end of Isla del Sol Bs15. Neither option includes a guide.

Currency Exchange: Banco Union (☎622 323), on 6 de Agosto. US$2 commission for up to US$200 in traveler's checks; 1% commission for US$250-500. The bank does not (officially) buy soles. **ATM** takes V and MC. Open daily 8:30am-6pm. **Cooperativa Multiactiva Virgen de Copacabana L.T.D.A.** (☎622 116), on 6 de Agosto next to the Hotel Playa Azul. Exchanges traveler's checks (1% commission). Open M-F 9am-1pm and 2:30-6:30pm, Sa-Su 9am-1pm. Many shops along 6 de Agosto and on the Plaza 2 de Febrero also exchange traveler's checks and sometimes soles.

Outdoor Equipment: Titicaca Tours (☎622 060), on the beach. Kayaks Bs20 per hr. Cata-marans Bs30 per hr. Motorcycles Bs50 per hr. Bicycles Bs10 per hr. Open daily 7am-7pm.

Police: (☎110), on the Plaza 2 de Febrero, across from the cathedral.

Hospital: (☎118), off Felix Rosa Tejda.

Telephones: ENTEL (☎622 331), on Murillo, just left of the cathedral. Allows calling card calls, toll-free calls, and cash calls. Open daily 8am-8pm.

Internet Access: @lfa-internet, Jáuregui on the Plaza Sucre. Bs20 per hr. Open daily 10am-2pm and 3-10pm.

Post Office: On Plaza 2 de Febrero. Open Tu-Sa 9am-noon and 2:30-6pm, Su 9am-3pm.

ACCOMMODATIONS

Nearly every block of Copacabana boasts a high-flying sign for an *alojamiento*, *residencial*, or *hostal*—there are always beds, though overcrowding can be a problem on holidays. Many hostel owners will want you and your backpack in by 10pm and out by 11am; read signs on the wall before heading out for the day.

Alojamiento Emperador, Murillo 235 (☎622 083), 1½ blocks behind the cathedral. The Emperador is paradise for the do-it-yourself backpacker—and there are always plenty of them hanging around. Extras include a kitchen and big sink for laundry. The welcoming owners can arrange trips to Isla del Sol and Isla de la Luna. Rooms Bs10 per person.

Residencial Boston (☎622 231), on Conde de Lemus, near the cathedral. Simple hostel, comfortable beds. Rooms Bs13 per person, with bath Bs25.

Residencial Copacabana, Oruro 555 (☎622 220), 2 blocks from the Plaza 2 de Febrero on Jáuregui. Maintains the basics. Rooms Bs10 per person, with bath Bs20.

Hostal Utama (☎622 013), on 3 de Mayo, 3 blocks from the Plaza 2 de Febrero on Jáuregui. Clean towels on the bed, a bottle of mineral water on the table, and new soap and toilet paper in the sparkling bathrooms anticipate every need. Rooms Bs40 per person, negotiable when business is slow.

Residencial Brisas del Titikaka (☎622 178), on 6 de Agosto, next to the port. Bright rooms, some with spectacular Titicaca views. Rooms Bs30 per person, with bath Bs40.

Alojamiento San José, Jáuregui 146, on the Plaza Sucre. Central and tidy. Plain rooms overlook an open courtyard. Rooms Bs10 per person.

Ambassador Hotel (☎622 216), on the Plaza Sucre at Jáuregui. Large selection of rooms surround a sunny patio. Bath and TV in every room. Rooms Bs35 per person.

FOOD

Copacabana boasts a sizeable restaurant population, particularly on main drags 6 de Agosto and Jáuregui, but as most offer indistinguishable menus, the town's actual culinary options prove somewhat limited. The local favorite, trout, appears in most *almuerzos* and *cenas* (Bs5-10). Stands around the market offer fare similar to the restaurants' at lower prices (under Bs4). And for sweet tooths, there's always a bag of *pansacaya* (Bs1), the light, chewy caramel popcorn-like snack sold on street corners. With its eager staff and views of the lake, the bright ■Restaurant Colonial, at 6 de Agosto and 16 de Julio, reaches above and beyond the Copacabana standard. The fish, in particular, is delicately prepared. Patio seating available. (Entrees Bs20-28. ☎622 160. Open daily 7am-11pm.)

SIGHTS

COPACABANA CATHEDRAL. In the 16th century, Franciscan missionaries forced most of Copacabana's population to convert to Catholicism. One man in particular, Francisco Yupanqui, took their lessons to heart and built a statue of the Virgin Mary with a baby Jesus in her arms. Unfortunately, the Franciscans did not approve of his likeness—both mother and child looked Aymara, native to the

> The area around Copacabana is not particularly well-lit at night, and a path that's slippery or hard to find during the day will only prove more trouble come sunset. When visiting sights in the area, allow time to return before dark.

area—and they ordered the artist to destroy his blasphemous creation. But Yupanqui was convinced that his people needed an image in which they could truly believe, so rather than start over, he covered his statue with a layer of gold and decorated it with elaborate religious images. The missionaries welcomed the new statue and built a church to house it. In time, legends sprung up about the statue's healing powers, and the church drew worshippers from around the region. Copacabana grew out of the life that surrounded that church—today's beautiful cathedral stands as the final product of centuries of community, construction, and art production. It continues to draw crowds, especially on religious holidays, though Yupanqui's "Dark Virgin of the Lake" is now shrouded in a small temple at the back of the cathedral, only to be seen by her people at the festival in her honor during the first few days of February. A small museum presents a scattering of religious artifacts and a well-kept garden to groups of 5 or more. *(Open daily 6:45am-9pm. Museum open M-F 9am-noon and 2:30-5:30pm; Sa-Su, and festivals 8am-noon and 2:30-6pm.)*

BAÑO DEL INCA. Amid the surrounding altiplano's parched dirt and hot rock, this spring-fountain in Kusijata takes on all of water's mythic properties: renewing, healing, life-giving. The Inca believed its waters could foretell the future and made it his bath (hence the name) in order to feel closer to the times to come. The surrounding garden blooms in the shade of its eucalyptus trees. *(Follow Junín toward the Plaza de Toros and out of town (1hr.), where it becomes a rocky downhill path that loads through the country to the small town of Kusijata. Bs5.)*

HORCA DEL INCA. Perched high above town on Cerro Sancollani, the Horca del Inca more likely served as a solar calendar than as an *horca* (gallows). This rock formation, constructed around 1700 BC and now covered in graffiti, draws Copacabana's citizens up the hill every winter solstice (June 21) to watch the sun rise. If the sun's rays shine on the correct area of the Horca, the onlookers celebrate the coming of a prosperous crop year; if the rays hit a dark crevice, Copacabana must begin to prepare for a barren harvest—the site's caretaker can point out the specific portentous spots. Some other large stones at the site indicate the four cardinal directions; still others, again with the help of the sun's telling light, remind people when the leap year is upon them. *(Start facing the entrance to the cathedral and take Murillo out of town; when you reach a fork where the dirt paths diverge, head straight and up the hill (30-40min.). Follow the arrows painted on rocks to the top. Bs10.)*

CERRO CALVARIO. Fourteen large crosses, each symbolizing a certain point in Christ's journey to his crucifixion at Calvary, mark the steep and rocky trek up Cerro Calvario. Some visitors decorate the bases of the crosses with stones as testament to their faith, and although such religious dedication is not required, these **stations of the cross** do allow periodical excuses to stop, breathe, and watch Copacabana shrink into the shadow of the hill. At the summit, a small stand sells miniature cars, houses, bags of pasta, boxes of laundry detergent, and even diplomas. On Sundays and holidays, worshippers scale the hill, make their purchases, and then sacrifice them at the individual altars scattered around the park; they believe that by burning these miniatures, they increase their chances of earning the real things. *(The path up Cerro Calvario begins behind the Capilla del Señor de la Cruz de Colquepata, a church at the top of Bolívar.)*

◪ NIGHTLIFE

Don't jump from your seat the first, second, or 50th time you hear a loud bang in the night—most likely it's just a group of kids experimenting with their never-ending supply of firecrackers. Wandering the town's streets and plazas, locals young and old enjoy Copacabana's brisk, fresh air as late as midnight every night. Most visitors seem sedentary in contrast, establishing themselves in one of the ubiquitous restaurants to drink beer or Irish coffee.

Tatú Carreta Pub, on Oruro off 6 de Agosto. An upbeat music mix brings this small, candlelit den to life. The energetic waitstaff serves meals too, but most customers come for the coffee (Bs5-8) and drinks (around Bs10). A great place to devour a book or make chill new friends. Open daily 6pm-2am.

Cafe Bar Sol y Luna, 16 de Julio 3 (☎ 622 094), an annex of the Hotel Gloria de Copacabana. The decor rides the line between artistic and rustic, but stays true to its theme—"*Sol y Luna.*" Expensive meals (Bs18-30), extensive drink list. Coffee Bs4-9. Cocktails Bs25. Milkshakes Bs7. Open daily 10:30am-4pm and 6pm-late.

Discoteque Migueliu's, on Cochabamba; follow the signs down Avaroa from Plaza 2 de Febrero. Migueliu's mixed-age clientele prefers drinking and dice-playing to dancing. Beer Bs7. Mixed drinks under Bs15. Open daily 6pm-2am.

Pacha Cafe (☎ 622 206), on 6 de Agosto. The jungle-themed vines and Bolivian art create an embracing environment where tourists can enjoy international food (Bs12-35), drinks (Bs3-20), and a book exchange. Open daily 7-11:30pm.

⚡ DAYTRIPS FROM COPACABANA

COPACABANA PENINSULA

Start walking out of Copacabana on Junín, then follow the dirt road that runs along the lake to Sicuani (3½hr.) and to Yampupata (4-5hr.). Bring sunblock, snacks, and water or a means to purify it, as there's no place to buy such things along the way. At the strait, continue on to Isla del Sol (boats 20min., Bs60; sailboats and rowboats 45min., Bs25).

Whether an alternate route to Isla del Sol or just an excuse to enjoy the fresh air, the walk to the end of the Copacabana peninsula provides a chance to encounter daily life on Titicaca's shores. Bicycle riders and sheep use this lakeside road—which winds around mountains, passing through the occasional tiny town—more than cars do. Note the small **temple** dedicated to the Virgin Mary which hides in a cluster of trees (after 1½hr.); below it, a grassy knoll is ideal for a picnic. Further down the road, along the shore, lies **Sicuani** (2hr. away). If this is as far as you want to walk, head for the billboard advertising Inca Thanki boat rides, and Señor Hilario Paye Quispe will soon appear. (If he doesn't, inquire at the restaurant next to the billboard, which Quispe's nephew owns.) Nostalgic Quispe conducts brief (10min.) excursions in his homemade totora reed boats as well as rides to the other side of the bay (30min.), where there are multiple camping sites. He even dons a native hat and poncho in an effort to present the old lake life. For all his services, he asks only that you "pay what you feel is appropriate." From Sicuani, the walk continues to **Yampupata** (45min.). There, sundry boats wait to ferry passengers across the Strait of Yampupata to the south end of Isla del Sol. Don't leave too late, as trying to navigate Isla del Sol in the dark can be frustrating and dangerous.

ISLA DEL SOL

Few would guess, from the humble lives lived now on Isla del Sol, that both Manco Kapac and Mama Ocllo, who together founded the Inca Empire, were born on its rocky shores. But from the views atop its ruin-speckled mountains, it's easy to imagine why one might be so inspired. Called "paradise" by many a visitor, Isla del Sol could be just that for those in search of peace, simplicity, and great walks.

■☀⚡ TRANSPORTATION. Tour companies in Copacabana transport tourists to Isla del Sol by **boat.** (2hr.; 8 and 9am, some at 1pm; half-day Bs25, full-day Bs35. Return trip from Callapampa at north of the island, 1pm; or Pilko Kaina ruins at the south, 10:30 and 11am and 4pm.) Most boats deposit at the south end of the island, by the Templo del Sol or the Escalera del Inca and the great Fountain. Many routes back to Copacabana stop at Isla de la Luna (see Sights, below). A half-day tour will cut down your time on Isla del Sol, but you can get around this by choosing one of the many open-ended tickets One-way tickets (Bs15) allow you to walk from Copacabana to Yampupata (see Copacabana Peninsula, above).

⚄ ACCOMMODATIONS AND FOOD. The best selection of accommodations lies on the south end of the island, though most still lack running water and electricity (candles are provided, flashlights suggested as back-up). Friendly, informative owners and sunrise views worth waking up for make **Hostal Inty-Wayra**, directly above the Iglesia de San Antonio, the pick of the pack. (Rooms Bs10-15 per person and up.) **Restaurants** number about five in the area, all serving simple meals at prices a bit higher than those on the mainland (*menús* average Bs10, entrees Bs20). Food shortages are common all over the island, so don't be surprised if it's the waiter telling *you* what you'd like for dinner.

The small village of **Challa**, a little more than halfway to the north end of the island, offers rustic, bathroom-less accommodations at the **Posada del Inca Hostal**, where enormous windows yield stunning shore-side views. (Rooms Bs10 per person.) There aren't any restaurants in Challa, so plan on walking 30-40 minutes to **Challapampa** for meals (bring a flashlight if you're going for dinner), or you can try to convince a local to row you. There, three identical **restaurants** serve breakfast and lunch; one also stays open for dinner—it's the one by the port with its lights on after dark. Challapampa also shelters one **hostel.** The beds are uncomfortable, but the rooms are large and warm. (Rooms Bs10 per person.) A popular housing alternative, unofficial **campsites** lie around Challa, along the shore in the less populated parts of Challapampa, by the Palacio del Inca, and on the western beaches.

⚄ SIGHTS. The biggest attraction on Isla del Sol remains the awe-inspiring **hike** from one end to the other. The hike, however, does not follow a rigid course; there are actually several routes by which one can walk the length of the island. Of the two best-trodden (3-3½hr. each), one follows the spine of the ridge of hills that stretches across the island, allowing for constant panoramic views of Lake Titicaca; the other treads a variable, lung-testing path on the eastern side of the island. Sheep and their herders have carved less popular paths all over the mountain— these wind in and out of every bay and allow hikers to explore ever more rustic scenery, but require up to six hours to navigate. If you select one of these routes, be certain to bring water.

The common destination of the two major routes is **Challapampa**, the northern port. From there, the **Museo Marka Pampa** (10min.) houses a small collection of ruins that date back to the time of the developing Inca Empire. But the north's main attraction is the **Palacio del Inca** (30-40min. away). This intricate network of crumbling stone rooms and four-foot doorways provides both entertainment and access to the sandy beach on the western shore. If you're lucky, you might also spot the **Titicaca Rock,** a grey boulder that looks like a puma when viewed from the north. In the south, three attractions dominate: the **Templo del Sol,** a decayed remnant of what was once a grand meeting place for worshipers from all over the island, the **Escalera del Inca,** a steep stone staircase, and the **Fuente del Inca,** which remains, as it has since ancient times, the main source of water on the dry island.

Isla del Sol's floating neighbor **Isla de la Luna** is little more than a serviceless rest stop on the way back to Copacabana—one many of the tour boats take. Once the residence of Iñak Uyu, the Sun Virgin, large clay walls are all that remain of this former refuge for select women from Isla del Sol. Camping is permitted, but rocks cover most of the shore.

HUATAJATA   ☎ 08

One of the many small towns on the lakeside route between the Straits of Tiquina and La Paz, Huatajata distinguishes itself by being the starting point for a trip into the past of Lake Titicaca. Huatajata itself has little to offer: a few hotels that are constantly falling in and out of business, and a string of small restaurants that stretch along the highway. The true jewels that draw most visitors lie beyond, in the dazzling blue water that laps the town's edge. There is nowhere to change or withdraw money in Huatajata. Accommodations average Bs20 per person, entrees in most restaurants Bs25, and trips to Suriqui and Kaluata Bs130-180, depending

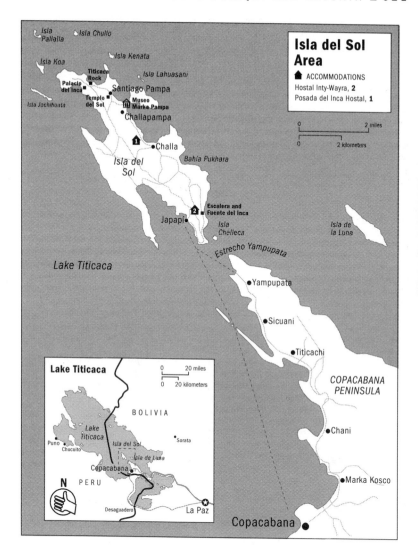

WESTERN BOLIVIA

on which islands are visited. Any bus headed toward Tiquina or Copacabana from La Paz can make a quick stop in Huatajata—catch a mini-bus (2hr., leaving when full, Bs6) at Aliaga and Bustillos in the Cementerio district. In Huatajata, ask to be let off in front of one of the hotels that advertise island trips.

NEAR HUATAJATA: ISLAS SURIQUI AND KALUATA

Nearly every owner of a hotel or restaurant owns a motorboat to shuttle visitors to and from their island. Many owners will even wait by the side of the road to make sure no tourists stray too far. A trip to Suriqui alone costs an average of Bs130, and Kaluata can be added for Bs40-50 more. Since most excursions are private boats that leave immediately upon your arrival, you can spend as long or as short a time on the island as is desirable.

SURIQUI. About 35 minutes across the lake from Huatajata remains a community of people who remain true to their roots—and very proud of them. A small entourage of boys will most likely be waiting on the landing to show you (and plead with you to buy) miniature versions of the **totora reed boats** that are this small island's claim to fame. Beginning in the first half of the 20th century, a Norwegian scientist by the name of Thor Heyerdahl decided to use the skills of the Suriqui people to prove his theory that the people of Asia could have quite possibly arrived to the continent of South America by means of small handmade boats still used on Lake Titicaca (see **Whatever Floats Your Boat,** p. 196). Heyerdahl continues these experiments, and the people of this dry, rocky island continue to make the reed boats essential to their livelihoods. A short visit to the **Centro Cultural** is rewarded by an honest introduction to the tedious method used to create the narrow boats in which the men of the island spend most of their days, fishing to feed their families and collecting more reeds to replace the boats as they slowly become water-logged. Every July 1st, the people of Suriqui take a break for the **Celebration of the Artisans,** when handicrafts from boats to woven goods to musical instruments are paraded through the street for all to appreciate.

KALUATA. Another 20 minutes from Suriqui (or about 35min. from the mainland) lies an island speckled with the physical remains of the Aymara culture that lived on the land 700 years ago—their work still amazes the most technically advanced architects of today. The name of the island was divined from these remains: "Kaluata" is Aymara for "stone house." Set back from the shore, sheltered a bit by the low surrounding hills from the wind that whips across the level plane of the altiplano mainland and the lake, still stand the low, **stone homes** that kept a population warm for hundreds of years. Right next to them are the towering *chullpas* that housed those same people in the afterlife.

In the hollow of the valley lie the barely identifiable, destroyed remnants of what was once a sacred temple and what is now the **greatest mystery of the island of Kaluata.** At the beginning of the 19th century, when archeologists began a feverish attempt to understand the history of the inhabitants, an entrance to a tunnel was discovered underneath the temple. Theories suggest that the tunnel leads to various other islands—and perhaps even to the mainland on the other side of the lake—but no destination has been discovered for certain. Why? Those who have returned from the depths of the tunnel have traversed it for miles without being able to locate an exit. Many more have entered, never to be heard from again. For this reason, the entrance was caved in, blocked by stones, and is now grown over by rough brush. Local legend has it that the power of the ancient pathway is so great that those wandering too close when the heat of the noon-time sun strikes may, too, be captured by the ancients who still inhabit the space of the temple.

THE YUNGAS

SORATA   ☎08

With varied terrain perfect for exploring, Sorata has become a mecca for outdoorsy types. Above Sorata hulks the solidly frigid Illampu; below rushes Río San Cristóbal; and on both sides, mountains are covered in everything from pines to grass to palm trees. Sorata isn't much in itself: it's small, and locals love to sit in the central plaza to await encounters. Once the gates on the plaza close after dark, inhabitants disappear into their homes and only the dense, cool fog remains.

⌐▪ TRANSPORTATION AND PRACTICAL INFORMATION

Buses from La Paz stop on the main plaza, **Peñaranda**. Most everything of importance in town is on the plaza or visible from it. The **Río San Cristóbal** lies downhill.

Buses: Transportes Unificados Sorata, Fernando Guachalla 132 (☎310 345). To **La Paz** (4½hr.; every hr. 4am-4pm, Sa 4am-6pm, Su 4am-5pm; Bs11). Trans Larecaja Tours (☎812 862), on the Plaza Pañaranda. Also to **La Paz** (4½hr., 9 per day 4:30am-3:30pm, Bs11). Buses *to* Sorata stop in Achacachi (2hr. from La Paz), where all foreigners must register with the police; have your passport available.

Tour Agencies: Several agencies cluster in and around the plaza; along with organizing tours and trips, these are a good resource for general tourist information. **Casa de Turista** (☎115 222; email info@skysorata; www.skysorata.com), 150m down from the Plaza Peñaranda—follow the signs. **Laguna Glacial** (3 days US$120, 4 days US$160). **Illampu Circuit** (7 days US$280, 14 days US$590). Prices include safety equipment, transportation, porters, and food. They also organize **bouldering** excursions. This is also the only place in town with **Internet access** (Bs25 per hr.). Open daily 8am-8pm. **Sorata Guides and Porters,** Sucre 302 (☎115 044; fax 115 218; email resorata@ceibo.entelnet.bo), on the Plaza Pañaranda. A reliable place to find equipment, guides, porters, and mules for any trip, from 1-20 days. Guides or porters Bs60 per day plus their food. Mules Bs50 per day. 2-3 person tent Bs20 per day. Sleeping bag Bs15 per day. Open daily 8am-8pm. **Illampu S.R.L. Eco-Turismo y Aventuras** (☎115 038), on Esquivel off the Plaza Pañaranda. Low prices for guides, mules, and porters for a the most popular treks. Also offers transportation to Illampu and Ancoma. Porters Bs40 per day plus food, mules Bs50 per day, guides Bs50 per day plus food (guide and mule together Bs50; the guide will cook meals for Bs15 more). Open daily 9:30am-8pm.

Emergency: ☎011.

Police: on 14 de Septiembre at the Plaza Peñaranda.

Hospital: At the top of Illampu, 1 block above the Plaza Bosque.

Telephones: ENTEL (☎115 038), in Hostal Panchita, on the Plaza Pañaranda. Open daily 8:30am-9pm.

Post Office: Escobol, on 14 de Septiembre at the Plaza Pañaranda. Open M 8-10am, W-Sa 10am-noon and 3-6pm, Su 9am-1pm.

▪ ACCOMMODATIONS

While Sorata's accommodations are very pleasant, many travelers are happy to camp in the town's beautiful surroundings. There are two **campsites**, both 20-minute walks out of town on 9 de Abril (en route to Gruta de San Pedro): **Altai Oasis** and **Cafe Illampu** charge Bs6 per person per night to pitch a tent. Camping here isn't exactly roughing it; enjoy hot showers, laundry facilities, fireplaces, book exchanges, hammocks, cafes, games, stunning views, and friendly company.

▨ **Residencial Sorata** (☎115 044; fax 115 218; email resorata@ceibo.entelnet.bo), at Villavicenio and Sucre. This mansion is over 120 years old and filled with entertainment of all sorts, from ping pong to nightly movie screenings. Restaurant. Knowledgeable owner. Rooms Bs20 per person, overlooking entrance or garden Bs30, with bath Bs40.

Hostal Panchita (☎115 038), on the plaza. Clean rooms, a colorful courtyard, and a welcoming manager make this a satisfying accommodation. Bs15 per person.

Hotel El Paraiso, Villavicenio 102. Modern rooms with paintings on the walls and pretty curtains over circular windows that let in plenty of light. All rooms (except #2) have hot showers. Laundry Bs7 per kg. Rooms Bs25 per person, with bath Bs30.

Alojamiento Sorata Central, on the Plaza Pañaranda. Spartan rooms with saggy beds, peeling paint, and worn floors surround a cement courtyard. Rooms Bs10 per person.

FOOD

■ **Restaurant Cafe-Altai,** Plaza Peñaranda 113. Fantastically flavorful vegetarian food as well as juicy steaks. Small book exchange (Bs2). The tables fill up quickly, but it's worth the wait. Open Tu-Su 8:30am-10pm.

Spider Bar Cafe (www.geocities.com/r_h_bryant), on Muñecas near Hostal El Mirador. Cheerful British owner. Relaxing environment. Instruments, books, board games, and puzzles. Drinks Bs3-20. Open daily 8pm-1am.

Pizzeria Restaurant Italia, on the Plaza Pañaranda. Sets itself apart from others on the plaza with fast, friendly service. Pizzas Bs16-48. Pastas Bs25. Open daily 9am-11pm.

SIGHTS

LAS CUEVAS. For some boulder-jumping, rock-skipping, trout-searching, branch-ducking fun, troop on down to the Río San Cristóbal and find all the elements necessary to be a kid again. The water is filled with rocks just big enough for a perfect perch above the roar and the foam. If the grip on your shoes is right and the surfaces dry, bouldering is a possibility: numbers painted in white on the largest of the land masses guide extremities to the foot-, hand-, and finger-holds that allow them to scale the steep rocks. The Casa de Turista can provide a written guide. *(From the Plaza Peñaranda, head downhill on Muñecas, past the Spider Bar Cafe, and along the rocky path 30min. The caves are all along the river side.)*

MUSEO ALCADÍA. A small room in a courtyard of governmental offices, this museum is just a small collection of relics from the time of Tiahuanuco, as well as some pretty but worn-out festival costumes from the town's early days. *(Upstairs in the Alcadía building, on 14 de Septiembre on the Plaza Peñaranda. Open daily 8am-5pm. Free.)*

LA GRUTA DE SAN PEDRO. A small hole in the side of a mountain descends quickly into a gargantuan, humid cave. The ceiling is etched with the signs of waves, but today the water has receded to a long, narrow channel whose end has yet to be discovered. Most of the scratches made on the roof's surface today are from the numerous resident bats. *(From the Plaza Pañaranda, facing downhill, take 14 de Septiembre to the right, until you see a large staircase downhill. Follow the stairs down, then take a right onto the dirt road which goes all the way to La Gruta (marked by the occasional blue arrows; 2½-3hr.). On Sunday mornings, camiones leave from the Plaza for La Gruta at about 7am to bring people in for market day. These trucks also drop people off around 3pm, and are often willing to take on extra passengers for a small fee. The entrance to La Gruta is manned daily from 8am-5pm, and a ticket costs Bs7. The person at the entrance will crank on the generators to light the cave for 40min. and no more. A warning black-out usually happens at 20min. and 5min.)*

INTO THE MOUNTAINS FROM SORATA

The landscape around Sorata can provide days of trekking fun. However, because many of the routes are quite long, traveling with a guide from one of the agencies in town, or at the very least talking to them in length about the route, is strongly suggested. The stops along the way are very few and far between.

LAGUNA CHILLATA. Climbing up into the hills behind Sorata, not only is this small lake a great place for fantastic views and a refreshing swim in the clear water, it is also an archeological site, home to many Inca ruins. The most popular schedule is for a daytrip: starting in the morning, breaking with a picnic lunch at the lake, and making it back to town before nightfall.

CAMINO DEL ORO. Unfortunately, *el camino* is becoming shorter and shorter as modern-day needs infringe on nature. The trail begins in Ancohum, a few hours' drive from Sorata (transportation is included in packages offered by Sorata guide companies), and ends in Guanay, which was once one of the biggest gold-mining towns in Bolivia. However, as time passes, the roads out of Guanay creep closer and closer to the path—what used to be a seven-day trip has now been cut to five because the road has overtaken and evened out most of the path.

CAMINO A MAPIRI. As its name suggests, this trek ends in Mapiri—after about seven days among lush hillsides. From Mapiri, those still excited by the looks of a dirt road can continue to Guanay (another day), or for those needing a change of scenery, a five-hour trip downriver can provide just as many pretty vistas.

CAMINO DE TRES LAGUNAS. The Camino de Tres Lagunas incorporates a visit to three lakes in the hillside high above Sorata: **Laguna Chillata, Laguna Glacial,** and **Laguna Illampu,** and the water gets colder as the climbing gets higher.

ILLAMPU CIRCUIT. If admiring the snowy whiteness of Illampu from afar doesn't give you all the goosebumps you crave, give the Illampu Circuit a try. For seven to eight days, you'll be tramping around in the icy coldness of this peak and the more humble summits that cushion it. A certain amount of equipment is needed to scale the slippery sides, and experience in ice climbing is suggested.

CARANAVI
☎08

If another hot bus ride has you pondering what could be worse than another dusty turn in the road lined with dust-coated plants, step off the bus in Caranavi, walk a few blocks, and witness paradise: a silver ribbon of river below, a lustrous orange sun above, and enough plantain trees to feed a *pueblo* for months.

Various bus companies use the Caranavi terminal and go to **La Paz** (8hr., frequent 7am-9:30pm, Bs23) and **Rurrenabaque** (12hr.; 5 per day 7:30-11am and 6:30pm; Bs45). Buses to **Guanay** (5hr., every hr. 7am-6pm, Bs13) leave from Mariscal Santa Cruz, in the market area, about 10 blocks from the bus station. **Mariscal Santa Cruz** runs throughout all of Caranavi. Upon entering the town, the first major landmark is the **bus station.** Looking down the avenue, the **river** is downhill on the left, along with everything in town. The **plaza** is downhill one block from the mayor's office. Services include: **Banco Mercantil,** Mariscal Santa Cruz 102 (open M-F 8:15am-12:30pm and 2:15-6:30pm); **ENTEL,** Mariscal Santa Cruz 104 (☎233 494; open daily 6:30am-11pm); the **post office,** on the plaza (open M-F 8am-noon and 3-6pm); and **Internet access** at Infonet, on Bolívar downhill from the plaza (Bs15 per hr.; open daily 8am-11pm).

Inexpensive lodgings line Mariscal Santa Cruz. **Residential Norte Paceña** is directly across from the bus station. Pillows are firm; showers are cold. (Rooms Bs10 per person.) **Hotel Landivar,** Mariscal Santa Cruz 106, lets you live like a king, with TVs, baths, towels, a swimming pool, a restaurant, and a game room. (Singles Bs60; doubles Bs90; triples Bs110.) **Residencial Caranavi,** on Mariscal Santa Cruz one block in the direction of the bus station from the plaza, has a friendlier feel than the other lodgings lining the streets. (Singles Bs15 per person, with double bed Bs20 per person.) Fried chicken and fixed menus are the only options for food. The omnipresent **plantain** takes on the role of bread, and fills about half the stands in the market. Bottled water is scarce; bring your own or learn to love soda.

GUANAY
☎08

In Guanay, coconut trees line every street, *heladeros* advertise their bounty from morning to night, rooster calls punctuate the darkness, and locals spend their afternoons running from one spot of shade to another. All modes of transport enter on the main road, which quickly runs into the main plaza, parallel to **Río Tipuani.** Connected to the main plaza by Comercio is another plaza, **Gutierrez Guerra.** Continuing past Guerra leads to the port. All bus company offices are on the Plaza Gualberto Villarroel. Turbus Totaí goes to **La Paz** (11½hr., 5:30pm, Bs35) and **Caranavi** (5hr., every hr., Bs15). TransBolivia also goes to **La Paz** (11hr., 6pm, Bs35). *Botes* (long, narrow wooden motorboats) leave the port every morning to **Mapiri** (7hr., 8-9am, Bs45). **Pahuichi Hotel,** on Comercio between the two plazas, is dependably staffed and securely protected against mosquitos. They offer clean common bathrooms, and squishy beds. (Rooms Bs15 per person.)

MAPIRI
☎08

Known to most travelers as the end of a seven-day trek from Sorata, there's not much in Mapiri to keep visitors hanging around once they've rested up. The stars are bright, the air is hot and moist, and refreshment comes from bottled soda, oranges, or a cold shower. A few reminders of the old gold-mining days linger—

mostly in the form of "Compro Oro" signs dangling over storefronts—but from the looks of things, no one has any to sell anymore. To leave Mapiri, you'll need a 4WD vehicle, or to expect to take the *bote* downriver to **Guanay** (5hr., 9am, Bs35) to get anywhere. If staying the night, the choice of where is made for you—**Alojamiento Mexico,** on Comercio, is all that's here. (Rooms Bs10 per person.)

COROICO
☎ 08

The descent from La Paz to this sub-tropical paradise is not only one of the most dangerous but also one of the most stunning rides in Bolivia. The trip breaks through layers of cloud and fog and emerges into a heat that makes most people forget the numbing cold of the altiplano. The land here is rich and fertile, the landscape tantalizing to both eyes and mouth—exotic fruits grow in every orchard, and coffee beans and coca leaves supply additional income. In midday's heat, every bench in the shade is occupied by lounging locals; at night, the town center echoes with the shrieks of children playing soccer in the central gazebo.

▐█▌ TRANSPORTATION AND PRACTICAL INFORMATION

The **main plaza** is the center of both town and of all activity in Coroico. The **church** is the largest landmark on the plaza.

Buses: Turbus Totaí, on the plaza. Flota Yungueña, ½ block downhill on Reyes Ortiz. Both have frequent service to **La Paz** (every hr. 3:30am-5:30pm; Bs15, Su Bs18).

Tourist Information: (☎(01) 597 309), on the plaza. Open daily 9am-6pm.

Tour Agencies: Vagantes Eco Adventures, Julio Zuazo Cuenca 019 (☎(01) 912 981). Transportation and tours to just about any region of interest around Coroico. Their motto: "make nature yours," from Cotapata National Park to the communities of Tocaña and Mururata to the Inca trails. During the rainy season, talk to them about rafting on the Coroico and Vagante Rivers. Open M-Sa 8am-noon and 3-6pm. **El Relincho** (☎(01) 923 814) rents well-behaved horses for touring Coroico (Bs35 per hr.) From the plaza, follow Julio Zuazo Cuenca up the hill and to the right, past Hotel Esmeralda, and follow signs to the "caballos" (15min.).

Bank: Banco Mercantil, R. Ortiz 2502. Open M-F 8:30am-12:30pm and 2:30-6:30pm.

Hospital: Facing the church, follow the street that passes by on the right up and out of the center. It's about a 15min. walk from the plaza.

Telephones: ENTEL, on the plaza (☎118 644), opposite the church. Open daily 7:30am-10:30pm.

Internet Access: Residencial La Casa (see Accommodations, below). Bs20 per hr. Open 8am-9pm.

Post Office: On the plaza, next to the information office, in the back of the building. Open Tu-Sa 8:30am-noon and 2:30-6pm, Su 9am-noon.

▟ ACCOMMODATIONS

Accommodations in the center of town tend to be simple, but if you walk a bit farther from the center, you will be rewarded with more spectacular views and more creative owners.

Residencial Coroico, Reyes Ortiz 507. The bathrooms couldn't have been cleaner when they were first installed, beds are firm, and the terrace is perfect for star-gazing. Rooms Bs18 per person, matrimonials Bs40; during holidays rooms Bs25, matrimonials Bs45.

Hostal Sol y Luna (☎(01) 561 626). From the plaza, follow Julio Zuazo Cuenca up the hill and to the right, past Hotel Esmeralda. From there, follow the colorful sun and moon signs. About a 20min. walk. Those who venture this far from town will be rewarded with a bamboo porch overlooking the jungle and delicious food. Reservations recommended. Singles Bs25; doubles Bs50; triples Bs75; cabañas for 2 with bath Bs80.

DANGEROUS CURVES AHEAD In some form or another, just about everyone's doing it. (No, it's not coca, the miracle drug.) It's the ride from La Paz to Coroico on what the Inter-American Development Bank dubbed, in 1995, the **World's Most Dangerous** road. That status may be a few years old, but the adrenaline rush has diminished not at all. The descent starts, in La Paz, at 4700m above sea level and drops an incredible 3500m, to the steamy jungle town of Coroico. You can do it by bus, by minibus, by bicycle, or by foot, but somehow, you've got to make it to the bottom, and there are a few rules of the road to keep in mind.

Because of the dangerous curves, vehicles tend to stay to their left for best visibility. A horn-happy driver may honk at every corner, whether it's blind or not, just to announce his arrival. Some drivers will also honk at other drivers they know, dogs in the road, trees, and rocks. Other drivers, more the silent type, prefer to search out dust clouds to perceive the oncoming traffic. True, there's little logic to it, but *you* can't honk the horn, so just hold on tight. According to statistics, large buses and trucks are the most common victims of the steep fall over the edge, but they also tend to proceed more slowly and cautiously to compensate. Despite the dangers, hundreds of people make this journey every day. Be aware, but be excited for some incredible views and a jumping, jarring ride that will only make you appreciate your destination even more. Flota/Minibus Yungueña, Yanacachi (☎213 513). **From La Paz to Coroico** (4½hr., departures approximately every 2 hours from 7:30am-5pm, Bs13).

WESTERN BOLIVIA

Hostal El Cafetal, (☎(01) 933 979), next to the hospital. The relaxed owner provides just as relaxed an environment—enjoy the hammocks and adjacent swimming pool in your spare time. The architecture fits the tropical atmosphere with reed wall coverings and bright, flowery sheets. Rooms Bs25 per person.

Hotel Esmeralda (☎116 017 or 116 434; email esmeralda@latinwide.com; www.latinwide.com/esmeralda), at the foot of the Calvario. Follow Julio Zuazo Cuenca (to the left of the church) uphill, staying to the right of the fork. Or, catch a ride with one of the Hotel Esmeralda taxis that circle the plaza. Pool. Hammocks. Lots of lounge chairs. Restaurant. Singles with bath US$15; doubles US$15, with bath US$25.

Residencial La Casa, Adalid Linares 3511 (☎116 024 or (07) 939 343; email: lacasa@ceibo.entelnet.bo), down the stairs opposite the church on the plaza. Comfortable and clean. Breakfast included. Rooms Bs20 per person; Bs50 during holidays.

Hostal Para-Ti. Facing the church, follow the street to the right down to the bottom; then take a left. 3 homey rooms Bs20 per person with either a view or bath.

Hotel Lluvia de Oro, Reyes Ortiz 506 (☎116 005). Wallpaper with poems and thoughts of past inhabitants spruces up these simple rooms. Pool. Rooms Bs20 per person.

Hostal Kory, Adalid Linares 6020 (☎(01) 564 050), down the steps on the side of the plaza opposite the church. Super clean rooms in a cool and shady location. Gorgeous pool with a view. Rooms Bs30 per person, Bs50 during holidays.

Residencial La Torre, on Julio Zuazo Cuenca. The rooms are simple and the windows don't let in much light, but the sunny courtyard's plentiful flowers more than make up for it. Rooms Bs15 per person.

FOOD

Restaurant La Casa, Adalid Linares 3511, downstairs from Residencial la Casa. The menu includes fondues, pastas, goulash, soups, and salads, all under Bs35. Breakfast also available. Open daily 8am-9pm.

Restaurant Las Peñas, on the plaza. Family-style atmosphere. Often crowded with locals and tourists around dinner. Bolivian staples Bs18-25. Vegetarian pastas Bs15-23. Fresh fruit juices Bs2.5-3.5. Open daily 8:30am-10pm.

Snack Hawaii, with your back to the church, follow the street on the opposite side of the plaza downhill to the left about ½ block. Great for breakfast (Bs5-8) or a light snack in the late afternoon. Sandwiches Bs3-10. Open daily 9am-10pm.

WESTERN BOLIVIA

👁 SIGHTS

CERRO UCHUMACHI. If you can manage the steep, two-hour climb to the top—the highest accessible point for miles—you'll be rewarded. Laid out below are numerous Yungas towns. Silver ribbons of rivers and hillsides covered with lush forests lie hidden in tiny creases of land that promise great rewards to those who dare to explore. *(From the plaza, head uphill on Julio Zuazo Cuenca, staying to the right until you reach the sign for Hotel Esmeralda. At this point, head up the hill on the left, following the green crosses; this will lead you to Iglesia Calvario. Head to the right of the church to find the path that borders the chain-link-enclosed telephone tower, which will lead you to the top.)*

CASCADAS. A precious resource for people all over the northern Yungas, these waterfalls are a good excuse to wander through the hills around Coroico. The path is level, and there are hundreds of butterflies—the most impressive is the large, radiantly-blue *morpho*. Some sections of the path appear not to have seen a visitor taller than a grasshopper in some time; wear long pants and bug repellent. The falls themselves, though interrupted by some machinery essential to water collection, slide swiftly down a wall of black rock. They are most impressive during the rainy season, but their cooling influence can be appreciated all year round. *(From the plaza, follow Julio Zuazo Cuenca up the hill, staying to the right until you reach the sign for Hotel Esmeralda. Here, veer left and follow the green crosses until you reach Iglesia Calvario. A path leads left from the church—follow it (don't diverge), and you'll arrive at the falls within 2hr.)*

❋ FESTIVALS

Bolivian Independence day is celebrated in a big way on August 6. Accommodations fill up very quickly—usually two weeks in advance—and may cost over twice as much as usual. But the excitement in the air is worth it, as all the bands in town practice for weeks with hopes of awing a crowd from miles around.

CHULUMANI ☎08

Fruit grows abundant in Chulumani, and a smile accompanies every word. Passing cloud-shadows dapple the hillsides. Carved into square fields, the land below could belong on a cozy patchwork quilt. And when the sun burns off the morning fog, light reflects off the flowers, roses and trees that line the streets. The main plaza is the **Plaza Libertad;** one block right lies the smaller, less populous **Plaza Martín Villalobos.** Transito A.T.L. Chulumani sends minibuses to **La Paz** (4½hr., leaving when full 6am-6pm, Bs15). Their office is on Junín, close to the police checkpoint at the entrance to town. Trans San Bartolome, on the Plaza Libertad, sends large buses to **La Paz** (5hr., 6:30am and noon, Bs15). Services in town include: **Banco Union,** on the Plaza Libertad (☎116 031; open M-F 8:30am-noon and 2:30-6pm, Sa 8am-12:30pm); the **police** (☎3) on Junín at the entrance to town; and **ENTEL** (☎116 801; open daily 8am-9pm). If the phone line at ENTEL is down, purchase an Unica Long-Distance card (Bs25) and use it in the **phone booth** outside the Cotel office (Bs25 per 5min.). Accommodations in Chulumani are either very basic or come complete with all the perks—there's not much in between. But even the simple ones are clean and friendly. **Alojamiento Chulumani II,** between Montoya and the Plaza Libertad, has simple rooms with soft mattresses and large windows—and traffic passing by at all hours. (Rooms Bs15 per person.) Another option is the **Panorama Hotel,** on Murillo at Andrade; from the Plaza Martín Villalobos, follow Murillo uphill. All the large rooms—with clean, cool tile floors—have baths, and there's a welcoming blue pool outside. (☎116 109, La Paz ☎(02) 783 849. F-M package Bs240, including meals; Tu-Th rooms Bs40 per person, including breakfast. Reservations recommended.) **Alojamiento Chulumani,** on Bolívar, ½ block up from the Plaza Libertad, is the place to go for peace and quiet—the flowery courtyard is perfect for reading and relaxing. (Rooms Bs15 per person.)

SOUTHERN BOLIVIA

Behind Bolivia's booming industrial centers—Cochabamba, Santa Cruz, even La Paz—lurk reminders of the nation's colonial past and long struggle for independence. **Sucre and Potosí** (p. 331), the country's first cities, house churches and colonial buildings that serve as evidence of a history dominated by Spanish aristocracy and indigenous subordination. Sucre remains the student, judicial, and cultural capital of Bolivia, while aging Potosí plays a lesser role in the face of modernity. The white-washed walls and broad sunny avenues of the first boast the original optimism of an independent republican government; with narrow winding avenues (built on the silver boom) attempting to shut out the chill altiplano wind, Potosí harkens back to a past of greed and spilt blood. Often visited together, their colonial legacies delight architecture buffs, enlighten history lovers, and make strolling around the center a pleasure for anyone missing the old world.

HIGHLIGHTS OF SOUTHERN BOLIVIA

MEANDER among second-capital **Sucre's** colonial buildings (p. 331).

DESCEND into the "Mouth of Hell," in the ancient **mines** of Potosí (p. 344).

DANCE the Dance of the Devils at Oruro's crazy yearly **Carnival** (p. 352).

CLIMB Bolivia's highest peak, **Nevado Sajama** (p. 354).

SLEEP in a hostel made of salt in the moonscape that is the **Salar de Uyuni** (p. 357).

IMBIBE fine Bolivian wine in Tarija's lush **bodegas** (p. 369).

Chill winds sweep across Bolivia's harshest climate, this "high plain" where the average altitude is 3800m—the tundra desert, hemmed by the Cordillera Real (or Oriental) and the Cordillera Occidental, does little to hinder them. With its brave settlements of cold but cheerful Aymaras, the **altiplano** (p. 348) is also home to the country's most stunning landscape. When the 60,000-sq.-km Lago Minchín flooded the area over 25,000 years ago, it left behind Lake Titicaca, Lago Poopó, and Lago Uru Uru. Another lake, Tauca, evaporated 10,000 years ago and left behind the world's largest salt deposit, now the area's most-visited site. In addition to an absurd amount of sodium, the altiplano overflows with volcanic activity: boiling mud pits and climbable craters beckon visitors strong enough to endure the altitude and eternally chilly weather. A study in browns and greys, only the lively Oruro Carnival and lower hills of Tupiza add color to the austere and dusty setting where llamas and alpacas seem to out-number people.

Infamous in Bolivian history for the losses to Paraguay incurred in the Chaco War (1932-35), southern Bolivia's third, inhospitable region contains few people and even fewer sources of water. Currently, Bolivia claims only a small section of the Gran **Chaco** (p. 365), stretching across Paraguay and Argentina and encompassing 725,000 sq. km of dense outback. An evaporative hotbed, possibly the country's hottest and driest area, the Chaco remained until recently home to only the Guarani people. And, although cosmopolitan Tarija has recently influenced the area's style, the Chaco remains a paradise for rugged adventure seekers.

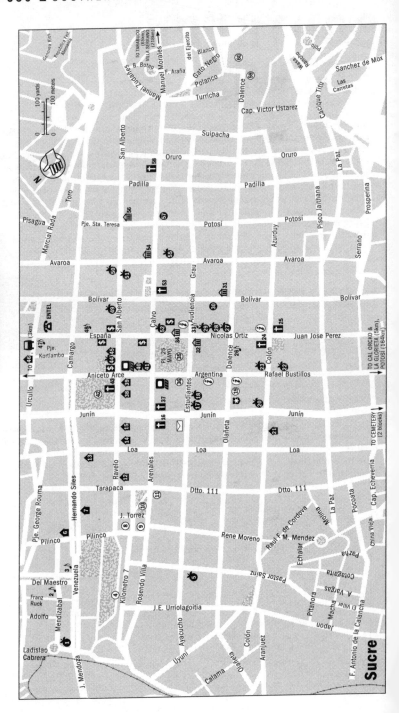

Sucre

SUCRE AND POTOSÍ

SUCRE ☎ 06

A city of countless names (including La Ciudad Blanca, the University City, the Athens of America, Chuquisaca, and the City of Four Names), most of which recall the pride *sucreños* feel in their wide colonial streets and white-washed walls, Sucre abounds with culture, tourists, and history. The carefully preserved buildings that tell the stories of Bolivia's colonial past beat with a youthfulness evident throughout this progressive student center. The home of Bolivia's first university, San Francisco Xavier (founded in 1624), Latin America's first cry for freedom (May 25, 1801), and Bolivia's first republican government (all but the legislative branch lost to La Paz in the short civil war of 1899), Sucre has many reasons to vaunt its rich history. It comes as no surprise that UNESCO named the city a "Patrimonio Histórico y Cultural de la Humanidad" in 1991.

▐ TRANSPORTATION

Flights: Aeropuerto Juana Azurduy de Padilla, 10km northwest of town. Accessible by micros 1 and F (Bs1), which run along Hernando Siles. Taxi Bs20. LAB, Bustillos 121 (☎454 599 or 454 994; toll free for reservations ☎0800 3001, for information ☎0800 43 21; fax 451 943). Open M-F 8:30am-12:30pm and 2:30-6:30pm, Sa 9am-noon. To: **Cochabamba** (30min., 1 per day, Bs265); **Santa Cruz** (40min., 1 per day, Bs301); **Tarija** (40min., 1 per day M and Th, Bs321); and **La Paz** (2hr., 1 per day, Bs414). Aerosur, Arenales 31 (☎462 141 or 460 737; toll free ☎0800 30 01). Open M-F 8am-12:30pm and 2:30-6:30pm, Sa 9am-noon. To: **La Paz** (50min.; M-F 11:55am, Sa 12:35pm, Su 4:55pm; Bs414). b Junín 742 (☎460 944). Open M-F 8:30am-noon and 2:30-6pm, Sa 9am-noon. To: **La Paz** (2hr., M 9:20am, Bs300) via **Cochabamba** (35min., Bs170); **Santa Cruz** (35min., F 3:15pm and Su 2pm, Bs210); **Villamontes** (3hr., Sa 10:20am, Bs310) via **Tarija** (40min., Sa 10:20am, Bs190).

Buses: Central **terminal** (☎41292), 3km from the center of town on Ostria Gutiérrez. Micro A, which leaves from Ravelo in front of the market (Bs1). Taxi Bs3. Buses run to: **Potosí** (3hr., every hr. 6:30am-6pm, Bs15); **Cochabamba** (11hr., 7 per day 6:30pm, Bs40); **Santa Cruz** (14hr., 7 per day 4-5:30pm, Bs60); **Oruro** (10hr., 3:30 and 5pm,

Sucre

♠ ACCOMMODATIONS
Alojamiento Central, **46**
Alojamiento El Dorado, **13**
Alojamiento La Plata, **39**
Alojamiento Potosí, **12**
Alojamiento Turista, **15**
Casa de Huespedes
  Colón 220, **21**
Grand Hotel, **40**
Hostal Charcas, **38**
Hostal Londres, **6**
Hostal Veracruz, **14**
Residencial Avenida, **7**
Residencial Bolivia, **45**

● FOOD
Biblio Café, **29**
Café Cultural Kaypíchu, **49**
El Germen, **51**
El Paso de los Abuelos, **22**
El Patio, **44**
Hacheh, **5**

Kultur Café Berlin, **55**
La Repizza, **27**
La Taverne, **41**
Las Cebollitas, **23**
Monte Bianco, **20**
New Hong Kong, **50**
Penco Penquito's, **17**
Piso Cerro, **1**
Restaurant Plaza, **52**
Restaurant Suiza, **28**
Salón de Té Las Delicias, **18**

🏛 ○ SIGHTS
ASUR Museo Textil-Etnográfico, **56**
Casa de La Libertad, **36**
Cathedral/Museo Eclesiástico, **32**
Cerro Churuquella, **59**
Corte Suprema de Justicia, **8**
Hospital Santa Bárbara, **11**
La Recoleta, **60**
Mercado Central, **42**
Museo de Historia Natural &
  Museo Gutiérrez Valenzuela, **34**
Museo Universitario Charcas, **31**
Museo-Convento Santa Clara, **54**

Parque Bolívar, **4**
Plaza 25 de Mayo, **35**
Plaza de Libertad, **10**
Plaza Zudáñez, **19**
Teatro Gran Mariscal, **9**

🏢 CHURCHES
La Merced, **25**
San Felipe de Neri, **24**
San Francisco, **43**
San Lázaro, **58**
San Miguel, **37**
Santa Mónica, **16**
Santo Domingo, **53**

♪ ENTERTAINMENT
Boomerang, **26**
Chili Pepper, **33**
Club Nano's, **48**
Micerino, **47**
Mitsu Mania, **3**
Up down, **2**

● SERVICES
Centro Boliviano-Americano, **57**
Laverap Laundry, **30**

Bs40); **La Paz** (18hr.; 2, 2:30, and 5:30pm; Bs60); and **Camiri** (18hr., 5:30pm, Bs80). **Camiones** leave from offices along Av. de Las Américas; **trufis** leave from a dirt field, uphill and around the corner. Both accessible by Micro C (Bs1) which stops in front of the market, or by taxi (Bs3). To: **Padilla** (6½hr., 3 per day 5:30-6pm, Bs20); **Villa Serrano** (7hr., 7am and 5pm, Bs15-20); **Mojocaya** (4-5hr., 10 and 10:30am, Bs15-17); **Tarabuco** (2hr., every hr. 7am-6pm, Bs6); **Azurduy** (13hr., 7:30am, Bs40); **Sopachy** (8hr., 8:30am, Bs25); and **Alcala** (8hr., 8am, Bs30). Other camiones and trufis leave from the Plazuela Tupaj Katori, on the road to the airport. To get there, take micro 1 or F (Bs1) and ask to get off at the "Parada De Camiones a Ravelo." Taxi Bs3. To: **Ravelo** (2½hr.; 2 per day, leaving when full; Bs5-7); **Ocuri** (6hr., 1 per day around 10am, Bs10); **Antora** (5hr., 1 per day around 10am, Bs10); **Llallagua** (12hr., Th 7am, Bs20); **Matcha** (8hr., F 10 or 11am, Bs15). Trufis to **Potolo** (3hr., leaving when full around 11am, Bs6) leave from farther up the street. Go to the end of Canelas and head up the dirt mound to the left.

Public Transportation: Micros Bs1. Popular lines 4, 5, 8, and A, B, and C come every 4min. and run 6:30am-10pm. Other lines stop at 7pm and come every 7min. Most can be picked up either in front of the market on Ravelo or anywhere along Hernando Siles.

Taxis: Anywhere in the city Bs3. Airport Bs20. Finding a cab is easy; you can also always call one: **Supremo** (☎442 444); **Cielito Lindo** (☎441 014); **Charcas** (☎460 000); **Bolivia** (☎442 222); and **Exclusivo** (☎451 414).

Car Rental: **Imbex Rent-A-Car,** Potosí 499 (☎461 222 or ☎01 762 634; fax 06 912 470; email info@imbex.com), at Azurduy. Credit card required. Min. age 25. Cars start US$50 per day. Open M-F 8am-noon and 2-6:30pm, Sa-Su 8:30am-12:30pm. V, MC, AmEx.

✴ 🔢 ORIENTATION AND PRACTICAL INFORMATION

Sucre's heart beats around one of Bolivia's most beautiful plazas, the Plaza 25 de Mayo, named for the day the city led the cry for freedom in 1809. Most streets change names a number of times, often in relation to the plaza; numbering starts over when the name changes.

Tourist Information: Tourist Office, Argentina 65 (☎451 083), in the Casa de la Cultura. Open M-F 8am-noon and 2-6pm. University-sponsored tourist office run by local students, on the Plaza de Mayo 25; another on N. Ortiz between Dalence and Colón. Closed during December, January, February, and parts of July. Buy poster-sized maps (Bs4) from the newspaper salesmen in the Plaza 25 de Mayo.

Tour Agencies: Eclipse, Avaroa 310 (☎/fax 443 960; email eclipse@mara.scr.entel-net.bo). Open M-F 8:30am-12:30pm and 2:30-6:30pm, Sa 8:30am-12:30pm. **Sur-Andes,** N. Ortiz 6 (☎452 632; fax 453 212). Open M-F 8:30am-12:30pm and 2:30-6:30pm, Sa 8am-12:30pm. **Seatur,** Plaza 25 de Mayo 25 (☎440 909). Open M-F 8:30am-12:30pm and 2:30-6:30pm, Sa 9am-noon.

Consulates: Brazil, Arenales 212-A (☎452 561), in the Solarsa office. Open M-F 11am-noon. **Paraguay,** Plaza 25 de Mayo 28 (☎422 999), in Capital Plaza Hotel. Open when the consul is in. **Peru,** Avaroa 472 (☎455 592). Open M-F 9:30am-2:30pm.

Immigration Office: Pastor Sainz 117 (☎453 647). Open 8:30am-4:30pm.

Currency Exchange: Few banks cash traveler's checks. **Casas de Cambio Ambar,** San Alberto 7 (☎461 339) changes traveler's checks; also gives cash advances on V and MC. Open M-F 9am-12:15pm and 2:30-6:30pm, Sa 9am-noon. **El Arca,** España 134 (☎460 189). Traveler's checks and V and MC cash advances. Open M-F 8:30am-12:30pm and 2:30-6:30pm, Sa 9am-12:30pm. Many shops and hotels nearby also buy and sell US dollars and bolivianos.

Banks/ATMs: Bisa, on España just off the Plaza (☎443 901). Changes AmEx traveler's checks at a rate 6% below the normal buying price. Open M-F 8:30am-noon and 2:30-6:30pm, Sa 10am-1pm. **Banco de Crédito,** on the Plaza (☎442 929), has one of the few ATMs servicing V, MC, and AmEx. **Banco Santa Cruz** (☎455 400), at España and San Alberto. V/MC ATM.

Western Union: Plaza 25 de Mayo 25 (☎441 204; fax 912 520). Open M-F 9am-12:30pm and 2-7pm, Sa 9am-12:30pm.

Cultural Centers: Centro Boliviano-Americano, Potosí 204 (☎441 608; email cba@mara.ser.entelnet.bo). Open M-F 9am-noon and 3-8pm. **Instituto Cultural Boliviano-Alemán,** Avaroa 326 (☎/fax 452 091; email gmielke@mara.scr.entelnet.bo). Open M-F 9:30am-12:30pm and 3-9pm. **Alliance Francaise,** Arce 35 (☎452 599). Open M-F 9am-noon and 3:30-7:30pm.

Spanish Courses: Centro Boliviano-Americano, Instituto Cultural Boliviano-Alemán, and **Alliance Francaise** all have classes.

Market: Bordered by Ravelo, Junín, Hernando Siles, and A. Arce.

Laundromat: Laverap (☎424 501), on Bolívar between Dalence and Grau. Clothes in 1½-2hr. Bs15 per load. Open M-Sa 8am-8pm, Su 9am-1pm.

Emergency: Police ☎110. Hospital ☎118. Fire ☎119.

Police: Plazuela 2 Udañez (☎453 152), Estudiantes between Junín and Argentina.

Pharmacy: Contact ☎110 or ☎118 for the *farmacia en turno* (open 24hr.).

Hospital: Hospital de Santa Bárbara (☎451 900), on the Plaza Libertad at Destacamiento III and Arenales.

Telephones: ENTEL, España 271 (☎455 820), 2½ blocks north of the plaza, just past Hernando Siles. Open M-Sa 7am-11pm, Su 8am-10pm.

Internet Access: Trebol Net, on the plaza. Bs6 per hr. **Internet 2000** (☎423 862), on San Alberto between España and A. Arce. **Cyber Café** (☎420 617), on Arenales between Junín and Argentina.

Post Office: Junín 699 (☎454 960), at Ayacucho. Open daily 8am-8pm. Send packages **DHL** (☎441 204; fax 06 912 520), on the Plaza 25 de May. Open M-F 9am-12:30pm and 2-7pm, Sa 9am-12:30pm.

▛ ACCOMMODATIONS

Sucre presents an incredible range of lodgings, although you'll often pay a little more here than elsewhere. Most cluster in the blocks around the Plaza 25 de Mayo and close to the bus terminal.

▨ Hostal Charcas, Ravelo 62 (☎453 972; email hostalcharcas@latinmail.com), between A. Arce and Junín. The foreign hub of Sucre, Charcas's rooftop terrace buzzes with road adventures, Spanish lessons, and travel tips. Super friendly and informative hosts. Simple but comfortable rooms. Laundry Bs8 per kg. Breakfast Bs6. Sunday bus to Tarabuco Bs16. Call ahead in the high season. Singles Bs40, with bath Bs65; doubles Bs65, with bath Bs100; triples Bs95, with bath Bs140; quads Bs120, with bath Bs155.

Casa de Huéspedes, Colón 220 (☎455 823; email colon@usa.net). The 7 rooms in this beautiful colonial house fill quickly during the high season; it's easy to see why. Extremely gregarious owner will do just about anything to guarantee a pleasant stay. All rooms with bath, optional TV, and breakfast, served overlooking the white-pillared courtyard. Call ahead June-Aug. Singles US$11; doubles US$17; triples US$23.

Grand Hotel, A. Arce 61 (☎452 461 or 451 704; email grandhot@mara.scr.entelnet.bo; www.statusprd.com/grandhotel), off the Plaza. Carpeted rooms with bath and cable TV. Two paradisiacal courtyard filled with palm trees, lawn chairs, and sunbathing guests. Breakfast included. Singles Bs90; doubles Bs110; triples Bs160.

Residencial Bolivia, San Alberto 42 (☎454 346; fax 453 388), between España and Arce, a block north of the Plaza. Simple rooms open onto a regal courtyard. Breakfast included. Singles Bs30, with bath Bs50; doubles Bs55, with bath Bs85; triples Bs75, with bath Bs120; quads Bs100, with bath Bs145.

Alojamiento Potosí (☎451 975), on Ravelo between Tarapuca and Loa. Although grimy on the outside, the bathrooms are actually quite sanitary, as are the well-swept wood floors in the rooms. Singles Bs15; doubles Bs30; triples Bs45; quads Bs60.

Hostal Londres, Hernando Siles 951 (☎454 792), between Pilinco and Tarapacá. Clean but spartan rooms. Singles Bs25, with bath Bs35; doubles Bs45, with bath Bs60; triples Bs65, with bath Bs85; quads with bath Bs110.

Residencial Avenida, Hernando Siles 942 (☎451 245), between Pilinco and Tarapacá. Cupboard-size rooms open onto the pink-painted courtyard. Sparkling baths. Singles Bs35, with bath Bs45; doubles Bs50, with bath Bs60; triples Bs75.

Alojamiento Central (☎462 634), on Ostria Gutiérrez across from the bus terminal. "Central" only if you plan to spend time around the bus terminal. A little musty, but still the best place to crash if you arrive too late to make it into the city center. Singles Bs20, with bath Bs25; doubles Bs34, with bath Bs45; triples Bs50, with bath Bs60.

Alojamiento El Dorado, Loa 419 (☎461 932). Nicer than the faded yellow bedspreads and slightly stuffy rooms is the sparse courtyard, lined with potted plants. Singles Bs25, with bath Bs40; doubles Bs40, with bath Bs60; triples Bs60.

Alojamiento Turista (☎453 572), on Ravelo between Loa and Junín. Bathrooms don't smell the sweetest, but the owners are very friendly. Laundry Bs5 per kg. Singles Bs20; doubles Bs32; triples Bs49; quad Bs64; quints Bs75.

Hostal Veracruz (☎451 560), on Ravelo between Loa and Junín. Rooms with bath are much nicer than those without; all beds afford a good night's sleep. Singles Bs30, with bath Bs70; doubles Bs50, with bath Bs100; triples Bs75, with bath Bs150.

FOOD

Sucre presents an array of international and local cuisine. The town specialty is *chorizos chuquisaqueños* (fried pork sausage), but Sucre is also known for its chocolate—satisfy your sweet tooth at shops around the plaza, especially off A. Arce and Arenales. In the market, the better food stands serve meals for Bs5.

Café Cultural Kaypíchu (☎443 954), on San Alberto between España and Bolívar. A haven for vegetarians and fresh-food lovers alike. Exquisitely prepared meals. Open, airy dining room with local paintings and peaceful classical music. Breakfast Bs9-17. *Almuerzo* Bs12. Dinner entrees about Bs13. Open Tu-Sa 7am-2pm and 5-9pm.

El Germen, on San Alberto between Avaroa and Bolívar. Vegetarian. Peaceful atmosphere. Entrees such as falafel, curry tofu, and greek salad Bs12-20. Mouth-watering cakes, cookies, and other pastries Bs3-6. Open M-Sa 8am-9pm.

Monte Bianco, Colón 149 (☎462 775). The place for pasta. Italian owner doubles as chef. Savory, though small, dishes Bs18-23. Cozy rooms straight out of an Alps ski-lodge. Tiramisu Bs6. Espresso Bs4. Open daily 7am-11pm.

Piso Cero, Venezuela 1241 (☎452 567), just south of the train tracks. A classy choice. Traditional, mostly meat, dishes. Lunch Bs13. Dinner Bs18-22. Open daily noon-3pm and 6:30-11pm.

Restaurant Suizo Arco Iris, N. Ortiz 42 (☎423 985), off the plaza. A gringo favorite. Very interesting decor. Fondue Bs23. Roeschti Bs15-19. Excellent pastas Bs10-15. Greek salad Bs12. Filling omlettes Bs10-12. Live music Sa. Open daily 6-11pm.

La Taverne, A. Arce 35 (☎453 599), off the plaza, in the Alliance Francaise. Well-prepared French classics. Beef bourguignon Bs25. Quiche Bs18. Succulent chocolate torte Bs3. Delicate crepes Bs5. French films every night. Open daily 8am-3pm and 6-10pm.

La Repizza, N. Ortiz 78 (☎451 506), off the plaza. One of the more popular pizza parlors in Sucre. Extensive buffet lunch Bs12. Nights bring pizzas (large Bs39-47) and droves of people to this mural-rich haunt. Live music F-Sa. Open M-F 12-2pm and 6-11pm.

Las Cebollitas, at Bustillos and Colón. Mexican, Bolivian-style. Tacos Bs4. Most beer Bs5. Heineken Bs7. Open daily 7-11pm (the afternoon restaurant is rented by different people and serves mediocre traditional Bolivian food).

New Hong Kong, San Alberto 242 (☎441 776), between Bolívar and Avaroa. As authentic as Bolivian chifas get. Hearty lunch Bs10-15. Meat (Bs20-25), rice (Bs10), and noodle (Bs16-20) dishes. Open daily 11:30am-2:30pm and 6-10:30pm.

Restaurant Plaza, Plaza 25 de Mayo 34 (☎455 843), 2nd fl. Known for incredibly huge portions. Limited, but lovely, outdoor seating overlooks the plaza. Traditional 4-course lunch Bs12. Steak Bs14-22. Open daily noon-midnight.

CAFES

Filled afternoon and night, Sucre's cafes offer cappuccino or espresso to the Nescafé-weary. Estudiantes, an area northwest of the plaza, houses many a busy one. Sucre also holds a larger-than-average number of shops devoted to the *salteña*.

Biblio Café, N. Ortiz 30, off the plaza. Biblio is always the place to be. Excellent Thai pasta (Bs25) and sweet crepes (Bs12), along with cappuccino (Bs5) and beer (Bs6), keep the crowd fully satisfied. Four daily lunch offerings (Bs13-20) range from the traditional Bolivian to international fare. Great live music F-Sa. Open daily 11am-2am.

El Patio, San Alberto 18 (☎454 917), 1 block from the plaza. If the omnipresent line outside this *salteñaría* doesn't clue you in, the tasty juices and *salteñas* will. Meat *salteña* Bs2. Chicken *salteña* Bs2.5. Open daily 9am-noon.

Kultur Café Berlin, Avaroa 324 (☎452 091), in the Instituto Cultural Boliviano-Alemán. Popular. Sandwiches Bs5. Müeslix Bs6. Cappuccino Bs4. Open daily 8:30am-midnight.

Salon de Té Las Delicias, Estudiantes 50 (☎442 502). Herds of locals follow the pastry scent to afternoon tea on glass tables, each with a small vase of delicate flowers. Lemon pie Bs2.8. Chocolate cake Bs2.9. *Empanadas* Bs2. Open daily 4-8pm.

El Paso de Los Abuelos, Bustillos 216 (☎455 173), 3 blocks southwest of the plaza. A friendly specialty shop filled with patrons munching on *salteñas* and *empanadas* (both Bs3). Open daily 9am-1pm.

Hacheh, Pastor Sainz 233 (☎462 818). A wooden salon fit with ornate magenta velvet chairs, regal chess sets, and offbeat music. The small menu includes coffee (Bs3), beer (Bs6), and burgers (Bs7). Worth the hike from the city center. Open daily 4-midnight.

👁 SIGHTS

CASA DE LA LIBERTAD. This white house, where the liberators signed Bolivia's **Declaration of Independence** on August 6, 1825, houses that document as well as General Sucre's sword from the fateful battle of Ayacucho, a famous portrait of El Libertador (Simon Bolívar) himself, and the first **Argentinian flag,** snatched when Bolivia was still under the jurisdiction of Buenos Aires. A haven for Bolivian history buffs and patriots in general. There's an historic art exhibit upstairs. *(On the plaza. ☎454 200. Open M-F 9-11:40am and 2:30-6:10pm, Sa 9:30-11:40am. Bs10.)*

ASUR: MUSEO TEXTIL-ETNOGRÁFICO. This convent-turned-museum holds an incredible collection of local **Jalq'a and Tarabuco weavings** and information on their cultural history. The museum highlights both past and contemporary designs, including traditional dress and men's attempts at weaving. Watch Jalq'a and Tarabuco women weave their intricate tapestries in the upper salon; these are sold in the museum shop—and although they're more expensive ($100-200) than those bought in the Tarabuco market, proceeds go to train weavers and support ASUR's advances (see Andean Renaissance, p. 336). *(San Alberto 413, at Potosí. From the plaza, walk 3 blocks southeast down Calvo and take a left on Potosí; the museum's on the corner. ☎453 841; email asur@mara.scr.entelnet.bo. Guides available.)*

CATHEDRAL. This dominating plaza fixture was begun in 1559, although not fully completed until the mid-1600s. It is most exciting from the outside, with a bell tower clock (imported from London in 1772) that rises 40m over all other city structures. The best ecclesiastical collection in Bolivia, the paintings displayed within the cathedral's Museo Eclesiástico are by far the most interesting in Sucre. The cathedral's treasure—and patron saint—lies in the chapel just off the main temple: **Virgin of Guadalupe** (1601), adorned with enough jewels to dull even the colored lights that surround her. *(On the Plaza 25 de Mayo; entrance on N. Ortiz 61. ☎452 257. Open for 7am mass. Museum open M-F 10am-noon and 3-5pm, Sa 10am-noon. Bs10. All guests must wait until the previous tour has finished before entering. All tours in Spanish).*

LA RECOLETA. Begun in 1600 by Father Francisco de Morales, the three cloisters of this monastery have sheltered countless monks, soldiers, and prisoners. In addition to many anonymous religious works, the exterior grounds shelter the **Cedro Milenario,** a thousand-year-old tree that was declared a national monument in 1965.

Its trunk was once so large that it took 12 people to encircle it; unfortunately, the tree has been besieged by local insects and shrunk to a slightly less impressive eight-person girth. Also worth visiting is the **choir room,** where wooden figures of the 1870s depict the martyrdom of Franciscans in Nagasaki, Japan during the 16th century. *(Polanco 164, on the Plaza Pedro de Anzúrez. ☎ 451 987. Open M-F 9-11:30am and 2:30-4:30pm; church open daily 5am and 6pm for mass. Tourists must wait for the previous tour to finish before being let in with a Spanish-speaking guide. Visits last about 45min. Bs8, Bs10 including photography rights.)*

MUSEO UNIVERSITARIO CHARCAS. The Universidad Mayor de San Francisco Xavier de Chuquisaca houses a number of collections. The colonial part includes paintings by some of Bolivia's greats, including **Melchor Pérez de Holguín** of the *mestizo* school. On the second level, a section devoted to anthropology emphasizes deformed and sacrificed **skeletons,** in addition to a less interesting, although nonetheless comprehensive, ceramics and tools display. There's also an ethnography and folklore section with traditional masks and costumes. More exciting is the third section, a collection of **modern art** by Cecilio Guzmán de Rojos and Solón Romero. *(Bolívar 698. From the plaza, walk southeast down Audiencia; turn left after a block; the museum's on the left. ☎ 453 285. Open M-Sa 8:30am-noon and 2:30-6pm. Bs10.)*

MUSEO DE HISTORIA NATURAL. One of the University museums, this collection houses a lot of stuffed birds and mammals in addition to an incredible Bolivian beetle collection. It's a good source for dinosaur track information, including Cal Orcko and a few other, more obscure sights. *(Plaza 25 de Mayo 23. ☎ 453 828. Open M-Sa 8:30am-noon and 2:30-6pm. Bs8.)*

MUSEO CONVENTO SANTA CLARA. Two rooms display a number of anonymous colonial religious paintings from the *mestizo* school, including a few works by Melchor Pérez de Holguín. The church, built in 1639, contains a restored Baroque organ from the 17th century in addition to other less sophisticated instruments. *(Calvo 212, 2½ blocks southeast of the plaza. ☎ 452 295. Open M-F 9am-noon and 2-6pm. Bs5.)*

ANDEAN RENAISSANCE Since the 1960s, Andean textiles have been in style, gracing the walls of the ethnically-interested and interior design-conscious. But those beautiful tapestries were probably originally *axsus*, an over-dress worn by women. The Jalq'a people of the Guquisaca area, specifically around Sucre, wove magnificent textiles for years until they woke up one day and realized that they had sold off all their rich designs to swindling dealers. So they stopped, and it seemed that the magic of their original fabrics was lost forever—until the arrival of anthropologists Gabriel Martínez and Veronica Cereceda. In search of the ancestors of the Chulpas, the first Andean people, the two stumbled upon the impoverished Jalq'as, about 25,000 in all. With the goal of once again producing original textiles, the couple created a system of workshops, classes, and community organizations to teach and facilitate weaving. Gradually the Jalq'a women recalled the mysterious and complicated designs of their mothers and grandmothers, and, after a few years, began creating designs of their own. This reclaimed element of their cultural heritage has brought about a complete renaissance within the Jalq's community. The textiles are on display and sold by Antropólogicos del Surandino (ASUR), the organization founded by Martínez and Cereceda, and each brings home the equivalent of a family's income, although the largest pieces take two to three months to compose. Because of this new-found source of sustenance, families have been able to stay together without men migrating south for work; the entire community has become involved with weaving, spinning wool, and managing the textile cooperatives, and women now have a significant voice within the community. Unlike other groups that have attempted to rejuvenate Andean textiles solely for their economic value, ASUR focuses on the community as a whole—a model of development that has proven successful and is now sought by ethnic groups attempting to save their distinct cultures throughout Bolivia.

MUSEO GUTIÉRREZ VALENZUELA. Upstairs from the Natural History museum, this one holds a collection of gold-plated furniture and ornate adornments left over from mining expatriates who emigrated to more refined France following the end of the French Revolution. *(Plaza 25 de Mayo 23. ☎ 453 828. Open M-Sa 8:30am-noon and 2:30-6pm. Bs8; Natural History Museum separate admission.)*

CAL ORCKO. In 1990, dinosaur footprints were discovered in Sucre—behind a cement factory! Perhaps 70 million years old, the tracks leads up an almost vertical wall for more than 100m. An international team of paleontologists speculate that the prints, from the cretaceous period, belonged to Saurópodos, Tetrópodos, or Anquilosaurios. *(5km north of Sucre, behind the FANCESA cement factory. Take the micro.)*

LA GLORIETA. This ornate mansion was built in the 19th century by Don Francisco Argandoña, a wealthy businessman who seems to have brought back a little of each European country he visited. The home now serves as a military school. *(5km south of the city, on the road to Potosí. Micro 4. Open M-F 8:30am-noon and 1:30-5:30pm, Sa 9am-noon. Bring your passport. Bs8, includes Spanish-speaking guide.)*

OTHER SIGHTS. Sucre's claim to fame is the **Corte Suprema de Justicia de la Nacion,** lies at the north end of Ravelo, about three blocks up from plaza. Well-dressed visitors are welcome to take a peek inside (M-F 9am-noon and 2-6pm). A block southwest, on Pilinco at the Plaza de Libertad, sits the lovely old building that now houses the **Teatro Gran Mariscal.** At the opposite side of the plaza, **Hospital Santa Bárbara** has a beautiful colonial *portada* from the 17th century. The city **cemetary** houses many rich, famous, and dead Bolivians. The entrance reads, "Today for me, tomorrow for you." *(From the Plaza 25 de Mayo, walk 2 blocks northwest up Estudiantes. Turn left and head all the way down Loa—6 blocks—to the entrance. For Bs5, local boys will give you a complete tour.)* For a great city view, check out **Cerra Churuquella,** behind La Recoleta on Dalence. The 10-minute uphill walk, following the stations of the cross, is a bit windy, but a nice escape from Sucre's busy streets.

CHURCHES

IGLESIA DE SAN FRANCISCO. Home of Bolivia's Liberty Bell, which first rang for revolution in 1809 and now sporadically announces the hour. Begun in 1540 as a shack where recently immigrated Franciscans could gather, the final product was finished in 1581 and remained as a place of God until war got in the way: 1809 signaled not only rebellion, but also the church's confiscation for military purposes. After serving as an army barracks, a customs house, and a market, the arch-filled edifice was returned to the Franciscans in 1925, gold-plated altar and all. *(At Ravelo and A. Arce, 1 block northeast of the plaza. ☎ 451 853. Open daily 6:30-10:30am.)*

IGLESIA DE SAN MIGUEL. Construction for this originally Jesuit church is thought to have begun in 1621, when the order first arrived from Potosí. Famous for its *mudejar* style, San Miguel also has a lovely silver altar and painted ceilings. *(Arenales 10, half-block northwest of the plaza. ☎ 451 206. Open only during 7am mass.)*

IGLESIA DE SAN LÁZARO. Built in 1538 of adobe brick and a straw roof, this relatively simple building is considered the first church of Sucre. A severe fire in the 16th century called for a 17th-century rebuilding. A series of perfectly white exterior arches guard the original interior silver altar. *(At Calvo and Padilla, 4 blocks southeast of the plaza. ☎ 451 448. Open daily for 7am mass.)*

IGLESIA DE SAN FELIPE DE NERI. An imposing stone structure capped by brilliant white belltowers and cupolas, this is one of the later colonial works in Sucre. Begun in 1795, it offers a panoramic city view along with a rose-filled courtyard. Visiting is rather difficult: the church opens only rarely for special festivities. *(N. Ortiz 165, 2 blocks southwest of the plaza. ☎ 454 333.)*

SOUTHERN BOLIVIA

OTHER CHURCHES. One of Sucre's best examples of colonial architecture is the now-closed **Iglesia de Santa Monica,** Junín 601, 1 block northwest of the plaza on Arenales. It's well worth a visit to check out the *portada*, made in the 18th century by indigenous artists. **Iglesia de La Merced,** at Azurduy and Pérez, boasts an ornate gold altar and a few works by Melchor Pérez de Holguín. *(Open daily for 7am mass.)* **Iglesia de Santo Domingo,** at Calvo and Bolívar, 1 block southeast of the plaza, is a local favorite popular for the 5pm Friday mass candle-lighting to honor the Santo de Gran Poder. *(Open daily for 7am mass.)*

✳ FESTIVALS

Since Sucre is known as a cultural center, the **International Culture Festival,** two solid weeks of singing, dancing, poetry, theatre, and just about any other artistic expression you can think of, comes as no surprise. It usually begins mid-September; contact the Fundación Cultural (☎445 553 or 445 558) for more details. Held around the same time is the **Celebration of the Virgin of Guadalupe,** patron saint of the city. Officially September 8, the parade featuring the cathedral's ornate image of the virgin happens on the weekend closest to the saint's day. Also quite important, especially to Sucre, are the **25th of May** Anniversary of the first shout for liberty in the Americas, and **August 6th,** Bolivia's independence day.

♪ ▧ ENTERTAINMENT AND NIGHTLIFE

Sucre's party scene follows the coming and going of the university students who enliven the city. When in session, check out the discos **Up-Down** (☎453 587), on Gregorio Mendizabal a block north of Mitsu Mania, and **Micerino** (☎443 777), at Bolívar and Urcullo. At any time of year, dancing rarely begins before midnight. For healthier fun, check out the **Sucre Tenis Club,** on Venezuela just south of the railroad tracks. (☎452 463. Bs30 for a morning or afternoon on the club's clay courts; Bs20 for 1hr. at night; racquets Bs5. Open M-F 6am-10pm.)

Chili Pepper (☎444 804), on N. Ortiz between Grau and Datence, south of the plaza. Unmarked—look for a door made of curtains and glass bricks. This small blue barroom plays US rock and fills with both locals and travelers on F and Sa. Beer Bs5-16. Mixed drinks average Bs17. Open daily until late.

Boomerang, on Datence between N. Ortiz and Bustillos, 1 block south and 1 block west of the plaza. Catering to the 16+ crowd, with a half-functioning discoball, flashing lights and occasional strobe action. Open Tu-F 9pm-2am, Sa 9pm-5am.

Club Nano's (☎424 288), on España between Camargo and San Alberto, 1½ blocks north of the plaza. An older (21+) local crowd. A great place to salsa on a packed dance floor. Open daily 8pm-3am.

Mitsu Mania (☎421 616), at Venezuela and Maestro, on the northern side of Parque Bolívar. It's hard to miss the flashing lights and well-dressed teenagers of this car dealership-cum-disco where the theme is auto racing. The cover (Bs20) is converted to Mitsu money, which can be used to buy overpriced drinks. Open Th-Sa 8pm-3am.

▨ DAYTRIP FROM SUCRE

TARABUCO

Tarabuco-bound camiones (2hr., Bs7) leave daily from the Plaza Huallparimachi. Catch either micro B or C from in front of the market on Ravelo to the plaza and wait for a bus to fill up. The same buses leave from Tarabuco's main plaza about once an hr. until nightfall (Bs7). Many tour agencies run buses to Tarabuco on Sundays. One of the best deals is through Hostal Charcas (2hr.; Su 7:30am, returning 1pm; round-trip Bs16).

Tarabuco's Sunday market overflows with woven goods and other market fare in possibly Bolivia's biggest tourist trap. A short 65km southeast of Sucre on a well-paved road, this small town is a little colder and a little higher (3284m) than Sucre. Many locals wear traditional dress—*monteras* (hats) and two layers of ponchos.

Women wear *axsus*, ornate dress-like coverings. The city's grandest festival celebrates the March 12, 1816 victory in the Battle of Jumbati over the domineering Spanish. Usually occurring in mid-March, locals from all over flock to dance through the city streets. The two statues in the plaza recall two men who ate Spanish soldiers' raw hearts to vindicate the rape of the area's women. This is the reason why *tarabuqueños* are also called *soncko mikus*, Quechua for "heart-eaters."

NEAR SUCRE: VILLA SERRANO

Camiones to Villa Serrano (7hr., 7am and 5pm, Bs15-20) leave from Américas. Buses returning to Sucre (6hr., 7am and 4:30pm, Bs15) leave from La Plata office on the plaza.

The capital of Chuquisaca folk music, Villa Serrano lies 218km east of Sucre, hidden by the surrounding hills and valleys. The birthplace of famous folk musician **Mauro Nuñez**, this isolated town carries on the tradition with lively music festivals. A Christmas celebration (Dec. 25-27) brings dancing and *folklórico* to the streets, repeated again for the **Festival de Charango,** held every year on September 21. People from all over the department flock with instruments in hand to honor traditional tunes with a three-week festival, culminating with the celebration of the city's patron, St. Miguel, on September 29. Of Villa Serrano's two *alojamientos*, **Misky Life,** just off the low end of the plaza, is the better choice. Bathrooms shine and rooms are comfortable, if remarkably simple. (☎912 346. Singles Bs20, with bath Bs25; doubles Bs40, with bath Bs50; triples Bs60; quads Bs80.)

NEAR SUCRE: CORDILLERA DE LOS FRAILES

Although somewhat expensive, it is best to visit the Cordillera with a guide, especially for longer trips or more obscure destinations. Many area villagers only speak Quechua and don't welcome strangers. Most agencies (see Practical Information, p. 332) run tours for US$20-30 a day, including all transportation, food, and basic lodgings; prices decrease with more people and longer excursions. Maps of the area can be bought at the Instituto Geográfico Militar, on A. Arce just south of Hernando Siles. Originals (Bs45) are scarce, but the photocopies (Bs35) aren't bad. Sucre (6536IV) and Estancia Chaunaca (6537II) include almost all feasible destinations; Potolo is on Anacoma (6436I). (☎455 514. Open M-F 8:30am-noon and 2:30-6pm.) Altitude remains relatively low for Bolivia, ranging from Sucre's 2700m to Chataquila's 3726m.

The ridge of hills and mountains rising up to the west of the city makes Sucre a great start to 1- to 10-day treks. Most begin at **Chataquila,** a small stone temple 25km west of Sucre on the road to Potolo. From here many choose to head north for a day to explore the ancient rock paintings in **Incamachay** (also called Pumamachay). Agencies also offer day trips here. From Chataquila almost anyone can handle the 7km (all downhill) along a precolonial road to **Chaunaca,** a small village of *campesinos*. The extremely ambitious head southwest, to **Potolo,** one of the centers for Jalq'a weavings, while others head south 8km to the town of **Maragua** and the maroon crater of the same name. Many groups choose to spend a few days exploring the many weaving villages and settlements nearby. Trips down further to the **Talula Thermal Baths** were quite popular until a geological shift stopped up the source, drying up the wells of steaming hot water. Rather than taking the western, longer route to Quila Quila, a pleasant village and also site of stone paintings, the dried baths encourage many to head straight south, about 10½km. A few distinct options arise from this point. Access to the summit of **Cerro Obíspo** (3453m) is only 5km away. Most agencies head directly back to **San Juan** (8½km), ford the Cachimayu River, and drive the rest of the way (18km) back to Sucre. Although the entire road between Quila Quila and Sucre is theoretically accessible by auto, during the rainy season (especially Dec.-Feb.), the river is impassable. But if you haven't gotten enough of the rock paintings, head to **Supay Huari,** or House of the Devil, for some bizarre but intriguing artwork. The easiest way to reach this extremely obscure site is to drive north 17km to Padilla and walk 2½hr. to the paintings, following the Mama Huasi river.

POTOSÍ ☎ 06

The source of Spanish opulence, dominance, and successive economic downfall, Potosí at one point overshadowed all other colonial endeavors in the Americas, claiming the titles of highest (4090m), largest (at its height in 1650 the city boasted more than 160,000 inhabitants), and wealthiest (by far) city on the two continents. Today the city remains the highest in the world, and its source of wealth, the mines of Cerro Rico (4824m), still tower in the background and are still ravished for tin, welfram, zinc, lead, and occasionally even silver. But the current population of 120,000 barely fills this space rich with ghosts of conquest, wealth, and suffering, and modern-day Potosí is merely a reflection of what this boom town once was, with colonial buildings and a plethora of churches grazing the disorderly streets of a city that grew more rapidly than it could be planned.

▌ TRANSPORTATION

Airlines: No flights leave from Potosí, but airlines have offices in the city. **LAB,** Lanza 19 (☎222 361), in the Hotel Turista, 1½ blocks south of the main plaza. Open M-F 9am-noon and 2-6pm. **Aerosur,** Cobija 25 (☎228 988 or 222 232), 1½ blocks west of the main plaza. Open M-F 9am-noon and 2:30-6:30pm.

Buses: Terminal on Antofagasta, in the northwest part of the city, a 20min. walk. Most micros (Bs1) head there; some include numbers 80, 90, 100, or letters "I" and "C." The information booth (☎243 361) is open daily in winter 6:30am-12:30pm and 2:30-8:30pm; in summer 6am-noon and 2-8pm. Bs1.5 exit fee. Buses run to: **La Paz** (20hr., 7 and 7:30pm, Bs80); **Cochabamba** (12hr., 7pm, Bs70); **Sucre** (3hr., 5 per day 7am-6pm, Bs15); **Oruro** (7hr.; 7am, 8, and 10pm; Bs50); **Tarija** (11hr.; 11am, noon, and 7pm; Bs40); **Tupiza** (7hr.; 7, 8, 9:30am, and 7pm; Bs60-70); **Villazón** (12hr.; 7, 8, and 9:30am; Bs60-70); and **Uyuni** (6-7hr., noon, Bs30-35). The majority of buses leave for **Uyuni** (5-6hr.; 11am and 6:30pm; Bs30) from farther down Antofagosta toward the city at the intersection with Villa Toledo, right near the train tracks. **Micros** leave from the Antofagosta side of the Plaza Chuquimia to: **Miraflores** (30min.; leaving when full, about every 30min. 7am-6pm; Bs3.5); **Totara** (30min.; leaving when full, every few hr. 7am-5pm; Bs3.5); and **Santa Lucia** (30min., 8:30am and 3pm, Bs3.5). From the other side of the Plaza Chuquimia, off América, micros leave from the office of Trans Norte to: **Bombori** (Th and F 11:30am, Bs50); **Colquechaca** (7hr.; M, W, F 11am; Bs30); **Macha** (5hr., 11:30am, Bs25); **Pocoata** (6hr.; Tu, Th, and Sa 11am; Bs27); and **Sucre** (F 11am, Bs30). Camiones and micros leave for **Sucre** from the northern end of the Final de Chayanta (3hr., leaving when full 7am-6pm, Bs10-15). Camiones also leave from the Plaza de Uyuni, at the northern end of the city. To: **Don Diego** (1hr., leaving when full 7am-5pm, Bs3); **Bentanzos** (2hr., 10 per day 8am-8pm, Bs5); **Huari Huari** (1hr., 4pm, Bs4.5); and **Sucre** (3hr., leaving when full 7am-6pm, Bs10-15).

Public Transportation: Micros of all different numbers and letters run throughout the city (Bs1). Most leave from around the central market.

Taxis: Within the city, including to the bus terminal, Bs3. Easy to pick up, but can also be called: **Imperial** (☎227 878); **Potosí** (☎225 257); and **Arco Iris** (☎223 123).

▓ ▌ ORIENTATION AND PRACTICAL INFORMATION

The heart is the **Plaza 10 de Noviembre,** abutted by the **Plaza 6 de Agosto.** The **central market** is a few short blocks northwest. Most streets change names at the plaza. Streets head uphill from west to east, rising toward Cerro Rico. **Antofagosta** runs northwest and is the major thoroughfare, passing through the **Plaza Chuquimia** and the **bus terminal** (an uphill walk back to the plaza).

Tourist Information: Most helpful is the **information booth,** above the Plaza 6 de Agosto in the Plaza Alonsa de Ibañez, which sells city maps (Bs2.5) and guidebooks (Bs25). Open M-F 8:30am-noon and 2-5:30pm. There is also a **university office,** next to the museum on Bolívar between Sucre and Junín. Open M-F 8:30-noon and 2-6pm.

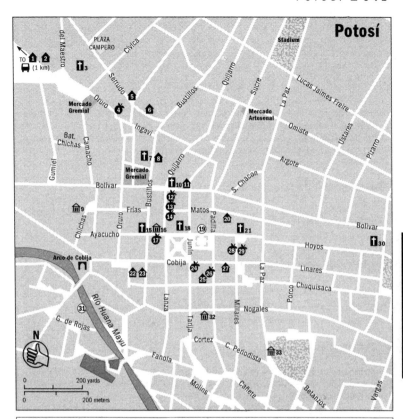

Potosí

ACCOMMODATIONS
Alojamiento Tumusla, **2**
Casa de Huespedajes Hispano, **20**
Casa de Huéspedes María Victoria, **22**
Hostal Carlos 16, **27**
Hostal Compañía de Jesús, **25**
Hostal Felimar, **11**
Hotel Central, **23**
Posada San Lorenzo, **8**
Residencial Copacabana, **5**
Residencial Felcar, **6**
Residencial Sumaj, **1**

FOOD AND DRINK
Café Cultural Kaypíchu, **28**
Candelaria Internet Café, **17**
Chaplin Café, **14**
Cherry's, **26**
Den Daske Café, **13**
El Mesón, **24**
La Manzana Mágica, **4**
Potocchi, **29**
San Marcos, **33**
Sumac Orcko, **12**

SIGHTS
Belén/Teatro Orniste, **19**
Catedral, **18**
Compañía de Jesús, **15**
Iglesia de Jerusalem, **3**
Iglesia de la Merced, **21**
Iglesia de San Agustín, **10**
Iglesia de San Lorenzo, **7**
Iglesia de San Martín, **30**
Ingenio Dolores, **31**
La Casa Real de la Moneda, **16**
Museo Santa Teresa, **9**
Museo-Convento de San Francisco, **32**
San Marcos Ingenio, **33**

Instituto Geográfico Militar, Chayonta 769 (☎226 248), 4 blocks north of the market, has good maps of Potosí's surrounding areas. Originals Bs60. Photocopies Bs45. Open M-F 8:30am-noon and 1-5pm.

Tours Agencies: Many different agencies offer tours of the mines, the city, and Kari Kari, among other destinations. Tour quality tends to depend more on individual guides than on the agencies themselves, making navigation through the companies difficult. Below is a smattering of the most popular agencies, listed cheapest to most expensive.

Carol Tours, Serrudo 345 (☎228 212; email santosm@cedro.pts.entelnet.bo), next to Residencial Felcar, 2 blocks north of the market on the right. Open daily 8am-12:30pm and 2-10pm.

Koala Tours, Ayacucho 5 (☎/fax 222 092), across from Casa de la Moneda. A portion of mine tour profits filter back to support miner's aid, such as health programs. Open daily 8am-7pm.

Sumaj Tours, Oruro 143 (☎224 633 or 222 495; fax 222 600), in the Jerusalem Hotel, 1½ blocks north of the market. Open daily 8am-noon and 2:30-7pm.

Banks: Banco Mercentil, Pasaje Boulevard 9 (☎228 085), on Padilla between Matos and Hoyos. Visa **ATM.** Open M-F 8:30am-12:30pm and 2:30-6:30pm, Sa 9am-1:30pm. **BNB,** Junín 6 (☎223 501). V and MC cash advances. Open M-F 8:30am-noon and 2:30-6pm, Sa 9am-1pm. **Banco de Crédito** (☎223 521), at Bolívar and Padilla. V, MC, and AmEx cash advances at 5% commission.

Immigration: Linares 35 (☎225 989), 2nd fl., just east of Padilla on the left. Open M-F 8:30am-4:30pm.

Cultural Center: Centro Boliviano-Americano, Chuquisaca 590 (☎225 556), between Padilla and Millares. **Internet access** Bs7 per hr.

Markets: Central Market within Bolívar, Bustillos, Oruro, and Chichas. **Mercado Artesanal,** at Sucre and Omiste, has artisan goods.

Emergency: ☎110 or 116.

Police: On the Plaza 10 de Noviembre (☎222 661).

Pharmacy: Call ☎116 for the *farmacia en turno* (open 24hr.).

Hospital: Cruz Roja, Camacho 127 (☎226 045), just below the Plaza del Estudiante.

Telephones: ENTEL (☎224 007 or 222 497), just south of Bolívar. Open M-Sa 8am-10:30pm, Su 8am-10pm.

Internet Access: C. Camex, on Bolívar between Bustillos and Quijarro. Bs6 per hr. Open daily 8am-10pm. **Internet Tukós Café,** Junín 9 (☎225 487), at Bolívar. Head up to the 3rd floor for what owners claim is the highest Internet access in the world. Bs6 per hr.

Post Office: Lanza 3 (☎222 513), 1 block south of the main plaza, between Cobija and Chuquisaca. Open daily 8:30am-7:30pm.

ACCOMMODATIONS

Lodgings abound in Potosí, but finding a place with heat requires time and money—look for someplace with at least four blankets. Most "hot" water runs about 7am-6pm.

Hostal Carlos V, Linares 42 (☎225 121), 2 blocks east of the main plaza. Don't let the beat-up street sign fool you; inside lie white stucco walls, wooden railings, and crisp bedspreads. Breakfast Bs12. Singles Bs30, with bath Bs40; doubles Bs60.

Residencial Sumaj, Gumiel 12 (☎223 336). From the main plaza walk 4 blocks west to Chiches. Head north 4 blocks to the Plaza de Estudiantes; Sumaj is on the far right corner. Rooms open onto a hallway full of travelers hanging out. Kitchen access. Singles Bs25; doubles Bs45; triples Bs60; quads Bs80; garage rooms Bs20 per person.

Residencial Felcar, Serrudo 345 (☎224 966). From the north side of the market, head 2 blocks up and take a right; Felcar is on your left about ½ block down. 24hr. gas-powered hot showers make up for the sparse blanket supply. Helpful owners. Breakfast Bs3.5-8. Laundry Bs8 per kg. Singles Bs25; doubles Bs40; triples Bs60; quads Bs80.

Casa de Huéspedes María Victoria, Chuquisaca 148 (☎222 132). Head 1 block south from the plaza to Chuquisaca and follow it 2½ blocks to the end. The beautiful colonial building, usually full of travelers, comes at a price: 6min. showers and an insistence on advance payment. Singles Bs25; doubles Bs50, with bath Bs60; triples Bs75.

Hostal Compañía de Jesús, Chuquisaca 445 (☎223 173), 1 block south and ½ block east of the main plaza. Copious blankets, 24hr. hot water, and Potosí's friendliest owners can keep anyone warm. Breakfast included. Singles Bs40, with bath Bs50; doubles Bs70, with bath Bs90; triples Bs120.

Posada San Lorenzo, Bustillos 967 (☎224 842), just north of the central market on the right. The cheapest place in town, with no hot water, an outdoor sink and shower, and thin blankets. Singles Bs12; doubles Bs20; triples Bs30; quads Bs40; quints Bs50.

Hostal Felimar (☎224 357), at Junín and Bolívar, 2 blocks north of main plaza. Low ceilings, especially in basement rooms, but oddly tall showers. Carpeted rooms with TVs. Singles Bs40, with bath Bs60; doubles Bs70, with bath Bs90; triples with bath Bs120.

Residencial Copacabana (☎222 712), at Serrudo and Chayata, 2 blocks north of the central market. Rooms open onto a hallway of windows with live ivy clinging to the ceiling, countering the aqua-green walls. Floors are a bit dusty, but toilets are spotless. Singles Bs25; doubles Bs40; triples Bs60; quads Bs80.

Casa de Huespedajes Hispano, Matos 62 (☎(01) 475 342), 2 blocks from main plaza. Sturdy beds. Glass-roofed courtyard. Motherly owner. Breakfast Bs6. Laundry Bs8 per kg. All rooms with bath. Singles Bs50; doubles Bs90; triples Bs110.

Hotel Central, Bustillos 1230 (☎222 207). From the main plaza, head west 1 block, take a left on Bustillos; it's a half block down on the right. Hot water 7am-6pm. Rooms are fairly large and breakfast (Bs4) is cheap. Singles Bs25; doubles Bs40; triples Bs60.

▒ FOOD

Traditional food in Potosí includes *lagua*, a spicy corn paste made from *choclo* (a type of corn) and served with little pieces of ham. *Calaporka* is *lagua* served with a hot stone in the middle that keeps it sizzling even on the table. For dessert, try *tahua-tahuas*, corn-based pastries topped with honey. For the cold morning savior (*api* with *pasteles*) or any cheap meal, head to the market.

La Manzana Mágica, Oruro 239, on the right side a block north of the market. A fruit haven, this meatless joint blends *licuados* (Bs3.5), fruit juices (Bs3), and fruit salads (Bs7) of all kinds. Munch on lunch or dinner (Bs10) at the dark wood tables. Burgers (of quinoa, cereal, veggies, and soy) Bs4. Spaghetti Bs7. Open daily 7am-10pm.

Sumac Orcko, Quijarro 46 (☎223 703), 1½ blocks north of the main plaza. Popular among tourists and locals alike. Vegetarian-friendly. 4-course lunches Bs13. Specialties include *viscacha* (a rabbit-like animal with a long tail native to the altiplano; Bs20), *lechón* (pork dish; Bs20), and Titicaca trout (Bs25). Open M-Sa 8:30am-10pm.

Potocchi, Millares 13 (☎222 759), 2 blocks west of the plaza between Hoyos and Linares. Both traditional (llama meat Bs18) and international (Roeschiti Bs18) cuisine. Great *peñas* M, W, and F 8pm, Bs10 cover. Open M-Sa 7am-11pm.

Candelaria Internet Café, Ayacucho 5 (☎226 467), 1 block west of the main plaza, across from La Casa de la Moneda. Travelers converge at here for Internet (Bs10 per hr.), a book exchange, and a diverse menu (llama meat Bs15). The sun-filled terrace overlooking the city is a great place for afternoon coffee (Bs1). Open daily 8am-10pm.

Den Daske Café (☎(01) 476 331), at Quijarro and Matos, 1 block north of the plaza. Gringo-oriented. Thai noodles Bs20. Chicken curry Bs20. Open daily 7:30am-10:30pm.

San Marcos (☎222 781), on La Paz just north of Periodistas. A posh restaurant set in an old factory. Customers eat on glass tables over the original machinery. *Filet flambê San Marcos* Bs30. Llama medallions Bs20. Open M-Su noon-11pm.

El Mesón (☎223 087), at Tarija and Linares, on the Plaza 10 de Noviembre. Quite possibly the best restaurant in Potosí. Tasty traditional dishes (most meat-based) Bs25-28. Mussels in a light cheese sauce (Bs12) or asparagus with ham pieces (Bs8) grace fine china, set with care at each hardwood table. Open daily noon-2pm and 5-10:30pm.

Cherry's, Padilla 8 (☎225 367), 1 block south of the Plaza 6 de Agosto. Small, but usually full, traveler's haunt. Cakes and pies Bs2.5. Piping hot tea or coffee Bs1.5. Granola Bs5. Open daily 8am-10pm.

Chaplin Café, at Quijarro and Matos, 1 block north of the plaza. A mix of herbivorous and carnivorous entrees for a crowd of hungry foreigners. Muesli with yogurt Bs8. Spaghetti with chicken Bs10. Tacos Bs6. Open daily 7:30am-noon and 4-10pm.

SIGHTS

MINE TOURS

It is only legal to visit the mines with an accredited guide. Make sure you receive a hard hat, protective clothing, boots, and a lamp. Mine tours involve scrambling, so wear old clothes. Because of the extreme depth and noxious fumes; these tours are not for the asthmatic or claustrophobic. Temperatures can reach 40°C. Trolleys of ore run up the tracks—be prepared to jump out of the way. For the full effect go M-F, as many miners don't work Sa-Su. Tours 4-5hr.; 2½-3hr. spent in the mines. US$10 or Bs50.

One of Potosí's touristic highlights—and a brutal glimpse into the city's harsh reality—is a tour of one of the many mines that weave through Cerro Rico. A visit into the depths takes any visitor back in time; working conditions here have changed little since the days of the Spanish. Men and boys (ages 8-16) work with primitive tools, pounding away at arsenic- and ore-ridden riches. Although the two governmental and six privately-owned mines work with modern technology, the 27 other mines are cooperatives, rented from the government for 6-8% of the mine's profits. In cooperatives, miners generally work six eight-hour days a week without ventilation, proper safety equipment, maps, or any forewarning of a cave-in (no engineers or geologists), at temperatures upward of 40°C. Over 7000 people (1000 of whom are children) carry over 1000 tons out of Cerro Rico daily. Most agencies offer tours and (usually) experienced guides, many of whom are ex-miners themselves.

All tours begin with gear-gathering and gift-buying. The miners have come to expect the cold drinks and dynamite that tourists lug down with them. However, most people buy dynamite and ammonium nitrate not for the miners, but to put on a show at the end of the tour. Fridays call for gifts of chicha—the 96-proof alcohol made from corn. And then it's off into the mouth of hell to experience the daily life of many *potosinos*. On the way down, visitors talk to the miners, many of whom are children. Conditions, especially on the cooperatives, are appalling; add softhearted to the list of people for whom this tour is not. The following guides have received good recommendations, although chances of getting a good guide are high no matter what: **Juan Mamani Choque** and **Eduardo García Fajardo** of Koala tours (which gives 15% of its profits to miners), or **Santos Mamani** and **Roberta Guitierrez** of Carol Tours. Almost all guides speak English; some can also give tours in German, French, or Quechua if you prefer.

INGENIOS. At the height of Cerro Rica's silver extraction (around 1660), 132 *ingenios* (ore refineries) existed on La Ribera, to the south of the city. Here the ore was pulverized by large stones or powered hydraulically by the Kari Kari lakes. Then mercury was added to the ground rock to separate the silver from the other minerals present. **San Marcos,** now a restaurant and partial museum, and **Dolores,** on Mejllones between Nogales and Bustillos, are both worth visiting as some of the best preserved examples of 17th-century refineries. Continue west along the Rio Huana Mayo; a few more pop up after the train tracks.

MUSEUMS

With a wealth of history in addition to its famous material riches, Potosí boasts a few excellent (and a few haphazardly-prepared) museums. Wear warm clothes—two-hour tours in unheated stone buildings tend to get chilly.

■ **LA CASA REAL DE LA MONEDA.** Ironically, this is both Bolivia's current treasure of a museum and a symbol of Spanish historical oppression. The original building was begun in 1572 as one of many of Viceroy Toledo's reforms, the purpose being to mint the Potosí silver locally in order to extract taxes. A new mint was constructed between 1759 and 1773; even after the 1825 revolution, the mint was used to forge the republic's currency until its founding as a museum in 1940. The Casa also had stints as a prison and as army headquarters. A three-hour tour yields some of Bolivia's finest treasures, including many paintings by master Holquin, the anonymous **La Virgen del Cerro,** and a grinning **Bacchus mask** on the entrance arch, placed in 1865 by French woodcarver Eugene Martí Mulón. More interesting are the **minting tools,** including three huge rolling mills imported from Spain in 1750, which take up two floors and were powered by mules in order to flatten the silver into sheets. The final rooms of the museum seem haphazardly organized, with smatterings of historical, minerological, and anthropological pieces. *(At Ayacucho and Quijarro.* ☎ *223 986. Open Tu-Sa 9am-noon and 2-6:30pm; Su 9am-1pm, but come at least an hour before closing to catch a tour. For a full tour, your best bet is to come at either 9am or 2pm. Guides in English, Spanish, and French. Bs10.)*

MUSEO-CONVENTO DE SAN FRANCISCO. Founded in 1547 by Fray Gaspar de Valverde, San Francisco was Bolivia's first church and monastery. What you see now, however, was constructed between 1707 and 1726; the original church was too modest for local Franciscans. The first courtyard holds a badly damaged 25-painting series of the life of St. Francis of Assisi (painted in the 17th century by Gregario Gamarra), but more interesting is Metchor Pérez de Holguín's most recognized painting, **La Erección de la Cruz.** The church's high, vaulted ceilings, painted to look like brick, house a statue of the city's patron saint, **Señor de la Vera Cruz** (supposedly, the statue grows human hair). Visitors also get a sneak peek into the church's **catacombs,** which are linked by unexplored and unrestored colonial tunnels to sights all over the city. Tours culminate with a spectacular rooftop view of the city, itself worth the entrance fee. *(Entrance at Tarija and Junín, 2 blocks south of the main plaza.* ☎ *222 539. Tours last 45min.; Spanish-speaking guides. Open M-F 9am-noon and 2:30-5:30pm, Sa 9am-noon. Bs10; Bs10 extra to take pictures (including from the rooftop).*

MUSEO SANTA TERESA. Founded in 1685 by Carmelites from Sucre, the convent was completed just seven years later. Almost all the original stone and woodwork (cedar imported from the Chaco region) remain within the pumpkin-hued building with one of the most notable *mestizo portadas* of the city. A tour of the museum presents a study of cloistered life more than anything else; highlights include the spiked windows through which family members talked with their daughters and sisters and the wooden turnstile that allowed nuns to sell goods without glimpsing the outside world. The extremely well-preserved convent also houses a few works by Bolivian master painter Holguín, in addition to collections of statues, altars, and an intricate moorish ceiling. Other works revere the Carmelite's favorite religious figures, including Santa Teresa de Avila, San Juan de la Cruce, San Joseph, and—of course—the Virgin of Carmen. At the end of the tour visitors can buy *quesitos* (the sweet marzipan candy still made by the nuns today) as well as other goods. *(At Ayacucho and Chichas, 4 blocks west of the main plaza.* ☎ *223 847. Tours 2hr.; Spanish only. Open daily 9-11:30am and 3-5:30pm. Bs15.)*

SAN MARCOS INGENIO. More a restaurant than a museum, San Marcos is the best-preserved ore refinery in Potosí. Check out the hydraulic wheel, 5m in diameter, used to power the 19th-century machinery. Next door is the annex museum, **Arte Textil de Catcha.** Like Sucre's ASUR foundation (see Andean Renaissance, p. 336) this shop sells traditional weavings of the Calcha people. *(At La Paz and Betanzos, 3 blocks east and 3 blocks south of the plaza.* ☎ *222 874. San Marcos has a restaurant open M-Sa 1-8pm.)*

CHURCHES

CATHEDRAL. Potosí's first major church, the cathedral was begun in 1564 but wasn't finished until the end of the 16th century. But it couldn't withstand the test of time, and collapsed in 1807. The larger, current edifice (completed in 1836) was constructed in its place. Inside lie a number of paintings and ornate decorations. *(On the Plaza 10 de Noviembre. Open daily for mass 7am and 6:30pm.)*

BELÉN/TEATRO ORNISTE. Originally part of the Church of the Bethlemites, who arrived in Potosí in 1700, this ornate facade now belongs to the Teatro Omiste. The church was a hospital before being overtaken by the Bethlemites and served as royalist headquarters in the war of Independence. Sometime in the 20th century, it also served as a movie theater, but restoration movements returned it to its theatrical grandeur. *(At Hoyos and Junín, across the street from Plaza 6 de Agosto.)*

IGLESIA DE SAN MARTÍN. Founded between 1592 and 1595, this was the last church built as part of Viceroy Toledo's massive reforms, using the labor of Indians from the Titicaca region as part of *la mita*, the system of forced labor the Spanish inflicted on Potosí's men. Although the adobe exterior has gone through a number of changes, the interior still holds its original treasures, which include oil paintings chronicling the life of the Virgin. *(On Hoyos between Pizarro and Diego de Almagro, 5 blocks east of the plaza. Open daily at 7am for mass.)*

FESTIVALS

Potosí's most interesting festival begins on August 24th. Officially called **Fiesta de San Bartolemé,** this three-day party is better known as **Ch'utillos.** People from all over the department flock to the city to partake in the folkloric parade, as well as drinking, frolicking, and general merriment. The city's other major festival is that which celebrates the **founding of Potosí** (Nov. 10).

ENTERTAINMENT AND NIGHTLIFE

When the cold nights hit, many *potosínos* prefer to take refuge in their warm beds than to hit the town. Nonetheless, gringos and students crowd into pubs and clubs on the weekend, drinking and dancing the chill away. Make sure to try the singani, a liquor that, in Potosí, is more popular than wine. For a dose of pop culture, try **Cine Imperial,** Padilla 31 (☎216 133), south of Chuquisaca, 1½ blocks south of the Plaza 6 de Agosto, which plays mostly US films with Spanish subtitles.

> **Pub La Casona,** Frias 41 (☎222 954). From the plaza, walk west past the Casa de la Moreda and turn right; after a block turn left. The pub is half a block down on the right. In the building that housed La Casa de Moneda's 1st administrator. Relaxed (and heated) atmosphere. Coffee Bs3. Potosina Bs7. Singani Bs8. Great trout Bs30. Sandwiches Bs5. Open M-Sa 6pm-midnight.

> **La Chatarra Pub,** on the Plaza Alonso de Ibañez, east of the main plaza. Another popular nighttime choice, because of both the heat and the soccer. Beer Bs10. Cappuccino and espresso Bs5. Margaritas Bs10. Open daily 7pm-midnight.

> **Estravagenze,** on Bustillos near the Casa de la Moreda. A *discoteca* popular among the university crowd. Music ranges from US pop to Latin beats, but salsa is king. Cover is your first drink. Open Th-Sa 8pm-2am.

> **U2,** on Matos, east of Padilla. From the main plaza walk 1 block north and 1½ blocks east. Whether named for the Irish band or not, the music definitely does not coincide; Latin grooves dominate this dancing, drinking crowd. Open Th-Sa 7:30pm-2am.

DAYTRIPS FROM POTOSÍ

TARAPAYA AND MIRAFLORES

Micros to Miraflores leave from the Plaza Chuguimia on the side next to Antofagosta (30min., every 30min. 7am-6pm, Bs3.5). The last micro back to Potosí leaves Miraflores at 7pm. To reach the Ojo del Inca, get off just before the bridge to the left. Cross the bridge and take the left fork. Either follow the road around or take one of the many trails marked into the hill (10-15min.). Baths Bs2.5 per day. Private baths are more costly— Miraflores is Bs15 per hr., Paraíso is Bs10, and Tarapaya is Bs5. Locals prefer the slightly warmer, indoor pools at Miraflores, while most tourists head to Tarapaya after a dip in the Ojo del Inca. All open daily 8am-6pm.

For a weekend dip, most *potosínos* head to the **thermal baths** north of the city. The Balnearios of Tarapaya, Paraíso, and Miraflores all fill with people grateful to make the 25km trek (on a paved road) to warmer waters. Although still valued for their medicinal properties—many claim the baths can fix aching muscles—most visitors romp through the many pools, both public and private, in perfect health. The most intriguing bathing is found in the perfectly round crater lake known both as the **Baño del Inca** and the **Ojo del Inca.** A favorite resting spot for Inca Huayna Cupac in his travels between Cusco and the southern reaches of the empire, the 30°C bath is also popular among weary travelers today. There are inexpensive lodgings (around Bs20 per person) in all the small towns; **camping** is also quite easy in this area, especially on the flat ground near the Ojo del Inca.

HACIENDA CAYARA

One bus leaves for the hacienda (1hr., 12:30pm, Bs7) daily from the Plaza Chuquisaca, on the Américas side. A bus returns to Potosí the same night when full, usually at 7:30 or 8pm. Radio taxis Bs70 round-trip, another Bs20 to wait. Call the office in Potosí (☎226 380), next to ENTEL on Camacho, to make reservations or to arrange a visit. US$3.

With the wealth of Spaniards drunk on silver, it's no wonder the area around Potosí holds the remains of many lavish haciendas. The best preserved, and most prepared for tourist visits, is the Hacienda Cayara, founded 20km west of the city in 1557, just 12 years after Potosí's own birth. The beautiful old house is a study in colonial architecture, with all original furniture, a 17th-century library, and a small museum collection. Perhaps more lovely are the surrounding grounds, a quiet retreat from bustling Potosí. The hacienda still functions today, producing dairy products—including excellent cheese—for Potosí. It also houses guests in expensive rooms. (Singles US$25; doubles US$50; triples US$75. Breakfast included.)

CAIZA

A daily bus leaves Potosí for Caiza (2hr., leaving when full 1-3pm, Bs7) from the Plaza del Minero. The flota returns to Potosí daily at 5am.

Two hours south of Potosí, in a significantly warmer climate and lower altitude, lies Caiza, a small town where quiet, unassuming villagers produce the **silver** goods sold in Potosí and La Paz. While it's often hard to find paper in this quiet, sleepy town, silver's everywhere—the shops are usually in the silversmiths' homes. However, there's no guarantee that any goods will be available for sale; most are shipped out to the larger cities regularly. But it's still worthwhile to ask around; you might be able to find a few silver spoons or some jewelry. The town's most important festival is in honor of the **Virgin of Copacabana** (Aug. 5), with music, dancing, and intensive drinking. Two *alojamientos* grace the peaceful streets of Caiza. The better option, **La Cabañita,** sits on the plaza, but it's usually locked up. Backtrack on the same street, toward the road to Potosí, to the owner's house at Bolívar 113, the rounded wooden door on the right. Rooms are simple and hot water scarce, but the owners are extremely congenial. (Bs10 per person.)

NEAR POTOSÍ: KARI KARI

To get to Kari Kari, head out to the Plaza Sucre or Pampa Ingenio (Micro M) or to barrio San Cristóbal (Micros F and 40), all on or close to the main thoroughfare heading left to Sucre and right to Tarija. Start walking to the right. After about 150m you should see a path on the left, across the road from 1 of the first ingenios, rising uphill between stone structures. After about 200m the path runs into the service road used to maintain the remaining functioning lakes. Take a right and after about 1km you'll come to the first lake, San Sebastián. From here, follow the trail up the crest of the growing mountain to a number of smaller lakes, about 2km to the summit at about 4700m. Coming down the other side of the mountain lie other lakes, including San Idelfonso, the largest. A small village also lies at the base of the mountain and is where most tours set up camp if hiking for more than the day. If just taking a daytrip, follow the maintenance road 2km down, back to the original trail. Two-day trips usually consist of heading deeper into the Cordillera for higher (5000m+) peak-bagging and a difficult, constant up-and-down trek to the thermal baths and the town of Chaquí. The last bus back to Potosí from Chaquí leaves at 5pm. Most tour agencies (see p. 340) offer one- or two- day treks for US$10-20 per day, depending on the group size. Going with a guide is recommended—villagers don't welcome foreign intrusions and usually speak only Quechua. There is also nowhere to rent equipment in Potosí. However, a map of the region can be bought at the Instituto Geográphicoo Militar (see Practical Information: Tourist Information, p. 340).

In order to power Potosí's many *ingenios*, Viceroy Toledo constructed a system of 32 artificial lakes in the **Kari Kari Cordillera** to the southeast of the city in 1574. The complex was constructed though the slave labor of 20,000 local people, cost 2,500,000 pesos, and was finished in 1621. The lakes, most of which are now abandoned, make a good hiking destination. The hike itself is difficult, but the altitude, which spans 4000-5000m with most of the hiking above 4600m, is the most trying element. Hikers need warm layers, water purification tablets, and food, along with a 4-season sleeping bag and tent if spending the night. Although most tours camp in a small settlement at the base of a peak, living conditions are basic at best. Also, hiking during the rainy season. (Oct.-Nov.), is particularly dangerous and difficult. If trekking alone in any season it's helpful to check in with the tourist booth in the Plaza Alonso de Ibañez for more information.

THE ALTIPLANO

ORURO ☎ 05

A whopping 3706m above sea level on the desolate southern altiplano, rough-and-tumble Oruro is a city of industry rather than entertainment. Oruro—the hispanicization of Uru Uru, an ancient people of the altiplano—rose out of the depths of the mines that briefly brought it fame and fortune, and which continue to coat it with incredible amounts of dust. Its residents' amiable nature, however, compensates for the city's dirt-encrusted exterior; foreigners stand out in Oruro, but only to be welcomed by the locals, most of whom are of Indian heritage, with curious questions and hospitality. Rarely a tourist destination, Oruro comes alive once a year when revelers flock from all over the world to celebrate Bolivia's largest festival, Carnival, with more color and splendor than is found in the city throughout the entire rest of the year.

▐ TRANSPORTATION

Trains: (☎ 274 605), at Velasco Galvarro and Aldana, 5 blocks east and 3 blocks south of the plaza. Open M-F 8:30-11:30am and 2:30-6pm, Su 9-11:30am and 3-6pm. Regular trains to **Villazón** (18hr., Su and W 7pm, Bs52) via **Uyuni** (8hr., Bs25), **Atocha** (10½hr., Bs32), and **Tupiza** (14hr., Bs43). Express trains to **Tupiza** (11hr., M 11am and F 3pm, Bs63) via **Uyuni** (6¼hr., Bs33) and **Atocha** (8hr., M 11am and F 3pm, Bs45); and **Villazón** (14½hr., F 3pm, Bs70).

Buses: (☎ 260 935 or 279 535), at Aroma and Baco Biz, 10 blocks north and 6 blocks east of the plaza. Open daily 6am-10pm, though some buses leave earlier or later than closing time. Bs1.50 exit fee. To: **La Paz** (3½hr., every 30min. 6am-10pm, Bs10); **Cochabamba** (4hr., every 30min. 6am-10pm, Bs15); **Potosí** (8hr., 8 per day 8am-8:30pm, Bs20); **Sucre** (11-12hr., 7 per day 8am-8:30pm, Bs35); **Uyuni** (8-9hr., 8 and 8:30pm, Bs20); **Challapata** (2hr., every hr. 7am-8pm, Bs8); **Huari** (2½-3hr., 20 per day 7am-7pm, Bs9); **Llallagua** (3hr., 17 per day 6:30am-7pm, Bs13); **Santa Cruz** (12hr., 8 per day 6am-3pm, Bs50); **Tarija** (17hr., 4 per day 8am-8pm, Bs70); and **Villazón** (15hr., 5 per day 8am-8:30pm, Bs60); **Arica, Chile** (8hr., 4 per day noon-1:30pm, Bs75); and **Iquique, Chile** (12hr.; M-Sa 5 per day noon-10:30pm, Su 4 per day noon-1:30am; Bs90). Note that the 10:30pm bus to Iquique must wait 4hr. for the border to open (9am-6pm).

Public Transportation: Minibuses, micros, and colectivos run all over the city 6am-11pm. Most pass every 4-6min. and can be flagged down anywhere, most easily on the northwest corner of the plaza. Many of the privately owned buses cover the same routes; these are labeled with their destination and the cardinal direction in which they're heading. Bs1.50-2.

Taxis: Any ride within Oruro costs Bs3, though drivers will try to charge more at night. Taxis roam the city center all day and night. You can also call a radio taxi to come pick you up. **Radio Taxi Oruro** (☎ 276 222), and **Radio Taxi El Faro** (☎ 254 444).

Oruro

⌂ ACCOMMODATIONS

Alojamiento Ferrocarril, **2**
Hotel Bernal, **1**
Residencial Gloria, **3**
Residencial San Salvador, **4**

Car Rental: It's expensive, but renting a car is often the best way to reach less popular sights on the altiplano. **SOS Rent-a-Car,** Vasquez 210 (☎241 005), at Lira, 6 blocks west of the bus terminal and 2 blocks north. Minimum rental age 25. Credit card deposit required. Standard, 4-door vehicles start at US$25 per day, US$.30 per km. Four-wheel-drive vehicles, which are usually necessary on Oruro Department roads, cost US$80 per day. Open 24hr. V, MC.

◼◼ ORIENTATION AND PRACTICAL INFORMATION

Semi-circular Oruro hugs the hills to its west, but its basic square grid makes navigation easy. Most businesses list their addresses as one street between two others, and street numbers rarely mean anything. Almost all action takes place in the city center, the area surrounding the **Plaza 10 de Febrero.** One of the main thoroughfares, **6 de Agosto** runs north-south and abuts both the bus station and the train terminal. At night, everyone sallies out onto **6 de Octubre** around **Bolívar.**

Tourist Office: (☎250 144), on the western side of Plaza 10 de Febrero, 3rd door from the south corner; also a booth (☎257 881), at Bolívar and Soria Galvarro, next to the ENTEL office. Extremely helpful, mostly Spanish-speaking staff. Free basic city maps. Office open Apr.-Sept. M-F 9am-6:30pm; Oct.-Mar. M-F 8am-6pm. Booth open Apr.-Sept. M-F 9am-12:30pm and 2-6:30pm; Oct.-Mar. M-F 8am-noon and 2-6pm.

Currency Exchange: Banco Unión (☎250 150), at Adolfo Mier and La Plata, changes US dollar traveler's checks at 1% commission. **Banco de Crédito** (☎252 421), at Presidente Montes and Bolívar, 5% commission. Both open M-F 8:30am-noon and 2:30-6pm, Sa 9am-noon. Many banks around the Plaza 10 de Febrero also have **ATMs.**

Markets: Mercado Fermín López, at Presidente Montes and Ayacucho, 3 blocks north of the plaza, and **Mercado Campero,** at Pagador and Bolívar. For **Carnival momentos,** head up La Paz between León and Villarroel. Most stores open 9am-noon and 2-6pm. Handmade masks Bs40-190. Clothes US$100-250.

Emergency: ☎ 110 in the city, ☎ 157 elsewhere in the Oruro Department.

Police: (☎251 921 or 251 920), at Bolívar and Presidente Montes, just west of the Plaza 10 de Febrero.

Pharmacy: To find out which is *en turno* call ☎ 115.

Hospital: State-owned **Hospital General** (☎275 405 or 277 408 for emergencies), at San Felipe and 6 de Octubre.

Telephones: ENTEL (☎250 302), at Bolívar between La Plata and Soria Galvarro, 1 block east of the plaza. Open daily 7:30am-10:30pm.

Internet Access: Abundant on 6 de Agosto between Bolívar and Ayacucho. **Rock'N'Net Cyber Cafe,** Bolívar 513 (☎257 417), between Soria Galvarro and 6 de Octubre. Bs7 per hr. Open M-Sa 9am-midnight, Su 3pm-midnight. **Full Internet** (☎270 785), on 6 de Octubre between Adolfo Mier and Bolívar, 2 blocks east of the plaza. Morning Bs4 per hr., afternoon and evening Bs5 per hr. Open daily 8:30am-11:30pm.

Post Office: Presidente Montes 5449 (☎251 660), between Junín and Adolfo Mier, 1 block north of the plaza. Open M-F 8:30am-8pm, Sa 8:30am-6pm, Su 9am-noon. **DHL** (☎250 252), at Presidente Montes and Sucre. Open M-F 8:30am-12:30pm and 2-7pm, Sa 9am-1pm.

ACCOMMODATIONS

Little differentiates accommodations in Oruro. Inexpensive establishments cluster around the train and bus stations; being closer to the city center costs more. Unless otherwise noted, all establishments have some semblance of hot water.

Hotel Bernal, Brazil 701 (☎279 468), just behind the bus station. This large hotel's supple beds and sparkling baths make it a fabulous deal for any traveler. Singles Bs25, with bath Bs60-70; doubles Bs40, with bath Bs60-70; triples Bs60; quads Bs80.

Residencial San Salvador, Velásco Galvarro 6325 (☎276 771), between Aldana and Murguía, across from the train station. The best deal for Bs15, San Salvador has 51 rooms and a common space on every floor. Hallways are dark but rooms are light. Singles Bs15, with bath Bs35; doubles Bs30, with bath Bs35; triples Bs45; quads Bs60.

Residencial Gloria, Potosí 6059 (☎276 250), between Adolfo Mier and Bolívar, 3 blocks west of the plaza. Centrally located. Rooms all open onto a sunny courtyard lined with potted plants. Rooms Bs20 per person, with bath Bs30.

Alojamiento Ferrocarril, Velásco Galvarro 6278 (☎279 074), between Sucre and Murguía, 1 block north of the train station. One of the cheapest finds in Oruro. Undergoing repairs, Ferrocarril should be even spiffier in 2001. Doubles Bs20; triples Bs30.

FOOD

The abundance of good restaurants in Oruro testifies to *orureños'* love of food. But only a strong-stomached visitor should try the local favorite, sheep's head. Whether boiled, called simply *cabeza*, or baked in full (*rostros asados*), this delicacy is generally served with potatoes, onions, and *chuños*—a dry boiled tuber grown at high altitudes. *Tostaditas*, fried lamb with potatoes and *chuños*, is another favorite. Most eateries keep flexible hours, depending on business.

El Huerto, Bolívar 359 (☎279 257), between Pagador and Potosí, 3 blocks west and 1 block south of the plaza. One of Oruro's two vegetarian restaurants. Low, low prices. Yoga classes upstairs. Lunch Bs7. Dinner Bs6. Open Su-Th 9am-8pm, F 9am-3pm.

Restaurant Chifa Rosa, on Bolívar at the Plaza 10 de Febrero, 2nd fl. The only Chinese restaurant in town, Rosa's knows how to cook rice at high altitudes, a skill other local eateries have yet to master. Heaping portions Bs12-20. Open daily noon-10pm.

Nayjama, Aldana 1880 (☎277 699), at Pagador, 1 block east of the train station. One of the oldest and most popular restaurants in Oruro, Nayjama may be right when it declares itself the "best food in town," Specialties include fresh-squeezed *tumbo* juice and homemade *chirimoya* ice cream. Open M-Sa 10am-9pm, Su 10am-3pm.

Govinda, 6 de Octubre 6071 (☎255 205), between Bolívar and Adolfo Mier, 2 blocks west of the plaza. Indian music plays as you enjoy your lunch (Bs10, Bs6 for a half portion). Pizza, pasta, and soy burgers Bs6-10. Open M-Sa 9:30am-10pm.

📷 SIGHTS

MUSEO ETNOGRÁFICO MINERO. This museum leads visitors into the depths of a mine shaft in order to illustrate the techniques of early mining. Following the tracks of the carts used to carry ore out of the mine, the exhibit guides you to glass cases that display old mining tools, ore, and other materials. At one end of the shaft sits El Tío, god of mining and minerals, offerings at his feet. Once upon a time, this mine churned out large quantities of tin, copper, silver, gold, and zinc. Now a huge part of Carnival, the museum marks the end point in the opening parade or *entrada*. The integration of mining and religion to which the Museo Etnográfico Minero testifies (a church was built atop the mine to honor the Virgen del Socavón), a tradition that the Incas began and the Spanish continued, is still prevalent in Oruran culture. *(On the Plaza de Folklore Socavón, 1 block north and 3 blocks east of the Plaza 10 de Febrero. Go through the main church doors, then head right to office labeled "Secretaria." Open M-Sa 9am-1:45pm and 3-5:45pm, Su 8:30am-12:30pm. Bs3.)*

MUSEO ANTROPOLÓGICO EDUARDO LOPEZ RIVAS. This small but interesting collection is dedicated to illustrating the Chullpa, and present-day Chipaya, way of life. Thought by some to have evolved from the Chullpas, who became extinct practically overnight, most of the remote and insular Chipaya people now live in one village (see Near Oruro, p. 353). This museum displays their woven goods, architecture, and most prominently, their burial rituals—Chullpa skeletons recline next to sets of skulls. There are also a few Aymara artifacts and a section devoted to Oruro's Carnival. One of the most interesting artifacts, a large round stone embedded with different rocks in a spiral formation, represents early Aymaran writing. *(At España and Urquidi. ☎274 020. Catch either the green A, green 2, green 5, red 102, or red 103 mini heading south (marked "sud") from the Plaza 10 de Febrero. The museum is on the right in a white stone building with an arch over the entrance. Open M-F 9am-noon and 2-6pm, Sa-Su 10am-noon and 3-6pm. Bs3.)*

CASA DE LA CULTURA MUSEO SIMON I. PATIÑO. The wealth that arrived in Oruro via the exploitation of its mines brought with it cosmopolitan excess and affectation. One of the most blatant examples of this is tin baron Simon I. Patiño's neoclassical mansion, which now houses Oruro's cultural center. "King of Tin" Patiño imported Venetian glass, gold mirrors, and Louis XV furniture with which to decorate his home. Built between 1900 and 1903, the house—and its finery—illustrates the vast chasm between life in the mines (exhibited in some of Oruro's other sights) and the lives of those who reaped their benefits. *(Soria Galvarro 5755, between Ayacucho and Cochabamba, in the pink building in the middle of the block, 3 blocks north and 1 block west of the plaza. ☎254 015. Open M-F 9am-noon and 3-6pm. Bs10.)*

MUSEO MINERALÓGICO. If rocks are your thing, this is your place. With over 7800 samples of minerals from around the world, including many from the altiplano itself, this museum is one of the four most important in the world for the study of minerology. Perhaps because it doesn't receive that many visitors, the guide across the hall is quite willing to walk tourists through it himself. *(In the Ciudad Universitaria. Take micro green A, 5, or 2, or red 102 or 103 south "sud" to the University stop. Walk straight through the gate on your right. The museum is on the left, through the doors labeled "ING. de Minas".* ☎ *261 250. Open M-F 8:30am-noon and 2:30-4pm. Bs7.)*

MINES. Should you feel the urge to visit the mines that for all intents and purposes created Oruro, you can. Two working mines, **Inti Raymi** and **Vinto,** also allow visitors, but you'll need permission from their offices. Ask at the tourist information booth for more details. To reach **San José,** which is no longer functioning, catch the yellow micro D—it says "San José" in its front window.

ZOOLÓGICO MUNICIPAL. Not for the soft-hearted animal lover, this local zoo exhibits such regal birds as the condor and the hawk, in cages barely large enough to encompass their wingspans. Other beautiful animals on display (in equally harsh conditions) include monkeys, *pécarides* (jungle pigs), pigeons, a llama, and Fido the lion. *(On Tomás Frias, behind the anthropological museum.* ☎ *274 841. Open daily Oct.-Mar. 8am-6pm; Apr.-Sept. 9am-6pm. Bs2.)*

⚡ OUTDOOR ACTIVITIES

Some of the best bouldering and **rock climbing** in Bolivia lies just 2km northwest of the city, in Rumi Campana. Head out on mini 12 north ("norte") on your own or with the **Club de Montañismo Halcones (CHM),** a local climbing enthusiast group which treks over to Rumi Campana almost every weekend. With gear available at no charge, in addition to help from experienced climbers, the CHM is a superb resource in Oruro. *(CHM* ☎ *240 398 or 247 090; CHM_ORURO@yahoo.com; www.geocities.com/Yosemite/Gorge/1177/deportival.html, most easily accessed through www.rockclimbing.com and the link for Bolivia. To go alone, take either mini 12, 4, or 15 to the northern end, then walk the short distance west to Rumi Campana.)*

🎭 FESTIVALS

Oruro's claim to fame lies in the wild celebrations that constitute its **Carnival,** a collision of local myth, indigenous culture, and Christian doctrine. With foundations rooted in so many aspects of Oruran history, the festival's exact starting date is difficult to pinpoint, though its honorees are not. Carnival is dedicated to the **Virgen del Socavón,** patroness of miners, and also pays homage to El Tío, god of mines and minerals. Carnival begins the Saturday before Ash Wednesday with its most important parade, **La Entrada,** at which more than 30,000 people dance through Oruro wearing intricate masks and costumes (many valued at over US$200). Throngs fill the stands on either side of the street as the procession moves west on Villaroel, south down 6 de Agosto, east on Bolívar, around the plaza, and north to its ending point: the Sanctuary of the Virgen del Socavón. Each dance of the many along the way symbolizes a different event or era in Oruran culture. The most cherished of these is the **Diablada,** or dance of the devils, a fight between good and evil in which good triumphs by the time the dancers reach the Sanctuary. For the rest of the week, different groups prance through the city and perform *challas,* pagan ceremonies in which such items as cigarettes, coca leaves, and llama fetuses are offered as homage to El Tío and the earth.

Oruro gets crowded during Carnival, and everything costs more; even bus tickets to the city triple in price. Accommodations raise their prices—a room that normally costs US$25 will cost US$100—and are also likely to be full. Call at least three months in advance to make reservations. Tickets are necessary to watch the parades; the best seats cost US$15-20. Call a month ahead to reserve them, either to the tourist office or the official Carnival office (☎ 246 919). Any questions concerning Carnival can also be directed to this number.

NIGHTLIFE

Oruro has a surprisingly swinging party scene for a town its size. Locals and gringos warm up at night, dancing and drinking in the packed clubs and bars.

Brujas, at 6 de Octubre and Junín, 1 block north of the Plaza 10 de Febrero and 2 blocks west. One of the only bars where men *and* women converge. Packed by 11:30pm F-Sa. Concerts sometimes. Beer Bs5. Open M-Th 6:30pm-12:30am, F-Sa 6:30pm-2am.

Sounder, Petot 1140 (☎255 915), between Cochabamba and Caro, 3 blocks west and 3 blocks north of the plaza. This disco welcomes all types, from La Paz professionals to young *orureños*. Sounder doesn't hit full swing until 1:30am. Beer Bs10, mixed drinks Bs15. Cover Bs20, includes 1 drink. Open Sa 10:30pm-4am.

Bunker (☎252 868), at Washington and Murguía, 1 block west and 2 blocks south of the Plaza. Deep in the south of the city, Bunker is truly a find. The only place to go after-hours, this tiny split-level bar and disco welcomes crowds at 4am. Classic rock to Latin pop; requests are always welcome. No cover. Open F-Sa 10pm-7am.

Champagne, Potosí 4990 (☎270 974), at Aroma. From the plaza, head 3 blocks west to Potosí and walk 10 blocks north until you see a huge neon cocktail. A disco on weekends, it fills Oruro's craving for karaoke during the week. Drinks are expensive (most around Bs20), but there's no cover. Open Tu-Sa 9:30pm-6am, Su 9:30pm-1am.

DAYTRIPS FROM ORURO

OBRAJES

To get to Obrajes, 23km northeast of the city, catch a mini (30min., leaving when full, more frequent in the morning and early afternoon; Bs3.50) at the corner of Caro and 6 de Agosto. Open daily 7am-6:30pm. Bs10 buys access to the warm pool and 30min. in slightly hotter private baths. Rooms in the adjacent hotel start at Bs75, including access to even nicer private baths, pool, and breakfast. Mountain bikes Bs50 per day. Call ahead for reservations. ☎051 12 106 or 051 12 107; fax 051 50 646.

For a relaxing dip, head to the Obrajes resort, an oasis on the cold, dry altiplano that's an antidote to any aching muscle. Powered by nearby **hot springs**—ask the manager for a tour—the pools stay wonderfully clean and clear, unlike other hotsprings in the area and despite the hordes of heat-seeking *orureños* who fill them on weekends. Fascinating **ruins** of the buildings in which the Chipaya once melted their mined gold into bars lie on well-marked trails nearby, and an hour's walk up the road leads to **Paria,** the first church the Spanish built in Bolivia.

LAGO POOPÓ

To get to Challapata, take any bus to Uyuni (2hr., Bs8). Four buses (Bs8) return to Oruro every morning—head 2 blocks west and 3 blocks south of the main plaza, and wait in front of the Pension Sud Chichas.

Dusty **Challapata** sits on the southern half of Lago Poopó, one of two extremely shallow lakes left by ancient Lago Minchín, which 25,000 years ago covered most of the altiplano. During the rainy season, Poopó's length expands to 90km, though the lake remains only 50cm-2½m deep. Since its contamination by Oruro mines, Poopó's bird population has shrunk, although summer months bring some species to water. A three-hour walk or half-hour drive west of Challapata, there's little to see, especially at high tide. It's just a cool natural phenomenon.

CHIPAYA

Buses leave Oruro for Chipaya (5hr., F-Sa 6am, Bs15) from the Mercado Walter Khon off España. Other buses leave daily for Arica, Chile and pass through Huachacalla (3½hr., Bs30) en route to the border town of Pisigia. From Huachacalla, either pay a townsman to drive you down the road to Chipaya (1½hr.) or wait by the side of the road and hop on a worktruck. One bus per week returns to Oruro from Chipa (5hr., M, Bs15).

An anomaly in the predominantly Aymara-inhabited altiplano, the Chipaya people bear no relation in civilization or language to the neighboring cultures. The actual village of Chipaya is a somewhat modern take on architecture. Traditional round huts have been replaced by square buildings, which now house trucks and other modern machinery to work the land. During the day, tourists are greeted only by old women, small children, and an extraordinary rooster population—the majority of the 1800 inhabitants are off herding animals and maintaining agriculture in the surrounding area. Beyond the village's rustic charm, there is little reason for travelers to linger here.

PARQUE NACIONAL SAJAMA   ☎08

Beckoning those with enough gall to attempt an ascent, inspiring awe in natives and tourists alike, Bolivia's highest peak, Nevado Sajama (6542m), welcomes all to its namesake national park. These 120,000 hectares were set aside in 1939 to conserve Bolivia's highest prize as well as to protect the plants and animals native to the altiplano and shelter the intense geothermic activities typical of volcanic regions. Wedged up against the Chilean border, the park shares two slightly smaller but still magnificently impressive eroded volcanos, Las Payachatas, with Chile's Parque Lauca. During colonial times this area was used by Spaniards as a rest stop between the two countries, which accounts for the decaying 18th-century churches scattered throughout the park.

TRANSPORTATION AND PRACTICAL INFORMATION. There are two ways to reach the Parque Nacional Sajama from within Bolivia. **From La Paz,** take a bus to Arica, Chile; tell the bus company that you are going to Parque Sajama and want to get off just before the Chilean border at Lagunas (4hr., 6:30 and 7am, Bs50). From Lagunas, it's 12km up the main dirt road to Sajama village, home to the park's information office—you may have to walk. From **Patacamaya,** there's one mini per day to Sajama (3½hr., leaving when full around midday, Bs17). The bus to La Paz leaves Lagunas daily at 10am; the bus to Patacamaya leaves Sajama daily at 7am. Coming from Patacamaya, the first building you'll see in Sajama holds the park's **information office.** (☎115 260. Radio frequency 8025 USB, Parque Nacional Sajama. Open daily 8am-6pm, though the two rangers live next door and often stay in the office 7am-9pm.) The extremely helpful, Spanish-speaking rangers distribute all the information they can, though the availability of park maps is low. They can also point out owners of four-wheel-drive vehicles who can drive you to view park sights. If you're interested in this option, it's best to arrange a car the day before to ensure that drivers are available and prices reasonable; trips should cost US$30-50 per day. Parque Sajama charges a Bs10 entrance fee.

ACCOMMODATIONS AND FOOD. Though quite small, Sajama village boasts a number of basic **alojamientos** along its main street. (Beds Bs10 per person.) Currently under construction, a new hotel should be open by November. You can also **camp** throughout the park, just make sure to bring a sturdy tent and winter gear. The only **hot bath** available during a park visit lies in a natural pool 5km north of the village. A few **restaurants** also grace Sajama's main road. (Open daily 7am-10pm. Lunch or dinner Bs6-7. Breakfast Bs2.50.) Beyond these and some similar resources in the town of Lagunas, there are no services available in the park.

MOUNTAINEERING. The primary reason people visit Parque Nacional Sajama is to ascend Bolivia's highest mountain, **Nevado Sajama** (6542m), one of the most difficult climbs in the Cordillera Occidental. Aspiring summiters must endure the violent winds and high altitude of the mountain locals call "Doctor Sajama" out of respect for the white blanket of snow it wears every day of the year. The summit can be reached by the south, west, or north side; allow three-four days to ascend and descend.

East of Sajama on the Chilean border rise reasons two and three to visit the park: **Parinacota** (6132m) and **Pomerape** (6222m), known collectively as Las Payachatas. Chile claims the eastern Pomerape, but the western Parinacota belongs to

Bolivia. Quechua for "lake of the flamingos," Parinacota was Bolivia's last active volcano and is best approached from the southwestern snow fields. When ascending from the Bolivian side, Pomerape, meaning "peak of the puma," is normally climbed via the western ridge. Both mountains take approximately two days to ascend and descend.

Mountaineering is only allowed in the winter (early Apr.-Oct.), when the ice is properly frozen. All supplies must be brought to the park, as there is nowhere to rent equipment. You should not attempt to summit any of these three volcanos alone. Local guides can be hired for about US$40, porters and mules for Bs70. It's best to call the park office a few days ahead of time to arrange an ascent.

◙ SIGHTS. One of the motivations behind creating Parque Nacional Sajama was to protect the area's **vicuñas,** a wild cameloid smaller, more delicate, and even more often hunted for its fine wool than its domesticated brothers, the llama and the alpaca. Visitors can catch a glimpse of whole herds if they head 20km north to **Patoca,** the valley region where the vicuñas feed. Other park animals (most noticeably birds) drink from **Laguna Huaña Kkota,** 12km northeast of Sajama. There's excellent birdwatching here in the summer, but the lake (one of the highest in the world) freezes during the winter. A park fostered on superlatives, Sajama also houses **the world's highest forest.** Sajama places a huge amount of value on the forest's very small and gnarly bush-like *keñua* trees, which were previously used to fire the engines of passing trains. Living at altitudes of up to 5200m, keñuas only grow about 2cm a year—the oldest reach 3 or 4m. Found on the entire eastern side of Nevado Sajama, the trees' small yellow flowers and red bark distinguish them from the surrounding tholares bushes. Finally, 8km northeast of Sajama steam 30 **geysers and pools,** spread out over this incredible geothermic area. Steam rising from the hot, sometimes boiling, algae-infested waters increases the surreal feeling prompted by this intensely active valley.

UYUNI   ☎ 06

Originally founded in 1889 as a railway hub between the north, south, and Pacific coast, Uyuni (3660m; pop. 12,000) still serves as a traveler's hub, with tourists from all over the world breezing in and out en route to the stunning salt plains that share the city's name. Although quite isolated from the rest of the country, Uyuni won national favor through its magnanimous support of soldiers who passed through town during Bolivia's war with Paraguay—it's been dubbed both the "Ciudad Predilecta de Bolivia" (favorite daughter of Bolivia) and the "Ciudad Benemérita" (Veteran City).

▐▀ TRANSPORTATION

Trains: Station, at Ferroviaria and Arce (☎932 320), across the street from the plaza. Open M-F 9am-noon and 2:30-5:30pm, Sa-Su 10-11am; also one hour before arrivals. To: **Oruro** (7hr., Tu and F 1:35am, Bs25; express 6¾hr., Tu 12:15pm and Sa 11:30pm, Bs36); **Atocha** (2hr., M and Th 2:35am, Bs11; express 2hr., M 5:20pm and F 9:25pm, Bs13); **Tupiza** (5½hr., M-Th 2:35am, Bs22; express 5hr., M 5:20pm and F 9:25pm, Bs28); and **Villazón** (9hr., M and Th 2:35am, Bs30; express 8½hr., F 9:25pm, Bs43) via **Avaroa** (4hr, Bs32) and **Calama** (6½hr., Bs41).

Buses: Terminal on Arce between Peru and Cabrera. All buses leave from same block. (Open M-Sa 8:30am-noon and 3:30-8pm.) To: **Potosí** (6-6½hr., 10am and 7pm, Bs20); **Sucre** (8hr., 10am and 7pm, Bs35); **Atocha** (3hr.; W and Su 9am; Bs15); **Tupiza** (8hr.; W and Su 9am; Bs25); **Tarija** (18hr., 10am, Bs60; change buses in Potosí); **Oruro** (8hr.; W 7 and 8pm; Su 6, 7, 8pm; Bs25); and **La Paz** (12hr.; W 7 and 8pm; Su 6, 7, 8pm; Bs45; change in Oruro).

Taxis: Don't pay more than Bs3 for rides within the city.

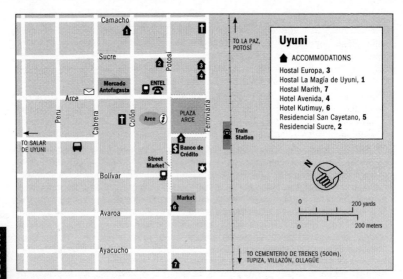

ORIENTATION AND PRACTICAL INFORMATION

Uyuni's resources are very close together, and the city's gridded streets make it easily navigable. At its center is the **Plaza Arce,** across the street from the train station. All valuable tourist offices, restaurants, and accommodations are at most two blocks in any direction from the plaza.

Tourist Information: (☎932 400), in the bottom of the clock at Arce and Potosí. The very knowledgeable, English-speaking representative of the **Eduardo Alvaroa Reserve,** Georgina González, can help with any information on Uyuni, the Salar, or the Reserve. Open M-F 9:30am-12:30pm and 2:30-6pm. The official **Reserve Office,** on Potosí between Arce and Bolívar, may be able to answer other questions. Open M-F 9am-12:30pm and 2-6:30pm.

Currency Exchange: Banco de Crédito (☎932 050), on Potosí between Arce and Bolívar. Open M-F 8:30am-12:30pm and 2:30-5pm. Changes cash only. Most **tour agencies** cash traveler's checks at terrible rates and a US$3 commission per check.

Immigration: (☎932 062), at Sucre and Potosí. Obtain exit stamps (valid for 3 days or longer with exact date of departure) to enter Chile from Hito Cajón or Avaroa.

Markets: Mercado Antofagosta, on Arce between Colón and Cabrera. Open daily 8am-dusk. Another nameless **mercado** on Potosí and Avaroa. Th and Su, a **street market** flows down Potosí from Arce to Bolívar.

Emergency: ☎110

Police: (☎110), at Ferroviaria and Bolívar.

Hospital: Hospital General Jose E. Perez (☎932 081), on Ferroviaria, 3 blocks northeast of Carnacho.

Telephones: ENTEL (☎932 111), at Arce and Potosí. Open daily 8am-10pm.

Internet: Not the most reliable. **Servinet,** between Bolívar and Potosí. Bs20 per hr. Open daily 8am-10pm, although usually closed for lunch. **Cafe Internet My M,** on Arce next to ENTEL. Bs20 per hr. Open daily 9:30am-noon and 2:30-8pm.

Post Office: (☎932 146), at Cabrerea and Arce. Open M-F 8:30am-7pm, Sa-Su 9am-noon.

ACCOMMODATIONS

Most buses and trains arrive in Uyuni in the middle of the night, but almost all hotel and hostel owners will take you in as long as you knock loud enough to wake them up. During the winter months, most places have hot showers only during the day. Heat is hard to find; just ask for an extra blanket.

Hotel Avenida, Ferroviaria 11 (☎932 078), across from the train station. 4-blanket warmth and hot water in this 80-bed behemoth. Luggage storage. Showers Bs5. Laundry Bs5 per load. Singles Bs20, with bath Bs40; doubles Bs40, with bath Bs80; triples Bs60, with bath Bs100; quads Bs70. 10% group discount with more than 8 people.

Hostal Europa (☎932 752), at Ferroviaria and Sucre, 1 block from train station. Kitchen access. Fire at 6pm. Pink bedspreads. Laundry Bs5 per 12 pieces. Singles Bs20, with bath Bs35; doubles Bs40, with bath Bs70; triples Bs60, with bath Bs105; quads Bs80.

Hostal La Magía de Uyuni, Colón 432 (☎932 541), 2 blocks north of the plaza. Currently the nicest stay in Uyuni. All rooms have baths, an endless supply of blankets, and classy wooden beds. Inner rooms are warmer. Breakfast included. Singles US$15; doubles US$20; triples US$25. Discounts for groups of 7 or more.

Hotel Kutimuy, at Potosí and Avaroa, 2 blocks southwest of the plaza. Spotless bathrooms. Warm internal rooms. Friendly service. Breakfast Bs10. Singles Bs20, with bath Bs40; doubles Bs40, with bath Bs80; triples Bs60.

Hostal Marith, Potosí 61 (☎/fax 932 174), just past Ayacucho if walking away from the plaza. Simple, tidy rooms. Breakfast Bs7. Laundry Bs1 per piece. Singles Bs20, with bath Bs40; doubles Bs40, with bath Bs80; triples Bs60, with bath Bs120; quads Bs80.

Residencial Sucre (☎932 047), on Sucre off Potosí, 1 block northwest of the plaza. Simple digs with 2 outdoor sinks and 1 shower pump hot water daily. Singles Bs18; doubles Bs30; triples Bs45; quads Bs60; quints Bs75.

Residencial San Cayetano (☎932 551), on Arce at the plaza. Central, with compact rooms surrounding a rather small courtyard. Singles Bs15; doubles Bs30; triples Bs45.

FOOD

Almost all Uyuni restaurants line the plaza on Arce. Food is uniformly mediocre and on the pricey side. Pizza, however, abounds.

Restaurante 16 de Julio, Arce 35 (☎932 171), on the plaza. Sunny and always overflowing. Breakfast Bs7-16. *Almuerzo* Bs15. *Cena* Bs10. Vegetarian noodles and omlettes Bs20-25. Open daily 7am-11pm.

Kactus Restaurant, Arce 45 (☎932 386), on the plaza. Fills at night with travelers warming themselves over the candles. Thick and hearty pancakes Bs8. Steaks Bs20-24. Pasta Bs12-20. Open daily 8am-11pm.

Pizzeria Arco Iris, Arce 27 (☎932 517), on the plaza. Gringos overlook pricey portions to bask in the dark glow of colorful hanging lamps, popular music, and jolly conversation. Medium pizzas Bs40-50. Open daily 3pm-midnight.

THE SALAR DE UYUNI

The Uyuni tour agency scene is a nightmare. Twenty-six separate offices adorn one square block in the town center, and they're all vying for your money—whatever it takes. The two most important aspects of a successful tour—a knowledgeable driver and a sturdy Jeep—fluctuate within all tour agencies from excellent to horrific. *Let's Go* cannot recommend any tour agencies; random selection may be more reliable than any calculated choice. However, there are a few things to look out for. Always demand a written itinerary including food and accommodations specifics, preferably the night before you leave. Most agencies include lodging and meals but not drinking water, showers, toilet paper, or admission to the Reserve. Nevertheless, it is important to hammer out the details before you book. The more insistent you are on having a knowledgeable guide (about both the Salar and the Jeep), the more likely you are to land a better one. Unfortunately, it is nearly impossible to meet your guide beforehand—most guides work every day, returning home only once every four nights. That said, they are paid comparatively little; tip a good guide and recommend him to the respective agency. Most agencies also provide free luggage storage (before you store, find out what times people will be in the office to collect belongings) and sleeping bags (US$5; warmth is variable). Nights can drop to -25°C; warm clothes are a necessity. Travelers also need sunglasses, sunscreen, toilet paper, and plenty of film. Altitude sickness is a serious risk, some locations are as high as 5000m. Don't forget plenty of water—the best defense against both acute mountain sickness and hypothermia.

During the high season (June-Sept.) and the rainy months (Dec.-Feb.), prices skyrocket to as much as US$120 a person for the typical 4-day tour, which during the off-season generally costs US$70. But prices fluctuate constantly, depending on conditions and tourist demand, so it is nearly impossible to confirm prices in advance. Fewer agencies offer tours in the rainy months. Although the shallow water that covers the Salar then is in some ways more magnificent than winter's blinding white floor, the dangerous combination of wet, mushy roads and salt makes Jeep travel difficult. Quite a few tours get stuck in the mud or washed away in the occasional flash flood. So you may have to wait a few days to get a group together. When booking a tour, ask how many other people have signed up. Jeeps hold six or seven people; often, agencies will dump you on a lesser agency at the last minute if they don't have enough to fill the vehicle.

Many people use the Salar tours as a route into **Chile** (on the third day). There is nowhere to stay within about 10km of the border in Bolivia and within 35km of the border in Chile. Rather than risk abandonment in this cold, waterless area, it is best to go with an agency that has a San Pedro de Atacama (the town across the border in Chile) office as well as reliable border pickup. Some of the more popular agencies are listed below. Almost all agencies claim to be open daily 8am-8pm, although many close from noon-2pm for lunch and have varied hours throughout the day. English-speaking guides are available in some agencies for a hefty price; up to US$25 more per day. Going to the Salar alone is impossible from Uyuni.

TOUR AGENCIES

Colque Tours (☎/fax 932 199; email colque@ceibo.entelnet.bo/tcolque@ctcinternet.cl), on Potosí between Avaroa and Bolívar. One of the largest agencies in Uyuni. A good choice if heading into San Pedro after a tour. Guide/driver Renato is excellent. Accepts traveler's checks, V, MC.

Tunupa Tours (☎/fax 932 823), at Ferroviaria and Arce. V, MC.

Toñito Tours (☎/fax 932 094; email tonitotours@yahoo.com), at Ferroviaria and Avaroa. Vegetarians accommodated. V, MC.

Olivas Tours (☎/fax 932 173), on Ferroviaria between Arce and Bolívar. V, MC, AmEx.

THE SALAR AND THE SOUTHWEST CIRCUIT

The incredible geography of Southwest Bolivia, including its salt deposits and glacier lakes, can be attributed to Lago Minchín, which once covered an area of about 60,000 sq. km and reached altitudes of 3760m. Minchín dried up about 25,000 years ago, only to be refilled by Lago Tauca thousands of years later; Tauca evaporated 10,000 years ago, leaving two large salt deposits, the Salars of Uyuni and Coipasa—Lago Poopó and Lago Uru Uru.

DAY I: SALAR DE UYUNI. Most tours enter the Salar from **Colchani** (pop. 300), 22km north of Uyuni. Here, people work in a cooperative, mining and refining salt for national consumption. At an average altitude of 3653m, this 10,000-12,000 sq. km salt field is the largest and highest in the world. Near Colchani, mountains of salt about three meters high are scraped together for human consumption while circular blocks are cut out by hand. The blocks display the seasons of rain (dirt) intermixed with pure salt, much like the concentric circles of a tree show its age. Nearby lie one group of **ojos de sal,** the weakest part of the Salar, where the layer of salt—sometimes up to six meters deep—has been worn away to reveal underground wells of water. These bubbling, sulfuric-smelling holes may look like hot springs, but are actually cold, mineral-filled pits that are red and pink because of the iron-rich ground.

After a 10-minute drive, two buildings as white as the land around them rise up out of the barren landscape. **Hotel Playa Blanca,** and its new competitor **Hotel Palacio de Sal,** cater to those craving complete salt immersion: the walls, beds, and tables—basically everything but the roof—are constructed of salt blocks. The hotels lie 30km outside Uyuni; rooms at Playa Blanca are US$20 per person; Palacio de Sal charges US$30 per person. Forty minutes and 76km later, you'll arrive at **Isla de Pescado,** a smooth drive straight across the Salar. Covered in ancient cacti, some up to 12m high, this arid landscape supports little more than a family-run ore business. It's possible to spend a frigid night here watching the sunset through a large rock window (Bs15) and continue, but for most, this otherworldly island serves as a mere lunch stop. The journey continues to **San Juan** (91km from Isla de Pescado), where the harsh white land opens to deep red hills, speckled with limited vegetation, all that can survive on the harsh altiplano. This town of about 400 people thrives on its tourists, with five different *alojamientos* that cater to tour groups. All rooms are dorm-style, with only one or two blankets per bed—it's a good idea to bring your own sleeping bag. (Semi-hot showers Bs5. Rooms Bs15 per person.) There is little to see in San Juan other than the town's simple colonial cemetery. Additional days can be taken to scale **Volcán Tunupa** (5432m), on the northern edge of the Salar de Uyuni.

DAY II: LAGUNAS AND THE EDUARDO AVAROA RESERVE. Day two begins with a short drive to **Chiguana,** the home of a less-impressive, thinly scattered Salar and a military checkpoint 31km south of San Juan. Most jeeps stop an hour or so down the road to admire distant **Volcán Ollague** (5865m), Bolivia's only active volcano. Shared with Chile, Ollague's summit technically belongs to Bolivia while its geothermic activity resides in Chile. Sixty kilometers from San Juan are a series of glacial lakes. Within a matter of kilometers the road passes by crystal-clear **Lagunas Cañapa, Hedionda** (meaning "smelly lake" for its strong sulfur composition), **Charkota, Honda,** and **Ramaditas.** The lakes are filled with flamingos, especially during the summer months; though they freeze partially in the winter, they still house smatterings of wildlife. During the 55km drive to Laguna Colorada, jeeps enter the **Eduardo Alvaro Bird Reserve** and the small but impressively sparse **Desert of Ciloli** (25 sq. km). See the **Arbol de Piedra,** or stone tree, composed of rocks worn away by thousands of years of the area's winds. This is also a good spot to spot *viscachas,* rabbit-like creatures with long tails.

Finally, the short but horrible road reveals the **Laguna Colorada** and the central office for **La Reserva** (4121m). Only about 80m deep, this shallow pool of bright pink and red water covers 60 sq. km. Winds whip unhindered, bringing the minerals and algae that contribute to the lake's color (and name) to the surface. It is better to purchase your entrance ticket (Bs30) here than from a tour agency. Do not lose it; tickets must be displayed when leaving. Founded in 1973, the reserve protects over 80 species of birds. The Andean, Chilean, and James flamingos are best seen at the Laguna Colorada. The reserve also protects the *vicuña* and other altiplano flora and fauna. A guide to the park's many birds, **Aves de la Reserva Nacional de Fauna Andina Eduardo Avaroa,** is available in the Uyuni tourist office. The reserve provides the best alternative for night two, although many agencies choose the shoddy *alojamiento* next door.

DAYS III AND IV: SOL DE MAÑANA AND LAGUNA VERDE. A very early start gets tourists to the geyser region, **Sol de Mañana,** 29km out of the Laguna Colorada, by sunrise. At 5000m, these bubbling hotsprings spit boiling water and mud while geysers shoot columns of steam 80 to 1000m into the air. Thermal baths are a short drive away; many tours stop there for a quick dip and breakfast. Head over a mountain pass, and 65km later the road opens to the final destination: **Laguna Verde** (4315m). By mid-morning both this emerald-green lake, whipped with small waves, and its sister **Laguna Blanca** appear before the hulking **Volcán Llicancabur** (5868m), an ascent of which is included in many 5- and 6-day packages. There is a refuge at Laguna Blanca, although the midday wind makes one shudder to even think about the nighttime conditions.

BORDER CROSSING: INTO CHILE

Many people file into Chile from this southernmost area of Bolivia—**Hito Cajón,** the Bolivian border town, is a desolate 10km from Laguna Blanca, with nowhere to sleep, eat, or exchange money. From the unguarded border, it's another 35km to Chile's first sign of life: **San Pedro de Atacama.** Most Uyuni tour agencies can arrange transportation between Laguna Blanca and the frontier (about 15min.) for an extra US$10 if not originally part of the tour. You must obtain an **exit stamp** from the immigration office in Uyuni, valid for up to three days (longer if you give officials an exact re-entry date). Once in San Pedro, Chilean customs throughly check all baggage; produce cannot be taken across the border. The drive takes about an hour from the border to the San Pedro checkpoint; Chilean customs take about 30min. It's then a short ride to the city center.

TUPIZA   ☎06

In the mid-16th century, King Charles V of Spain gave most of southern Bolivia to Diego de Almagro, in hopes that he and Francisco Pizarro would stop bickering over who would control Cusco. When Almagro's men arrived at the Río Tupiza, it was clear they had inherited their superiors' quarrelsome nature. The Spaniards argued over who would dip his foot in the water first, each one insisting "tu pisa," or "your step." The few nature enthusiasts who visit today's Tupiza (pop. 24,000) don't need similar urging to dive into their surroundings. Dramatic red rock formations rise from the valley to envelop the city center, and nearby mountains and riverbeds make for spectacular hikes. Best of all, Tupiza's dry, mild climate ensures that almost any excursion here will be a good one—even for those busy quibbling that it's more likely that "Tupiza" came from "Topejsa," a Chicha word for the area, than from a bunch of Spaniards shouting at each other to put their feet in the river.

▐ TRANSPORTATION

Trains: Station (☎942 527), at Avaroa and Serrano, 3 blocks east of the Plaza Independencia, across from the river. Ticket office open M-Sa 8:30-11am and 6-7:30pm, as well as an hour before any arrival or departure. To: **Oruro** (12½hr., M and Th 7pm, Bs43; express 11hr., Tu 7am and Sa 6:20pm, Bs68) via **Uyuni** (5hr., Bs19; express 5hr., Bs28) and **Atocha** (3½hr., Bs11; express 3hr., Bs15); and **Villazón** (3hr., M and Th 8:40am, Bs11; express 3hr., Sa 2:25am, Bs15).

Buses: Terminal, on Serrano, the easternmost street across from the river, 1 very long block south of Florida, the southern border of the plaza. There is a Bs1 bus terminal exit fee. To: **La Paz** (18hr., 10am, Bs60-90); **Potosí** (8hr.; 10am, 8:30, 9pm; Bs25-30); **Tarija** (8hr., 7:30 and 8pm, Bs20-30); **Uyuni** (9hr., M and Th 11am, Bs25-30); and **Villazón** (3hr.; 4am, 2, 3pm; Bs10). Prices vary by company and season.

▐ ▐ ORIENTATION AND PRACTICAL INFORMATION

Most resources lie within a few blocks of the **Plaza Independencia.** Three blocks to the east runs **Serrano,** beside the railroad tracks and **Río Tupiza,** which mark the eastern edge of town.

Tour Agencies: Tupiza Tours, Chichas 187 (☎943 001; fax 943 003). From the plaza, walk 2 blocks east, then head right for a half-block. Dominates the expanding agency market with the most extensive and best-established offerings. Full-day Tupiza tour, including lunch, US$15-18 per person, depending on number of participants. Half-day tour US$8-12 per person. Up to 4-day horse tours Bs120 per person per day. Jeep daytrips to Huaca Huañusca, site of Butch Cassidy and the Sundance Kid's final robbery, and San Vicente, site of their graves, US$60-100 per person, again depending on number of people in the jeep. Internet access Bs15 per hr. English book exchange. Changes traveler's checks with 4% commission per check. Owner Fabiola Mitru and her entourage also serve as the **unofficial tourist office** for Tupiza, doling out free hand-made maps and answering questions (for those who need an English speaker, ask for Beatriz). Open daily 8am-8pm. Tupiza's competition comes in the form of the **Hostal Valle Hermosa**'s impromptu and less recognized, but still competent, tour service (☎942 370; fax 942 592; www.Bolivia.freehosting.net; hostalvh@cedro.pts.entelnet.bo), on Serrano just past Florida, 3 blocks east of the plaza. Full-day tours Bs450 per jeep, which holds up to 6 people. Half-day Bs250 per jeep. Horse rides Bs18 per hr. Motorbikes Bs50 per day. Trips to Huaca Huañusca Bs540; to San Vicente Bs1750. Internet access Bs15 per hr. English book exchange.

Currency Exchange: Banco Crédito (☎943 765) and **Banco Mercantil** (☎943 541), both on the plaza, will only be useful if you already possess legal tender (either *bolivianos* or US dollars). Open M-F 8:30am-noon and 2:30-6pm. To get money off a credit card (V,MC) or to exchange traveler's checks, head to **Tupiza Tours** (4% commission per check) or **Hostal Valle Hermosa** (traveler's checks only).

Markets: Main market between Santa Cruz, Chichas, and Junín, 2 blocks east and 1 long block north of the plaza. Smaller market at Florida and Chichas, 1½ blocks east of the plaza. Th and Sa, a street market pops up at the north end of Serrano, about 1 block north of the plaza. All open daily sunrise to sunset.

Emergency Numbers: Police ☎110. Medical ☎119.

Police: At Avaroa and Sucre, just west of the plaza, next to ENTEL.

Pharmacies: Many around the center. To find out which is *en turno* call ☎119.

Hospital: Hospital Ferroviario Benigno Inchaustia (☎942 996), on Chichas between Florida and Avaroa, 2 blocks east of the plaza. Open 24hr.

Telephones: ENTEL (☎942 100; fax 942 121), at the corner of Aramayo and Avaroa, 1 block west of the plaza. Open M-Sa 8am-11pm, Su 8-11am and 3-10pm.

Internet Access: Both **Tupiza Tours** and **Hostal Valle Hermosa** have one sporadic computer each, but your best bet for a speedy (working) connection lies in a little machine at the back of a **wholesale soda business.** On Florida, 1½ blocks east of the plaza; look for the "Internet" sign in the doorway. Bs15 per hour.

Post Office: on Avaroa, just west of the plaza. Open M-F 8:30am-6pm, Sa 9am-5pm, Su 9am-noon.

ACCOMMODATIONS

Tupiza presents a pretty standard hotel scene. Many places claim 24-hour hot water, but chances are you'll have the best luck in the morning. Even the farthest hotels listed below are less than a 5-minute walk from the city center, so don't let location unduly influence your decision. The area's many *quebradas*, or dry river beds, make excellent **campsites** in the dry season but fill with water during heavy rains in the summer—you should be on the watch for flash floods at any time of year. See Sights, p. 362, for site inspiration.

▨ **El Refugio del Turista** (☎943 003), on Chichas south of Florida, next to Tupiza Tours, 2 blocks from the plaza. Tupiza's most popular hostel. Rustic benches and travelers fill the grassy courtyard. Kitchen access. Bs15 per person. V, MC, traveler's checks.

▨ **Residencial Valle Hermosa** (☎942 370; fax 942 592; www.bolivia.freehosting.net; hostalvh@cedro.pts.entelnet.bo), on Serrano just past Florida, 3 blocks east of the plaza. Currently revamping its 4 levels. Sitting rooms on each floor bring the sunny afternoon inside. Laundry service Bs5 per 12 pieces. Bs15 per person. V, MC, traveler's checks.

Hotel Mitru, Chichas 187 (☎943 001), next to Tupiza Tours, 2 blocks east of the plaza, south of Florida. Sets the standard for Tupiza lodgings. Clean rooms, friendly service, hot water showers included. Laundry service Bs5 per 12 pieces. Bs20 per person, Bs 40 with bath. V, MC, and traveler's checks. **Hotel Anexo Mitru** (☎943 002), on Avaroa, just around the corner from the train station, is identical but with a restaurant.

Residencial San Luis (☎943 040), on Junín between Santa Cruz and Chorolque, 1 long block north of the plaza. Not as run-down as its exterior suggests, but still the cheapest place in town. Rooms open onto a rather cluttered courtyard with plenty of showers to go around. Daytime hot water Bs5 for guests, others Bs6. Bs12 per person.

Residencial My Home, on Avaroa between Chorolque and Santa Cruz, just east of the plaza. My Home's enthusiastic staff keeps its spartan rooms neater even than your own home. The only thing bigger than the private baths is the large, bare courtyard. Kitchen access Bs2. Bs18 per person, Bs28 with bath.

Residencial Centro (☎942 705), on Santa Cruz just south of Avaroa, 1 block from the plaza. Flowers deck the stairs that lead from the courtyard to the simple second-level rooms. Singles Bs16, with bath Bs30; doubles Bs36, with bath Bs55; triples Bs54.

🍴 FOOD

Only a few formal restaurants grace Tupiza, but many small pensions line the plaza and nearby streets. As usual, the market vends the best breakfasts and cheapest food. For dessert, **Heladería Cremalin** and **Heladería Cramer,** both on the main plaza, serve good ice cream.

Il Bambino (☎943 903), at Florida and Santa Cruz, just east of the plaza. Excellent-value *almuerzo* Bs8, includes bread, soup, main course, dessert, and a drink. A la carte dish prices rise to Bs18. Lip-smacking *salteñas* Bs1.50. Open daily 8:45am-10pm.

Los Helechos (☎943 002), Avaroa between Chichas and Serrano, under Mitru Anexo. Den of gringos, but the food's well-prepared. Try the tasty dinner special (Bs25), usually a savory cut of chicken. Burgers and pizza slices Bs4-6, full dinner plates average Bs22. Breakfast Bs4. Open daily 8am-11pm.

Pension Doña Aurora, at Chichas and Avaroa, 2 blocks east of the plaza. Generous portions of traditional fare come cheap in Aurora's kitchen. Sit at a table outside, enjoy your *almuerzo* (Bs6), and people-watch over bites of fried meat. Meaty à la carte dishes run Bs10-15. *Cena* Bs5. Open daily 8am-10pm.

👁 SIGHTS

Various natural intrigues lie just outside the city; you can reach most by jeep, horse, or foot. Unless tracking Río Tupiza, be sure to bring water—the arid climate affords few drink stops. Both Hostal Valle Hermosa and Tupiza Tours distribute simple regional maps.

QUEBRADAS. South of the city, rock pinnacles line flat **Quebrada Palmira.** The grouping of large phallic formations on one side is known as the **Valle de los Machos** (Valley of Men), though the less modest sometimes call it the Valle de los Penes (Valley of the Penises). From Palmira, a narrow canyon winds through rocks of diverse colors. Scrambling over the 2km of boulders and river makes a fun, relatively easy hike. By contrast, hikes along the road north seem difficult, in large part because of the strong mountain winds. The most interesting of these follows the railroad tracks north about 2½km to the mouth of **Quebrada de Palala,** a wide stretch between the ascending road and walls of red rock. In the dry winter months, Aymara traders lead their pack-llamas through the area, exchanging Uyuni salt for southern grains.

OTHER SIGHTS. At the **Angosta,** 10km south of Tupiza, the south-bound road tunnels through red-rock walls full of parrot nests. *(From the bus terminal, cross the bridge over Río Tupiza and head south.)* Farther (12km) down the road a lookout point juts off to the right, affording a lovely view of **Entre Ríos,** the spot where the Río Tupiza and the Río San Juan del Oro merge. Walk down to the Tupiza's bank, pass under the bridge, continue for about 50m, and you'll reach **La Torre,** a huge rock pinnacle.

Heading north, the steep mountain road climbs 3700m to **El Sillan,** "the saddle" between two mountains. The pass yields great views of the surrounding area and makes the difficult climb worth it. Like a moon rock forest, otherworldly stone spikes rise out of the landscape below. Finally, die-hard Butch and Sundance fans can make the 40km trip to **Huaca Huañusca** (Dead Cow Hill), the site of the infamous duo's last hold-up (see p. 363). This, however, requires a jeep or an organized tour (see Tour Agencies, p. 360).

♫ ENTERTAINMENT

Sport aficionados will delight in Tupiza's outdoor **Tenis Club Ferrovaria,** at Avaroa and Serrano, across from the train station. Courts, rackets, balls, and games are always available. Stop in a day early to reserve a court (Bs25 per hr.).

NEAR TUPIZA: SAN VICENTE

Thought by many to be **Butch Cassidy's and the Sundance Kid's final resting places,** bleak, weather-battered San Vicente now houses only 50 people—and many empty buildings. Travelers enthusiastic enough to withstand a four-hour drive over arduous terrain to a ghost town 4300m high can visit Cassidy's final **Casa de Tiroteo** (shoot-out house) and the cemetery where the bandits are supposedly buried. Trucks run to San Vicente only about once a month, making hiring a tour company the easiest way to track Butch and Sundance. This, of course, will cost you—about US$80-100 per person, to be exact. Bring food, water, sunscreen, sunglasses, and wind protection. For the full experience, you can stay the night in San Vicente's one hotel, **El Rancho** (Bs10).

S O U T H E R N   B O L I V I A

DESPERADOS' DEMISE Some believe they had facelifts in Europe and lived out their days in the American West. Others claim they died in a bar brawl in the early 1900s, the late 1920s, the late 1930s, the early 1940s. Countless legends surround Robert LeRoy Parker and Harry Alonzo Longbaugh, better known as **Butch Cassidy and the Sundance Kid.** Evidence, however, places the outlaws' demise on November 6, 1908, in desolate San Vicente. By 1901, both men were wanted throughout the United States for robberies totalling over US$200,000 (US$2.5 million today), so Butch (named for a stint as a butcher and a teenage-reverence for vagabond cowboy Mike Cassidy) and Sundance (so called because he spent time in jail in Sundance, Wyoming) took refuge in Argentina's Cholila Valley. Here, the two most famous members of the group known as the Train Robbers' Syndicate, the Wild Bunch, and the Hole-in-the-Wall gang settled down to a peaceful ranching life. But when a warrant for their arrest surfaced in 1905, the boys headed up to Bolivia.

It was probably their ceaseless search for capital that brought Butch and Sundance to Tupiza in 1908. Mid-morning on November 3, Butch and Sundance intercepted money-carrier Carlos Peró halfway up **Huaca Huañusca,** at the beginning of his three-day journey to transport a miners' payroll to mine headquarters. Peró alerted authorities, who in turn telegrammed warnings all over Bolivia. By the time Butch and Sundance reached San Vicente, just behind a police squad from Uyuni, every unpaid miner in the area was looking for the two gringo bandits. After a final meal of sardines and beer, the men retreated to their room. Shortly thereafter, the Uyuni squad staged a shoot-out. Entering the room at dawn on November 7, they discovered the two men dead. It seems Butch shot first an already injured Sundance, to put him out of his misery, and then himself. The two were buried in the San Vicente cemetery. But then, in 1991, a team sponsored by PBS's NOVA exhumed the grave and removed one caucasian male skeleton, which forensic tests proved was neither Butch nor Sundance. While many claim the two lie somewhere else in the cemetery, the story's inconclusive nature encourages others to propagate, ever more, the myths of America's favorite bandits.

VILLAZÓN ☎05

More often a gateway between Bolivia and Argentina than an actual destination, Villazón is the quintessential dusty border town. Crossing the border here is easy, almost too easy: herds of people, goods strapped to their backs, strut between the two countries. But this *comercio de hormigos* (ant trade) interferes little with the traveler just passing through—unless she desires cheap electronic goods. Still, though not unattractive, Villazón leaves little reason to linger.

☞ TRANSPORTATION

Trains: Station (☎962 565), the end of the line, on República Argentina, about 8 blocks north of the border. Ticket office open M-F 8am-noon and 2-6pm, Sa 8am-noon and 2-3:30pm, as well as an hour before any arrival or departure. Express trains to **Oruro** (14½hr., Sa 3:30pm, Bs76) via **Tupiza** (3hr., Bs15), **Atocha** (6hr., Bs43), and **Uyuni** (8hr., Bs43). Regular trains to **Oruro** (16hr., M and Th 3:30pm, Bs52) via **Tupiza** (3hr., Bs11), **Atocha** (7hr., Bs19), and **Uyuni** (10hr., Bs29).

Buses: Terminal, on República Argentina, just north of the plaza. **Luggage storage** available (Bs1 per bag), though most bus companies let you ditch your pack in their offices anyway. To: **Tarija** (8hr.; M-W and F-Sa 8 and 8:30pm, Th and Su 11am, 8, and 8:30pm; Bs25); **Potosí** (10-12hr., 8 per day 8am-6:30pm, Bs40); **Sucre** (15hr., 8:30am and 5:45pm, Bs70); **La Paz** (22hr., 8:30am, Bs60); and **Tupiza** (2½hr.; M-Sa 7am, 2:45, and 3pm, Su 7 and 11am, 2:45 and 3pm; Bs10).

BORDER CROSSING: INTO ARGENTINA

Only the Río Villazón separates Villazón and its Argentinian counterpart La Quiaca. Crossing the border here is quite easy, and there are few lines. The Bolivian side is open daily 6am-8pm, though the Argentinian is open 6am-11pm. You don't need stamps if crossing only for the day—just pass on through. For longer forays, you'll receive a Bolivia exit stamp and an Argentinian entrance stamp, valid for three months. **Argentinian time is an hour later than Bolivian during daylight saving time (Apr.-Oct.).**

✳🛈 ORIENTATION AND PRACTICAL INFORMATION

Almost everything in Villazón, including the train station, bus terminal, central plaza, and border crossing, lies on **República Argentina,** which runs north-south through town. Parallel, on the opposite side of the train tracks, **Antofagosta** holds a few hotels and businesses, as does **Independencia,** one block east of República Argentina. The **Río Villazón** marks the town's border with Argentina; the main **plaza** is three blocks north of the border.

Consulate: Argentina, 311 Cornelio Sabedra (☎962 011), 1 block north of the border, 1 street east of República Argentina (right if facing the border). Open daily 10am-5pm.

Currency exchange: Many *casas de cambio* around the border on República Argentina. **Banco de Crédito** (☎963 848), on Antofagosta 1 block north of the plaza exchanges traveler's checks for a 1½% commission. Open M-Sa 8:30am-12:30pm and 2:30-5pm.

Market: 1 block east of the plaza.

Emergency: ☎110.

Police: ☎110, on the northeast corner of the plaza.

Hospital: San Rogue (☎962 555), 7 blocks north and 2 blocks east of the plaza.

Telephones: ENTEL, on República Argentina 1 block north of the plaza. Open M-Su 7:30am-10pm.

Post Office: On República Argentina 1 block north of the plaza, in the ENTEL building. Open M-Sa 9am-noon and 2-6pm.

ACCOMMODATIONS

More good accommodations line Villazón's dusty streets than one might expect. The cheapest places to stay lie in the north part of the city, on Antofagosta, across from the train station: **Alojamientos Mexico, Copacabana,** and **La Paz** each cost Bs15 a night with outdoor faucets and occasional morning hot water (Bs5).

El Cortijo Residencial, on Antofagosta, 2 blocks north of the plaza. Larger than it appears from the street, this enchanting old hotel also houses a restaurant/lounge nicer than any found within the town. Summer months bring water to the outdoor pool and blooming flowers all around. Showers Bs5. Singles Bs25, with bath Bs50; doubles Bs50, with bath Bs80; triples Bs75, with bath Bs120; quads Bs100, with bath Bs160.

Hostal Plaza (☎ 963 535), on the southern side of the plaza, is the nicest place in town. Inside a small glass-encased mall, the hallways overflow with green potted plants. Downstairs, a *comedor* serves breakfast (Bs4). All rooms with bath include cable TV. Singles Bs35, with bath Bs50; doubles Bs70, with bath Bs80; triples Bs105, with bath Bs130; quads Bs140.

Residencial Cristal, 1 block south of the train station, on Antofagosta, is a better value than the similarly-priced options listed above; flowers and drying laundry decorate the courtyard onto which the slightly musty rooms open. Rooms Bs15 per person.

Gran Palace Hotel (☎ 965 333 or 965 544), just behind the bus station. Though not as regal as its name implies, Gran Palace remains one of Villazón's nicer digs. Large rooms include cable TV and telephone. Clean common baths. Singles Bs25, with bath Bs50; doubles Bs50, with bath Bs100; triples Bs75, with bath Bs150; quads Bs100.

FOOD

Charquekan, behind the bus station, next door to the pizzeria. A hit with locals, cooking traditional food at good prices. Lunch or dinner Bs6.

Pizzeria Don Vicho (☎ 965 073), behind the bus station. Regular fare in a warm, red-checkered den. Pizzas around Bs24. Burgers Bs6. A la carte dishes (meat and chicken) about Bs17.

Chifa Jardin (☎ 965 058), near the middle of República Argentina, serves mediocre Chinese food expensive enough for the prices to be listed in dollars. Lunch US$5. Dinner US$4. Open daily until 1am.

THE CHACO

TARIJA ☎ 06

With its palm trees and rose-filled plaza, "the gem of the south" seems like paradise, shining between its chilly altiplano and dusty chaco neighbors. It's not hard to see why locals of both Bolivian and Argentinian heritage take pride in the oft-overlooked treasure that is Tarija (pop. 120,000). *Tarijeños* (or *chapacos*, as they call themselves) first displayed this pride in their city when they revolted against the Spanish in 1807. But it was not until ten years later that they were taken seriously, when Eustaquio "Moto" Méndez led local troops to victory over the conquistadors in the 1817 Battle of La Tablada. Although they enjoyed this autonomy, in 1825 the *chapacos* decided to join newly-liberated Bolivia, spurning the alternative, Argentinian citizenship. Now, though, many *tarijeños* claim mixed blood—their culture incorporates both national heritages, as the Argentinian-style meat restaurants and white faces attest. But Tarija belongs to Bolivia in more ways than name: maybe it's the mediterranean climate, the wine it produces, or the rich fare at Tarija's excellent restaurants, but life moves slowly down south. Slower, even, than in the rest of the country; lunch lasts three hours, and almost every establishment closes its doors each day for a long afternoon nap.

TRANSPORTATION

Flights: Airport (☎642 283), about 2km east on Victor Paz. Open 6am-7pm. Domestic flight **exit fee** Bs10. International flight **exit fee** US$20. It's best to go to airline offices in Tarija to purchase tickets. **LAB** (☎/fax 632 000, 642 195, or 645 706), on Trigo between Virginio Lema and Alejandro del Carpio, 1½ blocks south of the Plaza Fuentes. Open M-F 8am-noon and 2:30-6:30pm, Sa 9am-noon. To **Cochabamba** (55min.; M 5pm, Th 5:20pm, F 5:10pm, Sa 12:10pm, Su 5:15pm; Bs459) and **Sucre** (40min., M 11am and Th 4:15pm, Bs321). 10% discount to students, groups of 2 or more, and those over 60. **Aerosur** (☎630 894; fax 630 893), on Ingavi between Sucre and Daniel Campos, 1 block north of the Plaza Fuentes. Open M-F 8:30-noon and 2:30-6:30pm, Sa 8:30am-noon. To **La Paz** (1hr.; M, W, F 4:20pm; Bs647). **TAM** (☎/fax 642 734), on La Madrid just west of the Plaza Fuentes. Open M-F 8am-noon and 2:30-6pm, Sa 7-8:30am. To: **Sucre** (45min., M 8am, Bs190); **Cochabamba** (1¾hr., M 8am, Bs355); **La Paz** (3hr., M 8am, Bs455); **Villamontes** (30min., Sa 12:30pm, Bs190); and **Santa Cruz** (2hr., Sa 12:30pm, Bs320). **SAVE** (☎/fax 644 764), 15 de Abril between Méndez and Santa Cruz, 2 blocks west of the Plaza Sucre. Open M-F 8:30am-12:30pm and 2-6:30pm, Sa 7am-noon. To **Yacuibe** (20 min.; M, W, and Sa 9:20am; Bs595) and **Santa Cruz** (1½hr.; M, W, and Sa 9:20am; Bs595).

Buses: Station, on Victor Paz and Las Americas, 11 blocks east of the Plaza Fuentes. Set with an **ENTEL office,** little **post office** stop, **police,** and a very helpful **info booth.** (☎636 508. Open daily 6am-noon and 3-8:30pm.) To: **La Paz** (24hr., 6:30 and 7am, Bs90); **Cochabamba** (24hr., M and Th 5pm, Bs90); **Santa Cruz** (24hr.; M, Th, and Sa 7am, Sa 7am and 5:30pm; Bs80); **Bermejo** (6-7hr.; 7, 9, 11am, 4, 6:30, 8:30pm; Bs30); **Villamontes** (11-12hr., 6pm, Bs45); **Uyuni** (18hr.; 3:30, 4, 4:30pm; Bs50); **Sucre** (15hr.; 3:30, 4, and 4:30pm; Bs45); **Potosí** (12hr.; 3:30, 4, 4:30, 5pm; Bs40); **Villazón** (7hr.; 8 and 8:30pm, W and Sa also 7:30am; Bs30); and **Yacuibe** (10½hr.; 7:30am, 6:40, 7:30pm; Bs40). **Exit fee** Bs2.

Taxis: Hailable throughout the day; at night Tarija's taxis can also be called. A few radio taxis include: **Moto Méndez** (☎644 480); **Tarija** (☎644 378); **4 de Julio** (☎642 829); and **V.I.P.** (☎643 131). Rides to the airport Bs5; anything within the city Bs3.

BORDER CROSSING: INTO ARGENTINA

About seven hours from Tarija lie **Bermejo,** 210km south, and **Yacuibe,** 356km southeast, two popular places to cross into Argentina. Crossing is relatively easy; neither side charges fines and both remain open 24 hours daily. Both Bermejo and Yacuibe also have places to sleep and eat should you get stuck there, but because this border crossing is so easy, that's unlikely. **Remember that Bolivia is one hour behind Argentina during daylight saving time (Apr.-Oct.).**

ORIENTATION AND PRACTICAL INFORMATION

Tarija revolves around its two plazas, the main **Plaza Luis Fuentes y Vargas** and, two blocks east and one block south, the smaller **Plaza Sucre.** Activity in the northern part of the city centers on the **market** and **Domingo Paz.** Colón runs north-south and divides the city into east and west sides—addresses to its west contain an "o" for *oeste* and addresses to the east with an "e" for *este.* The **Río Guadalquivir** marks Tarija's southern border; Victor Paz, otherwise known as Las Américas, runs beside it.

Tourist Office: (☎631 000), on General Trigo, on the Plaza Fuentes. Free maps and information. Open M-F 8am-4pm.

Consulate: Argentina (☎644 273; fax 634 668), at Ballivián and Bolívar, 3 blocks west and 2 blocks north of the Plaza Fuentes. Open M-F 8:30am-12:30pm.

Immigration Office: (☎643 594; fax 644 521), on Bolívar between Ballivián and Saracho, 2 blocks north and 3 blocks west of the Plaza Fuentes. Open M-F 8am-4pm.

SOUTHERN BOLIVIA

200 yards
200 meters

N

Tarija

ACCOMMODATIONS
Alojamiento 8 Hermanos, 7
Gran Hotel Baldiviezo, 11
Hostal Carmen, 8
Hostal Miraflores, 3
Hotel América, 5
Residencial El Turista, 4
Residencial Guadalquivir, 13
Residencial Rosario, 9
Residencial Zeballos, 2

MUSEUMS
Casa Dorada, 10
Museo Nacional
Paleontológico
Arqueológico, 12

SITES
El Castillo, 6
San Roque, 1

Streets and landmarks:

Stadium

Parque Bolívar

Oruro

Cochabamba

Potosí

Santa Cruz

La Paz
Padilla
Ejército
Belgrano
Church of Villa Fátima
O'Connor
Junín
Issac Attie
Delgdillo
Méndez
Suipacha
Carpio
Avaroa
Colón

Virginio Lema
PLAZA SUCRE

Basílica de San Francisco

Banco Santa Cruz

Market

Banco Bisa

15 de Abril

Daniel Campos

Sucre

PLAZA SUS PUENTES Y VIÑAS

General Trigo

Campero

Cathedral

Juan Misae Saracho

Ballivian

Ramón Rojas

Sevilla

Capilla la Loma de San Juan

Ingavi

Bolívar

Madrid

Domingo Paz

A. Corrado

F. Mingo

PLAZA URIONDO

Río Guadalquivir

Mirador de la Loma

Parque Zoológico

TO CAMPESINO MARKET,
PARQUE DE LAS FLORES

TO PARQUE
LA TABLADA

TO ENTRE RÍOS (110km)

Terminal de Buses

TO 13
(1 block)

Currency Exchange: Banco Bisa (☎ 638 101), on the Plaza Fuentes. Exchanges AmEx traveler's checks at a rate of 5% lower than the current exchange. Open M-F 8:30am-noon and 2:30-6pm, Sa 9am-noon. **Banco Santa Cruz,** Trigo 942 (☎ 648 888), 3 blocks north of the Plaza Fuentes, exchanges traveler's checks for a minimum commission of US$20. Open M-F 8:30am-6pm, Sa 9am-noon. Also, between Daniel Campos and Sucre, Bolívar houses numerous *casas de cambios*.

ATMs: A number of ATMs lie on Sucre just north of the plaza. V, MC.

Market: 2 blocks north of the Plaza Fuentes, bordered by Bolívar, Sucre, Domingo Paz, and Trigo. Another, larger campesino market lies in northern Tarija, along Las Américas.

Emergency: ☎ 110.

Police: ☎ 110, on Victor Paz between Ballivián and Saracho.

Pharmacy: To find out which is *en turno* call ☎ 118.

Hospital: Hospital San Juan de Dios (☎ 645 555), on Santa Cruz, just north of Cocha-bamba. **ProSalud Clinic,** Ballivián 536 (☎ 637 459), 3 blocks west of the Plaza Fuentes and a half-block north, is a good, centrally located option.

Telephones: ENTEL (☎ 612 100), on Virginio Lema between Sucre and Campos, 1 block south of the Plaza Fuentes. Open M-Sa 7:30am-11:30pm, Su 8am-9pm.

Internet Access: Café Internet Pizzeria Europa (☎ 647 611), on Plaza Fuentes. Bs10 per hr. **Sur Net Internet Online,** on Plaza Sucre. Bs10 per hr. Check hostels also.

Post Office: (☎ 642 586; fax 632 710), at Virginio Lema and Sucre, 1 block south of the Plaza Fuentes. Open M-Sa 8am-8pm, Su 9am-noon.

▌ ACCOMMODATIONS

On the whole, basic lodging prices are higher in Tarija than in other parts of Bolivia. But the cost comes with benefits: almost universal 24-hour hot water, fabulous shower pressure, even hot water knobs on the sink. Visa and MasterCard are readily accepted.

▨ **Residencial Rosario,** on Ingavi between Ramos Rojas and Ballivián, 3 blocks west and 1 block north of the Plaza Fuentes. Lounge chairs await sunbathers in a courtyard full of roses. Well-kept and filled with children and dogs. Laundry Bs5 per 12 pieces. Singles Bs25, with bath Bs40; doubles Bs40, with bath Bs75; triples Bs60, with bath Bs105.

▨ **Hostal Miraflores,** Sucre 920 (☎ 643 355; fax 630 391), 3 blocks north of the Plaza Fuentes, across from the market. The unassuming facade opens onto a lovely colonial courtyard. Music plays from a lively common room. Slightly less exciting rooms, most with bath, telephone and cable TV, to round out the establishment. Internet access Bs8 per hr. Singles Bs25, with bath Bs75; doubles Bs40, with bath Bs100; triples Bs60, with bath Bs120; quads Bs80; quints Bs100.

Hostal Carmen, Ingavi 784 (☎ 643 372 or 644 342), 3 blocks west and 1 block north of the Plaza Fuentes. Doubling as a tourist agency, this hostel is a favorite among the area's gringo volunteers, who often fill the worn leather chairs in the TV den. All rooms come with bath, phone and TV. Breakfast Bs4. Singles Bs50; doubles Bs100.

Gran Hotel Baldiviezo, La Madrid 443 (☎ 637 711), just west of the Plaza Fuentes. Baldiviezo's central location and modern appeal attract many visitors, but if you're searching for individual flavor, move on. Laundry Bs15 per 12 pieces. Internet access Bs15 per hr. Singles US$15; doubles US$30; triples US$45.

Hotel América, Bolívar 257 (☎ 642 657), 3 blocks west and 2 blocks north of the Plaza Fuentes. Designed for pink lovers, the run-down rooms may smell a little funny but just open your windows onto the sunny courtyard for a breath of fresh air. Breakfast Bs3.50. Laundry Bs10 per 12 pieces. Singles Bs25, with bath Bs35; doubles Bs50, with bath Bs70; triples Bs75, with bath Bs105; quads Bs100, with bath Bs140.

Residencial El Turista, Bolívar 138 (☎ 643 102), between Colón and Daniel Campos, 2 blocks north and 1 block east of the Plaza Fuentes. Despite its name, El Turista's full of locals. The "courtyard" consists of a drain for the outdoor bathrooms. 10 cramped, but definitely cheap, rooms. Singles Bs15; doubles Bs30.

Residencial Zeballos, Sucre 966 (☎633 313 or 642 068), 3 blocks north of the Plaza Fuentes. A sea of green follows you to your room—the courtyard and hallways are so full of plants that Zeballos feels more like the jungle than the lowland valleys. Retreat from plant-havoc to the cafeteria and living room. Breakfast included. Singles Bs30, with bath Bs45; doubles Bs60, with bath Bs80; triples Bs90, with bath Bs120.

◪ FOOD

Vegetarians beware, and vegans run for cover. Argentina's on the horizon, which means meat and lots of it. As always, the market offers the cheapest eats.

▨ **El Solar** (☎638 785), at Campero and Virginio Lema, 2 blocks south and 1 block west of the Plaza Fuentes. Tarija's veggie haunt, creatively decorated. Free meditation class, daily 6pm. The food? Grains, fruits and veggies—although unfortunately only for lunch. Four-course *almuerzo* Bs10. Open daily noon-2pm.

▨ **Hostal La Costañera** (☎642 851), at Victor Paz and Saracho, 3 blocks south and 2 west of the Plaza Fuentes. Too expensive to stay at, this charming house serves a popular, surprisingly affordable vegetarian lunch. The four courses, highlighted by homemade juices, fresh bread, soft music, and quick service (Bs10), are a relaxing way to pass the afternoon. Open M-Sa noon-2pm.

Taberna Gattopardo (☎630 656), on the north side of the Plaza Fuentes. The place to meet other travelers, this cat's going for the brooding pub look. Choose from pizzas (Bs30), pastas (Bs20), and meat dishes (Bs25). A wide selection of dessert crepes (Bs9) and drinks top off a menu that caters to foreigners. Open daily 7:30am-1am.

Restaurant Chifa Hong Kong (☎637 076), on Sucre between Victor Paz and Alejandro del Carpio, 2 blocks south of the Plaza Fuentes. The excellent rice dishes (Bs10) at this classic Chinese restaurant could make a full meal. Traditional meat and noodle entrees Bs25. Untraditional fried wontons Bs10. *Almuerzo* Bs12. Open M-Sa 11:30am-2:30pm and 6:30-11:30pm; Su 11:30am-2:30pm.

Restaurant Don Pepe (☎642 426), at Campos and Victor Paz, 4 blocks south and 1 block east of the Plaza Fuentes. Long wooden tables fill the main room, and weekends bring the occasional *peña*. Su *criolla* buffet Bs25. Meat dishes Bs25. Open M-Sa noon-2:30pm and 6pm-1am, Su noon-2:30pm.

◪ SIGHTS

BODEGAS. No trip to Tarija is complete without a bodega visit. Many area bodegas offer demonstrations of their wine (and, at some, singani) production processes, give tours of their vineyards, and stage tastings. Keep in mind that the harvest takes place in February and March; the bodegas have little to display in the winter months. Only tour companies can get you to the Kohlberg, Aranjuez, and Casa Real wineries, far from town, but a city trufi suffices for the trip to La Concepción. *(From the Plaza Sucre take the bus marked "Concepción." Any tour agency will be happy to ferry you to and from the others for Bs50-100. Let's Go recommends guide Karen Méndez Montalvo. ☎642 145; email marikaren@yahoo.es. Bs40 per person with 3 people.)*

MUSEUMS. Museo Nacional Paleontológico Arqueológico houses an impressive collection of big bones and other artifacts from the region. *(At Trigo and Virginio Lema, 1 block south of the Plaza Fuentes. Open M-Sa 8am-noon and 3-6pm. Free.)* Gaudy turn-of-the century **Casa Dorada** now serves as the Casa de la Cultura, but was once home to the wealthy landowner Moisés Navajas and his wife Esperanza. Its highlights include magenta walls and ceiling frescoes. *(At Trigo and Ingavi, 1 block north of the plaza. Open M-F 9am-noon and 2:30-6pm. Donation requested.)* If ornate house-stalking is your hobby, go seven blocks right (if you start facing La Casa) and one block to the left on Junín to visit Navajas's other masterpiece, **El Castillo,** now privately owned.

REACHING NEW HIGHS Ah, fine wine. Produced in France, Italy, Chile, even California, but Bolivia? Who knew? When the Spaniards introduced wine grapes to Latin America in the 1500s, production flourished in the valley south of Potosí. But such tamely bacchanalian delights weren't enough for everyone; the miners wanted a brew strong enough to help them forget their harsh working conditions. After much contemplation and distillation, **singani,** a new white-grape firewater, was born. In recent years, the center of Bolivia's wine and singani production has shifted to Tarija's southern valleys, where visitors can witness Bolivian winemaking practices at vineyards such as La Concepción and Kohlberg. With these and other bodegas sitting between 1700 and 2600m, their wine may not be the world's priciest or most famous, but it's certainly the highest.

CHURCHES. The interesting **Basílica de San Francisco** occupies an entire block. If the Fathers are there (chances are better on weekdays), they can show you around the two wonderful old libraries. *(At Ingavi and Daniel Campos. To visit, knock on the first door down from Ingavi.)* Uphill, **Iglesia de San Roque,** named for the patron saint of dogs and Tarija, stands watch. The church's primary claim to fame, other than its supreme visibility, is its place at the center of Tarija's most important festival. *(From the plaza, head north and walk 5 blocks, past Casa Dorada. See Nightlife, below.)*

PARKS. Mirador de la Loma, a hilltop park, has beautiful sunsets. *(Head 5 blocks west from Domingo Paz.)* Peaceful **Parque de las Flores** boasts a little pond. *(From Mirador de la Loma, take a right out of the lower main gate and walk uphill until you can turn left; continue 2 short blocks.)* **Parque Zoológico** caters to children with a small pool, jungle gym, and a few animals. *(From Parque de las Flores, head south along Las Américas. Open M-Sa 7:30am-noon and 2:30-6pm, Su 7:30am-6pm. Adults Bs1, children 50 centavos.)* Pleasant lookout **Parque La Tablada** once saw Moto Méndez's famous victory over the Spanish. *(Far south along Las Américas, in Tablada; about 4km from the bridge. Follow the road uphill to the stone steps.)*

🎴 🎇 NIGHTLIFE AND FESTIVALS

Nightlife in Tarija is made mostly of *tarijeños* too busy cruising in their SUVs to stop and party, but numerous high schoolers do make it out to the karaoke bars. **Cine Gran Rex** (☎643 728), on La Madrid between Daniel Campos and Colón, and **Cine Eden** (☎633 803), on Virginio Lema between Daniel Campos and Colón, both play subtitled American films daily. **La Vinchuca,** Daniel Campos 147, just north of Victor Paz, four blocks south and one block east of the Plaza Fuentes, is a playful bar and gringo hangout, with giant "insects" decorating the windows. Live music, especially on weekends. Open nightly until 1am.

Tarija's most important **festival** is that of its patron saint, **San Roque.** The first Sunday in September, the city attends a 10am mass at Iglesia San Roque before following a procession lead by *chunchos*, traditional male dancers in turbans, veils, small ponchos, and long skirts. On August 15, a more somber festival in honor of the **Virgin of Chaguaya** takes almost 50,000 people from all over the country on a 70km pilgrimage to the town of Chaguaya. Also prominent is **La Pascua Flórida,** during the Easter Holy Week festivities. This celebration, which takes place mainly outside the city proper, begins on Saturday evening with traditional food and singani drinks. Sunday brings flower arches and the election of the Queen of Pascua Flórida. Less religious, the **Feria de Uva,** or Festival of the Grape, arrives with the harvest in late February or early March. It's held in the towns surrounding Tarija, most notably in Concepción. Vineyards display their best fruits and participants make wine *de patino*—through the traditional foot-stomping method.

ENTRE RIOS ☎ 06

Halfway between Tarija and Villamontes, both in distance and in altitude, lies Entre Rios (1230m), so named for its strategic location between bathing spots Santa Ana and Pajonal. Dominated by a rose-filled plaza, this small, serene village is surrounded by dense green hills and glorious scenery; visitors, lulled by the swaying trees and gentle wind, spend their time relaxing in town or exploring the easily accessible countryside. Its prime location gives this small town a to-die-for climate: hot summers, warm winters, and peaceful weather year-round. Mounted on the hill behind the hospital looms a gigantic **Christ statue,** which watches over the entire city and has a great panoramic view of the hillsides. From the church on the plaza, walk one block down and four blocks left, passing the soccer field to the steps and base of the hill. The folks at Hotel Tarija own a **farm,** El Alambrado, about 1km past the hospital, where they rent horses for half or full-day country jaunts (Bs10 per full day). Inquire at the hotel to arrange a trip. They can also point you in the right direction to go bathing in **Río Santa Ana** (30min. by foot) or to see the waterfalls along the way to the town of **San Diego** (2½hr. by foot).

Entre Rios encompasses about two blocks in every direction from the main **plaza,** the place where all buses arrive and depart. Buses go to: **Tarija** (3½ hr., 8 per day 4am-midnight, Bs18); **Santa Cruz** (24hr.; M, Th, and Sa 11:30am; Bs60); and **Chiquiáca** (4hr.; M, Tu, Th, Sa 3pm; Bs20). Flotas pass through town to **Villamontes** (9-10pm) and to **Yacube** (10:30-11:30am, 9:40-10:40pm, and 10:30-11:30pm). **Banco de Crédito,** on the plaza, isn't much help unless you have cash, but they will change US dollars to *bolivianos.* (☎ 118 057. Open M-F 8:30am-noon and 2:30-5pm.) Other services include: the **police,** two blocks from the plaza; 24-hour **Farmacia San Antonio,** one block to the right when facing the church in the plaza; **Hospital San Juan de Dios;** and **ENTEL,** one block from the plaza (☎ 119 500; open daily 7am-11pm.) For such a small town, Entre Rios has a surprising number of accommodations. For all hotels, reservations are only needed around the time of the town's most important festival, **Guadalupe,** on the first Sunday in October. Reserve one month in advance. The informative staff at **Hotel Tarija,** on the corner of the plaza, can set you up with a simple room off turquoise-blue halls. (☎ 118 052. Singles Bs15, with bath and TV Bs50; doubles Bs30, with bath and TV Bs50; triples Bs45.) **Alojamiento El Carmen,** one block down and to the left of the far church plaza corner, offers the lowest prices in town. (☎ 118 045. Singles Bs12; doubles Bs24; triples Bs36; quads Bs48.) The most luxurious lodging is presented by **Hotel Plaza,** right on the plaza. Stucco walls and wooden doors open to simple rooms and soft beds. Two outdoor lounge areas with iron tables and chairs support serious reading and sunbathing. (☎ 118 039. Singles Bs15, with bath Bs40; doubles Bs30, with bath Bs50; triples Bs45.)

VILLAMONTES ☎ 06

If you teach a man to fish, he'll head to Villamontes, where fishing is both a pastime and a valued export. Just follow the Río Pilcomayo, which cuts through thick, heavy brush and rolling hills, into the heart of the Chaco. You'll find dusty-hot days in these low, low lands (385m) and an August **festival** dedicated not to a patron saint but to the holy fish itself. A stronghold during the Chaco war, locals—many of Guaraní Indian descent—take pride in their home's historic role and stifling heat and live off its sacred fish industry. So what better way for a visitor to pass the time than **fishing** in the Chaco's wild heart? Popular spots to cast a line include **hoterma** and **peña colorada,** both fishing holes seven to 10km from the plaza along the **Cañon de Pilcomayo.** A number of waterfalls caress the river; **El Chorro Grande** lies about 20km out and is also full of fishermen. To reach any of these prime destinations, head out of town on the one and only road south, toward Tarija. The first spots can be hit in about a 30-minute walk. Some visitors try to hop any bus or truck headed in that direction, but *Let's Go* does not recommend hitchhiking. Taxis (Bs15) can also haul you and your gear to the river.

The town consists almost entirely of one very long main street, **Mendez Arcos,** although the name will be of little use. At the south end, beyond town, lies the way to Tarija and the Río Pilcomayo gorge (10km to prime fishing spots). A trip north passes by the **plaza, market, bus terminal, train station** (2km), and eventually the **airport** (15km). **TAM,** with an office on the plaza (☎722 135; open M-F 8:30am-noon and 3-6pm), has flights to **Tarija** (30min., Sa 8:30am, Bs190) and **Santa Cruz** (70min., Sa 3:30pm, Bs320). The **train station,** 2km north of the plaza (☎722 808; open M-Sa 9am-noon and 3-6pm) sells tickets to **Yacuiba** (2hr.; Tu, Th, and Sa 4:20am; Bs8) and **Santa Cruz** (11hr; Tu, Th, and Sa 7:30pm; Bs27). The **bus station,** 13 blocks north of the plaza (☎722 600; open daily 7:30am-noon and 3-6pm), sends flotas to: **Santa Cruz** (12hr., 10:30am and 7pm, Bs30); **Tarija** (11hr., 4am and 5:30pm, Bs40); and **Yacuiba** (1½hr., 6 and 10:30am, Bs15). Flotas to the border with **Paraguay** (10hr.) via Ibibobo, as well as trufis to **Camiri** (2hr., 5am-8pm, Bs25) and **Yacuiba** (1½hr., 5am-8pm, Bs15), which leave when full, depart from the **traffic stop,** 2 blocks toward the plaza from the bus terminal and one block west.

Services include: the **police,** two blocks west of the plaza (☎722 044); **Hospital Basico de Apoyo,** five blocks west of the plaza (☎722 475); **Internet access** at the I.C.T.C. office (☎723 111; open daily 8am-noon and 3-10pm; Bs15 per hr.); and **ENTEL,** one block west of the plaza (☎722 323; open M-Sa 7:30am-11pm, Su 8am-8pm). The tightly budgeted traveler might do best **camping** near the river. **Residencial Miraflores,** four blocks north of the plaza, away from Tarija, has 30 rooms, all with fans. Baths are rather rough but provide 24-hour hot water. (☎722 991. Singles Bs20, with bath Bs30; doubles Bs40, with bath Bs60; triples Bs60; quads Bs80.) One block east of the plaza, **Residencial Raldes** has a lively courtyard designed for *fiestas.* Rooms with bath include cable TV and A/C. (☎722 088. Singles Bs30, with bath Bs50; doubles Bs60, with bath Bs100; triples Bs90, with bath Bs150; quads with bath Bs200.)

BORDER CROSSING: INTO PARAGUAY

Within the Chaco region there are three ways to pass into Paraguay. Two roads from Villamontes head to **Esmeraldas** and to **Picada Sucre,** both on the border. The second route, which passes through Ibibobo, is more popular and more frequently taken by *flotas* coming through Villamontes from Santa Cruz. The infamously-rough Chaco road, which heads east from Boyuibe, is also taken by those heading south from Santa Cruz or Camiri. The Bolivian border station at **Hito Villazón** stays open until about 8pm, occasionally levying fees for passing travelers. If entering Bolivia from Paraguay, check in with Camiri immigration officials before heading on to greener pastures.

CENTRAL AND EASTERN BOLIVIA

In **Central Bolivia** (p. 373), you can still see the effects of the ancient conflict between the Inca and the Aymara. The Quechua-speaking Inca descended hundreds of years ago, and were very successful—their ruins dot the area, and it may help to learn a few essentials in Quechua if you plan to do much bargaining at the market. But they weren't completely successful—throughout the region, there remain small clumps of Aymara indians who don´t speak a word of Quechua, or Spanish. There, as well as in the Valles Alto and Bajo and the rest of the area around Cochabamba, agriculture characterizes a gritty lifestyle.

HIGHLIGHTS OF CENTRAL AND EASTERN BOLIVIA

CELEBRATE the **Fiesta de la Virgen de Urkupiña,** held every August 14th-16th in Quillacollo (p. 380), which lures hordes of visitors with its elaborate folklore dances.

SCREW Versailles—**Villa Albina** (p. 380), the vast grounds and elaborate, renaissance style mansions of tin baron Simon Patiño, is where it's at.

PLAY in the dinosaur footprints at **Parque Nacional Torotoro** (p. 383).

TRAVEL through the historic **Jesuit missions** (p. 399), and their beautiful 18th-century churches.

WONDER at **El Fuerte** (p. 396), a remarkable complex hewn from a single rock.

Eastern Bolivia (p. 385) is quite large—it includes Santa Cruz the department, Santa Cruz the city, the western mountainous regions, the Jesuit mission circuit, and the whole eastern frontier—a whole night train ride shy of the border with Brazil. It's diverse, too—Santa Cruz is a flat, semi-tropical city, but a short jaunt in any direction will show you something completely different. To the south, gigantic sand dunes encroach on the metropolis; to the northwest lie stretches of virgin jungle. Perhaps the region´s best kept secret is the old road to Cochabamba, whose first major stop is Samaipata, a charming mountain nook and home to El Fuerte, a sprawling complex of Inca, pre-Inca, and Spanish ruins.

CENTRAL BOLIVIA

COCHABAMBA   ☎ 04

The Cordillera del Tunari doesn't shield Cochabamba from the 21st century. Even the ancient Inca outposts in the areas surrounding the 5200m Cerro Tunari could have done little to prevent the entrance of dot-coms, cellular phones, and Pokémon. *Campesinos* still trek to the city to sell their wares, as they have for hundreds of years; but now instead of filling a simple unpaved road, they stack their wares in front of Tulio's Cybercafé. The popular tourist destinations of Cristo de la Concordia, el Palacio Portales, and the Archeological Museum are incredible, but they're only half the ticket—the subtle character of Cochabamba can easily be drowned out in the general roar of the city, and it may take a few steps and a trufi ride to reach, but you're certainly more likely to find it if you take the time to see more of this incredible city.

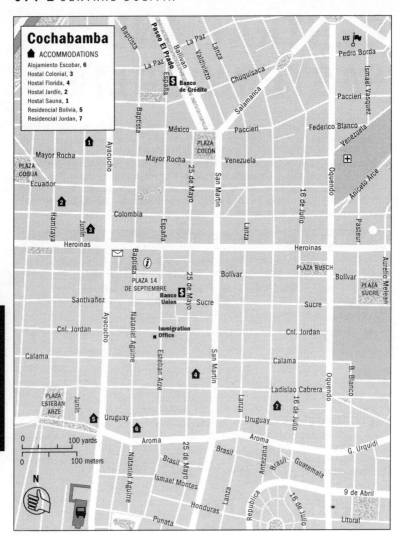

Cochabamba

🏠 ACCOMMODATIONS

Alojamiento Escobar, **6**
Hostal Colonial, **3**
Hostal Florida, **4**
Hostal Jardin, **2**
Hostal Sauna, **1**
Residencial Bolivia, **5**
Residencial Jordan, **7**

📧 TRANSPORTATION

Flights: Aeropuerto Jorge Wilstermann, southeast of center on Killman (☎ information 591 820). **Lloyd Aereo Boliviano** (☎ 230 325 or 230 327) on Heroínas between Ayacucho and Baptista. Open M-F 8am-12:30pm and 2-7pm, Sa 8:30am-1pm. **Aero-Sur,** Villarroel 105 (☎ 400 909), at Oblitas. Open M-F 8am-12:30pm and 2:30-6:30pm, Sa 8:30am-noon. Both head to: **La Paz** (35min.; 2-3 per day; Bs590 round-trip, Bs290 one-way); **Santa Cruz** (45min.; Bs750 round-trip, Bs380 one-way); and **Sucre** (2hr., 1-2 per day). There is a **Bs10 tax on national flights,** and a **US$25 departure tax on international flights.** To get to the city center, take a micro "B" (Bs1.4). Micros are not available late-night or early morning—take an airport taxi (Bs15-20).

Long-Distance Buses: Terminal (☎234 600), on Ayacucho, 1-2 blocks south of Aroma (within walking distance of most locations in the south); if you plan on going near the Plaza 14 de Septiembre or beyond, catch a taxi (Bs3-3.5) or micro "J," which passes by the station on Ayacucho, and continues on Ayacucho through the city center (Bs1.4). To: **La Paz** (7hr.; every hr. 6am-4pm and 7-10:30pm: Bs30, with beds Bs40-50); **Santa Cruz** (10-11hr.; 6-9am and 5:30-10pm; Bs35, with beds Bs50-55); **Oruro** (4hr., every hr. 5am-10:30pm, Bs10-15); **Potosí** (12-13hr., 6:30-8pm, Bs40); and **Sucre** (13-14hr., 7:30-8:30pm, Bs35-50).

Inter-departmental Buses: Buses leave from República and 6 de Agosto to: **Totora** (3½hr.; 1:30 and 3:30pm; Bs8); **Mizque** (4hr., noon, Bs15); **Aiquile** (6hr.; 1pm, M-Sa also 1:30pm, Su also 7pm; Bs15); and **Pocona** (3hr., Sa 1pm, Bs25).

Local Buses: Includes micros, trufis, and taxi-trufis. Micros are Bs0.50-1 more expensive than trufis. Trufi or taxi-trufi rides within Cochabamba Bs1.40. Micro routes can be determined by their letters, while taxis and taxi-trufis go by numbers (all vehicles list destinations on their windshields as well). Micros or trufis to **Quillacollo** (trufi Bs2), **Vinto** (trufi Bs3), and **Sipe Sipe** (trufi Bs4) can be caught at the corner of San Martín and Aroma in the southern part of the city, and at the south end of the intersection of Tumusla and Heroínas in the north end of the city. Trufis leave from Barrientos, near the intersection with 6 de Agosto, to: **Tarata** (45min.; every 10-15min.; Bs3.50) and **Cliza** (30-45min.; every 15-20min. until 7pm; Bs3.50). Finally, trufis to **Punata** (every 30min., Bs4) leave from the corner of La República and 6 de Agosto.

Taxis: Most are white with a blue or green stripe. At night, it's best to call a radio taxi or simply dial ☎195 from a local phone. **Radio Móvil Tropical** (☎259 999, 251 222, or 221 666). Taxi within the city center Bs3-3.50. Crossing the Río Rocha or going past Aroma Bs3.50 to Bs4. Taxis can also be hired by the hour (Bs20) for long trips, or for city tours; this rate is universal. **Karim Vargas** (☎361 508 or 262 378) is particularly friendly and knowledgeable about the routes throughout the Cochabamba region.

Car Rental: International Rent-A-Car (☎226 635), on Ayacucho, rents small Jeeps (US$30 per day) and larger Land Cruisers (US$40 per day) with US$0.40 charge per km. You can also pay a fixed amount (US$70 per 150km or per day) for a certain distance. Minimum age 25; driver's license, credit card, and passport or ID required. Open M-F 8:30am-12:30pm and 2-7pm. **J. Barron's Rent-A-Car** (☎222 774, ☎014 98 050), on Sucre near Antezana. Rents a variety of 4x4 vehicles (US$48-90 per day). Min. age 25; passport, credit card, and driver's license required. Open daily 8am-7pm.

ORIENTATION AND PRACTICAL INFORMATION

Once you get your compass bearings straight, Cochabamba is fairly easy to navigate. The main business and tourist districts, centered around the **Plaza 14 de Septiembre,** extends north from **Aroma** to the **Ramon Rivero,** and lies east of the **Río Rocha** to a little beyond **Oquendo.** Addresses on streets perpendicular to **Heroínas,** the main east-west road, include a N or S to denote whether the location is north or south of Heroínas; the first two digits of an address specify exactly how many blocks you are from Heroínas (for example, Junín S-0349 means that the location is three blocks south of Junín). The same method is used, except with "east" and "west," for the streets perpendicular to **Ayacucho** (which becomes **Libertador Simón Bolívar** north of the Río Rocha). Taxi drivers won't have a clue where to take you unless you provide them with an intersection, or the names of adjacent streets.

TOURIST, FINANCIAL, AND LOCAL SERVICES

Tourist Office: Dirección Departmental de Turismo (☎221 793), opposite the tourist office on the 3rd fl., offers brochures and candid advice. Open M-F 8am-4pm. Basic tourist maps are available at street vendors and hostels. For official city maps, you'll have to go to **Catastro** in the mayor's office (☎258 030), on Ayacucho between Mayor Rocha and Ecuador. Open M-F 8:30am-noon and 2:30-6:30pm, Sa 9am-noon.

Tour Agencies: Fremen, Tumusla 0245, between Ecuador and Colombia (☎259 392), has package tours to Torotoro National Park, Incallajta, Carrasco National Park, El Chapare, and many others. Offers private air transport to Torotoro. Prices drop sharply in proportion to the number of people involved. Open M-F 9am-noon and 2-6:30pm. **Caixa Tours,** E. Arce S-563 (☎226 148), between Jordan and Calama, offers similar tours to Chaparé, Torotoro, the Valle Alto and the Valle Bajo. Open M-F 9am-12:30pm and 2:30-6:30pm, Sa 9am-12:30pm. Both companies offer multilingual tour guides.

Consulates: Brazil, Edificio los Tiempos II, 9th fl. (☎255 860). Open M-F 8:30-11:30am and 2:30-5:30pm. **Chile,** Heroínas E-0620 (☎253 095). Open M-F 8:30am-1pm. **Peru,** Pando 1325 (☎240 296). Open M-F 9am-noon and 3-5pm. **Paraguay,** Edificio El Solar, 16 de Julio 211 (☎221 474). Open M-Sa 8:30am-12:30pm and 2:30-6:30pm. **Argentina,** Federico Blanco 929 (☎255 859). Open M-F 8:30am-1pm. **US,** Torres Sofer, Bloque A, Of. 601 (☎256 714). Open M-F 9am-noon.

Immigration Office: (☎225 553), on E. Arce and Jordan. Open M-F 8:30am-4:30pm.

Currency Exchange: Banco Ganadero (☎235 223), northeast corner of Ayacucho and Acha. Commission of US$10 per traveler's check; US$300 maximum. Open daily 8am-noon and 2:30-6:15pm. Money changers with rates similar to the banks gather at the intersection of Heroínas and Ayacucho next to the post office.

ATM: The **Banco de Crédito** (☎522 776), at the very top corner of España and Paseo El Prado, has a Visa/MC **ATM** on the Plaza 14 de Septiembre at the corner of Baptista and Bolívar. Open M-F 8:30am-12:30pm and 2:30-6:30pm.

English-Language Bookstores: Los Amigos del Libro (☎251 140), on Heroínas at the corner of España, stocks prominent English-language magazines.

Language Instruction: Centro Boliviano Americano, 25 de Mayo N-0365 (☎221 288), offers Spanish lessons. One-on-one (US$6 per hr.) or group lessons (US$4.50 per hr. for 2 people, price drops US$0.50 per hr. for each additional person). Organizes homestays with local families. Open M-F 8:30-11:45am and 2:30-7:15pm.

EMERGENCY AND COMMUNICATIONS

Emergency: ☎100 will connect you to the police.

Police: Call ☎221 793; daily 8am-4pm for tourist police (after hours ☎041 7496).

Pharmacies: Farmacia Boliviana (☎228 382), on the Plaza 14 de Septiembre, at the corner of Santivañez and N. Aguirre. Open M-F 8am-12:30pm and 2:30-8pm, Sa 3-7pm. Signs in pharmacy windows list which pharmacy is *en turno* (open all night).

Hospital: Hospital Viedma (☎533 227). Between Venezuela and E. Arce after the streets cross German Urquidi.

Telephones: ENTEL, at Ayacucho and Acha. Open M-Sa 7:30am-11pm, Su 8am-11pm.

Internet Access: ENTEL Internet (☎118 097), at Ayacucho and Acha. Bs7 per hr. Open daily 8am-2am. **Cyberland Café Internet** (☎230 903), in the Edificio Los Tiempos at Plaza Quintanilla. Bs4 per hr. for students. Open M-F 8:30am-10pm.

Post Office: Correo Central, Ayacucho S-0131 (☎230 979), on the southeast corner of Heroínas. Open M-F 8am-8pm, Su 9am-noon.

▌ ACCOMMODATIONS

Fairly inexpensive but comfortable hostels dot the market district and, more importantly, are very close to the bus station. If you have a few *bolivianos* to spare, consider the options in the north of the city.

Hostal Colonial, Junín N-0134 (☎221 791), on your right after taking a right off Heroínas. Travelers and locals alike flock here for the bright rooms, large courtyard, and friendly owners. Laundry service. Singles Bs30, with bath Bs40; doubles with bath Bs70; triples Bs90; quads with bath Bs140. Group discounts available.

Hostal Florida, 25 de Mayo S-0583 (☎257 911), going north on 25 de Mayo, on your right after crossing L. Cabrera. Internet access, ENTEL long distance service, and laundry service. Check in before midnight; check out noon. Singles Bs30, with bath Bs55; doubles Bs50, with bath Bs90; triples Bs90, with bath Bs135; quads Bs120.

Alojamiento Escobar, N. Aguirre S-0749 (☎225 812), ½ block south from the intersection of Uruguay and Aguirre. Despite poor lighting and the occasional mystery stain, solid locks and a central location make this a decent option. Rooms Bs17 per person.

Residencial Bolivia (☎250 086), on Aroma. Heading up Ayacucho with your back to the bus station, it is across the street on the left. Conveniently located near the bus station, with basic but comfortable rooms. Doors close at midnight; doorbell for stragglers.

Hostal Oruro, Agustín Lopez N-864 (☎224 345), between Montes and Aroma, just 2 blocks from the terminal. Simple and clean, with the best showers around. Rooms Bs20 per person, with bath Bs25.

Hostal Jardin, Hamiraya N-0248 (☎247 844), between Ecuador and Colombia. Ritzy by Cochabamba hostel standards. Breakfast included (7-8:30am). Singles Bs50; doubles Bs80, with bath and cable TV Bs110; triples Bs150; quads Bs175-185.

Residencial Jordan (HI) (☎228 069), on Antezana between Uruguay and L. Cabrera. A great deal if you have a Hosteling International card. Rooms include TV, telephone, bath, and breakfast. Rooms Bs25, non-members Bs60.

▐ FOOD

Cochabamba's typical plates—*silpancho, chajchu, pique de pollo*—can be found at almost any neighborhood *comedor* or in the market on the corner of Jordan and 25 de Mayo. The same dishes are available, albeit a little pricier, all along the **Paseo el Prado.** There, you'll find sidewalk cafes serving full *menús* (Bs7-15). Street vendors on Heroínas hawk greasy burgers with fries (Bs4-4.5).

▨ **El Chop las Américas,** J. Baptista 572, at Hernando Siles (☎241 817); taxi (Bs4). Specialties like *picante de conejo* (Bs26) available at dinner; lunch (Bs9-12). Open T-Su noon-2:30am. Friday *peñas* 8:30pm-3am. Las Américas also has a slightly cheaper **anexo** (☎221 590) at Antezana between Calama and L. Cabrer, which serves the same food, but with no music. Large plate of *chajchu* Bs10. Annex open M-Sa noon-2am.

▨ **Lacto Bar,** Jordan 0858 (☎500 244), between 16 de Julio and Oquendo; near the Universidad Mayor de San Simon. Run by and for a local orphanage. Oh-so-smooth smoothies (banana juice with milk, Bs3). Vegetable Omlette Bs4-5. Cheeseburger Bs8. *Flan Casero* Bs3. Open M-F 8:30am-10pm, Sa 8:30am-8:30pm.

Casa de Campo (☎243 937), on the Paseo Boulevard, the string of restaurants to the east of the intersection of Pando and Padilla. A local favorite, though a bit pricey. House special *pique de lobo* Bs31. Open daily noon-2:30am.

Taquiña Brewery Restaurant (☎288 676), north on the steep road starting at the *Cruce Taquiña.* Take trufi/taxi 101 or trufi 1 going north on Ayacucho and Heroínas to the *Cruce Taquiña,* then take a taxi up the hill. Great views. Taquiña serves 3-4 plates per day, often including *trucha* (trout, Bs35), or *pato bebé* (duckling, Bs49). *Cerveza* Bs8. Reservations recommended F-Su. Open M-F noon-6pm, Sa-Su noon-8pm.

Pizzeria La Leñas, San Martín 143 (☎500 674), on your left when heading east on Heroínas. *Pizza de choco* (pizza topped with chocolate and bananas, Bs18-44). Equally interesting pizzas, some topped with tuna or sweet corn Bs17-48. Sangria Bs6. Open daily 8:30am-1:30pm; pizza and pasta served 5:30-11:30pm.

Pension Vegetariana, 25 de Mayo 329. Heading south on 25 de Mayo, it's on your right after crossing Mayor Rocha; walk through the entrance to the Residencial Buenos Aires and to the end of the hall. Buffet *menú* Bs8. Open daily 7:30am-6pm.

▐ SIGHTS

▨ **CRISTO DE LA CONCORDIA.** A 40m statue perched atop the 275m Cerro de San Pedro to the east of Cochabamba, this Christ offers the best views of Cochabamba and the surrounding area. To reach the base of the statue, visitors can climb the hill by foot (20-30min.) or take the *teleférico.* Even when the statue is closed for viewing, many Cochabambinos hang out around the base, sharing a drink at the cafe (Bs3), viewing the city with a telescope (Bs2) or binoculars (Bs1), or convincing a member of the opposite sex that they are sensitive and romantic. *(To get to the base of the hill, take a micro marked #2 or "Cristo" or "Teleférico" from the corner of Lanza and Heroínas to near the end of Heroínas. To get to the teleférico take a left on Ruben Diario (Tu-Sa 10am-7pm, Su and holidays 9am-8pm; Bs4). Walk to the very end of Heroínas to take the footpath; you'll have to take the footbridge on your left to get to the base of the hill. Taxi to the base of the statue Bs30-40. Open on Sa-Su 9am-8pm. Bs1.)*

▨ MUSEO ARQUEOLÓGICO. It's one thing to see ancient Inca mummies on the glossy pages of *National Geographic;* it's quite a different experience to stare at them, face-to-face. Organized chronologically counter-clockwise, tours begin with 30-million-year-old dinosaur skulls, skip a few eons to the oldest human skeleton found in Bolivia (15,000-17,000 years old), and then trace the development of Andean civilization, starting with primitive tools, the first musical instruments, and, of course, the rise of recreational drug use. Tours culminate in the mummy room—many of the mummies still have most of their hair and flesh intact. The museum has a few special exhibitions every year; check the posters at the entrance of the Casa de la Cultura (corner of 25 de Mayo and Heroínas; ☎ 243 137) for dates and times. *(The museum is on the northwest corner of Jordan and N. Aguirre; a block south of the Plaza 14 de Septiembre. Open Tu-F 8:30am-6:30pm, Sa-Su 9am-noon. Guides in English or Spanish are free for groups of 5 or more. US$2; first day of each exhibition free.)*

PALACIO PORTALES. It took one French architect, numerous Japanese gardeners, and 40 European artisans over 12 years to build this eclectic complex, finally completed in 1927. Simon Patiño, the tin magnate who ordered the construction of the house, never had a chance to live in his dream house.

Today the Palacio can be divided into three parts: the gardens, the art galleries below the house, and the house itself. The **gardens** are large and well-kept. Once inside the **house** you can see, among other things, a room specifically designed to imitate a Vatican library. The basement houses the **Centro de Arte,** an art gallery displaying the work of the best Bolivian artists of the past 50 years. Works from famous artists like Remy Daza hang next to pieces by less famous artists, including Max Arequipa. *(Take micro "F" or "G" from the Plaza 14 de Septiembre (Bs1.40), or a taxi (Bs3-4), to the corner of Portales and Potosí. ☎ 241 337. Open M-F 2:30-6:30pm, Sa-Su 10:30am-noon. House, gardens, and gallery Bs10, including an English (M-F 5:30pm, Sa 11:30am) or Spanish (M-F 5pm, Sa 11am) guide.)*

CHURCHES. Although Cochabamba is not known for its churches, a few stand out from the rest. The **Convento de Santa Teresa,** on the small plaza near the corner of Baptista and Ecuador, is perhaps the most elaborate, with a golden sunburst pattern at the head of the church and an ornate, buttercup-like lectern. *(Open for mass daily at 8am; visitors are only allowed in the convent itself during Easter week, and for the occasional saints day.)* The **Catedral Metropolitana,** the largest church in Cochabamba, at the southeast corner of the Plaza 14 de Septiembre, features a large, wooden grotto dedicated to the Virgin Mary as well as a high, domed ceiling with frescoes of Christ's life. It's best to visit early in the morning; mass begins at 8am and services continue for one or two hours depending on the day. The **Convento de San Francisco,** on the northeast corner of 25 de Mayo and Bolívar, also worth a visit, was founded in 1581, declared a national monument in 1967, and housed Pope John Paul II in 1988. *(Covent open to visitors Easter week; church open M-F 7:30-11am.)*

MARKETS. Cochabamba's three largest markets are all south of the Plaza 14 de Septiembre. At the intersection of 25 de Mayo and Jordan, you'll find hordes of **food vendors.** Locals often refer to *la cancha;* in reality, there are two canchas with different names. **La Cancha de Calatayud,** located between Uruguay to the north, Aroma to the south, Lanza to the east, and San Martín to the west, and **La Cancha de San Antonio,** situated along Punata and Tarata, sell everything from chicken feet to top hats. An **artisan's market** cuts through the block to the northwest of the Plaza 14 de Septiembre, with entrances on Heroínas to the north and General Achá to the south. Here you'll find leather and silver work and the occasional bookseller.

FESTIVALS

The **Fiesta de la Virgen de Urkupiña** takes place in Quillacollo August 14-16th, and floods the entire Cochabamba region with tourists and visitors. The first day consists of an *entrada*, with over 40 *fraternidades folklóricas* dancing down Ramon Prada, doubling back on Martín Cárdenas, and ending up near the Plaza 15 de Agosto. The procession takes over eight hours from start to finish. The 2nd day is spent praying and participating in religious services, while the last day marks the *calvario*, when *campesinos* dig up rocks from a specific location, symbolizing prosperity. On the **14 de Septiembre**, Cochabamba celebrates its anniversary with a parade led by the President of Bolivia. **The Corso de Corsos**, on the Sunday following Ash Wednesday, is marked by a similar parade.

ENTERTAINMENT

Major events in Cochabamba are publicized on the painted murals that hang outside the **Casa de la Cultura** (northeast corner of 25 de Mayo) and the **Teatro Achá** (see below), or in *Los Tiempos*, Cochabamba's daily paper (M-Sa Bs 3, Su Bs5).

TEATRO ACHÁ. A convent during colonial times, in 1860 this building was converted into a small but elegant theater. It usually features local groups, but has hosted some big names, including the Moscow Ballet Company. (España S-0130, on the southwest corner of España and Heroínas; the entrance is on España. ☎258 054. Tickets Bs15-25. Box office open M-Su 3-8pm.)

GALERIA GILDARO ANTEZANA. See the painting, then meet the painter. There is no sign above the door, so just walk right in; with your back to the cathedral, it is the last door on your right. Almost every night, regional artists and art critics sit and chat; anyone is free to join them. Exhibitions change every two weeks. Every September 14, national artists submit their work to Cochabamba's national painting competition. The winning works are displayed here before moving to Casa de la Cultura. (On the north side of the Plaza 14 de Septiembre at the intersection of Bolívar and E. Arce. ☎227 561. Gallery open M-F 9am-noon and 3-9pm.)

FÚTBOL. The local soccer team, **Wilsterman**, is fairly popular around town; matches are usually held Saturdays and Sundays at the **Félix Capriles stadium.** (Tickets Bs15-35; go early to avoid long lines. Call *Los Tiempos* (☎254 561) for dates and times of upcoming matches.)

MOVIE THEATERS. Those in Cochabamba often show foreign flicks, which usually arrive at least a couple of months after their US releases (3 per day; 2:30, 6:30, and 9:30pm; Bs8-17). Try **Cine Astor**, Sucre, just east of the intersection with 25 de Mayo; or **Cine Avaroa** (☎221 285), on 25 de Mayo between Jordan and Calama.

NIGHTLIFE

Many warm up before their nocturnal exploits at one of the stylish cafes that line España. From there, a little jazz? Merengue? And hey, how about a little booty?

Automanía (☎286 383), northwest corner of Pando and Buenos Aires. Car racing has never been so young, hip, and booty-shakin' sexy. Drinks (Bs20-25) are named after prominent regional car racers. Arrive early. Cover F-Sa men Bs10; no cover for women. Open M-Sa 9am-2:30am.

Metrópolis (☎323 118), España and Ecuador. The place to loosen up with a *pisco sour* (Bs15) before hitting the clubs. Packed on weekend nights. Open M-Su 8am-2am.

Las Planchitas Originales (☎238 281), off a dirt road to the south of Laguna Alay; take a taxi (Bs4) and ask for Las Planchitas or "El Campo Ferial." Loud music, crowded dancing, and tons of food (F-Sa). Th karaoke, Su *música folklórica*. No cover. Open M-Th 11am-11pm, F-Su 11am-2am.

Trocadero Jazz Club, Paseo Boulevard 616 (☎224 901), next to the Casa de Campo. Watch young Cochabambino professionals let loose after a long day and maybe grab a Coltrane (vodka and grenadine) before they call it a night. Jazz drinks Bs20-25; women's drinks Bs20-22. Live music Th-Sa keeps it hopping. Open Th-Sa nights.

DAYTRIPS FROM COCHABAMBA

TARATA

Trufis leave for Tarata from the north side of Barrientos near the intersections with 6 de Agosto (30min., Bs3.5) and return from Leonidas Rojas (every 15min. until 7pm).

Located 33km southeast of Cochabamba, Tarata's appeal is historical. Just off the main square stands the neoclassical **Iglesia de San Pedro,** where the **ashes of Esteban Arce,** a Bolivian revolutionary martyr, are interred. A walk to the nearby **Iglesia and Convento de San José** affords a quick tour of town, passing some of Tarata's colonial architecture. From the main plaza, turn right at the Farmacia Vallejos II, walk down one block, and hang a left onto a tree-lined street. To get to the convent, turn right at the bridge. Going toward the convent, the path will bend to the left, and when you see a street on your right leading uphill to an orange building, take it to the top. The convent is open for visitors until noon; highlights of the convent tour include the tiny cell in which one priest elected to spend his entire life. The adjacent church contains a shrine to Tarata's patron saint, Severino.

QUILLACOLLO

Micros or trufis from Cochabamba deposit passengers at the north end of the Plaza Bolívar; you'll want to walk down Héroes del Chaco toward the more relaxed Plaza 15 de Agosto, near the church.

The **church,** at the far end of the Plaza 15 de Agosto, houses a **shrine to the Virgen de Urkupiña.** Here, devotees come every morning to pray, light a candle, or add a plaque thanking the Virgin for her support. Over the years, the entire front wall has been covered in these plaques; even Cochabamba's Wilsterman soccer team has placed two or three plaques, thanking the Virgin for helping them qualify for the Copa de Libertadores soccer tournament. (Open mornings for mass, but it's best to visit M-F 8-9am, when there are no scheduled services.) Every year from August 14-16th, people flock to Quillacollo during the **Fiesta de la Virgen de Urkupiña** to see the dancing *entrada* of the *grupos folklóricos,* the subsequent exposition of the statue of the Virgen, and the ceremonial *calvario,* a symbolic digging of rocks in hope of future wealth on the final day.

VILLA ALBINA

Trufi 211, which can be caught along with the other Vinto trufis in Quillacollo or at the corner of Albina Patiño and the road from Quillacollo, will drop those who ask a few meters away from the entrance (Bs1). ☎260 083. Tours M-F 3pm. Call ahead to make arrangements to see other parts of the estate, such as the gardens or the harvesting center.

The former *hacienda* of tin baron Simon Patiño and a **National Monument of Bolivia,** ▨Villa Albina is a testament to the wealth and power of one man. Compared to Villa Albino, Palacio Portales (Patiño's Cochabamba house) is small potatoes. A guided tour of the residence, built from 1920 to 1928, takes guests through the lower level of the mansion, carefully tended gardens dotted by shapely marble statues, and an island pagoda situated on a small artificial pond.

SIPE SIPE

From Cochabamba, take trufi 245 from the intersection of República and 6 de Agosto; it will drop you off at the Plaza 14 de Septiembre (30min., Bs4). For travel info, contact the Office of Human Development and Communication (☎260 932). Cabaña: Take trufi 245 past Sipe Sipe. Reservations required. Open F-Su. Rooms US$27 per person.)

Sipe Sipe, 29km from Cochabamba, got its name from the Sipisipis, a tribe that once inhabited the region. The city is struggling to make a tourist business out of the nearby Inkarakay ruins. The scenic path to the ruins, said to rival the site itself, takes 45 minutes by car and 2½ hours on foot. A trip to Inkarakay is best made with a knowledgeable guide, as the trail becomes unclear at times.

Every 21st of July, *grupos folklóricos* reenact what are supposed to be ancient Inca rites at the site of the ruins. To catch a glimpse of the proceedings, get up before dawn and hike the trail in time to reach the ruins by 7am; the ceremonies are memorable and include the ritual sacrifice of a llama.

Farther from Sipe Sipe is the **Cabaña de la Torre resort,** on Km32 of the Carretera Confital (the road that passes through Quillacollo and Vinto). With thermal spring baths, tennis courts, soccer fields, hiking trails, and a wood-and-wire footbridge spanning a nearby stream, the resort provides all facilities necessary to entertain a large, hyperactive family.

NEAR COCHABAMBA: PARQUE NACIONAL TUNARI

By car, head north on Paseo El Prado in Cochabamba and continue north on Libertador Simón Bolívar. At the Plaza Guzman, take Atahuallpa until you reach the Circunvalación Beijing. From there, take a left on Shakespeare, after passing Francisco de Quevedo on your left; take Shakespeare to the top. By micro/trufi, take either trufi 35 (Bs1.5) or micro ÑZ (Bs1.40) going north on San Martín; either will take you to the entrance of the park. For more info on the park contact Forest Ranger Manuel Savedra (☎ 242 688). Open daily 8am-4pm. Free; Bs10 to bring in a car.

Created in 1962 to protect a small sliver of forest north of Cochabamba, Parque Nacional Tunari has expanded to include 300,000 hectares, including the massive 5200m **Cerro Tunari.** The parts of the park that are now open to tourists contain trails affording dizzying views of Cochabamba below. Other parts of the park are occasionally used, somewhat illegally, for rapelling or hang-gliding expeditions.

The most popular and easily accessible portion of the park is a 10km trail that rises steadily higher as it continues north. To reach the trailhead, walk along the dirt road from the main entrance of the park. At one point, the major road will turn left, between two walls. Do not take this road; instead, keep straight along the smaller road. After 1½km, you will come to a *tranca,* or guardhouse. The trail begins at the wooden footbridge just past the *tranca.*

NEAR COCHABAMBA: VILLA TUNARI

With no terminal in town, if you're planning on going to Santa Cruz (7-8hr., 10am-12:30pm and midnight-dawn, Bs25), it's best to wait at the tollbooth—at the southwest end of the highway near the hospital—for the next bus. Transporte 7 de Junio has micros to Cochabamba (4hr.; M-Sa 8:30, 11am, 6pm, Su 1pm; Bs18).

Villa Tunari is gearing up to become a tourist town. The nearby **Carrasco National Park** is busy expanding its tours and services, and rumors abound with plans for a mega-hotel across the river. At present, though, there isn't much else to see but the jungle and wildlife; a visit to the nearby **Inti Wari Yassi Community** wildlife refuge is worth spending the night here. Hostels are clustered around the highway, and along Beni and Santa Cruz in the area north of the highway before it crosses the river Espíritu Santo. **Hotel Pilunchi** (☎ 114 164) sits at the end of Benigno Paz near the intersection with Beni. The cheapest and most colorful place in town. Rooms Bs10 per person; hot water Bs5. **Hostal Valle Grande,** at the corner of Pando and the highway, has triples (Bs45), and doubles (Bs30; with bath Bs60).

NEAR VILLA TUNARI: INTI WARA YASSI COMMUNITY

To get to Parque Machía, walk or take a cab across the bridge on the east side of Villa Tunari; the trail to the entrance is about 100m past the bridge, on the left. The park is open 9am-5:30pm; if the ranger is present you may have to pay a Bs2.5 entrance fee.

Covering only 36 acres and offering a mere 3½km of ecological trails, Parque Machía is definitely not one of the largest or most impressive of Cochabamba's parks. However, tucked in a little corner of the nature preserve is the Inti Wara Yassi Community refuge for wild animals. Working in cooperation with Bolivian law enforcement officials, this organization rescues animals taken illegally from the wild and reintroduces them into their natural habitats.

A visit to the facility is unforgetable. Within minutes of hitting the trail visitors can expect to be approached by a monkey or other creature eager to make friends. Among the guests of the Inti Wara Yassi are capuchin monkeys, spider monkeys, squirrel monkeys, toucans, parrots, eagles, a nutria, one anaconda, and a puma. A 3km ecological trail runs through a portion of the park, passing by the aviary. The park also has some other trails, but as any community volunteer will tell you, "those aren't protected from the puma." (Visitors are charged Bs15 for use of a still camera and Bs25 for use of a video camera.)

The center is open M-Sa 9am-5:30pm; it is also possible to volunteer for a minimum of 15 days. Community volunteers feed the animals, maintain the trails and perform general chores. Volunteers have access to a room in the volunteer lodging house (bed Bs15, tent Bs5). Those interested should present themselves to the Inti Wara Yassi director, Don Juan Carlos, early in the morning.

NEAR COCHABAMBA: INCALLAJTA

Reaching Incallajta can be quite difficult and expensive without private transportation. One micro leaves from Cochabamba for Pocona, about 20km from the ruins (Sa 1pm, Bs25). Taxis return to Cochabamba from Pocona (2am and about noon, Bs25). If conquering the road by car, a 4x4 is best (and essential during the rainy season).

Cochabamba's most important archeological site, Incallajta (city of the Inca) has often been ignored by scholars, the Bolivian government, and tourists. However, this remote site 130km east of Cochabamba contains a number of significant ruins, including the remains of a large stone building, probably the grand temple, and an astronomical observatory. Discovered in 1917 by Swedish ethnologist Erland Nordenskjöld, the site didn't become a center of academic research until the 1960s. For the casual traveler, this means unspoiled exploration, surrounded only by local people and hillside potato fields. The ruins most likely served a military function, defending Pocona from the fierce, man-eating Chiriguanas tribe and guarding the Inca Empire's southern flank. Local *campesinos* host an **Incallajta festival** on December 21 every year.

The closest place to sleep is in **Pocona,** about 20km from the ruins. However, a number of flat **campsites** can be found right around the ruins with easy access to the river below. Pocona, about 20km from the ruins, sells food and water in addition to housing a simple *alojamiento.* For more detailed information and a good site-map, check out either Jesús Larga's original study, *Inkallajta-Inkaraqay* (US$4), or Roy Querejazu Lewis' catalogue of research, *Incallajta y la Conquista Incaica del Collasuyu* (US$18), both available from the Los Libros del Amigo bookstore on the corner of Héroine and España in Cochabamba (see p. 375).

NEAR COCHABAMBA: TOTORA

Micros and buses leave for Totora from the intersection of República and 6 de Agosto, toward the southern end of the Cochabamba. Take one headed directly to Totora or to Aiquile (3hr.: 4 per day 1-3:30pm; return 3, 4, 6am and 10-10:15pm; Bs8).

The colonial town of Totora, characterized by red roofs and a plaza surrounded by blue arched buildings, was hit hard by a September 1998 earthquake measuring 7 on the Richter scale. The town has been slow to recover; although reconstruction continues, many edifices remain empty and crumbling. Originally founded as the Spaniards' gateway into the jungle, the town served as the administrative center for the region's coca (for the Potosí miners), coffee, and sugar cane operations. The only place to sleep, and one of the best places to eat, is in the **Residencial Colonial,** just south of the plaza. Huge rooms above the restaurant could shelter all Totora. (Rooms Bs15 per person.)

NEAR COCHABAMBA: MIZQUE

Buses leave from Cochabamba at República and 6 de Agosto (3½hr., noon, Bs15). From Mizque, buses return to Cochabamba (3pm, M 7pm, Tu 8am, F 8am and 7pm). Buses from Mizque run to Aiquile (1hr.; noon, 5, 7pm; Bs5). The two bus companies are on the plaza and 1 block away toward the market.

Mizque's location at the confluence of the Ríos Mizque and Tucana in the fertile Tucana valley accounts for the area's eye-popping plant life. Dark purple blossoms cascade off terraces lining the main plaza. The hills around town make hikes in search of Inca ruins very pleasant. Mizque is also one of the best places to see macaws soar over the soft rolling hills. The best place to stay is **Residencial Mizque,** two blocks from the market toward the road to Aiquile. (☎ 115 071. Singles Bs15; doubles Bs30; triples Bs45). Right on the plaza, **Residencial Plaza**, which doubles as a restaurant (lunch Bs6), has new, clean rooms. (Singles Bs15; doubles Bs30.)

AIQUILE

Halfway between Sucre and Cochabamba in the dry valley area (2242m), Aiquile's claim to fame is its status as home of the *charango*, a tiny guitar-like instrument found only in Bolivia and usually traced back to this town. Like Totora, Aiquile was hit hard by the September 1998 earthquake.

Buses run to: **Cochabamba** (6hr., 2 and 11am, Bs15); **Sucre** (5hr., 1 and 2am, Bs15); and **Santa Cruz** (12hr., 9 and 9:30pm, Bs30), all leave from offices along Bolívar. The town spreads north and south along **Bolívar;** the **main plaza** lies one block east of Bolívar on the first street on the north side (toward Cochabamba).

Banco Santa Cruz, one block east of Bolívar near the doctor's office, exchanges dollars for *bolivianos*. (☎ 114 938. Open M-F 8:30-11:30am and 2:30-5pm.) The **police station** (☎ 115 015) is 2 blocks north (toward Cochabamba) of the main plaza. The **Centro Medico Maria del Carmen,** on Bolívar, is marked with a large red cross. (Open daily 8am-noon and 2-8pm; 24 hr. for emergencies.) The **Farmacia Virgen de Copacabana** is just across the street (Open 24 hr.). A block up toward Cochabamba on Bolívar is the basic **post office**. (Open M-Sa 8am-8pm.) **ENTEL** is nearby on Bolívar. (☎ 114 927, 114 926, 115 026; Open daily 7am-10pm.)

Hotel los Escudos, on the northernmost end of Bolívar (toward Cochabamba), boasts the cleanest bathrooms with hot water, although the rooms do smell a bit musty. (Singles Bs20; doubles Bs40; triples Bs60.) Next door, **Alojamiento Italia** is a slightly cheaper option, located in the back of a woman's home. You probably won't want to spend too much time in the bathroom. A few cheap eateries sit toward the southern, Sucre end of Bolívar.

To buy a **charango,** check out the several shops on Bolívar and adjacent streets. Depending on quality of sound and detail of carvings, the instruments will run between Bs180-200 and about Bs250 for the more ornate, inlaid designs. The shell, now made of local woods, used to be constructed from an armadillo shell (before the armadillo became endangered). During the festival of **All Saints' Week,** beginning November 2 each year, Aiquile holds a **Feria of the Charango.** Also notable is the week beginning February 2, devoted to the **Virgin of Candelaría.**

PARQUE NACIONAL TOROTORO

Covering 162 sq. km of jagged peaks and deep ravines interspersed with crashing waterfalls, the valley of Torotoro offers a little bit of everything. The region of Torotoro, originally inhabited by the Aymara Indians, was incorporated into the Inca Empire and settled by Quechua-speaking conquerors. When the Spanish came looking for gold, they forced the Quechua into slavery. Ironically, when the Republicans arrived hundreds of years later, they too exploited the region's inhabitants as a free source of labor. In 1952 government-sponsored agrarian reform returned the land to the *campesinos*. Modernization has come slowly to Torotoro; until recently the region was inaccessible for much of the year. Electricity and a lone ENTEL telephone are other recent arrivals. In July 1989, a presidential decree officially founded Torotoro National Park. The village of Torotoro, at the head of the valley, makes an ideal springboard for exploring the park.

🖪 🔁 TRANSPORTATION AND PRACTICAL INFORMATION

Now that the roads leading to Torotoro have improved, the trip there is no longer a day-long bus trek. Getting there by private transportation or by a micro is feasible, so long as you don't mind the bumps in the road. To get to the park from Cochabamba, hop one of the few **buses** to Santa Cruz that take the old road through Tolata (7-8hr., M and F 6am, Bs15). To get to the Park by car (a 4X4, that is), take the same old road to Santa Cruz until about 30km before Tolata. From there, turn onto the road going south to Cliza; the park is 60km away just past the village of Anzaldo. It is also possible to fly in to the park (US$120). Contact **Don Eugenio Ferguson** (☎ 227 042 or 246 289) for more info.

It is not necessary to sign on with a private tour company to get the most from Torotoro. Hiring a local **guide** (which is what the tour operators will do anyway) is straightforward (Bs10 per person, min. 5 people). The director of tourism, Johnny Torrico Nogalus (☎ Torotoro (04) 113 927, Cochabamba (01) 731 639), speaks English and leads tours. Mr. Nogalus can also arrange trips with other guides. Technically speaking there are only a few spots in the park that can only be visited with a guide (including the Humangalanta Caverns and the El Vergel canyon) but guides are highly recommended; the few dollars you'll spend will make a world of difference in your understanding of the park and in insuring that you don't get lost. Travelers bent on going through a tour operator can contact Fremen Tours or Caixa Tours in Cochabamba. There is a one-time Bs20 entrance fee to the park.

There are technically three hostels in Torotoro. Only one, **Hostal Charcas,** has bathrooms and is open throughout the year. (☎ (04) 113 927. Rooms Bs10 per person.) Upon arrival, ask about the status of the other two, **Alojamiento Trinidad** and **Alojamiento Humajalanta**—when open, they are even cheaper. There are **no restaurants** in the area, but stores in Torotoro stock crackers, make sandwiches, and will cook for guests upon request. Families, particularly those who own shops, will invite visitors to join them for dinner (about Bs5).

🖸 SIGHTS

THE HUMAJALANTA CAVERNS. You will need a guide to enter the caverns, which lie about 10km southwest of the village. The path to the caverns begins at the top of the hill to the west of town off Santa Barbara. Along the way the trail crosses three dry stream beds and passes several dinosaur footprints. After 7km, you will see the Wayra Q'asa (or "Broken Wind") school on the right (north) side, recognizable for its shiny metallic roof. Continue along the road for another 1km. Here the path become less distinct. Looking at the mountains to the southwest, count in from the peaks on your right. You'll see a small peak to your farthest right, a larger peak to the left of it, and an even smaller pyramidical peak to the left of that. Continue towards the valley between the second and third peaks from your right. Walk southwest, cross two small, dry red clay riverbeds; climb a hill to the top of the valley, and stairs will lead you down to the cavern. Bring a strong flashlight or headlamp (no candles or torches allowed), and extra batteries.

EL VERGEL. Four kilometers northwest of town, El Vergel is legally accessible only through a guide. The path to El Vergel, which descends into a canyon, is steep and treacherous. Once in El Vergel, you'll see a series of small waterfalls and adjacent pools. Immediately before you reach El Vergel, you'll come to a point in the stream where you can see the edges of three different canyons in the distance.

PINTURAS RUPESTRES. The rock paintings, believed to date as far back as two thousand years, were made by the Aymara Indians on two panels of a wall adjacent to a stream. To get there, go directly north of town until you find a river. Continue downstream for 2km. Eventually, you'll see several stacked rock walls on the left bank. Climb to the side opposite this wall, and you'll see the small but distinct cave paintings. Some guides believe that the jagged zig-zag line that suddenly drops at its end resembles a sort of primitive map of the mountain range in the region. The rest, which consists of some sunburst patterns as well as other squiggly lines, is open to much speculation.

DINOSAUR FOOTPRINTS. Aside from the examples that lie en route to Humajal-anta, the next clearest specimens are just across town, and are even visible from the roof of the Alojamiento Charcas. Take the northeast path out of town, and where the road crosses the river, climb a few meters up the slope. The footprints are large and clearly visible. These prints are believed to have been made by a member of the Brontosaurus family. New prints are found every few months, when the mudslides or erosion of the wet season expose previously unseen bedrock. These discoveries have often been made during tours themselves; Torotoro is by no means fully charted territory. There are additional fossils south of the village near the Cerro de Siete Vueltas, or "hill of seven turns."

THE LLAMA CHAQUI RUINS. Archeologists believe that the two thousand year old Llama Chaqui ruins are the remains of a large military outpost. Although only the foundation remains, the fortress would have afforded a commanding position over the river valley below. The ruins are not easy to find. You must first walk 2km to the southeast, around the base of the Cerro. Once at the base of the eastern face, it's a 17km trudge to the top.

EASTERN BOLIVIA

SANTA CRUZ ☎03

Paceños (people from La Paz) and *cruceños* (those from Santa Cruz) will forever debate whose city is bigger or more central to the economy. In reality, any taxi driver puts it best: "Santa Cruz—now *that's* a city." The facts may say it even better: sitting at an easy-breathing 470m above sea level and bursting with 1,200,000 inhabitants, Santa Cruz is rapidly shedding its Andean roots. Here, the average person is more likely than his La Paz counterpart to know the going conversion rate for a dollar, and store owners always know what the competition is charging. Even the clouds move faster than normal—strong southern winds, known as *surazos*, hit the city cold and hard during the winter. Santa Cruz de la Sierra, as it is formally known, was founded in 1561 by Spaniard Ñoflo de Chavez. Economically, the Santa Cruz region benefits from large mineral and petroleum reserves as well as from very strong agricultural production. The *avión pirata*, a plane abandoned by drug smugglers, still sits in a city field—a sober reminder that Santa Cruz has also been home to a far more dangerous industry: cocaine.

⌨ TRANSPORTATION

Airport: Viru Viru Int'l Airport (☎852 400), 17km north of the city center. Take a taxi (15min., Bs40), or a micro (20-30min., Bs4.5), which leave direct for the airport every 20min. from the main bus terminal (at the intersection of Cañoto and Irala). The airport has an ENTEL station, car rental agencies, and luggage storage facilities. There's an **airport tax for foreigners**—Bs10 for national flights and US$25 for international flights.

Airlines: Aerolineas Argentinas (☎339 776), on Junín at the Plaza 24 de Septiembre, has 2 flights to **Buenos Aires** (4hr., US$249). AeroSur, Irala 616 (☎0800 30 30), serves: **La Paz** (55min., 3-4 per day, Bs643); **Cochabamba** (45min.; M-Sa 2 per day, 1 on Su; Bs377); and **Sucre** (35min., 2-3 per day, Bs643), as well as **Tarija, Trinidad, Cobija,** and **Puerto Suárez.** American Airlines, Beni 167 (☎341 314), between Avenales and Bolívar, goes to **Miami** (6hr.40min., 2 per day, US$425). Lloyd Aereo Boliviano, Warnes corner of Chuquisaca (☎344 625, info/reservations ☎0800 30 01), to: **La Paz** (55min., 3-4 per day, Bs643); **Cochabamba** (45min., 3 per day, Bs377); **Sucre** (35min., 1 per morning, Bs402); **Trinidad** and **Tarija,** both one flight per day. TAM Mercosur (☎371 999), to **Asunción** (2hr.; M, W, and Sa 3:30pm; US$217). Varig, Celso Castedo No. 329 (☎349 333), to **São Paulo** (30min., M-Sa 3:50pm, US$322).

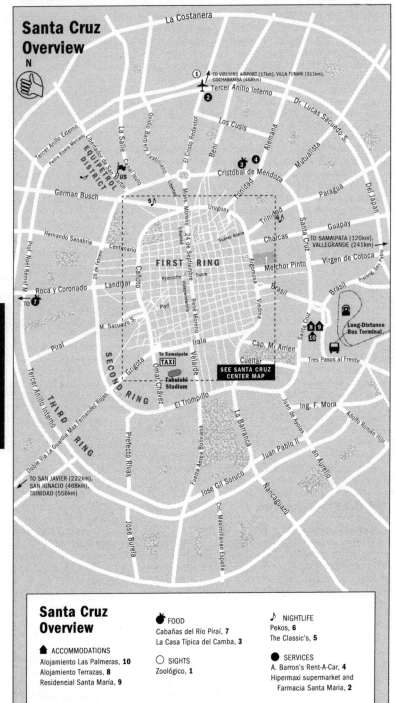

Santa Cruz
Overview

N

La Costanera

TO VIRUVIRU AIRPORT (17km), VILLA TUNARI (311km), COCHABAMBA (468km)

Tercer Anillo Interno

Dr. Lucas Sacuedo S.

Los Cusis

Tercer Anillo Externo

Pedro Rivera Mercado

Liberilso de San Martin

La Salle

Ovidio Barea

Justiniano

El Cristo Redentor

Beni

Alemana

Mutualista

EQUIPETROL
DISTRICT

Canal Isuto

Uberici

Cristóbal de Mendoza

Trinidad

Paragua

Del Jaban

German Busch

Mons. Moreno

Uruguay

Suárez Arana

Charcas

Trinidad

Santa Cruz

Guapay

TO SAMAIPATA (120km), VALLEGRANDE (241km)

Hernando Sanabria

Centenario

24 de Septiembre

Liberid

FIRST RING

Melchor Pinto

Virgen de Cotoca

Roca y Coronado

28 de Febrero

Landivar

Cañoto

Ayacucho

Suere

Independencia

Rene Moreno

Viedma

Argamosa

Brasil

Brasil

TO 7

M. Sacuedo S.

Pari

Irala

Santa Cruz

Long-Distance
Bus Terminal

Prolong. San Aurelio

Piral

Grigota

Omai Chávez

Velarde

Cap. M. Arrien

Cuellar

Tres Pasos al Frente

SECOND RING

To Samaipata
TAXI

Tahuichi
Stadium

El Trompillo

SEE SANTA CRUZ
CENTER MAP

Ing. F. Mora

Doble Via La Guardia

Max Fernandez Rojas

THIRD RING

Tercer Anillo Interno

Prefecto Rivas

Fuerza Aerea Boliviana

La Barranca

Juan de Ayolas

Juan Pablo II

an Aurelio

Adolfo Román Hijo

TO SAN JAVIER (222km), SAN IGNACIO (468km), TRINIDAD (556km)

Jose Gil Soruco

Rancaguari

Jose Bureia

Cnl. Maximiliano España

Santa Cruz
Overview

🏠 **ACCOMMODATIONS**
Alojamiento Las Palmeras, **10**
Alojamiento Terrazas, **8**
Residencial Santa María, **9**

🍎 FOOD
Cabañas del Río Piraí, **7**
La Casa Típica del Camba, **3**

◯ SIGHTS
Zoológico, **1**

♪ NIGHTLIFE
Pekos, **6**
The Classic's, **5**

⬤ SERVICES
A. Barron's Rent-A-Car, **4**
Hipermaxi supermarket and
Farmacia Santa Maria, **2**

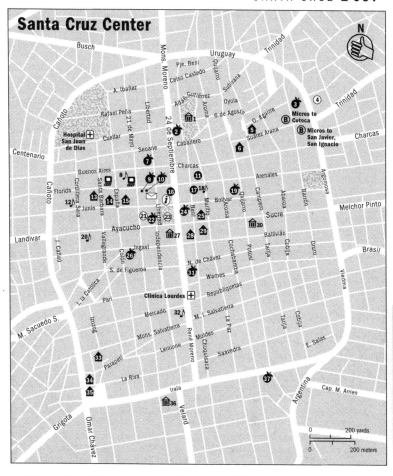

Santa Cruz Center

🏠 ACCOMMODATIONS
Alojamiento Acre, **5**
Alojamiento Los Angeles, **6**
Alojamiento Oriente, **13**
Alojamiento Santa Barbara, **14**
Hotel Bibosi, **15**
Hotel La Paz, **25**
Residencial Ballivián, **29**
Residencial Beni, **28**
Residencial Bolívar, **33**
Residencial Las Palmeras, **34**
Residencial Royal's, **35**

🍎 FOOD
Café Victory, **3**
Club Social 24 de Septiembre, **2**
El Galeón Peruano, **7**
Irish Pub (Café Irlandés), **9**
Los Lomitos, **10**
Mandarin, **19**
Restaurant Vegetariano, **22**
Rincón Brasilero, **24**
Super Extra, **26**
Super Florida, **31**
Tabernet Pizzeria, **37**

🏛 MUSEUMS
Museo de Arte Contemporaneo, **1**
Museo de Arte Religioso, **27**
Museo de Historia Natural Noel Kempff
  Mercado, **30**
Museo Etno-Folklórico and Parque Arenal, **36**

◯ SIGHTS
Avión Pirata, **4**
Casa de la Cultura Raúl Otero
  Reiche, **21**
Plaza 24 de Septiembre, **23**

♪ NIGHTLIFE
Café Kafé, **8**
Clapton's Club de Blues, **12**
El Muro, **20**
Insomnia, **18**
La Vitrola Pub, **32**

● SERVICES
Aby's Rent-A-Car, **11**
Rosario Tours, **17**
Todo Para Camping, **16**

Trains: The **train station** (☎463 388) is located at the end of Brasil, if you're traveling east from the first *anillo*. Micro #20 (Bs1.50), caught going north on Cañoto near the bus station, will drop you off at the front door. Ticket office open M-F 8am-noon, 2:30-6pm, Sa 8am-noon, 2:30-3:30pm. **Ferrobuz** sells tickets Su 4-7pm. Passports required to purchase a ticket. Classes are pullman, first, and second; and ferrobuz trains, which all provide breakfast, A/C, and dinner (and travel much faster than normal trains), are divided into *cama* and *semi-cama*—bed and semi-bed. To **Quijarro** (border with Brazil) via **normal** trains (18hr., 3:30pm, Bs42), via **ferrobuz** (12hr.; Tu, Th, and Sa 7pm; Bs205). To **Yacuiba**, Argentina (15hr.; M, W, and F 5pm; Bs36).

Long-Distance Buses: The terminal (☎340 772) is next to the train station. **Bolívar** (☎350 762), **Bolivia** (☎329 791), **Copacabana** (☎542 149), **Trans Copacabana** (☎362 057), and **El Dorado** (☎341 197) are the most popular lines. To: **Cochabamba** (12hr.; 7-9am and 5-9:30pm; Bs40); **La Paz** (18hr.; 7:30-9:30am and 5:30-7:30pm; Bs60); **Copacabana** (direct bus-cama; 15hr.; Bs70); **Sucre** (16hr.; 7:30-9:30am and 5-6pm; Bs40, bus-cama Bs60). Buses to **Torotoro** leave from the intersection of 6 de Agosto and República (7-8hr., Th and Su 6am, Bs15).

International buses: Flechabus Panamericana goes to **Buenos Aires, Argentina** (36hr., 5pm, US$90-100). Trans Bolpar (☎335 533) goes to **Aunción, Paraguay** (28hr.; Tu, Th, and Sa 7pm; US$60, includes breakfast, lunch, and drinks). Stel Turismo (☎378 706) to: **Asunción, Paraguay** (26-30hr.; W 6pm, Su 1pm; bus-cama US$75).

Local buses: Trufi-taxis leave for **Samaipata** from the corner of Omar Chavez and S. de Olguin when full (2hr., Bs15). Micros leave every 10-20min. for **Cotoca** from the corner of Suárez Arana and Barrón (40min., Bs2.50). To **San Javier,** micros leave from the opposite corner of Suárez Arana and Barrón (4hr., 4 per day, Bs25). To **San Ignacio** from the same corner (12hr., 6:30pm, Bs40).

Local Transportation: Local micros go everywhere (6am-10pm, sometimes later). Standard fare Bs1.50. To find out exactly which micros go where, buy a *Guía Santa Cruz* (Bs40); or just ask around. Micros are both numbered and labeled by destination.

Taxis: Any taxi ride from one destination in the first ring to another destination within the first ring is Bs5. From first ring to second, it's Bs6; from first to third, Bs7 and so on. A taxi to the airport costs Bs40; micros are a cheaper option. Rates may change with luggage or number of passengers. Radio taxi service is ubiquitous; try **Radio Movil America** (☎422 222) or **Radio Movil El Tucan** (☎333 222), respectively.

Car Rental: Rental places in Santa Cruz tend to have very similar prices. **A. Barron's,** Alemania No. 50 (☎420 160; fax 423 439; cel. 013 97511), on the corner of Tajibos just past the second ring, has a wide selection of vehicles starting at US$60 per day for a jeep; prices include 130km per day, taxes, and insurance. **Across Rent-A-Car** (☎852 190) and **Localiza** (☎852 418), both with offices at Viru Viru Airport, charge per km, often a better deal for shorter distances. Minimum age 25, passport, driver's license, and credit card (or cash deposit) required.

✦ 🔽 ORIENTATION AND PRACTICAL INFORMATION

Santa Cruz is one of the only cities in the world arranged in **concentric rings** (*anillos*). The original city structure, devised by a Brazilian designer in the 1800s, arranged the city into four quadrants, divided by two main roads. Unfortunately, as the city grew, so did the number of rings—up to 8 or 9 in some cases, though most places of interest to tourists lie within the first few rings. It's customary to give an address by saying the radial street, plus the two rings that the location lies between (i.e. Suárez Arana between the 1st and 2nd *anillos*). Street names downtown change after crossing the central streets they are perpendicular to. All east-west streets change after crossing the main north-south road, **René Moreno/24 de Septiembre,** and north-south streets change names after crossing the main east-west street, **Ayacucho/Sucre.** Many accommodations, restaurants, services, and sights are concentrated around **Plaza 24 de Septiembre,** the central plaza. The tourist information office on the main plaza issues maps (see below). RC Publicidad Ltda. publishes a good *City Guide Multiplano Santa Cruz*, free with any purchase at the Café Irlandés (see Food, p. 390). The *Guía Santa Cruz* (Bs40) contains detailed maps of the city, plenty of tourist info, and a list of micro numbers and their destinations.

TOURIST, FINANCIAL, AND LOCAL SERVICES

Tourist Office: Prefectura de la Municipalidad (☎369 595 ext. 41), on the north side of Plaza 24 de Septiembre. Dispenses maps and useful advice. Open M-F 8am-4pm.

Tour Agencies: Rosario Tours (☎369 977), on the corner of Arenales and Murillo, with subsidiaries in Sucre and La Paz, offers tours to: Samaipata (2-day tour US$137 per person for 4-7 people); Cotoca (half-day tour US$19 per person for 3-7 people); the Jesuit missions (2-day tour US$195 per person for 4-7 people); and the Parque Amboró (2-day tour US$135 per person for 4-7 people). **Neblina Forest-Bolivia,** Mojos No. 246 (☎336 831), is one of the few outfits that regularly offer trips to Noel Kempff Mercado National Park. **Forest Tour Operator** (☎372 042), on Cuellar between Libertad and 24 de Septiembre, offers longer tours to destinations both traditional (Amboró, Jesuit missions, etc.) and novel (Lago Rogaguado, Piso Firme). **Viru Viru Travel** (☎364 040), on Ballivían at the corner of Chuquisaca, specializes in international travel.

Camping Equipment: La Jara Caza y Pesca, Bolívar 458 (☎350 491). Open M-F 9am-1pm, 3-7pm, Sa 9am-1pm.

Markets: Los Pozos specializes in clothing and apparel. **Siete Calles** and **La Ramada** offer everything from haircuts to coca leaves (Bs38/kg).

Consulates: Argentina, Junín 22 (☎324 153). Open M-F 8am-2pm. **Brazil,** Busch 330 (☎344 400). Open 9am-3pm. **Chile,** Calle #5 Oeste 224, Equipetrol (☎434 372), open 8am-1pm. **Ecuador,** Velasco 700, Of. 301 (☎325 040). Open M-F 9am-6:30pm. **Paraguay,** Salvatierra 99, Esq. Chuquisaca, 1st fl., Of. 101. Open M-F 7:30am-1pm. **Peru,** Edificio Oriente, 2nd fl., Rm. 213 (☎434 940). Open M-F 8:30am-1:30pm. **US,** Guemes Este 6 (☎330 725), open M-F 9-11:30am.

Currency Exchange: Banco Santa Cruz (☎369 911), on the corner of Junín and 21 de Mayo, just off Plaza 24 de Septiembre, cashes AmEx traveler's checks (2% commission). **Citibank,** 140 René Moreno (☎340 211), cashes Citicorps traveler's checks.

American Express: Magri Turismo (☎345 663), on Warnes, corner of Potosí. Receives mail for American Express customers if sent to: *Recipient's name*, Magri Turismo Ltda., Warnes Esq. Potosí, P.O. Box 4438, Santa Cruz, Bolivia. Open M-F 8:30am-12:30pm and 2:30-6:30pm, Sa 8:30am-12:30pm.

English-Language Bookstore: Los Amigos del Libro, Ingavi 14 (☎327 937), between René Moreno and Independencia, sells magazines and a few paperbacks.

EMERGENCY AND COMMUNICATIONS

Emergency: ☎110.

Police: The **Policía de Turismo** (☎369 595) is at the Prefectura Departamental on the **Plaza 24 de Septiembre**. Open M-F 8am-4pm.

Pharmacy: Farmacia Santa Maria (☎372 352), at Irala and Vallegrande. Open 24hr.

Hospital: San Juan de Dios (☎332 222, emergency ☎118), corner of Santa Barbara and Cuellar, handles emergencies (consultation Bs24). Farther south, the **Clínica Lourdes,** René Moreno 352 (☎325 518), charges US$20 per consultation.

Telephones: ENTEL (☎350 055), on Warnes between Chuquisaca and René Moreno. Open daily 7:30am-11:30pm. One of the few places that permits calling card calls.

Internet Access: El Sitio Net, Santa Barbara 210 (☎ cel. (010) 18 642), on the corner of Florida. Bs7 per hr. Open daily 9am-11pm.

Post Office: On Junín near the corner of 21 de Mayo, off the Plaza 24 de Septiembre (☎347 445). Open M-F 8am-8pm, Sa 8am-6pm, Su 9am-noon.

▟ ACCOMMODATIONS

On average, accommodations here are more expensive and more likely to charge in dollars, but there are still plenty of good values to be found.

Residencial Ballivián (☎321 960), on Ballivián, between Chuquisaca and René Moreno. Very green, very bright, very spacious, and hey, Che Guevara once slept here. The neighborhood is close to the city center, but far enough to be calm and quiet. Bs30 per person; singles, doubles, triples, and quads available.

Residencial Bolívar (☎342 500), on the corner of Sucre and Beni. Clean, comfortable rooms, with hot water, hammocks, and the occasional toucan. Very popular with travelers. Quiet hours begin at 10pm, and the *residencial* is often full to capacity. Singles Bs45; doubles and triples US$6 per person. Call ahead for reservations.

Alojamiento Oriente, Junín 362 (☎321 976), on Junín between Santa Barbara and España. All rooms have fans during the hot season. Rooms with TV, bath, fans, and breakfast: singles (Bs50), doubles (Bs80), and triples (Bs105). Without the amenities: singles Bs35; doubles Bs60; and triples Bs75; prices lower if you stay over three nights.

Alojamiento Santa Barbara, Santa Barbara 151 (☎321 918), just north of the intersection with Junín—around the corner from the Alojamiento Oriente. One of the cheapest places in town. Shared baths only. Singles Bs30; doubles Bs40; triples Bs60.

Residencial Las Palmeras (☎342 199), on Suárez Arana between Quijarro and Campero—just in front of the south end of the **Los Pozos** market. Simple, cheap rooms in a busy part of town. Singles, doubles, and triples are all Bs20/person; singles and doubles with shared bath are Bs30 and Bs50, respectively. Fans provided on request.

Alojamiento Los Angeles, Campero 434 (☎328 279), ½ block above the intersection with Suárez Arana, facing the Los Pozos market. Hot water and a friendly owner compensate for the slight lack in cleanliness. Singles Bs20; doubles Bs30; triples Bs45.

Hotel Bibosi, Junín 218 (☎348 548), between 21 de Mayo and España. Good value for the money. Rooms come with cable TV, telephone, and breakfast. Facilities include a rooftop restaurant and several lounges. Singles Bs100; doubles Bs160; triples Bs200.

Residencial Royal's (☎368 192), in a back alley off Lemoine, near the old bus station. Singles Bs30, with A/C Bs80; doubles with A/C Bs120; triples with A/C Bs180

Residencial Beni (☎368 606), on Salvatierra, at the intersection with Cañoto, near the old bus station. Doubles with common baths Bs30-35. Often full.

Alojamiento Terrazas (☎464 575), on Montes, corner of Saturnino Saucedo, near the new bus station. Large, quiet rooms, some with balconies. Singles, doubles, and triples Bs15-20 per person, with bath Bs25-30 per person.

◖ FOOD

Santa Cruz is a big city, but the culinary selection can be pretty small; when it comes to food, *cruceños* do one thing and do it well—meat. For cheap chicken, try the *brasserias* along Cañoto near the old bus station The row of *churrasquerías* on the second anillo, between Alemania and Beni serve similar dishes in a more upscale setting. Signature dishes include *majadito*, a mix of rice, meat, potatoes, onions and tomatoes, served with egg and *plátano frito*—fried bananas.

Los Lomitos, Uruguay 758 (☎326 350), on the first *anillo*, near the intersection with Suárez Arana, across from the *avión pirata*. Come here expecting no-nonsense meat eating, and you won't be let down. True *gauchos* should try the *sandwich de lomito* (Bs10) or a *Biffe de Chorizo Argentino* (Bs45 for 1 person, Bs80 for 2). Open 8:30am-midnight.

Tabernet Pizzeria, Ñuflo de Chavez No. 24 (☎371 155), between René Moreno and Chuquisaca. Great food, good prices, and open late—a rare combination here. Welcoming service and well-prepared pizzas like the *Capriccio* (tomato, cheese, bacon, ham, onions, and mushrooms Bs25 for 2 people) will not disappoint. 4-course *almuerzo* Bs12. Open Tu 11am-3pm, W-Su 11am to midnight.

Irish Pub (Café Irlandés) (☎338 118), on the second floor of Shopping Bolívar on the Plaza 24 de Septiembre, with an annex, the **Shamrock Irish Pub (Bar Irlandés),** at 3er Anillo No. 1216, in between Banzer and the zoo. In the morning, the pub offers hearty Irish breakfast (bacon, eggs, and sausage, Bs18), in the afternoon, a full lunch (Bs18), and in the evening, strong whisky (Bs18) and other cocktails (Bs15). Irish Pub open 9am-1am; Shamrock Irish Pub open 6pm until 2, 3, or 4am.

Café Victory (☎322 935), on the corner of Junín and 25 de Mayo, on the floor above the post office. An eccentric artists' haunt. Has earned a reputation for its coffee (Bs4) and wide range of desserts. Open M-Sa 9am-midnight.

Las Cabañas de Río Piraí, at the very end of Roca y Coronado. Take micro #29 (Bs1.50) from in front of the church at the corner of Charcas and Beni; get off at the last stop. A series of restaurants lining the east bank of the Río Piraí. The Cabañas serve a variety of local specialties (*pacamuto*, Bs30; *picante de gallina*, Bs12). Different cabañas keep different hours; for the best selection, go at midday.

Restaurant Vegetariano "Su Salud," Quijarro 115 (☎360 168), between Arenales and Bolívar. Vegetarian versions of traditional dishes. Breakfast Bs4. Three-course lunch Bs10. Open Su-F 8am-9:30pm.

SIGHTS

ZOOLÓGICO. A zoo excursion requires some initiative; there is no set route nor literature to supplement the exhibits, which include **howler monkeys, ostriches,** and **sloths.** The lame horses worriedly grazing on the grass are destined to be tossed to the lions. (*The zoo is located between Radial 26 and Radial 27, between the inner and outer third anillos. To get there, take any micro marked Zoológico. The ticket office is open daily 9am-6pm. Zoo office ☎429 939. Bs7.*)

MUSEO DE ARTE CONTEMPORANEO. One of Santa Cruz's best kept secrets, the Museo de Arte Contemporaneo periodically holds highly acclaimed exhibitions. Keep a heads-up for the September 2001 XIII Bienal de Artes Plásticas, a national painting, sculpture, and photography competition that highlights some of the best up-and-coming Bolivian resident artists. (*☎340 926. On Sucre, near the intersection with Potosí. Open M-F 10am-noon and 3-7pm. Free.*)

MUSEO DE HISTORIA NATURAL NOEL KEMPFF MERCADO. Diehard naturalists will appreciate this cramped but comprehensive presentation of South American fauna, past and present. Highlights include a *piraña* exhibit and a collection of breathtaking butterflies. (*☎366 574. The museum is located on the south side of Irala, between Ejército and Velarde, right across from the 24hr. Santa Maria pharmacy. Open daily 8am-noon, 3pm-6:30pm. Bs1.*)

MUSEO DE HISTORIA. Although nominally a museum of history, the Museo de Historia crams a little bit of everything into its two floors of a colonial house. The first floor is to devoted to exhibitions by local artists. Every year (Nov.-Jan.), the museum holds its *ARTEFACTO* exhibit, commissioning twelve prominent national artists to create pieces that accentuate the *arte* in *facto*—that is, the art in everyday objects. The second floor has several temporary exhibits and a permanent collection of artifacts from the Chané (AD 100-800) and Guaraní (AD 100-1500) cultures that occupied western Bolivia. (*☎365 533. Junín 151, opposite the Banco de Santa Cruz and the post office, near the north side of the Plaza 24 de Septiembre. Open M-F 8am-noon and 3-6:30pm. Free.*)

CASA DE LA CULTURA RAÚL OTERO REICHE. Every 15 days the Casa de la Cultura features expositions on two different Bolivian artists. In June, the Casa de la Cultura holds the seven-day Festival Llama de Plata film festival which screens the previous year's most popular movies. (*☎345 500. On the west side of the Plaza 24 de Septiembre. Open M-Sa 8am-10pm, Su 10am-9pm.*)

OTHER SIGHTS. If you find yourself near the northeast corner of the first *anillo*, check out the **Avión Pirata,** a jumbo jet that, according to local legend, was deserted by drug-traffickers after an emergency crash landing.

♪ ENTERTAINMENT

The best way to find out about upcoming events is to visit the Casa de la Cultura on the Plaza 24 de Septiembre. Every year, APAC, the **Asociasión Pro Arte y Cultura** (☎ 332 287) puts on one of two international festivals in Santa Cruz: the Festival Internacional de Teatro, an international theatre festival, or the Festival Internacional de Música Renacista y Barroqua Americana, an American Renaissance and Baroque music festival. During these times, performance spaces are opened up across the city to accommodate a flood of musicians and artists from all over the world. The Festival Internacional de Teatro will be held in 2001; call APAC for more details, as dates have yet to be decided.

THEATER. The **Casateatro,** working in conjunction with the **Museo de la Historia** (☎ 365 533), is located next to the museum on Junín, across from the post office. Each year, the company produces three shows (presentations Th, Sa, and Su evenings). The **Paraninfo Universitario** (☎ 365 533 ext. 3903), across from the post office, functions as a theater and cinema. Look for posters in front advertising the theater and comedy troupes that frequent the venue. (Tickets usually around Bs10.)

SPORTS. Fútbol in Santa Cruz rests on the rivalry of the department's two biggest soccer clubs, the sky-blue **Blooming** and the green and white **Oriente Petrolera.** Big games take place in the **Tahuichi Stadium,** a few blocks south of the bus station. You can usually grab tickets (Bs15-40) 15min. before a game at the stadium itself—unless it's really a big match. Check out the **El Deber** newspaper (Bs2.5) for schedules and times. (Games W, Sa, and Su.)

FESTIVALS. Santa Cruz's biggest festival is **Carnaval,** celebrated the weekend before Ash Wednesday, with three days of dancing, drinking, and water balloon fights. At night, check out the east sides of Ballivián and Salvatierra, just before they cross the first *anillo*, for street dancing and drinking.

◪ NIGHTLIFE

Cruceños know how to party and there are clubs, bars, and cafes to suit everyone's tastes. When most locals are asked to furnish directions for a good time, most will shoo you in the direction of **Equipetrol,** the row of elegant bars and clubs that line San Martín between the second and third *anillos*. Cheaper venues can be found near the city center; you just have to look in the right places. For the latest listings, pick up a copy of **El Deber** newspaper (Bs2.5) on Friday morning. Inside, you'll find **La Guía,** a newspaper magazine with all the latest info on clubs, bars, concerts, and other events.

EQUIPETROL DISTRICT

Dress to impress–bouncers will be quick to turn away shabby-looking foreigners. Most clubs charge a cover, usually Bs10-20, paid at the door or in the form of a drink minimum.

> **La Roneria** (☎ 329 320) on San Martín. One of the oldest and most successful bars in Santa Cruz. The place features a pirate theme and doles out an awful lot of Old Parr whisky (Bs25). **Los Fanáticos** (the house band) plays a variety of fresh, danceable music on Th, F, and Sa. Open Tu-Sa, 4pm-2 or 3am.

> **Automanía** (☎ 377 265), on San Martín, between *Club Mad* and *La Roneria*. Like its subsidiary in Cochabamba, you'll still find the racing games, checkered flags, and drinks named after racing stars (Juan Pablo Hurtado, Bs20). This dance club, however, plays more typical Latin music. Open M-Sa 6pm-4am or whenever.

DOWNTOWN

Slightly less formal than a night in Equipetrol, a night in the city center can be just as fun. Clubs tend to be scattered around, so you'll probably need a taxi if you plan on doing some hopping. Late at night, taxis may try to charge you more, but the ride should still cost Bs5 within the first ring, Bs6 out to the second.

Clapton's Club de Blues, Murillo 169, between Bolívar and Arenales. Great jazz and blues and a cheerfully rowdy crowd. Hear the **Perros Rabiosos** (rabid dogs), the energetic **Marcela Gala Quartet,** or the lovely singer **Andrea Alberelli.** Beer (Bs10), *cuba libres* (Bs20). Bs20 minimum consumption cover. Open Th-Sa 10pm-3am.

Insomnia, Florida 517, at the intersection with Sarah. Young and friendly. Although a little crowded at times, the mostly 20ish crowd gives the place an inviting feel. Ideal for solo travelers. M-Sa opens 9-10pm, closes 3-4am. Live music F-Sa; cover Bs10.

El Muro, Independencia 416 (☎312 498), south of the corner with Mercado. A great cafe where you can have an actual conversation without having to shout. Warm up in the winter with a simple coffee (Bs3), a *cuba libre* (Bs12-15), or *el muro*, the house drink (gin, cointreau, OJ, Bs20). Open M-Sa 8:30pm-3am.

Pekos, Suárez Arana 278 (☎375 830), between the first and second rings. Good Latin music, in the style of Sylvio Rodriguez and Mercedes Soza. Live music on the weekends, when there is also a Bs10 minimum consumption cover. Open M-Sa 9pm-late.

DAYTRIPS FROM SANTA CRUZ

BOTANICAL GARDENS

Taxis leave when full from the corner of Suárez Arana and Barron (5-10min., Bs3.5). The park is marked with a large sign. Gates are open until 2pm. Free.

Located on Km8 of the road to Cotoca, the botanical gardens provide a pleasant respite from the drone of downtown Santa Cruz. You won't find any towering monuments or thrilling waterfalls—just a pleasant, mostly paved pathway weaving around a small lagoon, lined with palms and tree nurseries.

PARQUE REGIONAL LOMAS DE ARENA

To get to the park, take micro 31, labeled "CORTEZ," traveling south on Cañoto, just south of the intersection with Grigota (20-30min.). Ask to get off at "Las Palmas de Arena." From the gate its a 7km hike down a dirt road to the dunes. If you plan on going by car, you'll need a 4WD vehicle and a quick hand at the wheel. Entrance fee Bs2.5.

Just 17km south of Santa Cruz lies sprawling Parque Regional Lomas de Arena, known by locals as Las Lomas de Arena. Five giant sand dunes, all of which are open to visitors, dot an area of the park that includes ducks, *garzas*, and the occasional crocodile. On weekends, particularly during the summer months, families flock to the dunes to play in the sand and swim in the small lagoons nearby. The contrast between the sand dunes and the swamp land around them is jarring. During the summer months, a **restaurant** opens next to the dunes.

NEAR SANTA CRUZ: PARQUE NACIONAL NOEL KEMPFF MERCADO

*To visit a camp, contact FAN at their offices in Santa Cruz, on Km7 of the old road to Cochabamba (☎329 717), or go through one of the private tour operators that arrange tours of the region, such as **Neblina Forest-Bolivia** (☎336 831).*

Covering an area roughly the size of El Salvador and frequented by a few hundred people per year, the Parque Nacional Noel Kempff Mercado is as close to untouched as anyone is likely to get. The park, named in honor of a Bolivian biologist who was assassinated in 1986, covers a wide range of ecosystems, including dry forests, flooded savannahs, wetlands, Brazilian *cerrado*, and, of course, the Amazon rainforest. The biodiversity within these habitats is stunning: over 620 species of birds, 130 species of mammals, 250 species of fish, 162 amphibian species, 74 reptile species, and 12 types of orchids call the park home.

Under the administration of **FAN** (Fundación Amigos de la Naturaleza; ☎329 717), the park now maintains two camps offering rustic accommodations. Most visitors fly from Santa Cruz to **Los Fierros** (2hr., 400km), landing at the nearby indigenous community of Florida and then taking transport to the camp, 32km away. From **Los Fierros,** which can accommodate a maximum of 40 visitors (with running water and electricity), one can explore over **60km of footpaths,** visit the **El Encanto waterfall,** or attempt to climb the **la meseta de Capurú.** The park's other camp, **Flor de Oro,** has facilities for 35 guests and is a 2½hr. flight from Santa Cruz. From Flor de Oro, travelers can explore 40km of trails (some of which require a guide, hired in camp), visit **Las Torres** (two rock formations from which you can look out over the Río Iténez) and parts of Rondonia, Brazil, and take a boat to the **Arco Iris and Ahifeld waterfalls.**

PARQUE NACIONAL AMBORÓ

Lying between the old and new roads to Cochabamba, Amboró National Park has just started reeling in tourists. Encompassing 450,000 hectares of virgin forest, the park is teeming with wildlife, including 120 species of mammals, 830 species of birds, and countless insects. Among the park's rarer inhabitants are the Horned Curassow, the Andean "Cock of the Rock," and spectacled bears.

Parque Amboró, as it is now called, first came under government protection in 1974 as the **Reserva Natural Teniente Colonel Hernán Busch.** A *decreto supremo* in 1984 officially granted the land national park status, and expanded it to about 650,000 hectares. Expansion of the park angered local settlers; in response the government created the Area Natural de Manejo Integrado, also known as Area Multiple-Use, a 185,000 hectare section of the park that is open to "ecologically sustainable" development. There are two ways to enter the park: from Buena Vista to the north, or from Samaipata to the south. Buena Vista is the more established springboard, though entering from Samaipata is quickly growing just as popular.

BUENA VISTA. Buena Vista is the best place to prepare for an excursion into the north of Amboró National Park. Here you can purchase supplies and hire a local **guide** (US$20 per day) by asking around or visiting the park office a block from the main plaza. British ornithologist Guy Cox (email guy_cox@hotmail.com) has been living in the area for quite some time, and periodically guides trips to the park. He is the only guide in town who speaks English. Hiring a private guide is generally the least expensive way to see the park, but pricier, package tours are also a popular option. **Rosario Tours** (☎ 369 656, based in Santa Cruz) organizes all-inclusive 2-day tours (US$159 per person for 3 people, US$135 per person for 4-7 people). The smaller **Forest Tour Operator** leads tours through the less frequented Mataracu entrance; call ☎ 372 042 for prices. There are several budget options near the main plaza. Rooms at the **Residencial Nadia** are basic, but all have fans. (Rooms Bs25 per person, with bath Bs30-40.) Señora Delsi Antelo runs **La Casona,** near the *Alcadia*, and charges between Bs20-25 for a room with common bath. More expensive cabins are available at **Cabañas Quimori,** half a kilometer away, on the road to Santa Barbara (rooms US$10 per person). They also arrange full tours to Amboró.

ENTERING THE PARK. The are four entrances to Amboró near Buena Vista; three off the road heading south from town and another near Yapacani, to the north. The **Río Chouta** or **Río Saguayo** entrance is about 20km south of Buena Vista. From the entrance, it's about 8-9km to a suitable campsite. You can enter at the settler's commune of **Los Espejitos,** south of Buena Vista, and it's a long hike to a scenic *mirador,* but there are no established campsites, so you'll need to find a guide familiar with the area. Perhaps the most popular gateway to the park, the **Macuñucu** entrance lies several kilometers beyond **Las Cruces,** just past **Los Espejitos** on the road south from Buena Vista. From Las Cruces, it's 6-8km to the Río Surutú. There is a ranger camp 6-8km beyond the bridge, past the small community of Villa Amboró, where you may or may not have to pay an entrance fee. From the camp, you can stage one- or two-day trips into the jungle, following the Río Macuñucu. It is also possible to enter near **Yapacani,** northwest of Buena Vista. Most taxis that stop at Buena Vista continue on to Yapacani (1hr., leaves from the old bus terminal, Bs18-20). From Yapacani you can stage trips to natural pools, cascades, and other destinations.

SAMAIPATA ☎ 09

Samaipata, or "rest in the highlands," is a hidden jewel. Tucked away amid red clay mountains and rolling hills 120km west of Santa Cruz, the charming little town offers visitors plenty of diversions, inside and outside of town. Just when the highlands of Cochabamba or the friendliness and sociability of the Jesuit Circuit seem long gone, in Samaipata you'll find both—as well as a sizeable community of Europeans. In 1998, UNESCO declared Samaipata a Cultural Patrimony of Humanity. From here, you can ramble through El Fuerte—extraordinary pre- and post-Inca ruins, or swim and hike in the neighboring wilderness.

⌨️ TRANSPORTATION AND PRACTICAL INFORMATION

Most activity in town is centered around **Bolívar**, just above the plaza.

Micros: There is no bus company in Samaipata; ask locals when the next *micro* is expected. *Micros* and buses stop on the highway near the *surtidor* (opposite the gas station for Vallegrande, same side as gas station for Santa Cruz). A *micro* to **Vallegrande** (3-4hr., Bs25) passes through around noon; buses to **Santa Cruz** (3-4hr., Bs25-30) pass through most of the day.

Taxis: Taxis stop at the *surtidor*. To: **El Fuerte,** Bs50 round trip; and **Santa Cruz,** Bs100.

Tourist Information: Amboró Tourist Service (☎446 293), on Bolívar, is run by the former director of the Parque Nacional Amboró. Tours to **El Fuerte** (US$19 for 1-2 people, including transportation and guide), **Amboró** (1-day tour US$25 per person for 2 people), and other local destinations. The owner can also arrange bike rentals or horses. **The Roadrunners** has daily trips to El Fuerte and Amboró as well as canyoning tours to the Cataratas de Cuevas and the Mataral cave paintings, 60km to the west.

Banks and Currency Exchange: The **Cooperativa la Merced Ltda.** is on Campero just off the main plaza. Open M-F 8am-noon, 2:30-6pm, Sa 8am-noon.

Police: (☎110), just off the main plaza.

Hospital: (☎446 142) near the *surtidor* on the highway.

Pharmacy: Farmacia Claudia (☎446 198) on the main plaza. Open daily 8am-noon and 2-10pm, can be contacted any time in case of emergency.

Telephones: ENTEL (☎113 101), 2 blocks uphill from **Amboró Tourist Service,** open M-Sa 8am-noon and 3-9pm, Su 8am-noon and 3-7pm.

Internet: Amboró Tourist Service, on Bolívar. Bs15 per hr. Open nights.

🏠 ACCOMMODATIONS

Samaipata specializes in cabañas—little cabins, usually equipped with sleeping, eating, living, and cooking facilities. Most of the cabañas are located along the outer perimeter of town, a little higher than the rest of the pueblo.

RESIDENCIALES AND HOTELS

Residencial Don Jorge (☎446 086), on Bolívar, one block past the museum when walking away from the church. Popular backpacker haunt. Hot water available. Rooms Bs25 per person, with bath Bs30 per person.

Residencial Kim (☎446 161), one block away from the plaza, between Campero and Bolívar. Rooms are simple, bathrooms are somewhat clean, and the management claims there is hot water. Rooms Bs20 per person.

Hotel Casa Blanca (☎446 076), on Bolívar, across from the church. The nicest non-cabaña digs in town. TVs, private baths, garage parking, and continental breakfast make this place a step above the rest. Ground floor rooms US$7 per person; second floor rooms with balconies US$10 per person.

CABAÑAS

Cabañas Traudi (☎446 094), about 1km south of the main plaza, opposite **La Víspera**. Cabins have superior small cubbies, mezzanines, and grill out back. Owners also provide bug nets, potable water dispensers, clean bedding, and a swimming pool (Bs10 for non-guests). Singles US$5; cabins US$15 per person.

La Víspera (☎446 082), on a scenic hillside south of town. In addition to organizing popular excursions to El Fuerte, Amboró, and other local attractions, and running a successful organic farm, La Víspera has a wide range of rooms. Reservations suggested before *Carnaval* and New Year's. Rooms US$7; cabins US$25-70.

Cabañas Fridolín (☎323 768 in Santa Cruz). Some of the best cabins in town. Almost all have lofted bedrooms. Cabins house 6-7 people and are also equipped with a *churrasquería*. Cabins US$60.

Landhaus Cabañas (☎446 033). The Landhaus doesn't only cook and party on Sa nights, but you'll have access to a sauna (US$20 per use) and a pool. Rooms US$5, with bath US$10; cabins from US$25 for 2 people to US$60 for 7 people.

FOOD

Due to Samaipata's large international community, cuisine is quite varied. The best restaurants for *comida típica* are on the main plaza.

La Paola (☎446 093), on the plaza, has cheap, two-dish *almuerzos* (Bs5) and is open all day—knock on the door if it is closed. Open daily 8am-midnight.

Restaurant Rincón Samapateño, also on the plaza, has large *platos extras* like *milanesa* (Bs7) and is quite popular among locals.

Restaurant Pizzería Descanso en las Alturas (☎446 072), on the plaza, often called by its old name, the *chancho rengo*. Serves up a wide variety of tasty pizza pies, from the *Argentina* (Bs35) to the *Florentina* (olive, peppers, onion, and mushrooms; Bs50).

Landhaus Restaurant (☎446 033), by the *cabañas* of the same name, is the swankiest place in town. Regional and international entrees Bs20-24. Open Th-Su and holidays.

SIGHTS

EL FUERTE. A military, civil, and religious center for three civilizations, this complex of ruins hewn from a single giant rock is one of Bolivia's prime attractions. In fact, guides will repeatedly tell you that El Fuerte is second only to Incallajta near Cochabamba in importance and size. The complex is believed to date from at least 1500 BC when Amazonian tribes first decorated the 300m rock with reliefs, fountains, and the mysterious "priest's chair." During the 15th century the Incas built a military outpost on the site. Later still came the Spaniards, who built a house on top of it all.

Tours start at the **mirador,** a small hill overlooking the west side of the complex with views of the reliefs. All of the reliefs were carved by Amazonian tribes. The wall with three niches at the top was erected by the Incas. To the right of the boulder, indentations in the rock may have been the homes of Inca priests and bishops. Walking along the south of the wall, you'll reach the *kallanka,* a spiritual long house found at only a handful of sites in the Inca world. Its existence in El Fuerte suggests that the site was of profound symbolic importance to the Incas. A little farther along, you'll reach the base walls of a more recent building: the ruins of a Spanish colonial house. Past the house and down a hill is one of El Fuerte's most intriguing features, **La Chinkana,** a deep hole bored directly into the rock. Meaning "labyrinth where you lose yourself" in Quechua, the hole appears bottomless. During the wet season, vast amounts of water funnel into it, but the hole never fills. *(The ruins are 8km from the surtidor. It is not an easy or particularly scenic walk (1½-2hr.); hire a taxi (round-trip Bs50, an extra Bs10 to wait on-site). Tour guides can be hired at La Víspera, The Roadrunners, or Amboró Tourist Service, or at the ticket office, and usually cost US$10. Ruins open daily 9am-5pm. Bs20 entrance fee includes admission to the archaeological museum.)*

THE OFFICIAL STORY Though there is no such thing as a tried and true account of Che Guevara's last days, the following facts are fairly widely agreed upon. On October 7, 1967, the Bolivian army was in hot pursuit of Che and his international band of 16-17 guerillas. The next day in a morning gunfight in the Churro Ravine near La Higuera, General Prado's rangers (almost all of whom were US trained) confronted several guerillas. Both sides sustained injuries, and Che (code name Ramón) was hit once or more in the leg. His comrade, the Bolivian Simon Sarabia, "Willy," defended the wounded Che. Some claim that "Willy" was shot to pieces, while others, including most La Higuera eyewitnesses, hold that he was captured alive along with Che. They were taken to a one-room schoolhouse by the Bolivian forces, awaiting orders from higher command. The next morning, October 9, Felix Rodriguez, a Bolivian CIA operative, arrived in La Higuera. Che was interrogated by Rodriguez, who recounted that he was in poor physical condition. Rodriguez photographed Che, his diary, and his belongings. Other Bolivian soldiers spoke to Che, and report that he made defiant remarks and insisted he be killed while standing. Some among the Bolivian army claim that his last remarks were, "I am Che Guevara, and I have failed." However many hold that he said, "Shoot, coward! You are only killing a man!"

MUSEO ARQUEOLÓGICO. The archaeological museum, on Bolívar near the Hamburg Café, puts the El Fuerte ruins in historical perspective. Exhibits include a history of the Inca Empire's expansion and a full-scale model of the Mataral cave paintings. **Sonia Abilez,** the English-speaking resident archaeologist, is an expert on the ruins. (☎ 446 065. *Museum open daily 8:30am-6pm.*)

ENTERING THE AMBORÓ NATIONAL PARK. Since the approach to the park from Samaipata is less established than the Buena Vista entrances, it's wise to take a guided tour. The **Amboró Tourist Service** offers a variety of tours, from one-day excursions to 8- or 9-day adventures. The relatively cheap and popular one-day tours are US$25 per person for two people, US$17 per person for three people, and US$15 per person for four people.

VALLEGRANDE

A pretty town tucked into the hills 240km from Santa Cruz, Vallegrande has long been a magnet for Che Guevara fans. After his execution, Che's body was brought here and stored in the hospital laundry room. The people of Vallegrande put up remarkably well with Che-chasers, but they'd prefer that their town be known for its beautiful views and mellow atmosphere. Hot and dusty during the day, Vallegrande cools off quickly at night; bring warm clothes during the winter season.

▐▊ TRANSPORTATION AND PRACTICAL INFORMATION. Travelers will have little need to stray far from **Plaza 26 de Enero** in the middle of town. **Jumbo Bus Bolívar** (☎ 21 40), on Cacho a half block away from the Santa Cruz intersection (away from the plaza), has buses to **Santa Cruz** (7hr., 10pm, Bs30). **Trans Expreso Vallegrande** (☎ 22 89), on the main plaza, half a block past the Alcaldia, also has nightly service to **Santa Cruz** (7hr., 9:30pm, Bs30). **Expreso Guadalupe,** Santa Cruz N-119, between Sucre and Florida, serves **Cochabamba** (12hr.; M 6pm, F 7:30am; Bs30). Buses **to Vallegrande** leave from the terminal in **Santa Cruz** (Jumbo Bus Bolívar, 6hr., 11-11:30am, Bs35). A *micro* to La Higuera leaves every other day from near the hospital (8am, 3-6hr., Bs10). **Taxis** loiter around the market plaza, at the intersection of Santa Cruz and Sucre (Bs10 round-trip to Che's former grave under the airstrip; Bs130-150 roundtrip to **La Higuera**). Professor Carlos Soza at the Casa de la Cultura on the Plaza 26 de Enero is happy to provide **tourist information.** The owners of the **Cafeteria La Cueva** (see Food) can help arrange locally-guided trips to sights such as the *pinturas rupestras* (cave paintings) that dot the area. Change money at the **Banco Santa Cruz** on Señor de Malta (open M-F 8:30-11:30am and 2:30-5pm). The **policía nacional** (☎ 110) are located on the Plaza 26 de Enero, at the corner of Sucre and Escalante y Mendoza. For medical help, the **hospital** (☎ 21 21) is on Señor de Malta between Pucara and Virrey Mendoza.

THE UNOFFICIAL STORY According to locals, the first of Che's ragtag band of guerillas—who had been pursued relentlessly by the Bolivian military in the months preceding October 1967—visited a town near La Higuera on or before the 7th of October. Che and the others followed shortly thereafter, this time with the military close behind. On the 8th of October, Coco, one of Che's men, walked on a trail near La Higuera where the hidden army units ambushed and shot him; Che and his comrades ran to investigate. Although locals heard the gunshots that ensued, the accounts of the fight are from the military. After a long and bloody gun battle, Che was trapped in a ravine by three Bolivian soldiers. Che shot the soldier closest to him in the neck, killing him immediately. The soldier to Che's left hit Che in the leg, leaving him wounded and defenseless—or not?

The owner of the El Mirador in Vallegrande was allowed to inspect Che's weapons after his arrival, post-mortem, in Vallegrande. He claims that when Che turned himself over to the soldier, he was *not* at the end of his rope; Che had on him a fully-loaded and functional German pistol, a pistol he had used in the past. The soldiers themselves recount that, just before the soldiers were about to finish off the wounded Che, he pleaded, "No me maten, no me maten! Soy el Che Guevera, valgo mas vivo que muerto!" ("Don't kill me... I am Che Guevera, and I'm worth more alive than dead.")

▓▒ ACCOMMODATIONS AND FOOD. The **Residencial Vallegrande,** on Sucre half a block up from the central plaza, features fine furniture more befitting a mansion than a budget hotel. (☎21 12. Rooms Bs15 per person, with bath Bs20.) The **Hostal Teresitas,** half a block from the main plaza, has clean, tiled rooms. (Bs15-20 per person; parking included.) Across the street, the **Alojamiento Copacabana** has spacious rooms with a common baths. (☎20 14. Singles Bs20; doubles Bs30.) Finally, the **Hostal Vallegrande,** on Santa Cruz, between Chaco and Florida, has a range of rooms. (☎22 81. Regular rooms Bs25 per person; singles with bath and TV Bs40; doubles with bath and TV Bs70.) **ITEI Gaucho,** just around the corner from the Alojamiento Teresitas, has *churrascos* serving 1-2 people for Bs30. **Café la Cueva,** one block south from the market plaza, serves cheap pizzas (Bs8-13). **El Mirador** (☎23 41), at the top of Escalante y Mendoza, affords a great view of Vallegrande and dishes out trout, beef, pork, chicken, and goulash (Bs16-22). The owner, a friendly German, has pictures from when Che's body was brought in.

▣▷ SIGHTS AND ENTERTAINMENT. The **hospital laundry room** where Che was displayed following his death, now an abandoned shed behind the hospital, is on Señor de Malta. Here, Che's body was washed and put on display, in order to convince the public that Che really was dead. His body was then buried beneath the town airstrip; in 1997 it was unearthed and returned to Cuba.

Every year Vallegrande throws a **fiesta** for its patron saint the week before Carnaval (which, in turn, is the weekend prior to Ash Wednesday), with games, fireworks, and more questionable traditions like *el pato enterrado*, in which a live duck is buried up to its head and killed by a blindfolded contestant.

LA HIGUERA

Fifty-five kilometers south of Vallegrande is La Higuera, site of Che Guevara's last stand. The road to La Higuera passes through **Pucara,** a small village of little interest. There are no formal accommodations in La Higuera, and camping in town, which can get bitterly cold at night, is not recommended. If you get stuck overnight, ask at **Pensión Vivy** (*almuerzos* Bs4-5) on the main plaza for rooms to let— several villagers have extra rooms in which you can sleep for Bs15 per night. From Pucara, the road goes downhill to La Higuera. Once a respectable *pueblo* of 50-60 families, it's now a ghost town of under a dozen families who eke out a living from subsistence farming and tourist handouts. It's best to visit on a Thursday or Sunday when the man who tends the local **museum** is in town. This is also the best time to catch somebody at the radio post, which is located in the schoolhouse where Che was imprisoned and executed. Villagers of 50-60 years of age are most likely to provide an accurate account of what happened. Most will be more than happy to tell you what they know in exchange for a small tip. It is also possible to hire a local (2hr., Bs20-30) to take you to the *quebrada* (stream) where Che was killed.

THE JESUIT MISSIONS ☎ 09

There are few places on earth like the Jesuit missions of Chiquitania. Where else can you hear clips of Beethoven or Bach while walking the dusty streets of a South American *pueblo?* The six Jesuit missions in Chiquito province are widely regarded as the finest examples of colonial architecture in the country and are well worth the trip. Travelers without an interest in religious architecture can still appreciate the tranquil setting of the mountain towns that host the missions.

Jesuit priests first established a presence in Chiquitania a decade after the foundation of the first Jesuit mission (*reducción*) in Bolivia. Padres José de Arce and Antonio Ribas founded the **San Javier** mission in 1692. The next 80 years marked a golden age for Jesuits in South America, and five more major missions were founded in Chiquitania in **Concepción** (1708), **San Miguel** (1718), **San Ignacio** (1748), and **Santa Ana** (1755). Five of these churches were built under the watchful eye of a Swiss father, Martín Schmidt. The Jesuit *reducción* was more than just a center for proselytizing; it was church, an army barracks, a concert hall, and a public school as well. Trade between the missions flourished; unlike the Spaniards, who enslaved the native people, the Jesuits gave the citizens of the *reducción* ownership of their territory and allowed their chiefs to participate in governing the settlement. At the height of Jesuit influence in the 1750s, there were over 15,000 members of the Chiquitano missions.

The Jesuits' success angered their rivals, especially the Spanish, and the order became scapegoats for any problems that arose within indigenous communities. The Spanish accused the Jesuits of fomenting an indigenous uprising in Paraguay, and in 1773, under intense pressure from Spain and rival religious orders, Pope Clementine XIV expelled the Jesuits' from the region. Over the past 20 years, restoration efforts have helped reverse the effects of 200 years of decay, and the six surviving missions have become one of Bolivia's premier tourist attractions.

SAN JAVIER. Founded on New Year's Eve 1691, San Javier is the first mission of Chiquitos. Completed in 1752 under the direction of Father Martín Schmidt, the church itself is fairly plain compared to other churches on the circuit. The **Vicarito Apostólico de Ñuflo de Chávez,** as the church is now called, has remained in good condition, and recent restorations have helped preserve its original beauty. The church is open to visitors; just ask at the side entrance (small donation suggested).

All buses heading to or from the other missions pass through San Javier. Expreso Jenecheru, on the highway near the Alojamiento San Javier, has service to **Santa Cruz** (4hr., 1:30am, Bs25) and **Concepción** (2hr., midnight, Bs10), continuing to the other missions. Misiones del Oriente (☎635 082) also has service to **Concepción** (2hr., 11am and midnight, Bs15) and the other missions, and to **Santa Cruz** (4hr., 2am, Bs25). The town consists of a **plaza,** dominated by the impressive **church,** and the road continuing to the other missions. In the other direction, the road leads to Santa Cruz. Buses drop passengers off a few blocks before the plaza. For the **police,** call ☎635 167; for the **hospital,** call ☎635 072.

Almost all accommodations are in old-style colonial houses with large courtyards. The **Alojamiento Ame-Tauna,** on the main plaza opposite of the church, has spacious rooms with clean bathrooms and steady hot water. (☎635 018. Rooms Bs30 per person.) A few steps from the bus stop is the **Alojamiento San Javier,** well-equipped for large groups. (Rooms Bs30 per person.) The **Posada Pinto** and the **Alojamiento Hermano Añe** are both a block or two away from the church, and both charge Bs25 per person for simple lodging with shared bathrooms. A few popular eateries and food vendors line the main road and serve favorites like **salchipapas**—hot dog and fries—for just a few bolivianos. The **Restaurant Sede Ganadera,** open late and regarded by locals as the best place in town, is on the main plaza and serves mean cuts of beef from Bs8.

CONCEPCIÓN. Concepción, or "Conce," as it is called by locals, is about 300km northeast of Santa Cruz, set amid rolling tropical plains. The church, **Catedral del Vicariato Apostólico de Ñuflo de Chavez,** constructed by Father Schmid from 1753 to 1756, is one of the most ornate of the mission churches—the sides of the church pews have been carved with scenes from biblical passages and a brilliant *altar mayor*, or backdrop, makes up for the general darkness of the cathedral. The church was restored in 1982 and very little of the original structure remains; of the 121 columns standing today, only 15 of them are originals.

Linea Transporte 31 del Este (☎643 036) has service to **Santa Cruz** (5hr., 3 per day, Bs30). Misiones del Oriente (☎643 034), on the main plaza, also has service to **Santa Cruz** (6hr.; 11:30pm, also 11:30am every other day; Bs40) and **San Ignacio** (3hr.; 2am, also 2pm every other day; Bs25), continuing on to the other missions. Like most mission towns, Concepción is centered around the **main plaza.** The **Centro Médico y Farmacia Concepción** (☎643 094) is more central than **Hospital Cesar Banzer** up north. The **police** are near the main plaza, between the church and the **Apart Hotel Las Misiones.** The **tourist office** is on the plaza, on the corner just to the right of the church. The **Hotel Colonial** has very new, clean rooms with baths and hammocks. (☎643 050. Rooms Bs35.) At the **Hostal La Pascana,** a block away from the main plaza, the rooms all have private exits to the street and common baths with lukewarm water. (Rooms Bs25 per person.) The **Posada El Viajero** is the cheapest in town. (Bs15 per person.)

SAN IGNACIO DE VELASCO. San Ignacio, the capital of Velasco province, is a curious little town. Every morning, storeowners hold their own against the red sand—a battle no one pretends to be winning. At night, the grit creeps out of its little piles, and carefully wraps itself around the strangely bulbous trees in the main plaza. Locals have learned to accept their fate, but tourists can be spotted frantically batting their eyes or brushing off their clothes. The town's **church** was demolished in 1948. Only the altars and the pulpit were saved. A visit to the church can shed valuable light on how the structures were built. Talk to the priest or swing by the **Casa de la Cultura** for more information on the church and on San Ignacio in general. Aside from the church, locals are proud of the **Laguna el Guapomó.** On July 31st, the town throws a **fiesta** for its patron saint, San Ignacio de Loyola. The FAN (Fundación Amigos de la Naturaleza) office for **Noel Kempff Mercado National Park** is just off the main plaza, opposite the church. FAN urges travelers to check in before visiting the park, as parts of the park close unexpectedly. They can also help arrange transportation (by car or plane) and a guide for the park. (☎632 194; email sanignacio@fan-bo.org. Open M-F 8am-noon and 2-6pm.)

The San Ignacio **airport,** south of town, has only one regular flight—TAM arrives on Mondays at 11am, and leaves almost immediately for **Santa Cruz.** Call Sra. Erika at the Hotel Palace (☎642 063) to book a flight (Bs300). San Ignacio is a major **bus** hub. Several bus companies go to **Santa Cruz** (10hr., Bs35); **Santa Ana** (40min., Bs7); **San Rafael** (70min., Bs10); **San Miguel** (20-30min., Bs5); **San José** (5hr., Bs45); **Matias** (8-9hr., 50 Bs); and **Corumbá** (10am, Bs130). Most of the action in town is centered around (surprise!) the **main plaza.** The **Hospital Districtal** (☎632 170), one block from the plaza, has 24-hour emergency attention. **Police** (☎110) are near the market. **ENTEL** (☎632 117) lies three blocks from the plaza. **Banco Santa Cruz,** on the plaza, changes dollars. (Open M-F 8:30-11:30am and 2:30-5:30pm.) The **post office** is across the street from Restaurant Barquitos.

Casa Suiza, five blocks west of the center of town on Sucre, is well worth the short walk. Rooms include all meals and plenty of snacks. There's a thriving book exchange and you can rent horses from the owner's friends. (Rooms US$10 per person). The new **Residencial Bethania** has very clean facilities and comfortable mattresses. (☎632 307. Rooms Bs25 per person.) The slightly crumbling **Hotel 31 de Julio** on the plaza (rooms Bs20) and the family-run **Alojamiento 25 de Julio** (rooms Bs25) are both good and cheap and will reduce their price to Bs15 for groups of three or four. The **Princezhina Modas** on the main plaza charges Bs12 for a single plate *almuerzo*, Bs2 for various *empanadas*, and serves good Brazilian food too.

SAN MIGUEL. The *reducción* of San Miguel was founded in 1718, and the church was finished a few years later; the confessionals are inscribed with the names of the mission's "founding fathers." Not surprisingly, Father Schmidt is among them. Be sure to note the striking fresco on the ceiling above the front of the church. Bus companies Flota Chiquitano, Expreso Trans Bolivia, and 31 del Este all have offices in San Miguel and service to **Santa Cruz** (9hr.; 4:30, 5, 5:30pm; Bs35-40), with stops at **San Ignacio, Concepción,** and **San Javier.** Trans Bolivia also goes to **San Rafael** (30min., 2 per day, Bs5). Local micros leave for **San Ignacio** (30min., 3 per day, Bs5) from the main plaza. **La Pascana,** opposite the church, charges Bs25 per person for basic rooms. Next door, the **Alojamineto Pardo** charges Bs10 per person.

SANTA ANA. Santa Ana, founded in 1755, remains the least developed of the Chiquitos missions. The only church on the circuit with three front doors, Santa Ana's is also the only church that has never been restored. The design bears resemblance to the church in San Ignacio de Moxos up north. During the 18th century, skilled craftsmen were often "traded" between towns; one theory maintains that such exchange explains how Santa Ana ended up with three entrances. The town also boasts a rare 18th-century organ, though you may have to ask around to see it. Buses go to **San Ignacio** (30-40min., early in the morning and around 3pm, Bs7) and **San Rafael** (30min., 11:30am and 6 or 7pm, Bs5) Buses leave from the main plaza, opposite the church. The very friendly family at the **Pensión Pacú,** on the plaza near the church, has an extra room available (Bs15 per night).

SAN RAFAEL. San Rafael was the second mission, founded in 1696, and was the site of the first church constructed under the direction of Father Martín Schmid in the mid 1700s. By the 1960s, the church was in a sorry state; when renovations began in 1972, many of the pillars had sunk two meters into the ground. Today, the church is in fantastic shape—the *altar mayor* is coated in *pan de oro* and mica; the pulpit is also decorated with mica. The window on the right closest to the front of the church is surrounded by a mica-layered wall—some believe that this was how the original walls actually appeared. Every day, a bus leaves from the main plaza bound for **Santa Ana** (30min., early morning and 1 or 2:30pm, Bs5) and **San Ignacio** (1hr., early morning and 1 or 2:30pm, Bs10). Trans Universal passes through San Rafael on its way to **San José** (5-6hr.; M, W, F, and Sa 4pm; Bs30). Trucks load up in the main plaza bound for various destinations (**San Miguel, Santa Ana, San Ignacio**); ask the locals in front of the Bar 7 Copas for more information. **Hotel Paradita** on the main plaza has simple but comfortable quarters. (Rooms Bs20, with bath Bs25.)

SAN JOSÉ DE CHIQUITOS. The capital of Chiquitos province, San José is the largest and busiest of the mission towns but has managed to retain the friendliness and hospitality of its smaller neighbors. The main plaza here is bright and inviting; people-watching is almost as popular as karaoke-hopping on a Friday or Saturday night. The church, whose front façade alone takes up an entire side of the plaza, looks more like the Alamo than a traditional Jesuit church. The **church** is the only one on the circuit built entirely of stone; in fact it is one of the only remaining stone churches in Bolivia, Brazil, and Paraguay. The full complex includes the **Capilla de la Muerte** (Chapel of Death), built in front of the old cemetery and now overgrown with shrubs, the cathedral, the stone façade, and the *colegio jesuítico.* All were constructed using Chiquitano Indian labor in the mid-18th century. The large barracks-like building on the south side of the complex is the old **convent** (*colegio jesuítico*). Like the rest of the church complex, plans are in the works for extensive renovations, but nothing has come of them yet. On the side of the *colegio* not facing the courtyard, a set of stairs leads up to the roof. The tower, which used to have a stone balcony, contains an original bell from the first mission complex; visitors can to climb to the top.

BORDER CROSSING: INTO BRAZIL

Just across the border from **Puerto Quijarro** (a 20min. train ride from Puerto Suárez) is the beautiful Brazilian city of Corumbá. Getting there takes a little paperwork. Citizens of all English-speaking countries other than the UK must apply for a Brazilian entrance visa at the consulate in Puerto Suárez (open M-F 8am-2pm). Children under 10 must present a yellow vaccination card. Although Bolivian citizens are free to enter and exit Corumbá as they wish, **all other nationalities must get an exit stamp from Bolivian Immigration** when they cross the border (open M-Sa 8am-noon and 2:30-6pm, Su 9am-noon). Taxis from Quijarro or the Quijarro train station to the border cost Bs3 per person. At the border, you can change your *bolivianos* into *reals*.

As soon as you cross into Brazil you will need to get an entrance stamp at the **Rodoviária,** or the Polícia Federal. On weekdays take a mototaxi (3 reals) to the Rodoviária. The **immigration office** at the Rodoviária stamps passports from 8am-11:30am and 2-5:15pm. Travelers who cross on Saturday or Sunday must go to the Polícia Federal at the Praça de República. A bus (1 real) which leaves from the little parking lot on the left as you enter Brazil, can drop you off near the Polícia Federal (1 real). A mototaxi should cost 3 reais.

In Corumbá, change traveler's checks at the **Banco de Brasil,** just off the Praça da Indepencia, open daily 10am-3pm. The tourist office, **Sema Tours,** is in Porto Geral, open M 1:30-5:30pm and Tu-F 8-11am and 1:30-5:30pm.

The office of Flota Universal (☎722 198), the only bus company with regular service to and from **San José,** is just north of the gas station, but has **buses** that leave from the train station to **San Ignacio** (5hr., 7am, Bs45) and the other missions. Other buses go to **Quijarro** (7½hr.; Tu, Th, and Su 11:52pm; *cama* Bs143, *semi-cama* Bs122) and **Santa Cruz** (5hr.; M, W, and Th 2:15am; *cama* Bs186, *semi-cama* Bs159). The **train station** sits at the east end of Gallardo (24 hr. info: ☎722 005). Trains go to: **Quijarro** (10hr.; M-Sa 9:30pm; *pullman* Bs88, *primera* Bs28, *segunda* Bs22); **Santa Cruz** (6hr.; M-Sa 2am; *pullman* Bs48, *primera* Bs21, *segunda* Bs18); **Quijarro** (12hr., Tu and F 3:50am, Bs22); and **Santa Cruz** (9½hr., Th and Su 12:30am, Bs18). You will need your passport to purchase tickets. Tickets to Quijarro can only be bought one or two hours before the train arrives. Tickets to Santa Cruz can be purchased up to the day before. Don't expect anything too out of the ordinary. Activity centers around the pleasant **plaza central,** the railway station, and the *surtidor* up north. **Police** (☎110) are on the main plaza. The main hospital is **Hospital San José de Chiquitos** (☎722 111). The **pharmacy, Botica San Silvestre,** on Jesús Chavez, between Barbery and 9 de Abril, is open M-F 8am-noon and 2-7pm, Sa 8am-noon and 5-6pm. The **Banco Santa Cruz** will change dollars. **ENTEL,** two blocks behind the church on Santistevan, lets customers use **MCI, AT&T, and Sprint calling cards.** (Open M-F 7:30am-11pm, Sa and Su 7:30am-9pm.) **Hotel Victoria,** opposite the north flank of the church, is your best bet—simple rooms border a sunny courtyard. (☎722 136. Rooms Bs25 per person.) There is also a *pensión* in the courtyard serving decent food (*almuerzo* Bs8, *cena* Bs6). **Hotel Raquelita,** on the plaza, beats out its competition with its top-notch service. (Rooms Bs35 per person, with bath Bs50.) The **Posada Vallegrandina** is the cheapest in town. (Rooms Bs15 per person.)

PUERTO SUÁREZ   ☎09

Puerto Suárez is a typical border town. There's not much to do here, except maybe wait for a flight and apply for a Brazilian visa. Otherwise, the plaza is small, the streets are dusty, and the going's pretty slow.

Flights out of Puerto Suárez are limited. For **airport** information call ☎762 092 between 6am and 6pm. Airport taxes total Bs30. Taxis to the airport cost Bs10. LAB, La Paz 33 (☎762 744), AeroSur (☎762 581; open daily 8:30am-noon and 2:30-6pm), on Bolívar near the corner of Israel Mendia, and Transporte Aereo Militar

(TAM) (☎762 581), on Heroes del Chaco near the corner of Israel Mendia, service **Santa Cruz** (55min.; LAB and Aerosur M, W, F, Su 4:30pm, Bs549; TAM Tu 1pm and Sa 2pm, Bs350) with connections to **Cochabamba** (Bs595) and **La Paz** (Bs928). The **train station** is called *el paradero*, and is the second to last stop on the train from Santa Cruz. All trains pass through Puerto Suárez 20-25min. before arriving in **Puerto Quijarro** or after leaving it, so ticket prices are almost identical. Taxis to the station are Bs3 from central Puerto Suárez.

Almost everything in town is within a few blocks of the **plaza.** In emergencies, call the **police** (☎110) or the **hospital** (☎762 020). **Hotel Progreso,** on Bolívar near the corner of Santa Cruz, has the cheapest rooms, with clean common baths, and fans for Bs25 per person. **Hotel Beby** (☎762 700; Bolívar 110) and **Hotel Restaurant Puerto Suárez** (☎762 296; Bolívar 111) also have simple rooms with fans for Bs30. **Hotel Frontera Verde,** Vanguardia 24, off Bolívar, has an English-speaking owner and good rooms with fan, bath, and breakfast. (☎762 470. Singles US$8, with A/C US$15; doubles US$11, with A/C US$20; triples with A/C US$21.)

EASTERN BOLIVIA

THE BOLIVIAN ORIENTE

The Bolivian Oriente encompasses the north and west of Bolivia—the Beni, the Pando, and a northern slice of the La Paz departments—all told, almost seventy percent of the country's area. Yet that vast space can be divided into just two topographical categories: jungle and pampas. In other words, if you visit, you'll be either surrounded in green or soaked to your knees in brown—mud, that is. And this is most of what potential visitors know about the Bolivian Oriente. With a landscape so overwhelming, it's easy to forget that, in the late 1600s, the region was home to the first Jesuit missions in Bolivia and, before that, pre-Inca empires like the Patiti, who ruled the Trinidad region around AD 300.

HIGHLIGHTS OF THE BOLIVIAN ORIENTE

LOLL in a hammock in what might be the most **cosmopolitan corner** anywhere along the Amazonian riverways: Rurrenabaque (p. 404).

FROLIC with **pink river dolphins** and their friends on a tour of the pampas (p. 408).

CROSS the border into **Brazil** (p. 412 and p. 414). Wait! You might need a visa.

RURRENABAQUE ☎08

Twenty years ago, the incredible jungle and pampas around Rurre (as locals refer to their town) brought in only wealthy safari types and hardy Israeli backpackers. Nowadays, 2400-3000 tourists tramp through monthly (during the dry season, that is). This explosive tourism has had, for the most part, positive effects, and gringos will find very little hostility here. Locals just smile in amusement at the new styles and gadgets that foreigners lug in; if North Face has come out with a new internal frame, triple-reinforced, windproof, waterproof, high-altitude safari-trek backpack just a bit shinier than the last, it won't be long before it shows up in a hostel in Rurrenabaque. After all, however ridiculous it may appear, this travelers' parade keeps Rurre residents among the best-dressed small-town Bolivians around. But despite its monumental popularity, Rurrenabaque is not a tourist trap. It is a lucky village situated at the edge of two distinct but equally fascinating landscapes that can offer visitors unparalleled outdoor experiences at unbelievable prices.

▪ TRANSPORTATION

Flights: Airport (☎922 537), 2½km north of town. Open M-F 8am-noon and 2-6pm, Sa-Su 8am-noon. Bs6 **airport tax;** Bs6 **municipal tax.** Flights are often cancelled due to inclement weather; expect delays of 1-2 days. Mototaxi Bs5. **TAM** (☎922 398), on Santa Cruz between Abaroa and Comercio. To: **La Paz** (1hr.; M, W, and F 2 per day, Sa 1 per day; Bs320); **San Borja** (20min., Th 10:30am, Bs130); **Trinidad** (1hr., Bs200); and **Santa Cruz** (2hr., Bs380); and **Riberalta** (1¼hr., M 10am, Bs280) via **Guayaramerín** (1½hr., Bs280). Office open M-F 8am-noon and 3-6pm. **Servicio Aereo Vargas España** (☎922 144), at Santa Cruz and Bolívar. To: **La Paz** (45min., M 1 per day, Bs410) and **Trinidad** (45min.; Tu, W, and Sa 1 per day; Bs348) via **San Borja** (15min., Bs178) and **Santa Cruz** (1¾hr., Bs750).

Bus: Terminal, on Ayacucho, between Junín and 18 de Noviembre. Mototaxi Bs1.5. Flota Yungueña (☎922 112) goes to: **La Paz** (20hr., noon, Bs65) via **Yucumo** (3hr., Bs30); **Caranavi** (10hr., Bs50); **Trinidad** (16hr., Th and Sa 5am, Bs140); **Gua-**

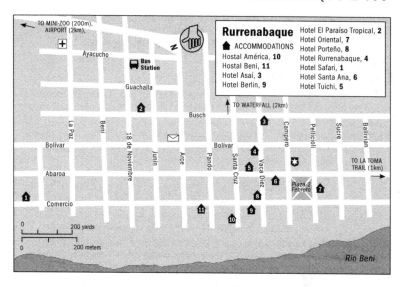

Rurrenabaque

🏠 ACCOMMODATIONS
Hostal América, **10**
Hostal Beni, **11**
Hotel Asaí, **3**
Hotel Berlin, **9**

Hotel El Paraíso Tropical, **2**
Hotel Oriental, **7**
Hotel Porteño, **8**
Hotel Rurrenabaque, **4**
Hotel Safari, **1**
Hotel Santa Ana, **6**
Hotel Tuichi, **5**

TO MINI-ZOO (200m),
AIRPORT (2km),

Ayacucho

Bus Station

Guachalla

La Paz

Beni

Bolívar

Abaroa

Comercio

18 de Noviembre

Junin

Arce

Pando

Busch

TO WATERFALL (2km)

Bolívar

Santa Cruz

Vaca Diez

Campero

Pellicioll

Sucre

Ballivian

TO LA TOMA TRAIL (1km)

Plaza 2 Febrero

0   200 yards
0   200 meters

Río Beni

yaramerín (22hr., 1 per day 8am-noon, Bs130) via **Riberalta** (20hr., Bs120); and **Cobija** (2 days, Th 1 per day, Bs180). Trans Totai and Turbo Totai go to: **La Paz** (20hr., 10:30-11am, Bs70) via **Yucumo** (3hr., Bs30) and **Caranavi** (10-11hr., Bs50). Trans Tours, on Abaroa, between Pando and Aniceto Arce, has **Jeeps** that go to **La Paz** (12hr., 6-7am, Bs125; min. 4 passengers). Arrange a day ahead. Open M-F 8am-6pm.

Mototaxis: Taxi stops: in front of the market at Abaroa and Pando, and at Santa Cruz and Comercio. Within town Bs1.5; airport Bs5.

Ferries: Ferries run to **San Buenaventura** (every 10-15min. 6:30am-11:30pm, Bs1) from the shore, close to the end of Santa Cruz on the river.

Micros: Micros to **Reyes** (1hr., leaving when full, Bs9) depart from the corner of Santa Cruz and Comercio.

◼🛈 ORIENTATION AND PRACTICAL INFORMATION

Unlike most towns, Rurrenabaque doesn't center around the plaza—the plaza's only noisy on Sunday nights. Most activity takes place around **Santa Cruz** (which runs roughly east-west), on and between **Abaroa** and **Comercio**. Across the **Río Beni** is **San Buenaventura**, a former mission town even older than Rurrenabaque. If you go north past Arce or south past the plaza, the Rurre you'll see will be largely indistinguishable from any other tropical town.

Currency Exchange: Red Express Oriental, on Abaroa between Arce and Pando. 3.5% commission on traveler's checks. Open daily 8am-noon and 2-6pm; knock if closed.

Immigration: (☎922 241) Visa extensions. Open M-F 8am-4pm.

Camping Supplies: Vendors on Pando between Abaroa and Comercio. Flashlights Bs10-20. Hammocks around Bs75. For foodstuffs, try the **Micro Mercado Masary,** at Santa Cruz and Abaroa. Open M-Sa 8am-12:30pm and 2:30-9:30pm, Su 8am-3pm.

Book Exchange: Café Motacú (☎922 219), on Santa Cruz between Abaroa and Comercio. Small English book exchange (Bs5). Open daily 8:30am-noon and 5:30-8:30pm.

Laundromat: Laundry Service Number One, at Vaca Diez and Abaroa. Bs8 per kg. Same day service Bs9 per kg. Open M-Sa 8am-8pm, Su 9am-noon and 6-8pm.

Police: (☎110), on Campero, off the plaza.

Hospital: Hospital Rurrenabaque (☎922 112), at Ayacucho and La Paz, north of town.

Telephone: ENTEL, at Abaroa and Arce. Open daily 8am-9pm. Most prefer the **magnetic-card payphones** at Santa Cruz and Comercio, or at the market.

Post Office: Correos Ecobal, at Bolívar and Arce. Open daily 8am-noon and 2-6pm.

▐ ACCOMMODATIONS

With so many people coming in and out, the most popular hotels are often booked solid. Fortunately, due to the booming tourist trade, there are plenty of other places to spend the night.

▐ **Hotel Oriental** (☎922 401), on the main plaza. Very clean, very new, and very inviting, with a colorful courtyard. A bit off the beaten path. All rooms have ceiling fans. Singles Bs20 per person; doubles with bath Bs80.

▐ **Hotel Santa Ana** (☎922 399), on Abaroa, half-block up from the plaza. Perks include a hammock rotunda, laundry facilities, and an area where you can take your camp stove and cook. Hot showers Bs5. Rooms Bs20 per person, with bath Bs30 per person.

▐ **Hotel Beni** (☎922 408), on Comercio, near Pando. Some basic rooms, some souped-up ones. Singles Bs20; doubles (some with TV, A/C, bath or toilet paper) Bs50-150.

▐ **Hostal el Paraíso Tropical** (☎922 123), on Busch, between Junín and 18 de Noviembre, 2 blocks from the bus station. Doubles are so spacious they'd be triples in the center of town. Great mosquito netting. Laundry facilities. Dorms Bs20.

Hotel Tuichi, on Abaroa between Santa Cruz and Vaca Diez. Serving Rurre's most international crowd, most of whom want to meet fellow travelers. Mornings can be loud. Sporadic hot water. Dorms Bs20; rooms with bath Bs25 or Bs30 per person.

Hotel Safari (☎922 210), at the north end of Comercio. The nicest place in town. Pool. Safari-mobile (a minivan that carts guests back and forth from town). Karaoke. Breakfast included. Singles US$20; doubles US$30; triples US$38; quints US$50.

Hotel Asaí (☎922 439), at Vaca Diez and Busch. The quietest place in town, 3 blocks from the foothills of the jungle. Rooms with bath and fan Bs30 per person.

Hotel Rurrenabaque, at Bolívar and Vaca Diez. Surprisingly well-equipped for a cheap hotel that's essentially an aging mansion. Restaurant. Laundry service Bs8 per kg. Limited hot water. Singles Bs30; doubles Bs50.

Hostal América (☎922 413), on Santa Cruz near Comercio. Halls are narrow and rooms slightly crowded, though well-kept. Upstairs lounge has a pretty view of the river. Doubles tend to be cleaner and more comfortable. Singles Bs20; doubles Bs30.

Hotel Porteño (☎922 558), at Comercio and Vaca Diez. Old colonial house. Decorations are sparse, but dorm rooms are large. Rooms with bath come with towels, fans, and hot water. Dorms Bs20; rooms with bath Bs40 per person.

Hotel Berlin (☎922 450), on Comercio between Santa Cruz and Vaca Diez. Rooms with bath are a bit disheveled. Rooms without have mosquito nets to compensate for the holes in the wall. Still, the staff is friendly, and this is the cheapest place in town. Singles Bs10, with bath Bs20; doubles Bs20, with bath Bs30.

◖◗ FOOD

Eating in Rurrenabaque can get expensive. The touristy restaurants offer the most varied menus and stomach-friendly dishes but are usually also fairly expensive—a meal can easily go for Bs20-30. Penny-pinchers need not despair, however; they, too, have some good options. The ▐**fruit juices** at the **mercado municipal**—two fresh mugs for Bs1.5—are out of this world. One floor up, you can get a decent, two-dish *almuerzo* for Bs5. Finally, for some good and cheap burgers (Bs2), try the vendors on Comercio and Arce.

▐ **Restaurant La Perla de Rurrenabaque,** at Vaca Diez and Bolívar. First on most locals' lists, serving good, two-dish *almuerzos* (Bs6), and a variety of large fish, beef, and chicken dishes (Bs15-20). The *surubí al ajillo* (Bs20) is great. Open daily 7am-10pm.

▨ **Club Social Rurrenabaque,** on Comercio, near Santa Cruz. Attentive waiters. River view. Locals recommend it for its meat dishes. Cheeseburgers Bs9. *Milanesa de carne* Bs20.

Restaurant Heladería Camila's Snack (☎922 250), at Avaroa and Santa Cruz. The best ice cream (banana split Bs11) and lasagna (Bs18) in town. Decent vegetarian options: vegetarian lasagna (Bs18) and vegetarian burritos (Bs7).

La Cabaña, at the west end of Santa Cruz, at the Río Beni. An open-air restaurant where you can watch the ferries pull in and out of port. Grilled fish Bs20. Sandwiches 2.5-4.

Café Motacú (☎922 219), on Santa Cruz between Comercio and Abaroa. The most vegetarian options. Dishes Bs2-10. Local *artesanía*, on sale. Book exchange (Bs5).

Restaurant Tacuara, at Santa Cruz and Abaroa. Feeding hungry tourists. Open later than most. Vegetarian-friendly. Entrees average Bs12.

Pizzeria Italia, on Comercio, half-block from Santa Cruz. Large pizza Bs50. Billiard table (free if consuming, Bs6 per hr. if not). Open M-Su 7am-10:30pm.

◗ SIGHTS

Almost everyone has a day in Rurrenabaque before or after a trip to the jungle or pampas. Most spend it wallowing in their hammocks, complaining about their delayed flight or about how there's nothing to do. While it's true that there aren't any spectacular sights immediately around Rurrenabaque, there are a few area walks and boat trips that will take you to interesting destinations.

WATERFALL. If you walk to the east end of Santa Cruz, away from the Río Beni shoreline, you'll find a small stream and a few paths that wrap back and forth around it. If you follow the creek upstream for about 20min., you'll reach a small brown sand clearing surrounded by rock on three sides; a light (or strong, depending on the season) waterfall, drops about 10m into the center of it. It's a quiet place, possibly good for a wet picnic or midday snack.

ROCK CARVINGS. About one kilometer along the Río Beni, on the same side of the shore as Rurrenabaque, you'll find a large rock. On two faces, you'll see a large carving of a serpent curling across it. Many stories accompany this ancient etching; the most interesting concerns a large cave that only surfaces during the dry season. If you've come during a very dry spell, you may be able to see a dark cave, just above water level, to the left of the carving. People suggest that the carvings were a warning—a prehistoric "beware of dog" sign of sorts, except in this case, Spot was some sort of bloodthirsty man-eating beast. *(To see the carvings, you'll have to hire a boat. They're quite near Rurre, and the boatman (whom you can hire around where the ferry leaves for San Buenaventura—at the west end of Santa Cruz) shouldn't charge more than Bs15-20 round-trip. Ask to be taken to El Serpiente.)*

CENTRO CULTURAL TACANA. Located in San Buenaventura, just across the river, and not all that well-publicized, the Centro Cultural Tacana is one of the few "intellectually stimulating" sites that the Rurrenabaque area has to offer. Through colorful exhibits and a native guide, you can learn more about the culture and history of the Tacana people, who, after the rise of the post-Jesuit Franciscan missions, were dispersed throughout 20 communities. If you don't have the time or money to visit an indigenous community (which the Centro Cultural can also arrange), you can learn about the spinning techniques and medicinal plants of the Tacana here. *(Take the ferry across the Río Beni from the west end of Santa Cruz. Bs1. Once you get to San Buenaventura, take Murillo to the plaza; walking up from the river, it will be on the far left side of the plaza. ☎922 394. Open M-Sa 8:30-11:30am and 2-5pm.)*

MINI-ZOOLÓGICO. If you're not going on a trip to the pampas or jungle, you can see some of their animals in this private zoo. It's a sad sort of place for the animals, which include spider monkeys, alligators, parrots, and a lonely-looking jaguar, as they don't have much space to romp or roam about. *(Walk north on the road to the airport. You'll see a big sign for the zoo on your right after a few minutes. ☎922 479. Open daily 8am-6pm, except when it rains. Bs2.5, students and children free.)*

🎵🖼 ENTERTAINMENT AND NIGHTLIFE

There are surprisingly few things to do in Rurrenabaque, particularly when the sun goes down. Among travelers, the main morning, afternoon, and early-evening activities seem to be **lounging in hammocks and reading travel guides.** If anyone mustered up the energy and a ball, you could go over and have a **fútbol** match in the little field at the Mini-Zoológico. The Pizzeria Italia, on Comercio between Santa Cruz and Vaca Diez, has a **pool table** (Bs6 per hr., free if eating). If it gets too hot out, take a dip at the **Balneario Amaiba;** it's open every day that's hot (Bs10 per person). Rurre's big fiesta takes place on **February 2,** with folk dancing and other festivities. In the way of nightlife, Friday, Saturday, Sunday, and very occasionally Thursday nights are the only times you'll find anything worth looking for. Outside of those days, it's all about **karaoke,** which seems to have a death-grip on Rurre. If you'd prefer to dance, head to one of the two fairly decent **discotecas** in town. One has no sign, but is on Arce, near Comercio, close to the river. (Cover Bs2. Open F-Su.) The other, **Taurus,** is on Abaroa, between Santa Cruz and Vaca Diez. Both play a good mix of Latin and international tunes, and are fairly friendly to travelers.

🌴 INTO THE JUNGLE OR PAMPAS FROM RURRENABAQUE

The prime activity in Rurrenabaque—the reason tourists visit—is to tour the surrounding wilderness. For years, these tours were directed at the **jungle,** the area to the west of Rurre, which includes some of the terrain of Madidi National Park farther north. Soon, people realized that the **pampas,** the savannah-wetlands that surround Reyes and Santa Rosa to the northeast, also had strong tourist potential.

JUNGLE. Jungle tours can last anywhere from three to 25 days and are oriented toward learning about and understanding the environment. You'll see plenty of exotic vegetation and learn which flowers, leaves, and trees have special medicinal (or toxic) properties. If you're lucky, you may see **spider monkeys, toucans, ocelet,** or maybe even a **jaguar** (only spotted by about five groups per year). Bring long-sleeved shirts and pants that you don't mind dirtying, along with strong insect repellent. Excursions to **Parque Nacional Madidi** are some of the most in-demand (thanks to a glossy **National Geographic cover article** in 2000). Within only five years of its creation, Madidi has acquired quite the wild mystique. Its 1,895,750 hectares span almost 6000m in altitude, and house 1000 different species of birds, 44 percent of all species of new world mammals, and almost 40 percent of all neotropical amphibians. The park, however, is not an uninhabited jungle; over 26 indigenous communities call it home. And people always have: extensive Inca and pre-Inca ruins pepper the region nearest the village of Apolo. Almost every tour company in Rurrenabaque runs tours to Madidi, usually for a minimum of 5 or 6 days, at the jungle tour rate of US$30 per person per day.

PAMPAS. The pampas are more standardized and dependable. Most three-day tour pampas tours encounter at least a few **alligators** and plenty of **garzas.** Sighted a little less often, though still common, are **sloths** and **squirrel monkeys.** If you go to the Santa Rosa area, you're more likely to see **pink freshwater dolphins** and **capybaras,** the largest rodents on earth. Almost all tours to the pampas, like tours to the jungle, involve some **fishing,** and you may be able to catch a **piranha,** if you're quick enough. You'll also look for an **anaconda,** and, if your guide is willing and tour group supporting, catch and examine a **baby crocodile.**

LOGISTICS. The first rule about planning a tour in Rurre is to leave yourself a day in the area to plan it. This won't be hard, as most tours leave at 8 or 9am, before most planes or buses arrive. When arranging a trip, you should definitely visit at least a few agencies. Ask them to explain exactly what you will be doing, and exactly how many will be going (steer clear of groups larger than 8 people—they scare away animals). If you are a vegetarian, or will need an English translator, indicate so immediately. While the number of animals you see may vary dramatically, the quality of food or service should not. In general, your tour company should be willing and able to cater to your needs; the services they offer are uniform enough that you probably won't lose if you choose a smaller company instead of a larger and vice versa. Also, you shouldn't have to haggle over cost—all of the tour agencies in town have agreed to standardize prices; both jungle tours and pampas tours cost US$30 per person per day. Tour companies ask their customers to bring the basics: usually long-sleeved shirts, a flashlight, toilet paper, insect repellent, and a liter of water. If you have a sleeping bag, bring it along; if not, blankets should be provided at no extra cost. The tour company should also provide mosquito nets.

 When choosing a tour, talk to as many people as possible about potential guides, as there have been several instances of women being raped by their guides. Women should be wary of going on tours alone.

TOUR COMPANIES

Lots of companies offer very similar, very good services.

Fluvial Tours (☎922 372) and **Amazonico Travel** (☎(01) 796 142), on Abaroa between Santa Cruz and Vaca Diez. Run by Father Tico Tudela and his son, respectively. Fluvial Tours is the oldest and probably the most popular agency in town. It maintains fully established camps with dormitories and running water. The only drawback may be its popularity—groups tend to be a little large, and thus less attention is paid to each individual. Two doors down, Amazonico Travel seems to be picking up the slack with an overly friendly staff. During the wet season, Amazonico organizes 5-day and longer tours to more secluded sections of Madidi. Both accept V, MC, and traveler's checks.

Flecha Tours (☎922 478), at Abaroa and Santa Cruz, and **Aguilar Tours** (☎922 476) at Vaca Diez and Abaroa. These two also share an owner. Both have a reputation for having good food. Flecha Tours has a variety of tours available for Madidi, with expeditions along the Ríos Tuichi, Escalón, Hondo, and Toregua in the Lower Madidi; 6-10 day trips along the Río Yariapu, in the Upper Madidi; and 3-week treks to places up north like Ixiamas. Both accept V, MC, and traveler's checks.

Chalalán Albergue Ecológico-Ecolodge. Although it's out of most backpackers' budgets, this intriguing option is a good thing to know about. The indigenous community of San José de Uchupiamonas has built this ecological resort deep in the jungle. Accessible only through a 5-hour boat trip on the Beni and Tuichi Rivers, the albergue has facilities for 14 people, including a professional kitchen staff and a library. Once at the resort, you can hike along 25km of trails, go on various canoe or birdwatching trips, or just hang with the community. There is one English-speaking guide, and all proceeds go to the development of the community itself. 4 day/3 night stays US$280, US$235 for children under 12. Each additional night US$100, children under 12 US$70.

REYES   ☎08

Reyes is basically a smaller Rurrenabaque, minus the tourists and the Río Beni. The city itself is the capital of the local province, and its main plaza is very well tended, even if the palm trees have been painted slightly unattractive colors. The church, the Catedral de los Santos Reyes, a garishly modern building, has a stone ceiling that looks more like a mausoleum's, and a platform above the altar, which, since it's suspended with very thin wires, appears to hover in mid-air. While visiting Reyes, you may want to check out the nearby **Laguna Copaiba** (round-trip mototaxi Bs20). Also, Flecha Tours recently opened an office on the main plaza, and will soon offer horseback riding, as well as boat tours of the nearby Río Yacuma and other lagoons. (Open daily 7am-9pm.)

Unlike in Rurrenabaque, all activity here centers around the main **plaza,** or the streets **Comercio and 24 de Septiembre,** both very near the main plaza. The **airport** is a Bs5 mototaxi ride from town. **TAM** has an office on 24 de Septiembre. (☎252 254. Open M-F 8am-noon and 2:30-6pm, Sa 8am-noon.) Flights arrive in nearby Rurrenabaque. The quickest way to **Rurrenabaque** (1hr., Bs9) is on the trucks that drive

BOLIVIAN ORIENTE

around the plaza looking for passengers from 8am to 6 or 7pm. The **bus terminal** is five blocks from the plaza (mototaxi Bs2). Flota Yungueña has service to **La Paz** (24hr., 10am, Bs75) and **Riberalta** (18hr., noon, Bs120) via **Santa Rosa** (2½hr., Bs20), continuing on to **Guayaramerín** (20hr., Bs130). You may also arrange in Rurrenabaque to hitch a ride with any of the tour companies that pass through Reyes, either continuing on to Santa Rosa or returning to Rurre. Other services in town include: **Banco Unión,** on the plaza (open M-F 8:30am-noon and 2:30-6pm), and an **ENTEL phone** in the Residencial 6 de Enero, on Comercio, just off the main plaza.

The best of the budget accommodations is the **Residencial de Enero,** on Comercio, half a block off of the plaza. (☎252 151. Rooms Bs15 per person, with bath and fan Bs25.) **Hotel Tropical** is surprisingly fancy for a town like Reyes. As you walk in, the wall to the left boasts expensive liquors. All rooms have private bath, frigobar, TV, and mini-toiletries. (☎252 053. Singles Bs60; doubles Bs100. To eat, there are a series of cheap *pensiones* along 24 de Septiembre; the most popular is the **Restaurant Esmeralda,** next to the TAM office, charging Bs5 for a good two-dish *almuerzo*. If there are a bunch of people with you, you may want to pay a visit to the **Snack Heladería el Pingüino,** on Comercio. For every three purchases greater than Bs5, you get a little treat; every five purchases will get you an ice cream cone.

RIBERALTA ☎08

If you're looking for a quaint Bolivian village, or some interesting jungle wildlife, Riberalta's not the place. It is, however, the place to be if you're on your way from one place to another and need somewhere to get a good night's sleep and some filling food. Riberalta (pop. 50,000-80,000) is big, but it's not pretty. A recent population boom has clogged the city rather dramatically; at this point, officials don't even know how many people live here. While stopping over, don't spend much time looking for the "nice part of town"—aside from Mario Vargas Llosa's classical houses, it doesn't exist. Still, Riberalta is not a bad place to stop for a night, eat some Brazil nuts (Bs1 from the vendors on the street), and be on your way.

⊟⊓ TRANSPORTATION AND PRACTICAL INFORMATION. All streets that surround the **main plaza** (the only one you'll want to visit) are in a grid pattern. The **Río Beni** lies three blocks north of the plaza. **Nicolas Suárez** is Riberalta's principal north-south road; it runs along the eastern side of the plaza. The **airport** is south of town, on Chiquisaca. (☎522 350. Bs10 airport tax. Mototaxi Bs2.) Airlines include: **Lloyd Aereo Boliviano,** at Martínez and Melardo Chávez (☎522 239; open M-F 8am-noon and 2-6pm, Sa 8am-noon); **AeroSur,** on the plaza (☎522 798; open M-F 8am-noon and 2-6pm, Sa 8am-noon); and **TAM** (☎522 646), on Chiquisaca, 1½ blocks east of Nicolas Suárez. All fly to: **Trinidad** (1¼hr.; 1-2 per day; Bs502, TAM Bs370); **Cobija** (55min., 5 per week, Bs405); and **Guayaramerín** (20min., 7-8 per week, Bs136). TAM also has direct service to: **La Paz** (3½hr., M 12:10pm and F 10:40am, Bs600) via **Rurrenabaque** (2hr., Bs290); **Cochabamba** (Tu 1pm and Th 12:10pm, Bs520); and **Santa Cruz** (2¼hr., W 11:30am and Su 10:45am, Bs600). **Servicio Aereo Vargas España** (SANE), Ejército 76 (☎523 343), 1 block off the plaza, flies to **Guayaramerín** (15min., Sa 1 per day, Bs136) and sometimes **Trinidad** (55min., Bs502). There is no central bus terminal. Three companies have regular service: Syndicato Unificado de Buses Guayaramerín/Guaya Tours, at Nicolas Suárez and Beni Mamoré (☎522 575; open daily 6am-8pm); Flota Yungueña, at Beni Mamoré and Juan Aberdi (☎522 511; open daily 8am-noon and 3-6:30pm); and Flota Trans Pando, Melardo Chavez 93 (☎522 294), which only has service to **Cobija**. Only Guaya Tours has service to **Guayaramerín** (2hr., 6 per day, Bs20). Guaya Tours and Trans Pando go to **Cobija** (14hr., 1 per day 7-8:30am, Bs90). Guaya Tours and Yungueña go to **Trinidad** (30hr., 10am, Bs160) via **Rurrenabaque** (20hr., Bs130), **Yucumo** (23hr., Bs140), and **San Ignacio** (27hr., Bs150). Yungueña has service to **La Paz** (36hr., 11:30am, Bs160), via **Rurrenabaque** (20hr., Bs130), and **Caranavi** (30hr., Bs150). **Taxis** within the city, including the airport, should cost Bs2. Services include: **Banco Mercantil,** on the main plaza (open M-F 8:30am-12:30pm and 2:30-6:30pm, Sa 9am-1:30pm); the **police** (☎110), just off the main plaza; a **hospital** (☎523 586); **ENTEL,** half-block off the south end of the plaza (open M-F 7:30am-11pm, Sa 8am-11pm, Su 8am-10pm); and **Correos Ecobal,** on the main plaza (☎523 100; open M-F 8am-noon and 2:30-6pm).

⌂⌂ ACCOMMODATIONS AND FOOD. If you're here, you're probably stuck for the night on the way from one place to another. There are plenty of places to stay, but the cheapest ones aren't exactly pleasant. However, few places are filthy, so if you don't mind very basic accommodations, go for the cheapest options. Otherwise, a slightly higher price tag can ensure a more comfortable stay. ▓**Residencial Los Reyes,** Sucre 393, just south of Chiquisaca, is much nicer than most places at this price level, with red curtains at the front door and plenty of newspapers at the desk. (☎522 615. Dorms Bs10; singles with bath Bs30; doubles Bs40.) Elegant **Gabriel René,** Plácido Mendez 95, half-block from the plaza, has a beautiful garden. All rooms have bath. (☎523 018. Singles Bs60; doubles Bs85; all rooms with TV Bs85; suites with TV and A/C Bs150-200.) At **Residencial Julita,** Santiesteban 374 (☎522 380), 2 blocks south of the plaza, half-block from Nicolas Suárez, humble rooms cost Bs15 per person, but can be bargained down to Bs10 per person with four people. In most cities, it pays off to go to the markets to eat. In Riberalta, however, the market charges Bs5 for a two-dish *almuerzo.* Take extra precautions like brushing your teeth with purified or mineral water and beware of drinks with ice cubes. Pleasantly resort-like, **Restaurant Club Náutico Naval,** at the northernmost end of Nicolas Suárez, serves a great *almuerzo* (M-Sa Bs5, Su Bs10)—they're very cheap and equally tasty. (☎523 019. Pool use Bs10, kids Bs5. Open daily 8am-midnight.)

GUAYARAMERÍN ☎08

Guayaramerín is more than just another Bolivian border town. Business thrives here, thanks to the duty-free "Zona Franca" that allows for tax-free shopping. Motorbikes zoom through the streets, adding to Guayaramerín's bustle. Across the Río Mamoré, just three blocks north of the main plaza, sits the Brazilian port town of Guajará-Mirim, Guayaramerín's ugly foreign cousin. For tourists, this is a well-kept and pleasant city from which to catch a boat down the Mamoré (perhaps all the way to Cochabamba's Puerto Villarroel) or to commence a visit to Brazil.

▐ TRANSPORTATION

Flights: Airport (☎553 271). Mototaxi Bs3. Taxi Bs5. Airport tax Bs12. **LAB,** 25 de Mayo 652 (☎553 540). **AeroSur Express** (☎553 594), on the plaza. **TAM** (☎553 924) at 25 de Mayo and 16 de Julio. All open M-F 8am-noon and 2:30-6pm, Sa 8am-noon (TAM also open Su 8am-noon). LAB and AeroSur have service to **Trinidad** (1hr.; M-Th and Sa 2 per day, F and Su 1 per day; Bs502); **Riberalta** (15min., 1 per day, Bs136); **Santa Cruz** (30min., 1 per day M-Sa, Bs880); and **Cobija** (1¼hr., 1 per day M-Th and Sa, Bs405). TAM flies to: **La Paz** (2hr., M and F 1 per day, Bs600) via **Rurrenabaque** (1¼hr., Bs290); **Cochabamba** (2¼hr., Tu and Th 1 per day, Bs520), Th via **Trinidad** (1¼hr., Bs390); and **Santa Cruz** (1hr., W and Su 1 per day, Bs600) via **Trinidad** (1¼hr., W, Bs390).

Buses: Terminal, at Avenida and San Borja. To: **La Paz** (38hr., 8am, Bs165) via **Riberalta** (2hr., Bs20), **Rurrenabaque** (14hr., Bs130), **Yucumo** (24hr., Bs140), and **Caranavi** (30hr., Bs150); **Trinidad** (30hr., 7am, Bs170) via **Riberalta** (2hr., Bs20), **Rurrenabaque** (14hr., Bs130), **Yucumo** (24hr., Bs140), and **San Ignacio de Moxos** (27hr., Bs160); **Cobija** (14hr.; M, Tu, Th, and Sa 6am; Bs110) via **Riberalta** (2hr., Bs20); and **Riberalta** (2hr., 6 per day, Bs20). The Syndicato de Autotransporte 8 de Diciembre (☎554 290) has **express taxis** to **Riberalta** (2hr.; Bs120 alone, Bs30 per person for 4 passengers).

Boats: If you plan on traveling by boat via the Río Mamoré, arrive at least 24hr. before your departure at the **Capitania del Puerto** (☎553 866), at Costanera and Santa Cruz. Bring your passport. From there, you can catch boats to **Trinidad** (6 days in motorboat; Bs150, with food Bs200), or all the way down to Cochabamba's **Puerto Villarroel** (10-12 days in motorboat; Bs300, Bs350 with food). Expect to wait up to 2 or 3 days to catch the right boat. Capitania open M-F 8am-noon and 3-6:30pm, Sa 8am-noon.

Ferries: To **Guajará-Mirim** leave from the docks above Federico Román and Costanera whenever full. 7:30am-6:30pm Bs5; 6:30pm-6am Bs7.

Taxis: Mototaxis Bs2 within the city, including the bus terminal and the airport. Regular **taxis** Bs5 within the city.

BORDER CROSSING: INTO BRAZIL

Any foreigner can take the ferry across the Mamoré to visit Guajará-Mirim for the day. If you plan on going farther into Brazil than Guajará-Mirim, however—or spending the night there—you must formally enter Brazil, which involves getting exit and entry stamps and a visa if necessary (as it is for US citizens, Canadians, Australians, and New Zealanders). If you need a visa but don't yet have one when you get to Guajará-Mirim, head to the **Brazilian Consulate** (☎553 766) at Beni and 24 de Septiembre. Visas take at least 24 hours to process and cost US$45 for US citizens, US$40 for Canadians, US$35 for Australians, and US$20 for New Zealanders. Open M-F 9am-1pm and 3-5pm. But wait! Before you leave Bolivia, you'll need to get an exit stamp at Bolivian immigration. (Open M-F 8am-4pm, Sa 8:30am-noon.) To get a Brazilian entrance stamp, you must have a **yellow fever vaccination certificate** that is older than 10 days and younger than 10 years. Once you arrive in Brazil, stop at the **Policia Federal** at Presidente Dutra and Quinchio—to expedite things, look presentable, and always address the officer, politely, as *mosso* (sir) or *mossa* (madam). If you have a visa, a yellow fever certificate, and a Bolivian exit stamp, the border police will stamp your passport at any time of day or night (knock loudly). They also keep regular office hours M-F 8am-noon and 2-6pm.

✦🛈 ORIENTATION AND PRACTICAL INFORMATION

On a full map, Guayaramerín looks huge; the parts a visitor will see are anything but. The city is laid out in a grid pattern with two plazas, the smaller lying eight blocks below the main one. Bordering both **main plazas** are the two main north-south streets, **Oruro** and **Federico Román.** The biggest street in town turns into **Alto de la Alianza,** simply known as "La Avenida," down south. Both streets end three blocks north of the main plaza, when they hit **Costanera,** which runs along the shore of the **Río Mamoré.**

Currency Exchange: Banco Mercantil, on the main plaza. Open M-F 8:30am-12:20pm and 2:30-6pm. The only place to change traveler's checks (and the last place you'll be able to if your next stop is Riberalta or Cobija) is the **Casa de Cambio,** 6 de Agosto 347 (☎553 555), in the Hotel San Carlos. Open daily 7:30am-noon and 2-6pm.

Market: On Federico Román, between Max Paredes and Tarija.

Police: (☎110), at Santa Cruz and 6 de Agosto.

Hospital: (☎553 007), on 22 de Septiembre, between Mamoré and 6 de Agosto.

Telephones: ENTEL, at Oscar Umzaga de la Vega and Mamoré. Open M-Sa 7:30am-11pm, Su 8am-9pm.

Post Office: Correos Ecobal, Oruro 239 (☎553 896). Open M-F 8am-noon and 2:30-6pm, Sa 8am-noon.

▛ ACCOMMODATIONS

Stick to the center of town; you'd think the hotels that are simpler, dirtier, and farther from the city center would be cheaper, but they aren't.

▧ **Hotel Santa Ana** (☎553 900), at 16 de Julio and 25 de Mayo. There's no beating the Santa Ana, and travelers know it. If it's hot out, the freezer's stocked with ice water; if it's cold, there's a thermos of sweet coffee. Rooms Bs20 per person, with bath Bs25.

Hotel Litoral (☎553 895), at 16 de Julio and 25 de Mayo. Rooms are a bit dark. Large lounge. Breakfast Bs5. Rooms Bs20 per person, with bath Bs25.

Hotel Central, Santa Cruz 235 (☎355 911), at 6 de Agosto. Grandmotherly owner. Quiet courtyard. Bug nets could use a little patchwork. Rooms Bs15 per person.

Hotel Plaza Anexo (☎553 650), on the main plaza. Not the most popular, but still a good budget option. Fans and towels in each room. Rooms Bs25 per person.

▛ FOOD

Guayaramerín sticks to what it knows: meat. There is a smattering of largely indistinguishable *churrasquerías* to the south. Those who are still feeling the pinch of high Brazilian prices across the border can save by sticking to the snacks on the main plaza—they almost all serve a decent burger for around Bs5. Street vendors provide yet another option—beefcakes, and lots of them (Bs0.50 each).

La Parrilla, Santa Cruz 161 (☎554 544). Stylish owner, stylish restaurant. Thatched. *Almuerzo* Bs7. A la carte dishes Bs25-35. Juices Bs5-15. Open daily 10am-midnight.

Restaurant Karla Greta, (☎(01) 682 109), on Federico Román, near the main plaza. *Almuerzo* Bs7. Excellent meat dishes for two, Bs25-30. Pleasant sidewalk seating. Booming stereo system. Open daily 8am-11pm.

Club Social Guayaramerín (☎553 918), on the plaza. For the meat-lover in everyone. Checkerboard floor tiles and chintzy colored lightbulbs. *Almuerzo* Bs10. A la carte dishes Bs20-25. Open daily 11:30am-midnight.

Restaurant y Churrasquería El Sujal (☎554 330), on Federico Román, near the bus station. A straight-shootin' *churrasquería*. Their massive *parrilladas*—pounds and pounds of meat—serves 8 (Bs120). Open daily 8am-3pm and 6:30-10pm.

COBIJA   ☎08

Cobija is not on most locals' future business or vacation stops. It's not slated for many travelers either. Even though Cobija is literally a stone's throw from Brazil (the winding Río Acre forms the border between the two countries), most decide to enter or exit Brazil from Guayaramerín. But it's a shame that the city is not more popular, because Cobija is cleaner, more attractive, and more fun than almost any other border town. It is also a city well-suited to introduce visitors to Brazil—if you're planning on spending some time here, it's a good idea to learn some Portuguese, watch plenty of soccer, and learn to *samba*.

▛ TRANSPORTATION

Flights: Aeropuerto Internacional Capitán Anival Arab (☎422 260), southeast of town. Airport tax Bs15. Mototaxi Bs5; taxi Bs10. **AeroSur** (☎423 132), on the plaza. Open M-F 8:30am-noon and 3:30-6pm, Sa 9am-noon and 3:30-5pm, Su 8am-noon. **LAB** (☎422 170), on Fernández Molina. Open M-F 8am-noon and 3-6pm, Sa 8am-noon. **TAM,** 9 de Febrero 59 (☎422 267). Open M-F 8am-noon and 3-6:30pm, Sa 8:30-11:30am. To: **Trinidad** (1¾hr., Tu-Th 1 per day, Bs706); **Riberalta** (1hr.; Tu-W 1 per day: LAB Bs405, TAM Bs260); **Guayaramerín** (1¼hr., Tu 10:30am, Bs290); and **La Paz** (1¼hr.; W 1 per day, F and Su 2 per day; AeroSur Bs854, LAB Bs726, TAM Bs550).

Bus: There is no terminal, just 3 companies: **Guaya Tours,** 9 de Febrero 177 (☎422 349), open daily 8am-10pm; **Flota Trans Pando,** on 9 de Febrero near the stadium (☎422 450), open daily 8am-9pm; and **Flota Yungueña,** across from Trans Pando (☎423 457), open M-Sa 8am-noon and 2-7pm. To **Riberalta** (12hr., Su-F 6:30am, Bs90) and **Guayaramerín** (15hr., Guaya Tours Tu and Th 6:30am). Flota Yungueña goes to **La Paz** (2½ days, Su 6:30am, Bs240).

Ferry: Across the Río Acre (6am-10pm, Bs2). Follow the walkway at the western end of Nicolas Suárez; the ferry leaves from the riverbank right behind the Fuerza Naval.

Taxi: Taxis and mototaxis Bs2.5 per person within town. Mototaxi to airport Bs5 per person. Taxi to airport Bs10 per person.

BORDER CROSSING: INTO BRAZIL AND PERU

You don't need to get your passport stamped to visit **Brasiléa,** the city opposite Cobija across the Río Acre, unless you're planning on more than just a daytrip. In that case, you'll need to get your passport stamped and, if you're an Australian, New Zealander, Canadian, or US citizen, a visa. The **Brazilian Consulate,** off the north side of the main plaza, across from the Banco Union, issues visas. The process generally takes at least 24 hours and costs US$45 for US citizens, US$40 for Canadians, US$35 for Australians, and US$20 for New Zealanders. (☎423 225. Open M-F 8am-1pm.) To enter Brazil, you'll need a **yellow fever vaccination certificate** that is older than 10 days and younger than 10 years. You'll also need to pick up an **exit stamp** from **Bolivian Immigration,** at the north end of Internacional. (☎422 081. Open 24hr.) There are two ways to get to Brazil from Cobija: by rowboat ferry at the end of Nicolas Suárez (daily 6am-10pm, Bs2); and by road on the Internacional. There is a Bolivian immigration post at the end of Internacional, but there is no post at the ferries, so if you need an exit stamp, you will have to go via taxi to the border at Internacional. Once you arrive at the Brazilian border, you can get a taxi (Bs10) to the **Policia Federal,** in Epitaciolándia. (Open daily 6am-midnight.) If you have an exit stamp, visa, and a yellow fever certificate, they should give you an **entrance stamp,** but don't risk anything—make sure you look presentable. From **Brasiléa,** it is possible to travel to Peru. Take a taxi to **Assis-Brasil,** then get another taxi to take you over very rough roads to **Puerto Maldonado, Peru.**

◆🛈 ORIENTATION AND PRACTICAL INFORMATION

The **Río Acre** wraps around the northern and western sides of town and serves as the border between Bolivia and Brazil. Most restaurants, hotels, and other important businesses gather around the **main plaza,** or on the two streets (**Fernandez Molina** and **9 de Febrero**) that run southeast of it, parallel to each other.

Tourist Information: Director of Tourism (☎422 235), on 9 de Febrero, in the Corte de Pando building, across from TAM. Open daily 7:30am-3:30pm.

Currency Exchange: Casa de Cambio Cachito (☎422 581), at Cornejo and 9 de Febrero. Open M-F 8am-noon and 3-6pm, Sa 8am-noon. **Casa de Cambio Horacio** (☎423 277). Open M-Sa 7:30am-12:30pm and 3-6:30pm. There is no place to change traveler's checks in Cobija. There is, however, a **Western Union,** 9 de Febrero 98 (☎422 800). Open M-F 8am-noon and 3-6pm.

Market: On Otto Felipe Braun, which connects 9 de Febrero and Fernández Molina.

Emergency: ☎110.

Police: ☎110. On Fernández Molina.

Hospital: Hospital Roberto Galindo (☎422 017), south of town.

Pharmacy: Farmacia Cruz del Sur (☎(01) 995 787), on the main plaza. Open daily 8am-11pm; 24hr. for emergencies.

Telephones: ENTEL (☎422 291), at Sucre and Bolívar, 2 blocks northeast of the plaza. Open daily 7:30am-11pm.

Internet Access: The **university** has a public access Internet parlor on Cornejo, just below the main plaza. Bs8 per hr. Open M-F 8am-10:30pm, Sa 8am-noon.

Post Office: Correos Ecobal (☎422 598), on the main plaza. Open M-F 8am-noon and 2:30-6:30pm, Sa 9am-noon.

ACCOMMODATIONS

Hotels here are a little more informal than usual—no standard room prices have been set, and most owners are open to a little friendly bargaining.

Residencial Cocodrilo (☎422 215), on Fernández Molina, near Sucre. The cheapest decent place in town, though the water smells a bit funny. Singles Bs30; doubles Bs40.

Residencial Exclusivo (☎423 084), at Cochabamba and 6 de Agosto, 2 blocks from Cornejo. A good value. Rooms downstairs tend to be cooler, but some walls don't reach the ceiling. Dorms Bs20; rooms Bs20 per person; with TV, bath and fan Bs35.

Residencial Frontera (☎422 740), on Beni. Always bustling. Rooms for 1 or 2 people Bs60, with TV Bs70, with bath, fan, and TV Bs80.

Hotel Avenida (☎422 108), at 9 de Febrero and Otto Felipe Braun. Rooms with bath, some with A/C, border a tiny courtyard. Reserve rooms with A/C in advance. Breakfast included. Rooms with fan Bs80; singles with A/C Bs120; doubles with A/C Bs150.

FOOD

Eateries in town are surprisingly good. Cobija even has an excellent bakery/coffeeshop: the **Panadería y Confitería Cobija,** opposite the mini-plaza to the south of the main plaza. For lunch, there's no reason to go to the market—restaurants serve better food for similar prices (around Bs6).

 La Esquina de la Abuela (☎422 364), at Sucre and Fernández Molina. By far the best restaurant in town, and the most popular, too, especially with locals. Sidewalk seating. *Lomo montado* Bs15. *Bife chorizo* Bs20. Open M-Sa 11am-midnight.

Restaurant Chifa Hong Kong, Emilio Mendizabal 754 (☎422 700), at the end of Fernández Molina closest to the plaza. Chinese specialties like sweet and sour pork or lemon chicken Bs10-15. Open M-Sa 11am-2pm and 6pm-midnight.

Heladería Nishi, on the plaza. Old men come here for hours on end, and young couples dart in and out throughout the night. Large speakers pump out the latest Brazilian and Bolivian tunes. Ice cream Bs5. Sandwiches Bs5. Open daily 9am-midnight.

El Meson de la Pascana (☎422 185), on Beni near 9 de Febrero. Old-fashioned Bolivian cuisine. *Almuerzo* Bs6. On Sundays, they only serve *salteñas* (Bs3.5) and ice cream (Bs5-10). Open M-Sa 8:30am-10pm, Su 7am-noon.

NIGHTLIFE

Lennon, a disco on 16 de Julio, about two blocks south of 9 de Febrero, draws only the largest and best-dressed crowds. You won't hear much Beatles here, however—it's straight salsa and *samba*. On Saturdays, old-timers take over, and the *discoteca* becomes, for the night, what people call a *viejoteca*. Don't go alone. (Beer Bs10 for 3. Open F-Su.) Other than Lennon, it's all about karaoke. The nicest place is **Don Gerardo**, at 6 de Agosto and Villamonte, with plush couches, plenty of blacklights to pick up any dirt on your clothes, and a relatively mature (30-50+) clientele. (Drinks Bs5-15.) For something a little younger, try **Las Palmas,** opposite Lennon. (Both open Tu-Su.)

YUCUMO
☎ 04

At Yucumo, the road from Trinidad runs into the road to La Paz, Rurrenabaque, and Guayaramerín. And the town is literally that: two dirt roads that run into each other—plus the auto parts stores, eateries, and cheap *alojamientos* that have sprung up to cater to the passing buses. Any bus north to Rurrenabaque, south to La Paz, or east to Trinidad must pass through here. To: **Rurrenabaque** (4hr., 2-3 per day 3:30-5am, Bs20); **La Paz** (12hr., 3-4 per day 2-3pm, Bs55); and **Trinidad** (8hr., 1-2 per day 7pm-2am). It's usually best to wait for buses at the tables where the roads cross. **Hotel Tropical,** the pink building you'll pass on your left if you're coming from Trinidad, is probably the nicest. (Rooms Bs15, with bath Bs30.)

SAN IGNACIO DE MOXOS
☎ 04

Known as the cultural capital of the Beni department, San Ignacio has more than its share of history and tradition. When Lima Jesuits founded it in 1689, it was the third largest mission in Moxos. But while much of San Ignacio still speaks the native dialect, Ignaciano, just about everything else has changed since its Jesuit years. For one thing, 47 years after its founding, the town shifted to its present position, near the shore of Laguna Isirere. Today, San Ignacio de Moxos attracts visitors with its 300-year-old church and the cool waters of Laguna Isirere, 1km from town. Moreover, San Ignacio's **Fiesta de San Ignacio de Loyola** is one of the largest and most recognized in all of Bolivia. The partying starts on July 30 with a massive *entrada folklórica*. Participants perform traditional dances, including that of the *machetero*, a symbol of the original tribe's struggle against nature. The eve of the 30th is capped off with fireworks and *peñas* throughout town. For most, the next three days of the fiesta pass in a blur. The **running of the bulls** starts on the first day and continues for the next two, and the *palo ensebao*, a large pole greased with oil and fat, with prizes waiting at the top for successful climbers, is raised on the first of August. Throughout all of these days, you are likely to see the **Achus,** dancers who, with their wrinkled face masks and warped canes, represent the elderly of San Ignacio. Things wind down on August 2, when a large procession exits the town. Prices during the fiesta can almost double, and the town is packed. It would be wise to reserve a room or bring your camping gear—some campers stake out in the area immediately in front of the church. Most of the action in town, including the market, takes place behind the church. Syndicato 31 de Julio (☎ 822 253) sends buses to **Trinidad** (2½-3hr., 8:30am and 2pm, Bs25). The Syndicato 1 de Mayo (☎ 822 168) goes to **Trinidad** (3hr., 8am and 1:30pm, Bs30) via **San Borja** (4hr., 1:30pm, Bs50), **Rurrenabaque** (10hr., Bs120), and **Guayaramerín** (23hr., Bs150). Services include: the **police** (☎ 110); **Hospital San Ignacio de Moxos** (☎ 822 110); and **ENTEL,** 1½ blocks from the plaza. There are no banks in town; ask around—many stores and hotels will change dollars. San Ignacio de Moros only has electricity M-Sa 9am-3pm and 6pm-1:30am, Su 10am-1pm, so you may want to bring candles or a flashlight and batteries. The best lodging is definitely at **Residencial Don Joaquín,** on the main plaza, which has a well-tended courtyard and fans in all rooms. The owner rents out horses. (☎ 822 112. Rooms Bs20, with bath Bs30.)

TRINIDAD
☎ 04

Some first impressions cast Trinidad as larger, dirtier, and more impersonal than it is. That said, Trinidad is a large, dirty, and impersonal city. The constant growl of motorcycles and scooters results in a noise level characteristic of cities ten times its size. And the open sewer system, with foot-deep drains lining every block, doesn't make it look any better than it sounds. But the place isn't all bad. It was one of the first Jesuit missions in all of Bolivia, and before that housed the Patiti Empire (around AD 300). Of course, that's about it. If we were you, we'd skip to the awesome options in the "Near Trinidad" section, p. 419.

☞ TRANSPORTATION

Flights: Airport (☎620 678), 5km from town. Airport tax Bs17. Mototaxi Bs5. Regular taxi Bs7. **LAB** (☎620 595), at Santa Cruz and La Paz. Open M-F 8am-noon and 2:30-6:30pm, Sa 8am-noon. To **Cochabamba** (35min., 1 per day, Bs339) and **Magdalena** and **San Joaquín** (40min., 1 per day M and F, Bs228). **AeroSur,** Cipriano Barace 151 (☎623 402). To: **Santa Cruz** (40min., 1 per day M-Sa, Bs402); **Guayaramerín** (1½hr., 1 per day M-Sa, Bs502); and **Riberalta** (1½hr., 1 per day M-Sa, Bs502). **TAM** (☎622 363), at Santa Cruz and Bolívar. Open M-F 8am-noon and 2:30-6:30pm, Sa 8am-noon. To: **Riberalta** (1¼hr., W-Th 10:30am, Bs390) via **Guayaramerín** (1½hr., Bs390); **Santa Cruz** (1hr., W-Th 2:30pm, Bs290); **Cochabamba** (1hr., Th 2:50pm, Bs295); **Rurrenabaque** (1hr., Bs200); and **La Paz** (2hr., Bs300).

Bus: Terminal, in the Barrio Fatima, at Viador Pinto Saucedo and Romulo Mendoza. To: **Santa Cruz** (12hr., 5-7pm, Bs20-60); **San Borja** (8hr., 9am, Bs80) via **San Ignacio** (3hr., Bs25); and **Guayaramerín** (29-30hr., 10am, Bs170) via **Rurrenabaque** (12hr., Bs120) and **Riberalta** (28hr., Bs160).

Boat: Although there are few passenger boats that navigate the Mamoré, you can hitch a ride on one of the many **cargo boats** that go up and down the river. There are 3 ports: **Puerto Almacen,** on the Río Ibare 8km to the south, **Puerto Varador** 10km away on the Laguna Mamoré, and the newest, **Puerto Los Puentes,** on the Río Mamoré. During the wet season, all three ports are in service, and the Capitanía del Río is at the Puerto Almacen. During the dry season, only Almacen and Varador function, and the Capitanía del Río is at Los Puentes. If you are interested in taking a trip, you should visit the navy's **Capitanía del Río.** Make sure you bring your passport (and entry slip), and the captain will give you all the information you want for boats going north to **Santa Ana** and **Guayaramerín,** and south to **Puerto Villarroel.** Then, you'll have to walk to the docks themselves and ask for the latest prices. A non-stop 6-day trip (or a 15-day trip that stops frequently) to Guayaramerín costs Bs150, Bs200 with food; direct 36hr. trip to Puerto Villarroel Bs50, Bs100 with food; the boat that docks at night takes 5 days. Work out specific arrangements with the captain, and be prepared for anything. Bring a hammock, bug spray, and a water supply or purification system. Trufi-taxis leave when full for all 3 ports (Bs5 to Almacen and Varador, Bs10 to Los Puentes) from the gas station at the south end of Pedro Ignacio Muiba.

Taxis: Mototaxis are cheaper and faster than regular taxis. Mototaxi in town Bs2, taxi Bs3. Prices rise by Bs1-2 after 10pm.

Motorcycle Rental: Moto Rental, at 6 de Agosto and 18 de Noviembre. **Alquilar de Motos Negrito,** at Nicolas Suárez and Bolívar. Bs10 per hr.; full tank of gas included.

☀☞ ORIENTATION AND PRACTICAL INFORMATION

A highway encircles Trinidad. It goes by different names, but the only one you need to know is **La Circumvalación.** The city is divided into *barrios*—most visitors stick to the **barrio central,** the area around the **Plaza Ballivián.** If you're coming in from the bus station, you'll arrive in the **Barrio Fatima,** which is connected to the rest by **Simón Bolívar,** a heavy-traffic road that runs northeast. Finally, the **Arroyo San Juan,** once a creek, now a glorified mud puddle, divides the town in half—you'll have to cross it going south to the Barrio Pompeya. Take extra precaution in Pompeya, especially at night.

Tourist Office: (☎620 665), in the prefectura, 1 block south of the plaza, on Joaquín de la Sierra. Open M-F 7:30am-3:30pm.

Tour Agencies: Turismo Moxos, 6 de Agosto 114 (☎621 141). Budget boat, birdwatching, and camping tours. Local guides and English translators are available for an extra US$20 per day. 3-day, 2-night boat tour US$180 per person for 2-6 people, less in larger groups. **Paraíso Travel,** 6 de Agosto 138 (☎620 692). Birdwatching tours. 4-day, 3-night all-inclusive tour for 4 US$530 per person. **Viajes Fremen** (☎622 276), on Japón. 3-day boat tour US$190 per person.

Immigration: (☎ 621 449), in the police building on Busch, half-block off the plaza. Grants 30- or 90-day visa extensions. Open M-F 8am-4pm.

Currency Exchange: Banco Nacional (☎ 621 034), on the Plaza Ballivián. Open M-F 8:30am-noon and 2:30-6:30pm, Sa 9am-1pm. **Banco Mercantil,** on Joaquín de Sierra half-block from the plaza. **Visa/MC ATM.**

Camping Equipment: Casa Williams (☎ 622 338) on the plaza. Flashlights, raingear, fishline, and other hunting-style equipment. Knowledgeable owner.

Laundry: Lavandería Pro-Vida (☎ 620 626), at Felix Pinto and Cipriano Barace. Bs6 per dozen. 1-day service Bs12 per dozen. Open M-F 8am-noon and 2-6pm, Sa 8am-noon.

Market: Mercado Municipal, 2 blocks south of the main plaza. **Mercado Seccional,** at Sucre and Cochabamba. **Mercado Fatima** is farther out, on the same block and adjacent to the bus station. **Mercado Pompeya,** down south, at Isiboro and Ibare.

Emergency: ☎ 110.

Police: (☎ 620 466). Open daily 8am-noon and 3-6:30pm.

Hospital: Hospital Presidente German Busch (☎ 118), on Bolívar between Carmelo López and Fabian Monasterio Claure.

Telephone: ENTEL, next to the post office. Open M-F 7:30am-11pm, Sa-Su 8am-10:30pm.

Internet: CambaNet (☎ 625 134), on the Plaza Ballivián. Bs15 per hr., students Bs10. Open daily 8am-midnight.

Post Office: (☎ 621 266), on the plaza. Open M-Sa 8am-noon and 2:30-6pm.

ACCOMMODATIONS

Make sure to check for mosquito screens.

Residencial Fatima (☎ 622 474), 1 block north of the bus station on Viador Pinto. The cleanest budget place near the bus station. The place has come under new ownership and is much improved. Rooms Bs20 per person, with bath Bs50.

Hotel Yacuma (☎ 622 249), at Santa Cruz and La Paz. The walls are crumbling, and the water sporadic, but Hotel Yacuma is a cozy sort of old. Gigantic upstairs rooms. English-speaking staff caters to largely touristy crowd. Rooms Bs20 per person, with bath Bs50.

Residencial Santa Cruz (☎ 620 711), on Santa Cruz between Sucre and Vaca Diez. Big rooms. Relatively cool. Complimentary soft drinks. Rooms Bs40, with bath Bs70.

Residencial 18 de Noviembre (☎ 621 272), on 6 de Agosto, near Santa Cruz. Nice courtyard with hammocks. Good bug netting. Fans in most rooms. Rooms Bs20 per person, with bath Bs25.

Beni Hotel (☎ 620 522), on 6 de Agosto between 18 de Noviembre and Nicolas Suárez. Rooms are equipped with bath, TV, telephone, fan, and hammock. Free water and coffee. Singles US$18, with A/C US$30; doubles US$23, with A/C US$35; triples US$25.

Hotel Copacabana, Villavicencia 627 (☎ 620 305), near Vaca Diez. Popular with Bolivians. Good mattresses and bathrooms. Dorms Bs33; rooms with bath Bs55 per person.

FOOD

At night, food vendors set up shop at La Paz and Santa Cruz and offer sausage-dogs and hamburgers (Bs1.5).

La Casona (☎ 622 437), on the Plaza Ballivián. Popular. Good meat and pasta dishes. *Almuerzo* Bs9. Dinner entrees Bs17-30. Open daily 8am-midnight.

Heladería Kivón, on the Plaza Ballivián. Somewhat expensive (soda Bs4), but the pleasant upper balcony is one of Trinidad's nicest hangouts. Open daily 7am-midnight.

Churrasquería La Estancia (☎ 620 022), across the Pompeya bridge, on Ibaré, between Ignacio Muiba and Hernán Velarde Rojas. Arguably the best *churrasquería* in town. *Churrasco* and *pacumuto* Bs25 per person. Open daily 4pm-midnight.

👁 🎵 SIGHTS AND ENTERTAINMENT

Even the tourist office will admit that there's not much to see in Trinidad. If you've got a few hours to kill in the city, check out the **Plaza Ballivián;** the water in the curiously decorated fountain actually contains several catfish and a baby crocodile. Also interesting is **Museo Ioticola** in the technical university. (Mototaxi Bs3.) There, you'll find hordes of fish and water-creatures, including the **piraiba,** the largest fish found in Amazonian riverways, which can reach up to 4m in length and 300kg in weight. You can also see freshwater dolphins or buy a dried piranha (Bs15) to take home. (☎621 705. Open M-F 8am-3pm.) Just a few kilometers from the southeast part of town, the **Laguna Suárez** is a pleasant place to spend a hot afternoon. It's dotted with resort-like establishments.

🎭 FESTIVALS

Trinidad's largest fiesta is the **Fiesta Santíssima Trinidad,** held the weekend before Corpus Christi; that Sunday, you can see folkloric dances, among them **los macheteros,** a dance unique to the region, which symbolizes the indigenous man's struggle against nature, performed by men wearing large, feathered headdresses. When they're not being used, you can check out these headdresses at the **Casa de la Cultura** (☎620 796), at Santa Cruz and Vaca Diez.

🎵 NIGHTLIFE

Trinidad nightlife hits its stride on Saturdays, and sometimes Sundays. For something true to the spirit of South American fiestas, try the **Quinta Show La Costanera,** on the southwestern side of La Circumvalación. They play dancing music—and the diverse revellers break out their dancing shoes. (☎625 929. Open F-Sa 10pm-late.) Trinidad's more affluent are more likely to end up at **Zodiac,** on the corner of Santa Cruz and Av. del Mar. (Cover F-Su Bs5. Open F-Sa 8:30pm-3am.) Another attractive locale is just down the block. The **Matehua Café,** at Santa Cruz and Bolívar, is the only true cafe in town. The owner, an amateur archeologist, sometimes shows regional archaeology videos or hosts poetry readings. (☎625 326. Beer Bs8. Live music Th-Sa. Open daily 3-8pm and 8:30pm-2am.)

NEAR TRINIDAD: SANTUARIO CHUCHINI

Trips to Chuchini are organized and led by the owner's family, and can range from a few hours to a whole week. Half-day US$35, full day US$70. Prices include all meals, guides, lodging, and pickup and drop-off from your hotel or the Trinidad airport. If you just want to visit for a few hours, perhaps to see the museum, you can hire a mototaxi; the round-trip, including the wait, should cost around Bs40-50. Bring good bug spray; you'll need it. For more information, contact Efrem Hinojosa Hieber, 18 de Noviembre 543, Casilla 89 (☎624 744 or 625 284).

Over 20 years ago, Efrem Hinojosa Hieber purchased what seemed to him and everyone else to be a miserable, mosquito-filled, and swampy 700-hectare plot, only good for logging. Deciding to brave the mosquitos to explore his new property 17km from Trinidad, Hieber noticed a curious system of hills, mounds, and land bridges—not to mention clay pottery and figurines that kept, literally, popping out of the ground. He decided to dredge the swamps to rid himself of the mosquitos, but that was a job that no sane local man would take. So, he hired 30 workers from surrounding departments, bought them rubberized suits, and set them to work. The result: a newly accessible, largely unexplored area of great archaeological and environmental interest.

Visits to Chuchini are custom-made; you can take a daytrip to the nearby **Laguna Media Luna,** which has a floating island of Yomomo trees, or to **"La Catedral,"** a giant Bibosi tree with vines you can climb and slide down. You can also travel deep into the jungle, maybe take a prolonged boat trip on the Mamoré, or, perhaps most interesting, decide to give your tour an archaeological twist and study the pieces in the Santuario's small but impressive **museum**. Inside, aside from seeing the remains of the *osito oro* (the smallest bear in the world, which would fit comfortably in the palm of your hand), and the gigantic *caimon negro* (a tropical alligator-like creature than can measure up to 7m long), you can admire ceramics and pottery left over from the Paititi Empire.

NEAR TRINIDAD: LAST FRONTIERS

Taxi Bs60. Contact the owners, Sarah and Celia Dieter (lastfrontiers@yahoo.co.uk).

What started out as an English-owned dairy farm 55km on the asphalt road to Santa Cruz has become the best access point for the **Reserva de Vida Silvestre Ríos Blanco y Negro** and 20,000-hectare rustic resort of sorts. As such, it is one of the best deals around, charging US$6 per person per night for camping, including three meals, soft drinks, use of hammocks and tents, and bucket showers. From there, you can go on horseback riding trips (US$28 per person per day). Or, if you've found a group beforehand, you can take a six-day tour of the reserve (dry season US$230 per person, wet season US$250-280). Tours are custom-designed and can include anything from birdwatching to hard-core jungle exploration.

ECUADOR

HISTORY SINCE INDEPENDENCE

CONSERVATIVES AND LIBERALS (1830-1947)

During its early, tormented years, various rivalries plagued Ecuador: Quito and the Sierra emerged as conservative and clerical; the cosmopolitan, commercial port of Guayaquil was ruled by a nouveau riche merchant class with much exposure to imported 19th-century liberalism; and the coastal bourgeoisie favored free enterprise and anticlericalism.

The liberal-conservative split made it impossible for Ecuadorians to agree peacefully on a national leader, although the most natural choice was **General Juan José Flores,** whom Bolívar appointed governor of Ecuador when it was part of Gran Colombia. As part of the *criollo* elite, Flores found his support among the conservative *quiteños,* while **José Vicente Rocafuerte** rose as his rival in liberal Guayaquil. For the next 15 years, the two politicians struggled for power, taking turns in the presidency. Starting with an overthrow of Flores' regime in 1845, Ecuador experienced another 15 years of chaos. One of the more powerful and influential military leaders, **General José María Urbina,** ruled from 1851 to 1856,

emancipating the nation's slaves once he came to power. By 1859, a year known in Ecuador as the **Terrible Year,** the country stood in a state of near-anarchy after one local *caudillo* stirred up anger by trying to cede Ecuadorian territory to Peru.

CONSERVATIVE REGIMES. A strong leader was exactly what Ecuador needed, and it got as much in 1860 in the figure of **Gabriel García Moreno,** hailed by some as the father of Ecuadorian conservatism and the country's greatest nation-builder. García Moreno's diagnosis: the nation needed cohesion. **Catholicism** became the magic ingredient in García Moreno's social cement. After beginning his authoritarian 15-year rule in 1860, García Moreno placed state matters such as education and social welfare within the Church's domain, hoping that religious order, hierarchy, and discipline would unify the nation's population. In 1873, the republic was officially dedicated to the **Sacred Heart of Jesus,** deviating from most other Latin American nations at the time, which had military dictatorships that passed anticlerical measures. Despite the conservative nature of García Moreno's ties to the Church, his accomplishments were often progressive. Nevertheless, García Moreno was **hacked to death with machetes** in 1875 by disgruntled peasants while standing on the steps of the presidential palace. Moreno's brand of conservatism lingered for the next 20 years until the liberals finally saw the chance to make their move. Led by General José Eloy Alfaro Delgado, the **Partido Liberal Radical (PLR)** stormed Quito, emerging victorious after a brief civil war.

ERA OF LIBERALISM. For the next 30 years, **General José Eloy Alfaro Delgado** (president 1897-1901 and 1906-11) was to liberalism what García Moreno had been to conservatism. One of his first moves as president was to create a new secular constitution removing many Church privileges, exiling prominent clergy, secularizing education, and ending the nation's dedication to the Sacred Heart of Jesus. Because of his close ties with the United States, Alfaro was said to be "delivering the Republic to the Yankees." The exploitation of *indígena* labor continued unchecked, and Alfaro's repression of political opponents proved just as ruthless as that of his predecessors. When he refused to step down after his second term ended in 1911, Alfaro was forced into exile in Panama. The new president died only four months later. When Alfaro returned, a lynch mob killed him.

In the next 13 years, government changed hands four times among liberal leaders and their respective constitutions. A group of coastal agricultural and banking interests known as **La Argolla** (The Ring) called the shots from Guayaquil. During World War I and the short economic boom following, **cocoa** became Ecuador's dominant export, and the country's economy briefly thrived. Disaster struck in the early 1920s when a fungal disease ravaged Ecuador's cacao trees and the British colonies in Africa became a major cocoa-growing competitor. The resulting inflation and unemployment hit the working classes especially hard. In the **July Revolution** of 1925, a group of young military officers overthrew the government in a bloodless coup, believing they could start a new program of national regeneration.

TURBULENT YEARS. Although many of the leaders of the July Revolution preached socialist ideology, the sentiment did not last; the 1926-31 military dictatorship of **Isidro Ayora** seized the nation with an iron fist. But the living conditions of the poor still did not improve. One critic said that Ayora's **public cleansing** reforms meant "prohibitions on entering markets, public buildings, schools, parks, and theaters without wearing shoes—but no reforms which gave the unshod means to buy them." With the **stock market crash** of 1929, nearly every Latin American government came crashing down, including Ayora's. Overthrown in 1931, Ayora was the first of 14 presidents to step down in the next decade. In fact, from 1931 to 1948, none of Ecuador's 21 presidents succeeded in completing a full term in office. Ecuador fared no better than the rest of the world during the **Great Depression.** The global demand for cocoa dropped drastically, the price fell by 58%, and Ecuador's exports decreased by nearly 50%. To add to the strife and instability, a four-day civil war broke out in Quito in August 1932.

The scene was perfectly set for a charismatic leader like **José María Velasco Ibarra,** who took on his first of five presidential stints from 1934 to 1935 (also 1944-47, 1952-56, 1960-61, and 1968-72). A master of 20th-century populist politics, Velasco later went on to create his own personal movement, **Velasquismo,** centered around his charisma: a carefully cultivated image of honesty and sincerity, expanded through fiery orations. The Velasco revolution would have to wait, however, since the military overthrew him after less than a year for trying to assume dictatorial powers. The nine years before he returned were marked by fiscal crisis, political coups, and fraudulent elections. **Carlos Alberto Arroyo del Río** claimed victory in the disputed 1940 presidential election, but the regime toppled when a border dispute with Peru became a disastrous 1941 military defeat. Peru's occupation of Ecuador continued until January 1942, when both countries signed a treaty known as the **Rio Protocol,** ceding 200,000 sq. km of Ecuadorian territory in the Oriente to Peru. This is still a cause of dispute between the two countries.

Velasco returned to power in 1944 with whopping bipartisan demonstrations of support. Fine-tuning his populist rhetoric, Velasco managed to enchant the masses, transcending individual ideology. Yet instead of dealing with the country's major economic problems, Velasco obsessed over restoring Ecuador's morality and social justice. Inflation and standard of living worsened; when he was ousted in 1947, Velasco had alienated so many supporters that few rose to defend him.

RISE OF THE MILITARY (1948-79)

Between 1948 and 1960, Ecuador experienced something with which it had little familiarity—a period of political stability brought on by the economic prosperity of a **banana boom.** Ecuador became the US's main banana supplier after disease ravaged the Central American crop in the late 40s. Prosperity led the people back to Velasco, re-elected in 1952, who became so popular that he publicly referred to himself as "the National Personification." By the time Velasco began his fourth term in 1960, low export prices led to unemployment and social discontent.

SEEING RED: COMMUNISM IN ECUADOR. The 1959 **Cuban Revolution** had profound reverberations throughout Latin America, making communism very real as a threat or an attraction. Steering toward communism, Velasco began including more leftists in his government and consciously antagonizing the US. In 1961, Vice President **Carlos Julio Arosemena Monroy** ousted his superior and immediately sent a goodwill mission to Washington, eager to renew favorable terms with the US; but repeated terrorist attacks made Monroy seem to be a communist sympathizer. In July 1963, a four-man military **junta** seized power, vowing to implement basic reforms and to take a hard line against communism. After a bloody attack on the students of Central University in Quito, the military reformers stepped down.

BUCARAM AND THE OIL BOOM. When in doubt, Ecuadorians vote for Velasco, and in 1968 this master of charisma began an unprecedented fifth term. Velasco assumed dictatorial powers with an **autogolpe** (a coup against his own government), and remained in this position until his overthrow by military coup in 1972. The coup was provoked by the army's fear that **Asaad Bucaram Elmhalim** might be elected after Velasco's term ran out months later. The leader of the populist **Concentration of Popular Forces (CFP)** and popular two-time governor of Guayaquil, Bucaram was considered by both the military and business community to be dangerous, unpredictable, and unfit for the presidency. The interim military leaders were not prepared for the 1970s **oil boom.** After joining the Organization of Petroleum Exporting Countries (OPEC), the minister of resources tried pricing the country's oil above the world price. The country's economic problems worsened.

The creation of a new constitution and the democratic election of a president was supposed to happen in 1976, but the process was delayed partly to ensure that Bucaram would not be elected. He was eventually barred from running, but the second-in-command of the CFP, **Jaime Roldós Aguilera,** with his reformist platform, won a run-off election in 1979 with 68.5% of the vote. **Osvaldo Hurtado Larrea,** leader of the **Christian Democratic Party (PDC),** stood as his running mate.

RETURN TO DEMOCRACY (1979-1996)

The Roldós-Hurtado regime began under auspicious circumstances. With the country's preferential treatment as part of the **Andean Common Market,** the oil boom was finally having positive repercussions for Ecuador. In 1981, Roldós died in a plane crash, and Ecuador's economy nose-dived in a similar fashion soon after. Oil reserves ran dry, and massive foreign borrowing led to a debt of almost US$7 billion by 1983. **El Niño** brought drastic climate changes in 1982 and 1983, resulting in nearly US$1 billion in infrastructure damage. Unemployment skyrocketed to 13.5%, and the **United Workers Front (FUT)** launched three riotous strikes during Hurtado's term in office.

Elected in 1984, the soon-unpopular **León Febres Cordero Ribadeneyra** supported free-market economics and a pro-US policy, trying to emulate and ingratiate his government to that of US President Reagan. Oil prices continued to fall, and Febres Cordero continued to face troubles with the National Congress and the military. A March 1987 earthquake left 20,000 homeless and destroyed a stretch of the country's main oil pipeline, forcing the president to suspend interest payments on Ecuador's US$8.3 billion foreign debt.

The next president, **Rodrigo Borja Cevallos,** made agreements with various paramilitary protest organizations, guaranteeing their civil rights in exchange for demilitarization of his government. One guerilla organization, **Montoneros Patria Libre (MPL),** refused and continued with violent action. Cevallos not only faced opposition from outside the government but from within it as well, as several internal coups were eventually unearthed. The National Confederation of the Indigenous Population of Ecuador (CONAIE) also planned a seven-province uprising, seizing oil wells and taking military hostages. Their demands included the return of various traditional community lands, recognition of Quichua as an official language, and compensation for the environmental damage caused by petroleum companies. Though the protests ended when the government agreed to consider CONAIE's demands, tensions heightened again in April 1992, when thousands of *indígenas* from the Oriente marched to Quito, demanding that their territorial rights be recognized (see **A Regional Overview: Indigenous Ecuador,** p. 13).

During his 1992-96 presidency, **Sixto Durán Ballén** dealt with many of these same problems on a larger scale. CONAIE and other indigenous movements caused an even bigger stir with widespread demonstrations in June 1994, when they objected to the **Land Development Law,** which allowed commercialization of indigenous lands for farming and resource extraction. Revelations of embezzlement by top officials led to numerous impeachments and even demands for Ballén's resignation, voiced by student demonstrations throughout 1995 and early 1996.

POLITICAL UNCERTAINTY (1996-PRESENT)

BUCARAM'S BACK. Abdala Bucaram (yet another Bucaram) of the **Partido Roldosista Ecuatoriano (PRE)** defeated Jaime Nebot of the Partido Social Cristiano (PSC) in the presidential election of July 7, 1996. Bucaram lost to Nebot in Ecuador's two biggest cities—Guayaquil (63% to 37%) and Quito (52% to 48%)—but overwhelmingly defeated him in the tiny towns and the Oriente. The conservative Nebot did not inspire enough confidence with his slogan, *"Primero La Gente"* (People First), which paled in comparison to Bucaram's *"Primero Los Pobres"* (The Poor First). Bucaram took office on August 10, 1996, and devalued the *sucre* a few weeks later; his popularity experienced a similar devaluation soon after. Surfacing reports of corruption earned the regime the nickname, "Ali Abdala and the 40 thieves," and by early January 1997, public discontent began bubbling up into pockets of often violent protest, and the man of *los pobres* found himself abandoned by the very constituency that had put him into office. Tensions culminated on February 5 and 6, 1997, when the public sector unions, the left-wing political group **Movimiento Popular Democrático (MPD)**, and the indigenous group CONAIE launched a united strike against the government.

Congress's response was swift and unprecedented. On February 6, 1997, the legislative branch ousted Abdala Bucaram from the presidency on grounds that he was mentally unfit (see graybox, below). Bucaram responded by barricading himself within the presidential palace. Insisting that a "civilian dictatorship" had been imposed, Bucaram fled the country and was granted political asylum in Panama. With military assistance, Vice President **Rosalía Arteaga** immediately assumed control even though Congress voted 57-2 that congressional head **Fabián Alarcón** would serve as Bucaram's heir. Arteaga accused Congress of a "coup against the constitution" but surrendered authority to Alarcón two days later.

ALARCÓN. From the start, Alarcón's role was limited to the temporary. Under fire from Arteaga and others who demanded that the president be approved by popular vote, Alarcón conceded to an election scheduled for August 1998. He then focused on creating stability through his proposed plan, **El Paquetito** (The Little Shock), which would reduce the deficit, increase import tariffs and electricity rates, reinstate an 8% income tax and a 10% across-the-board budget cut, and create a task force to reduce corruption in both customs and tax collection.

Despite ambitious predictions of economic recovery, however, conditions only worsened, and the regime's roster of scandals came to rival that of Bucaram's era. In the most stinging scandal, the president was linked to an operation that sold off donated clothing intended for the victims of El Niño for a profit.

"¿Y ESTE HOMBRE QUIERE SER PRESIDENTE?"

"No puede ser," cried the television commercials of the Social Cristiano candidate Jaime Nebot before his narrow defeat at the hands of *"El Loco,"* Abdala Bucaram. With an uncanny resemblance to Adolf Hitler—mini-mustache, arm sweeps, and all—Abdala marched on the campaign path with *"una sola ideología: derrotar a la oligarquía"* (only one ideology: tear down the oligarchy). His resemblance to Hitler may not have been coincidental: Abdala (he is known by his first name) once cited *Mein Kampf* as his favorite book. However, his antics put him in his own class entirely. In his unsuccessful 1988 campaign, Abdala once emerged from a helicopter dressed in a Batman costume. Traveling with a Uruguayan rock band on the trail, Abdala would pack the working class into squares and sing *boleros* on command. But when it came to speaking, Bucaram was all business: his charismatic content matched his throaty shouts, and he somehow motivated almost all of Ecuador's poorer areas to vote for him (in the provinces of Zamora and Morona-Santiago, he won by approximately three to one). One reason may have been the female vote: Rosalía Arteaga, his running mate, was the first female vice president of Ecuador, but once elected, she seemed to have little place in the actual running of the country. Abdala's brothers also received attention: one, who was rumored to be Abdala's new Minister of Finance, had studied to be a witch doctor, and another was detained in Guayaquil the day after the election for driving a stolen vehicle. Scared members of Ecuador's upper classes fled the country the day after the results were announced (one hour late, because exit polls revealed a difference below the margin of error). Perhaps they fled for good reason. It is revealing that the man actually lost two to one in the city he was mayor of, Guayaquil. Bucaram did not last long in office and was eventually exiled (see below). In Panama, Bucaram has been making headlines as vigorously as ever. He has cut a CD entitled, "Madman in Love," and has been spotted frequenting Panama City casinos.

1998 ELECTION. With Alarcón's record tainted, the presidential race became a contest between businessman **Alvaro Noboa** and **Jamil Mahuad,** mayor of Quito. Mahuad, educated at Harvard in public administration and supported by the **Popular Democracy Party,** was favored among the educated middle class but worried some with his recent, albeit minor, stroke. Noboa, a banana mogul and member of the country's wealthiest family, belonged to Bucaram's Roldosista Party and enjoyed the backing of *El Loco* himself, cheerfully exiled in Panama. Many feared Noboa would pardon Bucaram, and when Ecuadorians went to the polls on July 12, they elected Mahuad by a slim margin.

MAHUAD'S ADMINISTRATION. Mahuad inherited a severely troubled economy, and his administration took immediate and drastic measures—particularly in attempting to revitalize the nation's banking system. To make some of its improvements, Mahuad and his Popular Democracy Party were forced to forge an alliance with the populist **Social Christian Party.**

Despite Mahuad's reforms, the economy deteriorated significantly in late 1998 and the first half of 1999. Radical attempts on Mahuad's part to alleviate the dire economic crisis led to strikes by taxi drivers and bus companies throughout Ecuador; in Congress, Mahuad's erstwhile ally, the Social Christian Party, declared a "total frontal opposition" to the new policy.

Mahuad's popularity ratings rose a little with the October 1998 settlement with Peru's **Alberto Fujimori** over a long-standing border dispute between their two countries. In a desperate attempt to stabilize the economy, Mahuad made a January 9 announcement that Ecuador would replace the country's *sucre* with the American dollar (a movement known as **dollarization**). This announcement infuriated many Ecuadorians and ultimately caused Mahuad's demise. On January 21, 2000, a mass of Ecuadorian *indígenas* (supported by military officials and led by the Confederation of Indigenous Nationalities of Ecuador) stormed Mahuad's palaces and overthrew the president in a bloodless coup. He was quickly replaced by one of the military officials, but upon the US's warning that a military government would not be recognized, Mahuad's vice president, **Gustavo Noboa,** took office.

NOBOA GIVES IT A SHOT. Noboa has embraced rather than discarded Mahuad's plans to improve the economy, most conspicuously his controversial dollarization plan. As of June 2000, American dollars made up one-third of Ecuador's circulating money (a transition expected to be complete by September 13, 2000). Protests continued, however, as June also brought Ecuador a record annual inflation rate of 103.7%. Many Ecuadorians say the inflation rate is evidence of the damage dollarization will do to the nation. Noboa is willing to take a risk, however, and has gained much support from outside agencies such as the International Monetary Fund (IMF), who have agreed to aid the hurting country on a few conditions. Those conditions include cutting subsidies on fuel, gas, electricity, and water, however, and with already inflated prices, Noboa might do all he can just to stay in office without another coup.

Along with the IMF plan, Ecuador is receiving aid to construct a new oil pipeline; with it, investors hope, Ecuador's annual revenues could increase by US$700-800 million, though the pipeline's construction would eat up a year's worth of profits from the start.

As if Ecuador's domestic worries weren't bad enough, the country now has to worry about Colombia's. As the Plan Colombia (in which the United States will provide over one billion dollars to the Colombian military's effort to eliminate illegal coca growth and export) evolves, Ecuadorians worry that the disputes will cross the border into their country. As is obvious, Ecuador can't afford to have that happen, and has sent troops near its border with Colombia to prevent any chance of the war on drugs from taking place on their soil.

MODERN ART

Conveyed in a variety of styles and media, the theme that unifies the bulk of 20th-century art in the country of Ecuador is its indigenous subject matter, lending the movement the name **indigenismo. Oswaldo Guayasamín,** the most famous member of this school, is known for his politically charged depictions of suffering *indígenas,* as in his *Cabezas,* a series of portraits of anonymous heads, influenced by Picasso and the European cubist movement. Guayasamín worked with Mexican muralist José Clemente Orozco and produced some controversial murals of his own, including his 23 panels painted in the meeting hall of the Ecuadorian Congress in 1988. Next to portrayals of national historic events, Guayasamín placed a black-and-white panel of a Nazi soldier whose helmet bore the letters CIA. Diplomatic nerves eventually calmed and the mural was not touched. The best place to see Guayasamín's work today is at his museum in Quito (see **Quito: Museums,** p. 438).

Eduardo Kingman, another indigenist, is considered by some to be the trailblazer of the movement. The figures in Kingman's paintings are stylized and shadowy, depicting scenes of oppression. In *Mujeres y Santos* (1953), a downtrodden *indígena* wearing a bright blue shawl clutches an icon with Kingman's trademark gnarled, exaggerated hands. **Camilo Egas** was part of the early indigenist movement, although his style was much more varied and also influenced by French surrealist currents. **Manuel Rendón,** another well-known Ecuadorian painter, was not especially indigenist, but is still considered part of the movement. He grew up in Paris, the son of the Ecuadorian Ambassador, and (like Egas) was influenced by the modern art there. His works use various styles, such as cubism and pointillism.

Of the more recent generation of painters, **Ramiro Jácome** is the most famous, with his abstract human figures using deep colors. Paintings by Jácome and other modern Ecuadorian artists are on display at the Casa de la Cultura in Quito.

LITERATURE

Before the advent of writing, indigenous Ecuadorians established an oral tradition of stories, songs, poetry, and theater intimately linked with religious practices. With the arrival of the Spanish and the forceful conversion of the indigenous peoples to Catholicism, much of this tradition was lost. One notable exception is the preserved story of the war between Atahuallpa and his brother Huáscar for control of the Inca Empire just before the Spanish Conquest.

17TH AND 18TH CENTURIES. The first textual works were the writings of various clergymen during the 17th century, including poetry and discourse on social and political issues in the Spanish colony. The most well-preserved authors of the following century were three Jesuit clergymen, **Gaspar de Villarroel** (1590-1665), **Antonio Bastidas** (1615-81), and **Xacinto de Evia.** In the 18th century, bourgeois professionals began to express discontent with the state of affairs that eventually led to the independence movement. Called "the literature that did not yet have a country," these writings were the first to explicitly focus on what was to become Ecuadorian society. **Juan de Velasco** (1727-92), a historian and narrator, is considered by many to be the most talented writer of his time. A journalist, physician, and philosopher, **Eugenio Espejo** (1747-95) advocated societal reform and wrote on a vast array of topics including education, theology, politics, health, and the economy. He also started Quito's first newspaper, though it lasted only three months. **Juan Bautista Aguirre** (1725-86) is best known for his "Brief Design of the Cities of Guayaquil and Quito," which examines the still-present rivalry between the cities.

19TH CENTURY: MERA AND MONTALVO. The 19th century brought Ecuador its independence from Spain and, with that, a distinctive national literature established by the founding fathers, **Juan León Mera** (1832-94) and **Juan Montalvo** (1832-89). Though their Romantic style was influenced by Spanish literature, the content was anti-monarchical and aimed at creating Ecuadorian national identity. The most important work is León Mera's *Cumandá*, the first Ecuadorian novel. León Mera also published other short novels, poetry, and collections of Ecuadorian folklore. Montalvo, known as the favorite novelist of Ecuador's liberal movement, was a more political writer. His fictional *Chapters that Cervantes Forgot* narrates Don Quixote's adventures through the Americas and is dotted with criticism of intellectual and political enemies.

20TH CENTURY: INDIGENISMO AND BEYOND. Since the 19th century, Ecuadorian literature has taken on a life of its own, dealing with uniquely Ecuadorian social, political, cultural, and historical topics. One of the most marked differences between the writings of the 19th and 20th centuries is the move away from a romanticization of indigenous traditions toward a more realistic portrayal of the indigenous struggle. One of the first works to mark the movement known as **Indigenismo** is the 1934 *Huasipungo* by **Jorge Incaza** (1906-78), a story of indigenous resistance to exploitation. Another important work of the 1930s is a collection of short stories by different authors, *Los que se van (Those Who Leave)*. Subtitled *Tales of Halfbreeds and Hillbillies*, the stories use crude language and themes that deviated from traditional literary norms and shocked the readers of that time. **Pablo Palacio** (1906-47) was active during the 20s and 30s, laying the foundations of an ironic, existential, and traumatized writing style that would become more widespread in the 60s and 70s. Two authors of the 60s, **Miguel Donoso Pareja** and **Pedro Jorge Vera,** wrote anti-imperialist works reflecting Ecuador's frustration with its dependence on foreign powers. In 1978, the first Meeting on Ecuadorian Literature lent legitimacy to the growing literary movement, which has continued to flourish.

QUITO

☎ 02

Airplanes descending toward the 2800m plateau upon which Quito rests discover a sprawling metropolis bordered on all sides by green, cloud-cloaked peaks. From the sky, Quito's powerful landscape steals all attention from what humans have created. But then the plane lands, and visitors, still dizzy from the altitude, look around and begin to grasp the immensity of this capital. Part thriving modern city, part decaying colonial showcase, Quito is in every way the geographical, political, and historical center of Ecuador.

Quito's first residents were the Quitu, Cara, Shyri, and Puruhá peoples, who discovered inhabited the area from the 6th century. The Incas conquered Quito around AD 1500, then made it the northern capital of their empire. Pizarro and company invaded in 1532, and despite Quito's long legacy, the recognized date of its founding is December 6, 1534—the day the Spanish finally drove the Incas out. Quito was then home to 204 families; 1.5 million people live here now, divided along economic and ethnic lines into two areas: Old Town (*la parte colonial*) and New Town (*Quito moderno*). In 1978, the United Nations declared the colonial city a World Cultural Heritage site. As a result, Old Quito's appearance has changed little since colonial days. Streets remain narrow and cobblestoned, buildings retain their cool inner courtyards, and daily activity still revolves around the many plazas throughout the city. But Old Town's poor population and increasingly dilapidated buildings reflect Ecuador's worsening economy.

HIGHLIGHTS OF QUITO

JOIN the crowds at the **Plaza de la Independencia** (p. 438), the centerpiece of the colonial city.

TAKE IN the stunning view from nearby **El Panecillo** (p. 438).

GAWK at Quito's most impressive collection of ancient and modern artwork: **Museo Nacional del Banco Central** (p. 439).

DEFY the sierra's *tranquilo* reputation in New Quito's **nightlife** (p. 442).

CLIMB Volcán Pichincha (p. 443). It's spectacular.

COMMUNE with nature in Mindo's outdoor paradise (p. 446).

Meanwhile, New Quito expands up toward the sky 'and into the mountains. New Town is the capital's social and commercial engine, filled with students, business people, and a growing number of tourists. These last use the area as a base, returning to it after hikes through the Andes, jaunts out to jungle lodges, or cruises around the Galápagos. Consequently, the streets framed by Amazonas, 6 de Diciembre, and Cordero have become a gringo paradise, complete with hot shower and continental breakfast. Part of the appeal, of course, is Quito's climate, which remains remarkably constant throughout the year; the temperature usually hovers between 10°C and 25°C (50°F and 77°F), and seasonal variations hardly exist. If anything, the city experiences all four seasons in a day: the morning sky, usually clear and sunny, becomes overcast by midday. Showers in the afternoon are not uncommon, and the temperature drops at night. But if you come prepared for anything, Quito will not disappoint.

QUITO

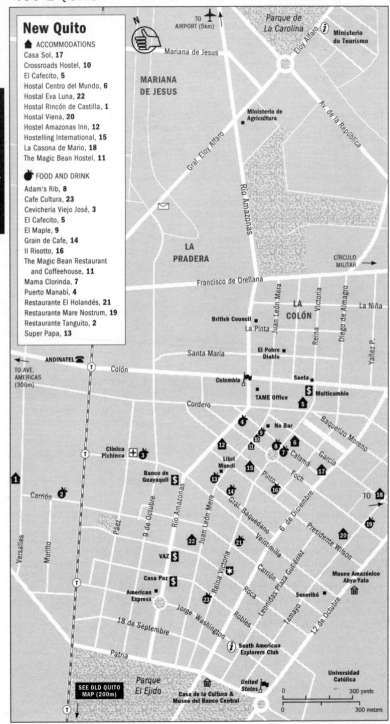

New Quito

⌂ **ACCOMMODATIONS**
Casa Sol, **17**
Crossroads Hostel, **10**
El Cafecito, **5**
Hostal Centro del Mundo, **6**
Hostal Eva Luna, **22**
Hostal Rincón de Castilla, **1**
Hostal Viena, **20**
Hostel Amazonas Inn, **12**
Hostelling International, **15**
La Casona de Mario, **18**
The Magic Bean Hostel, **11**

🍅 **FOOD AND DRINK**
Adam's Rib, **8**
Cafe Cultura, **23**
Cevichería Viejo José, **3**
El Cafecito, **5**
El Maple, **9**
Grain de Cafe, **14**
Il Risotto, **16**
The Magic Bean Restaurant
 and Coffeehouse, **11**
Mama Clorinda, **7**
Puerto Manabí, **4**
Restaurante El Holandés, **21**
Restaurante Mare Nostrum, **19**
Restaurante Tanguito, **2**
Super Papa, **13**

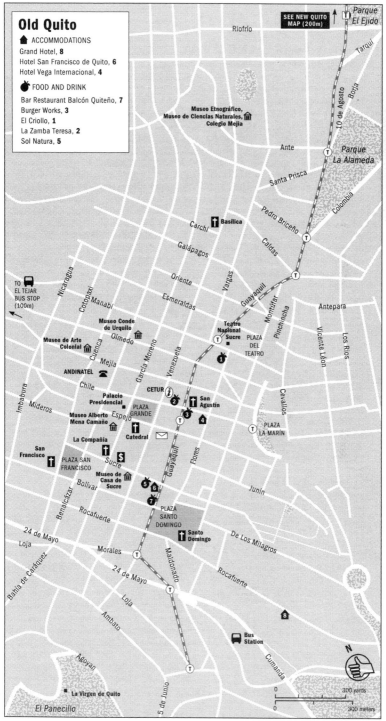

Old Quito

🏠 ACCOMMODATIONS

Grand Hotel, **8**
Hotel San Francisco de Quito, **6**
Hotel Vega Internacional, **4**

🍎 FOOD AND DRINK

Bar Restaurant Balcón Quiteño, **7**
Burger Works, **3**
El Criollo, **1**
La Zamba Teresa, **2**
Sol Natura, **5**

QUITO

SEE NEW QUITO MAP (200m)

Parque El Ejido

Riofrío

Tarqui

10 de Agosto

Borja

Museo Etnográfico,
Museo de Ciencias Naturales, 🏛
Colegio Mejía

Ante

Parque La Alameda

Santa Prisca

Colombia

Pedro Briceño

Carchi

Basílica

Galápagos

Caldas

Oriente

Vargas

Guayaquil

Antepara

TO
EL TEJAR
BUS STOP
(100m)

Nicaragua

Cotopaxi

Manabí

Esmeraldas

Montúfar

Pichincha

Vicente León

Los Ríos

Museo Conde
de Urquijo 🏛

Teatro
Nacional
Sucre

PLAZA
DEL
TEATRO

Museo de Arte
Colonial 🏛

Olmedo

Cuenca

Mejía

García Moreno

Venezuela

1

ANDINATEL ☎

Chile

CETUR 🛈

San Agustín

Cevallos

Palacio
Presidencial

PLAZA
GRANDE

2

Espejo

3

4

PLAZA
LA MARÍN

Museo Alberto
Mena Camaño 🏛

Catedral

Flores

La Compañía

San
Francisco

Sucre

PLAZA SAN
FRANCISCO

Museo de
Casa de
Sucre 🏛

5 **6**

7

Guayaquil

Junín

Imbabura

Mideros

Benalcázar

Bolívar

Rocafuerte

PLAZA
SANTO
DOMINGO

Santo
Domingo

De Los Milagros

24 de Mayo

Loja

Morales

Maldonado

Rocafuerte

Bahía de Caráquez

24 de Mayo

Loja

8

Ambato

Bus
Station

Agoyán

Cumandá

N

La Virgen de Quito

5 de Junio

El Panecillo

0   300 yards

0   300 meters

▛ TRANSPORTATION

GETTING THERE AND AWAY

Airport: Aeropuerto Mariscal Sucre, on 10 de Agosto to the north of town, near Florida. Taxi US$2 and up; set the fee before you get in. The bus marked "Aeropuerto" runs to the airport from Old and New Town; catch it along 12 de Octubre or Amazonas. The 10 de Agosto trolley (M-F 6am-midnight, Sa-Su 8am-10pm) also goes to the airport, but you will have to transfer onto the Rumiñahui *alimentador* route from Estación Norte in northern New Town. Airport **departure tax** US$25.

Airlines: TAME, Amazonas 1354 (☎509 375), at Colón. Open M-F 8am-7pm. To: **Cuenca** (40min.; M-Sa 7:15am, Su-F 4 or 4:15pm; US$50), **Lago Agrio** (30min.; M and F 10:30am and 4:40pm, Tu-Th and Sa 10:30am; US$54), **Guayaquil** (45min.; M-F 10 per day 7am-7:45pm, Sa 6 per day 7am-5:15pm, Su 7 per day 7am-6:30pm; US$60), and **Lima, Peru** (2hr., M-Sa 11:30am, US$179 and up). **ICARO,** Palora 124 (☎254 891), at Amazonas. To **Cuenca** (40min., Su-Th 2 per day 4:30-5:50pm, US$50). **TACA** (tickets must be bought through a travel agent) flies to **Lima** (2hr., M-Sa 8:30am, US$129 plus 12% IVA). **Ecuatoriana** (☎563 003), at Colón and Reina Victoria, in the Torns de Almagro building. Open M-F 8am-6pm, Sa 9am-12pm. **Lloyd Aero Boliviano (LAB),** associated with Ecuatoriana, flies to **La Paz, Bolivia** (Tu and Th 2pm, US$358 and up).

Trains: Station (☎656 142), on Maldonado. Take the trolley to the Chimbacalle stop, south of Old Town. Service often suspended for repairs. High prices for foreigners; some say the roof-riding opportunities are worth them (beware of branches and wires overhead). To: **Riobamba** (8hr., Sa 8am, US$15), **Latacunga** (US$15), **Ambato** (US$16). Another route runs to **Boliche**, near Cotopaxi (3hr., Su 7am, US$20).

Buses: Terminal, in Old Town, next to the highway at the end of 24 de Mayo. Take the trolley to the Cumandá stop, descend the stairs on the north side of the highway (away from El Panecillo and la Virgen de Quito), and keep walking. Buses go everywhere including: **Baños** (3½hr., every 30min. 5:10am-7pm); **Cuenca** (10hr., 12 per day 7:30am-10:45pm, US$6.80); **Esmeraldas** (6hr., every 30min. 5:50am-12:30am, US$4.40) via **Santo Domingo** (3hr., every 10min., US$1.60); **Guayaquil** (8hr., every hr. 5:30am-12:15am, US$5.60); **Ibarra** (3hr., every 15min. 6am-9pm, US$1.60); **Lago Agrio** (8hr., every hr. 4am-10:30pm, US$5.60); **Latacunga** (2hr., every 10min. 6am-7pm, US$1); **Loja** (14hr., every 2hr. 12:50pm-9:30pm, US$9); **Macas** (10hr., 6 per day, US$5.20); **Manta** (8hr., 16 per day 6:30am-10:30pm, US$5.60) via **Portoviejo** (8hr., US$5.60); **Otavalo** (2hr., every 20min. 6am-8:30pm, US$1.12); **Puyo** (5hr., every 30min., US$2.60); **Riobamba** (4hr., every hr. 7:30am-7pm, US$2.20); **Salinas** (10hr., 9:50 and 11pm, US$4); and **Tena** (5hr., 4 per day, US$3).

GETTING AROUND

Local Buses: There are 2 classes of bus: light blue **Servicio Popular** (US$0.10; pay as you get off) and red-and-white **Especial** (US$0.12; pay when you get on). Children, senior citizens, and handicapped passengers pay half-price. When you want to get off, say *"gracias"* or *"aquí, no más"* loudly. Buses that connect to the trolleys are green and white; *interparroquial* (to small towns outside the city) buses are pink and white. Buses post routes and destinations on their front windows. The **Old Town-New Town route** is served by the Colón-Camal (#2) bus on Versalles, the San Bartolomé-Miraflores (#10) on 12 de Octubre, the El Tejar-El Inca (#11) on 6 de Diciembre, and several buses on Amazonas. You can catch the "Aeropuerto" and "Estadio" (to Olympic Stadium on 6 de Diciembre and Naciones Unidas) buses at 6 Diciembre and Naciones Unidas.

Trolleys: The environmentally friendly *trole* system in Quito is fast, efficient, and crowded. You can't miss the glass-walled stops. The trolley runs along **10 de Agosto** in New Town and then into Old Town along **Guayaquil** and **Maldonado.** The C1 route travels the length of the city, from Estación Recreó to Estación Y. The C2 travels only the southern loop, from Recreó to Colón, while the C3 does only the northern loop, from Y to Colón. Operating M-F 6am-midnight and Sa-Su 8am-10pm. US$0.10, children under 18 and senior citizens US$0.06.

Taxis: City-taxi (☎633 333), **Central de Radio Taxi** (☎500 600), and **Tele-taxi** (☎411 119) offer 24hr. service.

Car Rental: Budget Rent-a-Car, Colón 1140 (☎237 026, airport 459 092), at Amazonas. **Avis Rent-a-Car,** Aeropuerto Mariscal Sucre (☎440 270 or 255 890). Must be at least 25. **Team Rent-a-Car,** Amazonas 1128 (☎562 436), at Foch.

⁊ PRACTICAL INFORMATION

TOURIST AND FINANCIAL SERVICES

Tourist Information: Ministerio de Turismo, formerly CETUR, has 2 locations in Quito. **Old Town office** (☎954 044), at Venezuela and Chile, accesible from the Plaza Grande trolley stop. **New Town office,** Eloy Alfaro N32-300 (☎507 560), at Carlos Tobar, across from Parque la Carolina. Both open M-F 8:30am-5pm. **The South American Explorers (SAE),** Jorge Washington 311 (☎/fax 225 228; email explorer@saec.org.ec; www.samexplo.org), at Leonidas Plaza. A great resource. The English-speaking staff can help you make the most of any vacation with trip reports, events listings, and a large selection of maps. Lending library. Storage. Membership US$40. Open M-W and F 9:30am-5pm, Th 9:30am-8pm.

Tour Agencies: Safari has 2 offices: Calamá 380 at León Mera, which specializes in climbing and jungle tours (☎552 505; email admin@safariec.ecuanex.net.ec; open daily 9am-7pm); and Roca 630 at Amazonas, which specializes in Galapagos trips (fax 220 426; open M-F 9am-6pm). The biggest climbing agency in Quito. Helpful English-speaking staff. Tours are a bit expensive (US$185 for a 2-day guided Cotopaxi climb, US$45 for most daytrips), but less pricey adventures come up periodically. Discounts sometimes available to SAE members. **G.A.L.A. Ecuador** (☎9 807 887; fax 2 230 922; email info@galasouthamerica.com; www.galasouthamerica.com) specializes in gay and lesbian trips. Rarely inexpensive, agencies in New Town offer package deals with transport, guides, and meals. Two reputable ones are **The Biking Dutchman,** Foch 714 at Juan Leon Mera (☎ 568 323; open M-F 9am-6pm and Sa 8am-noon), and **Adventours,** Calamá 339 at Reina Victoria (☎820 848; open M-F 9am-7pm, Sa 10am-2pm). Ask to see guides' state certifications.

Embassies and Consulates: For **Canada, Ireland, UK,** and **US,** see p. 26. **Bolivia,** Bosmediano 526 (☎446 450; fax 244 833), at José Carbo. **Colombia,** Colón 133 (☎228 926 or 222 486; fax 567 766), at Amazonas. Open M-F 9am-1pm and 2-5pm. **Israel,** Eloy Alfaro 969 (☎565 510; fax 504 635), at Amazonas. Open M-F 8:30am-4:30pm. **Netherlands,** 12 de Octubre 1942 (☎525 461 or 229 229; fax 567 917), at Cordero, in the World Trade Center, Tower One. Open M-F 9am-noon. **Peru,** El Salvador 495 (☎468 410; fax 468 411), at Irlanda. Open M-F 9am-1pm and 3-5pm.

Immigration Office: Dirección General de Extranjería (☎454 122), at Paez and Carrión. Take a trolley to the Santa Clara stop, then walk toward Parque El Ejido and turn on Carrión toward Amazonas. Tourism card extensions. Open M-F 6:30am-1:30pm.

Currency Exchange: Producambios, Amazonas 370 (☎564 500; fax 564 753), at Robles. Open M-F 8:30am-6pm. **VAZ,** at Amazonas and Roca, next to Hotel Alameda Real along Amazonas. Open M-F 8am-6pm, Sa 9am-1pm. **Multicambio** has 4 offices: at Amazonas and Santa María (☎561 734); Amazonas 363 (☎567 351), at Robles; Venezuela 731 (☎951 075), at Espejo; and at the airport (☎440 080). All open M-F 9am-2pm and 3-5:30pm.

Banks: Banks line Amazonas. Hours vary slightly, but most exchange cash M-F 9am-1:30pm. Reliable banks include: **Banco de Guayaquil,** at Colón and Reina Victoria, (☎566 800; open M-F 9am-4:30pm and Sa 9am-1pm); **Banco del Pacífico,** at Amazonas and Veintimilla, (☎437 537; open M-F 9am-5pm, Sa 9:30am-2:30pm); **Citibank,** at Rep. El Salvador and Naciones Unidas, (☎970 100; open M-F 9am-4pm).

ATMs: Plentiful in New Town and slightly scarcer in Old. V/MC ATMs at designated **Banco de Guayaquil, Banco del Pacífico, Banco de Prestamos,** and **Filanbanco** machines.

Credit Card Offices: MasterCard, Naciones Unidas 825 (☎262 770), at Shyris. Open M-F 8am-5pm. **Visa,** Shyris 3147 (☎459 303), at Tomás de Berlanga at Filanbanco. Open M-F 9am-5:30pm.

American Express: Amazonas 329 (☎560 488; fax 501 067), at Jorge Washington. Open M-F 8:30am-5pm.

LOCAL SERVICES

Bookstores: Confederate Books and Cafe, Calama 410 (☎/fax 527 890; email tommys@accessinter.net), at León Mera, has a great selection of used books. Open M-F 9am-8pm, Sa-Su 10am-7pm. The **SAE** (see Tourist Information, above) has Quito's best selection of English guidebooks, a variety of books available for borrowing (US$30 deposit), and a small book exchange. **Libri Mundi,** León Mera N23-83 (☎234 791), at Jorge Washington; (☎464 473), in Quicentro Shopping on Naciones Unidas and Shyris; and in Hotel Colón (☎550 455), at Amazonas and Patria. Though not cheap, this is the place to go for literature in Spanish, German, French, and English. Open M-F 8am-7pm, Sa 9am-1:30pm and 3:30-6:30pm; Quicentro location also open Su 10am-7pm.

Cultural Centers: British Council Amazonas N26-146 (☎508 282; fax 508 283), at Niña. Restaurant and tea room. (Open M-Sa 7am-8pm). Spanish language school. **Email** access (US$0.20 per hr.). Open M-F 7am-8pm. The **Asociación Israelita de Quito** synagogue (☎502 734), at 18 de Septiembre and Versalles. Open services F 7pm, Sa 9am, and Su 9am.

Supermarkets: Supermaxi, at the Multicentro on 6 de Diciembre and La Niña; the airport Centro Comercial; and El Jardín shopping center. All open M-Sa 9:30am-8pm, Su 9:30am-2pm.

Laundromats: Lavandería Lavanda Calama, Calama 244 (☎544 528), at Reina Victoria. Standard cleaning US$0.15 per lb. Dry cleaning US$0.15 per item. Open M-F 8am-8pm, Sa 8am-6pm, Su 8am-noon. If you'd rather do it yourself, **Opera de Jabón,** Pinto 325 (☎543 995), at Reina Victoria, has self-service. US$0.75 per wash load, includes detergent. Open M-Sa 7am-7:30pm, Su 9am-5pm.

EMERGENCY AND COMMUNICATIONS

Emergency: ☎911.

Police: ☎101. **Criminal Investigation Office,** in Old Town at Cuenca and Mideros. Open 24hr.

Pharmacies: Farmacia CYF, Jorge Washington 416 (☎555 438), at Reina Victoria. **Farmacia el Sol,** 6 de Diciembre (☎507 335), at Veintimilla. Both open 24hr.

Medical Services: Hospital Vozandes, Villalengua 267 (☎241 540), at 10 de Agosto, on the Villaflora bus line. Consultation US$2. **Hospital Metropolitano** (☎431 457), at Mariana de Jesús and Occidental, on the Quito Sur-San Gabriel bus line. Taxi US$1. Private medical practitioner **Dr. John Rosenberg,** Foch 476 (☎521 104; ☎09 739 734; pager 227 777), at Almagro, speaks fluent English, German, French, and Hebrew. **Dr. Wallace Swanson** (☎470 830) is an American doctor affiliated with the Hospital Vozandes. He can give referrals to specialty doctors. **Clínica Pichincha,** Veintimilla 1259 (☎562 408 or 562 296), at Paez, is recommended for emergency care.

Telephones: Quito is the easiest place in Ecuador from which to make international calls. This is not saying much. **ANDINATEL,** at 10 de Agosto and Colón, at the airport, at Benalcázar and Mejía, and at the bus station. **Bellsouth** and **Porta Ale** have phone booths throughout the city but require phone cards (domestic calls US$0.08 per min.); the catch is that your card only works on phones for the appropriate company. In general, international direct dial calls can be made from any direct-dial phone, including those in the lobbies of many hotels. Be careful the hotel you call from doesn't charge by the minute; you should be charged a reasonable flat rate for service (under US$0.50).

Internet Access: Tons along Calamá, Reina Victoria, and Juan León Mera. Expect to pay US$0.70-90 per hr. One convenient place to get connected is **Magic Roundabout Hipe Mail** (☎569 767), at Foch and Reina Victoria. Open daily 8:30am-9pm.

Post Office: Old Town Post Office, on Espejo between Guayaquil and Venezuela, half a block towards Guayaquil from the Palacio de Gobierno. Mark mail "Correo Central Lista de Correos" to have it sent here. Open M-F 7:30am-7pm, Sa 8am-2pm. **New Town Post Office,** Eloy Alfaro 354 at 9 de Octubre. If you want mail sent to this branch, mark it "Correo Central, Eloy Alfaro Estafeta SUC#21;" otherwise it will be sent to the Old Town office. Open M-F 8am-7:30pm, Sa 7:30am-2pm. **Packages** should be sent via **Correo Marítimo Aduana,** Ulloa 273 (☎546 917), at Ramírez Dávalos, next to the Santa Clara market. Open M-F 7:30am-4pm. **EMS** (☎569 741), next to the post office on Eloy Alfaro. Open M-F 8am-7pm, Sa 8am-12:30pm. **FedEx,** Amazonas 517 (☎569 356), at Santa María. Open M-F 8am-8pm, Sa 10am-2pm.

ACCOMMODATIONS

NEW TOWN

Many of the many hostels in New Town are gringo-run or at least gringo-populated. They tend to congregate centrally, between Amazonas and 6 de Diciembre. Budget hotels, on the other hand, tend to lie slightly off the main strips. Anywhere you stay, expect to pay a 10% IVA tax in addition to the cost of your room unless otherwise stated. Most also charge a 10-20% fee to pay with a credit card. Be sure you make clear that you want to stay in the same room for consecutive nights; if you don't, the hotel may shuffle you around.

Casa Sol, Calama 127 (☎230 798; fax 223 383; email casasol@ecuadorexplorer.com), at 6 de Diciembre. Bright, immaculate rooms, all with bath. Sunny courtyard. Superior service, though you do pay for it. Singles US$12, with bath US$15; doubles US$22, with bath US$26; triples US$32, with bath US$33. Discounts for long stays.

The Magic Bean Hostel, Foch E5-08 (☎566 181; email magic@ecuadorexplorer.com/magicbean/home), at León Mera. The best known of Quito's gringo hosteling hotbeds. Prime (though noisy) location. Great restaurant. Well-maintained dorms US$8 per person; singles US$22; doubles US$26; triples US$32.

La Casona de Mario, Andalucía 213 (☎544 036 or 230 129; email lacasona@punto.net.ec), at Galicia. A bit out of the way, but it's worth the walk to come home to the sweet dogs and delightful flowers. Patio. Kitchen access. Rooms US$6 per person; 10% discount on stays over 7 days and for SAE members.

El Cafecito, Luis Cordero 1124 (☎234 862), at Reina Victoria. Comfortable rooms with colorful wall hangings, upstairs from a popular cafe (where guests get a 10% discount). Canadian-owned and European-filled. Dorms US$6 per person with tax.

Hostal Centro Del Mundo, at Reina Victoria and García. Where the cool cats hang out. Generally clean and comfortable. Each bed has a locking chest. Delicious breakfasts in the small cafe (US$2-5). Dorms US$2.50-6; triples US$12 per person.

Hostal Amazonas Inn, Joaquín Pinto E4-324 (☎225 723), at Amazonas. Central, with comfortable rooms and private baths. Some 1st floor rooms have balconies. Singles US$5; doubles US$8; triples US$10; quads US$12; includes tax.

Hostal Eva Luna, Roca 630 (☎234 799), down an alley between León Mera and Amazonas. Quito's only women's hostel. Feminine wiles include a pink door and painted wall flowers. TV room. Rooms US$5 per person with tax; discounts for stays over 9 days.

Hostal Rincón de Castilla, Versalles 1127 (☎/fax 224 312), at Carrión. Spartan rooms are clean enough. Cheap and under 10min. from most New Town activity. Laundry service. TV. Kitchen access. Rooms US$3.60 per person with tax.

Hostal Viena, Tamayo N24-77 (☎235 418), at Foch, a few blocks up hill from 6 de Diciembre. An unmistakable aura of cleanliness surrounds this hostel and its various shrines to the Virgin Mary. Rooms US$5 per person.

Crossroads Hostel, Foch N5-23 (☎234 735; email crossrds@vio.satnet.net), at Juan León Mera. A favorite among adventure travelers. Basic rooms, but amenities include a basketball court and an opportunity to chat with the owner, Jeff, who can help plan excursions. Dorms US$5-6 per person; singles US$12; doubles US$20; triples US$30.

OLD TOWN

Staying in Old Town will bring you closer to the pulse of colonial Quito—during the day, that is. At night, there's little of interest in this part of town, and safety is a real concern; take taxis after dark.

Grand Hotel, Rocafuerte 1001 (☎280 192 or 959 411; email grandhotelquito1@hotmail.com), at Pontón. A great value. Everything a traveler could desire: Internet service, a cafe, laundry, Spanish school, cable TV in the common room, storage, and kitchen access. Rooms US$3-6 per person, with bath US$4-12.

Hotel San Francisco de Quito, Sucre 217 (☎287 758; fax 951 241; email hsfquito@impsat.net.ec), at Guayaquil, a block up from the Plaza Santo Domingo. Old Town elegance at very reasonable rates. Comfortable carpeted rooms, all with bath, some with iron balconies overlooking the charming courtyard. Singles US$6; doubles US$8-9; triples US$11; quads US$13; mini apartment US$15; includes tax.

Hotel Vega Internacional, Flores 562 (☎959 833; fax 954 327), at Chile. With a large courtyard, sun-filled hallways, and new TVs in rooms, Vega's a refreshing alternative to some of Old Town's gloomier establishments. All rooms with bath. Restaurant. Singles US$4; doubles US$7; triples US$8-10.

⚅ FOOD

Restaurants charge a 10% IVA in addition to your bill and sometimes another 10% for service. Using a credit card also sometimes results in a 10-20% service charge.

NEW TOWN

Predictably, New Town restaurants tend to be pricier than their Old Town counterparts, but it is still possible to eat well on a reasonable budget. After all, much of the extra cost at the fanciest New Town restaurants covers the frills around the edges: chandeliers, engraved china, waiters in black tie—but the food's not necessarily better than that in the *comedor* around the corner. For cheap eats, hit the *almuerzo* spots on the side streets off **Río Amazonas.** On Amazonas itself, **sidewalk cafes** allow for people-watching and a moderately priced drink or two, but be prepared to be bombarded by people begging or selling. **Restaurant Row,** the informal name for another strip of eateries, many of which are tourist-oriented, lies between León Mera and Reina Victoria, around Calama.

▨ **The Magic Bean Restaurant and Coffeehouse,** Foch E5-08 (☎566 181), at León Mera. Like the hostel upstairs, the Magic Bean restaurant is a gringo stronghold. Salads average US$3, but with 7 varieties of pancakes, this Bean is best known for its breakfasts (around US$1.50). Open daily 7am-10pm.

▨ **El Maple** (☎231 503), at Calama and León Mera. The "vegetarian food" sign tempts herbivores from afar. Plenty of plants and bright lighting make the atmosphere as fresh and healthy as the food. All dishes made with organic vegetables washed in boiled water. Entrees average US$2. Daily specials US$1.65. Open daily 11:30am-10:30pm.

Restaurante Tanguito (☎543 565), on Carrión between 10 de Agosto and Murillo. The locals know where to go—here. Mouthwatering *almuerzo* US$1. Open daily 8am-7pm.

Restaurante El Holandés, Reina Victoria 600 (☎522 167), at Carrión. Extensive vegetarian menu; not much atmosphere. Dutch, Indonesian, Hindu, Italian, and Greek platters start at US$2. Open M-F noon-9pm.

Super Papa, León Mera 741 (☎239 955), at Baquedano. Potato-lovers congregate here to celebrate this sacred food of the Inca. Baked taters (most US$2-3) come heaped with loads of hot or cold fillings. Seating both inside and out. Open daily 7am-9:30pm.

Cevichería Viejo José, Ventimilla 1274 (☎228 369), at Paez. Friendly music encourages high spirits, which are raised even higher by this delicious seafood. Appetizers US$0.50-$2. Special dishes US$2. Open M-F 8am-7pm, Su 8am-5pm.

Mama Clorinda, Reina Victoria 1144 (☎544 362), at Calama. Traditional dishes in a cozy space. A good place to try Ecuadorian specialties like cattle tongue (US$2) or figs with cheese (US$0.50) Open Tu-Sa 10am-10pm, Su-M 10am-5pm.

Adam's Rib, Calama 329 (☎563 196), at Reina Victoria. The name says it all. The BBQ sauce is so good they sell it to go. Dishes US$2. Open M-F noon-10:30pm, Su noon-9pm.

Puerto Manabí, Calama 433 (☎553 080), at León Mera. A fireplace gives this small meat restaurant a homey feel. Entrees US$1-2. Open daily 9am-9pm.

THE BIG SPLURGE

Restaurante Mare Nostrum, Foch 172 (☎237 236), at Tamayo. An outstanding seafood restaurant housed in a stunning 1930s mansion. Solid pewter plates, a suit of armor by the fireplace, and stained glass windows add to the ambiance. Order some Chilean, Spanish, or French wine and the bill may seem less painful. Seafood paella US$5. Crab crepes US$2. Daily specials US$4-12. Open daily noon-11pm.

La Choza, 12 de Octubre N24-551 (☎507 901) at Cordero. Farm equipment scattered about contributes to the elegant pastoral dining room. Stylish Ecuadorian meat and fish entrees US$3-13. Open M-F noon-3:30pm and 7-10pm, Sa-Su noon-4pm.

Il Risotto (☎220 400), at Pinto and Diego Almagro. Put on your best (or your cleanest) and enjoy the mahogany furniture, candlelight, and fresh flowers at this elegant Italian restaurant. Home-made ravioli, gnocchi, or fettucine US$3. Risotto in champagne sauce US$4. Open Tu-S 11am-3pm and 6:30-11pm.

CAFES

Usually small, crowded, and overflowing with trendy espresso drinks, the following coffeeshops can't be beat for a hip meeting place. But don't come hoping for any deals—they're notoriously expensive.

Grain de Café, Baquedano 332 (☎565 975), between Reina Victoria and León Mera. A huge selection of imported coffees, teas, and alcohol. Espresso US$0.45. Tequila shots US$0.75-2.20. Cocktails US$1.80-$2.45. Open M-Th noon-12am, F-Sa noon-1am.

Café Cultura, Robles E5-62 (☎224 271), at Reina Victoria. The place to go for high tea, complete with scones, jam, and clotted cream (US$1.75). Open daily 7am-9:30pm.

El Cafecito, Cordero 1124 (☎234 862), at Reina Victoria. This coffeeshop and vegetarian cafe proves that the trendy alternative scene has hit Ecuador. Mediocre coffee drinks. Desserts US$1-2. Open Su-Th 8am-10pm, F-Sa 8am- midnight.

OLD TOWN

Old Town's many small *almuerzo* and *merienda* restaurants make it the perfect area in which to seek a cheap and tasty three-course lunch. Look around for a spot free of flies and filled with locals, or try one of the dependable favorites below.

Bar Restaurant Balcón Quiteño, Bolívar 220 (☎512 711), at Guayaquil, on the top floor of the Hotel Real Audiencia on the Plaza Santo Domingo. Nowhere else can you dine with such an amazing view of the colonial city. English menu. Entrees average US$2.50. Open M-Sa 7:30am-2:30pm and 4-10pm, Su 7:30-10am.

La Zamba Teresa (☎583 826), at Chile and Venezuela, off the Plaza Grande. The lively little sister of the fanciest restaurant in Old Town. Sandwiches US$1-1.50. Traditional Ecuadorian dishes US$1.25-3. Pastries average US$1. Open daily 7am-7pm.

El Criollo, Flores 825 (☎219 811), at Olmedo. A traditional, gringo-frequented, Old Town restaurant with some classy touches. Omelettes and sandwiches under US$1. Open daily 8am-9:30pm.

Burger Works, (☎566 298), at Chile and Guayaquil, across the street from Iglesia San Augustín in the Centro Commercial. The food's about as Ecuadorian as the name. The combos (US$1-2) come with fries and a drink. Open daily 9am-7:30pm.

Sol Natura, Sucre 209 (☎951 879), at Guayaquil, next to Hotel San Francisco de Quito. Pleasant Andean music accompanies this high-mountain vegetarian food. Most plates hover around US$1. Fresh squeezed juices US$0.50 and up. Open M-Sa 7am-6pm.

◆ SIGHTS

There is always something to see or do in Quito. Unlike with other activities, sights revolve around Old Town, which is a sight in itself.

OLD TOWN (LA PARTE COLONIAL)

When the United Nations declared Old Quito a World Heritage Site in 1978, scores of 300-year-old plazas, churches, and government palaces were guaranteed both longevity and a high profile. Since then, strict zoning laws have kept much of Old Town looking more or less the way it did when Ecuador was a Spanish colony. However, travelers should exercise caution when exploring the area, even by day. Pickpockets roam the streets, particularly around the market and bus terminal. The streets get even more dangerous at night, at which time tourists should retreat to New Town. The best way to get to the center of Old Quito is on the trolley.

QUITO

■ **LA VIRGEN DE QUITO.** Visible from the Plaza del Teatro, as well as most other locations on the outskirts of Old Town, the majestic statue of La Virgen de Quito surveys her domain from the summit of **El Panecillo** at the far end of Old Quito. Views to both the north and south reveal why these hills have been so strategically important to the region's inhabitants for centuries. There's a *mirador* atop this one, just below the pedestal of the serpent-stomping virgin. The trip up El Panecillo involves a long and dangerous walk up the stairs at the end of García Moreno—even groups get robbed frequently; a safer bet is to have a taxi take you up and wait to bring you back down. *(Round-trip, including a 20min. wait at the statue, US$5. Open daily 9am-dark.)*

PLAZA DE LA INDEPENDENCIA. Also called the Plaza Grande, this plaza is the centerpiece of colonial Quito. Its stunning **Palacio Presidencial,** historic **Hotel Majestic** (colonial Quito's first hotel), and colossal **cathedral**—with green-and-bronze domes and a high white turret—enchant visitors. *(Cathedral open daily 8-10am and 3-6:30pm.)* However, the plaza is best-loved by *quiteños* as a relaxing retreat with shady palm trees and meticulously maintained gardens. Few realize the true historical significance of this favorite rest stop. Built in 1667, the cathedral contains the grave of **Antonio José de Sucre,** Independence hero and namesake of the country's fading currency; a statue commemorating Quito's Independence Day (August 10) dynamizes the plaza's center. Down the block from the Plaza Grande, at Chile and Guayaquil, the **Iglesia de San Agustín** contains the paintings of 17th-century artist Miguel de Santiago. *(Open daily 7:15am-noon and 3:30-6pm.)*

PLAZA SANTO DOMINGO. Though there's little to do in the plaza itself, the Plaza Santo Domingo serves as a good starting place for those interested in exploring the old city. The attendant 16th-century **Iglesia de Santo Domingo** stands out for its elegance and simplicity. *(Open M-Sa 6am-noon and 4-7pm, Su 6am-1pm and 6-7pm.)* Following Rocafuerte from the plaza, you'll pass **Carmen Alto,** the home of Santa Mariana. *(Open M-Sa 6:30am-5:30pm, Su 4:30-7pm.)*

PLAZA SAN FRANCISCO. Always well-populated, the Plaza San Francisco is flanked by the gorgeous and gigantic **Monasterio de San Francisco,** constructed between 1535 and 1605. *(Church open daily 7am-noon and 3-6pm. Free. Museum open M-Sa 9am-6pm, Su 9am-1pm. US$1, students with ID US$0.75. US$1 for a guide.)* **Catedral de La Compañía,** down Sucre a block away from the plaza at García Moreno and Sucre, is under renovation until 2002. Visitors can still appreciate its wonderful baroque facades, carved from volcanic rock, from behind the construction fences. Farther along the right side of García Moreno, the **Iglesia de El Sagrario** features a large stone portico and bright interior. *(Open M-Sa 8am-6pm, Su 8am-1pm.)*

OTHER SIGHTS. The **Plaza del Teatro,** three blocks down Guayaquil away from San Agustín and towards New Quito, is the backdrop for the **Teatro Nacional Sucre,** constructed in 1878 and under reconstruction in 2000. *(Three blocks down Guayaquil away from San Agustín, at Flores and Manabí.)* The most awe-inspiring church is the **Basílica,** on the corner of Venezuela and Carchí. It contains a cafeteria, library, and gift shop, but the coolest thing about the basilica is the tower (115m high). Though this lookout spot offers incredible views of Quito, the long climb up a tiny spiral staircase may terrify sufferers of vertigo. *(Open Tu-Su 9am-5pm. US$0.60 to climb.)*

MUSEUMS

Quito's diverse museums—with collections ranging from ancient artifacts to local reptiles—appeal to almost every visitor. If you're a student, be sure to show your ID at every opportunity—you may get a discount.

NEW TOWN

■ **FUNDACIÓN GUAYASAMÍN.** This museum opens onto a spacious garden with metal statues and white houses. The collection includes an extensive exhibit of pre-Inca artifacts and some 18th-century colonial religious art from the Quiteña and Cuzqueña schools. The rest of the museum is dedicated to the magnificent paintings of the foundation's namesake, Oswaldo Guayasamín, a leader of the indigenist movement, whose images capture the pain of racism, poverty, and class stratification in South America (see **Modern Art**, p. 427, and **Indigenous Identity**, p. 11). *(José Bosmediano 543. Take 6 de Diciembre north to Eloy Alfaro, where Bosmediano begins, and start climbing—the museum is way up the hill. ☎446 455. Open M-F 9am-1:30pm and 3-6:30pm. US$1.)*

MUSEO NACIONAL DEL BANCO CENTRAL. The recent consolidation of several separate Banco Central museums has created the most extensive and impressive museum in Quito. The enormous, winding rooms contain archaeological exhibits, pre-Hispanic gold, pre-Independence paintings, colonial religious portraits, modern art, and indigenous *artesanía*. *(At Patria and 6 de Diciembre. ☎223 258. Open Tu-F 9am-5pm, Sa-Su 10am-3pm. Foreigners US$2, with student ID US$1.)*

CASA DE LA CULTURA ECUATORIANA. In the same building as the Museo Nacional, this museum presents a collection of 19th- and 20th-century art, an ethnology display, and several unique musical instruments, including the *caperazon*, made from a tortoise shell, and the *pifono*, a flute made from an armadillo tail. An Amazonian shrunken head and indigenous regional garb mix with the sculptures and paintings. From time to time, the museum also shows movies and puts on plays. *(☎223 392. Open Tu-F 10am-6pm, Sa 10am-2pm. US$0.50, with student ID US$0.25.)* The **Galería** hosts temporary exhibitions. Call ahead to find out what the current exhibition is. *(6 de Diciembre 794. Open M-Th 10am-5pm, F 10am-6pm. Free.)* The complex also maintains a library. *(Open M-F 9am-7pm, Sa 9am-5pm.)*

VIVARIUM. This is not the place for people who fear snakes or other slimy reptiles. Iguanas, a small alligator, several turtles, and some tiny poisonous frogs all lurk in this reptile and amphibian zoo. Pythons, cobras, snapping turtles, and other potentially harmful animals are caged and labeled with color-coded information cards so visitors can tell which are venomous, which live where, and which want to eat you. Ask nicely to hold the boa. *(Reina Victoria N25-68, at Santa María. ☎230 988. Open Tu-Sa 9:30am-1pm and 2:30-6pm, Su 11am-1pm. US$1, children US$0.50.)*

INSTITUTO GEOGRÁFICO MILITAR. This institute boasts the best maps for every region of Ecuador. Political, topographical, sierra, oriente—you name it. Many are for sale or can be copied (starting at US$1), but be prepared to wait around a while. There is also a **planetarium** and a **geographical museum**, and great satellite photos of Ecuador's volcanic craters are on display in the main room. Spanish is helpful for getting past the military guards at the entrance. *(On Telmo Paz y Miño, at the top of a hill. You can only reach Paz y Miño from Telmo, which runs along the base of the hill. It's a 10min. uphill walk to the top. ☎502 091. Open M-F 8am-4pm. Planetarium shows M-F 9, 11am and 3pm, Sa 11am. US$1; passport required to enter.)*

VISITING HOURS For many, the notion of a women's prison in the developing world invokes images of automatic weapons, barbed wire, and questionable human rights practices. The **Carcel de Mujeres,** las Toronjas, New Quito, is a happier, if no less shocking, vision. On visitors' day, the prison yard becomes a circus of inmates, husbands, and children playing volleyball. Two unarmed female guards sit by, knitting. Many of the prisoners have children living in the jail with them, in blocks of rooms rather than cells. Most are poor *indígenas*, but there's also a handful of foreigners serving up to eight years for **drug possession charges.** These women—most from the United States—eagerly receive the English-speaking visitors who often bring gifts of food, cigarettes, and books in return for hearing some extraordinary stories. To get to the prison, take a northbound local bus on 6 de Diciembre to El Inca and ask the driver to drop you off at the prison. Follow El Inca and take a left onto las Toronjas. *(Visiting hours W, Sa, and Su 10am-4pm; passport required.)*

MUSEO AMAZÓNICO ABYA-YAL. A one-room exhibit on Oriente life, this museum features exhibits on Amazonian culture; wildlife, musical instruments, and photos of oil exploitation are all on display. Downstairs in the awesome bookstore, a huge variety of publications is available on the foundation's main interest: indigenous anthropology. *(12 de Octubre 1430, at Wilson. ☎562 633. Open M-F 8am-6pm. US$0.75.)*

OLD TOWN

Not surprisingly, many of the museums in Old Town are concerned with history. Colonial Quito comes alive at these exhibits, sometimes housed in buildings as old as the artifacts themselves.

MUSEO DEL CONVENTO SAN DIEGO. Spanish colonists established this religious institution 400 years ago, and the 40-minute guided tour through the complex (given in Spanish and necessary to enter the museum) reveals many intimate windows into the distant past: original murals, cooking facilities, and a chamber where bones are buried. The walls wear religious paintings; one depicts the Last Supper, with *cuy* (guinea pig) substituted for Christ's main course. *(Calicuchima 117, at Farfán. Follow Imbabura south from Old Quito until it dead-ends in the plaza in front of the convent. ☎952 516. Open Su 9:30am-1pm and 2:30-5:30pm. US$1.)*

MUSEO CASA DE SUCRE. This museum celebrates Ecuador's battle for independence in the house of one of its key participants, Mariscal Antonio José de Sucre. The museum includes a free house tour in Spanish, which provides a glimpse into Sucre's personal life—or at least his chapel, bedroom, and even his skull after his assassination. *(Venezuela 573, at Sucre. ☎952 860. Open Sa 8:30am-4:30pm. US$0.50.)* A continuation of the Museo Casa de Sucre, the **Museo Templo de la Patria** sits farther up the hill of Pichincha, under the monument to Ecuador's freedom fighters, at the spot where they triumphed and won independence in 1822. *(☎952 860. Open Tu-F 8am-4pm, Sa 8am-1pm, Su 10am-3pm. US$0.40.)*

MUSEO ALBERTO MENA CAMAÑO DE ARTE E HISTORIA. Currently closed for renovations, this museum should reopen by 2001. The permanent exhibit is a historical journey that descends into the maze-like basement, where wax figures lie in murdered positions. A ground-level room displays temporary art exhibits. *(Espejo 1147, at García Moreno. ☎510 272. Open Tu-Sa 9am-4:45pm. Free.)*

MUSEO DE ARTE COLONIAL. Quito's artlife began as a form of religious expression, as this museum, with displays from the 16th to early 19th centuries, shows. The collection includes old books, faded and gilded paintings, leather furniture, some colonial clothing, iron keys, and sundry other gems. *(Cuenca 901, at Mejía. ☎282 297. Open Tu-F 10am-6pm, Sa 10am-2pm. US$0.50.)*

MUSEO CONDE DE URQUIJO DE LA CASA DE BENALCÁZAR. Though located in the home of Quito's founder, this museum isn't devoted to the glorification of Sebastián de Benalcázar. Instead, through the Ecuadorian Hispanic Culture Institute, the small one-room exhibit houses an extensively decorated chapel, paintings, and a collection of sculptures from the 16th to 18th centuries, donated in 1966 by the Conde de Urquijo, then the Spanish ambassador. The art is religious, and the public library devoutly intellectual. *(Olmedo 968, at Benalcázar. ☎285 828. Open M-F 9am-1pm and 2-6pm. Free.)*

COLEGIO NACIONAL MEJÍA. The Colegio Nacional Mejía houses two separate museums behind its high walls. The **Museo Etnográfico** presents a series of life-sized dioramas of different indigenous Ecuadorians, as well as a taxidermy exhibit of animals that once roamed the country. *(On Ante between Vargas and Venezuela. ☎583 412. Open M-F 8am-noon and 2-6pm, Sa 8am-noon. Guided tours required. Free.)* The **Museo de Ciencias Naturales,** accessible via the school's main entrance, contains a thorough taxidermy collection, which includes brightly colored birds, turtles, and sharks. *(☎583 412. Open M-F 7am-3pm. Free.)*

SHOPPING

Quito's most cosmopolitan thoroughfare, New Town's **Río Amazonas,** is also the most popular (though not the cheapest) place to buy souvenirs and Ecuadorian handicrafts. If you plan to buy a lot, keep in mind that markets in neighboring towns such as **Otavalo** offer both lower prices and a more "cultural" shopping experience. Even so, visiting the shops on Amazonas, if only to browse, can give you an idea of the *artesanía* Ecuador has to offer in a setting more comfortable than the hectic local markets. Directed at tourists, these shops stock the most popular handmade Ecuadorian crafts: Panama hats, carved tagua-nuts, hand-painted pottery, and handwoven rugs, shawls, wall hangings, and bags. **Parque El Ejido** hosts a weekly craft market, another good place to get an idea of what's out there. (Su 10:30am-5pm). The **Santa Clara market,** walled in at Reina Victoria and Jorge Washington, is yet another option. Unless prices are marked or explicitly stated as fixed, bargaining is expected. The prices at the **El Jardín** mall are just that: marked and fixed, not to mention as high as they would be at home. With a giant Supermaxi and MIKASA department store as its foundation, this first-world fix houses multiple boutiques, food courts, and escalators, though very little *artesanía.* (Open M-Sa 10am-8:30pm, Su 10am-7:30pm.)

▣ ENTERTAINMENT

SPORTS

Amateur *fútbolistas* play in the parks. The pros play at **Estadio Atahuallpa,** at 6 de Diciembre and Naciones Unidas, near Parque La Carolina. To get there take the "Estadio" bus on 6 de Diciembre. (Intra-Ecuador games cost US$1, international games run US$3-4; purchase tickets 2-3 days in advance.) To watch bulls battle instead, contact **La Plaza de Toros,** at Amazonas and Ascaray—fights are very rare, however. (☎246 037. Tickets US$8.) Other diversions include go-karting at the **Speedway,** at Amazonas and Eloy Alfaro, around the corner from the Ministerio de Agricultura. (☎553 105. 5min., US$1.20; 10min., US$2. Open Tu-Sa 10am-7pm.) For some bright flashing lights, check out **PlayZone,** an arcade at Naciones Unidas and Chile. For some fresh air, join one of the aerobics sessions on Sunday mornings in **Parque La Carolina,** north of the city center on Amazonas between Eloy Alfaro and República. This park, with its roller-skating rink, horses, paddle boats, and tennis and basketball courts, is best (read: safer) in the mornings. The central **Parque El Ejido,** sandwiched between Old and New Town, has similar greenery. **Parque Alameda** in Old Town has an observatory and some monuments to science but lacks the relaxed atmosphere of La Carolina.

ECUADOR STRIKES GOLD July 26, 1996: a mild summer morning. But more than 80,000 people held their breath as 22-year-old Jefferson Pérez, in slinky shorts and professional walking shoes, entered the Olympic Stadium in Atlanta, Georgia, to claim the first gold medal of the 1996 Track and Field competition—**Ecuador's first Olympic medal ever.** Walking 20km in 1 hour, 20 minutes, and 7 seconds, he beat his best time by 1 second and the rest of the field by 25m. The closest Ecuador came to medaling before this was in 1972, when Jorge Delgado Panchama came in fourth in the 200m butterfly. In interviews, Pérez reminisced, "When I took the lead, I felt very tired, as if I was asleep. It felt like a dream. Then I thought that *this* is my dream. I have to go for it, even if I died." Back in Quito, patriots filled the streets, celebrating the momentous occasion into the wee hours of the morning.

QUITO

FILM

Quito's many movie theaters generally screen several-months-old American movies in English with Spanish subtitles. The best movie listings are in the newspapers *El Comercio* (in the classifieds) and *Hoy*. Some theaters have matinees, but most just screen twice during the evenings. (Tickets US$1.80-2; anything much cheaper is probably a porno.) The **Casa de la Cultura** sometimes also has film festivals. Theaters include: **Cinemark 7**, at Americas and República, on the Plaza de las Américas (☎260 301; US$1 shows M, W, F); **Multicines,** Japan 250 (☎259 811; US$1 shows W-Th); **Universitario** (☎230 280), at Américas and Vérez Guerrero at the Universidad Central; **Colón** (☎224 081), at 10 de Agosto and Colón; **Benalcázar,** at 6 de Diciembre and Portugal. **Bolívar** (☎582 486), at Espejo and Guayaquil in Old Town, is decent, though New Town theaters are generally of a much higher caliber.

THEATER

Although the **Teatro Nacional Sucre** was built to satisfy cultural Quito's dramatic desires, it has been under renovation for so long that no one can quite remember when the last real performance took place. Theatrical events have instead been relegated to a plethora of smaller theaters and *salas* around town. Check the cultural agenda in *El Comercio* for current listings.

◪ NIGHTLIFE

After dark, curls of cigarette smoke fill in for bus exhaust as the real world goes to sleep and young people throughout the city relax at Quito's wide range of bars and dance clubs. Stick to nightlife in New Town; not only is the scene hipper, but Old Town's streets are too dangerous for night wandering, especially if you're a bit drunk. That said, New Town's not such a safe haven either; recent reports of robberies and assaults have put revelers of the night on guard. Follow their example, especially around Reina Victoria, and take a taxi back to your hotel.

BARS

▨ **Café Sutra,** at Calama and León Mera, above Safari Tours. Follow the wooden boa to this trendy 2nd-floor coffeehouse/bar with soothing tunes on the stereo and odd drawings on the wall. Nightly cocktail specials (2 for US$1.50) complement healthful snacks such as hummus (US$1.20) and fruit salad (US$1). Open daily 8am-11pm.

El Pobre Diablo, Santa María 338 (☎224 982), at León Mera. At this 6-room cafe/bar, sounds of happy chatter and a crackling fire mix with jazz, blues, and latin music. Good coffee US$0.50-2. Pilsener beer US$0.75. Open M-Sa 4:30pm-2am.

Café Habana, Juan León Mera 134 (☎590 911), at Calama. The dance floor can get hot and sweaty, but the real draw are the great wicker couches. Open daily 5pm-2am.

Red Hot Chili Peppers, Foch 713, at León Mera. This dimly lit Mexican restaurant and bar may not be much to look at, but it serves incredible mixed drinks. Pitcher of strawberry daiquiri US$6. Guacamole US$1. Open daily 11am-11pm.

Reina Victoria Pub, Reina Victoria 530 (☎226 329), at Roca. The place for a pint of proper ale (US$1.25). Cozy fireplace. Serves standard pub fare like breaded fish on a roll (US$2) and not-so-standard banana chips (US$0.50). Open M-Sa 5pm-midnight.

Varadero (☎542 476), at Reina Victoria and La Pinta. Packed with locals, but anyone who appreciates rhythm and style should feel welcome. Live Cuban music F-Sa. Cover US$1. F-Sa. Open W-Sa noon-4pm and 7pm-2am.

Arribar, León Mera 1238 (☎228 545), at Lizardo García. Tempting customers with foosball, pool, comfy couches, reggae, a slide projector, and a full bar. Beer US$1.50. Tequila shot US$1.50. Happy hour 5-8pm. Open M-Sa 5pm-2am.

CLUBS

Starting around 11pm, the dance clubs around New Town fill with people anxious to get a groove on. One block north of Colón, **Santa María** claims some of Quito's most traveler-friendly nightclubs, including **Tijuana and Papillón.** Lesbian and gay travelers have options in Quito as well, but they are often difficult to find. Ecuadorian law only recently decriminalized homosexuality (see **Bisexual, Gay, and Lesbian Travelers,** p. 55); gay hangouts are a quiet, cautious phenomenon.

No Bar, Calama 380 (☎545 145), at León Mera, on Calama's Restaurant Row. Locals and travelers pack the floor at one of the trendiest nightspots in Quito. Happy hour M-W 6-10pm. Cover US$1.50 F-Sa, includes one drink. Open M-Sa 8pm-3am.

Seseribó, at Veintimilla and 12 de Octubre, downstairs in the Edificio El Girón; look for the flashing pink sign. Latin music lovers will find a lot to dance to here—to be specific, salsa, merengue, and rumba. Cover US$2. Open W-Sa 9pm-2:30am.

El Choque, Calama 317 (☎546 086), at Reina Victoria. The folks at El Choque move their hips—or wish they could. Live music and salsa lessons W. Open daily 8am-2am.

Bar-Ril, Lizardo García 356 (☎226 714), at 6 de Diciembre. Quito's first (and pretty much only) gay bar on a very cool spot. Shows on weekends and special occasions. US$2 drink min. on show nights. Happy hour 8-9pm F-Sa. Open W-Sa 8pm-2am.

▶ DAYTRIPS FROM QUITO

VOLCÁN PICHINCHA

The summit can be accessed from the volcano's southern base, through the villages of Mena Dos and Lloa, an hour's drive from Quito along Mariscal Antonio Jose de Sucre. To reach Lloa, take a "Mena Dos" bus south from the bus canopy at Américas and Colón, adjacent to the Seminario Mayor San José, where returning southbound buses make a U-turn (45min., every 15min. 6am-7:30pm, US$0.25). Take the bus until Angamarca, the main street and bus stop in Mena Dos. From here, camionetas or taxis go to Lloa (US$2); the farther up you walk, the less transport will cost. Alternatively, volquetas (multicolored trucks) run toward Lloa from the junction of Venidores and Angamarca, and will often give rides (5am-7pm, US$0.25). Angamarca leads up the hill into a street named Via Lloa, which leads to Lloa, but the walk to Lloa (1hr.) is not recommended because of recent muggings along the roadway. In Lloa, there is a road winding up to the refuge (by 4X4 1hr., by foot 5-7hr.), which sits just shy of the crater's edge. Without a 4-wheel-drive vehicle to take you to the refuge from Lloa, it will be difficult to complete the trip in a day, and transportation can be difficult to coordinate. Those planning to make it up and back in one day should start very early to beat the clouds which settle over the crater midday. It might be worth the money to go with a tour agency (see Tour Agencies, p. 433). Though most hikers do Pichincha as a daytrip, those wishing to spend the night should bring US$3 to stay at the refuge. From the refuge, the sometimes snow-covered summit is a 2-3hr. round-trip hike. It is not recommended to hike down into the crater, as some climbers were asphyxiated by gaseous emissions several years ago while camping inside.

One of the most awe-inspiring aspects of Quito is the surrounding terrain. The most impressive feature of this terrain is perhaps the double-cratered Volcán Pichincha. The younger, more energetic crater, Guagua Pichincha, erupted in 1660, 1881, and 1981, to name a few fiery occasions. But while the volcano rumbles alarmingly close to Quito, it does not pose an enormous threat; the closer crater, Rucu Pichincha, is utterly inactive and fires off in a western direction, away from the city. Pichincha's proximity to Quito makes it one of the most popular climbs in Ecuador. Less strenuous than some of Ecuador's other peaks, Pichincha provides fantastic views of Quito, the valley, and a slew of other mountains in the distance.

The closer crater, **Rucu,** tempts tourists to start scrambling up the hillside from the city. This is possible, but quite dangerous because of the sometimes-armed thieves that occasionally lurk at the foot of the mountain. Check with Safari or the SAE (see p. 433) for the present state of affairs. Because of the risks involved, *Let's Go* does not recommend visiting Rucu, especially with so many safer, and equally scenic, mountains nearby. **Guagua** outdoes Rucu in altitude, scenery, and safety, though one should be wary of dogs. From its peak, vistas stretch to the uninhabited west and south, and when clouds don't get in the way, climbers can see down into its crater.

STRAIGHT FLUSH When 18th-century French explorers came to Ecuador in search of the "middle of the Earth," they (or rather their huffing lackeys) hauled along the finest compasses and astrolabes that the king's court could provide. Their find wasn't worth all the fuss—the Frenchmen could have done the job with a bidet. Among the odd phenomena that occur at the Earth's equator, which include feeling lighter than at any other spot on Earth and being able to balance an egg on the head of a nail, is the strange fact that toilets don't know which way to flush. A toilet in a house to the north will flush counterclockwise, while a porcelain pal to the south will flush in the opposite direction. The query: what is a poor potty to do when it's set squarely in the middle? Scientists claim that something called the **Coriolis effect** causes the swirly switcharoo, but even they can't predict which way an equatorial whirlpool will turn. Rumor has it that, in order to dispel the mystery, a group of experts has set up a laboratory of 10 toilets, one bathtub, and a lava lamp in the basement of Mitad del Mundo's equatorial monument. These gurus of bowl mechanics follow a strict daily regimen (reposition toilet, pull cord, reposition, pull cord) in search of one thing—the mythical straight flush. No one knows if they've seen it—some claim they never will—but if you want to see for yourself, head to the closest w.c. and keep on flushin'.

MITAD DEL MUNDO

Flag down a pink-and-white interparroquial bus with a "Mitad del Mundo" sign in the window along Américas in New Town—try the intersection at Colón. Returning buses leave from the traffic circle in front of Mitad del Mundo (every 5min. until 6pm, 7pm on F).

Latitude 0°0'0". Yes, you're on the equator, Ecuador's namesake and a popular tourist attraction. Since the equatorial monument known as Mitad del Mundo (Middle of the World) was erected in 1979, equator-mania has transformed this spot into a center for Ecuadorian culture, history, and capitalist venture. Perhaps more than any other location in the country, Mitad del Mundo has become a bona fide, circus-style tourist attraction, visited by foreigners and nationals alike. Predictably, the major festival days in these parts fall on March 21 and September 23 (the equinoxes) and June 22 and December 22 (the solstices). But the overpriced tourist "village" houses bleached-white buildings, smooth stone pathways, and a sprawling complex of museums, restaurants, and gift shops that cater to visiting equator-philes all year long. In the center of it all, a 2.5-ton metallic globe tops a monument 30m high; this wide trapezoid is perfectly aligned with the cardinal points of the compass. From the monument, a yellow stripe extends to denote the equator itself, which an army of tourists straddles each day, enchanted by the notion of standing in both hemispheres at the same time.

INSIDE THE COMPLEX. From the parking lot (US$0.50 to park), the gates open to a gleaming pathway toward the globe. Bordering this walkway are busts of the 13 men from France, Spain, and Ecuador who explored and measured the equator from 1736 to 1744. While visiting the site itself is free, most attractions charge for admission. Tickets to the obelisk (US$2 for foreigners) are available from the office in front of the monument's entrance on the first floor of the main information building. A ticket for the obelisk allows you to take an elevator to the top of the monument and then, on the way down, see the **Ethnographic Museum** (☎394 806) that surrounds the winding staircase. The museum's exhibits detail the clothing, food, dwellings, and customs of many Ecuadorian indigenous groups. The same ticket also give you access to the **French Museum,** southeast of the monument, which explains the history of the equator's measurement. (Free tours in Spanish and sometimes English. Open M-Th 9am-6pm, F-Su 9am-7pm.)

Though these are the highest-profile, the Mitad del Mundo complex contains several more modest but interesting attractions. Back inside the complex, adjacent to the French museum, a spiffy **planetarium** waits for at least 15 tourists to arrive before beginning its shows. (38min. ☎395 795. Open Tu-F 9am-5pm, Sa-Su

9am-6pm. US$1, children US$0.25). Nearby, **Fundación Quito Colonial** houses **miniature city models** of colonial Quito, downtown Guayaquil, and Cuenca. (Open daily 9:30am-5pm. US$0.50.) A monument dedicated to the **Héroes del Cenepa**, near the entrance, honors the soldiers who died in the 1995 war with Peru. A **scale** across from the post office lures weight-watching tourists to marvel at the kilos they seem to lose on the equator (usually no more than 4kg). They haven't really trimmed any inches; the equatorial bulge brings them farther from the center of the earth, where gravity has a weaker pull and, consequently everything weighs less. The **Plaza de Toros** occasionally hosts **bullfights.**

OUTSIDE THE COMPLEX. Arguably the best site outside the Mitad del Mundo complex is the thatch-roofed **Museo de Sitio (en vivo) Inti-Ñan** ("The Path of the Sun" in Quichua), northeast of the obelisk. To get there, follow the equatorial line through the plaza, and continue down the hill along the path just to the left of the church. After exiting the complex, turn left and walk uphill past Restaurante Equinoccio. The museum's owners proudly guide visitors through exhibits on the sun's path, indigenous customs, and regional flora. Even if you don't speak Spanish, it's worth seeing the live guinea pigs and Galapagos tortoises on site, as well as shrunken heads and bottled snakes. Also look forward to demonstrations of the Coriolis Effect (see Straight Flush, opposite page) and dart-blowing. The museum also has the privilege of sitting on the current scientifically-measured latitude 0°0'0", where one can balance eggs on nails. (☎395 122. Open daily 9:30am-6pm. US$1.)

PULULAHUA AND RUMICUCHO. Visible from the equatorial monument 6km away, the rising ridge of volcanic crater Pululahua in the **Reserva Geobótanica Pululahua** (US$5) offers magnificent views. The crater, which has been inactive for over 3000 years, is great for hiking. Two paths head here from the Mitad del Mundo complex and then continue as trails to the crater floor. Both are well-marked and turn off the highway between San Antonio de Pichincha and the town of Calacalí, 8km to the west. The first path begins at the Sangría Restaurant. Follow the road up 2km, bearing left at the fork until you reach a lookout spot called **Ventanilla** (2900m). From here a footpath leads down into the crater. The second trail begins 3km past the first along the highway to Calacalí. Clearly marked, this 16km road leads uphill to lookout point Moraspungo (3186km) and down a very steep footpath into the crater. Bring sensible footwear; trails get muddy. As an alternative to walking, catch a bus that passes through Mitad del Mundo's traffic circle (15min., every 45min. 6am-7pm, US$0.10) on its way to Pululahua. Buses run back to Mitad del Mundo, often continuing to Quito, with the same frequency (5am-6:30pm). Taxis and camionetas can also run tourists to the first trailhead (under US$1) and later pick them up for the same amount. There is a **refuge** to the right of the crater's main road. Ranger Jorge Guzmán speaks flawless English and makes overnight visitors feel at home. (US$0.50 per person.) Bring food. Camping in the refuge is free for those who pay the admission fee to the reserve, but make reservations. For the most impressive views, go before noon; afternoons, a blanket of clouds often settles over the crater.

The other jaunt from Mitad del Mundo is to **Rumicucho** (which means "stone corner" in Quichua), a set of Cara ruins atop a hill to the northeast. However, since at one point locals took stones from the site to build their own homes and since there are still areas yet to be excavated, there aren't actually many ruins to see. But the view from the site, which includes the **Canyon of Guayllabamba**, is reason enough to visit. Free tours in Spanish are offered but are unpredictable; try after 1pm on weekdays or after 10am on weekends. (Open daily 7:30am-5pm. US$0.25.) The easiest way to get there to Rumicucho is by camioneta from Mitad del Mundo (US$0.35 each way). Alternatively, the walk leads through hot, dusty, and not-so-picturesque neighborhoods for over an hour. Take Equinoccial and make a left onto 13 de Junio, the principal strip of San Antonio de Pichincha that runs north-south. Stay on the road for 30 to 45 minutes. At the Rumicucho sign, take a right; the ruins are not far.

The safest and most efficient way to visit these two sights, however, is with a guide who can make up for sparse information and transportation. **Calima Tours,** in the main information building at Mitad del Mundo, can give visitors rides to the sights along with all the related details and history. Call ahead to arrange for guides in English or Spanish. (☎394 796. US$5 per sight, per person. Open daily 9am-6pm.) For a local perspective, go to **Centro de Información Equinoccio** and ask for José. His tour, in Spanish or rough English, includes discussions of medicinal plants and Cara history. (US$5 Pululahua, US$9 both sights.)

NEAR QUITO: BELLAVISTA CLOUD FOREST RESERVE

Bellavista's remote location is one of its greatest charms, but it can also be an obstacle to travelers on a tight schedule or budget. The only way to get there with public transportation is by taking a bus from the Quito bus terminal to Nanegalito (2hr., US$1); any bus going to Pacto, Puerto Quito, San Miguel de los Bancos, or Mindo passes through Nanegalito. In Nanegalito, ask at Viveres Paty for Don Raúl, or anyone with a camioneta to take you the remaining up the hill to the reserve (45min., about US$15 per truck load). Walking the 12km up to Bellavista is also an option (5hr.); ask the driver to drop you off at Km32, just beyond Café Tiepolo but before Nanegalito. Follow the road past a few trout hatcheries and through the village of Tandayapa to reach the lodge. Buses returning to Quito pass through Km32 (last bus 5:30pm); allow 3 hours for the trip back down the hill. Transportation (US$60 round-trip for up to 4 people) can also be arranged through the Bellavista office in Quito, Jorge Washington E7-23 (☎/ fax 232 313), at Reina Victoria. Contact the reserve itself at ☎ (09) 490 891 or 232 313.

Though commonly known as a bird-lover's paradise, almost anyone who has visited Bellavista agrees that it's on the stairway to heaven. Spanning 700 hectares at 1600-2500m above sea level, the reserve's lush forests are usually sunny in the morning until the clouds roll in midday, bathing the bromeliads, orchids, and moss in mist, and attracting at least 300 bird species. Come equipped with binoculars, good hiking shoes, rain gear, and snacks so that you can take in as much as possible. An extensive network of 15 well-maintained and easy-to-follow trails (1 easy, 8 moderate, and 6 difficult) makes various parts of the forest accessible to visitors. Rubber boots are supplied upon request when it rains and gets slippery.

Bellavista Lodge itself is a four-story, dome-like structure made out of bamboo, situated so as to offer occupants fantastic views of the surrounding cloud forest and the Tandayapa valley below. Visitors can take splendid meals in the first floor dining area (US$8 per meal) while watching hummingbirds feed just outside the windows. Some guests bring their own food to minimize costs and maximize time on the trails. On the second floor, rooms have balconies, baths, and sitting areas. (Singles US$32; doubles US$54; triples US$75.) Upstairs, budget rooms share baths and balconies. (US$14 per person.) Camping costs US$5 per person. Visitors can also volunteer at the research station, where tasks include trail-building and -maintaining, fence building, and light carpentry work, in exchange for reduced room rates. (US$5 per day for the first 20 days; min. 30 days.)

NEAR QUITO: MINDO

Buses to Mindo (2hr., every hr. 8am-6pm, US$1) leave from the Quito bus terminal. Buses back to Quito leave from the bus station on the main road; since there are relatively few buses, it is best to purchase a return ticket as soon as you arrive. The office is on the main road to the left as you enter the town, next to the Mindo-Nambillo office.

An amazing weekend getaway for anyone who's ever wanted to tromp through cloud forests, swim beneath waterfalls, follow a river in an innertube, or gallop through fields of orchids and butterflies, tiny Mindo attracts many who intended to stay for a day, then a week, then a month, and still haven't left. Choosing among the myriad outdoor activities promises to be the hardest part of your visit. You might bring good hiking boots, sandals, rubber boots, a rain jacket, binoculars, and a bathing suit to keep your options open. Although locals swear by the power of lemons or shampoo, you'll probably also want to bring some insect repellent. Check with the center run by **Fundación Pacaso y Pacaso,** at the end of the main road just before the plaza, to get the latest word on lodging, food, and guides. Or, to learn more about Mindo prior to your visit, check out the **Centro de Información de Mindo** (☎458 546) in Quito, Yumbos 133 at Cristóbal Sardoval, near the airport.

Hiking is a popular option, but since paths are sometimes hard to find and tresspassing onto private reserves a real possibility, a guide is recommended (from US$2 per day). One popular hike is to **Las Cascadas de Nambillo,** two and a half hours from the plaza. There are also several **bird-watching routes;** Mindo was commended by Birdlife International in October 1997. Choose your guide carefully, as they have varying degrees of knowledge about the local species. **Tubing** on the Río Mindo can also be arranged through the center (tube US$1). The El Carmelo de Mindo resort offers **horseback riding** (US$5 per hr.). To get there (about 30min.), follow the road that leads past the soccer field, which intersects the main road near the blue-and-white church about halfway into town. Walking straight leads you to the Mindo River bridge; go left and follow the signs to the resort. There's an **orchid collection** on the way (US$1). **Guides** can be arranged through most hostels.

Mindo's plethora of lodging options accommodate all budgets. Backpackers flock to **Gypsy Hostal,** in front of the soccer field, run by a British man and his Ecuadorian wife, with hot showers and lots of hammocks. Bag lunches, vegetarian food, guides, and activities can be arranged here. (☎351 061 or 352 805; email gypsyhostal@yahoo.com. US$3 per person per night, all included.) **Hostal Arcoiris,** on the left before the park, has bare rooms and hot showers. (Rooms US$1.50 per person, with bath US$2.) A popular option among visitors is the **Centro de Educación Ambiental,** 4km outside town. Located on 19,000 hectares, it encompasses the **Mindo River, Nambillo River,** and **Cinto River** and contains 450 species of bird and 370 species of orchid. Excursions to Las Cascadas de Nambillo, trekking, and tubing can be arranged for guests. Prices are steeper than in the rest of the town and there is no electricity or hot water in the cabins (US$75 per person including three meals and guide, US$15 to camp). For more information on the resort, contact the **Amigos de la Naturaleza** office in Mindo, on the left hand side of the main road before the plaza, or call the office in Quito (☎223 242; fax 221 628). Another choice is **El Carmelo de Mindo,** which is like CEA but cheaper (US$30).

NEAR QUITO: RESERVA MAQUIPUCUNA

The roundabout route from Quito to Maquipucuna goes through the towns of Calacalí, Nanegalito, Nanegal, and Marianitas, 4km from the reserve's entrance. Buses from Quito run to Nanegal (2½hr.; M 2pm, Tu-F 1pm, Sa 9am and 1:30pm, Su 9am and 1pm; US$0.75) from the San José de las Minas terminal near Parque Alameda on José Antepara and pass through the Plaza Cotocollao in north Quito. Get off the bus 2km short of Nanegal, at the big green-and-yellow house at the La Delicia crossing, beyond Nangalito. From here it's a 2km hike to Marianitas and another 4km to Maquipucuna. From December to May, excessive mud makes walking is difficult. Alternatively, truck drivers in Marianitas might be willing to go the remaining 4km (US$2). A milk truck leaves Marianitas each morning between 7:15 and 7:45am (catch it in front of the white store) and can give you a lift to Nanegalito (45min., US$0.25). In Nanegalito, buses pass on their way to Quito (every 30min. until 5pm, US$1).

In the northwestern Andes, just 70km from Quito, the Reserva Maquipucuna protects an ecological gem. Its borders contain 5000 hectares of land, eighty percent of which is primary cloud forest. Researchers have swarmed to the reserve throughout its twelve years of existence, and their work has produced numbers to brag about: within Maquipucuna's boundaries, there reside over 1300 species of plants, 45 mammals, 350 birds, and 250 butterflies. The warm-blooded creatures include pumas, bears, bats, agoutis, peccaries, tapir, and deer. In addition to wildlife, Maquipucuna shelters a number of archaeological sites left by the **Yumbo,** a people who inhabited this forest after the Incas.

Visitors to the reserve can go hiking, birdwatching and, if weather permits, swimming in the Río Umachaca (open daily 7am-6pm; US$5). Overnight guests stay at the **Umachaca Lodge,** an ecotourist oasis that can accommodate 18 people and offers hot baths and three meals per day (US$25 per person, children US$20). Guides are available through the Ecotourist center (US$10 per day). Bring boots, insect repellent, raingear, and binoculars. For more information, contact **Fundación Maquipucuna** in Quito, Baquerizo E9-153 at Tamayó, P.O. Box 17-12-167 (☎507 200; fax 501 201; email root@maqui.ecuanex.net.ec). They request that you call in advance to talk about Yunguilla, a sustainable-development, community-based project with organic gardens, recycled paper goods, and tagua nut crafts.

WESTERN ECUADOR

Ecuador's diverse **Pacific coast** (p. 449), a motley combination of beaches, mangroves, estuaries, and rocky shores, stretches almost 3000km from the town of San Lorenzo, near the Colombian border, to Huaquillas on the Peruvian border. While weather patterns are quite similar down the length of the coast (with a rainy season Dec.-Apr. caused by warm water currents offshore), changes in latitude mean changes in attitude. Those looking for constant partying race to Atacames and Montañita, where nights are spent in thatched-roofed beachside bars and days are spent recovering in the sun. A more mellow beach experience awaits elsewhere—in Playa Escondida, Same, Canoa, Muisne, or Alandaluz—where virtually untouched beaches stretch for miles. If you can't bear to leave the city behind, head for the coastal metropolises of Bahía de Caráquez, Manta, and Salinas, where sand meets skyscrapers and ecology sometimes finds itself sacrificed in the name of efficiency and modernization. Nature lovers can escape to the area around Puerto López to explore Parque Nacional Machalilla, which includes Isla de la Plata, the budget Galapagos experience. A cultural awakening awaits in the smaller, less touristed towns, especially in the African-influenced northern coast, where the fish and shrimp are more than just food—they're a livelihood.

HIGHLIGHTS OF WESTERN ECUADOR

LOUNGE on some of softest and least crowded beaches in South America: **Súa** and **Same** (p. 453).

SPOT wildlife at Parque Nacional Machalilla (p. 468), known as the "poor man's Galapagos."

CHILL in surf-central, **Montañita** (p. 470).

HOB-KNOB with Ecuador's elite in glitzy, beachside **Salinas** (p. 472).

PUSH your way into Guayaquil's **Jardín de la Salsa** (p. 486), along with the other 6000+ party animals.

SAVOR succulent ceviche on the beach of **Jambelí Island** (p. 489).

The fertile **lowlands** (p. 475), nestled between the Pacific coast and the western base of the Andes, have played a pivotal role in Ecuador's history. It was here that the first plantations were established during the 17th century. As agriculture's importance swelled, the forests that once shaded the fertile soil here were pushed farther and farther toward the perimeter of the lowlands and, in many cases, completely out and into extinction. Such is the price burgeoning Ecuador paid to develop what became its most prosperous industry, bananas. During the youthful era of independence, the liberal port of Guayaquil was the benefactor of newly booming agriculture. As the center of the Río Guayas maritime traffic, the city became the economic hub of the region, and the profits that poured in fueled further agricultural development. This self-perpetuating cycle of agricultural, commercial, and urban development continued well into the 20th century, though the 1970s discovery of oil in the Oriente decreased agriculture's economic significance. Today, Guayaquil and the lowlands continue to develop along same path as they have through Ecuador's history: Guayaquil as the commercial capital, and the lowlands as the agricultural machine that fuels it.

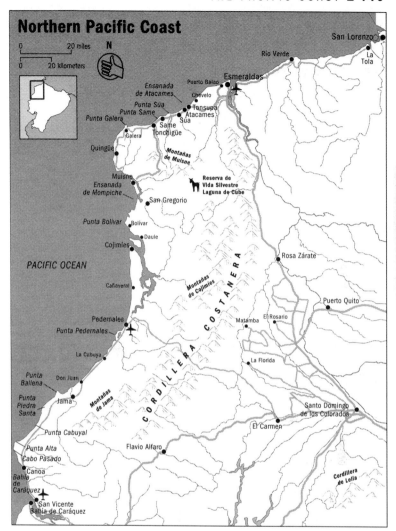

Northern Pacific Coast

0   20 miles   N
0   20 kilometers

San Lorenzo
La Tola
Río Verde
Esmeraldas
Ensanada de Atacames
Puerto Balao
Chevelo
Punta Súa
Tonsupa
Punta Same
Atacames
Punta Galera
Súa
Same
Galera
Tonchigüe
Quingüe
Montañas de Muisne
Reserva de Vida Silvestre Laguna de Cube
Muisne
Ensanada de Mompiche
San Gregorio
Punta Bolívar
Bolívar
Daule
Rosa Zárate
Cojimíes
PACIFIC OCEAN
Cañaveral
Montañas de Cojimíes
Puerto Quito
Pedernales
Matamba
El Rosario
Punta Pedernales
La Cubuya
La Florida
Punta Ballena
Don Juan
Punta Piedra Santa
Jama
Montañas de Jama
Santo Domingo de los Colorados
Punta Cabuyal
El Carmen
Punta Alta
Cabo Pasado
Flavio Alfaro
Canoa
Cordillera de Lelia
Bahía de Caráquez
San Vicente
Bahía de Caráquez
CORDILLERA COSTANERA

THE PACIFIC COAST

SAN LORENZO   ☎ 06

In the years since El Niño-induced mudslides paralyzed the Ibarra-San Lorenzo train line, tourism in San Lorenzo has plummeted. Nevertheless, adventurous visitors armed with plenty of insect repellent can look forward to impressive mangroves, beautiful tropical forest, and jungle excursions. Natives affirm the natural splendor of nearby ecological reserves such as **Cayapas-Mataje;** contact the regional director of tourism, Jaime Burgos (☎780 230), for information. Almost all services of interest to tourists can be found along the town's two main streets: **10 de Agosto,** which runs from the park near the dock into the center of town, and **Imbabura,** which stretches from the train station toward 10 de Agosto. Their intersection serves as a good point of reference for visitors. **Buses** go to **Ibarra** (8hr., 4 per day 4-11:30am, US$5) from the traffic circle along Imbabura, near the train station, and to **Esmeraldas** (6hr., 6 per day 5am-3pm, US$3.25) from the park. **Boats** go to the **Colombian border** (1½hr., 7am and 2pm, US$1.80). You can **exchange money** at the **Almacén Su Economía,** across Imbabura from EMETEL; ask for owners Olgapuco and Patricio. (☎ 780 272 or 780 422. Open daily 7am-8pm.) The **police,** by the park on 10 de Agosto, can stamp your passport and give information on crossing the border (open 24hr.). The **hospital** (☎ 780 189), on Divina Providencia, is a short trek outside town. **EMETEL,** on the street parallel to Imbabura and across from the playground, allows international calls with no surcharge. (Open M-Sa 8am-10pm, Su 8am-noon and 7-10pm.) The better places to stay tend to be away from the train station. **Hotel Tolita Pampa de Oro,** on Tásito Ortiz, the third left coming from the train station, is the cleanest and most modern of the options. Every room has a private bath, cable TV, fan, and mosquito net. (☎ 780 214. Rooms US$2.25.) **Hotel Gran San Carlos,** on Imbabura at José Garcés, across from EMETEL, is a similar option. (☎ 780 306. US$1.60 per person, with bath US$2.)

ESMERALDAS ☎ 06

When a throng of emerald-clad *indígenas* greeted the conquistadors arriving in Ecuador's north coast, the Spaniards concluded that the area must be rich with the rare green gems. They were wrong, but the name they assigned the town stuck nonetheless. In time, locals came to regard it as a compliment on the lush vegetation that surrounds their city. However, certain neighborhoods now shoulder reputations for being among the country's most dangerous, and most travelers who end up here press on quickly, making Esmeraldas little more than a transition stop en route to sunnier destinations. Ask around about safety before visiting any unfamiliar areas, and, after dark, avoid Malecón and all streets farther downhill. Most buses unload passengers either at the **bus terminal** on **Malecón** (Transportes del Pacífico and Cooperativo La Costeñita), or by the **Parque Central** (Transportes Esmeraldas). Bordered by parallel streets **Bolívar** and **Sucre,** and **10 de Agosto** and **9 de Octubre,** the Parque Central serves as a good reference point.

You can get just about anywhere from Esmeraldas. **Aeropuerto General José Rivadeneira** is 25km south of town. (Taxi US$4-5; Transportes Zambrano bus US$0.20.) **TAME** (☎ 726 863), at Bolívar and 9 de Octubre, goes to **Quito** (30min.; M, Tu, F, Su 4:30pm; US$24.28). There are four primary intraprovincial bus companies. (Open M-F 8am-1pm and 3-6pm.) **Transportes Esmeraldas** (☎ 721 381), on 10 de Agosto between Sucre and Bolívar, runs to **Quito** (6½hr., 18 per day 6:30am-12:55am, US$4.40) via **Santo Domingo** (3hr., US$2) and to **Guayaquil** (8hr., 16 per day 6:30am-12:15am, US$5.20). **Cooperativa La Costeñita** (☎ 723 041), at Malecón and 10 de Agosto, and **Transportes del Pacífico** (☎ 713 227), at Malecón and Piedrahita, alternate service for daily buses to: **San Lorenzo** (6hr., every hr. 6am-6pm, US$3.20); and **Muisne** (3hr., every 20min. 5am-9pm, US$1.04) via **Atacames** (1hr., US$0.40), **Súa** (1¼hr., US$0.50), and **Same** (1½hr., US$0.56). **Transportes Zambrano** (☎ 726 711), at Sucre and Piedrahita, services **Muisne** (3hr., daily 9am-8pm, US$1.04) and **Santo Domingo** (3hr., daily 6am-7pm, US$1.60). **Las Palmas** runs local buses around town (US$0.12). **Esmeraldas Tur** is at Cañizares 221 at Bolívar. (☎/fax 726 875. Open M-F 8:30am-1pm and 3-7pm.) **Banco Pichincha,** at 9 de Octubre and Bolívar, across from Parque Central, changes traveler's checks. (☎ 728 745. US$100 min.) **Western Union** is available on the first floor. Open M-F 8am-2pm, Sa 8:30am-2pm. **24hr. ATM** accepts Visa. **Police,** at Bolívar and Cañizares. (☎ 723 158 or 725 800. Open 24hr.) **Clínica Central,** on Espejo between Olmedo and Sucre. (☎ 726 520. Open 24hr.) **ANDINATEL,** at Montalvo and Malecón. (☎ 728 810. Open M-Sa 8am-10pm, Su 8am-4pm and 6-10pm.) **Compunet,** down Bolívar from the Parque Central, is on the right just after Cañizares. (☎/fax 728 670. US$0.04 per min. Netphone US$0.36 per min. Open M-Sa 8:30am-1pm and 2-7pm, Su 9am-5pm.) **Post Office,** at Montalvo and Malecón, 1st fl. (☎ 726 831; fax 726 834. Open M-F 8am-7pm, Sa 8am-2pm.)

EL NIÑO THROWS A TANTRUM

Known as the nastiest little boy to hit the Pacific, El Niño is a warm-water current that brings the rainy season to Ecuador's coastal region and the Galapagos Islands. Its deceptively diminutive name comes from its advent around Christmas, making it the second "boy child" of the season. Most years, El Niño is well-behaved, leaving on cue in late April or early May. However, in those fateful years when the child decides to act up, havoc ensues. The mention of the 1982-83 bout still brings shudders from those in the western lowlands, but the 1997-98 El Niño left a crippled and broken Ecuador in its wake. The Pacific coast was devastated; rivers flooded, destroying homes and buildings, clean water became dangerously scarce, and highways and other roads collapsed. Fishing and farming were severely affected as well, damaging the livelihood and economy of the region and, in turn, the country. However, even in the first few months following the brunt of El Niño's damage, Ecuador began rebuilding with unprecedented speed. Private companies were hired to repair the coastal highway and have made remarkable progress. While buses can now pass with relative ease through the coast, towns like Montañita are threatened by an ever-eroding shoreline, and potable water still must be brought in by truck; Ecuador can only wait to see what Santa brings next year.

Esmeraldas's hotels won't be the highlight of your trip. Hot water is hard to come by, and while few places offer mosquito nets, many have open-air vents. **Hotel Costa Esmeraldas,** Sucre 813, at Piedrahita. Large, clean rooms, private baths, a very accommodating staff, and new color TVs make this a real find. (☎723 912 or 720 640. Singles US$3, with A/C US$5; doubles US$6, with A/C US$10.) **Hostal Galeón,** Piedrahita 3-30, at Olmedo. The lobby's sea paintings build anticipation for ship-shape rooms, but the mattresses are flimsy and the showers tiny. Private baths in all quarters. (☎723 820; fax 723 821. US$2 per person, with A/C US$2.80.)

ATACAMES

☎06

As the most touristically developed beach on the northern Pacific Coast, Atacames has become quite the party destination. Some of the best maintained highways in the region pump visitors into town every weekend, filling the hostels, bars, and clubs. By day, the crowds swim, tan, and shop. By night, they hit the dance floor. Come Monday, Atacames exhales; blenders whir at half-speed and revellers rest up for the weekend. A great place to meet other backpackers, this hotspot may inspire solitude seekers to plant their beach umbrellas elsewhere.

▐ TRANSPORTATION

Buses: From the central stop on Principal, daily buses head to: **Muisne** (2½hr., every 30min. 5:30am-10pm, US$0.40) via **Súa** (15min., US$0.20), **Same** (30min., US$0.20), and **Tonchigüe** (1hr., US$0.20). **Cooperativa La Costeñita** sends 2 buses daily to **Playa Escondida** (1hr., 1:10 and 3:10pm, US$0.60). **Transportes Occidentales** (☎731 276), just beyond the river as you walk away from the beach, travels daily to **Quito** (6hr.; 11:50am, 2, 11:45pm; US$5.20) and **Guayaquil** (8hr., 11:15pm, US$5.60) via **Muisne** (1¼hr., US$0.60).

Taxis: Standard taxis are scarce and expensive—they're all based in Esmeraldas. You can get from Atacames to Esmeraldas for US$5, but getting from Esmeraldas to Atacames costs around US$10. Self-described "ecological tours" (actually just bikes with carts) also drive people around town for US$0.40 per person.

▐▐ ORIENTATION AND PRACTICAL INFORMATION

Buses stop anywhere along the main road, known as **Principal** or **La Carretera;** a sign that says *"parada"* and a long white bench in front of an ice cream bar mark the central stop. Facing the ice cream bar, the road that heads to the right, **Jorge Prado,** leads across a **footbridge** spanning the **Río Malecón** to **Malecón,** a strip of budget hotels, discos, and restaurants along the beach. Back in town, most services are concentrated around the Parque Central. With your back to the ice cream bar, walk straight and make a right on **Juan Montalvo;** the park is on the next block.

Currency Exchange: Banco del Pichincha (☎ 731 029), at Tello and Espejo, across from the park. Changes a minimum of US$500 in traveler's checks for a 0.3% commission. Open M-F 8am-8pm, Sa-Su 8am-2pm.

Laundromat: Zum Tuncán (☎ 731 191). Head away from the beach on Jorge Prado and make a left onto Luis Vargo Torres; the laundromat is on the left. US$0.35 per 1lb. Open M-F 10am-6pm, Sa 10am-2pm.

Police: (☎ 731 275), at La Acacia and Principal, in a blue-and-white building across from the Estadio Walter Aparicio Alomia.

Hospital: Centro de Emergencías (☎ 731 183 or 731 083). With your back to the ice cream bar, walk 100m from the bus stop. **24hr. pharmacy** located in the same building.

Telephones: ANDINATEL (☎ 731 050), at Montalvo and Tello. National and international collect and calling card calls. Open M-Sa 8am-10pm, Su 8am-2pm and 7-10pm.

Internet Access: Principal Librería y Papelería (☎ 731 521), at Montalvo and Tello, between the bank and ANDINATEL. US$0.06 per min. M-F 7:30am-8pm, Sa 9am-8pm.

Post Office: On Principal near Espejo. Open M-F 9am-6pm, Sa 8am-2pm.

ACCOMMODATIONS

At first, it might seem as though Atacames has too many accommodations. Then the weekend arrives, hotels fill with bikini-clad teenagers, and there is scarcely a room free in town. Despite the generally high level of comfort, noise from bars and clubs can sometimes prevent a good night's sleep. Low-season (Oct. to mid-Dec. and Mar.) or mid-week visitors may be able to bargain prices down.

Cabañas Los Bohios (☎/fax 731 089). Heading toward the beach, make a right after the footbridge, and you'll reach this pleasant cabaña cluster. Complete with TVs, clean private baths, and a guard to keep out late-night drunks. Cabañas US$4 per person.

Hotel Sambaye (☎ 731 410). From the Cabañas Los Bohios, walk to the beach. Make a right; Sambaye is on the right. Firm beds and clean bathrooms; secured locks ensure safety. Bottled water and sandwiches for sale at the desk. Rooms US$4 per person.

Residencial la Casa del Manglar (☎ 731 464), to your left after crossing the footbridge toward the beach. About 150m from the sand, this cozy *residencial* overlooking the Río Malecón offers a retreat from Atacames' nightlife scene. Relax on the terrace or in the cheery, well-decorated rooms. Rooms US$4 per person, with bath US$5.

Hotel Galería Atacames (☎ 731 149; fax 731 282), on the beach, to the right after you reach Malecón from the footbridge, 2nd fl. Fans and private baths almost compensate for the less-than-firm mattresses. Mosquito nets available upon request. Rooms US$4.80 per person.

FOOD

Atacames boasts a number of establishments offering international cuisine, though seafood still dominates most menus. Along Malecón, sidewalk chefs cook up shish kabobs and corn-on-the-cob.

Restaurant La Cena (☎ 731 203), on Malecón, 1 block to the right along the beach from the footbridge. Ceiling fans make this open-air eatery even cooler. Breakfast US$0.60-0.80; *encocados* US$1.40; salads US$1.20. Open daily 6am-12am.

No Name Pizzeria (☎ 09 821 565), on Malecón, 3 blocks to the right along the beach from the footbridge, 2nd fl. Accessible only by stepladder, this balcony restaurant offers a relaxed atmosphere and great people-watching, service, and pizza. 16 toppings (large pizza US$5-7). Salads US$1.20, pasta dishes US$1.80-3. Open M-Sa noon-late.

Da Giulio Restaurante, on Malecón, 1 block to the right along the beach from the footbridge. This white mission-style building hides delightful Spanish and Italian cuisine. Munch on *tapas* (US$1.80-2.60) or gorge yourself on a platter of *paella mejor* (US$4.80). Open daily 11:30am-6pm and 7-10pm.

🌊 BEACHES

Atacames's beaches are soft, unsullied, and extend very far in either direction. First-rate views of **Punta Esmeraldas** to the east and the jagged **Isla de los Pájaros** to the west frame the enormous expanse. Sunbathers and *fútbol* players coexist peacefully while **banana boats**—for rent on the south side of the beach (US$0.40 per person)—buzz by on the blue-green water. Though the beach is generally safe in the resort area, exercise caution if exploring less-populated stretches, and avoid leaving possessions unattended. The water stays warm for most of the year, but take care when swimming in the surf; the undertow can be quite strong.

🌃 NIGHTLIFE

With 39 grass-hut bars and a handful of discos, Atacames has something for everyone. Most places offer similar fruity drinks, thatched roofs, music, and prices (US$1-4 for cocktails), and keep the same hours (daily 4pm-2am). Malecón is well-lit and generally safe, but many locals agree that visitors should be cautious, especially when the streets are busy. Late-night beach walks are a bad idea.

> **El Oasis de Nagiba Bar,** just to the right of Principal along the sand. Swings hanging from the ceiling stand in for bar stools. The house specialty is the *nagiba* (made from Colombian fruits and rum; US$1.80). Live marimba Sa. Happy hour daily 8:30-9:30pm.

> **Scala Discoclub,** just after Nagiba Bar along Malecón. Partiers of all ages cram together under the neon lights that illuminate tributes to Elvis, Metallica, and Claudia Schiffer. Beer US$1. Cover US$1. Open daily 8pm-2am.

> **Sambaye Discoteca** (☎731 308), at the far end of Malecón; head right from the footbridge. With a capacity of almost 1000 people, this mega-plex is one of the hottest *discotecas* on the beach. Beer US$0.80. Cover US$0.80.

NEAR ATACAMES: SÚA

To reach Súa from Atacames, take a bus (15min., every 15min., US$0.20) or a mototaxi (US$0.60), or walk south along the beach at low tide (30min.).

While weekends bring fewer beachgoers than in Atacames, Súa's verdant hills attract hikers as well. South of the bay, a 30min. walk along a dirt path and up the side of a large green bluff yields a great view of Atacames to the north and less-developed coastline to the south. Quality accommodations in Súa don't cost much, though prices vary significantly on a seasonal basis and rise during Carnival in February. The **Hotel Chagra Ramos,** on the far north side of the beach, provides restful hillside villas and slightly older cabañas. The villas have private baths, and the screens on the windows of the basic but blemish-free rooms provide a cool, itch-free, and untroubled sleep. (☎731 006 or 731 070. US$2-3 per person.) Hotel Chagra's **restaurant** serves quality seafood (US$1.40-2.60) and salads (US$1-1.80) under palm shade. (Open daily 7:15am-9pm.) The French-owned **Hotel Súa Café/ Restaurant** is one of the first buildings on the left as you come from town. Though few seedy characters wander this neighborhood, Hotel Súa takes safety seriously, with sturdy door locks and strongboxes in each room. All have baths and ceiling fans. (☎731 004. US$1.60 per person.) The restaurant downstairs serves French, Italian, and local cuisine—all delicious. (Entrees US$1-3. Open daily 6am-9:30pm.)

NEAR ATACAMES: SAME

Same can be reached from Atacames by bus (30min., every 15min. 5am-10pm, US$0.20).

Same's virtually uninhabited beach 7km southwest of Súa stretches almost 3km in length, though it's never more than 20m wide. Its green surf, a refreshing 25°C (75°F) year-round, is said to be the best in the area. Graced with only a handful of low-key establishments, Same stresses quality rather than quantity. Unfortunately, because of the high proportion of North American and European visitors, prices are a little higher than those in the neighboring beach communities. The charming seafront cabañas of **La Terraza Quito** are just to the left as you reach the beach from the main road. Each comes with bath, fan, and porch with a hammock. (☎ 09 476 949. US$5 per person.) Adorned with giant turtle shells and dugout canoes, La Terraza's **restaurant** is the center of the Same social scene. Inside, an international crowd drinks cuba libres (US$2). Try specialties such as calamari (US$3.20), pasta dishes (US$2.20-2.60), and ceviche (US$2.20-2.50). (Open daily 10am-5pm and 7-10pm.) ☒**Hostal y Restaurant Sea Flower,** on the road to the beach just before La Terraza, complements its elaborate food and Pre-Columbian furnishings with congeniality. Even if the room prices (US$15 per person) prevent you from spending the night, it would be an injustice to your palate to miss the homemade bread, savory sauces, and delectable seafood and steak platters. Large portions and unbeatable service make up for the high prices. (Entrees US$7-9. Open daily 10am-10pm.)

NEAR ATACAMES: PLAYA ESCONDIDA

Playa Escondida is just south of Tonchigüe, along the dirt road that leads to Punta Galera. Any bus connecting Muisne and the northern beaches passes Tonchigüe, where the road to Playa Escondida and Punta Galera begins, but only 2 buses daily can drop you off at the resort's doorstep. Cooperativa La Costeñita sends them from Esmeraldas to Punta Galera (2hr., 1:10 and 3:10pm, US$0.60), via Atacames (1¼hr., 1:50 and 3:50pm).

This "Hidden Beach" sees more sand crabs than people. Situated in a bay between two points where the Ecuadorian hills meet the Pacific Ocean, Playa Escondida is a self-described ecological refuge. The swimming's best at high tide, but low tide brings resort-front tide pools—home to all sorts of marine creatures—as well as stretches of firm sand and flat rocks that allow for long walks along the cliffs and coast. The **Beachside Lodge,** the only place to stay at Playa Escondida, offers open-air rooms on the second floor or the larger third-story loft. Let the crash of the surf lull you to sleep as you relax on a mosquito-netted bed or any of the hammocks lining the common kitchen. Camping is also possible. The common cold-water shower and outhouse, complete with compost heap, make for a rugged beach experience. (☎ 09 733 368. US$8-10 per person; camping US$5 per person; 10% IVA tax.) On the other hand, the **restaurant** at the lodge is anything but simple. (Pancakes US$1.40; fruit salad US$1.80; fish or vegetable *platos fuertes* US$3-3.60.)

MUISNE   ☎ 06

Quiet island Muisne remains unmindful of other beaches' tourist-driven ways. Free of cars or cares, this seagirt town stands apart from its coastal counterparts. Bizarre weather patterns yield gray mornings, hot afternoons, and howling winds come nightfall; an insurrection last summer yielded a jobless former mayor and an island without local government. While this easygoing attitude sometimes manifests itself in a poorly maintained town and shoreline, it also accounts for the warm welcome its visitors receive.

▓▊ **ORIENTATION AND PRACTICAL INFORMATION.** Muisne-bound **buses** stop by the docks on the mainland. From there, **boats** run to the island (5min., every 5min., US$0.06), where **bicycle-taxis** offer rides to the beach (US$0.20). **Isidora Ayora,** the main street, leads inland from the island docks. From the mainland docks, **buses** go to: Esmeraldas (3hr., every 1½hr. 5:30am-9pm, US$1) via Same (1¼hr., US$0.24), Súa (1½hr., US$0.36), and Atacames (2hr., US$0.60). To reach Pedernales, take a bus to Salto and board a direct camioneta (3hr., US$2.60) or a Cooperativa La Costeñita bus (1½hr., US$1.20) heading toward Chamanga. From Chamanga, take a camioneta to Pedernales (1½ hr., US$1.40). There are **no banks** in Muisne. The **police station** is a blue-and-gray building on the street parallel to the main road, just before the central park. The **hospital** (☎ 480 269), on the right coming from the docks, has free 24 hour emergency care. The **ANDINATEL** office is on the left when coming from the docks. (Open daily 8am-10pm.) The **post office** is on the third cross-street to the left of the docks, around the corner from the municipal building. (Open M-F 9am-noon and 3-6pm.)

ACCOMMODATIONS AND FOOD. Muisne has few hotels, but those there are provide quality quarters and come equipped with mosquito nets (a must). **Hostal Calade,** on the beach, to the left of the main road, is just past the Hotel Playa Paraíso. Warm showers complement the warm hues on the walls—not to mention the video room, the Internet access, and constant tunes from the stereo. (☎480 276. Dorms US$3 per person; rooms US$4 per person, with bath US$5.) The new Italian owner has retailored the **bar/restaurant** around Italian cuisine (spaghetti US$2; *ensalada italiana* US$1.30). The English-speaking owners who run the bright pink **Hotel Playa Paraíso,** to the left as you reach the beach from the main road, treat guests like family. Rooms share well-scrubbed toilets and showers; a reasonably priced **restaurant** rounds out the experience. (☎480 192. Rooms US$3 per person.) **Cabañas San Cristóbal,** on the beach to the right of the main road, have fancy tiled rooms with private baths and mosquito nets. For safety's sake, some travelers prefer the cement cabins over wooden ones. (☎480 264. Cabañas US$4 per person.) Besides the excellent restaurants at Playa Paraíso and Calade, there are several other dining options, most by the water. On the main road just before the beach, **Restaurant Suizo-Italiano** operates out of an old building with "Pizza and Spaghetti" spray-painted on the outside. The Swiss-Italian owner makes phenomenal vegetarian pizzas. (Small US$2; large US$2.40-4. Open daily noon-9pm.)

BEACHES. Once lined with palm trees, El Niño did away with most of these during the winter of 1997-98. In an effort to save beachfront establishments from further harm, the government constructed a concrete wall along the boardwalk to hold back the surf. Luckily, the wall is short enough to avoid detracting from the splendid view. Muisne's beach extends for more than an hour's walk in either direction, especially at low tide (the difference from high tide can be as much as 70m). The water can get pretty rough; still, it's generally the small stinging jellyfish that bother most people. (Most stings are mild and can be healed with a dab of vinegar, found at any local restaurant.) Avoid the unlit areas of the beach at night; Muisne is a relatively safe town, but there has been some crime in recent years.

SIGHTS. Boating through the mangroves is possible and pleasurable, although there are frequent blemishes in the otherwise green landscape where *camaroneras* (shrimp farms) have sprung up. Rides through the mangroves sometimes aim for a destination, such as **Isla Bonita,** with its rolling green hills and rocky cliffs; other times, they meander aimlessly around the lush vegetation. If you plan to leave the sheltered area behind the Muisne Island, be prepared for rolling waves. Boats can be found at the port (around US$3 per hr.). Having a driver wait for hours while you hunt for seashells can get expensive; arrange for a pick-up later to avoid paying for the wait. Make sure to pay the driver *after* he picks you up, as Isla Bonita is uninhabited and probably a poor place to get stranded.

PEDERNALES ☎ 05

This bustling seaport takes advantage of its position in the center of things. Pedernales hosts the largest market on the northern coast and serves as an important center for the shrimp industry. But while locals may consider Pedernales crucial, most visitors view the town only as a key link in the coastline's chain of transport. Pedernales's central **plaza** sits at the intersection of the town's two most important streets: **López Castillo** and **Eloy Alfaro.** The town's lackluster **beach-cum-port** is at the west end of Alfaro. **Camionetas** arriving in Pedernales drop people off along Castillo; buses stop at their respective offices on Castillo and Alfaro. **Buses** go to: **Bahía de Caráquez** (3hr., every hr. 5:30am-5pm, US$1.40) via San Vicente; **Esmeraldas** (7hr., 5:20 and 8:20am, US$2); **Guayaquil** (9hr.; 6am, 12:15, 1:30pm; US$5.20); **Manta** (7hr., 7 per day 6-11am, US$3.20) via **Portoviejo** (6hr., US$2.80); **Quito** (6hr., 7:20am and 3:45pm, US$3.60); and **Santo Domingo** (3hr., every 20min. 8:20am-7pm, US$2). **Banco Pichincha,** on Alfaro two blocks from the plaza, has a 24-hour Cirrus **ATM.** (Open M-F 9am-3pm.) Pedernales has few enchanting accommodations. If you arrive late at night, it's probably best to find a place in town rather than stumble around in the dark down by the beach. The **Hotel Pedernales,** Alfaro 6-18 at Manabí, three blocks uphill from the plaza, has rooms with occasionally inoperable fans. Secure locks may keeps the crooks out, but screenless vents in some rooms will let in the mosquitos. (☎681 092. Rooms US$1.20 per person.)

BAHÍA DE CARÁQUEZ   ☎05

Many believe that Bahía was the first capital of the Cara people, who conquered the area some 3500 years ago before deciding to resettle in Quito. Now, hundreds of years after the Cara made their fateful move, *quiteños* have returned. Many of Ecuador's elite spend weekends and summers in the sparkling white highrises that decorate Bahía de Caráquez. The standard of living is high, thanks to significant investment during the presidency of Sixto Durán Ballén (1992-96), and though it has undergone tremendous development, this modern peninsular city strives toward environmental consciousness. In February 1999, Bahía declared itself an "Eco-city," signaling the importance of protecting delicate ecosystems, appreciating nature, and conserving ancestral culture.

🖃🔊 TRANSPORTATION AND PRACTICAL INFORMATION. Boats from San Vicente drop visitors off along the docks near the intersection of **Aguilera** and **Malecón,** the main street in town. Most services and accommodations are found within the grid marked by the parallel streets Malecón, Bolívar, Montúfar, and Morales, which all intersect Aguilera, Ante, Ascazubi, Riofrío, Arenas, and Checa. Visit the **AECA** office (☎690 377) on Aguilera and Malecón for precise information on flights out of **Bahía Airport** in San Vicente. While **buses** heading to and arriving from the Northern Coast are stationed by the docks in San Vicente, southernbound buses leave from the informal station along Malecón a few blocks up-river from the docks. Buses go to **Guayaquil** (6hr., every hr. 6:30am-11pm, US$3.40) via **Portoviejo** (2hr., US$0.80) and **Manta** (3hr., US$1.40). **Ferries** leave from the dock on Malecón and Aguilera for **San Vicente** (10min., US$0.12). **🖼Guacamayo Bahíatours,** Bolívar 906 and Arenas, offers Bahía info, maps, and local tour options. (☎690 597; fax 691 412. Open M-Sa 8am-7pm, Su 10am-2pm.) **Bahía Dolphin Tours** (☎692 097; fax 692 088; email archtour@ecua.net.ec), Bolívar 1004, is another option. Traveler's checks can only be changed at **Banco de Guayaquil,** Riofrío and Bolívar, which also has a Visa **ATM.** (☎692 205. Open M-F 9am-6pm, Sa 9:30am-1:30pm.) The **police** station (☎690 054) is at Sixto Durán Ballén and 3 de Noviembre. Medical services: **Clínica Viteri** (☎690 429), Riofrío and Montúfar. Make calls at **PacificTel,** at Malecón and Arenas. (☎690 020. Open daily 8am-10pm.) **Internet access** is available at **Genesis.net,** Gostalle and Padre Laennen (☎692 4001; US$0.10 per min.; open M-Sa 9am-7pm), or at **Bahía Bed and Breakfast** (US$0.12 per min.; open daily 8am-8pm). **Post office:** Aguilera 108 and Malecón (☎610 177; open M-F 8am-5pm.

THE ART OF CREATIVE RECYCLING In keeping with the surge of ecological awareness sweeping the country, numerous groups in Bahía de Caráquez have begun producing **ecopaper.** Paper is collected after having been used in local offices and schools, and then soaked in a mixture of seeds, stalks, leaves, and flowers. Ecopaper artisans initially use screens to form sheets of textured paper, then sun-dry, roll, and press the sheets by hand, all without the use of environmentally harmful chemicals. Flowers indigenous to the coastal lowlands, Amazon, and Andes—all collected according to the phases of the moon to preserve the plants' colors—are arranged on the fresh paper. These tedious techniques culminate in ecopaper's use in business cards, wedding invitations, and other products. Not only is ecopaper a work of art, but it is a small industry providing work for many *ecuatorianos.* Email ecopapel@ecuadorexplorer.com or call ☎5935 691 412 for more information.

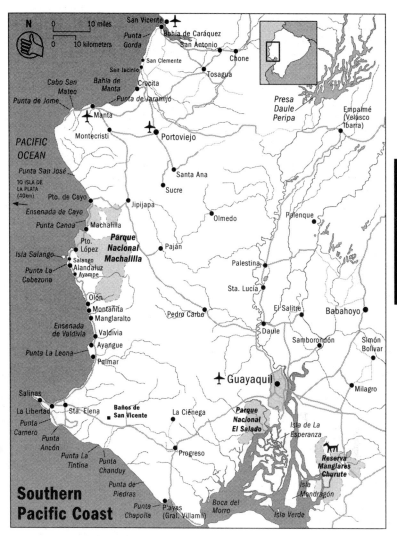

ACCOMMODATIONS AND FOOD. While the abundance of towering waterfront establishments gives the impression that accommodations here are all expensive, Bahía has a few reasonably priced hotels. One highly recommended option is ☒**Bahía Bed and Breakfast Inn,** Ascazubi 316 at Morales. This inviting bed and breakfast has neat rooms with fans, Internet access, and a gregarious English- and French-speaking owner. Creatively painted restaurant walls provide a great atmosphere in which to enjoy complimentary breakfast. (☎690 146. Rooms US$3 per person, with bath US$5.) **Bed and Breakfast Hostal Santiguado,** Padre Laennen 406 at Intraigo, is an equally pleasant alternative. While only some rooms have rocking chairs and terraces, all are clean and comfortable. (☎692 391. Rooms US$4 per person, with bath US$5.) There are plenty of excellent dining opportunities in Bahía, with a variety of inexpensive eateries by the docks. Expect the typical coastal entrees—seafood—along with gorgeous views of the marina and the bluffs of San Vicente. **La Terraza,** on Malecón by the docks, has a pretty covered terrace. (Good seafood US$1-1.60. ☎690 787. Open daily 10am-11pm.) **Muelle Uno,** on Malecón, across from Banco Manabí, has been taken over by Bahía bourgeoisie but still offers good prices and prime water views. The specialty is meat (US$0.80-3), but there are a few vegetarian dishes. (☎691 500. Open daily 10am-3am.)

🔯🍴 **SIGHTS AND BEACHES.** Situated off the coast of Bahía, both the **Islas Fragatas** and **Heart Island** are home to large colonies of frigatebirds. The former also contains over 30 other species of marine birds. The best time to visit these islands is from August to December, the frigates' mating season. The tour usually takes three hours, and departure times vary depending on the tides. Bahía's surroundings also offer diverse coastal vegetation. The nearby **Jororá** and **Punta Bellaca** make up all of the remaining one percent of Ecuador's tropical dry forest. From December to May, the forests are lush and green, while during the rest of the year, they become completely arid and void of vegetation, save the cactus and *palo santo* (whose wood is burned as a bug repellent). The forests are also filled with animals and bromeliads, and are interesting to visit any time of year. A walk through the forest takes four hours. At the other end of the tropical forest are the wetlands and mangroves. Dolphin Bahía Tours offers excursions to the nearby ruins of **Chirije.** For more local sights, check out **Miguelito,** the **90-year-old Galapagos turtle,** at the Miguel Valverde school up the hill on Ascazubi, or go to the **lookout point** at the top of the hill along Ascazubi to get an aerial view of the Bahía Peninsula and an occasional **humpback whale** (Jul.-Sept.). Surfers tend to cluster on the rocky shores at the western end of Malecón. Though Bahía itself does not have much of a beach, there is an excellent one not too far away. The relatively long walk is only possible at low tide, but cabs in town are eager to take people there (US$0.60) and will set a time to pick you up for the return trip.

🎭 **ENTERTAINMENT.** Though many of Bahía's residents may be on the older side, there is plenty to do at night for the young or young-at-heart. **My House,** Teniente Rodríguez and Hurtado, a few blocks from the tip of the peninsula, is the most popular of the town's *discotecas.* (Cover US$1.60. Open Th-Sa 10pm-2am.) For a mellower night, visit the bar at the **Hostal Santiguado,** located at Intraigo and Padre Laennen. The music is good, and the mixed drinks even better. (Open daily 7pm-2am.) For an even more low-key night, **Cínema Bahía,** Bolívar 1418 and Pinueza (☎690 363), projects VHS movies onto a huge, 15-foot tall screen.

NEAR BAHÍA DE CARÁQUEZ: CANOA

Buses depart frequently for Pedernales (2½hr., every 30min., US$1.40) and San Vicente (30min., every 30min., US$0.20). From San Vicente, a boat can be taken to Bahía de Caráquez (15min., US$0.12).

The uncrowded beaches of Canoa represent some of the Ecuador's finest. Los Aposentos, the **coastal caves** not too far from Canoa's beach, have been some of the town's major attractions. Though only two of nine remain after an earthquake on August 4, 1997, you can still visit the bat-caves by boat and see the wealth of blue-footed boobies in this area. There are two excellent (though somewhat expensive) hotels in this tiny town, one of which is 🏖**Hotel Bambú** (☎753 696), at the north end of the beach. Its restaurant offers healthy but tasty meals (crepe with banana and *coco* US$1; fruit salad with homemade granola and yogurt US$1). The main building offers spotless rooms, screened windows, large ceiling fans, and hot water during cooler months. Cabins are also available. Most high rises have private baths (US$6-8 per person) and are more expensive than the low rises and dorms, which have clean communal baths and toilets (US$4 per person). Camping is also available (with personal tent US$1.50 per person; provided bamboo tent US$3 per person). Stay awhile and start a volleyball game with other *huéspedes* or ride the waves on a rented surfboard. Another fabulous option is **La Posada de Daniel,** about 100m from the beach on the main road. With cabins overlooking the town and spacious rooms, you won't be disappointed. (☎691 201. Rooms US$5 per person.) **Restaurant Tronco Bar,** 50m from the beach along the main road, offers patrons a laid-back environment. Dine in a hammock set on a sand floor on the ground level, or, if you prefer a chair, climb a rope-ladder to the second-floor loft. (Open daily 9am-1am.)

race. (Good seafood US$1-1.60. ☎ 690 787. Open daily 10am-11pm.) **Muelle Uno,** on Malecón, across from Banco Manabí, has been taken over by Bahía bourgeoisie but still offers good prices and prime water views. The specialty is meat (US$0.80-3), but there are a few vegetarian dishes. (☎ 691 500. Open daily 10am-3am.)

🔯🏖 SIGHTS AND BEACHES. Situated off the coast of Bahía, both the **Islas Fragatas** and **Heart Island** are home to large colonies of frigatebirds. The former also contains over 30 other species of marine birds. The best time to visit these islands is from August to December, the frigates' mating season. The tour usually takes three hours, and departure times vary depending on the tides. Bahía's surroundings also offer diverse coastal vegetation. The nearby **Jororá** and **Punta Bellaca** make up all of the remaining one percent of Ecuador's tropical dry forest. From December to May, the forests are lush and green, while during the rest of the year, they become completely arid and void of vegetation, save the cactus and *palo santo* (whose wood is burned as a bug repellent). The forests are also filled with animals and bromeliads, and are interesting to visit any time of year. A walk through the forest takes four hours. At the other end of the tropical forest are the wetlands and mangroves. Dolphin Bahía Tours offers excursions to the nearby ruins of **Chirije.** For more local sights, check out **Miguelito,** the **90-year-old Galapagos turtle,** at the Miguel Valverde school up the hill on Ascazubi, or go to the **lookout point** at the top of the hill along Ascazubi to get an aerial view of the Bahía Peninsula and an occasional **humpback whale** (Jul.-Sept.). Surfers tend to cluster on the rocky shores at the western end of Malecón. Though Bahía itself does not have much of a beach, there is an excellent one not too far away. The relatively long walk is only possible at low tide, but cabs in town are eager to take people there (US$0.60) and will set a time to pick you up for the return trip.

🔲 ENTERTAINMENT. Though many of Bahía's residents may be on the older side, there is plenty to do at night for the young or young-at-heart. **My House,** Teniente Rodríguez and Hurtado, a few blocks from the tip of the peninsula, is the most popular of the town's *discotecas.* (Cover US$1.60. Open Th-Sa 10pm-2am.) For a mellower night, visit the bar at the **Hostal Santiguado,** located at Intraigo and Padre Laennen. The music is good, and the mixed drinks even better. (Open daily 7pm-2am.) For an even more low-key night, **Cínema Bahía,** Bolívar 1418 and Pinueza (☎ 690 363), projects VHS movies onto a huge, 15-foot tall screen.

NEAR BAHÍA DE CARÁQUEZ: CANOA

Buses depart frequently for Pedernales (2½hr., every 30min., US$1.40) and San Vicente (30min., every 30min., US$0.20). From San Vicente, a boat can be taken to Bahía de Caráquez (15min., US$0.12).

The uncrowded beaches of Canoa represent some of the Ecuador's finest. Los Aposentos, the **coastal caves** not too far from Canoa's beach, have been some of the town's major attractions. Though only two of nine remain after an earthquake on August 4, 1997, you can still visit the bat-caves by boat and see the wealth of blue-footed boobies in this area. There are two excellent (though somewhat expensive) hotels in this tiny town, one of which is **◪Hotel Bambú** (☎ 753 696), at the north end of the beach. Its restaurant offers healthy but tasty meals (crepe with banana and *coco* US$1; fruit salad with homemade granola and yogurt US$1). The main building offers spotless rooms, screened windows, large ceiling fans, and hot water during cooler months. Cabins are also available. Most high rises have private baths (US$6-8 per person) and are more expensive than the low rises and dorms, which have clean communal baths and toilets (US$4 per person). Camping is also available (with personal tent US$1.50 per person; provided bamboo tent US$3 per person). Stay awhile and start a volleyball game with other *huéspedes* or ride the waves on a rented surfboard. Another fabulous option is **La Posada de Daniel,** about 100m from the beach on the main road. With cabins overlooking the town and spacious rooms, you won't be disappointed. (☎ 691 201. Rooms US$5 per person.) **Restaurant Tronco Bar,** 50m from the beach along the main road, offers patrons a laid-back environment. Dine in a hammock set on a sand floor on the ground level, or, if you prefer a chair, climb a rope-ladder to the second-floor loft. (Open daily 9am-1am.)

MANTA ☎05

Dominated by an immense harbor, Manta has long been a hub of seafaring activities. In pre-Columbian times Manta was home to the Jocay, an indigenous community distinguished for their maritime accomplishments. Since the time of the Jocay, the town's convenient location on the coast has spurred speedy population and economic growth. Though its beaches aren't spectacular, this city is sure to cater to many of your practical and recreational needs: you can access myriad supplies and services downtown, catch a movie at the local cinema, dine along the beach, and party until dawn in the *manicentro*.

TRANSPORTATION

Flights: The **Eloy Alfaro Airport** is 5km northeast of the *centro*. A taxi should cost US$1.50. **TAME,** Malecón and Calle 14, has flights to **Quito** (1hr.; M-Sa 6:45am, Su 5:30pm; US$36.60, round-trip US$63.20).

Buses: The **terminal** is along 24 de Mayo/Calle 7 just past Av. 4. All buses to northern destinations will pass through Portoviejo, all buses south through Jipijapa. Buses go to: **Esmeraldas** (10hr., 4 per day 3:15am-9:30pm, US$4); **Guayaquil** (4hr., every hr. 3am-6pm, US$3.40); **Montecristi** (30min., every 10min. 6am-7:30pm, US$0.20); **Portoviejo** (1hr., every 5min. 3am-9pm, US$0.40); **Puerto López** (4hr., every hr. 6am-6:30pm, US$1.40); **Quito** (9hr.; 4:30, 7, 9:30am; US$4); and **Santo Domingo** (6hr., every hr. 4am-9pm, US$3.20).

Local Buses: The blue and white *selectivos* cross the city (US$0.08), usually starting from the terminal and traveling east toward El Paseo.

ORIENTATION AND PRACTICAL INFORMATION

Buses enter the city by way of **4 de Noviembre,** passing through **Tarquí** before crossing the **Río Manta** into downtown Manta. If you plan on staying in Tarquí (which has many budget accommodations), you can save yourself a hike by asking to be dropped off before the **bridge** that crosses into the heart of Manta. The **terminal** is located just west of the **harbor,** not far from the bridge over the inlet. In Manta's *centro*, the streets running parallel to the coast are **avenidas,** with numbers increasing the farther one gets from the water. Streets leading uphill away from the water are **calles,** numbered beginning at the Río Manta.

Tourist Information: Ministerio de Turismo, Av. 3 1034 and Calle 11 (☎622 944). Open M-F 8:30am-5pm.

Travel Agencies: Delgado Travel (☎620 049), Av. 2 and Calle 13, offers car rental, an international delivery service, and **currency exchange.** Open M-F 8:30am-1pm and 3-6:30pm, Sa 9am-1pm. **Manatours** (☎621 020), Malecón and Calle 13 in Edificio Vigía. Open M-F 8:30am-1pm and 2:30-6:30pm.

Banks: Banco del Pacífico (☎623 212), Av. 107 and Calle 103, Tarquí. 24hr. Cirrus/MC **ATM.** Open M-F 9:30am-2:30pm. **Filanbanco** (☎623 002), Av. 6 and 24 de Mayo, has a 24hr. Visa/Plus **ATM.** Open M-F 9am-2pm.

Laundromat: Lavamatic, Calle 11 604 and Av. 5 (☎610 154). Open M-Sa 9am-3pm.

Emergency: ☎101.

Police: ☎920 900, 4 de Noviembre and Calle J2, on the road to Portoviejo. Open 24hr.

Hospital: Hospital Rodríguez Zambrano de Manta (**emergency** ☎611 849 or 620 595), San Mateo and Calle 12, Barrio Santa Martha. Take a university bus headed along Malecón (US$0.08). Free 24hr. emergency treatment and ambulance service.

Telephones: PacificTel (☎622 700), Calle 11 and Malecón. Open daily 8am-2:30pm and 3-10pm. If it isn't crowded, the **Puerta Virtual** staff may let you use their phone.

Internet Access: Puerta Virtual (☎629 926), on Malecón between Calle 15 and 16. US$1.32 per hr. Netphone US$0.32 per min. Open M-Sa 9:30am-9pm.

Post Office: (☎/fax 624 402), Av. 4 and Calle 8. Open M-F 7:30am-6:30pm, Sa 8am-1pm.

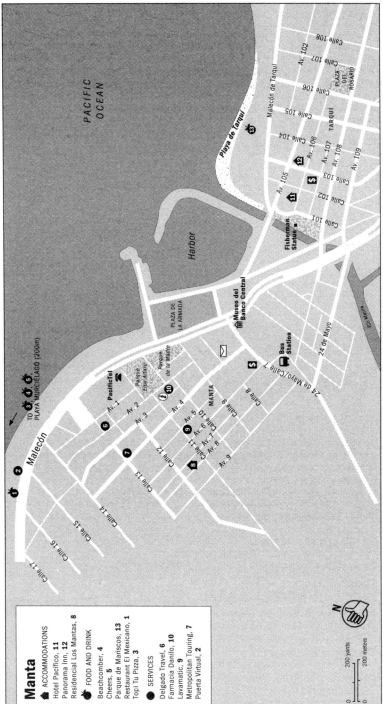

Manta

ACCOMMODATIONS
Hotel Pacifico, **11**
Panorama Inn, **12**
Residencial Los Mantas, **8**

FOOD AND DRINK
Beachcomber, **4**
Cheers, **5**
Parque de Mariscos, **13**
Restaurant El Mexicano, **1**
Topi Tu Pizza, **3**

SERVICES
Delgado Travel, **6**
Farmacia Danilo, **10**
Lavamatic, **9**
Metropolitan Touring, **7**
Puerta Virtual, **2**

ACCOMMODATIONS

The hotels in downtown Manta tend to be geared toward businessmen. You're likely to find concrete highrises badly in need of a paint job. Malecón de Tarquí, the beachfront avenue, monopolizes the hotel market.

Panorama Inn (☎/fax 611 552), Av. 105 and Calle 103. Though not the cheapest in town, clean bedrooms, private bathrooms, TV, fans, and a hotel pool might justify the cost. Rooms US$6.72, with A/C US$9, with A/C and cable TV US$13.44.

Hotel Pacífico (☎ 622 475 or 623 584), Av. 106 and Calle 101. While the unusual turquoise and mustard paint job may appear less than attractive, all rooms have private baths. Rooms US$5 per person, with A/C US$6.

Residencial Los Mantas (☎ 623 681), Calle 12 and Av. 8, is one of the only reasonably priced *residenciales* this close to downtown Manta. While bathrooms are not spectacular, rooms are generally clean and livable. Rooms US$1.60, with A/C US$2.40.

FOOD

All the restaurants clustered along Murciélago (identifiable by their matching green roofs and white walls) are referred to as **Malecón Escénico**—essentially a union of restaurants, all with the same menus and prices. Their counterpart along the Tarquí beach is **Parque de Mariscos,** where the owners' laid-back attitudes show in the hammocks and Pilsener signs that decorate their huts. These restaurants' claim to fame is one of the world's largest ceviches, made in September 1997.

Topi Tu Pizza (☎ 621 180), Malecón and Calle 15. Decorated with bamboo fixtures, illuminated ferns, and terrace, this pizzeria is all about atmosphere. Pizzas US$1.50-5.

Beachcomber (☎ 625 463), Flavio Reyes and Calle 20, should probably be called Ranchcomber—creatures of the sea don't appear much on the menu. The steak cut of the day (US$1.40) is meat-lover heaven. Open daily noon-3pm and 6pm-12:30am.

Restaurante El Mexicano (☎ (09) 749 551), Malecón and Calle 16, takes you out of Ecuador and into the heart of Mexico. Tacos US$1.08-1.20. Open M-Sa 10am-10pm.

BEACHES

There are two stretches of beach in Manta: **Playa Murciélago,** located in Manta just west of the *centro;* and **Playa de Tarquí,** farther east. A five-minute drive or 20-minute walk west of the *centro,* Murciélago has a good deal of soft sand, and its proximity to the Oroverde and other luxury hotels means that it is better-maintained than most public beaches. Tarquí's unpleasant, littered beach, on the other hand, could not be calmer. Placid as a lake at dawn, Tarquí's waters are a playground for **pelicans** and **frigatebirds** but offer little excitement for humans.

ENTERTAINMENT

Nights in Manta radiate with energy. The **Manicentro,** Flavio Reyes and Calle 24, is the focal point for a number of bars and clubs that coexist with a residential neighborhood. **K'chos,** Flavio Reyes and Calle 20, is definitely a weekend hot spot. Exquisitely dressed twenty-somethings crowd both the techno and merengue dance floors. (Cover US$2. Open daily 9pm-dawn.) Those seeking a more toned-down and romantic setting may appreciate the **Madera Fina,** Flavio Reyes and Calle 23. Dimly-lit coves encircle the small dance floor. (Cover US$3 per person, US$5 per couple.) A popular daytime destination is **El Paseo Shopping,** on the highway to Portoviejo. A Western-style mall, El Paseo has a food court as well as a **Supercines Post Office:** (☎/fax 624 402), Av. 4 and Calle 8. Open M-F 7:30am-6:30pm, Sa 8am-1pm.

PANAMA HATS ARE NOT FROM PANAMA

Forget the name. With its origins in the ancient straw hats of the Manabí, the Panama hat industry got its start in the 1830s, when the poverty-stricken inhabitants of Cuenca were forced to make hats for a living. Exports experienced a boost after the 1855 World Expo, when King Napoleon III, and subsequently the rest of Europe, fell in love with the hat. Fifty years later, when Panama Canal workers used the hats as protection from the sun, the craze hit the States and the wrong name stuck. The industry reached its peak in 1946, when the export of five million hats accounted for 20% of Ecuador's earnings. Presidents and Hollywood stars alike sported the stylish *sombrero*—an integral part of 30s and 40s American style. Gangsters even adopted the hat in the 20s; to this day a certain model is called the Capone.Meanwhile, the craftspeople worked for pennies, making hats that sold for a hefty profit in the States. The middlemen—factories, exporters, and retailers—all took their shares, leaving little for the actual artisans. These days, the hats are less popular, and imitation paper hats have taken a substantial bite out of the market. If their revenues continue to drop, the master artisans from the Montecristan countryside may have to put their straw away; while you're in the neighborhood, help save a dying art and buy yourself an Ecuador hat.

WESTERN ECUADOR

⊁ DAYTRIP FROM MANTA

MONTECRISTI

Buses arriving in Montecristi drop passengers off along the central plaza, bordered uphill by the streets 9 de Julio and Sucre, and the cross-hill streets 23 de Octubre and San Andreas. Buses passing by town en route to Manta or Portoviejo drop passengers off at the bottom of 9 de Julio; the plaza is a 20-minute walk uphill.

Between the rowdy giants of Manta and Portoviejo lounges Montecristi, patiently churning out its world-famous and sadly misnamed **Panama hats.** Though these high-grade hats have always been made in the countryside surrounding Montecristi, most of the ears their woven brims shelter have never heard of the place (see Panama Hats Are Not from Panama, p. 374). Still, industrial anonymity has its benefits; the town's streets remain tranquil and uncommercialized.

Shopping in Montecristi is about as fast-paced as a ride atop one of the town's many donkeys. Montecristi's principal street, 9 de Julio, presents many different *sombrero* shops (though these are found all throughout the town), all selling similar items at comparable prices. Hats start at US$10 for *gruesos* (made from the coarsest straw, usually taking 3 days per hat), US$20 for *finos* (softer and more delicate, processed in a single month), and become expensive with the *extrafinos* (US$200), which are the most carefully constructed and delicate of them all. Prices drop steadily the more hats you promise to buy. Along with the famed Panama hats, most of these shops sell straw handbags, baskets, and dolls. Few hats are made in town; the *almacenes* selling goods to the public only finish the hats. To fully appreciate the labor and patience required by the time-consuming weaving process, head out to the surrounding countryside. If you are interested in seeing the art in process, the **Artesanía Franco** (☎ 606 259) workshop, Eloy Alfaro and 23 de Octubre, gives demonstrations, provides a little background history, and offers some of the best prices in town.

Aside from markets, Montecristi offers some interesting sights. The impressive church of **La Virgen de Montecristi,** on the corner of Sucre and 23 de Octubre, houses the venerated statue of the Virgin of Monserrat, said to have miraculously cured various sickly *montecristianos*. A painting of the Sacred Family adorns the ceiling of the nave. This pleasant village is also home to two small museums. **Casa**

de Eloy Alfaro, Eloy Alfaro and 23 de Octubre, commemorates town hero and former president Eloy Alfaro with a selection of historical objects and a library. If you ask the librarians, they can provide you with a protracted description of Alfaro's assassination in Quito (the short story: he was dragged, dismembered, and burnt), as well as give you a brief tour of the exhibit. (Open M-F 8am-12:30pm and 1:30-5pm, Sa 9am-4pm.)

PORTOVIEJO ☎ 05

Originally situated on the coast, Portoviejo ("Old Port") moved 40km inland to its present land-locked locale to avoid continual pirate attacks. In spite of the move, Portoviejo has retained its name. Over the years the distance from the coast has become cultural as well as geographic—while its maritime neighbors seem more relaxed and carefree, Portoviejo's population plods along to the drone of its sober duties—commerce, industry, and education. However, although often regarded as the stiff-necked, straight-laced capital of an informal province, Portoviejo is well-respected by coastal residents.

Portoviejo seems huge, but anything a tourist needs is in the *centro*. Buses usually drop visitors off along the north-south **Universitaria,** at the intersection with **Ramos y Duarte,** before heading toward the **terminal** on the outskirts of town. From Universitaria and Ramos y Duarte, the **Parque Eloy Alfaro,** bounded by Universitaria and **Olmedo,** as well as by **Moreira** and **Alajuela,** is only two blocks away. The **Aeropuerto Reales Tamarindo** is about 3km northwest of the *centro*. (Taxi 5min., US$0.60). TAME (☎ 632 426 and 650 000), located on Chile and América, has flights to **Quito** (30min.; M, W, and F 11:10am; US$37). Open M-F 8am-12:30pm and 2:30-6:30pm. As a major coastal transportation link, a multitude of **bus** companies leave from Portoviejo's terminal. Buses go to: **Bahía de Caráquez** (2¼hr., every 45min. 5am-8:30pm, US$1); **Guayaquil** (4hr., every hr. 4am-9:30pm, US$2.80); **Jipijapa** (1¼hr., every hr. 4am-9:30pm, US$1.04); **Manta** (45min., every 10min. 4am-7pm, US$0.40); **Pedernales** (6hr., every hr. 4am-4pm, US$3); and **Quito** (9hr., every hr. 6am-11pm, US$4.20) via **Santo Domingo** (5hr., US$2.80). The **Ministerio de Turismo** is at Pedro Gual 234 and Montalvo, 3 blocks east of Morales. (☎ 630 877. Open M-F 8:30am-5pm.) **Banco del Pacífico,** 9 de Octubre and Rocafuerte, changes traveler's checks until 3:30pm. 24hr. Cirrus **ATM. Filanbanco,** Pacheco and Pedro Gual has a 24hr. Visa/Plus **ATM.** (☎ 630 455. Open M-F 9am-2pm.) **Police:** (☎ 630 343 or 636 944), 18 de Octubre between Sucre and Bolívar. **Regional Hospital de Portoviejo** (emergency ☎ 630 555 or 630 087), Rocafuerte and 12 de Marzo. **Correos del Ecuador,** Ricaurte 217 and Sucre. (☎ 632 384. Open M-F 6:30am-7pm, Sa 8am-2pm.) **Internet access:** Multiservicio del Sol, Rocafuerte and 9 de Octubre (☎ 631 222. US$0.04 per min., US$1.60 per hr.) **PacificTel,** 10 de Agosto and Pacheco. (Open daily 8am-9pm.)

Most budget places are situated between the town's two parks, while the more expensive places are located along Pedro Gual, especially around Chile. **Hostal Colón,** Colón 212 at Olmedo, a block south of Parque Central, has a lobby that looks like a beauty parlor, but the rooms' wooden furniture give off a more hotel-like feel. Don't expect to sleep late—there's an elementary school next door. (☎ 654 004. Rooms with bath, TV, and fan US$3 per person, with A/C US$5.) **Hotel Conquistador,** 10 de Agosto at 18 de Octubre, 2 blocks up and 2 blocks west of Parque Central, is one of the cheaper executive haunts. Huge cable TVs take up half the room; your backpack might take up the other half. Bathrooms are spotless. (☎ 651 472. Rooms with fan US$4 per person, with A/C US$6.) **Hotel Pacheco/Hotel Victoria,** 9 de Octubre at Morales, share a maze of halls and 70 stark sleeping chambers. Super-clean rooms have super-thin mattresses. Tiny skylights battle the darkness. (☎ 637 695. Rooms US$1, with bath, sink, TV US$1.80.) Portoviejo's cuisine is slightly different from that of its coastal neighbors. Though local *comedores* still offer many of the region's typical fish dishes, they concentrate more on beef and fowl. **La Fruta Prohibida,** Chile and 10 de Agosto, with another shop 1 block up the street, is a fancy *fuentes de soda*. The fruit might be forbidden, but it definitely is fresh (fruit salads US$0.48-1). Tasty sandwiches (US$0.40-1.40) too. (☎ 637 167. Open daily 9:30am-11pm.)

NEAR PORTOVIEJO: CRUCITA

Transportes Crucita buses from Portoviejo (1hr., every 15min. 5:30am-7pm, US$0.42) drop visitors off at the plaza, two blocks along the dirt road from the beach.

Only an hour's bus ride from Portoviejo, Crucita is the landlocked capital's favorite beachside getaway. Anyone arriving during high tide might wonder about this popularity, as there is almost no beach to be seen. But when the tide goes out, it leaves clean, firm sand bordered by relatively calm, green-blue water. Crucita is filled with reasonably priced hotels, the best of which is the **Hostal Rey David**, on the far north end of the boardwalk. This eight-room hostel is incredibly clean and nicely decorated, with new furniture and a clean pool. (**☎**676 143; fax 676 102. Rooms US$6 per person, with A/C US$11.) Another decent choice is **Hostería Las Cabañitas,** halfway down Malecón from the street that connects the beach and the highway. Basic cabañas with baths offer little excitement, but the popular restaurant in front serves as a diversion. (**☎**652 660. Rooms US$1.20 per person.)

JIPIJAPA   ☎05

Unfortunately, most of the fun associated with Jipijapa (pronounced "heepy-hoppa"), 60km south of Manta, comes from saying its name. Otherwise, this city of 60,000 only offers some of the practical facilities lacking in many coastal cities. Jipijapa chiefly serves as a stopping point and transportation hub for eager sun-seekers and anxious surfers shuttling back and forth to the sandy shores of communities such as Puerto López and Montañita. Deal with money matters while you're in town: there a.e few banks and ATMs between here and La Libertad. The **terminal** is a few kilometers west of the *centro*, near the traffic circle. **Buses** leave from the terminal bound for: **Guayaquil** (2½hr., every 30min. 7:30am-7:30pm, US$2); **Puerto López** (1¾hr., every hr. 6am-6pm, US$0.72); and **Manta** (2hr., every 15min. 5am-6pm, US$0.80). **Local buses** between the terminal and the center of town cost US$0.08; **taxis** cost US$0.28. **Filanbanco,** Bolívar and 9 de Octubre, has a 24-hour Visa **ATM.** (**☎**601 262; fax 600 455. Open M-F 10am-1:30pm.) Should you inexplicably find yourself staying in Jipijapa, you have few options for accommodations and food. **Hostal Jipijapa,** at Santistevan and Eloy Alfaro, provides clean and modern rooms with fans and private bath. (**☎**601 365; fax 600 783. Rooms US$4 per person, with A/C and hot water US$9.)

PUERTO LÓPEZ   ☎05

Puerto López isn't much of a tourist town. Packs of dogs roam its muddy streets, and an unusual species of aquatic swine (more commonly known as the "sea pig") has been spotted along its beach. However, the bright signs for travel agencies and restaurants remind visitors that this fishing town reels in its share of tourists as well, if only because of its proximity to Parque Nacional Machalilla.

▐ TRANSPORTATION

Buses travel north to **Manta** (3hr., every 2hr. 7am-7pm, US$1.40) and **Jipijapa** (1¾hr., every 30min. 6:30am-7pm, US$0.74). South-bound buses (every 30min., 6:30am-7pm) go to: **Salango** (15min., US$0.18); **Alandaluz** (30min., US$0.40); **Montañita** (1hr., US$1); **Manglaralto** (1½hr., US$1); **La Libertad/Salinas** (3hr., US$2); and **Quito** (11hr., 6pm, US$5).

▐▐ ORIENTATION AND PRACTICAL INFORMATION

The principal road in town, **Machalilla,** continues north to Jipijapa and south to La Libertad. Buses stop here on the corner of **Córdova.** The street closest to the river, **Malecón,** runs parallel to Machalilla two or three blocks to the west. The **Machalilla National Park Headquarters,** at Eloy Alfaro and Machalilla, has information and a park interpretation center (**☎**604 170; open daily 8am-5pm). Many tour companies in Puerto Lopez offer excursions to the park. **Exploratur,** Malecón and Córdova, has some staff with English experience. (**☎**604 123; www.exploratur.com. Open daily

7:30am-8pm.) Also recommended are **Machalilla Tour Agency,** on Malecón off Córdova (☎604 154; open daily); **Mantaraya,** on Malecón a few blocks north of Córdova (☎604 233; open daily 7am-8pm); and **Bosque Marino,** at Machalilla and Córdova (☎604 106; open daily 7am-9pm). There are **no banks** in Puerto López. The **police** are at Machalilla and Atahualpa. (☎604 101.) **Centro de Salud de Puerto López,** is at the end of Machalilla, eight blocks north of the *centro*. Walking away from the bus stop, veer right after the Tienda Rosita sign on the right side of the road. The **post office** sits at Atahualpa and Machalilla. (Open M-F 8am-noon and 2-5:30pm.)

ACCOMMODATIONS

There are plenty of places to stay here, but you may still want to reserve a room during high season (July-Sept.), when both the town and its lodgings fill up.

Hostal Villa Colombia (☎604 105), on the first right off Córdova after Machalilla when heading away from the beach; on the left. Hot water, laundry service, kitchen, and clean rooms. Bike US$4 per day. Dorms US$3; singles and doubles US$4 per person.

Hotel Pacífico (☎604 147), at Suárez and Malecón, 50m from the beach at the northern end of Malecón. Lush courtyard. Hammocks. Simple but clean cabañas. Dorm-style cabañas US$3; singles with bath and breakfast US$10.

Hostel Tuzco (☎604 132), at Córdova and Juan León Mera, 2½ blocks east of Machalilla. Tuzco's bright color scheme and immaculate housekeeping make up for the muddy road you take to reach it. Rooms fit up to 6. Dorms US$3.

FOOD

While many of Puerto López's restaurants are strikingly similar in appearance and menu offerings, a few provide much-needed variety.

Yubarta Café Bar, at the far northern end of Malecón. Walk past Hotel Pacífico for a few blocks, cross the bamboo bridge; it's on your right. Titanic baguette sandwiches. Succulent chocolate cake US$0.60. One of López's finest eateries. Play ping-pong or pool (US$1 per 30min.) to the tunes of Bob Marley. Open 5pm-late.

Whale Café, just south of Córdova along Malecón. Ocean view. Sandwiches with homemade bread (US$0.75-2). Half-pizza (US$1.50). Bilingual book swap. Open daily.

Restaurant Carmita (☎604 149), Córdova and Malecón, has been around for 28 years. Try the house specialty, *pescado al vapor,* a fabulous fish-and-vegetable dish (US$1.60). Vegetarian menu US$0.60-1.60. Open daily 8am-10pm.

SIGHTS AND BEACHES

Puerto López is an ideal base from which to explore the marvels of **Parque Nacional Machalilla** (see p. 468). Multiple tour companies offer trips to the park and battle for tourists' bucks with bigger and better bargains (see p. 465), especially to **Isla de la Plata,** 40km off the coast from Puerto López. The opportunity to see soaring **humpback whales** (late June-Sept.) comes with boat trips to Isla de la Plata. Fortunately, prices among most of the agencies are standardized, so you don't always have to shop around to get the best deal. Exploratur and Mantaraya offer **scuba** packages as well. If you'd rather keep your feet on solid ground, Puerto López's own **beach** (barely) meets the challenge with brown, rather dirty sand.

DAYTRIP FROM PUERTO LÓPEZ

SALANGO
Accessible by bus from Puerto López (15 min., US$0.18).

Situated 5km south of Puerto López, Salango sits patiently, like an old man with a story to tell. Salango's tale comes from beneath its sands, home to a massive collection of **archeological artifacts.** Dating back almost 5000 years, six different pre-Hispanic communities thrived here, leaving behind scatterings of everyday life as well as jewelry and artwork. Many of the pieces have been excavated and now fill Salango's archeological museum, but a large number remain trapped in the silent sand, buried beneath Salango's **fish factory.** The factory itself is the subject of another kind of story: the firing of the factory's Salangan workforce after a wage strike in 1989 and the hiring of people from neighboring towns to take their places. Salango has been hit hard by the layoffs, and most locals have returned to unpredictable—and often unprofitable—fishing and agricultural careers.

The **Museo a los Balseros del Mar del Sur** has a well-preserved and informative collection chronicling the six cultures found at the site. The **Valdivia** culture is the oldest, subsisting from 3000-2000 BC, followed by the **Machalilla** (2000-1500 BC), **Chorrera and Engoroy** (1500-500 BC), **Guangala/Bahían** (500 BC-AD 500), and **Manteño** (AD 500-AD 1000). For more information, see **The Earliest Inhabitants, p. 14**. Each culture has separate glass encasements, labeled with Spanish descriptions that present various artifacts from the areas of Salango, Isla de la Plata, Puerto López, Machalilla, and Agua Blanca. The museum also has, among other things, an example of the kind of balsa raft used by some of these cultures. (Museum open daily 9am-5pm. US$1, students US$0.80, children US$0.50.)

NEAR PUERTO LÓPEZ: PUEBLO ECOLÓGICO ALANDALUZ

Alandaluz is 6km south of Salango through Puerto López (30min., US$0.20). Practically impossible to miss on the west side of the road. Even without spending the night, a 10min. walk through the well-kept gardens provides an excellent feel for this place, and its beaches are worth a visit. Reservations recommended July-Aug. (☎ (04) 780 184).

Arranged like a garden-filled village, **Pueblo Ecológico Alandaluz** is a gorgeous beach resort just off the road between Puerto López and Montañita. It was recently rated as **one of the seven best socially responsible ecotourist projects in the world,** constructed wholly of rapidly growing, easily replenishable materials. Visitors can make their contribution by frequenting the bathroom, where waste is mixed with sawdust and dried leaves to speed up the decomposition process. The resort itself is set up like a tiny village. In addition to the two main buildings, there are several beachfront cabins, complete with bamboo patio-decks and ocean views. All of the pristine bamboo quarters are festooned with cheerful curtains and mosquito nets. The one exception is the **Cabaña del Arbol,** the honeymoon suite. It is built into a live tree—you can feel the structure sway as you and that special someone climb the tree-branch ladder into your lofty love nest. Check out the **Cabaña del Poeta** to see what a writer serious about tranquility and comfort seeks. Eco-conscious extravagance, even **camping,** has its price (US$3, with their tent US$4). From there, the prices climb. You can pay extra for private baths, ocean views, eco-toilets and/ or luxury non-cabin rooms. (Singles US$7-26; doubles US$9-37; triples US$11-44; quads US$46.) The center of the complex boasts plentiful amenities. Relax at a cozy bamboo **bar,** furnished with cushioned straw couches and an outdoor furnace. (Open daily 4pm-late). Near the bar, a first-class **restaurant** specializes in vegetable and seafood dishes. The chef uses an oven constructed of hardened fecal matter to create his pride and joy, the *viudo de mariscos* (an enormous serving of baked seafood inside a bamboo cane, US$2.40-3), or a variety of other chicken, fish, and vegetable dishes cooked in bamboo or coconut. (Breakfast US$1.60, lunch and dinner US$2.40. Open daily 8am-9pm.) Alandaluz's beach is beautiful and largely uninhabited, but the **surf** is monstrous, so a swim amounts to a salty pummeling. However, if you have a surfboard and know how to use it, the water is ideal. Generally slow-breaking, crumbling waves—with 5-7 ft. faces in summer and 9-10 ft. faces in winter—break in both directions. Alandaluz doesn't always have the hollow, echoing barrels of Montañita, but it also doesn't have the crowds. Alandaluz has an on-site travel agency, **Pacarina Travel,** in the main house, which offers tours by land or sea into Parque Nacional Machalilla. Prices are comparable to those in Puerto López (☎601 203. US$30 per person, including lunch.) Pacarina can also arrange tours to **Cantalapiedra,** Alandaluz's experimental organic farm (1½hr.; US$15 per person, including breakfast).

PARQUE NACIONAL MACHALILLA

Parque Nacional Machalilla's 55,000 hectares preserve archeological riches, one of the most pristine cloud forests in Ecuador, and the only protected virgin dry tropical forest in South America. The arid, sometimes colorless tropical forests may not be part of the most beautiful ecosystem around, but they provide for some of the most stunning beaches in the country. To make things even better, **Isla de la Plata** summarizes the Galapagos experience—sea birds, sea lions, seasickness—for only a fraction of the cost. Most visits to the park take the form of daytrips that leave Puerto López early in the morning and return in the afternoon. From Puerto López, **buses** make the 10km trip to the Los Frailes gate (US$0.20). From there, it is a 2km hike to the reception *cabañita* and the rest of the grounds. Most sites in the park cannot be visited without a guide, but relatively inexpensive trips can be arranged through any of the tour agencies in Puerto López (see p. 465). The park admission is good for at least a week (US$20). In general, trips are cheaper for bigger groups, so ask around at the agencies to see if a group is looking for another member. For more info on Parque Nacional Machalilla, visit the **headquarters** in Puerto López (see p. 465). Before embarking on a particular trip, find out what the day includes. Most land tours do not include food and bottled water—these are impossible to find inside the park, so bring your own. Though **camping** is allowed at San Sebastián and Agua Blanca (US$15 per day; food, guide, and transportation included), there are no facilities, so campers must provide everything themselves. Many also recommend bringing **snorkeling equipment,** as the supplies of tour agencies and boats are limited in numbers and of unpredictable quality.

AGUA BLANCA. This frequently visited hamlet is called home by 43 families who still carry on many of the customs of their ancient ancestors. A short bus ride from Puerto López leads to the park entrance where a dusty one-hour trail through the lowland dry forest to Agua Blanca allows for study of the varied flora. **Figs, laurels,** and **Kapok** trees are scattered loosely, while the lush beanstalks of the pea-like, perennially verdant **algarrobos** pierce the dry wasteland. Those dry-climate staples, **cacti,** abound. The tall, spindly **prickly pear** and the **pitahaya** (which sprouts a delectable yellow fruit Feb.-Mar.) are well-represented among the spines. Agua Blanca provides an interlude to the wilderness education, with both an **archeological museum** in the *pueblito* and the ruins of the **Manteña,** an indigenous group that resided here for the 1000 years preceding Spanish conquest. The museum brims with Manteña artifacts, including art, jewelry, pottery, religious pieces, and miniature replicas of their **balsa rafts.** The giant **pottery urns** on the way to the ruins were used as tombs for Manteña dead. A 30-minute walk uphill, the anticlimactic **ruins** are only the basic foundations of the Manteña's homes and places of worship. Guides are required for the trip to the ruins. (Guides US$15 per person; museum admission included, group discounts.)

SAN SEBASTIÁN HUMID FOREST. The trip from Agua Blanca to the humid forests of San Sebastián almost always requires two days and is often done on horseback. The trail takes six or seven hours each way, and during the course of the hike there, the land undergoes a striking transition from dry tropical to humid forest. The trip is well worth it—San Sebastián sports many **exotic animal species,** including tarantulas, giant centipedes, scorpions, coral snakes, armadillos, howler monkeys, *guantas* (agoutis), anteaters, and numerous bird species. This tour also requires a guide, which can be arranged in a Puerto López tour agency. Less expensive guides may be available in Agua Blanca, but they often have a much more limited knowledge about the area's plants and animals and are only able to show the way. (Two-day tours cost US$15 hiking, US$25 on horseback; both per person.) Some warn that slippery paths and occasionally weak horses can make the latter option a bit dangerous.

LAS GOTERAS. One alternative way to explore the humid forest without the expense and two-day time commitment is to visit the Las Goteras area (US$20). The entire trip takes five to six hours but is relatively difficult—the path to the humid forest is almost all uphill, and the forest itself is a slow trek through thick and slippery mud—but eventually provides gorgeous views of the surrounding mountains and, on a clear day, of the ocean far below. The vegetation gradually changes on the way up the mountain, as the trees become bigger and more lush. The humid forest itself hosts a variety of fascinating **flora and fauna:** coffee and mango trees, bright butterflies, spiders resting on glittering webs, plentiful birds, and maybe a monkey or two. Beyond the beauty of the forest, guides can point out the varied uses of different trees and plants—everything from brooms to jewelry.

LOS FRAILES. For still more environmental contrast, these secluded shores, located 2km north of the Agua Blanca gate, include **three beaches:** La Playita, La Tortuguita, and the star of the sandshow, Los Frailes. A guide is not required for the trip but is highly recommended (US$10 per person). The excursion starts at the Los Frailes gate on the road from Puerto López. About 100m past the gate, the road bends left at a *cabañita* (at which you can buy tickets for the park entrance), while a smaller dirt path leads to the right. The two trails are the different ends of the same 3760m trail. The trail on the left leads through dry forest to Los Frailes (30min.). Down the trail to the right, the tiny rock cove of **La Playita,** a 25-minute walk from the *cabañita,* is layered with **black sands** and lapped by calm waters perfect for waders and young children. This is also a great **snorkeling** spot, and sea turtles nest here from December to April. Walk five minutes farther and reach a cove festooned with curious rock configurations: **La Tortuguita.** Though its shallow, soft, whitish sand won't harm a soul, the two chaotic swirling swells breaking toward each other can be **dangerous;** swimming is not advised. Two paths lead from here to the third beach, **Los Frailes:** the easy low road and the overgrown high road. The high road leads to a platform with a spectacular view of the beaches and ocean. The immense, almost perfectly symmetrical rocky cove of Los Frailes waits at the end of the hike. Uninhabited except for a lining of greenery, the beach stretches in a golden arc of pure, solitary sand facing tranquil waters. These beaches are also often visited by boat trips taking passengers to a variety of good snorkeling spots (min. 2 people, US$20 per person).

 The boat journey from Puerto López takes two solid hours, and the sea swells are often large and turbulent. Anyone even slightly susceptible to motion sickness should take appropriate precautionary measures.

ISLA DE LA PLATA. The "Plata" in the name refers to the legendary lost treasure of pirate Sir Francis Drake. Supposedly, after liberating his booty from the Spanish galleons, Drake hid it somewhere on this 3500-hectare island, which lies just 40km off the shore of Puerto López. Today, the island is more popular with tourists admiring its pristine natural environment and diverse wildlife than with scavengers looking for lost treasures. After all, in the booby-watching Olympics, the Galapagos Islands take the gold, but Isla de la Plata is happy with the silver. The boobies in question include the outlaw **masked booby,** the nurturing **blue-footed booby,** and the small but abundant **red-footed booby.** In addition to the boobies, La Plata is home to many other species. The largest colony of **frigatebirds** in the world lives here, and from April to November the rare **waved albatrosses** wing in for fly-by-night mating season affairs. But the boobies and the other birds aren't the only wildlife to be found at this island party. A small off-shore colony of **sea lions** is occasionally spotted sun bathing, and from July to September, the waters teem with **humpback whales.** These amorous aquatics have complex and fascinating courting routines best seen during the rollicking boat ride from Puerto López to the island. The park office is at **Bahía Drake,** the island's only inlet and the docking point for mainland boats. From Bahía Drake, two different three-hour **trails** (each

3km) head up hills, over dales, and through nesting sites. Groups only do one of the two trails, and the decision is made in advance by the park office. One of the trails allows visitors to see albatrosses (Apr.-Dec.), blue-footed and masked boobies, sea lions, and tropical birds. The other excludes albatrosses and sea lions, but features all three booby varieties, as well as magnificent frigatebirds, pelicans, and some tropical birds. The all-day trip is a package deal, including guide, food, and snorkeling (US$25 per person). A slightly less expensive way to do the Isla de la Plata trip is to charter a boat yourself, which usually only requires assembling a group of eight people and arranging for food and a guide (US$15 per person).

MONTAÑITA   ☎ 04

Lying 65km north of La Libertad, Montañita throbs with the wave-crashing vibes of its seasonal international surfing crowds. During the high season (Dec.-Apr.), the streets become a barefoot parade, flowing with long hair, bronzed torsos, and the boards that go with them. The town calms down considerably in low season since the waves do the same, but a band of die-hard surfers resides here year-round. While days are spent in the surf, nights are full of beach parties, bonfires, and general seaside debauchery. Legends of this revelry are too intriguing to ignore; they attract hundreds of non-surfers to this all-around party town. In fact, Montañita attracts quite a bohemian crowd—nomadic artisans, left-over hippies, and trippy gringos mingle with locals, making for an unusual demographic medley.

◨◪ TRANSPORTATION AND PRACTICAL INFORMATION

Montañita is comprised of two distinct sectors a kilometer apart. The **pueblo** to the south houses most of the town's inhabitants, hotels, and restaurants. Here, **Rocafuerte** runs from the highway to the sand, while **15 de Mayo,** perpendicular to Rocafuerte, is the last street before the sand. There is a small **central plaza** on 15 de Mayo south of Rocafuerte. **Chiriboga** lies one street east of 15 de Mayo. **La Punta,** the other sector to the north, is named for the rocky bluffs that loom over its famous barreling break, and its one road, parallel to the beach, is filled almost exclusively with hotels and restaurants. Transportation is limited to **buses** to **Puerto López** (1hr., US$1). There are **no hospitals, police stations,** or **banks** in Montañita. You can, however, still check your email—**Internet access** is available at **Hostal Casa Blanca** and at **La Casa del Sol** (both US$2 per 30min.). **PacificTel,** on Chiriboga across from the central plaza, charges outlandish rates for international calls. You can try your luck with the erratic-houred **netphone access** at **Cafe Futura** (☎901 135).

▰ ACCOMMODATIONS

Montañita makes it cheap and comfortable to come for a night and stay for a week or two. An alternative to hotels, beach houses often offer rooms for rent. Clean, wood-panelled rooms, bamboo balconies, palm-thatched roofs, hammocks, mosquito netting, and lively, friendly surroundings are pretty much the standard.

▨ **Casa Blanca** (email lacasablan@hotmail.com), in the *pueblo,* 2 blocks north of Rocafuerte on Chiriboga. Airy rooms with high ceilings, balconies, fans. Internet access (US$2 per 30min., US$1 for guests). Surfboard rental (US$2 per day). Restaurant. Dorms US$2; singles US$3 per person, with bath US$4. Credit cards and traveler's checks.

Centro del Mundo, the towering building on the water at the end of Rocafuerte in the *pueblo,* reachable by walking through La Cabañita restaurant. Cozy lobby. Pool table. Restaurant. Simple but clean rooms. The dorm consists of an open-air attic and rows of mattresses and strongboxes. Dorms US$1.40; rooms start at US$3, with bath US$4.

La Casa del Sol (☎901 302; email casasol@ecua.net.ec) offers more financial, phone, Internet, and other services than the town of Montañita. An adjacent bar is open every night during high season. Rooms US$4 per person, with bath US$5.

FOOD

Montañita's restaurants are sure to replenish calories lost in the waves. For vegetarians, the menus are a refreshing break from ceviche-dodging.

La Cabañita, the last establishment on the right as you hit the beach on Rocafuerte. Despite the absence of blaring music and colorful signs, this low-key eatery draws a lot of customers. Seafood dishes US$1.12-1.32. Fabulous *empanadas* US$0.52-1.

Tres Palmas (☎ 755 717), right on the beach in *la punta*. Popular with both locals and tourists. In addition to the traditional enchilada (US$1.12-1.56) and *quesadilla* (US$1.12), this Tex-Mex joint offers a taste of the Caribbean with a Jamaican jerk chicken platter (US$4.40). Open W-Su noon-10pm.

BEACHES AND NIGHTLIFE

Though partially famous for its ability to reel in party-philes from all across the globe, the **surf** is what makes Montañita what it is. The beach stretches endlessly south, but looming, jagged cliffs with peculiar rock formations contain it to the north. These cliffs bring about the consistent 1-2m. swells with echoing barrels that break to the right, away from the point. During the off-season, the waves sometimes struggle (offering only 1m apologies), but on good days in both seasons, waves can pitch up to over the 1.5m. mark. During the *temporada alta*, the *pueblo*'s streets and bars are packed nightly. In general, Chiriboga north of Rocafuerte is the most social strip in this town. More specifically, **Bongo Beach Bar** and **Mahalo** are the most frequented bar-cafes. Hustlers can find their way to **Arriba** for a Pilsener and a game of pool. If you stay in Montañita long enough, you may even catch a spontaneous **house party.**

NEAR MONTAÑITA: VALDIVIA

A 25-minute bus ride south of Manglaralto, this pint-sized village—where 70% of inhabitants work in the footwear industry—offers little besides a bit of history and a small, quiet beach frequented mostly by fishermen. The **Valdivia people,** who lived here from 3000-2000 BC, were the oldest of the ancient cultures from this area. The **Museo Valdivia,** just off the main road in the center of town, displays originals and replicas of the culture's artifacts, from small figurines to funeral urns. The museum is small but attractive and well-organized, and includes stations demonstrating how replicas and crafts native to the area are created today. (Museum open daily 9am-6pm. US$0.32, children US$0.16.)

NEAR MONTAÑITA: AYANGUE

Although Ayangue is only 5km south of Valdivia, only mountain goats manage the walk. With a monstrous rocky point separating the two towns, motorized vehicles provide the only reasonable inter-village transport; they drop passengers off along the highway near a few "Welcome to Ayangue" signs. The paved road heading west leads into town; it's a five-minute *camioneta* ride (US$0.12) or a 30-minute walk. This road leads directly to Ayangue's **beach,** a pretty cove surrounded by high cliffs and filled with fishing boats. The currents can get strong, but when the water is calm it's a beautiful spot for a swim. During the low season, when the weather everywhere else on the coast is drearily overcast, Ayangue's cove is often magically sunny and the beach has few, if any, swimmers. The town itself offers limited food and shelter options. On the street parallel to the beach, **Hostal Un Millón de Amigos** (☎916 014) provides clean, comfortable rooms with fans and some private baths (US$5 per person). The hostel's restaurant fires its stoves up only when full pensions (3 meals and accommodations) are purchased. **Pensión 5 Hermanos** (☎916 029), on the main road right by the beach, has less-than-sparkling common bathrooms and less-than-impressive rooms (US$2), but does offer a breezy, open-air feel, some nice sea views, and even a resident monkey named Rocky.

SALINAS ☎ 04

Salinas screams hedonism with an unusual abundance of BMWs, yachts, highrises, beach bums, and party fiends—especially for Ecuador. Brimming with affluence, the town is packed with the luxurious vacation homes and condominiums of many of Ecuador's wealthiest residents. From December to April, the town is hopping, and the many discos and restaurants which are closed during the low season spring to life. At the westernmost tip of the Santa Elena Peninsula, 150km west of Guayaquil, Salinas boasts one of the prettiest beaches around—with its wealthy visitors and modern buildings, Salinas cannot help but adopt a cosmopolitan air.

▐ TRANSPORTATION

The town of **La Libertad**, a few km to the east, is the peninsula's transportation hub. However, **Cooperativa Libertad Peninsular** goes to **Guayaquil** from Av. 5 and Calle 17 (2¾hr., every 20min. 3am-7:10pm, US$1.60). There are three options when commuting between Salinas and La Libertad; **buses** and **vans** leave from Av. 3 (which becomes Av. 7) around the clock (US$0.12). **Taxis** could cost up to US$2. In La Libertad, several bus lines are based at 9 de Octubre and Guerra Barreiro. **Buses** go to **Guayaquil** (2½hr., every 10min. 3:30am-8:10pm, US$1.60) via **Progreso** (1¼hr., US$0.80); and **Quito** (10hr.; 10am, 8:30, 9:30pm; US$6.40). The rest of the buses that go through town leave from the **terminal**, several blocks away from 9 de Octubre. Walk up Guayaquil and bear right at the top of the hill. When the road forks, bear slightly right again, and then turn right as soon as you can. Walk two blocks, turn left, then left again; the terminal is on your right. From here buses go to: **Puerto López** (3hr., every 30min. 4am-4pm, US$2) via **Valdivia** (1hr., US$0.12) and **Manglaralto** (1½hr., US$0.80); **Jipijapa** (4½hr., every 30 min. 4am-4pm, US$1.50); and **Manta** (every hr., US$1.48). If a bus to Manta isn't available, take a bus to Jipijapa and catch one there.

◀▐ ORIENTATION AND PRACTICAL INFORMATION

While navigation through Salinas is difficult due to the lack of street signs; it helps to know that most facilities of general import are found on **Malecón** (**Av. 2**), **Gallo** (**Av. 2**), and **Av. 3** (which becomes **Av. 7**) east of **Calle 16**. *Calles* increase in number from west to east and run more or less perpendicular to the **beach** bordering the northern end of town. The **Salinas Yacht Club** divides the beach into two sectors.

Tour Agencies: Pescatours (☎ 772 391), Malecón between Calles 20 and 22, leads deep-sea fishing adventures (US$350-550 per day). Open daily 8am-noon and 2-6pm.

Banks: Banco del Pacífico (☎ 774 137), Gallo/Av. 2 between Calles 18 and 19. 24hr. MC/Cirrus **ATM**. Open M-F 8:45am-5pm, Sa 9am-3pm.

Police: (☎ 778 699), Espinoza and Calle 57, at the east end of town.

Hospital: Dr. Jose Garces Rodríguez (☎ 776 017), in Ciudadela Frank Vargas Pazoz, in the southeast of town, has a 24hr. emergency room and ambulance service.

Post Office: Calle 17 and Av. 2A. Open M-F 8am-noon and 2-5pm, Sa 9am-2pm.

Internet Access: Café Planet (☎ 775 500; email cafeplanet@porta.net), Gallo/Av. 2 between Calles 25 and 26. Internet US$2 per hr., netphone US$0.32 per min. and up. **Salinas.net,** Calle 19 between Malecón and Av. 2A. US$1.20 per hr.

Telephones: PacificTel, Calle 20 and Gallo/Av. 2. Open daily 8am-9:45pm.

▐ ACCOMMODATIONS

Salinas's budget accommodations congregate between Calles 22 and 27, on the parallel roads south of Malecón. You won't find anything lower than US$3.20 per person, but most rooms are well-maintained and have private baths.

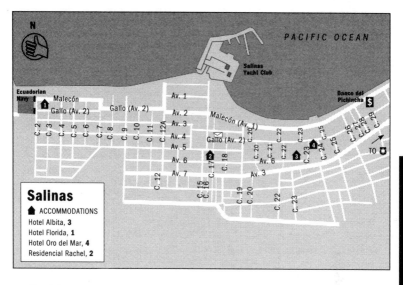

WESTERN ECUADOR

Hotel Oro del Mar (☎ 783 110), Gallo/Av. 2 and Calle 23. Large. Great location and quality rooms, with comfortable mattresses and clean baths. Rooms US$4 per person.

Hotel Albita (☎ 773 211, or 773 662), Av. 6 between Calles 22 and 23. Powerful fans and good window screens. Breezy balconies. Rooms US$3.20 per person.

Hotel Florida (☎ 772 780), Malecón and Calle 3. Well-lit rooms have fans; some also have large windows and ocean views. Rooms with bath US$7.32 per person.

Residencial Rachel (☎ 772 526 or 772 501), Calle 17 and Av. 5. Rooms have a hospital feel—in appearance and cleanliness. Rooms US$4 per person, with bath US$6.

FOOD

If ceviche is your thing, you've come to the right place. Enríquez Gallo between Calles 16 and 18 is packed with ceviche stands. Most other food options are found along Malecón. For cheap sandwiches, the chain *panadería* **Baguette** is located on Gallo/Av. 2 and Calle 18, with another up the street at Gallo/Av. 2 and Calle 8.

Cevichelandia, Gallo/Av. 2 between Calles 16 and 17, is a ceviche fan's wildest fantasy come true. The Salinas version of fast food, this large plaza is filled with ceviche stands. Although the prices and food options are similar throughout, **Don Kleber** and **Carmita** are among the most highly recommended. **Chelita** has a good juice selection. Ceviche US$2. *Batidos* and juices US$0.40. Most stands open daily 8am-5pm.

Restaurante Los Helechos (☎ 773 984), Malecón and Calle 23. Fern-filled, simple, and breezy diner. Diverse menu (US$1-3). Open daily 9am-midnight.

Trattoria Tony (☎ 772 609), Malecón and Calle 19. Tablecloths make indoor dining charming; outside diners get ocean views and breezes. Pasta US$1.60-2. Pizza US$2-4.

BEACHES

Salinas' two **beaches** are divided by a small peninsula that houses the **Salinas Yacht Club**. Salinas's main beach covers the stretch of sand to the east of the yacht club. Palm-laden and relatively unlittered, the sands are packed to capacity with sun worshippers. The water is even more congested, teeming with every kind of watercraft imaginable. Shallow water is safe for children and timid swimmers; the surface only stirs when a boat motors through. Join in the water diversions—a 15-minute **banana boat** ride costs US$1. **Paddle boats** fit up to four (US$1 for 30min.).

The chronically lazy can rent junior **motorboats** to go around the harbor (US$20 per hr.). Requiring less exertion on your part, **tour boats** cruise the harbor (US$30 per hr.). Never fear, high-speed enthusiasts, the sea's the limit on **jet skis** and **waterskis** (both US$20 per hr.). The less busy beach on the western side of the yacht club offers few of the aforementioned diversions, but it also provides peace and quiet.

 NIGHTLIFE

When the sun goes down, Salinas's sandy carnival moves inside, infiltrating the city's bars and *discotecas*. Nightlife in Salinas means bar-hopping; just follow the teeth-rattling music. Frenzied dance action is restricted to the weekends during the off season, but during the *temporada alta* the city gyrates with visitors almost every night. Ask around to find out where the party's at.

El Patio, Calle 27 and Enríquez Gallo, in Hotel Salinas Costa Azul, attracts such a large crowd that they stop letting people in to pacify the fire marshal. Head out back for needed fresh air and a game of pool. Cover US$1.20 includes 1 beer or cuba libre.

Choclo's Café Bar, Malecón and Calle 23. The ultra-friendly owner offers a hip atmosphere, coffee, and beer (US$0.75). Open Th and Su-Tu 6pm-midnight, F-Sa 6pm-4am.

Flintstone's Rockabar, Enríquez Gallo and Calle 25, was recently renovated and is better than ever. The Flintstone motif is subtle—Fred and Wilma lead the way into their respective restrooms but then leave room for a hodgepodge of other themes that somehow fit together. Mixed crowd. Cover US$0.80. Open Th-Sa 9pm-at least 4am.

BAÑOS DE SAN VICENTE ☎ 04

Situated 20km east of La Libertad, the Baños de San Vicente cater to those seeking unity with Mother Nature while they purify their bodies and relax their minds. Hailed as a miracle of natural healing, San Vicente's muddied volcanic crater contains an extraordinary amalgam of 18 minerals, a mixture found only in three places in the world—Germany, France, and Ecuador. Supposedly, the power of this blend of minerals creates a natural panacea for such ailments as arthritis and rheumatism. Those suffering from these afflictions, as well as health-conscious pleasure-seekers, flock to San Vicente to experience this rare form of physical therapy and to enjoy luxurious extras, including massages and steam baths. General admission to the park includes access to the **mud bath,** as well as two *piscinas tibias* (warm water pools) and a natural hot spring. Park employees will tell you exactly how long one should remain in each of these areas in order to attain the maximum overall benefits. (Park open daily 7am-6:30pm. US$0.60, children and senior citizens US$0.30.) **Massages** using mud or *savila*, a natural aloe, relieve tension (US$2), while **hydra-massages**—20 minutes of high-powered jacuzzi jets—soak you for US$1. The park also offers **internal purification,** which involves sweating away the evil buildup of everyday life in the eucalyptus and chamomile scented steam bath (US$1 for 20min.). Chances are they won't have any towels lying around, so you may want to bring your own. Should you decide to spend the night, **Hotel Florida** is just behind the park and has clean rooms with screened windows. (☎ (09) 620 933. Rooms US$3.20 per person; with 3 meals US$10.)

PLAYAS ☎ 04

As the closest beach resort to Guayaquil, Playas (named, not surprisingly, for its sandy beaches) inevitably receives masses of *guayaquileños* during the sweltering weekends. To top it off, it's cheaper than the other major beach resort, making Playas the sunbathing spot of choice for most residents of the southern Sierra. Frequent weekend invasions have left Playas somewhat over-visited and in disrepair—the beach is strewn with litter, the main streets are filled with more dust than sunshine, and the ocean view is obscured by bunches of ceviche stands. Nevertheless, for each weekend's gleeful vacationers, Playas more than suffices as an affordable and almost effortless escape from the city. Far from picturesque, the vast, treeless, litter-sprinkled sands of Playas are popular because there is room for everyone. Playas' nightlife rocks in the *temporada alta*, when clubs like **Mr. Frog,** on Aguilera west of the *centro*, light up the night. Choices are limited in the off-season, but try **Oh Sole Mío,** on Calle 9 before Aguilera heading toward the beach. There are no walls to conceal the wild partying that goes on. (Corona US$1. No cover. Open daily 8am-late.)

Coop Transportes Villamil, Pedro Menéndez Gilbert and 15 de Agosto, sends **buses** to **Guayaquil** (2hr., every 15min. 4am-7:30pm, US$1.15) via **Progreso** (30min., US$0.60). Transportes Urbano has local buses (US$0.10). Most of the town's practical facilities are found along the east-west **15 de Agosto,** Playas' main street. The **central plaza,** a good reference point, is located at 15 de Agosto and Calle 9. **Banco de Guayaquil** (☎760 040), 15 de Agosto and Gilbert, exchanges traveler's checks (on weekends) and cash, and has a Visa/PLUS **ATM.** (Open M-F 8:45am-7pm, Sa 9am-6pm.) The **police,** Asiselo Garay and 15 de Agosto, are on the right-hand side of the street as you head north. (☎761 375. Open 24hr.) **Farmacia Villamil** is on 15 de Agosto between Gilbert and Paquisha. (☎761 607. Open daily 8am-10:30pm.) **Hospital General Villamil Playas** (☎760 328) sits at 15 de Agosto, 1km east of town. Catch a bus to avoid the walk. The **post office,** Asiselo Garay and 15 de Agosto, is next to the police station. (Open M-F 9am-1pm and 3-6pm, Sa 9am-2pm.) **PacificTel,** Aguilera 800m west of town, allows collect and calling card calls for US$0.06 per min. (☎760 120. Open daily 8am-10pm.)

Budget options tend to congregate in the western end of town, along Malecón and Aguilera, but there are a few others dispersed along 15 de Agosto. Somewhat pricier hotels are scattered along Aguilera as it runs to the east from the *centro*. Note that **mosquitos** adore Playas—a fan or netting is essential. **Hotel Rey David,** Calle 9 and Malecón, is a well-lit, glass-enclosed hotel with roomy quarters, fans, firm beds, and clean baths. (☎760 024. Doubles US$10; triples US$15; TV US$5 extra.) For those in the mood for a bit more luxury, **Hostería el Delfín** is worth the walk and the extra dollars. Head east down Aguilera 1½km out of town to the sign for the hotel, then turn right. (☎760 125. Doubles US$14.80; cabañas US$20.88.) **Hotel Tropicana,** is on the left side of Paquisha heading away from 15 de Agosto toward Aguilera. You can't miss the huge sign. Though the hallway isn't particularly attractive, rooms are satisfactory with screened windows, firm beds, and clean baths. (Rooms US$2.40, with bath US$2.80.) The beach is lined with nondescript seafood establishments serving standard coastal dishes (ceviche US$1.60). Other restaurants cluster along Malecón, Aguilera, and Paquisha near the beach. **Sabory Yogurt,** lies on the northeast corner of Gilbert on 15 de Agosto. Feast on warm and scrumptious submarine sandwiches (US$0.30-0.75), yogurt (US$0.35-0.40), and fruit salad.

THE LOWLANDS

SANTO DOMINGO DE LOS COLORADOS   ☎02

Before giving in to concrete urbanity, Santo Domingo belonged to the *indígenas* who gave the city the second part of its name, the **Colorados.** The scant clothing and red bowl-cuts of this tribe are commonly exploited on postcards and store signs. Although you may spot someone from an outside village still sporting the telltale coif, the city today has little connection to its indigenous roots. **Buses** leave around the clock for **Quito** (3hr., US$1.80); **Esmeraldas** (4hr., every 20min. 4am-5:30pm, US$1.60); and **Guayaquil** (5hr., US$2.80). **Filanbanco,** on Quito and Tsachila, changes dollars and traveler's checks. (☎758 889. Open M-F 9am-4pm.) Make **phone calls** from the San Francisco de Asis building, 2nd floor, Quito 1200. (Open daily 8am-10pm.) Hotels are densely packed downtown, especially near 29 de Mayo; most are of the you-get-what-you-pay-for variety. At the lower end of the spectrum is **Hotel Amambay,** 29 de Mayo and Ambato, with basic but comfortable rooms. (☎750 696. Rooms US$1.60 per person.) **Hotel Unicornio,** 29 de Mayo and

Ambato, is around the corner from the movie theater. (☎ 760 147. Singles and doubles US$2, TV US$2.40 extra.) The nearby **Colorados** are considered the only true tourist attraction of Santo Domingo. Some live in hut villages not far from the outskirts of the city, along Quevedo. While the Colorados will let you observe their lifestyle and take pictures, they expect payment. For interesting info on hallucinogenic healing, check out shaman Marcelo Aguavil off the 7km mark from Quevedo. Round-trip taxis to the Colorado villages should cost US$6, including time to roam around and take pictures. Buses marked "Vía Quevedo" also travel along this route. Make sure to ask the driver if the bus goes to the "end of the line" ("*a la última parada*"); certain buses on Quevedo stay within city limits.

QUEVEDO   ☎ 05

Visitors who aren't looking for any special attractions, don't mind not having their tourist needs catered to, and happen to be in the area at nightfall are those you'll find in Quevedo. Bordering the Río Quevedo, the *centro* is typical—tall buildings, street-side commerce, and lots of noise. **Buses** from Quevedo go to: **Guayaquil** (3hr.; every 20min. 4am-6:30pm; US$1.48); **Quito** (5hr.; 6:30, 7:20, 8:50am, 5:15, 7:20pm; US$2.40); **Santo Domingo** (2hr.; 7:30, 10, 11:30am, 3, 4, 5, 6:30, 9pm; US$1.04); **Ambato** (6hr.; US$2.48); and **Cuenca** (8hr.; 9am and 9pm; US$5.20). **Filanbanco** has a 24-hour Visa/Plus **ATM** on Bolívar between Cuarto and Quinto. The **police** (☎ 750 361) are on Novena between Progreso and Cortes. The hospital, **Hospital Centro de Salud de Quevedo,** is at Guayacanes 400 (☎ 755 031). **Sandy.net,** 7 de Octubre and Primera, offers cheap **Internet service** (US$1.60 per hr.) and netphone for international calls (US$0.32 per min. and up). The **IETEL telephone office** is on 7 de Octubre and Décima Tercera, but is more expensive than using the netphone. (☎ 754 223. Open daily 8am-10pm.) Hotels in Quevedo are nothing to write home about, but they get the job done. **Hotel Imperial,** Malecón and Séptima, overlooks the market. Rooms provide basic private baths, fans, and concave beds. (☎ 751 654. Singles US$1.20; doubles US$2.40.)

GUAYAQUIL   ☎ 04

Once an indigenous settlement, Guayaquil (pop. 2,000,000) was conquered by the Spanish in the 16th century. Legend has it that before surrendering their beloved home (and with it, their pride), the native prince and princess committed suicide. His name was Guayas, her name Quil, and from their martyrdom was born the name of the most populous city in Ecuador. Guayaquil, the economic capital of Ecuador, attracts few travelers, but nonetheless brims with movement and energy. Here, wealthier neighborhoods offer modern malls, theaters, and gourmet restaurants, while *el centro* contains the dilapidated, albeit fascinating, 400-year-old, tin-roofed Las Peñas *barrio*. The downtown area houses grand government palaces, beautiful parks, skyscraping monuments, ornate churches, and interesting museums, along with the partially completed Malecón 2000 strip, the city's newest and largest attraction. *El norte*—comprised by neighborhoods north of the *centro* such as Alborada, Urdesa, and Kennedy—is replete with choice restaurants and neuron-jolting nightlife. Finally, the insane crowds at mega-disco El Jardín de la Salsa and the Bacchanalian revelry of the wandering *chivas* (party buses) that cruise the streets of this part of town have given Guayaquil's nightlife a reputation as the wildest, most memorable around.

▌ TRANSPORTATION

Airport: Simón Bolívar International Airport (☎ 282 100; fax 290 018), on Américas, about 5km north of the city. The airport has two terminals about 3km apart. The larger one houses national and international flights; the smaller is the place to catch *avionetas* (smaller planes) to national destinations. **Avionetas** run to **Machala, Manta, Bahía,** and **Portoviejo.** A **taxi** ride to the heart of the *centro* US$1.20-3. Numerous **buses** also go to the *centro* for US$0.15.

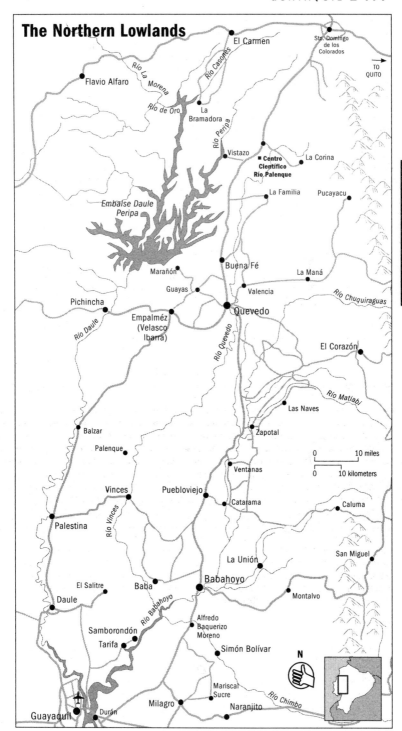

The Northern Lowlands

El Carmen

Sto. Domingo de los Colorados

TO QUITO

Flavio Alfaro

Río La Morena

Río Casones

La Bramadora

Río de Oro

Vistazo

Río Peripa

Centro Científico Río Palenque

La Corina

Embalse Daule Peripa

La Familia

Pucayacu

Marañón

Buena Fé

La Maná

Guayas

Valencia

Río Chuquiraguas

Pichincha

Quevedo

Río Daule

Empalméz (Velasco Ibarra)

Río Quevedo

El Corazón

Río Matiabí

Las Naves

Balzar

Zapotal

0   10 miles

0   10 kilometers

Palenque

Ventanas

Vinces

Puebloviejo

Caluma

Río Vinces

Catarama

Palestina

La Unión

San Miguel

El Salitre

Baba

Babahoyo

Daule

Río Babahoyo

Montalvo

Alfredo Baquerizo Moreno

Samborondón

Tarifa

Simón Bolívar

N

Mariscal Sucre

Río Chimbo

Milagro

Naranjito

Guayaquil

Durán

Guayaquil Centro

▲ ACCOMMODATIONS

Ecuahogar (HI), **1**
Hotel Alexander, **10**
Hotel California, **2**
Hotel Caprí, **6**
Hotel Delicia, **13**
Hotel Doral, **16**
Hotel Ecuador, **12**
Hotel Rizzo, **18**
Hotel Sander, **11**
Hotel Vélez, **7**

◆ FOOD

Cafetería El Malecón, **3**
La Canoa, **19**
Las 3 Canastas, **14**
Peña Restaurant Pailoteca, **9**
Restaurant Vegetariano, **8**

🏛 MUSEUMS

Ecuador Antigua Museo
  Arqueológico, **15**
Museo Antropológico, **5**
Museo de Arte Prehistórico, **4**
Museo Municipal, **20**
Museo Nahim Isaías B., **17**

Flights: TAME, 9 de Octubre 424 and P. Icaza (☎560 778), in the Gran Pasaje Building. Open M-F 9am-6pm, Sa 9am-noon. To: **Quito** (30min.; M-F 10 per day 7:45am-8:30pm, Sa 6 per day 8:30am-6pm, Su 7 per day 7:45am-7:15pm; US$92 round-trip); **Cuenca** (25min., 5:15pm, US$59); **Loja** (30min.; M, Th, F, Sa 5:45am; US$50); **Machala** (25min., M-F 8:15am and 3:30pm, US$44); and the **Galapagos** (1½hr.; 9:15 and 11:30am; round-trip Jan. 6-June 14 and Sept. 1-Nov. 30 US$295, June 15-Aug. 30 and Nov. 31-Jan. 5 US$340; student discount US$50 with ISIC). Ecuatoriana (☎326 724), Malecón and 9 de Octubre, offers international flights. Open M-F 8:30am-6pm, Sa 9am-noon. SAN/SAETA does not currently service flights to Galapagos, but may resume doing so in the near future; inquire at the airport.

Trains: Due to damage from El Niño, train service out of Guayaquil is no longer available. In order to catch the Devil's Nose "express," you will need to catch a bus at the terminal going to Alausí (4hr.).

Regional Buses: Jaime Roldós Aguilera Terminal Terrestre Américas, a few kilometers north of the airport. Tons of *boleterías* sell similarly priced tickets. To: **Quito** (8hr., 23 per day 12:15am-11:50pm, US$5.60); **Cuenca** (4 per day 1:30am-11:15pm, US$4); **Salinas** (2½hr., every 10min. 3:30am-10:30pm, US$1.60); **Playas** (2hr., every 10min. 4:30am-8:10pm, US$0.75); **Santo Domingo** (5hr., every 30min. 3am-8:15pm, US$2.55) via **Quevedo** (4hr., US$1.50); **Riobamba** (6hr., 2:45 and 8pm, US$2.60); **Manta** (3¾hr., every hr. 3:30am-11pm, US$2.40); **Machala** (3hr., every 30min. 4:30am-10pm, US$2.40); **Esmeraldas** (7½hr., 9 and 11am, US$5.20); and **Huaquillas** (4½hr., 11 per day 1:05am-11:05pm, US$3).

Travel Agencies: Guayaquil is bloated with travel agencies. However, there are not nearly as many offering Galapagos packages as in Quito. **Galapagos Discovery** (☎/fax 566 303; email mauponce@gu.pro.ec; www.galapagosklein.com), Chimborazo between 9 de Octubre and P. Icaza, not only arranges Galapagos tours (from US$110 per day) but also has an informative gray book in English about the archipelago. They also have an office in Puerto Ayora (see **Practical Information,** p. 584). Open M-F 9am-6pm. **Galasam,** 9 de Octubre 424 (☎304 488), on the ground floor of the Gran Pasaje Building, offers jungle tours, Galapagos tours, and tours around Quito, Cotopaxi, and Otavalo. Economical Galapagos tours last 1 week, visit 5 islands, and include 3 meals per day and a guide (US$500). Open M-F 9am-6pm, Sa 9am-1pm. **Guayatur** (☎322 441), Aguirre between Malecón and Pichincha, might also be able to arrange relatively inexpensive tours. Open M-F 9am-6:30pm. **National Tours** (☎322 374 or 321 705), next door to Guayatar, offers tours of the Galapagos, Sierra, and Amazon. Open M-F 9am-6pm, Sa 9am-noon.

Ferries: A boat leaves to **Durán** (20min., every hr. 10am-6pm, US$0.15) from the waterfront at Malecón (Sgt. Vargas) and Cuenca.

City Buses: The cheapest (US$0.15) and fastest way to get around. Routes are seemingly endless in number. Many buses take 9 de Octubre, Quito, or Malecón and travel throughout the *centro,* as well as to outlying *ciudadelas* such as Alborada, Kennedy, Urdesa, Garzota, and Sauces. Confirm that the bus stops exactly where you want to go as soon as you get on. They are usually too crowded to carry much luggage.

Taxis: Guayaquil's drivers are notorious for taking advantage of tourists; suggest a price and turn a driver away if he doesn't agree. Taxis within the *centro* US$1.20; taxis between the *centro* and the airport or outlying *ciudadelas* US$1.20-3. Try the dispatch **Taxi del Guayas** (☎301 393) or **Taxi Paraíso** (☎201 877).

Car Rental: Avis (☎395 554), **Budget** (☎288 510 or 284 559), and **Hertz** (☎293 011) have offices at the airport, outside the international departures entrance. Minimum age 25. A car is unnecessary and cumbersome in Guayaquil. US$26-115 per day.

▞ ORIENTATION

Guayaquil sprawls far to the north and south, but the two square kilometers comprising the *centro* next to the river is easy enough to navigate. **Malecón** is a bus-laden thoroughfare that parallels the **Malecón 2000** waterfront strip (see Sights, p. 482) on the east side of the *centro.* **9 de Octubre,** the main east-west boulevard in the city, starts at Malecón by **La Rotonda** and passes through the central **Parque Centenario**. The T formed by 9 de Octubre and Malecón outlines the most tourist-essential parts of the *centro*. Most places outside the *centro* are identified in terms of the neighborhood, or *ciudadela*, in which they are located. The safety of these suburbs varies a good deal. The upper-class neighborhoods of **Urdesa** and **Alborada** are generally safer than the downtown and can be easily reached by cab or bus.

> Guayaquil frequently hosts public demonstrations. Many of these occur in the *centro*. Unauthorized marches are often dispersed by the police with tear gas; if you find yourself in or near a demonstration, use your best judgement in deciding whether or not to hang around; *Let's Go* clearly recommends steering clear of any possibly dangerous demonstration.

PRACTICAL INFORMATION

TOURIST AND FINANCIAL SERVICES

Tourist Offices: Ministry of Tourism (☎568 764; fax 562 544; email infotour @telconet.net), Pichincha and Icaza, 6th fl., across the street from Banco del Pacífico. Several employees speak English; Alejandra is especially helpful. Open M-F 8:30am-5pm.

Consulates: Canada, Córdova 812 and Manuel Rendón, 21st fl., Office 4 (☎563 580; fax 314 562). Open M-F 9am-noon. **UK,** Córdova 623 and Padre Solano (☎560 400 or 563 850; fax 562 641; weekend emergency ☎(09) 723 021). Open M-F 9am-noon and 2-4pm. **US** (☎323 570; fax 325 286; 24hr. emergency ☎(02) 321 152), 9 de Octubre and García Moreno. Open M-F 8am-noon and 1-5pm.

Currency Exchange: The first several blocks of 9 de Octubre, starting from the waterfront, are loaded with banks and *casas de cambio*. **Cambiosa** (☎325 199 or 517 174), on 9 de Octubre, between Pichincha and Malecón. Open M-F 9am-5pm. **Banco del Pacífico** (☎328 333), near Malecón at Pichincha and Icaza. There is a **branch office** (☎329 831), west of the Parque Centenario at 9 de Octubre and Ejército. Both have 24hr. Cirrus/MC **ATMs.** Both open M-F 8:45am-4pm. **Filanbanco** (☎321 780), 9 de Octubre and Pichincha, has a 24hr. Visa/PLUS **ATM.** Open M-F 8:30am-6pm.

American Express: 9 de Octubre 1900 and Esmeraldas (☎394 984 or 286 900), 2nd fl. English is spoken. Open M-F 9am-1pm and 2-6pm. Send mail to: Ecuadorian Tours, American Express, 9 de Octubre 1900, Guayaquil, Ecuador.

Western Union: There are many Western Union operators scattered throughout the *centro*. The only 24hr. office (☎1 800 937 837) is in Alborada, Guillermo Pareja Rolando 565, in the *Edificio de Bronce*.

EMERGENCY AND COMMUNICATIONS

Emergency: ☎911. **Fire:** ☎102. **Information:** ☎104.

Police: (☎101), on Américas several kilometers from the *centro* toward the airport.

Pharmacy: Scattered throughout the downtown area. One popular chain is **Fybeca,** in Urdesa at Estrada 609 and Las Monjas (☎881 444; open 24hr.).

Medical Services: Hospital Clínica Kennedy (☎289 666 ext. 470, emergency ext. 100), across the street from the Policentro mall, is where tourists should go for emergency medical attention. **Clínica Guayaquil,** Padre Aguirre 401 and Córdova (☎843 487; **emergency** ☎322 308). **Red Cross** ambulance service (☎560 674 or 560 675).

Telephones: PacificTel, at Ballén and Pedro Carbo, in the same building as the post office. International calls require a deposit (US$2-6). Though they may say calling card and collect calls aren't possible, ask if they can dial one of the long distance operators (MCI ☎999 170; AT&T ☎999 119). Open daily 8am-9:30pm. Pre-paid phone cards for BellSouth and Porta pay phones can be purchased from stores around town.

A LEGEND OF QUIL Since the beginning of Guayaquil, sacrifices of women have helped define the city. Three hundred years after the indigenous princess Quil immortalized her memory by killing herself for her native home (see above), another woman, **Rosa Borja de Icaza,** immortalized herself through her dedication to social justice. As one of Ecuador's first and most prominent feminists, Borja, born in 1889, began working for the poor and publishing her first poems shortly after her 1916 marriage. After spending from 1920 to 1923 in Germany, Borja returned to her native Guayaquil and, along with some other young and gutsy women, dedicated herself to the improvement of opportunities for her gender. In 1929, Borja supported a women's conference at a Guayaquil university, causing a ruckus among those who preferred to limit a woman's role to the home. Borja herself, in 1932, founded the **Feminine Legion of Popular Education.** In the next several years, she worked for the education and safety of women and children. Borja racked up many important positions in the city and community, enabling her to further advance her work. Late in life, she published an autobiography and other books—such as *Impresiones,* a collection of her lectures at the Feminine Culture Club of Quito. Many attest that no one else has had such an influence on the Ecuadorian social conscience.

Internet Access: AllComp, on Quito and Velez, 2nd fl., offers cheap service (US$0.80 per hr.). **Ecuanet** (☎562 577), Icaza and Pichincha, 3rd fl. of Banco del Pacífico building, charges the same. Open M-F 9am-6:30pm, Su 11am-2pm. Though a bit more costly, **Express Internet Club** (☎306 159), Córdova and 9 de Octubre, offers netphone service (from US$0.08 per min.) and Internet service (US$1.50 per hr.). Open M-Sa 9am-10pm.

Post Office: On the west side of Pedro Carbo between Aguirre and Ballén. Open M-F 8am-5:30pm, Sa 9am-noon.

ACCOMMODATIONS

Guayaquil has many strengths, but budget accommodations are not among them. There's only one hostel in the city, and lower-end hotels aren't very cheap and are often in not-so-safe areas. The hotels in the busiest part of the *centro* are bursting with amenities but also are quite expensive.

Hotel Vélez Velez 1021 (☎530 356 or 530 311), between Quito and Pedro Moncayo. Safe and central *centro* location. Firm beds, spotless, cold-water bathrooms, TVs. 24hr. restaurant. Rooms US$5.90 per person, with A/C US$6.30.

Ecuahogar (HI) (☎/fax 248 357; email youthost@telconet.net; www.ecuahostellint.net), Isidrio Ayora in Ciudadela. Near the airport and bus terminal. Rooms are clean and have mediocre fans. Laundry service (US$2 per load), Internet (US$2 per hr.), safe deposit box, currency exchange. Breakfast included. Reservation through web site suggested. Dorms US$8; singles and quads US$10 per person; doubles US$11 per person; rooms with bath US$12 per person. HI/ISIC members US$1 discount.

Hotel Capri (☎517 880; or 530 093), Machala and Luque, provides plain but comfortable rooms; marble bed frames add pizzazz. All rooms have A/C, TV, and hot bath. Matrimonials US$6.75; dorm US$32.

Hotel California (☎302 538; fax 562 548), Urdaneta and Ximena, puts safety first. A/C, private bath, cable TV. Cafeteria open 7am-10pm. Singles and doubles US$6.60; triples US$7.70; extra bed US$2.10; refrigerator, phone, and hot water US$5 extra.

Hotel Alexander, Luque 1107 between Quito and Moncayo. A/C, color TV, hot water in private baths, and phones. Reservations suggested. Singles US$17; matrimonials US$20; doubles US$22; triples US$26; luxury suite US$30; 10% service tax.

Hotel Delicia, Ballén 1105 and Moncayo (☎324 925). Not the best area. Basic rooms have comfy beds. Bolted security gate. Singles US$2, with bath and TV US$4; doubles US$4.80, with bath and TV US$5.60; triples US$7.20, with bath and TV US$8.40.

Hotel Ecuador (☎321 460), Moncayo between Luque and Aguirre. Not particularly exciting, but cheap for the area. All rooms have TV and bath. Restaurant. Singles or doubles US$4, with A/C US$4.80.

Hotel Doral, Chile 402 and Aguirre (☎328 490; fax 327 088). Carpeted rooms have all the amenities. Offers a tasty complimentary breakfast. Singles and doubles US$30.

Hotel Rizzo, Ballén 319 and Chile (☎325 210). Simple rooms have tile floors, cable TV, and refrigerators. Includes complimentary breakfast. Singles and doubles US$10.

FOOD

THE CENTRO

Along the sidewalks of the *centro*, locals frequent the numerous, one-room restaurants whose few tables spill out into the streets. These similar *comedores* serve cheap *almuerzos* and *meriendas*. Often, though, price tags reflect food quality.

■ **La Canoa** (☎329 270, ext. 227 or 228), Chile between Ballén and 10 de Agosto, next to the Hotel Continental. Both the heavily-used cappuccino machine and chefs churn out goodies 24/7. Good, quick service. Salad US$0.90. Rice dishes US$1.40. French toast US$1.20. Pastries US$1.10-2.10. Coffee US$0.90. Open 24hr.

Restaurant Vegetariano, Moncayo 1015 (☎519 955), between Luque and Vélez. Carrot bread (US$0.40) and fresh juices are just a few treats served between the bright walls of this tiny restaurant. Soy substitution *almuerzos* US$0.80. Open daily 8am-10pm.

Peña Restaurant Pailoteca, Luque between Moncayo and 6 de Marzo, offers hefty meat dishes (US$1-1.20). Live music F-Sa. Open M-W 8am-10pm, Th-Sa 8am-1am.

Las 3 Canastas, Vélez and Chile, under the 10-story building with the DELI sign. Looking for *batidos?* You're in luck—this quick-service diner offers 38 flavors. Submarine sandwich US$0.40-0.60. Fruit salad US$0.70. Open daily.

Cafetería El Malecón (☎565 555), Malecón and Orellana, next to Hotel Ramada. Giant murals of aquatic life and well-dressed waiters. *Comida típica* US$1.65-3.55. Sandwiches US$2. Salads US$2.65. Open daily 6am-2am.

NORTH OF THE CENTRO

The eateries on Victor Emilio Estrada in the **Urdesa** strip tend to be a bit more expensive than many *centro* options, but several restaurants offer delicious food for reasonable prices. **Alborada** has a high concentration of fast food joints; look on Guillermo Pareja Rolando for higher-quality restaurants.

■ **Tsuji de Japon,** Victor Emilio Estrada 813 (☎881 183 or 882 641), between Guayacanes and Higueras in Urdesa. Cross the red-banister bridge to the first Japanese restaurant of this caliber in Guayaquil. Sit back, relax, and watch the cook grill up *parilladas* (US$5-13) at your table. Sushi bar US$0.65-1.90. Karaoke. Open daily noon-3pm and 7-11pm.

Lo Nuestro, Estrada 903 and Higueras (☎386 398 or 882 168), in Urdesa. The elegant and intimate ambiance makes dining feel like a special occasion; fabulous food just makes it better. Entrees US$1.80-3.60. Open daily noon-midnight.

La Parrilla del Ñato, Estrada 1219 (☎387 098), in Urdesa. You can't miss the gigantic sign or the smell of meat and chicken grilling on an open stove. Huge and popular with suburban *guayaquileños*. Servings are big. Hearty portions of pizza (US$0.60-0.75).

◉ SIGHTS

Few travelers make an effort to squeeze Guayaquil into their busy itineraries, and they're not missing too much. The city, however, is sprinkled with parks, museums, historic buildings, and other landmarks that make for a good sightseeing.

MALECÓN 2000. Spanning some 25 blocks along the Río Guayas waterfront, the grand-scale urban regeneration project known as Malecón 2000 has become the new major attraction of Guayaquil. Started in September of 1998, the entire chrome-gated strip, including the **ecological park** and **Museo Banco Central** to the north, should be completed by 2001. Much of the strip resembles the typical *parque*, with grassy areas, trees, benches, and beautiful **fountains** and **statues.** One of the principal sights is the awe-inspiring **Rotonda** at 9 de Octubre, which commemorates Bolívar and San Martín's secret 1822 Guayaquil meeting. Farther south by 10 de Agosto is the four-story **clock tower,** a Moorish-style structure traditionally used to call the city people to prayer. Situated across the street from the clock tower is the grand **Palacio Municipal** and the adjacent **Palacio de Gobernacion.** The two are separated by the **Parque Sucre,** which contains a monument of **Mariscal Antonio Jose de Sucre,** an independence-movement war hero. Along the boardwalk are *miradores* (lookout points), and toward the far southern end is a **commercial center** which parallels parts of the Bahía shopping plaza (see Shopping, p. 485).

IGUANA PARK. With the alternate aliases of **Parque Bolívar** and **Parque Seminario,** this attraction is commonly known by what it contains—loads of iguanas. They're big and small; they pace the walkways and climb the tree, gobble vegetation and pose for the cameras. While these reptiles are pleasant in their slow and methodi-

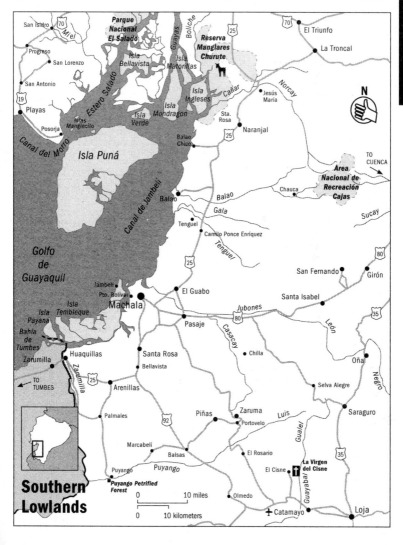

WESTERN ECUADOR

cal movements, these bad boys are notorious for spontaneously ejecting streams of liquid excrement from their tree-top hide-outs. Tourists aren't pooped on regularly, but it's wise to keep an eye out for flying bowel-pellets. When not dodging such projectiles, visitors appreciate the 43 species of flora and fauna, the **statue of Simón Bolívar,** and the massive **cathedral** across the street (see **Churches,** below).

CHURCHES. Some of Guayaquil's most beautiful buildings are its old Catholic churches. In addition to the Iglesia de Santo Domingo (see p. 485) at the north end of Rocafuerte, there are several beautiful churches in the *centro* as well. The most recent version of **La Merced,** on Rocafuerte and Rendón, was constructed in 1938, the same year as the most recent Santo Domingo renovation. Where Rocafuerte becomes Pedro Carbo, the *centro* opens up to a plaza dominated by the facade of the **Iglesia de San Francisco.** The altar of this impressive cathedral is covered with ornate gold work. The **Metropolitan Cathedral,** on Chimborazo between Balléen and 10 de Agosto, might be the most spectacular church in town, with a striking gray-and-white interior and spectacular stained-glass windows. The Metropolitan Cathedral overlooks **Iguana Park.**

MUSEUMS

MUSEO NAHIM ISAÍAS BARQUET. This museum has two large, square-shaped halls. The first displays regional artifacts from prehistoric Ecuadorian cultures; the other houses colonial religious painting and sculpture. English pamphlets are available. *(Pichincha and Ballén. ☎510 784 or 510 818. Open M-Sa 10am-5pm. Free.)*

ECUADOR ANTIGUO MUSEO ARQUAEOLÓGICO. The museum has a comprehensive archaeological collection with detailed explanations (in English and Spanish) that inform visitors about everything from developments during Ecuador's pioneering Formative era to shamanic hallucinogenic healing practices in the tropical forest region. The third floor is reserved for temporary exhibits of modern art. *(Ycaza 113, between Malecón and Pichincha. ☎566 010 or 563 744 ext. 5390 91; fax 564 636. Open M-F 9am-6pm, Sa-Su 11am-1pm. Free.)*

OTHER ARCHAEOLOGICAL MUSEUMS. Across town, the **Museo de Arte Prehistórico** is perched on the western side of the Parque Centenario on the sixth floor. *(9 de Octubre and Moncayo. ☎300 500 or 300 586 ext. 102. Open Tu-F 10am-6pm, Sa 9am-3pm. US$0.20.)* Larger and better displayed, however, is the **Museo Antropológico del Banco Central de Ecuador,** which contains detailed exhibits, an interactive computer display in Spanish and English, and a knowledgeable staff. *(9 de Octubre and José de Anteparra. ☎327 402. Open Tu-F 10am-6pm, Sa-Su 10am-2pm. US$1.)* The **Museo Municipal** has a permanent exhibition of paintings of Ecuador's presidents, as well as an archaeological exhibit, and temporary exhibits. *(Sucre between Chile and Pedro Carbo, attached to the library. ☎524 100 ext. 7401. Open Tu-Sa 9am-12:30pm and 1-5pm. Free guided tours Sa 10am, noon, 2pm. Free.)*

OF FIRES AND FORGOTTEN TIMES If it seems that an unusually high number of Guayaquil's buildings were constructed in the last 100 years or so, it's probably because only in this century has Guayaquil managed to avoid getting its behind whooped by a nasty, out-of-control fire. Although Guayaquil was struck by *incendios* in 1592, 1620, 1624, 1632, 1678, 1693... (and continued in that manner for another 200 years or so), the fire that has earned the coveted title of **Incendio Grande** swept through the city on October 5-6, 1896. Burning for almost 30 hours straight, it destroyed 92 blocks (a fifth of the city), including the Las Peñas neighborhood, reaching as far south as Aguirre. Over half of Guayaquil's population was rendered homeless by this fire and two earlier ones which occurred in February and August of the same year. But the *guayaquileños,* being as tough and as proud as they are today, fought *incendio* with *incendio*—with a blaze of rebuilding, that is. By the end of 1899, the *Cuerpo de Bomberos de Guayaquil* (association of fire-fighters) had finally been established, and with the exception of two large conflagrations in 1901 and 1902, Guayaquil has been nearly fire-free ever since.

NORTH OF THE CENTRO

LAS PEÑAS. The Las Peñas neighborhood, climbing the hills that begin at Malecón's northern end, contains Guayaquil's oldest houses. The product of over 460 years of development, Las Peñas has been destroyed and rebuilt several times since Guayaquil's devastating 17th, 18th, and 19th centuries. The lack of empty land and obvious non-existent urban planning testify to the area's age. Tin-roofed homes pile onto each other, some rising majestically at the water's edge. The higher one goes, the more spectacular the views of the city and the river become. Many important Ecuadorian artists and other heroic figures were born in this neighborhood, including the composer of the Ecuadorian national anthem. A number of the houses in the neighborhood have been turned into art galleries that became important exhibition centers during festivals. The local Ministry of Tourism office recommends taking a guide along when exploring Las Peñas; don't venture into this part of the city alone at night. Day explorations tend to be fairly safe, however. Contact one of the many travel agencies in town to see about a guide.

THE CEMETERY. Guayaquil's hillside cemetery, west of the Las Peñas neighborhood, faces the city from the north as well. Mausoleums and elaborate tombs crowd the slopes of this virtual city-of-the-dead like mini high-rises, and pathways wind like streets through the resting sites. The cemetery is sometimes called **La Ciudad Blanca** ("The White City"), because of its size and the preponderance of white marble. *(Take buses from the centro labeled "cementerio," or give it a quick look from taxis or buses on the way in and out of the centro.)*

ENTERTAINMENT

FESTIVALS

Guayaquil's serious disposition is left in the dust during its festivals. July is an exciting month, with Simón Bolívar's birthday on July 24 and the anniversary of the city's founding on July 25, both of which involve parades and concerts. October 9 is the anniversary of Guayaquil's Independence.

SHOPPING

Guayaquil has all the malls and specialty stores of a big city, so if you are looking for something, it's probably here. There are plenty of stores in the area between **9 de Octubre** and **Parque Bolívar.** For a more US-style shopping experience, take a bus or cab to the new **Mall del Sol**, north of the *centro*. Practically every sign and store name is in English, and there's a food court (with every kind of American fast food), an arcade, and a 24-hour restaurant. The **Policentro Shopping Center** in Ciudadela Kennedy provides quite the modern shopping experience as well. An **artisan's market** offers indigenous crafts on Loja and Baquerizo Moreno near Las Peñas (open M-Sa 9:30am-6:30pm). For very cheap (often contraband) items sold in a crowded, labyrinthine street market, head to the **Bahía**, in Pedro Carbo and Villamil between Olmedo and Colón.

MOVIES

Guayaquil has plenty of cinemas in the *centro*, in surrounding *ciudades*, and in malls and shopping centers. The most notable are **Cinemark,** in the Mall del Sol (☎ 692 013; US$0.80), **Albocines,** at the Plaza Mayor in Alborada (☎ 244 986; US$0.60); and the **Maya**, Las Lomas and Dátules in Urdesa (☎ 386 456; US$0.60).

◪ NIGHTLIFE

As the saying goes, spend your days in Quito and your nights in Guayaquil. The city might not draw a considerable number of tourists, but it certainly lures enough locals to its wild, exciting, and ever-changing nightspots. Clubs and *discotecas* in the *centro* light the sky in shades of neon until sunrise, but the downtown area can be dangerous and unpredictable. A safer option is to hit the clubs and bars out of the *centro*. Many hot spots lie along Victor Emilio Estrada in Urdesa, Francisco de Orellano in Kennedy Norte, and Guillermo Pureja Rolando in Alboraba.

▨ **El Jardín de la Salsa,** Las Américas 140 (☎396 083), between the airport and the terminal. The hottest night spot in Ecuador. With a capacity of 6000, this stadium-sized disco is packed with anyone and everyone. Pitchers of beer US$2.

Alto Nivel, in Urdesa Norte, next to the huge TV antennae, is worth the US$1.60 taxi ride from the *centro*. Dance, techno, salsa. Funky atmosphere. Cover US$4, includes unlimited beer and mixed drinks. Open daily until 4am.

Chappu's Beer, on Estrada, 1 block from Manantial in Urdesa, has patios overlooking the street. Bamboo banisters, stone walls, and a small dance floor add excitement to the laid-back atmosphere. Beer US$2. No cover. Open M-Th 6pm-midnight, F-Sa 6pm-2am.

KENNEDY NORTE

Kennedy Mall, off Francisco de Orellano, has a cluster of clubs and bars. Beer costs around US$0.80, and several are usually included in the cover. **Mr. Babilla Bar and Grill** has walls lined with picture frames, a bar, and a packed dance floor. (Cover US$3.20, includes 4 beers. Open Th-Sa 8pm-4am.) **Disco Bar Bananas** has the most spacious dance floor. (Cover US$2, includes 1 beer. Open W-Sa 8pm-4am.)

▨ CHIVAS

Guayaquil continues its tradition of over-the-top entertainment with its *chivas*. These huge trucks carry over 100 revelers: hanging out the windows, on the hood, and off the roof, where the Latin band plays. *Guayaquileños* rent these portable parties for birthdays or other occasions; although they certainly don't happen every night, travelers who happen to see them passing by can usually hop on (for a price). They can often be spotted in front of El Jardín de la Salsa.

MACHALA ☎07

The self-proclaimed "banana capital of the world," the growing town of Machala (pop. 250,000) takes its fruit seriously. As the second largest Ecuadorian export, the value of the banana is listed in daily newspapers, alongside the value of the dollar and the price of gold. Machala greets entering visitors with a huge statue of El Bananero, a larger-than-life banana grower carrying an eight-foot bunch. Locals extol the sacred fruit with a banana festival during the third week in September. Festivities include the selection of one lucky lady to receive the highest honor the city has to offer—the coveted Banana Queen title. Its lively atmosphere and proximity to the fresh seafood and clean beaches of Puerto Bolívar and Jambelí make Machala an good place to stop before braving the border crossing to Peru.

◰ TRANSPORTATION

Flights: The **airport** is a few blocks south of the main plaza on Montalvo. TAME flies to **Guayaquil** (30min., M-F 9:10am and 3:50pm, US$22) and **Quito** (1hr., US$72). Flights to Cuenca or the Galapagos from Guayaquil can be arranged at **TAME** (☎930 139), on Juan Montalvo between Bolívar and Pichincha. Open M-F 7:30am-4:30pm.

Buses: Ecuatoriano Pullman, at the corner of 9 de Octubre, between Tarquí and Colón; Rutas Orenses, 9 de Octubre 706; and CIFA all send buses to **Guayaquil** (3hr., every 30min.) from the corner of Bolívar and Guayas or 9 de Octubre between Tarquí and Colón. CIFA (☎933 735) also sends buses to the Peruvian border at **Huaquillas** (1hr. direct, 2hr. local; every 10min. 4:30am-7:45pm; US$1 direct, US$0.90 local) via **Santa Rosa** (40min., US$0.30) and **Arenillas** (1hr., US$0.60). Panamericana, on the corner of Bolívar and Colón, goes to **Quito** (12hr., 7 per day 7:45am-10:30pm; US$6.40), as does TAC (12hr., 8:15 and 10pm, US$4), on Colón between Rocafuerte and Bolívar. TAC (☎930 119) also travels to **Zaruma** (3hr., every hr. 4am-7pm, US$1.50) via **Piñas** (2hr.) and **Portovelo** (2½hr.). Both Coop Pullman Azuay, on Sucre between Junín and Tarquí, and Rutas Orenses, 9 de Octubre 706 go to **Cuenca** (4hr.; Pullman 1, 2, 3am and every 30min. 4am-10:45pm; Rutas Orenses 18 per day 5am-6:15pm; US$2.20). Loja Internacional (☎932 030) on Tarquí between Rocafuerte and Bolívar, travels to: **Loja** (6hr., 8 per day, US$3.40); **Zamora** (8hr., 9pm, US$4.80); and **Ambato** (8hr., 10:30pm, US$4.40).

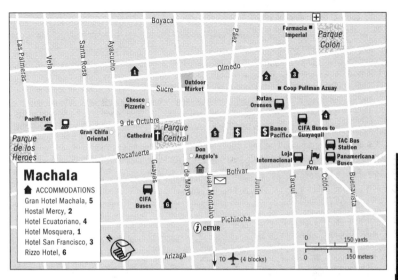

Machala

↟ ACCOMMODATIONS
Gran Hotel Machala, 5
Hostal Mercy, 2
Hotel Ecuatoriano, 4
Hotel Mosquera, 1
Hotel San Francisco, 3
Rizzo Hotel, 6

WESTERN ECUADOR

💥❔ ORIENTATION AND PRACTICAL INFORMATION

Streets in Machala use names and numbers. **9 de Mayo** is the main north-south strip, running past the **market** and the **main plaza,** where it intersects with busy **9 de Octubre.** The **church** spire on the west side of the plaza is a good landmark. Buses leave from the eastern six-block grid defined by Junín, Bolívar, Colón, and Sucre.

Tourist Information: CETUR (☎932 106), 9 de Mayo and Pichincha, 3rd fl. Spanish-speaking staff answers questions and offers a map booklet. Open M-F 8:30am-2:30pm.

Consulate: Peruvian (☎930 680; fax 937 040), on Bolívar near Colón in an unmarked gray building, 2nd fl., room 102. Open M-F 9am-6pm.

Bank: Banco del Pacífico (☎930 700), at Rocafuerte and Junín, is the only place that changes traveler's checks and cash. 24hr. **Cirrus/MC ATM.** Open M-F 8:45am-5pm.

Emergency: ☎101.

Police: (☎930 449; fax 933 911), 9 de Mayo and Manual Serrano. Open 24hr.

Pharmacies: Farmacia Imperial, Boyaca 601 (☎938 120). Open 24hr.

Hospital: Hospital Teofilo Davila, Buenavista and Boyaca 502 (☎937 581, emergency ☎939 099), in front of the Parque Colón.

Telephones: PacificTel (☎920 050; fax 922 666), 9 de Octubre between Anda de las Palmeras and Vela, handles collect and calling card calls. Open daily 8am-10pm.

Internet: Cyber@yogur, 9 de Mayo 2120 (☎939 962). US$1 per hr. Open M-Sa 8:30am-10pm. **@qui.net,** 9 de Octubre 1324 and Ayacucho (☎935 017; email aquinet@cue.satnet.net). US$1.20 per hr. Open M-Sa 8am-10pm, Su 8am-4pm.

Post Office: Correos, Bolívar 733 and Juan Montalvo (☎930 675; fax 931 908). Open M-F 7:30am-7:30pm, Sa 9am-1pm.

🏨 ACCOMMODATIONS

Because of the large number of tourists spending the night in Machala, budget accommodations abound. Anyone staying overnight in Machala should check for window screens or mosquito nets. Also make sure your room has a fan. Hotels closer to the center of town, while usually noisier, tend to be the safest.

Hostal Mercy, Junín 915 (☎920 116), at Olmedo and Sucre. Clean rooms with private cold-water baths and A/C. Sweet, grandparent-like owners. Rooms US$2 perr person.

HERE'S SOMETHING A'PEELING

Ripe *(maduro)* or unripe *(verde)*, cooked or raw, for dinner or dessert, *el banano* (or *el guineo*) and its less-sweet cousin, *el plátano* (plaintain), have inspired countless culinary wonders in the kitchens of Machala. Here's a mere sampling of dishes prepared with these most important, abundant, and delicious of fruits:

Empanadas de verde: *Empanadas* with a shell of ground, green plantain.

Chirriado: Cheese, fried egg, and mashed green plantain all rolled up in a ball.

Chifles: Thin slices of unripe plantain deep-fried.

Patacones: Thick, fried slices of unripe plantain.

Maduro con queso: Grilled, ripe plantain filled with cheese.

Maduro lampiado: Slices of ripe plantain covered in egg and fried.

Colada de guineo: A juice made with ground, dry, unripe banana.

Guineo cocinado: Boiled, unripe banana, usually eaten with meat.

Torta de Guineo: Banana cake.

Choco banano: Chocolate-covered bananas.

Banano verde con Maní: Boiled, unripe banana served with *maní*, a sweet honey-like peanut sauce.

Hotel Mosquera, Olmedo 1208 (☎931 752; fax 930 392), between Ayacucho and Guayas. The shining-but-basic rooms with private (cold-water) baths and TVs. Singles with fan US$4, with A/C US$5.60; doubles with fan US$6, with A/C US$7.20.

Gran Hotel Machala, Montalvo 2019 (☎930 530), at Rocafuerte. The iron gate puts guests at ease in the run-of-the-mill rooms; centrally located and inexpensive. Rooms with fan and private bath US$2.40 per person; doubles with A/C, TV, and bath US$6.40.

Rizzo Hotel, Guayas 1923 and Bolívar (☎921 511; fax 933 651), 2 blocks from the park. Treat yourself to luxury in rooms with A/C, TV, and hot bathrooms. Swimming pool. Casino and *discoteca*. Singles US$13.42; doubles US$18.30.

🕏 FOOD

Those in search of local flavor should visit Machala's sprawling **outdoor market,** centered around 9 de Mayo between 9 de Octubre and Pasaje, where fresh fruits and meats can be found from 7am to 6pm. Inexpensive *almuerzos* and *meriendas* are widely advertised around town, and provide a filling two- or three-course helping of *comida típica*. If it's seafood you're craving, join the locals at **Puerto Bolívar** (see below), only a five-minute cab ride away.

Chesco Pizzería, Guayas 1050 (☎936 418), with a second location at Pichincha and Ayacucho. A local hangout with music videos playing non-stop, serves the best pizza in town. US$1.20-6. Open M-Sa 11am-midnight, Su 3pm-midnight.

Geco's, Rocafuerte 855, is Machala's teeny-bopper hangout. To accommodate its clientele, this fast food joint serves drinks (US$0.10) and sandwiches (US$0.10).

Restaurant Gran Chifa Oriental, 9 de Octubre 1227. The biggest, best, and most authentic chifa in town. Noodle and rice dishes US$1.60-4. Open daily 11am-11pm.

Don Angelo's, 9 de Mayo 1907 (☎932 577). One of the most popular late-night restaurants. Large selection of liquors. Open M-Sa 7am-4pm, Su 7am-9pm.

🕏 DAYTRIP FROM MACHALA

PUERTO BOLÍVAR

Hop on the #1 bus from Machala's Parque Central, at the corner of Guayas and 9 de Octubre, or anywhere on 9 de Octubre. Get off when you see the street sign for Bolívar Madero Vargas (20min., US$0.10). Returning buses leave from Córdova and Municipalidad. Taxis US$1.

The international port at Bolívar, 6km west of Machala, was initially founded to ship the country's second largest export, the bountiful bunches of bananas. Puerto Bolívar's waterfront now doubles as a popular spot where locals come for **scrumptious seafood.** On weekends, Puerto Bolívar comes alive with lights, music, and swarms of people. Compared to the polluted harbor and inland streets, Puerto Bolívar's restaurants are refreshingly clean. Each tries to outdo its competition with a stronger superlative, but when multiple restaurants claim to make "the best ceviche in the world," it's hard to know where to turn. **Pepe's,** at the corner of Malecón and Rocafuerte, offers some of the best selections of seafood in town. (☎ 929 505. Open daily 8am-midnight.)

NEAR MACHALA: PUYANGO PETRIFIED FOREST

From Machala, take the 9am Loja Internacional bus headed to Ambato via the Bosque de Puyango (3hr., US$1.60). Another route entails taking a CIFA bus to Arenillas (1hr., every 10min. 4:30am-7:30pm, US$0.60) and catching a colectivo, taxi or local bus from there to the park (2hr.). No matter how you get to the park's entrance, you'll still have to stroll 5½km from the security checkpoint to the park offices; from there it's another 15min. walk to the park entrance. Hail down a bus from the checkpoint to get back to Machala or Loja. Since buses are somewhat sporadic in this area, ask about return times when buying your morning bus ticket. Finding information about the park is difficult, but the Puyango Administration Commission in Machala may be helpful. ☎ 930 012; fax 937 655. US$10; guide US$40. Museum open daily 7:30am-3pm.

The Puyango Petrified Forest, near Ecuador's border with Peru, celebrates both the living and the dead. The park's few visitors roam under the towering palms and creep through the giant ferns that grow alongside Puyango's 100-million-year-old petrified **Arcadia trees.** These stone-cold stumps are some of the largest fossilized trunks in the world; the biggest, known as "el gigante," measures 125m in length and 4.5m in diameter. Though they'd be hard-pressed to nest in these trees, over 130 bird species live in this small park. To fully appreciate and identify them, check out *Deirdre Platt's Bird Guide,* available in Spanish from the park administration. The trail through the towering trunks is mostly flat and well-maintained, with some tougher terrain and river crossings. Entry into the park is prohibited without the supervision of a guide (US$0.40) who will take you along the wandering paths and point out leaf and root impressions as well as the immense and lofty **Petrino.** The park admission includes access to a small one-room **museum** that exhibits interesting fossilized remains of shells, fruit, and animals. Making this a daytrip is difficult, so you might want to take advantage of Puyango's simple but sufficient **accommodations** in the caretaker's small lodge; camping is also available. (US$1.20 per person). A nearby store sells water, soda, and crackers (US$0.20 each). For something a bit more substantial, locals can prepare meals (US$0.40).

NEAR MACHALA: JAMBELÍ

To get to Jambelí, take a boat from Puerto Bolívar (30min.; M-F 7:30, 9, 10am, 1, and 4pm; US$1.40 round-trip. The return from Jambelí can be made every 30min., M-F 8:15am, noon, 3, 5, and 6pm). During peak season, boats depart when full in addition to and in between the scheduled times. Entrance fee US$0.10.

Unlike the Galapagos, the small island of Jambelí, 30 minutes by boat from Puerto Bolívar, has little in the way of exotic wildlife, unless one counts the species of Ecuadorian vacationers with a few gringos mixed in. Jambelí's palm-covered food stands and bell-ringing ice cream vendors congregate around a cement street that runs through the center of this small beach town. While music, bamboo benches, thatched roofs, swaying palms, warm water, and gentle waves give Jambelí a constant summer feel, some things do change with the seasons. Hot summer months bring mosquitos; tourists come in droves from August to October and during holidays, causing prices to rise to as much as three times the normal rates. Reservations during these crowded times are suggested, but messages will have to be left with the telephone operators (office open daily 11am-2pm and 7-9pm) as few locales have phone connections. If nobody answers, it's because the electricity (daily 11am-2pm and 7pm-2am) has been cut.

THE BANANA WARS Who would imagine that the innocent banana, so beloved the world over, could be the source of controversy, intrigue, and even bloodshed in Ecuador's "banana republic?" In the fertile lowlands of Southern Ecuador, the tasty yellow fruit is big business, generating more than US$600 million in annual export revenue. With all that money coming in, you'd think there would be enough to go around. But, as economists have long claimed and multinational corporations have demonstrated, human greed knows no bounds. Therein lies the source of conflict. This has most recently taken the form of a fight between foreign fruit companies and their local suppliers over what constitutes a fair price for a box of bananas. The exporters pay growers about US$2 per box, which workers complain is unjust, since the "going price" is US$4.20. In June 1997, contractual negotiations between the two parties broke down; banana workers took to the streets, blocking highways and generally wreaking havoc. The subsequent strike was said to have cost the country US$12-16 million per week. Government mediation temporarily restored order, but it is only a matter of time before the next battle in Ecuador's banana wars is ignited.

Not all visitors are daytrippers, and Jambelí has several options for those looking for a place to hang their beach hats. Despite its fun-in-the-sun atmosphere, accommodations here—while pleasant—are expensive and basic. The largest, best-maintained rooms are at **Hostería La Casa de la Luna**, at the northern end of the island. The airy and dreamlike beach house attracts many foreigners. The Dutch owner also runs a book exchange and offers snacks on the patio. (☎954 116; email jambeliluna@hotmail.com. Singles with bath US$5, doubles with bath US$8.) **Cabañas del Mar**, near Restaurant Costañita, has comfortable and well-equipped rooms (with porch, fan, private bath, and big windows) that fit five, but can be split into doubles (US$4 per person). At the other end of the island, the popular and inexpensive **Las Cabañas de Pescador**, offers doubles with shady porches and private baths. (☎964 113. US$2.40 per room.) Superb seafood is always the specialty of the day in Jambelí. **Restaurant El Niño Turista** (at the beachfront corner of the main street) and its neighbor **El Penguino** both serve fantastic, fishy, and frugal meals. (Both open daily 7am-8pm.)

ZARUMA   ☎07

Founded in 1536, just after the arrival of the Spanish conquistadors, the mountainous, gold-mining town of Zaruma (pop. 7,000) wears its age well. Most mines were combed clean long ago, and the only sign of the international mining giants today is the surprising amount of golden hair among the local population. Nevertheless, the conspicuous number of *"Compro Oro"* ("I buy gold") signs still found around town do have a target audience: small scale miners inject cash into the local economy and, unfortunately, mercury and gold waste into the local streams. Yes, several active gold mines are located just outside of town, and with a little research and persistence, it may be possible to visit one of them. The miners love to talk (and talk, and talk) about their experiences and the fascinating but complicated politics surrounding the gold industry. Nevertheless, despite the gold, Zaruma is not a rich town, and its narrow streets are still lined with aging but beautiful wooden buildings from the turn of the century.

🖅🏧 TRANSPORTATION AND PRACTICAL INFORMATION. Zaruma is easily accessible by bus either from Machala or Piñas. Most services cluster near the town plaza. **TAC** (☎ 972 156) and **Ciudad de Piñas** share an office on Honorado Márquez. Their buses travel to: **Quito** (12hr., 2 per day, US$4); **Guayaquil** (6hr.; 3 per day; US$3.60); **Cuenca** (5hr., 2 per day, US$3.60); **Loja** (6hr.; 3 per day; US$2.60); and **Machala** (2hr., every hr. 3am-7pm, US$1.50) via **Piñas** (US$.50).

Banco de Pichincha, on Pichincha past PacificTel, changes dollars but not traveler's checks (open M-F 8am-2pm). The **post office** is on the right when facing the church from the center of the park (open M-F 8am-4:30pm). **Pharmacies** line Bolívar just down from the church. **PacificTel** (☎ 972 104), at the corner of Pichincha and Luis Crespo, past the market, doesn't do collect or calling card calls (open daily 8am-10pm). Find the **police** (☎ 972 198) on Colón. The **hospital** (☎ 972 025), on Rocafuerte, offers 24-hour emergency service. **Telephone code:** 07.

⌐ ACCOMMODATIONS. Both of Zaruma's hotels have sacrificed a central location for spectacular views. On the main road into town, **Hotel Roland** (☎ 972 800), is well worth the extra money and uphill hike into town. All rooms have private hot-water baths, carpeting, and TVs. Most have splendid views of the mountain valley, but latecomers might have to suffer views more reminiscent of a mine shaft. (Rooms US$3 per person). The **Hotel Municipal** (☎ 972 179), on Sesmo (just uphill from the TAC terminal) near the mountain ridge, may inspire grumbling on the hike up, but the view silences any complaints. All rooms have private hot-water baths and many have spectacular views (US$3.20 per person).

▨ SIGHTS. Grab a pick-axe and hard hat, cross your fingers, and hope to strike it rich. Just outside of town, active **gold mines** inspire champagne wishes and caviar dreams. Those wishing to visit or learn more about the mines should inquire at the **Asociación de Mineros Autonomos Muluncay** (☎ 972 855), just uphill from the Hotel Roland. They might also be able to hook you up with a guide to take you into one of the smaller, less productive excavations, such as the **Sesmo Mine. Compañía Bira** (☎ 972 227), a gold mining outpost on the road into town, is the largest mining company in the area, employing 120 miners in four shifts for maximum productivity. Unfortunately, Bira is not able to take tourists into the active mine.

Those overcome with gold-plated, greedy thoughts may can make a hasty retreat to the stunning **Iglesia de Zaruma** in the center of town. Started in 1912, this intricate chapel took over 18 years to build, and the decorating still hasn't been finished. Two surprisingly life-like series of paintings have recently been added to its ceiling, depicting the creation of Adam and Eve and the life and times of Christ. Both murals end above the two-story altar that gleams with a thin, glittering layer of the very best of what Zaruma's mines have to offer. Also worth a visit are the walls of shrine-like sarcophagi at the **cemetery,** on the edge of town along Honorado Márquez. If you happen to be in town during the second week of July, enjoy the **Expo-Zaruma,** one of the town's biggest festivals.

PIÑAS   ☎07

In 1825, Spanish geologist **Juan José Luis** was given a large land grant for his work in the Ecuadorian gold mines near what is now the town of Zaruma. Eager to honor his homeland, the miner called his new ranch **Piñas** after his former home in Spain's pineapple region. Eventually, his big ranch became the small town of Piñas, with a current population of about 10,000. Uninterested in pineapples, however, the people of Piñas spend their time cultivating coffee and bananas in the surrounding blue-green mountains. If you talk to anyone in Piñas about their home, the word *tranquilo* will doubtlessly come up, as it is the town's unanimously agreed-upon adjective. The laid-back Piñas of today has few ties to its historical past, with the **Virgen del Cisne** and an accompanying pantheon of saints exerting far more influence than any of Juan's kinfolk. From the cross on top of the hill to the electric candle-lit pictures of Madonna and child at roadside shrines, Piñas's piety is prominently displayed. For a good workout and breathtaking mountain views, one need only walk the town's steep streets. Many roads and walkways slope up and down as much as 45 degrees. Along these streets, vistas of the surrounding mountains and brightly colored buildings—including a simple but charming church with a tiled, oddly ventilated steeple—provide plenty to please the eye. The hilltop cross is worth a visit for the spectacular view. Taxis will take you there; otherwise, the path is clearly visible from town.

Loja and **Sucre,** which merge on the Machala end of town, are the most active streets. The two **bus** companies, **Ciudad de Piñas** (☎ 976 167) and **TAC** (☎ 976 151), share an office on Sucre and Montalvo. Their buses run to: **Machala** (2hr., every hr. 4:30am-7:30pm, US$1); **Zaruma** (30min., every hr. 4am-7pm, US$.50); **Loja** (5hr.; 3 per day; US$2); and **Cuenca** (5hr., 1 per day, US$3). The **police** (☎ 976 134 or 976 433) may be found at Carrión and 9 de Octubre, at the bottom end of town (open 24hr.). **Policlínico Reina del Cisne** (☎ 976 689), on Loja near Olmedo, is a 24-hour clinic. **PacificTel,** (☎ 976 105; fax 976 990), Ruminahui and Suárez, two blocks uphill from the church does not allow collect or calling card calls (open daily 8am-10pm). The **Residencial Dumari** (☎ 976 118), Loja at 8 de Noviembre, on top of the hill, has the most comfortable beds and cleanest sheets in Piñas. (Rooms US$1.40 per person, with bath and color TV US$2.40.) **Hotel Las Orquideas** (☎ 976 355), on the corner of Calderón and Montalvo, in the lower end of town, has windows and not much else—rooms are basic, but clean and well-lit, with private baths and color TVs (US$1.50 per person). It's easy to find a chicken—alive or roasted—or a plate of meat in Piñas, but other type of cuisine may be a bit harder to find. Vegetarians will want to stick to the numerous *panaderías* or visit the **market** on Loayza and Juan Leon Mera to enjoy fresh fruits and vegetables. Restaurants with standard *meriendas* and *almuerzos* are scattered about Sucre, Loja, and Bolívar.

HUAQUILLAS   ☎ 07

On Ecuador's border with Peru, the small town of Huaquillas enjoys a fame that is strictly geographic. Because prices in Ecuador are lower than those in Peru, the main road becomes a virtual street market, swarming with Peruvian day shoppers,

Huaquillas

ACCOMMODATIONS
Hotel Gabeli, **3**
Hotel Rodey, **2**
Hotel Vanessa, **1**

money changers, and mosquitos. The border crossing is usually a painless (although somewhat bewildering) affair, and most travelers opt to keep moving rather than loiter in Huaquillas. The bus cooperativo CIFA (☎907 370), one block east from the only street light on República, two blocks from the immigration office, just off República, sends buses to **Machala** (1hr. direct, 2hr. local; every 20min. 6:30am-7pm; US$1 direct, US$0.90 local) via **Arenillas** and **Santa Rosa**; and **Guayaquil** (4hr., 8 per day 2:30am-4:15pm, US$2.80). Panamericana, at the corner of Cordovez 152 and Santa Rosa (☎907 016), goes to **Quito** (12hr., 5 per day 6:30am-9pm, US$7) via **Santo Domingo; Ambato** (10hr., 8pm); and **Tulcán** on the Colombian border (18hr., 4:30pm). Trans Santa, on Cordovez, also travels to **Ambato** (5:30pm, US$5.60) via **Riobamba** (US$4.80). **Pullman Azuay** (☎907 575), on Cordovez, has buses to **Cuenca** (5hr.; 5 per day 3:30am-6:30pm; US$2.80). Trans Caraimanga and Trans Nambija, both on Cordovez, go to **Loja** (11:30am and 12:30pm, US$3).

Everything of any importance, including the bus terminals, border crossing, and immigration office, is along one of Huaquillas's three main dusty thoroughfares: **Machala, Teniente Cordovez,** and **Central.** This last street transforms into **República del Perú** at the bridge between both nations, and is the most important for border-related procedures. Most bus companies are found on Cordovez. For financial and informational needs, the **Tourist Center,** just west of the bridge on the Ecuadorian side, changes soles and provides smaller denominations of dollar bills. Most banks will not exchange cash without proper Ecuadorian identification. Since dollars are accepted as Ecuador's new currency, tourists are advised to carry bills of small denomination. **Money changers** can also be found on the streets on either side of the border, but be especially wary of fake bills and fixed calculators. **Police** are ready at their station on the corner of República and Costa Rica, just beyond the street light. (☎907 341. Open 24hr.) Near customs (*aduana*) are the **post office** (open M-F 9am-4pm) and **PacificTel** (open daily 8am-10pm).

BORDER CROSSING: INTO PERU

Ecuador and Peru are separated by the Río Zarumilla, which is crossed by an international bridge. In crossing the border, everyone must pass through both Ecuadorian and Peruvian immigration during a 24-hour period. Leaving Ecuador, you must pass through **Ecuadorian Migraciones** (☎907 755), on the left side of República, about 3km before Huaquillas. Get there early, as the lines get longer throughout the day. After getting your stamp, take one of the waiting cabs to Huaquillas (US$1). Walk across the bridge into Aguas Verdes until you reach the mototaxi stop, two blocks from the border on República del Perú. These vehicles can take you to **Peruvian Migraciones** (3km., s/1), and may try to con you into paying extra for your luggage. After completing customary procedures, combis can be hailed as they head to the corner of Tumbes and Abad Puell in Tumbes (30min., s/1). All persons crossing the border in either direction must have a tourist **T3 card,** available at both Ecuadorian and Peruvian immigration offices, and a **valid passport.** Tourists are given up to **90 days** in Ecuador or Peru. Anyone who wishes to stay longer must get a visa extension (see **Documents and Formalities,** p. 27). All visas can be obtained at the Peruvian consulate in Machala (see p. 487). Occasionally, immigration officials ask for a return ticket out of the country or for proof of sufficient funds for each day travelers expect to spend there, but this is uncommon.

Huaquillas is probably not ⸱ place where most budget travelers want to hang out. Although spending the night here is not highly recommended, and is considered dangerous by some, travelers arriving late in the evening may find it necessary to check into one of Huaquillas' several hotels. **Hotel Vanessa,** 1 de Mayo 323 and Hualtaco, is slightly off the main drag but still easily accessible. The most comfortable and reliable choice in town for safety, spotlessness, and a good night's rest. Rooms have private bath, TV, phones, A/C, and fridges. (☎907 263. Singles US$5; doubles US$8.) **Hotel Rodey,** at the corner of Cordovez and 10 de Agosto, provides comfortable doubles with private baths, TV, and A/C as well as simpler, less expensive rooms with communal baths. (☎907 736. Singles US$2; doubles with amenities US$8.)

MACARÁ

☎07

The border crossing at Macará may be one of Ecuador's best kept secrets. Unlike the chaotic and sometimes dangerous experience of entering or exiting Peru at Huaquillas, going through Macará is not only painless but can even be quite enjoyable. The town's white-and-blue church sparkles against a gorgeous mountain background, as does the water in the central plaza's fountain. The Río Macará, forming the natural border between the two countries, is surprisingly clean; locals sometimes swim by the small "beach" on the Ecuadorian side.

The short distance between the **market** and the **central plaza** is covered by **10 de Agosto. Loja Internacional,** on J. Jaramillo behind the church, travels to **Loja** (5hr.; 1:30am, 4, 8:30, 9:45am, 1am, 4, 11pm; US$3) and **Piura** (3hr.; 4am, 1, 4pm; US$3.40). **Trans Unión Carimanga** (☎694 047), on Loja between Rengel and 10 de Agosto, also sends **buses** to **Loja** (6hr.; 12:30, 4:30, 5:30, 7:30, 11am, 1, 3pm; US$2.80). **Migraciones** and an **information office** are both located in the second floor of the **Municipalidad,** on the plaza. **INEFAN** (☎694 280) has a small office on the junction of C. Jaramillo, Rengel, and Veintimilla, at the Parque Amazonas; they can provide information on the nearby protected forests of **Susuco** and **El Tundo** ("bosque húmedo"). **Money changers** can also be found in the market in Macará. The nicest lodging in Macará is the **Hotel Espiga de Oro,** on Ante, off 10 de Agosto between the market and the plaza. Hanging plants and stunning views contribute to atmosphere, as do fans and baths in room. (☎694 405. Singles US$4; doubles US$6.80.) A 10-minute walk toward the border down the paved road at the end of Bolívar, leads you to **Parador Turístico.** Isolated from the bustling market, rooms have baths, and some have balconies. The large hotel also includes a restaurant, bar, disco, and swimming pool. (☎694 099. Rooms US$4.40 per person.) For travelers on a tight budget, the **Hotel Amazonas,** on Rengel near the Parque Amazonas, offers bare rooms with common baths (rooms US$1.20 per person).

BORDER CROSSING: INTO PERU

The bridge between Peru and Ecuador is about 3km from Macará; taxis and colectivos (US$0.20) leave from the market area on 10 de Agosto near Bolívar (ask for "la frontera"); or make the pleasant walk on foot (45min.) down the paved road at the end of Bolívar (after passing a small church, make a left on the main highway that leads to the border). Both the Peruvian and Ecuadorian **immigration offices** are ready to issue or receive your tourist **T3 card** and stamp your passport **24hr.** Soles and dollars can be exchanged on the Ecuadorian side at the **Banco de Loja** (☎694 247; open M-F 9am-6pm, Sa 8am-1pm) and the Peruvian side at **Banco Financiero** (open M-F 9am-6pm, Sa 9am-1pm). **La Tina** is the tiny settlement closest to the Peruvian border, but colectivos at the border run to its big brother **Suyo** (20min., 2 soles) or directly to **Sullana** (2hr., 10 soles). Although there are a number of hotels and restaurants in Sullana, it is also possible to take buses, colectivos, or combis from José de Loma to the nearby, larger city of **Piura** (45min., s/1-1.50-2).

WESTERN ECUADOR

CENTRAL
ECUADOR

The farther one strays from Quito, the more everyday life appears to slow down. In the northern highlands, **north of Quito** (p. 496), a network of indigenous communities lives amid sparkling lakes and thriving cloud forests. But both the people of the region and the natural landscapes find their existence endangered. In towns such as Otavalo, *indígenas* struggle to reconcile their traditional lifestyle with western values and technology. Locals speak Quichua on the street, wear traditional ponchos and fedoras, and specialize in the crafts of their forefathers. Much of this locally crafted *artesanía* is sold in Otavalo's famous Saturday market, packed with tapestries, leather, wood carvings, and paintings. However, the region has much more to offer than its market goods—most notably, the naturally wrought cloud forests that provide some of the last remaining havens for the most endangered flora and fauna in the northern Sierra.

HIGHLIGHTS OF CENTRAL ECUADOR

SHOP at **Otavalo's Saturday Craft Market** (p. 498), the most famous of its kind.

TREK among the brilliant **Lagunas de Mojanda** (p. 499).

VIEW the tallest active volcano in the world in **Parque Nacional Cotopaxi** (p. 511).

BATHE in the salubrious waters at **Baños** (p. 516).

RIDE atop the spectacular **Devil's Nose Train** (p. 528) as it chugs down to the coast.

FACE two historic cathedrals in **Parque Calderón** (p. 534), Cuenca's graceful and well-restored colonial center.

WALK the partially eroded **Inca highway** that still connects Cuenca's Pumapungo ruins to the religious center of Ingapirca (p. 534).

CANTER around sedate **Vilcabamba** (p. 544) on horseback.

Possibly the most beautiful part of the country, Ecuador's central corridor runs through treacherous volcanoes and knife-edged ridges. Almost half of the nation's population lives in this region; since pre-Hispanic times, farmers have benefited from its rich soil, fed by millions of years of volcanic eruptions. Many of these fire-spewers still simmer in the northern part of the corridor, the **"avenue of the volcanoes"** (p. 505)—a nickname courtesy of 19th-century German explorer Alexander von Humboldt. This still-volatile region extends from Quito down to Riobamba, flanked on the eastern side by Parque Nacional Cotopaxi and Parque Nacional Sangay, and on the western side by Volcán Chimborazo. As the road meanders farther south, rocky peaks soften into green hills. But the most spectacular scenery belongs to the routes descending from Cuenca and Alausí to the coast (El Triunfo and Guayaquil). Roads and train tracks alike dip 3000m, hugging cliffs and deep ravines as they pass through diverse vegetation zones, from mountain *páramo* to coastal jungle wetlands, descending into layer after layer of misty cloud cover en route to their muggy destinations.

The southern tip of Ecuador's sierra may lack the snow-capped volcanic peaks of the central Cordillera de los Andes, but the natural and man-made wonders of the **southern highlands** (p. 528) are equally impressive. Tourism hasn't hit the region as hard as other parts of the country; as a result, these cities, towns, and villages remain relatively peaceful and "authentic." Even Cuenca, the third largest city in Ecuador, manages to balance its cosmopolitan airs with its colonial history and atmosphere. A visit to the region is an opportunity to see everyday Ecuador at its best—serene, breathtaking, and glowing with character.

NORTH FROM QUITO

OTAVALO ☎06

Otavalo is one of the most prosperous and respected indigenous communities in Latin America, but its success hasn't come easily. Since the Inca invasion of 1496, the local *indígenas* have been persecuted by outsiders, suffering from oppression and racism. The Spanish colonists took the brutality to grim new heights, forcing *otavaleños* to work 15-hour days under dangerous conditions in textile sweat-shops called *obrajes*. Such extreme cruelty gradually became less common, and in 1964 an agrarian reform law returned much of the land to its indigenous residents. Most *mestizos*, however, still treated the *indígenas* like second-class citizens until the early 1980s, when local *indígenas* gained worldwide recognition for the beauty of their weaving and music. Now *otavaleño* products are sold internationally, and foreigners flock to Otavalo's Saturday market specifically to buy locally crafted goods. Modern Otavalo is a testament to the determination and talent of indigenous *otavaleños*. No longer solely weavers, many *indígenas* are now doctors, lawyers, and politicians, yet remain grounded in their traditions.

▐ TRANSPORTATION

Buses: Several major bus lines are based at the **terminal** on Atahuallpa and Ordoñez. Buses go to: **Quito** (2½hr., every 10min. 4am-6pm, US$1.10); **Ibarra** (1hr., every 5min. 5:40am-6:30pm, US$0.20); **Peguche** (15min., every 15min. 7am-7pm, US$0.08); and **Agato** (45 min., every 30 min. 5am-7pm, US$0.10).

Taxis: Taxis congregate around the parks and plazas, including **Taxi 31 de Octubre Otavalo** (☎920 485). **Cooperativo de Taxis el Jordan Otavalo** (☎920 298).

▐▐ ORIENTATION AND PRACTICAL INFORMATION

Buses usually drop visitors off in the southeast corner of town, in front of the **Plaza Copacabana**, on the corner of **Atahuallpa** and **Calderón.** Be prepared, however, to be dropped off anywhere along **Roca** (parallel to Atahuallpa) or at the **terminal.** If you get a bus that only drives by the city, not through it, get off at Atahuallpa and make the easy walk into town from the highway. **Sucre,** the major north-south avenue, runs past both the **Parque Rumiñahui** and the **Poncho Plaza,** the focal point of the famous Saturday market. The major east-west street is **Calderón,** which runs by the Plaza Copacabana.

Tour Agencies: A number of travel agencies offer tours to neighboring villages, lakes, and mountains. Daytrips usually cost US$15-30 per person. Several agencies are found along Sucre between Calderón and Salinas. ▧**Diceny Viajes,** Sucre 10-14 and Colón (☎/fax 921 217). Open M-Sa 8am-6:30pm, Su 8-9am and 4-5pm. **Zulay Tours** (☎921 176; fax 922 969), Colón and Sucre, 2nd floor. **Inty Express,** Sucre 11-10 and Morales (☎921 436; fax 920 737). Open M-Sa 8:30am-7pm, Su 8:30am-1pm.

Banks: Banco del Pichincha, Bolívar 6-16 and Moreno (☎920 214). **MC/Cirrus ATM.** Open M-F 8am-6pm, Sa-Su 8am-2pm. Open M 9am-1pm, Tu-F 9am-4:30pm, Sa 8am-3pm. **Banco Previsora,** Sucre 10-07 and Calderón (☎921 213). **Visa/Plus ATM.**

Laundromat: Laundry Lavandería, Colón 5-14 and Sucre (☎921 267). US$0.50 per kg. Open M-Sa 9am-7pm. **New Laundry Lavandería,** Roca 9-42. US$0.60 per kg. Open M-Sa 8am-1pm and 3-6pm.

Emergency: Policía Nacional (☎920 101).

Police: The **Policía Municipal** (☎921 179), at Sucre and García Moreno, in the municipal building. Open daily 8am-noon and 2-6pm. They have no telephone but can be seen on patrol or reached through the Comisera Municipal.

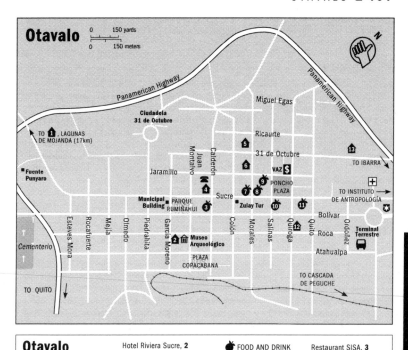

Otavalo

▲ ACCOMMODATIONS
Hostal Irina, **6**
Hostal Valle de Amanacer, **12**

Hotel Riviera Sucre, **2**
Jatún Pacha, **13**
La Luna Hostería, **1**
Residencial Santa Martha, **5**
Samay Inn, **4**

🍎 FOOD AND DRINK
Gemini's Restaurant, **10**
Mi Otavalito, **8**
Pizza Siciliana, **7**

Restaurant SISA, **3**
Sahara, **11**
Shanandoa Pie Shop
and Cafetería, **9**

Medical Services: Hospital San Luis de Otavalo (☎920 444, emergency ☎923 566), on Sucre at the northern edge of town. Ambulance service and free consultations. Emergency medical care available in the municipal building in the Parque Rumiñahui.

Telephones: EMETEL, Calderón between Sucre and Jaramillo. Open daily 8am-8:40pm.

Internet Access: Caffé.Net (☎922 969), on Sucre and Colón, offers Internet access until 7pm and Net2Phone. Internet US$0.80 for 30min. Open M-Sa 8am-9pm. **Micro Control,** Bolívar 14-22 and Ordoñez (☎/fax 921 587) charges US$0.04 per min. Open M-F 9am-1pm and 3-7pm, Sa 9am-1:30pm. **MTC Handicraft for Export** (☎922 893), Jaramillo and Quito, off the Poncho Plaza (US$0.04 per min.). Open daily 8am-6pm.

Post Office: (☎/fax 923 520), Sucre and Salinas, at the corner of Poncho Plaza, 2nd fl. Open M-F 8am-7pm, Sa 8am-1pm.

🚩 ACCOMMODATIONS

Most options in Otavalo are fairly congenial, inexpensive, and conveniently located in the triangle formed by **Poncho Plaza, Parque Rumiñahui,** and **Plaza Copacabana.** Most hostels include tax in quoted prices.

🏨 **Hostal Valle del Amanecer** (☎/fax 920 990), Roca and Quiroga. Constructed of avocado trees and bamboo ceilings, El Valle is a refreshing switch from the conventional plaster and cement. Great for sharing stories, a little noisy for going to sleep. Mountain bike rentals US$4 per day. Rooms US$2, with hot bath US$3.

Jatún Pacha (HI) (☎922 223), 31 de Octubre and Pan-American Highway. Tucked away from the tourist center of the city, this is the homiest of Otavalo's hostels. Large rooms have polished wood floors and balconies. Luggage storage. Bike rental US$3 per hr. Singles US$10, with HI or ISIC US$8; doubles US$18, with HI or ISIC US$16.

Hotel Riviera Sucre, García Moreno 380 and Roca (☎920 241). A pleasant, airy hotel with a patio, ping pong, and large suites. Rooms US$3 per person, with bath US$5.

Hostal Irina, Modesto Jaramillo 5-69 and Morales (☎920 684). Bright entryway leads to plain, clean rooms. Laundry, and shipping services. Rooms US$3 per person.

La Luna Hostería (☎/fax 737 415), 4½km on the roadway to Laguna Mojanda. This is the place to go for a tranquil rest in the Otavalan countryside. Restaurant, bar, and common room with cable TV. US$1.50 per carload to Otavalo. *Menú del día* US$3. Camping US$1.50; dorms US$3; doubles or triples US$6; doubles with bath and fireplace US$8.

FOOD

Otavalo's restaurants offer a variety of cuisine to suit all tastes. Though some spots serve traditional Ecuadorian cuisine, most places cater to a gringo clientele. There are several good restaurants around Poncho Plaza, but they get very busy.

■ **Restaurant SISA,** Calderón 409 and Sucre (☎920 154), 2nd fl. of SISA shopping center. The immaculate entryway, spiral staircase, fireplace, well-stocked bar, and leather-bound menus provide the backdrop for fine dining; all-around good food provides the substance. Grilled trout US$2.50. Salad US$0.80. Open daily noon-10pm.

■ **Sahara** (☎922 212), Quiroga between Bolívar and Sucre, is all about ambiance. Most nights, the cushions and straw mats on the floor are packed with backpackers enjoying *pipas de agua* (water pipes) with peach, mint, apple, or strawberry tobacco (US$2). The menu is limited but tasty. Entrees US$.060-2. Open daily 11am-midnight.

■ **Shanandoa, The PieShop/Cafeteria,** Salinas 515 and Jaramillo (☎921 465). Not your grandmother's pie, but just as tasty. Fillings include apple, strawberry, chocolate, and lemon; for a more Ecuadorian flavor, try the blackberry, pineapple, or *barbaro*. Pie US$0.60, with ice cream US$1.15. Open daily 7am-9:30pm.

Gemini's Restaurant (☎920 431), Salinas between Sucre and Bolívar. A bright, international restaurant. Spinach crepes (US$2.40) and meat dishes (US$3.20) fulfill the promise of "Nice Food" painted over the door. Open W-M 10am-11pm.

Mi Otavalito (☎917 132), Sucre and Morales, is a local favorite specializing in *criollo* delicacies and a few scrumptious international plates in a pleasant courtyard setting. *Trucha otavalito* US$1.80. *Menú del día* US$2. Open daily 8am-7:30pm.

SIGHTS

Otavalo is best known for its brilliant and sprawling market, which is most active on Saturdays but features vendors several days during the week.

THE MAIN MARKET. The uncontainable fanfare of the Saturday market starts in Poncho Plaza but overflows onto the surrounding streets, stretching for several blocks. **Local weavings** are concentrated in the plaza and all along Sucre, where many *indígenas* set up booths in front of their shops. **Wood carvings** and **leather goods** abound; some of the best are sold on Sucre and in the southeastern end of the market. The fried egg, pork, and potato aroma that permeates the entire market originates on Quiroga, where streetside stands cook up **market munchies.** Jaramillo, the most eclectic area, sells everything from "genuine" Air Jordans to traditional jewelry and hand-carved pipes. Be especially careful with valuables along Jaramillo. *(Open market days 6:30am-3pm.)*

MUSEO ARQUEOLÓGICO. This one-room museum houses over 10,000 archaeological relics found in different regions of Ecuador. It includes artifacts belonging to indigenous groups dating from BC 15,000; flutes made from condor leg bones manipulated at birth; and models of ancient astronomical observatories. *(Montalvo and Roca, on the 2nd fl. of Hostería Los Andes. Open when curator is there. US$0.20.)*

◪ NIGHTLIFE

Though not wild and crazy by any standard, Otavalo's nightlife is most easily found in a few quality **peñas** (with live music) that can spice up any weekend night. Most tourist-friendly establishments are concentrated along Morales between Jaramillo and Sucre. **Peña Amauta**, Morales and Jaramillo, wins the best atmosphere award. It also serves the mysterious and potent *guayusa*, made from fermented sugarcane with a touch of lemon (☎922 435. US$2.80 for a pitcher. Cover less than US$1. Open daily 8pm-2am. At **Peña La Jampa**, Jaramillo and Morales, groups boogie in the outdoor courtyard. (☎932 618. Cover US$1. *Peña* and live music Th-Sa 7pm. Restaurant open daily 9am-9:30pm.) The **Peña Tuparina**, Morales and 31 de Octubre, features local bands (F-Sa 9pm). One of the more traditional d*iscotecas* is **Peña Samay**, Morales and Sucre. (Open W-Su 8pm-2am).

▐ DAYTRIPS FROM OTAVALO

LAGUNAS DE MOJANDA

To walk to Mojanda, follow Sucre west to the outskirts of the city and cross the Panamerican Highway; a cobblestone road begins at the sign for the lagoons. Taxis US$8 round-trip with up to an hour wait at the lakes. A cheaper option is to take a cab there and hike back (3½hr.) or to take a camioneta both ways. Tours visit Mojanda, but they don't allow much time for walking around the lagoons (US$20 per day). Be advised that there have been several muggings in recent years at Mojanda—don't visit the lagoons alone.

These three peaceful lakes are tucked away between the extinct volcano **Fuya Fuya** and a range of smaller rolling mountains situated 16km south of Otavalo. The **hiking** trail begins uphill, to the right of **Laguna Grande**, the only lake immediately visible from the road. The path diverges at the far end of the lake. There is an oft-used dirt trail and a less-used path through the grass; the latter is on a steep bank and leads to another dirt trail. The trail that cuts to the left winds around the back of **Montaña Pequeña**, leading to an amazing view of **Laguna Negra**, named because it is tightly surrounded by cliffs that keep the waters eternally shadowed. The path to the right leads to a view of the less spectacular **Laguna Chiquita**, providing glimpses of the misty mountaintops of Fuya Fuya and Montaña Pequeña (45min. each way). From there the road forks a second time. Both paths go up Montaña Pequeña to Laguna Grande, but the right-hand one, though slightly longer, is less muddy. The total walk around the lagoons should take four hours.

LA CASCADA DE PEGUCHE

The bus line 8 de Septiembre routinely travels between the Plaza Copacabana in Otavalo and the central plaza of Peguche (30min., every 20min., US$0.08). Transportes Imbaburac has buses from the terminal in Otavalo to Peguche (30min., every 30min., US$0.08). Have the driver drop you off at Loma Pucará or Las Cascadas; the waterfall is straight up the hill (US$1).

Peguche, a name derived from the language of the *cayapa*, roughly translates as "sweet jumping of water." This undoubtedly describes Las Cascadas de Peguche, the well-shrouded, oasis-like waterfalls near the town entrance. Once at the ruins of Bohío at the top of the hill, take a right through the archway and follow signs for the waterfalls through the forest. If coming from the central plaza in town, take the aptly-named Calle Cascada out of town and keep on it through the arch, where signs for the waterfalls should appear (15min.). If coming from Otavalo, follow the main tracks—which turn into a road—out of town. A trail goes off uphill to the right as you pass the river (40min.). From the forest entrance, it's a five-minute walk until the waterfall emerges through the misty air, but there are also beautiful trails through much of the woods. **Thieves** have been known to lurk in the forest; check to see if other hikers are around in the woods before starting out alone.

COTACACHI

Buses going to Cotacachi leave from Otavalo's terminal; buses to Otavalo leave from the corner of Sucre and 10 de Agosto, or on Peña Herrera near the park (45min., every 15min. until 6pm, US$1.40).

Endowed with more leather than a sadomasochist's kinkiest dream, Cotacachi is Ecuador's leatherwork capital. Planted 12km northwest of Otavalo under the watchful eye of **Mount Cotacachi** (4939m), the eponymous town sells leather goods of sublime quality at relatively low prices. None of this is sold in Otavalo; the truly leatherhungry are forced to come here. **Craft shops** around town sell everything from leather jackets to purses to briefcases. Most accept credit cards, but give discounts of up to 10% to customers with cash. **El Palacio del Cuero,** 10 de Agosto and Bolívar, is among the largest. (☎915 378. Open daily 9am-6pm). The town's two parks, mostly concrete **Parque San Francisco** (along 10 de Agosto between Tarquí and Rocafuerte) and **Parque de la Matriz** (along Peñaherrera between Suárez and Bolívar), serve as geographical points of reference. **Banco Pichincha**, Imbabura and Tarquí, just off the Parque San Francisco, exchanges cash and traveler's checks. (☎915 456; fax 915 491. Open M-F 8am-6pm.) If you decide to spend the night in town, try the centrally located **Hostal Plaza Bolívar,** Bolívar 12-26 and 10 de Agosto. (☎915 327. Rooms US$3 per person.)

NEAR OTAVALO: INTAG CLOUD FOREST

Situated on the verdant western slopes of the Andes, this privately owned reserve protects a small portion of Ecuador's endangered cloud forests, over 90% of which have been destroyed. To combat the deforestation from agriculture and mining, proprietors Carlos and Sandy Zorilla have tried to purchase as much of the land as possible. Guests help out their cause with their room and board. With elevations of 1750 to 2800m and temperatures ranging from 12 to 27°C (55-80°F), Intag cloud forest is a dynamic place. Particular combinations of clouds, fog, and constant humidity produce an incredible variety of flora and fauna. There is a plethora of **epiphytes** (plants that grow on other plants and trees), including orchids, bromeliads, and araceas. Medicinal plants such as **sangre de drago,** only recently discovered by modern medicine to cure child respiratory viruses, also grow here amongst the ferns and mosses. The mammals that live in the region—spectacled bears, pumas, spider monkeys, and mountain tapirs—tend to elude observation, as most are nocturnal and afraid of humans. Plants and animals alike are threatened by deforestation and are in danger of extinction. While mammals are a rare sight, the forest is heaven for birdwatchers; about 180 different species of bird have been identified, including 22 species of hummingbird. A stay on the reserve includes lodging, vegetarian meals, and a bilingual guide. All beds come equipped with thick blankets, and solar-heated water flows from rustic outdoor showers. (US$45 per person per night; min. 2 nights.) The Zorillas require reservations and only accept groups of six or more: write or fax them a few months in advance at Casilla 18, Otavalo, Imbabura, Ecuador (☎/fax 923 392 in Otavalo). If you are looking for a group, the Zorillas will happily place you in one.

IBARRA ☎06

Ibarra maintains a peculiar balance between past and present. After an earthquake destroyed much of the city in 1868, the survivors were left with the monumental task of piecing the rubble back together. Whether by chance or intention, they built many of the public buildings and business centers in the southern half of the city and most of the colonial-style, white-with-red-tile homes in the northern half. This duality persists today; Ibarra's professionals and politicians race into modernity in their taxis, buses, and Mercedes, while the northern half of the city resounds with the clatter of horse-drawn buggies on cobblestone avenues. However, Ibarra is one of the few Ecuadorian cities where all three major ethnicities are successfully integrated: black, indigenous, and *mestizo*. Though not much of a tourist city, Ibarra does offer some peaceful parks and plazas, serves as a good central location for daytrips to La Esperanza or San Antonio, and is a good stopping point on the way to or from Colombia, Quito, or Otavalo.

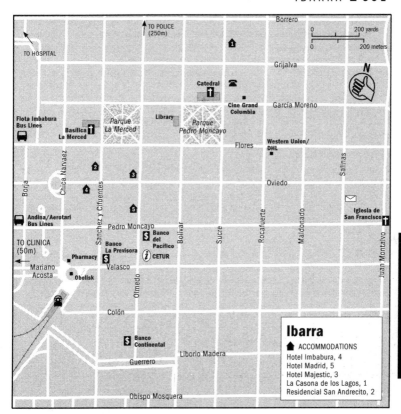

Ibarra

▲ ACCOMMODATIONS
Hotel Imbabura, 4
Hotel Madrid, 5
Hotel Majestic, 3
La Casona de los Lagos, 1
Residencial San Andrecito, 2

TRANSPORTATION

Buses: As a provincial capital and transportation hub, Ibarra has a number of bus lines with routes serving most of the northern highlands and the Ecuadorian coast. Buses usually leave from the headquarters of their respective company—most of them lie to the west of the obelisk. Buses leave to: **Esmeraldas** (9hr., 4 per day 6:45am-7:40pm, US$5.60); **Guayaquil** (10½hr., 7:30pm, US$6.80); **Otavalo** (35min., every 15min. 5am-8pm, US$2); **Quito** (2½hr., every hr. 1-10pm, US$1.40); **San Lorenzo** (6hr., 4 per day 6am-2pm, US$1.80); **Santo Domingo** (every 15min.; US$1.60 through Quito, US$3 direct); and **Tulcán** (2hr., every hr. 5:30am-1:30pm, US$1.40). 28 de Septiembre runs **local buses** up and down Mariano Acosta (US$0.08).

Taxis: In parks and near bus stations. **Cooperativo Pasquel Monge** (☎915 415), at the train station; **Cooperativo Los Lagos** (☎955 150).

✹🛈 ORIENTATION AND PRACTICAL INFORMATION

Buses from Quito and Otavalo drop visitors off along **Borja** and **Vacas Galindo,** on the western outskirts of town, or along **Mariano Acosta** near the market on **Guerrero.** If you are not dropped off in the *centro*, walk a short distance toward Mt. Imbabura and take a left on Mariano Acosta. The immense **obelisk,** visible from a distance, serves as a good landmark. Beyond the obelisk, the street changes names to **Velasco** and intersects **Olmedo, Bolívar,** and **Sucre,** which is home to most hotels and restaurants. Three blocks from the obelisk, lies **Parque La Merced** and, two blocks east, the **Parque Pedro Moncayo.** One block north of the obelisk, east-west **Pedro Moncayo** splits Ibarra into two manageable halves.

CENTRAL ECUADOR

Tourist Information: The **Ministry of Tourism,** Olmedo 956 (☎958 759; fax 958 547), between Moncayo and Velasco. Open M-F 8:30am-1pm and 2-5pm.

Banks: Banco La Previsora, Sánchez y Cifuentes 10-98 and Velasco (☎955 900; fax 957 295), doesn't accept traveler's checks. **Visa/Plus ATM** and Visa cash advances. Open M-F 9am-7pm, Sa 9am-2pm. **Banco del Pacífico** (☎957 728), Olmedo and Moncayo, has a 24hr. **MC/Cirrus ATM**. Open M-F 8:45am-4pm.

Emergency: ☎101. **Police:** Villamar 148 and Olmedo (☎950 444).

Medical Services: Hospital San Vicente de Paul, Luis Vargas Torres 1-156 (**emergency** ☎131, 950 666, or 957 272). **Clínica Mariano Acosta,** Mariano Acosta 1116 (**emergency** ☎043 136; main ☎950 924), is a 24hr. emergency clinic.

Telephones: EMETEL, Sucre 4-48 and Moreno. Open daily 8am-10pm.

Internet Access: Nov@net Cybercafe, Bolívar 969 and Colón, in the lobby of Hostal Ejecutivo (☎956 575 or (09) 696 486). US$2 per hr. Open M-Sa 7:30am-9:30pm.

Post Office: Salinas 664 and Oviedo (☎950 412; fax 958 038). Open M-F 8am-7pm, Sa 8am-1pm. **DHL** (☎957 766; fax 955 270), Rocafuerte and Flores, in the Intipungo. Open M-F 9am-1pm and 3-6pm, Sa 9am-1pm.

▌ ACCOMMODATIONS

While there is certainly no shortage of rooms in Ibarra, high-quality rooms at moderate prices can be hard to come by. Most budget accommodations congregate along Olmedo or near the train station.

▨ **Hotel Imbabura,** Oviedo 9-33 (☎950 155; fax 958 521), between Narváez and Cifuentes, 1½ blocks from the Parque La Merced. Wood-paneled floors and cots decorate barren rooms; the courtyard makes up for it. Internet access. Rooms US$2 per person.

La Casona de los Lagos, Sucre 350 and Grijalva (☎957 844; fax 951 629). One of the city's few old hotels. Courtyard. Outdoor patio. Other comforts include a tea room, pool table, and bar. Simple rooms all have bath and phone. Rooms US$3 per person.

Residencial San Andrecito (☎958 644), Cifuentes and Oviedo. You get what you pay for: virtually empty rooms leave space for large backpacks. Rooms US$1 per person.

Hostal Madrid, Olmedo 869 and Moncayo (☎643 903). Recently constructed and immaculate. Private bath and cable TV. Rooms US$3.20 per person.

▌ FOOD

Ask Ibarrans where to find a good restaurant, and they'll be as stumped as you are.

▨ **Helados de Paila Rosalía Suárez,** Oviedo 7-82 and Olmedo (☎958 778). A wooden cutout of Mickey Mouse welcomes you to this homemade ice cream shop and Ibarran tradition. Two scoops US$0.20). Open daily 7:30am-7pm.

▨ **Café Arte,** Salinas 5-43 and Flores (☎950 806), is both a cafe and gallery. Wooden menus contain a unique combination of coffees, Mexican specialties, and cocktails (US$0.30-2). Cultural films and concerts F-Sa. Open M-Th 4-11pm, F-Sa 4pm-late.

Café Coffee Kaffee, Moreno 404 and Rocafuerte (☎640 438 or 951 848). This redundantly named favorite is filled with an aura of romance. Cappuccino sprinkled with chocolate US$0.50. Burgers US$0.50. Open M-Th 4-10pm, F 4pm-1am, Sa 6pm-1am.

▌ SIGHTS AND ENTERTAINMENT

Ibarra is home to many interesting historical and architectural structures. Rising more than 30m high, the stunning white **obelisk** at Narváez and Velasco sticks out like a sore thumb in its surroundings. The landmark looks more like a monument to Cleopatra than to Miguel de Ibarra, who founded this Spanish colony in 1606. Ibarra has two peaceful parks, both surrounded by outstanding architecture. The **Parque La Merced,** on Flores between Cifuentes and Olmedo, exhibits a statue of

Dr. Victor Manuel Peñaherrera (1865-1930), an Ecuadorian Supreme Court judge. On the west side of the park, the **Basílica La Merced** supports a portrayal of the Virgin Mary adorned with a crown of silver (only sporadically open to the public). The eclectic **Parque Moncayo** is on Flores between Bolívar and Sucre. The surrounding architecture is exceptional, especially that of the **cathedral** and the municipal building. While the golden altar outshines most everything else in the cathedral, the building also houses huge portraits of all 12 apostles, painted by local artist Rafael Troya. Car-endowed Ibarrans escape to **Laguna Yahuarcocha** (Quichua for "Lake of Blood") for some fresh air and great views of the surrounding valley. Those not too frightened by the creepy name sometimes rent canoes (US$1 for 30min.) or jog around the rim of the lake, only 9km north of Ibarra.

On weekends, the **Cine Grand Columbia,** on Moreno between Sucre and Rocafuerte, sometimes shows cultural films; stop by to check a schedule. **El Encuentro,** Olmedo 959 (☎959 526), is a mellow bar. **Tequila Rock,** Oviedo 636 and Sucre, is much smaller. (Cover US$1, includes a drink.) **Café Arte** has live music on the weekends and occasional cultural movies (M and Th 8pm, Sa 4pm, Su 5pm).

🔁 DAYTRIP FROM IBARRA

SAN ANTONIO DE IBARRA

Cooperativo 28 de Septiembre and San Miguel de Ibarra labeled "San Antonio" both go up the hill to the park and can be caught on the obelisk, near the corner of Acosta and Chica Narvaz (10min., every 20min., US$0.08). A taxi from Ibarra should cost US$1.

With its economy firmly rooted in exquisite **woodcarving,** San Antonio de Ibarra caters to tourists with a hankering for carved chess sets or exquisite wooden sculptures. The town has little else to offer, but the work is of such quality that it has carved a place for itself among the South American *artesanía* elite. San Antonio's woodwork stands out because of its meticulous, stunning precision. People from across the Americas flock to San Antonio to witness the town's handiwork and buy a piece or two. Only recently has San Antonio become known for its craft worldwide, but already many shops sell pieces overseas, and the influx of foreign visitors continues to increase. San Antonio is west of Ibarra along the Panamerican Highway. The layout is simple. Most of the woodcarving galleries are either around the park or along 27 de Noviembre, the town's main street.

The **Unión Artesanal de San Antonio de Ibarra,** at the end of the Parque Calderón, is a set of 11 woodcarving cooperatives that sell pieces straight from the tables they're made on. Many shops carry very similar carvings, but there are always a few unique pieces to be found. (Open daily 9am-7pm. Visa.) To the east side of the park, the **Galería de Arte Luis Potosí** has several rooms and two floors of work a little finer and more detailed than the offerings in other shops. (☎932 056. Open daily 8am-6pm.) More shops line 27 de Noviembre toward the Panamerican Highway. Some of these galleries produce larger works, some as tall as 2m, and carry a multitude of abstract, modernist carvings.

NEAR IBARRA: LA ESPERANZA

Buses from Ibarra to Esperanza (30min., every 20min., US$1.20) can be picked up at the Parque Grijalva on the corner of Sánchez y Cifuentes and Toro Moreno, or at the southernmost end of Ibarra, on the corner of De La Torre and Retorno. Taxis US$2. If your boots are made for walking, the hike to La Esperanza is along Retorno, the main road (7km, 2hr.).

Life is more or less peaceful as you head out of Ibarra toward La Esperanza. The idyllic landscape, punctuated by Volcán Imbabura and other majestic mountains, encourages clear thinking and deep breathing. This tranquility is interrupted only by the groaning of buses struggling their way uphill and the occasional truck filled with military men rumbling toward the neighboring citadel. La Esperanza really has just one road, **Galo Plaza,** which runs towards Imbabura. Nearly all attractions in the town are accessed from this cobblestone roadway. 🔁**Casa Aida** is a green and yellow building on the right, far up the hill from Ibarra, consisting of a number of traditional dormitories as well as a five-person straw hut with two beds in a loft accessible only by step ladder. Thick brick walls and blankets provide plenty of warmth on frigid nights, and the kitchen and baths are impeccable. Common baths have 24-hour hot water. (☎642 020. Rooms US$1 per person.) Casa Aida also boasts a fabulous **restaurant**. For good day-hike, try getting to the top of **Loma Cubilche** (3826m; 3hr. up, 2hr. return.) Die-hard climbers use La Esperanza as a base before attempting **Volcán Imbabura** (4621m). To get to Imbabura, head toward Cubilche, but turn right on the street before the bridge. This road goes most of the way up, and various paths lead to the top. Esperanza has resident guides available for this hike (US$8 per day).

TULCÁN   ☎06

There are only three reasons to go to Tulcán: you are going to Colombia, you are coming from Colombia, or you know someone who lives in Tulcán. Most of the action can be found along parallel streets **Colón, Olmedo, Sucre, Bolívar,** and **Arellano.** In the center of things is the **Parque Principal** (sometimes called the **Plaza Central**). The bigger **Parque Isidro Ayora,** between Arellano and Bolívar, is two blocks southeast of the enormous **cemetery.** The **terminal** is located 1½km uphill from the *centro* on Bolívar. The **Colombian border** is northeast of town, 6km down **Brazil,** which begins at the northeast end of town. Only taxis and minivans go to the border. **Cooperativo Carchi** vans can be picked up on the Venezuela side of Parque Ayora and go to the border when they fill up (US$0.40). **Transportes Popular** buses run from the terminal to the **Parque Principal** (5min., US$0.15). Buses go down Sucre or Colón and return on Bolívar. Buses leave from the terminal to: **Quito** (6hr., every hr. 1:30am-10:30pm, US$2.60) via **Ibarra** (3hr., US$1.35) and **Otavalo** (4hr., US$1.60). **Ministerio de Turismo,**

> ### BORDER CROSSING: INTO COLOMBIA
>
> Crossing the border (*frontera*) between Ecuador and Colombia at the Rumichaca Bridge is usually fairly straightforward. Tourists are required to present a valid **passport,** to be stamped at the immigration office of each country, and to turn in and/or receive a 90-day tourist card. Very few nationalities need a visa to enter Colombia. Copies of passports, driver's licenses, birth certificates, library cards, and doctor's notes are not acceptable identification; officials are very strict about this. A **provisional passport** may be acceptable. Occasionally, backpackers will be asked to prove that they have sufficient funds (US$20, students US$10) for each day they plan to stay in the country. Officials may also ask to see a round-trip ticket proving that a visitor intends to leave the country within 90 days, the maximum amount of time a traveler can spend in either country in a one-year period. If you want to stay longer, you'll need to obtain a **visa** (see **Visas and Work Permits,** p. 27). Tulcán's border never closes, and the **Ecuadorian Immigration Office** (☎/fax 980 704) is open 24 hours. Ecuador charges a US$0.80 **exit tax.** If crossing from Colombia into Ecuador, be sure to get your passport stamped inside the Colombian immigration office, as thieves often pretend to be border officers.

in the CENAF building at Romicacha bridge. (☎983 892. Open M-F 8:30am-1pm and 1:30-5pm.) **Banco Pichincha** is at Sucre and 10 de Agosto. (☎980 529. Open M-F 8am-6pm, Sa 8am-2pm, Su 9am-1pm.) **Emergency:** ☎101 or 980 101. **Police:** Manabí and Guatemala, to the north. (☎981 321, 980 345.). **Post Office:** Bolívar 53027 and Junín. (☎980 552. Open M-F 8am-noon and 2-6pm, Sa 9am-noon.) Unless you want to spend more than US$4 per person, your accommodations in Tulcán will not be elegant. Sucre, just west of the Parque Principal, hops with lodgings. **Hotel Internacional Azteca,** Bolívar and Atahuallpa, one block west of the Parque Ayora, on the 2nd floor, has the cleanest rooms in town. Rooms have hot-water bath, phone, and TV. (☎981 447; fax 980 481. Singles US$1.90; doubles US$2.60.) **Hotel España,** Sucre and Pichincha, has big windows, hot water in the mornings, baths, and color TVs. (☎983 860. Rooms US$2.80 per person.) **Residencial Sucre,** Junín 396 and Bolívar, near plenty of restaurants. Where there are windows at all, they face walls, making rooms pitch-black. Perk up in the lobby with a fuzzy TV and comfy chairs. (Rooms US$1 per person.) A number of Colombian restaurants have made a place for themselves alongside the Ecuadorian establishments. To sample this international culinary excitement, visit eateries along Sucre and Bolívar, below 10 de Agosto.

AVENUE OF THE VOLCANOES

LATACUNGA ☎03

Between 1532 and 1904, Volcán Cotopaxi, the tallest active volcano in the world, would not stop erupting. Twenty-two times, the fire-spitter devastated and sometimes entirely destroyed the neighboring city of Latacunga. Each time, the citizens of Latacunga dutifully chose to return to their home and rebuild virtually everything. This leads to one of the classic Ecuadorian mysteries—why in the world did they keep going back? Maybe it was the fruit, coffee, sugar, cacao, rubber, and herds of cattle that are sustained on soil made rich by millennia of volcanic ash. It could have been the gold and silver discovered and mined there. Or maybe it was the incredible panorama—a crown of Andean peaks that surrounds the 2700m-high town—and the proximity to natural wonders that has made it a popular tourist base. And then again, perhaps it was Cotopaxi itself—its surreal, tranquil, white cone towering majestically on the northeast horizon. After years of relative geological stability, Latacunga has settled into the role of Cotopaxi province capital and regional transportation hub.

CENTRAL ECUADOR

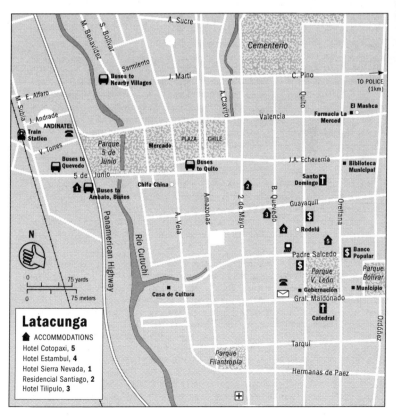

Latacunga

🏠 ACCOMMODATIONS
Hotel Cotopaxi, 5
Hotel Estambul, 4
Hotel Sierra Nevada, 1
Residencial Santiago, 2
Hotel Tilipulo, 3

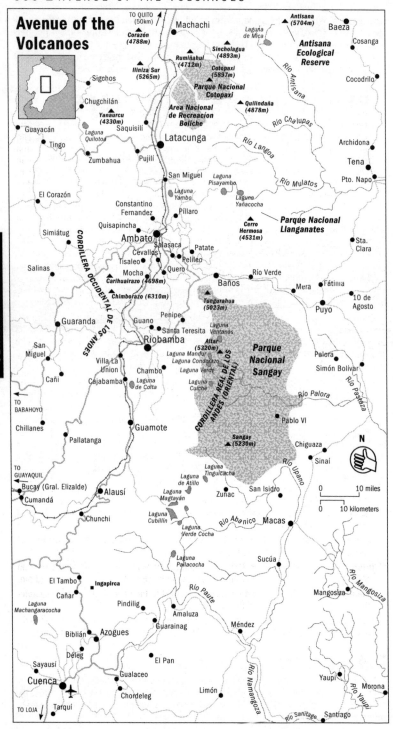

Avenue of the Volcanoes

TRANSPORTATION

Trains: The **train station** (☎960 115), M.A. Subia and J. Andrade, is on the far side of the Panamerican Highway. Trains go to **Riobamba** (6hr.; M, Tu, F, Sa 7am; US$8) and **Quito** (7hr., Sa 11:30am, US$8). Call ahead to confirm schedule and prices.

Buses: The best bus company is **Transportes Cotopaxi** (☎800 752). Main offices are on the Panamerican Highway across from J. Andrade, but most buses depart elsewhere; only tickets to Quevedo need to be bought at the office. Open M-Sa 9am-noon and 2-6pm. Buses to **Quito** (2hr., every 10-15min. 5am-7pm, US$0.90) leave from a parking lot next to the market at Amazonas and 5 de Junio (see map). Buses to **Ambato** (1hr., every 10-15min., US$0.60) and **Baños** (2hr., every 20-30min., US$1.10) leave from the Panamerican Highway. Other buses leave from 5 de Junio, 1 block west of the Panamerican Highway to: **Quevedo** (5hr., every 1½hr. 5am-7pm, US$2.10); **Pujilí** (20min., every 5min. 6:30am-8pm, US$0.20); **Zumbahua** (2hr., every hr., US$0.60); **Pilaló** (3hr., US$0.80); and **La Maná** (4 hr., US$1.60). Buses to the loop of small *pueblos* surrounding Latacunga line up along Benavidez, next to the river, starting at Simón Bolívar go to: **Saquisilí** (30min., every 10min. 5:30am-6:30pm, US$0.20); **Sigchos** (2½hr., every 30min. 9:30am-4pm, US$0.80); and **Chugchilán** (4hr., noon, US$1.10). On Thursdays, buses to Chugchilán and Sigchos leave from Saquisilí.

ORIENTATION AND PRACTICAL INFORMATION

The most heavily traveled part of Latacunga is along the **Panamerican Highway.** This strip has its selection of solid hotels and restaurants mostly concerned with the vehicular traffic passing through. On the other side of the **Río Cutuchi** lies the main part of the city, sloping up the mountainside in a grid-like fashion. Shops line the main drag, **Amazonas,** while the municipal and tourist sections are near the **Parque Vicente León** on **Quito** and **Quevedo.** Buses will take you across the river into the main part of the town; otherwise it's only a short walk.

Tourist Office: Latacunga doesn't really have a tourist office, but the owners of the **Hotels Cotopaxi, Estambul,** and **Tilipulo** happily provide info on the town. Likewise, many tour groups are knowledgeable about the subject.

Banks: Banco de Guayaquil (☎813 902), is at Sánchez de Orellama and Maldonado. It's best to exchange money before coming to Latacunga in Ambato or Riobamba. Open M-F 9am-6pm, Sa 9am-1pm.

Market: Essential to the Latacunga experience, the **mercado** lies between 5 de Junio and Clavijo, and is a tribute to random, cheap stuff, especially on Sa. Open daily from 7am-6pm. For general food supplies, try the **supermarket** next to Restaurante Rodelú.

Emergency: ☎101.

Police: (☎812 666), on General Proaño about 1km from the center of town. About a 20min. walk east from the cemetery.

Hospital: Hospital General (☎800 331 or 800 332), Hmas. Paez and 2 de Mayo, has ambulance service. Prices increase with distance.

Internet Access: ACCOMP (☎810 710; email accomp@uio.satnet.net), in the mall on Salcedo between Quito and Quevedo. US$1.20 per hr. Open M-Sa 9am-1pm and 3-8pm.

Telephones: EMETEL Maldonado and Queredo, next to the post office. Open daily 8am-9pm. **Andinate,** on Torres and the Panamerican.

Post Office: (☎811 394), Quevedo and Maldonado, a block from Parque Vicente León and next door to the EMETEL office. Open M-F 8am-noon and 2-7pm, Sa 8am-noon.

ACCOMMODATIONS

While Latacunga is not tourist-swamped, it does have its fair share of hotels. Several lie conveniently along the Panamerican Highway; others are in the midst of town across the river. Most fill up the night before Saquisilí's Thursday market. Many hotels will also arrange daytrips to Cotopaxi (US$20-30).

Hotel Cotopaxi (☎ 801 310), on Salcedo, next to Banco del Austro on the Parque León. Perks include private baths, very friendly staff (able to offer tour info.), hot water, a cafe, TV, luggage storage, a safe, and excellent views of the park. The central location brings with it the continual drone of passing buses. Rooms US$2.80 per person.

Hotel Estambul, Quevedo 6-44 (☎ 800 354) between Salcedo and Guayaquil. Situated in the city center it offers immaculate and comfortable rooms with shared or private bath and hot water. Enjoy the evening air in the courtyard, or a view of the city from the rooftop terrace. Laundry tub available. Rooms US$3-4 per person.

Hotel Los Nevados (☎ 800 407), on 5 de Junio, next to the bus stops for Ambato and Baños. Quiet. Cute bedcovers and birds painted on stained wood above the doors invite you to relax, take a warm shower and think about your laundry drying on the terrace. Singles US$1.60, with bath US$2; doubles US$2.80, with bath US$3.60.

Residencial Santiago (☎ 802 164), 2 de Mayo and Guayaquil. Large, comfortable rooms have TV, mirrors, and hot water in the sparkling, color-coordinated bathrooms. Common room has comfy chairs for reading or napping. Rooms US$2 per person.

Hotel Tilipulo (☎ 802 130), Guayaquil and Quevedo, on the corner 1 block north and 1 block west of the Parque León. Prides itself on being a friendly sort of place. Rooms have names like "the illusions" or the "the sunflowers." Rooms US$3 per person.

◖ FOOD

Latacunga's narrow streets are crammed with scores of typical restaurants that offer the standard *almuerzo* (US$0.50). Even cheaper meals can be found in the *mercado*, but hygiene is not guaranteed.

Restaurant Rodelú (☎ 800 956), on Quito between Salcedo and Guayaquil, under the hotel of the same name. Devour a divine pizza with roasted pepper or parsley pesto (US$1.20-1.40) while bopping to the tango music in the background. Pastas US$1.40 and up. Open M-Sa 8am-3pm and 5-9:30pm, Su 8am-3-pm.

La Casa de Chocolate, Amazonas and Guayaquil. Walls of pastel green and turquoise, gingham tablecloths, and a bright yellow fridge provide perfect ambiance for *telenovela* watching. Great Hot Chocolate US$0.40. *Empanadas* US$0.10. Open M-Sa 8am-9pm.

◉ ❀ SIGHTS AND FESTIVALS

Admittedly, most tourists coming to Latacunga are here to see sights outside of town. However, if you're here for the night, there are a few things to keep you busy. The **Molinos de Monserrat,** next to the waterfall at Vela near Maldonado, is the center of the province's **Casa de la Cultura** organization and houses a gallery of local artwork, a museum of ethnology, a small library, and a riverside amphitheater. Built by the Jesuits in 1756 and originally used as a grain millery, this colonial building now pays homage to the culture and traditions of the area's inhabitants. (Open Tu-Sa 8am-noon and 2-6pm. US$0.40, students US$0.10.) The **mercado** is impossible to miss; its mammoth offerings take up several blocks from the river to Amazonas. (Open daily 7am-6pm; Sa is the most popular day.) Visitors September 23-24 can see the traditional fiesta of **La Virgen de Las Mercedes,** in which *indígena* men dress up as black women and engage in a ceremony that involves squirting perfumed milk on bystanders. Then during the **Mama Negra** festival (Nov. 11) white men cross-dress and paint their faces black. This is also coincides with **Latacunga's Independence Day,** which is celebrated with parades, fairs, and bullfights and commemorates the day Latacungan patriots defeated Spanish royalists in 1820.

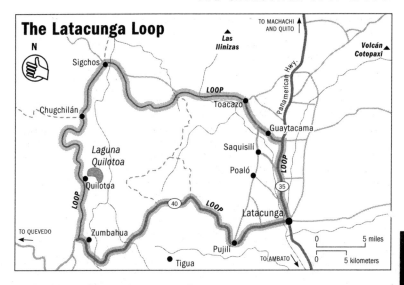

THE LATACUNGA LOOP   ☎03

To the west of Latacunga, narrow streets are replaced by fields of *chilco* and hay, and the area sometimes seems more populated by sheep than by humans. The small villages are hidden away among a patchwork farms and the vast, jagged-rock faces of the Andean peaks. Visiting them is an excellent way to take a trip off-road and submerge yourself in a foreign world, but expect to be a pioneer of sorts in finding your way. Hiking will probably be required on more distant trips, as the bus service to many of these out-of-the-way places is inconvenient and inadequate. The fairly reliable bus service to Sasquisilí and Pujilí is the exception (see Latacunga: Buses p. 507).

PUJILÍ

Frequent bus service to Pujilí from the corner of 5 de Junio and M.A. Subia, one block from the Panamerican Highway next to the railroad tracks in Latacunga (15min., every 5min. 6:30am-8pm, US$0.20). There is nowhere to stay in Pujilí—don't miss the last bus.

The first step in the loop, Pujilí, is effectively a suburb of Latacunga. The town's main attractions are the Sunday **market** at Rocafuerte and Pichincha and the world-famous pottery workshops at **La Victoria** (head uphill from where the bus stop at the statue of the welder). Come June 3-6 for the festival of **Corpus Christi**.

ZUMBAHUA

To get back to Latacunga, catch the Quevedo-Latacunga bus on the "highway" above Zumbahua (2hr., every hr. until 8pm, US$0.30).

As Latacunga and Pujilí fade slowly into the distance, the scenery becomes filled with fertile, black earth on the way up into the hills, and dusty grit on the descent. The capital of the local communities, Zumbahua hosts a large **Saturday market.** Several new hotels are trying to make Zumbahua more tourist friendly. **Hostal Richard,** offers rooms with luke-warm water adorned with local paintings (US$2 per person). One step up, **Hostal Cóndor Matzi,** also on the market plaza, provides bright rooms with neat beds, hot-water common bathrooms, and a wood stove downstairs. (☎814 610. Rooms US$3 per person, with breakfast US$6.) Hotels can arrange guided tours to Quilatoa and other nearby destinations.

LAGUNA QUILOTOA

There are several ways to get to and from the neighboring towns of Chugchilán (22km) and Zumbahua (14km). The bus from Chugchilán leaves around 4am. Trucks from Zumbahua or Chugchilán will take tourists to Quilotoa (US$6 and up). For a little bit more, many drivers will wait to bring you back. To hike from Zumbahua you must cross the Río Toa!chi Canyon and then head along the main road (5-7hr.). The owners of Cabañas Quilotoa can provide maps showing a strenuous off-road hike from Quilotoa to Chugchilán (about 5hr.). Warm clothes are key—it gets cold at 3800m, and the weather changes quickly. Alternatively, rent a horse to go from Chugchilán to Quilotoa (US$10).

At the top of the world, where the heavens meet the earth, lies the awe-inspiring **Laguna Quilotoa** (3854m), contained in an enormous crater which was once the colossal Volcán Quilotoa. One glance at this emerald lagoon will justify the arduous journey you endured to get here. Hikes down to the lake take 30 minutes or less, but the hike back up is quite steep and may take more than twice as long. Mules are available for hire to take you either direction (US$2). A walk around the edge of the crater takes about five hours—halfway around from the access road at the top of the crater, and you're already well on your way to Chugchilán. However, due to recent landslides, the hike has become a bit treacherous in parts. Near the access road, the town of Quilotoa is home to several family-run "hotels" which compete for the settlement's scanty overnight crowd. Because of the extremely remote location, these accommodations may test even the hardiest traveler's standard of comfort. The primary concern is warmth, as temperatures at this altitude plummet when the sun goes down. That said, **Cabañas Quilotoa** has common rooms complete with wool blankets, a wood stove, and hot water. (Rooms US$3; with meals US$5). The **Hostal Quilotoa** is simpler, with three beds (or a dirt floor) and no running water. (Breakfast US$0.80; dinner US$1. Rooms US$1.20 per person.)

CHUGCHILÁN

The daily bus to Latacunga (4hr.; M-Sa 3am, Su 6am; US$1.10) or Zumbahua via Quiltoa with more options depending on the day; the Black Sheep Inn has a schedule.

The tiny town of Chugchilán has seen more than its share of visitors in recent years. Part of it may be due to an oasis soaked in idealism: the ⊠**Black Sheep Inn,** located about 500m before Chugchilán on the road from Sigchos. A completely organic mountainside complex conceived and constructed by a young North American couple in the early 1990s, the inn seems to be more *of* the land than *on* the land. Ducks, llamas, and even an *oveja negra* (black sheep) roam the thoughtfully planned grounds, which include an organic garden, a composting toilet, and hot-water showers with strategically-placed windows that provide soap-dropping views of the Andean countryside. The price of a room includes two home-cooked vegetarian meals, served in the comfortable dining room with other travelers; tea, coffee and potable water are all free. (☎(03) 814 587; email blksheep@interactive.net.ec; www.blacksheepinn.com. Internet US$1.25 per 15min. Dorms US$15 per person; singles US$30; doubles US$36; triples US$51.) **Mama Hilda's,** a little closer to town, is cute and clean and run by a wonderful Ecuadorian woman. (Rooms US$7, includes 3 meals.) For cheaper and very basic rooms, **Hostal Bosque Nublado** is trying to establish itself. (Rooms US$4, includes dinner.) Because of the relative difficulty of transportation and the isolated beauty of the region, a multi-night stay in Chugchilán may be worthwhile. The owners of the Black Sheep Inn can suggest some excellent excursions in the vicinity varying in difficulty and commitment. For example, Quilotoa is not far off, and the **Río Toachi Canyon** is even closer. Following your nose in the other direction will lead to a **European cheese factory,** established decades ago by a Swiss entrepreneur and now run by local Ecuadorians. Some mysterious **Inca ruins** of the "circle in the ground" UFO variety lie three hours away by foot. A one or two-day descent leads into an awe-inspiring **cloud forest** on the western slopes of the Andes. Hiking maps of the area are provided by the Black Sheep Inn and trucks and **horses** are available for hire (US$10).

SAQUISILÍ

Frequent buses to Latacunga leave from Bolívar and Sucre (20min., every 10min. 5:30am-6:30pm, US$0.20) and once a week to Chugchilán (Th 11:30am).

One of the principle reasons for travelers to visit the Latacunga area is to shop at Saquisilí's acclaimed Thursday morning market. Come Thursday, Saquisilí explodes in living color, splashing its goods out among the various town plazas. Follow the crowds of people 1km north of the main market area to visit the livestock market. (Open Th until 10am.) Saquisilí's spanking new **San Carlos Hotel,** Bolívar and Sucre, offers private baths, matching bedspreads, clean tile floors, a cafe, and a garage. (☎721 057. Singles US$2; doubles US$3.90; triples US$4.) Two blocks down Bolívar back toward Latacunga, the **Salón Pichincha** welcomes guests like family. (☎721 247. Rooms US$1 per person.) Hotels in Saquisilí and Latacunga tend to fill up Wednesday nights, so call ahead to make a reservation.

PARQUE NACIONAL COTOPAXI

Cotopaxi, derived from Cayapa, means "neck of the sun;" in Quichua, it means "boundary of the moon." For years, the volcano has been worshipped by *indígenas*, mountaineers, and seekers of beauty. In a paradox of thermal *fumaroles* and glaciers, **Volcán Cotopaxi** (5897m) is the tallest active volcano in the world. While many visitors come to scale this lava rock, the park offers more subtle pleasures as well. The flower-filled *páramo* surrounding the peak is home to many of Ecuador's unique species. (Open daily 7am-6pm. US$10.)

WILDLIFE. Cotopaxi suffers from a variety of exploitations. Next to pine and eucalyptus timber sites, INEFAN conducts studies to nurture and preserve the llama population and the rest of the *páramo* residents. The park is hopping with white-tailed deer, who have made an impressive comeback under the watchful eyes of park management. Hot on their tails—literally—are the Andean pumas, whose numbers have slowly but steadily climbed since a low point in the mid-1970s. Other mammals, though seldom seen, are the Andean fox, the Andean spectacled bear, and the knee-high red brocket deer; most visible are the herds of wild horses. The park has received much attention as the last refuge of the endangered Andean condor (there are less than 100 remaining), but also nests such rarities as the Andean hillstar, the Andean lapwing, the Andean gull, the great thrush, and the tongue-twisting carunculated caracara. The innocent-looking lancetilla plant sucks water and nutrients from the roots of neighboring plants, while the arquitecta plant is still used as a diuretic.

MOUNTAINEERING. Without a doubt, the major adrenaline-inducing attraction of the park is the immense **Volcán Cotopaxi.** The first climbers to reach Cotopaxi's rim were the energetic German Wilhelm Reiss and Colombian Angel Escobar in 1872. Since then, thousands of world-class mountaineers and adventurers have made the icy ascent. The climb is strenuous and requires ice-climbing gear, but isn't technically difficult. Nevertheless, climbers of all abilities can benefit from a properly-qualified (INEFAN) guide who knows the peculiarities of the ascent and some of the natural history. Expeditions to the summit begin from the José Ribas refuge (4800m) at around midnight, to insure hard-packed snow and safer conditions. It usually takes six to seven hours to reach the top, but only about two to three hours to return to the refuge. Due to the necessity of an early start, it is imperative to stay in the refuge the night before. The 45-person shelter has bunk beds, clean water, and electricity (US$10 per person). Visitors must bring plenty of warm clothes, heavy sleeping bags, nourishment, and acclimatized lungs.

For more information on climbing Cotopaxi, check out one of the travel agencies in Quito, which are especially abundant along J. León Mera (see p. 433). Make sure your guide is certified by the **Ecuadorian Association of Mountain Guides (ASEGUIM),** the most respected association around. **Compañía de Guías,** Jorge Washington 425 and 6 de Diciembre in Quito, offers a two-day summit climb

(US$160 per person) complete with food, shelter, transportation, equipment, and an ASEGUIM-certified guide fluent in a number of languages. (☎/fax 504 773; email quismontania@accessinter.net; www.ecuaworld.com/guides. Open daily 9:30am-1pm and 3-6:30pm.) **Safari Tours,** Calama 380 and León Mera, also provides experienced, ASEGUIM-approved mountain guides fluent in a number of languages. Their two-day summit package (US$185 per person) includes food, shelter, transportation and equipment if you didn't bring your own. (☎552 505; fax 220 426; email admin@safariec.ecuanex.net.ec. Open daily 9am-7pm.) If you're already in Latacunga, **Expediciones Amazonicas** (☎03 800 375), Quito 16-67, has CETUR-qualified guides and similar services to the Quito-based companies. **The Biking Dutchman,** in Quito (see p. 433) offers mountain bike trips around the park.

HIKING AND CAMPING. From the plain at the base of the volcano, hikers equipped only with hiking boots, raingear, and a warm sweater can set off in almost any direction. The absence of trees and the ever-present Cotopaxi make navigation easy. A flat walk around **Lake Limpiopungo** takes about an hour—slightly more adventurous hikers can extend the walk by venturing into the low hills at the base of **Volcán Rumañahui** (4712m), on the opposite side of the lake from Cotopaxi (2hr. to the top). For those planning on spending the night, campgrounds within the park are about a 30-minute drive down the main road from the entrance gate. The road crosses a small bridgeless river. A sign for **campgrounds** will be on the left, and a short jaunt leads to a campsite fit for a king. Most people stay in tents, but there is a less reliable cabin as well; at least it has running water and is close to the shore of the immense Lake Limpiopungo. Up the road another 15 minutes is a second sign for **campgrounds** on the right. About as big as the other, this one comes with a view of Cotopaxi. There is a cabin here (US$0.10) but no running water. A tiny **museum** on the path up to the campgrounds is a tribute to the National Park and is furnished with stuffed wildlife, a 3-D representation of the park, and wall-to-wall info on the history of Cotopaxi. Outside the museum is a helpful map of the park, which shows trails leading to the base of Rumañahui and a garden.

TRANSPORTATION. It is a good idea to have some kind of four-wheel-drive transportation in the park since the main attractions are a not-particularly-scenic hike from the nearest bus stop on the Panamerican Highway (2hr. to the park entrance and 4hr. to the lake). Any of the buses going between Quito and Latacunga can drop you off right at the park's southern access road or 10 minutes farther south in the town of **Lasso** (from Latacunga, 30min., every 10min, US$0.30; from Quito, 1½hr., every 10min., US$0.80). Those who risk hitchhiking say that it is fairly easy to catch a ride into the park from the intersection of the entrance road and the Panamerican Highway. From Lasso, taxis and trucks take passengers into the park. If you want to go all the way to the refuge, it'll cost US$16, and you'll still need to hike about 45 minutes up from the parking lot. In Latacunga, the hotels Estambul, Cotopaxi, and Tilipulo can arrange transportation to the park, as well as group tours (starting at US$25 per person, not including entrance fee).

AMBATO   ☎03

Located 128km south of Quito, in the Province of Tungurahua, Ambato is another city surrounded by volcanoes and glaciated peaks. The city itself is warm, and even in late afternoon, stored-up heat radiates from the many stone walls. The modern mountain metropolis was built on a series of different plateaus and hills, giving the city a quirky topography. *Ambateños* pride themselves on being productive, hard-working people who have continued the centuries-old tradition of farming the region's rich land. Ambato's cultural rebirth has been as fruitful as its economic one, particularly in the area of South American literature. Called "the land of the three Juans," Ambato has been home to novelists **Juan Montalvo, Juan Benigno Vela,** and **Juan León Mera,** as well as several other intellectual figures whose names now meet at the city's street corners and in its impressive museums.

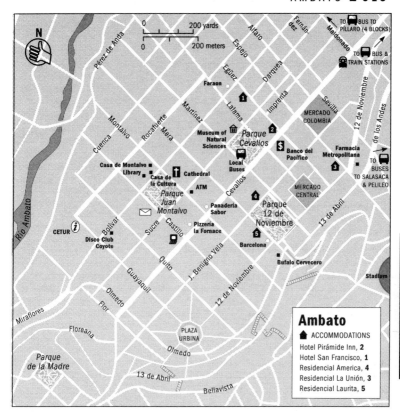

Ambato

▲ ACCOMMODATIONS

Hotel Pirámide Inn, **2**
Hotel San Francisco, **1**
Residencial America, **4**
Residencial La Unión, **3**
Residencial Laurita, **5**

TRANSPORTATION

Long-Distance Buses: Buses leave from the terminal to: **Guayaquil** (6hr., every hr. 7am-2:30pm, US$2.80); **Quito** (2½hr., every 15min. 6am-6pm, US$1.40); **Santo Domingo** (4hr., 15 per day, 8am-9:45pm, US$1.90); **Babahoyo** (5hr., every 30min. 6am-6pm, US$2.50); **Riobamba** (30min., every 45min. 5:30am-7pm, US$0.70); **Baños** (45min., every 30min. until 8pm, US$0.40); **Tena** (6hr., 12:30pm, US$2.80); and **Puyo** (3hr.; 9, 11am, noon; US$1.40). When the Baños road is open to Puyo, a faster bus runs from Baños to the Oriente (Su-M).

Local Buses: Buses to towns in the vicinity of Ambato depart from several places in the downtown area. From **Parque Cevallos,** buses depart to **Ficoa, Atocha, Ingahurro** and Super-maxi, and **Pinllo** (15-30min., every 10min. 6:15am-7:30pm, US$0.10). Buses leave from Los Andes and Tomás Sevilla to **Picaigua** (10min., every 10min. 6:30am-6:30pm, US$0.10) and **Pelileo** (35min., every 10min. 6:10am-6:10pm, US$0.20) via **Salasaca** (25min., US$0.10). Long-distance buses bound for Baños also stop here.

Taxis: (☎821 190), or hail one at any corner. A trip across town costs US$0.60.

ORIENTATION AND PRACTICAL INFORMATION

The **terminal** and **train station** are both in the northern end of the city, about 2km down **12 de Noviembre** from the *centro*, which is easily reached by taxi or bus. Turn right on the street in front of the terminal and walk uphill about 200m. At the first major intersection, catch the bus to the *centro* (US$.10). A slew of budget hotels border the **Parque 12 de Noviembre.** Two other important parks are found in the downtown area: **Parque Juan Montalvo** (the center of the city's government offices and agencies) and **Parque Cevallos** (the departure spot for many local buses). The downtown area is contained within a five-by-five block area.

Tourist Information: Ministerio de Turismo, formerly known as CETUR (☎821 800), Guayaquil and Rocafuerte. Armed with exhaustive lists of local accommodations and festivals. Occasional English spoken. Open M-F 8am-4:30pm. **INEFAN Office** (☎848 542), Quis Quis Caspicara, has information on the Parque Nacional Llanganates.

Tour Agencies: Metropolitan Touring (☎411 095), Rocafuerte and Montalvo. Open M-F 9am-7pm, Sa 9:15am-1pm. **Casatours** (☎825 842), on Cuenca and Latama.

Currency Exchange: Banco del Pacífico (☎844 942) is at Lalama and Cevallos. M-F 8:45am-4pm. There is a Cirrus **ATM** on Sucre and Montalvo, across from the cathedral.

Market: Sells mostly local produce and household items. Especially active on Monday. Partly indoors on 12 de Noviembre, between Martínez and Egüez, and a block up Vela in Mercado Colombia.

Laundromat: Química Automática (☎822 888), Vela 432 and Quito. Open M-F 8am-6:30pm, Sa 8am-noon.

Police: Atahuallpa 568 (☎101).

Hospital: Hospital Regional Ambato (☎821 059; emergency ☎822 099), Pasteur and Unidad Nacional.

Telephones: There are 2 **EMETEL** (☎820 034) offices: next to post office, and a block away along Castillo towards Rocafuerte. Both open M-F 8am-12:30pm and 1-10pm, Sa 8am-6pm.

Internet Access: Ciudadandina, Castillo 5-28 and Cevallos (☎822 242). US$0.80 per hr. Open M-F 9am-8pm, Sa 9am-7pm.

Post Office: (☎823 332), Castillo and Bolívar. Open M-F 7:30am-7pm, Sa 8am-2pm.

▚ ACCOMMODATIONS

▨ **Hotel San Francisco** (☎840 148), Egüez and Bolívar. Ecuadorians flock to this place on the weekends. If you can stand the noise penetrating the thin walls, the spacious rooms will do you good. Rooms US$2 per person.

Residencial America, on Vela near Mera. Run by a friendly family. Spotless rooms with high ceilings, hardwood floors, and large beds. Some rooms have small balconies with views of the park. Clean, common baths have hot water. Rooms US$1.60 per person.

Hotel Pirámide Inn (☎842 092), Cevallos and Egüez, above Pollo a la Brasa. Enjoy the tidy, carpeted rooms, colorfully tiled private baths equipped with soap and shampoo, and cable TV. Rooms US$5 per person and up.

Residencial Laurita (☎821 377), on Mera between Vela and 12 de Noviembre, screams simplicity. Except for the occasional cool ceilings and funky tiles, these stripped-down rooms contain walls and beds. Hot water. Rooms US$1.60 per person.

Hostal La Unión (☎822 375), 12 de Noviembre and Espejo, in the market district. Clean, basic rooms. Hot common baths. Rooms US$0.80 per person.

◖ FOOD

▨ **K'feteria Marcelo** (☎828 208), Castillo and Rocafuerte. Let the burgundy-clad man open the door for you, and enjoy a great meal. Great coffee and cappuccinos (US$0.24-0.36) and specialty sandwiches (US$0.44-0.96). Open daily 8am-10pm.

Panadería Sabor (☎825 378), on the corner of Cevallos and Montalvo. Mouth-watering pastries and buns (US$0.10-0.30) will satisfy your sweet tooth. The baked goods come in take out or sit down form. Open daily 6:30am-10pm.

Chocobanana, Rocafuerte 15-77 and Quito (☎826 344). *Ambateños* of all ages meet here for vegetarian sandwiches (US$0.50) and chocolate-covered bananas (US$0.25). Open M-Sa 10am-1:30pm and 4-10pm.

Restaurante Faraon (☎821 252), on Bolívar between Egüez and Lalama. For 25 years locals have kept coming back for excellent Ecuadorian dishes. *Desayuno* US$1. *Almuerzo* US$2. Open daily 8:30am-6pm.

Pizzería La Fornace, (☎823 244) Cevallos 17-28 and Montalvo. Everything about this place looks, tastes, and feels wonderful. A blast of heat from the brick oven and the smell of pizzas (US$1-1.80) greet guests. Takeout available. Open M-Sa noon-11pm.

👁 SIGHTS

▨ INSTITUTO TÉCNICO SUPERIOR BOLÍVAR (ITSB). The institute houses the **Museum of Natural Science,** which is by far the most arresting sight in Ambato. It starts slowly, with black-and-white photos of the Sierra at the beginning of the century (including a Cotopaxi eruption) and some indigenous musical instruments and clothes. The highlight of the museum, however, is its seemingly endless collection of preserved animals, including the world's largest insect species, the elephant beetle. Jaguars, birds, tarantulas, and snakes all preserve their final contorted poses, many in dioramas showing Ecuador's diverse habitats. This exhibit climaxes with the stuff bad dreams are made of—unfortunate **freak animals,** such as a two-headed goats and cyclops dogs. (*Sucre 839, on the Parque Cevallos, between Calama and Martínez. ☎827 395. Open M-F 8am-12:30pm and 2:30-6:30pm. US$1.)*

MONTALVO MANIA. Ambato provides plenty of opportunities to pay homage to its literary hero, **Juan Montalvo** (see **Literature,** p. 427). First there's the **park** that bears his name, well-groomed with bushes carved into topiary shapes. Next to the park, on the corner of Bolívar and Montalvo, is our hero's birthplace and lifelong home, the **Casa de Montalvo.** (*Open M-F 9am-noon and 2-6pm, Sa 10am-1pm. US$1.)* Inside are lots of his written books, including original manuscripts. You'll feel like you've met the man after pondering renditions, sculptures, pictures, the clothes he wore, and the places he knew well. A couple of kilometers from the *centro*, in the suburb of **Ficoa,** lies the **Quinta de Montalvo,** Juan's country residence. *(Take the Ficoa bus, leaving from the Parque Cevallos every 15min. Open M-F 7:30am-5pm.)*

OTHER LOCAL CELEBRITIES. Though Juan Montalvo certainly receives top billing in Ambato, several other *ambateños* may be of interest to visitors. The **Quinta de Mera** (home of **Juan León Mera**) and **Quinta de La Liria** (home of mountain climber **Nicolas Martínez**) in the suburb of Atocha. They are connected and provide a peaceful respite from the city under trees, by the river. *(For both, take the Atocha bus from Parque Cevallos (US$0.10); tell the driver where you're headed. Both open M-F 9am-4:30pm.)*

🎵 ENTERTAINMENT

Ambato doesn't offer much in the way of late-night revelry, but the weekend offers several worthwhile opportunities to join in the *fiesta* and enjoy what fun Ambato has to offer. The **Casa de Cultura** sometimes sponsors films and concerts. Otherwise, **Club Coyote** on Bolívar 2057 and Guayaquil is a nice, chill spot to sip a *cerveza* for US$0.40 (open Tu-Sa 4pm-2am). The rest of Ambato's nightlife sits along Olmedo, just above Parque 12 de Noviembre. A popular spot is the **Bufalo Cervecero,** Olmedo 681 and Mera, which attracts a young crowd and plays mostly Latin music and flashing neon lights. (☎841 685. Open Th-M 4pm-3am.)

NEAR AMBATO: SALASACA AND PELILEO

*Buses to Pelileo (30min., every 10min. 6:10am-6:10pm, US$0.20) via **Salasaca** (20min., US$0.10) leave near Los Andes and Iliniza in the Ferroviaria district. **Baños-bound buses,** leaving Ambato's terminal, also stop at these towns en route.*

The large volume of tourist traffic on the road to Baños creates great shopping opportunities but provides a challenge for those who want to experience more. **Salasaca** offers a wonderful **artisan fair.** The Quechua who live here specialize in making woven ponchos and tapestries. The Sunday market is best (open daily

8am-5pm). To learn about Salasaca and the surrounding area, contact **Alonso Pilla** (☎09 840 125), who gives tours (in Spanish) of the surrounding countryside for US$2. To track him down, walk back toward Ambato on the highway and there will be signs on the left. **Pelileo,** a significantly larger town with a rather turbulent history, is 10 minutes east of Salasaca. Destroyed by earthquakes in 1698, 1797, 1840, 1859, and 1949, it now rests several kilometers from its original spot. After Ambato, it has the most important **market** in the province of Tungurahua, held every Saturday. The strip closer to Ambato is the blue jean capital of Ecuador; they come in all shapes and with varying degrees of bells and whistles.

NEAR AMBATO: PICAIGUA, PATATE, AND PÍLLARO

Picaigua is a 15min. bus ride southeast of Ambato. Buses to Patate leave from the market in Pelileo (25min, every 30min., US$0.20). Buses run to Píllaro (35min., until 6pm, 4pm on Sundays; US$0.30) from across from the fire station in Ambato.

The smaller towns farther from Baños are less visited and more traditional. **Picaigua** demands respect for the jackets that locals sew and sell. The town of **Patate** lies across a golden valley from Pelileo. This fruit-producing marvel is home to the **Complejo Turistico Valle Dorado,** featuring conference rooms, saunas, a water slide, and other diversions. (☎870 253. Open Sa-Su 9am-6pm. US$1.) Far above the garbage dump you'll pass on the road north of Ambato, **Píllaro** bursts with agriculture, apples, and cattle galore. There's a big market on Sunday, but unlike other traditional villages, that's not even the most intriguing draw. Píllaro is the gateway to the brand new **Parque Nacional Llangantes,** where the emperor Atahuallpa supposedly buried his treasure. Nobody has found it—yet. To start searching, hire a camioneta at the park to take you to the end of the line at **Laguna de Tarrubo** or **Laguna Pisayambo,** about 40km away (US$10). Ask at the Municipio in Píllaro for more information. There's only one place to stay in Píllaro: **Hostal Pillareñita,** the tallest building in town. (Rooms with hot bath US$2 per person.)

BAÑOS ☎03

The legendary baños consist of pools of water geothermally heated by the same fiery god that created nearby **Volcán Tungurahua.** A towering wall of neighboring green mountains, including Tungurahua, provides easy access to everything from pastoral strolls to vigorous hikes. Resting in the eastern flank of the Andes, the town's popularity also comes from its status as a jumping-off point for jungle tours and exotic excursions. After Tungurahua erupted in late 1999, Baños became a ghost town and remained so until January 2000. Although some establishments remain closed, the town is starting to spring back into tourist action.

▮ TRANSPORTATION

Buses: The **terminal** takes up a block between Maldonado and the main road to Ambato. Buses from the terminal area travel to: **Quito** (3hr., every 30min. 4:30am-6:20pm, US$1.80); **Ambato** (1hr., every 10min. 4am-7pm, US$0.40); **Riobamba** (2hr., every hr. 6am-6pm, US$1); **Puyo** (2hr., every hr. 5:30am-8:30pm, US$1); **Tena** (7hr., US$2.80); and **Guayaquil** (7hr., 2am, US$2.80).

Taxis: **16 de Diciembre** (☎740 416), found at the parks.

▰▮ ORIENTATION AND PRACTICAL INFORMATION

The layout of Baños is quite simple. The main highway between Ambato and Puyo runs east-west across the northern end of town. From the **terminal** on the highway, it's about three blocks south along **Maldonado** to the **Parque Central.** East-west **Ambato** is the principle thoroughfare, passing the Parque Central, the municipal **market,** and the **Parque Basílica.** A huge **waterfall** on the southeast corner of town marks the location of the most popular hot springs.

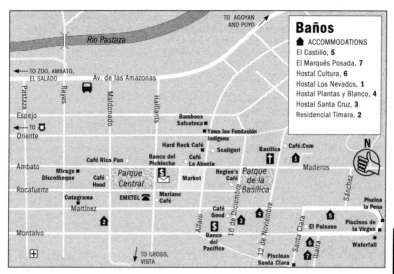

Baños

ACCOMMODATIONS

El Castillo, **5**
El Marqués Posada, **7**
Hostal Cultura, **6**
Hostal Los Nevados, **1**
Hostal Plantas y Blanco, **4**
Hostal Santa Cruz, **3**
Residencial Tímara, **2**

Currency Exchange: Banco del Pacífico (☎ 740 336), Montalvo between 16 de Diciembre and Alfaro, has a MC/Cirrus **ATM.** Open M-F 8:45am-4:30pm, Sa 9:30am-2pm.

Market: Boxed by Rocafuerte, Ambato, Alfaro, and Halflants. Open daily 8am-6pm. **Sunday** is the biggest day. An **open-air market** specializing in produce is on Ambato and Mera, on the western edge of town.

Emergency: ☎ 101.

Police: (☎ 740 367) On Oriente, 3½ blocks west of the Parque Central.

Hospital: (☎ 740 443), Pastaza and Montalvo. Open daily 8-11am and 2-4pm.

Telephones: EMETEL (☎ 740 104), Rocafuerte and Halflants, on Parque Central. Open daily 8am-10pm.

Internet Access: Cafe.com (see food). US$1.60 per hr.; US$1.20 per hr., with a food or drink order.

Post Office: Correos Central (☎ 740 901), on Halflants between Ambato and Rocafuerte, bordering the Parque Central next to the immigration office. Open M-F 9am-5pm.

▌▌ ACCOMMODATIONS

Baños offers great, inexpensive lodging. Hotels pile on top of one another along Ambato, and there are also dense patches on Montalvo toward the pools.

▨ **Hostal Los Nevados** (☎ 740 673), right by the Parque Basílica. From Ambato, take the 1st left past 12 de Noviembre. Both the rooms and the private baths are large and spotless, with reliable, 24hr. hot water. Services include a laundry service, message board, in-house travel agency, complimentary continental breakfast, roof-top bar, and 24hr. security. Reservations recommended. Rooms US$2 per person.

▨ **Hostal Plantas y Blanco** (☎ 740 044), Martínez and 12 de Noviembre, a block off the Parque Basílica. Good location. Laundry, phones, storage, rooftop bar/restaurant with great breakfasts and lovely view. Early morning "purifying" steam baths US$3. Loads of movies (US$0.20 each). Rooms US$4 per person, with bath US$6.

Residencial Tímara (☎ 740 599), Maldonado and Martínez, 2 blocks south of the Parque Central along Maldonado. Tímara includes simple rooms with psychedelic bedspreads, a clean communal bath blessed with hot water in the mornings and evenings, a sink for washing clothes, and free kitchen access. Rooms US$1.20 per person.

Santa Cruz Hotel (☎740 648), 16 de Diciembre and Martínez, 2 blocks south of the Parque Basílica. Sports a large central garden and open-air walkways. Big windows let in lots of light, showing off the clean rooms. Also has private hot-water baths, a cafeteria, and 24hr. security. Rooms US$6-7 per person.

El Marqués Posada (☎740 053; email ivonsol@uio.satnet.net), Montalvo and Ibarra. A few blocks from the *centro*. Clean, airy rooms with hot-water baths, a patio, and a friendly staff greet visitors. Body massages US$10 per hr. Rooms US$6.

Hostal El Castillo (☎740 285), Martínez and Santa Clara. Friendly owner. Simple rooms. Restaurant. Pleasant inner courtyard. Rooms US$2 per person.

◆ FOOD

Cheap restaurants surround the bus station; international cuisine fills the center. The **Quimicome** food kitchen on Martínez and Pastaza provides food for the less fortunate members of the community and welcomes volunteers and donations.

▧ Ristorante Scaligeri, Alfaro near Ambato. The food is as classic as the handmade, hand-stamped menus. Remarkably good pasta dishes (US$1.60) and real Italian salads (US$0.80-$1). Open Tu-Su noon-3pm and 5-10pm.

▧ Mariane Café/Restaurant (☎(09) 837 976), Halflants and Rocafuerte. Succulent, trout with tons of vegetables US$2.40. Filet mignon in a peppered cream sauce with vegetables and *papas au gratin* US$2.80. Chocolate crepe (US$1.40) and a half-liter of wine (US$3.50) provide the appropriate post-meal euphoria. Open daily 6:30-11pm.

▧ La Abuela Café (☎740 635), on Ambato, across from the market. This dark cafe is often full and for good reason. Homemade pies (US$0.50) and an extensive drink list (US$1.45-$2), pastas, and sandwiches satisfy any customer. Open M-Sa 7:30am-10:30pm, Su 6:30-10:30pm.

▧ Cafe.Com (☎740 309; email cafe_ec@yahoo.com), 12 de Noviembre and Oriente. This cybercafe "with a Swedish touch" specializes in a welcoming atmosphere and international cuisine. They even offer Swedish meatballs (US$2), along with tons of satisfying vegetarian food. Open M-Sa 8am-2am.

Mercedes Cafeteria (☎740 410), Ambato and Halfants. It's a breakfast kind of place—except that it serves it all day. The breakfasts (US$0.80-1.20) include some eclectic pancake flavors. Juices US$0.30. Open 6am-10pm.

Café Hood (☎740 573), Maldonado and Ambato, on the Parque Central, "where the food is good," the book exchange is the best in town, and the soul music warms the heart. *Platos fuertes* from around the world US$0.80-1.52. If it's full, head over to **Café Good** on Martínez and 6 de Diciembre where the food is the same and there are daily movies (8pm). Both open daily 8:30am-9:30pm.

Bamboo, Ambato and Alfaro, across from the *mercado*. Completely meat-free; almost gringo-free. Entrees US$1.60. Open daily 8am-10pm.

ON THE TRAIL OF DON SERGIO

It seems that almost every visitor to Ecuador comes home with at least a few stories of the miracles performed by Ecuadorian auto mechanics. Following in this grand tradition of tinkerers, an old man named Don Sergio decided in the late 1970s to build his own car. Seventeen years later it was finished, and in it, a 68-year-old Don Sergio set out to travel the country-side. Constructed mostly of scrap metal and old pieces of wood, Sergio's car resembles an old corrugated shack—and with a top speed of 5km per hour, it isn't much faster. But that's okay, he's not in any hurry; he simply enjoys the freedom of traveling the road and seeing the world. When the car breaks down, as it frequently does, Don Sergio simply parks on the side of the road for however long it takes for him to fix the problem. With his toothless grin and wild, white beard, Sergio is as conspicuous as his mechanical creation and has attracted national and even international attention.

👁 SIGHTS

Baños is one big sight. The tourist magnets begin at the hot spring pools and radiate outward to the volcanoes, the Oriente, and beyond. Locals soak themselves in the salubrious springs at sunrise; tourists who take a dip later miss the clean water and daybreak over the Andes. The pools are busiest on Fridays and Saturdays.

THE BAÑOS. The most popular spring is the **Baño de la Virgen,** at the eastern end of Montalvo. A waterfall cascades down the mountainside into this pool, and it's the only *baño* open at night to soothe sore hiking muscles. Several murky mineral-water pools, reputedly cleaned daily, are filled with the legendary hot, healing waters. *(☎ 740 462. Open daily 4:30am-5pm and 6-10pm. Daytime US$0.30; nighttime US$0.40; children US$0.20.)* Next door, **La Piscina Las Peñas** has a slide and specializes in screaming children and water fights. *(Open Th-Su 8am-6pm. US$0.30, children US$0.20.)* The **Piscinas Santa Clara** are at the end of the street with the same name. *(Open weekends. US$0.20, children US$0.15.)* Two other pools, visited mostly by locals, lie outside of town. **El Salado** is a 20-minute walk or a five-minute bus ride from the *centro*. Head west on the road to Ambato, then turn left at the sign to El Salado. Follow the road uphill until the end. Cleaned each day, the six pools include one cold, two hot, and one scalding. *(☎ 740 493. Open daily 6am-5pm. US$1.)* The **Piscinas Santa Ana** lie 20 minutes by foot or five minutes by bus on the road to Puyo. A sign points the way to the tree-enclosed pools. *(Open F-Su 8am-5pm. US$1.)*

THE BASÍLICA. Clean and beautiful like the waters themselves, the Basílica imposes its strange, zebra-like form upon the skyline of the city. The church was built in honor of the great **Virgen de Agua Santa,** displayed in all her neon-lit glory inside the church. There are numerous stories of exactly how this plaster sculpture began working her miracles. The official version is depicted in one of the church's many murals. Apparently, during a religious procession in 1773, Volcán Tungurahua suddenly threatened to blow its top once again. The people of Baños, in a fit of religious fervor, prostrated themselves before the image of the Virgin that they had been parading around the plaza. The eruption came to a sudden halt, and the rest, as they say, is history. The murals of the church illustrate the many miracles that the Virgin has since performed. A **museum** in the church houses a miscellany of religious items. *(Open daily 7am-4pm. US$0.20, children US$0.15.)*

🎵📺 ENTERTAINMENT AND NIGHTLIFE

In spite of Baños's 2am closing law, the town has some of the wildest nightlife in Ecuador. After dinner, tourists wander down Alfaro checking out the ample selection of bars and discos. **Pipas,** trying to make a name for itself, has an electric guitar, microphone, and bongos. (Open daily 8pm-2am.) Toward the river, **Donde Marcelo Al Paso** (☎ 104 427; open daily 2pm-2am), on Alfaro and Ambato, blasts out the beat, while **Rodeo's** on Alfaro and Oriente (open daily 7pm-2am) switches over to live *música folklórica* for an hour at 9pm on weekends. Across the street, **Bamboos Salsateca** provides salsa music at midnight and has a pool table. (Open daily 8pm-2am.) To escape from all the gringos, try the very Ecuadorian **Mirage Discoteca** on Ambato and Maldonado (cover US$0.80). A staple in the Baños **nightlife** scene, **▨Hard Rock Café,** on Alfaro between Ambato and Oriente, is probably awaiting a lawsuit for trademark infringement. (Open daily 6pm-2am.) In *peñas*, like **Volcán Peña Bar** across from Bamboo, *música folklórica* plays Thursday to Saturday. (☎ 740 576. Cover US$0.60 for live music. Open daily 8pm-2am.)

🏔 INTO THE WILDS FROM BAÑOS

On the major thoroughfare between Sierra and Oriente, Baños is one of the most popular and practical gateways to some of Ecuador's most amazing natural attractions. From here, you can explore nearby volcanic peaks, cloud forest, or jungle, and still be back in time for a gourmet meal and an evening soak in the hot springs.

CENTRAL ECUADOR

HIKING. The steep, green hills that surround Baños are visible from anywhere in town and beckon to hikers. To do the standard first hike, follow Maldonado toward the mountainside. Where the road ends, a path leads to the illuminated cross on top of the hill. It's about 45 minutes up to the top. The path continues beyond the cross, eventually looping back to Baños. To get an up-close view of some precipices, cross the main highway at the terminal and head toward the Río Pastaza, where the shaky San Francisco bridge crosses the churning gorge. From the other side, a path leads up the steep mountainside to the twin villages of **Illuchi Baja** and **Illuchi Alta.** For another escape from the tourist scene, take the dirt road on the right just before entering El Salado (see p. 519). Follow the path beside the river, which has views of the forest and the patchwork of farms across the valley. The trail also leaves from the highway to Ambato, a little farther back; a green sign on your right says Tungurahua and the road goes uphill to the left. The dirt path is the first thing you see on your right.

BIKING. Though bicycle touring is somewhat unheard of in Ecuador, low-quality bikes can be easily and cheaply rented from many places in Baños (US$1 per hr., US$5 per day). A popular trip goes 16km down the road toward Puyo to the town of Río Verde (see p. 520). The mostly downhill ride passes over, under, and through countless waterfalls, as well as through an unlit tunnel (a flashlight might be a good idea). From Río Verde you can hop on a Baños-bound bus and put your bike on the roof (US$0.60).

GUIDED TRIPS. Other excursions can benefit from the experience of a guide. Most are flexible about duration, number of people, and will try to do what you want to do. Baños is conveniently located between the mountains and the jungle so many options are available; dozens of tour agencies pack the streets. Just keep in mind that relatively few of these are legitimately registered, and serious problems have been reported with a number of them. Before spending a large sum of money, don't hesitate to ask for a guide's CETUR and INEFAN certifications.

One reputable agency is **Rainforestur,** right off the Parque Central on Ambato and Maldonado. General manager Santiago Herrera sets up trips to the mountains (Tungurahua, Cotopaxi, or Chimborazo) and the Oriente. Jungle packages come in many shapes and sizes. (☎/fax 740 743; rainfor@interactive.net.ec. US$25-40 per person per day for 3-4 days. Open 8am-1:30pm and 3-6:30pm.) **Geotours,** on Halflants and Ambato, which is easily contacted through the Hostal Los Nevados, also offers mountain packages as well as **"jungle river rafting"** trips of up to two days. (☎741 344. www.ecuadorexplorer.com/geotours. Rafting trips US$25-30 per day; horses US$15-20 per day. Open daily 8am-12:30pm and 2:30-9pm.)

A refreshing alternative for a jungle tour is offered by **Tsantsa Expediciones** which works with the non-profit **Yawa Jee Fundación Indígena** (☎740 957; email marco.moya@gmx.net), at Oriente and Alfaro. The *fundación* works with several native Shuar villages in the forest south of Puyo to promote sustainable agriculture and sanitation. They offer trips from Baños with an emphasis on education and cultural exchange. (3-4 days, US$45 per person per day.)

NEAR BAÑOS: RÍO VERDE

To get to Río Verde, take one of the Baños-Puyo buses (30min., US$0.10) from Baños.

Halfway between Baños in the highlands and Puyo in the jungle, the town of **Río Verde** seems to draw on the best of both worlds. A convergence of tropical weather and rugged terrain have made the town and its surroundings a veritable breeding ground for waterfalls. There are over 20 *cascadas* in the area, ranging from serpentine trickles to booming cataracts. As an added perk, a number of quality cabins in the area provide bases from which to enjoy the idyllic landscape. Near Río Verde, an implausible contraption, euphemistically called "the longest cable car in Ecuador," ferries fearless passengers across the abyss with a car motor. Río Verde proper is nothing more than a few convenience stores along the highway; the real attractions lie outside of town. The **Río Verde** itself gushes over smooth black volcanic rock at the **Cascadas San Miguel,** 250m from the highway. Showering you with mist and humility is the **Pailón del Diablo (Devil's Cauldron),** where the Río Verde roars off a cliff to join the Río Pastaza on its path toward the Amazon. At the falls, **El Pailon Café** serves drinks and asks an admission fee to help conserve the trails leading to the falls. Surrounding the *cascadas*, **Cabañas Restaurant Indillama** provides charming cabins with bath, hot water, and free breakfast. (☎ (09) 785 263; email indillamaO@hotmail.com. Rooms US$10 per person).

PARQUE NACIONAL SANGAY

In the Parque Nacional Sangay, which spans four provinces and 517,765 hectares, visitors can witness three of Ecuador's 10 highest peaks, including two active volcanoes. Excursions to Sangay's snow-capped summits and virgin forests are less commercialized than those to Chimborazo or Cotopaxi and are virtual pioneering expeditions through relatively undiscovered lands. With altitudes ranging from 5319m on the peak of Volcán Altar to 900m in the Amazon basin, much of the amazing landscape is simply impossible to traverse. This inaccessibility, combined with the park's main objective (to protect and conserve), bars visitors from reaching some of Sangay's more remote areas. First founded as a reserve in 1979, the park shelters a selection of flora and fauna almost as diverse as its geography and includes such rare and strange specimens as the endangered **Andean tapir** *(Tapirus pinchaque)*, also known as the *canta de monte*.

Though Sangay's unreachable areas may fascinate, the accessible ones are nothing to scoff at. The park is divided into two sections: the **zona alta** in the Sierra (1500-5319m) and the **zona baja** in the Oriente (900-1500m). The *zona alta* contains Sangay's main attractions; its entrance points are easily accessible from Baños or Riobamba. The *zona baja* entrance is most easily visited from Macas in the Southern Oriente. The four main attractions in Parque Sangay's *zona alta* are the relaxing **El Placer,** the towering fire-spewers **Volcán Tungurahua** (5016m) and **Volcán Altar** (5319m), and the remote namesake, **Volcán Sangay** (5230m).

LOGISTICS. Sangay's administrative body, **INEFAN,** is a tremendous resource for those planning to explore the park. In addition to providing information, the staff offers advice for finding guides. For more info, contact them at the Riobamba office (see Riobamba: Practical Information, p. 524). For more trip-specific information in English, consult the South American Explorers in Quito (see p. 433). Park admission is US$10.

EL PLACER. El Placer is a relatively low, swampy area with *aguas termales* for bathing. Most make this into a long daytrip, departing for Alao at daybreak (INEFAN leaves at 5:30am) and returning to Riobamba at dusk. **Atillo,** a picturesque lagoon, is a two-hour drive (from INEFAN, leaves at 8am). Some amazing species populate the park; the Andean tapir, visible from the Atillo and El Placer areas, is found nowhere else in the world. Plant and animal stalkers in the know head to **Playa de Sangay** and **El Palmar** for their observational kicks. Others take a walk on the wild side of the Oriente by heading to **Culebrillas** and the **Lagunas de Sardmayacu** *(zona baja)* in the neverending quest for still more jaguar and bear sightings. Both places are accessible from Palora and Macas (see **Into the Jungle from Macas,** p. 552), though El Placer itself is reached from the other side.

VOLCÁN TUNGURAHUA. This 10th-highest peak in Ecuador is currently off-limits due to its recent eruption. However, it still makes a nice day hike, and once it stops erupting, it may be safe to climb again. The road to Pondoa, which was once accessible by car, is now closed, so the hike begins from the green Tungurahua sign on the road back to Ambato from Baños. Some travel agencies offer horseback riding tours up Tungurahua (US$20).

EL ALTAR (LOS ALTARES). The highest mountain in the park, El Altar, collapsed in 1460 and is now partially covered by glaciers. Accessible from yet another park entrance at **Candelaria** (a 1hr. ride from INEFAN in Riobamba), the eight-hour climb to the crater is similar to the two-day Tungurahua ascent, although there is no worthwhile daytrip to a *refugio.* Trips cost US$35 per day, and guides are readily available in Candelaria (INEFAN officials will assist you). Equipment is needed for the climb to the crater. Camping is possible in a cave near the crater; you can also stay overnight at the park entrance.

VOLCÁN SANGAY. One of the most active volcanoes in the world, Sangay constantly spews ash and smoke to signal its presence. This lava-dripping monster has three deep craters at its summit. The park's mammoth namesake requires a minimum of six days to conquer. Begin the hike up Sangay from the entrance at **Alao,** on the western side of the park. Hiring a guide is a must, at least for the start of the climb. In Alao, you can find a guide (US$40 per day) and a mule for your luggage and equipment (US$10 per day). It is dangerous to climb all the way up to Sangay's crater; you might get in the fiery path of all that spewed ash and lava. Experience is another must, and visitors should only climb as far as guides recommend. INEFAN rides from Riobamba to Alao leave early—call to check times (☎963 779).

RIOBAMBA ☎03

Tranquil and relatively tourist-free, this quintessential Andean city (pop. 130,000) allows one to become immersed in Ecuadorian life without the fast pace and danger of a major metropolis. Cobblestone streets criss-cross plazas and parks, many with awe-inspiring views of snow-capped Volcán Chimborazo. These towering volcanoes keep watch over a city that bears the scars of its tumultuous past. After a devastating earthquake and landslide in 1797, the entire city (then the capital of Ecuador) was moved to its present site on a highland valley plain. As a result, the city's oldest architecture is neoclassical, with one notable exception: the cathedral on Veloz and 5 de Junio was transported stone-by-stone from its pre-quake location. Most visitors, however, don't come to experience the parks, plazas, and architecture. As with Latacunga to the north, Riobamba's main attractions lie outside of town. The city is known primarily as a departure point for daytrips, including Chimborazo and the jaw-dropping train rides to Alausí. Also common are visits to nearby indigenous villages and Parque Nacional Sangay.

▶ TRANSPORTATION

Buses: The main **terminal** is on León Borja (the western part of 10 de Agosto) and Daniela, about 1km to the northwest of the center of town. From there, buses head to: **Quito** (3½hr., every 15min. 2:15am-9pm, US$2.20); **Guayaquil** (5½hr., every 30min. 2:30am-9:30pm, US$2.70); **Cuenca** (6½hr., 7 per day, US$3.60); **Ambato** (1hr., every 15min. 4:35am-6:30pm, US$0.80); and **Alausí** (2hr., every hr. 5am-7pm, US$0.90). The **Terminal Oriental** (☎960 766), on Espejo and León Borja, north of town, sends buses to: **Baños** (2hr., every hr. 6am-6pm, US$1); **Puyo** (4hr., 6 per day, US$2); and **Tena** (7hr., 6 per day, US$3.60). The **Guano Terminal,** Rocafuerte and Nueva York (north of town), sends buses to **Guano** (25min., every 30min., US$0.20) and **Santa Teresita** (35min., every 30min., US$0.20). Buses for many nearby destinations leave 3 blocks south of the terminal (take the Control Sur bus from the bull-ring and get off at the 3-way intersection) and go to **Cajabamba** (20min., every 30min. 6am-7pm, US$0.20) via **Laguna de Colta** (25min., US$0.20) and **Guamote** (1hr., US$0.40). Additional buses leave on Thursday for the Guamote market. Buses to **San Juan,** the closest town to Chimborazo, leave from Unidad Nacional and Prensa (45min., every 15min. 6am-6:45pm, US$0.30). Many more buses traveling the Quito-Loja route stop in Riobamba; to catch one, wait *outside* the station.

Trains: The **train station** (☎961 909) is at 10 de Agosto and Carabobo. Office open daily 8am-7pm. After a long history of track-closing repairs, the magnificent **Riobamba-Guayaquil** route was reopened in 1999, but only with limited service from Riobamba to Aluasí. The locomotive has now been replaced with a converted monobus, but the cars are still old-school. You can choose to sit inside or on the roof. The train departs twice a week (11hr. round-trip; W and F 7am; one-way US$15). Check the schedule—it often changes. A **Riobamba-Quito** route (Su 8am, US$15) offers fantastic volcano views from the (real) train roof. Make sure to arrive at the station by 6pm the night before to ensure getting a ticket. (See also the Riobamba-Alausí-Bucay-Durán Railway, p. 528.)

Local Buses: Buses are unnecessary; Riobamba is eminently walkable.

Taxis: Taxis charge US$0.60 between any 2 points in the city.

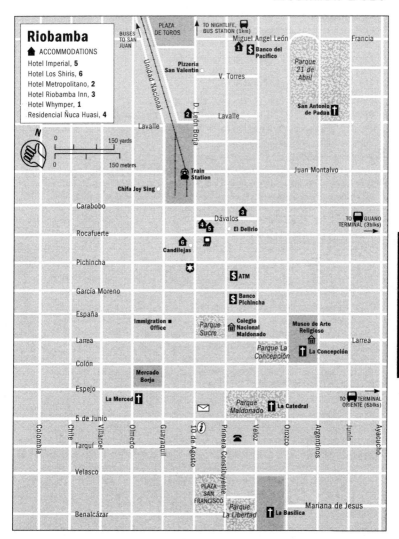

Riobamba

⌂ **ACCOMMODATIONS**
Hotel Imperial, **5**
Hotel Los Shiris, **6**
Hotel Metropolitano, **2**
Hotel Riobamba Inn, **3**
Hotel Whymper, **1**
Residencial Ñuca Huasi, **4**

0 — 150 yards
0 — 150 meters

PLAZA DE TOROS
BUSES TO SAN JUAN
TO NIGHTLIFE, BUS STATION (1km)
Miguel Angel León
Francia
Banco del Pacifico
Pizzería San Valentín
V. Torres
Parque 21 de Abril
San Antonio de Padua
Lavalle
Lavalle
Train Station
Chifa Joy Sing
Juan Montalvo
Carabobo
Dávalos
El Delirio
TO GUANO TERMINAL (3blks)
Rocafuerte
Pichincha
Candilejas
ATM
García Moreno
Banco Pichincha
España
Immigration Office
Parque Sucre
Colegio Nacional Maldonado
Museo de Arte Religioso
Larrea
Larrea
Parque La Concepción
La Concepción
Colón
Mercado Borja
Espejo
La Merced
Parque Maldonado
La Catedral
TO TERMINAL ORIENTE (6blks)
5 de Junio
Colombia
Chile
Villaroel
Olmedo
Guayaquil
10 de Agosto
Primera Constituyente
Veloz
Orozco
Argentinos
Junin
Ayacucho
Tarqui
Velasco
PLAZA SAN FRANCISCO
Parque La Libertad
La Basílica
Mariana de Jesus
Benalcázar

CENTRAL ECUADOR

⚡✱🛈 ORIENTATION AND PRACTICAL INFORMATION

Activity centers around the area squared off by **Argentinos** and **Olmedo** to the east and west, and **5 de Junio** and **Angel León** to the south and north. **Primera Constituyente** and **10 de Agosto** are the city's main thoroughfares. From the **terminal**, head right (south) for 1km on **León Borja**, which turns into 10 de Agosto at **Carabobo**, or simply hop on one of the passing city buses on the **control norte** route. The **train station** is in the center of town at 10 de Agosto and Carabobo.

> **Tourist Information: CETUR** (☎ 941 213), 10 de Agosto and 5 de Junio, will amiably distribute city maps and brochures. English spoken. Open M-F 8:30am-5pm.

> **Immigration Office:** España 10-50 and Guayaquil next to police (☎ 964 697). For affairs relating to visas and tourist cards. Open M-F 8am-12:30pm and 3-6:30pm.

INEFAN: (☎963 779), 9 de Octubre near Duchicela, at the **Ministerio del Cultura Agrícola (MAC)** in the northwest corner of town. Super-helpful staff, some of whom speak English, can suggest excursions to Chimborazo and Sangay. Open M-F 8am-4:30pm.

Banks: Banks include the **Banco del Pacífico,** Veloz and Angel León, and **Banco Pichincha,** Primera Constituyente and García Moreno. Both open M-F 9am-4:30pm. Banco del Pacífico has a Cirrus/Plus/MC **ATM**.

Emergency: ☎101.

Police: (☎961 913 or 961 951), Policia and La Paz, on the Vía al Chembo.

Hospital: The **Policlínico** (☎968 238), Proaño and Chile, is the most modern and highly recommended medical facility in town.

Telephones: EMETEL (☎943 036), Tarquí and Veloz.

Internet Access: Café Internet, Rocafuerte 22-30 3rd fl. (☎968 882; email net-cafe@laserinter.net), at 10 de Agosto. US$1 per hr. Open M-Su 9am-10pm.

Post Office: (☎966 006), 10 de Agosto and Espejo. Open M-F 7:30am-7:30pm, Sa 8am-noon.

▌ ACCOMMODATIONS

Hotel Imperial (☎960 429), 10 de Agosto and Rocafuerte, in the heart of Riobamba, still maintains vestiges of the hotel empire. Relax in spacious, airy rooms or lounge on the balcony. Management arranges Chimborazo excursions. Rooms US$2 per person.

Hotel Metropolitano (☎961 714), León Borja and Lavalle. Caters to a largely Ecuadorian crowd. A well-rounded option downtown, offering clean, rather small rooms with hot-water baths. Matrimonials US$2.40; discounts for groups of 10 or more.

Hotel Whymper, Angel León 23-10 and Primera Constituyente (☎964 575), next to Banco del Pacífico, is a bit outside the center of town. King-sized beds and hot-water baths. Breakfast included. The staff can arrange trips. Rooms US$4 per person.

Hotel Ñuca Huasi (☎966 669), 10 de Agosto between Rocafuerte and Dávalos. Old but clean, with tasteful decorations and terrace. Rooms US$1.20, with bath US$1.60.

Hotel Riobamba Inn, Carabobo 23-20 and Primera Constituyente (☎961 696), across from the Banco Central. Boasts immense private hot-water bathrooms, spotless bedrooms, and TVs in every room. Singles US$3.90; doubles US$7.20; triples US$10.80.

Hotel Los Shyris (☎960 323), Rocafuerte and 10 de Agosto. The clean, telephone- and TV-equipped rooms (local calls US$0.15 per min.) offer shampoo and soap for the cubicle bathrooms. 24hr. internet access. Rooms US$2, with bath US$3.

◖ FOOD

Come dinner time, locals crowd around outdoor stands that scoop various traditional dishes out of steaming bowls lit by little floodlights.

▩ **El Delirio** (☎967 502), Primera Constituyente and Rocafuerte. In Simón Bolívar's old house, with outdoor tables in a charming patio garden under blossoming trees. Meats US$4-8. Drinks US$1.50-3.50. Open daily noon-9:30pm.

Restaurant Candilejas, 10 de Agosto 27-33 (☎960 220), between Pichincha and Rocafuerte. The menu includes Kodachrome pictures of dishes. Try the *sopa de cebolla* (US$0.80). Open M-Sa 8am-8pm, Su 8am-2pm.

Ashoka, Carabobo between Primera Constituyente and Borja. A hip, warm, welcoming vegetarian cafe. Profits go to support street kids. Internet access US$0.80 per hr. Entrees US$0.80-1.20. Open daily 8am-9:30pm.

Chifa Joysing, Unidad Nacional 29-33 and Carabobo (☎961 285). The huge portions of savory cuisine at this typical Ecuadorian chifa will have you singing with joy. Vegetarian dishes as well as old favorites. Open daily 10am-11pm.

Pizzería San Valentín (☎963 137), Borja and Torres. Touted by some American expats as the best food in town. Young locals also enjoy the Mexican food (burritos US$0.72), ice cream (US$1), and pictures of scantily clad women. Open Tu-Sa 5pm-midnight.

■ SIGHTS

PARKS. Riobamba's scenic parks just cry out to be strolled in. One of the most colorful pleas comes from the **Parque 21 de Abril,** also known as **La Loma de Quito,** perched above the rest of Riobamba. At the northern part of town, the park is boxed in by Orozco, Argentinos, León, and Lavalle. Due to its auspicious position, this park monopolizes the best panoramic views and photo opportunities in the city. The park also houses a church, **San Antonio de Padua** (open Su-Tu 8am-noon and Th-Sa 2-5pm). The **Parque Sucre,** at España and Primera Constituyente, at the center of town, graces the inland city with a beautiful bronze **fountain** and **statue of Neptune.** Local men gather on the palm-tree-shaded benches, socializing and people-watching. The engaging **Parque Maldonado,** Primera Constituyente and Espejo, displays a monument to its namesake, Pedro Vicente Maldonado. This *riobambeño* historian and cartographer drew up the first political map of Ecuador. Big and bustling with weekend activity the **Parque Guayaquil,** Unidad Nacional and León Borja, provides the perfect opportunity to let your inner child roam free.

CHURCHES. The city's **churches** reveal the Riobamban penchant for atypical architecture. **La Basílica,** Veloz and Benalcázar, constructed from 1883 to 1915, gained fame as the only round church in Ecuador. The main **Cathedral,** Veloz and 5 de Junio by Parque Maldonado, is the oldest building in town (although it may not look like it). The sole remnant of Riobamba's pre-earthquake site, it was transported in 1797, one stone at a time.

MUSEUMS. Two **museums** of note grace Riobamba. **La Concepción,** or the **Museo de Arte Religioso,** Argentinos and Larrea, has a collection of religious art and artifacts from the 17th to 19th centuries. (☎965 212. Open Tu-Sa 9am-noon and 3-6 pm, Su 9am-12:30pm,. US$1.60, students US$0.60.) The **Museo del Colegio Maldonado,** also known as the Museo de Ciencias Naturales, is a tiny natural history and science exhibit inside the schoolhouse at the Parque Sucre. (☎970 275. Open M-F 8am-1pm. US$0.12.)

♫ ENTERTAINMENT

The **Saturday market** is a huge affair. The entire length of every street boxed in by España, 5 de Junio, Guayaquil, and Argentinos—as well as all the space in-between—fills with vendors, shoppers, and good old Ecuadorian energy. On Fridays, the **vegetable market** at La Valle and Esmeraldas promises to amaze through the sheer size of mountains of plant material. **Cockfights** can be seen Saturdays in a house at Almagro and Olmedo, mostly in April. Riobamba's biggest *fiesta*, **La Loma de Quito,** commemorates the city's founding. The actual holiday falls on April 21, but *riobambeños* get a head start on the 20th and party until the 22nd; fairs, bullfights, and parades swamp the streets. The high *páramo* around Riobamba is littered with lakes, villages, and stunning vistas. For those with well-acclimatized legs and lungs (and plenty of cash), a **bicycle ride** might be the best way to see this area. **Pro-Bici,** Primera Constituyente 23-51 and Larrea, runs trips into the surrounding countryside. While this does not include food or lodging for one-day trips, it does include a guide, support, and a good bike. (☎ 941 880 or 941 734. US$30 per day and up.)

▣ NIGHTLIFE

Riobamba is quiet during the week, but there are several options for weekend evening entertainment. Most discos cluster on León Borja between the terminal and Hotel Zeus at Duchicela, making a night of club-hopping all too easy. Some of the most dance-friendly discos are **Casablanca** and **Gens Chop** (☎ 964 325), at Borja and Duchicela, both open M-Sa 3pm-3am. Around the corner, on Duchicela, **La Che-V** is a slightly more formal, popular local bar. (☎ 945 644. Open daily 2pm-2am.)

DAYTRIPS FROM RIOBAMBA

GUANO

Catch the bus from Rocafuerte and Nueva York (30min., every 30min. 5am-7pm, US$0.20).

A quick bus ride from Riobamba, this tiny village offer an intimate glimpse into a rural Andean lifestyle that makes even tranquil Riobamba seem bustling. Guano specializes in rug-making and slow living. Numerous *artesanía* shops sell monstrous rugs, leather goods, and hemp items; many will custom-make any design you can communicate to them with pictures or broken Spanish. The central square houses a lovely **park** with a geometric garden, and a small **church** stands at Colón and García Moreno. One of the only restaurants in town, **El Oasis** dishes out the usual chow at Hidalgo and García Moreno, near the main plaza.

SAN FRANCISCO DE QUITO AND LAGUNA DE COLTA

Buses bound for Cajabamba and Laguna de Colta leave Riobamba from the area around Unidad Nacional and Bolívar (behind the bull ring). Both locations can be reached by bus (every 45min., US$0.10-0.40). Buses to Guayaquil also pass by San Francisco. Buses to Riobamba or Guamote can be flagged down anywhere on the highway until dark.

San Francisco de Quito, the first capital of Ecuador, has two major sites: La Balbanera church and the Laguna de Colta. Built in 1534 by the Spanish, **La Balbanera** was the first church in Ecuador. Plaques on the walls record the occurrence of a series of church-related miracles. Beyond the church and across the road to the left sits the large **Laguna de Colta.** While the lagoon is visible from the highway, there's also a road that wanders through several beautifully framed rural villages to the back of the lake. The backwoods route reveals rural settlements with indigenous farmers working fields on the slopes of picturesque, clouded hills. It should take about two hours to walk the perimeter.

NEAR RIOBAMBA: VOLCÁN CHIMBORAZO

Those up for a challenging hike can ask the driver of the Riobamba-Guaranda bus if he plans to use the Arenal route. If so, ask to be dropped off at the turn-off to the refugios. From the dropoff point it's a 7km hike up a dirt road to the second refugio. Four-wheel-drive vehicles travel this road, and some travelers hitch. Remember, hiking is much harder at this altitude; those unaccustomed to the altitude should not hike alone. On the way back, hop on a passing bus going from Guaranda to Riobamba. Park entrance US$10.

If Riobamba is the sultan of the Andes, Volcán Chimborazo (6310m) is the king of volcanoes. Explorers once mistook Chimborazo for the highest mountain in the world; while it lost this honor, its summit remains the farthest from the center of the earth (due to the earth's bulge at the equator). Snow-capped year-round, this dormant volcano peeks above the clouds into the silence of space. Chimborazo's second refuge, Whymper (5000m), offers stunning views, and can be reached in half a day without any climbing experience, equipment, or extreme expense.

Superb scenery graces the ride up the flank of the mountain. *Comunas* and *caseríos*—tiny villages without any government administration—dot the fertile farmlands and the hills in the shadow of Chimborazo. Tourists and local *indígenas* find each other equally foreign sights. Keep your eyes peeled for *vicuñas*; about a thousand of these deerlike creatures roam the park, usually herded by nimble farmers who scamper up a lot faster than you can.

INEFAN recently instituted an admission fee for the park, but it is collected irregularly. Some unscrupulous tour guides have taken advantage of the situation to collect the fee from tourists, and then pocket it. With this warning in mind, a relatively cheap way to reach the second refuge is through the **Hotel Imperial** (☎960 429) in Riobamba. Tell them the night before, and they'll set you up with a driver who can take you on the trip to the lower refuge (4800m). The driver will wait while you hike up to the second refuge. (2hr., round-trip US$15 per person, departing 7:30am and returning 1pm.) For a little more, the driver may go to the *aguas termales* north of the mountain (1hr.). The drive to Chimborazo can also be done by any 4x4 taxi in Riobamba or by guides arranged by a travel agency in town.

Most people stop at the second refuge, but experienced, adventurous climbers can take on the challenging ascent to **Chimborazo's summit** (8hr. ascent, 4hr. descent). Crampons, ropes, and other standard equipment are essential. Climbs leave at 11pm from the second refuge; a guide is a necessity. **Alta Montaña** (☎963 694 or 942 215) in Riobamba can provide qualified guides. (For information on guides, see Mountaineering, p. 511.) Both refuges on the mountain have basic food items, coffee, and tourist souvenirs. They also offer accommodations (US$6), but bring your own sleeping bag and stock up on plenty of extra water and food. If you stay overnight at a refuge, arrange for the 4x4 taxi to pick you up the next day (round-trip US$17). Besides its namesake, Chimborazo Park has other attractions as well: two **Inca Ruins** and **La Chorrera Canyon** are all within hiking distance from the road but may require some exploring. Inquire at INEFAN for details.

ALAUSÍ

A beautiful setting and a slower pace of life make Alausí a worthy stop for weary travelers moving up and down the central corridor. **Plaza Bolívar** and the **train station** are at the base of the *centro*, near Sucre and **5 de Junio**, the main thoroughfare in town. It takes five minutes to walk through the entire downtown area. **Buses** leave from the corner of 9 de Octubre and 5 de Julio and go to: **Riobamba** (2hr.; every 30min. 4am-5pm; US$0.90); **Quito** (5½hr.; 8:30, 9:30am, 4, 8pm; US$3); **Cuenca** (4½hr.; 7 per day; US$2.60); **Guayaquil** (5hr.; 9am, 1:30pm; US$2.80); and **Ambato** (3hr.; 4, 8, 10, and 11:30am; US$1.60). Buses traveling the **Quito-Cuenca** route pass along the Panamerican Highway at all hours of the day and night. Transportation may also be arranged to **Achullapas** (1hr.), from which it is a three-day hike to the ruins at Ingapirca (see p. 534). National phone calls can be made from the **EMETEL** office opposite the train station. (☎930 104. Open 8am-noon and 2-7pm.) The **post office** is at the corner of 9 de Octubre and García Moreno. **Banco de Guayaquil**, 5 de

THE RIOBAMBA-ALAUSÍ-BUCAY-DURÁN RAILWAY Before the El Niño storms of 1997-98, this exhilarating railway was a source of pride for Ecuadorians and a feather in the cap of railroad engineers everywhere. The line fearlessly traversed every climate zone in the land, beginning in the breathless highlands of Chimborazo province, plummeting through the *páramo* and cloud forest of the western Andes, and finally terminating in the steamy coastal jungle of Guayaquil. One section right after Alausí, La Nariz del Diablo (the Devil's Nose), was particularly inspiring. The train surmounted a perpendicular cliff by means of two amazing switchbacks—quite a feat of railroad acrobatics. In under 30km, the line descended from 2347m to 1255m, with heart-stopping horseshoe twists and turns revealing magnificent views of the countryside. However, in 1997-98, storms battered the tracks and left them in disrepair. Today, after considerable reconstruction, the railway is once again covered from head to toe with tourists (whose hefty tickets pay for the upkeep). Farmers and schoolchildren wave at the passing train and washerwomen come out of their houses to see it. The train departs several times a week along the old tracks, which run parallel to the Panamericana until the town of Alausí. Then, it slows to a snail's pace and tenuously descends La Nariz del Diablo. The train only traverses a small section of its original route, as its current purpose is simply a scenic ride for tourists (US$15).

Junio and Ricaurte, has good rates on dollars and traveler's checks. (☎930 160. Open M-F 9am-6pm.) **Hotel Americano,** García Moreno 51 and Ricaurte, is located above the Farmacia Americano and run by the same management. Quiet, cozy rooms have wooden floors, street views, and baths complete with actual bathtubs. (☎930 159. Rooms US$2 per person.) **Hotel Panamericano,** 5 de Junio near the bus stop, can provide information about the two-day hike along the Inca trail from Achupallas to Ingapirca. (☎930 156. Rooms US$2 per person, with bath US$2.40.)

SOUTHERN HIGHLANDS

CUENCA ☎07

Cuenca (pop. 320,000), seated in the Guapondélig Valley (2530m), serves as the heart of southern highland culture. Cuenca was built on the ruins of Tomebamba, a Cañari city destroyed by the Incas in their northern conquests. With the arrival of the Spanish, the conflict between the Cañari and the Incas resurfaced, and by the time Gil Ramírez Dávalos re-founded Cuenca in 1557, the mysteriously deserted Tomebamba lay in ruins. A lively locale bursting from the banks of the Río Tomebamba, cosmopolitan Cuenca offers adobe-tiled buildings, cobblestone streets, active nightlife, a plethora of language schools, and some of the best restaurants and museums in Ecuador.

▐ TRANSPORTATION

Flights: Aeropuerto Mariscal Lamar (☎862 203) on España and Elia Liut, a 5min. walk from the terminal or 10min. north of the city by taxi (US$1) or bus ($0.12). Make reservations for national flights at individual airline offices. **TAME** (☎843 222), Benigno Malo and Larga. Both open M-F 7:30am-noon and 2:30-5pm. TAME flights go to **Quito** (40min.; M-Sa 8:25am, Su 5:25pm; US$46.12) and **Guayaquil** (30min., M-Sa 6:30am, US$29.32). **Austro Aereo,** Hmo. Miguel 5-42 and Hon. Vásquez (☎832 677; fax 848 659), flies to **Guayaquil** (30min.; M-F 7:50am and 4pm, and F 7:50am; US$29.32). Reservations at the office M-F 8:30am-1pm and 2:30-7pm, Sa 9am-noon. **ICARO Express,** España 11-14 (☎802 700; jerg@cue.satnet.net; www.icaro-air.com), travels to **Quito** (40min.; T-F 6pm; T, Th 7:45am; M, Su 6pm; US$53) and **Guayaquil** (30min.; T-F 4:05pm; US$33). Open M-F 8am-1pm and 3-6:30pm.

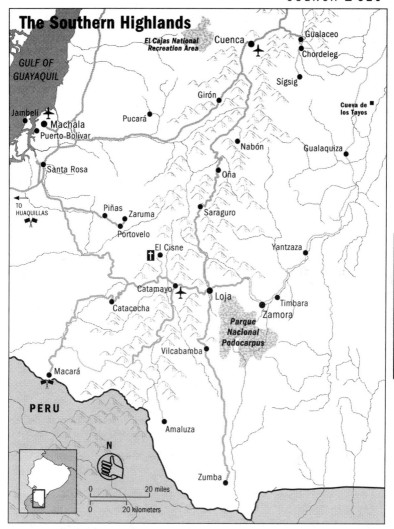

The Southern Highlands

Buses: The **terminal** (☎827 061), on España, is a 20min. walk northeast of the center of town. **Bus #40** (US$0.12) makes the journey back and forth between the terminal and the *centro;* taxis (US$0.80) can be hired to make the quick trip. If comfort is important to you, get on one of the better buses (usually the long-distance ones), even if you're only going a short distance. Buses go to: **Riobamba** (6hr., US$3.60) and **Ambato** (US$5.20) on the way to **Quito** (10hr., US$6-6.80); **Machala** (3hr., US$2); **Huaquillas** (4hr., US$2.80); **Guayaquil** (4hr., US$4); **Loja** (5hr., US$3.60); **Gualaquiza** (8hr., US$3.60); **Macas** (8hr., US$7.20); **Azogues** (30min., every 30min. 6am-10:30pm, US$0.32); **Cañar** (1.5hr., US$0.72); **Ingapirca** (2hr., 9am, US$1.08); **Cajas** (30min., US$0.80); **Gualaceo** (40min., every 15min. 5am-7pm, US$0.32).

Local Buses: City buses traverse all the city's districts. US$0.12.

Car Rental: International Rent-a-Car, España 10-50 (☎801 892; fax 806 688) across the street from the airport. Open M-F 7:30am-1pm and 2:30-7pm, Sa 7:30-1. US$42-94 per day. **Localiza Rent-a-Car,** España 14-85 (☎863 902; fax 860 174, email localiza@cue.satnet.net) has a conveniently located branch (☎803 198) by the airport. US$30-63 per day. Open M-F 7:30am-1pm and 2:30-6:30pm, Sa 7:30-12:30.

◀ ☀ 🛈 ORIENTATION AND PRACTICAL INFORMATION

Most of Cuenca's activity transpires in the 42-block area framed by **Mariscal Lamar, Honorato Vásquez, Tarquí,** and **Mariano Cueva.** Gran Colombia serves as the high-end commercial drag while Larga, with the *mercado*, offers cheaper options. The **Río Tomebamba** flows through town south of the *centro*, parallel to **Larga,** and its grassy banks look anything but urban. Less congested, suburban dwellings across the river provide refuge for the local elite. Another respite from everything urban, the **Parque Calderón** lies at the heart of the colonial center.

TOURIST AND FINANCIAL SERVICES

Tourist Information: Cámara de Turismo (☎868 482). Maps of the city. Lists of licensed guides, hostels, and agencies. Open daily 8am-10pm. **Ministerio de Turismo** (☎822 058), at the corner of Córdova and B. Malo, on the second floor of *edificio* San Agustín, supplies maps and brochures. Open M-F 8:30am-5pm.

Travel Agencies and Tours: Various agencies and hostels around the *centro* advertise guided group trips (US$30-45 per person, including entrance fees, transportation, and lunch) to **Girón, Gualaceo, Ingapirca,** and **Cajas.** Both **MontaRuna,** Gran Colombia 10-29 (☎846 395), in the *casa azul* opposite Santo Domingo (open daily 8:30am-1pm and 2:30-7pm), and **Río Arriba,** Hmo. Miguel 7-15 (☎840 031; email negro@az.pro.ec) and Pdte. Córdova (open M-F 9am-6pm) are recommended and organize daytrips or multi-day treks in Cajas. Alternatively, guides like **Genaro Palacios,** Borrero 5-90 (☎880 963; email gemapa@hotmail.com) can be hired independently. Both offer horseback riding adventures in the surrounding country. **Rock-climbing** aficionados can organize expeditions to Mt. Arquitectos or the Girón region.

Currency Exchange: Vaz Cambios, Gran Colombia 7-98 (☎833 434; fax 822 558), Cordero and Gran Colombia 7-98. Open M-F 9am-1pm and 3-5:30pm, Sa 9am-12:30pm. **Cambidex** has its main office at Gran Colombia 9-75 (☎829 572). Open M-F 9am-1pm and 2:30-5pm, Sa 9am-12:30pm. **M.M. Jaramillo Arteaga,** Bolívar 5-80 and Hmo. Miguel (☎841 980, fax 846 916). Open M-F 8:45am-5pm. **Western Union** has offices at Gran Colombia 5-96 and Hmo. Miguel (☎844 698); Sanguirma 2-64 and T. Ordóñez (☎827 941); and Borrero 8-44. Open M-F 9am-6pm, Sa 9am-2pm.

Banks: Banco del Pacífico, Benigno Malo 9-75 and Gran Colombia (☎831 144), has a **MC/Cirrus ATM.** Open M-F 8:45-5pm. **Banco La Previsora,** at the corner of Gran Colombia and B. Malo, has a **Visa/Plus ATM.** Open M-F 9am-7pm, Sa 9am-2pm. **MasterCard,** Crespo 1-777 and Estado (☎883 577). Open M-F 8:30am-5pm.

Consulates: Brazil (☎844 932) on Ordoñez. **Chile,** Gran Colombia 21-143 (☎840 061). Open M-F 8:30am-1pm and 3-6:30pm. **UK** (☎831 996), in the Plazoletta San Alfonso, 9A, at Borrero and Gran Colombia. Open M-F 8:30am-noon. **Centro Cultural Abraham Lincoln,** Borrero 5-18 and Vásquez (☎823 898) assists US citizens.

Immigration Office: Cordero 6-62 (☎831 020), in police headquarters. Open M-F 8am-noon and 3-6pm.

LOCAL SERVICES

Markets: Plaza Rotary, in the Machuca and Sangurima area northeast of the *centro*, sells everything. A smaller market dwells in the **Plaza San Francisco,** at Córdova and Aguirre. Prepared dishes and their individual ingredients can be found at **Mercado 10 de Agosto** on Torres and Larga, **Mercado 9 de Octubre** on Hermano Miguel and Lamar, and **Mercado 3 de Noviembre** on Talbot and Lamar. Thursday is the big day. **El Arenal** in the Plaza las Américas, on the far west of town, is busiest on Wednesdays.

Supermarkets: Popular, Córdova 7-23 and Cordero. Open M-Sa 8am-8pm, Su 8am-1pm. **Supermercados Unidos,** Cordero 11-05 and Lamar (☎830 815). Open M-Sa 8:30am-8:30pm, Sa 8:30am-1pm.

Laundromat: Fast Klin, Hermano Miguel 6-68 and Córdova (☎823 473). US$0.20 per lb. Open M-F 8am-7pm, Sa 8am-1pm. **La Química,** Borrero 7-34 and Sucre. US$0.24 per lb.; dry cleaning US$1 per item. Open M-Sa 8am-6:30pm.

WORLDWIDE CALLING MADE EASY

The MCI WorldCom Card, designed specifically to keep you in touch with the people that matter the most to you.

MCI WORLDCOM   WORLDPHONE.

1·800·888·8000

J. L. SMITH

www.wcom.com/worldphone

Please tear off this card and keep it in your wallet as a reference guide for convenient U.S. and worldwide calling with the MCI WorldCom Card.

HOW TO MAKE CALLS USING YOUR MCI WORLDCOM CARD

> **When calling from the U.S., Puerto Rico, the U.S. Virgin Islands or Canada** to virtually anywhere in the world:
1. Dial 1-800-888-8000
2. Enter your card number + PIN, listen for the dial tone
3. Dial the number you are calling :
   Domestic Calls: Area Code + Phone number
   International Calls:
   011+ Country Code + City Code + Phone Number

> **When calling from outside the U.S.,** use WorldPhone from over 125 countries and places worldwide:
1. Dial the WorldPhone toll-free access number of the country you are calling from.
2. Follow the voice instructions or hold for a WorldPhone operator to complete your call.

> **For calls from your hotel:**
1. Obtain an outside line.
2. Follow the instructions above on how to place a call.
   Note: If your hotel blocks the use of your MCI WorldCom Card, you may have to use an alternative location to place your call.

RECEIVING INTERNATIONAL COLLECT CALLS*
Have family and friends call you collect at home using WorldPhone Service and pay the same low rate as if you called them.
1. Provide them with the WorldPhone access number for the country they are calling from (In the U.S., 1-800-888-8000; for international access numbers see reverse side).
2. Have them dial that access number, wait for an operator, and ask to call you collect at your home number.

*For U.S. based customers only.

START USING YOUR MCI WORLDCOM CARD TODAY. MCI WORLDCOM STEPSAVERS℠
Get the same low rate per country as on calls from home, when you:

1. **Receive international collect calls to your home** using WorldPhone access numbers

2. **Make international calls with your MCI WorldCom Card** from the U.S.*

3. **Call back to anywhere in the U.S. from Abroad** using your MCI WorldCom Card and WorldPhone access numbers.

* An additional charge applies to calls from U.S. pay phones.

WorldPhone Overseas Laptop Connection Tips —
Visit our website, www.wcom.com/worldphone, to learn how to access the Internet and email via your laptop when traveling abroad using the MCI WorldCom Card and WorldPhone access numbers.

Travelers Assist® — When you are overseas, get emergency interpretation assistance and local medical, legal, and entertainment referrals. Simply dial the country's toll-free access number.

Planning a Trip?—Call the WorldPhone customer service hotline at 1-800-736-1828 for new and updated country access availability or visit our website:

www.wcom.com/worldphone

MCI WorldCom Worldphone Access Numbers

Easy Worldwide Calling

MCIWORLDCOM   WORLDPHONE

1·800·888·8000

J. L. SMITH

MCI WORLDCOM.

The MCI WorldCom Card.
The easy way to call when traveling worldwide.

The MCI WorldCom Card gives you…

• Access to the US and other countries worldwide.

• Customer Service 24 hours a day

• Operators who speak your language

• Great MCI WorldCom rates and no sign-up fees

For more information or to apply for a Card call:

1-800-955-0925

Outside the U.S., call MCI WorldCom collect (reverse charge) at:

1-712-943-6839

COUNTRY	WORLDPHONE TOLL-FREE ACCESS #
Argentina (CC)	
Using Telefonica	0800-222-6249
Using Telecom	0800-555-1002
Australia (CC) ♦	
Using OPTUS	1-800-551-111
Using TELSTRA	1-800-881-100
Austria (CC) ♦	0800-200-235
Bahamas (CC) +	1-800-888-8000
Belgium (CC) ♦	0800-10012
Bermuda (CC) +	1-800-888-8000
Bolivia (CC) ♦	0-800-2222
Brazil (CC)	000-8012
British Virgin Islands +	1-800-888-8000
Canada (CC)	1-800-888-8000
Cayman Islands +	1-800-888-8000
Chile (CC)	
Using CTC	800-207-300
Using ENTEL	800-360-180
China ♦	108-12
Mandarin Speaking Operator	108-17
Colombia (CC) ♦	980-9-16-0001
Collect Access in Spanish	980-9-16-1111
Costa Rica ♦	0800-012-2222
Czech Republic (CC) ♦	00-42-000112
Denmark (CC) ♦	8001-0022
Dominica+	1-800-888-8000
Dominican Republic (CC) +	
Collect Access	1-800-888-8000
Collect Access in Spanish	1121

COUNTRY	ACCESS #
Ecuador (CC) +	999-170
El Salvador (CC)	800-1767
Finland (CC) ♦	08001-102-80
France (CC) ♦	0-800-99-0019
French Guiana (CC)	0-800-99-0019
Germany (CC) ♦	0800-888-8000
Greece (CC) ♦	00-800-1211
Guam (CC)	1-800-888-8000
Guatemala (CC) ♦	99-99-189
Haiti +	
Collect Access	193
Collect access in Creole	190
Honduras +	8000-122
Hong Kong (CC)	800-96-1121
Hungary (CC) ♦	06*-800-01411
India (CC)	000-127
Collect access	000-126
Ireland (CC) ♦	1-800-55-1001
Israel (CC) ♦	1-800-920-2727
Italy (CC) ♦	172-1022
Jamaica +	
Collect Access	1-800-888-8000
From pay phones	#2
Japan (CC) ♦	
Using KDD	00539-121 ▶
Using IDC	0066-55-121
Using JT	0044-11-121

COUNTRY	ACCESS #
Korea (CC)	
To call using KT	00729-14
Using DACOM	00309-12
Phone Booths +	
Press red button ,03,then*	
Military Bases	550-2255
Luxembourg (CC)	8002-0112
Malaysia (CC) ♦	1-800-80-0012
Mexico (CC)	01-800-021-8000
Monaco (CC) ♦	800-90-019
Netherlands (CC) ♦	0800-022-91-22
New Zealand (CC)	000-912
Nicaragua (CC)	166
Norway (CC) ♦	800-19912
Panama	00800-001-0108
Philippines (CC) ♦	
Using PLDT	105-14
Filipino speaking operator	105-15
Using Bayantel	1237-14
Using Bayantel (Filipino)	1237-77
Using ETPI (English)	1066-14
Poland (CC) ♦	800-111-21-22
Portugal (CC) +	800-800-123
Romania (CC) ♦	01-800-1800
Russia (CC) ♦	
Russian speaking operator	747-3320
Using Rostelcom	747-3322
Using Sovintel	960-2222
Saudi Arabia (CC)	1-800-11

COUNTRY	WORLDPHONE TOLL-FREE ACCESS #
Singapore (CC)	8000-112-112
Slovak Republic (CC)	08000-00112
South Africa (CC)	0800-99-0011
Spain (CC)	900-99-0014
St. Lucia +	1-800-888-8000
Sweden (CC) ♦	020-795-922
Switzerland (CC) ♦	0800-89-0222
Taiwan (CC) ♦	0080-13-4567
Thailand (CC)	001-999-1-2001
Turkey (CC) ♦	00-8001-1177
United Kingdom (CC)	
Using BT	0800-89-0222
Using C & W	0500-89-0222
Venezuela (CC) + ♦	800-1114-0
Vietnam + ●	1201-1022

KEY

Note: Automation available from most locations. Countries where automation is not yet available are shown in Italic

(CC) Country-to-country calling available.

+ Limited availability.

★ Not available from public pay phones.

♦ Public phones may require deposit of coin or phone card for dial tone.

● Local service fee in U.S. currency required to complete call.

▶ Regulation does not permit Intra-Japan Calls.

* Wait for second dial tone.

‡ Local surcharge may apply.

Hint: For Puerto Rico and Caribbean Islands not listed above, you can use 1-800-888-8000 as the WorldPhone access number.

CENTRAL ECUADOR

Cuenca

ACCOMMODATIONS
El Cafecito, 14
Hostal Colonial, 5
Hostal Macondo, 1
Hostal Paredes, 2
Hostal Santo y Seña, 18
Hotel Milan, 12
Hotel Pichincha, 9

FOOD AND DRINKS
El Pedregal Azteca, 4
Heladería Holanda, 6
La Barraca Café, 7
Raymipampa Café-
   Restaurante, 11
Restaurant Vegetariano
   La Primavera, 10
Sanducheria Golosos, 3

MUSIC AND CLUBS
El Cafecito, 14
Kaos and Suava, 15
La Mesa, 8
Picadilly Bar, 13
Santo y Seña, 18
Santú, 17
WunderBar, 16

TO CEMENTERIO
MUNICIPAL

TO TERMINAL
TERRESTRE (3bks),

Olmedo

Juan León Mera

Huayna Capac

Manuel Vega

Estrella

Arriaga

Tomás Ordoñez

Mariscal Sucre

Pres. Córdova

Alfonso Jerves

Alfonso Malo

Vargas Machuca

Antonio Vega Muñoz

Mariano Cueva

Simón Bolívar

Juan Jaramillo

Honorato Vázquez

Larga

Museo de Sitio
de la Casa
de la Cultura

Museo del
Banco Central

PL.
ROTARY

Rotary
Market

Hermano Miguel

Gran Colombia

CETUR

Museo de las
Conceptas

Todos
los Santos

Pres. Borrero

Mariscal Lamar

VAZ

Instituto
Azuayo de Folklore

Planetario

Luis Cordero

Parque
Calderón

Pacifictel

Immigration
Office

Museo Remigio
Crespo Toral

Museo de Artes
Populares de
América

Bus to Baños

Benigno Malo

Larga

Padre Aguirre

Santo
Domingo

12 de Abril

Gral. Torres

Market   PL. DE
SAN
FRANCISCO

Torres

TO MIRADOR
TURI (2km)

Tarquí

Gaspar Sangurima

Museo de
Medicina

Colegio
Benigno Malo

Río Tomebamba

Juan Montalvo

Daniel Córdova

Salcedo

Aguilar

Estevez de Toral

Museo de Arte
Moderno

3 de Noviembre

Universidad
Estatal

Talbot

Mercado 3
de Noviembre

Miguel Vélez

Miguel Heredia

N

300 yards

300 meters

Book Exchange: The **Centro Cultural Abraham Lincoln,** a language school at Borrero 5-18 and Vásquez. Exchanges books M-F 3-6:30pm. **Wunderbar,** a popular bar on the Escalinata at Larga and Hmo. Miguel. Open T-Sa 11am-1am, M 11am-6pm. **Cuenc@net,** Hmo. Miguel 4-46 and Larga, 2nd fl. **Librería Siglo XX,** Cordero 6-85 and Córdova (☎823 689). Open M-F 8:30am-1pm and 2:30-8pm, Sa 8am-noon.

Spanish Schools: Numerous language programs provide personal or group instruction and can also arrange homestays. Program fees, which cost less with ISIC cards, generally include additional cultural lessons and excursions. **Estudio Internacional Sampere,** Hmo. Miguel 3-43 and Larga (☎823 960; fax 841 986; email sampere@samperecen.com.ec) instructs students 4-6hr. per day.

EMERGENCY AND COMMUNICATIONS

Emergency: ☎911.

Police: Central Office, Cordero 6-62 (☎101). **Tourist police** (☎841 319) are on the 2nd fl. Open daily 8am-noon and 3-6pm.

Pharmacy: *El Mercurio,* the local newspaper, publishes the 24hr. *en turno* schedule.

Hospitals: Clínica Santa Ines, Córdova Toral 2-113 and Cueva (☎817 888), on the far side of the river, just south of 12 de Abril. **Hospital Militar,** 12 de Abril 7-99 (☎827 606) and the **Centro de Salud del Azuay** (☎822 202) across the river, west of B. Malo.

Telephones: PacificTel, B. Malo 7-35 and Pdte. Córdova (☎842 122), 1 block from the Parque Calderón. Open daily 8am-10pm. **Etapa,** B. Malo 7-35 (☎831 900), across the street. Internet access US$0.64 per hr. Open daily 8am-9:45pm.

Internet Access: Cuenc@net, Hmo. Miguel 4-46 and Larga, with a **branch** at Larga 6-02 and Hmo. Miguel. In addition to providing Internet access (US$0.72 per hr.), Cuenc@net attracts pool and foosball players (US$1.20 per hr.). Open M-Sa 9am-10pm, Su 10am-9pm. **Compu Centro** (☎844 685), Bolívar and Hmo. Miguel, 3rd fl., offers cheaper service (US$0.60 per hr.). Open daily 8am-8pm.

Post Office: (☎838 311), at Borrero and Gran Colombia.

▛ ACCOMMODATIONS

Hotel pricing in Cuenca is a tricky business. Though accommodations are on the expensive side—by Ecuadorian standards—don't just make a mad dash for the cheapest place around; for a little extra, hotel quality increases drastically.

▨ **El Cafecito** (☎832 337; email elcafec@cue.satnet.net), Vásquez 7-36 and Cordero. An inviting sky-lit cafe by day, when the sun sets, the candles take over and a lively crowd filters in. Full restaurant/bar (open daily 8am-midnight) and nightly happy hour (5-7pm). Clean, colorful rooms. Dorms US$2; rooms US$3 per person, with bath US$4.

▨ **Hostal Macondo,** Tarquí 11-64 and Lamar (☎840 697; macondo@cedei.org.ec). Some claim this is the best hostel in Ecuador. Knowledgeable staff, beautiful lawns and gardens. Kitchen access. Singles US$8; doubles US$12. Singles US$180 per month; doubles US$220. Additional 10% tax; 10% HIYA member and ISIC discount.

Hostal Santo y Seña, 3 de Noviembre 4-71 (☎841 981), on Río Tomebamba, between the Escalinata and Puente Roto. A beautiful riverside mansion, the hostel features a large front yard, spacious hardwood interior, restaurant/bar (open daily 7am-9pm), dance floor, and live music many Th and F evenings. Rooms US$6 per person.

Hostal Colonial, Gran Colombia 10-13 at Padre Aguirre (☎841 644; email hcolonia@cue.satnet.net), on Plaza Santo Domingo. Rooms have refrigerator, bottled water, and wall-to-wall carpeting. Breakfast included. US$8 per person. 7% off with ISIC card.

Hostal Milan, Pres. Córdova 9-89 and Padre Aguirre. Most rooms have balconies overlooking the Plaza San Francisco. Pool tables on the roof. Rooms with bath, cable TV, and phone. Bicycle rental and tours of El Cajas (US$35 per person). Rooms US$2 per person; singles with bath and TV$4.50; doubles with bath and TV US$7.

Hotel Pichincha, Torres 8-82 and Bolívar (☎823 868). Dirt-cheap but dirt-free, in the center of town. Lounge has a huge TV. Rooms US$2 per person, with bath US$4.

Hostal Paredes, Cordero 11-29 (☎835 674). Antique furnishings in this mansion allow patrons to experience colonial living. Rooms US$4 per person, with bath US$6.

FOOD

With its attractive and diverse array of food, Cuenca is a great place to cure hunger pangs. From the numerous *típicos* with their traditional *almuerzos* to the costly world-class cuisine at El Jardín, Cuenca satisfies even the most selective stomach.

Raymipampa Café-Restaurante, Benigno Malo 8-59 (☎834 159). This lively restaurant hops with gringos and the local elite, especially around dinnertime. The view onto the Parque Calderón complements the casual, coffee-shop feel. Scrumptious dinner crepes US$1.20-1.80. Cappuccino US$0.32. Open M-F 8:30am-11pm, Sa-Su 8:30am-9pm.

Sanducheria Golosos, Gran Colombia 11-20 and Torres (☎827 312), across from Hostal Chordeleg. This small lunch counter makes some of the most innovative and finger-licking sandwiches in town. Hot turkey, chicken, or vegetarian subs (US$1-2) make for a good snack or nice picnic in the park. Delivery available. Open M-Sa 8:30am-9pm.

Heladería Holanda, Benigno Malo 9-51 and Bolívar (☎831 449). Widely acknowledged as serving the best ice cream in town. Delicious *copas* US$1. Open daily 8am-8pm.

Restaurant Vegetariano La Primavera, Hmo. Miguel 7-28 and Pdte. Córdova. Magnificent, meatless *almuerzos* (US$0.56). Yogurt, crepes, and fruit salads. Open M-F 8:30am-9:30pm, Sa 8:30am-4pm.

La Barraca Café, Borrero 9-68 and Gran Colombia (☎842 967; email gzuniga@az.pro.ec). In addition to a long list of alcoholic beverages and the snacks, there are flavorful meals (US$2) and crepes (US$0.80). Open M-Sa noon-midnight.

El Pedregal Azteca, Gran Colombia 10-29 and Padre Aguirre (☎823 652), dishes out some of the best Mexican food in Ecuador. No bargain basement, but authentic tacos, burritos, and enchiladas (US$1.75-2.50). Live music (M, W, F 8pm) enhances the dining experience. Open M 6-11pm, Tu-Sa 12:30-3pm and 6-11pm.

SIGHTS

Though the area's most compelling sights are out of town—at Turi, Ingapirca, Baños, Biblián, El Cajas, and the nearby markets—Cuenca proper has much to contribute. With a booming *artesanía* community (concentrated on Gran Colombia between Hmo. Miguel and Pdte. Borrero) and almost too many museums to count on your fingers, Cuenca serves up many cultural offerings.

MUSEO DEL BANCO CENTRAL. This museum houses Cuenca's most extensive collections of art and artifacts. The upstairs ethnographic exhibit takes you through the homes, lives, and handiwork of 22 indigenous cultures. The ground-floor archeology room explains the Cañari and Inca occupation of the Tomebamba (Pumapungo) ruins and documents the nearby site's recent excavation. Also prominent are collections of 19th century Ecuadorian art and—reflecting the interests of the management—a history of money in Ecuador. Visitors can also wander through the ancient city of Tomebamba, behind the Banco Central. After conquering the area, Sapa Inca Yupanqui converted this important Cañari site into a military outpost and then an administrative center. Traditional Inca architectural traits are visible over the earlier Cañari constructions, and some believe that this location served as Huayna Cápac's palace. *(Larga and Huayna Cápac. ☎831 255. Open M-F 8am-1pm and 2:30-6:30pm, Sa 8am-1pm. US$1.)*

MIRADOR TURI. From Turi, a treacherously high lookout spot four kilometers south of the city center, you can experience an avian outlook as only the high-fliers normally do. A 15-minute bus ride up a steep, pothole-ridden road pays off at the top, with a breathtaking panoramic view of Cuenca and its surrounding mountains. A cartographic tiled painting of the city matches the view and provides a guide to the scenery. Pay-binoculars (US$0.40) give a closer look. *(Getting up to Turi means taking either a bus, a cab, or a hike. Buses leave from 12 de Abril and Solano, south of the river (every 1½hr. 7:30am-4:30pm; US$0.08) and drop you off at the base of the hill upon which Mirador Turi is perched—a 30min. climb from the mirador. Taxis cost US$2.)*

CHURCHES AND PLAZAS. Cuenca has more churches per capita than most Ecuadorian cities. Cuenca's two most striking churches face each other across the Parque Calderón in the heart of town. Built in 1557 with stones from the Inca's Pumapungo Palace, the **Iglesia del Sagrario** (Old Cathedral) is under renovation until 2001. Across the street, the massively exquisite ■**Catedral de la Inmaculada Concepción** (New Cathedral; open daily 7am-4pm and 8-9pm) towers over the Parque Calderón and glows spookily by night. Initiated by Bishop Miguel León Garrido and the German Juan (Johannes) Bautista Stiehle in 1885, it was Bishop Manuel Maria Polit who gave the cathedral its current appearance in 1908. Officially, though, it remains unfinished. The cathedral is one of the most recognized churches in Ecuador; its ornate domes and brick face cover a cavernous marble interior, where brilliant rays of sunlight enter through the various windows and reflect off a four-column, gold-leaf canopy. **San Blas,** on Vega and Bolívar, was erected in 1575 in the form of a Latin cross using stones from Tomebamba. **San Sebastian,** Tálbot and Bolívar, with its single cupola, tower, and elaborately carved wooden portal, stands on the edge of a beautiful park.

OTHER SIGHTS. Cuenca promotes local arts and crafts through a variety of exhibition houses. The **Museo de Arte Moderno,** operating in the ancient House of Temperance, displays Ecuadorian modern art and hosts a biannual international art competition. *(Sucre 15-27 and Talbot, on Plaza San Sebastian. ☎831 027. Open M-F 8:30am-6:30pm, Sa-Su 9am-3pm; small tip.)* **Instituto Azuayo de Folklore** exhibits a fascinating array of local and regional *artesanía.* *(Cordero 7-22 and Córdova, third fl. ☎830 016; open M-F 8:30am-noon and 2:30-5pm.)* The **Museo de Artes Populares de América** has an equally impressive exhibit of handicrafts as well as the tools and materials that are used to make them. *(Hmo. Miguel 3-23 and Escalinata. ☎828 878. Open M-F 9:30am-1pm and 2:30-6pm, Sa 10am-1pm.)*

 ENTERTAINMENT

The large tourist contingent keeps Cuenca's bars and nightclubs open throughout the week. There's always a crowd enjoying happy hour drinks at **El Cafecito** and **Santo y Seña** (see Accommodations, p. 532). On weekends, there are even more options. The hippest disco in town is **Santú,** Larga and Jerves, which plays techno and house. For lively salsa dancing, try ■**La Mesa,** a favorite among locals and foreigners alike, on Gran Colombia at Ordoñez. For the uncoordinated and lethargic, **Kaos** and **Suava,** both at Vásquez and Hermano Miguel, are a little bit more laidback. Other bars without a cover charge include ■**Ego** on Unidad Nacional, **Picadilly Bar** at Córdova and Borrero, **WunderBar,** on the Escalinata at Hmo. Miguel 3-43 and **Larga** (☎831 274; open M 11am-11pm, T-Sa 11am-1am).

■ **FESTIVALS**

Fun-lovers flock to Cuenca's two prominent festivals. The week-long **El Septenario (Corpus Christi)** celebration—in which the main plaza explodes with fireworks and dancing—begins the second Thursday in June. Cuenca stretches its **Independence Day** celebration into a four-day cultural fair centered around November 3.

NEAR CUENCA: INGAPIRCA

Hardcore trekkers can make the difficult journey between Pumapungo and Ingapirca along Ingañan, which traverses the Cajas National Park, but a Cañari bus (2hr.; 9am, returns 1 amd 4pm; US$1.12) goes directly to the ruins from the terminal in Cuenca. Alternatively, buses can be taken to Tambo and then trucks or rancheras can take you the rest of the way. Lodging in the hotel near the ruins is much more expensive than more humble stays in hostels (US$2-3) in the nearby town of Ingapirca (5min. walk). Almuerzos

(US$1) and snacks available from restaurants at the site or in town. Admission to the ruins includes guided tours in Spanish or English and free access to the museum (US$5).

Located 85km north of Cuenca, Ingapirca lies along the now-eroded Inca highway (Ingañan) that ran from Pumapungo to the coast. Originally a Cañari settlement, the Incas transformed this site into an important religious center. Carefully constructed Inca edifices with trapezoidal doorways and pillowed stone blocks were built atop Cañari walls. The highlight of the ruins lies with the circular Temple of the Sun (37m by 15m). The celebrations of the annual Inti Raymi festival were believed to have been carried out at this summit. Interestingly, the rectangular structure atop the circular mound is of poorer construction. The site also contains *acllawasi* (Virgins of the Sun) residences, storerooms (*collcas*), and baths—no longer functional. And if you look carefully, you might be able to make out the face of an Inca carved in a nearby rock face. The **Museo del Sitio** exhibits the most precious artifacts found during recent excavations as well as a replica of the site.

NEAR CUENCA: GUALACEO

Santa Barbara and Santiago de Gualaceo buses leave from Gualaceo's terminal (☎255 730) on the main highway to Cuenca (40min., every 15min. 5am-7pm, US$0.32). Or visit jewelry merchants in nearby Chordeleg (15min., every 30min. 5am-7pm, US$0.12). Buses also journey to Azogues (45min., Sa 7:15am, US$0.32), Machala (5hr.; Sa 5am, Su 9am; US$2.60), Sígsig, and Paute.

Every Sunday, the center of activity in the Cuenca area shifts to the weekly market in this tiny village east of Cuenca, drawing bargain-hunters from neighboring mountain towns and even more rural settlements. Textile production ceases on this day and the week's output is brought into town. Heaps of handmade sweaters are sold to middlemen in the plaza by the bus station for resale in Otavalo and elsewhere. On any other day, you can visit the artisans in their homes, see the process, and buy souvenirs without any intermediary getting a cut of the price. Smaller versions of the market take place every Tuesday and Friday. Facing uphill in the bus station, the **indoor market, outdoor market,** and **main park** (in that order) lie diagonally ahead to the right. From the bus station, head up Cordero and turn left on Cuenca, or better yet, follow the herd. **Greentours,** 9 de Octubre 5-00 and Dávila Chica, on the plaza, provides maps of Gualaceo and offers tours of the surrounding villages and countryside. (Open M-F 9am-noon and 2-6pm.) For a place to stay, try **Hostal Carlos Andres,** Gran Colombia 2-03, two blocks from the main plaza (away from the market). A marble staircase accesses the four floors of clean and comfy rooms with baths and color TVs. (☎255 379. Rooms US$2.40 per person.)

NEAR CUENCA: CHORDELEG

Most buses heading back to Gualaceo (US$0.12) or Cuenca (US$0.44) leave one block uphill from the plaza (every 30min. 5am-7pm). Buses depart for Chordeleg from Gualaceo's terminal as soon as they fill up (15min.; every 30min.), and some buses coming from Cuenca to Gualaceo continue on to Chordeleg. The walk between Gualaceo and Chordeleg is beautiful, passing picturesque, rolling countryside and farmland. The downhill stretch from Chordeleg to Gualaceo takes about 1hr.; the return uphill can take 1½hr. On blind curves, be careful of cars hugging the right side of the highway.

While Gualaceo's market specializes in the daily necessities, the market at Chordeleg has a lock on the luxuries. The main plaza is absolutely studded with **jewelry** stores, sparkling with good deals thanks to all the competition (be wary of some of the great deals). Most jewelry merchants open their doors T-Su 9am-6pm, but close Mondays to buy their merchandise. Some artisan goods are also sold on the main plaza, but the best pottery shops, including the large and upscale **Centro de Artesanías,** are outside the center of town, toward Gualaceo on the main road. (Shops open daily 8am-1pm and 2-5pm.) While the modern church and main plaza are generally silent, a little more activity goes on a few blocks down at the market, a small-scale version of Gualaceo's. The small but info-packed **Museo Comunidad,** on the plaza, displays *artesanía* and ethnographic material (open daily 8am-1pm and 2-5pm.) There are no accommodations in this tiny town.

NEAR CUENCA: EL CAJAS NATIONAL RECREATION AREA

Buses headed straight for the information center leave from San Sebastian Park at Talbot and Mariscal Sucre in Cuenca (1hr.; 6 and 6:30am, return 2 and 3pm; US$0.80). If traveling on a weekend, arrive well before 6am to assure a seat for the crowded ride. San Luis buses to Guayaquil (1hr., 12 per day 5:05am-9:20pm, US$0.80) stop at the park. Ask to be let off at the information center. Return buses traveling the main road through the park pass by the Visitor Center throughout the day. Buses to the more isolated entrance at Soldados leave from El Vado square (1½hr., 6am). Admission to park US$10.

El Cajas National Park consists of water, rock, and bush. Their varied forms as well as the sheer magnitude of the landscape make this 29,000 hectare park a site not to miss. Peaks rise to a skyscraping 4450m, and nowhere does the altitude dip below 3150m; sheer cliffs, carved by glaciers, cut through rolling highlands; and from subterranean caverns, rivers rise to the surface and then resubmerge into fissures in the rock. Not to be outdone by the splendor of El Cajas' geological wonders, varied plants and flowers blanket the land with spring turf and splashes of color. Diminutive Quinua (Polylepis) trees, the highest-altitude trees in the world, sprout their gnarled trunks from the *páramo* covering most of the park's area. Virgin humid mountain forests cover the east and west ends of the area. El Cajas's unique climate makes it one of the few places where the rare cubilán, chuquiragua, and tushig plants flourish. Those with a little patience and luck may see some of the park's standard-issue wildlife such as deer, foxes, and rabbits, as well as the more distinctive spectacled bear, llama, puma, and *tigrillo* (little tiger). Birdwatchers can marvel at Andean condors, highland toucans, and hummingbirds. Pre-Hispanic ruins lie scattered throughout, and the ancient Inca Road of **Ingañan** stretches between Luspa Cave and Lake Mamamag in the center of the park. The best-preserved ruins are at Paredones, near Molleturo.

LOGISTICS. El Cajas has two main entrances at **Soldados** in the south and **Lake Toreadora** in the north. The latter lies right next to the highway that transects the park and is equipped with an information center (3778m). The small complex offers general info and basic shelter (*refugio*) with electricity but no running water. (US$0.20 per person.) Sparsely scattered restaurants serve tour groups a few kilometers from the refuge on the highway toward Cuenca. Before entering, fishing, or camping in Cajas, park wardens must be notified at either of the two entrances. The optimal time to visit is between August and January, but temperatures can drop to -5°C at night, so warm, waterproof gear is always essential. Dense fog often arrives in the early afternoon, and visitors without maps, compass, and experience have been known to get lost.

Seeing the park really requires a guide. **Río Arriba,** Hmo. Miguel 7-15 and Pdte. Córdova, caters trekking or horseback tours to the desires of travelers. (☎840 031; email negro@az.pro.ec. Open M-F 9am-6pm.) **Santa Ana**, Borrero and Pres. Córdoba, provide private transportation and the services of an English-speaking guide. (☎832 340. US$40 per person. Open M-F 9am-1pm and 3-7pm, Sa 11am-1pm.) **Apullacta Tours,** most easily contacted through the Hostal Macondo, offers daytrips (US$35 per person), as does **Aventuras Nomadas,** Hermano Miguel 6-91 and Pres. Córdoba (☎820 158). Both provide English-speaking naturalist guides.

The most popular trail is the loop (3-4hr.) around Laguna Toreadora, which affords great vistas of some of Cajas' 232 lakes. This is the only hike that can be done independently (after receiving specific directions from the park warden). Guided, two-day treks along the four kilometers of preserved Inca highway (between Cave Lupsa and Lake Mamamag) start at Tablón and end at the control post near Laguna Lanuco. Remnants of Inca buildings are concentrated near Laguna Mamamag, but more impressive ruins lie 3½ hours (or 2½hr. by horse) southeast of Molleturo at Paradones. Ecological tours can also be arranged to penetrate Quinua forests near the refuge.

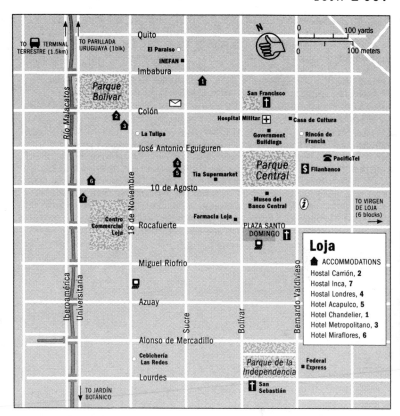

LOJA   ☎ 07

Always on the move, Loja (pop. 160,000) was relocated from the Catamayo area
in 1548 and was rebuilt twice following severe earthquakes. Loja, a gateway to
the Oriente, sits only a stone's throw from the most seductive and secluded
spots in the southern cordillera—Vilcabamba, Zamora, Saraguro, and the
Parque Nacional Podocarpus. Home to two universities, a law school, and a
musical conservatory, this small city has developed a sense of modern culture
that many other towns in the area lack; at the same time it has retained ties to
its historic and rustic origins. Colonial influences persist along Lourdes and
around the Parque de la Independencia, no buildings rise past the fourth story,
and the local Saraguros, in their traditional black dress, are a strong presence
throughout the city.

▮ TRANSPORTATION

Flights: La Tola airport, in Catamayo, is a 35km ride from Loja. Buses make the journey
to **Catamayo** (1hr., every 30min. 6am-7pm, US$0.56), and taxis (US$0.60) from the
main plaza go the rest of the way. TAME flights depart to **Quito** (M-Sa 6am, US$38) and
Guayaquil (M and Th-Sa 5:45am; US$25). Reservations can be made at their office
(☎573 030), on 24 de Mayo near Eguiguren. Open M-F 9am-4:15pm. ICARO (☎578
398), on Eguiguren near Olmedo, also flies to **Quito** (W, F, Su 6pm; US$60). Open M-F
8am-1pm and 3-6pm, Sa 8am-1pm

Buses: The **terminal** (☎579 592), located a few minutes north of the *centro,* is well staffed with a post office, telephone and Internet center, and information booth. A billboard lists all departure times. To: **Quito** (12hr., US$8); **Cuenca** (5hr., US$2.80) via **Saraguro** (2hr., US$1); **El Cisne** (2hr., US$1.12); **Catamayo** (1hr., every 30min. 6am-7pm, US$0.56); **Marcará** (5hr., US$3); **Guayaquil** (9hr., US$5.20); **Gualaqulza** (8hr., US$2.80) via **Zamora** (2hr., US$1.12); **Huaquillas** (6hr., US$3); **Machala** (6hr., US$3.40); and **Vilcabamba** (1hr., every 30min. 4:30am-7pm, US$0.60).

Taxis: Taxi Ruta, on Iberoamérica, crams 5-6 people into their cabs bound for **Vilcabamba** (50min., leave when full, US$0.60).

✴ 🛈 ORIENTATION AND PRACTICAL INFORMATION

Loja lies along two rivers. The main one, **Río Malacatos,** runs between (and underneath) **Universitaria** and **Iberoamerica** in town. **Río Zamora** parallels **24 de Mayo,** marking the eastern boundary of the city. The heart of the **centro** lies between these two rivers; the northern and southern boundaries are marked by **Quito** and **Lourdes.** The **terminal,** on Cuxibamba, is about a 15-minute walk, US$0.60 taxi ride, or US$0.08 bus ride north of the *centro* along Universitaria.

Tourist Information: The **Ministerio de Turismo,** Valdivieso 8-22 (☎572 964) and 10 de Agosto; and **Cámara de Turismo** (☎571 500), 10 de Agosto 15-46, provide info and maps. Open M-F 8am-noon and 3-5:30pm. The **Ministerio de Medio Ambiente, (INEFAN)** (☎571 534), on Sucre between Imbabura and Quito, administers Parque Nacional Podocarpus. Open M-F 8am-12:30pm and 2-5pm.

Tour Agencies: Biotours, on Eguiguren near Olmedo (☎578 398, email biotours@cue.satnet.net; open M-F 8am-1pm and 3-7pm, Sa 8am-1pm); and **Aratinga Aventuras,** Lourdes 14-80 near Sucre can customize 1-3 day tour packages. (☎582 434; email jatavent@cue.satnet.net. Open M-F 10am-12:30pm and 3-6:30pm, Sa 10am-12:30pm.)

Immigration Office: (☎573 600), at Argentina and Tebaida Alta, next to the police station. Open M-F 8am-noon and 2-6pm.

Peruvian Consulate: Sucre 10-64, 2nd fl. (☎571 668). Open M-F 8:30am-1:30pm.

Banks: Filanbanco, Valdivieso 7-56 and 10 de Agosto (☎578 647; fax 577 455), on the main park, has a **Visa/AmEx ATM.** Open M-F 8:30am-3pm. **MC ATMs** are at other banks around the Parque Central. **Banco de Loja** (☎571 682), on the corner of Bolívar and Rocafuerte. Open M-F 8am-4pm, Sa 8am-3pm, Su 8am-1pm.

Book Exchange: Biotours, on Eguiguren near Olmedo, has a large selection of books. Open M-F 8am-1pm and 3-7pm, Sa 8am-1pm.

Emergency: ☎115. **Police:** (☎560 500), Argentina and Tebaida Alta.

Hospital: Hospital Isidro Ayora (emergency ☎570 540), on Iberoamèrica near Quito.

Telephones: PacificTel (☎571 025) has two branches in Loja: at Eguiguren and Valdivieso, and on Iberoamérica 13-71 near Lourdes. Open daily 8am-9:30pm.

Internet Access: Triple C, Rocafuerte 13-41 (☎585 084; email triplec@loja.telconet.net), 3rd fl., also charges US$1.20 per hr. Open M-F 9:30am-1pm and 3:15-7:30pm, Sa 9:30am-1pm. **Cheaper service** is available at 18 de Noviembre 10-44 (☎570 037). US$1 per hr. Open M-Sa 9am-8pm, Su 10am-7pm.

Post Office: Colón 15-09 and Sucre (☎571 600), also offers **EMS** service. Open M-F 7:30am-7pm, Sa 8am-noon.

🛏 ACCOMMODATIONS

Loja has an over-abundance of hotels, most of which are clustered around 10 de Agosto and Sucre. Unless there is a local festival, availability is never a problem.

▨ **Hotel Metropolitano,** 18 de Noviembre 6-31 and Colón (☎570 007). Single-handedly keeping local lumberjacks in business, this place is a tribute to wood paneling. Color TVs, double beds, quiet surroundings. Singles US$4; doubles US$6.40.

Hostal Carrión, Colón 16-36 and 18 de Noviembre (☎584 548). Simple rooms satisfy basic living needs with a bed, table, and clean sheets; significantly snazzier private baths upstairs have color TVs. Singles US$2 per person, with bath US$4.

Hostal Inca (☎582 928), on Universitaria near 10 de Agosto, is a good deal. Clean rooms have hot-water baths and TVs. Rooms US$2 per person, with color TV US$3.

Hotel Chandelier, Imbabura 14-82 and Sucre (☎563 061). Carved pillars and a tiled courtyard create the slightly-run-down-mansion look. Rooms facing the street have better lighting but are noisier. Rooms US$2 per person, with bath and TV US$4.

Hotel Acapulco, Sucre 7-61 and 10 de Agosto (☎570 651). Luxurious rooms with color TV, desk set, free bath supplies. Singles US$8; doubles US$12; triples US$15.

◖ FOOD

Bread seems to be unusually good in Loja, and *panaderías* diffuse warm bakery smells on every block. **Panadería La Europa,** 18 de Noviembre 6-05 and Colón, sells sweet bread ($0.32; ☎573 116; open M-Sa 8am-1pm and 2:30-7pm).

■ **Trattoria Verona,** Imbabura 15-46 and Sucre. Palatable pizzas and pasta (US$2) are served by candlelight in a minimalist red-and-white room that pays homage to goddesses Marilyn Monroe and Shakira. Individual pizzas US$1-3, large US$5-8.

■ **Cevichería Las Redes,** 18 de Noviembre, at Mercadillo and Lourdes (☎578 697). This seafood joint offers more than just your average ceviche (US$1.80). Traditional Ecuadorian fare (US$1.80) and Chinese dishes too. Open M-Sa 8am-9:30pm, Su 8am-3pm.

Mero Mero, Sucre 6-22 and Colón. Serves up good Mexican fare: tacos, burritos, enchiladas, fajitas (US$0.64-1.64) Open M-Sa 10am-11pm.

Parillada Uruguaya (☎570 260), on Salinas near Universitaria, is a carnivore's paradise. This clean, bright restaurant is a local favorite and serves some of the best meat around. *Parilladas* are huge (US$8). Open M-Sa 6pm-2am.

◪ SIGHTS

The area that surrounds Loja is so scenic that every visitor ends up outdoors, whether admiring a view, visiting the city's parks, or trekking in the nearby hills.

■ **PARQUE DE JIPIRO.** A few blocks north of the terminal, this expansive park amuses children with miniature reproductions of the Kremlin and the Eiffel Tower. The Chinese dock rents **paddleboats** (US$1 for 30min.), the European castle offers **Internet** connections (US$0.20 per hr.), and the Islamic mosque doubles as a **planetarium.** (Open daily 8am-noon and 2-6pm. Adults US$0.80, children US$0.40.) There's also a pool (open T-Su 9am-5:30pm; adults US$0.24, children US$0.12) for swimming. *(Take a bus (US$0.08) north to Jipiro from Universitaria or walk a few blocks north of the bus station.)*

PARQUE UNIVERSITARIO LA ARGELIA. Run by the Universidad Nacional de Loja, the park is another outstanding outdoor experience. Full of beautifully maintained hiking trails, the park covers the hills across the Río Malacatos from the campus. There is a small **museum** and **info center** at the base of the trail, and a wooden sign outside illustrates the various hikes. The trail that heads left provides a complete two-hour loop through a flowered pine forest, full of tranquil mountain streams, and (depending on the time of year) squadrons of butterflies. *(Take any bus headed to Vilcabamba, or take a Argelia-Capuli bus running down Iberoamerica. Argelia-Pitas buses will drop you off at the university campus. From the campus it's a 15min. walk east across the Río Malacatos and down the highway. Open daily during daylight hours. US$0.32.)*

JARDÍN BOTÁNICO. Across the highway from the trail base at La Argelia, a botanical garden boasts 889 species of tropical plants as well as sections devoted to medicinal plants and orchids. *(Located in Parque Universitario La Argelia. Open M-F 9am-4pm, Sa-Su 1-6pm. US$0.32. For more detailed information on the plants visit **Fundatierra,** RioFrío 14-09 and Bolívar. ☎582 764. Open M-F 8am-noon and 2:15-6:15pm.)*

NIGHTLIFE

Nighttime entertainment is a bit scarce in Loja on weekdays, but the decor at the **Piano Bar Unicornio**, Bolívar 7-63 and 10 de Agosto, is amusement enough. (☎574 083. Open M-Sa 3-11pm.) On the corner of a five-way intersection at Prolongación 24 de Mayo and Segundo Cueva Celi, ▓**Free Days** tries to bring a bit of the US to Ecuador. (Open M-Th and Sa 4:30pm-midnight, F 4:30pm-2am). Nearby on Celi, **Siembra** is a romantic bar serving food and drink under a thatched roof to locals. (☎583 451. Open M-Th, Sa 4pm-12:30am, F 4pm-2am.)

NEAR LOJA: SARAGURO

Pullman Viajeros (☎200 164) and Sur Oriente (☎200 115), both located across the park from the church, have buses heading north to **Cuenca** *(3hr., US$2.40) and south to* **Loja** *(2hr., US$0.88), and stop on the main plaza about every 30min.*

A tiny stop on the Panamerican Highway between Cuenca and Loja, the town of Saraguro offers little other than typical small-town charm and untouristed solitude. Its main attraction is the **artesanía** of the indigenous Saraguros. Souvenir-hungry tourists will be able to find plenty on Sundays, when the market brings farmers into town from surrounding areas. On other days of the week, travelers can stop by **Maki Rurai** (☎200 258) near the church. The **traditional black dress** that is unique to this region of Ecuador represents mourning for the tragic end of the Inca Empire: men wear black ponchos and mid-calf black pants, while women wear black shawls with a silver pin called a **topo**. These pins are callbacks to pre-Hispanic times and are used to distinguish the marital status of its users: single women wear green, wives use blue, and widows don red. There are two hotels and a couple of eateries in Saraguro. **Residencial Saraguro,** at the corner of Loja and Fernando Bravo, has comfortable beds, thick adobe walls, and a garden. Extra blankets make up for plastic-covered windows. (☎200 286. Hot water US$0.20. Rooms US$1.20 per person.) A few doors down on Bravo, **Residencial Armijos** has less comfortable rooms that share hot-water showers (US$1 per person). **Bar Restaurant Cristal,** one block behind the church on Oro, serves some of the tastiest *almuerzos* and *meriendas* in town. (Open daily 7am-10pm.)

NEAR LOJA: CATAMAYO

Cooperativa Catamayo, Catamayo 3-32 near Isidro Ayora and the Parque Principal, has buses to Loja (1hr., every 30min. 6am-7pm, US$0.56). Transportes Santa on 24 de Mayo on the park travels to Quito (11hr., 1 and 7pm, US$7.80). Camionetas to El Cisne leave from the corner of Ayora and 24 de Mayo when full (1hr., US$0.60). Taxis to the airport can be hired from the plaza on 24 de Mayo (5min., US$0.40) or El Cisne (US$2).

Busy but uninspiring, Catamayo's main contribution to the traveler subculture is the **La Tola airport** (2½km away), the nearest spot for flights into and out of Loja. Briefly the site of the city of Loja itself, Catamayo has been untroubled by major happenings ever since the better-known metropolis moved 30km east in 1548, two years after its founding. Though the city may be unexciting by most standards, travelers with early-morning and late-evening flights may find this an adequate site to spend the night. **Hotel Turis,** Ayora near 24 de Mayo, is the best deal in town. A sunny courtyard and chirping caged birds compensate for dimly-lit surrounding rooms. (☎677 126. Rooms US$0.60 per person, with bath US$1.20.) The same owners provide linoleum-floors next door at **Hotel Rossana.** Rooms with bath have color TVs. (☎677 006. Rooms US$1.40 per person, with cold-water bath US$2.40.)

NEAR LOJA: EL CISNE

Buses leave for El Cisne from Loja's terminal. Transportes Catamayo has direct service (M-Th and Sa 4pm, F 9am and 4pm, Su 4, 7:30 and 8:30am). Another option is to take a bus to Catamayo (1hr., every 30 min. 6am-7pm, US$0.52) and then catch one of the camionetas to El Cisne (1hr., US$0.60), though they can be unpredictable.

High in the hills, the small village of El Cisne is home to an enormous **cathedral** with a bright, whitewashed exterior and a somewhat gothic feel. Inside the cathedral there is a statue of a virgin, **La Virgen del Cisne,** looking down at worshippers from behind a plate of glass in her ornate, gold-encrusted home. It is this statue, not the church, town, or gorgeous mountain scenery, that draws hordes of people to El Cisne every year. For four days every summer (Aug. 17-20), following a week of *fiestas,* a river of faith led by the famous statue pours into Loja from El Cisne. The local virgin, a common postcard image, floats on the shoulders of the hearty pilgrims who clog the 80km road to Loja. On November 1, she begins her crowd-surfing return to El Cisne, making temporary stops at the towns along the way. Chaucer-worthy pilgrims trek barefoot to the basilica from San Pedro, Catamayo, or even Loja. Outside of the fascinating procession, the town's best offering is the sanctuary itself, a building gargantuan in both scale and reputation. When you're done gawking at the spectacle within, buy a ticket in the clock tower's library to enter the **museum.** The small museum houses the Virgen's dresses as well as gifts and plaques given in her honor. (Open T-Su 8am-noon and 1-5pm. US$0.12 adults, US$0.08 children.) Despite regional Catholic significance, generally only the truly fascinated take the long daytrip between El Cisne and Loja. Pilgrims can spend the night at **Hostal Medina,** to the right before descending the stairs (rooms US$2 per person.) Restaurants line the plaza in front of the cathedral, though options at most of them are limited to the standard *menú* (US$1).

ZAMORA ☎ 07

Ecuador's city of gold, Zamora (pop. 9000) is a rustic jungle town that suddenly found itself in the center of things when Midas touched the nearby town of Nambija about 20 years ago. A mining frontier culture sprouted as quickly as the Oriente vegetation, resulting in inevitable turmoil and conflict between entrepreneurs and locals. Somehow, Zamora has adapted to these changes and come to exist between worlds: a newly-finished highway winds along pristine cliffs and waterfalls and through both highland cloud forests and jungle, while mining equipment and the tin roofs of gold-boom houses speckle the otherwise scenic valley. The town itself has become a "gateway" city, providing easy access to the Amazon basin via the Parque Nacional Podocarpus.

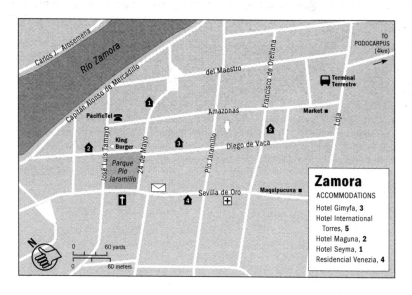

Zamora

ACCOMMODATIONS

Hotel Gimyfa, **3**
Hotel International Torres, **5**
Hotel Maguna, **2**
Hotel Seyma, **1**
Residencial Venezia, **4**

CENTRAL ECUADOR

TRANSPORTATION

Buses leave for: **Loja** (2hr., every 30min., US$1.12); **Gualaquiza** (5hr., US$1.72) via **Yantzaza** (2hr., US$0.60); **Machala** (9hr., US$4.20); **Cuenca** (7hr., US$4.40); **Zumba** (9hr., US$4.80); **Guayaquil** (8hr., US$6); **Quito** (17hr., US$9.20); and many smaller towns throughout the day.

ORIENTATION AND PRACTICAL INFORMATION

Activity in Zamora is divided between the main park, **Parque Pío Jaramillo,** and the **mercado**. The busy **Amazonas** and **Diego de la Vaca** traverse the three-block distance between the two centers. The **terminal,** opposite the market, adds to the commotion in the eastern part of town.

Tourist Information: Although there are no official information centers, **Vilcatur** (☎605 414), on Vaca near Jaramillo, may be able to answer questions. They can also send packages or cash to foreign destinations if requested. Open M-F 8:30am-12:30pm and 2:30-6:30pm, Sa 8:30am-12:30pm. **The Asociación Shuar** (☎605 820), on Jaramillo between Amazonas and Vaca, can supply useful information for those interested in making multi-day trips to the **Shuar communities at Alto Nangarita.** Open M-F 8am-noon and 2-6pm. **INEFAN** (☎605 606), on the highway from Loja, is an essential stop before Parque Nacional Podocarpus excursions. Open M-F 8:30am-12:30pm and 1-4:30pm. There are **no official guides** in the area, but locals with knowledge of the park can be hired (US$10 per day) to lead you through Bombuscaro. One such individual is Dr. Ramirez Reyes (☎606 067) who runs a furniture store at Vaca 4-103.

Banks: Banco de Loja (☎605 335), on Tamayo near Amazonas. Open M-Sa 8am 3:30pm, Su 8am-1pm.

Police: (☎101), at the corner of Orellana and Maestro.

Hospital: Hospital Julius Deepfuer (☎605 149), on Sevilla de Oro between Jaramillo and Orellana. Open M-F 8am-noon and 1:30-4pm.

Telephones: PacificTel (☎605 104), on Amazonas and Tamayo, one block from the main plaza, does not handle collect or calling card calls. Open daily 8am-10pm.

Internet: Opposite the bus station (☎605 697). Open M-Sa 8am-noon and 2-6pm.

Post Office: (☎605 546), on Sevilla de Oro near 24 de Mayo. Open M-F 8am-noon and 2-6pm.

ACCOMMODATIONS

Hotel Gimyfa Internacional (☎605 024), Diego de Vaca and Pío Jaramillo, has an appealing, modern design. Hot water, carpeted floors, cable TV, and an underpopulated downstairs disco launch it into comparative luxury. Rooms US$6 per person.

Hotel Maguna (☎605 113), on Vaca, past the park, offers equally elegant rooms with balconies. Other luxuries include cable TV, private baths, and a downstairs bar. Rooms US$4 per person.

Hotel Internacional Torres (☎605 195), on Orellana between Diego de Vaca and Amazonas, offers modern mirrored-glass with Greek columns and a semi-classical enclosed courtyard. Hot water, cable TV, and carpeting. Rooms US$4 per person.

Hotel Seyma, 24 de Mayo and Amazonas (☎605 583), near the plaza, is the essence of simplicity: bare wood floors, a hanging light bulb, and shared, cold-water-only bathrooms. Rooms US$2 per person.

Residencial Venezia (☎605 554) on Sevilla de Oro near Jaramillo, is even more minimalistic. Darkened rooms share cold-water baths in the rear garden of a family home. Rooms US$1.20 per person.

FOOD

Restaurants and *picanterías* offering *almuerzos* and *meriendas* (US$0.80-1) line Diego de la Vaca and Amazonas, especially near the bus terminal.

Las Gemelitas, on Amazonas, is particularly popular with a local crowd that consumes *almuerzos, meriendas,* and other entrees (US$1.20-1.40). Open daily 7am-8pm.

King Burger, across from the church on the corner of Vaca and Tamayo, was intended to be called Kim Burger. Señor Kim is still angry at the sign company but continues to grill beef for US$0.60-1.40. Open daily 8am-11pm.

PARQUE NACIONAL PODOCARPUS

ZONA ALTA (CAJANUMA ENTRANCE)

Layer upon layer of rolling mist obscure the scenery at the highest points in Parque Nacional Podocarpus. Miles of cliffside paths traverse this *zona alta*, a vibrant ecosystem which overcome harsh weather patterns to grow, flower, and breed at up to 3600m above sea level. Notoriously elusive high-fliers—the **toucan de altura,** the **quetzal,** and the Andean **cock-of-the-rock**—hide in the fingers of fog that cloud the Podocarpan sky. Threatened Romerillo (or Podocarpus) trees—Ecuador's only endemic conifer—dangle from the cliffs. It takes three or four days to reach the interior part of Podocarpus, but day-hikers need not feel deprived. Spectacled bear and puma tracks can be sighted near the *refugio*, and the surrounding trails have wildlife, views, and mud galore. For a list of the plants and animals that can be sighted in the park, visit the **Arco Iris Foundation** (☎577 449) at Segundo Cueva Celi 3-15 in Loja. The park is **staffed 24 hours** by wardens who issue entrance tickets; US$5 buys access to the entire park, including the camping cabins and resource-laden *refugio*, and is good for five days.

THE TRAILS. There are **four main paths** through beautiful mountain terrain, all of which begin at the **main refugio** (2750m). Mainly for children or families, **Sendero Oso de Anteojos** (Spectacled Bear Path) is a short 400-meter loop near the entrance. Although this trail gives a taste of the park's natural splendor, only the paths that go onward and upward provide climactic views. The more difficult **Sendero Bosque Nublados** (Cloud Forest Path) climbs higher; the 700-meter trail takes two hours to complete. **Sendero al Mirador** (Path to Lookout Point) captures the essence of Podocarpus, revealing a banquet of foggy *vistas* along the way. Birdwatchers can observe a feathered cabaret, and lucky hikers who smell strongly of food might glimpse a spectacled bear, mountain tapir, fox, or puma. The four- to five-hour loop, reaching 3000m at its apex, is muddy and misty in the summer, but clear and dry in the winter. Less ambitious hikers can opt out of the second part of the trail and do only the one-hour hike to the *mirador* and back. If Sendero al Mirador is a banquet, **Sendero Las Lagunas del Compadre** (Path of the Compatriot's Lakes) is an orgy. The 15km trail leads to shimmering lakes buried deep in the mountain forest. The total excursion takes seven hours, but most hikers choose to enjoy the journey over two or three days, camping at the halfway point or at Laguna del Ocho.

TRANSPORTATION. The park entrance is at **Cajanuma,** a barren stretch of highway about 15km from Loja on the road to Vilcabamba. Unfortunately, buses and shared taxis heading to Vilcabamba will drop you off on the highway, leaving an 8km uphill hike to the refuge, although regular taxis usually can go all the way up.

ZONA BAJA (ZAMORA ENTRANCE)

Tropical butterflies flutter across the trails in Parque Nacional Podocarpus's *zona baja*, a primary tropical rainforest along the **Río Bombuscaro** with trails winding past waterfalls and streams. Budding botanists can explore the Orquidiario, home to a dazzling diversity of plants. Highlights include over **40 varieties of orchids** as well as the **cascarilla tree,** the source of quinine, a key ingredient in both malaria remedies and tonic water. Wildlife is best in the heart of the park—mining has pushed most creatures away from the park's edges.

THE TRAILS. Several *zona baja* trails start from the Bombuscaro ranger station. The short trail to the **area de nadar** (150m) from the station follows a wooden staircase down to the river itself, where you can swim in freshwater except after recent rainfall, when currents are strong and swimming is prohibited. **Los Helechos** is a trail so short that spending 30 minutes on it requires self-control. INEFAN puts out an instructional brochure, available in Zamora or Loja, which lists **11 points of interest** along the trail. Among these are orchids, guarumo, helechos (huge trees), palms, and cascarilla. From point seven on the Helechos loop, a new route (1km) has been cleared to a **cascade.** Another waterfall, **Cascada La Chismosa**, is accessible on a short path (118m) before reaching the refuge from the parking area. The longest path, **Sendero Higuerones** (6km), is a three- or four-hour round-trip trek that encroaches on virgin forest. Another recent addition, the **Tarabita trail,** branches off from Higuerones before crossing the Río Bombuscaro. Bushwhacking and backwoods camping is illegal without the supervision of a guide.

TRANSPORTATION. Taxis for the journey from the bus station to the El Oso parking area cost about US$3.20 round-trip (arrange a pickup time with the driver in advance), but the four kilometer road also provides an easy walk amid cascading falls and lush vegetation. INEFAN trucks, often full, pass periodically.

OTHER ENTRANCES
There are various other entry-points, each equipped with a ranger station, which access less explored portions of the park. Another entrance to Podocarpus' *zona baja* is south of Zamora at a tiny town called **Romerillos.** INEFAN officials staff a refuge similar to the one at Bombuscaro but much smaller. *Rancheras* head to Romerillos from Zamora (2hr., 6am and 2pm) and return at 8am and 4pm. From the drop-off point it is a two-hour walk to the control post and the two uncleared trails. Additional access into the *zona alta* is possible near **Vilcabamba** (see p. 544); tours with destinations at the Laguna Rabadilla de Vaca or Laguna Banderillas enter the park through Río Yambala or Capamaco. **San Francisco**, located 23km en route to Zamora from Loja, is primarily a scientific station.

TOURS AND TOUR OPERATORS
All of Podocarpus is impressive, but as usual, the best parts are the hardest to reach. The easy-access fringes of the park, though overrun with tourists, miners, farmers, and the occasional grazing cow, will satisfy casual plant-lovers but will disappoint hard-core botanists and animal seekers. The **Arco Iris Foundation,** Segundo Cueva Celi 03-15, in Loja, can be reached by crossing the Río Zamora at Imbabura and heading downstream for one block on 24 de Mayo. This local nonprofit conservation group provides reams of information. (☎577 449; email fai1@fai.org.ec; www.arcoiris.org.ec. Open M-F 8:30am-12:30pm and 2:30-6:30pm.) **Biotours Ecuador** (☎/fax 578 398; email biotours@cue.satnet.net), on Eguiguren near Olmedo, and **Aratinga Aventuras,** Lourdes 14-80 and Sucre (☎582 434; email jatavent@cue.satnet.net) in Loja, have one- to three-day tours with all equipment, food, and park fees included (US$60 per person per day).

VILCABAMBA   ☎07

If most small towns in Ecuador are *tranquilo*, Vilcabamba is sedated. The warm weather, beautiful scenery, and recent gringo influence have turned this sleepy town into a place like no other; locals walk around in shorts and tank tops, every house has a hammock, and, from time to time, *fiestas* erupt in the town plaza for no reason at all. Throughout history, Vilcabamba has been seen as a mystical place, thought by the Inca, the Spanish, and recently by travelers from around the world to possess life- and conscience-expanding properties. There are many legends about residents who lived to ridiculously old ages in the clean air, mild climate, and unpolluted surroundings of the Valle de la Juventud Eterna (Valley of Eternal Youth). Inca elders used to make pilgrimages to the valley to engage in a longevity ceremony with the seeds of the local huilco tree. In this century, many *fiesta*-oriented foreigners have made a similar pilgrimage to sample the hallucinogenic properties of San Pedro, a psychotropic cactus endemic to the valley. But don't come to town looking to get high. Local opinion and law enforcement have recently united to decrease drug-related tourism, for which the town has become notorious. Because of this changing opinion, "daytrippers" may meet with a cold reception and encounter difficulty procuring their chemical muse. That said, the pleasant climate, resort atmosphere, and abundant attractive lodgings continue to make Vilcabamba one of the most popular destinations in Southern Ecuador.

▐ TRANSPORTATION

Buses: Vilcabamba Turis (☎673 166) **vans** leave for **Loja** (1¼hr., every 30min. 5:45am-8:15pm, US$0.60) from Sucre near Fernando de la Vega, just off the plaza. Sur Oriente buses (☎579 019) depart from the **terminal,** at the corner of C. Jaramillo and Eterna Juventud. To: **Loja** (1½hr., every hr. 5:30am-7pm, US$0.60); **Zumba** (6hr., 5 per day 9:30am-10:30pm); and **Yangara** (4 per day 10:30am-7:30pm).

Taxis: Taxi Ruta gets to **Loja** in 45min. but crams up to 6 people in a small car (US$0.60). Taxis leave from the terminal.

Bicycle Rental: Most hostels have bicycles to rent. **Fanny's Salon,** on the corner of Piscobamba and Vaca, rents out bikes for US$1 per hr. Open daily 8am-6pm.

✳ ▐ ORIENTATION AND PRACTICAL INFORMATION

Buses and taxis cruise in from Loja along **Eterna Juventud.** Activity in Vilcabamba's center crowds around a **main plaza;** the **church** is to the side. A slew of restaurants and tourist agencies crowd the plaza, and hotels are scattered for several kilometers on **Diego Vaca de la Vega** on the right.

Tourist Information: The **information center** (☎580 890) is on the corner of Diego Vaca de la Vega and Bolívar, on the park opposite the church. Provides helpful information in Spanish on accommodations, tours, and restaurants. Open daily 8am-noon and 2-6pm.

Tour Agencies: Aveturs, Vaca and Bolívar, is the umbrella organization for all the guides in town. **Centro Ecuestre** (☎673 151; centro_ecuestre@hotmail.com), a branch of Aveturs, is a good place to book a tour and get your questions answered in English. Open daily 8am-9pm. Most hotels and agencies advertise horseback-riding tours ranging from a few hours (US$10) to 3-day adventures (US$25 per person per day). New Zealander

CENTRAL ECUADOR

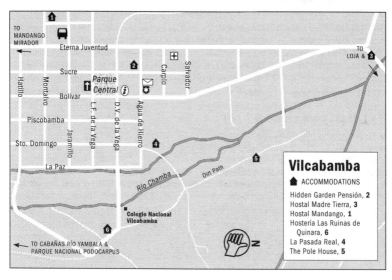

Vilcabamba

⚑ ACCOMMODATIONS

Hidden Garden Pensión, **2**
Hostal Madre Tierra, **3**
Hostal Mandango, **1**
Hostería Las Ruinas de
    Quinara, **6**
La Pasada Real, **4**
The Pole House, **5**

Gavin Moore (☎580 281; gavilanhorse@yahoo.com) includes gourmet food, drinks, and two nights of lodging at his 2500-meter-high mountain cabin in the nearby cloud forests. Open daily 9am-8pm. **Orlando Falco**, a bilingual zoologist, offers a selection of 1-day **cloud forest walks** (US$25-30 per person for groups of 5 or more).

Currency Exchange: There are no banks or *casas de cambio* in Vilcabamba, but most hotels and hostels are willing to change travelers checks and cash for their clients.

Laundry: Shanta's Café-Bar, a 5min. walk up Vaca, can deliver clean, dried clothes within the hour (US$2 per 5kg load). Open daily 8am-8pm.

Bookstore: Craig's Book Exchange, a 15-minute walk up Diego Vaca de la Vega, has books in a variety of languages. Open M-F 7:30am-6pm, Sa-Su 8:30am-6pm.

Police: (☎580 896), Agua de Hierro between Sucre and Bolívar. Open until 11pm.

Pharmacy: Farmacia Reina del Cisne (☎580 289), 1 block downhill from the plaza on Bolívar. Open 7am-10pm, 24hr. for emergencies.

Hospital: Hospital Kokichi Otani (☎673 128, fax 673 188), is 2 blocks from the plaza along Eterna Juventud. Open M-F 8am-4pm. 24hr. for emergencies.

Telephones: PacificTel (☎580 268), next to the tourist office on Bolívar and Diego Vaca de la Vega, allows AT&T but not MCI calling cards. Open daily 8am-9pm.

Internet Access: AdventurNet (☎580 281), on Sucre near Agua de Hierro, 1 block from the plaza, charges US$1.20 per hr. Open daily 9am-9pm. **Cyber Place,** on Sucre near Vaca, on the main park, has similar rates. Open daily 8am-10pm.

Post Office: (☎580 896), on Agua de Hierro, doesn't sell stamps. Open M-F 8am-noon and 2-6pm.

▶ ACCOMMODATIONS

Due to the steady stream of tourists, Vilcabamba has a bewildering array of excellent accommodations, ranging from full-service resorts to mountain lodges.

▓ **Hosteria Las Ruinas de Quinara** (☎580 314), Diego Vaca de la Vega, a 10min. walk from the park. Like summer camp. Pool (with slide). Jacuzzi. Basketball and volleyball courts. Foosball. Computer games. Direct TV and stereos in every room. Or, make an appointment with a beautician, masseuse, Spanish teacher, or dance instructor. Bike and horse rentals. Laundry, Internet access, and telephones. Breakfast and dinner included. Rooms US$9 per person, with bath US$11.

▓ **Cabañas Río Yambala** (email charlie@loja.telconet.net, www.vilcabamba.org/charlie), commonly known as "Charlie's." A free taxi service runs from the Vilcabamba bus station to the Cabañas. Otherwise, it's a pleasant one-hour hike down Vaca de la Vega and then along a dirt road forking to the left. Cabaña-style rooms in the Las Palmas nature preserve. Vegetarian meals. Equestrian or pedestrian tours of Podocarpus. Cabins US$3-10.

The Pole House and Ecolodge (email ofalcoecolodge@yahoo.com), near town but hidden in the Rumi-Huilco nature reserve. Take a dirt road off Agua de Hierro across the river and follow the first path on the left. Primavera Artesanía Shop (on the park at Sucre and Vaca de la Vega) knows directions and availability. Owners Orlando and Alicia Falco, both biologists and former Galapagos guides, are experts in local flora and fauna. Rooms US$4.50-7.50 per person; cheaper adobe cabins are also available.

Hosteria La Posada Real (☎580 904), on Vaca de la Vega, just before the first bridge at the edge of town, a short walk from downtown. A happy medium between full-service resort and jungle lodge. Comfortable rooms and hot baths. Rooms US$5 per person.

Hostal Madre Tierra (☎580 269), 20min. outside town toward Loja. Free taxi service from the terminal can save you the trek. A full-service resort with more than 20 buildings, including a restaurant and health spa—and plenty of *fiesta*-minded foreigners. Breakfast and dinner included. Rooms US$5.50 per person, with bath US$11.

FOOD

For such a small town, Vilcabamba offers an impressive selection of quality restaurants. Many hotels serve their guests delicious, homemade meals and snacks at all hours. **Panadería Paraíso,** on Bolívar near Fernando de la Vega, sells good picnic or daytrip supplies (open daily 6:30am-10pm).

Las Terrazas (☎580 295), on Vaca de la Vega and Bolívar, at the corner of the plaza. Serves up steaming Mexican, Thai, and Italian dishes (US$1-1.50), as well as homemade brownies and apple pie (US$0.50). Menu includes Thai stir-fry and chicken fajitas (US$1.50), hummus (US$1), and miso soup (US$0.90). Open daily 1pm-9pm.

Restaurante Huilcopamba (☎580 888), Vaca de la Vega and Sucre, right on the park. Arguably the best *típico* in town, this friendly place packs in both locals and visitors. Outside dining right on the park. *Almuerzo* US$0.64-1.44. Open daily 7am-9pm.

Manolo's Pizzería, a five-minute walk down Vaca de la Vega. Set apart from downtown, this Italian eatery dishes up pasta (US$1.40) and pizza (US$1-1.80) in a tranquil setting. Open daily 10am-10pm.

SIGHTS

The countryside provides all the sights and entertainment most Vilcabamba-goers could ask for. The sunny days are filled with leisurely strolls, hearty hikes, and horseback rides through the forested terrain. For those not staying at Las Ruinas de Quinara, the **Centro Recreacional,** a 20-minute walk along the paved section of Vaca de Vega, has athletic facilities and a pool. (Open daily 8am-6pm. US$0.40.)

HIKES. The hike up **Mount Mandango** to the **mirador** is a favorite. The trail starts just uphill of the bus station on Eterna Juventud and turns right just prior to the cemetery. The picturesque journey passes two crucifixes and some easily missed Inca ruins along the route. For a more forested experience, head to the opposite side of town to the **Cabañas Río Yambala** (see Accommodations, above). Several marked trails leave from the cabañas and head to swimming holes and elevated *miradores* in the Las Palmas nature reserve and Parque Nacional Podocarpus.

HORSEBACK TRIPS. Tours by horseback are extremely popular—and easy to come by—in Vilcabamba. They vary from several hours (US$10) to a few days (US$25 per person per day). Most tour companies advertise panoramic visits to several of the **lagos** in the Parque Nacional Podocarpus. For those more inclined to observe **archaeology and artesanal villages,** visits can also be made to the Inka Taraza ruins. **Centro Ecuestre** (☎673 151), on Vaca near the plaza, and **Caballos Gavilan** (☎580 281), on Sucre near the main park, provide superb service.

NIGHTLIFE

When the sun finally sinks below the Vilcabamban hills, nocturnal life begins to stir around town. On the roof of Hostal Mandango, the **Mirador Bar** lives up to its name with a thatched roof but no walls to obstruct the view. (Happy hour 8-9pm. Open daily until 2am.) **Shanta's Café-Bar,** a 15-minute walk down Vaca de la Vega, continues the thatched theme. **Sonic's,** on Santo Domingo near Hatillo, is the only nightclub in town, and serves up strong drinks to get the crowd dancing. (☎680 392. US$0.40 cover for men. Open Th-Sa 8pm-2am.)

THE ECUADORIAN ORIENTE

In the shadow of the Andes' sharply sloping eastern edge, leafy palms hide the clusters of flat concrete buildings and tin shacks that make up the tiny villages of the Oriente. Utility governs the architecture, and one road—the treacherous Oriente "highway"—traverses stretches of untamed wilderness at approximately 1000m above sea level, linking the small jungle communities of Ecuador's last and quickly disappearing frontier. This jungle wilderness—which encompasses thousands of acres of nationally protected lands—is home to countless plant and insect species, as well as larger, rarer animals, including sloths, monkeys, and crocodiles. The area is also home to a number of indigenous societies; among the largest are the Huaorani, Secoya, Siona, and Shuar peoples. Numerous agencies base themselves in the Oriente's larger towns, offering excursions into the forest.

HIGHLIGHTS OF THE ECUADORIAN ORIENTE

RELAX in **Gualaquiza** (p. 548), a tranquil jungle town with many nearby attractions.

BEFRIEND the indigenous **Shuar** people on a tour from Macas (p. 552).

RAFT the Class II-IV **rapids** in the many rivers around Tena (p. 559).

SWIM with the armadillos, river dolphins, and piranhas who live in the **Cuyabeno Reserve** (p. 567).

STEW in the **hot springs** near Papallacta (p. 568), which overlook lush mountains.

For centuries after the arrival of the Spanish, *indígenas* lived here in isolation, bothered only by occasional missionaries. Only at the beginning of this century did colonists from the highlands descend upon the jungle and begin to clear plots of farmland, hunt the wildlife, and intrude upon the *indígenas* who were already living there, including the Huaorani, Secoya, Siona, Quichua, Cofán, and Shuar peoples. The industrial growth surrounding the discovery of oil in the 1970s poses the greatest threat to these pristine natural areas and their indigenous communities. The oil companies continue to cut roads deeper into the jungle, not only destroying the forest but also opening it for colonization. Ironically, to facilitate the exploitation of the remote jungle, oil companies have indirectly acted to save it. The creation of an infrastructure to support employees has allowed environmentally responsible "ecotourism" to flourish from increased accessibility, helping to preserve and promote the region's natural habitats and populations. Likewise, tourism has provided more jobs and revenue that largely remains in the region rather than disappearing into the pockets of multinational petroleum companies. But tourism, however noble its priorities, has still taken its toll. It has been particularly intrusive on the indigenous peoples, who have reportedly been exploited by certain unscrupulous tour agencies.

THE SOUTHERN ORIENTE

GUALAQUIZA   ☎07

Hibernating deep in the heart of the Southern Oriente, the forgotten jungle town of Gualaquiza lies buried in a den of dramatic tropical hills. Although one of the largest towns in the area, Gualaquiza hears few foreigner footsteps on its cobblestone streets. The idea that people might come just to enjoy the tranquility and nearby attractions—deserted caves, a Salesian mission, undisturbed Inca ruins—elicits amused snickers from locals. Curious stares bombard the occasional deviant tourist who braves the Oriente "highway" to reach this hidden city. Although die-hard off-road travelers are attracted to Gualaquiza's remoteness in any season, the town's stunning setting is at its best from May to June and September to October, when the seasons are changing. The summer (Oct.-Apr.) tends to be swelteringly hot and humid, while the remainder of the year is rainy and fairly cool.

TRANSPORTATION AND PRACTICAL INFORMATION. Gualaquiza's **main plaza** is not the center of town, but close to hotels and restaurants. **24 de Mayo** and **Comín** each run opposite lengths of the park, and **Pesantez** and **Ciudad de Cuenca** run uphill along the other edges. Parallel to Comín are **García Moreno, Alfaro, 12 de Febrero,** and **Atahuallpa;** parallel to Pesantez is **Orellana. Buses** leave from the **terminal,** between Pesantez and Orellana, three blocks from the plaza, and run to: **Macas** (8hr., 3 per day, US$3.80); **Cuenca** (8hr., 3 per day, US$3); and **Loja** (8hr., US$3) via **Zamora** (5hr., US$1). Other services include: **Banco La Previsora,** on Pesantez opposite the bus

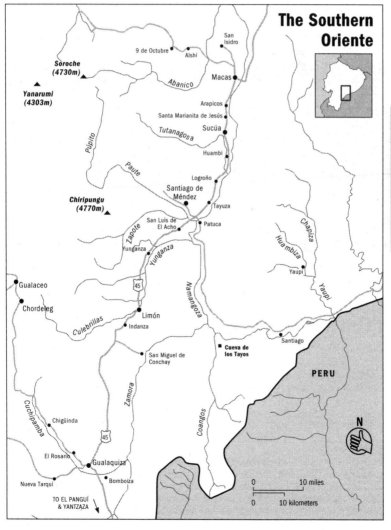

The Southern Oriente

station (☎780 001; open M-F 9am-3pm, Su 9am-1pm); the **police** (☎780 101), on Pesantez and 12 de Febrero, near the terminal; **Farmacia Central,** toward the church and near the school (☎780 106; open 24hr. for emergency service); the **hospital,** on Cuenca past the main plaza (☎780 106; open 24hr. for emergency care); the **post office** (☎780 119), at Cuenca 5-18 and Atahuallpa; and **PacificTel,** Cuenca and García Moreno, one block down from the park (open M-F 8-11am, 2-5pm, and 7-9pm).

█▐ **ACCOMMODATION AND FOOD.** **Residencial Amazonas,** Comín 8-65 on the plaza, has clean and airy rooms, an open courtyard, and a wonderfully aromatic bakery downstairs. (☎780 715. Rooms US$1.20 per person.) **Hostal Guadalupe,** Pesantez 8-16 and García Moreno, is better equipped, with fans, private baths, and a congenial common area with a large color TV. (Rooms US$1.40 per person, with bath US$2.) At mealtime, head to **Cabaña Los Helechos,** 12 de Febrero and Pesantez. The bamboo walls and palm-thatched roof resemble a Shuar hut, though few such abodes offer a bar with comparable selection (*almuerzo* or *merienda* US$1; open daily 8am-10pm).

▣ **SIGHTS.** While the town itself may not offer a ton of tourist attractions, many nearby adventures await just off the beaten path. Head for the hills and explore the **deserted caves of Nueva Tarquí,** 15km west of Gualaquiza. Though some folks in Gualaquiza may know how to find them, it's easier to find knowledgeable people in Nueva Tarquí. The **16 de Agosto** bus company travels to Nueva Tarquí and Provedía. Another nearby attraction, the **Salesian Mission of Bomboiza,** is a wooden bastion that holds its own against the jungle. This easy-to-reach sight lies just one km off the highway en route to Zamora. Buses traveling this road drop off passengers and often stop to pick them up. There are relatively unexplored Inca ruins in the nearby town of **Aguacate.** Nature walks can lead to the **caves of La Dolorosa** or the **waterfalls** at Kupiambritza and Guabi. For more information and a guide, talk to **Rodrigo Ituma** (☎780 716) at Restaurant Oro Verde. For all these destinations, ask for directions at the bus station, the Municipalidad, or the library (near the plaza).

MACAS
☎07

With a population of 33,000, the capital of the Morona-Santiago province is sometimes referred to as the "Oriental Emerald" because of its stunning beauty. Macas maintains the quiet, friendly atmosphere of smaller jungle towns while offering more of the amenities of a larger city, such as an airport with a paved runway and hotels with hot water. For tourists, Macas serves largely as a launch pad for trips to pristine stretches of the Amazon, visits to traditional Shuar villages, and the tremendous Cueva de los Tayos. Much, however, can be learned about the surrounding area from within Macas itself. Many townspeople tell fascinating tales—recounted with pride and passion—of their experiences in the jungle.

▐ TRANSPORTATION

Flights: TAME, Amazonas and Cuenca (☎701 162), at the airport, has flights to **Quito** (30min.; M, W, F noon; US$54). Open M-F 8am-noon and 1-5pm.

Buses: Cuenca (11hr., 7 per day, US$4.20); **Quito** (11hr., 6 per day, US$4.20); **Morona** (8hr., 6pm, US$3.40); **Puyo** (5hr., 8 per day, US$2.60); **Gualaquiza** (9hr., 12:30pm, US$3.80); and **Sucúa** (1hr., every hr. 6:15am-7:25pm, US$0.50).

▚▐ ORIENTATION AND PRACTICAL INFORMATION

The **airstrip** forms the western boundary of town. The Copueno River borders on the east, behind the cathedral. **Domingo Comín,** leading up to the cathedral, is the town's busiest street, especially around the intersection with **Amazonas.** The **terminal** is on 10 de Agosto, just west of Amazonas.

Tourist Information: Orientravel, 10 de Agosto and Soasti (☎700 380; fax 700 371; email orotravel@cue.satnet.net), is good for general information and also recommends guides. Open M-F 8:30am-6pm, Su 9am-1:30pm.

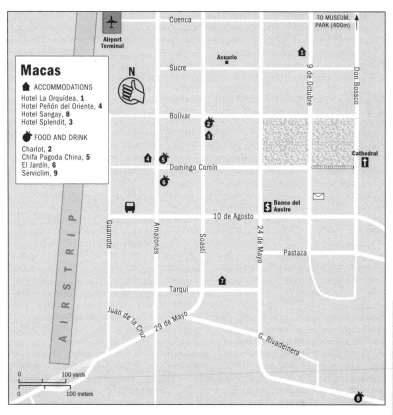

Macas

ACCOMMODATIONS

Hotel La Orquídea, 1
Hotel Peñón del Oriente, 4
Hotel Sangay, 8
Hotel Splendit, 3

FOOD AND DRINK

Charlot, 2
Chifa Pagoda China, 5
El Jardín, 6
Serviclim, 9

Currency Exchange: Banco del Austro (☎ 700 216), 24 de Mayo and 10 de Agosto, makes Visa advances. The nearest place to exchange is Puyo. Open M-F 8am-6pm.

Emergency: ☎ 101.

Police: There is a small police station (☎ 701 958) at the bus station.

Hospital: Emergency ☎ 701 898. The **Clínica Jervés,** 10 de Agosto 7-34 and Soasti (☎ 700 007).

Telephones: PacificTel (☎ 700 104), on 24 de Mayo, between Cuenca and Sucre. International service but no collect or calling card calls. Open M-F 8am-9:30pm, Sa-Su 8am-noon and 7-9pm.

Internet: Worldcyber (☎ 700 606). US$1.60 per hr. Open M-F 9am-11pm.

Post Office: Correos (☎ 700 060), 9 de Octubre, near D. Comín, 1 block from the central plaza. Open M-F 7am-6pm.

ACCOMMODATIONS

Rooms of the same price may differ in quality; try to look at several possibilities before choosing one, especially when shopping in a lower price range.

Hotel Peñón del Oriente (☎ 700 124; fax 700 450), Amazonas and D. Comín. Nestled between a bakery, ice cream shop, and restaurant under the same name. Great balconies. Deluxe rooms (hot water, TV, and rug) US$4. Cheaper rooms available.

Hotel La Orquídea (☎ 700 970), Sucre and 9 de Octubre. Airy, clean rooms. Rooms US$2 per person, with hot water US$2.20, with TV US$2.40.

Hotel Splendit (☎ 700 120), Soasti between D. Comín and Bolívar. The new half of the hotel offers color TVs and reliable hot water (US$4 per person). The older rooms are not quite as luxurious, but are reasonably priced. Rooms US$2-4 per person.

Hotel Sangay (☎ 700 457), 6-05 Tarquí between Soasti and 24 de Mayo. Mattresses are thin, and communal baths are not terribly clean, but the low prices and appealing atmosphere make for a great value. Rooms US$1 per person.

FOOD

Chifa Pagoda China (☎ 700 280), Amazonas and D. Comín. Large, clean, and tasty. Offers rice with vegetables and Inca Kola for US$1.40. Open daily 9:30am-10:30pm.

El Jardín (☎ 700 573), Amazonas and D. Comín. Provides a congenial atmosphere and a good selection of salty food. Entrees US$0.32-2. Open daily 7am-10pm.

Charlot (☎ 700 120), Cuenca and Soasti. Local dishes at low prices. Packed at meal times, and said to have the best coffee in town. Open daily 7am-3pm and 5:30-9pm.

SIGHTS AND ENTERTAINMENT

The **cathedral** in Macas is a large modern building whose main tourist appeal is the series of 12 elaborate stained glass windows that tell the story of la Virgen Purísima de Macas, the town's patron saint. Festivals dedicated to the virgen are celebrated on August 5 and February 18. Five blocks north of the cathedral on Don Bosco, just past Riobamba, the small **Museo Arqueológico Municipal** contains several rooms with ceramics, tools, instruments, and other remnants of the **Upano, pre-Upano, Shuar,** and **Sangay** traditions. Behind the building is a lush, well-maintained park with a view of the river below. Museum admission is free, but there are no regular hours; go in the morning when the librarian next door can open it for you.

Macas rages by jungle standards. Dance all night at the **Discoteca Acuario,** on Sucre between 24 de Mayo and Soasti. **Ten's Chop,** 24 de Mayo and Tarquí, is a happening tropical bar with dance floor, colored lighting, a big-screen TV, and cheap tap beer by the pitcher. (☎ 700 280. Open W-M 2-6pm and 8pm-2am.) For an ear-blasting experience, try the Cuban **Bar La Randimpa.** (Open daily 10am-11pm.)

INTO THE JUNGLE FROM MACAS

Macas is the most convenient town in the southern Oriente from which to begin a jungle jaunt. While the northern Oriente sees more tourists, the jungle east of Macas affords some unique opportunities. As in the north, hundreds of thousands of hectares remain undeveloped; large tracts of primary forest are still intact.

JUNGLE EXCURSIONS. This area is home to Ecuador's second-most-populous indigenous group, the **Shuar.** While many Shuar around Macas and Sucúa have abandoned their traditional ways, more isolated communities in the jungle east of Macas continue to live as they have for centuries. Many of the longer (4-6 day) tours from Macas visit these communities. While the Shuar have not expressed as much distaste for this kind of tourism in the way the Huaorani and other *indígenas* to the north have, the visits cannot help but affect their traditional way of life. If you decide to visit one of these communities, do so with a guide who has a **contract** with the people you will be visiting, to ensure that they are accepting of tour groups. Ask to see the contract if you are uncertain. When proper arrangements are made, you will find the Shuar to be welcoming hosts. Accommodations vary; some guides arrange a stay with a Shuar family, while others bring camping equipment. It will likely be possible to eat with the Shuar, and if you're lucky you may even be offered **chicha de yucca,** an alcoholic drink made from the yucca plant, fermented with the saliva of an older Shuar woman. It is polite to bring a small gift from home—even just a postcard—as a token of appreciation for their hospitality.

PARQUE NACIONAL SANGAY. Macas and its environs offer access into the **zona baja** of **Parque Nacional Sangay.** It's a good entrance to the Playas de San Luis, some *lagunas,* and lesser-known mountains, if you venture deep enough. One of the most jungle-intensive excursions around, its trails climb hills and weave through primary rainforest. Cable cars span the otherwise impassable rivers, Sangay and Upano. Though really best with a guide, there are entrances at Pamora, 9 de Octubre, and San Isidro, which can be reached by bus from Macas.

CUEVAS DE LOS TAYOS. Another commonly visited site near Macas, the **Cueva de los Tayos** is an enormous (85m deep) pitch-black cave that can only be explored with a guide. Its name comes from the large colonies of oilbirds (*tayos*) that reside in the cavern. Like bats, the oilbirds are nocturnal fruit-eaters; they also use sonar to stake out their location in the pitch-black environs. *Tayos* used to be captured and boiled for the oil harvested from their fat-rich flesh. Many tours leaving from Macas include Cueva de los Tayos and other *tayos* caves in their itineraries, but the caves can also be explored from **Morona,** a village on the Peruvian border with accommodations for 10 people (10-11hr. from Macas). Serious spelunkers should contact Marcelo Churuwia, head of the Sociedad Ecuatoriana de Espeleología (email churuwias@hotmail.com).

TOUR COMPANIES

The many tour companies leading trips from Macas offer a wide variety of packages. Most guides will work with the client to customize the tour. Tours usually run one to eight days and can include one or more of the sights described above, some smaller attractions, and canoeing, hiking, horseback-riding, and fishing. The tours are usually all-inclusive (food, lodging, transport, wisdom, medicinal plants, etc.), but it may be possible to hire a guide and pay for everything a la carte. Transportation is another key consideration. Some companies use small planes to quickly transport people to remote parts of the jungle, while others rely on walking, boating, horses, and buses. Tour prices vary with group size and duration; the larger the group, the less each person pays per day (generally US$30-70). To arrange a tour, visit several guides to see who can best meet your needs. Cheaper trips can be found by hiring an independent guide.

Tsunki Touring CIA (☎ 700 371; fax 700 380), ask in Orientravel. Owner Tsunki Marcelo Cajecai is Shuar, multilingual (Shuar, Achuar, English, Spanish), and specializes in rafting, though he offers other trips too. Prices vary depending on tour duration, destination, and group size (4-person 3-day tour US$40 per person per day; 2-person 5-day tour US$50 per person per day).

Winia Sunka Expeditions Cia. Ltda. (☎ 7003 088; email visunka@juvenilemedia.com). Amazonas and Pasaje Turístico owner Pablo Rivadeneira's guides are Shuar, his forests are primary, and his focus is on ecotourism and flexibility. Pablo's clients travel in Shuar canoes or rafts and visit any of the aforementioned areas. Tour discusses natural medicine, sacred rituals, and the like. Cabaña for 20 people and food and transportation included. 1 and 4-6 day tours; US$25-50 a day.

Tunkiak (☎ 700 185; email tuntiakexpediciones@hotmail.com), 10 de Agosto just west of Amazonas, in the terminal. This company is Shuar-run. Owner Carlos Arcos Tuitza focuses on ethnotourism in the central Amazon. He offers trips for 3-5 days or more, traveling by plane to visit the "real" Shuar people (those less affected by urbanization). Similar prices as other companies; vary with traveler and/or group.

Ikiaam (☎ 701 690; fax 700 380 or 700 450), on Amazonas next to the Hotel Peñon. Run by friendly, knowledgeable Shuar guides. English-speaking interpreter available. They offer a Shuar trip, a "buena esperanza" trip more focused on ecotourism, an excursion into Sangay National Park, or a daytrip around Macas and Sevilla Don Bosco. US$35-US$60 per person; trips generally last 4-8 days.

ECUADORIAN ORIENTE

🖪 DAYTRIP FROM MACAS

SUCÚA

Buses cruise up and down Comín, and head to Macas (1hr., every 30min. 5:45am-6:45pm, US$0.50).

The central office of the **Shuar Federation,** three blocks south of the park, is Sucúa's claim to fame. An aboriginal group of the Central and Southern Oriente, the **Shuar** lived in relative isolation until the beginning of this century. Long considered a "savage" people because of their religious traditions of headhunting and head-shrinking, the Shuar of today have abandoned these customs. Unfortunately for those interested in learning about the Shuar Federation, the central office is more an administrative hub than a cultural center. Ironically, the best place (outside of the Shuar villages) to learn about the culture is in Quito's museums. (For more information on the Shuar and their Federation, see **Indigenous Identity,** p. 11.)

THE NORTHERN ORIENTE

PUYO   ☎ 03

At the eastern foothills of the Andes, a harrowing two-hour ride from the valley of Baños, the Río Puyo passes through the town Puyo just as it enters dense Amazonian rainforest. Inhabited as early as 4000-3500 BC, by the time the Spanish arrived local tribes had united into a group called the Záparos. But in the years that followed, disease decimated 85% of the Záparo population. In contrast with towns in the Southern Oriente, most of Puyo's *indígenas* are Quechua. Today, whether out of pride or simply for tourism, Puyo nurtures its jungle-town image. Puyo itself is no more than a cluster of urban blocks that surrenders quickly to the surrounding wilderness; a very real, untamed rainforest canopy stretches to the east.

🮮 TRANSPORTATION

Buses: The **terminal** (☎885 480) is a 20min. walk or a short cab ride (US$0.60) west of the *centro*. Take 9 de Octubre downhill past the market to the traffic circle with a bronze bust, then turn right on Alberto Zambrano and follow it 1km. The terminal serves arrivals and departures until 11pm, after which buses drop off downtown. Evening and night trips leave from Transportes Touris San Francisco, on Marín 10m west of where Atahuallpa joins it. Buses go to: **Ambato** (3hr., every hr. 4am-7pm, US$1.40) via **Baños** (2hr., US$0.80); **Quito** (5hr., 20 per day 7:30am-5:45pm, US$2.60); **Riobamba** (4hr., 9 per day 3:45am-5:15pm, US$2.20); **Macas** (5hr., 12 per day 6am-5pm, US$2.60); **Tena** (3hr., every 30min. 5:45am-11pm, US$1.40); **Coca** (9hr., 6:30am and 9:30pm, US$5.20); and **Guayaquil** (9hr., 6:15am and 11pm, US$4.80).

◼🮮 ORIENTATION AND PRACTICAL INFORMATION

The road from Baños comes from the west to the **terminal.** From there take a bus (US$0.10), taxi (US$0.60), or walk 1km northeast into town. The **centro** is defined by the east-west **Ceslao Marín** and **Atahuallpa,** which are intersected by **9 de Octubre** and **27 de Febrero.** Most hotels, *comedores,* and shops cluster near 9 de Octubre and Atahuallpa. Muddy **Río Puyo** borders the eastern edge of town.

Tourist Office: CETUR (☎884 655), on Marín in the *centro shopping carmelita.* Provides info on tourist facilities throughout the Oriente and a decent map of town. Open M-F 8:30am-12:30pm and 2-6pm, Sa 8am-noon.

Currency Exchange: Casa de Cambios Puyo (☎883 219), on Atahuallpa between 9 de Octubre and 10 de Agosto. Open M-Sa 8am-8pm, Su 8am-noon. **Banco del Austro** (☎883 924), farther down Atahuallpa between 10 de Agosto and Dávila, provides Visa advances. Open M-F 8am-6pm, Su 9am-1:30pm.

Police: (☎885 101), 9 de Octubre, past the park.

The Northern Oriente

Pharmacy: Farmacia Ferr-ade, Marín 187 (☎883 892), is open 24hr.

Hospital: Hospital de la Brigada 17 (☎883 131), Alfaro and Pindo. In nearby Shell,

Telephones: EMETEL (☎883 104), Orellana and General Villamil, one block west of the market. Open daily 8am-10pm.

Post Office: (☎885 332), 27 de Febrero and Atahuallpa. Open M-F 8am-6pm, Sa 8am-3pm.

■ ACCOMMODATIONS

▨ **Hotel Araucano** (☎883 834), Marín 576 and 27 de Febrero. Clean rooms and hot-water showers. The helpful owners offer tours of their private jungle reserve (US$15 per person per day). Rooms US$1.60-2.80 per person.

Hostal El Colibrí (☎883 054), Manabí (on the way to Tena) and Vacas Galindo. A new, clean hostel with private baths. Laundry and cafe service. Rooms US$2 per person.

Hotel Granada (☎885 578), 27 de Febrero and Orellana, 2 blocks downhill from Atahuallpa next to the market. A no-frills, low-cost option. Bare but reasonably clean, with cold-water baths only. Rooms US$0.80 per person, with bath US$1.20.

◖ FOOD

▨ **Pizzería/Restaurant Cha-Cha-Cha,** Marín 249 (☎885 208), just past the Hotel Turingia. Wooden, painted menus on the walls and cardboard cutouts point you toward your meal. Personal pizzas US$2.40. Open M-Sa 8am-10pm.

La Carihuela (☎883 919), on Zambrano east of the terminal. The cloth napkins and classy decor contrast sharply with the Baños bikers crowd. *Filet mignon* US$2.40. Pastas US$1.20. Pizzas US$2-3.60. Open M-Sa 11am-10pm, Su 11am-4pm.

Yama Puma (☎883 787), 9 de Octubre and Atahuallpa. *Comida típica* in a jungle atmosphere. *Mantos* (fish cooked in a big leaf; US$1.60). Soups with *plátano* or yucca and fish (US$1). Worms and ants too. Open M-Sa 7am-8pm.

◉♫ SIGHTS AND ENTERTAINMENT

Puyo does justice to its jungle surroundings. Several institutions are dedicated to informing visitors about the local flora, fauna, and indigenous cultures.

PARQUE PEDAGÓGICO ETNO-BOTÁNICO OMAERE. This educational park speaks to the ethnobotanist in everyone, providing a wealth of information on how different indigenous groups use plants. The park lies on the Río Puyo, across a rope footbridge. A number of traditional *indígena* homes are scattered throughout the forest. Tours in English or Spanish. *(On the south end of 9 de Octubre. From the main plaza, walk 20min., or take a bus (US$0.10) headed for Obrero from the church. ☎883 001. Open Th-M 8am-5pm. US$2, includes a 3hr. tour.)*

HOLA VIDA. A self-service jungle experience can be found at the Hola Vida reserve. The reserve has basic cabins *(US$1 per person per night)* and food *(US$2 per meal)*, as well as 40 hectares of primary rainforest out of the 115 hectare whole. To see the area through the eyes of an experienced guide, contact AGSET or Amazonia Touring. *(27km south of town. ☎883 219. Taxis US$6. 3 days, 2 nights tours with Amazonia Touring run by Hola Vida US$15-20 per day. Buses leave Puyo for Hola Vida W 5am, Sa-Su 5:30am (1hr., US$0.60); return from Hola Vida W, Sa, Su at 2pm.)*

ORGANIZACIÓN DE PUEBLOS INDÍGENAS DE PASTAZA (OPIP). The OPIP is a worthwhile alternative to the scenic package an umbrella organization that can set you up directly with an indigenous guide. Ask at CETUR or Hotel Araucano for details. *(☎883 875. OPIP's office on 9 de Octubre and Atahuallpa. The Shuar and Huaorani tribes also have tourist offices in Puyo.)*

NIGHTLIFE. New Bar, 27 de Febrero and Atahuallpa, is a mellow bar lulled by purple lights and the sounds of American *música romántica.* (☎885 579. Beer US$0.60. Open M-Sa 4pm-3am.) For the lounge lizard in you, check out **Discoteca Rodeo** on Zambrano, past the bus station. (Open M-Sa 8pm-2 or 3am.)

TENA ☎ 06

Known as the "green heart of the Amazonia," Tena, 197km southeast of Quito, sits at the fast-flowing union of the Ríos Tena and Pano, part of the headwaters of the Amazon. East of Tena spreads the jungle, while the city's western panorama is dominated by the jagged silhouette of the mighty **Cordillera de los Llanganates.** Founded by the Spanish in 1560 as a daring foothold in the Oriente, the capital of Napo Province is now forging ahead with plans to become a center of Oriente ecotourism. Tena's entrepreneurs have developed a jungle playground here, with bamboo cabañas, spelunking, whitewater rafting, kayaking, and every other adventure a cement-weary urbanite could hope for.

▐ TRANSPORTATION

Buses: The **terminal** is easy to miss; look closely along the west side of 15 de Noviembre, 1km from the bridges. To: **Sacha** (US$5) via **Coca** (6hr., 9 per day 4:30am-11pm, US$4); **Lago Agrio** (8hr., 6:30pm, US$5); **Quito** (6hr., 14 per day 5:30am-3am, US$3) via **Baeza** (2½hr., US$1.40); **Ambato** (6hr.; every hr. 2am-6pm, 9, 11pm, midnight); **Riobamba** (7hr., 2am-6pm, US$3.40); **Misahuallí** (1hr., every 45min. 6am-7pm, US$0.40); and **Ahuano** (1½hr.; 8 per day 6am-5:30pm; US$0.20).

▚▐ ORIENTATION AND PRACTICAL INFORMATION

When visible, the mountains to the west are a useful landmark. The center of town lies at the confluence of the Ríos Pano and Tena. To the west, **Tena centro** spreads across an irregular grid, from **García Moreno** on the riverfront, to **Montalvo,** two blocks west, and from the **main plaza** along **Mera** to **Bolívar,** four blocks farther north. A pedestrian bridge crosses the river from Mera. East-west **Olmedo** becomes a bridge that takes a right on the opposite bank and becomes **15 de Noviembre.** The best hotels and restaurants are here, as is the **terminal.**

Tourist Office: CETUR (☎886 536), on Bolívar near Amazonas, in the *centro,* provides information on activities in the province. Open M-F 8am-4:30pm. The **Municipio** is also helpful. The **Dirección de Turismo** should have an office next to the river next year.

Currency Exchange: Banco del Austro (☎886 446), 15 de Noviembre between the bridges does Visa advances and has an **ATM.** Open M-F 8am-1:30pm.

Market: Amazonas and Bolívar, small but fairly active on F-Sa 6am-5pm.

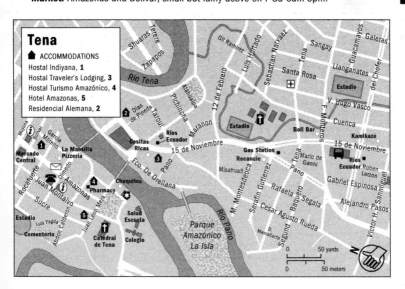

Tena

♦ ACCOMMODATIONS
Hostal Indiyana, 1
Hostal Traveler's Lodging, 3
Hostal Turismo Amazónico, 4
Hotel Amazonas, 5
Residencial Alemana, 2

Emergency: ☎101.

Police: (☎886 101), on García Moreno and the main plaza.

Hospital: The private **Clínica Amazonas** (☎886 515) is at Tena and Vasco. Walk toward the bus station on 15 de Noviembre and turn left at Banco del Pichincha.

Telephones: EMETEL (☎886 105), Olmedo and Montalvo. Open daily 8am-10pm.

Post Office: (☎886 418), Olmedo and Amazonas. Open M-F 8am-5pm, Sa 8am-3pm.

ACCOMMODATIONS

■ **Hostal Traveler's Lodging,** 15 de Noviembre 438 (☎886 372), next to the footbridge landing. Welcome to gringo central. Restaurant. Tour agency. Electric hot water, fans, and orthopedic beds in all rooms. Rooms US$2.50-US$4.

Hotel Amazonas (☎886 439), Mera and Montalvo, just off the main plaza. Floors swept daily, but common baths pose more of a challenge. Rooms US$1 per person.

Hostal Indiyana (☎886 334), Bolívar and Amazonas, across the street from CETUR. All the comforts of Traveler's Lodging without the gringos and with more plants. This brand new hostel offers private hot-water baths, cable TV, and fans. Rooms US$4 per person.

Residencial Alemana (☎886 409), Díaz de Pineda and 15 de Noviembre, next to the vehicle bridge. Hot and cold water in the private baths and private cabins or apartment-style rooms (which are really the same inside). Rooms US$2.30-6.70 per person.

FOOD

Vegetable stands and *panaderías* line 15 de Noviembre between the terminal and the footbridge.

■ **Pizzería Bella Selva,** down 15 de Noviembre from the car bridge. With high chairs facing the road and an open window on the river, this place makes a mean pizza. Pizzas US$0.80-3, toppings US$0.20-0.40. Open daily 7am-10pm.

■ **Kamikaze** (☎887 616), 15 de Noviembre, just past the terminal, opposite the Coke distributor. Krazy open-air, cabaña-style eatery with funky furniture. Jungle-sized pancakes US$0.80. *Camarones a la plancha* US$1. Open daily 7am-7pm.

Chuquitos (☎887 630), Moreno and the Parque Central, next to the police station. Hearty portions of Ecuadorian food in a tranquil setting between the Parque and the river. One of Tena's finer establishments. Open M-F 7:30am-9pm, Sa 7:30am-4pm.

SIGHTS AND ACTIVITIES

While some of Tena's attractions exist Oriente-wide, others can be found nowhere else. Most outdoor activities require a guide of some sort, but there are hikes you can do on your own. Before setting out, though, discuss the route with someone knowledgeable and leave a route plan with somebody in town; orientation is difficult, and getting lost in the jungle is serious business. For guided trips, agree on a price beforehand, and don't pay in full until you're safely back in town.

PARQUE AMAZÓNICO LA ISLA. A logistical no-brainer because of its central location, this park is impressive nonetheless. An island occupying 22 hectares between Río Tena and Río Pano, *la isla* connects to Tena via a bamboo bridge 50m upriver from the main footbridge behind Hostal Traveler's Lodging. Monkeys and birds inhabit the park's sprawling forest, which melts into sandy, soft beaches. Lots of *chozas* and swimming areas dot the river banks, and a lookout tower affords a panoramic view of Tena. *(Open daily 8am-5:30pm. US$1.)*

CUEVAS DE JUMANDI. These caves, which lie between Archidona and Cotundo (north of Tena) provide another unchallenging experience. The area is quite built-up (the waterslide out of the mouth of the cave is great). A resort has recently opened here and makes a convenient base for daytripping tourists who wish to explore the caves. Be prepared to get wet. *(Take a bus to Archidona from Amazonas and Olmedo (20min., every 15min. 6am-7pm, US$0.15) and then catch the bus from Archidona to Cotundo and ask to be let off at "las cuevas," US$0.10. Open daily 9am-5pm. US$0.80.)*

CASCADAS GRÁN EDÉN. On a nice day you can cross the river easily at these waterfalls (though you'll get a bit wet). On a rainy day, the river rises, but there's a muddy trail which takes you a fair amount up to the banks of the river Lata. *(US$1. Take the Misahuallí bus 40min. and the trail will be on the left. The trip to the waterfalls takes little over an hour. You can rent rubber boots in limited sizes for US$0.40.)*

FEATHERED SERPENT PETROGLYPH. A *serpiente emplumado* is just one of dozens of rock carvings in the area northwest of Tena (CETUR has an exhaustive list; see p. 557). Most are on private property, and the owner will charge a nominal fee to show you around. Nobody knows much about who made these carvings or why. *(On the same road as Cuevas de Jumandi between Archidona and Cotundo. US$0.20.)*

LA CASCADA DEL GRAN CANYON. Past Cotundo, a trail on the right leads up to La Cascada del Gran Canyon. The challenging three-hour hike (each way) is best done with someone who knows the trail; the waterfalls at the end are reported to be worth the effort. *(Buses headed north from Tena pass the trailhead. 50min., US$0.40.)*

NIGHTLIFE

On the weekend Tena goes disco. The most popular spot to boogie is **Discoteca Canambo** on Orellana and the river. There are cool paintings outside, pool tables, two floors of sitting or dancing space, and glow-in-the-dark stars on the ceiling. (☎886 320. Beer US$0.80. Open F-Sa 9pm-2am.) Around the corner is the new **Las Camelias,** with a louder, techno feel. (Beer US$0.60, other drinks US$1.40. Open Th-Su 8pm-2am.) For more mellow options, cruise the **Malecón Iluminado,** the area bordering both sides of the river between the two bridges, and hone in on whichever beat best suits your mood. Several dance clubs and watering holes line 15 de Noviembre toward the terminal. Of these, **Boli Bar,** just before the terminal, with its open-air cabaña feel, is most likely to bring out the jungle creature in you. (☎887 966. Open Su-F 6pm-3am, Sa noon-4am. Discoteca on weekends.)

INTO THE JUNGLE FROM TENA

RAFTING. Probably the biggest adrenaline rush in Tena—and maybe all of Ecuador—comes from its killer whitewater rafting. Only recently discovered by the world's whitewater enthusiasts, the river-filled region around Tena in the western Oriente is a truly amazing find. These rivers, the headwaters of the Amazon, rush down from the Andes through canyons, over waterfalls, and past rocky banks. Because of the unique topography and sheer volume of water, the density of whitewater rapids is higher here than almost anywhere else in the world. Moreover, it's always high season; the rapids churn year-round. ⊠**Ríos Ecuador** (☎887 438; email info@riosecuador.com), in Tena, across from Cositas Ricas, runs trips under the watchful eye of its owner, Gynner, a 28-year-old kayaking and rafting pro with nine years of guiding experience. The congenial entrepreneur is a native Ecuadorian, but he speaks perfect English. With multilingual, professional guides and modern equipment, the company leads exhilarating, safety-conscious trips. A one-day rafting trip is US$50 per person for Class II and II+ rivers (novice/moderate). In October a Class IV/IV+ trip is offered for US$65. One-day kayaking trips are also available (US$60 per person). Prices include transportation from Tena, guides, a tasty beachfront lunch, and maybe even a side trip to the jungle. Ríos Ecuador also periodically offers a four-day kayaking course for US$250. Make reservations through the Quito or Tena office. Qualified and experienced individuals may rent kayaks and gear without a guide (US$30 per day).

JUNGLE LODGES AND TOURS. For a more tranquil wilderness experience, spend some time at one of the many cabaña complexes scattered along the rivers. As cabañas open and close with unpredictable frequency, you might want to check with CETUR in Tena for ideas. CETUR recommends that you **only go with certified guides.** Tours typically travel by boat or car to a lodge which serves as a base for daytrips into the surrounding jungle. The best known tour company, **Amarongachi Tours,** operates out of the Hostal Traveler's Lodging (see Accommodations, p. 558). Other reliable agencies are **Expediciones Jarrín** (☎ 887 142), though their trips leave from Coca (see p. 562). For information on indigenous guides, go to their headquarters at **Recancie** (☎ 887 072), 15 de Noviembre and Serafín Gutierrez, where Pano and 15 de Noviembre merge; the group is a cooperative of ten Quechua and Huaorani communities. **Sapo Rumi** (☎ 887 896), 15 de Noviembre across from the pizzeria, offers *suave* or *fuerte* trips (US$25-35). It's Quechua-run and visits Quechua communities. **Hostal Iniyana** has also recently been certified.

MISAHUALLÍ   ☎ 06

The monkeys loitering in Misahuallí's town plaza should dispel any lingering doubts that this is *real* jungle—if the charitably-termed "road" into town hasn't done that already. A solid wall of trees lines the far bank of the muddy Río Napo, which fades into a swirling mist in the distance, while emerald parakeets and iridescent butterflies flutter among the orchids just outside of town. Except for the occasional intrusion of an outboard motor propelling camera-toting tourists to jungle lodges, the only sound to be heard in Misahuallí is the squawking of wild parrots. No road continues downstream on the north bank of the Río Napo, making Misahuallí the primary point of departure for many jungle tours. The tours are generally of rainforest exploration and few see indigenous villages.

⚏⁊ TRANSPORTATION AND PRACTICAL INFORMATION. The road comes to town from the west. Some hotels, restaurants, and shops congregate around the plaza. **Buses** leave the central plaza for **Tena** (1hr., every hr. 7:30am-4pm, US$0.45). Though Ahuano is only 15km downstream, no direct road connects it to Misahuallí. The cheapest way to **Ahuano** from Misahuallí is to cross the river in a **motorized canoe** (US$0.20), walk 30 minutes away from the river (on a dirt track) to the Tena-Ahuano road, and flag down a bus headed for **Ahuano Punta** (US$0.32). At La Punta, re-cross the river (canoe US$0.20) and walk for 20 minutes along the road from the canoe station to Ahuano. Alternatively, motorized canoes travel directly from Misahuallí to **Ahuano** (45min., US$35 per boat) or **Coca** (6hr., US$160 per boat). Although there is nowhere in town to officially change money, the Albergue Español occasionally changes cash and traveler's checks. The blue-and-white Registro Curl office houses vestiges of a **police** force (open Th-F). The only phones in town are at **ANDINATEL,** by the river between Hotel Marena and the Albergue Español. (☎ 584 965. Open daily 8am-1pm and 3-8pm.)

▞⛝ ACCOMMODATIONS AND FOOD. Prices of reasonably comfortable lodgings tend to be slightly inflated, reflecting the foreign clientele. The **Hotel Albergue Español,** on the right just before you enter town, is impeccably clean, with private hot-water baths, screens on the windows, and laundry service. (☎ 466 925. Rooms US$5 per person.) The **restaurant** uses only boiled water and choice meats (US$3-4). Ninety minutes downstream is **Jaguar Lodge.** Within 1000 hectares of primary forest are 10 cabañas with private bath, lights and hot water thanks to solar energy. (Complete package US$30-35.) **Hotel Marena** is between the Albergue Español and the main plaza. Immaculate rooms have stained-wood furniture, fans, and mini-bar fridges. (☎ 887 584. Rooms US$3 per person.) In town, **Hostal Sacha** is the best deal. It's average both in architecture and room quality, and offers kitchen access. (☎ 886 679. US$1-2 per person.)

🗟 INTO THE JUNGLE FROM MISAHUALLÍ. Most people use Misahuallí as a starting point for jungle tours. Trips down the river can last from a day to a fortnight and include anywhere from two to 20 people. Packages are flexible, but the important part is getting a satisfactory guide. Key guide qualities include Englishspeaking ability (depending on your Spanish), wilderness experience, familiarity with the area, and a CETUR license. Most of the guides in Misahuallí are weak on the English. **Ecoselva,** on the plaza, is run by the English-speaking biologist Pepe Tapia. In the evenings Pepe offers *charlas* (informational chats) about the local indigenous groups and jungle fauna. Itineraries can be tailored to fit a group's size and interests. (Tours US$20 per day for up to 10 people, discounts with bigger groups.) **Clarke's Tours,** also run by biologists, out of the Marena Hotel, has 30 hectares of private rainforest downriver, including a fenced-in **Muestrario,** where jungle animals roam in higher concentrations than they would in the wild. Some guides speak some English. Clarke's has customized three- to six-day expedition packages to their land. (☎ 887 584. US$25-35 per day.) **Fluvial River,** run by Hector Fiallos, is based out of Hostal Sacha. Like the hostel, it might be the best deal in town at US$20 per day. Now an independent company, **Expediciones Sacha Amazónica** runs off the beaten path. After 20 years of service, they change routes every year. They too are right on the central park in Napo, or can be contacted at the Tena bus station. (☎ 887 979; email sachamazonica@yahoo.com. US$25-50 per day.)

NEAR MISAHUALLÍ: JATÚN SACHA

Buses from Tena to Ahuano can drop visitors off in front of Jatún Sacha (1¼hr., US$0.75).

Quechua for "big forest," Jatún Sacha, eight kilometers east of Misahuallí, is still 80% primary growth. Refreshingly enough, Jatún Sacha, a 2000-hectare tropical rainforest reserve, is completely Ecuadorian-owned and run and was named the world's second International Children's Rainforest in 1993. Founded in 1986, the reserve aims both to conserve the incredible biodiversity of the land and to provide a window into it for researchers, especially Ecuadorian ones. The forest is first and foremost for scientific study, and large groups of visitors are not permitted. Casual visitors can, however, benefit from the facilities—well-marked paths meander through the forest past an incredible variety of carefully documented flora. Maps are available at the main office. The birds seem to love this peaceful place as well—to get a better view of Jatún Sacha's winged inhabitants, ask to be allowed up the station's 100-foot-high bird observation tower, or pay a visit to their canopy bridge woven from vines. (US$6. US$1 for self-guided information packet.)

The facilities can accommodate 25 visitors and 13 long-term residents at once. (Bunk beds in screened **cabañas** with nearby latrines, showers, and a supply of rainwater for hand-washing; beds US$25, includes 3 meals and admission, US$15 for student-scientists.) A new part of the complex, the **dining hall,** offers three relatively safe *and* tasty communal meals each day (US$1). Those looking for an unconventional experience can volunteer at the reserve for a month or more. Volunteers work with the local Quichua community on sustainable development projects, or they help maintain the reserve, though they rarely get involved in primary scientific research unless they have a specific project in mind. (Volunteers pay US$225 per month for food and lodging.) Rejected non-scientists and travelers seeking more comfortable lodgings can shack up at the solar-powered **Cabañas Aliñahui,** three kilometers down the road to the east of Jatún Sacha (follow the signs; 1hr. walk). With an office in Quito at Río Coca 1734 and Isla Fernandina, the cabañas help fund the reserve. The eight spacious cabins, raised on stilts above a hammock-blessed patio, each have two rooms that share a cold-water bath. Facilities including a conference room, bar, and library are all included. (☎ 253 267; fax 253 266. Jan-May US$42 per person, plus 20% in taxes; includes 3 meals per day; June-Dec. US$30 per person, tax included.) To contact the reserve, find out about the volunteer program, or make research reservations, the Quito address is: **Fundación Jatún Sacha,** Casilla 17-12-867 (☎/fax 453 583; email jatsacha@jsacha.ecuanex.net.ec; www.jatunsacha.org). Address in Tena: Casilla 15-01-218.

COCA ☎ 06

The easternmost urban outpost of the Orellana province, Coca (also known as Puerto Francisco de Orellana) has suffered the fate of many oil towns around the world. The original Coca developed in the early 20th century, when its pioneer residents built a hospital, schools, and churches, and grew to a whopping population of 300. Everything changed in the pivotal year of 1969 when foreigners from the north discovered a wealth of "black gold" bubbling underground. Within a few years, Coca's population exploded and its landscape changed forever. Roads tore into the jungle and newly-erected pumps drained the land, filling the pockets of oil entrepreneurs and transforming Coca into a gritty, dirty, riverside pit. The town's name reflects another aspect of its unflattering past: the booming cocaine trade that has now retreated into some of the city's poorer *barrios*. Regardless of the city's sorry aesthetics, Coca is significant for travelers, as many deep jungle tours often begin and end at this Oriente outpost.

▐ TRANSPORTATION

Flights: The **airport** (☎880 188) has one runway that goes almost into downtown. To get to the terminal, follow Labak for 1km toward Lago Agrio. Take a taxi from the center (US$1), or catch the *bus urbano* which runs from downtown to the terminal (US$0.10). Aerogal (☎881 452) offers flights to **Quito** (45min.; M-W, F-Sa 11:30am, Th 9am; US$54). Tickets can be purchased at the terminal before departure.

Buses: The **terminal** is on Napo, 8 blocks north of the river, but night buses go to and from Napo and Bolívar, just north of the *centro*. Trans Esmeraldas goes to **Lago Agrio** (2hr., 8:30pm, US$1.60) and **Quito** (8:30pm, US$6.80). Baños goes to **Ambato** (11hr., 6:30 and 8:15pm, US$8) via **Baños** (10hr., US$6) and **Puyo** (7hr.; 12:45, 4am, and 6:30pm; US$5.20). Baños will also take you to **Lago Agrio.**

Boats: Also known as **Puerto Francisco de Orellana,** Coca's marina sees its share of boat traffic. Most tourist traffic on the river comes from organized tours, so travelers generally don't have to worry about prices or times. All boats on the river, whether coming or going, must record the names and passport numbers of all foreign passengers at the **Capitañia,** a government office right on the water at the end of Amazonas. Destinations are **Hacienda Primavera** (US$1.20); **Pompeya** and **Limoncocha** (US$1.60); **Panacocha** (US$4.60); **Tiputini** (US$6.25); and **Nueva Rocafuerte** (US$7.45). Schedules and prices change due to variation in demand and water conditions. Hiring a boat is possible but not economical unless with a group.

Taxis: Outside the market, 7 blocks north of the *centro* (US$1 for a trip in the *centro*).

✦ ▐ ORIENTATION AND PRACTICAL INFORMATION

From the **terminal** in the north, **Napo,** the principal mud-laden tourist drag, extends eight blocks to the **Río Napo,** the town's southern boundary. **Amazonas,** which dead-ends at the dock a block east of Napo, parallels **Tena-Lago Agrio Road,** which enters town from the north and eventually straightens out one block east of Amazonas. It then crosses the river to the **military camp.**

Tourist Office: For the most reliable information on wilderness areas and the agencies that tour them, head to **INEFAN** (☎881 171), by the airfield on Amazonas and Bolívar. Open M-F 8am-5:30pm.

Currency Exchange: Hotel El Auca exchanges cash.

Market: Fruits and veggies galore can be found across Napo from the *municipio*, 500m north of downtown. Open daily 6am-5pm. **Outdoor market** downtown.

Emergency: ☎880 101.

Police: Policía Nacional (☎880 525 or 880 101), at Napo and Rocafuerte.

Pharmacies: Farmacia Clínica Sinai (☎880 401), across the street from Hotel El Auca on Napo. Open 24hr.

Medical Assistance: Clínica Sinai (☎880 362), at Napo and Moreno.

Telephones: EMETEL (☎880 104), at Eloy Alfaro and 16 de Diciembre, under the big tower. Open M-F 8am-4pm and 5-9pm, Sa-Su 8-11am and 5-8pm.

Post Office: (☎881 411), at the southern end of 9 de Octubre, by the river, 3 blocks west of Napo. Open M-F 8am-4:30pm.

ACCOMMODATIONS

A few respectable hotels cluster on Napo around the Hotel El Auca, while dank, simple cheapies hover close to the waterfront. The only other frequently touristed area is just down Malecón, the street that veers off to the left before the bridge, where the **Hotel Oasis** and the luxurious **Hostería La Misión** set up their quarters.

▓ **Hotel El Auca** (☎880 127; fax 880 600), Napo and García Moreno, 6 blocks south of the terminal. The rooms are safely guarded behind a row of hammocks, *guayaba* trees, and roaming *guatusas*. Rooms vary in size, but all have fans and hot-water baths. Rooms US$5 per person.

Hostal Oasis (☎880 164; fax 880 206), on Malecón on the river, 50m down the narrow left branch before the bridge. Beds are fluffed, floors spotless, and cold-water baths (in all rooms) well-scrubbed. Fans in all rooms. Rooms US$4 per person.

FOOD

Pretty much everything here has chicken in it; dash off to the market for exciting fruits and veggies. Most eateries lie on **Napo** or off it on a street near the river.

Restaurant Dayuma (☎880 127), in Hotel El Auca, is the only place with a wide variety. A gringo magnet. American breakfast US$1.40. *Almuerzo* and *merienda* US$1.80. Open daily 6:30am-10pm.

Restaurant Medianoche (☎880 026), Napo and Rocafuerte. Immaculate and bright, Medianoche is a favorite for take-out or late-night meals. *Caldo de Gallina* US$1. Fried chicken US$1.20. Open daily 6pm-2am.

INTO THE JUNGLE FROM COCA

Coca's location, farther *al oriente* than Tena or Misahuallí, makes it an ideal base for trips to the more isolated parks, reserves, and deep-jungle communities of the indigenous **Huaorani.** The still-untamed region east of Coca is home to some of the most remote indigenous communities and densest biodiversity in the world. But as a mixed fortune, it is also home to Ecuador's most lucrative natural resource in the technological age—oil—and all the concomitant development and pollution.

NATURE RESERVES
In most of the reserves, unless you really know what you're doing (e.g. you're a professional ethnobotanist) INEFAN requires that you go in with a guide. A handful of villages and natural areas down the Río Napo are favorite tour destinations from Coca. A relatively short distance downstream, the **Reserva Biológica Limoncocha** and the mission towns of **Pompeya** and **Limoncocha** often make their way onto tour groups' itineraries. These days you don't even have to float to get there, courtesy of the road that the oil industry has cut past Limoncocha into "pristine oil country;" *petrolero*-inflicted damage is reported to be quite severe in this area. Most groups charge US$30 per day to visit Limoncocha, including entrance fees. Most trips last about three or four days and might include swimming or night hikes to look for reptiles. Farther west is the **Parque Nacional Sumaco-Galeras,** virtually unexplored and untouched. The incongruous Volcán Sumaco soars to over 3500m in the middle of 207,000 hectares of dense vegetation and swamps where, rumor has it, man-eating anacondas lurk in the shadows. To attempt the four- to six-day summit climb, go to the village of **Huamaní** and ask for Don Chimbo. To the south of Coca is the village of **Tiputini,** one of the closest Huaorani communities and one of the most touristed. (Nature reserves US$10.)

BOSQUE PROTECTOR PAÑACOCHA. *"Cocha"* is Quichua for lagoon, and *"paña"* means piranha—exactly what to expect when visiting this swamp and lake area. Surrounding the Río Napo, the *bosque* hosts enough plant and animal species to make any biologist's millennium. Commonly observed animals include **monkeys, freshwater dolphins, crocodiles,** and, with luck, a **toucan** or a **sloth.** To see the park's namesake, just toss a small piece of fish or meat into the river and watch the water churn. Despite the abundance of piranhas, the guides swim fearlessly in the water, and often invite visitors to join them for a dip. Reportedly, the risk of getting bitten is low if you have no trace of blood on you (women, take note). **Cabañas Pañacocha** offers housing for tours and has a high bird and wildlife observation tower. Visitors planning a tour should take into account that transportation takes almost two full days. (Park admission US$10.)

PARQUE NACIONAL YASUNÍ. Coca is the push-off point to mainland Ecuador's largest national park, the 982,000-hectare Parque Nacional Yasuní. This is **Amazon Basin** country, with the Tiputini, Nashiño, Cononaco, Yasuní, and other tributaries coursing through the park's enormous expanse. Yasuní has three major habitats: dry land, sometimes-flooded land, and always-flooded land. While the rainforest is understandably wet year-round, the region's seasons still alternate between dry (Dec.-Mar.), rainy (Apr.-July), and unstable (Aug.-Nov.). Founded in 1979, Yasuní includes the greatest biodiversity in the country. The **Huaorani tribe,** first peacefully contacted in 1958, is as natural a part of the park as the wildlife. They share this land with boa constrictors, alligators, jaguars, eels, parrots, toucans, piranhas, capybaras, monkeys, sloths, and myriad other species. Today, much of the park's once-pristine territory is criss-crossed by pipelines and roads for drilling. INEFAN has yet to organize a management system for the *parque;* a force of only 10 rangers controls activity within the sprawling park. To further complicate matters, the park is not really open to tourism yet. Due to recently opened drilling sites, the park is now accessible by land, though the majority of entrances are still off the river Napo. The far edge of the park lies on the Peruvian border, with an entrance at the town of **Nuevo Rocafuerte,** eight to 11 hours downriver from Coca. In order to penetrate beyond the heavily damaged northwestern section of the park, most tours last 10 days or more. There are southern entrances from Shell and Puyo, as well. Tours generally run US$60 per day (including entrance fees).

TOUR COMPANIES

Tours offered from Coca vary greatly in price and quality. Part of the expense is the **entrance fee** (usually US$10) for each protected nature reserve on the tour. Some guides calculate their prices with this amount included, while others clearly state that it is additional. Either way, the INEFAN office in Coca (see Practical Information, p. 554) strongly suggests that at least one person from your group accompany the guide to INEFAN to pay the required amount. Check out a number of tour companies to find one that seems reputable. Ideally, a tour should have a guide with expertise in either natural history or local anthropology.

Several Coca-based companies offer multi-day jungle packages. Unlike in Misahuallí, each tour group offers something a little different. An important factor to consider before choosing a group is the region. Ask to see a map, preferably one with oil pipelines, to ascertain whether you're heading to primary rainforest or oil country. The Pañacocha and Sumaco region are nearly the only virgin areas left. Most tours leave between Friday and Monday. INEFAN-recommended guides include: **Luis García,** who works out of Coca but may be contacted through **Emerald Forest Expeditions** (see below) and **Juan Medina,** who may be contacted through Baños's **Vasca Tour Travel Agency** (☎(03) 740 147). Indigenous guide **Ernesto Juanka** and his son **Patricio** are also very good; they may be found through Hotel Auca.

>   **Witoto Tours,** Espejo, across from El Gran Chaparal. Co-owned by 3 Quechua relatives, their "eco-jungle" tours will take you to Reserva Puconacocha (US$30), Limoncocha (US$30), Pañacocha (US$50), Territorio Huaotani Shiripungo (US$60), or Tiputini-Parque Nacional Yasuní-Añangu (US$60). Prices include entrance and camping fees, with discounts for students. Trips run 3-12 days and can be tailored to suit your needs.

Emerald Forest Expeditions (☎881 155; email emerald@ecuanex.net.ec; www.ecuador-explorer.com/emerald), on Napo near the river. Most tours are organized through the Quito office, Amazonas N24-29 and Pinto (☎(02) 541 543), but travelers may easily hop on a tour in Coca. *El jefe,* **Luis García,** runs all-inclusive trips to most wilderness areas, including hard-to-reach Yasuní National Park. He speaks English well and has years of experience. Trips run US$30-40 per person per day.

Expediciones Jarrín Alomia Hnos. (☎880 860; fax 880 251), across from the Hotel Oasis, near the bridge. In Quito, at Reina Victoria and Veintimilla (email exjarrin@impsat.net.ec). Julio Jarrín and his family of guides take groups to his jungle lodge on the edge of Pañacocha. Julio speaks English and is very friendly, and specializes in natural history. The package includes boat transport, cabins, food, fishing gear, entrance, and hikes (US$100 per person for 4 days or US$35 a day for 2 people, student discounts).

Yuturi Jungle Adventure (☎880 164; email yuturi1@yuturi.com.ec), run out of Hotel Oasis (see p. 563) with a Quito office at Amazonas 13-24 and Colón (☎(02) 504 037). Runs tours to 2 sets of cabañas downriver, Yuturi and Yarina. Yuturi boasts a birdwatching tower, private baths, experienced guides, and good food. Both options offer full itineraries, including night hikes and/or canoe rides. Trips leave M or F unless you have a group of 3 or more. You can add a day or two if you wish, with special student/group discounts. Five-day tours cost US$200 at Yarina Lodge and US$300 at Yuturi Lodge.

Paushi Tours (☎880 219), best contacted through Hotel El Auca. Quito office: Calama 354 and Juan León Mera. Darwin García and his brother Edwin lead the only tours into the Sumaco region. The family lived for 30 years among a local Quechua tribe and now works with them on demonstrations of shamanism and storytelling. They keep the groups small (8 people max.) and the service good. Tours include an English-speaking guide, panning for gold, stone petroglyphs, and jungle wildlife. Cabañas come with bath/shower. Food, lodging, gear included. 2-10 days US$40 per day.

LAGO AGRIO ☎06

As late as the 1940s and 1950s, this was the heartland of the **Cofán,** a people almost completely isolated from contact with other indigenous groups, not to mention Europeans. Revered by surrounding tribes for their sophistication with medicinal and hallucinogenic plants, the Cofán spoke a language unrelated to any other. However, in the 1960s, Texaco hit the oil jackpot here. As bulldozers cleared the land (of the Cofán), Texaco executives decided to name the new city after their first big success in Texas: Sour Lake. Thus, the Spanish *Nueva Loja* was replaced by "Lago Agrio"—the name isn't the only mark the *petroleros* left. Once numbering more than 20,000, the Cofán and their knowledge of the forest are almost gone. The few hundred remaining have moved further east, where some forest remains. Today the city consists of strips of three-story banks, hotels, restaurants, and grocery stores. Most foreigners only pass through on their way into the jungle.

▐ TRANSPORTATION

Flights: The **airport** is located 5km east of the city center (US$1 taxi ride). TAME (☎830 113), Orellana and 9 de Octubre, has flights to **Quito** (30min.; M-Sa 11:30, M and F also 5:30pm; US$54). Open M-F 8-11am and 2:30-5pm.

Buses: The **terminal** is a short taxi ride (US$1) northeast of the *centro.* Daytime buses often go through downtown on their way to or from the *terminal.* Between 11pm and 6am buses only stop at their offices, all within a block of Hotel D'Mario. Buses go to: **Quito** (8hr., every hr., US$6) via **Baeza** (6hr., US$3.60); **Coca** (3hr., every 20min., US$1.60); and **Loja** (24hr., 1pm, US$12.60).

Taxis: Trips within town cost US$1.

⚡ ☷ ORIENTATION AND PRACTICAL INFORMATION

Lago Agrio's main road is the east-west **Quito,** which runs 3km east from the **airstrip** and forks at the market, forming the northern branch of **Río Amazonas.** The **market** is a triangular area formed by the fork of Quito and Amazonas and the north-south **12 de Febrero** one block to the west. **Francisco de Orellana** is parallel to, and one block west of, 12 de Febrero. The downtown area is generally safe during the day, but **it's not wise, especially for women, to explore any secluded areas alone or at night.**

Tourist Information: INEFAN (☎830 139), 10 de Agosto and Manabí, 6 blocks north of Quito. Open M-F 8am-noon and 1-5pm. Also check out the **Cámara de Turismo** (☎848 248) in front of Hotel Guacamayo for info on tour agencies.

Immigration Office: Quito and Manabí, in the police station.

Colombian Consulate: Quito 441 (☎830 084), next to Hostal Ecuador, across from Hotel D'mario, has info concerning the dangerous Colombian border crossing 20km north of Lago Agrio at Punto Colón. Open M-F 8am-4pm.

Currency Exchange: Banco del Pichincha (☎831 612), 12 de Febrero and Quito, has exactly one cashier who will change traveler's checks M-F mornings. Next door, Hotel Cofán will change money for an exorbitant fee.

Police: (☎830 101) Quito and Manabí across from the market. Considered to be more competent (read: heavily-armed) than many of their counterparts elsewhere in Ecuador.

Medical Services: Clínica Gonzáles (☎830 133), Quito, near 12 de Febrero.

Telephones: EMETEL (☎830 104), Orellana and 18 de Noviembre. Open M-Sa 8am-10pm, Su 8am-noon.

Post Office: (☎830 115), Rocafuerte, off 12 de Febrero. Open M-F 8am-noon and 1-5pm. Some travelers have reported mail from Quito taking several weeks to arrive.

▟ ACCOMMODATIONS

▨ **Hotel D'Mario,** Quito 175 (☎830 172; fax 830 456), 50m east of the fork. Unlike Lago Agrio itself, this hotel is clean, relatively safe, and friendly, and the street-level restaurant makes it a tourist hive. A/C and TV. Rooms US$6-13.

Hotel Secoya, Quito 222 and Amazonas (☎830 451), at the fork. All the action's on the second floor, all the foliage is on the first. Chill out on the landing with patio, TV area, and rows of spacious, fan-equipped rooms. Singles US$1.60, with bath and TV US$2.

Hotel Guacamayo GranColombia (☎831 032), Quito, 100m east of the fork. The new rooms are spotless and luxurious. The old Guacamayo rooms are a bit musty, but cheaper (US$2.80). New rooms come with A/C and fridge. Singles US$8; matrimonials US$10; doubles US$12; triples US$16.

◖ FOOD

▨ **Marisquería Delfín,** Añasco and Pasaje Gonzanama, around the corner from Oro Negro. The music makes you feel like jumping off the wooden benches and the ceviche makes you feel like you're on the coast. Open daily 9am-midnight.

Restaurante Los Guacamayos (☎831 032), on the other side of D'Mario from Hotel Los Guacamayos. Sidewalk dining with a slightly smaller menu than its neighbor (see below). Chicken US$2-2.80. Breakfast US$1. Open daily 7am-10:30pm.

Pizzería Restaurant D'Mario (☎830 172), Quito, in the hotel of the same name. This sidewalk restaurant feeds most of the gringos in town. Pizza (personal US$2.60, large US$6). Open daily 7am-11pm.

🏋 INTO THE JUNGLE FROM LAGO AGRIO

Lago Agrio's charm lies not in its black, sticky oil, but in its mind-boggling natural surroundings. To the east of town, vast expanses of jungle resonate with the cries of monkeys, calls of birds, and chirps of insects. Rivers flow silently throughout the rainforest, swallowing the ripples left by alligators and monkey-munching anacondas. Though tours from Lago Agrio are generally wildlife-based, there are a few opportunities to visit indigenous groups of the area. These groups tend to be more isolated, however, and if your interest truly lies in a more anthropologically-based excursion, you might want to head south where the tribes are fairly integrated into the economic process of tourism. Jungle tours often cruise the **Río Aguarico,** which runs near the city and then on to more remote areas, passing some indigenous villages along the way. The lagoons of **Lagartacocha** (Alligator Lagoon), **Limoncocha,** and **Pañacocha** satisfy visitors particularly interested in spotting wildlife; the latter two are also accessible from Coca.

RESERVA DE PRODUCCIÓN FAUNÍSTICA CUYABENO. When God created the animals of the earth, He must have stopped for a picnic in Cuyabeno, looked at what He had made—capybaras, ocelots, over 515 bird species, giant armadillos, boa constrictors, electric eels, alligators, freshwater dolphins, spiders, monkeys, tapirs, land tortoises, and piranhas—grabbed a beer, and took the afternoon off. Far to the east, past the Limoncocha mission and the Pañacocha lagoon, this 603,400-hectare wildlife reserve claims a substantial chunk of the Sucumbíos province. Besides the amazing fauna, the flora blooms and thrives as well, from joltingly colorful fruits and splashy flowers to enormous green leaves and fronds. A network of tributaries stems from Río Aguarico and Río Cuyabeno, and parades of wildlife follow the rivers as they flow into the reserve's 14 lagoons. The park also encloses the homelands of indigenous communities such as the Siona, Secoya, and Shuar. The other human presence in the reserve has come as a consequence of the oil industry, which has continued to exploit the land despite its protected status, though the damage here is reportedly less severe than in Parque Nacional Yasuní to the south. (*From Lago Agrio, the drive by truck or bus through Tarapota to Puenta Cuyabeno is a rough and dusty 2½hr. This method is often used to access the popular lagoons deep in the bush. Some tours launch into the Río Aguarico, then travel by water through the upper or lower regions of the reserve. Park admission US$20.*)

TOUR COMPANIES. The most dependable way to plunge into the jungle east of Lago Agrio is to hire a tour guide from a reputable agency in Baños or Quito. This expensive proposition often disheartens budget travelers. A few cheaper tour operations are based in Lago Agrio; some are unlicensed or unqualified (and technically illegal). INEFAN officials have been known to check for credentials when tour groups enter nationally protected areas; unapproved tours are routinely turned away, and even if you make it into the park, a second-rate guide won't be of much value. Of the licensed companies, the current favorite in trips to Cuyabeno is 🖾**Native Life Tours,** Foch E4-167 and Amazonas, in Quito. **Fabián Romero,** the head guide, has a good track record and is passionate about his job. He speaks English, is quite fond of birds, and likes to flow slowly down the river to look for flying things in the forest. (☎(02) 550 836; email natlife@natlife.com.ec. Groups run 2-12 people for 3-10 days, generally M-F or F-M. Trips US$40 per person per day, with a 10% discount for SAE members.) **Kapok Expeditions,** Pinto E4-225, in Quito, is a new company that emphasizes the educational aspects of its tours. (☎(02) 556 348. US$50 per person per day, plus US$20 Cuyabeno admission.) For an experience like no other, inquire in advance at Hotel D'Mario about the **Flotel Orellana,** a floating hotel in the Aguarico reserve. Travelers recommend **Green Planet,** Juan Leon Mera N2384 y Wilson (☎520 570; email greenpla@interactive.net.ec), US$200 for 5 days. For tour advice, SAE members may consult trip reports in Quito about jungle tours in the Sucumbíos province. For the most up-to-date info and additional questions, check INEFAN offices in Lago Agrio (see Practical Information, p. 566), in Tarapoa en route to Cuyabeno, or at the bridge entrance to Cuyabeno.

BAEZA

Officially a part of the Oriente, Baeza puts on the convincing facade of a sierra hamlet. The quiet village sits at the junction of three roads, known as the **Y of Baeza.** One road leads northwest to Quito, one south to Tena, and the last northeast to Lago Agrio. Deliciously cool at night and not oppressively hot during the day, Baeza provides a perfect climate for day hikes and pleasant sleep. Not far from Quito and a pleasant pitstop on the way to or from the jungle, Baeza offers nothing to do but enjoy the coolness and scenery of the mountains. It is also a good base for those venturing to **San Rafael Falls.**

⌷⎆ TRANSPORTATION AND PRACTICAL INFORMATION. Baeza is a 40-minute walk from the Y junction, along the Quito-Tena road. First, two roads turn off to the right from the main one, leading through several old buildings to a plaza and a small church, which constitute **Baeza Vieja.** The main road twists over Río Machángara and eventually leads to **Baeza Nueva** as it becomes **Quijos,** which later turns into the Tena highway. Most people arriving in Baeza get dropped off at the Y, unless the bus is heading to Tena, in which case you should ask the driver to let you off at the Baeza Nueva bus stop. From the Y, about 35 minutes downhill from Baeza Nueva, flag down one of the *camionetas* heading up the road (US$0.20). **Buses** pass by the Y every 45 minutes heading to: **Quito** (3hr., US$3.80); **Tena** (2½hr., US$1.20); and **Lago Agrio** (6hr., US$3.60). There are no currency-changing banks in town. The **police** are in a white building at the Y. The **Hospital Estatal Baeza** (☎320 117) is 200m downhill of Quijos, near Hotel Samay. **EMETEL,** Quijos and 17 de Enero in Baeza Nueva. (☎/fax 580 651. Open daily 8am-1pm and 2-8pm.)

⌘ ACCOMMODATIONS. Hostal San Rafael, at the bottom of new town's Quijos, on the right coming from the Y, has a clean, energetic atmosphere with tiled floors and nifty perks including a video/music room and kitchen/restaurant. (☎320 114. Rooms US$2.20 per person, with bath US$2.60.) **Hotel Samay,** on the right side of the road toward Tena, has light, wooden rooms, and communal baths. A hot shower is available. (Rooms US$1.60 per person.)

NEAR BAEZA: SAN RAFAEL FALLS

Las Cascadas de San Rafael are another display of natural beauty on the Baeza-Lago Agrio road and are the **highest waterfalls in Ecuador.** They dive about 1km west of the starting point of the Río Reventador, about two hours east of Baeza or four hours west of Lago Agrio. Bus drivers generally know where to let you off if you ask for *las cascadas;* there is a sign and a little hut at the start of the road on the right side if you are coming from Baeza. The trail descends from there, continuing past a bridge over a small waterfall and a little house marked "Guardia" where you pay an entrance fee (US$0.60). The trail continues on to a group of **casitas.** The black arrows to the left of the *casitas* indicate where the path enters the jungle.

PAPALLACTA

It's been exhausting and messy wherever you've been; you're dirty and drained; it's time for Papallacta. The baby-Baños of Ecuador, this steaming sanctuary hides away in a spectacular Andean valley, one hour west of Baeza and two hours east of Quito. The cloud forest greenery and blue pools of steaming hot water pretty much define Papallacta. Though the town itself may not be much to look at—worn sheet metal buildings have a tough time competing with the surrounding Andean mountains for attention—Papallactans have no trouble luring visitors from all over with their beautiful and surreal bathing facilities.

RIBBIT Poster children of the fight to save the South American jungle, **Amazonian tree frogs** are doted on throughout the world for their psychedelic coloring. In the Amazon itself, animals and humans alike have learned to keep their distance from these cute little fellows—their skin contains a poisonous chemical that acts as a metabolic suppressant, slowing down the bodily functions of whatever creature has been fool enough to meddle with them. Over the years, the indigenous people of the Oriente have learned to take advantage of this powerful toxin for hunting purposes. Tranquilizer darts dipped in a concoction made with "frog skin juice" are launched through a long tubular blow gun with a carefully timed puff of air. The blowguns are about seven feet long and extremely heavy, and yet hunters often hold them up for hours, waiting for the perfect opportunity to strike. Not all of the jungle's beautiful tree *ranas* contain this potent drug, but it's best to leave them all alone, for your own safety as well as theirs.

Papallacta itself is a handful of small buildings along the main Quito-Baeza road. **Buses** to **Quito, Lago Agrio,** and **Tena** run frequently along this road and can easily be flagged down in front of the **police station,** the gray-and-blue checkpoint on the right as you walk down the hill after entering town from Quito, or other obvious spots. By far the best, and most expensive, place to stay in Papallacta is the **Hostal Posada de Montaña,** near Las Termas. Several hot pools serve guests that are too lazy to walk the 45 seconds to Las Termas. A fireplace in the common room, a patio, soft fluffy towels, and free passes to Las Termas are included in the deal. (In Quito: Foch E6-12 and Reina Victoria #4A. ☎ (02) 557 850; email papallc@ecnet.ec; www.papllacta.com.ec. Rooms US$16, with bath US$33.) For food, **La Choza de Don Wilson,** at the foot of the road to Las Termas, is the best option in town. Enjoy the local specialty—farm-fresh *trucha* (trout; US$1.55)—in this thatched-roof, bamboo-walled restaurant. (☎ 657 094. Open daily 7am-9pm.)

THE HOT SPRINGS. At the base of the town itself are the piping hot **Coturpas** (blue pools), or *piscinas modernas.* Changing stalls, mandatory hot-water showers, and baskets for belongings are provided. (Open M-F 7am-5pm. Sa-Su 6am-6pm. US$0.60, children US$0.40.) Folks might think nothing could be more perfect, unless they hiked the 2km up to ■**Termas de Papallacta** and **Jambiyacu,** the genuine hot springs. The road to these *piscinas* veers off the main highway to the left just before you enter the town from Quito (there's a big sign). The first half of the walk is steep, but it flattens out and is well worth it once the springs appear, on the far side of a Japanese-funded trout farm. Both sets of pools have the same water source (38-42°C) and views. But the slate-floored Termas de Papallacta pools have a more natural, elegant feel, while the Jambiyacu ones resemble swimming pools. (Termas open daily 6am-10pm. US$2, children and senior citizens US$1. Jambiyacu open W-Su 8:30am-3pm. US$1.50 for kids and senior citizens.) The company that runs the hot springs also offers horseback riding (US$4 per hr.) and has several trails through the nearby mountains and cloud forest (US$0.60 per person; US$5-10 per person for a 4-6hr. guided tour W-Su.)

THE GALAPAGOS ISLANDS

There are few places in the world where humans are truly second-class citizens. In the Galapagos Islands, however, a national park is more than simply an isolated area within the realm of human activity; rather, 97% of the land area is protected territory, and humans can only tiptoe around this veritable miracle of nature. From the amazing amiability of the animals to the tranquil beauty of the landscape, these islands form an archipelago of fairy tale magic. On an ordinary day, one might swim with sea lions or observe frigatebird courtship on sandy beaches surrounded by cliffs, volcanoes, and the shimmering expanse of the Pacific Ocean.

But just as visitors marvel at their own insignificance within the natural world, they learn about nature's fragility. Along with discussions of unique geology and wildlife come tales of ecosystems disrupted by the carelessness of human settlers. Even after the 1959 declaration of the Galapagos National Park, whole species remain threatened by rats that came with the earliest settlers and by feral goats, which were originally brought to the islands for food.

While the interests of humans and other animals may be contradictory, the interaction between the two has been one of the Galapagos' most unique aspects. In its lava lizards and its legends, the islands seem to hold a key to the most mysterious aspects of natural history—secrets which have not gone unnoticed by its visitors. Charles Darwin made observations here that would help substantiate his then-radical evolutionary views; 60,000 tourists now come here each year to feel a bit closer to nature. Whether it's because they've learned everything they'd ever want to about marine iguanas' mating patterns or because they've been mesmerized by the sunset over a never-ending stretch of ocean, all who visit these enchanted islands will remember the trip for the rest of their lives.

THE GALAPAGOS: AN OVERVIEW

HISTORY

All the flora and fauna on the Galapagos mysteriously crossed nearly 1000km of ocean to reach the islands; the first human inhabitants also arrived with the help of auspicious waves. Pottery shards found on various islands suggest that pre-Inca *indígenas* spent time on Santa Cruz and Floreana—likely the result of their balsa rafts floating astray. But the first Galapagos tour to be recorded in history set sail around 1485, when the Inca prince **Tupac Inca Yupanqui** sent his army to explore.

In 1535, **Fray Tomás de Berlanga,** the archbishop of Panama, and his Peruvian-bound ship didn't think it too propitious when a week-long storm and a six-day drift carried their boat far off course. This voyage is considered the official "discovery" of the Galapagos. When the islands were first included on maps 35 years later, they were given the name Galapagos (Spanish for "turtles") after the enormous shelled specimen that Berlanga described.

For the next few centuries, **pirates** used the islands (most notably Isla Santiago's Buccaneer Cove and James Bay) as hideaways and launching pads for surprise sea attacks. The lava tunnels that snake beneath the islands are rumored to have been hiding spots for the pirates' booty—keep an eye out for buried treasure while spelunking. Raiding and pillaging can be hard work, and when hungry pirates discovered that the Galapagos tortoises could survive for months with little food or water, they began storing them in their ships to use as a fresh meat source on voyages. When this trend caught on, the tortoise population began to dwindle at an astonishing rate; at the time of **Charles Darwin's** 1855 visit, he reported that pirate ships would take as many as 700 tortoises with them at a time. In subsequent years, hunters continued to harvest the animals for their meat and for the oil prepared from their fat (used in Guayaquil's street lamps).

Darwin only stayed in the Galapagos for five weeks, but his visit would ultimately determine the historical path of the archipelago and its precariously endangered namesakes. Darwin's writings about the islands and their purported impact on his theory of evolution eventually won the archipelago worldwide recognition. Ecuador had claimed the islands only a few years before Darwin arrived and used them as a penal colony. But due to the Galapagos's fame and importance in the scientific and ecological world, a few areas were declared wildlife reserves in 1934, and in 1959 all non-colonized areas officially became the **Parque Nacional Galapagos.** In the following decades, tourism steadily increased. In the 1990s, the islands hosted 60,000 visitors each year, at least 75% of them foreigners.

GEOLOGY

The first Galapagos island was formed over 4 million years ago, and new islands have been forming ever since. The islands were made by underwater volcanos that expelled lava onto the ocean floor, building themselves higher and higher until they finally broke the water's surface. Volcanically active islands such as Fernandina have continued to add new territory even within the last decade.

Tectonic theory proposes that the surface of the earth is made up of a number of **tectonic plates** that are suspended on the **magma** (molten rock) that lies below them. These tectonic plates are constantly moving, each one being pushed and pulled by the plates around it. The Galapagos are located on the **Nasca plate.** The "hot spot," a stationary area beneath the Galapagos, melts the Nasca plate into magma that bubbles onto the surface of the earth through volcanos, and consequently formed the islands. The Nasca plate is moving to the southeast, taking the older islands with it and leaving the hot spot to form new islands to the northwest. Española in the southeast is the oldest island in the archipelago, while Fernandina and Isabela to the northwest are the youngest and most volcanically active.

THE GALAPAGOS

A FISTFUL OF FINCHES
In 1831, **Charles Darwin** was a 22-year-old medical school drop-out and mediocre theology student. Young Charles looked forward to a simple life as a country parson indulging in his true passion—natural history. One of Darwin's professors, **John Stevens Henslow,** recognized that the bright young man was more interested in worms than in the Edict of Worms, so he hooked him up with a job as a ship's naturalist on the **H.M.S. Beagle** and as "gentleman companion" to the captain, **Robert Fitzroy.**

The Beagle set off on a five-year, around-the-world voyage, during which Darwin's observations and collections of flora and fauna from South America, the Pacific Islands, and Australia made him something of a scientific celebrity when he returned to England. But young Charles had done more than observe and collect. After examining multiple, disparate ecosystems, Darwin began to see a certain set of patterns. An eager reader of **Charles Lyell's** *Principles of Geology,* Darwin was willing to see the natural world as a product of constant change. Evolution was not a new idea—by the 18th century, geologists had developed the fossil record sufficiently to see convincing evidence for change—what Darwin provided was a mechanism. His idea that the brutal competition to survive and reproduce writes its story in the offspring of the victor—the survival of the fittest—was as insidiously persuasive as it was in contradiction to conventional views on natural history and man's place in the universe. Upon the 1859 publication of **The Origin of Species,** a scientific and social firestorm broke out across the literate world, altering biology and philosophy forever.

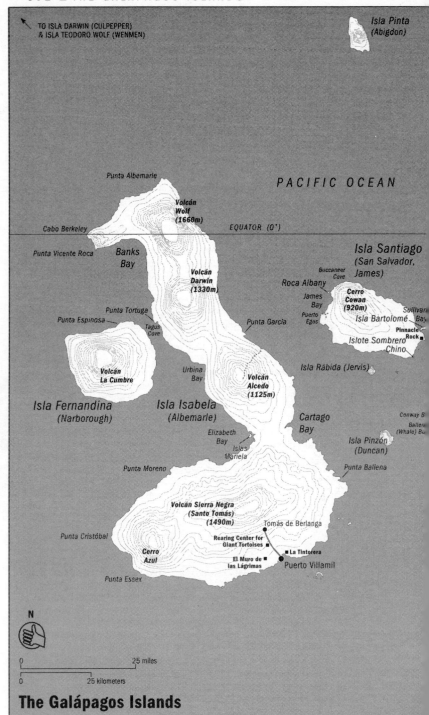

TO ISLA DARWIN (CULPEPPER)
& ISLA TEODORO WOLF (WENMEN)

Isla Pinta
(Abigdon)

Punta Albemarle

PACIFIC OCEAN

Volcán Wolf
(1660m)

Cabo Berkeley   EQUATOR (0°)

Punta Vicente Roca   *Banks Bay*

Volcán Darwin
(1330m)

Isla Santiago
(San Salvador, James)

Buccaneer Cove
Roca Albany

James Bay
Puerto Egas

Cerro Cowan
(920m)

Isla Bartolomé

Sullivan Bay

Pinnacle Rock ■

Punta Tortuga
Punta Espinosa

Tagus Cove

Punta García

Islote Sombrero Chino

Isla Rábida (Jervis)

Urbina Bay

Volcán La Cumbre

Isla Fernandina
(Narborough)

Isla Isabela
(Albemarle)

Volcán Alcedo
(1125m)

Cartago Bay

Conway B
Ballena
(Whale) Ba

Elizabeth Bay

Islas Mariela

Isla Pinzón
(Duncan)

Punta Moreno

Punta Ballena

Volcán Sierra Negra
(Santo Tomás)
(1490m)

Tomás de Berlanga

Rearing Center for
Giant Tortoises ■

■ La Tintorera

Punta Cristóbal

Cerro Azul

El Muro de
las Lágrimas ■

Puerto Villamil

Punta Essex

N

0   25 miles
0   25 kilometers

The Galápagos Islands

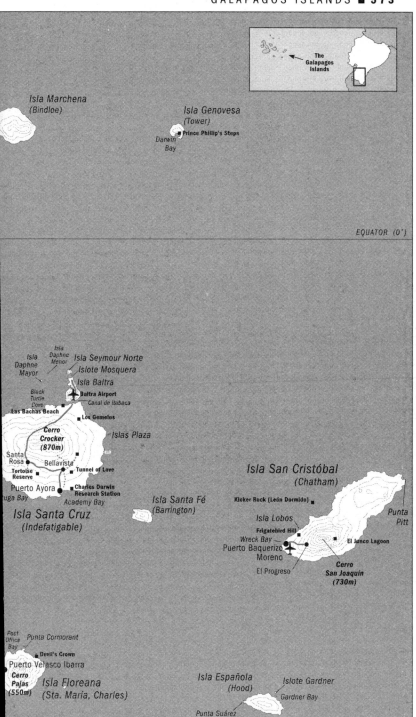

The Galapagos Islands

Isla Marchena
(Bindloe)

Isla Genovesa
(Tower)

Darwin Bay ■ Prince Phillip's Steps

EQUATOR (0°)

Isla
Daphne
Mayor

Isla
Daphne
Menor

Isla Seymour Norte
Islote Mosquera

Isla Baltra

Black
Turtle
Cove

✈ Baltra Airport
Canal de Itabaca

Las Bachas Beach ■

■ Los Gemelus

**Cerro
Crocker
(870m)**

Islas Plaza

Santa
Rosa ●

● Bellavista

■ Tunnel of Love

**Tortoise
Reserve**

Puerto Ayora ●

■ **Charles Darwin
Research Station**

uga Bay

Academy Bay

**Isla Santa Cruz
(Indefatigable)**

Isla Santa Fé
(Barrington)

Isla San Cristóbal
(Chatham)

Kicker Rock (León Dormida) ■

Isla Lobos

Frigatebird Hill

Wreck Bay
Puerto Baquerizo
Moreno ✈

■ **El Junco Lagoon**

Punta
Pitt

El Progreso

**Cerro
San Joaquín
(730m)**

Post
Office
Bay

Punta Cormorant

■ **Devil's Crown**

Puerto Velasco Ibarra

**Cerro
Pajas
(550m)**

Isla Floreana
(Sta. María, Charles)

Isla Española
(Hood)

Islote Gardner

Gardner Bay

Punta Suárez

FLORA AND FAUNA

BACKGROUND

At some point 4.5 million years ago, bacteria rode air and ocean currents to the recently hardened volcanic rock off the Ecuadorian Pacific coast. These micro-organisms facilitated the decomposition of rock into soil, providing a nutritious foundation for plants. Soon birds, insects, and other animals showed up, using the plant life for food and shelter. Presumably, many organisms that came to the islands died because they were "unfit," and failed to develop survival techniques.

The animals that completed the journey and prospered found a large area of land with lots of fish and little competition. Isolated from the mainland by about 1000km and from each other by up to 200km, the Galapagos Islands provided a secluded environment for rapid and undisturbed species expansion. Interrupting the evolutionary development and balance of the archipelago, humans began introducing a slew of animals, including goats, rats, cats, and dogs, which inevitably disrupted local ecosystems by destroying habitats and depleting food supplies.

An active park service is now making strides in curbing the contamination of ecosystems, despite the constant flow of typically destructive tourists. The purity is unique and extraordinary; the biological distinctions, complex connections, and remarkable adaptations among the animal and plant species never fail to incite intrigue; and the unbelievable amiability of the animals doesn't cease to amaze visitors. Preserving this purity is the responsibility of all who visit the Galapagos.

RESPONSIBLE ECOTOURISM

The islands' ecosystems are fragile. The regulations of the National Park Service are designed to protect these areas for future generations and should be followed: stay on the trails, don't bother wildlife, don't take or leave anything, and respect what your guide tells you. The importance of following these rules can never be over-emphasized. The perfect photograph is not worth the insidious damage that clumsy feet and harassment will have on the animals. At the most basic level, the mere presence of tourists on the islands contributes to their contamination; recognize that these islands are a unique natural treasure as well as an opportunity for the adventure of a lifetime. The only evidence of visitor presence should be light footprints and tourist dollars.

BIRDS

Ornithologists love the islands. Not only are birds the most prominent and diverse type of animal on the islands, but they usually allow up-close observation and don't shy away from camera-toting tourists. Even more alluring is the fact that many species are endemic—found nowhere else in the world. The different bird species found in the Galapagos are presented here grouped by habitat.

BIRDS OF THE SEA. The endemic **Galapagos penguin** is an aberrant member of its cold-water family. These shy birds (long-lost relatives of the penguins of southern Chile and Antarctica) live mainly around the Bolívar Channel between Isabela's western coast and Fernandina. They are also found in various places near the Isla de Santiago. Some of the most well-known birds in the Galapagos are the **boobies,** of which there are three types: the **blue-footed, red-footed,** and **masked.** The highest concentration of red-footed boobies is on Genovesa. They are the only boobies that nest in trees or bushes. Blue-footed and masked boobies nest on the ground, surrounding their territory with a circle of bodily waste.

Another famous endemic seabird, the **flightless cormorant,** is found only on the westernmost islands of Fernandina and Isabela. These cormorants were originally a flying species, but lack of predators or food on land meant that big wings were a waste of energy; selective pressures favored the strongest divers. Those with webbed feet, powerful legs, and small wings survived, and the species conformed through the millennia. Today, the birds rely mostly on their powerful legs for swimming. Cormorants have light bones—appropriate for flying but not for diving deep down into the water; in order to weigh themselves down to reach deep, fish-filled waters, flightless cormorants swallow small stones which give their light bodies the extra ballast needed to get down deep. Cormorants nest in small colonies on sheltered shores; when a bird returns to its nest, it brings some new decoration and the nests evolve into eclectic masses of seaweed, stones, and shells.

Some of the largest and most notable birds on the islands are the cleptoparasitic **great** and **magnificent frigatebirds.** The male of both species boasts an inflatable red pouch below the beak. A frigate's wingspan can reach 2.3m, giving it the largest wingspan-to-weight ratio of any existing bird. Mating occurs on San Cristóbal and Genovesa from March-April, and on Seymour Norte throughout the year. Perhaps the rarest bird in the Galapagos, the **waved albatross** is endemic only to Española. The largest birds in the archipelago, weighing over four kilograms with a wingspan of 2.5m, these albatrosses only stay on the island from April to December and spend the rest of the year around the South Pacific. Other seabirds include the **brown pelican,** the **swallowtail gull,** the **lava gull,** and five kinds of **petrels.**

BIRDS OF THE SHORE. Of the shorebirds, the **flamingoes** are by far the most rare and famous; a mere 700 specimens currently inhabit a few lagoons around the islands. They feed on small, bright pink shrimp larvae and pink marine insects, hence their pinkish hue. They can be seen on Isla Rábida, in lagoons near Puerto Villamil on Isabela, at Punta Cormorant on Floreana, and at Espumilla beach on Santiago. A much more common shorebird is the **heron,** of which there are several types: the **great blue, lava,** and **night herons,** to name a few. Another Galapagos shorebird is the **oyster catcher.** There are also a healthy number of **egrets, gallinoles, turnstones, whimbrels,** and **black-necked stilts.**

BIRDS OF THE LAND. Because of their isolation from other landbird populations, the residents of the Galapagos compose the greatest percentage of endemic species (76%). Most famous are **Darwin's finches,** of which there are 13 types. These tiny sparrow-sized birds all look very similar and can only be differentiated by beak morphology and feeding habits; Darwin himself didn't recognize them as distinct species until after he'd left the archipelago. While some live on seeds or fruits, the elusive **carpenter finch** uses a stick to dig insects out of trees, and the **"blood-sucking" vampire finch** of Wolf Island uses its sharp beak to suck the blood of red-footed and masked boobies. Other notable endemic landbirds include the **Galapagos mockingbird** on Santa Fe and Genovesa, the **hood mockingbird** on Española, the **Galapagos hawk** (the largest land predator on the islands), the **Galapagos dove,** the **Galapagos martin,** and the **Galapagos rail.** Some of the more striking land birds are non-endemic. The **vermillion flycatcher,** a red-and-black bird found in the humid highland forests of the central islands, is a favorite, as is the nearly universal **yellow warbler.** Lastly, the islands are populated by two subspecies of **barn owl** and **short-eared owl.**

REPTILES

TORTOISES AND TURTLES. The undisputed king of the Galapagos reptiles is the **giant tortoise.** These are the animals that really set the islands apart from other parts of the globe (only one other island in the world has a tortoise population). How the tortoises first came to inhabit the islands is still a mystery. Their closest relative is a species of tortoise native to Argentina; it is possible that the big guys (up to 250kg) got stuck on some floating vegetation that carried them out to sea and eventually to the Galapagos.

As a result of human interference, the tortoises aren't as plentiful as they once were. Three of the original 14 sub-species are now extinct, and introduced animals such as rats, dogs, and goats continue to threaten the remaining populations. While each animal can live to be over 150 years old, they do not reproduce often, and when they do the vulnerable hatchlings have low chances of reaching maturity. The **Galapagos National Park** and the **Charles Darwin Research Center** (see p. 584) are doing what they can to prevent predation and boost the head count, by harvesting eggs, raising the hatchlings to four years of age, and then releasing them back into their natural habitat. Some preservation efforts are not so progressive, as seen with the captive Pinta Tortoise in Puerto Ayora and the captive Cerro Paloma tortoises at the Breeding Center in Puerto Villamil. The **largest tortoise population** is found on Isabela, concentrated around the crater of Volcán Alcedo. Elsewhere in the islands, wild tortoises can be observed at the **tortoise reserves** on Santa Cruz (see p. 588) and Española (see p. 604). Captive tortoises can be viewed at the Darwin Research Center on Santa Cruz (see p. 588) and the **Breeding Center for Giant Tortoises** on Isabela (see p. 596).

Marine turtles are also common. Four of the eight existing species of marine turtle have been seen on the Galapagos, but none are endemic (given their great mobility). The **black turtle,** a sub-species of the Pacific green turtle, is the most common. They lay their eggs in nests on the beach, burying them to incubate in the hot sun. While they can lay eggs year-round, it is most common from January to June. For a day or two after the eggs are laid, visitors may observe tracks leading from the sea to the nest and back again. Night visitors may even catch a turtle in the process of laying eggs. In these cases, it is fine to watch quietly, but do not disturb the animals, especially not with the beam of a flashlight.

IGUANAS. One of the most bizarre and unique reptiles of the Galapagos is the **marine iguana,** the only aquatic iguana in the world. Related to the land iguanas of the American mainland, marine iguanas have evolved to eat green algae that grows underwater. They can swim to a depth of 20m, stay underwater for up to one hour at a time, are able to rapidly discharge excess absorbed salt out of their unusually square noses (an amusing spectacle), and their tails are tailored for efficient swimming. The largest marine iguanas (on Isabela) can grow to be 1m long. Like other reptiles, these creatures are **ectothermic,** meaning that their body temperature is determined by the temperature of their surroundings. Consequently, they are often seen piled on top of each other, sunning their black, spiny bodies on rocks.

Two species of **land iguanas** also inhabit the islands; while their genus is endemic to the Galapagos, the land-loving lizards seem less exotic than their water-borne counterparts. They can also grow to 1m in length, but their noses are more characteristically pointed. Keep an eye out for the **prickly pear iguanas** on Santa Fe and South Plazas, the rare **hybrid iguana** on South Plazas, and the **crested canolophus pallidus** land iguana species, only in the Galapagos on island Santa Fe.

OTHER REPTILES. Long ago, through some heroic feat of seamanship, **snakes** also reached the islands. On land, the non-poisonous Galapagos **land snake** slithers in search of small prey to crush with its constrictive power. Found on all but the northernmost islands, these brown or gray snakes have yellow stripes or spots and may grow to 1m long. Seven species of **lava lizard** are also endemic to the islands. They are gray, and females have eye-catching red-orange throats. They are very territorial, but most confrontation takes the form of bouncing up and down on the forelegs; fights between lizards are seldom serious but especially entertaining.

MAMMALS

While **Homo sapiens** have arrived only recently on the Galapagos, they have had a great impact on the ecology. The number of people that call the islands home fluctuates regularly but is rising. It is unclear whether the population can continue to grow at this rate without damaging the islands beyond repair. Humans have also increased the mammal contingent of the islands by introducing varieties of dog, cat, goat, and rat, which have multiplied faster than their primate counterparts.

A less disturbing large mammal found in astonishing abundance in the Galapagos is the endemic **Galapagos sea lion.** Relatives of the sea lions of California and Peru, they live in colonies on the beaches of most of the islands. Males are much larger than females and can weigh up to 250kg. They are highly territorial, holding their turf and the females that come with it for a month at a time, aggressively defending them from any kind of intruder (usually other males). Mating occurs in the ocean, but females give birth on land, and the pups are suckled for up to three years before being weaned. The animals are playful and are commonly seen surfing or showing off for tourists.

Another related but quite distinct species is the **Galapagos fur seal** (or fur sea lion). Technically, fur seals are not seals at all but rather a species of smaller sea lion with pointed ears and an extra layer of fur. Their short snouts and thick necks have earned them the nickname "Galapagos sea bears." These features result from their ancestors: they came from the south of South America where their small surface-area-to-size ratio and extra layer of insulating fur kept them warm in the chilly waters. These animals' rich pelts were once much desired, causing them to be hunted nearly to extinction by European fur traders; one boat in the Galapagos killed 50,000 in a period of three months. The little "bears" are much more shy than their personable sea lion cousins, most likely because of their unpleasant history with humans. These timid creatures are also prey for sharks; when the moon is full and visibility high, you'll find them seeking refuge on dry land.

The only other mammals on the islands that were not introduced by man are **bats** and **rice rats**. Two species of bat eat insects on the islands of Santa Cruz, Floreana, Isabela, and San Cristóbal, while the brown rice rat searches for vegetation. Lately, the rice rat population has been decreasing due to the introduction of the **black rat**, which competes with the rice rat for food. Before the black rat arrived there were seven species of endemic rice rat; today, there are only two remaining.

MARINE LIFE

The waters of the Galapagos are truly tropical, teeming with just about every form of marine life. The islands are fed by three nutritious **currents:** the Humboldt, the Cromwell, and El Niño, which bring a large supply of species and nutrients from all over the Pacific. Among the 16 species of **whale**, you'll find the **sperm, humpback, blue, and killer whales.** The **common** and **bottle-nosed** are the most prevalent of the seven species of **dolphin,** which are concentrated off the west coast of Isabela.

Twelve species of **shark** also inhabit these waters. By far the most common is the white-tipped reef shark, but **black-tipped reef sharks, hammerheads, Galapagos sharks,** and **tiger sharks** are common as well. Less common are the **Lorn shark** near Espinosa and the monstrous **whale shark,** found near the distant Darwin and Wolf islands. There are five species of **ray,** including **stingrays, eagle rays,** and **manta rays.** Before the most recent visit of El Niño, **coral reefs** used to surround many of the islands, but the inhospitable temperature extremes caused by this pesky weather phenomenon destroyed most formations. Galapagos marine life is resilient, however, and numerous species such as **lobster, squid, octopus, starfish,** and **shellfish** of all kinds abound. **Crab** species are numerous, the most striking being the **sally light-foot crab,** which is bright orange and white with a touch of blue. The **sea cucumber,** or *pepino*, continues to struggle against its status as a delicacy in Japan.

Because of this diversity, the waters in and around the Galapagos, an area of 70,000 sq. km, form part of a marine reserve established in 1986. While the area is protected and fishing is frowned upon, regulated commercial fishing of some species is allowed; before dropping a line, consult the locals or your trusty tour guide.

PLANT LIFE

The Galapagos support **seven vegetation zones** that are home to over 600 species of plant, approximately 170 of which are endemic. The zones range from dry and low to high and moist. The area right on the coast—the **littoral zone**—is dominated by plants that have adapted to the presence of salt, such as **red mangroves.** The **arid zone** is the driest region and is just above the littoral in altitude. Generally on the side of the island opposite the prevailing winds, the region is dominated by cacti and other dry-weather plants. The **opuntia cactus,** with bright yellow flowers, is the only endemic species of cactus and also is the most common. It is often a shrub, except on islands where it is threatened by herbivorous animals; there, these cacti can grow trunks up to 5m tall. Other species are the **prickly pear cacti** on South Plazas and the **lava cacti** on Bartolomé. The **Palo Santo** tree is also native to this zone. Producing only small leaves in the wet season, the branches of these stark gray trees are often burned for their incense-like odor. The tree (its name means "Holy Stick") is so named because of the small white blossoms it sprouts around Christmas. The **Palo Verde** is a similar looking tree with draping green leaves year round.

The next highest zone, which is also more humid, is the **transition zone.** The most common inhabitants are the Palo Santos, as well as the **pega pega** (which translates literally as "it sticks, it sticks"), which has spread-out branches and a short trunk. The next zone is very humid and has been called the **scalesia zone** for the endemic and common scalesia trees which can grow up to 10m tall; many **mosses, ferns,** and **grasses** also thrive here. The three remaining zones are the **brown, miconia,** and **pampa zones.** The brown is named for the prominent **brown liverwort mosses** found here. The miconia zone gets its name from the endemic and shrubby **miconia plants,** which look somewhat like flowering cacao plants. The highest and wettest vegetation zone is the **pampa,** dominated by mosses, ferns and grasses; few trees or shrubs grow in this hyper-humid region.

ESSENTIALS

BUDGET GALAPAGOS: FACT OR FICTION?

The Galapagos are not a budget destination. Even when leaving from the relatively nearby cities of Quito or Guayaquil, it costs US$400-500 in airfare and park fees to enter the islands. Once there, tourism-inflated prices and tours could easily push a two-week vacation to over US$2000. Yet the exotic animals and landscape remain the same whether observed by the craftiest budget traveler or the guy on a US$300-a-day cruise ship. With a little savvy, negotiation, and patience, an incredible two-week adventure can materialize for around US$1000.

The most logical way to budget travel through the Galapagos is by devising a plan involving both independent travel and relatively inexpensive boat and land tours. The independent traveler can access inhabited islands via *avioneta* (small plane) or *fibra* (fiber-glass motor boat), visit sights utilizing *camionetas* or horses, and mingle with the local *galapaqueñas* for substantially less than those tourists opting for high-cost cruises and luxury tours—you might even get a better, more realistic, glimpse at wildlife on the islands. However, to experience the magnificence of many of the uninhabited islands (such as Bartolomé) and the splendor of hard-to-access sights (such as Elizabeth Bay off Isla Isabela), tours and guides are usually necessary. Guided land tours are arranged through travel agencies in Puerto Ayora, or at local hotels in Isabela. Boat tours come in two categories: *tours diarios* (daily tours), and *tours navegables* (multi-day tours).

Although daytrips, independent or guided, often cost less per day than package multi-day tour boats, they only include lunch (tour boats include full room and board) and daytrippers visit one site a day (tour-boaters visit two). Although a Galapagos trip usually revolves around the sights reached primarily by boat, time spent in the towns and nearby attractions prove an enjoyable (and inexpensive) complement to the tour boat scene. Another way to cheaply visit the Galapagos is to take advantage of low-season deals on airfare and tours—your chances of booking a last-minute tour bargain in Puerto Ayora are very good.

WHEN TO GO

The relative stability of the equatorial climate ensures a rewarding Galapagos experience year round, but the region has two distinct seasons. Warm ocean currents cause hot, rainy weather from January through April, while the rest of the year the islands dry out and cool down. Neither season is ideal—during the rainy months, the ocean water refreshes at a comfortable 75°F (24°C), but heavy rain showers often disturb the tropical tranquility. Likewise, while rain may fall rarely during the dry months, the sky is often overcast, the water a chilly 70°F (21°C) or lower, and the waves choppy from winds. **The ideal visiting months,** climate-wise, are between seasons—March through May, when rainfall lightens, and November and December, as the climate warms up. Note also that some animals are only around at certain times, so research nesting patterns to avoid disappointment.

The Galapagos **surfing** season is December through February. Puerto Baquerizo Moreno, on San Cristóbal, is headquarters to the annual pilgrimage of devoted surfers during this season, and it is not uncommon for hotels to rent multi-person rooms for an affordable monthly rate.

During the busy months of July, August, and December, finding a boat is challenging, bargaining nearly impossible, and prices significantly higher—book flights and boat tours well in advance. October is not a busy month, but many boat owners choose to make repairs then and put their vehicles out of commission. All things considered, the best month is May: tourism hasn't yet picked up, the climate is moderate, and the seas are calm. July and August tend to be the worst times to go because tourism peaks and the seas are cold and rough. During the sweltering months from January to April, consider splurging on a boat with air conditioning.

The Galapagos Islands are one hour behind the Ecuadorian mainland and six hours behind Greenwich Mean Time. Daylight Savings Time is not observed.

USEFUL ORGANIZATIONS

Charles Darwin Foundation, Inc., 100 N. Washington St., Suite 232, Falls Church, VA 22046, USA (☎(703) 538-6833; fax (703) 538-6835; www.darwinfoundation.org). Mailing address: Casilla 17-01-3891, Quito, Ecuador. A non-profit membership organization promoting conservation, education, and research in the area. Publishes a newsletter, the *Galapagos Bulletin*, 3 times annually and maintains an informative website.

Corporación Ecuatoriana de Turismo (CETUR), Eloy Alfaro 1214 and Carlos Tobar, Quito (☎(02) 507 555; fax 507 564; www.cetur.org). A government-run tourist agency with valuable facts about hotels and transportation. Provides maps and info as specific as animal mating seasons and the best sites for spotting certain wildlife. CETUR offices are in all major cities in Ecuador, including Puerto Ayora (☎526 179), on Charles Darwin.

South American Explorers Club (SAE), Jorge Washington 311 and Leonidas Plaza. Mailing address: Apartado 17-21-431, Eloy Alfaro, Quito, Ecuador (☎/fax (02) 225 228; email explorer@saec.org.ec; www.samexplo.org). A non-profit organization with info on traveling, working, volunteering, and researching in Latin America. Their "Galapagos Packet" of practical info about the islands is updated every few months. SAE has reports on the various boats operating in the Galapagos; check them out.

GETTING THERE

As of July 2000, **TAME** provides the only available flights to the Galapagos. **SAN/SAETA** has currently stopped servicing flights to San Cristóbal and the rumor is that **Ecuatoriana** will take their place. All flights start in Quito, stop in Guayaquil one hour later, then take another 90min. to reach the islands. Fares fluctuate depending on the season. During the high season (June 15-Aug. 31 and Dec. 1-Jan. 15), round-trip tickets cost US$378 from Quito and US$224 from Guayaquil; low-season fares dip to about US$324 from Quito and US$190 from Guayaquil. Getting last-minute flights to and from Puerto Ayora can be hard during the high season and just before and after these dates; flights are also usually overbooked, and buying a ticket does not assure flying on a specific day. Try to get a reservation, or *cupo*, for the day you want to fly. Otherwise you'll be put on the waiting list, which makes getting on a flight a matter of luck (and of how early you get to the airport that morning). Always re-check flight information a few days before traveling.

TAME (☎(02) 509 383; fax (02) 554 907), Colón and Reina Victoria in New Quito; 9 de Octobre and P Ycaza in Gran Pasaje Building in Guayaquil, runs the only flights to the Galapagos, departing daily from **Quito** at 8 and 10:30am, and from **Guayaquil** at 9:15am and 11:30am. Planes land on Isla Baltra, with easy access to Isla Santa Cruz and Puerto Ayora. Returning flights leave **Baltra** at 10:30am and 2:20pm. TAME also offers student discounts with valid university ID and an international student ID (☎(02) 554 900 or (04) 560 778 in Guayaquil). Even if Ecuatoriana begins servicing flights to Puerto Baquerizo Moreno, flying into Baltra with TAME is best, since most practical and tour-arrangement resources are found in nearby Puerto Ayora.

THE GALAPAGOS

GETTING AROUND

Galapagos inter-island travel is formidable at best. Islands are only reached by guided boat tour, small boat (*fibra*), or small plane. Island-hopping is time-consuming whether or not you're on a tour, and plane and *fibra* schedules are irregular. Independent inter-island travelers should not expect to follow rigid itineraries.

> When first arriving in the Galapagos (Isla Baltra or Isla San Cristóbal), everyone must pay a US$100 park admission fee in cash. Credit cards and traveler's checks are NOT accepted. It's necessary to keep the receipt if traveling between islands. A passport is also required to enter the Galapagos.

PACKAGE TOURS AND CRUISES

While independent inter-island travel has its advantages, partaking in at least one boat tour is a necessary ingredient for the complete Galapagos experience. Tours come in many lengths, from daytrips to three-week cruises. The most common are **three- to eight-day trips.** The SAE recommends the following tour companies:

Angermeyers Enchanted Excursions, Foch 726 and León Mera in New Quito (☎(02) 569 960 or 504 444; fax 569 956).

Safari Tours (☎(02) 234 799; fax 220 426), Pasaje de Roca in New Quito, between Amazonas and León Mera.

Moonrise Travel Agency (☎(05) 526 589 or 526 348; ☎/fax 526 403), in Puerto Ayora on Darwin, facing the Banco del Pacífico.

TOUR BOATS AND GUIDES. There are three main classes of **tour boats:** economy, tourist, and first-class. **Economy** boats tend to be small with limited facilities, unremarkable food, and mediocre guides. Many of these boats are acceptable, but some are downright primitive. Getting an up-close view of the boat is probably out of the question, so ask to see a picture—tourist brochures are available for most boats. **Tourist** boats tend to be a little bigger (averaging 16 passengers), with private baths, palatable food, and better guides. Some tourist class boats are also equipped for voyages to more distant islands such as Genovesa. **First-class** ships are even nicer, but the comfort is reflected in their price tag. These boats rock less in the waves, have space for privacy, and handle longer voyages, enabling them outer islands such as Fernandina.

The quality of **guides** also matters; there three categories of guides: **Naturalist I** is a regular, usually Spanish-speaking guide with general knowledge of flora and fauna; **Naturalist II** has more in-depth knowledge and is guaranteed to speak English; **Naturalist III** is an bona fide biologist who may speak up to three languages, including Spanish and English. A guide can make or break the trip but a little prior study of the Galapagos can salvage a visit ruined by a mediocre naturalist. While more expensive boats come with better guides, it is possible to get a good Naturalist III guide on a tourist boat; guides on economy boats tend to be less knowledgeable. Try to get information about a trip's guide before booking a tour.

FINDING A TOUR. When shopping for Galapagos tours, remember this principle: **the closer you are to the sailing date and the boat when you reserve, the lower the price.** The trade-off is uncertainty—those who wait run the risk of not finding a suitable boat. Yet the best deals are in Puerto Ayora, and one can sometimes see the boat before deciding on it. It may also be wise to compare the many agencies along Darwin before booking with one of the first places you pass. Puerto Ayora prices per day tend to be as follows: economy (US$65-70); tourist (US$70-80); and luxury (US$100-400). Prices rise during high season, becoming more negotiable during low season.

An alternative is to book through a travel agency in Quito or Guayaquil. These agencies can often arrange very cheap passage on boats that are set to leave in a few days but have empty spaces. Quito is packed with agencies—Amazonas seems to have two or three on every block. Agencies that directly represent their own boats may be able to negotiate a lower price. Guayaquil has less agencies booking

Galapagos tours than Quito, but with a little patience, deals may be found there. To alleviate the burden of flight reservations, boat companies usually reserve airplane seats for their passengers—another reason to arrange a tour in advance.

LIFE ON THE BOAT. Life on a multiple-day tour boat is very relaxed, but a few precautions should be taken to ensure that your trip runs smoothly. To avoid seasickness, come stocked with motion-sickness medicine. Although not a major concern, minor theft has been known to occur—bring locks to secure valuables in your bag, lock your cabin if given a key, and keep money and traveler's checks on your person. Almost all tour boats follow a similar routine. Days start early (breakfast 7am) and generally include visits to two sites, either on the same island or on two nearby ones. Since boats cannot dock right at the shore of the islands, it's a **panga** (dinghy) ride to the shore—one quickly learns the difference between a **"wet landing"** (onto a beach—water generally about knee-deep) and a **"dry landing"** (onto a man-made or natural dock). Most days also include an opportunity to swim, snorkel, or kayak.

It is standard to **tip** the crew on a tour boat US$25-50 per week, depending on the quality of the service. Crew members work hard and aren't paid well (especially on economy boats), so this is probably not the best place to economize. The guide usually gets paid about twice as much as the crew, but it is appropriate to tip the guide as well. If an "anonymous tipping" box is not provided toward the end of a boat trip, pooling money with other passengers and giving it to the captain for distribution may be the least awkward way of going about it.

INTER-ISLAND TRAVEL

BY BOAT. The municipally-owned **Estrella del Mar 2** travels between **Isabela and Puerto Ayora, Santa Cruz.** (Isabela to Santa Cruz Tu 7:30am; Santa Cruz to Isabela W 11am; US$15.20.) Captains Juan Mendoza and Humberto Gil alternate shifts, so to reserve a place find either one by the *Muelle* dock in Puerto Ayora or through the municipal office in Isabela (see p. 595). Reserve before noon (on either island) the day before travel. Fishermen and navy members sometimes let passengers on their speedy *fibras* (**fiberglass boats**) when they travel between Isabela, Santa Cruz and San Cristóbal. Cost varies and there is no schedule. Ask about departures at the Wreck Bay dock in San Cristóbal, the *Muelle* dock in Puerto Ayora, or the *Capitania* in Puerto Bagquerizo Moreno. The government-run **INGALA** currently does not have trips between Santa Cruz, San Cristóbal, and Floreana because the main boat sank; service may resume when they get another boat.

BY PLANE. EMETEBE (☎ 526 177 in Santa Cruz, ☎ 520 036 in San Cristóbal, or ☎ 529 155 in Isabela) has small planes that travel between San Cristóbal, Santa Cruz, and Isabela in various combinations. Though the foreigner fee for any one-way trip is quoted at US$90, the price is usually a negotiable US$50-70. The schedule varies due to poor weather conditions or a "sick" pilot (there is never more than one available to fly out of an island). Flights take up to 45min. and carry up to 10 passengers. See "Practical Information" sections for the major cities to get specifics.

DAYTRIP OPTIONS

The cheapest daytrips cost around US$70 and include both lunch and a guide (who may not have received a Naturalist II badge yet). These trips go from Santa Cruz to: North Seymour, South Plazas, Bartolomé, Santa Fe, Floreana, and a few other nearby sites; book these at any travel agency. The luxurious **Delfin 2** offers more expensive trips (US$100-150) from Santa Cruz. Destinations include: Bartolomé (M); Santa Fe South Plazas (Tu); Rabida Island, Cerro Dragón (Th); North Seymour, Bachas (F); and Floreana (Sa). The boat's occasional two-site-per-day trips partially justify the high cost. Arrange trips through Moonrise Travel Agency in Puerto Ayora (☎ 526 348 or 526 589; fax 526 403; email sdivine@pa.ga.pro.ec), or contact Willy Timm at the Delfin Hotel (☎ 520 297 or 520 298) before 6pm at least a day prior to travel. Daytrip options in San Cristóbal and Isabela are limited but not unavailable. From Puerto Baquerizo Moreno, contact Rosita Restaurant for expensive daytrips to Leon Dormido and other nearby sights.

PRACTICAL INFORMATION

MONEY AND BARGAINING

US dollars are now the standard Ecuadorian currency, and are especially prominent in the tourist-laden Galapagos. It is a good idea to have a large quantity of cash and traveler's checks on hand when paying for a tour after getting to the islands, since travel agents usually charge a 10-20% service charge for credit card transactions. **Credit cards** are a somewhat impractical currency on the islands, and very few establishments accept Visa or American Express. **MasterCard** is preferred everywhere, but be prepared to still pay at least a 10% service charge. Locals routinely overcharge tourists; always ask the price beforehand and **bargain,** especially in the low season. Currently, **Banco del Pacífico,** in Puerto Ayora and Puerto Baquerizo Moreno, is the best place to **exchange money.** The banks' **ATMs** are convenient ways to access cash, but they do not accept Visa cards. Stock up on cash, especially before heading to Isabela, where there is no ATM; carrying large amounts of money in the Galapagos is less of a concern than on the mainland.

PACKING

Stores in the Galapagos tend to be souvenir oriented, so bring everything you'll need. Carefully consider footwear; for wet landings and easy hikes, a pair of sturdy sandals will suffice. However, hiking boots or sturdy shoes are a must for rockier or more difficult trails. Bring along some insect repellent and, rainy season or not, the sun's rays will likely scorch, so stock up on sunscreen and bring sunglasses and a wide-brimmed hat. For cool evenings, bring a sweatshirt and pants, though, it's best to prepare for any kind of weather with a couple of T-shirts, a pair of shorts. A light raincoat is a necessity during the rainy months (Jan.-Apr.), but may be useful anytime. Finally, bring snorkeling or scuba diving gear if you've got it. Most tour boats have a supply of masks on board, but there's no guaranteeing their quality (or quantity). One can also rent masks, snorkels, and flippers in Puerto Ayora. For those spending a long period of time in the dry season's chilly water, a short-sleeved wetsuit may ease the plunge. Most towns in the Galapagos shut off power during the night, so bring a flashlight. Also, a disposable underwater camera is a nice way to capture your snorkeling memories.

SCUBA DIVING, SNORKELING, AND KAYAKING

The Galapagos touts some of the best **scuba diving** sites in the world—Darwin Island, Wolf Island, and Gordon Rocks, to name a few. While strong currents reserve these sights for experienced divers, introductory dives in calmer bays are also available, and both offer the exceptional opportunity to swim with enormous schools of beautifully colored fish, mysterious rays, harmless hammerheads, playful sea lions, and (on occasion) the elusive white shark.

The most established diving outfit in Puerto Ayora is **Galapagos Sub-Aqua** (☎526 350 or 526 633, in Quito ☎/fax (02) 565 294; email sub_aqua@accessinter.net; www.Galapagos_sub_aqua.com.ec), on the left side of Charles Darwin, just after Piqueros heading away from the town center. Diveleader Fernando Zambrano is professional, friendly, licensed as a Naturalist Guide, and speaks English. Sub-Aqua offers daytrips from beginner to divemaster level. (US$80-120; including all gear, tanks for 2 dives, lunch, free drinking water, snacks and a divemaster guide.) "All-inclusive dive packages" include lodgings, two meals, and diving. (US$150-190 per night; multi-day dive excursions to Darwin and Wolf Islands, sights Zambrano has labeled "super-paradises," are cost more.) The only diving opportunities for non-certified divers are at Academy Bay (US$80). Also, **Galapagos Scuba Iguana** (☎/fax 526 497, in Quito (02) 260 608; email mathiase@pa.ga.pro.ec; www.scuba-iguana.com), is 20m past the green "Darwin Research Station" sign on Darwin, next to the Hotel Galapagos. Mathias Espinosa, a certified divemaster and instructor with over 5000 Galapagos dives, is a naturalist guide and fluent in Spanish, English and German. Iguana has daytrips (3-7hr.; US$78-110; includes dive gear, tanks for 2 dives, a divemaster guide, and a box lunch for 7hr. trips). They also rent underwater cameras (US$10 per day, with film US$20).

Unlike scuba diving, there are no special certifications or guide companies needed for most **snorkeling** adventures. For the most part, you just need a mask, a snorkel, pair of rubber flippers, and a desire to explore the world below. Most beaches on the islands allow snorkeling, and time is usually budgeted into tour boat schedules to accommodate passengers' fish-watching desires.

Kayaking is also an option. Some tour boats provide kayaks and allow time for brief excursions, or you can rent your own in Puerto Ayora (US$15 per day at **The Manglar Adventure,** on Darwin just before the turnoff to the Research Station).

ISLA SANTA CRUZ

Known also by its English name of Indefatigable, Isla Santa Cruz's never-ending diversity—its myriad wildlife, radically varied geology, and scores of international visitors—is indeed tireless. Tourism in the Galapagos revolves around this hub, near the geographical center of the archipelago. Nearly every visitor stops here, whether to schmooze with the tortoises or just to stock up on supplies, as Puerto Ayora is the largest and most developed town on the islands, and Santa Cruz is a conveniently close first stop if you arrive at the Baltra Airport.

On the trip from the airport to Puerto Ayora the entire landscape is covered with lava rock, cacti, and wind-blown trees. After a boat ride across shimmering, turquoise waters, visitors enter the central highlands of Santa Cruz, where the bus jostles its way through greenery. From there the bus descends to the port town.

Landlubbers will be in heaven here—Santa Cruz is one of the few islands in the Galapagos where many sites can be reached without a boat. In addition to the Charles Darwin Research Station and the beautiful beaches near Puerto Ayora, the lush scalesia forests of Santa Cruz's highland region provide ample opportunities for horseback riding, hiking, and exploring Santa Cruz's geology and wildlife.

PUERTO AYORA   ☎ 05

The constant influx of tortoise-happy tourists has given the port town of Puerto Ayora a vaguely cosmopolitan air, a high standard of living, and a happy-go-lucky attitude. However, it has also made Puerto Ayora more expensive than mainland Ecuador and brought strings of souvenir shops and bars. Despite the number of Galapagos T-shirts and sea lion figurines for sale along the main streets, however, the town maintains a very genuine feel. It exudes subdued contentment—the streets bustle, but only with people strolling casually. In the bars, streets and restaurants, locals and tourists mix and mingle, and everyone seems to appreciate the friendliness of the people and the beauty of the surroundings.

▐▀ TRANSPORTATION

Airport: To get to Puerto Ayora from the Isla Baltra airport, take the free shuttle bus to the boat to Santa Cruz (10min., US$0.16). A bus takes passengers across Santa Cruz to Puerto Ayora (50min., US$1.50). Buy bus tickets at the airport. The bus arrives and departs in the center of town. **TAME** (☎ 526 165), Darwin and 12 de Febrero, will arrange tickets and flight reservations. Try to reserve return flights as soon as possible during the high season (Dec.-May). Open M-F 8am-noon and 1-5pm, Sa 9am-noon.

Inter-Island Boat Travel: As of July 2000, the only destination is **Isabela**. The boat, Estrella del Mar 2, leaves from the Muelle dock in Puerto Ayora (W 11am; returns following Tu 7:30am; one-way US$15.20). Register your name and passport with Heriberto in Puerto Ayora by the docks. Pay when you arrive in Isabela.

Inter-Island Flights: EMETEBE (☎ 526 177), in the same building as the post office (2nd fl.), flies to **San Cristóbal** and **Isabela** (30min., US$80-90). Schedules vary. Flying is the cheapest way to San Cristóbal—boats cost more and are less convenient.

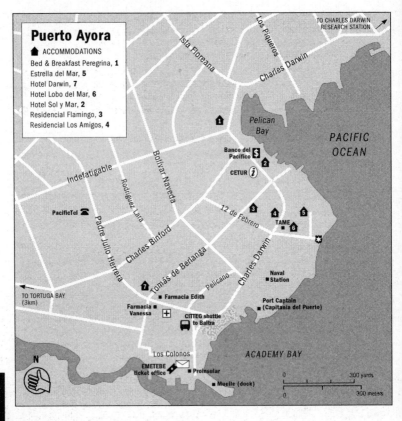

Puerto Ayora

⌂ ACCOMMODATIONS

Bed & Breakfast Peregrina, **1**
Estrella del Mar, **5**
Hotel Darwin, **7**
Hotel Lobo del Mar, **6**
Hotel Sol y Mar, **2**
Residencial Flamingo, **3**
Residencial Los Amigos, **4**

TO CHARLES DARWIN
RESEARCH STATION

Los Piqueros

Isla Floreana

Charles Darwin

Pelican
Bay

PACIFIC
OCEAN

Banco del
Pacífico 💲 **2**

CETUR ⓘ

Indefatigable

Bolívar Naveda

Rodríguez Lara

PacificTel ☎

12 de Febrero

3 **4** **5**
TAME ■ **6**

✚

Padre Julio Herrera

Charles Binford

Tomás de Berlanga

Pelícano

Charles Darwin

Naval
■ Station

TO TORTUGA BAY
(3km)

7

■ Farmacia Edith

Farmacia ■
Vanessa ✚

CITTEG shuttle
to Baltra

Port Captain
■ (Capitanía del Puerto)

Los Colonos

EMETEBE
ticket office ■ Proinsular

■ Muelle (dock)

ACADEMY BAY

N

0   300 yards

0   300 meters

✳ⓘ ORIENTATION AND PRACTICAL INFORMATION

The **center of town** is marked by a triangular median adjoining **Charles Darwin, Padre Julio Herrera,** and the short street leading to the **Muelle** dock area. The park and its volleyball courts are here, as well as the main **bus stop.** Blue taxis, yellow taxis, and white *camionetas* run frequently along Darwin and Herrera.

Tourist Information: Ministerio de Turismo (☎526 174), directly across from Hotel Sol del Mar on Darwin between Berlana and Binford, will give you a free blurry map and basic info in Spanish. **CAPTURGAL** (☎/fax 526 206; email cptg@pa.ga.pro.ec), on the left side of Darwin just before B&B Peregrina, heading away from the center of town, is better. A member of the *socios* tourism network, they have good maps (US$1), detailed information about tour boats, hotels, and restaurants in the Galapagos, and an interesting and informative book on Isabela (English text; US$1). A unique resource, the **Charles Darwin Research Station** (☎526 146 or 526 147; fax 526 651; email: cdrs@fcdarwin.org.ec) is less than 20min. from town along the path that branches to the right of Darwin heading away from the town center. The station is a worthwhile stop; English-speaking staff, written literature, and visual aids will provide answers to most questions about the *Parque Nacional de Galapagos.* Open daily 7am-noon and 1-4pm.

Travel Agencies: Several agencies in town arrange boat tours, daytrips, and inland excursions. **Moonrise Travel Agency** (☎526 589; fax 526 403; email sdivine@pa.ga.pro.ec), on Darwin across the street from Banco del Pacífico, is a very helpful English- and German-speaking agency recommended by the SAE. Open M-F 7:30am-6pm, Sa 9am-

THE GALAPAGOS

5pm. **Galapagos Discovery** (☎/fax 526 245), on Herrera in front of the hospital, also rents bikes (US$1 per hr.), surf boards, and snorkel equipment; **Galapatour** (☎526 581; email aagalap2@uio.satnet.net) is on Darwin by the volleyball court in the DHL/Western Union building. Both have English-speaking staffs.

Bank: Banco del Pacífico (☎526 282; fax 526 364), on the right side of Darwin past the Hotel Sol y Mar when walking away from the center of town has a Cirrus/MC **ATM** and MC cash advances. Open M-F 8am-3:30pm; window services Sa 9:30am-noon.

Market: Proinsular Supermarket (☎526 120), across from the Muelle dock. Open M-Sa 8am-8pm, Su 8am-noon.

Restrooms: Public restrooms are located on Darwin near the park.

Laundromat: The **Peregrina B&B,** on Darwin, runs a *lavandería* (US$0.72 per kg, including dryer service). Open M-Sa 8:30am-6pm.

Police: (☎526 101). By the water on 12 de Febrero, beside Lobo del Mar. Open 24hr.

Pharmacies: Farmacia Edith (☎526 487) is open daily 7am-11pm. **Farmacia Vanessa** (☎526 392) is open daily 7am-1pm and 2pm-midnight.

Hospital: Hospital República del Ecuador (24hr. emergency ☎526 103), on Herrera, less than a block from the center of town.

Telephones: PACIFICTEL (☎526 104 or 526 105), on Herrera, 5min. from the center of town, handles international phone calls, **faxes,** and **telegrams** for a fee. Fax daily 8am-noon and 2-4pm; telephone daily 7am-11pm. You can also make international collect or calling card calls from **Galapatours** (see above).

Internet Access: Several internet cafes line Darwin. **Galapagos.com**, on Darwin across from Banco del Pacífico, gives 15min. free with 1hr. use. US$5 per hr. **Pelik@n.net,** on the corner of Darwin and Indefatigable, also charges US$5 per hr.

Post Office: The **Correo Central** (☎526 575), on the ground floor of the Proinsular shopping center on Darwin, near the Muelle dock. Open M-F 8am-1pm and 2-6pm, Sa 9am-noon. **DHL/Western Union** (☎/fax 526 186; email pelicanb@pa.ga.pro.ec), on Darwin across from the park and next to El Rincón del Alma.

ACCOMMODATIONS

Given the number of wealthy tourists who visit the Galapagos, Puerto Ayora caters to those seeking a familiar level of luxury. However, penny-pinching budget travelers can find affordable clean lodgings with great views. Towels, toilet paper, and clean sheets are fairly standard. Mosquitos are not usually a problem, but most hotels and hostels have screened windows to combat the pesky few that plague this paradise. An ocean view may cost you US$5 more than the hotel down the street, but if you've gone to all the trouble to get to the island, it's worth it.

■ **Hotel Lobo del Mar** (☎526 188; fax 526 569), 12 de Febrero, just off Darwin, next to the police station. Spacious 2nd and 3rd floor rooms with clean baths and balconies overlooking the bay. Friendly staff, comfortable TV lounge. It's the best deal in town, hands down. Singles and doubles US$8.

Estrella del Mar (☎526 427 or 526 080), right next to the ocean. Make a left at the end of 12 de Febrero by the police station and follow dirt path. This *estrella* twinkles with airy rooms, clean baths, a TV lounge, and fantastic ocean views. Hot water in cold weather. Group discounts available. Rooms US$7 per person, with view US$10.

Peregrina Bed and Breakfast (☎526 323), on Darwin just after Indefatigable coming from the center of town. Though lacking ocean views and hot water, partitioned rooms for 4 are pleasant. Include clean baths, toilet paper, and towels. Breakfast US$1. Laundry service US$0.72 per kg. Rooms US$5 per person, with A/C US$7 per person.

Residencial Los Amigos (☎526 265), Darwin and 12 de Febrero, attracts backpackers with its balance of price and quality. Shared bathrooms and rooms for four. Singles US$4; doubles, triples, and quads US$3 per person.

Hotel Darwin (☎526 193), on Herrera, past the hospital, 1 block from the ocean. A weathered, palm frond-covered patio separates guests from Herrera. Bathrooms and thin mattresses betray their years, despite their cleanliness. Rooms US$2 per person.

Hotel Sol y Mar (☎526 281), on the right side of Darwin, just before the bank, coming from the center of town. The hefty price tag may not guarantee an ocean view, but expect a clean room, a hot water bath, and lounging iguanas. Group discounts for over 3 days. Doubles and matrimonials US$20, with view US$45; rooms for 6 people US$10 per person; extra person US$5.

FOOD

Restaurants are as abundant on Darwin as diving pelicans. Those on the first few blocks are moderately priced; most restaurants here and on Herrera are open most of the day and serve a set *desayuno, almuerzo,* and sometimes *merienda.* These places attract the tourists fresh off the boat and are a great spot to meet other visitors and arrange boat tours. Farther toward the Research Station, more expensive restaurants cater to those ready to splurge. For typical fare, check out Charles Binford, just off Herrera, where locals get cheap, fresh meals from wooden kiosks. Of these, **William's** is highly recommended.

■ **Capricho,** just after Floreana walking away from the center of town. No *comida típica* here, but superb veggie dishes (US$1.40-2.80), great sandwiches (US$1.20-1.60), and take-out lunches (US$3). Wash down a piece of chocolate cake (US$0.60) with natural juice. English, French, and German book and magazine exchange. Open daily 7am-8pm.

Servi-Sabrosán, on Berlanga between Herrera and Naveda, 2nd floor. A great environment for enjoying *almuerzo* or a *merienda* (US$1.20), topped off with a tasty dessert (US$1.60). Open daily 7:30am-3pm and 6-9:30pm.

La Garrapata, on Darwin, between 12 de Febrero and Berlanga, is hailed by many locals as the premier establishment for a romantic and relaxing dinner; worth the price. An eager-to-please staff and high-quality food make it one of the best digs among Puerto Ayora's pasta-and-meat dinner establishments. Delicious pasta with mushrooms (US$3.80) and gigantic T-bone steak (US$5). Well-stocked bar. Open daily 6:30-10pm.

El Rincón del Alma (☎526 196), facing the park on the waterfront, has both indoor and patio seating. Set menus and entrees, from soup of the day to typical meat and seafood dishes, are all reasonably priced (US$0.72-4.80). Open daily 8am-9pm.

El Chocolate Galapagos, on Darwin between Binford and Berlanga, directly across from Banco del Pacífico, serves up hefty hamburgers (US$1.40). For the early birds, they have a nice breakfast selection as well (US$1.40-1.80). Open daily.

Media Luna Pizza, on Darwin between Piqueros and Floreana. Offers delicious pizza and sandwiches; try the stellar avocado sub. Locals, tourists, and families alike appreciate Media Luna's homey feel and incredibly friendly staff. Open W-M noon-10pm.

Panadería La Selecta, Herrera between Indefatigable and Berlanga, across the street from PACIFICTEL. Baked treats and creamy yogurts. Open daily 6am-1pm and 4-11pm.

SIGHTS

THE CHARLES DARWIN RESEARCH STATION. The Research Station is a veritable complex of Galapagos and conservation-related information, as well as the headquarters of the **Galapagos National Park.** The helpful **Office of Tourism** as well as the office of the conservation program are here. This is also the place to pay the US$100 National Park fee for those who arrived on boats. *(Easy 15min. trail branching off to the right of Darwin one block from Piqueros coming from the center of town. Galapagos National Park, ☎526 189 or 526 511; fax 526 190; email png@ga.pro.ec. Information booth open daily 7am-noon and 1-4pm.)* For more info about the Galapagos, the Research Station, and its projects, visit the station's **library.** Although its resources are mainly used by students and researchers, the library is open to tourists. If you have a specific interest or question, ask Gail Davis, the station's extremely helpful librarian who came to the islands years ago on a research project and never left. There is also a tiny but beautiful **beach,** where sunbathers lounge and gaze across the turquoise waters of the harbor. While swimming doesn't appear too inviting, a wealth of coral and seashells on the shore, make a dry beach excursion rewarding. *(Library open M-F 7:30am-4pm. Beach open daily 7am-6pm.)* Up the road a bit, you can visit the **administrative building,** a good place to pick up a map of the park. *(☎526 146 or 526 147; fax 526 651; email cdrs@fcdar-win.org.ec. Open daily 7am-noon and 1-4pm.)*

VAN STRAELEN EXHIBIT HALL. Farther along the main road and up a short path is the Van Straelen Exhibit Hall, which has information on the islands' natural history and focuses on both threats to the ecology of the islands and on current efforts to counteract them. This is a great place to learn facts and figures which will make the next stop on your tour of the station far more rewarding. A 12min. video about conservation programs is available and shown to anyone interested. The center is run by an enthusiastic staff who can usually be found in the hall's tourist office. Roslyn Cameron, coordinator of public support, can answer most tourist-related questions about the park. *(Open daily 7:30am-noon and 2-5pm.)*

TORTOISE REARING CENTER. A shady path leads to the tortoise rearing center, with pens containing baby giant tortoises, from newborns to kids just a couple of years old. To get a good look at the cute little *galapaguitos,* visit between 7am and 4pm on a weekday, when the covers of their pens will be open. The animals in this area were originally kept by islanders as pets, so they really do like people and very rarely retreat into their shells like the wild ones do. Even though it's acceptable to get close enough to the tortoises to pose with them for those priceless pictures, touching them is a big no-no. Also, be careful not to walk across or stand on the tortoise feeding platform (a large cement slab covered with partially chewed vegetation), as this may contaminate their food with harmful organisms. There are many informative signs throughout the area to enhance the experience for both you and the tortoises. If you still aren't in awe after seeing all the miniature dome-shelled dinosaurs, wait till you get a glimpse of the albino tortoise. The Center keeps him indoors because of his obvious sun-sensitivity, so put in a request at the administrative building and they might let you see him.

THE GALAPAGOS

LONESOME GEORGE George is an 88kg tortoise who lives at the Charles Darwin Research Center. But George isn't like all the other tortoises. He isn't like any other tortoise anywhere—sadly; George is the last of a dying race.

Found in 1971, George was the first **Pinta tortoise** *(Geochelone elephantopus abingdoni)* to be seen in 65 years. Tragically, the story of George's race is all too reminiscent of tales of endangered species the world over; exploited by man until they were nearly extinct, the tortoises were left with an uphill battle for survival. The dwindling Pinta tortoise population suffered another blow when introduced goats drastically affected the island's habitat, further contributing to the demise of George's tragedy-stricken race.

Some think that George, who is probably 60 or 70 years old (halfway through his expected life span), should live out the remainder of his days on his home island of Pinta, now goat-free. Currently, George remains at the research center, comfortably housed with two lovely lady tortoises from Isabela, genetically his closest relatives. But sadly, George is apparently far too depressed to think about sex; the females just don't arouse his interest. Researchers are offering a US$10,000 reward to anyone who can supply a female Pinta tortoise, so keep an eye out. Unfortunately, the Pinta is not the only tortoise species in danger. Of the 14 species that originally inhabited the Galapagos Archipelago, five others are in danger and may soon join the three extinct species.

To catch a glimpse of Lonesome George, it is best to come early in the morning; as the day becomes hotter, he tends to retreat under the trees and out of visitors' sight.

TORTUGA BAY. Pristine white sand, a scenic, rocky background, and a foreground filled with giant cacti and yellow warblers make this perhaps the most beautiful beach in the Galapagos. This seaside eden gets its name from the large number of sea turtles that come here to lay their eggs. Sharks and marine iguanas also call Tortuga Bay home. Swim only in the designated swimming area in the cove about 50m to the right after initially hitting the beach from the 2.5 kilometer path—there can be unusually strong currents. As you lounge, keep your camera close by, as iguanas, pelicans, swallow-tailed gulls, and various species of crab are visible residents of Tortuga. *(Getting to the beach takes about 45min. Walk past the hospital on Herrera to Binford, turn left, and follow the dirt road out of town for 200m to a Galapagos National Park sign and an observation tower standing high on a sheer rock cliff. This is the beginning of a pleasant 2½km hike to the beach; check in with the guard—the passport numbers and names of all visitors must be recorded. Beach open 7am-6pm.)*

BOAT TOURS. Aqua Tours offers comprehensive tours of Academy Bay in its exclusive **glass-bottomed boat.** The boat sports four floor windows for sub-sea level observation. Some of the sights include the reef sharks at Shark Channel, the golden rays at Franklin Bay, and the sea lions at Isla Lobería. Short land excursions on Dog's Beach permit views of dog crabs. *(For more information, inquire about tours at Galapagos Discovery on Herrera or contact Aqua Tours directly by phone (☎ 526 234), or by the main dock next to Savavidas Restaurant.)*

🎵 NIGHTLIFE

As the hub of the Galapagos, Puerto Ayora offers the most lively late-night scene. Clubs and bars play everything from salsa to techno, dish up a variety of cocktails, and come furnished with pool tables. While there's usually a warm body in the house most evenings, things really get going on the weekends when locals join the tourists for wee-hour partying. Pilsner beer is sold everywhere (US$1-1.20).

La Panga, on Darwin and Berlanga. Sharks shoot pool, loungers sip *caipiriñas* (US$1.20), and jitterbugs grace the dance floor. No cover. Open daily 9pm-3am.

Discoteque Five Fingers, on Darwin across from the Port Captain on the 2nd floor, is adorned with comfy chill-out cubbies. Join that special someone (or recently met hostel pal) for a dance and watch the floor light up—literally. No cover. Open daily 8pm-3am.

Café Limón, on the corner of Darwin and 12 de Febrero, owner George attracts many passers-by, welcoming patrons in Spanish and English. Open daily 6pm-midnight.

Café Iguana, on Darwin and Floreana. Low-key atmosphere with wave-like walls and surfing videos. Try a creamy Blue-Footed Booby (no, not the bird). Open daily 8pm-midnight.

📌 DAYTRIPS FROM PUERTO AYORA

THE TORTOISE RESERVE. Chilling with the *tortugas* at the Darwin Station is fun, but it can't match the visceral satisfaction of meeting these guys on their own turf. Here, the reptiles are as wild as 250kg tortoises can get, which is evidenced by their trails—although slow, these reptiles are powerful green bulldozers, leaving behind flattened vegetation and collapsed fences in their path. A guide is now required to visit the reserve, and doling out the extra dollars for a knowledgeable one is highly recommended. These beasts are elusive and tortoise sightings cannot be guaranteed, but a good guide knows where to look. Hiking through the dense, low-growing vegetation can be challenging. Highland tortoises have large, dome-shaped shells that enable them to burrow through Santa Rosa's plant growth; for those without such natural advantages, wear sturdy shoes and long pants.

LOS GEMELOS. These "twins," on either side of the road to Baltra, just outside of Santa Rosa, are a pair of crater-shaped magma chambers. Each is approximately 30m deep, filled with lush vegetation (most of which is endemic scalesia forest), and truly monstrous. The area around Los Gemelos is home to Darwin's finches, the vermillion flycatcher, and the occasional short-eared owl. *(The National Park Administration has declared that Los Gemelos can be seen only with a guide. Inquire at the National Park Office (see p. 586) or at one of the travel agencies in town to arrange a tour.)*

LAVA TUNNELS. The island of Santa Cruz is riddled with **lava tubes** *(los túneles)*, the remains of ancient magma flows that helped to form the Galapagos. The outer crust of these molten streams hardened as they cooled, but the liquid magma within continued flowing. When the flow ceased, these enormous, hollow tubes were left behind. There are several tunnels around the island, but the most frequently visited is Bellavista's 800m **Tunnel of Endless Love,** named not for what could potentially go on in its dark chambers, but for the heart-shaped hole in the tunnel's roof. A rickety banister provides support, but visitors must tread carefully over the loose rocks on the descent. The sheer enormity of this tunnel and the strange, magma-carved designs on its inner surface serve as reminders of Ma Nature's creativity. The number of tubes and caves open to the public varies. Another set of lava pathways are **Furio's Tunnels,** off the road to Baltra between Bellavista and Santa Rosa. The tunnels are lit, but a flashlight may be useful. The tunnels are divided into different levels, connected by slime-coated ladders. Wear sturdy shoes and prepare to get dirty. The pretty but expensive **Restaurante de Furio** lies at the mouth of the tunnels (lunch US$14-18). *(The Bellavista tunnels are 7km outside Puerto Ayora—take the Baltra shuttle to Bellavista and ask for directions; or take a camioneta, which will get you directly there. US$4; flashlights US$0.50. Furio's tunnels can be reached by the Baltra shuttle. US$4. Contact Restaurante de Furio a day in advance; hotels and travel agencies in Puerto Ayora can radio them.)*

THE HIGHLANDS

The verdant interior of Santa Cruz offers a multitude of land excursions. Many of these places can be visited independently of tour groups or guides, though arranging trips through tour companies is, predictably, both more convenient and more expensive. The small towns of **Bellavista** (6km north of Puerto Ayora) and **Santa Rosa** (8km northwest of Bellavista) are ideal starting points for nearby hikes. Two popular peaks are **Media Luna,** a crescent-shaped volcanic cinder cone 5km from Bellavista, and **Cerro Crocker,** 3km beyond Media Luna. **El Mirador** is the lookout point near Santa Rosa that offers an impressive view of the southern coastal area. Luna, Crocker, and El Mirador are all reachable by camioneta (round-trip US$12).

Guided tours of the highlands usually include trips to **Los Gemelos,** the **Lava Tunnels** and the **Tortoise Reserve,** and can cost US$30 per person. Some agencies charge a flat rate for the car and guide, making it more affordable if you're part of a large group. Shop around and bargain; tour agencies are usually flexible, especially at the last minute before a tour. **Camionetas** (pickup trucks) are an alternative mode of transport to sites in the highlands and can be found anywhere in town, especially near the park and the CITTEG office. They are expensive but charge a flat rate for the truck—bigger groups might end up getting a good deal.

The most stylish way to see the highlands is atop your very own horse. **Amalca Horse Trekking** offers horse trips through a **finca** (highland farm; US$3). **Camping** is available at nearby **Butterfly Ranch.** Contact the Moonrise Travel Agency (see Travel Agencies, p. 584) in Puerto Ayora to arrange excursions. (Trips through a *finca* for 2 to 4 people US$15 per person; camioneta to the ranch US$6.)

To reach the highlands via bus, you'll need to purchase a ticket to the Baltra airport ferry from the CITTEG office in the center of town on Darwin. Passengers may get off the bus at any point on the route, so just let the driver know where you'd like to be let off (7:30 and 10:30am, US$1.50). Lower fares to Bellavista and Santa Rosa do not exist, so if your group is large, finding a camioneta might be cheaper. One shouldn't depend on taking this shuttle back to town, as it is often full with new arrivals and might not stop. Though *Let's Go* does not recommend hitchhiking, it's not unusual for trucks to stop and pick up passengers for a fee (approx. US$6). Head out early in order to catch a ride back into town before dark.

NORTHWESTERN SANTA CRUZ

The far northwest side of Santa Cruz boasts beautiful bays and beaches that can be reached by boat. Some daytrips to these areas leave from Puerto Ayora, but they are more often visited as part of larger, multi-day boat tours.

LAS BACHAS BEACH. Near the Baltra Airport, this beach makes for a refreshing swim. Bring bug repellent, though, to ward off stinging flies. Many visitors are happy lounging in the sand amid the outcroppings of lava rock. However you can try to catch a glimpse of a flamingo or two in the nearby saltwater lagoon. Other wading birds, such as black-necked stilts, can also be seen here. Marine iguanas and sally lightfoot crabs scamper along the beaches. On the way to the lagoon, visitors can see the remains of two barges, which were beached and abandoned by a sore US military when its attempt to occupy Baltra was cut short in the 1940s.

CONWAY BAY AND BALLENA BAY (WHALE BAY). On the island's west coast, both beaches remain untouristy, due to their lack of animal inhabitants. **Cerro Dragón,** on the northwest coast between Las Bachas and Conway Bay, is recently-opened and gets its name from the imposing hill that resembles a bumpy green dragon. Tour boats too large to visit tiny islands such as South Plaza often stop here. Its summit is a 2km hike up, and the more commonly used trail winds through scrubby vegetation and reveals dragons of another sort—monstrous, cactus-eating land iguanas. Visits to Cerro Dragón are often made as part of trips to Isla Rábida, an island to the northwest of Santa Cruz. The Delfin 2 daily tour boat goes to Bachas on F and Cerro Dragón on Th (approximately US$115). Contact Moonrise Travel Agency (see Travel Agencies, p. 584) to make arrangements.

THE CENTRAL ISLANDS

ISLAS PLAZAS

Of the tiny twin islands off the eastern coast of Santa Cruz, only **South Plaza** (a mere 1.3 sq. km) is open to visitors. **North Plaza** remains off limits due to scientific research (and the high rocky cliffs surrounding the island). The desert-like interior of South Plaza can be viewed from the rocky trail that winds its way around the sloping island. **Prickly pear cacti** are the dominate vegetation on this arid rock.

THE SEA LION COLONY. Travelers to South Plaza are greeted by barking female **sea lions** and their pups, basking in the sun and frolicking in the surf. The sea lion population on South Plaza, as on most beaches, is very territorial. During the **mating season,** which begins in May, the bulls join the females on the northern shore, each controlling a **harem** of females, patrolling and fighting with other males. After the tiring mating season, during which the bulls often do not even take time to eat, they retreat to the **bachelor colony** on the southwestern side of the island. The bachelor colony on South Plaza is one of the largest in the Galapagos.

> Sea-lion bulls, or *los machos*, bite several tourists each year, making them statistically more dangerous than sharks. Remember to keep your distance.

BIRDS AND IGUANAS. South Plaza is replete with birdlife. **Blue-footed** and **masked boobies, frigatebirds** and **lava gulls,** may be seen perched on the cliffs of the sea lion bachelor colony. Look for the **swallowtail gull,** with its striking white-and-gray body and red-ringed eyes. Gargantuan **prickly pear land iguanas** can be found lurking beneath the prickly pear cacti. The male iguanas and cactus fruit bear the same yellow hue, and share a scintillating tale of evolutionary intrigue. Long ago, the reptilian culprits devoured low-growing flowers. The only cacti able to reproduce were the taller, tree-like plants with large trunks that the chubby iguanas couldn't climb. Today, the sky-scraping prickly pears prevail, and the diminutive dragons must wait for their succulent treats to fall to the ground. Besides the land iguanas, South Plaza's physical layout makes it the best place in the Galapagos to see **hybrid iguanas**—the result of male marine iguanas (smaller with black skin) and female land iguanas overcoming their habitat differences and getting down and dirty. The geography of South Plaza leads itself to this phenomenon; the gradual, rocky coastline, with cacti very close to the shore, brings land iguanas near the water. When marine males decide to come onto shore, they use their comparatively large and strong tails to stand their own against land iguanas defending territory. Hybrid iguanas are difficult to find, so keep those eyes open.

ISLA SANTA FÉ

Isla Santa Fé keeps its treasures hidden; a walk along the beach here hardly assures sighting much animal life. Still, exploring the island is a great way to see the quieter, more elusive animals of the Galapagos. One of the best-concealed island creatures, the crested **land iguana** *(Conolophus pallidus)*, lives nowhere else in the world. Hide-and-seek champions with patience and time stand the best chance of spotting one of these devious creatures. The **prickly pear land iguanas** found on South Plaza also call Santa Fé home, but here they are a richer golden color here; they commonly measure 1m long, with some much larger.

To experience Santa Fé to its fullest, take one of the two easy **hiking trails.** There is a short 300m path and a longer 1½km trail that extends into the highland region. Both are somewhat rocky; the longer trail has a relatively steep uphill that might be difficult for inexperienced hikers but offers a better chance of seeing iguanas, and a breathtaking view of the island and shimmering ocean. The trail is also an excellent place to birdwatch and look for the **Galapagos snake** and **rice rat. Galapagos hawks,** finch species, and curious **Galapagos mockingbirds** frequent the area.

Santa Fé features a beautiful, sheltered **cove** in its northeast bay. While **snorkeling** bring a friend for safety. Sea lions often join snorkelers' fun or swim up close to anchored boats. Even if you don't get to snorkel with these friendly creatures, the flashy, fluorescent fish swimming around the bay provide excitement.

ISLA SEYMOUR NORTE

North Seymour Island, just north of Baltra, is a common tour boat stop that features not-so-common wildlife. This island is a must-see for any devoted ornithologist. The largest colony of **magnificent frigatebirds** in the Galapagos nests here, and Seymour is also one of the spots where both fabulous subspecies (the magnificent and the smaller **great frigatebird**) nest side-by-side. At first glance it's hard to tell these two birds apart, but there are a few simple distinctions. Magnificent female frigates have blue rings around their eyes, while great female frigates boast red ones. For the males, magnificent frigates have a purplish sheen in the feathers on their back, while great frigates have a greenish gloss. Also, magnificent frigates make only clicking, rattling, and grunting sounds, while great frigates' calls are more high-pitched. Some Seymour visits navigate through a **mangrove forest. Marine turtles, rays,** and **white-tipped sharks** swim near the surface. Come on a sunny day when the rays reflect off the fluorescent fish, and witness a dive bombing foray of **blue-footed boobies** as they pelt the water for these fishy snacks. Of all the islands, Seymour is one of the best for spotting *piqueros patas azules*. **Snorkeling** near Seymour Island is always a treat, with plentiful schools of brightly colored fish, the occasional stingray, and, of course, sea lions.

ISLOTE MOSQUERA

So small that it is often referred diminutively as "islet," Mosquera hides between Baltra and Seymour Norte. Its proximity to Baltra Airport, however, makes it a convenient first or last stop for tour boats. Reached via a wet landing, the island lacks hiking, swimming, or snorkeling, but is home to a large sea lion colony.

THE GALAPAGOS

ISLA SAN CRISTÓBAL

Isla San Cristóbal, despite its airport, closest location to the mainland, and position as the administrative capital of the islands, is perpetually a distant second to Santa Cruz for Galapagos tourism. Although many of its attractions are mediocre by Galapagos standards, it's one of the islands you can explore without being on a tour boat. Possibly the oldest of the islands, San Cristóbal was formed by the towering volcano Cerro San Joaquín (730m) and low-lying lava flows that fill out the southern regions of the island. The northern part of the island is dry and rather barren, but the lowlands are kept moist by humid southern winds. The island's first settlers founded the towns of Puerto Baquerizo Moreno and El Progreso to take advantage of the fertile soil and favorable climate. Today the island has a naval base and the Galapagos' first radio station. Puerto Baquerizo Moreno has plenty of comfortable places to stay. Interesting daytrips can be made by boat to **Isla Lobos, León Dormido, Punta Pitt** (the easternmost point in the Galapagos), and several other sites. Keep in mind, however, that these daily boat excursions will cost you a pretty penny if you're not part of a large group.

PUERTO BAQUERIZO MORENO ☎05

Puerto Baquerizo Moreno supports the seafaring interests of both surfers and fishermen. Arriving in droves between December and March when the swells are significant, ocean moguls make their way to the famous nearby surf spots of Carola, Canyon, Lobería and Tonga Reef. Despite the seasonal surfing craze, this port town exudes a more pronounced level of tranquility than its bustling inhabited neighbor, Puerto Ayora. The port's congestion with *pangas* and pelicans quickly reveal Baquerizo's status as a fisherman's town. Power is shut off at midnight.

▐◄ TRANSPORTATION

Flights: SAN/SAETA office (☎520 156), at the **airport** at the end of Alsacio Northia, doesn't currently fly in and out of San Cristóbal, but may in the future. **Ecuatoriana** may replace them and service regular flights. For flights within the Galapagos, **EMETEBE** (☎/fax 520 036; at the airport at the end of Alsacio Northia) flies to **Puerto Villamil** (35min., US$90) and **Baltra** (20min., US$90). Prices are negotiable and schedules change often. Open M-Sa 8am-1:30pm and 3-5:30pm.

Taxis: **Camionetas** line Darwin between the post office and Española, and go to the **airport, El Progreso,** and **Junco Lagoon** (round-trip US$8).

Inter-Island Transportation: Since **INGALA**'s (☎520 172) main boat sank, taking a *fibra* is the only option. Departure times and prices vary. Otherwise, fly (see above).

▐ PRACTICAL INFORMATION

Tourist Information: CETUR, on Darwin by the dock stationed across the street from Discoteca Blue Bay, is rarely open. For reliable service and good information, try **CAPTURGAL** (☎/fax 520 592) on Darwin between the bank and CETUR, next to Farmacia Jane. Open M-F 8am-5pm and Sa 9am-noon.

Bank: Banco del Pacífico (☎520 365; fax 520 368), on Darwin near José de Villamil, next to the ocean. Cirrus/MC **ATM**. Open M-F 8am-3:30pm, Sa 9am-12:30pm.

Laundry: There's a *lavandería* (☎520 333) on Alsacio Northia near the cathedral. US$2 per basket for wash and dry. Open daily 9am-9pm.

Police: Policía Nacional (24hr. emergency ☎520 101 or 520 129), Darwin and Española. In a blue and gray building.

Pharmacies: Farmacia San Cristóbal, Jose de Villamil, 1½ blocks from Banco del Pacífico. Open M-F 7:15am-1pm and 3-10pm; irregular weekend hours.

Hospital: Hospital Oskar Jandl (☎ 520 118), Quito and Alsacio Northia, near the Cathedral and museum.

Post Office: (☎/fax 520 373), at the end of Darwin just past the municipal building, provides fax service. Open M-F 8am-noon and 2-5:30pm, Sa 8am-2pm.

Telephone: Central Telefónica San Cristóbal (PacificTel; ☎/fax 520 104), Quito, 4 blocks past Darwin. Look for the mural of boobies and girl-with-cell-phone. No charge for collect and calling card calls, but connection may be cut off. Open daily 8am-10pm.

ACCOMMODATIONS

Although foreign tourists rarely take advantage of them, Puerto Baquerizo's hotels offer a decent alternative to cramped ship's quarters. Camping is permitted, but only at the beaches at the Galapaguera; check with the **National Park Information Site,** just out of town on Alsacio Northia toward the Cabañas de Don Jorge.

Hotel Chatham (☎/fax 520 137), on Alsacio Nortia at the edge of town heading to the airport, has spacious rooms, hot water, and a courtyard. Enjoy cheap meals (*desayuno* US$1; *merienda* US$2) and make free collect and calling card calls from the office. Special monthly rates. Singles US$7; doubles US$10; triples US$15; TV US$1 extra.

Cabañas de Don Jorge (☎/fax 520 208; email cterena@ga.pro.ec), on Alsacio Northia on the east side of town; follow Alsacio Northia as it veers to the left out of town. These ecologically-inspired cabins are popular with Isabela's surfers (Dec.-Feb.), but also provide excellent accommodations for families or long-term visitors. Private bathrooms have hot water. Breakfast US$2. Lunch US$4. Singles US$12; US$120 per month.

Hotel Mar Azul (☎/fax 520 384), on Alsacio Northia past Hotel Chatham when coming from the airport. Rooms have ceiling fans and common baths have hot water. Singles US$4; doubles US$6.

Residencial San Francisco (☎ 520 304), on Darwin just across from Banco del Pacífico, is one of the cheapest places in town. Cluttered indoor courtyard. Rooms have private baths, fans, and TVs. Rooms US$2 per person.

FOOD

Cheap *almuerzos* are available on almost every block, juicy morsels abound in the many fresh fruit stands scattered across town, and bread-lovers can start their day with cheap, delicious goodies from a *panadería*. For more formal dining options, go down Villamil from Darwin; you'll find a string of bar *cevicherías* (ceviche US$2.80) and Cabaña El Grande, which serves a large fruit salad (US$1) and a good *desayuno* with a *batido* of choice included (US$1.20). Try house salad (US$1) and veggie dishes on request (US$1-2) at family-owned **Casablanca Snack Bar,** the big white building with the table umbrellas across from *Muelle turístico* on Darwin. (☎ 520 392. Open daily 8am-10pm.) Two blocks up Vallejo, off Alsacio Northia, charming **Soda Bar Nathaly's** hamburgers (US$0.80; with egg and cheese US$1.20) are the biggest attraction. (☎ 520 018. *Batido* US$0.60. Open daily 8am-11pm.) There are tons of a la carte *comida típica* options, but, as usual, the cheapest meals are the set *desayuno*, *almuerzo*, and *merienda* (US$2) at **Restaurante Rosita,** Villamil and Ignacio de Hernandez. (☎ 520 106. Open M-Sa 8am-10pm.)

SIGHTS AND ENTERTAINMENT

INTERPRETATION CENTER. This impressive, relatively new complex is one of San Cristóbal's biggest attractions, by far surpassing the educational offerings in Puerto Ayora. The architecture and environment of the center are treats in themselves: wooden walkways wind through modern buildings amid lush plant life and ocean views. The center's informative exhibits trace the geological and human history of the islands and combine an appreciation for human life in the archipelago with a concern for the islands' conservation. Stories of the Galapagos' past inhabitants are fascinating. *(Down Alsacio Northia past the Cabañas de Don Jorge. ☎ 520 358. Open M-F 7am-noon and 1-4pm, Sa-Su 8am-noon and 1-5pm.)*

MUSEUM OF NATURAL HISTORY. Enter this small museum to find a huge whale jawbone, model reconstructions of Galapagos birdlife, and bottled sea life floating in formaldehyde (the morbidly scientific exhibit). There is a poster on "hot spots" and tectonic plates, and Pepe, an 88-year-old tortoise out back. *(On Alsacio Northia next to the cathedral. Open M-F 8:30-11:30am and 3:30-5:30pm, Sa 8:30am-noon. US$1.)*

LAS TIJERETAS. For an incredible view of the surrounding scenery, hike up the high hill where both the magnificent and great frigatebirds nest. The red roofs of Puerto Baquerizo Moreno stretch out to one side, and the bright white sand and lava rock beaches line the other. There is also a good view of León Dormido in the distance. *(Start at the Cabañas de Don Jorge and continue along the same dirt road for 5-7min. Two trails lead from an opening in a stone wall on the right-hand side at the end of the road, both of which lead to the summit. The first one goes through the woods before the foot of the hill; the second heads through woods and then along a beach. Wear hiking boots. 30min. to the top.)*

OTHER SIGHTS. The rocky and un-touristy beach of **La Lobería** offers tranquility, the sound of waves, and sea lions. *(Take Alsacio Northia out of town toward the airport. Turn left at the airport and then stay to the right at any forks in the road. 30min. walk. Taxis (10min., US$1.60).)* Head to El Progreso to see **La Casa del Ceibo,** a large bamboo cabin built 12m off the ground in a gigantic 200 year-old *ceibo* tree. Visitors enter via a rickety suspension bridge made of vine-covered bamboo. The two-story house is completely furnished with two bed mats, a hot-water bathroom, a fridge, and a soda-and-beer bar. *(☎ 520 248. (The house is on the way to El Progreso and is best reached by camioneta (round-trip US$2). Rooms US$1 per night. Tour US$1.)*

NIGHTLIFE. The club scene in town is rather dull, but there are still a few party places. *Discotecas* **Blue Bay** and **Neptunus** are across the street from the *muelle turístico* on Darwin, serve Pilsner (US$2), and play latin and other dance tunes. (Both open Th-Sa 8pm-3am.) Though located in distant El Progreso, **Quita d'Cristhi** is a very popular weekend destination. Take a camioneta there (US$1 one-way).

▓ DAYTRIPS FROM PUERTO BAQUERIZO MORENO

EL JUNCO LAGOON. Earth, wind, fire, and water came together millions of years ago to form Junco Lagoon, the largest freshwater lagoon in the Galapagos. A road winds up the verdant sides of an extinct volcano, until, at the summit, it reaches a beautiful mist-enshrouded lagoon formed by hundreds of years of rainwater collecting in the *caldera*. If at first the fog is too heavy, never fear—a wispy zephyrs will soon come along, lift the haze and reveal the erstwhile hidden lagoon. Frigatebirds use the lake as a bathtub, gliding through the mist and cleaning themselves in the fresh water. A narrow trail winds its way around the rim, past numerous birds, and overlooks nearly all of San Cristóbal. A small portion of the coastline is obstructed, however, by the looming **Cerro San Joaquín** (at over 700m, the highest mountain on San Cristóbal). Visitors do *not* need to be part of a tour group to visit the highlands, though tours can be arranged in town (ask at Restaurant Rosita or CAPTURGAL). *(The highlands can be reached by foot or by hiring a truck in town (no more than US$8 round-trip). To reach the lagoon by foot, head out of town on Quito or 12 de Febrero and follow signs to the town of El Progreso. From here, it is 10km farther to El Junco. Follow the highway until you can make a right onto an uphill dirt road.)*

GUIDED TOURS ON ISLA SAN CRISTÓBAL. All of the following sights can only be visited with a guide; for those not already part of a larger tour, contact CAPTURGAL (see p. 592) or Restaurant Rosita (see p. 593) in Puerto Baquerizo Moreno for daytrip information. With a group of 6-10 people, expect to pay up a total of US$500 for a daily tour (divided by the number of people in your group). A multi-day tour booked in Puerto Ayora may make more sense and cost less.

Isla Lobos is about one hour northeast of Puerto Baquerizo Moreno. Separated from San Cristóbal's shore by a small channel, the tiny, rocky island has a white sand beach where blue-footed boobies nest and sea lions sunbathe. **León Dormido,** another hour northeast of Lobos, gets its name from its resemblance to a sleeping lion. **Scuba diving** and **snorkeling** here are prime—beware the Galapagos sharks that live in the waters offshore, and watch out for dangerous currents. To the north, **Cerro Brujo** is a beautiful beach made from finely ground white coral.

The easternmost point in the archipelago, **Punta Pitt,** is home to red-footed, blue-footed, and masked boobies. Beyond the landing, a trail leads up the mountain, through booby territory and providing lofty views of the rocky shore below (20min. each way). **La Galapaguera,** where giant land tortoises roam free, is just down the shore from Punta Pitt (2hr. each way).

THE WESTERN ISLANDS

When the *Beagle*, carrying Charles Darwin on his fateful journey, crossed the Bolívar Channel between Isla Isabela and Isla Fernandina, Darwin marveled at what he called the "immense deluges of black, naked lava, which have flowed either over the rims of the great caldrons, like pitch over the rim of a pot in which it has been boiled, or have burst forth from smaller orifices on the flanks." This channel remains an exciting place—boats often visit the volcanically active Western Islands often see dolphins and whales surface from this region's deep waters.

The Western Islands of Isabela and Fernandina are usually only visited by large or fast boats, or those on extended tours, as the sights are far away from each other and from the rest of the archipelago. However, these more remote islands have a remarkable display of natural wildlife and serene beauty.

ISLA ISABELA

Much of Isabela's attraction derives from its powerful geology; the island (shaped like a sea horse), comprising over 58% of the archipelago's land mass, resulted from the fusion of six volcanos by lava flows. Eruptions have occurred on Volcán Wolf, Sierra Negra, and Volcán Alcedo in recent decades, and in September of 1998, **Cerro Azul** erupted with a blaze of red-orange magma and fire. The series of giant volcanos looms grandly between the ocean and sky. Besides the hard-to-reach western coast, once can explore much from the southern **Puerto Villamil.**

PUERTO VILLAMIL

In Puerto Villamil (pop. 1500), which is relatively free of commercialization, there is no tourist office, no supermarket, and, in lieu of a newspaper, people make announcements from a loudspeaker in the center of town. Prickly pears serve as fence posts, and only the moon and stars light the town after midnight. Outsiders are an uncommon sight in this distant town, so be prepared to receive many a curious look as you stroll along the sandy avenues. The people are friendly; don't be surprised if an islander invites you in for a chat, as everyone here has a story.

▆▉ TRANSPORTATION AND PRACTICAL INFORMATION. The **airport/land-ing strip** is 3km out of town, and while hitchhiking is not recommended by *Let's Go*, trucks can take you into town if you're not up for the leisurely walk (US$1.20). Captain Juan Mendoza takes passengers by his **boat,** the *Estrella Del Mar,* to Puerto Ayora (Tu 7:30am, US$15). Buy tickets at the **municipal offices** across the street from the health center on Mondays before 1pm. **Fletas,** chartered motorboat rides, are also available from the port. The **Capitania** (☎529 113), in the center of town by the *muelle embarcadero* and across from EMETEBE, knows when boats leave. The **EMETEBE** office, on the corner of Las Fragatas and Conocarpu, across the street from the Capitanía, arranges flights to **Baltra** (20min.; Tu, Th, and Sa; US$80) and **Puerto Baquerizo Moreno** (35min.; M, W, F; US$90), but schedules vary.

If the phones aren't working, the office can contact TAME or SAN via radio. (☎529 155. Open M-F 7am-noon and 2-6pm, Sa 7am-3pm.) Hotel proprietors, especially Dora at the **Hotel Ballena Azul,** can help with questions. In an **emergency** call ☎101. The **police** are also across the street from EMETEBE. There is a **health center** on 16 de Marzo and Antonio Gil, a block from the police station. (Emergency ☎529 181. Open M-F 8am-noon and 2-6pm.) Make calls from the **PACIFICTEL** office, on Las Escalecias, three blocks away from the beach.

⌔ ACCOMMODATIONS. Lodging in Puerto Villamil verges on excellent. **Hotel Ballena Azul** and the adjacent **Cabañas Isabela del Mar,** on Conocarpus at the edge of town, are easily two of the best places to stay in the Galapagos. The large, rustic rooms have hot water and ocean views. Dora, the Swiss mistress of the house, loves to sit down and chat—in English, Spanish, French, or German. (☎/fax 529 125 for both; email isabela@ga.pro.ec; www.pub.ecua.net.ec/isabela. Laundry approx. US$0.25 per piece. Ballenza Azul rooms US$2, with bath US$10. Cabañas doubles and triples US$10 per person.) The nearby **La Casa de Marita Bed and Breakfast** is visible from afar with its towering yellow and red building. This familiar *casa* offers kitchen facilities and ocean views, while outside lie hammock-laden sandy terraces. Backpackers are usually given a break with lower-than-normal rates; ask. (Singles US$10; doubles US$20-30; triples US$25-35; quads US$40-50.) **Hotel San Vicente,** Cormorantes and Pinzón Artesano, has basic, clean rooms with baths. (☎529 140 or 529 180. Singles US$3; doubles US$6. Free **camping.**)

⌕ FOOD. The restaurant at the **Hotel Ballena Azul** serves up high quality local and international meals. The menu includes a breakfast of fresh fruit, bread, eggs, homemade jam, and coffee (US$1); lunch and dinner offerings include rice, meat, salad, and vegetables (US$2). Ballena Azul prefers advance notice if you plan to have lunch or dinner. **La Casa de Marita B&B** offers delectable international cuisine and vegetarian options (meals up to US$4). If you just want some good ol' roadside *comida típica*, head to one of the restaurants near the Municipio. **Ruta, Costa Azul,** and **Rosita** all serve *desayuno, almuerzo,* and *merienda* (US$1.20 each).

⌖ DAYTRIPS FROM PUERTO VILLAMIL

VOLCÁN SIERRA NEGRA. After an hour of bruising your fanny on the back of a horse, the mist parts, your jaw drops, and you tell your bum that it was worth it. The dark, ominous *caldera* extends in all directions, refusing to be framed by even the widest angle lens. Volcán Sierra Negra is the oldest and largest of Isabela's six volcanoes; with a diameter of 10km, it is the **second-largest volcanic crater in the world.** Adventurous travelers may follow a trail westward along the crater rim to the **sulfur mines.** Just inside the crater, three levels of sulfur formations bubble and steam. The trip to the sulfur mines is longer and more difficult than the daytrip to Sierra Negra, and those who are planning on doing both might consider **camping** at the crater rim, which will allow time to see everything. Before camping, talk to the park officials in Puerto Villamil (☎529 178), on Antonio Gil. Fires are not permitted and trash must be carried out. Tents can be rented from Hotel Ballena Azul; bring long pants, long sleeves, and a rain coat. It's not safe to visit the volcano without a guide; however, the people who rent the horses to visitors will send someone who knows where he's going along with the group. Many tours stop at **Volcán Chico.** After walking across the Mars-like landscape, winded trekkers come upon steaming *fumeroles* and an amazing view of Fernandina in the distance. *(Daytrips are arranged through Hotel Ballena Azul and usually include a visit to neighboring Volcán Chico (camioneta, horse, guide US$35 per trip). This trip is more affordable in large groups.)*

LA GRIETA DE LOS TIBURONES. After a short walk, the rocky black lava trail approaches a large channel beside a lagoon. Small fish swim around the channel entrance, but farther up lurk **white-tipped reef sharks.** Far from aggressive, these docile creatures glide in and out of the channel in groups. **Sea turtles** and **spotted**

eagle rays occasionally appear. The trail continues to a small beach area where **sea lions** often rest in the shade of the mangroves just up from the water. **Penguins** also reside in this area. *(You might be able to find a panga willing to take you, but chances are it will be difficult, so it's better to arrange it through Hotel Ballena Azul (10min.). A group tour should cost approximately US$20. Includes 2hr. stay and boat ride back to town.)*

THE BREEDING CENTER FOR GIANT TORTOISES. Run in conjunction with the National Park Service, the center provides up-close looks at thousands of Galapagos tortoises in every size from small to extra-extra-large. The center focuses on rearing two breeds of Isabelan tortoise. While navigating this labyrinth of controlled tortoise proliferation, be mindful of the unusual number of **wasps** buzzing around. *(Follow Antonio Gil past the health center to the edge of town, where a sign points to the station, 1km away. National Park Office ☎ 529 178. Open daily 7am-6pm.)*

EL MURO DE LAS LÁGRIMAS (THE WALL OF TEARS). This wall, in accordance with its name, commemorates Isabela's past as a penal colony. In June 1946, then-President José María Velasco Ibarra decided to move 300 prisoners and 30 guards from Guayaquil to the base of a hill called La Orchilla, 5km outside of Puerto Villamil. With no other means of employing the prisoners, the penal colony's chief decided to construct a jail with the only substance available—lava rocks, piled on top of each other without cement. The extreme variety in the shapes of the rocks prevented efficient stacking, so the result was a tall pile 9m high with sloping sides. The grueling hours in the sun and back-breaking labor broke many men's spirits, stealing away their wills to live. Over time, it came to be known as the place "where the cowards died and the brave wept." Construction of this "wall of tears" ceased when the sadistic chief was transferred away and the colony moved to the highland agricultural area. The colony was abolished in 1959 after a major rebellion in which prisoners seized the camps and fled to the continent in a stolen yacht. *(To get to the Wall of Tears, follow Antonio Gil past the health center to the outskirts of town. At the huge pink house, the same location of the sign pointing toward the Breeding Center, continue straight along the sandy path. Pass all beaches and lagoons until you hit the open field with the wall. 2-3hr. walk.)*

TAGUS COVE AND PUNTA TORTUGA

Tagus Cove is the most frequently visited attraction on Isabela, and, incidentally, it gives a taste of much of what Isabela has to offer. A beautiful *panga* ride takes visitors here from their tour boat, and cruises along Isabela's cliffs past **penguins, iguanas, pelicans,** and the rare flightless cormorant. Up a series of wooden steps begins the upward path that eventually overlooks **Darwin Lake,** a body of water with a higher salt content and water level than the sea. The view just keeps getting better as the trail continues. At its summit, if visibility is good, one can see Volcán Darwin and Volcán Wolf to the north (both of which lie on the equator), and Sierra Negra to the south. Isla Fernandina also looms in the distance. Near Tagus Cove, the rarely visited **Punta Tortuga** boasts the only habitat in the world that supports the **tool-using carpenter finch.** Endemic to Isabela and Fernandina, these talented birds explore tree bark using sticks or cactus spines held in their beaks. When they find a particularly good tool, they stash it away for later use; the birds are nearly impossible to spot using their tool-wielding tactics.

URBINA BAY

Urbina Bay's attractions are big and tough. The bay is home to some gigantic wildlife—monstrous land iguanas frequent this area, as do those slow-but-steady *tortugas*. The tortoises come down from nearby **Volcán Alcedo** in the rainy season to lay their eggs, so they normally can't be seen here once the dry season hits. Urbina Bay also has some big coral formations that arose from the sea when it was uplifted by tectonic shifting in 1954, a phenomenon locally known as the *levantamiento*. Until that year, this entire area had been underwater. The trail consists of an initial wet landing onto a black beach and a short hike to a second beach, which was the shore of the island before the uplift.

THE GALAPAGOS

ELIZABETH BAY

On the western side of Isabela is Elizabeth Bay, a marine neighborhood rife with aquatic and land-based activity. There are no landing sites, so get out those binoculars and hope for a clear day. To the north of the bay lie the **Mariela Rocks**—a landscape of rugged cliffs and gnarled Palo Santo trees. Some tours offer **snorkeling** around these rocky isles, and oversized **starfish** and fishing **penguins** are the reward for plunging into the remarkably cold water caused by the Cromwell current. Boats continue past the Marielas into an aquatic **mangrove forest,** which creates a maze of watery channels that wander lazily among the lush green leaves and red roots of the mangroves. The dense mangroves serve as breeding grounds for **green sea turtles** as well as **rays** and **white-tip reef sharks** that often make rounds in search of a quick meal; the bay is also a favorite spot for the **flightless cormorant.**

PUNTA MORENO

Punta Moreno can be one of the most memorable stops on an entire tour. The juxtaposed craggy lava rocks and small, idyllic lagoons scattered across the landscape are home to a variety of birds, including **blue herons** and **flamingoes**. If you visit around mating season, the flamingoes' coloration is particularly vivid, with some birds sporting uncharacteristically dark red feathers. The colors that greet visitors' eyes are practically unreal—the black lava field is dotted with holes of blue water, each surrounded by a ring of green vegetation and speckled with pink flamingoes. Near Punta Moreno, some groups visit a series of coastal pools, one of which is known as **Derek's Cove.** While it is illegal to go ashore, these pools are an excellent place to observe **sea lions** and **sea turtles** from a boat (though the extra trip might not be worth it, as they are fairly common throughout the Galapagos).

ISLA FERNANDINA

An island of superlatives, Fernandina is the newest island in the archipelago, the westernmost link in the Galapagos chain, and the most volcanically active. The last eruption, in January 1995, was of **Volcán La Cumbre,** a smaller volcano on the island's southwest corner. One of the parasitic cones—the smaller volcanoes which sprout from the sides of larger volcanoes—could erupt again anytime. Perhaps most notable is Fernandina's lack of introduced plants and animals, a distinction that prompts many to award it the most impressive superlative of all: "the most pristine island in the world."

PUNTA ESPINOSA

Fernandina has only one visitor sight, **Punta Espinosa.** A geological baby formed by tectonic uplift in 1975, it is reached by a wet or dry landing, depending on the tide level. **Penguins** and other friendly wildlife are often spotted sunning themselves near the landing spot. The area also boasts the **largest colony of lava cacti** in the Galapagos.

Several different visitor paths jut out from the national park monument near the landing, none of which are particularly long. To the left, a path winds its way over and near dry fields of *pahoehoe* and *aa* lava, which take their names from similar flows in the Hawaiian islands. On the path to the right of the monument, hoards of large **marine iguanas** are often seen basking in the sun. These anomalous reptiles are much larger than their brethren on other islands. The iguana nests lie on either side of a very narrow sandy path, where **blue herons, Galapagos hawks,** and other predatory birds look to make a quick meal of their hatchlings. Be careful where you step; any visitor that strays from this path can kill the iguanas before the birds even get a chance. Nesting sites are quite fragile; the weight of a human being could easily crush an entire nest. This path also leads to the best place on the island for viewing the rare **flightless cormorant.** The cold Cromwell current that brings nutrient-filled waters into this part of the archipelago makes the ocean here particularly rich with fish; **snorkeling** around Fernandina is superb. Numerous **sea turtles** gracefully glide about the underwater volcanic rock formations, and the small **horn shark** can also be seen here.

ISLA SANTIAGO

Santiago's history has been less than serene. Human commercialism and a great deal of volcanic action have disrupted the island time and again, making it one of the most interesting, and thus frequently visited, spots in the Galapagos. Santiago's volcanic cones, beachfront lava spires, gentle *pahoehoe* lava flows, and black sand beaches are reminders of the island's explosive past. The first humans to inhabit the island were 16th-century pirates hiding out in the sheltered coves. It wasn't until the 1880s, when four rather amorous goats were abandoned on the island, that irreparable damage was done. Their population ballooned to over 100,000, and the gluttons ate everything in sight. Since then, environmentalists with voracious appetites for conservation have managed to keep the population in check. The island was further sullied in the 1920s and 1960s by two commercial salt mines that unsuccessfully attempted to profit from the island's salt-lined crater. Despite its turbulent past, there is much to see and do on Santiago. Its central location makes it easily accessible, so most Galapagos boat-trippers will get a taste of all Santiago has to offer.

PUERTO EGAS

Puerto Egas, located on Santiago's western shore, packs a lot into one fun-filled visitor site. A black beach, the remnants of the area's human history, amazing geology, and unique wildlife all cluster in Santiago's **James Bay.** The brown, layered tuff stone and black basalt volcanic rock that make up most of the landscape form a masterpiece of apertures, crevices, and natural bridges.

The visitor's trail first leads along the coastline to one of the best tide pool areas in the Galapagos. The black lava towers, basins, and craters are filled with crystal-clear sea water. As with all tide pools, the marine treasures of Puerto Egas' are only visible when the tide is out. Sea birds, such as **great blue herons, lava herons, ruddy turnstones, oyster catchers,** and **terns,** often gorge enthusiastically on the tasty shellfish, crustaceans, and small fish that reside in these easy-access tide pools. The lava rock along the tidal area is very slippery—be careful when walking.

Past the tide pools, water laps in and out of the **grottoes,** what many find as the highlight of the island. These deep pools, which all belong to a connected system of collapsed lava tubes, are constantly filled and refilled by the open sea. One pool, appropriately dubbed **Darwin's Toilet,** fills with a particularly noisy flushing force. The grottoes are an especially good spot to find the **Galapagos fur seals.** Once hunted to the brink of extinction for their thick, insulating fur, these diminutive sea lions have made a comeback. They reside in large numbers but are much more timid than their sea lion cousins. They are also excellent climbers, and use the shady ledges of the grottoes to keep the sun off their extra-thick fur. The impact of human activity on Santiago is quite apparent in both the historical and current uses of Puerto Egas. The remains of buildings and equipment from salt mine companies stand abandoned on the shore among the lava rock and vegetation.

PLAYA ESPUMILLA

Espumilla Beach, reached via a wet landing at the north end of James Bay, was a good spot to see flamingoes until the 1982-83 El Niño and a change in weather patterns. Since that time, flamingoes can no longer be found in the saltwater lagoon behind the beach, but the 2km inland trail is still a good place to observe other bird species; watch for **Darwin finches, Galapagos Hawks,** and **vermillion flycatchers.** The long, sandy beach is also a great swimming spot, but be careful where you step; sea turtles often lay their eggs here.

SULLIVAN BAY

The beach of **Sullivan Bay** is quite unlike the sandy areas lining many Galapagos shores. Instead, the shore of eastern Santiago is made up of a fresh (100-year-old) *pahoehoe* lava flow, producing solid black fields of rock. Pockets of gases trapped beneath the surface of the lava, known as *hornitos* (little ovens) have erupted as "mini volcanoes," producing the wrinkles that break up the smooth, black span. Also notice the *kipukas*, tuff cones that were once their own autonomous rocky isles before the sudden attack of Santiago's quick-flowing lava. A trail loops around the bay and takes about 1½ hours to hike.

BUCCANEER COVE

An impressive reminder of the renegade pirates that used to dwell here, Buccaneer Cove is located at the northwest end of Isla Santiago. Pirates frequented this cove in the 1600s and early 1700s, later followed by visiting whalers. Fresh water was often available in depressions in the lava rock, and the cove was also a convenient place to maintain boats. Although today tour boats don't land in the cove, many take the time to pass by slowly, letting passengers enjoy the area's towering cliff walls and impressive rock formations. The shoreline is now populated by feral goats that do as much damage to the landscape as the pirates did on the high seas. Its rock formations are remarkable—sailors watched the passing pinnacles and outcroppings with the same imagination people use when looking at clouds.

ISLA BARTOLOMÉ

Although only 1.2 sq. km in size, Isla Bartolomé's striking geology makes it one of the most visually stunning to visit—deep reds, blues, and shimmering blacks mingle and shift, creating a kaleidoscopic landscape. Dominated by an ancient volcano of stark and imposing beauty, this barren island consists of ash and porous lava rock on which colonizing plants are just beginning to grow. The *isla* boasts two visitor sites: the **summit** of the volcanic cone and the **twin crescent beaches,** location of the famous Pinnacle Rock, and home to the only colony of Galapagos penguins this side of Isabela.

THE SUMMIT

The trail to Bartolomé's summit begins as a dry landing at a set of stairs that sea lions often claim for their own. Farther along the trail, lava lizards dart back and forth, rarely stopping long enough to allow spectators to get a good look. The main part of the trail is a wooden staircase (over 370 stairs) built by the national park to limit the island's erosion. Although the climb can be tiring, the view from the top on a clear day enables climbers to grasp the immensity and uniqueness of the archipelago. A 180-degree turn while standing on this same peak will reveal why Bartolomé itself is often compared to the surface of the moon—unearthly craters coated with black ash surround the volcano. Nearby, the various colors of the **lava cactus's** banana-shaped stalks show the relative ages of the different parts of the plant—the oldest are gray, the younger green, and the youngest bright yellow. **Tiquilia** is another plant that has adapted to Bartolomé's severely arid climate.

THE TWIN BEACHES

Double your pleasure with Bartolomé's twin shores, on either side of the island. Many groups visit only the North Beach, where **swimming** is permitted, as powerful tides and currents, wandering sharks, and stingrays make the South Beach daunting for swimming but top-notch for nature-watching. Look for **nesting sea turtles** from late December to early March and **great blue herons** year-round. **Pinnacle Rock,** the most photographed Galapagos land formation, points majestically to the sky. This "rock" is made up of tightly packed sand shaped by the wind and sea. As with everything in the Galapagos, Pinnacle Rock is still changing; the Swiss-cheese holes caused by the wear-and-tear of the elements will eventually send the rock crumbling into the sea. Before it tumbles, take a moment while swimming to stop beneath the rock and stare at its immensity from below. **Snorkeling** is gorgeous at Bartolomé; brightly-colored tropical fish and the occasional white-tipped shark can be seen wandering among the submerged rock formations here. The oceanside base is also a popular place to try to spot the **Galapagos penguin.**

ISLA RÁBIDA

Though Isla Rábida, just south of Santiago, is certainly not conspicuous in size, its striking color, central location, and wide variety of wildlife keep it from being easily forgotten. After a wet landing, the northern beach glows a deep maroon color, and visitors usually encounter sea lions and marine iguanas resting on or close to shore. The salt bush area behind the beach is a nesting site for the brown pelican, one of the largest birds in the Galapagos. Behind this vegetation lies a small lagoon occasionally inhabited by **Galapagos flamingoes.** A visit to Rábida is not complete without a glimpse of the unique landscape from above. A short trail from the beach leads to a viewpoint overlooking the ocean, lagoon, and striking scarlet cliffs. This portion of the island is a great place to watch **blue-footed boobies.** Also, **snorkeling** off Rábida's beach is an enjoyable excursion—the water is clear, the fish are exceptional, and elusive **sharks** and **manta rays** are occasionally seen.

ISLA SOMBRERO CHINO

Isla Sombrero Chino, a tiny island off the southeastern coast of Santiago, is so named because of its uncanny resemblance to a Chinese hat. Though it is not visited as frequently as many of the other central islands and is not a daytrip destination, Sombrero Chino's proximity to various islands makes it possible for even those visitors who do not stop there to appreciate its unique landscape from a distance. Sombrero Chino's wet landing site is a beautiful, white beach where sea lions greet visitors. Because of the fragility of the lava rock that makes up most of the island, the visitor's trail does not go to the summit of the volcanic core; it does, however, head up a short distance to a point where visitors can "ooh" and "aah" at the waves. **Snorkeling** between Chino and Santiago provides ample opportunity to see **penguins** and **white-tipped reef sharks.**

THE SOUTHERN ISLANDS

Española and Floreana, the southernmost of the archipelago, have several visitor sites each, providing full days of boat-tripping fun. Getting to the islands isn't difficult—many tour companies offer tours that take visitors south to see both islands.

ISLA FLOREANA (CHARLES)

Although Galapagos visitors today may distinguish the islands from one another mainly by their animals and landscapes, the various legends that have arisen since the discovery of the archipelago give many of them a unique personality beyond the usual lava formations and divebombing boobies. Isla Floreana, the first inhabited island, does not allow its history to be easily forgotten. The remains of a Norwegian fish cannery at Post Office Bay and the well-known and sordid saga of the island's German colonists (see Sex, Lies, and Dentures, p. 602) loom over the island to this day.

PUERTO VELASCO IBARRA

With about as many people as a mid-sized hotel, the town of Puerto Velasco Ibarra (pop. 70) is quiet and unassuming, even with the occasional influx of tourist ships. Those choosing to disembark for a night won't find endless choices of where to eat and sleep, but they certainly won't be left hungry and homeless. The small **Pensión Wittmer** (☎ 520 150, in Guayaquil (04) 294 506) is the only place to stay on Floreana. Rooms with private baths, hot water, and an ocean view are priced far below their more popular competitors on other islands (rooms US$1.60). You don't have to go far to eat—the owners also serve breakfast (US$0.60), lunch, and dinner (US$0.80). Four Wittmer generations, one of the original German families to inhabit Floreana, reside under this friendly hotel's roof. Pensión Wittmer also sells autographed copies of original inhabitant Margret's book, *Floreana,* and stamps letters for the post office barrel.

Just outside of Puerto Velasco Ibarra is the **Asilo de Paz,** the site of the island's original settlement town. A number of mysterious, hand-carved "caves" were hewn out of this mountainside by the German settlers when they arrived, but exactly what they intended them for is uncertain. Perhaps they were primitive dwellings meant to heighten the idealistic colonists' communion with Nature. Or, perhaps, they were the product of the settlers having too much time and a whole lot of mountain on their hands.

POST OFFICE BAY

In 1793, a British whaling captain erected a post office barrel on the quiet bay of the uninhabited island, later named Floreana. For years, its barrel was the only postal facility for hundreds of miles. Whaling ships from around the world left their letters in the barrel and picked up those that they could deliver in their travels. Although the first post-barrel is now long gone, the tradition is kept up by the island's many visitors each year, who arrive via a wet landing at a brown beach on Floreana's northern shore. Today's barrel is quite different from the original one: no longer content to leave letters, numerous visitors have added signs, pictures, and other wooden messages to this growing piece of public art. Drop off a postcard, letter or hastily written note and see if any are addressed to an area near you. When you get home, deliver them personally if you can.

PUNTA CORMORANT

While many people come to Floreana for its history, Punta Cormorant gives other reasons: its glistening green stones, red mangroves, gray hillsides, pink flamingoes, white sand, and blue water. Visitors arrive here via a wet landing at the northern end of the island, on a beach littered with thousands of small, green beads. This unique crystal, known as **olivine,** was formed centuries ago as a volcanic by-product. The olivine gives the sand a greenish tinge; scoop up a handful and you'll easily see the smooth, green crystals. A short walk inland leads to **one of the largest flamingo lagoons** in the Galapagos. The rare *Leococarpus Pimatifícles*, or **Cutleaf Daisy,** can be seen here as well. This unusual flower grows **nowhere else in the world.**

Another site at Punta Cormorant, **Flour Beach,** gets its name from its strikingly soft white sand. Shadowy gray **ghost crabs,** bright red **sally lightfoot crabs,** and green **sea turtles** frequent this beach. Because of the **sometimes-dangerous stingrays** that live in the shallow waters offshore, Flour Beach is not a swimming or snorkeling spot, but Floreana's **Devil's Crown** more than fulfills these needs.

SEX, LIES, AND DENTURES
On September 19, 1929, a ship arrived on Isla Floreana with two people and a whole lot of boxes—the island hasn't been the same since. **Friedrich Ritter,** a German doctor and devoted follower of Nietzsche, retreated from society with **Dora Strauch,** his patient and lover. Their goal? To create an untainted community of two, dedicated to the healing powers of the mind. Before coming to the island, Ritter insisted that both he and Dora have all their teeth removed and **stainless steel dentures** made; one pair was soon lost, so the couple had to share. Over the next five years, more and more Germans moved to the isolated isle. The temperamental **Baroness von Wagner de Bosquet** blew into Floreana like a hurricane, dressed in riding pants and tall leather boots, with a revolver in one hand and a **whip** in the other (presumably to keep her lovers in line). Of course, she could have used it to crack the tension in the air when she proclaimed herself **"Empress of Floreana,"** a declaration that enraged Ritter and his dreams of intellectual isolation. But in 1934, the Baroness suddenly disappeared with one of her lovers, and the body of another was found on the beach of Isla Marchena. Soon after, Dr. Ritter, a vegetarian, mysteriously died from poisoned chicken. Onlookers say he cursed Dora with his dying breath; she moved back to Germany and lived only long enough to write the book *Satan Came to Eden* before falling victim to that curse. Today, one of the less eccentric of Floreana's original residents, **Margret Wittmer,** still lives on the island.

DEVIL'S CROWN

At one time, this underwater formation, just off the coast of Punta Cormorant, was a submerged volcano. Subsequent eruptions and the powerful ocean have eroded the cone into a jagged ring of black lava spires rising from the sea floor. Thanks to currents that bring in tons of fish, Devil's Crown offers some of the **best snorkeling** in the islands. But these same currents can be dangerous; snorkelers should be cautious. Sharks are perhaps the biggest attraction of the Corona del Diablo. The probability of seeing the elegant creatures is relatively high—both **white-tipped reef sharks** and **hammerheads** frequent the area. While hammerheads have been known to attack humans elsewhere in the world, the abundance of food in the Galapagos makes the sharks in these parts uninterested in, and even wary of, curious snorkelers. For the best odds of seeing a shark, remain calm and quiet.

ISLA ESPAÑOLA

The southernmost island in the archipelago, Española's distance from the rest of the chain may well be its greatest asset. Its remote location has largely prevented genetic flow between Española and other islands, thus, many of its animals are found nowhere else in the archipelago (or the world). Española's most unique fauna are its birds; the **waved albatross** itself makes many tourists glad to have made the trip. Don't let Española's distance deter you; a visit to this remote island proves to often be the highlight of island tours.

PUNTA SUÁREZ

Boats reach Española via a dry landing on Punta Suárez, an area covering the island's western tip. A large colony of **sea lions** loll about on the sandy beaches here, sometimes playfully posing for pictures and other times barking at pesky humans who disturb their peace and quiet. **Marine iguanas** are often found warming themselves on the black rocks that separate the sections of beach. Those endemic to Española are the only species that **change color** during breeding season. Though young iguanas are all black, adults have a reddish tinge and take on an additional greenish hue during the breeding season.

The endemic **española mockingbird** boldly greets Española's visitors in a display of inter-species camaraderie and friendship, or so it seems. This welcome wagon is actually more interested in those crystal-clear, gleaming bottles of universal solvent attached to your knapsack. Española has no natural source of drinkable water, so the mockingbirds do everything they can to quench their thirst, including trying to steal a sip from the humans that visit their territory. Slightly larger than its relatives on other islands, the Española subspecies also has a longer, curved beak and is the only carnivorous mockingbird species; they feed on sea lion placentas, sea turtle hatchlings, and insects. They've even been known to peck at and drink the water-rich blood of baby boobies.

Continuing along the recently-renovated pathway, visitors can see more of the unique bird species which distinguish Española. **Blue-footed boobies** caress the rocks with their sensuous blue feet, honking and whistling. The **swallow-tailed gull** also can be seen along this path; the charcoal-and-crimson beauty is one of five seabirds species endemic only to the Galapagos.

The most famous wildlife spot on the island, however, is the nesting area of the **waved albatross,** another endemic seabird whose habitat can be found nowhere else in the world. Albatrosses breed here between mid-April and mid-December. This striking bird combines elements of grace and ungainliness in a way only the albatross can. If you're lucky, you'll get a glimpse of these birds performing their comical **mating dance,** a spectacle which can last five days and involves strutting, stumbling, honking, and a good deal of beak-fencing.

One of the trails from Punta Suárez provides a prime view of the island's famous **blowhole.** A seaside cliff on the south end of the trail provides the perfect vantage point to watch spray soar over 25m into the air, as incoming waves are forced out of a narrow volcanic fissure in the rock. The rainbow-colored mist produced by this spectacular geyser tends to incite a frenzied camera-clicking craze.

A TIDIER TORTUGA TALE The giant tortoises of Isla Española came dangerously close to the same sad end as Pinta's Lonesome George (see p. 587). However, some luck and raging tortoise hormones have brought about a much happier ending to this story than to that of George and his poor Pinta pals. Feral goats had been doing their usual damage to the tortoise population on Española. Over two decades ago, only two male and twelve female tortoises were found on Española, and these were taken to the Darwin Station in Puerto Ayora. None of the tortoises, however, were reproducing. Just when scientists were beginning to fear extinction, an Española male was miraculously identified in the San Diego Zoo. This Californian had a mysterious—and fortunate—effect on the rest of the pack, since shortly after his arrival many of the tortoises began to reproduce. Now that the Española goats have been eradicated, some of the tortoises have been returned to their island, leading to more happy news: Española has become the first island on which repatriated tortoises have begun to reproduce in the wild, perhaps boding well for future programs to reverse the damaging effects of introduced animals.

GARDNER BAY

While Punta Suárez's animal attractions draw Española's tourists, boats often visit Gardner Bay, located on the northwestern side of the island. Although white sand, white sand, and more white sand is the majority of what you'll find here, gigantic waves and dancing **sea lions** provide another reason to venture to this pristine beach. Divided into two sections by an outcropping of lava rock, the long, open shoreline is one of the few places in the Galapagos that is completely safe to explore without a guide. Visitors planning to walk the entire length of the beach should bring sturdy shoes. **Snorkeling** is possible in Gardner Bay but is usually more rewarding nearby at the aptly named **Tortuga Islet,** which gets its name from being shaped a lot like everyone's favorite Galapagos creature. Look for **sea turtles, stingrays,** and **colorful parrotfish** while you're under water.

THE NORTHERN ISLANDS

The Galapagos' distant northern islands are rarely visited by one-week tour boats because the sail here from the central islands takes at least six hours and the seas are usually rough. **Isla Genovesa** (often known as **Tower Island**) is the only one of these islands visitors can set foot on; **Pinta** and **Marchena,** as well as **Darwin** and **Wolf** to the far northwest, are visited only by diving tours. However, a visit to Isla Genovesa is definitely worth the trip.

ISLA GENOVESA

Genovesa has two major tourist sights, both accessible via **Darwin Bay** on the east end of the island. This gigantic bay, which often gives visitors the impression that they are completely surrounded by land, is a partially submerged **caldera,** or collapsed volcanic crater. Most boats choose to enter and leave the bay in daylight, as only a small segment of the opening is deep enough to allow boats to pass. In order to assist boats in this complicated maneuver, two illuminated solar panels have been installed across the bay from the opening. Boats can only enter the bay at an angle that makes these two panels line up perfectly.

DARWIN BEACH

Most of Darwin Bay is lined with 20- to 30m-high cliffs, making the small, white-coral-covered **Darwin Beach** stand out near the middle of the bay. After a wet landing here, many visitors are amazed by the sheer number of birds that glide over the shore and rest on the rocks and vegetation on the beach. Although the birds on

Genovesa are rarely frightened by people, it is still important to remain at least 2m away from them, so as not to interfere with them or their nests. Isla Genovesa's remote location has prevented it from being a home to land iguanas, lizards, or snakes, transforming it into a bird-lover's paradise. **Masked boobies** whistle, **great frigatebirds** display their gigantic red pouches near the landing site, and **mockingbirds** dart along the sand. Boobies and frigates here have a less-than-peaceful relationship. Since they compete for nesting space, boobies destroy frigates' nests, while frigates steal boobies' eggs. After leaving the landing site and passing a tidal pool, the trail enters a wooded area of salt-bushes and mangroves, which is home to a **red-footed booby** colony. Birdwatching fun just goes on and on; Darwin Beach is the place to see **sharp-beaked finches, large ground finches,** and **large cactus finches,** as well as **Galapagos doves** and **swallow-tailed gulls.**

PRINCE PHILLIP'S STEPS

Genovesa's other visitor site, **Prince Phillip's Steps,** is also an excellent birdwatching area. This dry landing leads to a steep set of natural stairs which are the only access to the high cliffs that surround Darwin Bay. The rocky trail winds its way through several colonies of nesting sea birds to a wooded area of lush green **lava morning glories,** stark **palo santo** trees, and the occasional green and yellow **lava cactus.** Among the vegetation on the interior of the island, red-footed boobies, nests, and some species of **Darwin finches** can be seen as well. Eventually, the trail leads to a flat, rocky area formed by lava flows. Here, the air is filled with small black-and-white **storm petrels,** which nest in cracks in the hardened lava. Look for the elusive **short-eared owl,** which, in the absence of hawks, feeds diurnally. These birds, however, are well-camouflaged and difficult to find. Genovesa is also a popular destination for **scuba** divers. As is the case in much of the Galapagos, the current here is quite strong; only experienced divers should explore the depths.

THE GALAPAGOS

CLIMATE

To convert from °C to °F, multiply by 1.8 and add 32. For a rough approximation, double the Celsius and add 25. To convert from °F to °C, subtract 32 and multiply by 0.55. For a rough approximation, subtract 25 and cut it in half.

°CELSIUS	-5	0	5	10	15	20	25	30	35	40
°FAHRENHEIT	23	32	41	50	59	68	77	86	95	104

AV. TEMP. AND PRECIPITATION

	JANUARY			APRIL			JULY			OCTOBER		
	°C	°F	mm	°C	°F	mm	°C	°F	mm	°C	°F	mm
Galápagos	26	79	20	22	72	18	24	75.5	0	23	74	0
Guayaquil	26.2	79.2	224	26.7	80.1	288	24.0	75.2	2	24.4	75.9	3
Quito	13.2	55.8	113	13.2	55.8	176	13.2	55.8	20	13.0	55.4	127
Lima	22.2	72.0	1	20.5	68.9	0	16.3	61.3	4	17.0	62.6	2
Cusco	13.1	55.6	149	12.5	54.5	38	10.0	50.0	4	13.6	56.5	47
Iquitos	26.3	79.3	11	25.9	78.6	12	14.1	57.4	6	19.8	67.6	9
La Paz	9.9	49.8	130	9.4	48.9	47	6.9	44.4	9	10.2	50.4	40
Sucre	16.2	61.2	102	15.4	59.7	11	13.8	56.8	1	10.2	50.4	19
Cochabamba	18.9	66.0	200	17.9	64.2	29	14.1	57.4	11	19.8	67.6	49

HOLIDAYS AND FESTIVALS

Consult the tourist offices in each city for the dates of art exhibitions, theater and music festivals, and sporting events. Where possible, *Let's Go* lists specific 2001 dates in individual cities. Be aware of them, as hotels fill up quickly and banks, restaurants, stores, and museums may all close, potentially leaving you homeless, broke, and hungry. Regional holidays listed below are only a small sample of the many fiestas that take place in Peru, Bolivia, and Ecuador almost every week.

Semana Santa, the Holy Week immediately preceding Easter, occasions the most parties in these Andean nations. Ayacucho and Cusco in the Peruvian highlands are regarded as the best places to experience this celebration; in Bolivia, Copacabana welcomes the crowd of hundreds walking from La Paz on Good Friday; in Ecuador, Quito is the popular point of pilgrimage. However, large festivals can be found in most cities, especially in the highlands. As one would expect, **Navidad** (Christmas) on December 25 is another religious holiday of great importance. However, instead of a capitalist onslaught of Christmas trees and clearance sales, processions of the Christ child largely predominate. Although the celebration of **Carnaval,** the week before Lent, does not reach Mardi Gras proportions, it has its own flair: in Ambato, Ecuador, the streets fill with a cornucopia of flowers and fruit; in Cajamarca, Peru, and other highland cities, townspeople run around flinging water, paint, oil, and other liquids at each other (and especially at gawking tourists); in Oruro, Bolivia, the classic Andean celebration erupts; and in Santa Cruz, Bolivia, festival-goers participate in a tropical pageant and similar celebration to that of Rio de Janeiro. **Día de los Difuntos** (Day of the Dead; Nov. 2) combines the Catholic tradition of All Souls' Day with *indígena* burial rituals. Offerings of food, along with little bread renditions of people and animals, are laid on top of the graves of relatives. Many highland towns also hold a **Corpus Cristi** (Body of Christ) celebration around the second week of June, most notably in Cuenca in southern Ecuador. Though the religious significance is vague at best, the week-long festival has enough sweet pastries, fruit candies, and *castillos* (large towers of fireworks that explode every night with dangerous vigor) to supersede any traditional explanation.

Not all fiestas in Peru, Bolivia, and Ecuador have their roots in Catholicism; especially in the highlands and in the jungle regions, locals continue to celebrate holidays dedicated to non-Christian deities. The most famous of these is undoubtedly the festival of **Inti Raymi** ("Festival of the Sun" in Quechua), celebrated in Cusco on June 24. A tribute to the Inca sun god Inti, the solstice festival involves colorful parades, traditional dances, live music, diverse expositions, and an oration in Quechua given at the archeological complex of Sacsayhuaman. This celebration, attracting hordes of tourists to the Andean city, is reputedly the second biggest festival in Latin America after the carnival of Rio de Janeiro. One of Bolivia's biggest festivals, **Phujllay,** is celebrated in the market town of Tarabuco, and marks the 1816 local triumph over the Spanish.

Most towns celebrate an **Independence Day** associated with the date on which they were liberated from Spain. Quito's (August 10), Guayaquil's (October 9), and Cuenca's (November 3) are Ecuadorian national holidays and entail concerts, sporting events, parades, and other spectacles. Peruvians go all out for their **Fiestas Patrias** on July 28-29; even in the smallest towns, schoolchildren begin practicing weeks in advance for the parades. Bolivians celebrate their independence on August 7, and **La Paz Day** is July 17.

Many of the lesser-known celebrations take on more of a local flavor. Chincha Alta, on Peru's southern coast, is known for its colorful **Verano Negro** festival at the end of February, featuring all sorts of displays of local and cultural pride. In Ecuador, Esmeraldas's festivities (Aug. 3-5) include African music and *marimba* dancing. **Regional festivals,** such as those dedicated to patron saints, often originated as indigenous feast days before they were assimilated into the Catholic tradition. They are usually celebrated with drinking, dancing to local music, and occasional beauty pageants. In the Peruvian capital, the residents have been paying homage to **Santa Rosa de Lima,** the patron saint of the city, every August 30th since 1671. In Bolivia's **Santisisma Trinidad,** the holy Trinity is celebrated with processions and a bullfight. In Ecuador, men doll up in drag and blackface for Latacunga's **La Virgen de las Mercedes** holiday on September 24, in honor of the city's dark-skinned statue of the Virgin Mary, known as La Mama Negra (see p. 508).

Check in tourist offices when you get to a new city or town, since there's almost always bound to be some sort of festival going on in the area. When traveling on or around major festival days, reserve accommodations well in advance.

DATE	FESTIVAL	
January 1-6	El Año Nuevo	New Year's Day, with festivals throughout the week
January 6	Festividades de los Reyes Magos	Festival of the Three Kings (Epiphany)
January 18	Aniversario de la Fundación de Lima	Anniversary of the Foundation of Lima (Peru)
early February	Fiesta de la Virgen de la Candelaria	Festival of the Virgin of the Candelaria (Lake Titicaca, Peru and Bolivia)
February 12	Aniversario del Descubrimiento de los Ríos Amazonas	Discovery of the Amazon River
last week in Feb.	Verano Negro	Black Summer (Chincha, Peru)
February 27	Recordación de la Batalla de Tarqui, Día del Civismo y la Unidad Nacional	Commemoration of the Battle of Tarqui, National Unity Day (Ecuador)
early March	Phujllay	Celebrating the Battle of Lumbati (Tarabuco, Bolivia)
early March	Carnaval	Carnival (throughout South America, but in particular Oruro, Bolivia)

DATE	FESTIVAL	
April 9-15	Semana Santa	Holy Week
April 19-21	Feria Agrícola, Ganadera, Artesanal, e Industrial	Farming, Cattle, Handicraft, and Industrial Fair (Riobamba, Ecuador)
April 12	Jueves Santo	Holy Thursday
April 13	Viernes Santo	Good Friday
April 15	El Día de Pasqua	Easter
May 1	Día de Trabajador	Labor Day
May 2-3	Fiesta de la Cruz	Festival of the Cross
early May	Fiesta del Durazno	Peach Festival (Gualaceo, Bolivia)
May 11-14	Feria Agrícola e Industrial de la Amazonía	Agricultural and Industrial Festival of the Amazon
May 24	Fiesta Cívica Nacional	Battle of Pichincha (Independence Day, Ecuador)
late May-early June	Festividad de Nuestro Señor Jesú Poder	A celebration of Jesus Christ (La Paz, Bolivia)
June 14	Corpus Christi	Corpus Christi
June 24	Fiesta de San Juan/Inti Raymi Fiesta del Maiz y del Turismo Gallo Compadre, Vacas Loca, Castillo, y Chamiza	Saint John the Baptist's Day/Festival of the Sun (Cusco, Peru) Corn and Tourism Festivals (Sangoloqui, Ecuador) Rodeo Day (Calpi, Ecuador)
June 29	Festividad de San Pedro y San Pablo	Saint Peter's and Saint Paul's Day
July 16	Celebración de la Virgen del Carmen	Celebration of the Virgin of Carmen
July 23-25	Aniversario de Fundación de la Cuidad de Guayaquil	Anniversary of the Foundation of Guayaquil (Ecuador)
July 24	Fiesta del Chagra	Festival of the Chagra (Machachi, Ecuador)
July 24	Nacimiento de Simón Bolívar	Birth of Simón Bolívar
July 28-29	Fiestas Patrias	National Holidays (Independence Day, Peru)
August 3-5	Independencia de la Cuidad de Esmeraldas	Esmeraldas's Independence Day (Ecuador)
early August	Fiesta de la Virgen de las Nieves	Festival of the Virgin of the Snow (Sicalpa, Bolivia)
early August	Festividades de San Lorenzo Fiesta de San Jacinto	San Lorenzo Festivities (Pillaro, Bolivia) San Jacinto Festivities (Yaguachi, Bolivia)
August 6	Independence Day	Bolivia
August 10	Aniversario de la Independencia de Quito	Independence of Quito (Ecuador)
August 12-20	Aniversario de la Fundación de Arequipa	Anniversay of the Foundation of Arequipa (Peru)
late August	Fiesta de San Luís Obispo	Festival of San Luís Obispo
August 30	Fiesta de Santa Rosa de Lima	Celebration of Santa Rosa, patron saint of Lima (Peru)
early September	Fiesta de Yamor Festividades de la Virgen del Cisne	Festival of Yamor (Otavalo, Ecuador) Festivities for the Virgin of El Cisne (Loja, Ecuador)
late September	Feria Mundial del Banano Festividades de la Virgen de las Mercedes	Banana's World Fair (Machala, Ecuador) Festivities of the Virgen of Mercy (Latacunga, Ecuador)
October 8	Fiesta de Angamos	Battle of Angamos (Peru)
October 9	Aniversario de la Independencia de Guayaquil	Independence of Guayaquil (Ecuador)
October 12	Aniversario del Descubrimiento de las Americas	Discovery of America
November 1	Día de los Santos	All Saints Day
November 2	Día de los Difuntos	All Soul's Day
November 3	Aniversario de la Independencia de Cuenca	Independence of Cuenca (Ecuador)

DATE	FESTIVAL	
December 6	Aniversario de la Fundación Española San Francisco de Quito	Foundation of San Francisco de Quito (Ecuador)
December 8	Concepción Inmaculada	Immaculate Conception (Peru)
December 25	La Navidad	Christmas Day
December 28	Los Santos Inocentes	All Fool's Day
December 31	Incineración del Año Viejo	New Year's Eve

LANGUAGE

Even if you speak no Spanish, a few basics will help you along. Any attempts at Spanish are appreciated and encouraged, and you'll find that many people in the tourism industry and in larger cities understand some English.

Spanish pronunciation is very regular. Vowels are always pronounced the same way: *a* ("ah" in father); *e* ("eh" in escapade); *i* ("ee" in eat); *o* ("oh" in oat); *u* ("oo" in boot); *y*, by itself, is pronounced like i. Most consonants are the same as English. Important exceptions are: *j* ("h" in "hello"); *ll* ("y" in "yes"); *ñ* ("gn" in "cognac"); *rr*, (trilled "r"); *h* is always silent; *x* has a bewildering variety of pronunciations. Stress in Spanish words falls on the second to last syllable, except for words ending in "r," "l," and "z," in which it falls on the last syllable. All exceptions to these rules require a written accent on the stressed syllable.

Quechua, or Quichua in Ecuador, was the offical language of Tawantinsuyu, the Inca Empire. It is still spoken today by an estimated 12 to 16 million people in the Andean region, primarily in Peru and Bolivia, but also in Ecuador, Colombia, and Argentina. On the altiplano, Ayamara is the primary indigenous language. In Bolivia, Peru, and Chile there are 1.5 million Aymara speakers, with the highest concentration in Bolivia. Quechua and Aymara have only three vowels, and as in Spanish, the stressed syllable is normally the next to last one. In the case of a contraction, the last syllable is stressed. (The link between Quechua and Aymara is rather slim. While they share 190 words, it seems more likely that this resulted from geograhpic interaction rather than a common origin.)

SPANISH GLOSSARY

aduana: customs
agencia de viaje: travel agency
aguardiente: strong liquor
aguas termales: hot springs
ahora: now
aire acondicionado: air-conditioned (A/C)
ají: red Peruvian chili used in criollo cooking
ajo: garlic
a la plancha: grilled
albergue (juvenil): (youth) hostel
al gusto: as you wish
almacen: (grocery) store
almuerzo: lunch, midday meal
alpaca: a shaggy-haired, long-necked animal in the cameloid family
amigo/a: friend
andenes: agricultural terraces
arroz: rice
arroz chaufa: Chinese-style fried rice
artesanía: arts and crafts
avenida: avenue
ayllu: a kinship-based Inca clan
bahía: bay
baño: bathroom or natural spa
barato/a: cheap
barro: mud
barrio: neighborhood
batido: n: a shake (fruit and milk); adj.: whipped or beaten
biblioteca: library
bistec/bistek: beefsteak

bocaditos: appetizers, at a bar
bodega: convenience store or winery
boletería: ticket counter
bonito/a: pretty/beautiful
borracho/a: drunk
botica: drugstore
bueno/a: good
caballero: gentleman
caballo: horse
cabañas: cabins
cabildos abiertos: colonial era town councils
cajeros: cashiers
cajeros automáticos: ATM
caldera: coffee or tea pot
caldo: soup, broth, or stew
caldo de balgre: catfish soup
caldo de pata: hoof soup
calle: street
cama: bed
camarones: shrimp
cambio: change
camino: path or track
camioneta: small, pickup-sized truck
campamento: campground
campo: countryside
canotaje: rafting
caneliza: a drink made from boiling water, aguardiente, cinnamon and lemon juice
canta de monte: Andean tapir
cantina: drinking establishment, usually male dominated

carne asada: roast meat
caro/a: expensive
carretera: highway
carro: car, or sometimes a train car
casa: house
casa de cambio: currency exchange establishment
casado/a: married
cascadas: waterfalls
caseríos: hamlet/small village, often unregulated by govt.
casona: mansion
catarata: waterfall
cena: dinner, a light meal usually served after 8pm.
centro: city center
cerca: near/nearby
cerro: hill
cerveza: beer
ceviche/cebiche: raw fish marinated in lemon juice, herbs, veggies
chica/o: girl/boy
chicha: a liquor from the Oriente made from fermented yucca or maize plant and human saliva
chicharrón: bite-sized pieces of fried meat, usually pork
chifa: Chinese restaurant
chuleta de chancho: pork chop
chompa: sweater
chupa: shot
churrasco: steak
churriguerresco: rococo (in the style of the 18th century Spanish architect Churriguerra)
ciudad: city
ciudadela: neighborhood in a large city
coche: car
colectivo: small municipal transit bus or shared taxi
coliseo: coliseum/stadium
colonia: neighborhood in a large city
colpa: macaw lick
combi: small bus
comedor: small restaurant (Ecu.); dining room (Peru)
comida criolla: regional, Spanish-influenced dishes
comida típica: typical/traditional dishes
con: with
consulado: consulate
correo: post office
cordillera: mountain range
corridas: bull fighting
corvina: sea bass
criollos: people of European descent born in the New World
cruz roja: Red Cross
cuadra: street block
cuarto: a room
cuenta: bill/check
cuento: story/account
curandero: healer
desayuno: breakfast
descompuesto: broken, out of order; or spoiled/rotten food
despacio: slow
de turno: a 24hr. rotating schedule for pharmacies
discoteca: dance club
embajada: embassy
emergencia: emergency
encebollado: stew flavored with onions
encocados: seafood cooked in coconut milk

encomiendas: estates granted to Spanish settlers in Latin America
estrella: star
extranjero: foreign/foreigner
farmacia: pharmacy
ferrocarril: railroad
fiesta: party, holiday
finca: a plantation-like agricultural enterprise or a ranch
frontera: border
fumar: to smoke
fumaroles: hole in a volcanic region which emits hot vapors
fútbol: soccer
ganga: bargain
gordo/a: fat
gorra: cap
guineo: banana
habitación: a room
hacienda: ranch
hervido/a: boiled
iglesia: church
impuestos: taxes
indígena: indigenous, refers to the native population
jarra: 1-litre pitcher of beer
jirón: street
jugo: juice
kilo: kilogram
kuraka: the chieftan of an Inca clan (see p. 37)
ladrón: thief
lago/ laguna: lake
lancha: launch, small boat
langostino: jumbo shrimp
larga distancia: long distance
lavandería: laundromat
lejos: far
lente(mente): slow(ly)
lista de correos: the general delivery system in most of Ecuador and Peru
llapingachos: potato and cheese pancakes
loma: hill
lomo: sirloin steak
mal: bad
malecón: pier or seaside thoroughfare
máneje despacio: drive slowly
mar: sea
mariscos: seafood
menestras: lentils/beans
menú del día: fixed daily meal often offered for a bargain price
mercado: market
merienda: late afternoon snack/early dinner
mestizo/a: a person of mixed European and indigenous descent
mirador: an observatory or look-out point
mita: a system of forced labor imposed upon indigenous communities by the colonial Spaniards
mordida: literally "little bite," bribe
moto/mototaxi: small, 3 wheeled taxis adapted from motorcycles
muelle: wharf
muerte: death
museo: museum
nada: nothing
obra: work of art/play
obraje: primitive textile workshops
oficina de turismo: office of tourism
paiche: jungle fish
palta: avocado (Peru)
pan: bread
panadería: bakery

panga: motorboat
parada: a stop (on a bus or train)
parapente: paraglide
parilla: various cuts of meat, grilled
paro: strike
parque: park
parroquia: parish
paseo turístico: tour covering a series of sites
payaso: clown
pelea de gallos: cockfighting
peligroso/a: dangerous
peninsulares: Spanish-born colonists
peña: folkloric music club
pescado: fish (prepared)
picante: spicy
pisa de uves: grape-stomping
pisco: a traditional Peruvian liquor made from grapes
pisco sour: a drink made from pisco, lemon juice, sugarcane syrup, and egg white
plátano: plantain
playa: beach
policía: police
pollo a la brasa: roasted chicken
pozas: thermal bath
pueblito: small town
puerta: door
puerto: port
quebrada: dry river bed
rana: frog
reloj: watch, clock
ropa: clothes

sala: living room
salchipapa: french fries with fried pieces of sausage
salida: exit
salsa: sauce (can be of many varieties)
salsa/merengue: Latin dances
seco de cordero: pieces of lamb in a flavorful sauce
seco de gallina: pieces of chicken in a flavorful sauce
seguro/a: n.: lock, insurance; adj.: safe
selva: jungle
semana: week
Semana Santa: Holy Week
shaman/chaman: spiritual healer
SIDA: the Spanish acronym for AIDS
sillar: white, volcanic rock used in construction
sol: sun/Peruvian currency
solo carril: one-lane road or bridge
soltero/a: single (unmarried)
sucre: Ecuadorian currency
supermercado: supermarket
tarifa: fee
terminal terrestre: bus station
tienda: store
tipo de cambio: exchange rate
trole: trolley (Quito)
trucha: trout
vicuna: a usually wild animal in the camelloid family

SPANISH PHRASEBOOK

ENGLISH	SPANISH	ENGLISH	SPANISH
		BASICS	
Hello	Hola	Goodbye	Adiós/Hasta luego/Chao
Good Morning/Afternoon	Buenos días/Buenas tardes	Good Evening/Night	Buenas noches
Yes/No	Sí/No	How are you? (formal)	¿Cómo está Usted?
I don't know	No sé	How are you? (informal)	¿Qué tal?
Sorry/Forgive me	Lo siento	Cool!/Awesome!	¡Chévere!
Please	Por favor	Thank you	Gracias
Excuse me	Con permiso/discúlpeme	You're welcome	De nada, a la orden
Who?	¿Quién?	What?	¿Qué?
When?	¿Cuándo?	Where?	¿Dónde?
Why?	¿Por qué?	Because	Porque
		PHRASES	
My name is...	Yo me llamo....	I am from...	Soy de....
What is your name?	¿Cómo se llama?	It's a pleasure to meet you	Mucho gusto concocerle
What's up?	¿Qué pasa?/¿Como está la vaina?	Pardon/me	Perdón/perdóneme
How much does this cost?	¿Cuánto cuesta?	Let's Go	¡Vámonos!
Go away/Leave me alone	¡Déjame en paz!	Stop/enough	Basta
Could you tell me?	¿Podría decirme?	Is (Lara) available?	¿Está (Lara)?
I don't understand	No entiendo	Could you please repeat that?	Otra vez, por favor/¿Podría repetirlo?

ENGLISH	SPANISH	ENGLISH	SPANISH
Please speak slowly	¿Podría hablar más despacio, por favor?	How do you say...?	¿Cómo se dice...?
Could you help me?	¿Podría ayudarme?	Help!/Help me!	¡Socorro!/¡Ayúdame!
I am hot/cold	Tengo calor/frío	Where do you live?	¿Dónde vives?
Are there rooms?	¿Hay habitaciones?	Are there student discounts?	¿Hay descuentos para estudiantes?
I want/would like...	Quisiera/Me gustaría...	I'm looking for...	Busco...
I have...	Tengo...		

DIRECTIONS

(to the) right	a la derecha	(to the) left	a la izquierda
next to	al lado de	across from	en frente de
straight ahead	todo derecho	to turn	doblar
near	cerca	far	lejos
above	arriba	below	abajo
traffic light	semáforo	corner	esquina
street	calle/avenida/jirón	block	cuadra
How do I get to...?	¿Cómo voy a...?	How far is...?	¿Qué tan lejos está?
Where is...street?	¿Dónde está la calle...?	What bus line goes to...?	¿Qué línea de buses tiene servicio a...?
When does the bus leave?	¿Cuándo sale el autobús?	Where does the bus leave from?	¿De dónde sale el autobús?
I'm getting off at...	Bajo en...	I have to go now	Tengo que ir ahora
Where is the bathroom?	¿Dónde está el baño?	I'm lost	Estoy perdido(a)

NUMBERS

one	uno	twelve	doce
two	dos	fifteen	quince
three	tres	twenty	veinte
four	cuatro	twenty-five	veinticinco
five	cinco	thirty	treinta
six	seis	forty	cuarenta
seven	siete	fifty	cincuenta
eight	ocho	one hundred	cien/ciento
nine	nueve	five hundred	quinientos
ten	diez	one thousand	un mil
eleven	once	one million	un millón

FOOD

breakfast	desayuno	lunch	almuerzo
dinner	cena/merienda	dessert	postre
drink	bebida	water (purified)	agua (purificada)
bread	pan	rice	arroz
vegetables	legumbres/vegetales	chicken	pollo
meat	carne	milk	leche
eggs	huevos	coffee	café
juice	jugo	tea	té
wine	vino	beer	cerveza
ice cream	helado	fruit	fruta
cheese	queso	vegetarian	vegetariano(a)
soup	sopa/caldo	cup	una copa/taza
fork	tenedor	knife	cuchillo
spoon	cuchara	Bon Apetit	Buen provecho
napkin	servilleta	the check, please	la cuenta, por favor

ENGLISH	SPANISH	ENGLISH	SPANISH
		TIMES AND HOURS	
morning	la mañana	afternoon	tarde
evening	tarde, noche	night	noche
today	hoy	yesterday	ayer
tomorrow	mañana	week	semana
month	mes	year	año
midday	mediodía	midnight	medianoche
early	temprano(a)	late	tarde
open	abierto(a)	closed	cerrado(a)
What time is it?	¿Qué hora es?	When is it open?	¿Cuando está abierto?
		OTHER HELPFUL WORDS	
embassy	embajada	consulate	consulado
post office	correo	hospital	el hospital
alone	solo(a)	friend	amigo(a)
good	bueno(a)	bad	malo(a)
happy	feliz, contento(a)	sad	triste
hot	caliente	cold	frío

QUECHUA AND AYMARA PHRASEBOOK

ENGLISH	QUECHUA	AYMARA
	PHRASES	
Hello	napaykullayki	kamisaraki
Good bye	ratukama	jakisiñkama
How are you?	allillanchu?	kunjamaskatasa?
Please	allichu	mirá
Thank you	yusulpayki	yuspagara
Yes	arí	jisa
No	mana	janiw
Where?	may?	kawki?
Distant (Close)	karu (sirka)	jaya (jak'a)
Down (Up)	uray (wichay)	aynacha (alaxa)
How much?	Maik'ata'g?	K'gauka?
What?	iman?	kuna?
Why?	imanaqtin?	kunata?
Water	unu	uma
Food	mihuna	manq'a
Lodging	alohamiento	qurpa

NUMBERS

ENGLISH	QUECHUA	AYMARA	ENGLISH	QUECHUA	AYMARA
1	hoq	maya	20	iskay chunka	pätunka
2	iskay	paya	30	kinsa chunka	kimsa-tunka
3	kinsa	kimsa	40	tawa chunka	pusi-tunka
4	tawa	pusi	50	pisqa chunka	phisca-tunka
5	pisqa	phisca	60	soqta chunka	suxta-tunka
6	soqta	suxta	70	qanchis chunka	paqalqu-tunka
7	qanchis	paqalqu	80	pasaq chunka	kimsaqalqu-tunka
8	pusaq	kimsaqalqu	90	isqon chunka	llatunka-tunka
9	isqon	llatunka	100	pachak	pataka
10	chunka	tunka	1000	waranqa	waranqa

INDEX

MAPS INDEX

ABOUT LET'S GO

FORTY-ONE YEARS OF WISDOM

As a new millennium arrives, *Let's Go: Europe*, now in its 41st edition and translated into seven languages, reigns as the world's bestselling international travel guide. For over four decades, travelers criss-crossing the Continent have relied on *Let's Go* for inside information on the hippest backstreet cafes, the most pristine secluded beaches, and the best routes from border to border. In the last 20 years, our rugged researchers have stretched the frontiers of backpacking and expanded our coverage into Asia, Africa, Australia, and the Americas. This year, we've introduced a new city guide series with books on San Francisco and our hometown, Boston. Now, our seven city guides feature sharp photos, more maps, and an overall more user-friendly design. We've also returned to our roots with the inaugural edition of *Let's Go: Western Europe*.

It all started in 1960 when a handful of well-traveled students at Harvard University handed out a 20-page mimeographed pamphlet offering a collection of their tips on budget travel to passengers on student charter flights to Europe. The following year, in response to the instant popularity of the first volume, students traveling to Europe researched the first full-fledged edition of *Let's Go: Europe*, a pocket-sized book featuring honest, practical advice, witty writing, and a decidedly youthful slant on the world. Throughout the 60s and 70s, our guides reflected the times. In 1969 we taught travelers how to get from Paris to Prague on "no dollars a day" by singing in the street. In the 80s and 90s, we looked beyond Europe and North America and set off to all corners of the earth. Meanwhile, we focused in on the world's most exciting urban areas to produce in-depth, fold-out map guides. Our new guides bring the total number of titles to 51, each infused with the spirit of adventure and voice of opinion that travelers around the world have come to count on. But some things never change: our guides are still researched, written, and produced entirely by students who know first-hand how to see the world on the cheap.

HOW WE DO IT

Each guide is completely revised and thoroughly updated every year by a well-traveled set of nearly 300 students. Every spring, we recruit over 200 researchers and 90 editors to overhaul every book. After several months of training, researcher-writers hit the road for seven weeks of exploration, from Anchorage to Adelaide, Estonia to El Salvador, Iceland to Indonesia. Hired for their rare combination of budget travel sense, writing ability, stamina, and courage, these adventurous travelers know that train strikes, stolen luggage, food poisoning, and marriage proposals are all part of a day's work. Back at our offices, editors work from spring to fall, massaging copy written on Himalayan bus rides into witty, informative prose. A student staff of typesetters, cartographers, publicists, and managers keeps our lively team together. In September, the collected efforts of the summer are delivered to our printer, who turns them into books in record time, so that you have the most up-to-date information available for your vacation. Even as you read this, work on next year's editions is well underway.

WHY WE DO IT

We don't think of budget travel as the last recourse of the destitute; we believe that it's the only way to travel. Living cheaply and simply brings you closer to the people and places you've been saving up to visit. Our books will ease your anxieties and answer your questions about the basics—so you can get off the beaten track and explore. Once you learn the ropes, we encourage you to put *Let's Go* down now and then to strike out on your own. You know as well as we that the best discoveries are often those you make yourself. When you find something worth sharing, please drop us a line. We're Let's Go Publications, 67 Mount Auburn St., Cambridge, MA 02138, USA (email: feedback@letsgo.com). For more info, visit our website, www.letsgo.com.

Will you have enough stories to tell your grandchildren?

Yahoo! Travel